Y0-BCW-092

EPIC

of the

Greater Southwest

New Mexico ◆ Texas ◆ California
Arizona ◆ Oklahoma ◆ Colorado
Utah ◆ Nevada

Rubén Sálaz Márquez

Dedication

For my "new" Grandchildren: Brandon, Randall Raymond Dimitri, María Raquel, Aleksey Alyosha; and to the valiant women of New Mexico like Dolores, Millie, Conchita, Rozanne, Pátryka, Polly, Corine, Rebecca, Diane, Patricia, Bernadette, Amber, Linda, Rosemary, Loretta, Jody, Luguie, Irene, Annalee, MaryJane, etc.

Copyright 2004 by Rubén D. Sálaz
All Rights Reserved.

Design and production by David Wilson.

Limited First Edition.

Sálaz Márquez, Rubén
Epic of the Greater Southwest:
New Mexico, Texas, Arizona, California, Oklahoma, Colorado, Utah, Nevada
Includes:
1. Introduction to precontact Amerindians and their societies. 2. Spanish exploration of the Southwest. 3. Founding of Hispanic New Mexico, Texas, California, Arizona. 4. Spanish Institutions: Missions and Presidios; biographies of Kino, Margil, Serra, Anza. 5. Hispanic Society. 6. Indian Affairs in the Hispanic Southwest. 7. American Period of the Southwest: Mexican War; Civil War; Indian Affairs in the American Southwest. 8. Railroads. 9. Frontier law and order: Lawmen and Outlaws. 10. Statehood and Americanization of the Southwest. 11. Land Tenure. 12. Education in the Southwest. 13. Touring the Southwest. 14. Timelines. 15. Historical Essays. 16. Annotated Basic Bibliography. 17. Index.

Manufactured in the United States of America.

ISBN 0-932492-06-1

Cosmic House
P.O. Box 7748
Albuquerque, New Mexico 87194

WORKS by RUBEN SALAZ M.

Tabloid
Tierra Amarilla Shootout

History
Cosmic: The La Raza Sketchbook
New Mexico: A Brief Multi-History

Educational Materials
Cosmic Posters (bilingual)
Indian Saga Posters

Children's Books
The Cosmic Reader of the Southwest - For Young People

In Spanish
La lectura cósmica del suroeste - para los jóvenes

Short Stories
Heartland: Stories of the Southwest

Novels (trilogy)
I am Tecumseh! (Books I and II)

Dramas
Embassy Hostage: The Drama of Americans in Iran
Tonight or Never!

Essays
USA Today (Guest Editorials)

Anthologies
Included in: *The Language of Literature* (McDougal Littell);
Cuento Chicano del siglo XX (Universidad Nacional Autónoma de México,
Ediciones Coyoacán, New México State University);
Voces: An Anthology of Nuevo Mexicano Writers (El Norte Publications);
Tierra: Contemporary Short Fiction of N.M. (Cinco Puntos Press);
Mexican American Short Stories (Reclam, English-German)

Table of Contents

PART ONE: PRECONTACT   *Notes*
Chapter 1: PRE-COLUMBIAN CIVILIZATIONS....................................1   7

PART TWO: SPANISH PERIOD
Chapter 2: FIRST EUROPEANS IN THE SOUTHWEST........................18   24

Chapter 3: FIRST EUROPEAN COLONY and SETTLEMENTS
   COLONY: New Mexico, 1598 28   45
   SETTLEMENTS: San Antonio, Texas, 1718...............................50   53
                San Diego, California, 1769.................................55   61
                Tucson, Arizona, 1776 63   64

Chapter 4: SPANISH INSTITUTIONS
   Missions...65
   KINO 69   72
   MARGIL..74   76
   Presidio..77   79
   ANZA 80   93
   Ranching...95   99
   New Mexico 99   101
   Texas..101   103
   California...103   105
   Arizona..105   106

Chapter 5: SOCIETY in the HISPANIC SOUTHWEST
   New Mexico 109   159
   Texas..163   179
   California...182   226
   Arizona..235   238

Chapter 6: INDIAN AFFAIRS in the HISPANIC SOUTHWEST
   New Mexico 240
      Acoma War 240   243
      Jumano War 244   245
      St. Lawrence Day Massacre 245   250
      Reconquest of New Mexico 252   253

Table of Contents

Chapter 6 continued   *Notes*
      Comanche War and Peace................................. 254   257
      Cebolleta and the Navajo Frontier 258   260
   Texas..262   265
   California.. 265   269
   Arizona... 269   270

PART THREE: AMERICAN PERIOD
Chapter 7: THE MEXICAN WAR

  Synopsis...274   282

Chapter 8: The Mexican War in

      Texas.. 287   291
      New Mexico...292   295
      Arizona.. 296   297
      California.. 297   307

Chapter 9: THE CIVIL WAR in the Southwest...............................314   319

Chapter 10: INDIAN AFFAIRS IN THE AMERICAN SOUTHWEST

  Texas..321   328
  California...330   342
  Nevada.. 345   347
  Colorado 348   355
  Utah 356   359
  Oklahoma 360   366
  New Mexico 372   385
  Arizona... 388   402

Chapter 11: RAILROADS..412   421

Chapter 12: FRONTIER LAW AND ORDER 422   429
  Texas..430   436
  California...437   445
  Oklahoma 446   451
  New Mexico 451   457
  Arizona...458   461

Chapter 13: STATEHOOD AND AMERICANIZATION   *Notes*

Texas–1845 463   474

California–1850 477   505

Nevada–1864 511   518

Colorado–1876 519   528

Utah–1896 530   537

Oklahoma–1907 538   543

New Mexico–1912 543   557

Arizona–1912 560   566

Chapter 14: LAND TENURE 572   582

Chapter 15: EDUCATION IN THE SOUTHWEST 584

Chapter 16: A PERSONAL TOUR OF THE SOUTHWEST 589

ANNOTATED BASIC BIBLIOGRAPHY 591

EPILOGUE 602

TIMELINES

European Exploration of the Americas 7   14

Denominational Christianity 309   313

King of the Plains 368   371

HISTORICAL ESSAYS

History or Propaganda? 62

Land Grants 106   108

On Texas History 181

On California Historiography 233

On New Mexican Indian Affairs 261

On the Spanish Era 270

The Dred Scott Decision 284

On California Indian History 343

Morality Aside 404   410

Myth & Media in Western History 567

INDEX 603

Foreword

HISTORY is the most dangerous field of study in American society. There are many reasons for this observation and all have profound implications that should be explored in a genuinely mature fashion. The American psyche has a penchant for fantasy, which has given rise to industries like movies and television, and this is certainly for the good as far as "Entertainment" is concerned. But entertaining fantasies have been woven into the fabric of American Historiography, which isn't a positive effect when it comes to a sense of reality. While fantasy is very human, it shouldn't be the basis for writing History because the historical record and interpretation of present realities will be distorted. Correcting a fantasy historical record is where trouble erupts. Let us submit "King Arthur and the Knights of the Roundtable" as an example. Neither King Arthur nor his Knights ever existed. All stories from the "Arthurian cycle" are creations grounded in pure fantasy. Many writers will not broach this heavy truth because they don't wish to be targeted as spoilers, whistle blowers, or *revisionists*. So most people believe in King Arthur as a real person and learn next to nothing about historical personalities like Charlemagne, one of the few towering medieval kings, or El Cid, the most famous knight of the Middle Ages.

The popular mind doesn't concern itself much with fact or fancy until the matter is closer to home discussing issues like "American heroes." Were Daniel Boone, Zebulon M. Pike, John C. Fremont, Kit Carson, Davy Crockett, etc., "heroic frontiersmen/explorers/pathfinders"? How much of their histories is fact, how much fantasy? And since the written record of the Southwest began in 1540, what of the Hispanic personalities who came before our 19th century Southwest heroes? Can the American historical record do justice to such a diverse history? How do realities like *presentism* (to interpret historical facts by imposing contemporary ethics and/or sensitivities on people and events of the past) or *analysis* impinge on American historiography? If someone writes documented history that proves to be "unpopular" should he be labeled a *revisionist*? Should the "revisionist" refer to his accusers as the "Sweep-It-Under-the Rug" school? While mature minds could be expected to see through mere propaganda that wouldn't necessarily be the case with high school students studying History. According to an article titled "Remaking History" in *U.S. News & World Report* (November 25, 2002, page 46), if a book is accepted for use in Texas schools it will generally be approved in the rest of the USA. How does the adoption process work? A "line by line" scrutiny of the text, use of acceptable terms like "enslaved person" instead of "slave," and/or deletion of information like that there were "some 50,000 prostitutes" working in the Old West. "Traditionalists" want to glorify Democracy and "free enterprise" while "Progressives" refuse to exclude women and minorities. "Textbook wars" don't emphasize the fact that American students score lower in History than in any other discipline, "including Math." It would appear that a textbook is created for its "best seller" potential, not its veracity. [See *Lies My Teacher Told Me: Everything Your American History Textbook Got Wrong* by James W. Loewen.]

Upon reading this volume it will be obvious that published works are of necessity "major players" in *Epic of the Greater Southwest* because what has (or perhaps hasn't) been done must be addressed or confronted. For example, Dr. David J. Weber writes in his book of essays titled *Myth And The History Of The Hispanic Southwest* (Chapter 5) that the history of the Southwest from 1821 to 1850 is "...*notably unbalanced, ethnocentric, and incomplete.*"

Consider the often cited work *The Cattle On A Thousand Hills: 1850-1880* by Robert G. Cleland. The title states "1850-1880" as if the "cattle" industry had nothing to do with Californios who, in fact, put those hundreds of thousands of cattle on those "thousand hills" before "1850" when California became a State in the Union. Take another example: *The Decline Of The Californios* by Leonard Pitt. Did the people of Hispanic California suffer a mere "decline" or did they go from riches to rags at the hands of newly arrived (American) "California pioneers"? While studying Southwest History are we actually digesting someone's "interpretation" or "personal analysis" instead of History? If so, this is little more than propaganda shrouded as "History" (which I herein refer to somewhat facetiously as *propagandistory*). Besides being plagued with misleading strategies like presentism and "interpretation," there is also the Orwellian specter of "double speak," to say something in such a way that people will not understand but the writer can assert that's what he said. For example, if American beliefs concerning the Iraqi War of 2003 conflict with actual facts, you can phrase it by saying "Americans may be avoiding having an experience of cognitive dissonance."

What is it in the American psyche that demands conformity to whatever popularity asserts? What caused MSNBC and NBC to fire Peter Arnett (March, 2003) for reporting Iraqi perspectives during the Iraqi War? This behavior is nothing new. In 1975 Texas scholar Carmen Perry was targeted with fury when she translated a manuscript that contradicted the popularly held belief (i.e., the movie version) of how Davy Crockett died. Observations like these, addressed in the *Discussion Notes* sections, will not be popular in some quarters and might be combated with typical charges of *revisionist*, or worse, but they should be discussed openly if any study of Southwest history is to be complete. Whether considered polemical or not, these issues must be addressed, if for no other reason than to be able to refute them.

The intent of *Epic* is to lay an introductory historical foundation for what is herein referred to as *The Greater Southwest: New Mexico, Texas, California, Arizona, Oklahoma, Colorado, Utah, Nevada.* The work is intended for the person who wants to investigate History, regardless of academic background. No effort has been made to overwhelm the reader with erudition or staggering bibliography. Highly utilitarian scholarly forms like ibid (*ibidem*: in the same place), op.cit. (*opere citato*: in the work cited), passim (in various parts of the book; here and there), etc., have not be employed in this work.

While the Southwest is the oldest section of the present USA and there exist mind boggling amounts of historical information in the Spanish as well as English languages, the reader is provided with basic references that aren't treated as an end in themselves. Documentation is cited as an avenue for further study, which is highly encouraged. It is also paramount that differing perspectives be discussed in a mature, tolerant manner in order to enrich all participants, whether speaking or listening. While everyone

Foreword

maintains that one does not have to agree with a particular point of view, the reality of the situation is that individuals who question accepted precepts are often targeted for retribution, overt or covert. That's what makes the study of History *dangerous*. The historical facts and/or ideas presented in *Epic* might seem controversial but it should be considered important to understand these perspectives which might not have been studied in the past. Such is the way to personal growth and maturity. It behooves American society to value maturity because, among many other reasons, it controls more weapons of mass destruction than all the other countries in the world combined.

A debt of thanks is owed to Dr. Richard Griego and Dr. Henry J. Casso who read the manuscript and made very insightful comments. Dr. Griego's written commentary was typically professional and might well have been included as an appendix.

CHAPTER 1

Pre-Columbian Civilizations

It has been written that Paleolithic hunters and their families walked into what is now referred to as North America some 10,000 or perhaps more than 20,000 years ago. These bands of hunters found large, Ice Age mammals like mammoths, camels, horses, and ground sloths, all of which were hunted with atlatls. There is archaeological evidence that around 1000 B.C., people were harvesting a variety of corn and this is described as a transition from food gathering to food producing. (Archaeological digs are the only key to knowledge about people in the Southwest before the arrival of Hispanic people on the scene.)

By around the birth of Christ, assuredly by the years A.D. 100-200, the big game hunters had disappeared or their descendants had evolved into pottery making societies in the area now referred to as the American Southwest. While the hunting of small game had not been abandoned, the people lived more by gathering or nurturing wild plants for food. Seeds, fruits, and greens were now an important part of the diet.

It has been said that the Anasazi, Hohokam, and Mogollon people laid the foundations to the historic American Southwest. No study of the Southwest would be complete without introductory information on these three cultures but it must be remembered that knowledge about these ancient peoples is based on archaeological and anthropological discoveries, not written documentation.

ANASAZI

The Anasazi were the pioneers of the Colorado Plateau area and their settlements ranged from the Rio Grande Valley to the Grand Canyon. At first they lived in pit houses but later built imposing, above-ground structures. Their ceremonial kivas remained at least partially underground.

Religion dominated the daily life of the Anasazi people. It linked human beings to the world of nature as well as to families, clans, and community. It has been written that the Anasazi were/are direct line ancestors of *Pueblo* (Spanish for "village") people of the Rio Grande valley.

Archaeological evidence indicates that between 600 B.C. and 550 B.C. the early Anasazi lived in small groups that migrated into lowlands during the summer when they planted. After they harvested their crops they returned to the highlands for piñon nuts and various other foods that grew wild. It appears their agricultural and foraging activities were governed by the seasons. They used baskets as containers and they are often referred to as the "Basketmakers" during this period.

By around of 550 A.D. the Anasazi developed permanent communities close to water sources like rivers and streams. Pithouses were still dominant on the Colorado Plateau in Northern Arizona but the people in Chaco Canyon in northwestern New Mexico and those in Mesa Verde in southwestern Colorado built stone Pueblos that contained hundreds of rooms. Bows and arrows were now used for weapons. Turkeys were domesticated and beans became a staple in the diet. Pottery appeared and by ca. 950 A.D. there existed a sophisticated style with black-on-white and red-on-black designs for decoration.

Anasazi communities were mobile due to necessity. When resources were used up it was time to move. Towns lasted for some 30 to 80 years, depending on access to water and arable land.

HOHOKAM

The second dominant society to develop was the Hohokam. Where did the Hohokam come from? No one knows. Is it possible they came from Central America? Or is it that people from Central American cultures traded with the Hohokam? No one really knows.

These desert dwellers were masters of canal irrigation and this enabled them to master the desert. With little more than wooden digging sticks, the Hohokam excavated canals that could be 10 ft. wide and 15 ft. deep. They had hundreds of thousands of acres of desert land producing food for them. Settlements developed along the major canals that were built. The Hohokam dug more canals and moved more water than any other precontact society in North America. The Hohokam also controlled the flow of arroyos and created hillside terraces to control the flow of water. The Hohokam became known for their agricultural diversification. This was in addition to what the desert produced natively. They also hunted deer, bighorn sheep, rabbits, and the larger rodents like prairie dogs.

Despite alternating periods of drought and flood between A.D. 700 and 1150, the Hohokam produced a dominating red-on-buff pottery and recreated on some 200 earthen ballcourts–situated about 5.5 kilometers apart--that were found throughout Hohokam country. It has been suggested that trade fairs were held along with the games that people came to watch.

After A.D. 1100 to about 1450 there appear to have been forces that caused more centralization in Hohokam society. While cooperation was still necessary, force has been signaled as an important factor in daily living. Perhaps this was a reaction to necessary security measures. No one knows.

MOGOLLON

The Mogollon culture ranged from southeastern Arizona, southwestern New Mexico, and northern Mexico (the area known as "Apachería" when Athabascan groups moved into it at a later date). As with the Anasazi and the Hohokam, the Mogollon people made the transition from hunting and gathering to agriculture and by A.D. 200 they were at least semi sedentary and living in pit houses on high grounds above canyon valley floors. Changing weather required frequent moves by most Mogollon communities. They practiced small scale irrigation but also dry or runoff farming. They created terraces on mountain slopes and small dams to control the flow of water. Settlements grew larger after around A.D. 750 and perhaps by the year 1000 above ground stone dwellings were built in northern areas. Some archaeologists believe these northern Mogollon were absorbed by the Anasazi.

Southern Mogollon people maintained their distinct identity and their relatively large communities (from ca. 1000-1150) flourished. These settlements often consisted of at least six clusters of stone buildings which contained some thirty rooms per cluster. Large kivas gave way to plazas, probably to accommodate larger participation in ceremonial activities. Small kivas reappeared, perhaps used more or less exclusively by religious leaders.

The Mogollon produced unrivalled pottery by around 1000. Mimbres Valley potters created sophisticated pottery which proved them masters of design, employing geometric figures as well as representations of animals of the time. But by around 1150 this Classic production ended and was replaced by inferior efforts accompanied by differing architectural and communal customs. No one knows exactly why but various factors like changes in climate or social conditions have been postulated by archaeologists.

CHACO ANASAZI

It has been written that the Chaco Anasazi created perhaps the grandest precontact society in what is now the Southwest. These achievements took place around 900 to 1100 and were all but gone by 1200. Perhaps an in-depth study of Chaco Canyon will shed light on precontact people and their cultures.

Chaco Canyon has been described as a New World Heritage site. It dominated 40,000 square miles of land in the semiarid Four Corners region. It was also a vast and powerful alliance of some 10,000 and to 20,000 farming communities and perhaps 100 district towns referred to as "Great Houses" by archaeologists. Hundreds of miles of developed roadways connected the entire area.

The word "Anasazi" is a Navajo word that translates the phrase "ancestors of our enemies." The Anasazi knew how to use fire, had domesticated dogs. They had created simple tools from stone, bone, and wood. Their clothes were made from animal skins. When they came across from Siberia they did not have the bow and arrow. They used the atlatl. They hunted large game animals like the mammoth, bison, camel, horses, and the large elk. They also hunted small game and gathered edible plants. When the climate changed the great animals of the Ice Age vanished and were replaced by smaller ones, like deer, elk, antelope, bear, and bighorn sheep.

CLIMATE

From around 10,000 B.C. to about 5000 B.C. the climate of the Southwest was changing gradually, so gradually that people hardly noticed. Life was slow paced, highly mobile, and tradition ruled society. After about 5000 B.C. the Southwestern climate changed rapidly, becoming much more seasonal. The climate began on to warm up and dry out. The Four Corners area became hotter and this caused definite changes in society. By 4000 B.C. grass was sparse and a buffalo herds went north into Colorado Wyoming and Nebraska. People had to adjust and were forced to rely more and more on edible plants. Gathering became more important than hunting. The size of families became smaller due to abortion and infanticide.. The yucca root became a staple in the diet. The basic cooking technique was to heat stones over coals in the fire pit then the hot stones were put in water in which was put the food to be cooked. Life was difficult and survival no simple feat.

When the climate became wetter the grasslands reappeared and the larger game animals returned. Deer became the game animal of choice by around 3000 B.C. and the people still had their many edible plants. With a more favorable climate and a better food supply the population increased. Abortion and infanticide did not have to be used to control population growth. Then there were a couple of fortuitous occurrences: the climate got wetter and it has been estimated that abundant rainfall occurred between 2000 B.C. to 500 B.C. Second, corn was introduced from Mexico. Along with squash and later beans, these new staples became basic to the development of the Chaco Anasazi civilization.

BASKETMAKERS

The "Basketmaker" period goes roughly from A.D. 1-750. As yet there was no pottery, just beautifully woven baskets, sandals, bags, etc. The Basketmakers included experimentation in culture and economics. Foraging and hunting continued in some areas while rudimentary agriculture dominated others. Foods like corn, beans and squash were stored in baskets. Then somewhere the grinding stone *metate* and the one hand *mano* became larger in size. Better axes enabled people to cut timber. Small settlements of perhaps five dwellings were built. Pit houses of from 300 to 400 square feet in size were built in a circular figure eight pattern. These early houses also contained fire pits. Cooking with hot stones continued.

Hunting technology improved with the appearance of the bow and arrow some time between A.D. 1 and 300 but agriculture was gaining in importance.

Pottery came to the people of the Four Corners at around A.D. 300 to 400 and in time it revolutionized cooking technique because it was comparatively simple to place a cooking pot on the fire instead of heating stones and maneuvering them into skins for cooking. Food staples were corn, beans, squash, yucca, prickly pear, piñon, acorn, rabbits, rodents, and a rare deer or elk. Turkeys had been domesticated for their eggs and feathers but were rarely eaten because they were so valuable.

The "community house" emerged around A.D. 800, probably a response to the need for community organization as more families were included in society. But life continued difficult for everyone. Farming and grinding were difficult work without technological aids and most people died in their 20s, 30s, or 40s. Few people lived to the age of 50 or 60 because overwork was so common. Osteoporosis and malnutrition with its concomitant infections were common causes of death.

VILLAGES

Upland territories were most desirable for agriculture as well as foraging. Favored localities filled up and newer arrivals had to develop basin locales. It has been written that it took these foragers and hunters some 25 generations to establish semi sedentary villages and these settlements were expanding until around A.D. 800. It is believed people had to band together behind palisaded communities for security purposes. It isn't known who the invading "enemies" were. Villages were regularly abandoned after 30 or 40 years of use. In the late 800s Anasazi society moved to lower elevations.

From around 850 to 1000 the Anasazi farmers in the San Juan Basin area were having to adjust to climactic exigencies. They moved often, founded new villages, expanded wherever they could find land and water sources suitable for farming. It has been estimated that some 10,000 farmsteads were worked during these 150 years. Farmsteads were a result of "following the rains." Life was still generally difficult, characterized by overwork, seasonal hunger, broken bones, worn down or bad teeth, etc. Meat became even more scarce in farming districts as populations expanded.

GREAT HOUSES

Around the year 1000 the climate turned benevolent and stayed that way for some 130 years. Sufficient rains for farming were more or less constant. This gave rise to the "Chaco phenomenon:" great-houses were built and widely separated farming communities were connected by "roads," ritual, trade items, and sharing of culture as well as agricultural products approximately from the years 1020 to 1130. It has been postulated that the "Chaco phenomenon" developed because of open communities that valued trade and rituals that connected them. Perhaps religious ritual was the foundation for society and religious leaders became the elite members of society who were supported by everybody else.

Chaco communities have been characterized as consisting of a large sandstone kiva or great house surrounded by farmsteads. Daily life centered around seasonal activities like planting, watering, weeding, foraging, hunting when possible, and harvesting. Formal roadways were constructed after 1050 in order to connect centers of these communities.

Chaco Canyon has been described as the heartland of this Anasazi world. By 1100 there were nine great houses on the canyon floor (Pueblo del Arroyo, Pueblo Bonito, Peñasco Blanco, Una Vida, Casa Chiquita, Kin Kletso, Chetro Ketl, Wijiji, and Hungo Pavi) as well as three on top of the mesa (Pueblo Alto, Tsinkletzin, New Alto). It has been estimated that some 100,000 square meters were under roof and perhaps 215,000 trees were used for beams. This was labor intensive building because the logs had to be carried from 20 to 30 miles to the Chaco area.

Pueblo Bonito has been described as the most lavish of the great houses. It contained some 700 rooms and the floor area covered perhaps five acres. It had a total of 33 kivas, the largest one measuring around 52 feet in diameter and some 12 feet deep. Buildings were for ritual, residence, and storage but they also captured essential cycles or movements of the sun and moon. Life made few if any distinctions between the religious and the mundane but it has been postulated that Chaco had more to do with religious practice than with the secular world. But when drought hit around the 1090s the Chaco world was witnessing the beginning of the end. By 1140 it was over.

PEOPLE

Archaeological data suggests that the people of Chaco continued with the building or expansion of the great houses while ordinary farmsteads decreased or ceased altogether. It has been postulated that the people pertaining to each life style grew apart and possibly became uncommitted to each other. Farmers apparently lost their need to support elites. Ordinary farmers worked very hard and enjoyed few if any luxuries. They grew varieties of corn, squash, and gathered edible plants. When available, they ate deer, antelope, occasional turkey eggs, but more often than not the meat available was from jackrabbits, prairie dogs, and other rodents. Health conditions were poor. Burial sites indicate large numbers of children perished. At "luxurious" Chaco Canyon, children under five years of age comprised some 26% of all burials. In outlying districts the figure is around 45%. Anemia, parasites, diarrhea, and general malnutrition took the lives of young children due to crowded conditions, unpurified water, constant animal contact, and a serious lack of dietary protein and vitamins to overcome such realities. In some districts it is possible that only 50% of young people made it to age 18. Further, it has been written that 60% of those who made it past 18 were dead by 35, a disproportionate number being women in their prime child bearing years.

Women suffered from anemia, indicating an irregular food supply. They also suffered from severe dental cavities as well as arthritic conditions of the spine caused by overly demanding stoop labor or carrying too heavy loads. On the average men lived some seven years longer than women. But around 80% of all adults suffered from severe dental cavities, tooth erosion due to sandstone grit in cornmeal, and rampant periodontal disease.

Anthropological investigations indicate that the "elites" in the Chaco Canyon great houses lived much better. They were one or two inches taller so they must have enjoyed a better diet. Only slightly under 10% of their children under five died. Burial offerings like pottery or turquoise beads were often generous while they were almost non-existent in the farmsteads.

When the drought of 1090 dragged on for four years Chaco society began to decline but when the rains returned the power elites responded with traditional activities of road building, more great houses, and more ritual. But the drought that began around 1130 was the final blow, the beginning of the end. Farmers couldn't grow crops so they abandoned their farmsteads and without the farmers to grow the food there could be no "elites."

VIOLENCE

There had never been a "warrior class" in Chaco society. In the 1100s there are conclusive indications that death by violent means became a constant threat to the general population. Society appears to have fallen into chaos and there have been found mass graves of people who died violently. People moved to highland areas like Mesa Verde during these violent times but the shorter growing season and large numbers of migrants also proved a threat. Groups fought to the death in bitter hand to hand battles and sites have been excavated revealing remains of dismembered and decapitated bodies: men, women, and children, all done with flint knives or stone weapons. After the collapse of Chaco, archaeologists have estimated that some 60% of adults and perhaps 38% of children died violent deaths in the Gallina highlands. The period was one of sudden death, fear, brutality, chaos, hunger. According to archaeologists, these violent realities didn't begin to abate until around 1170.

By around 1200 society seemed to have stabilized, perhaps because it attended to defense as in the "cliff palaces" built out of protective stone. Despite the shorter growing season due to climate in the highlands, farmsteads were created and trade was renewed. Beginning around 1230 Anasazi people labored to entrench themselves in the mesa lands but enemies, intent on killing them or driving them off, were a constant threat. Life remained difficult, characterized by overwork and malnutrition. By 1300 only sites with sufficient water were still occupied.

RIVER SITES

It is estimated that from 1300 to 1500 the Anasazi permanently abandoned the San Juan Basin and moved to river sites where they built pit house communities that became villages. Each village was totally independent from the others, self sufficient and self contained like a sovereign nation. Using the land signified land ownership and boundaries were guarded against all enemies. Labor produced corn, beans, squash, as well as cotton, tobacco, and turkeys. Wild edibles like greens, seeds, roots, berries, and nuts were also gathered. The basic meats were rabbits and rodents with occasional large game like deer, antelope, or elk. Harvest festivals were held for the entire community and there were regular religious ceremonies along with group chants and various dances.

It is possible that the year 1500 was a zenith for *Pueblo* (Spanish for "village") people and their culture. There were many large villages (some generalize the number was between 100 and 200) and living conditions have been described as easier and more stable than ever before. After the brutal horrors of the 1100s and the droughts of the late 1200s it is thought that populations increased dramatically. While life was still difficult, the people wove cotton, made pottery, and created certain styles of jewelry, all of which have been described as *"a zenith in quality and variety never to be surpassed."*

CONFORMITY

In Pueblo society conformity came to be regarded as basic behavior. The village, the customs of its people and their rules came first. Those who refused to conform were driven out of the village, forced perhaps to begin a settlement of their own. The ancient clan system was still in force. While certain leaders like kiva elders, hunting captains, and medicine society elders might be described as a sort of societal elite, their status wasn't based on wealth but rather knowledge and community respect. The entire community shared good times or bad. Cooperation was the key, whether during a community hunt, cleaning out irrigation ditches, or defense against marauders. Everyone had a place through obligation to kin, ceremonial ritual, and village life.

DISCUSSION Notes *for* PRE-COLUMBIAN CIVILIZATIONS
There is a wealth of literature on precontact Amerindians. See *Those Who Came Before* by Robert H. Lister and Florence C. Lister; *Emil W. Haury's Prehistory Of The American Southwest* edited by Jefferson Reid and David Doyel; *The Chacoan Prehistory of the San Juan Basin* by R. Gwinn Vivian. *Anasazi America* by David Stuart provides perspectives that tie precontact people to the modern world, though his views on the Spanish "intrusion" are along the "Tree of Hate" school of American historiography.

Timeline: EUROPEAN EXPLORATION OF THE AMERICAS
790 A.D.
It is said that **Irish monks** reach Iceland while searching for retreats and new missionary lands.

874 A.D.
Norsemen (Vikings) led by **Eric the Red** settle in Iceland.

986:
The first Norse colony is planted on **Greenland.**

1000:
It is believed that **Leif Ericsson,** son of Eric the Red, stumbles upon the American continent when (it is sometimes said) he is blown off course while sailing from Norway to Greenland. He names the area Vinland (Wineland), now thought to have been Nova Scotia, because of the grapes he finds growing there.

1003-1006:
Thorfinn Karlsefni sets out from Greenland with three ships to settle Vinland. It is said he and his colony spent three winters somewhere on the American mainland–anywhere from Labrador to Florida–but no one is certain as to where.

1420s:
The **Norse colonies have disappeared** by around this time.
[The principal source for Norse exploration is derived from the *Norse Sagas* which are as often filled with tales of the fantastic. Artifacts have also been uncovered. For example, the Kensington Stone, found near Kensington, Minnesota, in 1898, records that Norsemen visited the area in 1362 – by which one would have to accept a probable route from Hudson's Bay up the Nelson River to its source at Lake Winnipeg and then crossing by a series of lakes and portages to central Minnesota. Depending on the writer, the Kensington Stone and various other artifacts have been labeled as authentic or forgeries.]

PORTUGAL, 1447-98:
Portugal under **Prince Henry the Navigator** (1394-1460) is mistress of the seas. (It is possible that by 1448 Portuguese mariners knew about the existence of South America.) The Portuguese **caravel,** a small vessel with broad bows, a high narrow poop (a raised deck at the stern of a sailing ship) and triangular lateen sails which aided sailing more efficiently against the wind, was crucial in this period of discovery, along with other inventions like the **magnetic compass,** the **astrolabe,** and **hydrographic charts** referred to as *portolani.* Henry sends expeditions down the west side of the African continent and also occupies the Azores, the Canaries, and Madeira.

1488: **Bartolomé Días** reaches the **Cape of Good Hope** (the southern tip of the African continent).

1498: **Vasco da Gama** sails around the Cape of Good Hope and reaches India, returning by the same route.

SPAIN, 1492:
Under Isabel of Castile and Fernando of Aragón, Spain sponsors *Cristóbal Colón,* **Christopher Columbus,** "Admiral of the Ocean Sea," to encounter the Orient by sailing west. Columbus and his men stumble across the Americas on October 12, 1492, changing the history of the world for all time because in the Americas people of enterprise would have opportunities that in Europe were more or less controlled by the aristocracy. [See Note #1. *Notes begin on page 14.*]

SPAIN, 1493:
Columbus makes his second voyage to the New World. The expedition has 17 caravels and 1500 men

in it.

ENGLAND, 1497:

Giovanni Caboto, usually referred to as **John Cabot**, a wealthy merchant from Genoa and Venice who had been living in England for some seven years, sends out expeditions that sail around southern Newfoundland in search of spices and other trade goods. [See Note #2.]

ENGLAND, 1498:

John Cabot (Giovanni Caboto) and his son **Sebastian** sail to Greenland, then Labrador, and possibly around the area of what is now referred to as Delaware in New England. (Their trading efforts aren't "successful" and John Cabot is never heard from again after 1499. Their expeditions apparently were authorized by "letters patent" from the English government.)

SPAIN, 1498:

Columbus makes his third voyage to the Americas.

SPAIN, 1499:

Peralonso Niño and **Cristóbal Guerra** lead an expedition to Venezuela where they discover the Pearl Coast. They return to Spain laden with pearls.

SPAIN, 1499-1500:

Alonso de Ojeda leads an expedition to the New World. With him are the famous pilot **Juan de la Cosa** and **Amerigo Vespucci**, the latter an employee of a Medici banking firm, now living in Seville. The mouth of the Amazon River is discovered.

PORTUGAL, 1499-1501:

Joao Fernandes, a noted seaman and small land owner of the rank of *"llavrador,"* from which is derived the name "Labrador," sails to the Greenland area. In 1501 **Gaspar Corte-Real** got to Labrador and Newfoundland then got lost, which also happened to his brother **Miguel** when he came looking for Gaspar.

SPAIN, 1500:

Vicente Yáñez Pinzón reaches the coast of Brazil.

PORTUGAL, 1500:

Pedro Alvarez Cabral reaches the coast of Brazil.

SPAIN, 1501:

Rodrigo de Bastidas explores the coast of South America from Maracaibo to the Gulf of Darien

PORTUGAL, 1501-02:

Amerigo Vespucci, now sailing for Portugal, sails to the Cape Sao Roque area then reconnoiters the coast of what is now Argentina. In the published account of the voyage he describes the area as a "New World." [See "Analysis," Note #1.]

ENGLAND, 1501-05:

It is presumed that the "Anglo-Portuguese" group known as the "Company of Adventurers to the New Found Lands" makes annual fishing voyages to the coasts of what is now New England, and possibly down the coast to what will be known as the Middle Atlantic States. [See Note 4 #2.]

SPAIN, 1502:

Columbus makes his fourth – and last – voyage to the Americas.

FRANCE, 1504:
French fishermen harvest fish from areas like Newfoundland.
SPAIN, 1508:
Sebastián de Ocampo circumnavigates Cuba, proving it isn't part of the American mainland.
SPAIN, 1508-09:
Vicente Yáñez de Pinzón and **Juan Díaz de Solís** explore the coasts of Honduras and Yucatán.
SPAIN, 1513:
Juan Ponce de León discovers Florida. [See Note # 3.]
SPAIN, 1513:
Vasco Nuñez de Balboa pushes across the Isthmus of Panama and discovers the Pacific Ocean, the first European to see that body of water.
SPAIN, 1516:
Juan Díaz de Solis sails to the mouth of the Río de la Plata in Argentina.
SPAIN, 1517:
Francisco Hernández Córdoba and **Antonio de Alaminos** explore the Yucatán Península of Mexico.
SPAIN, 1518:
Juan de Grijalva explores the Mexican coast from Yucatán to the Pánuco River.
SPAIN, 1519:
Alvarez Pineda explores the Gulf of Mexico from Florida to Vera Cruz.
SPAIN, 1519-21:
Hernando Cortés conquers Mexico with the aid of Indian allies like the Tlaxcalan warriors.
SPAIN, 1519-22:
Ferdinand Magellan, (*Fernando Magallanes, Fernao de Magalhaes*) sails out of Spain intent on finding a strait to the Moluccas. In time he enters the *Mare Pacífico* and makes it to the Philippine Islands where he is killed in a skirmish with natives. Under the command of **Sebastián del Cano**, one of his ships, the *Victoria*, makes it back to Spain, completing the first ever circumnavigation of the globe.
SPAIN, 1521:
Francisco de Gordillo explores the Atlantic coast from Florida to South Carolina.
SPAIN, 1524:
Esteban Gómez explores the Atlantic coast from Florida to Nova Scotia.
FRANCE, 1524:
Giovanni de Verrazano (*Jehan de Varrasanne*) is sent to find a waterway across the American continent. He reaches New York Harbor, Narraganset Bay, and Nova Scotia before returning to France.
SPAIN, 1524-25:
Pedro de Quexos explores up the Atlantic coast as far as 40 degrees N.L.
SPAIN, 1526-30:
Sebastian Cabot sails to the Río de la Plata then explores the Paraná and Paraguay Rivers.
ENGLAND, 1527:
The English ship *Mary Guildford* explores the North American coast from Labrador to the West Indies.

SPAIN, 1528-1536:

An expedition led by **Pánfilo de Narváez** lands in the area of Tampa Bay, Florida, with a group of some 400 colonists. After unspeakable hardships, they decide to return to Mexico but suffer a shipwreck. **Alvar Nuñez Cabeza de Vaca** is among the handful of survivors who traverse (what is now) the southern USA to make it back to Mexico City. The account of his adventures causes great interest in northern exploration.

FRANCE, 1534, -35, -36:

Jacques Cartier explores south from Newfoundland, discovers the St. Lawrence estuary and what is now **Canada**, proceeds to the future sites of Quebec and Montreal. The fur trade is begun.

SPAIN, 1539:

Fray **Marcos de Niza**, a Franciscan, and a few men, including **Esteban** who had survived with Cabeza de Vaca, approach the Zuñi villages in New Mexico. They believe they have found the fabled "Golden Cities" of Cíbola.

SPAIN, 1539-43:

Hernando de Soto lands an expedition of some 600 men in Florida and proceeds to explore the country as far west as Oklahoma.

SPAIN, 1539-42:

Francisco Vásquez de Coronado leads a force from Mexico into unknown territories as far north as Kansas. His men are the first to explore (what is now) northern Mexico, Arizona, California, New Mexico, Texas, and Oklahoma, the first to view sights like the Grand Canyon, new animals like the buffalo, and the Great Plains.

SPAIN, 1540:

Hernando de Alarcón sails from Acapulco up the Gulf of California (Sea of Cortés) and into the Colorado River in support of the Coronado expedition.

SPAIN, 1542:

Ruy López de Villalobos takes possession of the Philippine Islands for Spain.

SPAIN, 1542:

Juan Rodriguez Cabrillo sails up the California coast as far as San Francisco Bay and takes possession of the country for Spain. [See Note # 4.] Upon Cabrillo's death, **Bartolomé Ferrelo** (Ferrer) continues as far north as Oregon.

SPAIN, 1564:

Legazpi takes possession of the Moluccas Islands. He founds Manila in 1571.

SPAIN, 1565:

Pedro Menéndez de Aviles founds the settlement of St. Augustine in Florida. Knowing that scurvy was a threat to the health of his crew during passage to the Americas, Aviles loads plenty of LIMES into his boat in the Canary Islands in order to combat the health menace. [See Note # 5.]

ENGLAND, 1576-1606:

Martin Frobisher makes three trips to the New World, looking for gold and the *Northwest Passage*. He finds neither. **John Davis** also makes three trips, with no success. **George Weymouth** and **John Knight** also make unsuccessful trips.

ENGLAND, 1577-80:

Though England and Spain are not at war, England's grasping Queen Elizabeth sends out **Francis Drake** to steal as much gold as possible from Spanish ships and settlements. Since the attacks are unexpected, Drake is successful in his thieveries and circumnavigates the globe in the process of fleeing from Spanish retribution and returning to England. (So Drake duplicates the earlier feat of Magellan in 1519-22.)

SPAIN, 1596:

Sebastián Vizcaíno establishes a colony at La Paz.

1602: He reexplores the entire California coast and discovers Monterey Bay.

SPAIN, 1598:

Juan de Oñate leads a colony to New Mexico, *San Juan de los Caballeros* (Knights of St. John), some 1400 miles from Mexico City and perhaps 700 miles from Santa Barbara, the next closest Hispanic settlement. The settlement is surrounded by around 40,000 Pueblo Indians and much more numerous Navajo and Apache nations. Oñate explores the area from Kansas to the Gulf of California. *Santa Fe* is founded by around 1607-08.

FRANCE, 1603:

Samuel de Champlain makes his first voyage to Canada.

1604: Champlain makes his second voyage to Canada, leading a group of "gentlemen traders" interested in developing the fur trade.

1605: Champlain and his colonists build the first French settlement in North America on the shores of Port Royal Bay.

1608: *Quebec* is founded by Samuel de Champlain.

ENGLAND, 1607:

Jamestown, Virginia is founded as a trading center.

HOLLAND, 1609:

Henry Hudson is employed to search for the (non-existent) Northwest Passage. He explores coastal areas from Newfoundland to Virginia. In 1610 he sails through Hudson Strait and explores the east side of Hudson Bay.

SPAIN, 1629:

Father **Juan de Salas**, accompanied by Fr. Diego López and three soldiers, travels some 112 leagues east of Albuquerque (into what is now Texas) and makes contact with the Jumano Indians.

1632: Fr. Salas goes to the Jumanos once again, finding them by a stream of water named the *Nueces* (a branch of the Colorado River, probably the Concho), some 200 leagues southeast of Santa Fe.

FRANCE, 1642:

Montreal (*Ville Marie de Montréal*) is founded by settlers led by a devout young woman named Jeanne Mance and the valiant soldier Paul de Chomedey, *Sieur de Maisonneuve*.

SPAIN, 1659:

The Mission, Nuestra Señora de Guadalupe, is founded in *El Paso*, Texas, by **Fray García de San Francisco.**

FRANCE, 1673:

Louis Jolliet and **Father Marquette** go down the Mississippi as far as Arkansas.

FRANCE, 1678-82:

René Robert Cavelier de **La Salle** explores the area traversed by the Mississippi River, establishing important outposts like Fort Frontenac and Saint Louis in the process. France could now claim the interior of the North American continent, referring to it as "*Louisiana*" in honor of King Louis.

SPAIN, 1690:

The first Spanish settlements are established in Texas (El Paso was a part of N.M.), near the Nueces River.

RUSSIA, 1728-1741:

Vitus Bering, "a Dane in Russian service," makes a series of voyages in which he discovers the Bering Strait, explores the Aleutian Islands, discovers and names Mt. St. Elias.

SPAIN, 1768:

Fray **Francisco Hermenegildo Garcés**, a Franciscan, is the first European to visit the Pápagos at their Gila River village. He travels alone.

1770: Fray Garcés visits more Pápagos villages.

1771: Fray Garces makes contact with the Yuma Indians and their great chief Salvador Palma. (Garcés crosses the deadly desert land twice.)

SPAIN, 1769:

Father **Junípero Serra** founds Mission San Diego, the first Spanish European settlement in the (Alta) California mission system, the beginning of modern California. [See Note # 6.]

SPAIN, 1774:

Juan Bautista de Anza leads an expedition from Sonora to Mission San Gabriel (CA.), thence over Portolá's trail to Monterey, California.

1776: Anza returns to Tubac and leads a successful colonizing expedition over burning deserts and snow-clad mountains to San Francisco, California.

[See Note # 7.]

SPAIN, 1776:

Father Silvestre de **Escalante** and Father Francisco A. **Dominguez** lead a 2,000 mile expedition ("*without noise of arms*") that explores regions of the Great Basin (now known as Colorado, Utah, and Arizona).

SPAIN, 1787:

Pedro Vial and **Cristóbal de los Santos** blaze a trail from San Antonio, Texas, to Santa Fe, New Mexico.

1787: José Mares, **Cristóbal de los Santos**, and **Alejandro Martin** duplicate Vial's feat in reverse, from Santa Fe to San Antonio.

SPAIN, 1792:

Pedro Vial, accompanied by **Vicente Villanueva** and **Vicente Espinosa**, blaze a trail to San Luis (St. Louis), Missouri. (Their route later becomes famous as the "*Santa Fe Trail*.")

ENGLAND, 1793:

Alexander Mackenzie crosses the North American continent from east to west (from the Montreal area

to what is now British Columbia) and back again, the first Britisher to reach the Pacific Ocean overland.
UNITED STATES, 1803-06:

The **Lewis and Clark** Expedition, referred to as the "Corps of Discovery," goes down the Ohio River and up the Missouri. The men winter in the region of the Mandan Indians (near present Bismarck, N.D.). By November of 1805 they are in view of the Pacific Ocean and are back in St. Louis by September of 1806. [See Note # 8.]

DISCUSSION Notes *for* EUROPEAN EXPLORATION OF THE AMERICAS

Note # 1

Because of the letters written by Amerigo Vespucci, a geographer named Martin Waldseemüler suggested the New World should be named "*America, because Americus discovered it.*" Though it wasn't true, the name "*America*" caught on as the label for the New World, named after a bank clerk who happened to make a couple of voyages to the new lands discovered by Columbus.

Note # 2

A steady tenet of American historiography is that anyone now speaking English, no matter what nationality/ethnicity, is referred to as an "Anglo" if being written about in English and pertaining to the USA. Use of the ethnic label "Anglo" or "Anglo American" must be understood when studying Southwest history.

People who speak languages that evolved out of Latin are described as "Latins." English, Norwegian, Icelandic, Swedish, Dutch, Afrikaans, Flemish, etc., developed out of German and are referred to as "Germanic languages" so why aren't the people referred to as "Germanic"? The preferred label is *Anglo*, which supposedly connects someone to the (Germanic) tribe of Angles who entered England around the 5th century. When studying Southwest history one is certain to run across the phrase "Anglo-American" applied to all kinds of people, whether German, Irish, Italian, French, Czech, Latvian, Lithuanian, etc. Is this merely a device to establish a "majority/minority" system? The implication that whole groups of immigrants, most of whom have Ellis Island as a heritage, are descended from the Germanic tribe of *Angles* who settled in England in the 5th century A.D., is ludicrous. The Angles were just one of the many Germanic groups who settled northern Europe. Saxons from Germany also went into England. Celts, Visigoths, Ostrogoths, Vandals, Suevi, etc., are just a few of other examples of Germanic groups who are ignored by using "Anglo" as if it was the only acceptable Germanic tribe. Is it anti-German prejudice that doesn't permit American writers to use "Germanic" to describe themselves or other people from northern Europe? The "Anglo" connection to England is made even more tenuous when we observe that the people of England refer to themselves as "Brits," not *Anglos*.

Why don't we see "Hispano-Portuguese" or "Franco-Italian"? The Orwellian (from **George Orwell** who wrote the "classics" *Animal Farm* and *1984* in which the use of language is recognized as powerful as any weapon of mass destruction; Orwell structures, referred to as "Doublespeak" and "Doublethink," are "employed to make lies sound truthful and can give wind the appearance of something solid") and psychology aren't applied to paladins from other countries. Further,

English language writers generally point out that heroes like Ferdinand Magellan was really *Fernao Magalhaes*, a Portuguese who *merely happened* to be sailing for Spain. Likewise, *Jehan de Varrasanne*, a Florentine by birth who sailed under the French flag, is written about as Giovanni de Verrazano, while *Giovanni Caboto*, an Italian who sailed for England, is promoted as *John Cabot*.

It must be pointed out, especially when dealing with the Hispanic Southwest, that the "Anglo American" caricature is an Orwellian device intended to imply a connection with England, which is basically fantasy, as well as a sense of *"We're the superior majority"* racism.

The preceding points aren't intended as mere polemics. These perspectives should be discussed in an open, tolerant manner because they are as basic as they are crucial to understanding Southwest History.

Note # 3

One of the popular fantasies of American historiography is that Ponce de León was searching for the "Fountain of Youth" when he discovered Florida. This historical hoax is more indicative of Hispanophobia and is tantamount to asserting he was looking for Disney World. Youthful vigor has probably been a desirable trait throughout history but "Fountain of Youth" myths and legends can be found in "King Arthur" fantasies but should never be promoted in valid historiography. Might it be an effective device in *propaganda?*

Note # 4

American historiography is often suspect because of its propagandistic cultural bias. A case in point is information provided in the *Encyclopedia Of American History*, 1965, edited by Richard B. Morris with Henry Steele Commager as Chief Consultant Editor. On page 23 we are told in Orwellian fashion that in 1542 Juan Rodríguez Cabrillo *"…sailed up the California Coast to Drake's Bay and took possession of the country for Spain."* Francis Drake (1543?-1596) might have been one year old at the time of Rodriguez Cabrillo's discovery so how is it that reference is being made to "Drake's Bay" some 37 years before Drake might have been on it? This ploy could be described as popular scriptography. It certainly isn't valid historiography. It should also be clarified that the so-called "Drake's Bay" (described by eye witness Francis Fletcher as having *"white bancks and cliffes, which lie toward the sea"* and quoted by Charles E. Chapman in *A History Of California: The Spanish Period*) is neither Bodega Bay nor San Francisco Bay.

Note # 5

Thus it was that Spain's "Manila galleons" conducted trade with the Orient. Voyages were long, the food was bad, and scurvy was terrible until *"…galleons sometimes stopped on the Sinaloa coast to find relief from citrus fruits"* writes H.E. Bolton. Then he adds: *"The story that the cure was first discovered by Captain Cook in 1776 is ANOTHER ENGLISH MYTH. In fact, two centuries earlier, Menéndez de Aviles, on his way from Spain to found St. Augustine in Florida, stopped at the Canary Islands for a supply of LIMES to prevent the ravages of SCURVY."* (Emphasis mine.)

It is at once astounding and appalling at how some writers have confused the historical record, endowing the people of England with achievements effected by people from other countries. It is so serious that this form of propaganda could be described as a recognizable pathology. Stuart

Udall, author of *Majestic Journey*, writes that the Reverend Richard Hakluyt, author of *Principal Navigations, Voyages and Discoveries of the English Nation*, was a master of this type of propaganda, so adept at it that he could be considered the "Father of English Propaganda."

Note # 6

There are writers who have stated that California belonged to England by right of discovery because Drake supposedly was around San Francisco Bay in 1579. Few people are familiar with "the rest of the story" because if you investigate the historical record Drake was in reality the Osama bin Laden of the 16th century, stealing from and destroying Spanish ships and settlements, killing untold numbers of innocent people during his robberies.

England and Spain were not at war but England's Queen Elizabeth I, an unsavory personality who, among other personal habits, bragged she had taken a bath only twice in her life, but routinely portrayed as good for the country, sent Drake out to steal Spanish gold and silver wherever possible on the high seas or coastal settlements. Since no state of war existed, the pickings were easy, much like the 9-11 attacks on the World Trade Center. Francis Drake, billed as a "swashbuckler" to soften his record of thieveries, was a product of state sponsored terrorism. When Francis Drake returned to England his Queen made him a "Knight of the Realm" because he had been such a successful thief. Indeed, the stolen loot enabled the formation of the Bank of England and the East India Company so perhaps in England he was a "hero," much like Osama bin Laden has been to his terrorist cohorts. "Sir" Francis Drake's "swashbuckling" thieveries have been glossed over due to cultural bias, a bias that continues into the present day.

The Spanish Armada attacked Britain in 1588 because so many English pirates were preying on Spanish shipping but today Spanish motivation is generally attributed to "religious wars" in order to deflect England's state sponsored terrorism of the day. Was Drake a hero because he stole from Spain and killed Hispanic people? Was Osama bin Laden because of 9-11-01?

English history has been protected by American historiographers so few people understand that England was the leading slave-trading nation of the Western world because she ruled the seas and slave trading earned huge profits.

The East India Company began shipping opium to China in 1773 and within some fifty years was making a profit of some four million pounds sterling a year from this drug trade. The Chinese government prohibited the importation or sale of opium but the British government did everything it could to promote it. [See page 125 in *Gunfighters, Highwaymen, and Vigilantes* by Roger D. McGrath.] By the 1830s the British treasury was earning three and a half million pounds sterling from the immoral trade. When the Chinese government made serious efforts to stop the influx of opium in 1838-39 the English waged the Opium War (1840-42) which resulted in an English victory. In the Treaty of Nanking, China was forced to open more of her ports to the English and cede Hong Kong. The British now had a base from which to pour opium into China.

English atrocities in places like Ireland, in the American colonies, India, etc., are unpublicized and the popular mind is led to believe that Spain and institutions like the Spanish Inquisition have been the principal perpetrators of the world's enormous, inhuman cruelties. As Philip

Wayne Powell has written in his classic *Tree of Hate*, the printing press has been the most effective of all propaganda tools.

Note # 7

Anza's achievement, blazing a trail to California then returning to Mexico and leading a colony to San Francisco Bay, is unparalleled in American history. H.E. Bolton and his school of historians are among the few who laud this great knight of the Southwest.

Note # 8

Black Legend literature generally reports information on the European diseases contracted by Native Americans basically where Spain and its people explored/settled. The issue of diseases appears to be reserved for Hispanic people in Spanish lands and is studiously avoided east of the Mississippi. For example, the smallpox carried within the Lewis and Clark expedition, which all but exterminated the Mandan Indians, is seldom mentioned and never publicized.

CHAPTER 2

First Europeans In The Southwest

The first organized incursion by Europeans into what is now called the "American Southwest" was led by **Francisco Vásquez de Coronado**. [See Note # 1. *Notes begin on page 24.*] This reconnaissance in force included some 336 soldiers, most of them mounted. There were five religious, one of whom was Fray **Marcos de Niza**, who had brought back tales of rich lands to the north. Three women were in the expedition: **María Maldonado**, who served as a nurse; **Francisca de Hozes**, wife of a shoemaker; and the "native" wife of Lope Caballero. There were also some 700 Indian auxiliaries who performed various duties and herded the large numbers of livestock brought along for food or transport. The jumping off point was in the locale of Compostela some 500 miles northwest of Mexico City. All participants were mustered and sent off on February 22, 1540. [See Note # 2.]

VÁSQUEZ DE CORONADO

Francisco Vásquez de Coronado, Captain General of the expedition, was around thirty years old. He was of a noble family from Salamanca but he was the *segundón* (second son; the first son generally inherited all titles and lands) so he voyaged to the New World to make his fortune, arriving with America's first Viceroy, **Antonio de Mendoza**. Vásquez de Coronado married **Beatriz de Estrada** in Mexico. Francisco had held various posts in government when Mendoza selected him to lead the northern exploration into new lands.

MENDOZA

Viceroy Mendoza was a devout Christian as well as a friend of Bishop **Bartolomé de las Casas**, Spain's herculean Protector of the Indians. [See Note # 3.] Mendoza was determined the *entrada* (entry) would be a Christian effort, not a butchery as had occurred under some leaders in other places. [See Note # 4.] This is one of the reasons why he selected Vásquez de Coronado to lead the expedition, instructing him to treat the Indians as if they were Spaniards, i.e., Christians. He also ordered that Indians in the expedition not be used as carriers for equipment and supplies. Spaniards were a mining people but while the quest included the search for gold and other such riches, Mendoza understood that missionary efforts were of equal importance: Christianity would be brought to pagan people to prepare them for everlasting life in Heaven. [See Note # 5.] **Pedro de Castaneda**, a soldier who was also a talented chronicler, recorded the history of the expedition (and became the "Father of Southwest History" in the process).

Mendoza went to Compostela to be part of the final ceremony. On Sunday he joined everyone at mass then took part in the parade. He made a speech in which he emphasized the importance of God, their King, and their Captain General. If the venture was a success there would be benefits for everyone. Vásquez de Coronado was sworn in then each soldier did the same by placing his right hand on a cross and prayer book and swearing to serve God, King, and Francisco Vásquez de Coronado *as a gentleman should to the best of his ability and intelligence.*

With Viceroy Mendoza accompanying the expedition along the trail for two days before turning back for home, thus began the northward march, the longest of the 16th century. [See Note # 6.]

THE TRAIL

The trail north from Compostela took the expedition through five different life zones, from semi-tropical to alpine. These valiant sons of Spain went from marshes at sea level through the forbidding Sonoran Desert to mountain pine forests in Arizona.

VANGUARD

Captain **Melchor Díaz** entered the picture when he brought Vásquez de Coronado a message from Viceroy Mendoza. Díaz also informed the Captain General that the Cíbola Indians he had encountered knew nothing of gold or other precious metals, the first indication casting negative light on "Cities of Gold." Because of his versatile talents ranging from mayor of Culiacán to expert frontiersman, Díaz was selected to be the vanguard for the expedition.

Díaz alerted Vásquez de Coronado to the fact that a deadly desert area, referred to as a *despoblado* (unpopulated wilderness), lay beyond the presently bountiful land so food would be scarce to non-existent. Vásquez de Coronado decided to lead 80 horsemen and a group of foot soldiers into Cíbola while the main expedition under the direction of **Tristán de Arellano** made its way to a camp in the Valley of Hearts area (in the Sonora Valley of Mexico between Ures and Babiacora) to await further orders.

ARIZONA

Vásquez de Coronado and his contingent were in the desert country of (present day) Arizona southeast of Tucson in late May of 1540. They made their arduous way to a place called *Chichilticale* by the local Indians then headed toward the Gila River and its surrounding "impassable" mountains. Beyond the Gila range were treeless grasslands and tablelands leading to the rocky ledges of the Nantack Ridge where the horses became so exhausted *"...they could not endure it."* But when this latter obstacle was conquered the group made it to a comforting pine forest with plenty of water and grass.

ZUNI

After a much needed rest, Vásquez de Coronado led his men to Zuñi (Hawikuh) where they encountered the first Indian village in the land called Cíbola. The men were almost out of food so the young

García López de Cárdenas was sent ahead to see if a trade could be set up while also precluding a surprise attack. López de Cárdenas made camp at a spot known as "Bad Pass" because the Zuñis made a midnight attack on the encampment (the first skirmish between Europeans and Native Americans in what is today referred to as the American West). The ambush was repulsed and the next day the group made its way to where they could catch a glimpse of the "golden city." The view wasn't promising for the village appeared to be ordinary buildings thrown together haphazardly.

Vásquez de Coronado now took charge and made his way to the sacred cornmeal line that the Zuñis had made outside the village. He offered gifts and spoke for conciliation. The Zuñis launched an attack (July 7, 1540) whereupon the intrepid Vásquez de Coronado let loose the traditional Spanish war cry: ¡*Santiago y a Ellos*! (St. James and at them!) A battle royal raged for perhaps an hour, the gallant Captain General being the foremost target for Zuñi arrows and rock missiles. The warriors succeeded in knocking Vásquez de Coronado off his horse and he would have been killed had not García López de Cárdenas and Hernando de Alvarado thrown themselves on him, taking all blows from more rocks, then dragging him away to safety. While the Zuñis, using their weapons with skill and determination, had great numbers as their advantage, Spanish valor and weaponry routed them, the Indians fleeing to the hills. The Spaniards then went into the village where they found great storehouses of corn and beans, at the moment worth much more than any gold or silver.

No signs of precious metals were to be found. Vásquez de Coronado wrote to Viceroy Mendoza that nothing fray Marcos de Niza had said was true, *everything was the reverse.* There were no "cities of gold" if Zuñi was any indication. Fray Marcos had allowed his imagination to run away with him, it appeared. The young Captain General was probably as disappointed as his men. He also had to contend with his serious head wound. But Vásquez de Coronado proved why he was the Viceroy's new "Cortés." Fray Marcos was sent back to Mexico but don Francisco didn't behave harshly toward him nor was there an effort to make him a scapegoat. He wrote to Mendoza that there was little chance that farmer Indians in this part of the world would have gold or silver. Was the expedition a failure? Yes, since there was no gold, but perhaps there were other discoveries to be made. There would be no immediate return to Mexico City. If there was something to be found, he would search for it and at the least he would explore this portion of the New World brought into European orbit by the gallant sons of Spain and their Amerindian auxiliaries. The report was sent on August 3, 1540.

EXPLORATION

Vásquez de Coronado went about the business of exploring most of what is today referred to as the "American Southwest." His captains led expeditions to northern Sonora, California, the Grand Canyon, the Río Grande Valley, the Texas plains, and up to (what is now) Kansas. (The year was 1540 and no other expedition approached covering as much territory until centuries later with Lewis and Clark in 1804-06.)

CAPTAINS

Melchor Díaz, a fearless, energetic "commoner" (described by Stuart Udall as "heroic," America's "first frontiersman," "our first mountain man") was perhaps the most stalwart of Vásquez de Coronado's valiant captains. One of his men described Diaz as a *"beloved leader who accomplished what he did because of merit."* He was a talented individual who excelled as a frontiersman as well as in his administrative duties as Mayor of Culiacán. After the battle of Zuñi (Hawikuh), the Captain General told Díaz to return to the Sonora Valley and instruct the waiting army to move into Cíbola country. Then he was to go west into unexplored desert territory, locate the supply ships commanded by **Hernando de Alarcón**, and transport all supplies to San Gerónimo, the new base of operations in Sonora.

After alerting the army as to their new orders, Díaz led his men to the Colorado River where he found the message **Hernando de Alarcón**, captain of the flotilla, had ensconced in a tree some two months ago before returning to Mexico, without leaving the supplies because there was no one to safeguard them. It is believed Díaz explored up the mighty Colorado for some fifty leagues. He became the first European to step onto California soil. Somewhere on the trail Melchor Díaz suffered a mortal wound when a lance he had thrown somehow resulted in an injury that took the life of this intrepid paladin a few days later.

Pedro de Tovar was sent to the Hopi (Tusayan) villages. In his retinue was "the fighting friar," fray **Juan de Padilla**. At Antelope Mesa the Hopis warned the Spaniards to leave and a line of cornmeal was made in the sand. Words gave way to a scuffle then to a spirited attack by both sides. Indian clubs and arrows couldn't vanquish Spanish steel and the warriors were soon routed. Hopi elders then came up with gifts and asked for peace. Tovar and his men were then permitted to visit the other Hopi villages, probably including Old Oraibi (Third Mesa, which has been described as the oldest continuously inhabited town in the USA, along with Acoma and Taos). The basic discovery made by Tovar was that there existed a large river west of Hopi country.

Upon receiving this information, Vásquez de Coronado decided to send **García López de Cárdenas** at the head of a larger force to locate the river and discover if it lead to the South Sea (Pacific Ocean). García López de Cárdenas and his men returned to the Hopis and acquired guides who knew the trail to the big river. In short order they were viewing the (South Rim) Grand Canyon. The river far below appeared to be a mere stream but a party of rock climbers, led by **Pablo de Melgosa,** was instructed to descend and fill some water containers. They got about a third of the way down before they decided the descent was too great a task from the present location. The Hopis warned them that there was no other water available in the area so García López de Cárdenas returned to Zuñi (Hawikuh) and presented his report to the Captain General.

A couple of natives, nicknamed *"Cacique"* and *"Bigotes"* by the Europeans, entered the Spanish encampment and offered to serve as guides if the Captain General wished to see the villages in the Río Grande Valley or the immense herds of wild cattle to the east of those settlements. **Hernando de Alvarado** was given twenty men and eighty days to go and return. Fray Juan de Padilla was in Alvarado's contingent.

ACOMA

Alvarado's first stop (August/September, 1540) was at Acoma. Fortified in their "Sky City," the Acomas were considered the *"combative eagles of Puebloland."* With the *"tall, robust…"* gregarious Bigotes as mediator, the Acomas descended peacefully from their fortress and held a ceremony where gifts were exchanged. A few Spaniards were taken up to see the village itself. Friendship was established.

ISLETA & RÍO GRANDE VILLAGES

Next the Alvarado contingent was led to the area of Isleta Pueblo where camp was made. Bigotes went upstream to make contact with the twelve villages, called Tiguex Province by the Spaniards. The following day Bigotes reappeared with a number of chieftains and ordinary people who marched around with a man playing a flute. A spokesman presented Alvarado with gifts of food, cotton cloth, and skins. Once more, friendship was established and the Hispanic contingent obtained permission to travel through the Tiguex area (approximately from Isleta to Bernalillo). It was harvest season and Alvarado noted in his journal that the valley farmlands were heavy in corn, beans, melons, turkeys, as well as groves of cottonwood. He also noted that the people were apparently dedicated to agriculture and not war.

The visitors continued up the Río Grande Valley to the villages (now called) Santo Domingo, San Felipe, Cochití. They made their way into the Española Valley and visited San Ildefonso, Santa Clara, San Juan, and San Gabriel. By October they were in Taos, the most populated of all the villages according to Alvarado. It was getting cold so Alvarado returned to the Tiguex area and sent riders to inform Vásquez de Coronado that winter camp should be made there instead of northern areas like Taos.

Alvarado now turned east to investigate the cattle Bigotes had talked about. They got to Pecos Pueblo, Bigotes' home town, and were once more greeted with a friendly ceremony inside the fortress city. It was larger than the other villages and contained houses "*four or five stories high.*" Pecos controlled the route used to get to the plains where the wild cattle provided sustenance for successful hunters.

QUIVIRA

Bigotes selected two captives being held by the Pecos, **Sopote** (an Indian from the Quivira country) and **El Turco** (a Kansas Indian), to guide the visitors to the buffalo country. When the Spaniards gazed upon the immense herds of animals they were astonished at their numbers, Alvarado comparing them to "…*fish in the sea.*" Trying to get around a herd was all but impossible because there were so many animals. The bulls had "wicked horns" and killed several horses until the men learned the pike "…*was the best weapon to use against them, or the musket when this misses.*" The meat was described as better than beef.

While on the buffalo plains, the Turk began talking about a rich land far to the east, a land full of "*gold, silver, and fabrics, an abundance of everything.*" He mentioned that Bigotes back at Pecos had a golden bracelet he had gotten from the Quivira country. Alvarado decided to end his exploration and return to Pecos, determined to inform Vásquez de Coronado of this new development. Alvarado apparently believed the Turk when he said Bigotes was hiding gold and information on it.

ARMY at TIGUEX

Vásquez de Coronado brought up his army from its southern encampment to the province of Tiguex where a southern village, Alcanfor, was ordered vacated for the Spaniards to occupy as a base of operations. (No one knows why it was necessary to have the army spend the winter in this colder climate.) The army necessitated more supplies and these were requisitioned from the Pueblo people who became resentful of the newcomers taking advantage of their largesse. Furthermore, the Captain General's mediator and envoy extraordinary, Bigotes, was now in chains, accused of "holding out" riches from the people he had befriended.

Captain **Tristán de Arellano** led the army (the men might have been the first Europeans to see *El Morro*, Inscription Rock) into Alcanfor in December of 1540. Skirmishes between Indians and Spaniards had already occurred. It is puzzling that the Captain General had established friendly relations with the Zuñis but somehow this changed at Tiguex. The Spanish demanded winter clothes or took them at will. Resentful Indians killed horses. Cárdenas led an assault against the village of Arenal. European weaponry defeated native arrows and war clubs. Some thirty warriors were burned at the stake in typical 16th century European fashion.

Unconditional surrender was now demanded from all Tiguex villages. Many warriors retreated to Moho, their strongest village, and prepared to fight for their lives. Vásquez de Coronado himself took command and laid siege to the village for the entire winter. When the war finally ended it had cost some 200 Indian dead, at least ten Spaniards, and twelve villages burned or abandoned. Trust was now absolutely destroyed.

[With the exception of the incomparable Hernán Cortés, Conqueror of Mexico, Francisco Vásquez de Coronado has been described as the most humane and generous of Hispanic leaders dealing with Amerindians during this brutal century. As far as rationale, motivation, result, etc., are concerned, the Tiguex War is inexplicable. See Note # 7.]

CORONADO to KANSAS

In the spring of 1541 Vásquez de Coronado prepared to travel east to the buffalo country. When the contingent of thirty men, including the gallant fray Juan de Padilla, hit the trail that summer the Captain General was awed by the bison a few days out of Pecos: "*There was not a single day that we lost sign of them…*" such was their numbers. The Querecho Indians were encountered living close to the herds, their belongings pulled by large dogs (domesticated wolves?). They lived entirely off the buffalo and traded surplus buffalo items with the village Indians to the west.

The Turk and the Querechos became guides for the Spaniards while they explored the *Llano Estacado*, "palisaded plains," so named because from a distance table lands appeared to be stockaded villages, [See Note # 8.] a flat, featureless landscape that reminded Vásquez de Coronado of the sea because "*…there was no stone, tree, shrub, or hill*" to serve as a marker. It would be extremely easy to lose one's way in this country teeming with bison, antelope, and wolves. Nevertheless, the enterprising Captain General sent out his "*…captains and men*" in many directions to explore the country to see what value it held.

The Hispanic explorers made their way to the Arkansas River in the Quivira country (to the area of what is now Ford, Kansas). It was learned that an Indian trail traversed the country from Quivira to Pecos Pueblo. The Quivira Indians were friendly, hunted the buffalo, grew corn and lived in permanent thatched houses throughout the year. The men were very tall, some approaching seven feet, and the women looked more like Moors than Indians. Vásquez de Coronado wrote his King that "*the country is the best I have seen for producing all the products of Spain.*" Juan Jaramillo described Quivira (Kansas) as good as any he had seen in Spain, Italy, or France. He also felt there was a "*…profit to be made in the cattle…which are in such quantity that it could only be imagined.*"

ACCIDENT

Francisco Vásquez de Coronado suffered a serious concussion when he was out riding and his saddle girth broke. A hoof hit the Captain General in the head as he fell. All believed he was at the point of death. His recovery was as slow as it was doubtful but he pulled through.

After some twenty-five days of exploring the Captain General took a vote and the contingent decided to head back for home in Tiguex in April of 1542. Vásquez de Coronado reported to his King that his men had endured all sorts of hardships on their 3,000 mile trek. It was now a certainty that there was no gold or precious minerals of any kind in this remote land. And it was too far away to establish colonies. A few wanted to stay and hold the country but the Captain General refused to divide his forces.

FRANCISCANS

The Franciscan friars were not bound by civil authority so friar **Juan de Padilla**, who had explored as much new country as any other individual, declared his intention to stay and work for bringing the Indians to Christianity. The elderly lay brother fray **Luis de Ubeda** decided to stay with Padilla, making the Pecos village his home base. (Ubeda's fate is unknown but Father Juan de Padilla was quickly martyred in the spring of 1542 when he returned to the Kansas country, becoming the first Christian martyr of the Southwest.)

The expedition made it back to Tiguex without incident and within two months all were back in Culiacán where the group was disbanded. Thus closed the first European incursion into what is now the American Southwest. It was 1542 but no other exploration would approach it in scope or valor, lifting the curtain on this great expanse of land for the European world. [See Note # 9.]

DISCUSSION Notes *for* FIRST EUROPEANS IN THE SOUTHWEST

Note # 1

For positive treatments of don Francisco and his expedition see *Coronado: Knight Of Pueblos And Plains* by Herbert E. Bolton and *Majestic Journey: Coronado's Inland Empire* by Stewart L. Udall.

Note # 2

Stuart Udall writes that American history forged by Spaniards has been ignored by American historians, *"robbing us of our Spanish century."* It should be added that when it isn't ignored, it's often denigrated. For example, consider the *"requerimiento,"* the required notification to newly encountered Indians. This gave notice that fealty to the King was required and that Indians would now be accepted into the Christian Faith. This requirement, read in Spanish unless there was someone who could speak the Indian tongue, is often ridiculed by English language writers. There are probably many reasons for such a response, some of them valid, but is it possible the overriding motivation is that Indians east of the Mississippi, who were either exterminated/exiled to Oklahoma by the English and later Americans, were never extended even this modicum of respect? English Sir Jeffrey Amherst considered Indians *"an execrable race"* fit only for extermination so he fought them by giving them gifts of smallpox infected blankets. At a later date

American General Sheridan remarked: *"The only good Indians I know are dead,"* providing the basis for the motto of Manifest Destiny. Salvador de Madariaga put it succinctly: Spain had to be wrong so that its enemies could be right.

Note # 3

No other country produced as herculean a defender as Bartolomé de Las Casas. No one with enough authority defended the Indians against extermination under England, exile or extermination under the USA. In more recent times, no one dared stand up to the Nazis in their extermination of Jews and in the USA Japanese Americans were removed from their west coast homes and forced into barbed wire compounds in the interior without anyone speaking up for constitutionally guaranteed civil rights. Las Casa and his fellow missionaries stand virtually alone for their moral courage in the modern world.

Note # 4

Spaniards are often portrayed as cruel and ruthless, no matter what documented evidence exists to the contrary. As various writers have observed, American historiography is written in terms of "heroes and villains," resulting in pervasive cultural bias when depicting "villainous, Catholic Spain" and its people. See *Truth In History* by Oscar Handlin, especially chapters 3 and 13. See also Phillip W. Powell, *Tree Of Hate: Propaganda and Prejudices Affecting United States Relations with the Hispanic World*.

Note # 5

Queen Isabel took seriously her responsibility to propagate the Christian Faith. She decreed that the Indians of the New World would be proselytized into Christianity in order to enable them to achieve everlasting salvation. Bartolomé de Las Casas became the Queen's champion and fought his countrymen when victorious Spaniards demanded that Indians be made slaves for the economic gain of the owners. (See *The Spanish Struggle For Justice In The Conquest Of America* by Lewis Hanke.) He combated any Spaniard, whether from a high station in life or low, in defense of the Indians, which caused much hatred to be directed at him personally. It has been said that if the conquistador was on one side of a Spanish coin, the missionary was on the other. Missionaries proved as heroic as the conquistadores because Spanish religiosity empowered them to defend Amerindians against determined men who sought to use the defeated to enrich themselves. Las Casas is one of Spain's most heroic personalities, an individual who should be lauded by all Christendom. There was no Las Casas in the English colonies on the eastern seaboard to defend the Indians so they were mostly exterminated. There was no American Las Casas so Indians in the USA were forced to choose between extermination or exile to reservations. And there was no Las Casas in Nazi Germany to prevent the wholesale extermination of the Jews.

Note # 6

The herculean feats of Spanish discovery, exploration, and settlement are often excluded from the realm of "American History." Charles F. Lummis wrote in "The Miracle of San Felipe" (from his *A New Mexico David And Other Stories*):

"*I hope some day to see a real history of the United States; a history not written in a closet, from other one-sided affairs, but based on a knowledge of the breadth of our history, and a disposition to do it justice, a book which will realize that the early history of this wonderful country is not limited to a narrow strip on the Atlantic seaboard, but that it began in the great Southwest; and that before the oldest of the Pilgrim Fathers had been born, swarthy Spanish heroes were colonizing much of what is now the United States; in their little corner of which they suffered for three hundred and fifty years such awful dangers and hardships as our Saxon forefathers did not dream of. I hope to see such a history, which will do justice to perhaps the most wonderful pioneers the world has ever produced, but it has not come yet …*

Europeans have always valued monetary riches. Spaniards were not alone in that but they were unique in that they also valued Christianizing the aborigines. With the possible exception of the Catholic French, no other European people held Christianizing Amerindians as a priority. The motivation was propagated by the pious Queen Isabel (Elizabeth) of Spain. (See *Isabella Of Spain: The Last Crusader* by William T. Walsh.)

Note # 7

Hernán Cortés is considered the most talented and accomplished of the Spanish conquistadores, the personification of an immortal Spanish hero. Because of cultural bias, Cortés is little known by the American public, and what has entered the popular mind is often negative. (See *Conquistadors In North American History* by Paul Horgan.) Cortés was a warrior as well as a diplomat, a military general and man of letters, a ferocious enemy and usually a magnanimous conqueror, a sincerely religious man who kept his word and came to be trusted by the Native American people whom he led when he marched on Mexico City. The Aztec empire was conquered by Spanish led Mexican Indians, due mostly to the all around abilities of Hernando Cortés who became "…the idol of the Indian population." (See Chapter 3 in *Many Mexicos* by Lesley Bird Simpson.) Further, if we cast aside cultural bias and invoke comparative history, the horrendous atrocities of the 16th century don't begin to compare to those of the 20th.

Note # 8

Translations and mistranslations are a huge factor when studying English language history about Spanish speaking people. One can only wonder as to what the original Spanish language source actually says. For example, primary researcher Dr. Eloy Gallegos has said he can believe next to nothing until he sees the original Spanish document for himself.

Note # 9

Stewart Udall writes that American historiography must pluck *"our Spanish century from the wastebasket of history."* He is correct. American (European) history begins chronologically with Ponce de León in Florida in 1513, not Jamestown, Virginia in 1607. Further, America's true story continues in the Southwest with the founding of New Mexico in 1598, also before Jamestown. Udall continues by writing that *"…in five swift decades…the Spanish…produced exploits and discoveries that will never be excelled."* While the venerable Mr. Udall has documented history on his side, he also acknowledges that a *"campaign of defamation lasting centuries has been waged…against Spain…"* and its people.

It appears that the denigration of Hispanic people is woven into the fabric of Southwest history and can't be avoided. Neither can the penchant for just leaving out historical achievements. A cursory look into a high school library came up with a book titled *The Pioneer Spirit* published in 1959 by American Heritage: The Magazine of History. De Soto and Vásquez de Coronado are given a page and a half then written off in their *"quest for gold."* The "real" heroes turn out being men like Francis Drake "the captain," Richard Hakluyt "the promoter," Sir Walter Raleigh "the colonizer," and the "Remarkable Captain John Smith." Would it be *cultural treason* to observe that documented history declares Drake was knighted for being successful in stealing gold from Spanish ships, Hakluyt was a master propagandist adept at promoting "The Big Lie," Raleigh's colony failed so he was beheaded by order of James I, and John Smith is often described as little more than a colossal liar? What are the consequences upon learning that what one thought to be valid history is in reality nefarious propaganda?

CHAPTER 3

First European Colony: New Mexico, 1598

The first colony and settlement of European people in the Southwest was New Mexico in 1598. The leader of the colonizing enterprise was **Juan de Oñate** (1549?-1626), son of **Cristóbal de Oñate** and **Catalina de Salazar y de la Cadena**. Cristóbal was one of the Basque miners who discovered the Zacatecas silver mines, which made the Oñate family wealthy. The bonanza town of Zacatecas became second in importance only to Mexico City.

JUAN DE ONATE

Because of their wealth and dedication to community, the Oñate family wielded considerable influence in their society. Juan de Oñate grew up in the Zacatecas mining frontier as much as in cosmopolitan Mexico City. [See Note # 1. *Notes begin on page 45.*] He received a good formal education while he also absorbed skills necessary for life on the frontier. He was to prove himself a good soldier and born leader of men. It is possible the rigors of frontier life imbued him with a serious disposition.

The Chichimeca wars began about 1550 and lasted for around half a century. These Indians, who were virtually naked except for "exotic" body paint, were typical of many stone age groups living in Mexico. They moved around from place to place, hunting and gathering *tunas*, the fruit of the prickly pear cactus, living in crude shelters or scooped out holes in the ground. They were also fierce, cannibalistic warriors who fought with the lance, sling, club, bow and arrows. [See Note # 2.] Oñate quickly learned that the Chichimecas were a powerful, ruthless enemy who routinely tortured and scalped their captives before decapitating them. Captive (enemy Indian) children were forced to witness the execution of their parents then the children were forced to drink the blood and eat the brains of their murdered parents who were then roasted on spits and eaten by the tribesmen.

It is believed that teenaged Juan accompanied his father on expeditions against the Chichimecas. By his early twenties he not only commanded some expeditions but paid for them with his own money (as was common for leaders in that era). He fought bloody encounters with the Chichimecas for some twenty years, becoming adept in dealing with them whether in peace or war.

As a product of a mining family and society, Juan de Oñate was also motivated to develop new mines, which he did. For example, Oñate discovered Charcas around 1574 when he was perhaps twenty-two years of age. He started the town, brought in miners, then Franciscan friars from Zacatecas while he built up defenses against the *Guachichiles*, an extremely ferocious group of Chichimecas who claimed the land as their own. He acquired much valuable experience while he explored, led his men against the Indians, prospected, and built towns.

Oñate and the people of his era labored greatly for worldly riches but they also sincerely believed opening the way for Christianity was inextricable from their mission in the New World. While Church and Crown were paramount there was also the concept of Spanish personal Honor. [See Note # 3.] Hardship during one's quest came to be considered a virtue. Juan de Oñate could have lived off his wealth or that of his family. By the age of thirty he was wealthy in his own right and could have lived an easy life in the opulent society of Mexico City. Instead he actively explored, prospected, developed mines, and built towns where Christians could live. [See Note # 4.] Destiny seemed to be preparing him for some great crusade.

It is believed that Juan de Oñate married **Isabel de Tolosa Cortés Moctezuma** (granddaughter of Hernán Cortés and Isabel Moctezuma, daughter of the last Aztec King, Moctezuma II) in the late 1580s when Oñate was in his late thirties. In time they had two children, Cristóbal and Mariquita (María de Oñate y Cortés Moctezuma).

NEW MEXICO

Word got out that Viceroy Velasco was looking for some stalwart individual to lead a colonizing endeavor into New Mexico. Several well known personalities vied for the colonizing contract but despite machinations by various parties it was finally awarded to Oñate in September of 1595. [See Note # 5.] Don Juan began preparations immediately for the *entrada* (formal entry into new territory) by enlisting friends and kin to help him in launching the expedition. Two **Zaldívar** nephews, **Juan** and **Vicente**, were picked as second in command *Maese de Campo* (Field Marshall) and *Sargento Mayor* (Lieutenant Marshal), respectively.

Oñate had committed to leading some two hundred people but in the excitement of the day as many as 500 signed up. People joined the venture because they sought fame and fortune, plenty of land, and they wanted encomiendas which required Indians to pay tribute. It was decreed by the King that all who went to New Mexico and fulfilled their contract would receive a patent as an *hidalgo* (*hijo de algo*, the bottom rung in the hierarchy of Spanish aristocracy). After five years of residency in New Mexico every head-of-household would qualify as a *Caballero* (Knight) on par with the Knights of Castile and would be empowered to use *"Don"* (an acronym for *de origin noble*) before his name. He would also be exempt from taxes and could never be arrested for debt. Within weeks the expedition was ready to hit the road north.

DELAYS

Viceroy Velasco was then unexpectedly reassigned to Peru and replaced by Viceroy Zúñiga y Acevedo. The new viceroy was in no hurry to send Oñate on his way, demanding to study the contract and then deciding to change it here and there. This caused years of exasperating bureaucratic delays of the expedition. Oñate wrote to the King, describing how the delays were deleterious to him and everyone involved, some even changing their minds on going.

In the spring of 1596 bureaucratic delays seemed to end so the expedition moved to **Santa Barbara**, some four hundred miles from Zacatecas, the last frontier outpost and designated departure area for the new entrada. Parties of recruits, many with entire families, arrived at Santa Barbara. All members of the expedition were mustered and informed they were subject to military discipline, that Oñate could impose required punishment for all transgressions, up to and including capital punishment for serious crimes. All troops, arms, and supplies were reviewed. While waiting for the final inspection there were tournaments and much partying.

Five Franciscan priests and one lay brother also joined the expedition. They were led by Father **Rodrigo Durán** and included fray **Cristóbal de Salazar**, one of Oñate's cousins.

Then on September 9, 1596, a royal courier dashed up with urgent dispatches: the expedition was to halt until further notice. Reason: the King had received an offer from Pedro Ponce de León to conduct the entrada into New Mexico and the Viceroy ordered a complete halt to the Oñate expedition pending an investigation. (It has been written that jealous rivals were behind these orders.) Not wanting the settlers to lose hope, Oñate didn't share the new information with them. It would be sixteen months of perseverance, during which time Oñate had to pay all expenses. Numbers of recruits decided to escape their contracts (causing frictions which would become virulent at a later date). During those months, even the Franciscans returned to Mexico City, except for Fr. Salazar and Fr. Márquez, the latter of whom was also recalled before setting out. It was January 26, 1598, before the expedition was free to make the entrada into New Mexico.

THE TRAIL

As luck would have it, the Conchos River was (probably) in flood stage when the expedition reached it. Crossing it looked impossible. Oñate stepped forward and addressed his people, ending with the exhortation: *Come, Noble Soldiers, Knights Of Christ, here is your first opportunity to show your courage and prove that you are deserving of the glories that await you.* [See Note # 6.] Oñate then brought out one of his best horses, mounted up and plunged into the swollen river which swept them downstream until horse and rider made it to the opposite shore. Then the *"Adelantado"* rode along the shore until he went into the river once more, making his way safely to the group on shore. Then Oñate prodded the first yoke of oxen into the river, the others following his example until all were across except the sheep, who would be pulled down if their wool was saturated with water. Oñate then ordered that a bridge be constructed across the river. The solid wooden wheels of the carts were removed from axels and strung in line across the water. Logs, branches and such were then placed in support of the wheels, which in turn were covered with earth, whereupon the flock of sheep crossed the river. [See Note # 7.] By nightfall the entire expedition had made the crossing. The following morning a mass was celebrated. Later Oñate told his people: *Hardships and misfortunes are the lot of men adventurous and brave. Perhaps they prepare us for the glories which await our enterprise.*

Oñate was informed that the Franciscan friars assigned to the expedition were on the trail behind him so he sent some troops under the command of **Marcos Farfán de los Godos** to bring them in safely. While waiting he assigned Vicente Zaldívar and a detachment of troopers to scout ahead for a suitable trail through the desert which lay ahead.

Vicente Zaldívar, twenty-five years old, was a product of the Zacatecas frontier but the trail north was more dangerous than even he expected. Indian guides became lost and the whole scouting party became disoriented, wandering in a circle for days, the final three without water. Some of the men suggested turning back but Vicente refused. Finally some smoke from an Indian village was sighted and four natives were captured. Vicente promised them their freedom and rewards if they would guide him to the Río Grande. The Amerindians accepted.

The group went in a northeasterly direction, experiencing severe shortages of water and food. Vicente picked half of his men to return to Oñate and inform him of their progress. He instructed the returnees not to speak of the hardships of the trail to the colonists. Then he continued blazing the trail, arriving at the Río Grande on February 28, 1598. Vicente rested his men a bit then headed back to make his report to Oñate.

The Captain General had by now sent out a relief column led by Gaspar de Villagrá. When they linked up the Zaldívar contingent was in dire straits, one Juan Rodriguez described as *more dead than alive.*"

On March 3, 1598, Captain Farfán de los Godos arrived at Oñate's encampment with the ten Franciscan priests, led by Fray **Alonso Martínez**, and lay brothers. Oñate received the Franciscans by forming his army into columns that marched smartly to greet them formally. Once in the encampment, the missionaries were seated under shady boughs structured by the river for the occasion and served a marvelous banquet.

On March 10, 1598, the Zaldívar reconnaissance party rode into camp and informed Oñate of the best trail north. The *Adelantado* issued orders to strike camp immediately. The only fanfare must have been the excitement felt by all as the caravan, perhaps more than two miles long, surged north. Despite the ever present dust, the gold and crimson standard of the King led the way, followed closely by that of Oñate. Then there were many other pennants waving in the wind, along with lances, halberds and such. Some eighty wagons and oxcarts, most of them covered with thick white canvas, formed the caravan. There were about 7,000 head of livestock (horses, mules, donkeys, beef cattle, oxen, sheep, goats).

COLONISTS

Oñate's settlers numbered around 500 or so. The men's ages ranged from the mid-teens into the sixties with the largest percentage in their twenties. For example, **Pedro Robledo** was sixty years old, his four red-headed sons ranged in ages from 27 to 18. There are indications there were some 129 fighting men among these pioneers.

Adult males generally sported "manly" facial hair like beards. Some had battle scars or cheeks pitted by smallpox. None were obese or described as over fed. The impression is that of a group of hardy, battle ready pioneers. Oñate and his stalwarts brought much body armor with them. There were various styles of helmets, cuirasses for upper body protection, steel gauntlets for the arms, greaves for the legs. Spanish stallions, which were the preferred mounts, were also protected by armor. Along with pole arms, swords, and daggers, most of the men also used the heavy matchlock rifles which had to rest on an iron fork during use.

It is difficult to estimate how many females and/or children were in this group of pioneers. One well known woman, doña **Eufemia Sosa Peñalosa** (wife of Francisco), made her presence known when she came forward to bolster the prospective colonists when bureaucratic delays jeopardized the entire entrada back in November of 1597. She delivered a magnificent oration in which she asked: *Where is your courage? Defection is not the action of Spaniards!!*

While none of the other females were identified by name, it has been written there were some 130 families with Oñate. [See Note # 8.] For example, the family of *Alférez* (Ensign) **Juan Pérez de Bustillo** included a wife, seven daughters, and two sons. The Spanish government understood that only the family unit could give stability to a frontier community so the role of women must have been great with the Oñate pioneers. The family related work along the trail had to be handled by the distaff side of the expedition and one can imagine what evening camps must have been like, women being the center of family or group campfires.

Others about which little is known are those individuals hired as servants, drivers, herders, packers, etc., described as *"assorted shades of mestizos, mulattos, and Indians."*

EASTER

On March 20, 1598, Oñate ordered a halt at a river he named *Río Sacramento* because it was encountered on Holy Thursday, feast of the Blessed Sacrament. A temporary chapel was constructed and all men were called to evening services where they prayed on their knees, wept over their sins and begged forgiveness of their Christian God. The women and children then joined their men in prayer. In a traditional Spanish observance of Holy Week, some of the men began scourging their backs in atonement, *"Laying their backs open on one side, And on the other with cruel whips."* Oñate himself left the praying throng around the chapel, found a secluded spot and lashed his back until it bled profusely. [See Note # 9.] Tears and blood were an integral part of Spanish religiosity.

Water grew scarce past the Sacramento River and into desert country. A few small springs were located but the trail was long and mostly lacking in water. Then on April 1, 1598, a "heaven sent" downpour created large pools of water, succoring all men and beasts.

By April 19, 1598, sand dunes were seriously impeding all wheeled vehicles so Oñate ordered that oxen be double hitched to get through the sand. When they made it through, the oxen were driven back to retrieve the other half of the caravan. Within one more day the whole group was at the Río Grande River (some twenty-five miles from present El Paso, Texas). The *Adelantado* informed everyone they could rest at this site for an entire festive week.

The campsite on the Río Grande proved happy and restful. Food was plentiful, what with fish and ducks from the river. Cottonwood trees at the water's edge provided shade for relaxing and pleasant conversation. There was plenty of grass for the stock to graze on. There was an abundance of wood so bonfires were plentiful at night, various people relating stories of this adventure or that. Vicente de Zaldívar informed his listeners about the desert up ahead and Oñate openly praised the courage of the scouts who were serving the people.

THANKSGIVING

On **April 30, 1598,** the Río Grande was crossed and Juan de Oñate proclaimed the time had come to take formal possession of New Mexico. [See Note # 10.] A chapel was constructed with tree branches and a solemn high mass was celebrated by all. Father Martínez delivered the sermon. Later that morning, with all soldiers in shining armor and on horseback, Don Juan read for all to hear the official act of possession. When the reading was ended the soldiers fired their muskets into the air, trumpets blew, and everyone shouted for joy. Oñate signed the possession document and the King's banner waved proudly above the throng. New Mexico was now officially part of the Spanish Empire.

The rest of the day was spent in celebration. Among the festivities was an original drama Captain Farfán de los Godos had written for this day and it was acted out by members of the expedition. [See Note # 11.] The drama had to do with missionaries entering the Pueblo world and being received kindly, which was one of the goals of the entrada.

TRAIL HARDSHIPS

The pioneers hit the trail the next day and met groups of friendly Indians who repeated "*manxo*," which sounded like the Spanish word "*manso*" (tame as opposed to wild; peaceful ones) and these Indians were thus bestowed the "Manso" name.

On May 12, 1598, Oñate sent **Pablo de Aguilar** to scout the trail ahead up to the first Indian village he encountered. Aguilar was not to make contact with the Indians for fear they might abandon their village and not be around to trade for grain and other foodstuffs now desperately needed by the Spanish colonists. Aguilar and his party rode off, returning in eight days with information that they had entered the first village. Oñate would have had Aguilar executed for disobeying orders and jeopardizing everybody had not his fellows begged for leniency. So Aguilar got off with a stern rebuke but Oñate understood that starvation was a certainty if more food supplies weren't obtained.

On May 21, 1598, **Pedro Robledo** died and was buried (at what has come to be known as *Paraje de Robledo*). It is possible the hardships of the trail were the prime reasons for Robledo's death. His four sons were heartbroken and the rest of the expedition sobered to hard realities.

Because of Pablo de Aguilar's disobedience Oñate now decided to take some sixty men and ride to the Indian village and assure them the colonists came in peace. The trail (later to be referred to as *Jornada del Muerto*, Dead Man's Route) was a waterless desert and all "*fared badly from thirst.*" Water had to be searched out, mostly toward the mountains, and progress was slow. Fr. Martínez began to suffer from a severe gout condition, adding to Oñate's concerns.

The Piro village of *Qualacu* was finally sighted but by the time the Christians arrived all the villagers had fled. Oñate sent riders with gifts and in time convinced them that there was nothing to fear so they returned to their village. While the Christians traded for food a courier came up to the village with word that there was serious trouble developing back in the main wagon train, that only Oñate himself could stop the dissension. So the Captain General rode back and calmed his individualistic, assertive Hispanic colonists.

By June 12, 1598, Oñate was back at Qualacu and within a couple of days his small force hit the northern trail once more. One afternoon a mighty storm came in from the horizon and drenched everyone in a downpour filled with such lightning and thunder that Villagrá wrote *"...we felt an awesome amazement."*

The storm passed and the world seemed renewed with pure air and blue skies. The reconnaissance party came upon another deserted village, with empty storerooms, so the men rode on. At the next village the Indians were standing on rooftops, gazing toward the newcomers, when one of their leaders, *Letoc*, came forward and signaled that he wished to be friends. He offered the Spaniards a great supply of corn and Oñate named the place *Socorro* (Help; Assistance) in gratitude.

Continuing north the Christians came upon a village they called *Nueva Sevilla* (New Seville). Despite their small numbers and large numbers of Indians, the Oñate group stayed there for about a week while the Zaldívar brothers were sent east through a pass called *Abo* where some villages were said to be located on the edge of plains country. Upon their return everyone hit the trail once more, passing through this village and that. At one village, dubbed San Juan Bautista, and Indian came forward and said, *"Jueves, Viernes, Sábado, Domingo"* along with the names *"Tomás"* and *"Cristóbal."* It was learned these two men were living in a village further up the trail. Oñate needed someone who could speak local languages so he would look for these two men.

BERNALILLO

At *Puaray* (near present Bernalillo, New Mexico), a large village, the Indians welcomed them. The Franciscans were quartered in a room that had just been whitewashed. The next day when the walls were dry the drawings under the whitewash revealed how the previous Franciscans, Fr. Agustin Rodriguez and Fr. Francisco López, had been stoned to death in Puaray in 1582. Oñate ordered his angry men to remain quiet and all left the village immediately. An Indian war at this time would have been catastrophic.

It was reported that "Tomás and Cristóbal" were in the village of (now) Santo Domingo up ahead. In the wee hours of the morning the Christians entered the village and, sure enough, located Tomás and Cristóbal, who had arrived with the Castaño de Sosa expedition and had decided to stay and live. Both were married and living contently in the village. Oñate enlisted them as interpreters and their services proved invaluable.

While at Santo Domingo the *Adelantado* decided to conference with all interested Indian leaders to explain his colonization venture. The well attended meeting was held on July 7, 1598, everyone crowding into the large central kiva. With Tomás and Cristóbal explaining Oñate's words, the General told the congregation that the Christians had arrived in their country to teach them the way to Everlasting Salvation. The leaders were amenable for they acknowledged obedience to King Philip II of Spain and the Holy Father in Rome, at least according to participants writing in Spanish. (There is no way of knowing what the Indians felt at the time.)

KNIGHTS OF ST. JOHN

After six days at Santo Domingo the Spaniards made their way to the valley of San Juan (today's Española Valley) which was to be the general site for settlement. On **July 11, 1598**, Oñate and his men reached *Okhe*, San Juan Pueblo, and selected it as the capital for the new colony. The site was named *San Juan de los Caballeros*, **Knights of St. John**. [See Note # 12.]

While waiting for the main caravan to arrive, Oñate selected a group of horsemen and set out north to familiarize himself with the country. He met leaders from other Indian villages as well as inspected the land for possible mining ventures. He visited Pecos to the west at the foot of the buffalo plains. Then he went in a southwesterly direction. The party visited turquoise and lead mines which had been worked by the Indians since ages past. He met the caravan at Santo Domingo Pueblo and it must have been a joyful meeting during the short respite at the village. While the caravan rested for a few days, Oñate and his contingent headed west to the Jémez mountains where he made contact with Towa-speaking villagers. Then he returned to *San Juan de los Caballeros*. He estimated there were some 60,000 Indians living in New Mexico. [See Note # 13.]

The wagon train arrived at *San Juan de los Caballeros* on August 18, 1598. The weary colonists were informed they must start preparing immediately for a cold winter which would soon be setting in. While the villagers were willing to share buildings for shelter, and trade for corn, blankets and buffalo robes, a significant number of colonists, including some forty-five officers and soldiers, more than a third of the expedition's men, expressed their dissatisfaction with the country along with Oñate's leadership. Oñate (later) reported that the would-be mutineers were dissatisfied because they found no "bars of silver" lying on the ground for them to pick up, that they resented not being able to use the Indians to enrich themselves. Since no quick bonanza had been discovered it is possible that some of the mutineers had intended to traffic in Indian slaves, even if it was outlawed by the Spanish government.

The oath which they took at the beginning of the entrada did not seem to bind them, even if it was to be enforced as in the military. Oñate arrested three ringleaders, two captains (one of whom was Aguilar, who narrowly avoided execution before for disobeying orders) and a soldier, and ordered their execution. After pleadings from the friars and virtually the entire army, Oñate withdrew the order. Being an experienced leader of men, Oñate realized the matter wasn't ended so he wrote: *"A spark of this great fire remained hidden in the ashes."*

On August 21, 1598, there was a ceremony of "peace and atonement" for the entire colony. A chapel was built and in use within two weeks and its dedication celebrated on September 8. Father Martínez celebrated mass and Father Salazar delivered the sermon. That afternoon and the rest of the week there were ritual battles between Christians and Moors, followed by various games and other recreation like jousting, bullfights, and a drama composed for the celebration. At weeks end the festival concluded with volleys of artillery which thundered out across the land.

During the festive week Oñate remained active. He assigned individual missionaries to various Indian villages and entertained visiting delegations from the pueblos. Absent were representatives from Acoma, located atop a peñol to the southwest of *San Juan de los Caballeros*.

One day when Oñate was having lunch he heard a tremendous mournful cry coming from the plaza. He went to investigate the commotion and learned the Indian's crops were withering in the fields because no rain had fallen, despite their beseeching rituals. Father Martínez told the Indians to cease their wailings, that he would pray for rains to come and rescue the withering plants. At the same time the next day the heavens darkened with clouds and released torrents of rain, insuring there would be a good harvest. (Villagrá reports the Indians were awed by the bountiful mercies of the Christian God.)

DESERTERS

On September 12, 1598, Juan de Oñate was informed that four men had stolen horses and fled south toward Santa Barbara in Nueva Vizcaya. The four had been involved in the conspiracy of a few weeks ago. Desertion was an offense punishable by death, as was the stealing of horses. Oñate sent out Captain **Gerónimo Márquez** and Captain **Gaspar de Villagrá** to overtake the deserters and *execute them* on the spot. [See Note # 14.] The colony must be preserved so discipline had to be enforced. (Márquez and Villagrá caught up with the deserters and executed two of them. The other two somehow escaped execution.)

BUFFALO HUNT

Also in September there occurred the arrival of a native named **Jusepe**, an Aztec from Mexico who had been with the (illegal) Leyba de Bonilla expedition of 1593. Jusepe related that the eastern plains were alive with "wild cattle" and the Captain General saw a way to feed his people for the winter. So he sent his nephew, Vicente de Zaldívar, with sixty horsemen to bring in an ample supply of buffalo meat. By September 15 the "buffalo hunters" were on their way east with Jusepe as guide.

The soldier-colonists now becoming buffalo hunters met groups of *"Vaquero Apaches"* on the plains. These sociable people followed the buffalo herds, carrying their belongings on dog travois. They provided a fellow to lead them to the wild cattle which were soon located.

The men were intrigued by the animals whose *"…shape and appearance are so amazing or amusing and frightening that one never tires of looking at them."* **Vicente de Zaldívar** ordered that an immense corral be built to hold the buffalo but the animals proved so wild that none could be driven into it despite the fact that the men were master horsemen. Calves were captured by roping but they fought so hard they died from exertion. The hunters then realized they would have to treat the buffalo as wild game. Within a few weeks they laid up an enormous store of buffalo meat and tallow. By November the party set out for home with enough meat to supply the colony through the winter.

DIPLOMACY and EXPLORATION

On October 6, 1598, Oñate set out to make contact with Indian villages on the eastern slopes of the Manzano Mountains as well as prospect for possible minerals. In the (present) Estancia Valley he found lakes containing "excellent white salt," an immensely valuable commodity.

Perhaps the salt discovery kindled an old desire to find the *South Sea* (Pacific Ocean) because the indefatigable Oñate decided to head west until he encountered the ocean. He sent a messenger instructing his nephew, *Maese de Campo* Juan de Zaldívar, to wait until Vicente returned to San Juan from the buffalo hunt, then to pick thirty men and follow him westward to the sea. Oñate then hit the trail through the Río Grande Valley and on to Acoma. The Christians camped at the base of the huge rock mesa, *"…the best situated Indian stronghold in all Christendom"* which protected its inhabitants like no other in New Mexico.

ACOMA

Unknown to the Hispanos below, Acoma war leaders were engaged in a serious argument as to how to handle the invading newcomers. The war faction, led by a chieftain named **Zutucapán**, wanted to exterminate them. But other leaders demanded a peaceful resolution and they prevailed. Therefore many Acomas descended from their stronghold with gifts for the visitors. The Acomas were genuinely interested in these strange, armored men with faces full of hair. They were also fascinated by the horses, who neighed nervously all the while. The visitors were then invited to climb the peñol and meet the other villagers. The Christians made the laborious climb to the top then fired a thunderous salute with their "fire sticks."

One of Zutucapán's warriors took Oñate by the arm and led him to the entrance of an underground kiva. A ladder protruded toward the blue sky from the underground darkness below. The warrior urged Oñate to descend the ladder, trying to communicate that something marvelous awaited below. Experienced frontiersman that he was, Oñate politely declined the invitation then led his men back down to the valley floor. (It was learned later that a dozen warriors lay in wait in the kiva, intent on assassinating the Captain General in order to force a war of extermination against the Spaniards.)

It was late October when Oñate departed from Acoma, stopped to get water at El Morro, then traveled toward the friendly Zuñi villages where the expedition made camp for a week. Captain Farfán de los Godos was sent to investigate a salt lake which proved to be *a wondrous thing.* Also during the week some soldiers were sent out to bring back horses that had strayed off during a snow storm. They chanced upon Captain Villagrá, who had almost become a casualty while returning from his assignment concerning the deserters. He was taken to Oñate and Villagrá related the following story:

Riding his purebred horse, Villagrá goes west looking for Oñate but while approaching Acoma he encounters a war party, led by Zutucapán, guarding the trail… *"like so many crouching tigers ready to pounce upon their prey."* The Acomas are ready to attack so he quickly rides away because *"they were out for blood."* It snows early the next morning and Villagrá fails to see the camouflaged trap the Acomas had set, a deadly pit in the middle of the trail. Horse and rider plunge into the pit, killing the horse immediately, though Villagrá isn't wounded. He believes the Acomas will soon be after him so he sets out on foot, walking for four days until by chance he is encountered by Oñate's soldiers looking for stray horses.

For whatever reason, the situation at Acoma didn't cause Oñate to reconsider his plans. On November 8, 1598, Oñate and his men left Zuñi for the *Moqui* (Hopi) villages where they were received peacefully and cordially. After the visit Oñate decided to return to Zuñi and await the arrival of Juan de Zaldívar and his reinforcements. On December 12, 1598, Oñate realizes Christmas is rapidly approaching and there is still no word from his nephew Juan so Oñate decides to return home so his men can celebrate the holidays with their families and then later set out for the South Sea.

AMBUSH

On their way to Acoma, **Juan de Zaldívar** had instructed his 31 men to treat all Indians with utmost courtesy and respect when they stopped to trade hatchets, hawk bells and other items for provisions like flour. Unknown to Juan and the Spaniards in general, Zutucapán and the war faction have gained dominance in the village and the intent is to exterminate the Christians.

The Acomas met the Zaldívar party and invited them up to their Sky City. Zaldívar and 18 men climb to the top only to be told the flour is located at various houses in the Pueblo so the men have to separate. *"The Indians led us through small plazas and narrow streets."* Suddenly the Acomas rise in large numbers and attack the Spaniards from all sides and terraces, warriors shooting arrows, men and women hurling stones and wielding war clubs, all of which had been prepared beforehand. Zaldívar orders that no one should fire at the Indians, but to shoot their harquebuses into the air to scare them in order to calm them with *"words and kindness."* Then Zaldívar receives an arrow in the leg and the Christians realize they must fight back in order to preserve their very lives. They are forced against a rock wall and fall in bloody hand-to-hand combat. This includes Juan, Oñate's nephew, not yet 30 years of age, who receives the final blow from Zutucapán. (Survivors later were to testify they saw the Spaniards who had fallen to the ground had their heads split open with large stones.)

Only five Hispanics survive, some by jumping from the top of the Sky City and landing on sand dunes below. Bodies of dead Christians are hurled down the cliff where a small number of men are guarding the horses. The victorious Acomas are wearing the helmets, coats of mail, and brandishing the swords of the dead Spaniards when they jeer from the top of their stronghold. The Christian survivors hurry to where iron articles and horse shoeing materials had been cached only to find the items gone. When couriers go to seek Oñate in the Zuñi country some horses are killed with arrows by the warriors. The survivors link up with their Captain General at El Morro and break the news of the ambush at Acoma.

At *El Morro* (Inscription Rock) Governor Oñate heard the news about his nephew Juan de Zaldívar and the deadly ambush at Acoma. He retired to his tent then asked Captain Villagrá to construct a Christian cross out of branches and place it on the tent floor. All through the night he wept and prayed in front of the cross. The following morning, though his grief was heartfelt, Oñate realized that Hispanic New Mexico was now teetering on the brink of extermination if other Indian nations united with Acoma to wipe out the small colony of Christians. The reality of the situation was that there were thousands and thousands of Indians and only a few hundred Hispanics, most of which were women and children. The last thing in the world that he needed was an Indian war. The following morning he gathered his men and addressed them, his eyes red and swollen: *¡Caballeros! We have lost our valiant comrades in arms and Heaven knows they cannot be replaced for they had no equals. Our companions met a terrible fate, beaten and torn to pieces like the martyrs they were. They gave up their lives for our God and King. Their labors were not in vain for their work will continue… There is no one here who is not worthy to be considered a true soldier for Christ. Let your Christian spirit nourish you. Whatever comes, whether it be death, hardship, or suffering, we shall meet all as brave men who trust in the Almighty Creator…*

Oñate decided that all must return immediately to San Juan to prevent the colonists from being wiped out in another sneak attack. He had learned the lesson of wariness at the cost of his men's lives. *If he had sent a warning to his nephew, maybe all would still be alive!* During the seven day return journey to San Juan scouts went ahead and brought up the rear to protect the expedition. Sentries kept watch at night for attack was possible if the thousands of Indians united to exterminate them. But they made it home without incident.

CHRISTMAS

New Mexico's first Christmas was one of gloom and heartfelt sadness. [See Note # 15.] The pageantry of Christmas Mass in the church of San Juan Bautista was a ray of optimism that worked to alleviate the grief-stricken community. Christian spirit illuminated the path toward New Mexican survival. As always, it was up to Oñate to voice what everybody was feeling. He addressed the group: *Heaven knows my heart bleeds at the loss of our valiant comrades. In the deaths of our Maese de Campo and his companions we have suffered an irreparable loss. They cannot be replaced for they had no equals. We have heard how nobly they died in the service of their God and their King. Their work is done. It is essential now that our labors should continue. I know of no one present who is not worthy of the name of a true soldier of Christ. We have heard from eyewitnesses who came to us, grievously wounded in body and soul, the terrible fate our comrades have met. They were beaten and torn to pieces. They died like martyrs. My soldiers, let us keep a true Christian spirit. Whether death, hardship or suffering come, we shall meet them as behooves brave man. Let us lay aside our sorrow and place our trust in Almighty God.*

COMMUNITY COUNCIL

Christian spirit helps illuminate the path toward survival but everyone realizes that Hispanic New Mexico is now teetering on the brink of extermination if other Indian groups unite with Acoma to exterminate the small colony of Christians. [See Note # 16.]

In January of 1599, a tribunal convenes to decide if a justified war can be waged against Acoma. [See Note # 17.] Oñate weighs and considers all testimony and recommendations:

Capt. **Gerónimo Márquez** states that if Acoma is not captured "*...there will be no security in all New Mexico, nor can it be settled as the natives of other Pueblos are watching what we do at Acoma and whether we punish them...*"

Juan de Olague (who saved his life only by leaping onto the sand dunes below) testifies under oath that the Acomas have acted with treacherous premeditation in order to kill the Spaniards.

The friars testify that Oñate may wage war because the Acomas have sworn allegiance to the King and as subjects have no right to revolt; but war for revenge would be illegal.

Several married soldiers testify that unless the rebellion is crushed immediately they will be forced to ask permission to take their women and children back to New Spain for there will be no security for them in N.M.

The vote is unanimous against the unprovoked attack. The decision being agreed to democratically by all present, Juan de Oñate declares that *guerra de sangre y fuego* (a no-quarter war of fire and sword) will be waged against Acoma and he will lead it personally. But the colonists declare the Captain General mustn't participate in the attack for in case of failure he will have to lead everyone out of New Mexico. The Governor sees the logic in what his people are saying so he selects his other nephew, **Vicente de Zaldívar,** to lead the Christian army. While war is always war, Oñate's frontier experience enables him to include in his general orders: "*Make more use of clemency than severity if it should turn out that the Acomas have committed their crimes more from incapacity of reason than from malice ... If you should want to show leniency after they are arrested you should seek all possible means to make the Indians believe that you are doing so at the request of the friar with your forces. In this manner they will recognize the friars as their benefactors and protectors and come to love and esteem them, and to fear us.*" [See Note # 18.]

ACOMA WAR

Sargento Mayor Vicente de Zaldívar, 25 years of age and the fate of Hispanic New Mexico hanging in the balance, leads 72 men to Acoma where, through the interpreter Tomás, he states he wants to make peace and demands to know why they have killed the Spaniards. From atop their Sky City the Acomas jeer and insult (*llorones, cornudos*) the tiny army far below, promising to annihilate it, their puny colony, and all "*the Queres and the Tiguas and everyone at Zía because they have failed to kill Spaniards.*" Zaldívar demands surrender the required three times then, upon continued jeering, informs the Acomas to prepare for battle.

Meanwhile, back at San Juan de los Caballeros, scouts inform Oñate that many Pueblos are massing for an attack on the tiny Hispanic colony. All men prepare for its defense and the women of the colony, led by **Doña Eufemia,** wife of E. Sosa Peñalosa, have a meeting with Oñate in which they volunteer to fight if the Indians attack. Don Juan expresses his heartfelt respect and appreciation. Henceforth the women appear on the rooftops alongside their men throughout the crisis, thus giving the impression that there are more defenders at Knights of St. John than there really are. Aware of Spanish readiness, the Indians delay their attack until they receive news from Acoma.

On January 21, 1599, Vicente de Zaldívar discussed strategy with his soldiers in an effort to convince them that the Acoma stronghold wasn't impregnable. Defeat was not an option for it would be "*a serious blot upon our honor as Spaniards.*" The plan was simple: the bulk of the army would deploy in full view of the Acomas while Zaldívar and eleven picked soldiers would climb to the top and gain a foothold inside the village itself.

Like El Cid and other Spanish knights of old, Zaldívar rode up to the base of the Sky City and shouted to his enemies to prepare themselves for they were going to be attacked and no quarter would be given or expected. The Acomas had wanted war and it was now upon them, the fate of the entire Hispanic colony hanging on the outcome. Defeat meant that the people back in the Knights of St. John settlement would be attacked, perhaps exterminated.

On the afternoon of January 22, 1599, a blare of trumpets signal an all out assault along the principal path leading up to Acoma. The warriors answer the challenge and converge against the invaders. Zaldívar and his commandos make it to the top from another side, but once there are immediately discovered and targeted by hundreds of warriors armed with clubs, knives, bows and arrows. There are three days (January 22-24, 1599) of desperate, bloody, hand-to-hand fighting at Acoma but the Spaniards succeed in bringing up cannon to neutralize warrior numbers. Among the many incidents of the battle, Vicente spies a warrior wearing his brother Juan's clothes so he fights his way to him and slays him with a mighty swing of his sword. At first the Spaniards are on the verge of being overcome by sheer numbers but once again Hispanics prove themselves fierce fighters and the tide is turned against the valiant warriors. (Indians were later to testify that *Santiago*, St. James, appeared and turned the tide of battle.) With so many warriors killed Zaldívar sends the interpreter Tomás to urge the chiefs to surrender, "*promising that he would do justice to all who surrendered and placed themselves in his care.*" The leaders reply that they and their women and children want only to die, that the Spaniards are scoundrels, and they attack Tomás with arrows and stones. The Spaniards set fire to the houses to force the warriors outside. The battle continues until the Acomas realize they are defeated so they ask for peace. By now hundreds of Acomas have perished, and they blame Zutucapán and the war faction for the tragedy.

Zaldívar accepts their surrender and incarcerates them in their kivas. But the Acomas *"broke away through many tunnels and mines concealed in the estufas and which opened out into adjoining houses … Indians ran from house to house and killed each other without sparing their children, however small, or their wives."* Zaldívar orders the battle to resume, setting fire to all houses, and orders that *"all Indian women and children who could be found should be taken prisoners to save them from being killed by the Indian warriors."* Some 500 Acomas, men and women, young and old, are saved by Zaldívar's action. Acoma is then destroyed to prevent it being used as a fortress for rebellion.

COURT TRIAL

On February 9-12, Oñate holds court at Santo Doming Pueblo and Acoma survivors are put on trial for the murders of 27 Christians. Captain **Alonso Gómez Montesinos** is put in charge as Defense Attorney for the accused Acomas. Testimony is taken from all concerned:

Caoma, a native from Acoma, testifies through the interpreter Tomás that he was not present when the Spaniards were killed but they were killed because they asked for such large amounts of provisions.

Cat-ticati testifies the Christians were killed because they asked for maize, flour, and blankets. Some Acomas had not wanted to fight.

Taxio testifies that he was at home when he heard shouting and went outside where he saw the Spaniards were being killed.

Xunusta testifies that the Spaniards first killed an Indian and then the Indians became very angry and killed them.

Excasi testifies that it was said the Spaniards were killed because a soldier either asked for or took a turkey.

Caucachi testifies that the Spaniards wounded an Acoma and the people became angry and killed them.

Captain Alonso Gómez Montesinos pleads for clemency on the grounds that these Acomas were absent when the Spaniards were killed, that Indians aren't "civilized," that they should be acquitted, set free, allowed to go wherever they wish, and order compensation for the expenses resulting from their arrest. But the rebels are found guilty by the Captain General and sentenced according to the law. [See Note # 19.]

No Acoma is given a death sentence. Twenty-four (24) males over the age of twenty-five are sentenced to have **puntas de pies** cut off (*toes, not feet*, according to researcher/author E.J. Gallegos, who declares he inspected the actual Spanish document in Mexican archives) and then must render 20 years of servitude; two Moquis (Hopis) in the fight are to have a hand (*fingertips?*) cut off then set free; males 20 to 25 years of age are condemned to servitude for 20 years; females over 12 years of age are condemned to servitude for 20 years.

Oñate then states: *"All of the children under twelve years of age I declare free and innocent of the grave offense for which we punish their parents. And because of my duty to aid, support, and protect both the boys and girls … I place the girls under the care of our father commissary, Fray Alonso Martínez, in order that he, as a Christian and qualified person, may distribute them in this kingdom or elsewhere in monasteries or other places where he thinks they may attain the knowledge of God and the salvation of their souls. The boys under twelve years of age I entrust to Vicente de Zaldívar Mendoza, my sargento mayor, in order that they may attain the same goal. The old men and women, disabled in the war, I order freed and entrusted to the Indians of the province of the Querechos where they may be supported and may not allow them to leave their pueblos…"* [See Note # 20.]

PRECARIOUS COLONY

Governor Oñate understood the situation of his colony in New Mexico. The numerous Indian groups could wipe out the Christians at any time if they united in a war of extermination. So he wrote to the Viceroy and asked for more colonists, describing New Mexico's potential for mining, possible riches in pearls if he could get to the Pacific Ocean, generous supplies of excellent salt beds, and the super-abundance of meat and hides from buffalo on eastern plains. The letter was sent off with loyal couriers which included Gaspar de Villagrá, Farfán de los Godos, and Juan Pinero in March of 1599. (The relief caravan with new colonists arrived in New Mexico on Christmas Eve of 1600 and the event was one of great rejoicing. For whatever reasons, Gaspar de Villagrá, Farfán de los Godos, and Juan Pinero opted not to return to New Mexico.)

SAN GABRIEL

At around this springtime of 1599 the colony was moved a quarter mile to *San Gabriel*. Oñate had wanted to build a regular community in traditional Spanish fashion. It appears the colonists refused to work on the project due to their privations and dissatisfaction with the land. Nevertheless, San Gabriel, an established Indian village with perhaps 400 rooms, was remodeled into a U-shaped structure. Doors and windows were built into the ground floors and outdoor *hornos*, dome-shaped ovens, were built for baking. [See Note # 21.] A goal was to build a regular church in the new settlement. [See Note # 22.]

After staying alive, the basic activities in New Mexico were laboring to convert the Indians to Christianity and prospecting for mines. There must also have been serious efforts in agriculture.

JUMANO WAR

At around this time the Governor decided to send Vicente de Zaldívar to search for the ocean to the west. Vicente led his men to the Jumano villages in central New Mexico to collect provisions for the journey but instead of corn he was given stones. Zaldívar withdrew but sent a courier to inform his uncle as to what the Jumanos had done.

The Governor led some fifty soldiers to the Jumanos and demanded cotton blankets. He got perhaps a dozen. The next day he informed the Indians that the insult of giving Zaldívar stones to eat wouldn't be tolerated. A corner of the village was burned and onlookers standing on a rooftop were fired on, killing perhaps half a dozen. Two warriors were hanged and when the veracity of the interpreter was questioned, possibly speaking against the Spaniards while supposedly interpreting, the man was also hanged. This appeared to quiet the Jumanos.

During the Christmas season of 1600 a group of five Christians were riding by a Jumano village on their way south to Santa Barbara when Jumano warriors attacked the party and killed two Spaniards. When word got back to San Gabriel the colonists thought another Acoma rebellion was in the making.

Even the friars urged Oñate to make a strike against the Jumanos in order to discourage a province-wide rebellion. During the spring of 1601 Vicente de Zaldívar, now *Maese de Campo*, led a punitive expedition which resulted in a series of bloody skirmishes until the main village was taken by the soldiers and burned. (Fray **Juan de Escalona**, who had arrived with the colonists of Christmas Eve, 1600, and later became one of Oñate's bitter enemies, has been described as writing to the Viceroy that some eight hundred Jumano men, women, and children lost their lives during the war and that three Jumano villages were burned. Documentation for this charge hasn't been found in the archives.)

EXPLORATION and DISCONTENT

On June 23, 1601, Oñate marched off with some seventy picked men to reconnoiter the Quivira Country (Kansas). While he was gone on his almost 600 mile exploration, the festering discontent among the colonists burst into public debate. What was the purpose of this "grandiose New Mexico colony," where even food was hard to come by?! Even with corn and beans from the Indians, starvation was at hand. Many had sold their estates in Mexico, believing they would soon be a part of a new, silver-rich kingdom on the Río Grande. What illusion! The fine clothes they had brought were of no earthly use in this God-forsaken wilderness. And the weather! Drinking water in pottery on the kitchen table would freeze overnight. If starvation didn't get you the freezing temperatures would! Where were the promised encomiendas?! And the silver…what silver?! The land was poor, even for cattle. The only real reward was the title of "*Hidalgo.*" What purpose would it serve if you starved to death? On September 7, 1601, Fray Francisco de San Miguel orated in church that all colonists had a right to leave if they so desired. The moral right to do so, he maintained, rested on the fact that injustices being inflicted on the Indians were preventing their conversion to Christianity, one of the principal reasons for colonization. All the friars, except Oñate kinsman Fray Francisco de Velasco, who was with Oñate, joined the deserters.

Some of Oñate's veterans sided with those who would leave, as did some of the colonists. A small group of Oñate partisans refused to join them. They declared it wasn't bad luck that was destroying New Mexico but rather mutiny, cowardice, and disloyalty. They wrote and signed a document for the Viceroy in Mexico City and sent it posthaste with the faithful Captain Gerónimo Márquez.

DESERTION

The dissidents departed in early October, 1601. Some twenty-five soldiers and their families, remained behind. A portion of those who departed had gone through and helped themselves to some of the belongings of various soldiers with Oñate and they also took horses which weren't theirs. Due to their lack of numbers, those who remained were unable to oppose them.

Oñate and his men rode into San Gabriel on November 24, 1601, only to find a remnant of the Christian colony. After the initial shock a tribunal was set up and military leaders of the *traitors* group were condemned to death by beheading. Vicente de Zaldívar was sent at the head of a fast contingent to carry out the sentence and return the others to New Mexico.

But it was too late. The deserters made it to the safety of Santa Barbara and immediately wrote impassioned letters to the Viceroy (Count of Monterrey), denouncing Governor Oñate in every way possible. He also received letters from Oñate's partisans, so it would be difficult to come to a decision amid such conflicting reports. So he selected a council of jurists and theologians to weigh the evidence and recommend a solution. After serious deliberation, the council found that the people involved were colonists first, soldiers second, so they should not be held to stringent military law regarding desertion. Neither should they be required to return to New Mexico. Further, the serious allegations against Governor Oñate should be investigated.

Authorities in Mexico City were not all against Oñate. The Franciscan Order declared the friars who abandoned New Mexico were unworthy, possibly cowardly individuals. Historian Fray Juan de Torquemada wrote that the deserters were trying to fix the blame on everyone except themselves. But in the final analysis and in spite of the fact that back in Spain the King bestowed the title of *"Adelantado"* on Juan de Oñate, as Governor of the province most of the blame fell on his shoulders.

Four new Franciscans were sent to New Mexico around 1603. During that same year there was trouble at Taos Pueblo but Oñate squelched it immediately. In 1604 Fathers Velasco, Escalona, and Escobar were sent to Acoma in an effort to build on peace. They were cordially received.

EXPLORATION

On October 7, 1604, Juan de Oñate set out for the fabled Pacific Ocean. By late January of 1605 they reached the estuary of the Colorado River, the Gulf of California, which they thought was the South Sea. Oñate waded into the water and took possession for the King. Brother Juan de San Buenaventura took possession in the name of Holy Mother Church. After resting a few days, the expedition headed for home. The harbor was good and there were many Indian groups for Christianization but there were no pearls or other signs of wealth.

By mid-April the group was at El Morro where Oñate inscribed the following message on the sandstone rock:

Pasó por aquí el adelantado don Juan de Oñate del descubrimiento de la mar del sur a 16 de abril de 1605.

The men were back at San Gabriel by April 25th.

FRONTIER REALITIES

The new Viceroy Montesclaros back in Mexico City had studied the documentation relating to New Mexico. There were no valuable mines and such but the province couldn't be abandoned while there were Christian Indians there. Oñate's conquest was unspectacular. The Viceroy recommended that the Governor be removed from office.

By 1606, Indian villages and the settlement of San Gabriel itself was being attacked by hostile Apaches and Navajos. They killed villagers and burned homes with impunity. Retaliatory attacks were waged against these raiders but there weren't enough colonists to put a stop to the raiding.

On June 17, 1606, King Philip III ordered that Oñate be replaced in New Mexico with a "discreet, Christian" individual. By the time order got to Mexico City in early 1607 don Luis de Velasco, who had awarded Oñate his original contract, was once again the Viceroy.

Juan de Oñate finally understood that the New Mexico of his hopes and dreams would not come true. Though unaware of the order coming from Mexico City he resigned his post as Governor, stating to the Viceroy: *"Finding myself helpless in every respect, because I have used up on this expedition my estate and the resources of my relatives and friends, amounting to more than 600,000 pesos, I find no other means than to renounce my office, which resignation I am sending your Excellency."* He continues that no one in authority has bothered even to acknowledge the monumental sacrifices made by his soldiers, friars, and colonists. The deserters of 1601 not only haven't been punished but have used their freedom to spread lies, justify their treason, and attack his personal honor. He will hold his colonists only until the summer of 1608 then he will release them from all obligations to remain.

SANTA FE

It is thought that perhaps in 1607 or 1608 the capital was moved some twenty miles south from San Gabriel to a narrow valley unoccupied by Indians, a place now called *La Villa Real de la Santa Fe de San Francisco de Asís*, **Santa Fe**. (Oñate's replacement, **Pedro de Peralta**, formally established Santa Fe in 1610 but scholars believe Juan de Oñate was the principal force behind its founding as early as 1607 or 1608.)

Viceroy Velasco accepts Oñate's resignation in 1608 but orders him to remain in his post until a replacement is sent.

The stalwart Captain Gerónimo Márquez is in the escort that brings Pedro de Peralta to govern New Mexico in early 1610. The change of administrations is made amicably. In a short time Don Juan de Oñate, his son Cristóbal, and some of his closest friends leave New Mexico for the last time. Perhaps their departure was bitter-sweet. The ex-Governor was back in Mexico City by April 30, 1610 and the first phase of New Mexican history was at an end. [See Note # 23.]

DISCUSSION Notes *for* COLONY: NEW MEXICO
Note # 1
See *The Last Conquistador: Juan de Oñate and the Settling of the Far Southwest* by Marc Simmons, a short volume that is generally available for interested readers. *Don Juan de Oñate, Colonizer of New Mexico, 1595-1628*, by G.P. Hammond and A. Rey, the longer study on the subject, is available basically in Special Collections of large libraries. The Hammond and Rey work appears to have shortcomings, especially as related to the supposed "foot cuttings," now said to be toes, and it is uncertain that the sentences were actually carried out.

As Stuart Udall has mentioned previously regarding Vásquez de Coronado, the hispanophobic pattern of American historiography continues: *American histories generally don't credit the heroic Oñate and his colonizing pioneers for their epic achievements in New Mexico and the Southwest.*

Udall isn't alone in observing how American historiography is often closed to events transpiring away from the east coast or east of the Mississippi. Toward the end of the 19th century Charles F. Lummis wrote "The Comanche's Revenge" in *A New Mexico David and Other Stories* which contains the following viewpoint: *If the true story of New Mexico could be written in complete detail, from the time when the brave Spanish conquistadores planted there the first European civilization in all the vast area now embraced by the United States, it would stand unparalleled in all the history of the world. No other commonwealth on the globe has met and conquered such incredible hardship, dangers, and sufferings for so long a time…"*

Note # 2

Because Indian groups east of the Mississippi in what is now the USA were mostly exterminated by the English or exiled under threat of extermination by the Americans, the American popular mind is generally sympathetic to Native Americans, so long as they don't live close by. Amerindian groups encountered by Spanish people are often portrayed as worthy while those under British or American domination are described as *savages*. Documented history shows that Indians fought with each other just as viciously as Europeans did in the Old World. Further, most of the many nation groups of Indians in Mexico were cannibals. The Aztecs are probably the best known group of cannibals. The other Indian nations hated the Aztecs because of their bloody rituals which necessitated a daily human sacrifice.

Note # 3

The Spanish sense of Honor is often referred to as "exaggerated" by some English language writers. No one explains why it is considered "exaggerated," perhaps because the process would have to be comparative?

Note # 4

Contrast this behavior with that of American CEOs who looted their corporations at the expense of ordinary workers and/or stockholders. The former believed only in amassing tremendous fortunes for themselves while the plight of the workers interested them not a whit.

Note # 5

New Mexican scholar Dr. Miguel Encinias believes that Isabel, Oñate's wife, died in the 1590s, perhaps motivating him to look northward, away from this heartbreak. See Encinias' *Two Lives For Oñate*.

Note # 6

See *Historia De La Nueva Mexico, 1610*, by Gaspar Pérez de Villagrá, Spanish/English edition translated and edited by Miguel Encinias, Alfred Rodríguez, and Joseph P. Sánchez, UNM Press, © 1992. Villagrá was a soldier who was also a talented chronicler, in epic poem form, no less. The work is excellent history but sometimes denigrated as poetry. No such work exists in American history and one can only wonder how the *Historia* would be lauded if such a work had been written in English about English speaking colonists..

Note # 7

These heroics are fully documented. They aren't the product of a script writer or "patriotic Orwellian historian."

Note # 8

See *History Of Arizona And New Mexico, 1530-1888* by Hubert Howe Bancroft. There is a popular misconception that Spanish women didn't come to the New World, that Spanish men married only Indian women. Spanish women were colonists after military campaigns pacified the land and in New Mexico they were an integral part of the expedition. It is a documented fact that the 1607 settlers of Jamestown, Virginia, had no women with them. Did English settlers marry Indians? The John Rolfe/Pocahontas relationship is well known.

Note # 9

Spaniards as a group have been described as sincerely religious people. Some people find this hard to understand but it is a necessary consideration when discussing Southwestern history.

Note # 10

April 30, 1598, is the first Thanksgiving celebrated by European people in what is now the USA.

Note # 11

Farfán de los Godos is thus the first dramatist of the USA. Regrettably, no copies of the drama are extant.

Note # 12

Oñate and his people had now lengthened the Camino Real (Royal Road, King's Highway) by around six hundred miles, for a total distance of almost two thousand miles from Mexico City. Oñate and his pioneers thus blazed in 1598 the longest road in North America until the opening of the Oregon trail in the 19th century. It must also be pointed out that no other Europeans in North America ever settled that far away from "civilization," again until the 19th century Oregon Trail. Why did Hispanics venture out while the English hugged their coastal settlements?

Note # 13

Modern researchers now assert there might have been around 40,000, not 60,000, Indians at the time. Whichever figure is correct, it was a tremendous feat of courage for some 500 people to settle in an area dominated by so many thousands of Indians. This colonization is unparalleled in the American annals of England, France, or the USA.

Note # 14

One of the defects in American historiography is the penchant for *presentism*, to judge historical incidents as if they were happening today. Oñate is described as "harsh" in ordering that the deserters be executed despite the fact that desertion from the military and/or stealing horses have usually been a matter for capital punishment.

Note # 15

A close parallel to how the settlers must have felt after the surprise ambush is the 9-11 terrorist strike on New York in 2001.

Note # 16

With the Indians numbering around 40,000 and the Christians at about 500, one can only marvel at the courage of these Hispanic pioneers. In the entire history of the USA no other European people settled so far from a previous settlement or in such a geographical center of Indian populations.

Note # 17

According to Mark Simmons in *The Last Conquistador*, contrary to what *"many writers would have us believe,"* Spaniards weren't reckless or given to unprovoked reprisals. The King's law and Church doctrine required rational deliberation. A *"highly formalized and legalistic procedure"* was in place by this time and it had to be observed before launching a war.

Note # 18

This type of psychology is typically Spanish and all but unknown during wartime in other American areas settled by Europeans. Yet propagandistic writers consistently portray Spaniards as "cruel."

Note # 19

It is important to neutralize the American penchant for "presentism" in describing situations like these. If this isn't done then "History" becomes mere hispanophobic propaganda, what Philip W. Powell has described in his *Tree Of Hate*.

Note # 20

These punishments, especially the dismemberments if they actually occurred, must be understood in the context of the historical age in which they transpired. As mentioned above, *presentism* must be neutralized if we truly wish to understand the historical record. Physical mutilation was a legal, customary avenue at that time. For example, if a Pueblo woman was found guilty of adultery the Pueblo punishment was to have *her ears and nose cut off*. Such brutalities were also an integral part of the European legal process and in 1692, almost a century after Oñate, women were being tortured and executed on the (now) ridiculous charge of being *witches* in Salem, Massachusetts.

Paleography, the art of deciphering communiqués from centuries ago, in this case in the Spanish language, also has its pitfalls. First it must be pointed out that there are popularly accepted mistranslations that have made their way into academic circles as well as the popular mind. Perhaps the best know example is *"llano estacado,"* mistranslated into English as the "Staked Plains." Llano estacado means "palisaded plains" or "stockaded plains," so named by Spanish explorers because from a distance mesa table lands appeared to be villages protected by stockades. This might be considered to verge on poetic license in the present day but more far fetched, accepted by many English language writers, is that the early explorers hammered wooden stakes into the ground to be used as guideposts in order not to lose their way on the trackless plains. Common sense requires a few questions: Where did the Spaniards get enough wooden stakes to mark the land from New Mexico and Texas to as far north as Kansas? From how far away could you see a stake in the ground? How were so many stakes carried around?

Author and researcher Dr. Eloy Gallegos has declared it was *puntas de pies* (toes), not *pies* (feet), that were ordered to be cut off. G.P. Hammond and A. Rey assert in *Don Juan De Oñate, Colonizer of New Mexico, 1595-1628*, that it was "feet" ordered cut off and that the sentence was carried out. Historian, researcher and founder of the Vargas Project at the University of New Mexico Dr. John Kessell spoke in Santa Fe on April 2, 1998 ("A Foot for a Foot"), stating that neither he nor his team of professional researchers has found any document to prove that the sentence, whether it was feet or toes, was actually carried out. Archival documentation indicates that the friars, with or without the prompting of Oñate, went to the Governor with pleas to suspend the dismemberment, that Oñate was thereby encouraging the Pueblos to seek out Christian friars as protectors while saving face but instilling respect for Spanish law. Spaniards have been described as the *best record keepers in the world* and if the sentence had been carried out, especially one of that magnitude, it would have been recorded as required by law and custom. Despite professional concerted efforts no such record has surfaced, according to Dr. Kessell.

Common sense tells us that a man sentenced to twenty years of servitude would be of little value with only one foot. Chroniclers after the Acoma war make no mention whatsoever of seeing (Acoma) Indians walking around on crutches and one foot.

As for New Mexico's Acomas they escaped their servitude and by 1604 rebuilt their Sky City, which suggests that if they were not forced to abide with the servitude portion of their sentence, it is quite possible the dismemberment never took place either but was used as a strategy to impress the Indians. Acoma still exists as one of the most popular tourist attractions in New Mexico to the present day. J. Simon Ortiz, a well known writer from Acoma, has written that New Mexico is the only State where Indian nations survived basically intact. The other extreme is the virtual extermination of east coast Indian nations, an extermination so complete few Americans even realize there were extremely large numbers of Native Americans living there when the English began settling in 1607.

Note # 21

Today these structures are often referred to as "Indian ovens" and tourists generally believe they are products of Indian culture.

Note # 22

Archaeological digs have uncovered portions of the San Gabriel settlement but the New Mexico Office of Cultural Affairs hasn't seen fit to recreate the village as a tourist draw.

Note # 23

The saga of Juan de Oñate continued in Mexico. Documentation shows that he was in Zacatecas in 1613, tending to his mining enterprises which had suffered much during his sojourn in New Mexico. In a few months he got his mines back into profitable production. On June 1, 1613, the King ordered Viceroy Diego Fernández de Cordoba to investigate the allegations made against Oñate while Governor of New Mexico. He was arraigned on some thirty charges and held under house arrest in his home in Mexico City. Chief witnesses against Oñate were the deserters of 1601. Oñate countered that these were the persons who almost destroyed the New Mexico colony with their desertion, that they had broken their contracts, that they were under a death sentence for doing so, and that's why they were giving false testimony to the court. Eighteen charges were dismissed but Oñate was pronounced guilty on twelve others on May 13, 1614. His sentence was perpetual exile from New Mexico, a fine of 6,000 Castilian ducats plus court costs, and a four year exile from Mexico City. (Historians have described the judgment as extremely light if indeed he had committed the grave offenses of which he was adjudged guilty. Oñate had no interest in returning to New Mexico, he could certainly live in Zacatecas for four years, so the only real punishment was monetary.)

Oñate complied with the sentence but in 1617 he filed a formal appeal to the King, asking that the sentence be lifted. There was no answer so in 1621 Oñate set sail for Spain in order to petition the King in person. Young Philip IV occupied the Spanish throne and took no action to grant Oñate exoneration by lifting the banishment and returning his titles. Oñate didn't give up and by royal order of August 11, 1623, Oñate was reimbursed for the 6,000 peso fine he had had to pay. This was vindication, to a degree. He asked for the title of marquis and that the *Adelantado* designation be granted in perpetuity. These were denied. But King Philip IV did ask him to serve as Spain's Mining Inspector, which he accepted, in 1624. Oñate was also honored in 1625 by induction into the prestigious Military Order of Santiago. He was now listed with acknowledged, herculean heroes of the Spanish people and his personal vindication was complete.

During the first part of October of 1625 Oñate fell seriously ill and was confined to bed for several weeks. He recovered well enough to resume his duties inspecting mines in the Guadalcanal area north of Seville. Around June 3, 1626, he went in to inspect a mine, collapsed, and died.

The heroic Spanish knight Juan de Oñate, "Father of New Mexico," isn't neutralized by the fact that he was also very human in his failings. He blazed the *Camino Real* from Santa Barbara (in present southern Chihuahua province) into New Mexico. He must be credited with introducing Christianity to the Southwest through the Franciscan missionaries. Native Americans were not exterminated and this fact owes much to the leadership of Oñate. He and his colonists introduced livestock, horses, cattle, goats and sheep, etc. to the new country, creating the basis for the ranching industry of the West. He introduced an advanced Hispano mining industry. He explored the Southwest and contributed to a true understanding of its geography. By leading colonists to New Mexico he established a new kingdom for Spain and its Christian Church. He undoubtedly played a paramount role in the founding of Santa Fe, the oldest capital in the USA.

The legacy of Don Juan de Oñate is memorable and will endure for as Marc Simmons has observed: *"To the end, the Last Conquistador remained true to his vision."* Contemporary New Mexicans are a living part of that vision.

Settlements

SAN ANTONIO, TEXAS, 1718

What is today referred to as "West Texas" was commonly known as *"Apachería"* and later *"Comanchería"* during the early 1700s. The New Mexico settlements were far away and the road north was beset with palpable obstacles and dangerous warlike Indians. Excluding New Mexico, the northernmost settlement was the presidio/mission complex known as *San Juan Bautista del Río Grande*, founded in 1700. The Crown felt a need for a military presence in Texas so experienced Spanish commander **Martín de Alarcón** was selected to cross the Río Grande River in 1718 at the head of an expedition, consisting of a group of seventy-two people in which there were various types of artisans (engineer, blacksmith, stone mason, etc.), along with large numbers of horses (548), mules, cattle, sheep, goats, and poultry. On April 1, 1718, he founded the mission *San Antonio de Valero* (known today as "The Alamo") and named it after the Viceroy, Baltazar de Zúñiga Guzmán Sotomayor y Mendoza, Marqués de Valero. On April 5, 1718, Alarcón founded the *Villa de San Antonio de Béxar* (also *Béjar*; known today as San Antonio,

Texas.) [See Note # 1. *Notes begin on page 53.*]

Plans for this first permanent European occupation of Spanish Texas actually began in 1709 when **Fray Antonio Olivares** joined an exploratory expedition that crossed the San Antonio River near a place called San Pedro Springs. The area struck everyone as being an ideal spot for location of a Spanish mission and settlement. [See Note # 2.] When Fr. Olivares went to Mexico City in 1716 he petitioned the Viceroy for the formation of a mission, *presidio* (fort), and settlement on the *Río de San Antonio*. The Viceroy approved his requests and appointed the Governor of Coahuila, **Martin de Alarcón**, to the post of Governor of Texas. Fr. Olivares was exasperated that the founding took so long to be accomplished but when finally done there was elation and then much hard work to make the effort a success. The *Villa de San Antonio* started with perhaps ten families but some twenty more came in a short time later.

By June of 1718 there were six missionaries at San Antonio Mission: Olivares, Núñez, Mesquía, Guerra, Céliz, and Brother Maleta. Among early important incidents were that the chiefs of 23 tribes came to the mission and offered their allegiance. A mission, small fort and *villa* (legal settlement) had been established when Alarcón resigned early in 1719 because more soldiers weren't sent to the province.

Lipan Apaches attacked some settlers in 1720, beginning the era of Apache depredations against Béxar. The Apaches planted crops in the spring then followed the bison in the autumn but now they were being forced out of the eastern plains by the numerous, fierce Comanches, so the Apache groups moved south. Apache attacks against Béxar/San Antonio continued until 1726. The missionaries spoke up against retaliatory expeditions, saying their peaceful means would prove more effective in the long run.

Brigadier General Pedro Rivera visited San Antonio in 1727 and reported that conditions were good at the presidio, garrisoned by a captain and 53 soldiers, and the mission currently housed some 173 resident Indians. In 1728 **Fr. Juan Salvador de Amaya** arrived at the mission and served until his death on November 17, 1752.

In 1731 some fourteen families, around 55 people, arrived from the Canary Islands (often called *Isleños*, Islanders) to help colonize the area. They were settled near the presidio in an area called *San Fernando de Béxar*, supplied with land, seeds and farming tools. They established a fairly independent government, built permanent homes, founded a church, and the first school in Texas. Frontier or not, they realized the value of education. [See Note # 3.] These Islanders were also described as complaining against the Indians, the missionaries, the presidio captain, and the other forty-nine families settled in the area.

Apaches began raiding again by 1731 in a difficult period that lasted until 1749. The presidio, missions, and settlement were threatened. The missionaries still didn't want to deal with the Apaches militarily because they hoped to Christianize them. Because of presidial cuts in east Texas, three missions were relocated to the San Antonio area: *Nuestra Señora de la Purísima Concepción, San Juan Capistrano*, and *San Francisco de la Espada*.

Because peace with one or two Apache bands wasn't binding on other Apache groups, Captain Urrutia launched a campaign in 1749 that capitalized on the strategy of taking large numbers of captives, treating them well, then negotiating peace with the chieftains involved. The military/humanitarian strategy worked for a number of reasons, among which was because the Apaches wanted the *Tejanos* (Spanish settlers) to help fight the Comanches and other *Norteño* (Northern) Indian enemies. The peace held for some ten years but Indian attacks proved to be a basic characteristic of life in early San Antonio.

The founders of San Antonio were typical people of New Spain's northern frontier. The small group of Canary Islanders was added to the mix, along with a small group criticized by Fray Olivares as "*mulattoes, lobos, coyotes, and mestizos, people of the lowest order, whose customs are worse than those of the Indians.*" [See Note # 4.]

Spanish colonization efforts always centered around the family so the typical Béxar household consisted of the family unit of husband, wife, and children. Infant mortality was high, the frontier environment was dangerous, but illegitimacy was not substantial in the community. Mixed parentage was common and because of frontier dangers the usual designations came to mean very little unless people became angry and wanted to insult each other. Even priests who recorded racial designations applied terms like *mestizo, coyote, español*, etc., to members of the same family, depending on what they were told. There were some laws which were more harsh on individuals considered "non-white" but generally there seemed to be an accommodation as to who was considered "white" in this "racially mobile" frontier society.

By 1749-1750 the population of Béxar/San Antonio was about 560 men, women and children. The presidio had a force of 43 soldiers and the community included some 57 men capable of bearing arms. Considering the thousands of Apaches and thousands of Comanches who could descend on the settlements, the *Bexareños* were a courageous lot.

All heads of households were given their own land as well as use rights to *ejidos* (commons land). Land was awarded more or less democratically to rich or poor, male or female, young or old, newcomers (*agregados*) or established residents (*primeros pobladores*) alike. All that was necessary was to prove need. Ownership was acknowledged through use. Water rights often caused difficulties and in the 1730s the Canary Islanders monopolized much land and water. The situation was rectified over time and people learned that it was better to work things out with your neighbor than to go to court in Mexico City. Land ownership was democratically widespread among Bexareños. They built their rectangular homes, planted vegetable gardens, fruit orchards, and crops (sugarcane, corn), and grazed their livestock on the land. Not utilizing the land in these ways was grounds for canceling the grant.

Though ownership of cattle was common in Béxar, the ranch industry got off to a slow start during the first half of the 18th century. Deterrents to the growth of ranches was hostile Indians who slaughtered stock during raids, land claims made by the missions, and the uncertainties of getting legal title to land. A large grant of land for stockraising was made to **Francisco Hernandez** in 1736 but there were few others before the second half of the century. But the settlers laid the foundations for the ranching industry because cattle were so important, meat being basic to everyone's diet. In 1748 one **Mateo Pérez** wrote in his will that he owned 200 head of cattle and fifty horses. Jerked meat, candle tallow, and hides became exports to areas as far south as Saltillo, Mexico. Even wild cattle became a factor in the local economy.

Horses were also basic in the new settlement. In 1734 one **Miguel Núñez Morillo** sold horses to the military for six to seven pesos a head. A good horse was worth whatever you could get for it whether in money, land, or cattle. It is also clear that hostile Indians did their utmost to acquire horses so in that sense there was very real danger involved in horse ranching.

The development of labor pools were begun around the 1720s when soldiers were assigned to help the missionaries. The Canary Islanders worked for others until they were able to employ men to help them. Newcomers often started out as laborers until they were able to make their own way in the community. Labor was plentiful at times, scarce at others, but it appears manual labor was rewarded with a subsistence (minimum) wage. Mission Indians were recruited as laborers but missionaries protested, filed a lawsuit, and the matter was settled out of court in 1745.

Working with livestock was better rewarded. In 1735 stockmen who hired one **Matías Trevino** paid him three reales (twelve pesos) per day, corn worth another peso per week, and a horse from each stockman whose cattle he cared for.

Military service was another option for those who didn't work in agriculture or cattle industries. Enlistments were for ten years but for the first few decades of the Béxar settlements it was difficult to recruit from the native population due to its small numbers. This was to change in later decades.

Civilian "Town Council" government was established in Béxar in 1731. The Town Council (*cabildo*) was comprised of six councilmen (*regidores*) who served for life, a constable (*alguacil*), attorney (*síndico procurador*) and a notary (*escribano*).

The Cabildo annually elected two men to serve as mayor (*alcaldes*).

Elections for governmental posts began in the 1730s. When any of the Town Council members died the others elected a new one to serve. By 1733 the agregados ("newcomers") were demanding to be considered as members of the community (*vecinos*) on par with the Isleños (Canary Islanders). In the 1740s the first non-Isleño was elected to the post of alcalde and some agregados made it into the Cabildo. Politics continued to be hotly contested until the community blended into one basic group.

Practicing religion was a unifying factor in early San Antonio. By 1738 it was decided that a regular church should be built and donations were needed from everybody. Isleños, presidio soldiers, and agregados donated from one to ten pesos each. **Miguel Núñez Morillo**, retired soldier turned rancher, donated thirty pesos, the single largest contribution. During the formal laying of the corner stone, Father **Juan Recio de León** declared: *"In the exercise of my ecclesiastical jurisdiction I pronounce this said building the parish church of this villa and the royal presidio of San Antonio."* Work proceeded as funds permitted but by 1745 the edifice was only half completed. At one point Alcalde **Antonio Rodriguez Mederos** declared that all citizens, no matter of what group, caste, or station, would be required to contribute or be fined twenty-five pesos along with fifteen days in jail. Despite the problems, the church was completed in 1755 and represented efforts from the entire community.

It is discernible that by the 1750s a bond of community was developing in San Antonio de Béxar. [See Note # 5.]

DISCUSSION Notes *for* SAN ANTONIO, TEXAS, 1718
Note # 1
See *San Antonio De Béxar: A Community on New Spain's Northern Frontier* by Jesús F. De

La Teja.

While there is a wealth of material on Texas history, four basic, recognized volumes will be referenced and referred to in the Texas sections of *EPIC*. For purposes of brevity they will be signaled as the "YRFF cycle" and are:

Yoakum, Henderson K. History of Texas, From Its First settlement in1685 to Its Annexation to the United States in 1846. (New York, 1855.)

Richardson, Rupert Norval. Texas: The Lone Star State. (New Jersey, 1943.)

Frantz, Joe B. Texas: A Bicentennial History. (New York, 1976.)

Fehrenbach, T.R. Lone Star: A History of Texas and the Texans. (New York, 1983.)

American historiography is fortunate to have Jesús F. De La Teja and his *San Antonio de Béxar*. The YRFF cycle contains little to no information on the founding of San Antonio, Texas, and neither the names nor the accomplishments of its pioneering 18th century settlers are mentioned.

Note # 2

See *The Alamo Chain Of Missions: A History of San Antonio's Five Old Missions* by Marion A. Habig, O.F.M.

Note # 3

See *Hispanic Culture In The Southwest* by Arthur L. Campa. For a "Black Legend" introduction to Spanish Texas see *Lone Star: A History of Texas and the Texans* by T.R. Fehrenbach.

Note # 4

Missionaries throughout northern New Spain, referred to as the "Borderlands" in American historiography, were often critical of ordinary soldiers and/or settlers. This could be due to the missionaries' highly disciplined Christian lifestyle, efforts to guard Indian neophytes against what they considered to be "un-Christian" examples in daily living, competing for resources like labor and/or land, etc. It is also possible that some settlers didn't approve of the missionaries and their efforts as Amerindian champions, or perhaps they resented Christian discipline as opposed to frontier "freedoms." Historians have often selected negative commentary to cast shadows on people or historical incidents.

Note # 5

While there are a number of nationally renowned Texas writers, the following body of work is also highly recommended because it provides perspectives which should be considered basic to the study of Texas history: *Tejano Origins In Eighteenth Century San Antonio* and *Tejano Journey, 1770 to 1850* edited by Gerald E. Poyo; *Tejanos And Texas Under The Mexican Flag, 1821-1836* and *Tejano Empire: Life On The South Texas Ranchos* by Andrés Tijerina; *The Texas Revolutionary Experience: A Political And Social History, 1835-1836* by Paul Lack; *A Revolution Remembered: The Memoirs And Selected Correspondence Of Juan N. Seguin* by Jesús F. de la Teja; *The Alamo Remembered: Tejano Accounts And Perspectives* and *Tejano*

Religion And Ethnicity: San Antonio, 1821-1860 by Timothy M. Matovina; *Defending Mexican Valor In Texas: José Antonio Navarro's Historical Writings, 1853-1857* by Timothy M. Matovina and David McDonald; *Anglos And Mexicans In The Making Of Texas* by David Montejano;

Tragic Cavalier and *Knight Without Armor* by Felix D. Almaráz, Jr.; *Tejano Legacy: Rancheros And Settlers In South Texas, 1734-1900* by Armando C. Alonzo.

SAN DIEGO, CALIFORNIA, 1769

The history of the founding of (Alta) California settlements is inextricably linked to the heroic Franciscans, especially friars **Junípero Serra, Francisco Palóu, Juan Crespi,** and **Fermín Lasuén.** [See Note # 1. *Notes begin on page 61.*]

FATHER SERRA

The future "Father of California," *Miquel Joseph Serra* was born on November 24, 1713, at Petra de Mallorca off the coast of Spain. (His name is *Serre* in Mallorca, *Serra* in Catalan, *Sierra* in Castilian. He used the *Serra* form.) In 1729 Serra was taken to the capital city of Palma and entrusted to the Franciscans for his education. By 1730 he was invested with the Franciscan habit. In 1731 he became Fray *Junípero Serra.* (The original *Junípero*, which name meant *"Jester of God,"* had been a companion of Francis of Assisi.) He spent six years studying philosophy and theology, preparing for ordination into the priesthood, which occurred around 1737. Due to his powerful mind and personal discipline he was made a professor by 1740, he received his doctorate by 1742, and in 1743 he held the Chair of Scotistic Theology at the Lullian University in Mallorca. He proved himself as accomplished in teaching as in oratory. In 1748 the diminutive academic (it is said he was five feet-two-inches tall), revered and lauded in his world, asked to be assigned as an apostolic missionary in the Americas, along with his fellow **Fray Francisco Palóu** (who would become the "Father of California History"). The request was granted and they were on their way to the West Indies by May, 1748.

Fray Junípero realized what he was leaving behind aging parents, his beloved homeland, friends of his lifetime, his treasured books, the university, his cloister and community. He asked that his parents be told of his *"great joy at becoming a missionary, that he knew they would encourage him to go forward always. Let them rejoice that they have a son who is a priest, though unworthy and a sinner, who daily in the holy sacrifice of the Mass prays for them with all the fervor of his soul and on many days applies the Mass for them alone, so that the Lord may aid them. I know they are advanced in years but let them recall that life is uncertain and in fact may be very brief. Strive to merit from God, our Lord, that if we see each other no more in this life, we may be joined forever in future glory."* Fray Junípero clearly understood that henceforth his home and final resting place would be in the Americas.

FIRST CALIFORNIA GOVERNOR

Leader of the 1769 expedition that brought Junípero Serra and Spanish civilization to Upper California was **Gaspar de Portolá**, California's first Governor. [See Note # 2.] On July 1 of 1769, the Portolá expedition reached the site named *San Diego*, to be the first mission/settlement in California. The supply ships *San Carlos* and the *San Antonio* were at anchor in San Diego Bay, a sight that heartened the weary members of the expedition. Fray Junípero recorded in his journal: *"…it was a day of great rejoicing and* *merriment.*" The friar, eight thousand miles from his native Mallorca, was finally "home." Portolá rested a couple of weeks then gathered the remaining able-bodied men and set off to locate Monterrey Bay. Fray Junípero was left to create a mission/settlement as best he could.

FRONTIER HARDSHIPS

The first order of business was building an infirmary because most of the remaining members of the expedition were ill. Of the 219 men who had departed from Lower California a little more than a hundred were still alive. Burials had to be performed on site because twenty-one sailors and even some soldiers had finally succumbed to scurvy. Provisions were insufficient and Fray Junípero wrote: *"Let those who are to come here as missionaries not imagine that they come for any other purpose but to endure hardships for the love of God and the salvation of souls."* He understood that survival would be no simple feat. The pioneers would have to depend on the supplies they brought with them and whatever they could provide for themselves in San Diego.

FIRST MISSION

On July 16, (Feast of Our Lady of Mount Carmel) 1769, Father Serra blessed the cross raised by soldiers on Presidio Hill and Mission *San Diego de Alcalá* was born, the first Christian foothold in California.

CALIFORNIA INDIANS

There were some twenty Indian villages in the area of San Diego. They didn't appear to be as primitive as the Indians of Baja California (who lived solely by hunting, fishing, and gathering; there was no architecture, agriculture, or formal education; their food included rats and mice).

The California Indians (estimated to number from 350,000 to 600,000) were products of tribal life and all seemed to have their own distinct customs. They spoke more than 200 languages/dialects. Some of the men lived totally naked (except for elaborate body paintings), though the women wore scanty skirts. During colder weather some Indians plastered themselves with mud in an effort to stay warm. They were often at war with each other and the men were considered brave and strong. Some tribes were so fierce that women sometimes went on war parties with the warriors.

At first the Indians around San Diego were curious about the newcomers but the novelty quickly wore off and they became unfriendly. Then when they showed up they would take whatever caught their fancy. Father Serra forbade the use of weapons on them until they appeared en masse, obviously intending to attack. A few volleys from guns drove them away but missionizing was now all but impossible.

EXPLORATION and TENSION

Gaspar de Portolá returned to San Diego without knowing he had located Monterey Bay. (He had found the area but hadn't recognized it.) Food and other critical supplies were so low that Portolá felt the new settlement might have to be forsaken if aid didn't arrive by the middle of March (1770). The Indians appeared to raise no food so trading wasn't feasible. There was some wild game but ammunition supplies were low and had to be saved for a possible Indian attack. A few days before the deadline the *San Antonio* supply ship put into the harbor amid a tumult of cheers and rejoicing. San

Diego was saved, for the moment.

MONTEREY

Within some three weeks Gaspar de Portolá once more set off to find Monterey Bay, this time including the hardy **Fray Juan Crespi** in the overland group. Fray Junípero's leg injury back in Vera Cruz had become ulcerated so he sailed toward Monterey aboard the *San Antonio*. The two pronged expedition was successful and Serra arrived in Monterey on June 1, 1770, eight days or so after the overland group with Portolá. It was observed that Monterey Bay appeared to be merely a circular lake. A religious ceremony was celebrated and the Spanish flag was raised for the first time. Because of the plentiful timber in the area in a short time a church was built along with the military presidio. Rough as it was, compared to the brush and mud shelters of San Diego, Monterey prospered and quickly became Father Serra's favorite locale. *San Carlos Borromeo de Carmelo* mission was founded on June 3, 1770, and became his headquarters for the California mission chain which came to be identified with the ringing of Church bells calling everyone to prayer, work, or special events. The presidio was founded a few days later and in time the mission was moved to the bay of Carmel some four miles away from the presidio.

GOVERNOR FAGES

In July of 1770 California's first Governor, Gaspar de Portolá, was replaced by Lieutenant **Pedro Fages**. Slowly the relationship deteriorated between Fray Junípero and Governor Fages. The Governor believed civil authority must be held supreme and Serra felt all was lost if the work of God didn't come above all else. After many disagreements, Father Serra decided to go to Mexico City, accompanied by a few faithful friends like the Indian **Juan Evangelista**, and present his case in person to Viceroy **Antonio M. Bucareli.**

VISIT in MEXICO CITY

Serra and his companions were in Mexico City by February of 1773. Viceroy Bucareli received Father Serra with much cordiality for he recognized the friars as stalwart champions of peaceful conquest. At the close of their talks he advised Serra to make a complete written report and informed the missionary that he would do everything possible to cooperate in what Father Serra suggested.

Academician that he was, Junípero Serra created a *Representación* (Report) that included twenty-one points of information that turned out being the basis for most significant legislation relating to early California. It affected everyone from the Indians to the Governor to the Council of the Indies. For one thing, Governor Fages had to be replaced if the development of missions was to continue. Furthermore, management, command, education, or punishment of baptized Indians must be the sole responsibility of missionaries, not civil authorities, excepting for violent crimes of blood. There were also other powers, like the missionary requesting that "immoral soldiers" be removed from all mission areas. Viceroy Bucareli accepted Serra's suggestions and henceforth the "Father of California and President of Missions," had a strong ally in Mexico City.

While still in the huge metropolis, Serra had **José de Paéz,** one of the more famous painters of the time, do oil paintings of the patron saints of the already established missions. When Serra was preparing for his return to California the good friars at the College of San Fernando were extremely worried that the frail *Presidente*, at times hardly able to stand, might not survive the return trip. Before leaving Father Serra asked permission to perform an act of humility and esteem toward his assembled fellow friars by kissing the feet of all in atonement for his human faults. In so doing, *"he touched the hearts of all in such a way that they shed copious tears."* Perhaps they also realized this would be the last time they would ever see the *Presidente* in this world.

Upon leaving Mexico City Father Serra wrote to his nephew: *"I am restored to health and going back… ready to set out on my journey back to that vineyard of the Lord."*

RIVERA DE MONCADA

After a forty day voyage, Junípero Serra was in San Diego by March 13, 1774. Governor Pedro Fages was replaced by **Fernando Rivera de Moncada** (on May 23, 1774). The padres in San Diego had worked tirelessly in Father Serra's absence, the spiritual harvest had improved, the wheat crop was good, stock numbers had increased, and products like milk were in abundance.

ANZA and GARCES

On March 22, 1774, an unexpected expedition arrived at San Gabriel, led by the valiant Captain **Juan Bautista de Anza**, and including the indomitable **Fray Francisco Garcés**. Back in Mexico City Viceroy Bucareli had asked Serra what he thought about an overland route from Sonora to California and Serra had endorsed it with enthusiasm. And now it was a reality: because of Anza, settlers could now travel overland instead of having to trek to the western coast of Mexico then risk an ocean voyage.

On April 28, 1774, the two great Hispanic knights for God and King met and discussed the California that was being created. Both were now very optimistic for this *"Kingdom of the Bells."*

FUTURE HOPES

The *Presidente's* hope for the future of California was its native children. He wrote that *"…seeing a hundred young children of about the same age, praying and answering one by one all the questions asked regarding Christian doctrine, hearing them sing, playing happily and fully clothed, is a moving experience for which God is to be thanked."*

The harvest of 1774 had the Indians of Carmel Valley working in the field, orchard, and woodland. During the harvest it happened that large schools of sardines appeared in Carmel Bay and the Indians wanted to catch them. So a compromise was worked out: the harvest would be worked in the morning and the people would fish in the afternoon, which arrangement lasted for some twenty days until enough sardines were caught. The bountiful fish were dried in the sun for future use. Harvested grain and other foodstuffs were also issued to all mission Indian families.

The baptismal register at San Carlos Mission in 1774 and 1775 shows that Father Serra added historical notes to the baptismal records. By the end of 1775 Serra had personally performed 171 baptisms. Father Serra honored visitors as well as people from the community as sponsors for those to be baptized into the Christian fold. He would ask soldiers, servants, workmen, wives, visitors, etc., to act as sponsors and everyone appreciated the honor in this emerging society whose motto was

"*¡Amar a Dios!*" (Love God!).

COOPERATION and DISAGREEMENTS

Father Serra understood that success in California depended upon the cooperation of the Governor and the missionaries. While the *Presidente* was always optimistic he was also realistic enough to know that not every one shared his enthusiasm. Governors often had disputes and misunderstandings with the missionaries. For example, Serra wanted to found as many missions as possible because his goal was to convert all Indians to Christianity. He wanted to build some 10 or 11 missions while he still lived. (He often referred to each new mission as a "rung on a ladder.") Governor Rivera thought the risk of new missions was too great so he refused the petitions. (The name of Governor Rivera doesn't appear in the baptismal books.) The two did not get along because when Serra proposed something Rivera habitually refused it. After a delay of a month or so then he would accede.

By 1775 Father Serra was determined to establish new missions between Monterey and San Diego. In June of 1775 the order arrived for the establishment of a mission and presidio in the San Francisco Bay area. Captain Anza was coming for that purpose with soldiers, settlers, and supplies. Father Serra received the news joyfully and now everyone acknowledged that more missions had to be established.

MARTYRDOM

Everyone understood that when working with California Indians martyrdom was a real possibility at any time. The night of November 4, 1775, was bathed in moonlight at around 1:30 a.m. when some 600 warriors went into the San Diego Mission compound, took what they wanted, then set fire to the buildings. The two missionaries, the guards and Christian converts woke up to see their community in flames. **Fray Luis Jayme**, from Mallorca like Father Serra, walked up to the rampaging Indians and greeted them with the standard salutation: "*Amar a Dios, hijos!*" (Love God, my children!) The rampaging mob seized him, carried him off, stripped him of his clothing then riddled him with arrows. As he lay in his final agony his face was struck again and again with war clubs, rendering him unrecognizable except to those who knew it was Fray Luis. A few shots from muskets finally dispersed the attackers who quickly withdrew when their own lives were in danger.

Father Serra and the other missionaries demanded to know why the soldiers at the presidio hadn't reacted quickly to the attack but the Indians would not suffer retribution because Father Serra believed in the ancient saying "*The Blood of the Martyrs is the Seed of the Church.*" Immediately he wrote to Viceroy Bucareli, reminding him that Serra himself had gone on record "*that in case the Indians, whether pagans or Christians would kill me, they should be pardoned.*" Despite the brutal murder of the good Fray Luis Jayme, the missionaries would not permit retribution or extermination of the Indians by the military. Fray Luis' mangled body was buried in a quiet ceremony in the presidio then later removed to the mission church, the "First California Martyr" who gave his life laboring for Christ to bring pagans into the Christian Church.

Junípero Serra went to San Diego in the summer of 1776 to re-establish the mission. Governor Rivera suspended the work when he received indications that the Indians were gathering for another attack. Serra occupied himself by searching out items that might have survived the fire. On September

16, 1776, he began a new baptismal register and included a brief history of San Diego's early days. He also noted that military reinforcements arrived in September, for which everyone rejoiced. Church bells were rung in honor of the arrival. Three letters from Viceroy Bucareli also arrived and one decreed that the Indians guilty of the massacre were to be pardoned and treated with kindness. Work resumed on rebuilding San Diego Mission with adobe bricks before the rainy season set in.

NEVE ARRIVES

In 1778 Father Serra received authorization to administer the sacrament of Confirmation to California converts. A new political unit was formed for the northern provinces with **Teodoro de Croix** in charge. A new Governor, **Felipe de Neve**, also arrived.

Serra traveled to the various missions, confirming Indians and a few Hispanics. In time he recorded that he had confirmed 1,897 people. Problems were common, as when Governor Neve demanded that Serra produce the official papers authorizing him to administer Confirmation, papers which were in Mexico City. Neve instructed Serra to cease confirmations until the official papers arrived and Serra complied instead of fighting the Governor publicly.

PESOS for the AMERICAN REVOLUTION

When the American Revolution began Spain backed the colonies' bid for freedom against England. As the President of Missions, Father Serra was asked to pray for the Americans and collect one peso for the war effort from each Indian who could afford it.

FRONTIER LIFE and DEATH

By December of 1780 Fray Junípero received written verification that he was authorized to administer Confirmation, ending the impasse with Governor Neve.

Though Serra and the missionaries believed California was not yet ready to establish civilian villages, saying they would compete too much for limited resources, the *Pueblo de Nuestra Señora la Reina de los Angeles del Río de Porsiúncula* (Town of Our Lady the Queen of the Angels by the Porsiúncula River) was founded on September 4, 1781. Serra visited there in March of 1782.

On January 1, 1782, Serra's student and long time companion from Mallorca, Fray **Juan Crespi**, passed away after a brief illness. The sorrow was felt by every missionary in California.

Junípero Serra continued with his hectic schedule though he suffered severely from his swollen leg and serious chest pains. Back in 1770 when Serra had founded San Carlos Mission he had written in the burial register: *"We all die and like waters that return no more, we fall down into the earth."* Death never held terror for the President of Missions. On August 27, 1784, Father Serra celebrated a High Mass and delivered the oration. He returned to his cell and called for the presidio carpenter to prepare his coffin before visiting with Father Palóu. That evening he was anointed then passed most of the night praying on his knees. He seemed to feel better the following morning but in the early afternoon of August 28, 1784, Father Palóu performed the honor of closing the eyelids of his friend and superior, Fray Junípero Serra, the Father of California.

DISCUSSION Notes *for* SAN DIEGO, CALIFORNIA, 1769

Note # 1

See *The Life And Times Of Fray Junípero Serra* by Msgr. Francis J. Weber for a popular introduction to this era of California history. In this category are also *California Missions* edited by Ralph B Wright and *Saints Of The California Missions* by Norman Neuerburg.

Note # 2

See *California: A History* by Andrew F. Rolle for an accessible general history of California which also contains ample sections on *"Suggested Readings."* In one such section author Rolle advises readers that "A serious adulatory treatment of Serra and his fellow Franciscans has been written by a member of the order, Father Zephrin Engelhard, *The Missions and Missionaries of California*." Such "cautions" are by no means rare but how common is it to be warned in advance that such-and-such a book or author is hispanophobic or anti-Catholic? Is Rolle implying the Engelhard work could be misleading? If a "member of the order" might not be reliable, who might be? By the same token, what about "patriotic Americans" writing "American history"?

The psychology of denigration, perhaps directly or indirectly a product of the Black Legend, is often in the fabric of American historiography when dealing with Spain, its people, or the Catholic religion supposedly beset by *"papists and popery."* For example, an often quoted work in Southwest history is *Cycles Of Conquest*, 1962, by Edward H. Spicer. In the section titled "Bibliographic Notes to Chapters," Chapter One, page 587, Spicer refers to the work *Early Jesuit Missions In Tarahumara* by Peter Masten Dunne in this fashion: *"Dunne may be recommended, but with the reservation always that he is a Jesuit writing about, primarily, Jesuit activities. He inevitably exhibits a Jesuit bias in his selection and emphasis. It is not easy to find a corrective for this, for the only other broad narrative accounts of the period are also by Jesuits, Decorme and Alegre. Within the limits of secondary sources, the best correctives that can be recommended are Bancroft, Saravia, and perhaps West."* If this rationale is valid, should we expect "Americans" to exhibit an "American bias" when writing about "American activities" or about anything which they might happen to resent culturally? Can we believe in the work of Francis Parkman, an "American" writing on American themes? The renowned Dr. Walter P. Webb is a proud Texan. Should his histories of Texas therefore not be considered valid history? [See the essay at the end of this Notes section.]

James A. Sandos writes in Chapter 8 of *Contested Eden* that some writers have accused the Franciscans of genocide, that they have compared Father Serra to Adolf Hitler, that the California missions were like the Nazi death camps (of Auschwitz, Dachau, Treblinka?), *"thereby confusing results with intent."* (Results? Does this imply veracity of the accusations?) Then he states that "for an extreme statement of the anti-mission school..." see Rupert and Jeannette Henry Costo, eds., *The Missions Of California: A Legacy Of Genocide* published by the Indian Historian Press, 1987.

Essay: HISTORY OR PROPAGANDA?

The short volume, *Monterey In 1786: Life In A California Mission: The Journals Of Jean Francois De La Perouse* is worthy of study. The "Introduction," written by Malcolm Margolin, comprises almost half of the book and provides what is generally termed as "analysis" in American historiography. The reader is treated to the "Introduction" and its "analysis" instead of the original French language journal. While most Americans can't read French there is no other choice but to read what has been provided. No mention is made as to who translated the Pérouse journal into English so one has to rely on the veracity of the translation. The same is true when the author quotes Hispanics like Junípero Serra and governors like De Neve, who spoke and wrote in the Spanish language: no Spanish language sources are cited in the Margolin work. While writing and/or reading in three languages is no simple feat, scholar Salvador de Madariaga provides documentation and bibliography in various languages for his English language version of *The Rise Of The Spanish American Empire*. Madariaga's citations in French (despite limitations of my keyboard) and Italian will suffice for purposes of scholarship: "See for instance: Contribution á l'Ethnographie Précolombienne du Mexique. Le Chimalhuacan et ses Populations avant la Conquete Espagnole par M. Léon Diguet, Journal de la Sociéte des Américanistes de Paris, Nouvelle série, Tome 1, num. 1. Paris, 1903, p. 14." In Italian: "Giordano Bruno. La Cena de le Ceneri descritta in cinque Dialoghi per Quattro Interlocutori con tre Considerationi circa doi suggetti, 1584. G.B., A.W., p. 146: che quando vede un forastiero sembra per dio tanti lupi, tanti orsi che consuo torvo aspetto gli fanno quel viso, che saprebbe far un porco ad un, che venisse a torgli il tinello davanti."

So the reader of Margolin's La Pérouse is "informed" (is this really what La Pérouse wrote or is it "mostly Margolin"?) concerning items like the following: Monterey mission and its presidio were in "destitute condition" when visited by La Pérouse. Further, "…two monks and a handful of soldiers were expected to reproduce European civilization with the Indians of California as its citizenry." (Monterey has somehow become California.) "Admirers" praise Junípero Serra while "detractors" wonder if "there were not internal demons from which he was fleeing with such desperation." We are told that "Spaniards" didn't have much appreciation for the complexities of "Indian" (unnamed) hunting skills, government, justice systems, religion, cultures. "Indians" are represented as one people while in reality they were quite different as reflected by the more than 200 languages/dialects spoken by California Indian groups. The "historical analysis" in *Journals* appears to be that mission Indians were "in virtual slavery," suffered "horrendous" death rates due to diseases brought by the "newcomers," resulting in "unrelenting misery for he (sic) Indians," and therefore "The missions of California were places of defeat and death," an observation supposedly supported by La Pérouse and what others have said, if one is "reading carefully between the lines." It would appear clairvoyance is a vital component of Margolin's work but according to Margolin's La Pérouse there is no doubt the California mission resembled "a slave plantation of Santo Domingo…" which was of course French, while those like Barbados, among the most profitable of slave plantations in the British empire, aren't even mentioned. (See *Africans In America: America's Journey Through Slavery* by Charles Johnson and Patricia Smith.)

Orwellian thrusts are common when dealing in "American Historiography." For example, when discussing San Francisco Bay in *California: Land Of New Beginnings* by David Lavender, the reader is informed that "John Charles Fremont…would name it (the inlet; "La Boca" in Spanish language chronicles of the day) the Golden Gate…" as if anxious to get on with the real story. As Stewart Udall has suggested, unless history was made by English speaking participants, many writers feel there really isn't much "History" that needs to be recognized. This is one of the basic faults of American Historiography.

TUCSON, ARIZONA, 1776

On August 20, 1775, Comandante General **Hugo O'Conor** chose and marked off the site of a new *presidio* (fort) at a place called *San Agustín de Tucson* some ten miles north of San Xavier Mission. The area was chosen because the Santa Cruz River could be utilized by pioneer soldiers and settlers, who would also provide protection against the Western Apaches. Of prime importance would be to protect the overland trail to California blazed by Captain Anza.

The settlers (*vecinos*) and presidio soldiers who rode into the Tucson Basin in 1776 came from *San Ignacio de Tubac*. They were already people who knew the desert and how on live on it. [See Note # 1. *Notes begin on page 64.*] They knew where to find water and where they wouldn't, knew the Pimas and Pápagos were their allies, and understood the Apaches were their common enemy. [See Note # 2.] Some individuals were American born Spaniards while others were products of the racial/ethnic mixtures common to Spain's northern frontiers. [See Note # 3.]

The "*Tucsonenses*" were desert dwellers who utilized established Hispanic settlement patterns, adobe building materials, irrigation ditches (*acequias*), and productive farming and stock raising techniques. Their horses and cattle were as tough as the Hispanic pioneers themselves. Everything and everybody had to adapt to the desert as well as the Indians. Accommodations were made to the cultures of friendly Indians. Along with corn, beans, and squash there would now be wheat, grapes, various kinds of melons, fruit trees, etc., but they also learned to appreciate the edible parts of the *nopal* and the *saguaro*. They made flour out of mesquite pods for *pinole* since there was no coffee available. There was *mescal*. But now there would also be horses, cattle, sheep, mules, burros, goats, etc., a tremendous improvement to the food supply from pre-European days. The people learned to deal with their isolation, made their subsistence living through farming and stock raising, developed vital procedures for cooperation. Theirs was a society of pioneers based on self-reliance, hardship, and the will to survive.

According to writers like **Jesus García**, the men adapted their clothing to the hot weather by wearing breechclouts like the Indians. During the cooler months they wore pants, jackets or blankets with a hole in the middle (ponchos). Shoes were often *teguas* (moccasins made of buckskin) or *guaraches* (sandals).

Women wore long skirts and blouses, along with scarves or shawls (*rebozos*). They washed clothes along the river's edge by scrubbing them against rocks, always accompanied by armed guards.

Presidial soldiers on campaign wore *cueras*, leather jerkins which reached to the knee. These men, who came to be known as "*soldados de cuera*" or "**Leatherjackets**," received protection from Indian arrows because of their cueras, an important frontier item which was often in short supply.

Because of the danger from Apache attacks the presidio itself was surrounded by thick adobe walls. Homes were built inside the fort with houses built against the walls. They had flat roofs which weren't as high as the protective exterior walls, thus forming a protective parapet from which defenders could combat attackers.

By 1831 there were some 465 Hispanic people living in Tucson. There were no doctors so people treated themselves with various herbs and roots. Drinking water was obtained from the community well inside the presidio. The only regular contact with the rest of Sonora came by pack trains. Close contact was kept with Indian friends: Gila Pimas to the north and Pápagos to the west. These stalwart Indian tribes often participated in expeditions against the Apaches and it is doubtful Tucson could have survived, due to its small numbers compared to the Apaches, without the Pimas and Pápagos.

The *"Apaches Mansos"* also became important in defense of the frontier. Called *"Tontos"* (crazies; fools) by hostile Apaches, the Mansos under their able leader **Antuna** served as scouts and guides for the Tucsonenses, supplying valuable information necessary for survival of the Hispanic, Pima, and Pápago communities.

So it was that pioneering frontier families with names like **Romero, González, Gallegos, Urrea, Castro, Burruel, Comadurán, Pacheco, Pesqueira, Ruelas, Sosa, Zúñiga**, etc., and individuals like **Teodoro Ramírez** and **José de Urrea**, helped to establish the first settlement of European people in what is now southern Arizona.

DISCUSSION Notes *for* TUCSON, ARIZONA, 1776

Note # 1

See *Los Tucsonenses: The Mexican Community In Tucson*, 1854-1941, by Thomas E. Sheridan. For an introductory approach to Arizona history see *Arizona: A Cavalcade Of History* by Marshall Trimble. Don't miss *Arizona: A History* by Thomas E. Sheridan for a more in-depth treatment of certain issues.

Note # 2

In Hispanic societies in what is now the Southwest there were *"good Indians"* and they didn't have to be *"dead"* to prove it. Despite bitter warfare when necessary, Spanish policy never demanded the extermination or exile of Indian groups, including hostile Apaches. This reality is usually ignored in much of American historiography

Note # 3

As in other areas, Hispanic frontier society was influenced to a degree by European traditions but the need to have help from one's neighbors during times of danger served to level society into a more democratic organism. One didn't care if a "white" or "non-white" saved your life, so long as it was saved. Many writers using the English language focus on "the Spanish caste system" because there were so many racial/ethnic designations available. Hispanic frontier societies generally promoted cooperation much more than discrimination/segregation.

CHAPTER 4

Spanish Institutions

Major contributions of Spanish culture to (what is now) the Southwest would include the mission, the *presidio* (fort), and industries like ranching and mining.

THE MISSION

Missions are often described as the most important institution of the Spanish frontier. [See Note # 1. *Notes begin on page 72.*] In contrast to the later English settlements and American westward expansion from the east coast, Spanish missionaries either preceded, accompanied, or followed the *conquistadores* in their discovery, exploration, and settlement of the Americas. [See Note # 2.] The only real moral authority enjoyed by Catholic Spain in the Americas was the 1493 papal bull of Alexander VI which proclaimed in part that aboriginal people should be Christianized and not harmed.

In 1504 **Queen Isabel** (Elizabeth) of Spain decreed that the grant made by Pope Alexander VI obligated the Spanish Crown and all its citizens to convert the Indians *"…to our holy Catholic Faith, to teach and instruct them in good morals, and to do it with great diligence … and that they should not permit or give an occasion that the Indian citizens and dwellers of the said islands and firm land, acquired or to be acquired, receive any harm in their persons or in their possessions, even more they must order that they should be well and justly treated, and if they have received any harm they should amend it and see to it that in no way they should go beyond what is urged and commanded to us by the apostolic Letters…And I say and declare that this is my will…And so that this be firm and there be no doubt … I sign it with my name before witnesses and I order it to be sealed with my seal.* (sig.) **I, the Queen Isabel**

Queen Isabel was absolutely sincere in her responsibility to bring Christianity to American aboriginal peoples and subsequent missionary history in the Americas is testament to that fact. [See Note # 3.] These intrepid missionaries also became pioneers of European civilization and frontiersmen in the highest sense.

GOVERNMENT POLICY

Spanish governmental policy was also committed to converting, civilizing, and utilizing the Amerindian in Hispanic society. The *encomienda* system was created for those purposes. An *encomendero* (trustee) was granted a specific group of Indians which he must protect, Christianize, and civilize. As his reward, the encomendero was empowered to have the Indians work or produce for him, the profit from which the trustee must share with the King. Christian and civilizing instruction had to come from friars/missionaries, whom the trustee was required to support.

While the encomienda system was intended to benefit everyone, including the Amerindian, it soon became mere slavery. [See Note # 4.] This is when men of the cloth like **Bartolomé de las Casas** came forward as *Protectors of the Indians*. While they were fought tooth and nail by those who wished to enrich themselves by exploiting Indian labor, they were successful to the point that, except in the Caribbean islands, Indians were not exterminated in the Spanish Americas.

MISSIONARIES as INDIAN AGENTS

In what is now called the Southwest, the missionaries became the "trustees" responsible for Indian protection, conversion, and civilization. For all practical purposes, they became the Indian agents serving both God and King because their activities were also political: the country had to be held if it was going to be Christianized. [See Note # 5.] So these religious paladins served political as well as religious ambitions when they entered the wilderness ahead of or beside the conquistador, soldier, trader, prospector, miner, or cattle man. These "Soldiers for the Cross" embodied the highest qualities of manhood, qualities like spirituality, mental and physical courage, moral character, intelligence, resourcefulness, good health, willingness to endure all manner of hardships, including loneliness, and even to give up one's life if necessary to bring the Faith to groups of people who knew it not. Martyrdom wasn't sought as an end in itself but the distinct possibility of such a death wasn't a deterrent to heroic missionary activity. If martyrdom became the price it was accepted because it merely fanned the apostolic flame for a new Christian champion who would come on the scene.

Franciscan missionaries and missions became so successful that they were in all Spanish lands from California to Florida. (Other orders included the Jesuits and Dominicans.) First and foremost the missions were responsible for converting Indians to the Faith. When this was accomplished, generally within a period of ten years, the missionaries were to put the Christian Indians in possession of mission lands then move on to other areas and repeat the process. With some tribes the process needed more time but individuals who wanted to grab the land demanded the missionaries leave after completing ten years. The missionaries understood the situation and generally resisted secularization of the missions.

Beyond imparting the Christian Faith, which they sincerely considered an inestimable European gift, the missionaries were also agents of (European) Spanish civilization. They left behind them their families, their European society and amenities, to became explorers, chroniclers, teachers, scientists, doctors, geographers, cooks, artisans, ranchers, blacksmiths, architects, builders, painters, farmers, musicians, linguists, choral conductors, writers, stockmen, cowboys, etc., whatever was necessary to improve the lot of Christian Indians and attract new converts. It is almost incomprehensible that these tremendous intellects, schooled in university disciplines like Theology, Mathematics, Philosophy, who were teachers and founders of colleges, writers of informational books on a wide variety of subjects, could also be found in every-day activities like cooking, washing clothes, plowing, planting and hoeing fields, harvesting crops, handling stock animals, making adobes, building houses and churches, serving as doctors and nurses as well as veterinarians. In other words, they were on par with university professors as well as hard-working "blue collar" peasants.

PAYING EXPENSES

Mission expenses were generally paid by the Spanish Government at around $450 pesos per year per missionary. The Crown also shouldered expenses related to soldiers who protected the missionaries. Older missions were expected to help pay expenses for the new ones and this happened regularly if finances permitted. Private endowments were also an important factor. For example, **Pedro de Terreros** contributed to the founding of Apache missions in Texas and added to the **Pious Fund** (*Fondo Piadoso*) in California. In time the Indians themselves were expected to be self-sufficient and pay their own way. Some Indians became wealthy from ranching or agriculture. The missionaries received no share of that Indian wealth.

INDIAN ALLIES

Christian Indians became an integral part of Spanish expeditions against warlike tribes. By 1700 the alliance between Hispanic New Mexicans and the Pueblo people was easily discernible. In the same century the expeditions out of San Antonio, Texas, against hostile Apaches and Comanches included warrior mission Indians. In Sonora/Arizona Father Kino could be counted on to enlist his Pima converts to fight hostile Apaches.

CHRISTIAN ETHICS & LIFESTYLE

Mission life could be described as based on personal discipline. The missionaries believed in strict codes of behavior regarding religion, personal morals, social activity, and work ethics. Indians living in villages were easier to work with so the push was for prospective converts to live in one central location. This proved efficacious with people like the Pimas and Pueblos but not with some California Indians or the nomadic bands like Apaches or Comanches. Neophytes had to be controlled and living in the mission or nearby village was the simplest way to achieve that control. Few people in any age accept discipline so some Indians ran away. Whenever possible, soldiers brought them back, by force if necessary. In California Governor De Neve asked Father Serra to minister to the Indians in their own *rancherías* (encampments) but Serra pointed out there would be no control possible out in the wilds. De Neve didn't want to provide additional (expensive) soldiers at Santa Barbara so this caused a serious feud with Father Serra.

The typical, fully developed Spanish mission was many things but first and foremost a Christian seminary. Christianity was the most important avenue to assimilation. Despite the super abundance of Indian languages/dialects, missionaries were required to use them during instruction and many of them did but it was soon learned that Christian concepts couldn't be conveyed in most Indian languages. So Spanish was often used, through interpreters at first, then by the friars. Children were worked with assiduously for they learned the quickest and were the future. While serious efforts were made to teach these youngsters Spanish, speaking, reading, and writing it, none was made to prevent them from speaking their native tongues.

Imparting Christianity necessitated a daily routine of prayers, catechism, and church music. Talented youngsters were trained as altar boys then as catechists when they got a little older. Requirements were attendance at Mass, regular prayers, confession, celebrating Church holidays with processions and other pageantry. Religious fiestas also included secular activities like matanzas, horse races and even foot races. One Jesuit decided to race his Indian charges, he on horseback and the Indians on foot: the Indians won.

Church bells called everyone to Mass in the morning. Indian helpers would go through the village and call children and unmarried persons to services. At the end of Mass all recited prayers and the Apostle's Creed with the priest. The bells rang again at sunset and prayers were recited at the door of the church and sometimes a rosary was said. On Sundays and feast days all village men, women, and children were required to attend Mass dressed in their best clothes. Musical instruments like harps or violins were a part of the celebration, and the choir sang. Palm Sunday was celebrated with a procession.

MISSION & COMMUNITY COLLEGE

The mission had to be more than a school for religion if it was to succeed. Necessity forced it to become an industrial training school staffed by the missionaries. Missions worked with hundreds, sometimes thousands of Amerindians. It was during the teaching/learning process that neophytes became civilized, i.e., assimilated into European (Spanish) culture. Indian women were taught to cook in the European style, to sew, spin, weave. Men were taught to blacksmith, work leather, the wine press, *all the trades and polite deportment* of European life. They learned how to irrigate and harvest their crops old and new, tend to their horses, cattle, sheep, goats, hogs. While the missionaries managed the mission operations the goal was to make the Indians self-sufficient and the goal was often reached to an amazing degree considering the situation.

Father Kino of Sonora/Arizona wrote in 1710 that he saw many Indian gardens with onions, garlic, lettuce, mustard, etc., vineyards, fields of wheat and corn, orchards of European fruits like apples, peaches, apricots, oranges, pomegranates, quince, figs, etc., sweet cane for syrup and panocha, etc. He described ranches stocked with cattle, sheep, and goats. There were horses, mares as well as stallions, mules for pack animals. Wool products, tallow, suet, and soap were manufactured by the neophytes.

Central locations had to be chosen with the nomadic tribes and the Indians induced to settle permanently in that one place. Called *reducciones* (which meant "reductions of barbarism"), these efforts were not usually successful because the nomadic tribes preferred freedoms of the wild even if they had to live in caves or temporary huts. If the Indians already lived in villages the mission was established in the village, the "reduction" already accomplished.

The mission complex was often an imposing structure and mini-community. Each one had a church and *convento* which housed the religious. Generally structured around a patio, there could be individual cells for visiting missionaries, offices for business purposes, a kitchen and dining hall, spinning and weaving rooms and other workshops for activities like wine-press, carpentry, masonry. A granary and warehouses were required for storage. Reading, writing, and music could be taught anywhere, including in the church itself. There were corrals for the stock, fields for growing wheat and corn, along with irrigation ditches where necessary.

Indian housing was often built close to the mission as in San Antonio de Valero. Indian homes at San Antonio were built of stone and had regular doors and windows. There was a plaza with a fresh water well along with a small irrigation ditch at a distance for watering fruit trees. The entire area was surrounded by a wall and one gate provided entrance or exit, with a strong tower above it with emplacements for cannon and other firearms.

The Laws of the Indies required and the missions provided training for self-government. Activities were for the potential future rather than present realities. The representative of the King, whether governor, captain, or alcalde, appointed native officers and acknowledged title to the (typical) four league Indian land grant. After initial appointments Amerindian officers would be selected by the Indians themselves, under supervision of the missionaries and approved by the Spanish officer in charge. These Amerindian governments had varying degrees of success but it is certain that the effort was made by the Spanish government. [See Note # 6.].

As mentioned at the beginning of this section, missionaries like Juan Padilla, Alonso de Benavides, Andrés Juárez, Esteban de Perea, Eusebio Kino, Francisco Garcés, Antonio de Jesús Margil ("The Apostle of Texas"), Antonio de San Buenaventura y Olivares, Francisco Hidalgo, Benito Fernández de Santa Ana, Junípero Serra, Fermín Lasuén, Juan Crespi, Francisco Palóu, , etc., are herculean figures in the histories of the Southwest but few are studied in the present day. The following section on Eusebio Kino will serve as a basis for further study of North America's noblest pioneers.

"You Are and Ever Will Be My Dearest Master."

Eusebius Kino (also written as *Chini, Chino, Chinus*) was born in the little town of Segno, Italy, a short distance northwest of the famous city of Trent in the Tyrolese Alps. [See Note # 7.] Kino's parents were well-to-do villagers in Segno. Their native language was Italian. Eusebio decided to enter the Jesuit College at Trent and proved himself a most serious student. Next he attended the Jesuit College of Hala (Hall), near Innsbruck. In 1663 Eusebio was stricken with a mortal illness. He made a vow to his patron San Francisco Xavier, Apostle of the Indies, that if he recovered he would enter the Jesuit Order and make his life as a missionary in foreign lands. Miraculously, Eusebio recovered. True to his vows, he joined the Jesuit Order and when his training was complete asked for overseas duties in China.

STUDY IN GERMANY

Eusebio began his novitiate in 1665 and spent twelve years in academic studies and rigorous Jesuit discipline. During that time he attended the best German colleges: Innsbruck, München, Freiburg, Ingolstad, Oettingen. It was during this period that he added *"Francisco"* to his own name, in honor of his patron San Francisco. In 1677 Eusebio studied Philosophy for three years at Ingolstadt. In 1670 he was assigned to teach at Innsbruck for three years and then he returned to Ingolstadt for another four.

Eusebio became especially interested in mathematics, perhaps due to his professor Father **Adam Aigenler**, a cartographer. He also developed a deep respect for Father **Scherer**, a geographer and map maker. Eusebio became so proficient in mathematics that the Duke of Bavaria invited him to become a professor under the Duke's personal patronage. He declined the offer because he intended to do missionary work. In 1677 he went to Oettingen to complete Jesuit requirements and then he was ready for his life's work. [See Note # 8.] Now he was ready to go to the Orient, preferably China. He was certain he could succeed because, among other things, Chinese rulers treasured the Jesuits because of their expertise in mathematics. He and his fellow missionary Father **Antonio Kerschpamer** waited and finally the appointments came in: one missionary would go to the Philippines, the other to Mexico. Father Eusebio told Father Antonio to make the first choice. But Father Antonio was just as gallant so he refused. They hit upon the idea of drawing lots so two slips of paper were prepared, one with *"Mexico"* written on it, the other with *"Philippines."* Father Antonio drew the latter so Father Eusebio Francisco Kino's destiny was to be in Mexico.

The jumping off point was in Spain where the Jesuits arrived in 1678. After years of delays in Spain, which time Kino used to perfect his knowledge of the Spanish language, Father Eusebio and seventeen other missionaries set sail from Cadiz on January 27, 1681. The Atlantic passage had its very real dangers and discomforts but the missionaries were in Vera Cruz in early May and Mexico City by early June. Kino was assigned to work in Lower (Baja) California, which he did until all missionizing was suspended in that locale. He was then assigned to the Sonora/southern Arizona area, also known as *Pimería Alta*, arriving there in March of 1687 and getting to the work of exploration, conversion, and mission building immediately, efforts which he would make for the next twenty-four years.

PIMERIA ALTA

Based at the frontier mission of Concurpe, Eusebio Kino quickly learned that Pimería Alta was inhabited by different divisions of the **Pima** nation: those living in the valleys made by the Gila and Salt Rivers; the *Sobaipuris* living in the valleys of the San Pedro and Santa Cruz rivers; and the **Pápagos** (*Papabotes* to the Spaniards). Further to the northwest were the powerful Yuman groups (Yumas, Cocomaricopas, Cocopas, Quiquimas) who were unrelated to the Pima nations.

The Pimas, and to a lesser degree the Pápagos, grew corn, wheat, beans, squash, melons, etc. through irrigation, also raised cotton from which they made their clothing.

MISSION DOLORES

At the Indian village of Cosari, some fifteen miles north of Concurpe, Father Kino established the mission of *Nuestra Señora de los Dolores* (Our Lady of Sorrows) on the San Miguel River. Mission Dolores was to be Kino's headquarters and the "mother mission" for Sonora and Arizona. By 1695 the indefatigable Kino had founded a chain of missions throughout the valleys of the Altar and Magdalena Rivers as well as northeast of Mission Dolores. In April of 1700 he founded San Xavier del Bac and shortly thereafter Tumacácori and Guebavi.

EXPLORATION & GEOGRAPHY

Exploration went hand in hand with Kino's spreading the Faith. He was the first European to map Pimería Alta on the basis of first hand exploration. He criss-crossed the area several times, from south to north as well as east to west, traveling as far as (present) Tucson six different times, in his forty to fifty expeditions during his twenty-four years of service.

One of Kino's passions was the geography of California. He had been taught at the University of Ingolstadt that California was a peninsula and many had said it was an island. In 1700 he reached the Yuma Junction and learned he was at the head of the Gulf of California. He returned in 1701 and again in 1702 then declared that California definitely wasn't an island so an overland route to it was definitely feasible. (This was a first that laid the groundwork for the overland route which was to be blazed by Anza.)

RANCHING

In all his missions Kino started the ranching industry, in person or under his supervision. Supplied from his own established missions, Kino often drove as many as a hundred horses to a new site, along with as many cattle. Within fifteen years he implanted the ranching industry in the valleys of the Magdalena, the Altar, the San Pedro, and the Sonóita rivers. He was easily the cattle king of his day though he himself didn't own a single animal. These highly successful efforts in nineteen (19) different areas of the map established economic prosperity and independence for the mission Indians.

He also shared the wealth with other missions in which he wasn't directly involved. He sent more than a hundred cattle and a like number of sheep to Father Saeta in Caborca. In 1700 he sent some 750 head of cattle to San Xavier del Bac with a like number to Father Salvatierra at Loreto in sterile Baja California, a gift which Kino made several times.

It must also be pointed out that during his explorations and ranching efforts he was usually accompanied almost exclusively by his Indian charges. Only twice did he have soldiers with him and most often there was no other European in the group. An Indian uprising was always an imminent possibility. In 1695 Father Saeta was martyred at Caborca by the very Indians who later helped Kino drive a herd of cattle and flock of sheep to Tumacácori, Arizona.

KINO as COWBOY

Kino the mathematician, student of Theology and Philosophy, was also a cowboy whose endurance in the saddle could hardly be rivaled. At the age of fifty-one (1695) he rode to Mexico City, some 1500 miles away, in fifty-three days (which included stops like Guadalajara along the way). On his numerous missionary tours he could average some thirty miles a day on horseback for thirty straight days. All the while he would make stops to baptize newborns or seriously ill Indians, preach to assembled natives, supervise the erection of buildings or butchering of beeves, and distribute presents. In 1701 when he was almost sixty years old he rode some 1100 miles in thirty-five days.

PERSONAL COURAGE

Kino's physical courage might have been equaled by the legendary conquistadores but it is doubtful even they ever surpassed it. His life in the Americas was spent working with Indians who could have killed him at any moment. As mentioned previously, when the Pimas rose up in revolt in 1695 they murdered Father Saeta at Caborca along with seven helpers from Caborca and Tubutama. Missions were burned and stock killed throughout the Altar and Magdalena valleys. Some three hundred warriors swept down on San Ignacio and an Indian who saw the smoke rising raced to Mission Dolores to inform Kino the rampaging marauders were headed his way. Lieutenant **Manje** sped to get more soldiers and Kino was left alone. The following day Manje returned with help but Kino refused to leave, saying he would await his fate with his Christian Indians. The soldiers begged him to leave but he wouldn't so they stayed with him. By chance, the hostiles didn't go to Mission Dolores. When Kino later wrote about the uprising he didn't even bother to mention his personal situation in Dolores. Lieutenant Manje is the one who wrote about it in his report or it would have gone unrecorded.

KINO the MAN

Born in Italy, educated in Germany, missionary in the Spanish Americas, what kind of person was this Christian paladin? There are no portraits of Father Eusebio Francisco Kino so there is no certainty as to what he looked like (except as represented by Chini family descendants). Kino was more slight of body than muscular. He was described by contemporaries as an academic, medieval type who would pray many times a day, as gentle as he was humble. When he read from his prayer book he often wept. He liked good conversation, invoking the beauties of Jesus and Mary throughout. He was always inspired by the lives of the Saints and preached their virtues to Indians and Europeans alike. He could be exceptionally stern when chastising a sinner but when targeted by virulent disrespect in person he embraced his accuser and replied *"You are and ever will be my dearest master."*

No one ever saw him indulge in any sort of vice. He never smoked, never took snuff, nor drank wine except in celebrating Mass. He owned only two shirts because he gave away his clothing to the poor. He ate sparingly and took his food without salt. He slept perhaps four hours a night, and this generally on his saddle blanket for a mattress and pack saddle for a pillow. He lived in absolute poverty and never uttered a single complaint about it. These bits of information are known because others recorded them. Though Kino's historical writings, especially his *Favores Celestiales*, make him the foremost historian of Pima Land (and therefore Arizona), the good Father didn't write much about himself.

Around the middle of March in 1711 when Kino was sixty-six years old he rode to Magdalena to dedicate a chapel to San Francisco. Flowers were in bloom but during the ceremony Father Eusebio suddenly became seriously ill. He died around midnight. Suddenly all was gloom for the great missionary, this sterling pioneer of Christian European civilization, could never be replaced and everyone knew it. He had proved himself an indefatigable missionary and church builder, an expert mathematician and cartographer, a renowned Indian diplomat and explorer, superb diarist and historian, a highly successful frontiersman and rancher/cowboy. His reward for twenty four years of labor for his Christian Saviour, as phrased by another Jesuit, was: *"He is now resting in the Lord."* Father Eusebio Kino never desired any other reward.

DISCUSSION Notes *for* THE MISSION; FATHER KINO
Note # 1
For a positive view see *"The Mission as a Frontier Institution in the Spanish American Colonies"* in *Bolton And The Spanish Borderlands* edited by John Francis Bannon. For a contrary opinion

see *New Spain's Far Northern Frontier: Essays On Spain In The American West, 1540-1821*, edited by David J. Weber, for the article by Odie B. Faulk titled *"The Presidio: Fortress or Farce?"* Professor Faulk writes: *"For the most part, however, the mission system was a failure…"* because Western Apaches and the Comanches couldn't be induced into village living. Then he states the *"only successes"* were among sedentary tribes in California, Arizona, New Mexico, and East Texas. One might well ask how the "failures" neutralized the "successes." Is this the *papists and popery syndrome?*

Note # 2

By contrast, English policy didn't include proselytizing the Indians found in possession of the land. The English King gave away Indian holdings to Court or business favorites as if it was vacant land. See *Land Title Origins: A Tale Of Force And Fraud* by Alfred N. Chandler, who writes that the land was "bought" for trinkets from Indians who never understood they would never again be able to use the "sold" lands. By way of analogy, Europeans believed no one could "own" the oceans, and Indians held the same belief concerning land. Every schoolboy knows the story of Manhattan Island being *"bought"* from the Indians, some know the price was around $24 dollars in trade goods, but few realize the "trinkets" were given to Canarsees Indians who didn't own or live on the land they were *"selling."* The Weckquaesgeeks lived on it and therefore "owned" it but as far as Dutch policy was concerned payment to "whatever" Indians was sufficient title to any land they desired because they could use deadly force to enforce their "rights." See *Lies My Teacher Told Me: Everything Your American History Textbook Got Wrong* by James W. Loewen.

Note # 3

One often suspects that the Black Legend school of American historiography is fueled by anti-Catholic bigotry. So it is common to portray Catholic monarchs of Spain as "religious fanatics." There are exceptions: one of the better works on Europe's noblest queen is *The Last Crusader: Isabella Of Spain, 1451-1504* by William Thomas Walsh. (It is worth noting that the great Spanish Queen was named "Isabel," not "Isabella." The confusion might have been caused by referring to her as *"Isabel la Católica."*)

Note # 4

The history of American CEOs who looted their corporations and cared not a whit about investors or employees is nothing new.

Note # 5

Historian Herbert E. Bolton writes that Spain *"was equaled in humanitarian principles by that of no other country…looked to the preservation of the natives, and to their elevation to at least a limited citizenship."* See "The Mission as a Frontier Institution in the Spanish American Colonies" cited above.

Note # 6

Some writers have described Amerindian governments as farcical. Is there an implication that extermination was the only realistic alternative? One can only wonder if the motivation actually stems from the belief and/or practice that *"The only good Indian is a dead Indian."* In New Mexico, the State with the longest period of Spanish governance, the Pueblo people still have their own village governments patterned by initiatives first begun in 1598. And it must be pointed out that the Pueblo people were not exterminated, despite the atrocities (neutralized by use of "The Pueblo Revolt" to hide them) of the St. Lawrence Day Massacre. Compare that historical fact to any similar situation in Virginia, Plymouth, or just about anywhere east of the Mississippi.

Note # 7

The most complete biography on Father Kino is *Rim Of Christendom* by Herbert Eugene Bolton who also wrote *Kino's Historical Memoir Of Pimería Alta* and *The Padre On Horseback*. All are highly recommended for students of the good *padre*. The introductory "Kino in Pimería Alta" by H.E. Bolton can be found in *Bolton And The Spanish Borderlands* edited by J. F. Bannon.

Note # 8

Kino was later to write that he was now as much German as Italian. He must also have become quite Spanish, missionizing for twenty-four years in Spanish lands. Eusebio Kino is a hero for the ages and is in Statuary Hall representing Arizona.

APOSTLE TO TEXAS and the AMERICAS

Antonio Margil de Jesús (1657-1726), an early missionary to Texas who ranks with Perea (New Mexico), Kino (Sonora/Arizona), Serra and Lasuén (California) in the missionary history of the Americas, was born in Valencia, Spain, on August 18, 1657. His parents, **Juan Margil** and **Esperanza Ros**, were humble parishioners of the church of San Juan del Mercado. Antonio had two sisters.

Margil attended school and was a serious student though he was distinguished more by his peaceful and gentle personality as well as his abject humility. It is said that by the age of seven he would sometimes deny himself bread in order to take it to some of the poorer students at his school. Even as a youngster he referred to himself as *Nothingness Itself*, a label he used even into adulthood when he would sign his correspondence with "*La misma nada*, Fr. Antonio Margil de Jesús."

HOLY ORDERS

In his early teens Margil expressed a desire to become a Franciscan. On April 22, 1673, he received the order's habit at *La Corona de Cristo* in Valencia. He furthered his education with the study of philosophy and theology. At the age of twenty-five he received (1682) Holy Orders and soon accepted the challenge of missionary work in New Spain (Mexico) under the tutelage of Father Linaz.. He departed Spain on March 4, 1683, with 17 other priests and 4 lay brothers. All arrived safely at Veracruz on June 6. Walking two by two, the Franciscans walked toward Mexico City and Querétaro in the style of the first religious to enter Mexico after Cortés, without even a knapsack, barefoot, poverty stricken, living on alms given to them along the way, sleeping in barns or corrals along the way, armed only with a cane, the Crucifix, and a breviary. When the skinny missionaries entered a village they sang hymns and held their crucifixes high, people rushing out to meet them happily because they represented the living Gospel, the spirit of Christ. Father Margil was to become known as el *fraile de los pies alados* (Friar of the Winged Feet) because he walked, barefooted, so energetically that some found it difficult to keep up with him. Fray **Melchor López de Jesús** was for many years Margil's constant companion in his peripatetic apostolic labors.

In Mexico Margil was assigned to the missionary College of *Santa Cruz de Querétaro*, from where he spent several years as a missionary in Yucatán, Costa Rica, and Guatemala during a ministry that would last some 43 years. During that time he would take the light of the Gospel on an itinerary that today staggers the imagination because he went from the bay of Espíritu Santo by the Mississippi to Boruca on the Isthmus of Panama, throughout the center of Mexico and its innumerable villages, cities, and uninhabited areas, from Yucatán to Guatemala, singing as they traveled, always on foot, preaching to Hispanics and Indians, the vanguard of evangelists in remote, inhospitable, and dangerous mountains, jungles, and deserts. And wherever Margil and Melchor (as well as most missionaries) thought suitable, they would raise a wooden cross, as large as they could manage, and recite prayers before it. Then they would be on their way and in this manner they traveled as far south as Nicaragua.

In Chiapas the Indians were so impressed with this pair of missionaries, so happy and yet so poverty stricken, that afterward when they saw a Franciscan arriving they would go out and receive him with gifts of flowers because they were "brothers of Margil and Melchor."

FIRST GUARDIAN
Margil returned to Querétaro in late 1706, then traveled in early 1707 to Zacatecas to found and preside as Guardian over the newly created missionary College of *Nuestra Señora de Guadalupe de Zacatecas*. He was to have accompanied Domingo Ramón into Texas in 1716 in order to found Franciscan missions in East Texas but an illness at San Juan Bautista prevented his entrance on the scene until after the founding of the first four missions.

TEXAS
He arrived in Texas in July of 1717 with three other priests and two lay-brothers. The Margil group founded the missions *Nuestra Señora de los Dolores* among the Ays, *San Miguel de los Adaes* among the Adays, which with the previously established *Nuestra Señora de Guadalupe* among the Nacogdoches, completed the missions under the control of the Zacatecan Franciscans. When the French destroyed these missions, Father Margil withdrew to the Rio San Antonio and remained near the present city of San Antonio for more than a year. He then returned with his friars to the scene of his former activity, restored the missions, and even gave his attention to the "former enemy" French settlers in Louisiana. In February of the following year Margil founded at San Antonio the most successful of all Texas missions, *San José y San Miguel de Aguayo*.

In 1722 Margil was elected Guardian of his college and therefore required to leave his beloved Texas Indians. At the close of his three year term (1722-25) of office he resumed missionary work in Mexico.

HABITS
Antonio Margil de Jesús always walked barefooted, fasted almost every day, avoided meat and fish when-

ever possible, and, in imitation of the sufferings of Christ, unmercifully applied to himself the discipline as well as other instruments of penance. He slept very little, passing most of the night in prayer, as well as the time allotted for the siesta. The result was that his efforts for the salvation of Indians and colonists were crowned with extraordinary effort and success. Padre Margil was a highly developed personality, many sided and wonderful. He attracted the lowly and the most distinguished alike. He was comfortable just about anywhere.

ACHIEVEMENTS

In addition to his being an untiring and most successful worker for his Lord Christ, Father Margil was also a most capable leader, an executive of rare ability, a spiritual empire builder, a dreamer who had the power to make his dreams come true. Accordingly, he supervised or built roads, founded missions and villages, organized and led exploring expeditions, worked the soil and taught the Indians the advantages of European technologies of the day. Quite a developed linguist, during the time he was in the missions of Texas Father Margil created a dictionary of the various dialects spoken by the Indians of Texas.

He founded three colleges that would carry on with the work of Christ. In 1687 he founded and became the First Guardian or Superior of the famous college of Santa Cruz de Querétaro, Mexico. In 1701 he founded the celebrated College of Christ Crucified in Guatemala. And in 1704 he founded the famed College of Our Lady of Guadalupe in Zacatecas, Mexico. He died in Mexico City at the church of San Francisco on August 6, 1726, after some 43 years of labor in his Lord's vineyard.

Antonio Margil de Jesús was the most famous missionary to serve in Texas and is often referred to as "Apostle to Texas" or "Apostle to the Americas" because of his tremendous contributions for the welfare of Hispanic and Native American people. Margil wrote an excellent firsthand description of the Tejas Indians, part of a body of information written by missionaries and described by Donald E. Chipman as "…truly remarkable." Of such stature that he is claimed by many people, in time there were signs in various places that read "Fray Margil was here." In all his years of service he never took a vacation and was fond of saying; "To rest in the joys of God we have an eternity but to accomplish something in His service and for our brothers there is little time until the end of the world." [See Note # 1.] While his career in Texas was brief he served as an inspiration to his Zacatecan missionaries who assumed control of all Texas missions in 1773. The hard working Margil also wrote *Cronica Apostolica*, "the standard history of the colleges of Propaganda Fide of the Franciscans of New Spain" and it has been said to be the best description of missionary activities in New Spain's northern provinces, an invaluable contribution to the history of early missions in Texas. In 1836 his virtues were declared heroic by Pope XVI. "The memory of him shall not depart away, and his name shall be in request from generation to generation." The Lone Star State can be justly proud to lay claim to the knightly "soldier of the Cross," Antonio Margil de Jesús.

DISCUSSION Notes *for* APOSTLE TO TEXAS and the AMERICAS
Note # 1
Of valiant stature even during his lifetime, Antonio Margil de Jesús remains under consideration

---

for sainthood by the Vatican. For information on Margil see the classic *Our Catholic Heritage In Texas* by the stalwart Carlos E. Castañeda. The more accessible *Spanish Texas, 1519-1821* by Donald E. Chipman has some introductory information on him but not enough really to study the man or his achievements. Eduardo Enrique Ríos' work *Life Of Fray Antonio Margil, O.F.M.*, translated by Benedict Leutenegger, is difficult to obtain unless a large library with a strong Special Collections unit is close at hand.

THE PRESIDIO

The Royal Regulations of 1772 recognized that *presidios* (forts) were necessary to pacify and/or protect the northern frontiers of New Spain. [See Note # 1. *Notes begin on page 79.*] The strategy was to establish a cordon of twenty presidios, some forty leagues (one league was about 2.6 miles) apart, from California to the Gulf of Mexico, all of which would be under the command of a Commandant Inspector, the first one being **Hugo O'Conor** in 1772. [See Note # 2.] (While serving as provisional governor of Texas from 1776-1770, his red hair had given him the nickname "*Capitán Colorado,*" Captain Red.) O'Conor worked diligently to realign the presidios, abandoning some, moving others, and constructing new ones where necessary.

STRUCTURAL STYLE

New presidios were built in similar practical fashion along the frontier. First they were located on high ground but as close as possible to good farming land. Adobe was generally used, buildings were structured around a square or rectangle, and to form a natural parapet buildings abutted exterior walls which were some three feet thick. *Torreones* (towers, bastions) were located at diagonal corner walls and constructed for gun emplacements. Inside the presidio there was a chapel, barracks for military personnel, storage facilities, etc. The main gate was the only way in or out.

SOLDIERS

As is common throughout most cultures in the world, wealthy people didn't generally enlist in the Military. The sons of poor or impoverished families saw military service as a way to improve their station in life. It was an opportunity for upward mobility by which they could earn social status. For example, while officers were literate, some very highly so, many frontier soldiers could not read and write because Education was quite a luxury on the frontier compared to, for example, horsemanship or raising stock animals. While some soldiers could barely sign their own names, they generally wanted their children to have access to schooling with private tutors when available. [See Note # 3.]

"*Reared in freedom and accustomed to independence*" according to Viceroy Bernardo de Gálvez, presidio soldiers were often born on the frontier. This gave them advantages like being accustomed to the climate and dealing with different kinds of frontier people, including recognizing different kinds of Indians. Of even greater importance was that no equestrian in the Americas was a more expert horsemen. [See Note # 4.] While their frontier appearance might suffer compared to their European counterparts, in 1776 Hugo O'Conor himself complimented presidial soldiers for their *"hardiness, courage and steadfastness…They will endure risk, hunger, and fatigue"* causing Dr. Weber to describe them as *"skilled horsemen, courageous, and remarkably tough."* There was a price to pay: high adult male deaths were common throughout frontier areas so there were many widows as heads of families, numerous orphans, and remarried widows with their children making a life with step-fathers.

SALARY

A new enlistee earned (depending on the locale) between 290 to 400 pesos per year, a fourth of which he received in cash for the subsistence of himself and his family, the remainder kept to pay for expenses like uniforms, weapons, horses, and necessary equipment. (One of the weaknesses of this system was that commanding officers could conspire with paymasters or suppliers of goods to drive up prices for items a soldier had to buy, thereby promoting their own profiteering.) A sum of twenty pesos was also withheld annually for five years in order to be given to the soldier upon discharge. The soldier could usually acquire land near the presidio, he had retirement benefits including a pension for his wife if he was killed, access to medical services, and promotion through the ranks was an established fact in frontier areas.

WEAPONS

Weapons carried by soldiers included the lance, an *espada ancha* (wide sword), an escopeta (short-barreled carbine), and two heavy pistols. Training was rigorously prescribed but often ignored in isolated outposts. A soldier also carried an *adarga* (shield), wore a *cuera* (leather jacket which weighed about eighteen pounds), and *botas* (leather leggings). These offered protection against arrows but they were also hot and bulky.

FRONTIER SOCIAL MOBILITY

While European traditions of blood lines and racial superiority/inferiority were part of everyday culture, the Hispanic frontier military establishment became an avenue for upward social mobility. Life threatening dangers from hostile warriors encouraged solidarity in the field and concomitant social equality back home. Perhaps due in part to immediacy, ability became more important than race. Officers and soldiers therefore tended to become good friends who depended on each other in most situations. Even the aristocratic Bernardo de Gálvez once remarked: *"What does it matter to the Sovereign whether the one who serves him well be white or black…"* when the only thing that really mattered was *"…the nobility of his heart…"* Frontier egalitarianism didn't exist in the regular Army, which was more subject to European traditions.

MISSIONARIES vs. SOLDIERS

Another factor in the lives of presidial soldiers was the power enjoyed by missionaries who demanded that soldiers lead Christian, God-fearing lives as examples to Indians they were trying to convert. The missionaries knew soldiers were an absolutely necessary lifeline but they demanded soldiers who were Christian men with wives and families who valued a Christian lifestyle. They combated hard drinking, hard living types who, among other things, "preyed" on Indian women. [See Note # 5.] These missionaries weren't just isolated voices in the wilderness: they were cornerstones of Spanish society, "Knights of the Cross" who were listened to by civil authorities in Mexico City.

ADVERSITIES

Frontier hardships can't be minimized when discussing the life of a presidial soldier. Payrolls were often late and it was easy to get into debt due to no salary for a period of months. There were often shortages of every kind, from food to horses to gunpowder to iron. Corn was generally a basic dietary component and when it ran out people were forced to search out edible roots. Low morale was as common as attacks from hostile Indians.

REORGANIZATION of the FRONTIER

In 1776 the Crown established the **Interior Provinces**, separating them from the viceroyalty of New Spain, and putting them under the direction of **Teodoro de Croix,** who would report directly to the King. [See Note # 6.] Comandante General Croix studied the situation and concluded that presidios were typical products of European military theory but hostile Indians utilized a "hit and run" strategy which tended to neutralize presidio effectiveness except as a base of operation. He listened to his experienced frontier officers and made modifications suited for frontier conditions. He agreed with his men that defending an 1800 mile border with fewer than two thousand soldiers was mostly fantasy so he constantly appealed to the King and Viceroy for more soldiers. (He was successful to the degree that at one time he had 2,840 stalwarts to defend the frontier against Apaches, Comanches, Navajos, etc., any one of which greatly outnumbered the soldiers in any area.) He understood that presidios some forty leagues apart enabled hostile raiders to ride between them without detection so in 1778 he created the special force known as *tropa ligera* (speed/light troops) which operated without leather jackets, shield, or lance. As with the "Leather Jackets," these soldiers were among the best cavalry in the Americas.

DISCUSSION Notes *for* THE PRESIDIO

Note # 1

See *New Spain's Far Northern Frontier: Essays On Spain In The American West, 1540-1821*, edited by David J. Weber , for an article by Odie B. Faulk titled *"The Presidio: Fortress or Farce?"* Perhaps as a corollary to the title Professor Faulk writes that the layout of the presidios was a pattern *"learned from the Moors,"* that civilians living around the presidios were *"timorous, impoverished peasants,"* that soldiers were of the *"lower class,"* and *"troops preferred to stay behind the security of presidial walls...the wonder is not that the presidio largely failed in its military objectives as a frontier institution but that it succeeded as well as it did."* A student of Southwest history might well ask if Spanish people were successful in anything they did in the area, especially if one believes American historiography is credible. What is the message here?

Note # 2

Born in Ireland, Hugo O'Conor enlisted in the Spanish army in hopes of fighting the English who had committed horrendous atrocities against his Irish Catholic people. He arrived in New

Spain in 1765. See *The Spanish Frontier In North America* by David J. Weber.
Note # 3
See *Literacy, Education, and Society in New Mexico*, 1693-1821 by Bernardo P. Gallegos. It appears that on the frontier it was not crucial to be able to read and write so long as you had access to someone who could.
Note # 4
Many writers maintain that the American plains Indians were the best horsemen. As marvelous as they were, especially compared to English speaking riders, Hispanics had centuries old traditions on horseback before the Amerindian acquired the horse after 1680.
Note # 5
Letters and diaries written by missionaries, as well as those composed by military leaders, have often been used to denigrate people living during Spanish colonial times. A researcher can find commentary on just about any point of view and it seems the more denigrating is generally emphasized by some writers. An equivalent today would be perhaps to base History on testimony given in a court of law.
Note # 6
Teodoro de Croix was a Frenchman, a veteran of almost thirty years in the Spanish service. He served as Comandante General from 1776-1783. See *Teodoro De Croix* by Alfred Barnaby Thomas.

The GREAT CAPTAIN

The Spanish Borderlands have no dearth of personalities who merit fame in the annals of Southwestern history. There are sterling explorers, colonizers, Viceroys, Governors, trailblazers, diplomats, frontiersmen, leaders, etc., like Alvar Nuñez Cabeza de Vaca, Francisco Vásquez de Coronado, Antonio de Mendoza, Juan de Oñate, Diego de Vargas, José de Escandon, Gaspar de Portolá, Teodoro de Croix, Pedro Fages, Antonio Bucareli, José de Zúñiga, Fernando Rivera y Moncada, Gabriel Moraga, Martín de Alarcón, Marqués de San Miguel de Aguayo, Domingo Ramón, Teodoro Ramírez, José de Zúñiga, José de Urrea, Manuel Antonio Chaves, etc. Representative of these frontier paladins is **Juan Bautista de Anza**.

THREE ANZAS

The Anza family produced three men who are in the historical annals of the Spanish Borderlands. All were named *Juan Bautista de Anza*. Grandfather Anza served for thirty years as a Lieutenant and Captain at Janos. Anza Sr. was a Captain at Fronteras for twenty, along with serving as temporary Governor of Sonora for a short period. Among other things, he was a staunch supporter of the Jesuits and their missions and it was he who first expressed a desire to blaze an overland route to California. Juan Jr. figures in the histories of Sonora, Arizona, California, and New Mexico.

SILVER BONANZA

Anza Sr. was at Fronteras in 1736 when a rich silver mine, referred to as *Bolas de Plata* (Silver Balls) or *Planchas de Plata* (Silver Slabs), was discovered at a place called *Arizonac* (immediately south of the border of present day Arizona). Anza wrote to the Viceroy in 1737, describing the temporary bonanza and urging the government to secure the area by working with the Indians. There might well be great mineral wealth to the north. (It was at this time that Anza Sr. suggested opening an overland route to the Gila and Colorado Rivers.) Nuggets of almost pure silver, the largest said to weigh some 3500 pounds, were discovered near the surface and miners rushed to the area. Captain Anza maintained since the silver was *"hidden treasure,"* not really a mine where only one-fifth had to be turned over to the King, *it all belonged to the Crown*. The Viceroy ruled against Anza's decision, the Crown reversed the decision in 1741, but by then it was too late and the silver deposit was all but exhausted.

AMBUSH

In May of 1740 Anza Sr. and his soldiers were reconnoitering the area near the mission of Father Keller at Soamca. Father Keller had warned Anza that hostile Apaches had been seen scouting the area so the experienced frontiersmen took necessary precautions. On May 9, 1740, as Anza rode up a little ahead of his troops, he had no way of knowing that Apaches lay in ambush, camouflaged by the chaparral. Many rifle shots rang out and Captain Anza fell dead from his horse. The hostiles rushed in and took his scalp. [See Note # 1. *Notes begin on page 93.*]

ANZA the MAN

Very little is known about the personal life of **Juan Bautista de Anza.** He was born in 1735 or 1736 into the military family at Fronteras (or possibly in Cuquiarachi) in the province of Sonora, Mexico. His mother's name was **María Rosa Bezerra Nieto** of the town of Fronteras, province of Sonora, Mexico. Juan Jr.'s paternal grandparents were Antonio de Anza (a pharmacist) and Lucia de Sassoeta of Hernani, Guipuzcoa, Spain. His maternal grandparents were Antonio Bezerra Nieto (presidial captain) and Gregoria Gómez de Silva of Janos, Chihuahua, Mexico. As indicated above, Juan Jr. was without a father at a very tender age. It is unknown if he had brothers and/or sisters. It is believed young Juan's education was imparted mostly by the Jesuits, whom his father admired greatly.

Following the family tradition, Juan enlisted (1753) in the army at around the age of 18. Anza worked diligently under the guidance of his brother-in-law, **Gabriel de Vildosola.** By 1755 Anza was promoted to Lieutenant. He petitioned the government to lead an exploration party overland to California but was refused due to Indian uprisings. In 1758 he campaigned against the Apaches to the Gila River. In 1859 he was promoted to Captain.

TUBAC

In the year 1760 Juan was assigned as Commander of the Tubac, Arizona, presidio. Upon arriving at his post he learned that prices at the Tubac presidio were sky high. Presidial soldiers were required to take part of their pay in government supplies so this was a tremendous sore point with the men who were serving their country. One of Anza's first orders was to lower the exorbitant prices. He immediately became popular with his men.

Other settlers arrive to live at Tubac, including a sister of the post chaplain, **Ana María Pérez Serrano**, whom Anza married on June 24, 1761. Nothing else is known about Ana except that she was destined to survive her husband.

HOSTILE FRONTIER

In 1766 Juan leads expeditions against the warlike Apaches and Seris. He plays an important part in Elizondo's conquest of Sonora. Anza's life revolves around fighting hostile Apaches, Pimas, Seris, Pápagos, and Suaquis. He defeats the chief of the Pápagos in hand-to-hand combat, thus winning their fealty. Despite his fame as an Indian fighter and memories of the death of his father at the hands of hostiles, he never becomes an Indian hater. He is recognized for his personal courage, his ability to fight hostile Indians and/or deal with them diplomatically.

GARCES

In time Anza comes to know and admire **Father Francisco Hermenegildo Garcés**, a dedicated missionary as well as pioneer/explorer/frontiersman.

OVERLAND to CALIFORNIA

After riding 1,000 miles a soldier named **Juan Valdez** brings orders (1773) that Anza is granted permission to find an overland route to California. The dream of Anza Sr. now fell to the son. Viceroy Antonio Bucareli, whose task it was to carry out the policies of Charles III, was instrumental in helping Anza realize his expeditions. The intrepid **Fray Francisco Garcés**, an explorer in his own right, was delighted to accompany Anza, along with **Father Juan Díaz** who would win fame among the Pimas. Juan Valdez is also in the group as is **Sebastián Tarabal**, a native of Lower California who had gone with Portolá and been given a Christian name in Mission San Gabriel. Tarabal had traversed the area so he would prove an invaluable guide, though Anza planned to go directly to Monterey, not San Gabriel. There would also be twenty *"Leather Jacket"* soldiers, an additional soldier who had been with Serra and Portolá so he knew some of the trails into California, an interpreter of the Pima language, a man who was a carpenter by trade, five muleteers, two Anza staffers, thirty-five loads of provisions, sixty-five head of cattle, and one-hundred-forty saddle horses would be needed. [See Note # 2.]

Anza made careful plans because he understood that meticulous preparations were absolutely crucial in blazing a new overland trail across burning deserts and snow capped mountains. Then hostile Apaches raided the Tubac corrals and drove off many of the horses intended for use on the expedition. Instead of going north to the Gila then west/northwest across the desert they would now have to follow a route along established presidios/missions back down into Sonora to the town of Altar in order to acquire more horses.

The expedition departed from Tubac on January 9, 1774. Anza, Garcés, and Díaz kept journals of all events on the trail. By January 17 the group made it to the presidio in Altar. The only real inconvenience on the trail thus far was being unable to travel for two days due to a storm of rain and snow. Worn out horses were exchanged for fresh mounts and the expedition hit the trail for Caborca, reaching it in three days. Unfortunately, no horses or mules were available, which is why they had gone out of their way in the first place.

The expedition took a northwesterly direction toward the Colorado River. Grass and water became more and more scarce and the hills were bare of vegetation as the trailblazers entered the land of the Pápagos. On occasion they found springs of fresh water and sighted villages of heathen as well as Christian Indians but most of the time the trail was solitary and water could be had only by digging in arroyo sands. Now deep in the Sonoran Desert they encountered the strange forests of saguaros. By January 28, 1774, they were in sparsely settled Sonóita. Up ahead there would be no water for man or beast for at least fifty miles. The area also contained lava beds, known as the *"Sea of Broken Glass,"* and the travelers would have to depend on collected rainwater in the hollows of rock formations for survival. As a precaution, Anza held back the pack animals for one day while the rest of the train searched out water sources. The following day a water tank, *El Aguaje Empinado* (water tank high in the mountain) in the Pinto Range was reached, rescuing everyone for the time being.

Ahead of the expedition now lay the land of the **Yuma nation.** They were a *"tall, handsome, light skinned"* people whose friendship would prove crucial if this overland trail was to be a viable road to California. A Pápago Indian came into camp saying the Yumas wanted to attack the Spaniards and take their horses but the following day, February 6, a Yuma subchief and eight companions, all riding horses and totally naked, arrived with news that all would be welcomed by **Chief Palma**. The Spaniards rode into the village the following day, the Indians smiling and throwing dirt into the air to express their friendship. Chief Salvador Palma arrived and informed Anza that the people who had wanted to kill the Christians weren't his people but rather from another tribe and he had put them out of Yuma territory.

The Yuma men went about without any clothes at all but with elaborate coiffures of which they were very proud. The women wore clothes. Both men and women painted their bodies black and red, wore earrings and also small feathers in perforated nose cartilage. Father Garcés wrote in his journal that the Yumas were highly adept at taking items with their feet, thefts which they performed as easily as with their hands.

Captain Anza spoke to a gathering of Yumas, asked if they acknowledged Salvador Palma as their Chief, and since all said yes Anza also acknowledged him as Chief in the name of the King of Spain. Palma then received a coin bearing an image of the King, wearing it henceforth with a red ribbon around his neck. Anza embraced Palma and all in attendance were joyful at the demonstration of respect and affection. Anza also orated that henceforth the King wished for all to live in peace, that all should live without killing one another as in the past. Palma promised to live in peace. Gifts were later distributed where Chief Palma had his personal residence.

Anza hit the trail once again, forded the Colorado and stepped into California. The entire group, including horse and cattle herds, was across by the next day. They were now in the Colorado Desert where Mojave Indians warned the Captain that water would be extremely difficult to find and the animals would suffer greatly. Father Garcés, who had explored in this area back in 1771, wanted to continue as planned but Anza listened to the Mojaves and changed his plans to head straight for Monterey.

The expeditionary force encountered a range of north/south sand hills, some fifty miles long and five miles wide. This barrier, along with the delta of the Colorado, were among the most serious obstacles of the march. They walked through the land of the Kohuanas (Cojats) then got to the more unfriendly Cocopas. On February 15, 1774, Anza wrote in his journal that Tarabal pointed out the blue mountains in the distance as California from whence he had come. Father Garcés suggested finding an Indian village he had named San Jacome where there was ample water and pasturage for the animals. Anza followed this advice but the village was never found (because it had been abandoned due to lack of water). He sent a messenger to Chief Palma who arrived within a couple of days to meet the Captain at a place called Santa Olaya (February 25-28). Anza entrusted Palma with half of the animals in the pack train, which would be collected when Anza returned from Monterey. The expedition now rested for several days in the midst of hundreds of Indians. The biggest attraction was the violin played by one of the soldiers. The Indian women especially loved dancing the *seguidillas* which the soldiers taught them.

Not being interested in such frivolity, Father Garcés got permission to go down river and find friends he met back in 1771. As before, he carried his own "banner," a large canvas painted with the Virgin Mary holding the Christ Child on one side and a man burning in the flames of Hell on the other.

By March 2nd the greatly reduced expedition started out again in a west-southwest direction. They encountered many Cojat villages but pushed on into the desert and through a pass in the sterile Cocopa Mountains. They were deserted by their Cojat guides and suffered from lack of water but they finally encountered grass and water. On March 8 they camped at a place which they named Santa Rosa of the Flat Rocks (now Yuha Wells) because of its marvelous water. Tarabal now began to recognize the country and everyone realized the expedition would be successful.

Anza felt the worst was over but he knew they weren't home yet because the desert was still before them. They encountered some marshy springs, named them "San Sebastián," and encountered lands of the Kamias Indians. Some 400 Kamias had been camping in San Sebastián and some recognized Father Garcés and Tarabal. On March 10, 1774, Anza told the Kamias of the peace the Yumas had agreed to, the two groups being in constant war with each other. The two Yumas with Anza verified their commitment to peace with the Kamias and all rejoiced.

Father Garcés was ecstatic in this land so suitable for missions. It was also learned that Governor Fages of California had traversed the area in 1772 so Anza was not the first European leader to explore this particular area. [See Note # 3.]

The expedition continued to Borrego Springs (March 12) and then Coyote Canyon which led them into the mountains. Rain and snow flurries now pelted the dauntless trailblazers who continued to climb until they found (March 15) an opening which they named *Puerto Real de San Carlos*, Royal Pass of San Carlos. They spied the Cahuilla Valley and the entrance to southern California. While not intended, the trail would lead them to San Gabriel Mission where they arrived on March 22, 1774. They had spent seventy-four days on the trail after leaving Tubac.

No one had informed the friars concerning Anza's overland trail blazing but the men were received joyfully, the bells ringing out and the missionaries chanting the *Te Deum* to celebrate their arrival. Food supplies were short so Anza sent a contingent to San Diego for more provisions. Monterey was still some four hundred miles away. But San Diego didn't have much to offer and the men returned almost empty handed.

Juan B. Valdez, the courier who had originally brought Anza the news that he had orders to accomplish his overland trail blazing, was now sent to Viceroy Bucareli in Mexico City (some 2300 miles) to inform him of the success. Anza and four soldiers, along with two men from San Gabriel who knew the road, went on into Monterey where they spoke with **Governor Fages** about the possibilities of establishing mail and freight routes from Sonora to San Francisco, of building a chain of missions along the way, and building up a good intermediate harbor for the Manila Galleon trade.

Anza was back in Tubac by May 26, 1774. He had been absent for some four and a half months and traversed, riding or walking, more than 2000 miles. Then he was instructed to come to Mexico City to make a personal report to **Viceroy Bucareli.**

On November 13, 1774, Juan Bautista de Anza rode into the *Plaza Mayor* in Mexico City to report to Viceroy Bucareli. He was received cordially and with great respect for the good Viceroy understood he was dealing with one of Spain's greatest frontier personalities. Would the Great Captain be willing to lead colonists to Monterey then on to San Francisco to form a permanent settlement with some forty families? Most certainly. He would prove that women and children could cross the deserts and mountains to get to California, thus opening up the continent for more settlements. And, oh yes, Anza would be promoted to the rank of Lieutenant Colonel.

RECRUITMENT of COLONISTS

Anza relished his new assignment and began to recruit colonists immediately in Culiacán, Sinaloa, and Fuerte in the province of Sonora. People needing to make a fresh start were recruited because the wealthier classes had no desire to trade their comforts for pioneering hardships. The colonization of California was a venture of whole families, each unit averaging some four children. (Two families had nine each.) Money and clothing were provided as inducements to brave the trail to California where no colonists had ever traveled. Protective leather jackets (of seven thicknesses) were provided for the men, along with carbines, swords, and lances. Attacks from hostile Indians were understood as distinct possibilities but still the plucky pioneers signed up for the California venture.

Anza led his people from Culiacán across Sonora to the presidio at Tubac, a distance of more than six hundred miles, adding new settlers as he went. Others signed on at Tubac until the expedition numbered some 250 people.

PIONEERING PERSONNEL

With Anza as supreme commander, other notables included Fray **Pedro Font** as chaplain (and historian for his journal was to prove invaluable), priests **Francisco Garcés** and **Tomás Eixarch,** second-in-command *alférez* **José Joaquín Moraga,** Sgt. **Juan Pablo Grijalva,** ten Tubac soldiers who were to return upon completion of the mission, twenty-eight soldiers who were to remain in California, twenty-nine wives of officers/soldiers, and 136 family members of both sexes and all ages. [See Note # 4.] There were fifteen muleteers, three cowboys to control the stock, three servants for the *Padres* and a staff of four with Captain Anza, five interpreters who knew Indian languages, as well as **Sebastián Tarabal,** an Indian from Mission San Gabriel serving as guide, and a commissary.

At the outset Anza's leadership was already trusted by his pioneering families. They believed the Great Captain would get them through safely. At Horcasitas the expedition acquired the last of its necessities but while there it was learned that Apaches had run off with some 500 horses at Tubac, horses needed for the journey. (The same thing had happened before his first expedition into California.) There was a delay while other horses were rounded up for replacements.

On October 22, 1775, Padre Font celebrated Mass and all prayed for success of the new colonizers. The sermon he took from the Gospel, comparing them to the children of Israel going through the Red Sea to the Promised Land. The following day, **October 23, 1775,** the pioneers hit the trail, 240 people, 155 of them women and children, along with 165 pack mules, 302 cattle, and 340 horses for the saddle. [See Note # 5.] There were also adequate supplies of farm tools, seeds, grains, etc., to assure a permanent colonization. Eleven camp tents were provided for the soldiers, ten for the family units, one for the religious. For cooking for such a large group there would be iron frying pans, copper camp kettles, and large pots for luxuries like hot chocolate. [See Note # 6.] Because the trail was not developed, there were no wagons so everything had to be carried by pack animals which had to be loaded every morning and unloaded every night.

At the first night's camp a woman named **Manuela Pinuelas** paid the supreme price for motherhood, dying in childbirth. The baby survived. On October 27th a couple of muleteers decided to desert but they were caught and whipped.

PADRE FONT

Padre Font and the other religious were influential, Font writing that he constantly "...*exhorted everybody to have patience in the hardships of the journey and above all concerning the good example which they must set for the heathen, as a mark of Christianity, without scandalizing them in any way.*" Font had his own affliction, probably malaria, to contend with and there were constant rumors that Apache bands were watching the long caravan.

PROCLAMATION

Anza issued a proclamation so that everyone would understand the penalties to be suffered by anyone who would violate women, especially including Indian women, or steal from heathen or Christian. No one was to use weapons against any Indian except in self defense at the Commander's orders. The Indians were to be treated well and all Christians were to set a good example of Christian culture.

TRAVEL ROUTINE

Trail procedure quickly fell into the following routine: at a certain hour the order was given to drive in the horses and mules to be used that day. Each soldier, muleteer, servant, family, etc., would catch his own animals, bridle and saddle them. Padre Font would then celebrate Mass. When everything was ready the commander would shout: "*Everybody mount up!*" and the march would begin. Four soldiers always went ahead as scouts, then the commander, and the religious. Next came the men, women, and children, followed by the rest of the soldiers. The lieutenant was with the rear guard who looked after the pack mules, riding horses, and cattle. It was a very long caravan.

When a suitable camp site was reached at the end of the day a veritable village was established. The families ended their day by saying the Rosary in their tents and singing the *Alabado* or *Salve.*

The colonists met all sorts of Indians along the way: Pápagos, Gila Pimas, Maricopas (Cocomaricopas, Opas), Yumas, Cajuenches, Jalchedunes, the Dancers, etc. No problems were encountered.

On November 27, 1775, Chief **Salvador Palma** arrived in the camp of the Christians and happily embraced Captain Anza. Palma informed Anza that the peace had been kept as promised and the entire expedition was welcome to settle on Yuma lands. Anza explained these Christians were assigned to other lands but Padres Garcés and Eixarch would missionize in Palma's country. The following day camp was made at the junction of the Gila and Colorado after crossing the Gila. The Yumas displayed their hospitality by bringing in great quantities of calabazas, corn, wheat, beans, etc., and watermelons aplenty.

On November 30 the dangerous **Colorado River** was forded and completed the following day without loss of life or equipment. Padre Garcés was ferried across by three Yumas, Garcés stretched out as in a coffin, with two Yumas at his shoulders and one at his feet,

Once out of Yuma country the expedition got to Santa Olaya and the difficult Colorado delta area. The weather turned extremely cold and water and pasturage became scarce. There was a real risk of freezing to death and much stock would be lost. By December 9 the expedition was at Carrizal where enough water was found to supply all needs. Much firewood was needed to combat the severe cold. On December 12 a severe snow storm that lasted for days covered the desert floor. The colonists, unaccustomed to snow, asked what weather they could expect in the northern country of San Francisco if it was *snowing in the desert*. But they marched on valiantly despite the deaths of many animals. Second-in-command **Moraga** suffered severe pains in his head and ears (from which he later became deaf).

Whenever necessary Captain Anza would stop the caravan so people could rest. He would also call a halt for babies to be born, making their birth an informal celebration. On December 17, 1775, he allowed his soldiers to hold a dance, despite the objections of chaplain Font. On Christmas Eve the caravan halted once more to await the birth of a child as well as to celebrate the Child's Birth. Anza also issued an order permitting each soldier a pint of liquor and allowed them a celebration of singing and dancing, again over Padre Font's objections.

On December 26 a four minute earthquake was felt by the pioneers.

The colonist's basic concern now was the snow and cold weather climate for which they had no preparation. Some of the women asked Anza: *"With so many animals dying of the cold and the people near dying in places where there was less snow, how will it be where we see so much of it?"* The Captain assured them this was a once in a lifetime occurrence.

Eight months after leaving Culiacán, the principal point of assemblage, and seventy-four days on the difficult frontier trail from Tubac, so arduous that some hundred head of stock died from the hardship, these Hispanic pioneers arrived in San Gabriel in southern California on **January 4, 1776**. A woman had died in childbirth the first night on the trail but three new babies had been born along the way for a total of 242 stalwarts, two more than at the start. Mission San Gabriel bells rang out joyfully at their arrival. [See Note # 7.]

ANZA and GOV. RIVERA MONCADA

Anza met Monterey Commander **Fernando Rivera y Moncada** who was in San Gabriel to investigate the uprising by some 600 Indians at San Diego on November 5, 1775. They had burned down the mission and murdered the unresisting Father Luis Jayme along with two workmen. Captain Anza, perhaps the most able military leader in northern New Spain, volunteered himself and his soldiers if Commander Rivera y Moncada needed help. In the whole coastal strip of Spanish California, more than 400 miles, there were only 75 soldiers guarding five missions and two presidios so the Commander accepted. Rivera and Anza led some 35 soldiers to San Diego. Padre Font was in the group and later recorded his impressions in his journal. Father Serra insisted that no military retribution be taken so when some of the culprits were caught they were merely whipped and released.

NEW HOMELAND

While at San Gabriel, Padre Font's health improved noticeably and noted in his journal how beautiful the country had become. He carved the following inscription in a large sycamore tree: "In the year 1776 came the San Francisco expedition."

On February 21, 1776, Anza and seventeen soldiers, along with their families, continued northward to Monterey, reaching it on March 10, 1776. Moraga came in later with the other settlers. The colonists began to love the country, losing their fears of desert snow and ice-clad mountain peaks. As always, Anza and Font recorded all important events and impressions in their journals. While Padre Font had been highly critical of various Indian groups, as well as of Anza at times, the good Father wrote (March 11, 1776): *"For what purpose have we come? To gain Heaven by suffering trials in this world and assisting in these lands by setting a good example of Christianity in the conversion of the heathen, whose souls are the precious pearls sought by that celestial merchant, Jesus Christ…Let us give thanks to Almighty God and I, in the name of God and King, give thanks to our commander, Don Juan Bautista de Anza, for the patience, prudence, and good conduct which as leader he has shown in commanding this expedition, and I promise him that God will reward him for his labors."*

SAN FRANCISCO

After a short illness the Great Captain led a contingent of soldiers out of Monterey in fulfillment of his orders to *"explore the port of San Francisco."* By March 28 Anza and his men had erected a giant cross, blessed by Padre Font, on the eastern end of San Francisco Bay. Though not given to exaggeration, Anza praised the area in the most complimentary of descriptions. As he surveyed the area, Padre Font recorded that although in his travels he had seen much beautiful country… *"I saw none which pleased me so much as this…if settled like Europe there would not be anything more beautiful in all the world…the port of San Francisco is a marvel of nature and may be called the port of ports."* The group carried out inspections for presidio and mission sites then returned to Monterey on April 8, 1776.

ANZA'S DEPARTURE

Anza's work was done so he decided to depart and make his report to Mexico City. Lieutenant **José Joaquín Moraga** would escort the colonists to San Francisco but the settlers were heartsick to see their Great Captain leave them forever. Anza himself was quite moved for on April 13 he wrote in his journal:

"This day has been the saddest ever experienced by this presidio since its founding. When I mounted my horse in the plaza, the settlers whom I have led from their homeland, to which I am returning, remembering the treatment good and bad which they experienced at my hands while they were under my command, most of them, especially the women, came to me sobbing with tears which they declared they were shedding more because of my departure than their situation, filling me with compassion. They showered me with best wishes, embraces, and praises which I told them I didn't merit. But I shall never forget them and in the gratitude which I feel for all of them, the affection which I have had for them since I recruited them, I do now compliment them for their faithfulness. Up to this moment there has been not even a sign of desertion from those settlers whom I brought to remain in this wilderness. It is my honor to record the praise of these people who, as time goes on, will serve their King at the cost of leaving their relatives and homeland, which is of their essence." [See Note # 8.]

Anza was back in Sonora by June 1, 1776, then he rode to Mexico City once more to make his personal report to Viceroy Bucareli. It is believed he remained in Mexico City until February of 1777 before returning home where he has now been promoted to Commander of the Armed Forces of Sonora.

GOVERNOR of NEW MEXICO

In 1777 Anza received word he had been appointed Military Commander and Governor of New Mexico but his orders are to stay in Sonora until he quells an Indian uprising. When peace is assured he attends a meeting in Chihuahua during the summer of 1778 where a council of prominent officials gather to discuss frontier defenses. Chaired by General Teodoro de Croix, Commander General of the Interior Provinces of New Spain, whom Anza had met in Mexico City, the meeting is also attended by retiring New Mexican governor **Pedro Fermín de Mendinueta.** The situation is grim. Because of Indian hostilities New Mexico was on the verge of total collapse. In July of 1774 a thousand Comanches raided the Chama Valley and the area around Santa Clara Pueblo, killing seven people, wounding many more, and kidnapping three boys. Later that month 200 Comanches attacked in the Albuquerque area, killing Hispanics and Pueblos alike, taking a huge flock of sheep and Albuquerque's entire horse herd. There was little defense because the militia was away campaigning against the Navajos. In 1775, from May to July, forty-one people were killed during attacks by Comanches, Gila Apaches, and Navajos. Thirty-three of the forty-one were from Sandía Pueblo. Villages and Pueblos lost their horses to the raiders. Up and down the Río Grande people were forced to abandon their ranches. The population of Santa Fe more than doubled due to the refugees. Fray **Francisco Atanasio Domínguez**, who inspected New Mexico's missions in 1776, described Taos Pueblo as so heavily fortified that it was like the "walled cities with bastions and towers described to us in the Bible." [See Note # 9.]

STRATEGY

If New Mexico was lost to hostile Indians there would be nothing to prevent them from swarming into rich southern territories like Chihuahua. It is now Anza's responsibility to prevent that from happening. Croix suggests a basic stratagem: defeat the Comanches in battle then bring them into alliance with Hispanics and Pueblos in order to wage war against the Apaches. [See Note # 10.] Simple, yes, but could it be effected?

FRONTIER FAME

When Anza assumes his duties in New Mexico (it is believed he might have settled in Santa Fe toward the end of 1778) he is 42 years of age and a heroic figure in the Spanish Borderlands, famous in Sonora, Arizona, California, and soon to be in New Mexico. New Mexicans come to know him quickly: he is American born and reared on the Sonora frontier. He is a frontiersman who can negotiate diplomatically or fight hand-to-hand as the situation demands, embrace a Comanche or smoke with a Navajo. Unlike some of his predecessors, he can tell the difference between a Pueblo and an Apache just by meeting them.

NEW MEXICO SURROUNDED

Defense against hostile Indians was the major problem in New Mexico. Hispanic and Pueblo settlements were surrounded by Utes to the north, Comanches to the east, Apaches to the south, and Navajos to the west. Even combining Pueblo and Hispanic populations, the warrior tribes easily had the advantage of numbers. As efforts to ameliorate the situation, Anza informed outlying settlers to move back into fortified towns and ordered that the number of outlying missions be reduced. This caused much antagonism to the point that a delegation of settlers and some missionaries went to Arizpe and complained to the new Commander General **Felipe de Neve**, who occupied the office due to Croix's death. Neve gave credence to the delegation's charges. [See Note # 11.]

COMANCHES and CUERNO VERDE

Anza's orders included opening a route from New Mexico to Sonora but the situation with the Comanches-Apaches-Utes-Navajos in New Mexico was so desperate the decision was made to address this menace first. The most formidable antagonist appeared to be a chieftain known as *Cuerno Verde* (**Green Horn**, for whom the Colorado mountains are named) because he wore a green buffalo horn on his headdress. Anza wrote to Croix describing Cuerno Verde as the *"scourge of New Mexico"* who had exterminated hundreds of Hispanic and Pueblo New Mexicans, including captives which were executed in cold blood. Cuerno Verde's hatred appeared to stem from the fact that his father had been killed in battle against New Mexicans. [See Note # 12.] Anza's strategy was to invade the Comanche homeland in Colorado and the eastern plains of New Mexico. This had never been done so perhaps it was possible to surprise the marauding raiders as never before. Then, if victory should be his, he would strive to make them allies.

TRAIL NORTH

Despite the fact that they seldom had modern weapons, New Mexicans had achieved fame as Indian fighters throughout the centuries so the call was issued to meet at San Juan Pueblo in the middle of **August, 1779**. Anza's professional Regulars from Santa Fe were prepared for battle but the volunteer militia, Pueblo and Hispanic, were poorly equipped so the Army had to provide proper horses and weaponry. When the expeditionary force departed from San Juan Pueblo there were some 600 stalwarts ready to take on Cuerno Verde and his Comanche raiders. Previous campaigners had taken the trail east of Taos to get to Comanche country so their presence was quickly detected. Anza led his men north on the west side of the Rockies, the mountains thus hiding his movements. The expedition then cut to the east below *El Capitán* (now called "Pike's Peak") and came upon Comanche encampments from a northerly direction, totally surprising and capturing many Indians easily. There was so much booty it took more than a hundred horses to load it. It was learned that Cuerno Verde was raiding in the Taos area and would soon return to his main camp below the Arkansas River where a big victory celebration would be held. Anza immediately set his expeditionary force to move on the Comanche encampment.

BATTLE

When Cuerno Verde spied his enemies coming toward him the chief rode toward them on his curveting horse, ready to do battle. Too late the chieftain realized his warriors were totally surrounded. They killed some horses and used them as a barricade from which to fight. Cuerno Verde refused to surrender and even exposed himself to heavy fire. The New Mexicans charged in and the warriors and their chieftain fought to the last man. All were killed in the blood battle: Cuerno Verde, his son, four sub chiefs, the group's medicine man, as well as every last warrior. Anza was given Cuerno Verde's headdress with the green buffalo horn, which he took to Santa Fe to send to Commander General Croix. It was the symbol of the most decisive defeat of Comanche warriors in New Mexico's long history of frontier warfare. The Great Captain had now won enduring fame in New Mexico.

SONORA TRAIL

While waiting in 1780 to see what the Comanches would do next Governor Anza created an expeditionary force of some 150 men to blaze a new trail to the Sonora settlements. The only way into or out of New Mexico was the *Camino Real*. Because of this Chihuahua merchants held a strangle hold on all commerce, forcing New Mexicans to buy at the highest prices possible and sell at the cheapest. A road to Sonora could break their monopoly. Anza led his men in a southwesterly direction, crossed a waterless desert and climbed the San Luis Pass, finally reaching Arizpe, the capital of Sonora. The march was almost six hundred miles long and the new trail turned out not being feasible due to its difficulty so a new road wasn't established.

HOPI

Also in 1780 Governor Anza led an expedition to the Moqui (Hopi) villages in the western edges of New Mexico. Hopi land had been stricken by drought for three years so the Great Captain took them ample supplies of food in another effort to bring them into the New Mexican fold, efforts which had always been rejected in the past. Most of the Hopis sided with their cacique (Head Priest) who refused any form of help because they believed it would jeopardize their independence. Anza would not use force on the Hopis. The Governor distributed supplies to all who would accept then the only choice left open to him was to depart, with Hopi independence intact, privations notwithstanding.

THE COMANCHE PEACE

Back in New Mexico the end of Comanche warfare was in sight but to Anza and the people of the day the menace of sudden hostilities was still very real. Various Comanche bands conducted horrible raids in Texas but attacks in N.M. were repulsed with such heavy Comanche casualties that they finally come into Taos in 1786 to ask for peace. Anza had been working through diplomatic channels since the defeat of Cuerno Verde so now he told the chiefs that all bands must come in and sign a treaty or there would be none with anybody. A leader named **Chief Toroblanco** insisted on making war while **Chief Ecueracapa** spoke for peace. The intransigent Toroblanco was killed and the peace faction held sway.

In February of 1786 one of the most significant ceremonies in Southwest frontier history was about to take place. Comanche chieftain **Ecueracapa** led his people to Pecos Pueblo and ordered that they set up their tipis in peace. The chief was then escorted to Santa Fe where he was received by Governor Anza amid festivities and honors due any chief of state: a military escort, the town council in attendance, and the assembled crowd applauding at every turn. Governor Anza understood how important ceremonial ritual was to Native Americans and he provided it with all possible splendor, combining Hispanic frontier as well as Indian protocol.

Ecueracapa was enchanted and his greeting of Gov. Anza took at least 10 minutes. Then they went indoors where a Ute delegation (their "mortal enemies; *'Comanche'* is a Ute word for *'enemy'* and *'wants to fight me all the time'* ") accepted peace *"if Ecueracapa does."* He did and there are three days of conferencing and festivities. With the Utes now at peace with the Comanches, everyone adjourns to Pecos to sign the peace document.

On February 28, 1786, New Mexican Hispanics, led by Gov. Anza, and Comanches, led by Chief Ecueracapa, hold a peace conference at Pecos.

In solemn but colorful council Anza declares that Ecueracapa is the "General of the Comanche Nation" in the eyes of the "King of Spain, who gives him a Staff of Office." Anza then gives his own sword and banner to Ecueracapa for display to leaders of other bands not in attendance.

Ecueracapa and various Comanche chiefs, along with some Utes, respond with stirring oratory, thanking the New Mexicans for forgiving past hostilities. All promise to keep the peace as honorable men and to wage war against hostile Apaches until they make peace. They dig a hole then ritually refill it to symbolize the end of all wars against New Mexicans.

The Comanches at Pecos crowd around Anza at every opportunity. *"All, one by one, come up to embrace him with such excessive expressions of affection and respect … and rub their faces against his."* Governor Anza is at his diplomatic best and he has lunch with the Comanche captains in their camp.

The next day being Ash Wednesday, Anza receives ashes at service, along with all the Comanche and Ute captains in attendance. Then a trade fair is declared with the Governor proclaiming set rules to prevent cheating the Indians.

The formal Treaty of Peace contains the following terms: Comanches may come into Santa Fe whenever they wish; free trade fairs will be established at Pecos Pueblo; Comanches may move closer to the N.M. settlements while they are hunting or looking to trade; they will keep the peace with all nations friendly to N.M.; Comanches will help fight the Apaches; the Governor of N.M. will endorse whomever the Comanches select as chiefs.

By April, 1787, all three branches of the Comanche nation had signed peace treaties with Governor Anza and New Mexico. A real bond was formed between New Mexicans and Comanches. And in the process allies like the Jicarilla Apaches and Utes, former blood enemies of the Comanches, weren't alienated. The foundation for an alliance with the Navajos was also created.

Comanches are now described by Hispanic writers as robust, good-looking, and very happy people. Their faces display their martial, honest, and generous character. Their clothes are fashioned from buffalo skins and they paint their faces with red ochre and other colors, their eyelids with vermilion. They love to adorn themselves with anything that shines brilliantly, intertwining beads, ribbons, gold trinkets, etc., in their hair, which they often wear braided. While there would be individual problem situations that developed during trading, there are no general hostilities between New Mexicans and Comanches until well into the American period of New Mexican history. The Comanche Peace (from 1786 to 1846 and continuing somewhat into the beginning of the U.S. period of domination) stabilized New Mexico because Comanches and New Mexicans honored the treaty. It enabled both groups to survive then prosper. Despite the replacement of Anza due to ill health, the death of Ecueracapa, hostilities of other Native Americans, etc., the peace forged at Pecos stood unbroken for generations and the alliance was second in importance only to that with the Pueblo people.

The Comanches become stalwart allies, much like the Pueblo people, and a deep bond formed between Hispanic New Mexicans and the warrior Comanches, who were scrutinized by other warlike nations of the Plains to see how they fared. Comanchero traders, Hispanic and Pueblo, were now able to take their wares to the plains and it became big business for the time and place. New Mexican Hispanic *ciboleros* harvested buffalo on the plains, utilizing virtually the entire animal, and *mesteñeros* went out to capture wild horses to train to the saddle for the ranching industry. [See Note # 13.]

Due to ill health, in 1787 Juan Bautista de Anza asked to be relieved of his post as Governor of New Mexico. Upon the arrival of his replacement, **Fernando de la Concha**, in November of 1787, Anza handed over the reins of government. It is thought he accompanied the annual (November) caravan going to Chihuahua. He was made Provisional Commander of the Armed Forces of Sonora and Captain of the presidio of Tucson. But his health didn't improve. The Great Captain died on December 19, 1788, in Arizpe. He was buried in the church of Nuestra Señora de la Asunción.

So ended the life of the Southwest's greatest combination of Indian Fighter, Diplomat and Peacemaker; Explorer, Trailblazer, Colonizer, and Writer of Journals; Founder of San Francisco, California; Military and Civil Governor of New Mexico; Father of the Comanche Peace. To students of Southwest History, *Juan Bautista de Anza* will always be *The Great Captain*. [See Note # 14.]

DISCUSSION Notes *for* THE GREAT CAPTAIN

Note # 1
See *Quest For Empire: Spanish Settlement In The Southwest* by Donald Cutter & Iris Engstrand.

Note # 2
The master work on Anza still remains the five volumes written by Herbert E. Bolton titled *Anza's California Expeditions*. These volumes aren't generally available to the ordinary reader. For a con-

densation of Bolton's monumental work see *Anza Conquers The Desert: The Anza Expeditionms From Mexico To California And The Founding Of San Francisco, 1774 To 1776* by Richard F. Pourade. Among many other sources, see also *A History Of California: The Spanish Period* by Charles E. Chapman. Invaluable is *Forgotten Frontiers: A Study Of The Spanish Indian Policy Of Don Juan Bautista De Anza, Governor Of New Mexico, 1777-1787* by Alfred Barnaby Thomas.

Note # 3

R.F. Pourade hammers away at Anza's not mentioning Fages' previous exploration. Is this omission an important historical point? If "giving credit where credit is due" is crucial to American historiography, how many books on the history of the West point out that Hubert H. Bancroft *never* gave credit to his staff of researchers and writers who did most of the work on his 39 volume history series?

Note # 4

Since wealthy people seldom venture out as frontier settlers, these colonizers were from the impoverished elements of Spanish colonial society. "Poverty" of Hispanic people in the Southwest is a steady theme in English language historical literature. Were any groups of pioneers wealthy? The following joke was told in church by an Anglican minister: In coming to the West, the Catholics came on foot, the Baptists by covered wagon, the Anglicans by Pullman.

Note # 5

Along with the Juan de Oñate colonization and the others lead by Diego de Vargas into New Mexico, this journey is considered one of the most significant in the history of North America.

Note # 6

Even though Anza protested the disparity, Charles E. Chapman writes that the bill for these pioneers' food came to $1957 while that of Anza and Padre Font was $2232.50. Chapman refers to it as an *"undemocratic note"* in the expedition. What standards are being employed in historiography like this?

Note # 7

Charles E. Chapman writes: *"When one considers that scores of (American) lives were lost in the days of '49 over these same trails, Anza's skill as a frontiersman stands revealed."*

Note # 8

On June 17, 1776, amid pealing church bells from Monterrey Mission, the pioneers hit the trail to San Francisco. Led by José Joaquín Moraga, they selected a site (different from Anza's) for the presidio after reconnoitering the area. Formalities were celebrated on September 17, 1776, and for the mission on October 9. These pioneers had traveled some 1700 miles to found *Yerba Buena* which was to become the *"Beautiful City by the Bay."* Their arrival had doubled the numbers of Hispanic people living in California. Within the next five years more would arrive over the Anza Trail and in the future great herds of cattle and horses would flourish on California ranchos. According to C.E. Chapman, Anza's colonization was the most important event in the history of California up to that time and would have enduring importance for all time.

Note # 9

See *New Mexico: A Bicentennial History* by Marc Simmons.

Note # 10

It is easily discernible that neither extermination nor exile of hostile Indians was ever Spanish policy in the Borderlands. The plan was to defeat the Comanches militarily then make them friends. Simple, yes, but could it be effected?

Note # 11

It has been written that Commander General Neve was jealous of Anza's achievements in California and New Mexico. He even wrote the King that Anza should be removed from office. The next Commander General, Jacobo Ugarte y Loyola, countermanded Neve's assertions, thus setting the record straight.

Note # 12

See *Forgotten Frontiers: A Study Of The Spanish Indian Policy Of Don Juan Bautista De Anza, Governor Of New Mexico, 1777-1787*, for original documents translated, edited, and annotated by Alfred B. Thomas.

Note # 13

See *History Of Arizona And New Mexico, 1530-1888* by Hubert Howe Bancroft who, inexplicably, writes about Anza "*...yet with all his energy he effected but slight change for the better in New Mexican affairs.*" Bancroft is the giant of Southwestern historiography but such commentary/analysis doesn't emanate from the historical record. Anza defeated Comanche hostiles then forged the Comanche Peace. Those achievements were not "slight."

Note # 14

Professor A.B. Thomas writes that Anza "*faced issues from which he emerges as an empire builder.*" Students of American history are aware of the praise heaped on personalities like Sevier in Tennessee, Boone in Kentucky, Austin in Texas, Carson in the Southwest. Marc Simmons has written that Anza's "*...career as a frontiersman easily rivaled that of Boone, Crocket, or Carson.*" H.E. Bolton writes that Anza's historical record shows him to be "*...a man of heroic qualities, tough as oak, silent as the desert from which he sprang...,*" that there is no one in "*Anglo-American annals with whom to compare*" Anza.

RANCHING

Christopher Columbus and his Spaniards brought the first cattle to the Western Hemisphere in 1494. This second voyage of Columbus also included some 24 stallions and 10 mares. Horses and cattle were to alter the Americas like nothing except the introduction of Christianity and the future Industrial Revolution. **Cortés** (1485-1547) landed the first horses on the North American continent in 1519 and **Gregorio de Villalobos** introduced cattle in 1521. After the conquest of Mexico, completed in 1521, cattle ranching developed in Mexico and it was there that the vaquero/cowboy was born. From Mexico ranching spread throughout the Americas, including into what is now the American Southwest and the USA. [See Note # 1. *Notes begin on page 99.*]

CATTLE

The Spanish cattle brought to the Americas were "tough animals with long, low-swinging heads, formidable horns, narrow sides, and long legs." Tending toward a feral nature, they adapted readily to a frontier environment. They were accustomed to roaming at will, taking care of themselves without the need of human beings. The cattle varied in colors from differing shades of yellow to dun, deep brown, red, and black. Their meat was stringy but their hides were tough and above all these cattle knew how to survive.

While raising cattle as part of agriculture was common in Europe, only in Spain was there cattle *ranching*, where large numbers of cattle roamed over extensive grazing grounds. It was in Spain where the equipment and techniques necessary for ranching were first developed. For example, the mounted herdsman was standard in Spain, rare in countries like France or England. The branding of cattle in Spain dates back to the tenth century. The *silla de campo*, work saddle, was created to aid the mounted herdsman in his work. The roundup for branding, separating strays, etc., and the cattle drive were standard ranching activities. Cattle had to be driven to different grazing lands, depending on the season, so techniques were developed to facilitate the movement of large numbers of animals. Land was also used collectively by stockmen.

HORSE CULTURE

The European horse culture was most highly developed in Spain. The Spanish horse was famous for his speed and quality long before the Arabs took over the country starting in 711. There is no denying that the Arabs were products of the most highly developed horse culture in the world when they entered Spain. They added their Arabian horses, knowledge of husbandry, and equestrian techniques to what already existed on the Iberian Peninsula.

MESTA

The stockmen's association known as the "*Mesta*" was already a powerful Spanish institution by the early Middle Ages. Castilian stockmen would meet two or three times a year to discuss enforcement of ordinances pertaining to pastoral industries, including the raising of sheep. Herding large numbers of sheep from one pasture to another, as from mountains to plains, was carefully regulated by the Mesta. [See Note # 2.]

The Town Council of Mexico City established the Mesta association on June 16, 1529, pattered after the organization in Spain. Henceforth the Mexican Mesta had the power to call all stockmen to meet twice annually to discuss matters pertaining to their animals and to strays, etc., and required all stockmen to have their own brands which had to be registered with Mesta authorities in Mexico City. This would be the first "book of brands" in the Americas.

TRADITION and LAW

In 1533 when *Nueva España*, "New Spain," was proclaimed an official Spanish colony, common grazing grounds were established for livestock. This applied to animals owned by Hispanics or Indians.

Removing cattle from agricultural areas worked to reduce disputes and lawsuits as well as further the growth and development of the ranching industry. But removal of cattle to less populated areas also enabled rustlers to steal cattle and alter brands to cover up their crime. Stockmen demanded that rustlers be brought to justice. In 1537 the Crown ordered **Antonio de Mendoza**, the first American Viceroy, to establish the Mesta throughout New Spain and enact ordinances which would benefit and increase the herds of animals, and to remedy and/or punish all frauds and crimes committed against stock owners.

By July 1, 1537, the first code of the Mexican Mesta was issued. [See Note # 3.] The Mesta did much to develop Mexican ranch culture. It decreed, among other things, that all brands had to be different in order to quickly identify animal ownership; if two stockmen happened to come up with the same brand, the Mesta would assign each one a brand of their own; cropping the ears of animals was strictly forbidden because it encouraged fraud and deception, etc. All stockmen owning any combination of 300 animals, including sheep, goats, hogs, or at least 20 horses, mules, burros, cows, had to be members of the Mesta. Each member was required to attend Mesta meetings in person or send a verified representative. Well advertised meetings were held in February and August. Members were expected to bring all strays to Mesta meetings in their locality in order to return the animals to their rightful owners. If the strays couldn't be identified or their owners couldn't be found then the animals were sold and the money put into the royal treasury.

Mexico and its ranch people created ways to layout ranches, construct fences, corrals, etc. Roundups and branding techniques came into being. Mexican ranching also developed methods for handling horses, cattle, and sheep. Along with saddles they developed or refined bridles, bits, spurs, chaps, hats, boots, rawhide or horsehair ropes, hobbles, hackamores, etc., and the vocabulary necessary for all these items. Floral decorations of leather items like saddles also started in Mexico.

The Mesta governed virtually every aspect of animal husbandry. For example, it had rules on handling grains with which to feed livestock. It decreed what kind of dogs could be used in raising sheep and how many could be owned. Regulations were specific: one dog was allowed for each thousand sheep. Rules were applied equitably whether one was a small stockman, farmer, or large land owner with hundreds animals. It collected fines from anyone who violated its ordinances.

By 1540, when **Vásquez de Coronado** made the first European reconnaissance of what is now the American Southwest, there were so many cattle in New Spain that the "on the hoof commissary herd" of some 500 animals taken by the great conquistador was easy to gather. While passing through Sinaloa a number of exhausted cattle were left in the area and twenty-five years later **Francisco de Ibarra** recorded that "thousands of wild cattle" were roaming the country. It is believed the rest of the cattle with the Vásquez de Coronado explorations were used up to feed the gallant band of explorers so none remained in the lands visited.

HORNED SADDLE

As ranching gained prominence it was quickly apparent that roping technique had to be improved. A vaquero would lasso a steer and control the animal as best he could by anchoring the rope *under the horse's tail.* This was difficult to do and required much time to bring the steer under control. So the "*silla vaquera,*" the cowboy horned saddle, was created and henceforth a vaquero could rope a cow and turn the rope around an "anchor horn" built into the front of the saddle. This roping technique using the horned saddle came to be known as "*dale vuelta*" (give it a turn) and provided a tremendous impetus for the development of the ranching industry.

By the 16th century saddle-making in New Spain became a prestigious craft dominated by professionals called *talabarteros* (craftsmen who manufactured saddles and/or harnesses). Guilds were organized in the larger cities and the largest saddle shops developed there. These shops employed many saddle-makers, apprentices, and related specialty craftsmen. Because a vaquero spent many hours in the saddle, it was necessary to make it as comfortable as possible. More leather was used to cover it, thus providing needed padding. The rider's personal touches were often added to it if he could afford them. The stirrup straps became longer so the knees could provide a slight grip and the legs wouldn't tire as quickly. Stirrups were made, usually out of oak if available, to enable easy access to booted feet.

The "Santa Fe Saddle" evolved in northern Mexico (and later made its way into New Mexico and Texas). The "tree," the saddle's foundation wooden structure, came to be covered with a large piece of leather (*mochila*) with reinforced holes for the large horn and the cantle (the back of the seat). [See Note # 4.]

ROPE

After the saddle, *la reata*, the rope, became a vaquero's basic tool. Most of the time the vaquero would make his own reata. He would cut a cowhide into strips, soak them in water then stretch them before braiding the now pliable four to eight strands into a (typical) sixty-foot rope (though some could be a bit over a hundred feet long). The completed reata was then stretched further and oiled to the vaquero's liking. A vaquero could throw a *lazo*, lasso, from 25 to 60 feet to bring a steer under control.

CLOTHING

A vaquero's clothes were dictated by necessity. His hat was wide brimmed to protect against the hot sun. Generally constructed of leather, it had a low flat crown and wasn't intended to be decorative. Bandanas were sometimes tied around the head or the neck, the latter raised up to the nose when needed to protect against dust. Shirts were made of cotton or wool but sometimes of tanned leather, which was waterproof. Jackets were of leather. Pants, usually laced up the sides, were often made of tanned leather, sometimes of wool or cotton. From the knee down the vaquero usually wore *botas* which were leather leggings which reached to the top of his buckskin footwear, on which were strapped iron spurs. These made a pleasant, small bell-like sound when he walked. A vaquero was proud of his spurs for he considered them a badge of his profession which he felt was something of rank. Boots with enlarged heels became a necessity to anyone working on the ground and struggling to control an animal on the end of a rope.

PROLIFERATION

Wealthy Mexican land owners, called *hacendados* because they owned large *haciendas*, often became cattle raisers. When rich silver deposits were discovered, as at Zacatecas in 1548, Pachuca in 1552 and Guanajuato in 1558, mining camps burgeoned into villages, towns and/or cities. [See Note # 5.] Miners, their families and all others had to be fed so cattle drives were made to each new strike then the ranching industry took root in that area. Livestock in most Mexican climates "multiplied unbelievably" so the hacendado hired numbers of vaqueros to work his animals. He generally provided a place for the vaqueros to sleep and married cowboys were often permitted to build a house on ranch land. The hacendado generally hired an *estanciero*, overseer, to manage the ranch while he spent most of his time in the city. The estanciero delegated various duties to his *caporal*, who was in close contact with the working vaqueros.

Wild cattle were also common by the 1550s. Rounding them up became known as a *rodeo* (from Spanish *rodear*: to surround or encircle). Vaqueros would drive cattle toward their ranch or designated area where strays were then separated and new calves branded. Thus it was that roundups and cattle drives became commonplace in Mexico.

Vaqueros generally preferred to ride stallions because it was believed they were more powerful than mares. Because there were so many stallions there was a tremendous proliferation of wild horses by 1550. Anyone could own a horse merely by catching and training it to the saddle.

Thus it was that by around 1600 the ranching industry was firmly established in Mexico. It would provide a rich legacy of horses, cattle, equipment, techniques for working livestock, legal codes, stockmen's associations, folklore, and vocabulary.

DISCUSSION Notes *for* RANCHING

Note # 1
See *Cowboy Culture: A Saga Of Five Centuries* by David Dary. See also "The Ranching Frontier: Spanish Institutional Backgrounds of the Plains Cattle Industry" by Sandra L. Myres in *New Spain's Far Northern Frontier* edited by David J. Weber.

Note # 2
See *The Mesta: A Study In Spanish Economic History, 1273-1836* by Julius Klein.

Note # 3
See *The Mexican Mesta: The Administration Of Ranching In Colonial Mexico* by William H. Dusenberry.

Note # 4
See *King Of The Western Saddle* by Timothy H. Evans.

Note # 5
See *A History Of Latin America, From The Beginnings To The Present* by Hubert Herring.

RANCHING In NEW MEXICO

Large numbers of horses, cattle, and sheep were in the **Francisco Vásquez de Coronado** expedition into New Mexico in 1540. Chronicler **Pedro de Castañeda** wrote there were 1,000 horses, 500 cattle, and 5,000 sheep in the heroic exploratory venture. Two of the intrepid missionaries in the expedition, Fray **Juan de Padilla**, who chose to return to Quivira and Fray **Luis de Escalona**, who made Pecos Pueblo his headquarters, were supplied with sheep. Padilla and Escalona were soon martyred and there is no evidence that their sheep survived either.

The **Juan de Oñate** colonization of New Mexico in 1598 brought some 1,000 cattle, 1,000 goats, 150 mares and colts, and around 4,000 sheep to begin stock raising in New Mexico. [See Note # 1. *Notes begin on page 101.*] A spokesman for Governor Oñate testified in 1601 that cattle and sheep had increased to more than 3,000 head but another witness testified that neither cattle nor sheep were doing well due to the barren country of New Mexico. When Oñate resigned the governorship his replacement (1610), **Pedro de Peralta**, received 1,000 sheep and goats as part of the official governmental transition.

SHEEP

Farming and ranching became the most important occupations in New Mexico. Sheep quickly proved the most important ranch animal because the species could survive in the various landscapes peculiar to New Mexico. Governmental authorities, ordinary citizens, as well as Franciscan friars and their churches got into the sheep raising business. By 1634 Fray **Alonso de Benavides** wrote that mission agriculture and sheep raising were the principal sources of food during periods of scarcity or depression. The friars also used sheep and food products to pay workers for building churches at the various Pueblos. The good friar Benavides also recorded that woolen cloth was being produced by the friars and their Pueblo pupils.

In 1639 the Santa Fe Cabildo (Town Council) protested to Mexico City authorities that the friars at the Pueblos had 1,000 to 2,000 sheep while ordinary citizens had far fewer. During this period Church and State authorities were constantly feuding with each other but these complaints and counter-complaints provide facts and figures regarding the sheep ranching industry. The friars stationed in eastern Pueblo villages like Abó and Quivira, areas that were particularly vulnerable to Apache attacks, wrote (ca. 1659-60) that they had lost more than eight thousand sheep to Apache raiders.

So it was that between 1620-1670 the number of sheep increased significantly in New Mexico. It is also clear that markets to the south in Nueva Vizcaya, especially the mining district of Parral, were recognized as established markets for New Mexican stockmen, which included Church and State authorities as well as ordinary citizens.

The St. Lawrence Day Massacre of August, 1680, drove all surviving Christians into El Paso in (at that time) southern New Mexico. [See Note # 2.] One of the avowed purposes of the slaughter was to eliminate all vestiges of Hispanic culture but it appears that horses, cattle, and sheep, obvious products of Hispanic culture, were excluded from the decree because herds and flocks were found when Hispanics returned in 1692. During the fighting around Cochití Pueblo in 1694, Hispanics and their allies captured some 900 sheep. The valiant Diego de Vargas gave some 200 sheep to reestablish missions at Pecos, Zía, Santa Ana, and San Felipe while another 100 went to the missionaries in Santa Fe. Also in 1694, the Franciscans brought in some 500 sheep and cows. In 1695 around 1000 sheep and goats were brought in from El Paso.

STOCK DISTRIBUTION

In 1697 civilian authorities brought in large numbers of stock for distribution to New Mexican families, bachelors, single women, widows, and orphans. [See Note # 3.] During the livestock division some

1,000 New Mexicans received around 4,000 sheep, 170 goats, 500 cows, 150 bulls, etc. Acknowledged leaders like Fernando Durán y Chaves, Diego Arias de Quirós, Jacinto Peláez, etc., received no more than their fair share.

In the married group was **Fernando Durán y Chaves** who took his thirty ewes and returned to settle in the Bernalillo area (from where his descendants were later to distinguish themselves as soldiers, merchants, and politicians in New Mexican history). Among the single men was the Frenchman **Santiago Grolle** (*Jacque Grolet*, member of the La Salle expedition to Texas in 1684-1687) who became progenitor of the *Gurulé* family of New Mexico. Also in the "single" category was **Miguel de la Vega y Coca,** a young widower who parlayed his thirteen ewes into the famous hacienda *"Rancho de las Golondrinas"* between Santa Fe and Albuquerque. The record of the distribution ends with payment for the five Indian herders who had guided the stock from Nueva Vizcaya.

Due to the Spanish Government and the dauntless leadership of Diego de Vargas, the New Mexican sheep industry was now back in existence as of 1697. New Mexican stockmen went out to resettle areas like Santa Cruz de la Cañada, Bernalillo, Albuquerque, etc., expanding their ranching domains.

DISCUSSION Notes *for* RANCHING IN NEW MEXICO

Note # 1

See *Las Carneradas: Sheep Trade In New Mexico, 1700-1860* by John O. Baxter. See also *Quest For Empire: Spanish Settlement In The Southwest* by Donald Cutter and Iris Engstrand.

Note # 2

In the Spanish language documents of the time the "Pueblo Revolt" was referred to as *"El Día de San Lorenzo"* and therefore had no relation to most of what is implied in the English phrase. When one considers that out of the approximate 400 dead Hispanics, fully 300 or so were non-combatant women and children, the word *massacre* applies.

Note # 3

In contrast to the European traditions made into law east of the Mississippi, Hispanic females were legally entitled to own land and livestock in New Mexico.

RANCHING in TEXAS

The *haciendas* of northern Mexico were owned by rich and powerful miners, businessmen, and politicians of tremendous influence. These great estates of Nueva Vizcaya, Coahuila, and Nuevo León were enormous properties generally containing whole villages with living quarters, company stores, and permanent labor forces. The hacienda system didn't make its way into Texas for a number of reasons. The area which would come to be known as San Antonio de Béxar was founded on April 25, 1718, by seventy-two people led by **Martin de Alarcón**, Knight of the Order of Santiago and an experienced frontiersman. By the time Alarcón departed some of these had already abandoned the colony. By 1720 Apache attacks began, prelude to depredations which would continue in cycle throughout the century. The Comanches also entered the area and forced the Apaches out of their traditional domain, exacerbating the Apache problem.

PADRES as RANCHERS

Missionaries were the first ranchers in Texas, dating from the 1720s. These "Renaissance" *padres* managed mission lands, were the intellectuals of their society, and they had Indians to train in the arts of ranching. [See Note # 1. *Notes begin on page 102.*] The good *padres* gathered stock that had survived on the land from expeditions starting as early as the 1680s. They knew stock raising so animals multiplied prodigiously. Many became mostly wild. The missions would hold joint roundups, cattle would be divided equitably between the five missions, then mission brands would be applied. More than twenty priests and a number of lay brothers labored at the missions. Among the most prominent were Fathers Benito Fernández de Santa Ana, Francisco Mariano de los Dolores y Viana, José Ganzábal, and Alonso Giraldo de Terreros.

FIRST CATTLE DRIVE

The **Marques de San Miguel de Aguayo**, newly appointed Governor of Texas and Coahuila, must be credited with the very first "Texas cattle drive" in 1721 when his expedition herded in 4800 cattle, 2800 horses, and 6400 sheep and goats. Previous *entradas* always contained livestock but the huge herds brought in by Governor Aguayo were the real beginning of the Texas livestock industry.

HOSTILITIES, COLONISTS, & GROWTH

Governor Aguayo reinforced the San Antonio presidio by more than twenty soldiers in 1722. The presidio now had fifty-four stalwarts with which to defend Texas against hostile Apaches and Comanches. As incredible as it might seem, an improved stability was evident by 1727. The Apache problems began again in 1731 and lasted to 1749. These hostilities, though horses were the main target for raiders, were not conducive to cattle ranching.

On March 9, 1731, there occurred in San Antonio de Béxar the arrival of fourteen (fifteen?) families of Canary Island colonists, a total of some 55 persons. Captain **Juan Antonio Pérez de Almazán** of the presidio permitted them to settle in lands close to the fort. While the increase in population was in many ways advantageous, problems continued with the Apaches, who were in turn targeted by the Hasinai tribes of eastern Texas, the Tonkawa of central Texas, and especially the powerful Comanches (first reported to the Viceroy in 1743). These groups, as well as other smaller Indian groups, came to be referred to as *Norteños*.

By 1749-1750 the Spanish population of San Antonio de Béxar was approximately 560 men, women, and children. Mission ranches had already been established but "civilian" *ranchos* were more or less independently owned rural farms with a house and perhaps other necessary buildings. There were a few exceptions: the grant of land made to **Luis Menchaca**, 65,000 acres, was referred to as a "rancho."

Cattle ownership was common among *Bexareños* but only a few families owned enough animals to justify a need for additional pasture land. Problems in acquiring more land continued to be Indian hostilities, claims made by missions, and the expense of going to court to validate land titles. Notwithstanding these obstacles, some families expanded into the countryside between 1751-1768 but hostile Indians again became a basic danger until peace was made with the Comanches and other Norteño groups in 1785. But then Apache hostilities in 1789-1790 once more curtailed the development of the ranching industry. [See Note # 2.]

Despite all vicissitudes, Béxar's most important agricultural products became cattle and corn. The plucky *Tejano* pioneers were stockmen from the beginning, even if on a small scale for some. Ranching was encouraged by the Government. For example, each of the Canary Island families received five breeding cows, a bull, five mares and a stallion, as per their colonization contract. Ordinary Tejanos quickly became talented stockmen. For example, the 1748 will of **Mateo Pérez** listed ownership of more than 200 head of cattle along with 50 horses.

While many horses, mules and sheep were raised, by the early 1750s the economy was based on cattle. By the late 1760s some Tejanos owned five to six thousand head. Meat, including that from wild cattle, was the most important element in everybody's diet. There was so much of it that the mule trains that brought in trade items like flour, chocolate, cloth, etc., into Béxar returned to places as far south as Saltillo with jerked meat, candle tallow, and hides.

Common interests fostered by ranching worked to promote a sense of community solidarity. The various groups intermarried so kinship ties were also a factor but it was the agricultural and ranching economy which united Tejanos above all else. [See Note # 3.]

By the 1770s Tejano cattle herds were being driven to the Río Grande and Coahuila settlements, to annual fairs in Saltillo, and to mining areas where silver miners provided a lucrative market for Tejano beef. There were even cattle drives to Louisiana where in time Spanish forces would be fighting British armies who wanted to squelch the American War for Independence.

DISCUSSION Notes *for* RANCHING in TEXAS

Note # 1
See *Spanish Texas, 1519-1821* by Donald E. Chipman.
Note # 2
See *San Antonio De Béxar: A Community On New Spain's Northern Frontier* by Jesús F. De La Teja.
Note # 3
See *Tejano Journey: 1770-1850*, edited by Gerald E. Poyo.

RANCHING in CALIFORNIA

The first few livestock in California arrived by boat in 1769. The *San Carlos* sailed out of La Paz in Lower California on January 9, 1769. Its destination would be San Diego. Lieutenant **Pedro Fages** and some twenty-five volunteers were onboard to handle any difficulty with hostile Indians. The *San Antonio* sailed later on February 15. All were intent on achieving their goal: planting missions and presidios in California.

The overland expedition from Loreto in Lower California to what would be San Diego was led by

Captain **Fernando Rivera y Moncada** and included Fray **Juan Crespi**, close associate of Fray **Junípero Serra**. The Rivera y Moncada group herded larger numbers of horses and cattle. The second overland effort, led by **Gaspar de Portolá**, accompanied by Father Serra, also had livestock with it. Of the 300 or so valiants in the expeditions, more than a third paid with their lives.

While accompanying Portolá to what would be Monterey, Fray Juan Crespi wrote in his journal (January 4, 1770): "The country is beautiful, covered with grass…wonderful pasture for the livestock."

By 1773 there were five missions in California and each had perhaps 40-50 head of cattle. When the Great Captain, **Juan Bautista de Anza,** arrived with his colonists in 1776, some 350 cattle came with them, along with around 700 horses.

MISSION RANCHING

A total of twenty-one missions were established in California and all had livestock. [See Note # 1. *Notes begin on page 105.*] At first the cattle were relatively tame because they had been around people but as they multiplied they had to be set out on mission pasture lands. By around the late 1770s cattle began to grow more wild from being on the open range. There weren't enough vaqueros to care for them so the missionaries had to train reliable Indian converts to work the livestock. There was a law against permitting Indians to ride horses but in isolated California necessity required that Indians be trained to the ranching industry. The mission *ranchos* were so successful that by around 1821 they owned some 500,000 cattle.

INDIAN COWBOYS

Indian vaqueros had great teachers and they had the abilities to become excellent students. They were taught how to build branding fires, how to heat the branding iron and keep it hot, how to apply the hot iron without injuring the animal. They were taught how to saddle a horse, rope cattle from horseback, etc. Use of the braided rawhide *jáquima* (halter) was widespread in early California until metal bits became more readily available. The *mecate* (reins) was made of horsehair. While mission horses were branded as quickly as possible, no attempt was made to train them to the saddle until they were at least three years old.

Those Indian vaqueros who showed greater promise were apprenticed to blacksmiths at one of the presidios (four were in existence in early California) where they learned how to work with iron and, among other things, make horseshoes and branding irons.

Some vaqueros went into saddle making. While beginning efforts were rather simple, when expert *talabarteros* (saddle makers) were later brought to California, saddle quality improved and developed into what today is still referred to as the "California Saddle."

CIVILIAN RANCHING

In 1775 Governor Rivera y Moncada made a grant of land to one **Manuel Butrón**, said to be California's first private rancher. In 1786 individual grants of land were made to Juan José Domínguez, Manuel Nieto, and the sons of "the widow of Ignacio Carillo." These were among the first non-mission ranchers in California. Rancheros were required to construct necessary buildings and to stock the land with at least 2,000 cattle.

Manuel Nieto was a professional soldier. When he retired in 1795 he devoted the rest of his life to building up his *Rancho Santa Gertrudes*. By 1800 the rancho contained some 150,000 acres with at least fifteen to twenty thousand head of cattle and horses. When Nieto died in 1804 he was considered one of the wealthiest Californios.

Juan José Domínguez had some 75,000 acres in his *Rancho Domínguez*. Juan José lived in San Diego while a *mayordomo* (manager) ran the ranch for him. It has been written that Domínguez' horses weren't properly controlled so they ran wild, mixing with animals from missions and other ranchos, as well as roaming free.

When one ranchero bought cattle from another the cattle drive would be made, usually in the spring when nature provided grass for the stock. Roundups were held in the spring and fall in order to brand calves, strays were separated from the owner's herd, and animals were cut out of the herd for butchering. Beef was the principal element in the Californio diet.

Early California ranch lands were granted in sizes of 6 ½ square miles. Labor was generally done by the men in the family with help from hired Indian vaqueros if necessary. *Californio* ranchers became famous for their ranching skills and they have been described as the best horsemen of the Americas. Californios rarely walked if they could ride. Stallions were preferred over mares for all riding, even if women were doing the riding. Californios made ropes, reins, and halters from the tails and manes of their mares. (A stallion's hair was not cut.) On occasion different colored hair was used to create a particularly beautiful rope. The Californios' skill with the rope was especially remarkable for they could hunt deer, elk, and even *grizzly bears with ropes*. Certain horses were trained specifically for bear hunting but California horses in general were highly trained for working cattle.

Ranching was the principal industry in early California and provided an attractive outdoor life style on horseback for all amid rolling hills, little valleys, flowing creeks, wooded canyons, meadows painted natural green with lush grasses. Each rancho was a veritable community in and of itself. Houses were built in an especially favored location. Orchards were planted nearby and gardens were popular. While there were also thousands of sheep, horses and cattle were the principal basis for California's people.

DISCUSSION Notes *for* RANCHING IN CALIFORNIA
Note # 1
See *California: A History* by Andrew F. Rolle for an introduction to many aspects of California history. See also *Cowboy Culture* by David Dary for specifics on Californio ranching. For personal reminiscence based on the life of cowboys and Western ranching see *Californio!* and *Trail Dust And Saddle Leather* by Jo Mora.

RANCHING in ARIZONA

Father **Eusebio Kino** (-1711) was the first rancher in Arizona. Working from his mission headquarters in Dolores, Father Kino and a few colleagues planted the ranching industry as far north as the Gila

River near present-day Phoenix in the north and from the San Pedro River on the east to the Colorado River on the west. (He also introduced winter wheat, which added much to the Pima diet of corn, beans, and squash.) But ten years before Kino and his faithful companion **Juan Mateo Manje** explored the Pimería Alta, **José Romo de Vivar** was grazing cattle at the southern end of the Huachuca Mountain. Vivar was a prominent rancher and miner from Sonora who would qualify as Arizona's first Hispanic pioneer. [See Note # 1. *Notes begin on page 106.*]

ARIZONAC

It was the discovery of silver in 1736 in the area of a mining camp that came to be called *Arizonac* that provided the motivation for settlement and later development of what is today southern Arizona. It was an amazing discovery: large chunks (*bolas*) and slabs (*planchas*) of silver were found lying on the ground a few miles southwest of (contemporary) Nogales. The strike started Arizona's first mining boom and it brought people streaming into the area. Those who stayed after the silver was depleted had names like **Covarrubias, Bohórquez, Gallego, Ortega**, etc., and made their living by farming and ranching. The cattle have been described as little more than "horns and hide" but they knew how to survive the desert, isolation, and hostile Indians.

Survival on the Arizona frontier was no simple feat. While hostile Apaches were a constant menace to ranching and mining, in 1751 the "friendly" Pimas (O'odham) led by **Luis Oacpicagigua** rebelled, killed two priests and more than a hundred unsuspecting Hispanic settlers. A presidio was established at Tubac in 1753 in an effort to prevent future uprisings. Tubac thus became the first permanent Spanish settlement in Arizona and the northernmost outpost of Spanish Sonora until the presidio was moved to Tucson in 1776. Families with names like **Burruel, Castro, Gallegos, Pacheco, Ruelas, Romero, Sosa, Telles**, etc., raised their cattle, grew their crops, and survived Indian attacks to tell their story for all future generations to appreciate. [See Note # 2.]

DISCUSSION Notes *for* RANCHING in ARIZONA
Note # 1
See *Arizona: A History* by Thomas E. Sheridan.
Note # 2
H.H. Bancroft writes in *History Of Arizona And New Mexico* that early Arizona history is woefully lacking in information. It appears that problem is still prevalent.

Essay: LAND GRANTS

To understand the history of land grants in the American Southwest it is necessary to establish a background in Spanish customary law. Accepted custom was the basis for Spanish jurisprudence regarding land usage. [See Note # 1. *Notes begin on page 108.*] Laws regarding the use of land, including concepts of individual as well as community property rights, common ownership of pastures and woodlands, and councils of local citizens with authority over community land usage, were regulated by councils. These councils also regulated irrigation water usage. Arabic irrigation practices influenced Spanish customary law and provided much vocabulary (*acequia, noria, atarque, zanja*, etc.) still used in the Southwest.

The Moslem invasion of Spain (711) was more or less complete by the year 800. Only the northernmost section of Asturias remained in Christian hands and it was from this northern area that the Reconquest began. In order to reward Spanish leaders who fought the invading Moslems, Christian kings paid these "conquerors" with grants of (conquered) land, exemption from taxes, or titles of nobility. These grants were the historical forerunners of private land grants in the Southwest.

The grant of land to a community evolved in similar fashion. When a Christian village was founded, a way to hold the land permanently as well as use it as a springboard colony to drive further into Moslem strongholds, the King granted surrounding village land to the entire community. These lands, to be used in common by all, were administered according to local custom as described above. Village lands, the *commons*, were owned by the community as a whole. These common lands could be referred to as *ejidos, montes, pastos* (pastures) *abrevaderos* (watering places), *leña* (firewood), *árboles frutales* (fruit trees) *caza* (hunting lands), *pesca* (fishing areas), etc. Individuals had user rights, not ownership of the land, which remained with the village/town/city itself. While private land grants could be sold after ownership requirements were met, no individual could sell a community grant because all he was entitled to under customary law was user rights.

In 1681 the legal code known as *Recopilación de las Leyes de los Reynos de las Indias* was put into force in New Spain. These laws regulated the establishment of new settlements. Typically, each *vecino* (citizen; head of a family; colonist) received a lot (*solar de casa*) sized 50 square *varas* (a vara was around thirty-three inches), a piece of land on which to grow a garden (*suerte*) and one or two plots of land on which to grow field crops (*caballerías*, around 105 acres) like wheat or corn. Pasture land could also be awarded for the vecino's sheep (*sitio de ganado menor*), cattle and/or horses (*sitio de ganado mayor*). Above and beyond all this, the village/town owned land (ejido) for usage by all. The grants were in perpetuity so long as the owner lived on or used the land. [See Note # 2.]

It is a popular misconception that "the King of Spain awarded land grants." Grants were made by officials like the Governor through the local *Alcalde Mayor*. An individual would set the process in motion by petitioning the Governor as to the land that was being asked for, stating the petitioners qualifications, and declaring there were no other claims on the land being sought. The Governor would decide on the situation if he was familiar with the land in question but most often he would refer the petition to the local *Alcalde Mayor* for recommendations. The Alcalde would investigate if the land was indeed free of all claims, if the petitioner had the proper qualifications. If the matter was for a community grant, it would have to be decided if the land had enough pasture land, water, fire wood, etc., for everyone. Neighbors, whether Pueblo Indians or Hispanics, were informed to step forward and testify if the grant would be an encroachment on their own lands. If everything was favorable the Governor would make the grant and the Alcalde would be directed to conduct the ceremony of delivery of possession. The grantee would meet the Alcalde and a Notary, wherever possible, on the land itself, with perhaps neighboring land owners in attendance. This was the last opportunity for anyone to protest the grant. If everything was in order the grantee(s) and Alcalde would perhaps walk the boundaries of the land, mark boundaries with mounds of rocks or perhaps a cross. The grantee would pull up some natural grass, throw a stone or two as far across his property as possible, and all would declare "Long Live the King!" The written document (*expediente*) was then given to the grantee and a copy (*testimonio*) was kept by the Alcalde. [See Note # 3.]

In order to perfect one's title to the land, certain requirements had to be met, like having to live on the land for a specified period of time, having to own horses and weapons, grant land couldn't be sold for a period of from four to ten years, etc. Another land grant couldn't be obtained without relinquishing title to the first one. When the grantee had complied with stipulations like living on the land for the required number of years, the final document was issued if this was the local custom.

The Hispanic land grant system was tailored to fit the challenges of life in a frontier environment. [See Note # 4.] Despite disagreements, disputes, and hostile Indian raids, the system worked for Hispanic people as well as Pueblo Indian society in places like New Mexico.

The farmer-rancher-soldiers of the Spanish Borderlands settled their families on the land and wrested a living from it. These European pioneer populations had to be courageous as well as self-sufficient for New Mexicans, Tejanos, and Californios were isolated from their countrymen in the rest of New Spain. But the land system must also be credited because variables like land forms, water and other resources were made available for each family unit. Farmers had private as well as communal rights to arable land, despite its scarcity in desert areas, and ranchers were provided with communal rights to grazing lands throughout the year because mountain grazing was available during the spring and summer then stock was driven to lower altitudes for the winter. The community-based economy *worked*.

DISCUSSION Notes *for* LAND GRANTS
Note # 1
See *Landgrants And Lawsuits In Northern New Mexico* by the paladin Malcolm Ebright.
Note # 2
See *Los Paisanos: Spanish Settlers On The Northern Frontier Of New Spain* by Oakah L. Jones, Jr.
Note # 3
See *Mercedes Reales: Hispanic Land Grants Of The Upper Río Grande Region* by gallant Victor Westphall.
Note # 4
See *Land, Water, And Culture: New Perspectives On Hispanic Land Grants* edited by Charles L. Briggs and John R. Van Ness.

CHAPTER 5

Society In The Hispanic Southwest

NEW MEXICO

New Mexico was founded in 1598 and is the oldest colony of European people in what is today the USA. [See Note # 1. *Notes begin on page 159.*] The story of New Mexico centers around it being the northernmost reach of the Spanish Empire and has been referred to as a frontier area for most of its history. **Charles F. Lummis** asserted in his *A New Mexico David and Other Stories*:

I hope some day to see a real history of the United States; a history not written in a closet, from other one-sided affairs, but based on a knowledge of the breadth of our history, and a disposition to do it justice, a book which will realize that the early history of this wonderful country is not limited to a narrow strip on the Atlantic seaboard, but that it began in the great Southwest; and that before the oldest of the Pilgrim Fathers had been born, swarthy Spanish heroes were colonizing much of what is now the United States; in their little corner of which they suffered for three hundred and fifty years such awful dangers and hardships as our Saxon forefathers did not dream of. I hope to see such a history, which will do justice to perhaps the most wonderful pioneers the world has ever produced, but it has not come yet … When that history is written you will find thrilling matter in the story of New Mexico…"

"If the true story of New Mexico could be written in complete detail, from the time when the brave Spanish conquistadores planted there the first European civilization in all the vast area now embraced by the United States, it would stand unparalleled in all the history of the world. No other commonwealth on the globe has met and conquered such incredible hardships, dangers, and sufferings for so long a time…" [See Note # 2.]

ISOLATION

As with all European pioneers, the New Mexicans arriving in 1598 were far removed from European settlements, customs, traditions, and amenities. While the New Mexico settlement was large in numbers for the time and place and could depend on its own resources for a while, it was fortunate for the new colonists that the settled Pueblo people of the area were relatively advanced in their civilization and willing to aid the newcomers. The small group of Europeans, numbering perhaps around 600 souls, with some 129 qualifying as "soldier-colonists," could have been wiped out by the Pueblos, with a population of some 40,000 or so, not to mention the uncounted thousands of Apaches and Navajos living within striking distance.

OÑATE COLONISTS

Who were these first pioneers of a European-American culture? [See Note # 3.] Here are the names of the colonists who accompanied Governor **Juan de Oñate** to *San Juan de los Caballeros* (Knights of St. John; shortly they moved to San Gabriel and then around 1607-1608 to Santa Fe), New Mexico, many of them with families:

A:
Pablo de Aguilar; Araujo; Ascencio de Archuleta; Ayarde;

B:
Dionisio de Bañuelos; Bartol; Juan Benitez; Bibero; Juan Gutiérrez de Bocanegra; Juan Pérez de Bustillo (with his wife, María de la Cruz, a son, and three daughters);
[See Note # 4.]

C:
Cesar Ortíz Cadimo; Juan Camacho; Esteban Carabajal; Carrera; Juan de Caso; Bernabé de las Casas; Castillo; Juan Catalán; Cavanillas; Gregorio César; Cordero; Juan Cortés; Marcos Cortés;

D:
Pedro Sánchez Damiero; Juan Díaz; Juan Pérez de Donis;

E:
Felipe Escalte; Juan Escarramal; Marcelo de Espinosa;

F:
Marcos Farfán de los Godos; Juan Fernández; Manuel Francisco;

G:
Alvaro García; Francisco García; Francisco García; Marcos García; Simón García; Luis Gascón; Bartolomé González; Juan González; Juan Griego; Guevara; Francisco Guillén; Antonio Gutiérrez;

H:
Gerónimo de Heredia; Antonio Hernández; Francisco Hernández; Gonzalo Hernández; Pedro Hernández; Antonio Conde de Herrera; Cristóbal de Herrera; Juan de Herrera; Alonzo Nuñez de Hinojosa;

I:
León de Isati;

J:
Jiménez;

K:

L:

Diego Landin; Francisco de Ledesma; Juan de León; Domingo de Lizana;
Cristóbal López; Juan López; Alonso Lucas; Lucio;

M:
Mallea; Francisco Márquez; Gerónimo Márquez; Hernán Martín; Juan
Martínez; Juan Medel; Medina; Monroi; Alonso Gómez Montesinos;
Baltazar de Monzón; Morales; Juan Moran; Munera;

N:
Naranjo; Diego Nuñez;

0:
Juan de Olague; Cristóbal de Oñate; Juan de Ortega; Ortiz;

P:
Regundo Paladín; Simón de Paz; Juan de Pedraza; Pereya; Simón Pérez;
Juan Pinero; Francisco de Posa y Peñalosa;

Q:
Alonso de Quesada; Francisco Guillén de Quesada;

R:
Martín Ramiréz; Juan Rangel; Rascón; Pedro de los Reyes; Pedro de Ribera;
Alonso del Río; Diego Robledo; Francisco Robledo; Pedro Robledo (*the
first colonist to die in NM*) with his wife, Catalina López; Pedro Rodríguez;
Sebastián Rodríguez; Bartolomé Romeros; Moreno de la Rua; Capt. Ruiz;
Juan Ruiz;

S:
Lorenzo Salado; Juan de Salas; Alonso Sánchez; Cristóbal Sánchez;
Francisco Sánchez; Antonio Sarinana; Juan de Segura; Serrano; Sosa;

T:
Capt. Tabora;

V:
Francisco Vaca; Varela; Francisco Vásquez; Jorge de la Vega; Juan Velarde;
Francisco Vido; Juan de Victoria Vido; Gaspar Pérez de Villagrá; Villalba;
Villaviciosa;

Z:
Juan de Zaldívar; Vicente de Zaldívar; León Zapata; Zubia; Zumaia.

DISCONTENT

These pioneering settlers quickly became disenchanted with their new homeland because there were
shortages of every kind, especially food. The only thing in plenty was unrelenting hard work required
to keep body and soul together. They succeeded in introducing Christianity to the Indians, along with
the wheel, adobe, log housing, fireplaces and outdoor ovens, etc., also crops new to the area: wheat, chile,
watermelon, carrots, onions, etc., and European livestock: horses, cattle, goats, sheep, hogs, etc. The
Indians were to benefit greatly from all these gifts but what were the settlers getting out of it? Just a lot

of hard work and the right to use *don/doña* with their name. There was talk of abandoning the colony and returning to Mexico but their contract, similar to that of being in the Military, required colonists to remain in the new land.

On December 24, 1600, Capt. **Bernabé de las Casas** arrived at San Gabriel with new soldiers, colonists with families, six Franciscans, new stock and supplies. The Christmas of 1600 was a joyful celebration. Among the new colonists were:

Cristóbal Baca (with wife Ana Ortiz, their three grown daughters and one son; Cristóbal is the progenitor of the Baca family in NM);

Pedro Durán y Chaves (with wife Isabel de Bohorquez Baca and children; Pedro and Isabel are the progenitors of the Chávez clans in *NM*);

Cristóbal Enriquez; Alvaro García Holgado; Domingo Gutiérrez; Antonio Hernández; Juan de Herrera; Juan Jorge; Juan López Mederos; Juan Luján;

Juan López Holguín (0lguín);

Bartolomé de Montoya (with wife María de Zamora and family which includes three boys and two girls, all under 16 years of age);

Alonso Naranjo; Juan Rodríguez Bellido; Juan Ruiz Cáceres …

(There are "…*some 45 wives, sisters, children, and servants*" in this group.)

DESERTION

By October of 1601 most of the colonists have had enough so while Governor Oñate was away exploring the Quivira country east of New Mexico, they deserted the colony, fleeing south to Santa Barbara. When the Governor returned in November he found some 25 soldiers remaining and realized the Indians could exterminate all Christians if they wished. A quick tribunal was convened and the deserters were found guilty of mutiny and treason, offenses punishable by death. A detachment of soldiers was sent to capture the deserters, now with a death sentence on their heads, but they made it to Santa Barbara where Governor Oñate had no authority. They used their energies to defame Oñate and were successful in defending their behavior, perhaps because there were still powerful forces that had worked to defeat the effort for Oñate to be awarded the contract to settle New Mexico in the first place.

FRONTIER LIVING

Despite defections, the remaining intrepid settlers made a life for themselves in the new land. Most of the pioneers wore clothes made of *gamuza*, buckskin, the soft, tanned hide of deer or antelope. Gamuza became so valuable that it was used like money. The finest buckskin was used for religious paintings which hung in churches.

In 1603 there was an uprising at Taos Pueblo but it was quelled immediately. The following year Governor Oñate sent a peace mission to the newly reestablished village at Acoma. The missionaries reported that the serious wounds of the Acoma War now had to be healed. [See Note # 5.]

INSCRIPTION ROCK

Governor Oñate led an expedition west to map a trail to the South Sea (Pacific Ocean). On his return journey he left an inscription at El Morro (Inscription Rock): *Pasó por aquí el adelantado don Juan de Oñate del descubrimiento de la mar del sur a 16 de abril de 1605.* (This is the oldest European inscription in the USA.)

OÑATE RESIGNS

By 1605 a *cabildo*, Town Council, was established by the colonists. Serious Indian problems were beginning to develop by 1606 because Apaches and Navajos were attacking outlying Pueblos and even San Gabriel itself. But the most important fact of the year is that Governor Oñate sent his letter of resignation to Viceroy Velasco in Mexico City in 1607, citing that his personal fortune had been depleted by the colonization of New Mexico, that the monumental sacrifices of the heroic colonists had gone unrecognized, that the deserters of 1601 had used their liberty to justify their treason with his political enemies and spread lies to attack his personal honor. (It is possible that Oñate had a hand in the founding of Santa Fe in 1607-1608. Most scholars believe it was certainly in existence by 1608.) Oñate's resignation was accepted but he was ordered to remain at his post until a replacement could be found.

Serious discussions were now held by Viceroy Velasco and his advisors, including clergymen. All colonists could be recalled, that would not be difficult. But what would happen to the Indians who had converted to Christianity? It was finally decided that New Mexico would be retained as a missionary field under the direction of blue robed Franciscans. Furthermore, the Crown would pay all expenses until the missions were self-sufficient.[See Note # 6.]

CARAVAN

In 1608 Viceroy Velasco sent the first caravan to New Mexico, at royal expense. It included wagonloads of clothing and other needed supplies, along with 500 head of horses, cattle, and sheep. The wagons were the large, iron wheeled variety that carried tons of goods. (This caravan was the first of many to make its way into isolated New Mexico. In time its appearance became a joyful part of colonial life.)

HISTORIA DE LA NUEVA MEXICO

New Governor **Pedro de Peralta** arrived in 1610 to replace the valiant pioneer Juan de Oñate. During the same year was published in Spain *Historia De La Nueva Mexico* by **Gaspar Pérez de Villagrá.** (It is the first history of any part of the USA and the only founding chronicle in the world to be written as an epic poem along the lines of "The Iliad," "The Odyssey" and "The Aeneid.")

CHURCH & STATE

In 1612 the caravan from Mexico City brought much needed supplies along with **Fray Isidro Ordoñez**, first Franciscan prelate as well as Commissary of the Inquisition. Fray Isidro took his duties seriously and lived by the credo that service to God was the real reason for living. He informed Governor Peralta that using unpaid Indian labor to construct municipal buildings was contrary to the laws of God and men. He orated that anyone who wished to leave New Mexico could do so. When a number of people departed, Governor Pedro de Peralta warned Ordoñez that weakened defenses could very well lead to the destruction of the entire colony. The feuding, centered around political power, the rights of religious doctrine, use of fields and pastures, use of Indians, along with other economic matters, escalated to the point that one Sunday Fray Isidro ordered Governor Peralta's canopied chair be thrown out of the church into the street. Peralta does nothing except have some of his men recover the chair and place it in the back of the church where he sits with the Indian portion of the congregation.

Franciscan **Andrés Juárez** believed that Ordoñez had gone much too far in exercising religious authority. He planned to travel to Mexico City and inform his superiors but Fray Isidro learned of the "plot," intercepted Juárez and returned him to Franciscan headquarters at Santo Domingo where he was kept under house arrest for months. Ordoñez wrote to his superiors that a terrible *godlessness exists in New Mexico.*

In 1613 Fray Isidro denounced the tribute levied on Indians as much too burdensome. Additionally he charges that several soldiers have sexually abused some Indian women. Governor Peralta is ordered to correct all abuses or he will be excommunicated. Peralta replies that Ordoñez has no authority over secular matters. Fray Isidro excommunicates Don Pedro. He also threatens to excommunicate anyone who aids the governor. At his wits end, Governor Peralta decides to go to Mexico City and plead his case to the Viceroy. Fray Isidro and a group of partisans "arrest" the governor at Isleta Pueblo and hold him prisoner for nine months during which Ordoñez is the ecclesiastical as well as secular head of New Mexico. Governor Peralta finally makes good his escape in November of 1614 and after a complete investigation is fully exonerated in 1617. Fray Isidro Ordoñez is recalled and forbidden ever to return to NM. [See Note # 7.]

Feuds between governors and religious authorities of New Mexico thus became the single most detrimental characteristic of society until the St. Lawrence Day Massacre of 1680.

MISSIONIZATION

Missionizing the Indians continued to be a basic activity in New Mexico. Many churches were built between 1607-1640. But there is significant resistance to Christianity. The most heated objection from Pueblo Indians is the prohibition of polygamy. Pueblo men are unwilling to give up the practice for a number of reasons, including that having several wives provides status in Pueblo society. Missionaries also feel impelled to combat various aspects of Pueblo ritual and custom, especially dances where Pueblo men hold a live snake with their mouth and hand (considered a "rain dance" because the writhing snakes are thought to resemble clouds and rain). They also condemn what they describe as "pagan sexuality," along with brutal practices like cutting off the nose and ears of women adjudged to be adulterous. Medicine men especially resent the missionaries because they were losing their power to the Christian clergy. (Some 43 missionaries were martyred by the Indians of NM, 21 of them in the single tragedy of the St. Lawrence Day Massacre of 1680.)

Other efforts are channeled into establishing town government in all established Pueblos, with the election of Governor, Sheriff, mayordomo, etc., all supervised by the friars. Silver crowned canes are given to all governors as symbols of leadership. Each one has a Christian cross engraved on it, signifying a blessing from Holy Mother Church.

Efforts to missionize the Navajos are completely unsuccessful.

FATHER of the NEW MEXICAN CHURCH

Fray Estevan de Perea began his New Mexican ministry upon his arrival in 1610 and labored until his death in 1638. Among his many accomplishments is his petition to King Philip IV of Spain that Pueblo people be exempted from paying tribute or rendering personal service to any governmental authority. Philip IV signs the petition into law. As agent of the Inquisition Father Perea investigates charges related to religious subjects, but mostly matters concerning love potions and powders, witch curses, visions, bigamy, etc. Because they are new to the Faith, all Indians are exempt from prosecution by the Holy Office. (Because of those labors he is acknowledged as the "Father of the New Mexican Church.")

Among other herculean missionaries, the intelligentsia of NM, was the indomitable **Fray Alonso de Benavides** who promoted NM missions with great success in the New World and in the Old. Another paladin was **Fray Andrés Juárez** who supervised building of the Pecos Pueblo church, the grandest in all NM. By the time the church was completed in 1625 the men of Pecos Pueblo had won fame as carpenters and were in demand throughout the province.

LIFESTYLES

By 1638 there were some 800 Hispanic people living in NM. Around 200 are soldier/colonists capable of bearing arms. They hold the balance of power in the highly charged quarrel between Governor **Luis de Rosas** and Father Custos **Juan de Salas.** Father Salas closed the church at Santa Fe and ordered all Franciscans to gather at their Santo Domingo headquarters to decide what course of action to take against Governor Rosas. The Franciscans remained at Santo Domingo until a new governor was appointed.

EVOLVING TRADITIONS

Life continued and identifiable NM traditions began to evolve. Hair was worn long, males forming their hair into two braids, females into one and tied at the back of the head. These hairstyles came to symbolize personal honor and virtue. Cutting one's hair short was a punishment reserved for criminals so cutting off one's hair is a most severe punishment. Males work their farms/ranches while women maintain the home. Weaving is often done in the home, footless (tube) socks and blankets being popular items for manufacture. Along with Christianity, horsemanship is basic for all New Mexicans, even women sometimes becoming excellent riders. The first trade fair appeared around 1650 (probably in the Taos Valley area) and New Mexicans enjoy it so much that such fairs become a joyous tradition.

When harvests are good people live happily but they also have to contend with hardships like drought, resultant famine, or smallpox epidemics. There are also small scale Indian uprisings and hostile raiders take their toll on livestock, especially sheep. If apprehended, guilty Indians are hanged, whipped, put in stocks, etc. But the office known as "Protector of the Indians" is created to insure that justice is done and it becomes basic to protecting Indian rights, especially to their land, in NM. [See Note # 8.]

By 1670 there were some 2,000 Hispanos living in the strife-ridden New Mexican colony. Governors and Franciscans can't stop feuding with each other. The subsistence economy isn't strong enough to support the population during times of crisis. Apache raiders, sometimes also Navajos, are taking their toll on all settlements, Pueblo and Hispanic. Pueblo Indian rituals, especially those which include venomous snakes or human body parts like scalps, are targeted as pagan rites. Medicine men promote the idea that Hispanic people are the cause of all woes. Worst of all, the drought will not let up.

ST. LAWRENCE DAY MASSACRE

On **August 10, 1680**, St. Lawrence Day in the Christian calendar, the Pueblos rise up intent on killing every Hispanic in NM. The carnage is beyond belief and three out of every four of those slaughtered are noncombatant women and children. [See Note # 9.]

Ordinary New Mexicans weren't expecting an Indian attack but they were targeted for extermination. At least 400 Hispanics were slaughtered, some seventy-five percent of them women and children. Survivors retreated to El Paso, at that time a part of southern NM, where they lived for twelve years. According to Pueblo traditions, a delegation of Pueblo leaders went to El Paso and asked (1691-92) the Christians to return to the Río Grande settlements. Not only had the drought not ended when Hispanics departed in 1680, mounted Apache raiders were now destroying the Pueblo people.

DIEGO DE VARGAS

Now there appeared on the scene the herculean figure of Diego de Vargas, one of America's greatest heroes, not only for his warrior personal courage but for his willingness to make peace without revenge. When appointed as Governor of NM he vowed to restore the country to Spain and Christianity, without exterminating the Indians in the process. Vargas is the man for the job: he is able to lead and effectively manage different types of people, whether Hispanic, Indian, African, etc. And he didn't have to prove that he was as courageous as any conquistador who set foot in the Americas because he was.

By 1692 Vargas found the New Mexicans living in El Paso in terrible conditions. Soldiers of the garrison had neither swords nor leather jackets and there were only 132 horses available for military use. The hundred or so families owned no cattle, perhaps 200 horses, and maybe 600 sheep. He immediately requests more supplies of every kind and decides to lead a reconnaissance expedition into Santa Fe. By August of 1692 Vargas rides back toward Santa Fe with 50 presidial soldiers and their officers, 10 armed civilians, 3 Franciscan friars, and around 100 tough Pueblo Indian auxiliaries. The expedition is small considering that its goal is to conquer and resettle NM but everyone has faith that Diego De Vargas can accomplish the task if anyone can.

On September 11, 1692, the Vargas expedition entered Santa Fe unopposed. On the 16th the **Tupatú brothers, Luis** and **Lorenzo,** from Picurís Pueblo arrived to confer with Vargas and the missionaries over cups of hot chocolate. They swear allegiance to Spain and are pardoned for their role in the St. Lawrence Day Massacre. On the 21st the expedition, now expanded by 300 warriors from Picurís and led by the Tupatús, goes to the large Pecos Pueblo on hearing that the Pecos intend to fight. But when the Christians arrive they find the Pecos have deserted their village. Vargas now decides to work for peace: he orders the expedition to return to Santa Fe and leave without doing damage to the Pecos' village or taking their food supplies. Within a short time Pecos leader **Juan de Ye** arrives to offer his allegiance to Vargas, Spain and the Christians because his unprotected village hadn't been burned or pillaged. Juan de Ye understood that Vargas and his Christians could be trusted.

Within four months twenty-three villages of some ten different Indian groups were once again friends instead of enemies. Diego de Vargas is the toast of New Spain when he reports to the Viceroy that the *entrada* has been bloodless. He writes that some 500 families need to be sent to recolonize NM and at least 100 professional soldiers to secure the Reconquest.

VARGAS COLONISTS

Vargas worked diligently to recolonize NM. Among the settlers who returned to make their lives in the province are the following:

[The groups didn't all arrive at the same time. It must be kept in mind that names may and usually do have variant spellings. It should also be pointed out that carrying the mother's surname, generally written after the father's surname, is an Hispanic tradition. An "M" abbreviates *María*, a "J" for *José*]:

A:

Abalos: Antonio; Abrego: Francisco; Francisca; Acosta: María; Aguila: Miguel Gerónimo;

Aguilar: (Capt.) Alonso;

Aguilera: Pedro, M. Luisa;

Agular: J. Benito Isari; Antonio Isari;

Aguliar: Miguel Gerónimo;

Alamais: Manuela Antonia;

Alatia: María;

Alcalá: J. de Atienza;

Alemán: M. de la Cruz;

Almazán: Ana;

Anaya: Antonio de; Ana de; Juana; Francisco de Anaya; J. Salvador de Anaya; M. Josepha de;

Altamirino: Felipa Lechuga; Juan Tafoya; Anaya: Ynes; (Capt.) Francisco; Nicolasa; Luis; Ancizo: Juana; Angel: Miguel Ángeles: Catalina de los; Antonio: Juan;

Anzures: Bartolomé; Gabriel, Juana; Teresa; Apodaca: Cristóbal; Francisco; J. Gonzáles;

Aragón: Juan de Pedrasa; Antonio; Catalina Varela; Cristóbal; Félix; Francisco; Ignacio; Josefa Gonzáles; Juan; Juan Antonio; Juana; María;

Aranda: Mateo; Archuleta: Juan; Juana; Pablo; Pasquala; Juan; Andrés; Leonora; Juan; Cristóbal;

Aretia: (Capt.) Francisco;

Argüello: Juana;

Aris: Phelipa; Diego; J. Mateo; Joseph; Juana; Martín; Armijo: Antonio;

Arratia: Antonia; Juan Antonio; Mathais; Phelipa;

Arroyo: Diego; Arteaga: Felipe; M. López, Miguel;

Arvizu: Felipe; Tomás;

Aspeltia: Inés;

Atencia: Calstano; Francisco; Ignacio; Juan; María;

Atienza: José; Juan;

Avalos: Antonio; Juana; Pedro; Avila: María; Pedro Ayala: Diego Márquez; Antonio; Miguel; Azate: Juan;

B:

Baca: Cristóbal; Felipe; Ignacio; Lenora; Manuel,
Bachiniva;
Balanegra: Simón;
Barba: Domingo Martín;
Barbosa: Simón;
Bejarano: Tomás;
Belásquez: Miguel;
Bernal: Francisco;
Betanzos: Andrés; Diego;
Brito: Agustín; Francisco; Joseph; Juan León;
Brixida: María;
Brusales: Juan;
Bustillos;
Busto: Juan de la Paz;
C:
Cabrera: Josefa; M. de Medina;
Cáceres: (Sgt.) Juan Ríos;
Caldana: Mateo; Camarillo: Diego;
Candelaria: Blas de la; Feliciano de la;
Carabajal: María;
Caras: Juana de Aras;
Cárdenas: Petronia;
Careres: Juan Ruiz;
Carrera: Tomás Gutiérrez de la;
Carrillo: M. Nicolasa;
Cásares: Juan Ruiz;
Casitias: Joseph;
Castillo: Isabel López del; José Cortez; Lucía del; (Sgt. Mayor) Diego del; Pedro López del; Castro: María; María Rodarte de; Cervantes: Juan Manuel Martínez; Manuel; María Zuniga y; Chávez: (Capt.) Fernando Durán y; Joseph Durán y; María; Pedro Durán y; Christina: Juana; Cisneros: María;
Coca: Miguel de la Vega y;
Concepción: Pascuala de la; San Juan de: María de la;
Contrertas: Joseph; Cordero: Juan Ruiz;
Córdoba: Antonio Coronanda: María;
Cortés: Juan;
Cortez: José;
Cortinas: Pedro;
Crisostomo: Juana;
Cruz: Tomás de la; Ana de la; Cecilia de la; María de la; Miguel de la;
Cruzate: (Capt. Gen.) Domingo Jironza Petriz de;

Cuellar: Cristóbal;

Cueva: Petronila de la;

Cuitar: Alonso Rodríguez de la;

D:

Dios: Juan de;

Domíníguez: Antonio; Francisco; José; Juan; Juana; Petrona; Petrolina; Joseph; Antonia; Durán: Antonia; Antonia Ursala; Antonio; Bartolomé; Catallina; Cristóbal; Diego; Francisco; Felipe; Josepha; Juana; Lázaro; Luis; María; Miguel; Salvador; Ysabel;

E:

Encarnación: María de la;

Escalante: Antonio Gonzáles;

Esperaza: Catallina Montoya;

Esparza: María;

Espindola: Catalina; Francisco;

Espinosa: Nicolás;

Esquibel: Juan Antonio; Esteban: Juan;

Estrada: Juan;

F:

Farfán: Fray;

Félix: Antonio;

Fernández: Diego Manuel de la Santísima Trinidad de;

Florida: Geronima Días;

Fontes: Cristóbal; Francisco; Josepha;

Foranco: Ygnacio de Santa María;

Fragua: Pedro;

Francisco: Matías;

Fresque, Ambrosio;

Fresqui: Mariana;

G:

Gaitán: Isabel; Joseph;

Gallegos: Joseph;

Gamboa: Antonio;

Ramírez; Manuel; Miguel; Juan; Phelipa;

Garas: Juana;

García: Ana María; Alonso; (Ensign) Alonso; Antonia; Antonio; Casilda; Cristóbal; Diego; Elvira; Esteban López de; Felipe; Francisca; Francisco Jurado de; Ignacio López de; Juan; Juan de Noriega; Juan Esteban López de: Juan Jurado; Juana; Lucía; Luis; María; María Francisca; Miguel; Nicolás; Ramón; Theoria; Vicente;

Geuterero: Juana;

Gilteme: Joseph;

Girón: Rafaél Tellez;

Godines: Antonio; M. Luisa de Villaviecencio y; M. Luisa;

Godo: (Sgt. Mayor) Juan Lucero;

Godoy: Juan de Dios; Juan Lucero; María Luzero; Francisco Luzero; Nicolás Lucero;

Gómez: Antonio; Catalina; Diego; Domingo; Francisco; Josepha; Juan; Laureano; Manuel; Marcial; Margarita; M. de la Rosa; María; Thomana; Ursala;

Góngora: Cristóbal; Francisca; Gregoria; Juan de; Juana de; Juan Joseph; M. Gertrudis;

Gonzáles: Andrés; Antonia Blas; Catalina; Cristóbal; Damiana; Diego; María; Estefana; Francisco; Francisco de la Rosa; José; Josepha; Juana; Juan; Melchora de Los Reyes; Pedro; Petronia; (Councilman) Sebastián; Sevastián; Ysabel;

Granillo: Domingo; Josepha; Juan; Luis; María; (Sgt. Mayor) Luis; Gregoria: Antonia; Juan;

Greimaldos: Diego Sánchez;

Griego: Ana Martín; (Ensign) Blas; Agustín; Catalina; Francisco; Juan; Lenor; María;

Grola (Gurule): Santiago;

Guadalajara: Jacinta;

Guatamala: Juana;

Guebara: Pedro;

Guerrero: Felipa,

Guerro: Juana;

Guevara: Juan de Fernández de Atienza Ladrón de; Miguel Ladrón de;

Guido: Juan;

Gutiérrez: Ana; Antonia; Juan Rogue (Roque); Miguel; Phelipe; Rogue;

H:

Heras: María de las;

Hernández: Francisco; Gertrudis;

Herrera: Antonio; Domingo; Gertrudis de la Candelaria; Josepha; Juan; Juana; Luisa; M. Tapia; Miguel; Sebastián; Ynes;

Hidalgo: (Ensign) Diego; Pedro;

Hinojos: Diego; Fernando; Josepha; Nicolás Ruiz;

Hita: Tomás;

Holguín: Cristóbal; (Capt.) Salvador; Juan; Juan López; Tomás;

Hurtado: Andrés; Catalina; Diego; Juan Páez; María; Mariana;

I:

Iñigo: Francisca Sánchez y; Jacinto Sánchez de; Pedro Sánchez;

Isasi: Antonio de Aguilera;

J:

Jaramillo: Cristóbal Varela; Lucía; Lucía Varela; Juan Varela; María; Yumar Varela;

Jirón: Diego; Isabel; Joseph Telles; Nicolás; Tomás; Jorge: Antonio; Jurado: J. García; Francisco;

K:

L:
Lara: Ana Morena de;
Larea: Isabela;
Layba: Pedro; Juana;
Lechuga: Pedro;
León: Cristóbal;
Leyba: Francisco; Juana;
Linares: Miguel;
Lobato: Bartolomé;
López: (Ensign) Pedro; Angelo; (Capt.) Francisco; Carlos; Cristóbal; Francisco; Jacinto; José; Joseph; María; Nicolás; Pedro; (Sgt. Mayor) Diego;
Lorenzo: Francisco;
Losada: Juan Cristóbal; Lucía Varela; María Varela; Magdalena Varela; Pedro Varela;
Lucero: Antonio; Catalina; Francisco; Juan de Dios; Nicolás; (Sgt. Mayor) Diego; Luis: (Capt.) Juan;
Luján: Agustín; (Capt.) Juan Luis; Cristóbal; Diego; Domingo; Isabel; Josefa Juana; Juan; Matis (Matías?); Miguel; Pedro;
Luna: (Capt.) Diego; Diego; Juan;
Lusana: Clara,
Luxan: Agustine; Francisco; Luis, María;

M:
Machuca: Juan de Vargas;
Madrid: Francisco; (Capt.) Juan; Jacinto; José; Joseph; Juan, Juana; Lorenzo; Pedro; Rogue; (Sgt. Mayor) Lorenzo;
Maes: Luis;
Maese: Alonso; Alonso López; Luis; Miguel;
Magdalena: María;
Mandragón: Sebastián Monroy de;
Mantaño: José;
Manzanares: Ana de Sandoval y; Juan Mateo Sadoval y; María Sandoval; Sevastiana de Sandoval y; Marcelino; Cristóbal;
Marcos: Lucas;
Marín: Francisco;
Márquez: (Capt.) Antonio; Bernabé; Diego; Francisco; Juan; Juana Jaramillo y Zamora; Pedro;
Martín: (Ensign) Pedro; Antonio; Apoliar; Cristóbal; Diego; Domingo; Francisco; Hernando; Juan; Juana; Lucía; Luis; María; Pasquala; Pedro; Sevastián;
Martínez: Gerónimo; Juan de Dios Sandoval;
Mascareñas: J. Bernardo;
Mederos: (Capt.) Pedro López;
Medina: Alonso; Juan; Micaela; Manuela;

Méndez: Thomas;

Mendoza: Antonia; Antonio Domínguez de; Francisco Domínguez de; Juan Domingo; María; Tomé Domínguez;

Mestas: Tomás;

Miguel: José;

Miranda; Miguel;

Mizquia: Lázaro;

Molina: Sebastián; Simón;

Montalvo: Rogue;

Montaño: Antonio; Catalina-, Lucas; María;

Montero: Pedro;

Montesuma: Ysabel Caso;

Montiel: José;

Montoya: Ana María Griego; Antonio; Diego; Felipe; Francisca; Josepha; María; Onafre; Phelipe;

Mora: Francisco de la; María;

Moraga: Ana; Antonia; Felipe; Lázaro; María;

Morales: Francisca;

Moreles: Juan;

Morán: Agueda; Miguel;

Moriello: Cristóbal;

Moya: Antonio;

Munier: Pedro;

N:

Naranjo: Pasqual;

Negrette: Manuela; José Jaramillo; Mateo;

Nevares: (Capt.) Joseph; José;

Nicolás: María de San;

Nieto: Cristóbal;

Noriega: Juan García de; Juana García de;

Nuñez: José;

0:

Ocanto: María;

Ochoa: Juan;

Ojeda: Antonio; Juana;

Olivas: Isabel; Juan de la Cruz y;

Olives: Juan Bautista;

Ontiveros: Francisco;

Órgano: Magdalena;

Orozco: Mariana Salas;

Ortega: Andrés; Dionisio; Josepha; María; Nicolás; Nicolás de; Pablo; Simón; Tiburcio;

Ortíz: Juana; María; Nicolás de; Nicolasa; Sebastiana;

Osuna: María;

Oton: Nicolás; Margarita;

P:

Pacheco: Acencio; Juan; Silvestre; Padilla: Joseph de; Páez: Agustine;

Palocios (Palacios): María de Encarnación; María de;

Palomino: Tomás; Papigochu;

Parades: Ganzalo de;

Parra: Gregorio Cobos de la; Pasqual Covos de la; Paz: Juan de la; Manuela de;

Pedraza: Miguel; Francisco Romero;

Pedroza: Lázaro de Artiaga y;

Pelaez: Jacinto;

Peralta: Juan Bautista Anzaldo de;

Perca: Agustine; Antonia Varela; Isabel; Juan; Juana; Phelipe;

Porras: Francisco; Posada: (Capt.) Pedro Romero;

Q:

Quebara: Pedro;

Quintana: Miguel;

Quiros: Diego Aris de; José; Juana;

R:

Ramiréz: Gregorio; Nicolás; Petrona;

Ramos: Marcos; Miguel; Juan;

Reina: Juan;

Reinoso: Ana;

Rey: Nicolás Rodríguez;

Reyes: Agustine de los; Inés de los; María de los; Sebastián de los;

Ribera: Ana; Juan; Salvador Matías;

Rincón: Antonio Francisco;

Río: Alonso del; (Capt.) Alonso del; (Capt.) Juan del;

Ríos: Juana de los;

Riva: Miguel García de;

Rivera: Francisco; Josefa; Teresa;

Robledo: Ana María; Bartolomé Gómez; Francisco Gómez;

Rodon: Francisco Palamino;

Rodríguez: Agustín; Alonso; Francisca; José; Juan Severino; Manuel; Nicolás; Sebastián;

Rojas: Phelipa Rica de;

Romero: Baltazar; Bartolomé; Catalina; Diego; Felipe; Francisca; Francisco; Juan; Juan Antonio Juan Francisco; María; Phelipe; Salbador; Salvador;

Rosa: Antonia de la; María de la;

Roxas: Josepha Rico de; Ysabel Rico de;

Rueda: Juana;

Ruiz: Gregoria; Elena;

S:

Salas: Sebastián;

Salazar: Agustine; Baltazar Romero; Miguel; Francisca Ramiréz; Francisco; Isabela; Lucía; María; Pedro; Martín Serrano;

Samano: María; San Juan de Concepción;

San Nicolás: María;

Sánchez: Felipe; Juan; José; Pedro;

Sandoval: Phelipa; Tomás de Herrera y;

Santiago: Francisco; José; Julián;

Santos: Juan de los;

Sayagoa: Antonia;

Sedana: Antonia; Josefa;

Sedillo: Felipa Rico de Rojas; Joachin Rico de Roxas; Juan Rico de Rixas; María de Nava; Pedro; Pedro de;

Senorga: María Luisa de;

Serna: Antonia de la; Cristóbal de la; Felipa de la;

Serrano: Fernando Martín; Sevastián Martín;

Sevillana: Gertrudis;

Sierra: Nicolás;

Silva: Antonia;

Sisneros: Antonio

Solís (Ensign); Sonora;

Soria: Felipe;

Soto: Diego; Pasquala;

Sotomayor: María;

Suazo: Juan;

Susana: Clara,

T:

Tapia: Ana; Angela; Cristóbal; Lusía; María;

Tenorio: Miguel; Todos Santos San Bartolomé;

Torreón: Valle de;

Torres: Cristóbal: Francisco; Juana;

Toscano: Juan;

Trinadad: María;

Trujillo: Cristóbal; Cristóbal de (Elder); Cristóbal de (Younger); Damián; Diego; Bernadina de Salas y; Estafana; Gertrudis; Gregoria; Joseph Joaquín; Juan; Nicolás; Pasqual;

U:

Ulibarrí: Gertrudis Bautista de;

V:

Vaca: (Sgt. Mayor) Ygnacio; Valdés: J. Luis;

Valencia: Francisco, Juan; Juana; Juana de;

Valenzuela: Antonia;

Valle: José del;

Vallejo: Manuel;

Vendura: Francisco;

Varela: Cristoval; Diego; Teresa; Francisco; José; Petrona; Polonia; Rogue;

Vargas: Diego; Eusebio; Manuel; Vicente;

Vega; Francisca de la; Juana de la; María de la; Miguel de la;

Velasco: Cristóbal; (Capt.) Cristóbal de; Francisca; José; Micaela; Miguel García;

Velásquez: José;

Vera: Ana Jorge; Antonio; Isabel Jorge de; Melchor de; Vigil: Francisco Montes;

Villapando: Carlos; Juan;

Villasur: Pedro;

W:

X:

Xaramillo: Pedro Varela; Xavier: (Capt.) Francisco;

Ximénez: Phelipa;

Xirón: (Capt.) Joseph Telles; Rafaél Telles;

Y.

Yñigo (Iñigo): Jacinto Sánchez; Pedro Sánchez; Ysabel: Bernardina;

Z:

Zambrano: Josepha; Zamora: Juan; María de Mora

Zarate: Miguel;

Zepidia: María de;

Zevin: Diego.

DECISION to FIGHT

Scouts now reported that various Pueblos had changed their mind and were planning to attack the colonists before they could resettle the area. The Pueblo Indians, mindful of the atrocities they had committed on Hispanic non-combatants, didn't believe they would be pardoned. They decided it would be better to die fighting than be tortured to death.

The Tano and Tewa Indians who had taken over Santa Fe refused to surrender the town to Vargas' people who were at the gates, half-starving and shivering in a sudden snowfall. The Governor parleyed with their leaders but the Indians refused to withdraw. Vargas appealed to them for the last time to withdraw peacefully as they had promised, to no avail. With Pecos *"indios de guerra"* at the side of the Christians a ferocious battle for Santa Fe was begun on December 29, 1693. After two days of bloody fighting the city of the Holy Faith was once again in Christian hands.

Vargas and Juan de Ye became close friends and comrades in arms until the Pecos leader was assassinated by the Taos Indians in 1694. Vargas sincerely mourned the loss of his friend and ally.

The following pioneers, known as the *Españoles Mexicanos* from the City and valley of Mexico, arrived in NM in June of 1694 [names may have variant spellings as indicated above]:

A:

Aguila, Miguel Gerónimo del (with spouse Gerónima Días Florida, one child);

Aguilera, Pedro de (with spouse Juana de Torres, four children);

Aguilera Isasi, Antonio (with spouse Gertrudis Hernández, one child);

Anzures, Gabriel (with spouse Felipa Lechuga de Altamirino, one or two children);

Aragón, Ignacio (with spouse Sebastiana Ortiz, three children);

Atienza, Juan (widower, two children);

Atienza, José (with spouse Estafana de Trujillo and her two brothers, Damián and Joseph Joaquín Trujillo);

Atienza Alcalá, José (with spouse Gertrudis Sevillana);

B:

Betanzos, Andrés (widower, with two sons);

Betanzos, Diego (with spouse María Luisa de Senorga);

Busto, Juan de La Paz (with spouse Manuela Antonia de Alamias, two children);

C:

Cárdenas, Andre (with spouse Juana de Avalos, two children);

Castellanos, José (with spouse Manuela de Paz and their five children);

Cervantes, Manuel de (with spouse Francisca Rodríguez);

Cortés, Juan (spouse Juana de Aras [Caras?] with one, Perhaps three children);

Cortés del Castillo, José (with spouse María de Carbajal, two children);

D:

Dios, Juan de (with spouse and son);

E:

Esquibel, Juan Antonio (with spouse María de San Nicolás, two children);

F:

Fernández de Atienza Ladrón de Guevara (with spouse Teresa de Rivera, one child);

G:

Gamboa, Juan (with spouse María de Zepidia, three children);

Gamboa, Manuel (with spouse Ysabel Caso Montesuma);

Gamboa, Miguel (with spouse);

García Jurado, José (with spouse Josepha, de Herrera, and their two sons);

García de Riva, Miguel (with spouse Micaela Velasco and their five children);

Godines, Antonio (widower, with daughter);

Góngora, Cristóbal (with spouse Inés de Aspeitia);

Góngora, Juan (with spouse Petronila de la Cueva, five children);

H:

Herrera y Sandoval, Tomás de (with spouse Pascuala de la Concepción, two children);

J:

Jaramillo Negrete, José (with spouse María Sotomayor, three children);

Jirón, Diego (with spouse María de Mendoza, two children);

Jirón, Nicolás (with spouse Josefa Sedano);

Jirón, Tomás (with spouse Josefa Gonzáles de Aragón, two children);

L:

Ladrón de Guevara, Miguel (with spouse Felipa Guerrero, one child);

Leyba, Francisco;

Lorenzo, Francisco (with spouse and one child);

Luján, Juan (with spouse Petrona Ramiréz, one child);

M:

Marcelino, Cristóbal (with spouse Juana de Góngora);

Márquez de Ayala, Diego (with spouse María de Palacios, two children);

Martínez de Cervantes, Juan Manuel (with spouse Catalina de los Ángeles and a maid Cecilia de la Cruz;

Mascareñas, José Bernardo (with spouse María de Acosta, two children);

Medina, Juan (with spouse Juana Jaramillo y Zamora Márquez);

Medina, Juan de (with spouse Antonia Sedana, a sister of Josefa Sedana above married to Nicolás Jirón);

Molina, Simón (with spouse Micaela de Medina);

Moya, Antonio (with spouse Francisca Morales);

Nuñez, José (with spouse Gertrudis de la Candelaria Herrera);

O:

Ortiz, Nicolás (with spouse María Coronada, six children);

P:

Palomino, Tomás (with spouse Gertrudis Bautista de Ulibarrí, two children);

Porras, Francisco de (with spouse Damiana Gonzáles, one child);

Q:

Quintana, Miguel (with spouse Gertrudis de Trujillo, sister of Estafana Trujillo above);

R:

Rodríguez, José (with spouse María de Sarnano, three children);

Rodríguez, Manuel (with spouse María de la Encarnaci6n Palacios, one child);

Rincón, Antonio Francisco (with spouse Antonia de Valenzuela, three children);

Romero, Juan Francisco (with spouse María de Avila);

Rosa Gonzáles, Francisco de la (with spouse Antonia de la Serna);

Ruiz Cordero, Juan (with spouse María Nicolassa. Carrillo);

S:

Salas, Sebastián (with spouse María García);

Sánchez de Hita, Tomás Fulano (with spouse Antonia Gutiérrez, one child; Tomás died in Zacatecas and Antonia continued to NM where she married

Juan de Archibeque in 1697);

Sánchez, José (with spouse Josefa Gómez de Rivera, with father-in-law José Cortez);

Sayago, Antonio (with spouse María de Mora Zamora, two children);

Silva, Antonio (with spouse Gregoria Ruiz, one child);

T:

Trujillo, Nicolás (with spouse María Luisa de Aguilera, four children; returned to Mexico City in 1705);

V:

Valdés, José Luis (with spouse María de Medina Cabrera, two children);

Valle, José del (with spouse Ana de Ribera, with adopted child Bernardino Sena);

Vallejo, Manuel (widower, one child);

Velasco, Francisca (widow, with nephew Miguel García Velasco and niece Manuela);

Velasco, José (with spouse María de Tapia Herrera, one child);

Vega y Coca, Manuel de la (spouse Manuela Medina and mother-in-law Josefa de Cabrera).

[Three Frenchmen had been captured before the Pueblo Revolt and now returned to NM with stripes on their faces: Pedro Munier, Santiago Grola, and Juan de Archibeque.]

In May of 1995 Capt. **Juan Páez Hurtado** arrives in Santa Fe with more livestock and some 45 new families. The new colonists are from the Zacatecas- Sombrerete area of Mexico and include:

Aranda, Mateo (with Teresa de la Cruz and María Rodríguez);

Arellano, Cristóbal (with his sister and niece);

Armijo, Antonio (with spouse Manuela Negrete and Antonio's brother Marcos);

Camarillo, Diego (with spouse Antonia García);

Cortinas, Pedro (with spouse María Ortiz and a son);

Crisóstomo, Juana (with Toribio Nicolás and Juana Nicolasa);

Durán, Catalina (widow with three children);

Espinosa, Nicolás (with a sister and brother);

Félix, Antonio (with spouse Francisca Valencia, one son and two nephews);

López, José (with spouse María Osuna, one daughter);

Marcos, Lucas (with Juana de Guadalupe and Juan Nicolás);

Gómez, Laureano (with spouse Josefa Cruz and a nephew);

González, Francisco (with two cousins, Baltazar Rodarte and Terese de Jesús Rodarte); Guerro, Juana (with a son and daughter);

Guido, Juan (with spouse Isabel de los Reyes Ribera and a son);

Hernández, Francisco (with spouse Juana García and one son);

Lobato, Bartolomé (with spouse Luisana Negrete and one son);

López, Angela (and her two brothers Juan and Antonio Ortiz);

Martínez, Jerónimo (with spouse Antonia de la Rosa and a daughter);

Méndez, Tomás (with spouse María de la Cruz and one daughter);

Montalve, Roque Pantoja (with two other people, Miguel Gutiérrez and his sister Natiana);

Montes Vigil, Francisco (with spouse María Jiménez Armijo);

Montes Vigil, Juan;

Morillo, Cristóbal (with Sebastián Canseco and María Gutiérrez);

Miranda, Miguel (with a daughter and son);

Negrete, Mateo (with spouse Simona Bejar and one daughter);

Olivas, Isabel (with daughter and her brother José Rodríguez);

Olives, Juan Bautista (with spouse Magdelena Juárez and daughter);

Quiros, José (with a daughter and a nephew);

Quiros, Juana (with a son and nephew);

Ramos, Marcos (with spouse Isabela Larea);

Ramos, Miguel (with sister Antonia and a servant Josefa de la Rosa);

Reina, Juan (with spouse María Encarnaci6n and a nephew);

Reinoso, Ana (with daughter and son);

Reyes, Inés de los (with a daughter and son);

Reyes, María de los (with daughter María Canseco and nephew Nicolás Ararmujes);

Ribera, Salvador Matías (with spouse Juana Rosa and one son);

Rodríguez, Agustín (with spouse Nicolasa Ortiz);

Rodríguez, Sebastiana (widow with three children);

Romero, Juan Antonio (with two nieces and one nephew);

San Nicolás, María de (with a son and daughter);

Santos, Juan de los (with spouse Josefa Cristina Durán and a nephew);

Soria, Felipe (with spouse María Castro and one son);

Tenorio, Miguel (with a daughter and Cristóbal Rodríguez);

Trinadad, María de la (widow with two sons);

Zarate, Miguel (with spouse María de la Rosa and a son).

[It has been observed that New Mexicans of the 17th and 18th centuries became "one big family" through intermarriage. Common greetings often used the words *primo/prima* (cousin) when saying hello.]

LAND USAGE

For all practical purposes, the NM colony was started anew under the leadership of Diego de Vargas. Governor Vargas provided stable leadership and promoted economic recovery of the province. Unlike the situation east of the Mississippi, there was no vengeful retribution against the Pueblo people for the St. Lawrence Day Massacre of 1680. Among many other things, Vargas distributed vacant land to settlers, including women. (Unlike northern European societies, Hispanic law enabled women to own land.) Grants of land were of two basic categories: private or community. A private grant is made to one individual who owns the entire grant and can sell it after possession requirements are met; community grants are made to a group of people who each receive a *solar de casa* (plot of land for a house), *suerte* (an irrigable plot), and rights to use the common lands (unassigned grant land) for pasture, watering, logging, collecting firewood, hunting, fishing, rock quarrying, etc. **Common lands** in NM, referred to variously as *ejidos, montes, pastos, abrevaderos, leña, árboles frutales, caza, pesca*, etc., were owned by the community and couldn't be sold under Hispanic law since they belonged to everyone. [See Note # 10.]

CUBERO

New Mexican society continued to develop with typical human strengths and weaknesses. **Pedro Rodríguez Cubero** replaced Vargas in 1697, charged him with cruelty to the Indians and kept him under house arrest for three years. The two became bitter political enemies but in 1703 Vargas was exonerated and once more appointed as Governor, now with the title of *Marqués de la Nava Braziñas*. The gallant Diego de Vargas served until April 8, 1704 when he died after a short illness. The entire province mourned the death of this heroic Christian knight. [See Note # 11.]

COMANCHES and HOSTILES

Comanches were observed to be coming into the area as of 1705. This large warrior nation began to displace Apaches living in eastern NM. From 1702 until 1719 the New Mexicans were raided by Navajos, eastern Apaches, Utes, and Comanches. **Roque de Madrid** went against the Navajos and defeated them in 1705 but the Diné were raiding again from 1708-1714. The Utes and Comanches were allies against NM from around 1706 until 1747.

ALBURQUERQUE

In 1706, Alburquerque, which had been referred to as *Bosque Grande de Doña Luisa*, was founded by pioneer families, about 252 persons, 12 of which live in the [present] Old Town area, the others along the river in settlements called *"Ranchos"* such as "Ranchos de Alburquerque," Los Varelas, Los Duránes, Los Poblanos, Los Griegos, Los Candelarias, etc., and on the west side of the river and downstream were Los Corrales, Atrisco, Armijo, etc. Into the Sandía Mts. were Carnué and San Antonio. A list of heads of Albuquerque families includes: Juan Barela; Cristóbal Barela; Xavier Benavides; Francisco Candelario; Sebastián Canseco; Pedro Durán y Chávez; Francisco García; Tomás García; Antonio Gutiérrez; Martín Hurtado; Cristóbal Jaramillo; Pedro López y Castillo; Juana López y Castillo; Nicolás Lucero; Andrés Montoya; Juan Pineda; Baltazar Romero; Bernardina Salas y Trujillo (widow); J. Sebastián Salas; Joaquín Sedillo; Antonio Silva.

HUMANITARIAN CAMPAIGN

In July of 1706 Governor **Francisco Cuervo y Valdés** decided to address the plight of the people from Picurís Pueblo who had fled during the 1696 revolt but now had often asked for help of the Spanish because they had been enslaved by the Apaches after their flight. Cuervo decides to fight the **Apaches** (who live around present Pueblo, Colorado) and rescue the Picurís. **Juan de Ulibarrí** is put in command of the expedition to this *tierra incognita* where **Lorenzo Tupatú,** son of Luis Tupatú, is chief of the Picurís. Using his main scouts, **José Naranjo,** famous Pueblo leader from Zuñi, and **Juan de l'Archebeque,** a Frenchman from the La Salle expedition, the Picurís are located in scattered *rancherías* (encampments), destitute and without horses. The people, between 62 to 74 in number, are returned to their pueblo.

(This humanitarian campaign is the highlight of the Cuervo administration.) Ulibarrí claimed the area (Colorado) for Spain and the large peak *El Capitán* (now **Pike's Peak**) is identified.

PUEBLO/HISPANIC ALLIANCE

Hispanic garrisons were withdrawn from Santa Clara, Cochití, Jémez, and Laguna because Cuervo believes they weren't necessary any more and the Viceroy had so ordered. The alliance between Hispanic and Pueblo people, probably the strongest and most enduring in the history of what is now the USA, was strengthened by the bonds of Christianity and self-preservation.

CAMINO REAL

The comercial trail from *Santa Fe/Taos to Chihuahua* was referred to as the *Camino Real de Tierra Adentro* and traversed the towns/villages of Santo Domingo, Algodones, Bernalillo, Alameda, Albuquerque, Isleta, Peralta, Tomé, Belén, La Joya, Socorro, San Marcial, Fray Cristóbal, Laguna del Muerto, Ojo del Perrillo, Robledo, Doña Ana, Las Cruces, El Paso del Norte, Isleta del Sur, Socorro del Sur, San Elizario, Ojo de Lucero, Jesús María, Ojo de Gallego, Encinillas, El Sauz, Chihuahua, etc., to Mexico City.

RAIDING

Raids by hostile Indians are a basic reality of New Mexican life. **Apaches** raid Spanish and Pueblo settlements in 1708, killing many people, stealing livestock and horses. Governor Chacón attacked them vigorously and an unstable peace was achieved by November.

    Navajos had been at peace for over two years but now begin raiding again. In 1709 five separate campaigns are directed against the Navajos, who have been raiding the pueblos of Santa Clara and especially Jémez, where they sack not only houses but the church itself, taking sacred vessels and ornaments.

SCALP DANCE

Gov. Chacón denounces Pueblo ritual associated with the Scalp Dance. He believes it is un-Christian for Pueblo dances to use human body parts in any function. It appears he achieves some success or the Indians go underground with their ritual practices.

TRADE FAIRS

By 1710 trade fairs began to pop up all over NM. In time the most popular is the October gathering at Taos because of its size, noise, color, pageantry, and the wide variety of people and nations that it attracts. New Mexicans grow to love their trade fairs because it is an excellent opportunity to trade, meet different kinds of people and function in different cultures, hear different languages, dance, celebrate, etc. French merchandise appears at these fairs because the Pawnees trade it to the Comanches who bring it to NM.

VILLASUR EXPEDITION

In 1720 an expedition under the command of **Pedro de Villasur** is sent out of Santa Fe to investigate possible French incursions into Spanish territories. The reconnaissance party makes it to the Platte River in central Nebraska where it is ambushed by Indians, probably Oto, Optata, and Pawnee. Forty-five men are killed, including Villasur, scout José Naranjo, interpreter Juan de l'Archeveque, and Fray Juan Mínguez. The survivors report no evidence of French settlement in the area, though they might have armed the Indians to fight the Spanish. A painting depicting Villasur's defeat is created back in Santa Fe. (The painting is named the "Segesser Hide Painting" for the person who collected it. While the artist of the painting isn't known, an unnamed Franciscan friar and a shoemaker named **Francisco Xavier Romero** are believed to have done most of the religious paintings on hide that decorated churches and chapels of that time. The "Segesser Hide Painting" is the earliest extant painting drawn in NM and therefore what is now the USA.)

TAOS TRADE FAIR

By 1723 the **Taos Fair** was formally established as the chief trading event for all the plains and mountain tribes. Because of the universally recognized "Truce of God," all participants are accorded "safe conduct" so that business can be conducted without fear of being attacked. Pueblos, Utes, Comanches, Navajos, Apaches, etc., as well as Hispanics love the trading atmosphere with its constant bartering, horse races, drinking bouts, cooking of different foods, shopping around for a desired item, and amorous encounters. From the Native American side, **Comanches** are acknowledged as the most important participants, and the most volatile. During one fair the Comanches put a group of women up for sale and when no one buys them they are butchered on the market ground. When the Spanish King hears of the incident he orders the creation of a mercy fund to ransom such captives and give them Christian guidance afterward. (Knowing that captives would be ransomed, Comanches took more captives for eventual sale in Taos.)

MONETARY EXCHANGE

By 1724 New Mexicans making annual trading trips to Chihuahua are a basic part of the culture. Business men buy or trade for items like chocolate, ironware, etc., which they can't grow or manufacture themselves. [See Note # 12.] The monetary unit is the *peso* but in actual use it has four sliding concepts of value: *peso de plata*: a silver coin with the value of *eight reales* [which standard was later adopted by the United States for silver dollars]; *peso* of six *reales*; *peso* of four *reales*; *peso de la tierra* of two *reales*.

Chihuahua merchants pay New Mexicans with the *two real peso* and require that they buy in *pesos de plata* (eight *reales*). New Mexicans know they are being dealt with unfairly but at that time there is no other available market.

GOVERNMENTAL STRUCTURE

In 1726 the chain of authority from Spain to NM was as follows for items which were not an emergency:

King, who has direct dealings with the Council of the Indies,
Viceroy, Audiencia of Guadalajara;
Council of the Indies deals directly with the Viceroy;

Viceroy and Audiencia of Guadalajara deal directly with the Commandant General; Commandant General deals directly with the Commandant Inspector; Audiencia of Guadalajara and Commandant Inspector deal directly with the **Governor** of New Mexico.

The Governors' documentation to superiors had to be in duplicate or triplicate; the Governor worked directly with the **Alcalde Mayor;** the Alcalde Mayor worked directly with the **Teniente Alcalde** in handling minor local matters.

Duties of the Alcalde included military and police activities when necessary; examining applications for land grants and placing grantees in possession of a grant if approved by the Governor; recording of cattle brands; judicial responsibilities regarding minor matters; initiating and preparing the paperwork relating to serious incidents (called the *sumaria*, which includes a statement of charges, preliminary testimony by witnesses, declaration by the accused, all of which are passed on to the governor); summoning residents of each Hispanic and Indian town to the central plaza and proclaiming all royal edicts, laws, or decrees; seeing to Indian welfare; etc.

RELIGION and SANTERO ART

The Church continued as a basic, integral factor in New Mexican life. During the 18th century three bishops from Durango made visitations to NM:

1730: Benito Crespo (the first Bishop to set foot in NM);
1737: Martín de Elizacoechea;
1760: Pedro Tamarón.

In 1730, New Mexico's first native priest, **Santiago Roybal**, returned to serve in his native land after many years of study in Mexico City.

New Mexicans of the 18th century were sincerely religious people. They believed Christianity was basic to life itself. Churches were built in the few major towns like Santa Fe but for the most part churches existed basically in the Indian villages so private chapels attached to homes became common with people who could afford them. Hours of praying in these family chapels were a common occurrence. The demand for religious images with which to practice one's faith gave rise to what has become known as "Santero Art." According to historians, Santero Art is identifiable at least by 1750 and considered a "rare, truly indigenous art form" which became most highly developed in NM. [See Note # 13.]

"Santero Art" wasn't considered "art" by New Mexicans but rather an expression of Faith. Religious images and representations weren't intended for art museums or merely making money. They were necessary in order to "live the Faith," so to speak. In this sense, no piece was "complete" before being blessed by a priest. The images became such integral parts of living that it was as if they were members of the family.

Religious images didn't have to be beautiful in the style of the Renaissance. Indeed, visitors from outside NM often described the images as crude or even ugly. The NM frontier landscape was often harsh, menacing, forbidding, and Santero Art reflected those realities, along with the medieval religiosity represented by Franciscans of the day. What the religious images had to have was *power*, power to enable Christians to survive in a harsh land so full of dangers, physical as well as spiritual. Religious images came to represent New Mexican endurance, suffering, and survival in an often hostile world surrounded by palpable dangers that could be combated only by family effort and the inestimable gift of Christianity. New Mexico was a land of extended families where religion was a family celebration structured around the Holy Family, Christ, Mary, and the Saints. Large numbers of images were necessary because every family included them in their life style.

The three basic creations of NM Santero Art are:

Retablo, a painting made on a pine wood panel, sawed at the top and bottom, the surface hand-azed then covered with gesso, mixture of gypsum and glue, and painted with watercolors. (Small retablos are often taken along on journeys or for use while in camp.)

Bulto, a statue carved from cottonwood root then covered with gesso and painted, sometimes clothed ornately, especially the *Virgin Mary*.

Reredo, altar screen, a large structure of panels, finished like retablos, placed behind and above a church altar.

Although they take stylistic liberties, New Mexican saint makers draw on traditional Christian iconography from illustrated missals, bibles, devotional cards, etc., as well as paintings and sculptures brought up from Mexico. Main subjects favored in *Santero* art are:

The Trinity: God the Father, Christ (*Nuestro Padre Jesús*), the Holy Spirit;

The Holy Family: Joseph is the strongest of human father figures; the Christ Child appears often with Mary and also alone as the *Santo Niño, Santo Niño de Atocha, el Niño de Praga, el Niño Perdido*;

Mary with various titles: *Nuestra Señora de los Ángeles, de las Candelarias, de la Purísima Concepción, del Socorro, del Rosario, de los Dolores, de la Soledad*, etc.

Angels: (often "elder brother protectors") Gabriel, Michael, Raphael, and the Guardian Angel;

Saints (patrons and protectors, male and female): Joseph, Francis, Isidore, John Nepomucene, Raymond Nonnatus, Rita, Rosalia, Veronica, Jerome, John the Baptist, Agnes, Anthony, Ann, Rosalie, Stanislaus, Aloysius Gonzaga, Lucy, Apolonia, Lawrence, Bárbara, Ignatius, etc.

These figures are familial intermediaries and if they don't "deliver" what is prayed for they could be "disciplined" by turning them to the wall or putting them in a trunk to "teach them a lesson." Religion was lived day to day.

There was also an allegorical "santo" named *doña Sebastiana who*

represented *Death*, utilized as a chilling reminder of human mortality. Christians knew that life in this world was very temporary, a mere prelude to Eternity.

A santero was considered something of a holy man, a person dedicated to portraying higher beings *and their power*, a humble servant who rarely even signed his name to his creations. He works according to tradition and doesn't innovate except for his particular style. He generally gathers his own materials from around the area where his village is located and he crafts his own tools. A *santero* is highly respected by New Mexican community because he enables Christians to live their religion. It is a rare, noble calling and there are precious few in the province. (Among the most accomplished historical santeros were B. Miera y Pacheco, Fr. A. García, 18th Century Novice, Laguna Santero, R.A. Fresquis, A. Molleno, José Aragón, "A.J.," Quill Pen Santero, Santo Niño Santero, J. Rafael Aragón, Arroyo Hondo Santero, J. de G. Gonzáles, J.M. Herrera, J.R. Velázquez, J.B. Ortega.)

INQUISITION & MIGUEL DE QUINTANA

While NM society relied on a religious base, citizens could have serious disagreements with religious leaders. In 1734 **Miguel de Quintana** from Santa Cruz was well recognized for his writing abilities as notary public, practical lawyer, public scribe, and playwright for religious or community theater. Two Franciscans, friars **Manuel de Sopeña** and **Joseph Irigoyen**, denounced him to the Inquisition as a *"hypocrite and heretic."* [See Note # 14.] This caused an investigation (and preservation of Quintana's writings) by the Inquisition. Being an accomplished literary man for the time and place, Quintana defended himself by asserting that Sopeña and Irigoyen were driven by jealousy and personal differences unrelated to religion. He cited that in 1726 Sopeña had ordered him not to write any more Christmas plays for the community, an order which Quintana ignored because "inner voices" encouraged him to continue. He added that these "voices" also caused him to write poetry which was also "dictated" to him by the "voices."

The Inquisition, always thorough before rendering a decision, investigated for five years. A lengthy file of evidence was accumulated, weighed, and considered by the Holy Office in Mexico City. In 1735 it ruled that Quintana did indeed seem to be suffering from some sort of mental malady, thus negating the charge of heresy. The Inquisition ordered him to stop discussing this "nonsense" about "voices" and "dictated poetry" or he would be subject to the full force of canonical law.

The decision didn't reach Miguel de Quintana until 1737 and he stated he would abide by the findings of the Holy Office. Then he wrote a new barrage of prose and poetry as his final defense. It is believed he died around 1748. (His work would be unknown today had it not been for the investigation by the Inquisition.)

COMANCHES & PECOS PUEBLO

Comanches were now the most implacable enemies of New Mexicans, whether Hispanic or Pueblo. In 1748 at least 100 mounted Comanche raiders swooped down on Pecos Pueblo intent on wiping it off the face of the earth. Unknown to the Comanches, Governor **Joaquín Codallos y Rabal** was in the village with armed forces ready to fight. The defenders, led by the Governor himself, marched out to meet the attackers. The Comanche cavalry advances, war cries piercing the sky, but Governor Codallos orders his men to continue their march, in square formation, into them. He gives the order to fire when the Comanches are within point blank range then the lancers and bowmen decimate the attackers. The Comanches quickly withdraw out of range momentarily. A group of older Pecos men had walked out of the village to view the action when suddenly two new contingents of Comanches ride up and slaughter eleven of the old men. The reinforcements now give the Comanches about 300 warriors, horses prancing with the raiders just out of musket range, preparing for the final cavalry charge intent on destroying Pecos Pueblo which now would certainly be successful. Governor Codallos orders everyone to fall back to the village, Indians first, soldiers still in formation. Suddenly there appears on the road from Santa Fe another column of Christian soldiers, banners waving and extra horses in tow, giving it the appearance of being larger than it actually is. The Comanches decide to withdraw. When the Comanche withdrawal is verified the Pecos people thank and embrace Governor Codallos "a thousand times" for delivering them from their enemies the Comanches who would most certainly have killed or enslaved them had it not been for Codallos and his Christian soldiers.

SHEEP RANCHING

Hispanics in NM numbered some 4,353 by around 1750. Sheep ranching was becoming New Mexico's most important industry. The *partido* system was widely used and the churro breed thrives everywhere. Sheepherders, known as *pastores* or *borregueros*, who lived mostly in isolation and depend mostly on their own resources, were masters of sheep husbandry. Highly trained sheep dogs are indispensable to the industry because they could do the work of three men on horseback in rough country.

Goats, used as *marcaderos*, markers, were always mixed in with flocks of sheep, usually on a ratio of 1 to 100, to facilitate counting the sheep. Because of their intelligence, goats were good leaders as well as lookouts for predatory animals. Goats also supplied milk for orphan lambs as well as herders.

ARRIERO – Transporter of Goods

While most people made their livings by farming or ranching, there were other professions which become an integral part of New Mexican culture. Among the highly regarded professions was that of *arriero*, the respected transporter of goods in NM via the packing of mules, burros, and sometimes horses.

Arrieros became famous for their honesty and dependability, their feelings of brotherhood for one another, their skill in packing and transporting all kinds of goods, their knowledge of and care for the animals they work, and the courage with which they face all dangers on desert and mountain trails. Arrieros earned reputations as men who never turned their backs on friend or foe, who cared for their animals, and never robbed or cheated anyone. Personal honesty was especially important because arrieros handled all monies when goods are bought or sold.

Packtrains (*recuas*) which often consisted of hundreds of animals, were usually divided into strings (atajos), were under the direction of the *patrón* (owner) or the pack master, *mayordomo*, who was responsible for the men, animals, and cargo. The head loader, *cargador*, was the mayordomo's second-in-command who supervised the loading and unloading of all pack animals, usually mules.

Arrieros worked in pairs when loading or unloading. The animal to be loaded is blindfolded with tapojos (cloth of wool or even silk, with the mule's name embroidered on it). The *jerga* (a square saddle blanket) is placed on the animal, then a pad of sheepskin upon which a packsaddle is secured, to which is tied the pack of goods being transported, which is protected with a petate (cover) against the elements. Loading an animal is accomplished within three to five minutes. Animals are unloaded at the end of every day, packs and packsaddles arranged so that the same animal receives the same load the next day.

If there is no professional cook each arriero takes his turn at cooking the evening meal for the group after which the men socialize around the campfire with singing, somebody playing the guitar, harmonica, or accordion, etc., and relating stories of various adventures, special animals, memorable personalities, etc.

Arriero holiday outfits included high-heeled top boots with tiny spurs, a silken sash wrapped around the waist two or three times, an embroidered shirt, a cone-shaped hat with a silver snake around the crown, the brim trimmed with silver braid. Equipment was decorated with carved figures of birds and animals. Pack saddles were beautifully stamped and carved while bridles were inlaid with gold and silver if the arriero was well off and wished to impress his society.

The Comanche Peace was established in 1786 by Governor Juan Bautista de Anza and Chief Ecueracapa of the Comanche nations. Peace gave rise to the professions of *mesteñero, cibolero,* and *comanchero.* [See Note # 15.]

MESTEÑERO – Mustanger

Mesteñeros (mustangers; men who make a living from capturing wild horses on the plains) were an important factor in New Mexico's economy and culture as well as its ranching history. Equine power was crucial because it provided the energy that turned the wheels of this frontier society.

Like the arrieros, mustangers operated under highly developed techniques and traditions typical of a "horse culture." Some mustangers worked in a family unit but often "mustang outfits" worked in large groups of 100 or 200 men under the direction of a captain whose leadership was unquestioned because capturing wild horses depended on cooperation. Supplying needed horses to ranches was rewarding but if the wild mustangs escaped capture there would be no remuneration so the mustangers had to depend on each other for success. Expeditions to the plains were also challenging due to lack of firearms and ammunition, sudden changes in the weather, hostile Indians, accidents, etc.

Mustangers had to be self-sufficient while plying their trade. They made their own lariats of rawhide, wove their girths, bridle reins, and hackamores from roached horsehair. They roped wild cattle and javelinas for meat. They had to survive on their skills and supplies. Items like coffee and sugar (*piloncillos*) were luxuries on the plains. But the successful quest was worth every deprivation: the "wild and free" mustangs with bones like ivory, muscles of steel, fleet as the wind and all the spirit of ingrained liberty. [See Note # 16.]

It is unknown how Hispanic mustangers of the Southwest developed their knowledge and techniques on capturing wild horses but some information is available. Early in June mustangers built or repaired circular corrals at known watering places on the plains east of NM Each corral was located in a strategic place like the bank of a creek used by mustangs as a crossing, at brushy hollows, or in canyons. No corral was considered complete until it was named (*Las Comas, Las Animas,* etc.), often dedicated to a saint, and a cross put at the entrance.

The horses used by the mesteñeros were generally at least on par with their wild brethren on the plains. Mustangs were driven into the corral by using tried and tested techniques developed by Hispanic mustangers but cooperation is basic because some mustangs are splendid specimens who can be captured only by, for example, relays of well mounted riders.. The captured horses were then trained to the saddle by mustangers working in pairs. This in itself was no simple feat because a mount had to be trained to the saddle but a horse with a broken spirit was worthless. The New Mexicans trained the animals until they were ready to be sold to ranchers. Proper training of saddle horses also required well developed techniques.

Mesteñeros had distinctive traditions of their own. For example, custom decreed that two out of every hundred mustangs sold would go to pay for masses for dead mustangers, a duty called *El Lazo de las Animas* (Lariat Bond of Souls). The captain of the group was responsible for effecting this tradition.

There were many mustangers on the plains but few have been studied or written about in detail. The **Trujillo** brothers, **Pedro and Celedón,** from Las Vegas, NM, were among the most famous mustangers on the Great Plains. The Trujillos specialized in capturing colts. Their summer expeditions to the plains often included women and children, many burros, milk cows, dogs, etc. and wagons loaded with equipment. **Teodoro Gonzáles** was also a renowned mesteñero so accomplished he made capturing mustangs appear to be a simple frontier sport.

Mustangers become real-life folkheroes of NM and the Southwest. The mustanging era ended when the open range was fenced off by large American cattle owners who slaughtered most of the wild mustangs to make way for their cattle.

CIBOLERO – Buffalo Lancer

As with capturing wild horses, buffalo hunting became a basic part of the New Mexican economy. Ciboleros, *"rugged, daring, and picturesque…"* were Hispanos who hunted buffalo with the lance and were considered among New Mexico's "super stars" for their horsemanship, personal courage to charge into a stampeding herd of fleeing buffalo, and their success as hunters. [See Note # 17.] The buffalo of the plains were a rich resource for New Mexicans and virtually every part of the animal was utilized. The meat was tastier than beef, the bones were used to enrich soups in cooking, the hides were made into leather for any number of uses, the hair was used for mattresses or spinning into coarse cloth, and even the horns were used for ornamentation.

Most New Mexicans worked their farms but after the fall harvest was in, hunters from various settlements organized and banded together for expeditions to the eastern plains to secure a winter's supply of meat. While a buffalo hunt was undoubtedly enjoyed by most participants, obtaining an adequate meat supply went far beyond mere sport. Most villagers were aware of the serious nature of the hunt but the ciboleros' departure was often celebrated with a dance for the entire village (and feted with another upon their return).

As with most other group activities in New Mexico, cooperation was necessary for success. A *Comandante* was democratically elected by members of the hunting expedition and all participants vowed to obey his orders. Hunters and helpers gathered at favorite cibolero rendezvous like Taos, Lucero (*Placita de los Ciboleros* in the Mora country), Santa Cruz, San Miguel del Vado, Manzano, and as far away as El Paso. There was very much work involved so cibolero groups were large, sometimes more than 150 men. What with their horses, wagons, carts, etc., the caravans into the eastern plains created or followed well worn trails.

Ciboleros wore buckskin clothes. They typically used a leather shirt and leather pants that went just below the knees. On the feet were *teguas,* hard soled moccasins. On the head was a leather cap, usually pyramid shaped and often adorned with a curved feather. Many hunters didn't use a saddle preferring instead a sheepskin because it enabled the rider to guide his horse with knee pressure.

Little is known about how New Mexicans bred their horses but cibolero horses were the best in the villages. They were highly trained and had to be as courageous as their riders to charge into a herd of stampeding buffalo, guided only by knee pressure. They were never used in farm labors.

While some hunters employed guns or the bow and arrow, the lance was the ciboleros' favorite hunting tool. It was a wooden shaft 6 to 8 feet long with a double-edged, razor sharp blade of 12 to 16 inches affixed at the end of it. Hunting technique was deceptively simple: the horse would be guided up close to the fleeing buffalo and the rider would thrust the blade into the buffalo's heart or lungs. The animal would often tumble "head over hooves" so the horse had to be able to avoid colliding with the huge beast and recover quickly enough to line up for another kill. All this transpired in the midst of a stampeding buffalo herd.

Upon arriving at a suitable location on the plains a base camp or campsite was selected. Once camp was made, riders were sent out to find the herds. When buffalo were sighted the hunters utilized a basic strategy: if at all possible, the men formed a half moon line around the herd, the fastest horses at the ends in an effort to "corral" the buffalo. The hunters started their horses at a walk then a trot then when the stampede was on they raced into the herd at required speed. A good horse and hunter could down 20 to 25 buffalo in a run of about three miles.

Helpers, *los siguidores*, would come behind the hunters and bleed the downed buffalo after which the carts arrived with the butchers who cut up the carcasses and hauled them back to camp. Everyone in camp, including the Comandante and hunters, famous or not, worked on processing the meat, which was cut into long, thin strips to dry as *tasajo* (*charqui*, jerky) on rope stretched between carts. The hides had to be stretched and salted, the tongues (which brought a peso each in Chihuahua) preserved. Tallow had to be for use in greasing cart and wagon wheels and the making of soap and candles, the latter being an important export item in the NM economy. *Chicharones* were made for treats during long winter nights and the choice marrow bones were preserved for use in stews back home. Horns are sawed off and buffalo hair is gathered.

After a successful buffalo hunt the journey home was a high-spirited affair, the men from different villages visiting and playing musical instruments like the guitar, harmonica, etc., often singing in chorus around campfires. New songs are also composed spontaneously, along with *corridos* telling of personal adventures and those of famous hunters. But even on the way home there were still dangers: sudden blizzards or other storms could be dangerous and hostile Indian war parties might be encountered. The Indians often demanded some of the meat harvested from their plains and usually the Comandante would gift them with a certain amount. If hostilities broke out the New Mexicans formed a defensive circle with their wagons and carts.

Upon arriving in their home village the ciboleros and their helpers were feted with community dances and lots of good food.

COMANCHERO – Indian Trader

New Mexicans, both Pueblo and Hispanic, who invested in trade goods and went out to barter with plains Indians were referred to as *comancheros*. The traders plied their wares in the plains of Texas, Oklahoma, Kansas, etc., even up to the South Platte River, doing business with the Comanche, Kiowa, Cheyenne, Arapaho, Crow, Ute, Shoshone, etc. While comanchero trading expeditions weren't as large as those of other plainsmen discussed above, these business people would generally get together and form groups where a *Comandante* would be selected as leader. Each individual agreed to cooperate for success because trading with the Native Americans could be very dangerous if disagreements broke out on the plains where Indians were the masters. Indians with whom to trade weren't easy to find because they were constantly on the move, following the buffalo herds. A trading expedition could be on the plains for around three months.

The most popular months for trading were August and September. Typical comanchero trade items included wheat flour, corn meal, salt, lances, tomahawks, strips of iron with which to make arrow heads, blankets, dry goods, barley meal, sugar, saddlery, dried apples, plums, apricots, pumpkins, etc., onions, tobacco. One of the most popular items was "Comanche bread," a hard bread baked and rebaked by the women back home until it was almost imperishable. But when dipped in coffee or water the bread became "*light, porous, and sweet...a perfect luxury with a cup of coffee by a mountain fire.*" The Comanches liked it so much that a sack of it would get the trader a good horse.

Pueblo comancheros specialized in bread, flour, and cornmeal as trade items. Pueblo wives would grind whole loads of meal for the men to take to the plains. It was common for several women to get together and grind at night. They would grind the corn on three to four metates ranging from rough to smooth, starting with kernel corn and reducing it to fine flour by the last, toasting the flour after each grinding. As the women worked, the men sang the grinding song or beat a rhythm on the drum, the women keeping time with slow, regular strokes until the job was done.

Among many other items used for trade during the Territorial period were butcher knives, steel files, shirts, red and white flannel, tea, sugar, lead and gunpowder. Liquor made its appearance later but it was a dangerous item to be trading.

The Comanches and other plains nations traded items like guns, ammunition, horses, mules, buffalo robes and buffalo meat to the New Mexicans. Ransoming captives also became a comanchero activity (especially during the Territorial period).

Like other New Mexican plainsmen, the comancheros were adept at tracking. When an Indian trail was discovered, especially if there were indications that women and children were in the group, expectations ran high but enthusiasm had to be tempered with great care. When the traders were close to the Indians the Comandante would give the order to make camp close to the nearest available water source. Then he would go to the highest point and make a smoke signal which the Indians were bound to see.

The following morning the Indians made camp next to the traders, women doing all the work. The children and dogs made all kinds of noise. At first the Comanche children were shy but after a few days they became very friendly, asking for this-or-that item. The Comandante had instructed all comancheros to be on their best behavior and treat all Comanches with respect. They were also advised to be on guard because serious, sometimes deadly disagreements could arise. But the Comanches wanted the trade goods also so they generally treated the comancheros amicably.

As a preliminary a feast was held and attended by both groups. With this formality out of the way, serious trading began. But the festivities weren't all business because different kinds of contests were set up. Horse racing was a favorite and the Comanches liked to bet on their horses. As good as they were, the New Mexican horsemen usually crossed the finish line first, while everybody watched and rooted, winning many articles from the Indians.

The Comanches traded for a few days then moved on to new grounds, generally following the buffalo herds. The comancheros packed up and followed them, making a new camp wherever the Comanches did. At every encampment various contests were set up between Hispanics and Comanches, sporting events like foot races or wrestling matches. There were also bow and arrow shooting contests as well as activities like breaking horses.

When all trade goods had been bartered the comancheros informed their Comanche hosts that they would soon depart. The Indians selected stalwart warriors to escort the traders toward New Mexico for around three days just in case hostile Apache or Navajo raiding parties were in the vicinity (as they often were). While most trading expeditions remained mutually peaceful, there were instances when some Indians demanded the return of all items traded to the comancheros. There is one incident involving the Kiowas and some Pueblo traders who were informed that all Kiowa items had to be returned. The Pueblos refused and the Kiowas were readying an attack when Comanches rode in, ascertained the cause of the problem, and ran off the Kiowas.

On occasion there were individual problems between a comanchero and a Comanche, as the fight between Capitán Vigil and the Comanche known as Capitán Corona, but generally relations were positive between Comanches and the traders.

Back in their villages there was considerable anxiety as well as excitement waiting for the traders to return. As everyone knew, death was a constant possibility in the far off plains and some Hispanos never returned. When the returning expedition was sighted there were often people on the roof tops, counting the number of riders to see that all came back safely. The returning comancheros were received with much happiness in their villages. Then there were feasts and dances in honor of the celebrated *comancheros*, festivities which became a hallmark of New Mexican life.

JOSÉ TAFOYA

Comanchero trade was a big frontier business at least by 1820 and what started as bridle paths were full fledged cart roads by the 1840s. Because of the magnitude of his trade with Comanches and other plains Indians, José Tafoya became known as the *"Prince of Comancheros."* There were many other well known comancheros, acknowledged masters of the trackless plains, a list which would include Facundo Melgares, Vicente Romero (from Córdova), Julian Baca, Manuel Gonzales, Guadalupe Márquez, José Medina, Polonio Ortiz, Manuel Chávez, José Antonio Vigil (*El Capitán Vigil*), Juan Lucero, Juan Pieda, Rafael Chacón, etc.

Due to the nature of the work done by arrieros, mesteñeros, ciboleros, and comancheros, New Mexicans came to be considered as among the best horsemen in the world, "a race of centaurs" unsurpassed in their abilities as equestrians. [See Note # 18.] They also became master plainsmen who could find their way in a land so lacking in prominent geological features that later travelers would compare it to the ocean. New Mexicans became "people of the great outdoors," men and women who loved being out on the land, riding their horses, hunting and fishing, working their farms and livestock, trading with friendly Indians when the opportunity availed itself. When recalling those days, Vicente Romero from Córdova was quoted as saying: *"Blessed be God, those were the days!"*

TOMÁS VÉLEZ CACHUPIN

The first administration of Tomás Vélez Cachupín, one of New Mexico's best governors, was during the years 1749-1754. Comanche raids were devastating the province. For example, in the summer of 1751 some 300 Comanches rode against the village of Galisteo in an effort to sack it. Defenders repulsed the attack, killing six of the raiders and wounding many others. Governor Vélez Cachupín learned that only some of the Comanche bands held a deadly grudge against Pecos and Galisteo. In September he led an expeditionary force against the warring factions. A major battle was fought, some 100 warriors were killed, all women and children were allowed to surrender. Captured Comanche horses, saddles, weapons, etc., were awarded to the Pueblo warriors in the expedition. Within a short time the Comanche bands let it be known they wanted peace and Vélez Cachupín was lenient with them in hopes of forming a lasting peace. The Governor also forged a peace with the Faraón Apaches and the Utes. He saw clearly that making peace hinged upon active personal diplomacy backed by military force to be used only when absolutely necessary, as well as a plentiful supply of gifts and opportunities to conduct trading. Ever aware of the frontier environment, Vélez Cachupín also established an extensive "early warning system" (said to be the first in what is now the USA) which worked to identify hostile raiders before they made it to the NM settlements, either Hispanic and Pueblo. At the end of his term as Governor, the Pueblos petitioned the Viceroy to have Vélez Cachupín remain for another five years but the request was denied because he was needed elsewhere.

MIERA Y PACHECO

In 1757 the famous Bernardo Miera y Pacheco drew a map of NM on which he also recorded the following information: *There are 5,170 Spaniards living in NM; they own some 2,543 horses, 7,832 cattle, 47,621 sheep and goats. The Pueblo and Hopi Indians number around 9,000, they own 4,813 horses, 8,325 cattle, and 64,561 sheep and goats.*

MINING

Mining was carried on in some sectors. In 1762 **Tomás A. Sena** and two others registered the *Nuestra Señora de los Dolores* gold mine.

CACHUPIN RETURNS

Tomás Vélez Cachupín was reassigned to NM for the years 1762-1767 during which he once again restored peace with the plains Indians, a peace which held for the rest of his administration because he was as talented as he was moral. For example, in 1763 two *genízaras* (Indian women of plains nations living in a Hispanic community; the Pueblo people would not generally accept genízaros into their villages) sought and got an audience with the Governor to air grievances against their Spanish master. They informed Vélez Cachupín that the women were forced to herd sheep, a man's job, and while out in the fields one of them was raped. The Governor investigated then ruled that the women hadn't been properly cared for nor had they been instructed in Christianity so he removed them from the offending household and placed them in homes *"where they will be given instruction in Christian doctrine and custom, along with lodging, food, and clothing in return for performing household chores."*

COMANCHE HOSTILITIES

In 1768 The Comanche chieftain **Cuerno Verde** was identified as the undisputed leader of his band of Comanches. He wore a distinctive headdress that protruded a green horn at the forehead. (Cuerno Verde was to become New Mexico's most implacable enemy after, it is said, his father was killed while raiding in the province. During the years 1769-1775, some 50 people were killed by Comanches in Pecos Pueblo alone. In 1771 some 500 Comanches descended on El Valle on the Las Trampas land grant and killed many settlers. In 1774 expeditions had to be sent against raiding Navajos. In 1775 five *torreones* [defensive towers] had to be built for use against Comanches raiders. In 1776 Comanches attacked Tomé and killed some 23 people. New Mexicans, Hispanic and Pueblo, had to become adept Indian fighters just to survive against Indians who outnumbered them and were often better armed.)

FIESTA

Despite frontier vicissitudes, life continued for the hardy pioneers who constantly had to defend themselves and their families. For example, **Josefa Bustamante**, the wealthiest woman in NM, was instrumental in 1769 in reestablishing the Confraternity of *Nuestra Señora del Rosario* and the annual fiesta in her honor.

DOMÍNGUEZ-ESCALANTE EXPEDITION

In July of 1776 the Domínguez-Escalante Expedition started out of Santa Fe when two Franciscan friars, **Francisco A. Domínguez** and **Silvestre de Escalante** led a party of nine explorers, one of whom was the famous **Bernardo Miera y Pacheco**, in an effort to blaze a trail to Monterey, California. [See Note # 19.] Without military escort, the little expedition for the first time explored the western slope of the central Rocky Mountains, the beautiful canyon country of the upper Colorado River, and the seemingly endless deserts of the Great Basin area. They were unable to get to Monterey but their "great circular tour" enabled them to map the area from Santa Fe to western Colorado, central Utah, northern Arizona, and western New Mexico, a route which would later be utilized in part as the *"Spanish Trail"* to California.

THE GREAT CAPTAIN

By 1778 NM was on the verge of collapse because it has been suffering a serious drought and the Comanches were raiding at will. (In 1779 it is estimated that numbers of sheep, New Mexico's basic wealth, had declined by some 40% since the 1757 numbers supplied by Miera y Pacheco.) Then one of North America's greatest heroes was assigned as Governor: **Juan Bautista de Anza.** Arriving in the province at the age of 42, he was American born and reared on the Sonora frontier. He already owned a sterling reputation as a frontiersman, a tested Indian fighter as well as diplomat. Unlike some of his predecessors, Anza could tell the difference between an Apache and a Pueblo upon meeting them. He could parley with Comanches, smoke with a Navajo, or fight hand-to-hand if so challenged. Now as Governor he had to prove his administrative skills. He concluded the most imminent danger was from Comanches so he decided he must first defeat them in battle before he could win them over as allies. [See the section on Indian Affairs for Anza's history in the Comanche War.]

SMALLPOX

In 1781 a smallpox epidemic devastated NM, killing some 5,025 people, around a quarter of the population.

PEDRO VIAL

In 1787 the premier trailblazer of the West, **Pedro Vial**, mapped a trail from San Antonio, Texas, to Santa Fe. [See Note # 20.] During the last leg of this historic journey, Vial, born in France and acculturated to Hispanic society, was escorted as far as Pecos Pueblo by Comanche warriors. (**José Mares**, well known New Mexican soldier and scout, then duplicated Vial's feat by going from Santa Fe to San Antonio, accompanied by valiant **Cristóbal de los Santos** and **Alejandro Martín**.) In 1788-89, Vial traversed and mapped a trail from Santa Fe to Natchitoches to San Antonio and back to Santa Fe, a journey of some 2,377 miles in fourteen months. The heroic Vial was accompanied by several men on this expedition, two of whom, **Santiago Fernández** and **Francisco X. Fragoso**, kept journals. In 1792-93 Pedro Vial blazed a trail from Santa Fe to San Luis (St. Louis) Missouri. Accompanied by **Vicente Villanueva** and **Vicente Espinosa** on his way east, the trio was captured by Kansas Indians, kept naked to prevent their escape, and threatened with death for six weeks. They were finally released and completed their journey to St. Louis, thus establishing the basic route of the famous **Santa Fe Trail** which would be used by so many travelers to the West. (Loomis and Nasatir summed up the contributions of this paladin when they wrote: *"He it was who blazed the trail that was followed a few years later by…all that great galaxy of prairie men…But of them all, perhaps none is better qualified for immortality than Pedro Vial…who had shown that it could be done."*)

HISPANIC SOCIETY

New Mexican society in 1790 was characterized as self-sufficient and hard working. Author Ramon Gutiérrez has written that modern statistical analysis shows that 93% of all NM households held neither slaves nor servants. Hispanic people were proud to work their own family land and because of their sense of community they were happy to help their neighbors when customary. There were some 16,358 Hispanic people living in NM according to the 1790 Census. By the end of the decade records show that women outnumbered men by a ratio of 10 to 8. While New Mexicans have seldom been equaled as Indian fighters, defending the land had taken its toll on the male population. But settlements continued to sprout up throughout NM history. [See Note # 21.]

Homes were furnished with distinctive New Mexican style chests, chairs, benches, tables, cabinets, writing desks, and beds, often decorated with carvings. [See Note # 22.]

Despite NM being in existence alongside large, often hostile Indian groups for almost two centuries, "Indian Affairs" were still an integral part of living history. The Comanche and Kiowa nations, traditional enemies, made peace in 1790, a peace that was never broken. Apaches also came into Santa Fe and spoke for peace with Governor Concha. He settled a band of Apaches at Sabinal between Belén and Socorro then ordered Hispanic settlers from Albuquerque and Bernalillo to help the settlement by contributing money and livestock for the Apaches, their former implacable enemies. The settlers complied with the Governor's request. Toward the end of the century baptismal books in northern NM showed that large numbers of Comanches and other plains Indians were being baptized into the Church.

MINING

In 1800 Col. **José M. Carrasco** discovered a fabulous deposit of copper in southwestern NM. It came to be known as the Santa Rita Mine.

EDUCATION

In 1803 **Nemesio Salcedo** of Chihuahua mandated the establishment and maintenance of schools. Required subjects were Christian doctrine, reading, writing, and counting. (In 1808 there were 140 children attending classes in the presidio school.)

LAND GRANT

In 1804 the Cebolleta land grant in western NM was made to thirty families.

VACCINATION

Vaccination against smallpox was introduced in NM in 1805.

SPY MISSION

Zebulon M. Pike was sent into NM on a spy mission by President Thomas Jefferson in 1807. Pike told New Mexican authorities that he was "lost" though he was actually instructed by Jefferson to assess the possibility of taking NM into the American Union. Pike and his men are marched to Mexico City then released.

SHRINE

The legend and shrine which comes to be known as the *Santuario de Chimayó* begins in 1810. Also by this year there is a regular postal convoy (separate from the famous caravan) in operation from Santa Fe to points south.

NEW MEXICO DESCRIBED

Pedro Bautista Pino, delegate to the Spanish *Cortes* (Parliament), writes his *Exposición sucinta y sencilla de la provincia del Nuevo Mexico* in 1812 and is published in Cadiz. He informs the people of Spain and the world that:

⋅ There are about 40,000 people in New Mexico, living in 3 villas, 102 plazas, and 26 Indian towns. There are public schools in Santa Fe, Albuquerque, Taos, Belén, San Miguel, and Santa Cruz. There are 22 friars in the province. No bishop has visited the province in over 50 years. There is only one physician in NM Medicinal herbs are widely used by Natives and Hispanos alike.

⋅ NM agricultural products include the famous El Paso wines. Hostile Indians and great distances make it impossible to export fruits and vegetables.

⋅ Hunting is a profitable business. Buffalo are the most important because of their great abundance, superb meat, and utilitarian hides. There are a variety of deer, especially elk. There are many wild horses, rams and ewes.

• Wool and cotton items are the basic manufactures in NM, though bits and spurs are also made. The government should lift bans on free production of manufactures. Any exports are at the expense and risk of the merchants themselves.

• Groups of at least 500 men gather at La Sevilleta (La Joya) during the month of November to caravan to southern markets. Such force and numbers are necessary to repel Indian attacks.

• New Mexican spirit and loyalty have endured continuous warfare with 33 hostile tribes for 118 years and has not lost one span of land from its original boundaries. After acquisition of the Louisiana territory the United States has tried to win over the New Mexicans in order to own the land and invade the interior of Mexico. They have built forts on the New Mexican frontiers and given firearms to hostile tribes opposed to us in order to break us, to no avail.

• A voluntary militia of about 1,500 men (three companies) defends the province, without salary and at their own expense, and there are only 121 professional soldiers paid by the Crown. Five presidios need to be established. Sons of the province are discriminated against when it comes to selecting officers in the Army.

• Government monopolies on the manufacturing of tobacco, gunpowder, and playing cards are counterproductive because more tax could be collected if these items were produced in NM

• New Mexicans are basically on their own when it comes to education, health, commerce, manufacturing, and national defense. Some people can't even sign their own name.

• New Mexicans are in dire need of the following: establishment of a bishopric in Santa Fe; a seminary college for secondary studies and public schools; uniformity in the military service and the additional presidios; establishment of a civil and criminal high court no further than Chihuahua.

• *"Sire, I hope that Your Majesty will also become aware and be attentive to the fact that the United States having bought Louisiana has opened the door to the Americans as much for arming the wild Indians and inciting them against us, as for invading the province themselves."*

• New Mexicans have land, which is probably the reason why there are no poverty-stricken vagrants and beggars as found in other territories.

• Pueblo Indians live in multistoried housing much like the people of Cádiz. Pueblo people wear clothes, shoes; the women are endowed with natural grace and beauty, dressing much like the ladies of Cádiz.

• Apaches are a numerous people with several different bands. They are generally a traitorous people, warlike, and cruel. But they fear the brave and honorable Comanches.

• Comanches are known for their robust and graceful presence, a frank martial air, modest dress, particularly the women, and other commendable qualities. They are the most powerful militarily, accepting no quarter but granting it to those they conquer. They have been friendly to New Mexicans since the Comanche Peace was established by Governor Juan Bautista de Anza.

• Navajos are now given to farming and manufacturing since they fought Hispanos in the three-year war when don Fernando Chacón was governor. Their woolen goods are the most valuable in NM, Sonora, and Chihuahua.

- Utes are very interested in material goods and they will steal if necessary.
- Giving gifts to the Indians has been immensely successful diplomacy.
- Indian women use certain herbs to abort unborn children, thus diminishing the native population.

MR. SOUTHWEST

Manuel Antonio Chaves (New Mexico's greatest frontiersmen of the 19th century) is born on October 18, 1818.

INDEPENDENCE

As of September 27, 1821, Mexico won its independence from Spain and became a sovereign nation. New Mexico was now part of the Mexican nation. In a short time all Indians were officially recognized as citizens of Mexico and the use of *"genízaro"* is officially dropped.

In 1822 **Francisco Xavier de Chávez** from Belén became the first native New Mexican to serve as Governor. (Married to **Ana M. Castillo,** two of their sons also got to serve as governors of the State and four grandsons later served as Delegate in the U.S. Congress.)

FOREIGNERS ENTER NEW MEXICO

Due to Mexico's more liberal policy on permitting foreigners to enter NM, numbers of fur trappers (often referred to as "mountain men") were in NM by the 1820s. New Mexico became a popular base for the fur trade (though beaver were trapped to near extinction by 1835).

In 1821 a Frenchman named **William Becknell,** looking for Indians to trade with on the eastern plains, was chanced upon by some New Mexicans and invited to bring his trade goods to Santa Fe. He did, made a good profit, then in 1822 became the first trader to use wagons instead of pack mules on the road that became famous as the *"Santa Fe Trail."* (This is the trail first blazed by **Pedro Vial** and his companions in 1792.)

Carlos Beaubien, a genial French-Canadian from Missouri (representative of a number of French immigrants to the area), arrived in NM in 1823. Within four years he acculturated to New Mexican life, married **M. Paula Lobato,** then later became a Mexican citizen on the road to wealth and influence.

TRADE on the SANTA FE TRAIL

In 1824 Chihuahua merchant **José Escudero** led a delegation of some 25 Santa Fe businessmen to various points in the Mississippi valley. This event marked the beginning of significant commerce on the Santa Fe Trail. American merchants from Missouri, encouraged by the Escudero delegation, then brought in some $35,000 worth of trade goods, almost doubling it the following year, glutting the market. American traders were then encouraged to take their wares to Chihuahua, which was almost twice the size of Santa Fe. Chihuahua was a rich mining center where a mint was in operation, stamping out more than 500,000 pesos worth of coin each year. It quickly supplanted Santa Fe in importance as a trading center. Also in 1825 **Manuel Simon Escudero** was sent to St. Louis to negotiate military protection on the American side of the Santa Fe Trail because the USA wasn't protecting traders from raiders. Mexican troops protected trade caravans on Mexican territory but no one was taking on the responsibility on the American side. After years of demands for protection by American traders, in 1829 Washington authorities finally provided soldiers for protecting trade caravans. The only problem was that soldiers of the Sixth Infantry couldn't pursue mounted hostile raiders because the *soldiers were on foot*. American authorities, though not products of a horse culture, finally agreed that horses were needed "out West" so they ordered that soldiers be issued horses. The **U.S. Cavalry** was born.

With the 1825 Escudero party was a pack train of around 500 mules laden with trade goods. The *Franklin Intelligencer* newspaper reported on the trading expedition and observed that the effort "*may be considered as a new era*" in trade between Mexico and the USA. [See Note # 23.]

WEDDINGS

Among the greatest causes for celebration in NM were *bodas*, weddings. These celebrations were generally highly ritualized but festive occasions in NM village life. Marriage was one of the most serious steps anyone could take because it was for life. Weddings were often joyfully celebrated by extended families and friends. Procedure was set by tradition and "proper" behavior was considered a mark of good breeding whether one was rich or poor. The ritual included:

La pedida de la novia (Asking for the Bride):

The young man (*novio*) informs his parents that he wishes to marry. If the parents approve they speak (or write, depending on distance) to the parents of the young lady (*novia*) and if they are in favor of the marriage, items like the dowry and wedding arrangements (like the banns that have to be read for three Sundays) are discussed. (Oral tradition has it that an Hispanic suitor is expected to give filigree jewelry to his fiancée.)

El prendorio:

A *fiesta* (party) is sponsored by the bride's family, complete with food and dancing, in which the other party's relatives meet the bride and groom-to-be by attending and giving them presents. The novio gives jewelry to the novia.

La boda:

The wedding is held in church, relatives and friends from near and far making special efforts to attend in order to celebrate. A wedding dance is held after the church ceremony and there is much good food to enjoy.

La entriega:

The newly wedded couple is taken to both sets of parents and verses are sung or recited on the sacredness of their marriage, the responsibilities to each other, etc. Everyone dances far into the night, even if the newlyweds leave before the dance is over.

FOREIGNERS IN TAOS

Between 1826-1850 the village of Taos seemed to be the center for men from outside NM to congregate. There were some 218 non-Hispanic names listed in N.M. church records for this period: French: 87 names, 77 of whom were living in Taos; United States: 125 names, more than 75 in Taos; German: 2 (in Taos); English, Irish, Scotch: 1 from each country (all living in Taos); and one Simon Levi, origin unknown.

ARMIJO & SPANISH TRAIL

In 1829 **Antonio Armijo** from Abiquiú decided to take a trading expedition of at least 30 people to California. Armijo didn't wish to go as far north as the route blazed in 1776 by the Domínguez-Escalante expedition so he pioneered a westward route that skirted the north rim of the Grand Canyon. No one had ever attempted that route but the Hispanos were determined to make it to California, blazing sands notwithstanding. Everyone survived the harsh Mojave Desert, though they had to eat horse and mule meat when food supplies ran short. On December 25, 1829, a reconnaissance party went out and returned without (teenager) **Rafaél Rivera** who somehow got separated from the group. Rafael wasn't reunited with the group until January 7 after having explored some 506 miles and discovered the Las Vegas Valley in Nevada (the first non-Indian to see *Las Vegas*). The Armijo expedition made it to San Gabriel and then Los Ángeles where they traded their woven woolen goods like serapes, blankets, and quilts for horses and mules from the California ranchos. The venture was profitable so the two-month journey became a yearly event. Wives and children of the traders often accompanied the caravan on what came to be called the *Old Spanish Trail*. In time Antonio Armijo decided to take up permanent residence in Solano County, California. Other New Mexicans like Hipólito Espinosa, Manuel Baca (for whom *Vacaville* was named), Julian Chaves, etc., also stayed in California. (When the 1850 Census was taken, some 213 NM Hispanos were living permanently in California, 172 of them in Los Ángeles.)

TRADE

In 1831 there was signed a "treaty of amity and commerce" between the USA and Mexico in which the USA was categorized as a "*most favored nation.*"

NEW MEXICO DESCRIBED

In 1832 visitor **Antonio Barreiro** writes *Ojeada sobre Nuevo México,* (A Glimpse At New Mexico) a detailed social and economic report, generally critical, in which he states: "*Whoever has a slight conception of the ignorance which reigns in this country, will not require other colors to paint vividly the deplorable and doleful state in which the administration of justice finds itself.*" [This meant N.M. was a society functioning without lawyers. To lawyer Barreiro this was "deplorable."]

Sheep have increased with incredible numbers and N.M. would enjoy prosperity if peace could be made with hostile tribes. A few families dominate the sheep industry.

Ciboleros, Hispanic buffalo lancers, are harvesting from 10,000 to 12,000 buffaloes annually. Favorite rendezvous sites for cibolero hunters include Taos, Santa Cruz, **Lucero** in the Mora country is nicknamed *La Placita de los Ciboleros* because it is such a popular gathering place for hunters, San Miguel del Vado, Manzano, etc., to as far south as El Paso.

PRINTING PRESS

Ramón Abreú, Secretary of the Legislature, buys a printing press and with the aid of Jesús María Baca, a printer from Durango, Barreiro publishes (1834) the first newspaper in N.M, *El Crepúsculo de la Libertad* (The Dawn of Liberty).

[The press is acquired in 1835 by Father Martínez of Taos who uses it to publish items used in his private school. Two other newspapers are later published on it, *La Verdad* and *El Payo de Nuevo México*.]

EDUCATION

Schools are operating in Santa Fe, San Miguel del Bado, Santa Cruz de la Cañada, Taos, Albuquerque, and Belén, but he says *"The schools are in deplorable condition. No noticeable results are achieved by primary instruction, a condition which is due both to the neglect, carelessness, and ignorance of many of the teachers and to the lack of interest shown by the authorities."* He states no one is better paid than the teachers of the province.

Crafts *"are in the worst state imaginable."* There is very little iron and metal tools are difficult to come by. Nails are at a premium. There is no machinery with which to spin fine yarn or fine cloth. Foreign artisans are the only hope for development of the crafts and he identifies foreign "tailors, carpenters, blacksmiths, tinsmiths, gunsmiths, hatters, cobblers," etc., working in N.M. [See Note # 24.]

CUSTOMARY LAW

There were no lawyers in N.M. (except for the visiting Antonio Barreiro mentioned above). The **legal system** was based on Spanish *customary law* and its emphasis on conciliation. Litigants each appointed an *hombre bueno* (a good man) to recommend a fair solution to the *Alcalde*, who rendered a decision on the matter at hand if the *hombres buenos* could not agree on a settlement. If litigants accepted the Alcalde's decision the matter was closed. If they didn't then written testimony was taken, reviewed by the Alcalde, then passed on to the *Ayuntamiento* or finally the Governor himself for a final decision.

SHEEP KING

In 1832 **Mariano Chaves y Castillo** of Los Padillas made marketing history by sending 30,000 head of sheep to Durango (the largest delivery sent south by a single individual during the Mexican period of N.M. history).

DANGERS

By 1837 the Department of New Mexico is threatened on all sides as well as from within. While American traders in Santa Fe are a reliable source of revenue for the government, and some traders are stable, *"cultivated or useful men,"* others are typical frontier American riffraff *"…shameless smugglers, and their teamsters are rough and rowdy…"* frontier types, *"… always armed, often drunk, the source of trouble at dances and public gatherings."* [See Note # 25.] Across New Mexico's northern boundary of the Arkansas River there are American trading posts, considered to be possible bases for a military invasion of NM by the USA. Though the Comanche nation helps to keep the peace in NM, the trading posts supply modern guns to Plains Indians and (unofficially) encourage them to raid throughout Mexico. To the east is the new slave **Republic of Texas,** officially recognized by the USA, whose leaders claim NM to the Río Grande, often declaring their intention to secure their claim, by invasion if necessary. (Slavery is illegal in N.M. and the rest of Mexico but in Texas and the Southern American states the brutal institution is a pillar of society.) To the west are the **Navajos** who can be fierce raiders or trading partners during periods of truce. To the south are warriors of the Gila and Mescalero **Apaches** who can wage war and block communication with Mexico at their will.

MAIL CARRIERS

At least by 1837 a system of mail carriers, the solitary horseman referred to as an *extraordinario violento* (*volante?*), was used to correspond with people and authorities in Mexico. [This system was later referred to as the **Pony Express** when the U.S. entered the Southwest.]

CHIMAYÓ REVOLUTION

In August of 1837 a revolution breaks out in the Chimayó-Santa Cruz area over the issue of imposing additional taxes on the people of NM. It is led by the *alcalde* **Juan José Esquibel** and supported by a 12 member council referred to as *El Cantón de la Cañada*. Their avowed purpose is to sustain God, the nation, the faith of Christ; to defend N.M. to the last; not to allow the Departmental Plan or any tax associated with it; and to stop the excesses of those who try to carry them out. An army is gathered.

Governor Pérez decides to talk to the rebels until he learns how big the movement really is. Then he issues a call to arms but can collect only about 200 militiamen, many of them Pueblo warriors from the Río Abajo area. With two cannons, the little army marches north, but Pérez still has hopes of negotiating differences.

At La Mesilla government forces meet four groups of insurgents numbering from 1,500 to 2,000 men. Negotiations stop when the rebels open fire and disorder reigns. The two cannons are captured along with much of the Governor's force.

Governor Pérez doesn't have enough soldiers to quell the uprising so he flees south but is stopped on August 8th in the vicinity of Agua Fria road southwest of Santa Fe. Pérez puts up a heroic personal resistance and when his horse is shot from under him he fights on foot with his pistols. When he is out of ammunition he fights with his dagger, killing several of his assailants. Finally he is seriously wounded and killed.

Others of the Pérez party are hunted down and executed, including Santiago Abreú (who was brutally tortured before dying), and Jesús María Alaríd. In all, 17 men die, 6 of them soldiers.

José Gonzáles, a highly successful and therefore popular cibolero, is chosen as Governor of N.M. by the *Cantón*. Governor Gonzáles is totally against the Departmental Plan so he suggests to **Elisha Stanley**, an American trader, that all American traders join the *Cantón* movement and ask the *United States to annex N.M. to the American Union*. Stanley refuses to become involved.

Rebel unity now begins to unravel as does support for the cause when the *Cantón* comes out against Gonzáles' moderate goals. Opponents are jailed and threatened with death. Now there are two rebel factions: those with Gonzáles and those with the *Cantón*.

September 8: The Curate of Tomé, **Francisco Ignacio de Madariaga**, invites influential men of the Río Abajo to meet with him and formulate a strategy to stop the revolution in the north. The **Plan de Tomé** manifesto is issued by **Manuel Armijo** and others, decrying the anarchy. Though not a military man, Armijo is named to lead a liberating army.

September 11: Governor Gonzáles is informed of the Plan of Tomé and ordered to surrender, which he does with the *"greatest enthusiasm."* He is put in the Santa Fe jail.

September 14: Manuel Armijo arrives with his liberating army from the Río Abajo. Rumor has it that the Cantón army of 3,000 rebels would soon be descending on Santa Fe. Manuel Armijo states he is not a trained soldier, that he knows nothing of battle tactics, so he asks Colonel Juan Esteban Pino to take command of the Río Abajo army. September 19: Col. Pino declines Armijo's request, pleading advanced age and illness. So Armijo must shoulder the responsibility.

September 21: Armijo lets it be known that he wants to negotiate with Cantón leaders like Pablo Montoya, former *alcalde* of Taos, because he feels innocent people have been duped into joining the rebellion out of ignorance or fear. An agreement is signed and the rebels disband, thus ending the conflict. Some leaders like José Gonzáles and Pablo Montoya are granted amnesty.

AMERICAN VISITOR

Visitors from the USA are no longer rare in NM. Among such personalities is **Matt Field** who travels to N.M. in 1839 and publishes articles in the *New Orleans Picayune* relating his impressions about the land and its people. His first view of the *"mud built city of Santa Fe"* appears to be *"…an assemblage of mole hills…"* but upon closer inspection of the housing he is impressed with the practicability of local architecture. [See Note # 26.] He concludes that *"…a Santa Fe dwelling is even preferable to an American brick or frame residence. "*

⋄ N.M. blankets are *"…handsome (sometimes really beautiful …) with their brilliant colors and weaving so fine they can hold water."*

⋄ The dark-eyed Señoritas looking at him are *"…more delightful than the exhilaration of the wine bowl…"* though he finds them *"…dark complexioned, some of them pretty, but many of them plain, and most of them Ugly-but slightly removed from the Indians-and they paint their faces like the Indians, with vermilion, by way of ornament."* [Field is unaware of the protective facial masque.]

⋄ Amusement in Santa Fe centers around dancing and the game of monte, a card game. Field is fascinated by the most famous monte dealer in town, "Señora Toulous." American *"Traders often lose the profits of a whole season in an hour's play…."* at monte with La Tules, who appears to despise *"…both her fools and the tools by which she ruled them."*

⋄ He describes a richly attired *"cavallero (sic) … a fine gentleman of Santa Fe-with an enormous sombrero corded with gold … a jacket of black cloth covered with frogs and braid-pantaloons with the outside seam of each leg left open from the hip down, for the purpose of exposing the white drawers beneath … silver espuelas-with saddle and other gear gorgeously decorated with silver, and little bells and ornaments jingling…"*

⋄ One of the drivers in Field's caravan wants to buy Santa Fe from three ladies walking out of a store. He tells them: *"I'll give a heap of paysos for Santa Fe just for your sakes, though its a monstrous low place. Your houses are all in one story, like a pack of thieves; built of mud, too, so they ought to be dirt cheap. Madame, will you have a cigar? Miss, I beg pardon, I don't know your name-0, I remember-seenyora-Miss Seenyora … Six months since I've seen a gal, so help me Cupid, and I'll marry are [sic] a one of you-I'll marry the whole bunch of you right off…"*

⋄ The arrival of a caravan in Santa Fe is always an event: *"…the drivers, reckless and insolent fellows, cracking whips and jokes simultaneously.... the pass whiskey began to operate, and groups of noisy American drivers were heard singing, shouting, and rioting in every street..."*

• Field goes to a wedding dance where the bride is *"...smoking her chupar. She would pass for handsome among all who do not consider a fair skin absolutely indispensable to beauty...music is a guitar and violin...One waltz ... represents a battle ... exciting and delightful. Few Americans can partake in this dance, as it requires a rapidity of movement which they find by no means easy to acquire ... the people could not exist without the waltz ... With all this unrestrained freedom of manners they seldom quarrel, and the harmony of an evenings amusement is seldom broken unless by some imprudent conduct of the Americans themselves..."*

PENITENTE BROTHERHOOD

The *Brothers of Our Father Jesús*, often referred to as the Penitente Brotherhood, had become an important part of N.M. village life by 1840 because there was a serious shortage of priests, especially in the more isolated hamlets. This fostered the emergence of a kind of "folk religion" in the province, the *Penitentes*. This Brotherhood fellowship was created by the people themselves in order to fill a need for the *"devoutly Catholic and of necessity stoutly independent pioneer people..."* of Hispanic N.M.

The Brotherhood was natively referred to by various names: Brothers of Our Father Jesús, Brothers of Light, Fraternal Order (Pious Fraternity, etc.) of Our Father Jesus of Nazareth, Third Order of St. Francis, etc. Duly elected officers conducted all matters relating to the Brotherhood: *Hermano Mayor* (Elder Brother), Warden (sergeant-at-arms), Agent (keeps members informed), Teacher of Novices, Treasurer, Clerk, Nurse, Reader of prayers, Flutist, etc.

The *morada* is the lodge or meeting place for the Penitente Brotherhood. It contains (at least) two rooms, a capilla (chapel) and a meeting hall. (*"The immaculateness of the interior of the morada always is remarkable, with spotless whitewashed walls, packed earth floors clean enough to eat from, and white lace curtains..."*) It is decorated with santero religious art (and in time the Brotherhood is the chief patron of this folk art form).

Membership in the morada signifies separating oneself from the outside world, submitting to authority of the Elders (Brothers of Light), welcoming self-sacrifice that sustains the Brothers and their community. There are three ranks in Brotherhood membership: Brothers of Blood (individuals engaged in active penances, like novitiates), Brothers emerging from Darkness, and Brothers of Light (officials of the morada). Serious transgressions of Brotherhood rules result in expulsion, lesser wrongdoings by penance. Women are not members of the Brotherhood, though they can serve as *Auxiliadoras* (Auxiliaries) who help with various duties. They are also referred to as Verónicas, Carmelitas, or Terceras.

Purpose of the Brotherhood is to practice fellowship, community responsibility, and piety. Brothers must attempt to emulate His life by living simply and morally and by performing unobtrusive good deeds. Throughout the year members are required to render *"...service to God through Christ's teachings; observance of the Ten Commandments; leading a humble life like Jesus; avoidance of discord; shunning worldly temptations such as saloons; and charity and mutual love toward Brothers by setting a good example, aiding in times of illness or anguish, pardoning, tolerating, and respecting one another."*

Activities of the Brotherhoods include to conduct *velorios* (wakes) after seeing to the needs of the bereaved, preparing the body for burial, digging the grave, etc.; gather for group prayer for special (e.g., serious illness of a member) as well as religious occasions; own flocks of sheep with which to meet expenses; invite the community to the morada for certain ceremonies; hold (religious) processions in which the villagers may partake; commission santeros for the production of bultos, retablos, reredos, etc., with which to grace their moradas; serve community needs; enact spiritually beneficial rituals.

Brotherhood devotions are expressed through ritual, prayer, discipline, music and singing of *alabados* (hymns), and humility. [See Note # 27.] Lent (*La Cuaresma*) and Holy Week (*Semana Santa*) are observed universally by the Brotherhoods but there are also other devotional celebrations: Corpus Christi (Thursday after Trinity Sunday), Assumption (August 15), All Saints Day (Nov. 1), All Souls Day (Nov. 2), the day of the morada's patrón saint, as well as traditional celebrations which vary from village to village (days of St. John, St. James, St. Anne, Holy Cross, La Porsiúncula, the Twelve Days of Christmas, etc.).

During Holy Week observances [described as *"…a folk equivalent of the Catholic Mass"* [See Note # 28.] the Brothers retreat in their morada, from Palm Sunday through Holy Saturday, or more frequently, from Holy Tuesday to Good Friday. During retreat villagers are welcomed into the morada and time is spent praying and maintaining vigils. Public processions and Stations of the Cross are celebrated. Women from the community donate meatless meals called *charolitas* (Lenten dishes), like *torta* and *panocha*, for the Brothers.

Penitential exercises include walking on one's knees, carrying large crosses, self-flagellation with whips (called *disciplinas*), the most common form of penance, wrapping yourself in rope or chain, etc. All penances are under strict control at all times by the *Hermano Mayor* (Elder Brother). Individuals doing penance, wearing *vendas* (hoods) to insure humility, are accompanied by helpers and persons who pray, sing *alabados*, play the flute, or carry sacred images.

Major processions are held on Wednesday (Procession of Sorrows), Thursday (Procession of the Holy Cross), and Friday (Procession of the Blood of Christ).

The *Las Tinieblas* ceremony, usually held at night on Holy Thursday and preceded by a rosary service in which villagers participate, involves a candelabrum of 13 to 17 candles, each candle or pair of candles being extinguished after the singing of an alabado. When the last single candle is extinguished there is utter darkness and then loud noises from chains, matracas, drums, screams, etc., fill the air. The tumult alternates with periods of silence during which *sudarios* (prayers for those departed, said while covered with a blanket) are recited. A single candle, representing Christ as the light of the world, is relighted, then the other candles from it.

Good Friday is a day of universal mourning. Matracas, wooden clackers, are used in place of bells in all activities. It is on Good Friday that the individual selected to reenact the symbolic crucifixion of Christ is bound to a cross for a short time, after which he is brought down and taken into the morada. [See Note # 29.] This ends Holy Week activities.

TEXTILE PRODUCTION

New Mexican textile exports peaked during 1840 when more than 20,000 items were shipped to Mexico. The textiles were of three basic types: *sabanilla*, a plain-weave wool cloth used in clothing, mattresses, and backing for colcha embroidery; *jerga*, a coarsely woven cloth used for saddle blankets, floor coverings, etc.; Río Grande blankets, in a variety of patterns, used for bedding, seating, etc. These items were very welcome in Mexico.

TEXAN-SANTA FE EXPEDITION

The Texan-Santa Fe Expedition begins in the spring of 1841 when President Lamar of Texas decided to bring the rich Santa Fe trade into Texas. Texas claimed the Río Grande River as the western boundary of Texas is as signed over to the Texans by General **Santa Anna** so he outfits an expedition of about 300 men under the command of brevet Brigadier-General **Hugh McLeod** to go to N.M. and invite the people to unite under the Texas flag of freedom or at least to trade. Cannon are part of the military equipment with the men in the expedition, who refer to themselves as "Texian Invincibles."

Governor Armijo and New Mexico authorities have long heard rumors that Texans will invade N.M. because they demand the eastern half of N.M. for Texas. Ordinary New Mexicans believe Texans offer "freedom" as a way to make them slaves like the blacks whom they victimize in accordance with Texas law. Governor Armijo puts out word of the impending invasion and instructs anyone living in eastern N.M. to report all information on the invaders. The strategy works: three spies are taken, escorted into Santa Fe and instructed to stay in the capital, but after they escape and are recaptured they are executed.

Militia forces are called into service on the eastern frontier. Five men from the Texan expedition are captured, disarmed, and put in a Santa Fe jail. Another group of 94 Texans surrender at Antón Chico, their property is taken from them and they are marched under guard to Mexico City. The main body of Texans under McLeod, about 200 men, surrender to Armijo on the 5th of October and, as invaders, they too experience the cruel march to Mexico City.

George W. Kendall, editor for the *New Orleans Picayune* newspaper, is among the captured invaders. He relates his experiences in the newspaper (1842) then the generally derogatory sketches appear in the (1844) *Narrative of the Texan Santa Fe Expedition* which is widely read in the U.S. [See Note # 30.]

After their defeat the Texans swore vengeance and plans were made to raise a force that would bring "*freedom*" to N.M. and Chihuahua to boot. Col. **Jacob Snively** was directed to raise 800 men, "*...the only difficulty being to keep the number down...*" to liberate the land under "*...the banner of freedom.*" The grand scheme somehow fizzled out and the Texans took their vengeance by raiding on the Santa Fe Trail.

The Santa Fe Trade was made more difficult after the Texan-Santa Fe Expedition because some New Mexicans now felt American traders were also working as spies for the United States until it could invade and take the country.

ISOLATION

In 1844 Governor Chávez wrote: *'We are surrounded on all sides ... by many tribes of heartless barbarians, almost perishing; and our brothers in Mexico instead of helping us are at each other's throats in their festering civil wars."* New Mexicans are becoming alienated from the Mexican government to the degree that when Mexico City wants to shut down the Santa Fe Trail they insist on keeping it open.

TRADE

In 1844 goods taken over the Santa Fe Trail are valued at $200,000. In the month of August alone some eight Mexican merchants bought $90,000 worth of imported goods for resale in Chihuahua, Durango, Aguascalientes, etc. In 1845 trade goods were valued at $342,000. Most of the trade was now going to the interior of Mexico and trade goods were coming from New York, Philadelphia, etc.; Liverpool, England, and Hamburg, Germany. Some 32 wholesale houses in the eastern U.S. entered the trade directly, importing from Europe and using their own agents for selling to the caravans. Mexican merchants who traded directly with the U.S. did much business with the Spanish firm of **Peter Harmony, Nephews and Co.,** New York importers of English, French, German, and Venetian items. Trade items included a "bewildering variety" of goods. Indians valued bottles of all kinds and would trade their agricultural products for them. By 1846 trade was valued at $1,000,000 with a record 363 wagons crossing the plains, of which 315 continued to El Paso, Chihuahua, Durango, Zacatecas, Aguascalientes, etc., and eventually to Mexico City. Many merchants became well known in the Santa Fe trade, among which were Juan Otero of Peralta, Samuel C. Owens of Kentucky, James (Santiago) W. Magoffin of Kentucky, Albert Speyer of Prussia; David Waldo, Edward J. Glasgow, Henry Connelly, etc.

POPULAR BOOK

It has been said that *Commerce Of The Prairies* (1844) by **Josiah Gregg** was one of the most widely read books by Americans of the day interested in the West. The work has survived into the contemporary period and makes commentary like the following:

• Gregg describes a *cibolero* met on his caravan's approach to Santa Fe; a *fandango* (dance) is held to celebrate the arrival of a caravan;

• Oñate, founder of N.M., is an example of *"…that sordid lust for gold and power, which so disgraced all the Spanish conquests in America; and that religious fanaticism, that crusading spirit, which martyrized so many thousands of aborigines of the New World under Spanish authority…"* The pacific and docile aborigines of NM *"had neither intelligence nor spirit to resist…"* Oñate's settlers.

• New Mexicans prepare the best chocolate in the world; their horsemanship and ability with the lazo (rope) are remarkable; the arrieros are extremely skillful transporters of goods; sheep raising is the most important industry and Mexican sheepdogs are highly trained.

• *"…The New Mexicans appear to have inherited much of the cruelty and intolerance of their ancestors, and no small portion of their bigotry and fanaticism. Being of a highly imaginative temperament and of rather accommodating moral principles-cunning, loquacious, quick of perception and sycophantic, their conversation frequently exhibits a degree of tact-a false glare of talent, eminently calculated to mislead and impose. They have no stability except in artifice, no profundity except for intrigue: qualities for which they have acquired an unenviable celebrity. Systematically cringing and subservient while out of power, as soon as the august mantle of authority falls upon their shoulders, there are but little bounds to their arrogance and vindictiveness of spirit.."*

• Northern Mexicans…"*have often been branded with cowardice: a stigma … of the wealthier classes… though the rancheros … and yeomanry … possess a much higher calibre of moral courage. Their want of firmness in the field, is partially the result of their want of confidence in their commanders… and inefficacy of their weapons…"* The *"Mexicans, like the French, are remarkable for their politeness and suavity of manners…"*

⁺ Gregg writes that *"Goldsmiths and silversmiths are perhaps better skilled in their respective trades than any other class of artisans whatever...."*

⁺ Mexicans harbor a variety of gross superstitions that are *"...fantastic and improbable in idolatrous worship..., the most popular being the apparition of the Virgin of Guadalupe. The superstitious blindness of the people causes them to believe in a legion of saints and this ...abject idolatry sometimes takes a still more humiliating aspect, and descends to the worship of men in the capacity of religious rulers..."* as on the occasion of Bishop Tamaron's visit to Santa Fe when *...the infatuated population hailed his arrival with as much devotion and enthusiasm as if it had been the second advent of the Messiah."* The padres lead the people in vice and get away with it because *"...the Romish faith is not only the religion established by law, but the only one tolerated by the constitution, a system of republican liberty wholly incomprehensible to the independent and tolerant spirits of the United States..."*

⁺ Indians boast they *"would long before this have destroyed every sheep in the country, but they prefer leaving a few behind for breeding purposes, in order that their Mexican shepherds may raise them new supplies."*

HISPANIC SOCIETY

On the eve of the American takeover of NM custom and tradition were basic guidelines for Hispanic life in the province. Individualism was strong but exhibited in basically the same consistent fashion. Men were expected to be *muy hombre* and live by their *palabra de hombre*, which assured honesty and dependability. A man's word was his bond and written documentation was unnecessary. Males learned and refined the skills of planting, hunting (especially the buffalo), building, animal husbandry, harvesting, etc., and, above all else, *horsemanship*.

Partly due to religious personalities like Mary and the female Saints, Hispanic women were heirs to a special status at home and in social circles which gave them certain freedoms and responsibilities in society. Females learned the arts of home and family for the day they would be wives. They were taught to be stable, responsible (*muy mujerota*) hearts of the family. Many females also helped on the farm/ranch whenever necessary and those who chose to generally became good equestrians.

Hispanic law and tradition enabled women to own property separately from that of their husbands and utilize or dispose of it as they choose. A husband couldn't alienate his wife's land without her consent. [See Note # 31.] Husbands could make no claim to their spouse's property if it was owned before marriage. (This "Hispanic tradition" of female land ownership became the basis for the concept of community property in modern American law.) Wives could not be held accountable for their husband's debts. Women could sue and be sued in court.

The extended family was part of Hispanic community living. Blood relations were the nucleus of family life but there was also the *compadrazgo*, which included godparents (*padrinos*) as responsible kin in the event that something happened to the parents of one's godchild, parents and godparents referring to each other as *compadre* or *comadre*. [*Primo/prima* is often used when addressing someone because most New Mexicans are related by blood.] Women outnumbered men in settled, older communities like Santa Fe, Abiquiú, etc., but in most settlements the ratio was fairly equal. (It has been estimated that just before the American invasion from 45% to 50% of New Mexicans were under sixteen years of age.)

The mutual assistance tradition known as *peonada* (from *peón*, worker) was common among farmers and rancheros in N.M. For example, when spring came around and many hands were needed to clean out irrigation ditches everyone was expected to pitch in. When harvest time demanded intensive labor a farmer would alert his neighbors who sent available *peones* (workers) to help until the harvest was in. The farmer then reciprocated by providing workers when his neighbors needed them.

Most villages had at least one patriarch referred to as *"patrón"* as a sign of personal respect. The patrón was generally among the wealthiest citizens in the village (though it wasn't necessary to have been born to wealth). The patriarch provided jobs for ordinary people, whether it be herding sheep, working in a trading post or weaving shop, financing a cibolero hunt, working orchards and/or farm lands, taking trade goods to southern markets, etc. He would often loan money or goods to family and friends. The patriarch generally lived in a large house (sometimes containing a dozen rooms) filled with much quality furniture and often many santos, owned large amounts of agricultural land, storehouses for agricultural products, much livestock, etc., and he often supplied funding for purchase of necessary items for village fiestas/holidays. [See Note # 32.]

When it came to recreation the dance was still the most popular of social gatherings and the happiest way to celebrate an event. The highly accomplished Rafael Chacón wrote in his autobiography: *"During the entertainment no one had quarrels or fights, all had respect for their betters and consideration for their equals. Before the arrival of the Americans...the people lived simply and very contentedly."*

While physical isolation from the rest of the Hispanic world was still a fact of life, professional troops of *maromeros* (rope walkers, acrobats, actors, musicians, etc.) traveled north from Mexico to entertain New Mexican villagers. They also introduced new dances such as the quadrille, the *contradanza*, and variations of the waltz.

Horse racing, bullfighting and cockfighting were popular. New Mexicans continued to be described by visitors as among the best horsemen in the world.

In literary spheres New Mexicans were passionate over verbal skills like oratory and poetry. Extemporaneous poets known as *trobadores*, men and women who could improvise rhymed verse, were popular throughout N.M. and lionized, especially at social gatherings. Lauded by their society, these poets also composed and excelled in:

adivinanzas (guessing word games);

alabados (religious hymns and chants especially popular with the Penitente Brotherhood and religious gatherings);

autos (short plays on religious themes);

canciones (songs, the most popular of all forms);

coplas (poetry in the form of a four-line stanza);

corridos (narrative ballads descended from romances);

cuandos (accounts of adventures like buffalo hunting, always starting with "when");

cuentos (short stories);

decimas (popular poetry structured in an introductory quatrain called a *planta*, then followed by four 10 line stanzas, each of which ends with a line from the planta, respectively);

dichos (sayings, proverbs);

folk theater;

inditas (witty and amusing variants of corrido forms, characterized by dancing between sung verses and the use of drums and Native American Indian rhythmic patterns; among others, sheepherders often composed inditas);

love poetry;

romances (narratives sung to a catchy melody; one of the oldest New Mexican romances is *La Aparición*, "The Apparition," which tells about a bereaved husband's encounter with his wife's ghost who counsels him that he must adjust, find a good wife and seek happiness).

Among the many famous *trobadores* are Tomás Quintana, Juan Bautista Vigil y Alaríd, Antonio Martínez, Juana Marchanta, Vicente Maestas, Jesús María Gonzáles, J.B. Vigil y Alaríd, etc.

After years of threatening rumors that the USA was planning to invade NM and take the land from Mexico, the invasion finally materialized in 1846. New Mexico would be changed for all time.

DISCUSSION Notes *for* NEW MEXICAN SOCIETY

Note # 1
St. Augustine Florida, founded in 1565, was a garrisoned settlement, not a colony.

Note # 2
It must be pointed out that the Lummis narratives have often been dismissed as *"adulatory,"* *"laudatory,"* etc., by many writers using the English language, supposed mere "promotion of the Southwest for tourism" and such. One things is certain: Lummis did not fit into the "Black Legend" or "Tree of Hate" school of writers.

Note # 3
Stewart Udall writes in *The Forgotten Founders: Rethinking The History Of The Old West* that genuine American pioneers are usually ignored in favor of "celebrity" fantasy, in the case of the West, gunmen and/or outlaws. As usual, the venerable Stewart Udall promotes a sane approach to the writing of History.

Note # 4
It is a popular misconception that Spanish women didn't colonize new lands with their men. H.H. Bancroft states that in the NM colony there were some *"...400 men, 130 of whom were accompanied by their families."* Yet D.J. Boorstin and B.M. Kelley wrote in their popular classroom textbook *A History Of The United States*: "Nearly all" Spaniards who came to the Americas were males. *"Unmarried girls"* weren't *"allowed to come to America alone"* so Spanish settlers *"married Indian women."* The Spanish government understood that the basic unit of any society was the family. A married man was required to bring his wife with him or post a bond until he did so. Human personality being what it is, there is little doubt that people on the frontier "mixed" with people already there. This includes English, Scotch, Irish, German, etc., as well as Spanish, though some writers promote "mixing" with the latter while ignoring the same with the former.

Note # 5

It has been promoted that among the punishments against 21 Acoma rebels was to have a foot cut off and much has been made of this "cruelty" by various writers. According to primary researcher Dr. Eloy Gallegos, the order had to do with cutting *puntas de pies*, toes, not feet. Translation from Spanish into English is an obvious pitfall when writing about the colonial Southwest. Further, the fact of the matter is that after the Acoma war not a single observer of the time ever recorded that he saw a "footless" Acoma anywhere in New Mexico. The sentence was probably intended to prevent further uprisings but it is likely that it was never carried out because its victims would have been noticed and remarked on by writers of the day. It would certainly have been emphasized by Oñate's enemies. Furthermore, many Acomas had been sentenced to 20 years of servitude but by 1604 Acoma village was reestablished. If the 20 year sentence wasn't enforced it is quite likely the same happened with the dismemberments. John Kessell and his Vargas Project researchers have stated that an order to cut off feet has never been found, despite their efforts. Hammond and Rey say the order to cut off "feet" was carried out.

Note # 6

The responsibility of the Spanish government to introduce Christianity and the opportunity for Everlasting Salvation to the Indians was no pretense. That responsibility was considered basic to all Hispanic colonization.

Note # 7

See *Kiva, Cross, And Crown* by John Kessell.

Note # 8

See *The Protector De Indios In Colonial New Mexico, 1659-1821* by Charles R. Cutter.

Note # 9

The slaughter of August 10, 1680, is promoted by most English language writers as "The Pueblo Revolt" and has also been described as "The first American Revolution!" or "A blow for religious freedom!," etc.. There were a number of Indian uprisings on the east coast before 1680 so the tragedy in NM couldn't be "the first American Revolution." Further, Spanish language sources refer to it as "*el Día de San Lorenzo*," which I translate as "The St. Lawrence Day Massacre" to convey more accurately the essence of the bloody, unexpected uprising in which 3 out of 4 fatalities were ordinary women and children. Some writers like Paul Horgan and J. Manuel Espinosa have used "massacred" when referring to those slain in the surprise uprising.

Note # 10

See *Land Grants And Lawsuits In Northern New Mexico* by Malcolm Ebright.

Note # 11

The best study on Vargas and his era is the monumental *Journals Of Don Diego De Vargas* researched by John Kessell, Meredith D. Dodge, Rick Hendricks.

Note # 12

See *New Mexico's Royal Road: Trade And Travel On The Chihuahua Trail* by Max L. Moorhead.

Note # 13

See *Santos And Saints* by Thomas J. Steele, S.J.

Note # 14
See the essay "Miguel de Quintana: An Eighteenth-Century New Mexico Poet Laureate" by Clark Colahan and Francisco A. Lomelí in *PASO POR AQUI*, edited by Erlinda Gonzales-Berry.

Note # 15
See *New Mexico: A Brief Multi-history* by Rubén Sálaz Márquez.

Note # 16
See *The Mustangs* by J. Frank Dobie.

Note # 17
See *A History Of New Mexican-plains Indian Relations* by C.L. Kenner who remarks in "The Ciboleros" chapter: *"It was wonderful to be a successful cibolero."*

Note # 18
Robert M Denhardt, author of *The Horse Of The Americas* says of the New Mexicans: *"They were one of the greatest horse people of the 17th and 18th centuries, their only competitors being the Arabs and Comanches. So devoted were the vaqueros of Nuevo Mexico to equestrian exercise that they were termed 'a race of centaurs' by contemporary observers."*

Note # 19
See *Without Noise Of Arms: The 1776 Domínguez-Escalante Search For A Route From Santa Fe To Monterey* by Walter Briggs.

Note # 20
See *Pedro Vial And The Roads To Santa Fe* by Noel M. Loomis and Abraham R. Nasatir.

Note # 21
See *The Hispano Homeland* by R.L. Nostrand.

Note # 22
See *New Mexican Furniture, 1600-1940* by Lonn Taylor and Dessa Bokides.

Note # 23
A case might be made that Manuel Simon Escudero is the "Father of the Santa Fe Trade," an honor usually accorded to Frenchman Charles Becknell because it is said he was the first to use wagons instead of pack animals. Escudero is definitely the personality who led the way to significant trade on the Trail.

Note # 24
Antonio Barreiro's criticism was typical of many visitors to the isolated frontier province which was undoubtedly quite a contrast to society in large urban centers to the south. Few visitors weighed the frontier factor, even though they were aware of realities like Indian hostilities/depredations.

Note # 25
See *Rebellion On The Río Arriba, 1837* by Janet Lecompte.

Note # 26
See *Matt Field On The Santa Fe Trail* by J.E. Sunder, ed.

Note # 27
See *Hermanos De La Luz / Brothers Of Light* by Ray John de Aragón for a good collection of

alabados.
Note # 28
See *Santos And Saints* by Fr. Thomas J. Steele, S.J.
Note # 29
See *Brothers Of Light, Brothers Of Blood* by Marta Weigle. According to Ms. Weigle there is no substantiated evidence that nails have ever been used in the crucifixion.
Note # 30
Kendall vilifies Governor Armijo, asserting that it was Manuel Armijo who secretly fomented the rebellion of 1837 for his own advantage. Kendall further states that Armijo went to the rebel camp to claim the governorship but they ignored him because he hadn't been active in the fighting. When Armijo routs the rebels at the battle at Pojoaque, Kendall writes that Armijo ordered the execution of the leaders *"…more to prevent disclosures than for any crime they had committed."* Armijo sentenced to death *"…many of the persons who had aided him with money and arms…and caused many others to be privately assassinated."* One can only wonder as to how he acquired all this information while being marched to Mexico City. Kendall's diatribe is worthless as history, as are many other publications of the time. The story of Armijo's complicity in the rebellion of 1837 exists only in the writings of Kendall, Josiah Gregg, and W.W.H. Davis, who are the principal vilifiers of Governor Armijo. The vilification has been perpetuated by many historiographers.

Other writers have provided their viewpoints on the Texan-Santa Fe Expedition:

♦ *"They were simply armed invaders, who might expect to be attacked, and if defeated, to be treated by the Mexicans as rebels, or at best--since Texan belligerency and independence had been recognized by several nations--as prisoners of war,"* writes H.H. Bancroft

♦ *"The evidence is overwhelming that the Texan-Santa Fe expedition was intended only as a trading venture"* but that if the people of N.M. wanted to be a part of Texas as had been reported an attempt would be made to take over the area, writes W.A. Beck, who adds that Governor Armijo used the situation to refortify his waning popularity.

♦ Noel M. Loomis wrote a book called *The Texan-Santa Fe Pioneers*, published by the University of Oklahoma Press.

Note # 31
Dr. David Weber contrasts this with *"American or British women who lost control over their property as well as their legal identity upon marriage"* in his *The Mexican Frontier, 1821-1846: The American Southwest Under Mexico.*
Note # 32
See *Land, Water, And Culture: New Perspectives On Hispanic Land Grants* by Charles L. Briggs and John R. Van Ness.

TEJANO SOCIETY: SAN ANTONIO DE BEJAR

Governor **Martín de Alarcón** officially founded the "*Villa de Béxar*" (also spelled *Béjar*) on May 5, 1718, on a site by San Pedro Creek about three quarters of a league from the San Antonio River. While paper titles were not executed, Alarcón's colonists were granted "…lands, pastures, water, woods…" for their use and land titles were perfected by settler possession and labor. The Tejano pioneers cleared their lands and planted crops immediately but rodents destroyed them before harvest time. Irrigation proved troublesome so in January of 1719 the colonists began work on *acequias*, irrigation ditches, with which to water agricultural fields belonging to the settlers as well as the mission San Antonio de Valero. (By the end of the century the presidio San Antonio de Béxar, the town San Fernando de Béxar, and the secularized mission San Antonio de Valero were basically the community referred to in this section as "*San Antonio*.") Among these early colonists were families named Barrera, Carvajal, Castro, Chirino (Quirino), De La Garza, Flores, Galván, Guerra, Hernández, Maldonado, Menchaca, Sosa, Pérez, Valdés, Ximenes. [See Note # 1. *Notes begin on page 179.*]

TEJANO FRONTIER

As with most frontier communities, pioneering soldier-settlers of San Antonio had to perform unceasing labor to create homes in the wilderness as well as contend with hostile Indians. In the latter case the hostiles were Lipan Apaches who in 1720 attacked two settlers looking for their missing horses. The Lipan groups planted crops in the spring then hunted the buffalo in autumn and winter but the larger Comanche groups were quickly dominating Apache territories and taking the land for themselves. The semi-sedentary Apaches were targeted by advancing warrior Comanche bands so the former had to survive as best they could, which included raiding Spanish settlements. Apache hostilities began in 1720 and lasted until 1726 when the Hispanic population was estimated at 200. In 1722 new Governor **San Miguel de Aguayo** (Joseph Ramón de Azlor) reinforced San Antonio with more than twenty soldiers, the presidio then having some 54 stalwarts with whom to protect the community. Also in 1722 Fray **Antonio Margil de Jesús**, leader of the missionaries (from Zacatecas), petitioned the Governor for permission to construct a new mission for Indians living in central Texas. When permission was granted the mission was named *San José y San Miguel de Aguayo*. In 1723 Captain **Nicolás Flores y Valdez** led a force of soldiers and mission Indians on a two-month expedition which punished Apache raiders: 30 raiders were killed, 20 women and children were captured, and more than 120 horses were reclaimed. Missionaries protested that military attacks would not accomplish as much as gentler strategies so a planned military expedition for 1725 was abandoned. This substantiates that efforts to bring Christianity to Native Americans were not mere propaganda and missionizing was basic to Tejano society. By 1727 when Inspector General **Pedro de Rivera** arrived to inspect presidial defenses a discernible stability was apparent in the San Antonio area.

PIONEERS

Among the first colonizers, soldiers, and later 18th century settlers of the San Antonio area were individuals/families like the following (an "M" abbreviates *María*, a "J" for *José*; many names can have alternate spellings; most people carried the names of both father and mother):

A:

Amangual, Francisco; Armas, Ignacio; Armas, Martín Lorenzo; Arocha, Fernando; Arocha, Francisco José de (had 15 children with wife Ana Curbelo);

B:

Banul, Juan; Bethencourt, Maria Robaina de; Bueno de Rojas, Joseph; Bustillo y Zevallos, Antonio;

C:

Cabrera, Ana; Cabrera, José; Cabrera, Marcos; Cabrera, María; Cadena, Joseph; Cantú José; Cantún, Juan; Carbajal, Bernabé de; Carvajal, Feliciana de; Carvajal, Manuel de; Carvajal, M. Concepción de; Carvajal, Manuel de;

Carbajal, Mateo; Carvajal, Ignacio de; Castro, Joseph (with wife & daughter); Castro, Lucas (with wife & son); Castro, Marcos de; Charo, Francisco Luis; Chirino (Quirino), Lázaro; Córdova, Cristóbal de;

Córdova, Juan José; Cortinas, Juan; Curbelo, Joseph Antonio; Curbelo, Juan; Curbelo, Juana; Curbelo, M. Ana; Curbelo, Rafaela

D:

Decal y Musquiz, Francisco;

De la Garza;

Delgado, Francisco;

Delgado, Lucas;

Delgado, Juan;

De Niz, Josefa;

De Niz, Manuel;

De Niz, Sebastiana;

Durán, Luis Antonio;

E:

Esparza, José M.

Estrada, Francisco de;

Estrada, M. Concepción de;

F:

Falcón, Josefa;

Flores, Antonio;

Flores (de Abrego), Domingo;

Flores, Gerónimo;

Flores, Pedro;

Flores, Gertrudis;

Flores, Francisco;

Flores, Josepha;

Flores, Juan;

Flores, Miguel;

Flores, Rita;

Flores y Valdés, Capitán Nicolás;

Flores y Valdés, M. Josefa;

Flores y Valdés, Rosalía;

Fuente, Joseph de la;

Fuentes, Fr. Pedro

G:

Galindo, Joseph;

Galván;

Garza, Juliana de la;

Garza, Rafaela de la;

Gonzales, Domingo

Gonzales de Ynclán, Ignacio;

Gracia, María;

Granado, Juan Francisco;

Granado, Paula;

Granado, Pedro;

Guadalupe, Asencio

Guerra, Antonio;

Guerra, Gertrudis;

Guerra, Rosa;

Guerrero, M. Luisa;

H:

Henríquez, Diego Irineo;

Hernández, Brígida;

Hernández, Clemencia;

Hernández, Lucía (Catarina)

Hernández, Plácido
Huizar (Guizar), Pedro
L:
Leal, Catarina;
Leal, Joseph;
Leal Goraz, Juan;
Leal Goraz Jr., Juan;
Leal, Mariana;
López, Alberto;
M:
Maldonado, Joseph (and family);
Martines, Rosalía;
Martínez, José;
Medina, Juan Antonio de;
Menchaca, Diego;
Menchaca, Francisco;
Menchaca, José Félix;
Menchaca, Joseph;
Menchaca, Joseph Antonio;
Menchaca, Luis Antonio;
Menchaca, Luis Mariano;
Montemayor, Joseph de;
Montes, Plácido;
Montes, Rosalía;
Montes de Oca, Joseph
Morales, Alberto;
Muñoz, Ponciano;
N:
Nis (Niz), Manuel de (see also De Niz);
Navarro, Angel;
Nuñez Morillo, M. Ignacia;
Nuñez Morillo, Miguel;
O:
Olivarri, José;
Olivarri, Plácido;
P:
Padrón, Joseph;
Padrón, Juan Joseph;
Padrón, Juana Francisca;
Peres (Casanova), Joseph Antonio;

Peres (Casanova), Phelipe;
Peres, Cayetano;
Peres, Xavier;
Pérez Cabrera, María;
Pérez, Ignacio;
Pérez, Joseph;
Pérez, Joseph Antonio;
Pérez, Juan Ignacio ("Colonel Pérez")
Pérez, Phelipe;
Prudhomme y Umpierre, Gracia;
R:
Ramón, Antonia;
Ramón, Diego;
Ramón, Domingo;
Ramón, Teresa;
Rincón, Florencia;
Río, Marcelino del;
Rodríguez, J. Antonio;
Rodríguez Mederos, Antonio;
Rodríguez Granado, Juan;
Rodríguez, Isabel;
Rodríguez, Rosalia;
Rodríguez, Salvador;
Rojas, Juan José Bueno de;
Ruiz;
S:
Salinas, José María;
Sanabria, M. Francisca;
Sánchez, Gertrudis;
Sánchez Navarro, Josefa;
Sánchez Navarro, Teresa;
Santos, Ana de los;
Santos, Antonio de los;
Santos Coy, Cristóbal de los;
Sartuche, Juan ("the *Alférez of Texas*")
Saucedo, Antonio Martín;
Saucedo, Marcial (and wife);
Seguín, Bartólo;
Suárez de Longoria, María
T:

Travieso, Tomas;
Travieso, Vicente Álvarez;
Treviño, Manuela;
U:
Urrutia, Ignacio;
Urrutia, Juana de;
Urrutia, M. Luisa de;
Urrutia, Toribio;
V:
Valdés, Marcelo;
Valdez, Lt. Juan;
Vidales, Antonia;
Valle, José del;
Veramendi, Fernando de;
X:
Xavier, Francisco;

Ximenes Valdez, Ana María;
Ximenes, Antonio;
Ximenes, Diego Santiago;
Ximenes, María A.;
Ximenes, Nicolasa;
Ximenes, Teresa;
Ximenes Valdez, Diego;
Y:
Yturri;
Z:
Zambrano;
Zapopa, María;
Zerda, José Feliciano de la;
Zerda, Gertrudis de la;
Zimenes (Ximenes, Jiménez), Nicolasa.
[See Note # 2.]

MISSIONS & RAIDERS

Indian raids broke out again in 1731 and were major problems until about 1749. Raiders targeted horses but they would take other livestock, metal goods, guns and ammunition to use against the encroaching Comanches, etc., if they could. San Antonio de Béxar and its five missions populated basically by Coahuiltecan Indian groups who had been past Apache enemies, were major targets. Unlike most other European pioneers in the Americas, even the Apaches had champions like Fray **Benito Fernández de Santa Ana**, who wanted a mission established for them. In 1745 Captain **Toribio de Urrutia** led a spring campaign against the hostiles for which the Apaches retaliated. Tejano life seemed to be one of raid and counter raid.

CANARY ISLANDERS

In the midst of hostile raiders the Tejano community had to make other adjustments. In 1731 the East Texas missions and all their personnel were relocated to the San Antonio area. Further, on March 9, 1731, colonists from the Canary Islands founded the town of *San Fernando de Béxar* next to the presidio by permission of Captain **Juan Antonio Pérez de Almazán.** The expanding community now had identifiable groups of missionaries, military personnel, established civilian settlers (around 25 families), and the new Canary Islanders (*Isleños*; said to be comprised of 14 or 15 families, some 55 people). Despite frontier dangers, these disparate groups bickered and feuded with each other, and it has been written that Isleños were especially combative. [See Note # 3.]

FRONTIER STRATEGIES

Indian affairs were complex. Missionaries wanted to use humane methods to win them over while military personnel had to rely on defensive or offensive measures to protect the community. Making peace with one band of Apaches wasn't binding on the numerous others. In 1748 Captain Urrutia tried a new strategy: during retaliatory expeditions his soldiers were instructed to take as many captives as possible and would be kept in Béxar until chieftains made efforts to repatriate them. Once in town, chieftains were treated like visiting dignitaries and convinced that all captives had received good treatment, that the benefits of peace were much better than constant war. Apache leaders saw Tejanos as potential allies against the Comanches so perhaps peace was a good thing all around.

The Apache peace brought another problem: Apaches had always warred against the Hasinai (in which groups were the *Tejas* or Cenis Indians) of eastern Texas, Tonkawa of central Texas, as well as the Comanches (all referred to collectively as *Norteño* Indians). The Norteños took note of what they perceived as a Tejano alliance with their enemies, the Apaches, so Norteños took to attacking Tejanos as of 1758. Settlers were now caught in the middle: no matter where they turned, they were exposed to raids from dissident Apaches or Norteños. Outlying ranches were attacked, ranchers killed (causing abandonment of the land until peace could be reestablished), horses were taken, livestock slaughtered, causing Bexareños to accuse government officials of indifference to their very serious problems. Defense of their community thus became at least a part time occupation for all Tejanos. [See Note # 4.]

FAMILY

The basic social unit in Béxar was the family consisting of husband, wife, and children. As with all Spanish planning regarding settlements, the family unit was the essential aspect of society. Soldiers brought their wives and children to Béxar as soon as possible. Between 1720-1724 eight daughters of Béxar residents married soldiers from the presidio. For example, **Cristóbal Carabajal** and his wife **Juana Guerra** had three daughters and two of them married soldiers. Four widows married soldiers during those same years. By 1730 there were some 40 married couples in the settlement, perhaps 22 of them had married locally. Unlike many frontier areas, the ratio of men to women was fairly close so the pattern of marriage was established quickly in Béxar. Neither did widows nor widowers stay single for long.

Infant mortality was high. Losing half of all children born was not rare. For example, **José Cantú** and his wife **Florencia Rincón** had ten children between 1750-70 and only two lived beyond their second birthday. A total of 929 legitimate births were recorded between 1719 through 1760 and there were recorded 168 burials for children under ten. Illegitimacy was not prevalent: of the 442 recorded births between 1733-1761, only 31 were labeled illegitimate. (One widow, referred to as "*La Vieja*," gave birth to five.) Fifteen of the 31 were identified as coming from "mixed bloods," the rest from "Spanish" parents.

FRONTIER LEVELING

The San Antonio frontier became a racially mixed area by the end of the 18th century. The European caste system, while still a factor in some minds, didn't work on a frontier dangerous and demanding. Indian raids and isolation tended to make people work together because, simply put, they needed each other for defense. While there were a few people born in Spain, most Tejanos were American born. Marriage partners often came from outside one's own group and it appears marriage was more attractive than living single because there was no mate "of equal stature." So in time the Bexareños mixed with each other and tended to claim most groups as their own, often winding up labeling themselves "*español.*" When people became angry with someone there could be heard "epithets" like *mulato* (European-African mixture), *mestizo* (European-Indian), *coyote* (mestizo-Indian), *lobo* (Indian-African). "Negro" seems to have been used rarely (until late in the century) and was usually associated with slavery. Racial identities tended toward working to be considered "*español*" because it held the highest advantages. For example, in 1751 the penalty for slaughtering cattle outside of certain areas was 25 pesos for *Españoles* but 200 lashes for mixed bloods. Racial mobility seemed to be accepted, especially if an individual became respected in his/her community. Sculptor **Pedro Huizar** (Guizar?) arrived in Bexar in the 1770s, sculpted various items for Mission San José, earned respect as an able carpenter, worked as a land surveyor, etc. In the 1779 census he was listed as a *mulato* but by 1793 he was designated as "*español.*" [See Note # 5.]

RELIGIOUS LEVELING

Tejano society also tended to be leveled by religious practices. Religious obligations were for everyone, whether born high or low, so when in 1738 a new church had to be built, the Isleños in control of the government were more than willing to ask for help from the entire community. Soldiers from the presidio and ordinary citizens contributed money and labor for the church. Retired soldier **Miguel Núñez Morillo** led the way with a contribution of thirty pesos. The work progressed as finances permitted but the church was only half complete by 1745 when an exasperated Alcalde **Antonio Rodríguez Mederos** called on all citizens, caste status not being taken into consideration, to contribute or be fined twenty-five pesos plus a fifteen day jail term. Despite such efforts, the project wasn't completed until around 1755 but when finally accomplished it was a victory for the entire community. Our Lady of Guadalupe was selected as patroness. Organized religious feasts now gained renewed community popularity and celebrations were soon being held for Our Lady of Guadalupe, San Fernando Rey de España, Our Lady of Candlemas, St. Anthony of Padua, the Immaculate Conception, Corpus Christi, etc. Since there were no religious brotherhoods (*cofradías*), the Cabildo selected captains and assistants, whose main function was to pay all expenses, to handle the feast days. Among the paladin captains was **Juan José Montes de Oca** who sponsored the Feast of San Fernando for over ten years beginning in 1761. December became the most festive month for the San Antonio community. Aside from the religious celebrations, bullfights and equestrian games/activities were held in the plazas during the day then everyone attended dances at night.

EXTENDED FAMILY TIES

Another aspect of the community influence was the practice of *compadrazgo* (*padrino/madrina*; sponsors; co-parent relationships: *compadre/comadre*) The rituals of Baptism, Confirmation, and Holy Matrimony required sponsors who in turn became closer to family because of the honors and obligations involved. For example, when godparents (*padrinos*) baptized a child they could be expected to raise and educate the child if the biological parents died. Most "*compadre*" and "*comadre*" sponsors were carefully selected from the same social class though on a few occasions higher station individuals were asked to stand as witness to these important ceremonies.

LAND, FARMING & RANCHING

Land ownership is crucial to every community. In frontier San Antonio grants of land were made for home sites, whether a rude jacal or built of adobe or stone, but also to include a corral and garden. The size of lots varied from 2400 to 6400 square varas. Once the era of Isleños land monopoly passed (certainly by 1750), land was awarded very democratically, to pioneering residents as well as newcomers, to rich and poor, young and old, male or female. Home construction was basically rudimentary for most of the century and even stone houses were only valued at between 200 to 500 pesos, though the **Fernando de Veramendi** "Palace" home cost some 1,880 pesos to build. While the architecture of San Antonio was often criticized by visitors (like Nicolás Lafora, Father Agustin Morfi, etc.), the pioneers' gardens, orchards, even their lands growing corn or sugar cane, must have been pleasing to the eye.

Farmland was adjacent to the village and its value depended on the availability of water. The first acequias were dug out by soldiers and a few Indians. The work was subsidized by the Governor. When the Canary Island settlers arrived they were given lands which had been developed by presidio soldiers. The land and water (twenty-four hours of irrigation) apportioned to each Isleño family was valued at around 200 pesos. The Islanders demanded that land boundaries and water rights be specified legally, the absence of which caused much dissension in the community. By 1745 there were some 49 non-Islander families in Béxar and only four owned agricultural land, which they had purchased from the Isleños. The former banded together to demand their shares of land and water but it wasn't until 1776 that things began to improve.

Subsistence farming and capturing wild livestock were basic to the development of San Antonio. Corn was the basic grain, preferred over wheat, because it grew much better, produced greater yields, and could be utilized in more ways even before it was completely ripe, as in "milk corn." [See Note # 6.] The farming year began in January-February with the mending of fences and cleaning out irrigation ditches. March saw the planting of corn, beans, peppers, sugarcane, which generally could be grown without having to irrigate. March-April saw the planting of vegetable gardens. In May-June were planted late corn and beans. June-July brought the first harvest of corn, peppers, and beans, then the rest of the summer and fall brought in the vegetables. While this was going on the Bexareños were collecting their cattle for the September cattle drive to Saltillo. Late crops like potatoes, cotton, beans were harvested in November and late corn in December-January.

The "hacienda" didn't develop in Texas as it did in other areas of Mexico. The Tejano "rancho" was generally a farm with a house or small group of houses on it. While the 1759 rancho of **Luis Menchaca** contained some 65,000 acres, most ranchos weren't particularly large. The factors impeding development of ranching as a industry were hostile Indians, conflicting claims to the land, and the uncertainties of going to faraway courts to settle disputes. Indians were battled as necessary and 18th century Tejanos learned to settle their land disputes through compromise, which tended to solidify community.

Tejano ranches were in the San Antonio area at least by 1750 and some Tejanos owned horses, cattle, mules, (*ganado mayor*) and sheep numbering in the thousands. Large cattle drives in the 1770s were directed to Louisiana as well as the Río Grande settlements, Coahuila, and the September fair in Saltillo. Furthermore, the harvesting of wild cattle for meat and other related products (soap, candles, soldiers' leather doublets called *cueras*, and shields called *adargas*) was large enough for export to as far south as Saltillo. Arrieros took mule trains laden with *charquí* (jerky; dried beef), hides, tallow for candles, pecans, etc., and returned with wheat flour, chocolate, textiles, ironware, etc. Among the Bexareños who developed commercial proclivities were the families Arocha, Travieso, Menchaca, Zambrano.

CATTLE & HORSES

It soon became apparent that wild cattle were not an inexhaustible resource and by 1751 Alcalde **José Padrón** issued an ordinance forbidding the slaughter of wild cattle within an eighty mile radius of San Antonio. There also developed acrimonious relations between settlers and missionaries, each group claiming ownership of unbranded as well as wild cattle. Rancheros declared the animals were descended from those brought by their blood ancestors and the missionaries countered that the religious developed the first ranches in the area so the animals rightfully belonged to them. When Commandant General **Teodoro de Croix** arrived in Béxar in 1778 he "settled" the matter by asserting that all wild or unbranded stock belonged to the *Crown*. He ordered stiff fines for anyone slaughtering unbranded stock and required that a license must be bought in order to export cattle and a half-peso tax paid for each exported animal. Lawsuits were filed but it only delayed the inevitable until 1795 when Croix's ordinance was made into law. Henceforth anyone killing wild cattle without a license could be fined four pesos for the first offense, eight pesos for the second.

Despite the conflicts, cattle ranching was developing into a major industry. Between the years 1779-1786 there were 68 (legal) drives involving some 18,000 head of cattle, for which the half-peso tax was paid, to neighboring provinces like Coahuila and Nuevo Santander. By the 1790s wild cattle became more scarce and measures were taken to grow their numbers.

Raising horses also became an important, though secondary, adjunct to ranching. An impediment to obtaining sufficient numbers of horses was horse raids conducted by hostile Indians who depleted the supply. The military market for horses remained stable throughout the 18th century because soldiers had to have mounts. Large numbers of horses were being purchased in Nuevo Santander by 1780. Wild horse roundups were common at least by 1784 when more than four hundred animals were captured.

Sheep and goats were apparently of lesser importance in the San Antonio area during the 18th century. In the 1760s the missions owned some 5,000 head of sheep. In 1779 **Luis Antonio Menchaca** owned around 1500 sheep and goats but in general it appears Bexareños were more interested in cattle and horses than *ganado menor*.

LABOR

The labor supply in 18th century San Antonio fluctuated from scarcity to plentiful. At first mission Indians were employed as laborers but this ended in 1745 when missionaries protested. Laws were enacted requiring all able-bodied men to have some sort of employment, whether it be as servants (*sirvientes*), hands (*mozos*), field laborers (*campistas*), or day laborers (*jornaleros*). Typically, manual laborers were paid a minimum wage of a quarter peso (*dos reales*) per day. This was quite a contrast from men who worked livestock. In 1735 one **Matías Treviño** earned three reales per day, two *almudes* of corn per week, and a horse from each rancher who hired him, for a total of around thirteen pesos per month. By the 1770s a daily wage of one peso per day was an accepted standard for roundups and/or cattle drives.

Rancheros and their sons often did much of the work on their ranches. Rancheros also helped their neighbors during peak seasons and most cattle drives included animals from a number of ranchers as a cost saving device. In true democratic fashion, the owner, his sons or other blood family relatives, worked alongside hired vaqueros whether they were mission Indians or mixed bloods. In 1779 a full third of all men hiring themselves out to do ranch or agricultural work in San Antonio were *Españoles*. [See Note # 7.]

To a degree, slave labor also existed in San Antonio. Captured young Indian boys and girls (*criados*, literally "brought up;" domestics raised in a family setting) were often baptized, raised alongside blood family members, and used for work. People from various ethnic/racial groups could work as servants. This included people categorized as Spanish, mulatto, Indian, or mestizo. African and mulatto slaves were a minor part of life in Béxar. In 1777 there were fifteen slaves in the area, the same number as in 1796.

FIRST TEXAS HISTORY

Father **Juan Agustín Morfi**, a Franciscan, wrote *History Of Texas, 1673-1779* upon returning to Mexico. He wrote positively concerning the work of missionaries in Texas but was generally critical of most civil and military authorities and their soldiers. Despite the negative bias, Father Morfi provided valuable historical insights into life in Texas missions, presidios, and villages, along with information on Texas Indian groups. (Today Father Juan Agustín Morfi is considered the "Father of Texas History.")

MILITARY SERVICE

Service in the Military became more popular toward the end of the 18th century. When San Antonio was founded there was a real shortage of military personnel but as the civilian population grew the Military became attractive to those who weren't interested in ranching or farming. In the 1770s a soldier's annual pay was around 400 pesos (though this was reduced in 1729 and hit the low of 290 pesos by 1772). By the last quarter of the century the Military was San Antonio's principal employer. Military life differed little from the civilian on the frontier. Married soldiers generally lived in town, acquired house lots, raised gardens. Construction work relating to the presidio was generally assigned to soldiers. Soldiers guarding a horse herd had to know how to deal with stock. Those escorting caravans had to have skills of muleteers when circumstances demanded. Defending the town or campaigning against raiders was usually a joint military and civilian undertaking.

While the Military, ranching, and farming industries were filled mostly by local people, craftsmen generally emanated from other areas like French Louisiana, Spain, France, as well as Mexico. A carpenter named Francisco Guadalupe Calaorra was from Ireland. Another well known carpenter and practical surgeon, Juan Jupier, was from France, as was the blacksmith Juan Banul. The tailor José Lambremon was from New Orleans. The blacksmith Marcos Ruiz was from Querétaro. Juan Leal was one of the few native blacksmiths in San Antonio.

FREIGHTING

Arrieros (muleteers) were the brave transporters of all kinds of goods through the use of mules. Freighting on the frontier was a dangerous occupation. In 1770 four arrieros were killed by hostile Indians and mules themselves were highly prized by raiders. Freighting charges were therefore high (considering the place and time) and, among other things like Indian hostilities, the poor quality of goods, inflated prices and excessive profits due to monopolies, etc., this impeded San Antonio's commercial activity to the degree that full time merchants didn't appear until the 1760s. **Antonio Rodríguez Baca**, born in Béxar, made a name for himself as a merchant to the point that he was elected to be one of the sponsors for the Feast of the Virgin of Guadalupe for 1789. **Marcos Vidal** came in from the south and though he didn't stay long, dealt in brandy, wine, bananas, textiles, chocolate, flour, raisins, and soap, among other things. Other merchants included Santiago Villaseñor, Angel Navarro, Juan Baptista de Isurieta, Manuel Berasadi, José de la Santa, etc., but it is said the most successful was **Fernando Veramendi** from Pamplona, Spain. Born in Pamplona in 1743 or -44, he was in La Bahía (Goliad) by around 1770. He had many business dealings in San Antonio, where he married **María Josefa Granados,** descendant of the Isleño community. He opened a store in San Antonio which specialized in selling cloth and related items, loaned money, and bought land at every opportunity. He was killed by hostile Apaches in Coahuila in 1783.

LEGAL SYSTEM

The Tejano system of justice was the typical Spanish tradition of trial by conciliation. When a dispute landed in court each party selected an honorable, respected person to represent each litigant. These *hombres buenos* considered the case with the alcalde then rendered a decision which they believed fair to both parties. This form of arbitration usually settled the matter but if it didn't the case could be appealed to the Governor himself. (In 1824 Stephen F. Austin created a civil code for his colonists which was basically accepted Tejano legal procedures.) Trial by jury was begun as of 1834 (and the office of *Alcalde* was to evolve into the District Court).

Tejano water law, based on ancient Spanish law and custom, decreed that everyone in society owned water and its sources. Land units lacking water could be very large but each land owner was entitled to an equal share of necessary water, a concept that included Indian rights to water. No private individual or entity could own any water source.

By the end of the 18th century the Tejanos of San Antonio had all become *vecinos*, citizens of Texas who had shared and been forged by family, frontier hardship, celebration, poverty, isolation, religion, fighting, harmony, war and peace, birth and death. [See Note # 8.] These forces molded them into a vibrant community.

THE 19TH CENTURY

The new century brought Tejanos two new, especially significant influences. In 1821 Mexico won its independence from Spain and became a nation on its own. Perhaps the best known Tejano statesman during this period was José Erasmo Seguín. Don José was born (1782) and bred in Béxar where he became an intellectual and political leader. He loved books, collected them along with historical documents, and took many of them with him when he served as Congressman in Mexico City. He encouraged his son, Juan Nepomuceno Seguín, to study and acquire as much knowledge as possible. José Seguín was vitally interested in education, he served in city government as well as Postmaster for Texas. He was generally conservative in his views and his primary concerns were the safety and welfare of his community. When he was representing Texas in Mexico City in 1827 he wrote to his wife back home: *"I haven't much money but I'm not hungry and when I am I will not request help from my province because she exists for us to serve and not to serve us."*

ENGLISH SPEAKING COLONISTS

Stephen F. Austin and his colonists also arrived in Texas in 1821. (English speaking illegal immigrants from the States first came into Texas in 1816 and settled with their slaves at Pecan Point south of the Red River.) The Texas of that year consisted basically of three Tejano areas: the regions of Nacogdoches, the Béxar-Goliad settlements along the San Antonio River, and the ranching areas between the Río Grande and Nueces Rivers. The Austin colony, established in the general area of what came to be called "Washington County," grew like no other Texas community. Among the "**Austin 300**" pioneers would be people like the following [See Note # 9.]

A:

Alcorn, Elijah; Alcorn, James D.; Allen, Martin; Alley, John; Alley, Rawson; Alley, Thomas & William; Alley, William; Alsbery, Charles G.;

Alsbery, Harvey; Alsbery, Horace A.; Alsbery, Thomas; Anderson, Simon Asa; Andrews, John; Andrews, William; Angier, Samuel T.; Austin, John;

Austin, Stephen S.;

B:

Baily, James B.; Barrett, William; Battle, Mills N.; Bayless, Daniel E. Beason, Benjamin; Beard, James; Belknap, Charles; Bell, Josiah H.; Bell, Thomas B.; Berry, Manders; Best, Isaac; Betts, Jacob; Bigham, Francis; Bloodgood, William; Boatwright, Thomas; Borden, Thomas H.; Bostick, Caleb R.; Bowman, John; Bradley, Edward R.; Bradley, John; Bradley, Thomas; Breen, Charles; Bridges, William B.; Bright, David; Brooks, Bluford ; Brotherton, Robert; Brown, John; Brown, William S.; Brown, George; Buckner, Aylett C.; Burnet, Thomas; Burnham, Jesse; Bunson, Enoch; Byrd, Micajah;

C.

Callahan, Morris; Calvit, Alexander; Carpenter, David; Carson, William C.;

Carter, Samuel; Cartwright, Jesse; Cartwright, Thomas; Castleman, Sylvanus; Chance, Samuel; Charles,. Isaac Nidever; Chrisman, Horatio;

Clarke, Anthony R.; Clarke, John C.; Coats, Merit M.; Coles, John P.;

Cook, James; Cooke, John; Cooper, William; Crier, John; Croce, Jared E.;

Crownover, John; Cummins, James; Cummins, William; Cummins, John;

Cummins, Rebecca; Cummins, James; Curtis, Hinton; Curtis, James;

Curtis, James, Sr.;

D:

Davidson, Samuel; Davis, Thomas; Deckro, Daniel; Demos, Peter;

Dewees, Bluford; Dickenson, John; Dillard, Nicholas; Duke, Thomas; Duty, Joseph; Dyer, Clement C.;

E:

Earle, Thomas; Edwards, Gustavus E.; Elam, John; Elder, Robert;

F:

Falmash, Charles; Fenton, David; Fields, John T.; Fisher, James; Fitzgerald, David; Flannekin, Isaiah; Flowers, Elisha; Foster, Isaac; Foster, John; Foster, Randolph; Frazier, James; Fulcher, Churchill;

G:

Garrett, Charles; Gates, Amos; Gates, Samuel; Gates, William; George, Freeman; Gilleland, Daniel; Gilbert, Sarah; Gins, James; Gorbet, Chester S.; Gouldrich, Michael; Grey, Thomas; Groce, Jared E.; Guthrie, Robert;

H:

Hadden, John; Hady, Samuel C.; Hall, John; Hansley, James; Hall, William; Hamilton, David ; Harris, Abner; Harris, David; Harris, John R.; Harris, William; Harris, William J.; Harris, William and P.; Harrison, George; Harvey, William; Haynes, Thos. S.; Hill, George H.; Hodge, Alexander; Holland, William; Holland, Francis; Holliman, Kirchen; Hope, James; Hudson, Charles S.; Huff, George; Huff, John; Hughes, Isaac; Hunter, Eli; Hunter, Johnson;

I:

Ingram, Ira; Ingram, Seth; Irions, John; Isaac, Jackson; Isaacs, Samuel; Iramas, John;

J:

Jackson, Alexander; Jackson, Humphrey; Jameson, Thomas; Johnson, H. W. & Walker; Jones, Henry; Jones, James; Jones, Oliver; Jones, Randall;

K:

Keep, Imla; Keller, John; Kelley, John; Kennedy, Samuel; Kennon, Alfred; Kerr, James; Kew, Peter; Kew, William; Kincheloe, Willi; Kingston, William; Knight, James; Kuykendall, Abner; Kuykendall, Brazillia; Kuykendall, Joseph; Kuykendall, Robert;

L:

Lakey, Joel; Leayne, Hosea H.; Linsay, Benjamin; Little, John; Little, William; Long, Jane H.; Lynch, James; Lynch, Nathaniel;

M:

Marsh, Shubart; Martin, Wyley; Mathis, William; McCloskey, John; McCormick, Arthur; McCormick, David; McCormick, John; McCoy, Thomas; McFarland, Achilles; McFarland, John; McKinney, Thomas F.; McKensie, Hugh; Mclain, A. W.; McNair, James; McNeil, Daniel; McNeil, George W.; McNeil, John; McNeill, John G.; McNeil, Pleasant D.;

Society in the Hispanic Southwest

McNeil, Sterling; McNutt, Elizabeth; McWilliams, William; Milburn, David H.; Miller, Samuel R.; Miller, Samuel; Miller, Simon; Millican, James D.;

Millican, Robert; Millican, William; Mims, Joseph; Mitchell, Asa; Monks, John; Moore John W.; Moore, Luke; Morrison, Moses; Morser, David;

Morton, William;

N:

Nelson, James; Newman, Joseph; Nuckels, M. B.;

O:

Orrick, James;

Osborn, Nathan;

P:

Park, William; Parker, Joshua; Parker, William; Payton, Jonathan C.;

Pennington:, Isaac; Pentecost, George S.; Pettus, Freeman; Pettus, William;

Petty, John; Phelps, James A. E.; Phillips, Isham B.; Phillips, Zeno; Picket, Pamela; Polley, Joseph H.; Powell, Peter; Print, Pleasant; Pryor, William;

Q:

R:

Rabb, Andrew; Rabb, Thomas; Rabb, William; Raleigh, William; Ramey, Lawrence; Randon, David; Randon, John; Rankin, Frederick; Rawls, Amos;

Rawls, Benjamin; Rawls, Daniel; Reels, Patrick; Richardson, Stephen; Roark, Elijah; Robbins, Early; Robbins, William ; Roberts, Andrew;

Roberts, Noel F.; Roberts, William; Robertson, Edward; Robinson, Andrew;

Robinson, George; Ross, James; Rubb, John;

S:

San Pierre, Joseph; Scobey, Robert; Scott, James; Scott, William; Selkirk, William; Shelley, David; Shipman, Daniel; Shipman, Moses; Singleton, Phillip; Singleton, George W.; Sims, Bartlett; Smith, Christian; Smith, Cornelius; Smith, John; Smithers, William; Sojourner, A. L.; Spencer, Nancy; Stafford, Adam; Stafford, William; Stevens, Thomas; Stout, Owen H.; Strange, James Strawsnider, Gabriel; Sutherland, Walter;

T:

Talley, David; Taylor, John D.; Teel, George; Thomas, Ezekiel; Thomas, Jacob; Thompson, Jesse; Tone, Thomas J.; Tong, James F.; Toy, Samuel;

Trobough, John; Tumlinson, Elizabeth; Tumlinson, James;

U:

V:

Van Dorn, Isaac; Varner, Martin; Vince, Allen; Vince, Richard; Vince, Robert; Vince, William;

W:

Walker, James; Wells, Francis F.; Westall, Thomas; White, Walter C.;

Whitesides, Henry & Bouldin.; Whitesides, James; Whiting, Nathaniel;

Williams, John R.; Williams, Samuel M.; Williams, Solomon.

AMERICAN RACISM & SLAVERY

Austin's colonists, as well as those of other empresarios, have been described as representative of the Southern United States. Among other things, this means they brought their black slaves into Texas. Furthermore, the new arrivals soon made it known that they had no interest in blending or assimilating with Tejanos, whom they quickly came to regard as inferior due to miscegenation. [See Note # 10.]

The Mexican Congress began to discuss and contemplate the emancipation of slaves in 1824 and in July Decree No. 412 prohibited forever "the commerce and traffic in slaves in Mexico under any pretense whatever." It also stated that all slaves were free the first time they set foot on Mexican soil. S.F. Austin's colonization contract had not forbidden slavery so Austin protested the emancipation of any slaves, declaring it would do serious damage to his slave owning colonists. J. Erasmo Seguín counseled Austin to work at the State level for demanding slavery at the national level was a losing cause. A compromise was reached: there would be no immediate manumission but henceforth no one in Texas would be born a slave. Additionally, after six months of publication of the Coahuila/Texas constitution there could be no more introduction of slaves to Mexican soil. Austin felt it was a fair resolution.

IMMIGRATION FROM USA

Illegal immigrants from the USA poured into Texas in numbers which astonished Mexican authorities. By 1825 Austin's colony numbered around 1800 and included some 443 slaves, by 1834 there were more than 20,000 American immigrants in Texas (legal and illegal), a number which also included thousands of Africans. Not all immigrants were of the desirable kind. H. Yoakum writes in his *History Of Texas* that by 1823-24 the Austin colony was *"infested by robbers—men who had fled from justice in the United States…"* At first the miscreants were caught and whipped but things got worse and in time those guilty of murder were executed on the spot and their heads set on poles as a warning.

CREATING "THE WEST"

These first English speaking pioneers, who came to refer themselves as *"Texians,"* suffered typical frontier hardships but they also became Texans in the process of learning how to live in this new Tejano environment which would become the basis for "the American West." [See Note # 11.] There was much for the newcomers to learn. For example, the new colonists had no experience with cavalry. When militia companies targeted hostile Indians, as in 1824, they "marched" into combat with a "fifer and two drummers." While modern weaponry was powerful against Indians who didn't have rifles, militiamen on foot couldn't catch mounted Indians. So Texians took to riding horses while chasing hostile Indians.

On the home front the prevalent Tejano ranching lifestyle, quite different from American stockraising as an adjunct to agriculture, was a new experience for these English speaking settlers. They had never used horses as a working platform, the horned saddle was new to them, and they had no experience with wild cattle. Many a new settler tried roping in the Tejano *"da le vuelta"* style but some paid the price by losing their thumbs because they couldn't remove them from between the saddle horn and the rope before it was brutally pulled by the steer on the other end. They quickly took to tying the rope to the saddle horn *before* they roped the steer.

COMPANIA VOLANTE-FLYING SQUADRON

By 1832 Tejano militia squadrons were developing into formidable, highly efficient cavalry along "flying squadron" models. **Carlos de la Garza** was in command of the *Guardia Victoriana* (Victorian Guards) for the Victoria area, Mariano Rodríguez organized the San Fernando Rangers who defended the Béxar area, along with other squadrons led by paladins like **Juan N. Seguín** and **Salvador Flores.** The leader in Nacogdoches was **Vicente Córdova** while south of the Nueces a sixty-man squadron was led by **Enrique Villareal.** [See Note # 12.]

TEXAS RANGERS

Texians were ordered to create militia units for self protection against hostile Indians, which they finally did in 1832. The Texas Rangers were first organized in 1835 but men like Abner Kuykendall, Jack Hays, Ben McCulloch, Henry McCulloch, and Tom Green had already served as Rangers, which group was patterned after the Tejano *"Compañia Volante"* or "Flying Squadron." Rangers were a combination of military and civilian, relatively few in number for reasons of mobility as well as economics, they took a *caballada* ("cavyard") for remounts while in pursuit, and their equipment consisted of a pistol, rifle, knife, reata, Tejano saddle, Tejano blanket tied behind the cantle, and *pinole* ("panoln," parched corn) to eat. Rangers were among the first Texians to become capable riders though it would be decades before they could rival the superb Tejano horsemen, many of whom also served as Rangers. [See Note # 13.]

RACIAL/CULTURAL ANIMOSITIES

Tejanos of the 1830s generally welcomed Texian colonization but there soon developed difficulties and resentment between the two groups. Texians came to be perceived as "crude, rude, and unwashed," brutal slavers who nevertheless considered themselves so superior they contemptuously refused association with Tejanos. Texians looked at Tejanos as products of miscegenation, mongrels and halfbreeds "...*degraded and vile; the unfortunate race of Spaniard, Indian and African, so blended that the worst qualities of each predominate.*" [See Note # 14.]

American racism was alive and well among the characteristics of Texian culture, this despite the fact that leaders like S.F. Austin described the Hispanic-Mexican land policies of Mexico as the "*most liberal and munificent government on earth to emigrants.*" Austin went on record as opposing the annexation of Texas by the USA due to the latter's "illiberal" land policies. A basic premise of Mexican federalism of the day was that each State, not the federal government, owned its own public domain. The State also owned subsurface minerals along with possession of intestate property. As a legacy from the monarchs of 15th century Spain, Fernando and Isabel, a man's oxen, work animals, or work tools could not be seized for payment of debts in 19th century Texas. Further, unlike American law, women could own land, trade it, or sue for it in a court of law (the basis for later American community property legal concepts).

With regard to religion, English speaking colonists were required by law to be "Catholic" but Mexican authorities allowed the immigrants to qualify by professing to be "Christians." No Texians were ever harassed or persecuted if they practiced their own denominational form of Christianity so long as they didn't do it openly in defiance of the authorities. In 1834 Article 10 of Decree # 272 stated: "No person shall be molested for political or religious opinions, provided he shall not disturb the public order."

A well known, influential personality of the day was **Rafael Antonio Manchola** who had served as presidial Commander, State Deputy, and Alcalde (1831) of Goliad. As the military commander he had personally seen many illegal activities carried on by the Texian community. When **Green DeWitt** was granted an empresario grant Manchola expressed his disgust for DeWitt because he and his colonists were "libertines" who accepted no law but their own unless it suited them otherwise and "…no faith can be placed" in the Texian colonists because of their audacity and refusal to live by the law. Manchola recommended that detachments of soldiers be placed in Texian settlements in order to insure that laws were obeyed.

Other Tejano observers of the day reported their negative impressions of the Texians: that empresario Green DeWitt was little more than *"a drunk in the streets…adventurer,"* that a kind or courteous Texian was a rarity and that most were *"a lazy people of vicious character."* [See Note # 15.] In 1830 a law was passed prohibiting any more immigration from the USA into Mexico. It still permitted immigration from Europe, forbade importation of black slaves, provided for military installations in Texian colonies, and terminated all empresario contracts not fulfilled as of 1830.

CONVENTION

In 1832 **Horatio Chriesman** and **John Austin** called for a convention of all Texian representatives in order to draw up a list of demands to send to the government. Among the demands were that American immigration continue along with the importation of black slaves. Influential Bexareños gathered in their own convention that same year, led by younger leaders like **Juan Nepomuceno Seguín, Ambrosio Rodríguez,** and **Balmaceda.** Among the protests voiced were the illegal activities of colonies like those of Green DeWitt.

Texians held another convention in 1833. New leaders were now in the picture: **Sam Houston, William** and **John Wharton, David G. Burnet.** Some of the sentiments now being expressed were that "Austin's policy of conciliation and forbearance with Mexico" was a dire mistake. Austin defended himself by saying his critics were "…*demagogues, pettifoggers, speculators, and schemers.*"

CENTRALISTS & FEDERALISTS

In 1834 S. F. Austin was arrested in Mexico City where factions known as the Federalists and the Centralists were battling each other. Led by Santa Anna, the Centralists came to power in May of 1834 but the Federalists still had enough power to convulse the country in the ensuing power struggle. In 1835 Santa Anna's army crushed a Federalist citizens' army and this discouraged revolts elsewhere.

TEXAS REVOLUTION

Texians decided they would support neither the Federalist nor the Centralists, instead desiring to create their own Republic. In 1836 Santa Anna took the Alamo and Goliad but the Texas Revolution was a reality. On April 21, 1836, Sam Houston's army destroyed Santa Anna's unsuspecting forces at San Jacinto. Santa Anna was forced to sign a peace treaty in order to save his life.

Tejanos during the Texas Revolution were targeted by both sides. Mexican Centralist forces suspected Tejanos of treachery as did later Texian commanders. Victorious Texians robbed and plundered Tejano homes, driving out native families who fled to places like Coahuila, Nuevo León, Tamaulipas, or Louisiana. Texians flooded in and took Tejano ranches, livestock from the Béxar, Goliad, and Nacogdoches areas, through kangaroo court lawsuits, sheriffs' auctions, and other such swindles, all condoned by the victorious Texian authorities. If Tejanos resisted their ranches would be burned down, the Tejanos would be brutally murdered, and all livestock would be "put on the market" for a tidy profit. Tejanos like Juan N. Seguín, Vicente Córdova, and Carlos de la Garza, reputable individuals who sincerely believed in the freedoms espoused by Americans, finally realized that all were mere strategies to deprive them of their land and liberty in favor of the marauders who, sanctioned by Texian authorities, robbed or killed their victims merely because they were "*Mexicans*" who possessed attractive or desirable forms of wealth coveted by the "liberators." [See Note # 16.]

DISCUSSION Notes *for* TEJANO SOCIETY
Note # 1
For reasons/motives he didn't explain, Fray Antonio Olivares described Béxar's pioneers as "*mulatos, lobos, coyotes, and mestizos, people of the lowest order...*" As is typical in many works by various historians, such commentary has been widely publicized. Governor Alarcón's reply, and its implications, that settlers weren't available from seminaries, is generally ignored by the same writers.
Note # 2
Names are mostly from *San Antonio And Its Beginnings* by Frederick C. Chabot, graciously supplied by Esther Hardin of the San Antonio Genealogical and Historical Society. An intensive study needs to be done on this subject of early Tejano pioneers.
Note # 3
See *San Antonio De Béxar* by Jesús F. De La Teja.
Note # 4
See *Spanish Texas, 1519-1821* by Donald E. Chipman.
Note # 5
Jesús de la Teja writes that the use of "*español*" was more a "social label" than an indicator of race/ethnicity. Such an observation could be made for all societies unless DNA can actually be investigated in a laboratory. Since race reporting by appearance is always imprecise, to be labeled "white" or "European" is and always has been more "social" than anything else. Beyond that, genome discoveries assert that human DNA is 99.9% exactly the same for the entire human species so social status always had more to do with one's society than actual human ability or worth. It is certain that *racism* would accept no such conclusion.
Note # 6
It was better economics to obtain wheat from Coahuila than grow it in San Antonio. Governors coming in from southern areas criticized Bexareños as "lazy" because they didn't grow much wheat. Denigrating remarks like these are often perpetuated in histories written by individuals

like T.R. Fehrenbach, author of the well known *Lone Star*. Fehrenbach writes in Chapter Four, p. 57, of: "...an 18th century resident of San Antonio, who described his youth in these words: *'We were of the poor people...to be poor in that day meant to be very poor indeed...But we were not dis-satisfied...There was time to eat and sleep and watch the plants growing. Of food, we did not have over much---beans and chili, chili and beans.'* " There is no citation with this "quote" so only Fehrenbach knows its source. Would a product of Hispanic society say "chile" or "chili"? Is it logical that prod-ucts of a ranching society would have no beef to eat? The word "barbeque" grew out of the Spanish *barbacoa*. Fehrenbach doesn't assert that "chili and beans" were barbecued.

Note # 7

See *San Antonio De Béxar* by Jesús F. de la Teja.

Note # 8

Andrés Tijerina has written that this period in Texas history is often depicted as *"a mere prelude to the Anglo-American rescue of the region from barbarism."*

Note # 9

While the New Mexican colony had existed since 1598 and Tejanos had been in Texas for over a century, these 19th century American colonists to Texas were the first English speaking im-migrants in what is today the Southwest. They qualify as "pioneers" because they settled where no other European-based people were living. The names are from the work titled *Austin Colony Pioneers* by Worth S. Ray, graciously provided by Esther Hardin of the San Antonio Genealogical and Historical Society.

Note # 10

See *They Called Them Greasers: Anglo Attitudes Toward Mexicans in Texas, 1821-1900* by Arnoldo de León.

Note # 11

See the essay "On Texas History" below.

Note # 12

Andrés Tijerina has written in *Tejanos And Texas Under The Mexican Flag, 1821-1836*, that the Tejano flying squadrons *"influence and their very existence has scarcely been acknowledged."*

Note # 13

See Chapter 5 in *Tejanos & Texas Under The Mexican Flag, 1821-1836* by Andrés Tijerina who writes that works on the Texas Rangers, especially the most famous by Dr. W. P. Webb, don't mention that Tejanos served as Rangers.

Note # 14

See Chapter I in *They Called Them Greasers* by Arnoldo de León. Howard Zinn writes in his *A Peoples' History Of The United States* that while American historiography emphasizes things like *Liberty!!* and *Progress!!* the actual basic theme of American life is *racism*. The YRFF cycle of Texas historians don't touch upon Zinn's observation when they write about Texas.

Note # 15

See Chapter VII in *Tejanos And Texas* by Andrés Tijerina.

Note # 16

These perspectives have been written into the historical record by historians like Jesús de La Teja, Arnoldo De León, Gerald E. Poyo, Andrés Tijerina, Félix D. Almaráz, Jr., and, to a degree, Donald E. Chipman. Similar perspectives are basically lacking in the YRFF cycle of Texas history. H. Yoakum seems to be more concerned with national or international events and influences than 18th century Tejano history. R.N. Richardson's *Texas* survey supplies no information on founding pioneers like Fr. Antonio Margil de Jesús, the "Apostle of Texas." The amusing style of J.B. Frantz still promotes emphasis epitomized by the title of his Chapter 6: *"Mexican Texas: Epilogue to the American Revolution."* T.R. Fehrenbach is quick to inform (p. 84) his readers of the liberty loving slave masters who founded English speaking Texas: *"No one was less fitted by rationale to make human chattels of other men than the Anglo-Americans…"* except for prevailing complications of *"economics, social factors, and race."*

Essay: ON TEXAS HISTORY

There is a stark dichotomy in Texas history beginning when American immigrants enter Texas. Very few historians have written in the vein of Donald E. Chipman that writers like T. R. Fehrenbach have "misunderstood or misrepresented" the Hispanic founders of Texas. Fehrenbach implies that with just a little effort San Antonio could have become "a flourishing community" (Chipman quoting Fehrenbach). While it is impossible to detail an entire book or school of historians let us take a brief look at Fehrenbach, T.R. *Lone Star: A History of Texas and the Texans*. New York: American Legacy Press, 1983. The Chipman quote above is from page 55 so let's investigate the information on just that one page. Fehrenbach informs the reader (there isn't a single footnote or citation for documentation on page 55) that for the King of Spain to grant the immigrant Canary Islanders the use of *"Don,"* a sign of lesser nobility, was "in accord with Spanish desperation to settle the frontier…" and a "considerable mistake." What is being communicated here? That the "Spanish" were desperate and didn't know what they were doing? According to Fehrenbach the Islanders, a self-styled upper class but without money, expected to find a town peopled by individuals who would support them. Fehrenbach can discern the *"attitude"* of Juan Leal Goraz when he signed his name: *"I, Juan Leal Goraz, Spaniard and noble settler by order of his Majesty…in this Royal Presidio of San Antonio de Béjar and Villa of San Fernando, Province of Texas…and also farmer."* Fehrenbach informs the reader that the occupation of *farmer* is *"tacked on at the end, almost as an afterthought"* so that it would *"do the least social damage."* Are these amazing powers of clairvoyance to relate with such detail the psychology of Tejanos who lived in the 1730s? And how could a farming/ranching society look down on *farmers?* Fehrenbach then mentions Fray Morfi relating a story of a father who taught his son it was unnecessary to work and that the son transmitted the "philosophy" to his own family. By way of ending page 55, Fehrenbach states that instead of creating a "flourishing community," the Canary Islanders became *"hunters, fishers, loafers, and in some cases, thieves."* The "Spanish" could enjoy the climate and scenery while they grew *"a few beans"* and somehow took the *"ubiquitous Spanish cattle"* in the vicinity.

Incidentally, page 55 is in the chapter titled "The Faith and the Failure: The Missions." The tone is altogether different for *Lone Star's* Chapter 6: "The Anglo-Celts." It would appear that the "Anglo Celts" emanated from the *"unbearable"* British Isles, as a *"swarm of dissidents, diehards, and refugees"* who developed a society that was *"rational and ethical...inherently liberal."* The only *"dark cloud"* in the society they developed was "Negro slavery," the cornerstone of Southern society (slavery was tried in the North but due to weather conditions slaves weren't profitable enough) because someone had to do the work. Fehrenbach assures us however that *"No one was less fitted by rationale to make human chattels of other men than Anglo Americas..."* but (somehow) it couldn't be helped because of the complications of *"economics, social factors, and race."* That was written by T. R. Fehrenbach, not George Orwell.

The "Anglo-Celts" label is still intriguing. According to Fehrenbach they were the *"mixed race of Dane, Gael, and Saxon of the Teutonic Scottish south."* Thousands of these people, Presbyterians who hated Catholics, were transported to northern Ireland where they were referred to as " Scotch-Irish." There was a mixing with Huguenot and Irish blood, to which was added English and Germanic in America. By 1730 thousands of them were in America where they were known for their "thrift, self-reliance, and industry" as well as a simply phenomenal birthrate. They migrated to frontier areas because that is where the vacant land was. Fehrenbach doesn't elucidate Scotch-Irish dealings with Indians. The S-I have been described as the most brutal of Indian-hating frontiersmen who considered Native Americans as animals to be exterminated by fair means or foul. Neither does he say there were Presbyterian missionaries laboring to preserve the Indians. This *"...riotous, yet curiously disciplined horde"* made their way West where the Anglo-Celts (Germanic tribes but it isn't proper American historiography to refer to them as "Germanic") would found American Texas.

Lone Star is a powerful work but there are many others written in the same heroic Orwellian vein. A work published by the Library Committee , Daughters of the Republic of Texas At the Alamo, titled *The Free State Of Béjar* and written by Jack C. Butterfield states that *"Spaniard and American represented divergent types of civilization differing in language, appearance, culture, habit of thought and viewpoint on practically every known subject."* The *"adventurers and pioneers from the United States"* would have no peace until they *"had wrested the town of San Antonio from its founders."* While Fehrenbach says these heroes were "Anglo-Celts," Butterfield tells us *"They were gallant men, those filibusters of the 1800s...typical of the Anglo-Saxon who made the United States his own."* They were such heroes (these Scotch-Irish-Anglo-Saxon-Celts) that even the *"Spanish General Toledo remarked 'Give me a thousand such men and I could conquer all Mexico.'"* Further, there is *"No wonder that the names of Travis, Bowie, Crocket, and Bonham are known to every red-blooded man..."* for in the history of the world there is nothing to compare with the Alamo. Is this History?

CALIFORNIO SOCIETY

Presidio Hill in San Diego is the cradle of Christian civilization in California. On July 16, 1769, when Mission San Diego was founded by raising a Christian cross, there were some twenty Indian villages within a radius of ten leagues. The "California Indians," estimated to number at around 310,000, were in reality different groups of people who spoke possibly as many as a hundred mutually unintelligible languages. Much like Europeans, they constantly fought each other.

TRIBAL GROUPS

The (Alta) California tribes which would be missionized were a wide variety of basic groups like the: Ajachmen (Juaneño); Cajilla; Chumash; Cupeño; Esselen; Luiseño; Kawaisu; Kitanemuk; Konkow; Kumeyaay; Miwok; Miwok (Coast); Miwok (Lake); Mono (Western); Mono (Paiute); Nisenan; Ohlone (Costanoan); Patwin; Pomo; Salinan; Serrano; Shoshone (Panamint); Tataviam; Tubatulabal; Tataviam; Tongva (Gabrielino); Kumeyaay; Wappo; Washo; Yokuts (Foothill); Yokuts (Northern Valley); Yokuts (Southern Valley); Yuki. These groups were different people with different languages, customs, rituals, etc., therefore difficult for missionaries to work with.

CHRISTIAN MISSIONS

The missions which would be founded to integrate California Indian groups into Christian society were, in the order of founding:

San Diego de Alcalá, July 16, 1769;
San Carlos Borromeo de Carmelo, June 3, 1770;
San Antonio de Padua, July 14, 1771;
San Gabriel Arcángel, September 8, 1771;
San Luis Obispo de Tolosa, September 1, 1772;
San Francisco de Asís (Dolores), October 9, 1776;
San Juan Capistrano, November 1, 1776;
Santa Clara de Asís, January 12, 1777;
San Buenaventura (Ventura), March 31, 1782;
Santa Bárbara, December 4, 1786;
La Purísima Concepción, December 8, 1787;
Santa Cruz, August 28, 1791;
Nuestra Señora de la Soledad, October 9, 1791;
San José de Guadalupe, June 11, 1797;
San Juan Bautista, June 24, 1797;
San Miguel Arcángel, July 25, 1797;
San Fernando Rey de España, September 8, 1797;
San Luis Rey de Francia, June 13, 1798;
Santa Inés, September 17, 1804;
San Rafael Arcángel, December 14, 1817;
San Francisco de Solano (Sonoma), July 4, 1823.

MISSION FRONTIER

The beginnings of California were joyful. For the first few days of the missionaries' optimistic quest to bring European Christianity and civilization to the Indians of California the situation was one of rejoicing and happiness. The soil was fertile, the waters were pristine, grapes would grow in abundance, and the country was beautiful. Reality quickly set in and the wilderness soon required the padres to *"sustain themselves with the bread of affliction and the waters of distress."* Many of the sailors from the ships and some of the soldiers were sick and had to be cared for in a makeshift infirmary. A tight stockade of poles had been erected for protection but if the Indians had turned hostile the Europeans wouldn't have had a chance at survival. While many of the men in the San Diego expedition were sick, this did not prevent **Gaspar de Portolá** from leading a small expedition to found Monterey. The *"Camino Real"* had its beginnings in the trail blazed by the Portolá expedition which didn't recognize Monterey Bay until the second time they went in search of it. Father Serra was with the second expedition to Monterey and founded Mission San Carlos Borroméo. Portolá then placed the governorship of California in the hands of **Pedro Fages** and returned to Mexico.

INDIAN DISINTEREST

While the missionaries were eager to impart Christianity the Indians weren't much interested in the foreigners or their way of life if desirable gifts like beads ran out. Shy at first, they soon became curious and welcomed all efforts if gifts were involved. Material benefits were the inducements to the teachings of Christianity. When there were no gifts they could become sullen or even take whatever they pleased, gifted or not. Despite their unpredictability, missionaries championed the Indians, demanding that the Hispanic population, mostly military, allow the religious time to bring the Amerinds into the Christian fold. They understood it would take much time and labor to get native people, who, for example, in that time and place still didn't even wear much in the line of clothing, to become "civilized" to the degree to which they could understand Christianity, which was the basic avenue into the "advanced" European culture which ruled the Western world.

DIFFICULT REALITIES

Imparting European Christianity and civilization to California was no simple feat for many reasons. Junípero Serra, the *Father President*, had to work with the King of Spain, the Viceroy in Mexico City, the Council of the Indies, the Commissary General of the Indies, the Board of Trade, the head of the Apostolic College of San Fernando, the military governor, the local presidio commander, and in many cases the soldiers and colonists in the areas of the missions. [See Note # 1. *Notes begin on page 226.*] There was no getting away from having to work with all these forces. Relations were sometimes harmonious, as with Serra and Viceroy Bucareli, but, reflecting the human condition, they were often at variance. Disagreements in interpretation of orders or laws couldn't be rectified quickly because the California wilderness was a tremendous distance away from decision makers in Mexico City or Madrid, Spain. It could take a year or so to ask an important question and receive the answer. In the meantime, life had to continue in the wilderness.

COLONIZERS

The European California pioneers, who came to be called *Californios*, were very human individuals with foibles like anyone else but their pioneering activities made them hardy frontiersmen and settlers, whether in uniform or habit, bearing arms or shouldering the Cross, in the service of God and King. [See Note # 2.]

California missionaries like Father Serra, one of the most highly developed intellects of his day, were as much men of action as any member of the military establishment. Serra once said: *"I do not demand that everything be done in one day but I do believe a ship should sail when the wind is favorable."* It took as much intellectual courage as it did physical to champion and work with Indians. Baptisms were relatively few in the early years and catechizing was generally a long, arduous process. It has been written that no baptisms were performed in San Diego during the first year of its existence and possibly very few before 1771. [See Note # 3.] But mission bells continued to ring out their hope along the California coasts and valiants like Junípero Serra would live the call of *"Come, come to Holy Mother Church; come and receive the Faith of Jesus Christ!"* [See Note # 4.] In time the common greeting in California would be *"Amar a Dios."* And it was uppermost in the missionaries minds, based as well on corroborating decrees from the King of Spain, that Indians had natural rights, especially to their aboriginal lands. [See Note # 5.]

LOCATION & REALITIES

Mission sites were selected according to the proximity to Indian villages (or encampments referred to as *rancherías*) and the availability of necessary resources like water and wood. While the wilderness was beautiful, new missions were impoverished, not imposing sights. In the beginning bells were hung on trees and mass was celebrated on improvised *enramada* altars *"with all the neatness of holy poverty."* Missionaries and other European-Hispanic pioneers lived in tents until shelters were made from poles. In time buildings were made with adobe or rock. All supplies had to be brought in by ship or mule back until foods could be grown on mission lands.

Father Serra never endeavored to mask missionary life in the incipient California missions. In a letter written to his superiors at the Apostolic College of San Fernando, the Father Presidente stated quite bluntly: *"Those who come here dedicated to so holy a work must undergo real sacrifice…in all distant parts one must expect to suffer hardship…which will be even more burdensome to those who seek convenience and comfort."* In California the only enticements would be *"…mutual encouragement, security and solidarity"* from fellow apostles working to bring Christianity to the Indians. It was a daunting goal because frontier California suffered from a lack of provisions, trade goods, cattle and horses, soldiers, and a dependable supply route. Christian knights like Junípero Serra, Francisco Palóu, Juan Crespi, and Fermín Lasuén were equal to the task.

FEUDS

An additional basic problem in early California was authority. Father Serra believed that Governor Fages had no jurisdiction over the friars or, within reason, their activities. It was conceded that Governor Fages had charge over the half dozen or so soldiers guarding the missions but that was all. Fages held that since he was responsible for mission security, he should have a voice in their founding or his limited number of soldiers wouldn't be able to protect or provision the missions and their personnel. In 1770 there were only forty-three soldiers to protect the area from San Diego to Monterey where there were literally thousands of Indians who could turn on the newcomers at any time with the slightest provocation. (By 1773 the number of stalwart soldiers had increased to sixty-one.)

Governor Pedro Fages didn't despise the missionaries. He helped them at every opportunity when he saw it as his duty. In 1772 the supply ships were late in reaching San Diego and famine was a certainty in the northern settlements if provisions didn't arrive. Fages organized *"the most celebrated bear hunt in California history"* in the San Luis Obispo area. Bear meat saved the settlers until pack trains of provisions could be sent from San Diego. As a further reward, the Indians were happy for the killing of so many bears which often menaced or injured them.

FARM & RANCH

Efforts at agriculture were begun almost immediately. But farming took time and agricultural wealth couldn't be depended on during the first few years. By 1773, though a mere four years after the July, 1769 founding of San Diego, only San Gabriel was giving promise of what was to come. [See Note # 6.]

Stock raising was as crucial as agriculture because cattle were needed for food and equine stock were necessary as beasts of burden. As with everything else in the early years, supplies of livestock were insufficient. Breeding animals were scarce and milch cows couldn't be butchered because their milk was the staple on which most people survived. California was the land of privation and at the start of 1774 there were only some 616 head of livestock (cattle, sheep, goats, pigs, donkeys, colts, horses, mules) at the five missions. The presidios at San Diego and Monterey also had stock but it appears they weren't in significant numbers.

POPULATIONS

At the time of first European contact the aboriginal population throughout California is estimated to have been around 310,000. During the California Spanish colonial period (1769-1821) there were created the settlements of 21 Franciscan missions, 4 military presidios, and 3 civilian towns. In comparison to Indians, Hispanics continued to be a very small minority. It has been estimated that in California coastal areas the Indians outnumbered Hispanics 59,700 to 150 in 1770. In 1780 the ratio was 57,000 to 480. In 1790: 43,600 to 1,060. In 1800: 35,850 to 1,800. In 1810: 25,900 to 2,300. In 1820: 21,750 to 3,400. [See Note # 7.]

As in most Hispanic frontier areas, which spanned two continents from Santa Fe to Buenos Aires, California needed more settlers. The California Hispanic population at the beginning was a handful of soldiers, 11 missionaries, plus an occasional artisan brought in by the government on a temporary assignment. Six soldiers had married Indian women but the others had no wives in California. More soldiers and permanent colonists were needed but the dedicated missionaries demanded these be men with families and good Christians who would set a proper example for the Indians. [See Note # 8.]

SUPPLY ROUTES

Another major obstacle to California development was the absence of a reliable supply route. The sea lane from San Blas on the Mexican coast was treacherous and ships were too small and frail for families of colonists or herds of livestock to trust them. For example, in 1771 the *San Antonio* took 68 days to get to San Diego and when it finally arrived almost all aboard were sick with scurvy. There was no overland route but even if there was it would require some 1500 mules and 100 *arrieros* (muleteers) to bring in supplies in sufficient quantities. And what was there to eat and drink on the way across the desert? In 1773

Viceroy Bucareli (?-1779), one of New Spain's greatest, wrote that the province of California might have to be abandoned. The only possible ray of hope was blazing a suitable overland route from Sonora. So Bucareli sponsored he Anza expeditions of 1774 and 1775-76 which blazed the trail over which colonists journeyed into California as far as San Francisco. Spanish California was now a permanent reality.

LAWS & PERSONALITIES

Father Serra's visit to Mexico City in 1773, which had as one of its basic purposes the removal (successful) of Governor Fages, also served for supplying Viceroy Bucareli with information on the realities of needs in California. Serra's many talks with Bucareli over the months that the Father President was in Mexico City provided the basis for the *Reglamento Provisional de 1773*, the first "California Code," that was drawn up by **Juan José de Echeveste** and made official by Bucareli 's decree. Among other things it called for a total of eighty-two (82) soldiers, four carpenters, four blacksmiths, four muleteers, etc., all salaried by the government. It encouraged emigration to California by providing free passage from San Blas, free rations for five years, and wages similar to those of a sailor for two years. In California all such émigrés were expected to work in the field of agriculture. Also, special attention was to be given to colonizing and developing the area around San Francisco Bay.

What with personalities like Gálvez, Bucareli, Portolá, Anza, Neve, etc., there is no lack of herculean heroes in the founding of California. The missionaries of the era were just as valiant and deserving of remembrance. Father Serra is among the best known and most widely publicized. It must be pointed out that Serra's heroics in the quest of bringing Christianity to the Indians would be little known had it not been for the biography written by his friend and co-worker, **Francisco Palóu,** the "Father of California History." Friars Juan Crespi and Pedro Font were also among those who labored and wrote about what was happening. They were among the writers who recorded items like the goodbye letter (made a part of history by Palóu; like Father Kino, Serra never sought fame for himself) Father Serra wrote (1749) to Francisco Serra, his blood relative and brother Franciscan: "*…I lack words to tell you how much sorrow I feel in leaving you, and please repeat the same thing to my family, who, I have no doubt, must also feel grief and at seeing me leave. I would like to impress upon them the great joy I feel. I intend to pledge myself to go there [America] and never return. The vocation of the apostolic preacher, especially under the present circumstances, is the best which one could desire to go into. His life may be long or brief, but it he knows how to compare its length with eternity, he will say clearly that, in any event, it could not be more than an instant. Such is the will of God, and I shall render him the little assistance I can. If he does not wish us to be together in this life, he will unite us in immortal glory. Tell them that I am very sorry not to be with them as I was before, to comfort them, but they ought to have in mind also that the principle thing must be held first, and that is the will of God. For nothing else but the love of God would I have left them.*" [See Note # 9.]

LASUEN

The other monumental figure in the establishment of California missions was **Father Fermín Francisco de Lasuén** (who as of yet hasn't been studied by a biographer like Palóu). It was Lasuén who continued and finished Serra's great work for the Indians of California.

Fermín Francisco de Lasuén was born around 1720 in Vitoria, located in the Basque province of

Alava. He became a Franciscan, went to Mexico where he missionized in the area between Tamaulipas and Querétaro. In 1767 he joined Father Serra to work in the missions the Jesuits had been forced to abandon. Father Lasuén was assigned to manage San Francisco de Borja in Baja California where he served as the only missionary for five years under the most trying of circumstances. Despite serious obstacles like scarcity of water and suitable agricultural land, Lasuén grew cotton, planted vineyards, as well as fig and pomegranate trees. This Christian champion was also human for he asked for a second missionary to be assigned to Borja because Lasuén, a very learned man like most missionaries of the day, craved intellectual companionship. [See Note # 10.] But he served alone until 1773 when he was assigned to San Gabriel in Alta California, despite his petition to be permitted to retire. He humbly obeyed the orders of his superiors. Unknown to him at the time, his ministry in California would span thirty years and he would never leave the province. It is ironic that this co-founder of California never desired to stay in California.

When Father Lasuén took over the leadership of San Gabriel in September of 1773 the area was in the throes of famine and no relief would arrive until March of 1774. Lasuén proved to be the right man at the right time and fortuitously, out of all the missions San Gabriel happened to be the best site for future pastoral and agricultural development. But the present had to be borne with patience: Lasuén wrote in a letter that the Indians probably accepted him because his tattered clothes, which he had mended and re-mended until they couldn't be patched anymore, resembled those of the Indians themselves.

The first **Anza** expedition arrived in San Gabriel on March 22, 1774. While this caused an even further shortage of supplies, San Gabriel became more important politically because the mission was established as the first settlement to be reached by travelers using the overland route from Sonora.

Under the direction of Fermín Lasuén, San Gabriel became the most prosperous of missions by the end of 1774 and Indian problems were decreasing significantly. A new challenge now came Lasuén's way: found a mission between San Gabriel and San Diego in order to work with the Indians in that area and further improve communications between the two missions. Father **Gregorio Amurrio** accompanied Lasuén and with Lieutenant Ortega, identified the site that would become *San Juan Capistrano*.

The bloody uprising at San Diego in 1775 caused Father Lasuén to be assigned to minister at San Diego. There was now significant friction between Fr. Serra's missionaries and Governor Rivera. The former wished to pursue a policy of conciliation with the "rebellious" Indians while the latter wanted to deal with them militarily. The dispute finally went to the Viceroy who sided with the missionaries. Lasuén remained at San Diego for the rest of Fr. Serra's presidency and Palóu's short succession to the office on Serra's death. Palóu soon retired and Fermín Francisco Lasuén was appointed as President of Missions on February 6, 1785 (but not received until September).

Father Fermín threw himself wholeheartedly into his new assignment. More missions were needed because there were Indian souls to save and the land had to be developed to feed everyone. Serra's dream had been to build missions in the populous Santa Barbara Channel region. The last of Serra's nine missions had been San Buenaventura (1782) so the new Father President," now 66 years old, set to work in completing his predecessor's goal. Mission Santa Barbara was dedicated in December of 1786 as was Purísima Concepción in 1787 (although work didn't start on it until the following year). Mission Santa

Cruz was dedicated in August of 1791 and in October the cross was raised at Soledad.

California's governors and religious had always been interested in founding missions further inland, not just along the coast. Governor Borica (1794-1800) cooperated and worked actively with Lasuén who asked for permission to found five new missions, which were approved by the Viceroy. Lasuén spent most of the year 1795 making careful explorations for mission sites. After detailed planning everything was ready by 1797: from June to September four missions were dedicated with a fifth coming in June of 1798. Father Lasuén, aged around 78, was present at the dedication of each: San José, San Juan Bautista, San Miguel, San Fernando Rey, San Luis Rey, traversing some five hundred miles in the process. Founding so many missions was indeed a superlative achievement yet Lasuén never made mention of it in his writings.

While this Christian knight was a superb founder of missions he has also been described as a superlative administrator. Older missions had to be maintained while new ones were being brought into the system and Lasuén did both without injuring either. Additionally, Father Fermín was granted the rights of Confirmation, which he performed on some 9,000 persons (beginning in 1790). In 1795 he was assigned as Commissary of the Inquisition of Mexico. In fulfillment of priestly duties, in 1796 the Bishop of Sonora authorized Father Lasuén to administer customary sacraments to civilian as well as military personnel. He was also appointed as an ecclesiastical judge for situations in which a church court might be needed. Father Lasuén was a "hands-on" leader who went wherever necessary when there was something important to be done. His headquarters were at San Carlos in Monterey but because of his schedule he was seldom there for long. In 1797 an unabashedly admiring Governor Borica complimented the venerable missionary, saying he must have rejuvenated himself by bathing in waters of a different kind of Jordan.

The mission system begun by Father Serra blossomed under Father Lasuén. While there had always been an immediate focus on agriculture and stock raising, under Lasuén the missions provided instruction in various trades in order to prepare the neophytes (baptized Indians) for making a civilized living. In 1787 Governor Fages asked the Viceroy to send carpenters, smiths, masons, etc., to California to aid the missionaries in teaching their Indians charges. Mostly between 1792 and 1795, some twenty artisans were sent, at government expense, on four to five year contracts. Mission economics improved noticeably because of these master craftsmen, a few of whom remained permanently in California. It is quite possible the "mission style" of architecture began to develop at this time through the efforts of these master craftsmen and missionaries of the Lasuén period.

A basic characteristic of the Spanish colonial "Southwest" is the conflict between governmental/military and religious authorities. Not even the incomparable Father Serra could avoid these serious feudings. Fermín Lasuén has been described as the most tactful of all religious leaders and this skill generally avoided serious confrontation with civil or military authorities. The governors with whom Lasuén had to deal, personalities like Fages, Roméu, Arrillaga, Borica, Alberni, were generally good men who had also been instructed to cooperate with the missionaries. In 1779 Governor Neve recommended that missionaries exercise only spiritual supervision over their neophytes and that only one missionary serve at each location. Lasuén wrote to his superiors that he would accept their decision but that he would also invoke sacred Franciscan law and retire because *"For me the solitude of this occupation is a cruel and terrible enemy…I escaped from it, thank God, after evident risk of dying on account of it, and now I see its shadow again…which I fear worse than death…that of being alone in this ministry…I shall offer myself for any kind of suffering and to die in these parts, as soon as God may order it, but I am certain there will never be a man who can convince me that I must subject myself to that solitude in this ministry."* Lasuén made his point without quarreling and Neve's recommendation died a natural death. Further, Governor Fages wrote in highly complimentary ways about the missionaries in his 1787 report, summing up by saying: *"…the rapid, gratifying, and interesting progress, both spiritual and temporal, which we fortunately are able to see and enjoy in this vast new country, is the glorious effect of the apostolic zeal, activity, and indefatigable ardor of their religious."* Even when Lasuén didn't win he was able to accept an adverse decision as in 1797 when the village (*pueblo*) of Branciforte (Santa Cruz) was founded "too close to the mission" (according to the missionaries).

Because of his personality Father Fermín maintained harmonious relations with almost everybody, native and foreigner alike. French navigator **Jean François de La Pérouse** visited Monterrey in 1786 and though he compared the missions to the French slave plantations of Santo Domingo, he wrote that *"Father Fermín de Lasuén…is one of the most worthy of esteem and respect of all the men I have ever met. His sweetness of temper, his benevolence, and his love for the Indians are beyond expression."* The English navigator **George Vancouver** visited in December of 1792 and wrote as follows: "Our reception at the mission could not fail to convince us of the joy and satisfaction we communicated to the worthy and reverend fathers…the Rev. Fermín Lasuén…together with the fathers…came out to meet us…[Lasuén] was about 72 years of age, whose gentle manners…fitted him in an eminent degree for presiding over so benevolent an institution." The Spanish commander of ships on a voyage of discovery, Alejandro Malaspina, visited Monterey in 1791 and wrote of Lasuén: "He was a man who in Christian lore, mien, and conduct was truly apostolic, and his good manners and learning were unusual…"

Lasuén's missionary zeal was fueled by his love of the Christian faith. While fulfilling the duties of President of Missions he served those many years without pay. Missionaries at each mission received an annual salary from the Spanish king but those in the supernumerary category, in which group was Lasuén, served without pay. As Lasuén himself put it, he lived upon the alms of his Franciscan brothers. This created a hardship for the Father President because his sister Clara needed his financial help.

The greatest achievements of Reverend Fermín Francisco Lasuén began at an age when most men would be contemplating retirement. He lived to the age of 83, retaining his faculties and rendering effective service to God and King until the end. He became ill, had to stay in bed for twelve days, then died at San Carlos Mission on June 26, 1803.

CHRISTIAN KNIGHTS

It was indeed fortunate for California to have not one but two great champions to commence its written history. The incomparable Father Junípero was followed by the equally incomparable Father Fermín. Both "Christian Knights" were peerless founders of missions where Native Americans were taught the arts of Christianity and European civilization. Both traveled from mission to mission, baptizing Indians and performing other religious duties. Each one was successful in his goals, Father Serra establishing the mission system and Father Lasuén perfecting it. Because of the time period in which he labored,

Lasuén helped make the missions an economic success as well as to create the architecture which is so famous in the present day. No one ever surpassed these founders of California in missionary zeal or Christian spirit, and through it all, serving without pay or material gain whatever. H.H. Bancroft summed up: *Padre Fermín was physically small, of a vivacious expression though always dignified. He was candid, a kind-hearted old man who made friends everywhere. Foreigners or Spaniards alike were impressed with him and his quiet force of character. He held serious opinions but he worked harmoniously with everyone, even those who opposed him. No one had a firmer will and he never hesitated to express his views. He was an excellent man of business as his management of the missions attests. His writings were concise in style. His piety and humility were agreeable, unobtrusive, and blended with common sense. His life was one of duty, purity, kindness, and courtesy. Padre Fermín was the model of the ideal padre.* [See Note # 11.]

MISSION LIFE

It has been reported that in 1806 there were some 20,355 Indians living in California missions. In 1824 (under Mexican suzerainty) there were 21, 066, the highest number ever for California Franciscan missions. Directly or indirectly, California mission life created the basis for California society so it is necessary to discuss life in a California mission.

The mission was a place where Indians were introduced to Christianity through activities like religious instruction and structured work activities through which Indians would be enabled to earn a living after they no longer needed direct guidance from Christian missionaries. At the beginning agricultural production was slow but by 1775 some missions were on the road to self sufficiency with their harvests of wheat and corn. (The Father President of Missions, Junípero Serra, candidly remarked that he was indeed a *"manager of farms."*) Newly established missions were helped by the older ones and by 1778 the missions were capable of sustaining themselves. By 1805 there was a surplus of wheat, corn, barley, beans, etc., and missions helped each other as necessary. There were lands for orchards and gardens. Fruit trees included pear, apple, peach, orange, lemons, pomegranates, cherry, figs, quince, etc., and from the gardens came various kinds of vegetables, melons and watermelons, cabbage, lettuce, radishes, mint, parsley, etc., and the all important grapes. (Mission San Luis Rey had five big gardens in various areas of its district.) Foodstuffs were sold to the presidios at first until other markets could be opened up. Basic mission products were hides, tallow, butter, bearskins, chamois leather, wine, brandy, olive oil, corn, wheat, beans, and bull horns. These were sold/traded for items like clothing for the neophytes, linen, hats, coffee, sugar, chocolate, muskets, etc.

Raising livestock was also basic to mission life. The first small herds of cattle, from Lower California and Sonora, multiplied slowly but with missionary expertise and care the numbers increased. In 1773 five missions held a total of 204 head of cattle, by 1775 the number was 427. By 1805 mission livestock numbered at some 130,000 sheep, 95,000 cattle, 21,000 horses, 1,000 mules, 800 hogs, and 120 goats. Indians learned how to work and/or handle livestock in the mission environment.

Amerindians were also taught various crafts and trades in the missions, community colleges of their day. They learned how to make soap, boots and shoes, saddles, candles, blankets, beds, coffins, etc., all under the guidance of missionaries or experts brought in to teach the neophytes. Some 20 skilled artisans were sent (1791-95) to California on four- to five-year government contracts to teach blacksmithing, carpentry, brick masonry and adobe construction, shoemaking, tanning, pottery making, etc., and one **Antonio Domínguez Henríquez** taught textile arts throughout California. Indian workers learned these trades from the talented Mexican artisans, the first such professionals in California, and practiced them long after their teachers returned to Mexico. The missions, now generally as well stocked as any frontier general store could be, had the market cornered because supply ships had proved unreliable and there was no other source of supply.

Missionaries and their missions set the tone for California hospitality. Alfred Robinson wrote in his *Life In California* that any stranger traveling through the country could stop at any mission, for months if desired, and be fed and housed at no expense to himself. When he was ready to leave he had only to inform the padres and they would provide him with a horse and provisions for the road, including wine or brandy, for which he was required to pay nothing.

In an effort to offset presidio dependence on missions the Spanish government ordered the founding of civilian communities: San José (1777), Los Ángeles (1781), and Branciforte (1797, near present-day Santa Cruz). Agriculture was especially productive in the San José area. Spanish economic policy forbade the colonists selling their foodstuffs other than to presidios. Governor Diego de Borica (1794-1800) championed the colonists bid to sell to other markets like the San Blas supply ships. Permission was granted and the colonists were successful until the War for Independence interrupted all commerce.

Another basic reason for mission control of the economy is that missionaries controlled the Indian labor force. [See Note # 12.] There were very few Hispanic settlers to begin with so they couldn't personally have worked the agricultural land and livestock to any significant degree. [See Note # 13.] The highly disciplined missionaries believed that Christianity and honest work were the road to salvation, eternal and societal. Indian savagery had to be combated through prayer and work. The mission work schedule was regimented because, the missionaries believed, Amerindians needed "structure and discipline" if they were going to gain their way into civilized (i.e., European) society. Benefits? The supreme gift was eternal salvation through Christianity and while in this world, living on beef was more stable than trying to survive on acorns. So it was necessary to learn how to pray as well as raise cattle.

A typical mission day started by ringing the bells as a call to prayer. At around eight or nine o'clock all able bodied adults would report to their work duties and labor until around eleven o'clock when the workers would eat lunch. Afterward they would return and work until about an hour or so before sunset when the neophytes again reported for prayers. So the Indians worked five to eight hours a day, five or six days a week. There was no work on Sundays or religious holidays, which could number as many as ninety-two days on the Catholic calendar. Working at the missions was unpaid but the Indians were provided with food, clothing, housing, and religious instruction. All able-bodied Indians, regardless of age or gender, were responsible for some sort of work. Women could be assigned to grind a set amount of corn or weave a certain amount of cloth. Men could be assigned to make a certain number of adobes. Children could be assigned to chase birds out of the garden or pull weeds.

Neophytes often became quite skilled as vaqueros, carpenters, shoemakers, masons, gunsmiths, soap makers, blacksmiths, weavers, etc. (In 1822 one **José Chaquiles**, a shoemaker, petitioned for permission to leave Soledad Mission on the grounds that he had the skills to support himself. Permission was granted and within a short time he was making shoes in San José.) Despite specialization, workers also answered the call for seasonal necessities whether it be branding livestock, shearing sheep, producing lime or salt, making roof tiles, etc. Communal work didn't prevent specialization to any discernible degree.

The workload was not so demanding that it injured the neophytes. Able bodied Indians who refused to work would be scolded. If they persisted they could be whipped, put into stocks, or a makeshift jail. Because of this some Indians ran away but soldiers could be used to bring them back if they could be found. Indians weren't force to register at a mission but once they took that step it was considered a contract like in the military. [See Note # 14.]

Mission Indians who labored in mission fields or workshops didn't cease their own customary activities like gathering roots or acorns for food. They also continued to hunt game, fowl, or go fishing. Adjusting to European labor, which brought them gifts like beef and wheat to eat, didn't cause Indians to forget their own basic lifestyles.

The Indians proved good workers and were soon in demand at the presidios. If soldiers were assigned to build on to or repair crumbling presidios there were too few of them to handle most projects. They also protested that they were soldiers, not construction workers, that when there was an emergency society looked to them for protection which was what they had been trained for. [See Note # 15.] So missionaries supplied mission Indians to work for wages at the presidio. Mission Indians often used their free time to work at the presidios in activities like construction, cooking, washing clothes, milling grain, gathering wood. Workers were paid with food, blankets, beads, etc. Indians convicted of crimes could also be sentenced to work details at a presidio. Non-mission Indians also hired themselves out for presidio contract work.

Hispanics in California, always short in numbers, thus came to depend on Indian workers. The settlers in San José and Los Ángeles hired Indians as vaqueros, servants, cooks, arrieros, water and wood haulers, etc. Indian field workers could earn a third to half of the crops they harvested. Missionaries protested that Indians working in villages were being led into non-Christian behavior because settlers cared nothing about Christianizing them or teaching them to lead Christian lives. Father Lasuén wrote that the settlements were a *"hindrance to conversion…give a bad example, scandalize them…"* and tell them Christianity isn't necessary. [See Note # 16.]

QUEEN OF MISSIONS

Santa Bárbara, the first mission to be established by Father Lasuén, has been described as the "Queen of the Missions." The mission began its history with a simple rite conducted by Lasuén on December 4, 1786, the Feast of St. Barbara. A more formal ceremony, now with Governor Fages in attendance, was held on December 16 in a brush shelter (*enramada*) where a high Mass was sung and a sermon delivered for the occasion.

Initial log structures were occupied by May 21, 1787 and baptisms of Indians were recorded for the first time. Christianization was generally slow because there was no rush on the part of the Chumash to take up the Faith and missionaries didn't approve of mass conversions. The "strenuous years of evangelization" at Santa Barbara were from 1786 to 1804 and by 1812 most of the coastal Indians were baptized if they were going to be.

By 1793 when the English captain **George Vancouver** visited Santa Barbara it had the *"appearance of a far more civilized place than any of the other Spanish settlements."* The white buildings were well constructed with roofs of red tile. During shore leave sailors were provided horses to ride about the valley and **Archibald Menzies** was permitted to study the botany of the area. All sailors were required to return to their ship for the night but otherwise all were treated with Californio hospitality. The mission as well as citizens of the village supplied the visitors with meat, fowl, and garden vegetables. Menzies was impressed with the mission as a *"…laudable plan of civilization…with 500 to 600 Indian converts…"* living in the area, *"…clothed and maintained by the fathers"* whom he described as having been *"wonderfully successful"* in their efforts to become Christians but also in *"teaching them the useful arts and occupations"* necessary for life in a European community. Menzies was given a catch of fish in the village of Siujtu where he described the Indians as *"comely in appearance…clean…the men going about naked, the women covered from the waist down…"* their long, jet black hair giving *"…a peculiar grace to their persons."* They were expert in maneuvering their canoes and the baskets (*"astonishing"*) they made were so closely woven they could hold water. All told, the Vancouver visit was a splendid example of Californio hospitality and international good will (which Vancouver articulated in his 1798 *Voyage of Discovery* and Menzies later in his memoirs).

Mission building was a long process and Santa Barbara didn't take on its finished form until 1833 after being damaged by earthquakes and floods. It is believed that one **José Antonio Ramírez**, master mason and carpenter, was the principal architect and building superintendent at Santa Barbara. It appears his fame was so well known that he was referred to simply as "José Antonio the carpenter."

As with all missions, Santa Barbara was a farming community. Staples were, in order of importance, wheat, barley, corn, beans, peas, and horsebeans. The banner year of agricultural production was 1821 when some 12,820 bushels of the items named were harvested. The entire community labored for the benefit of all but deserving Indian workers were given private plots of land to raise chickens, melons, and vegetables of their own choosing.

Raising livestock was second only to agriculture at Santa Barbara. At the end of 1787 the mission had 24 cows, 20 horses, 27 sheep, etc. By 1803 there were 11,221 sheep and by 1809 there were 5,200 cattle. By 1814 there were a total of 16,598 head of livestock. There was so much activity with livestock that Santa Barbara acquired eight "ranchos" to manage its industry. From these stock ranches were obtained meat for the table, tallow for soap and candles, leather for shoes, boots, and saddles, as well as hides which were sold (along with tallow) to foreign ships.

The Chumash Indians proved to have discernible mechanical abilities so the missionaries imparted what knowledge they had then hired proficient laymen as teachers in certain arts and crafts. A soldier was hired to teach shoemaking and the famous José Antonio Ramírez was contracted to teach carpentry and masonry. Since the neophytes were new to European technologies of the day, the work schedule was not burdensome and considerations were made for age, gender, and individual abilities. The usual Santa Barbara work day for neophytes began around eight or nine o'clock in the morning and paused around 11:15 for lunch then work continued until about 3:45 p.m.

Women would usually be assigned to grind wheat and corn for the atole or they might bake bread. Pregnant women were never assigned to the grinding, unless it was herbs, because it was considered too heavy. (Indian men sometimes laughed at the padres, saying did they not see pregnant gentile women grinding corn and carrying wood?) Instead they might wash wool or clean wheat on the threshing floor. Ordinary women also helped in transporting bricks and tiles for building. Children over nine years of age were often assigned to combing wool or assisting weavers at the loom.

Weaving cloth was also a basic Santa Barbara piece-work industry and in full operation by 1796. The mission had three looms at which worked some sixty-five neophytes. Cloth was woven for shirts, skirts, and loin cloths. Each weaver had a particular amount to complete and if they did extra they were paid, in kind, for it. Carders and spinners also had preset allotments to complete. Once done, the rest of the day was of their own choosing. Every six months each mission male received a new loin cloth, every seventh month a new shirt and the women a new skirt. All neophytes, without distinction, were given a new blanket every year. If gentiles came in to have a child baptized the padres generally gave them clothing.

Manufacturing tiles and adobes was also important and also assigned on a piece-work basis. Nine men were assigned to produce 360 adobes a day and to accomplish this they rarely had to work beyond 11:00 in the morning, seldom on Fridays and never on Saturdays because they had completed their assignment for the week. To make tiles there was a group of sixteen men, aided by two women who handled the straw and sand, who made 500 tiles a day. They were as efficient as the adobe makers so they too enjoyed much leisure time.

The missionaries often complained of the *"gente de razón,"* charging that they were lazy, prone to constant idleness, and considered work as "dishonorable" because they were always hiring Indians to work for them. Conversely, it was no rarity for a civil or military authority to criticize the missionaries in regard to treatment of the Indians. In 1800 the presidial Captain **Goycoechea** charged that the Santa Barbara Indians were not receiving enough food. Father **Estevan Tapis** refuted these charges by stating that the neophytes were given three meals a day, which consisted of meat, corn, beans, etc., as well as *atole* (porridge made of corn) in the morning, *pozole* (comprised of wheat and corn) at noon, and atole again at night. Further, most of the neophytes raised chickens, given to them by the mission, so they had fowl and eggs. [See Note # 17.] This year (1800) the neophytes had received some 202 cows and calves slaughtered to provide them with beef and from which they kept the fat with which to trade. Despite the many new foods brought in by the mission fathers the neophytes were permitted to go fishing, gather acorns and wild fruits, and to go hunting for deer, rabbits, squirrels, rats, etc., as in the old days. (In 1813 Father Ramón Olbés reported that for the Indians *the entire day is one continuous meal* for they ate everything available at every opportunity.)

CHUMASH

While at the mission, evenings, most of Saturday, all Sundays and church holy days were "free time" for the Chumash of Santa Barbara. Their diversions included dancing, playing their music, certain guessing games, as well as hunting and fishing.

The Chumash loved to sing and play musical instruments. Under Padre **Narciso Durán** (1833-36), the greatest of the missionary musicians, the Santa Barbara choir flourished and his original compositions of *Misa de Cataluña* and *Misa Vizcaína* became well known as performed by his neophytes.

In a game resembling a sort of hockey/lacrosse, two teams consisting each of from 200 to 300 Indians vied to get a small wooden ball past opponents into a winning position. Everyone playing or watching became very excited in this game.

The Indians loved to gamble and play cards, which they learned from soldiers, but this had to be made illegal because they would bet everything, including their clothes, in hopes of winning. Other Chumash vices, according to the missionaries, were theft, promiscuity, and lying. Single women had to be locked in a room at night to prevent them from making amorous rendezvous with men. Women were rarely punished beyond being placed in stocks at Santa Barbara but men could also be whipped or shackled if they refused to desist in negative behavior like running away. Food was never denied to those being punished.

The Chumash continued to use their own language while the brighter neophytes were encouraged to become literate in Spanish, but it was not forced on them. Most young people learned it readily while the older generation never did.

By 1800 a pattern had definitely been set for activities as mentioned. Additionally, each Sunday after mass the padre would read out a fifth of the names of the Indians and these were given permission to visit their native villages if they wished, furloughs from one to two weeks in length. These periods enabled neophytes to visit relatives as well as serve to attract gentiles to the mission. The fact that most Indians returned to Santa Barbara speaks well of the mission system. [See Note # 18.]

PIONEERS

The Spanish Empire grew through the development of presidios to defend, missions to civilize and Christianize, towns to populate, ranches to feed, and mines to acquire wealth. It was common throughout the Empire for missionaries to feud with military and/or civilian authorities, as has been mentioned. Another basic California missionary lament was the "quality" of colonists who emigrated but it must be understood that the missionaries were highly disciplined Christians who might well have been in a class by themselves, judging by their enormous contributions to society, and could be rivaled by very few groups in history. While all colonists couldn't possibly be groups of Serras or Lasuéns, they were of sufficient heroic quality to tame the wilderness of California.

Following is a list of the pioneers who settled in California from 1769-1800. [Names are from H.H. Bancroft's *Inhabitants Of California, California Pioneer Register & Index* published by the Genealogical Publishing Co., Inc. of Baltimore, Maryland.] Strangely, female names are missing. Names can have alternate spellings (González-Gonsález-Gonzales) and still be the same family. Traditionally, males were often given the honorific name *José* then their actual name (as in *José* Antonio); the same for females with *María* (as in *María* Teresa)].

A:

Abella, Ramón

Acebedo: Francisco Antonio ; José Antonio; Julián;

Acedo, José;

Aceves, Antonio; José María; Antonio;

Quiterio; Pablo;

Acosta, Antonio; Acosta, José;

Aguiar, Francisco;

Aguila, José; Aguila, Juan José;

Aguilar: Francisco Javier; Luis Antonio;

Alanís: Antonio; Eugenio Nicolás; Isidro;

Máximo;

Alari, José;

Alberni, Pedro;

Alcintara, Pedro;

Alegre, Antonio;

Alegría, Norberto;

Alipás, Juan N.;

Altamirano: José Antonio; Lucas Domingo; José Marcos; Justo Roberto; Lúcas; Juan;

Alvarado, Juan B.; Bernardino; Ignacio; Francisco Javier; Juan B.; Francisco ; José Vicente; Juan José; Juan N. D.;

Álvarez: Juan; Joaquín; Luis; Pedro; Felipe; Doroteo; José; Juan; José.

B:

Bernal: Francisco; José Dionisio; Juan Francisco; Manuel Ramón; Apolinario; Juan; Ramón; , Bruno; Joaquín; José Agustín; José Cipriano; José C. Cipriano;

Bernardo, José; Nicolás A.;

Berreyesa: Juan José; José Nazario; José de los Reyes;

Blanco: Juan; Miguel;

Bojorges: José Ramón; Hermenegildo; Pedro Antonio; Francisco H.; Ramón;

Borica, Diego de;

Boronda, Manuel; Canuto José;

Bosch, Buenaventura;

Botello, Joaquín;

Bravo, José Marcelino;

Briones: Ignacio Vicente; José Antonio; Ignacio Vicente; José Joaquín; Felipe Santiago; Nicolás María; Marcos; Manuel;

Brito, Mariano; Miguel;

Bruno, Francisco;

Buelna, Eusebio José J.; José Antonio; Ramón; Eusebio J. J.; José Raimundo; José María;

Bulferig, Gerónimo;

Bumbau, Francisco;

Bustamante: José; Manuel;

Butrino: Manuel; Sebastián.

C:

Caballero: José; Calixto; José;

Calvo, Francisco;

Calzada: José Antonio; José; José Dionisio; José Antonio;

Camacho: Tomás M.; Juan Miguel; Anastasio; Antonio;

Camarena, Nicolás;

Cambon, Pedro Benito;

Camero, Manuel;

Campa, Pedro;

Campa y Coz, Miguel;

Campo, José;

Campos: Francisco; Cañedo, Albino;

Cañedo: José Manuel; Juan Ignacio;

Cañizares, José;

Cano, José;

Cantua, Ignacio;

Capinto: José M.; Mariano;

Carabanas: Joaquín; Nicolás;

Caravantes: José Salvador; Ventura;

Carcamo, José;

Cárdenas: Melchor; Cristóbal;

Cárdenas y Rivera, Tadeo;

Cariaga, Salvador;

Carlon, Hilario Ignacio;

Carnicer, Baltasar;

Carranza, Domingo;

Carrillo: Guillermo; Mariano; José Raimundo; Anastasio José; Carlos Antonio; Domingo Ant. Igna.; José Antonio E.; Luis;

Casasallas, Simon;

Casillas, Juan Manuel;

Castañeda: José; José Ruiz;

Castelo, Agustín;

Castillo: José; José;

Castro: Antonio; Ignacio; Joaquín; José; Isidro; José Macario; José Simon J. N; Mariano; Mariano de la Cruz; Agapito; Francisco; José

Joaquín; José S. T.; Simeon;
Cavaller, José;
Cayuelas: Francisco; Francisco; Pedro;
Cervantes: Juan Pablo; Guadalupe; Cervantes, Pablo Victoriano; Marcos; Pedro R.; José; José Luis; Salvador;
Chamorro;
Chaves, José; José Mateo;
Chavira: José Antonio; José;
Cibrian: Pablo; Leocadio; Pablo Antonio; Smith;
Ciprés, Marcelino;
Cisneros, José;
Clua, Domingo;
Contreras: Luis; José;
Cordero: Joaquín Ignacio; Francisco; Mariano Antonio; José E.; Fermín; Manuel; José Domingo; Miguel E.; Pedro;
Córdoba, Alberto;
Comejo, Casimiro;
Corona, Francisco;
Coronel, Juan Antonio;
Cortés: Juan Lope; José Antonio; Nicolás; Nicolás Felipe;
Costansó, Miguel;
Cota: Antonio; Pablo Antonio; Manuel Antonio; Roque; Guillermo; Juan Ignacio; Mariano; Nabor Antonio; Bartolomé José; Francisco Atanasio; José Manuel Ma.; José Valentín; Juan Francisco; Manuel; Pedro Antonio;
Crespí, Juan;
Cruz, Faustino José;
Cruz y Sotomayor, Juan;
Cruzado, Antonio;
Cuevas, Luis.
D:
Dandricu, Andrés;
Dantí, Antonio;
Dávila: José; Manuel; J. (soldier); José Antonio;

Delgado, Alonzo;
Díaz, Joaquín;
Domínguez: Juan José; José Dolores; José Antonio; José Ma. D.; Cristóbal; José Antonio; José Asunción; José Francisco; Remesio;
Duarte: Alejo Antonio; José Ma.; Pascual; Francisco Javier; Juan José; Leandro;
Ducil, Sebastián;
Dumetz, Francisco;
E:
Encarnación, José;
Enríquez, Antonio; Antonio Domingo; Sebastián;
Escamilla, Antonio Santos; José; Tomás;
Escribano, Sebastián;
Esparza, José Lorenzo;
Espí, José de la C.;
Espinosa: Antonio; Joaquín; Juan; Gabriel; José Miguel; Salvador; Tomás; Cayetano; José Gabriel; José Ma. E.; José Pío; Juan Antonio J.;
Estevan: Pedro de S.; José; Antonio;
Estrada, José Bonifacio;
Estudillo, José María;
F:
Fages, Pedro;
Faura, José;
Feliciano: Alejo; Hilario;
Félix: Claudio Victor; Anast. Ma.; Doroteo; José Vicente; José Francisco; Juan José Ignacio; Antonio Rafael; Victorino; Fernando de la T.; José; José Luciano; José Vicente Valentín; Juan; Juan José de G.; Leonardo Ma.; Pedro Antonio;
Fernández: Gaspar Antonio; José Rosalino; Pedro Ignacio; Rafael Ma. De la C.; Víctor; Gregorio; José Ma.; Manuel;
Feyjoo, José;
Ferrer, Pablo;
Figuer, Juan;
Figueroa: Manuel; Salvador Ignacio;
Flores: Hermenegildo; Victoriano; José Miguel;

José María; José Teodosio; Bernardo; Diego; Francisco; Isidro; José Ma. De la T.; Leandro José; Pedro;

Font, José;

Fontes, Luis Ma.; Pedro;

Fragoso, Luis Ma.; Rafael;

Franco, Juan; José; Pablo;

Fuster, Vicente;

G:

Galindo: Nicolás; Francisco A.; José Rafael; Alejandro Fidel; José Leandro; Juan Crisostomo; Claudio; José Carlos; Venancio;

Gallego, Carlos;

Gálvez, Diego;

Gámez, Teodoro;

Garaicoechea, José;

García: Diego; Felipe; Francisco Bruno; Francisco Ma.; Francisco P.; José Reyes; Juan José; José Antonio; Pedro; Pedro González; Carlos Ma.; José Antonio Inoc.; José Hilario Ramón; José de las Llagas; José Ma. Cancio; José Ma. Desiderio; Julián; Luz; Nicolás; Pedro Antonio; Pedro Gonz.;

Garibay: José Joaquín; Vicente;

Garracino, Pedro;

Gerardo;

German: Cris. Ant.; Isidro; Faustín J.; Manuel Ignacio; Juan; Juan (child);

Gíol, José;

Gili, Bartolomé;

Giribet, Miguel;

Gloria: Jacinto; Gloria, José Ma.;

Gómez: Francisco; Nicolás; Francisco; José Antonio; Rafael; Rafael; Francisco;

Góngora, José Ma.; José Antonio;

Gonopra, José Ma.;

González: Antonio Alejo.; Inocencio; Cirilo; José Antonio; José Romualdo; José Manuel; Mateo Jacobo; Ramón; Nicolás; Alejandro; Bernardo; Diego; Felipe; José Eusebio; José Feliciano; Mateo Jacobo, Tomás; Alejo; Francisco (soldier); Francisco (padre); José; José Rafael M.; Ciriaco; Juan; Pedro; Rafael, Gerardo; Rafael; José Leandro;

Goycoechea, Felipe;

Grajera, Antonio;

Grijalva, Juan Pablo;

Guerrero: Juan José; Joaquín; José; José Antonio; Julián; Mateo;

Guevara: José; José Canuto; José Sebastián; Sebastián; José Francisco;

Gutiérrez: Felipe; Manuel; Francisco;

Guzmán: Isidro; Juan Ma.; Toribio;

Guztinzar, Manuel;

H:

Haro, Felipe;

Hechedo, José Francisco;

Henríquez, Antonio Dom.;

Heredia: Bernardino; José Bernardo;

Hernández: José Rafael; Vicente Antonio; Justo; Juan José Antonio; Felipe; Felipe; José Antonio; José; J. José de la Luz; Antonio; Juan María; Juan;

Herrera, José;

Higuera: Joaquín; José Atanasio; José Loreto; José Manuel; Juan José; José Ignacio; Bernardo de la Luz; Juan José; Salvador; Tiburcio; Tiburcio Javier; Gregorio Ignacio Ma.; Hilario; José; José; José Carlos Salv.; José Gerónimo; José Ma.; José Policarpo; José Antonio; José Joaquín; Manuel; Nicolás Antonio; Salvador;

Horchaga, José Hilario; José Manuel; Manuel;

Hores, José;

Horra, Antonio de la C.;

Hortel, Juan;

I:

Ibarra: Francisco; Andrés Dolores; Gil María; José Desiderio; Juan Antonio; Ramón; Albino; Antonio; Calixto José Antonio;

Igadera: José; José Gordiano;

Iñiquez, Juan;
Islas, Miguel;
Isvan, José Albino;
Iturrate, Domingo S.;
Izquierdo, José;
J:
Jaime, Antonio;
Jaume, Luis;
Jiménez: Francisco; Hilario; Pascual Antonio;
Juárez: Francisco; José Joaquín;
Juncosa, Dom.;
L:
Labra, Juan Antonio;
Ladrón de Guevara, José I.;
Landaeta, Martín;
Lasuén, Fermín Francisco;
Lara: José; José Sostenes; Julián; José Antonio Seferino;
Larios, José Ma.;
Lasso de la Vega, Ramón;
Leal, Isidro José;
Leiva: Anastasio; Agustín; José Andrés; José Antonio Ma.; Juan; Miguel; José Antonio; José Rafael; Manuel Ramón; Rufino;
León: José Ma.; José Manuel;
Lima, José;
Linares: Ignacio; José de los S.; Mariano de Dolores; Francisco; Ramón; Salvador;
Lineza, Miguel;
Lisalde: Diego; Félix; Juan Crisos. Antonio;
Lizalda, Pedro Antonio;
Llamas, Antonio;
Lledo, Rafael;
Llepis, José Mariano;
Lobo: José; José Basilio; Cecilio; Pedro;
López: Baldomero; Jacinto; Juan Francisco; Francisco; Ignacio Ma. De Jesús; Gaspar;
Joaquín; José Ma.; Luis; Pedro; Sebastián A.; José Antonio Gil; José Ma. Ramón; Juan José; Melchor; Juan; Cayetano; Claudio; Cornelio Ma.;

Ignacio; Estevan Ignacio; Juan José Trinidad;
Lozano, Pedro;
Lugo: Luis Gonzaga; Francisco; Ignacio; José Ignacio; Seferino; José Antonio; Salvador; Ant. Ma.; José; José Antonio; Juan Ma.; Juan; Miguel; Pablo José; Ramón Lorenzo;
Lujan, José;
M:
Machado: José Antonio; José Manuel; José Agustín Ant.; José Hilario; José Ignacio Ant.;
Machuca, José;
Malaret, Domingo;
Maldonado. Juan;
Mallen, Manuel;
Manrique, Sebastián;
Manríquez, Luis;
Manzana, Miguel A.;
Mario, Antonio;
Mariné y Salvatierra, J.;
Mariner, Juan;
Mario, Tomás;
Márquez: Francisco Rafael; José;
Marron, Rafael;
Martiarena, José Manuel;
Martín, Juan;
Martínez: Luis Antonio; Pedro Adriano, Luis María; Toribio; Dionisio; José Ma.; Juan Ignacio; Norberto; Antonio; Bartolomé Mateo; Gregorio; José; José Leocadio; José Ma.; Manuel; Máximo; Máximo Ramón; Reyes;
Medina, José;
Mejía, Pedro;
Mejía: Francisco Javier; Juan;
Melecio, José;
Mendoza: Manuel; José de los Reyes; Manuel; Mariano; Mariano, José; Miguel;
Mequías, Juan Alberto;
Mercado, Mariano;
Merelo, Lorenzo;
Merino, Agustín;

Mesa: Nicolás Ma.; Valerio; Dolores; Ignacio; Juan Antonio; Luis Ma.; José Antonio; José Julián Antonio; Juan José;

Miguel, José;

Miranda: Juan Ma.; Alejo; Antonio; José Antonio; Apolinario; José Hilario; José Mariano; José Santiago; Juan Crisóstomo; Vicente Manuel;

Mojica: José Ma.; Vicente;

Molas, José;

Molina, Joaquín; Pedro;

Monreal, José Antonio Nicolás;

Mona, José;

Montaban, Laureano;

Montaña, Antonio;

Montaño, Antonio;

Montero: Cesareo Antonio; Manuel;

Monteverde, Francisco;

Montial, Juan Andrés;

Moraga, José Joaquín; Gabriel; Vicente José;

Moreno: F. S.; Felipe Santiago; Felipe; José; Juan Francisco; Manuel;

Morillo, José Julián;

Moumarus, Luis;

Muñoz, Manuel;

Mugártegui, Pablo;

Murguía, José Ant.;

Murillo, Loreto; Francisca; Juan;

Muruato, José;

N:

Navarro: José Antonio; José Clemente; José María;

Nieto: José Manuel; Juan José Ma.; Manuel Pérez; José Antonio Ma.;

Noriega, José Ramón; José Raimundo;

Noboa, Diego;

Nocedal. José;

O:

Obaye, José Antonio;

Oceguera, Faustino;

Ochoa: Francisco Javier; Felipe;

Ojeda, Gabriel;

Olivares: José Miguel; José Francisco B.; Pedro Alcántara;

Olivas, Juan Matia; Olivas, Cosme;

Olivas: José Herculano; José Lázaro Ma.; José Nicolás; Pablo;

Olivera: José Ignacio; Juan María; Ignacio; Antonio Lúcas Ma.; Diego Antonio de la Luz; José Desiderio; José; José Leonardo M.; José Ma. Matías; Máximo José; Tomás Antonio; Higinio; José Ant. Secundino; Rosalina Ma.;

Oliveros, Lúcas;

Olvera: Diego; Francisco;

Ontiveros: José Antonio; Francisco; Juan de Dios; Juan Ma.; Pacífico Juan; Patricio;

Orámas, Cristóbal;

Oribe, Tomás C.;

Orozco, José Manuel;

Ortega: José Francisco; Ignacio; José Francisco Ma.; José Ma.; Juan; Juan Cap. Ant. M. H.; José Ma. Martín; Juan Cap.; Miguel; Ortega; José Miguel; José Quintín de los S.; José Vicente; Antonio; Matías; Miguel;

Ortel, Juan;

Osequera, Faustino;

Osio, José Ma.;

Osorio, José;

Osorno, Pedro;

Osuna: Juan Ismerio; Juan Luis; Miguel; José Joaquín; José Ma.; Juan Nepomuceno;

Otondo, Felipe;

P:

Pacheco: Juan Salvio; Bartolomé Ignacio; Rafael; Miguel; Bartolo; Francisco; Ignacio;

Padilla: Juan; Jacinto;

Parrajales;

Palafox, José;

Palomares; José Cristóbal; José Ramírez;

Palóu, Francisco;

Panella, José, padre;

Parra: José; José; José Antonio; José Miguel Sabino;

Parron, Fernando;

Parrilla, León;

Paterna, Antonio;

Patron, Antonio José;

Patiño, José Victoriano;

Payeras, Mariano, padre;

Pedraza, José Antonio;

Pedro: José Antonio Ma. De S. T.; José Francisco de S. T.;

Pedro y Gil, Rafael;

Peña: Francisco Ma.; José Antonio; Gerardo; Luis; Eustaquio; Peña, José; Peña, Teodoro;

Peña y Saravia, Tomás;

Pengues, Miguel Sobrevia;

Peralta: Gabriel; Juan José; Luis Ma.; Pedro Regalado; Hermenegildo Ignacio; Juan; Pantaleón;

Pérez: Juan; Crispín; José Ignacio; Antonio Irineo; Antonio Ma.;Estevan; José Ma.; José Ma.; Juan Bautista; Luis Manuel; José;

Pérez de la Fuente, Pedro;

Pericas, Miguel

Peyri, Antonio;

Pico: Santiago de la Cruz; Francisco Javier; José Dolores; José Ma.; Juan Patricio; Joaquín; José Antonio Bernardo; José Vicente; Mariano; Miguel; Patricio;

Pieras, Miguel;

Piña: Juan Máximo; Mariano; Pedro Rafael; Juan María; Pinto, Pablo; Pinto, Marcelo;

Planes, Gerónimo;

Plenelo, Valentín;

Pliego, José;

Polanco, José;

Pollorena: Pedro; Juan; Rafael Eugenio;

Portella, Francisco;

Portolá, Gaspar de;

Preciado, Venancio;

Prestamero, Juan;

Puga, Joaquín;

Puyol, Francisco;

Prat, Pedro;

Puig, Juan;

Q:

Quesada, Manuel (soldier); Manuel;

Quijada: Ignacio Ma.;Vicente; José Nazario de la T.; José Lorenzo; Simon;

Quintero: Luis; Clemente; Teodosio

Quinto, Simon Tadeo;

R:

Ramírez: Francisco; Bernardo; José Antonio, José Guadalupe;

Ramos: José; José; Pablo Antonio;

Rasa, Lorenzo;

Rey: Cristóbal; José; Juan del;

Reyes: Juan Francisco; Martín; Francisco; José Jacinto; José; José (saddler) Máximo Julián;

Río, Francisco del;

Rioboo, Juan Antonio García;

Ríos, Feliciano; Julián; Cayetano; Silverio Antonio Juan;

Rivera: Tadeo; Joaquín; Salvador;

Rivera y Moncada, Fernando;

Roberto: Justo; Matías;

Robles: Juan José; Manuel Ma.; José Antonio;

Roca: Carlos Pedro José; José;

Rocha: Juan Estevan; Cornelio (settler); Cornelio; José; Juan José Lor.;

Rochin, Ignacio;

Rodríguez: Manuel; José; Rodríguez, Pablo; Vicente; Alejo Máximo; Inocencio José; Joaquín; José Antonio; José Fran. Ant. L.; José Ignacio; José de Jesús I.; José León; José Ma.; Sebastián; Alejandro; Rodríguez, Felipe Antonio; José del Carmen S.; José Brigido; Rodríguez, Juan; Juan Francisco; Juan de Dios; Manuel; Matías;

Román, José Joaquín;

Romero: Antonio; Felipe; Anselmo José

Ignacio; José Domingo; José Estevan; José Ma.; Basilio F.; Juan María; Pedro; José Ant. Estevan; José Gregorio; José Man. Secundino; Juan Ma.; Luis; Rafael;

Rosales: Bernardo; Cornelio; José Cornelio; Rosalío, Eugenio;

Rosas: Juan Estevan; Alejo; Baltasar Juan José; Basilio; Carlos; José Alejandro; José Máximo; José Máximo; Gil Antonio; José Darlo; José; José Antonio; José Antonio; José Antonio Doroteo; León María; Luis María;

Rubio: Ascensio Álvarez; Bernardo; José Carlos; Juan Antonio; Carlos; Fran. Ramón de la L.; Mateo; José Antonio; Luis Ma.; Rafael Felipe; Francisco;

Rubí. Mariano;

Rueda, Pedro;

Ruelas: Fernando; Francisco; Venancio;

Ruiz: Antonio Vicente; Alejandro; Juan Ma.; Diego Ma.; Francisco Ma.; Efigenio; Fructuoso Ma.; Juan Pedro Jacinto; Nervo Pedro; Pedro José; Estevan; Ignacio; José Hilario; José Joaquín; Manuel; Santiago; Toribio;

S:

Sáez: Nazario; Justo; Juan; Miguel;

Saenz, Ignacio;

Sajo, José;

Sal: Hermenegildo; Ignacio Francisco; Domingo;

Melitón; Alonso Isidro;

Salas, Francisco;

Salazar: Doroteo de la Luz; Doroteo; José Loreto; Juan José; Miguel; José Marcos; José; Miguel;

Samaniego: José Ma. Gil; Pablo Ant. Nemesio; Tiburcio Antonio; José del Cármen;

Sánchez: Francisco Miguel; Joaquín; José Antonio; Juan; Francisco; José Tadeo; José Segundo; José Antonio; Juan; Juan Ma.; Vicente; Vicente Anastacio;

Sangrador, Miguel;

Sandoval: Antonio; Gregorio Antonio;

Santa Ana, José Francisco;

Santa Catarina y Noriega, M.;

Santa María, Vicente;

Santiago, Juan José;

Sarmiento, Francisco;

Sarco, José Joaquín;

Segundo, Angel;

Segura, Gregorio;

Señan, José Francisco de P.

Sepúlveda: Rafael; Juan José; Francisco Javier; Enrique; Francisco Javier; José Dolores; José Enrique; A.; José de los Dolores; Patricio;

Sebastián;

Serra, Junípero, padre.'

Serrano: Francisco; Leandro José; José María;

Servin, José Isidro;

Sierra, Benito;

Silva, José;

Silva: José; Hilario León José; José Manuel; José Miguel; Juan de Dios J. S.; Rafael; Hilario León José; José de los Santos; José Ma.; José Manuel Victor; Teodoro;

Sinova: José; José Francisco;

Sitjar, Buenaventura;

Sola, Faustino;

Soberanes: José Ma.; Agustín; José Ma.;

Soler: Juan; Nicolás; Pablo;

Solis, Alejandro;

Solórzano: Francisco; Juan; Juan Mateo; Pío Antonio;

Somera, José Antonio F.;

Sorno, José Nolasco;

Sorde, José;

Sotelo: Francisco Antonio; José Antonio; José Gabriel; José Ma.; José Antonio; José Ma. Tiburcio; Ramón;

Soto: Mateo Ignacio; Alejandro; Damaso; Francisco José Dolores; Francisco Ma.; Ignacio;

Isidro; Francisco Rexis; Guillermo; Ignacio Javier; José Joaquín; Mariano; Antonio; José Ma. Ant.; Juan; Miguel; Rafael; Tomás;

Sotomayor: Alejandro; José Crisóstomo; José Doroteo;

Suárez, Simon;

T:

Talamantes;

Tapia: Felipe Santiago; Bartolomé; Cristóbal; José Bartolo; José Francisco; Francisco; José Antonio; Mariano;

Tapinto, Mariano;

Tapis, Estevan;

Tejo, Ignacio Antonio;

Tico: José Joaquín; Fern. José Ma. Ign. M.;

Tobar, Albino;

Toca, José Manuel;

Toral, José;

Torres: Victoriano; Narciso; Nicolás;

Torrens, Hilario;

Trasviñas, Antonio;

Trujillo, José;

U:

Ulloa, José Santos;

Uribes, Miguel;

Ursetino, José;

Uría, José Antonio;

Usson, Ramón;

V:

Valderrama, José Cornelio;

Valdés: Juan Bautista; Valdés, Antonio Albino; Antonio Ma. De Sta. M.; Eugenio; José Basilio; José Lorenzo; José Melesio; Juan Melesio; Luciano José; Máximo Tomás; Antonio; Crecencio; Francisco; Gregorio; José Rafael;

Valencia: José Manuel; Francisco; Ignacio; Juan Ignacio; Juan Vicente Cris.; Manuel; Miguel Antonio; José Antonio; José Manuel; Agustín; José Julián; Rafael; Angel; Antonio Ma.; Gaspar José; José; José Antonio Me.; José Manuel;

Antonio de Gr.; Joaquín; José Antonio Ma.; José Candelario; José Ignacio; José Rafael; Juan; Juan Angel; Juan Ma.; Máximo; Pedro; Simeon Máximo; Vicente; Vicente Antonio; José Ma.; José Matías; José Miguel; José Pedro; José Ramón; Segundo;

Valero, Ignacio;

Vallejo: Vicente Ferrer; Juan José; José de Jesús;

Vanegas, Cosme;

Varelas: Casimiro; Juan; José Cayetano; José Manuel; Juan;

Vargas, Manuel;

Vázquez: Gil Anastasio; José Francisco; Juan Atanasio; Juan Silverio; José Tiburcio; Antonio; José, Faustino; Felipe; Félix; Hermenegildo; José Antonio Pablo; José Timoteo; Julio Ma.;

Vega, José Manuel;

Vegas, Matías;

Véjar: Pablo; Salvador;

Velarde: José Jacobo; José Ma.; Agustín; José Luciano.4

Vegerano, José Ma.;

Velasco: Fernando; José Ignacio Mateo;

Velázquez: José; José Ma.;

Vélez, José Miguel;

Velis, José;

Verdugo: Joaquín; José Ma.; Francisco Ma. De la Cruz; Mariano de la Luz; Florencio; Ignacio Leonardo Ma.; Juan Diego; Juan Ma.; Leonardo; Manuel José; Anselmo José; Joaquín; José Francisco; Juan Andrés Dolores; Julio Antonio José; Melitón José;

Verduzco, Anastasio Javier;

Viader, José;

Victoriano;

Vila, Vicente;

Villa: José; Vicente Ferrer; Eleuterio; José Antonio Doroteo; José Francisco Antonio; Pascual; Rafael;

Villalba, Onofre;

Villagomez, Francisco;

Villalobos: José; José Ma.;

Villaseñor, José;

Villavicencio: Rafael; José Antonio; Antonio; Félix; Pascual; José;

Villarino, Félix Antonio;

Villela: Juan Manuel; Marcos;

Viñals, José;

Virjan, Manuel;

Vizcaino, Juan;

Vizcarra, José;

Y:

Yorba: Antonio; Francisco Javier; José Antonio;

José Domingo; Tomás

Z:

Zambrano, Nicolás;

Zayas, José Salvador;

Zúñiga, Pedro B.; Pío Quinto; José; José Antonio; José Valentín Q.; Serapio Ma.; Guillermo A.; José Manuel; Ventura.

PRESIDIOS

Presidial villages/towns were first established in San Diego (1769), Monterey (1770), San Francisco (1776), and Santa Barbara (1782). At first these were little more than a square enclosure surrounded by a ditch and a rampart of earth. Inside could be found a little church, barracks for the military, some civilian dwellings, storehouses, workshops, etc. When the area was safe enough, houses were built outside the square, gardens were planted and fields developed for crops. Pasture land was designated for livestock.

Soldiers, referred to as *"soldados de cuera"* (leather jacket soldiers) because they wore thick leather jackets to the knees for protection against arrows, were poorly equipped. Muskets were used when available but gunpowder was always in short supply. There were a few bronze cannon but no powder for them. Any well equipped ship of war would have more firepower than a California presidio. Soldiers explored, hunted for the presidio, returned runaway neophytes, carried the mail, etc., but they protested having to work on construction details, saying it wasn't military and they hadn't signed on for such work.

GABE MORAGA

The most famous explorer-soldier to come out of Spanish California was **Gabriel Moraga** (1767-1823). Born to the military tradition, his father was José Joaquín Moraga who served as second in command during the Anza colonizing expedition of 1776. It was José Joaquín who finally led the Anza colonists to the place where they built their homes in San Francisco and where J. Joaquín became first commandant of the presidio.

Gabriel was born at Fronteras, Sonora. He and his mother were with the Rivera Moncada expedition to California in 1781 and narrowly missed being victims of the Yuma Massacre. Moraga was a "Leatherjacket" by the age of 16 and in time became a renowned Indian fighter but his achievements in explorations of California surpassed even his fighting abilities. Gabriel enlisted as a private in 1784, was made a corporal in 1788, sergeant in 1800, alférez in 1806, brevet-lieutenant (1811) then finally lieutenant (1818). During his forty-one years of military service Gabriel was on forty-two (possibly forty-six) expeditions/campaigns, most of them successful. [See Note # 19.] Among his many trail breaking expeditions he explored the entire length and breadth of the San Joaquín Valley, penetrated to the foothills of the Sierra Nevada a number of times, identified rivers like the Sacramento and Kings rivers, visited the Russian Fort Rus (Ross) thrice, and possibly went into Nevada.

Gabriel Moraga has been described as a tall, well built outdoorsman, his skin darkened by the sun, a brave fighter of hostiles but also gentlemanly in behavior, *"honest, moral, kind-hearted, popular, and very energetic."* Even today he is considered the best soldier of his time. He died at Santa Barbara on June 15, 1823, and was buried in the mission graveyard. [See Note # 20.]

CIVILIAN VILLAGES

The first civilian communities to be established in California were **San José** (1777), **Los Ángeles** (1781), and **Branciforte** (near Santa Cruz, 1797). Like the missionaries, Hispanic pioneers in the wilderness first lived in brush shelters. Then huts were built by driving poles into the ground to form walls and roofed over with tules or grass smeared with mud or clay. It took time before the settlers could build with adobe and/or stone.

Each settlement was granted four square leagues of land. A large plaza (central square) was laid out and facing it were built the church, government offices, warehouses, jail, dwellings, shops, etc., in the usual way. As with the missions, agriculture was the principal activity and the market was the presidios. Within a few years San José was producing a large surplus of wheat, corn, and beans. As of 1790 supply ships from San Blas no longer brought in flour, corn, or beans because of village productivity. Production fell after 1796 with the establishment of Mission San José which gained control of Indian laborers for the mission. Impressive amounts of corn were harvested in the Los Ángeles area but this too diminished after 1800 due to the policy of allowing settlers to sell only to presidios. Governor Diego de Borica (1794-1800) petitioned his superiors that colonists should be allowed to sell beyond the presidios, for example, to the San Blas supply ships to take to Mexico. The petition was granted in 1801 and proved a resounding success when large supplies of flour and wheat were shipped. The California-San Blas trade was disrupted after 1810 because of civil war and the war for independence from Spain.

ECONOMIC DEVELOPMENT

Along with supporting the development of missions, presidios, and settler villages, the Spanish Crown promoted measures intended to strengthen the economic development of California, which included the hunting of sea otters for their pelts, the cultivation of hemp, and the sending of skilled artisans to California to promote manufactures in the area. The hunting of sea otters was encouraged because otter pelts were highly prized in China and commanded good prizes. Even more important, in Canton the furs could be traded for mercury which was crucial in silver mining. By 1786 Crown representative Vicente Vasadre y Vega was in California to direct the gathering of otter pelts. Within a few years bureaucratic obstacles impeded this industry and by 1790 the Crown terminated it, although pelts continued to be gathered on a smaller scale.

The cultivation of hemp in California was an effort to revitalize the colonial economy. Some of the northern Franciscan missions had experimented with the growing of hemp as of 1791 but for once the multi-talented missionaries didn't have the expertise (or much time for studying it) for its agriculture. In 1795 growing instructions were sent up from Mexico but it wasn't until Joaquín Sánchez, a marine sergeant, was sent up from San Blas that the situation began to improve markedly. Sánchez decided that the Los Ángeles area was superior to San José so he moved south. In 1806 exports of hemp went over 1,800 pounds and by 1810 a huge 222,000 pounds were produced. Hemp was now recognized as an export staple that could be produced in California. But the exhilaration was short lived: the wars for independence from Spain disrupted the San Blas supply line and in 1811 Governor Arrillaga (1800-1814) instructed Sánchez to produce only enough hemp for California needs.

Between 1791-1795 the Crown brought in some twenty skilled artisans to teach mission Indians carpentry, pottery making, tanning hides, the textile arts, blacksmithing, shoemaking, how to build with stone and brick, etc. The artisans worked on four- or five-year contracts and their highly successful efforts left a lasting imprint on California.

There were relatively few Hispanic people in California, much too few to handle the work that needed to be done in labor intensive industries like agriculture and ranching. It has been estimated that by 1800 there were around 1,800 Hispanics and some 35, 800 coastal Indians living in settled areas of Spanish California. [See Note # 21.] Because there were so few Hispanics, labor was performed mostly by Indians, for wages, in the settlements. The missionaries protested the use of Indian laborers, saying the settlers were "too few and too lazy" to do their own work while settlers and/or civilian authorities countered that missionaries were using Indians like virtual slaves. (As already indicated, these charges and counter charges provide the basis for much English language "history" that was to follow.)

Most of the settlers living in San José and Los Ángeles were retired military. Most were no longer young so they hired Indians to work for them. As early as 1782 the military established issued strict guidelines on how Indians could be hired to work, what they had to be paid, and what jobs could be performed by Indian women. In 1787 Governor Fages (1782-1791) issued laws that regulated the use of gentile Indian laborers: they could be cowboys, cooks, muleteers, water carriers, domestic servants, etc.; agricultural workers had to be paid a third to half of the crops they harvested. Gentiles could not live in the Spanish villages (like Hispanics couldn't live in Indian villages) nor were they permitted to enter their employers homes, especially the women. But there was much acculturation between the two groups. Many learned the other's language, the Indians dressed like their employers, sporting shoes, sarapes, hats, etc., and some single men married Indian women.

INDEPENDENCE and the MEXICAN PERIOD

The struggle for independence from Spain, which started in 1810 and ended in 1821, was costly both in Mexican lives and prosperity. In November of 1818 a Frenchman by the name of **Hippolyte de Bouchard**, commanding the vessel *Argentina*, and an Englishman named **Peter Corney**, commanding the *Santa Rosa*, arrived in the Monterey area with "...*some 350 cutthroats, thieves, and revolutionists...*" bent on looting California under the pretext of revolution against the King of Spain. The *Santa Rosa* opened fire on the Monterey presidio then Bouchard arrived in the *Argentina* and demanded surrender on the basis that resistance was useless because the vessels were mightily armed while the forty or so Californio presidial soldiers had only some eight dilapidated cannon. Not having enough soldiers to combat Bouchard's and Corney's cutthroats, Governor Solá retreated inland to Rancho del Rey (near present Salinas). The citizens of Monterey were in near panic as they gathered what belongings they could and fled to the missions of San Antonio and San Juan Bautista. The pirates sacked Monterey then burned the town and presidio. Even gardens and orchards were destroyed by these villains who maintained they were promoting "liberty." The pirates then sailed down the coast, burning Rancho del Refugio, robbing San Juan Capistrano of its wines, then finally sailing away.

While there was no legitimate revolutionary fighting in Alta California the independence movement ended state support for all missions and presidios. Neither missionaries nor soldiers could count on their salaries nor the goods brought through the San Blas supply line. In 1821 when **Agustín Iturbide** promulgated his *Plan de Iguala* the news spread that Mexico was indeed independent of Spain. Governor Solá (1815-22) and other California officials took an oath of allegiance to the new government, as did some of the missionaries. In short order a native Californio, **Luis Antonio Argüello**, was chosen as governor (1822-25), the first in California history. While the province escaped the bloodletting, political turbulence, and personal rivalries taking place in Mexico during the revolution for independence, California governors during the Mexican period had to confront lack of funds, political conspiracies against them as well as certain Mexican policies of which the Californios disapproved.

RAISING MONEY

In 1824 Governor Argüello invited a group of prominent military, civil, and clerical personalities to discuss how best to raise money for school, civic, and government expenses. It was decided that branded cattle and agricultural crops would be taxed. Customs duties would also be collected at all ports. The religious refused to permit mission products to be taxed, saying everything had been intended to promote Indian welfare right from the beginning. Further, as Indian properties, the missions and their products were untaxable. The debates raged but the missions and padres continued much as they always had.

TRADERS & SETTLERS

During Argüello's administration relatively large numbers of traders and some settlers arrived in California. Argüello had been friendly with the Russians since the days when **Nikolai Rezanov** had courted his beautiful sister, **Concepción Argüello**. The governor signed a trade agreement with the Russians and in 1824 some 677 sea otter skins were delivered to government authorities. Englishmen (like Hugh McCulloch and William Hartnell in 1822) and Americans (like Henry Gyzelaar and William Gale, already recognized because they had been successful smugglers from Boston) also came to establish trade relations for what was to become known as the "hide and tallow trade." American middlemen like Abel Stearns, William H. Davis, Alfred Robinson, Nathan Spear, John Cooper, etc., were to become somewhat famous in California. Some were able to blend Californio and American cultures, married California women, became Mexican citizens, and obtained valuable land grants. Some of these men came to be considered as *hijos del país* (native sons).

NORTH vs. SOUTH

Discernible jealousies cropped up between Californios living in the north as opposed to the south as of the administration of **José María de Echeandía** (1825-31) when the governor moved the seat of government from Monterey to San Diego. There continued frictions between native born Californios and authorities sent from Mexico. The mission padres also resented having to supply the presidios without being paid properly and they had the impression people mistrusted them for being Spanish born.

One of the most bitter Californio complaints was the attempted Mexican policy of sending convicts to California. Some 80 convicts arrived in 1829 with another 50 or so in 1830. [On the east coast Ben Franklin once criticized the English practice of sending convicts to the American colonies, saying "If they're going to send us their criminals we should have the right to send them some of ours."] There was such a public outcry that the practice ceased.

SECULARIZATION OF MISSIONS

The most significant event of Echeandía's administration was the 1831 proclamation for secularization of the missions. The missions were to become villages/towns, each Indian family would receive a share of mission land and livestock, and the padres would remain as curates in the villages. The "controversial" plan would be fought but eventually mission properties would be broken up.

ILLEGAL IMMIGRANTS

Also of important future significance for California was the appearance of illegal immigrants like **Jedediah S. Smith** and other fur trappers from the USA. In 1826 Smith led an expedition of trappers from the Bear River Valley in northern Utah to Mission San Gabriel. [See Note # 22.] The padres at the mission received the *"uncouth-looking strangers"* with typical California hospitality, supplying them with food, drink, and lodging. In return, *"…the trappers provided the friars with bear traps to be used to catch Indians who poached oranges from mission groves."* [See Note # 23.]

Smith went or was summoned to San Diego where Governor Echeandía demanded to know what he was doing in California. Smith replied that he and his men had merely "stumbled" into the province while trapping whereupon the governor placed him under arrest as an illegal immigrant. [See Note # 24.] Smith was finally set free and ordered to take his men and leave California at once and never return. Showing his contempt for Mexican officials who had released him from jail, Smith and his men made a base camp in the San Joaquín Valley in order to trap along the Stanislaus and Kings rivers. He left most of his men there and returned to the Great Basin of Utah. In July of 1827 Smith decided to return to California with another nineteen men. Along the way ten were killed by Indians and when they finally made it to Mission San José they were warned to leave immediately by Father Durán who said the Americans were trying to get the Indian neophytes to abandon their mission life. Governor Echeandía arrived and once more arrested Smith but then relented and released him for a second time. Smith and his men headed north, trapping whenever possible. In July of 1828 the group was attacked by Indians and only Smith and two others survived the slaughter. On May 27, 1831, Smith was on the Santa Fe Trail when he was killed by hostile Comanches. [See Note # 25.]

The "mountain men" like Jedediah Smith have been lauded for their roles in "opening the West." Robert G. Cleland wrote in *This Reckless Breed Of Men* that they *"…were destined to live for generations in the history and heroic tradition of the race–Jim Bridger, Thomas Fitzpatrick, Andrew Henry, James Clyman, Milton and William Sublette, Hugh Glass, Etienne Provost, David E. Jackson, Daniel T. Potts, and perhaps half as many more–a company that constituted 'the most significant group of continental explorers ever brought together.'* " [See Note # 26.]

James Ohio Pattie was another trapper who made it into the history of California after Jed Smith. Pattie wrote a book, *Personal Narrative* (1840) in which he relates his various "adventures," like after getting out of jail a smallpox epidemic broke out in northern California (late 1820s) and he just happened to have some vaccine with him so he became a "hero" when he vaccinated some 10,000 people, including Indians. [See Note # 27.]

PIONEERS

The last group of Hispanic pioneers to arrive in California were the colonists brought in by José María Padrés, who was backed by the prominent José María Hijar. This group of superior colonists included artisans as well as doctors, teachers, lawyers, goldsmiths, blacksmiths, etc. [See Note # 28.] They are known as the "Hijar-Padrés Colony" (sometimes referred to as the Farias Colony; Farias was the acting president of Mexico at the time of colonization) and they included:

Abrego, José. Age 22. Single.
Adrián, Juan Antonio. Single.
Aguilar, José María. Single. Aguilar, Santiago.
Alanis, Felipe.
Álvarez, Alvina. Teacher.
Andrade, Antonio.
Angela, María (this may not be her full name). Age 12.
Arana, José.
Araujo, Buenaventura. Naval officer.
Ayala, Juan Nepomuceno. Age 20.

Baric, Charles (French). Age 27. Teacher.
Berduzco, Francisco (sometimes spelled Verduzco). Age 22. Merchant.
Bonilla, José Mariano. Age 27. Teacher.
Bonilla, Luis (brother of José Mariano Bonilla). Single. Teacher.
Bonilla, Vicente (brother of José Mariano and Luis Bonilla). Single.
Brown, Charles. Joined the Farias colony in California.

Cabello, Martin S. Revenue officer who came out with the colony.
Camarillo, Juan.
Carranza, Francisco. Age 14. Single.
Castellón, Bárbara.
Castellón, Isidoro. Age 19.
Castillo, Doña Jesús. Teacher.
Castillo Negrete, Francisco Javier. Single.
Castillo Negrete, Luis (brother of F. J. Castillo Negrete), Age 35,. Married; 6 children.

Cepeda, Pedro (also spelled Zepeda).

Coronel, Antonio Franco. (son of Ignacio Coronel). Age 16.

Coronel, Guillermo. Teacher.

Coronel, Ignacio. Age 39. Married. Teacher.

Coronel, Josefa. Age 18. Single.

Coronel, Manuel. Age 2.

Coronel, Micaela.

Coronel, Soledad. Age 8.

Cosío, José María.

Covarrubias, José María.

Dávila, Agustín. Age 30. Single. Painter of saints. Dávila, Antonio (brother of Agustín Dávila).

Desforges, Auguste.

Díaz, Guadalupe (wife of Nicanor Estrada). Age 22.,

Díaz Argüello, Benito. Age 20.

Enriquez, Petra. Teacher.

Esparza, Juan Bautista (also known as Victoriano Vega). Age 24.

Espíndola, María Paz.

Estrada, Elena (daughter of Nicanor Estrada). Born on voyage to California in 1834.

Estrada, Nicanor. Age 28.

Estrada, Umesinda (daughter of Nicanor Estrada). Age 7.

Fernández, Dionisio. Teacher.

Fernández, Francisca. Teacher.

Fernández, José Zenón. Teacher.

Fernández, Juan Alonso. Died on voyage from San Blas to San Diego on the *Natalia*.

Fernández, Doña Loreto. Teacher.

Fernández, Manuela. Teacher.

Fernández, Máximo. Teacher.

Fernández, Sabás. Teacher.

Flores, Francisca.

Flores, Gumersindo.

Franco, Encarnación.

García, Francisco.

Gardano, Guadalupe (wife of José de Jesús Noé).

Garraleta, Antonio.

Garraleta, Justa. She is said also to have had a sister with her.

González, José de Jesús. Age 21.

González, Manuel María.

Guerrero y Palomares, Francisco.

Gutiérrez, Anacleto. Single.
Gutiérrez, José María.

Híjar, Carlos N. (nephew of José María Híjar). There is also a
Miguel Híjar listed, which might be another name for Carlos N. Híjar.
Híjar, José María.

Janssens, Agustin. Age 17. Single.
Jiménez, Cayetana.

Lara, Romualdo. Single.
Llano, Mariano.
López, José Rosas (known as "el clarín López"). Age 20.
López, Mariano. Single.

Madariaga, Doña María Enciso.

Meneses, Agustín.
Meneses, Florencio. Single.
Montes, José. Single.
Mora, Regino de la.
Morales de Castillo Negrete, Josefa (wife of Luis Castillo Negrete. Age 24.
Muñoz, Juan Antonio. Single.

Noé, José de Jesús.
Noé, Miguel. Infant, 1 year old.
Noreña, Antonio (also spelled Moreña). Teacher.

Ocampo, Francisco. Single.
O'Donoju, Simón. Single.
Olivier, Pierre.
Olvera. Agustín (nephew of Ignacio Coronel). Age 13
Ortega, Antonio. Single.
Ortez, Hilario. Age 22. Single.
Oviedo, José María. Teacher.

Padilla, Juan de Dios. Widower. Retired army captain.
Padrés, José María.
Padrés, Rafael (brother of José María Padrés).
Paz, Ignacia. Teacher.

Peña, Carmen (daughter of Cosme Peña). Age 10.
Peña, Cesaría (daughter of Cosme Peña). Age 6.
Peña, Cosme.
Pino, Braulis del. Single.
Prudon, Victor. Age 25. Teacher. (He married Teodocia Bojorques.)

Ramírez, Antonio.
Revilla family. 3 women, 2 boys, and Felipe de Revilla. Possibly the latter was the head of the family. His daughter, María Joaquina Revilla, was engaged to be married to Buenaventura Araujo.

Ríos, José. Single.
Rojas, Feliciano. Age 14.
Romero, Balbino.
Romero, Francisca (wife of Ignacio Coronel). Age 35.
Romero, José Mariano. Teacher.
Rosa, José de la.
Rosa, María Dolores de la (wife of José de la Rosa).
Rosas, Daría. A brother is also mentioned, whose name is given as *Eduwiges*.
Rosel, Francisca. Teacher.

Sabici, Matías.
Salgado, Tomás.
Santa María, José. Single.
Serrano, Florencio. Age 25. Teacher. He says he brought with him to California a widowed sister and a child.
Serrano, Rita (wife of Florencio Serrano).
Solís, Juan. Terán, Miguel.

Torres, Francisco. Age 28.

Valverde, Agustín. Age 22.
Vargas, Francisco.
Vargas Machuca, Miguel. Age 43.
Vidal, Bartolomé.

Zárate, Ignacia. Teacher.

SETTLERS & VISITORS

Many other types of people came to California, including from outside the Hispanic world. *Johann Augustus Suter*, now known as **John Sutter**, fleeing his native Switzerland to avoid debtors' prison as well as an angry wife, arrived around 1839. [See Note # 29.] Due to liberal Mexican land policies, Sutter established his estate, *New Helvetia*, in the area of what is now Sacramento. Among other things, it became a haven for illegal immigrants from the USA.

Richard Henry Dana was a young American sailor who worked on the New England hide-and-tallow ship *Pilgrim* during the years 1835-36 and wrote a book about his impressions. His often cited work, *Two Years Before the Mast*, was published in 1840 and lauded the beauty and fertility of California. Of the Californios he had almost nothing good to say. According to Dana, at the top of society were a few upper class families who intermarried with each other. *"From this upper class they go down by regular shades, growing more and more dark and muddy, until you come to the pure Indian."* Of the justice system Dana exclaimed: *"…they know no law but will and fear."* He portrayed Californios as *"idle, thriftless people,"* victims of "California fever," by which was meant *laziness*. He said the men were addicted to gambling, pride, and extravagance. The women, some of whom were quite beautiful, *"had little virtue…and their morality, of course, is not of the best."* [See Note # 30.] While the moral views of an American sailor on the men and women of California might be challenged in many ways, Dana's book provided information to the American reader who had little else with which to compare it. The trading ships carried *"…everything under the sun…to entice the gullible Californio elite…"* at markups of three hundred percent. Dana's puritanical New England background appears to have been the base for most of his observations, making remarks like that the Californios sold hides because they were too lazy to make shoes for themselves. The women's' fondness *"for dressing…is excessive and often their ruin…A present of a fine mantle or of a necklace or pair of earrings gains the favor of the greater part of them."* He criticized the men who bought fancy clothes for their wives, and he didn't much approve of buying them expensive furniture, jewelry, etc., or any other such frivolities. He ridiculed placing a richly canopied bed on a dirt floor. He laughed at people buying pianos when no one in the family knew how to play. [See Note # 31.] Dana remarked that various English and/or American traders married some of the women but if *"California fever"* spared the first generation of children *"it always attacks the second."* The reading public might well have questioned how Dana, who was at sea for a couple of years and trading along the California coast for a relatively short period of time, came to acquire such knowledge, including genealogy, on all that he professed. Richard Henry Dana didn't seem much impressed with Californio ranching, mission life to preserve the Indians, genuine hospitality, superb horsemanship, etc., but he did express an ominous sentiment when he wrote: *"In the hands of an enterprising people, what a country this might be!"*

The 1841 party led by a twenty-year-old school teacher named **John Bidwell** is often referred to as *"the first emigrant train to California."* (It is possible the party was the first from the USA.) Russell R. Elliott has written that the expedition's "inexperience was exceeded only by their foolhardiness." They departed from Missouri, experienced tremendous hardships because they weren't frontiersmen, didn't know how to handle their animals because they were not products of a ranching environment, ran short of food and had to eat their oxen and mules, were abandoned by their supposed leader (a man named Bartleson) and his cronies, whereupon Bidwell took over, were often lost because they were unfamiliar with the country of burning deserts or mountain snows. That they even survived is credited by Elliott to a chance addition of Father **Pierre Jean De Smet** and two other Jesuits who were going to Idaho with Thomas "Broken Hand" Fitzpatrick as guide. The Bidwell party of illegal immigrants reached the John

Marsh ranch after some six grueling months on the trail. [See Note # 32.]

CALIFORNIO LIFESTYLE

It is necessary to present a portrait of life in California before it was taken over by the USA in order to contrast the very negative opinions of various American writers like Richard Henry Dana or Thomas Jefferson Farnham, the latter of whom stated in his *Life and Adventures in California* that Californios were "*...an imbecile, pusillanimous race of men...unfit to control the destinies of that beautiful country.*"

RANCHING & CATTLE

As already stated, California had its beginnings as a series of Christian missions but by the Mexican period of its history it was dominated by ranching. [See Note # 33.] Almost everyone who wanted pasture land could comply with requirements to obtain it. A small *rancho* contained four square miles but a large one often had as many as thirty. Start-up cattle could even be borrowed on the condition that the same number would be returned within a period of a few years. The missions often loaned cattle in this way. Because the climate was mild there was no need to build shelters for cattle or sheep. Working cattle, sheep, or horses was second nature to Hispanic Californios for such were their cultural heritage. [See Note # 34.] They taught Indians to work livestock and they became adept in the ranching industry which by nature was a healthy activity which became demanding mostly at peak times like round-ups, branding, shearing, etc.

Cattle were of the "large bodied, long horn variety" who had been allowed to run free for so long that they returned to a wild state. These cattle were fierce and couldn't be approached by a man on foot so the Californios captured them from horseback. (**John Bidwell**, who had experienced running for cover from a raging bull, wrote that wild bulls were more dangerous than grizzly bears. **J. Ross Browne** scampered up a tree to watch a mortal combat between a wild bull and a grizzly, both antagonists dying in the contest.) Ranch culture included the *rodeo* (roundup), mandatory brands for ownership and sale, a Book of Brands Registry, *juez de campo* (field judge) to settle all disputes, matanzas (slaughterings), along with singing and dancing at most gatherings.

Ranching was the big business of California, especially between 1828 and 1846, because there was a market for hides and tallow. The Lima trade began in 1813 with the arrival of the ships *Flora* and *Eagle* loaded with manufactured goods to be exchanged for hides, tallow, and mission products like grain and wine. Salted beef was also shipped but for some reason this item didn't prove profitable so it never became a major export. Ships from New England, many from Boston, began arriving in 1822.

The Californios used their cattle in many ways. Beef was basic to the Californio diet. Some mutton was consumed but pork and bear meat were never favorites. Customary law enabled even a weary traveler to kill a beef if necessity required, so long as the hide was left where the cattle owner was certain to find it. For every day needs, the choicest cuts of beef were generally kept for family consumption. Strips of cattle skins were woven into *reatas*, indispensable for a vaquero's work. Many people tanned their own leather and made shoes, using cowhide for soles and deerskin for the covering. Cattle hides were worked for use in the tops and floors of oxcarts, for saddles, horse blankets, stirrup covers, knapsacks, etc., even as mattresses for beds. From tallow the Californios also manufactured candles and soap both for trade (to the Russians in Alaska) and their own use.

EQUALITY in SOCIETY

California society was basically egalitarian because if you owned land and raised cattle you were accepted as part of the "landed gentry," whether you owned four thousand or forty thousand acres. Assuredly, grandees like don **Mariano Vallejo** were at the top since at one time he owned around 175,000 acres on which he ran some 12- to 15,000 cattle, 2- to 3,000 sheep, 7- to 8,000 horses. [See Note # 35.]

BUSINESS & HONOR

The Californios came to be known as men who kept their word in business matters. Merchants and ship captains delivered whatever goods a ranchero asked for then waited in the harbor until the specified number of hides and/or amount of tallow were prepared and delivered. The ships were from South America, Britain, "Boston," France, Germany, Sweden, Russia, etc., and there are no records of anyone being cheated or swindled, nor did the rancheros have difficulties with the various nationalities. The variety of goods brought to California included silk, linen, wool and cotton goods, dresses, shawls, silk stockings, sarapes, lace, window glass, hardware of all kinds, farm machinery, furniture, nails, iron pots and kettles, etc.

WESTERN LIVING

Life on a California ranch was western living in the grandest sense. Each *rancho* had a distinguishing name based on religion, a significant event, or geography. According to William Heath Davis, there were some 1,045 ranches parceled out to Californios by various governors, some 800 of which were stocked with a grand total of some 1,200,000 cattle. He asserts that the department of California "*...was the richest country...*" in the whole Spanish empire. The *don* on a large ranch was like a feudal baron, though Mariano Vallejo once stated "*We treat our servants rather as friends than as servants.*" Most work was done by Indians and the larger ranches could have a hundred Indians or so employed at various tasks. They were paid in kind and beef also became basic to their diet. The Californios were not hard task-masters because they understood they needed native Indians because there weren't enough Hispanics to perform all necessary work. (Californio families were rather large. While one ranchero was said to ride out to work each morning with his *sixteen sons*, all at least six feet tall, this was not the typical Californio family.) The ranchero and his wife were always addressed as *don* (also *patrón*) or doña (*patrona*) as a sign of respect and respect was central to Californio culture. The richest dons also demonstrated their respect for less affluent neighbors.

RANCH HOUSE

Established ranch houses were built of adobe, with thatched or tiled roofs, according to the owner's wealth. Flowers were generally planted close to the house and fruit and/or shade trees were also popular. Doors had no locks because there were no thieves. Homes of the dons were generally designed around a principal room or hall large enough for dancing, the Californios most popular amusement. A house full of guests often stayed for several days, visiting during the day and dancing far into the night.

LABOR

A typical work day began for the *patrón* with a cup of hot chocolate and a tortilla for breakfast. Then he would mount his favorite horse and ride out to inspect his flocks of sheep, herds of cattle or horses, and ascertain that his workers were doing their jobs. At home the *patrona* would supervise the household help in their chores of sweeping, cleaning, cooking, sewing, embroidering, etc., and when there was time playing the guitar or other such musical instrument.

FAMILY

Walter Colton wrote (in *Three Years In California*) that Californios thoroughly enjoyed living, whether rich or not, and faced each new day with a *"genuine gladness of heart."* They abounded in good health, their homes were full of love, children were respectful, and all had something to keep them occupied whether it was work they enjoyed or some form of entertainment. The family was the basis for living and many foreign visitors remarked on the happy familial attachments exhibited by the Californios. They were relatively few in numbers and intermarriage occurred so often that almost everybody was related to everybody else. It became common for people to call each other *"primo"* or *"prima"* even if it happened they weren't directly related. When families visited each other all women worked at household duties as if they were in their own home. The men went out and slaughtered a fat calf with which to feed everyone. After eating there was always music, singing, and dancing. All property was considered communal because it would be repaid in kind when the hosts became guests.

Birth of a child was a serious yet festive occasion. It was considered a singular honor to be asked to stand as godparents for the ceremony. The tradition of standing as godparents for newborns also strengthened the bonds of community. *Padrinos* (godparents) were duty bound to care for their godchildren if something happened to the parents. Further, padrinos became acknowledged by parents as *compadre/comadre* (co-father/mother) because of the children they baptized.

On a rancho when a newborn was ready for the baptismal ceremony he was given to the padrinos who took him on horseback to the mission church. The ceremony concluded, the entire party rode back to the ranch and two things had been accomplished: there was a new Christian in the world and the baby had experienced his first ride on horseback, where he would spend much of his life.

Many names were given to newborn babies but it was customary, due to the religious faith of the Californios, to name most male babies *"José"* in honor of St. Joseph and the females *"María"* for the Virgin Mary. These were ceremonial names and their actual names followed as in José **Antonio**, María **Teresa**, etc. (Sometimes males were named "José María.")

Children were taught to have great respect for their parents and elders in general. While mothers were usually permissive and indulgent, fathers were generally strict disciplinarians. A youngster could be "punished" by being required to eat a Spartan meal alone in a corner while the rest of the family ate normally at table. The other children weren't permitted to ridicule the penitent. As soon as the father finished his meal and went outside the rest of the family rushed to the "miscreant" with regular food and much sympathy. Obedience from children was required even into adulthood. No son could wear a hat in the presence of his father (unless working on the ranch). Males couldn't take their first shave until permitted by the father. At dances you had to request permission to begin the first dance. You could not smoke in front of your parents no matter what your age. Californios into their twenties were required to be in by eight o'clock at night if they lived on their parent's ranch.

Though obedience was required, tenderness for children was a California trait. There was no need for orphanages in Californio because there was always someone who stepped up to care for youngsters if parents died. Due to communal bonds, rearing an orphan wasn't considered a burden but rather a privilege.

COURTSHIP

Courtship and marriage are popular in all societies but they were especially so in Hispanic California. Girls were often married at the age of 13 or 14 and various strategies were developed to conduct courtship despite the watchful eyes of parents or stern *dueñas* (chaperones). The *novio* might serenade his *novia* by playing the guitar and singing from under her window. They might exchange whispered messages at a dance or flashing eyes full of passion while riding or even in church. There was also a language of flowers: a red Indian cress conveyed the message: "my heart is bleeding;" tuberose: "I wait for you;" red rose: "you are the queen of women;" white rose: "you are the queen of purity;" dahlia: "I love only you;" the nasturtium "I wish to be a nun;" passion flower: hatred; turnsole: "I don't even want to look at you," etc.

MARRIAGE

If a young man wanted to marry his sweetheart he, or his parents, must first ask permission of the girl's parents. That was considered "proper" among the *gente de razón*. The prospective groom's father usually opened negotiations, which could often take a week or two. If the answer was in the affirmative then preparations were made for a grand celebration. The first thing the groom had to do was acquire the best horse possible along with the richest saddle he could buy, beg, or borrow because horses is what the wedding party would ride. The groom was also required to purchase the trousseau, which in California meant six articles of each kind of woman's clothing for his bride. He would also have to provide everything necessary for the wedding feast.

On the wedding day the finest horses were saddled and the groom's godmother (*madrina*) was placed to ride in front of the groom, the godfather (*padrino*) having the bride ride likewise in his luxurious saddle, her white satin shoe resting in a loop of gold or silver braid, while he sat behind on a bearskin covering. They rode to church, generally in silence. At the church door all were met by family and friends, usually with music. The ceremony was conducted by the good padre and afterward gaiety is the word. The wedding couple get on the groom's horse, the padrinos on theirs, and all make their way back to the bride's parent's ranch in happy cavalcade. Wagons in the party are often decorated with colored cloth, silk hangings, flowers. But most of the men and some of the women are on horseback, some of the young horsemen performing maneuvers to demonstrate their famous equestrian skills. The horses are richly caparisoned, more so than for any other celebration.

Upon arriving at the ranch the groom's buddies grab his boots and make off with his spurs (which could be redeemed only with a bottle of *aguardiente*.) When the wedding couple enters the ranch house they are received by their relatives, some of the females in tears, and kneel in front of her parents to ask for their blessing. After the blessing the groom signals the musicians to play and the celebration lasts from a few days to a week.

A California marriage was generally based on love and it was for life. Divorce was extremely rare and divorce settlements were utterly unknown. Love and devotion was expected from both sides and, while difficult to believe in the present day, few were disappointed.

HOSPITALITY

Of all the Californio social customs perhaps the people's *hospitality* was the most noted by visitors. This was true from founding years right through the lavish days of the dons. Almost everyone received a warm, uncalculating welcome. Foreigners were impressed with the Californios to the degree that they wanted to become residents. Men and women were honest and their word was their bond. There were *"no courts, no juries, no lawyers, nor any need of them."* José Arnaz writes in his *Recuerdos (Reminiscence; a manuscript collected by H.H. Bancroft): A traveler was received gladly and all of the best was prepared for him, including horses or servants to help him on his way. During the time of the missions a traveler could go from one end of California to the other without having to pay for anything. This hospitality was continued by most rancheros after the missions lost their power.*

Job F. Dye wrote in his "Recollections of California" (Bancroft manuscript) that once learning the language and getting to know the Californios he could travel from San Diego to Sonoma without a horse or any money whatsoever. *"Never was there a more hospitable, generous, and kindly people on the face of the earth than the native-born Californian."* **Walter Colton** wrote in much the same way in his *Three Years in California* but added *"…If I must be cast in sickness or destitution on the care of the stranger, let it be in California; but let it be before American avarice has hardened the heart and made a god of gold."* **William Heath Davis** wrote in his *Sixty Years in California* about don **José Martínez** who constantly favored the people of his area with help when they needed it, whether it be a horse, steer, or money.

Genuine hospitality wasn't reserved only for friends and relatives. When foreign ships came into port they were provided with all kinds of necessities (beef, milk, poultry, vegetables, grain, etc.) and lavish feasts were held in honor of officers and their crews, whether Catholic or of the various Christian denominations.

CRIME

There were very few thieves in California and crime was rare before the arrival of large numbers of Americans and other foreigners. **José Arnaz** wrote that from 1840 to 1843 he never heard of but one murder and one robbery for all of California, that people were secure whether in town or on the road. **James M. Guinn** has written that *relatively few capital crimes were committed in Spanish or Mexican California, that the era of crime began with the 1849 discovery of gold. There was no Joaquín Murieta or Tiburcio Vásquez before the days of '49.* The alcalde system and customary procedure using *hombres buenos* (good men) was considered to provide better justice *"…than in the courts of the present day, with all their elaborate machinery and prolonged course of proceedings"* according to William H. Davis.

Banishment was a popular penalty, Monterey prisoners generally being banished to San Diego, and those from San Diego to Monterey.

GOVERNMENT COSTS

The cost of government was paid for by taxes on sales of town lots, liquor shops, fines for activities like gambling, etc. Revenues were also obtained through the sale of wine and brandy, licenses for saloons and other places of business, tariffs on imports, permits for daces, etc. There were no taxes on land.

CLOTHING STYLES

Wealthy Californios wore a distinctive style of clothes. Men generally wore a broad brimmed hat (lined with silk), usually of a dark color, a distinctive band around the crown; a short jacket of silk or calico, an opened necked shirt, often a waistcoat (rich looking if he wore one); pants made of broadcloth or velveteen and trimmed with gold lace, open at the sides below the knee, or short breeches with white stockings; a red sash around the waist; shoes were generally made of deer skin and highly ornamented. The final garment was a serape (poncho) made of black or dark blue broadcloth, trimmed in velvet by the wealthy. The less affluent wore various colored ponchos.

Don **Tomás Yorba** could be considered representative of how a wealthy California dressed for special occasions. On his head he wore a broad sombrero under which he wore a black silk handkerchief tied in such a way as to have the four corners hanging down behind his neck. His shirt was heavily embroidered, "…*a cravat of white jaconet tastefully tied…*," a vest of blue damask, short breeches of crimson velvet, a jacket of bright green cloth and silver buttons, a brightly colored sash, shoes of deerskin. His sword hung at his waist as he sat astride his magnificent horse. The Yorba saddle, bridle, and spurs were decorated with silver plate.

California women wore gold necklaces and pearl earrings, short sleeved gowns of silk and calico for formal occasions, loose in the waist and without a corset; brightly colored belts or sashes; shoes were of kid or satin. Hair was worn loose or in long braids hanging down the back though married women often coiled it on top of the head where they fastened it with a high comb of tortoise shell (imported from Peru at around $600 each) or horn. The ladies wore hats mainly when they were out on horseback. While walking here and there they used a parasol to protect themselves from the sun and the parasol was every bit as common as the fan.

DIET

The Californio diet was built around beef, fresh or dried (*charqui*, "jerky"). Breakfast generally consisted of hot chocolate (or coffee) and a tortilla. Lunch was the biggest meal of the day. Soups and stews were basic, as were *tortillas*, *frijoles*, and *chile*. Garden vegetables were popular, as were fish and other seafoods where available. Jams and jellies were always popular. *Tamales* and *enchiladas* were always welcome though they required much preparation. Wine was sometimes taken at meal time but generally water was the only drink. Pastries were extremely rare. Probably due to their diet and love of the outdoors, Californios were an extremely healthy population.

SALUTATIONS

Greetings were often ceremonial in Spanish California. Father Serra taught mission Indians to greet each other with *¡Amar a Dios!* (Love God!) and the phrase spread throughout the province. Hispanics removed their hats and addressed each other as *Primo, Compadre,* or *Amado Amigo* when they met each other. When a son wrote a letter to his father the message generally began with *"Mi muy estimado padre."* Good manners were considered basic to the life style of the *gente de razón* in which most people wanted to be included.

RUBRIC

The Hispanic custom of the *rúbrica* was common throughout California for it took the place of an official seal. The rubric's loops, circles, and zigzag lines following one's name were part of a person's legal signature, with as much validity as a cattle brand.

WOMEN

Foreigners who came to California, most of whom were males, lauded the women (over the men) of the province for their abilities to work, moral character (with the exception of sailor **Richard H. Dana**), and their common sense. **William H. Davis**, who married a California woman, wrote in his book: *"During my long and intimate acquaintance with Californians, I have found the women as a class much brighter, quicker in their perceptions, and generally smarter than the men. Their husbands often looked to them for advice and direction in their general business affairs."* **Alfred Robinson** wrote in his *Life in California* that nowhere can there *"...be found more chastity, industrious habits, and correct deportment than among the women..."* of California. **J. M. Amador** wrote that they were famous *"...for their excellent conduct as daughters, sisters, wives, and mothers. They were virtuous and industrious, devoted to their families..."* **C. H. Shinn** agreed that *"The grace, modesty, and beauty of the women of the time were the admiration of every visitor."* Some women worked in gardens and fields as well as in the home, chopped wood, carried water from streams, etc., as well as prepared all food for the family. They usually sewed and embroidered, ironed and cleaned. Women generally combed and braided the long hair of their male relatives. The women were neat in appearance, charitable and hospitable, tender as mothers and affectionate as wives. They were often described as excellent swimmers and expert equestrians. [See Note # 36.]

Fermina Espinosa, the owner of Rancho *Santa Rita*, worked like a man, breaking colts, lassoing cattle, etc., and was widely respected for her managerial abilities. One **V. Avila** of *Rancho Sal-Si-Puedes* is said to have had four blue-eyed daughters who wore men's clothes and did all ranch work like men, used oxcarts to bring in timber from the mountains, and "rested" while doing things like making cheese. Only one of them is said to have married, the other three staying on the ranch to care for their father.

EDUCATION

Missionaries were the most educated class in Hispanic California. For most of the rest of society, working cattle and land didn't require literacy nor was it necessary to the outdoors Californio life style. How to defend yourself against a grizzly bear or an attacking wild bull couldn't be learned in books anyway. Nevertheless, a number of Californios became quite learned because it was their nature to value books and the education they provided. Men like **Mariano Vallejo, Juan B. Alvarado, Juan Bandini**, etc., built up impressive libraries considering the time and place.

Californios have been described as having a natural talent for the use of their language which gave them such a graceful manner that few would have guessed they could neither read nor write. In their own way they were polished, especially when compared to the crude behavior of Americans and other foreigners who little by little came into the province. **Josiah Royce** and **Bayard Taylor** wrote that Californios had a ready wit and many wrote "with ease and force." Women were "fascinating" conversationalists, even when they had received no formal schooling. Californios, men and women, seemed to take naturally to music, playing instruments like the guitar and violin without formal instruction. Many could sing exceedingly well and all danced with highly developed grace. Some boys and girls who lived in towns were taught the basics of reading and writing in various people's homes. Small children were taught to recite their prayers. José María Amador (*Memorias sobre la historia de California*) wrote that when he was born (1794) there were no schools so he learned to read and write from his mother, María Ramona Noriega, who also taught his siblings, various neighborhood children, and a few soldiers who wanted to become corporals in the Army.

Governor Borica made an effort to begin a public school system in 1794. The main problems were a lack of teachers and funds with which to pay them. His efforts were modestly successful, however, so Borica must be considered the forerunner of public education in California. A retired sergeant named Manuel de Vargas began the first primary school in California, housing it in the public granary in San José in 1794.

Pablo Vicente Solá became Governor in 1822 and was committed to improving education. Students had only their catechisms to read so he offered the more advanced readers copies of Cervantes' immortal *Don Quijote*. He opened schools at various places in the province and out of his own pocket founded schools for boys and girls in Monterey. Most Californios continued apathetic and Solá ordered that parents who refused to send their children to school be punished. Mariano Vallejo later wrote that schools were little more torture on the young for most teachers believed in the old adage of "spare the rod and spoil the child."

Teachers continued to be very few and hard to attract until the Hijar colonists arrived in 1834. One of the more famous teachers in the group was **Ignacio Coronel.**

BOOKS

Being a frontier area, there was a tremendous scarcity of books in California. The mission libraries held some 3,000 volumes and the Hijar colonists brought books with them but there grew such a demand that smugglers started bringing them in. By 1846 there were a number of personal libraries owned by men like Mariano Vallejo, Francisco Pacheco, John Marsh, William Hartnell, Capitán de la Guerra, etc. Of the native Californios, Mariano Vallejo, Juan B. Alvarado, and José Castro have always been designated as among the most learned men in California.

PERSONAL HEALTH

Visitors often remarked on how healthy Californios were. The principal occupations being ranching and farming, people worked out of doors and the climate was salubrious. **Walter Colton** remarked that tuberculosis was all but unknown and he highly recommended the outdoor Californio lifestyle. **William H. Davis** wrote that the men were *"…a race of men of large stature and of fine, handsome appearance."* Historian **H.H. Bancroft** believed that Californios were *"…probably as healthy and athletic as any people in the world…California bred a fine race."* Californios were described as being about five-foot-six in height ("tall" for those days), muscular, with good features under their pink to white skin. The women *"…were as fair as those of New York and had rosy cheeks, jet black hair…beauty which was by no means of an inferior order."*

Health seemed to encourage large families, ten children being the average but twenty was not uncommon. Living to the age of eighty or ninety was common and some lived to be over a hundred. Furthermore, many old people still had all their teeth.

There was disease in California. The first explorers/settlers of 1769 were plagued by scurvy and some ninety individuals with the Portolá expedition died of it. The situation might have gotten worse had it not been for Dr. **Pedro Prat**, the surgeon with the group, the first resident doctor in California history. The famous Dr. Pablo Soler was the second.

"Bleeding" as a treatment was outlawed by Governor Borica in 1799 but further quackery was by no means prevented. American and British foreigners, "from faraway places" often set themselves up as "doctors," doing much *"evil…quackery,"* according to **Nellie Van De Grift Sánchez**. Conditions worsened during the Mexican period of California history because that is when foreigners began to enter in large numbers, bringing smallpox, scarlet fever, measles, cholera, etc. [See Note # 37.] Unfortunately, there were epidemics in California as there were in other areas. Smallpox first appeared in 1798 but in 1834 an epidemic broke out that is said to have wiped out some 12,000 Indians. (Vaccination was enforced as soon as it was brought into California.) In 1838 the disease came down from Fort Ross and is said to have wiped out perhaps three-fifths of the Indians in the Sacramento Valley. In 1834 and 1849 there were outbreaks of cholera.

Indian medicine men were often asked to effect cures when no doctor was available, which was most of the time. These Indian healers utilized their traditional knowledge of herbs, along with chants, to help those afflicted with disease. They also utilized sweathouses.

Some foreigners were doctors. Among the best known were the Americans John Marsh, James L. Ord, (Irish) Richard Somerset Den, (English) Edward Turner Bale. The latter is also remembered because he fought a sword duel with **Salvador Vallejo**, uncle of Bale's beautiful wife, **M. Ignacia Soberanes**. It appears Bale was jealous of Ignacia's familial affection for her Uncle Salvador. Not understanding that such was the family tradition in California, hotheaded Bale challenged Vallejo to a duel. Considering the family ties, it is difficult to believe that Bale didn't know that Salvador Vallejo was considered California's most accomplished swordsman. Vallejo defeated Bale, without hurting him, as if playing with a child. Enraged, Bale then tried to shoot Vallejo but this only landed the Englishman in jail for a time.

RECREATION

Californios have often been described as people who knew how to enjoy life for they understood that nothing but work (the *rat race* of the modern era) was in the end unhealthy and self-defeating. Festivals, picnics, and dances were held as often as possible. A foreign ship in the harbor often invited townspeople to come aboard ship and dance all day. Then at sunset all would go ashore and dance until the wee hours of the morning. Work activities like roundups often ended with a grand ball because the people were so fond of dancing, which was an integral part of their Hispanic culture.

AN EQUESTRIAN SOCIETY

Californios went everywhere on horseback because they were great equestrians who depended on their horses almost like a friend. All were expert on a horse or throwing a lasso because they were on horseback even as young children. Described as among the best horsemen in the world because of their hard work, strength, and agility, Californios could ride at full speed and swoop down to pick up a coin or handkerchief laying on the ground. They could light a cigarette at full gallop. Horses were often so well trained they didn't need reins to guide them, knee pressure sufficing. The greatest gift from one Californio to another was to give him your best horse.

Palominos were favorites for wedding caravans but California horses were beautiful animals, descended from Arabian lines. They were relatively small in size but powerfully formed, full chested, small head, ears, and feet, large eyes, flowing mane and tail. They were very intelligent, which made them invaluable when working cattle. They could be trained to run at full speed then stop instantly, bracing themselves on all four legs to receive the pull of the lasso even when the other end held a grizzly or elk. Californio horses were very healthy and often lived for around twenty-five years. Their only real enemies were Indians who loved to eat horsemeat or the puma which would attack colts.

Horses were a matter of pride for Californios as were their saddles and associated trappings. The Californio saddle was large with a high tree fore and aft, the large apron of fancy leather often stamped in gold or silver by the wealthy *dons*. The bridle was generally silver mounted. Wood stirrups were covered in leather. Ceremonial spurs with rowels of four or five points were often inlaid with silver. (People loved their horses and no Californio used large spurs to inflict pain on their animals who were considered among their "best friends.") Wealthy Californios often spent a few thousand dollars in outfitting their horses.

HORSE RACING

They loved horse racing, "the sport of kings." Large sums were often wagered on favorite horses. Next to horse racing the *carrera del gallo* was extremely popular. A live rooster would be buried in the ground with only his head showing. At a given signal, riders would rush to the spot and try to pull the rooster up by the head.

BULLS and BEARS

Bull baiting was popular. Sarapes were waved in front of a bull to make him run around the ring. When he was tired out horsemen would come out of a gate and chase him, each rider trying to catch the bull's tale, twist it and throw him to the ground. Men and horses were often injured in the collisions that ensued.

Reminiscent of the Roman Coliseum, bull-and bear fights (which sometimes took place in the wild) were held and many enjoyed the brutal spectacle. The two animals were tied to each other, the bear by a hind leg, the bull from a foreleg. The beasts fought to the death, sometimes the bear winning, sometimes the bull. The fight was staged inside a strong wooden fence, a high platform erected for women and children, horsemen armed with shotguns and reatas ready in case either of the antagonists made it over the fence.

HORSE GAMES

The game of the rod, *juego de vara*, was a popular activity that required good horsemanship. Riders formed a ring, all facing the middle of the circle. One rider rode around the outside of the circle until the stick he was carrying was passed on to a rider forming the circle. The new rod carrier immediately chased the rider who had given him the stick and if he got close enough he was free to whip the fleeing rider about the shoulders until the latter was able to make it into the circle. The stick was then passed on to another, with the same rules applying.

MUSIC

Californios loved music, singing, and dancing. Music was a part of their lives from baptisms to weddings to funerals. Most men and women could play the guitar, often the violin, after learning it mostly on their own. (Pianos were owned by José Abrego, Eulogio Célis, and Mariano Vallejo.) Most people sang, songs being mostly from Sonora. Some could improvise songs in honor of guests or to poke fun at politicians. Folk songs were always popular, sometimes comic but often romantic. All were learned and passed on from memory.

HUNTING

Hunting was one of the principal sports of Californios. Relying mostly on the lasso, men would hunt the grizzly, huge elk, wild horses, or bulls. Bear hunting was done mostly for sport because bear meat wasn't popular for eating. The ferocious grizzly was a formidable antagonist for horse and rider but superb courage exhibited by both, along with expert use of the lasso, almost always gave victory to the Californio. The severest test for a horse was his behavior during a bear fight because by instinct the horse knew he should avoid a bear.

José Ramón Carrillo became famous as a hunter of grizzlies. When he located his bear he would dismount, take his bull-hide shield in his left hand, a large hunting knife in his right. The snarling bear would come in for the fight, charging the "puny" human animal. Carrillo would deflect the charge with his shield and plunge the knife into the grizzly. [See Note # 38.]

Elk hunting was also a passion. They were huge animals, immensely strong, agile, fast, and courageous fighters. They were so numerous in central and northern California that at one time they were hunted for their hides and tallow. As large and strong as the animals were, two Californios could bring an elk into a rancho by controlling it with their hand made reatas.

Wild horses often provided an exciting chase but a wild bull often tested the courage, strength, and skill of both Californio horse and rider. A well trained horse seemed to enjoy a bull hunt as much as his rider, approaching the bull cautiously, nostrils expanded, eyes full of expectant excitement, planting and bracing all four legs at just the proper time when the bull, much more powerful, pulls on his end of the lasso before he falls defeated to the ground.

OUTINGS

The picnic, *merienda*, was immensely popular, either with couples or whole families. Sweethearts would often climb on a horse, the lady in front, and ride off to some secluded spot to enjoy lunch. When whole families (and sometimes neighborhoods or small villages) decided to go on merienda all kinds of good foods were packed and all mounted their prancing horses or drove creaky *carretas* (wagon carts) and went to the seashore, hills, a favorite stream, or mountains. The people conversed, played the guitar, sang, raced horses, etc., enjoying themselves and their natural world.

RELIGIOUS CELEBRATIONS

Religious festivals were very popular, Christmas being the biggest celebration of the year, *La Noche Buena* (Christmas Eve) being at once sacred and merry. The religious drama *Los Pastores* (The Shepherds) was generally performed by young people dressed in biblical costumes. Performances of *La Pastorela* were also popular.

FORMAL BALLS

The *Cascarón Ball* was always held the week before the beginning of Lent. Long before the final dance before Lent egg shells were saved after having the contents removed through a small hole on one end of the egg. The shells were thoroughly cleaned and before the celebration all eggs were filled with shiny bits of paper or a bit of water laced with sweet smelling cologne. The holes were then sealed. During the course of the Cascarón Ball a person, whether man or woman, would walk up behind a favored one and lightly smash the eggs over the special one's head. The shiny paper gleamed on dark hair or cologne scented it, to the gaiety of all.

According to writers like **William Heath Davis**, life in California was wonderful. The Spanish Californios "*...were as sincere a people as ever lived... of manliness and simplicity ...a contented people.*" But Californio society was going to be changed forever with the arrival of an aggressively expanding United States of America.

DISCUSSION Notes *for* CALIFORNIO SOCIETY

Note # 1

See *The Life And Times Of Fray Junípero Serra* by Msgr. Francis J. Weber. This easily accessible volume is based on the monumental *The Life And Times Of Fray Junípero Serra, O.F.M.* by Reverend Maynard J. Geiger. For testimonials and other primary materials on Indians and many other California personalities see *Lands Of Promise And Despair: Chronicles of Early California, 1535-1846* edited by Rose Marie Beebe and Robert M Senkewicz.

Note # 2

Positive commentary about Hispanic pioneers is often represented as "adulatory" or "emotional" or other such Orwellian barb. Rare is a work like *Lands Of Promise And Despair*, edited by Rose Marie Beebe and Robert M. Senkewicz, that presents both sides of an issue. If comparative history is invoked, what California pioneer from any other culture, American or European, equals or even begins to rival individuals like Junípero Serra or Fermín Lasuén? Is the mission period of English language California history laced with bias against "papists and popery"?

Note # 3

See Chapter 19 in A *History Of California* by Charles E. Chapman.

Note # 4

See *Time Of The Bells* by Richard F. Pourade.

Note # 5

This Spanish royal attitude was not held by English monarchs who held sway east of the Mississippi where Native Americans had no rights of any kind if the English didn't wish them to.

Note # 6

Various English language writers claim that Hispanic people refused to work in activities like agriculture. The Hispanic founders of New Mexico, Texas, California, and Arizona, not products of slave societies, disprove such assertions because most worked right alongside their hired hands if they had any. Wealthy individuals didn't, which is rather typical in any human society. (Did John D. Rockefeller work at pumping gas after he made his millions?) Charges like these should be investigated in an academic setting. It is also important to read Spanish language accounts on issues like these and compare them to what has been written in English translations. Even the generally reliable Charles E. Chapman writes (page 248) that *"the Spaniards…were not acquainted with farming…"* despite the historical certainty that missionaries in California and the Hispanic Southwest would rank among the most highly successful agriculturalists and ranchmen, skills which they passed on to those who wished to learn them, including Indians and American immigrants.

Note # 7

See Chapter 5 in *Contested Eden: California Before The Gold Rush*, edited by Ramon A. Gutiérrez and Richard J. Orsi. While the author of this essay, Steven W. Hackel, seems quite reliable, these figures are estimates that might be investigated because the 1820 figure nearly coincides with the number of registered Indians living in the missions. There were many *gentiles* (unbaptized Indians) who were never a part of mission life.

Note # 8

Missionaries were quick to champion Indian females who asserted that this-or-that soldier had forced his attentions on her. This type of charge has been embellished by various American writers and should be investigated from original Spanish language sources. It must also be kept in mind that in general histories rape charges are rare to non-existent when one studies English colonization on the eastern seaboard. Is there a double standard in American historiography? Well known Oscar Handlin, a Harvard University professor and author/editor of works like

Truth In History and *Readings In American History* doesn't even mention "rape" as a topic in these two books. Is the venerable Oscar Handlin an exception? Not at all. There is no entry for "Rape" in the index of *The Beards' New Basic History Of The United States*, (1960) by Charles A. Beard, Mary R. Beard, and William Beard, though they do have the moral courage to state (p. 39) that *"the barbaric greed and brutality of innumerable whites* [the Beards don't say "English," preferring the more oblique, circuitous "whites" label] *led them to rob, murder, betray, and try to enslave Indians."* No "Rape" entry exists in *The Oxford History Of The American People* (1965) by Samuel Eliot Morison nor in *The Vineyard Of Liberty* (1991) by James MacGregor Burns. But study the Spanish Southwest and it's quite a different story. *The Spanish Frontier In North America* (1992) by David J. Weber has the following index entries (p. 573): "**Rape**. See Sexual Assault." On page 575 is the entry "**Sexual assault**: of Indian women by soldiers, 16, 48, 51, 54, 247, 262, 330; by Spanish employers, 125, 127." In the work *Spain In The Southwest* by John L. Kessell there is an entry (p. 459) for "**Sex**: concubinage, 200; **rape by Spaniards**, 5, 40, 51, 240, 320; restraint by Karankawas, 143; solicitation of, 278, 333." Might there be at least a Ph.D. dissertation somewhere on this subject of a double standard or is Orwellian historiography all we have? The same rationale holds true for items like "Diseases." Would the reader or students be given the impression that maladies like smallpox or syphilis didn't exist among Europeans east of the Mississippi but were common in Hispanic lands?

Note # 9

This apostolic dedication and zeal might be said to be analogous to the herculean motivation in contemporary American society to acquire money.

Note # 10

See Chapter 19 in C. E. Chapman's *A History Of California – The Spanish Period* where he quotes Bancroft: *"We can image the desolate loneliness of a padre's life at a frontier mission* [like the mission Borja in Baja California] *but the reality must have been far worse than anything our fancy can picture. These friars were mostly educated, in many cases learned men, not used to nor needing the bustle of city life, but wanting, as they did their daily food, intelligent companionship. They were not alone in the strictest sense of the word, for there were enough people around them. But what were these people?—ignorant, lazy, dirty, sulky, treacherous, half-tamed savages, with whom no decent man could have anything in common. Even the almost hopeless task of saving their miserable souls must have required a martyr for its performance."* This excerpt provides insight into the work of frontier Hispanic missionaries as well as American attitudes towards Indians.

Note # 11

The herculean figures of the Southwest during the Spanish colonial period would have to include Oñate, Father Estevan Perea, Vargas, and Anza (the last of whom was a significant factor also in Arizona and California) of New Mexico; Father Kino and Father Garcés of Arizona; Father Margil of Texas, and Fathers Serra and Lasuén of California. None could be classified as "Indian haters," even when they had to fight them, and the missionaries would have to be counted as among the foremost champions of Native Americans in any lands now comprising the USA.

Note # 12

See "Indian Life at San Luis Rey" written by Pablo Tac in *Lands Of Promise And Despair* for a missionized native's view.

Note # 13

Some missionaries criticized the civilian population for asking for mission Indians to work for them. Despite caustic remarks, the missionaries usually sent working Indians to labor for civilians because the mission got a percentage of the salary paid the workers. Some writers now maintain that the Californios were basically lazy, that as "typical Spaniards" they refused to perform labor because they considered it demeaning, that they considered themselves a "superior upper class," etc. For the purpose of investigation, the Californios were "lazy" as compared to whom? Comparative history impels us to point out that if Californios were "lazy" because they needed Indian labor, what of exploiting newly arrived immigrant laborers, indentured servants, and black slaves?

Note # 14

Was the mission system another form of "plantation slavery"? Historical facts don't substantiate such a view. First of all, Indians were not required to live in a mission unless they so chose, with the understanding that the choice was permanent like a contract in the Military. American black slaves had no such choice. Indians were encouraged to become literate in the Spanish language. In the American South it was illegal to teach a black person to read or to write. Mission Indians were intended one day to be owners of the land they worked. Black slaves had no such hopes. Missionaries strived to imbue Indians with Christian morality. African slaves were encouraged to have as many children as possible in order to enrich the master with the birth of new slaves. Mission punishments were those sanctioned by basic laws regarding whipping, stocks, shackles, or jail time. Black slaves could be punished in any way the master chose, from whipping to castration to execution. (See *Africans In America: America's Journey Through Slavery* by Charles Johnson, Patricia Smith, and the WGBH Series Research Team.) There is no real comparison between the two systems.

Note # 15

As already noted, this type of situation is often reported with comments like "Spanish people were averse to manual labor." Is this propagandistory or should anyone be able to function in any capacity if he is so ordered? Did George Washington build Mount Vernon with his own hands?

Note # 16

Like the "averse to labor" charges above, commentaries from these disputes and arguments have been very popular among various writers when interpreting California and the Hispanic Southwest. Are they being utilized out of context for propaganda purposes?

Note # 17

See Chapter 10 in *Mission Santa Barbara, 1782-1965* by Maynard Geiger, O.F.M.

As mentioned above, feuds between missionaries and military/civilians have been used by various writers to promote negative views.

Note # 18

A majority of the Chumash never became Christians. For a scholarly denigration of the mission system and most things Hispanic see the essay "Between Crucifix and Land: Indian-White Relations in California, 1769-1848" by James A. Sandos in *Contested Eden*. To his credit, Sandos states that portraying missionaries as "monsters," accusing Franciscans of genocide, comparing Father Serra to Hitler and the missions to Nazi death camps, is "an extreme statement of the anti-mission school" and in the bibliography he cites *The Missions of California: A Legacy of Genocide* published by the Indian Historian Press (now defunct) of San Francisco. Comparing Father Serra to Adolph Hitler is more than "*an extreme statement.*"

Note # 19

See *Quest For Empire: Spanish Settlement In The Southwest*, Chapter 12, by Donald Cutter & Iris Engstrand. See also *A History Of California: The Spanish Period*, Chapter 32, by Charles E Chapman.

Note # 20

Charles Chapman relates that historian H.H. Bancroft, while writing very positively about Gabe Moraga, referred to this California pioneer as "illiterate" though the great pathfinder Moraga kept journals and wrote descriptions during his expeditions. Writing valid history is no simple feat.

Note # 21

See Chapter 5, an essay written by Steven W. Hackel, in *Contested Eden*.

Note # 22

Popular historiography depicts Jed Smith as heroic, a notable personality who helped open the West. In all fairness it must be pointed out that Smith himself never made such claims but certain writers have bestowed the mantle of greatness on him and his achievements. Andrew Rolle writes in his *California: A History*, © 1963, Chapter 11, that "*...Smith became the first white person to reach California overland...*" Has it been forgotten that Captain Juan Bautista de Anza led an overland expedition to California in 1774 then duplicated the approximate 2,200 mile feat with colonists in 1775-76? Is the detail on Smith *misinformation*? If cultural bias enters the mix might this be *disinformation* since Rolle discusses Anza in a previous chapter? If so, what is the purpose of the *disinformation*? In the "Revised and Expanded Fifth Edition" of the same book, © 1998, we are informed in Chapter 10, page 70, that Smith "*...became the first Caucasian to reach California overland from the eastern United States.*" Jed Smith was "*...of New England parentage, became the pioneer who blazed a trail from the newly formed United States to southern California.*" Smith was working for William H. Ashley out of St. Louis, Missouri (yes, now part of the "*newly formed*" USA because of the Louisiana Purchase) in the 1820s and in 1826 made it to northern Utah from where he went into southern California. The statement that Smith "*blazed a trail*" from the USA is disingenuous at best. Lewis and Clark went before and Alexander Mackenzie before them. It is agreed that they didn't go into southern California but then, Captain Anza had done so almost a half century before. Of course, Anza's pioneers had not emanated from the "United States." Such are the convolutions of Orwellian propagandistory.

Note # 23

How credible is this information concerning bear traps? Mission padres were Indian champions from the beginning days with Father Serra. Even when the Indians murdered Father Jayme there was no retribution against the murderers because Father Serra wouldn't permit it. Is it conceivable that by 1826 missionaries would use a bear trap against Indians who went into an orchard to take a few oranges? Is this misinformation or culturally biased disinformation?

Note # 24

Some writers maintain that Jed Smith was jailed because he was a "Protestant," preferring that rationale rather than the reality of being an illegal immigrant and taking wealth (furs) from the province. The "Protestant" subterfuge can be traced at least as far back as Philip II's attack against England in 1588 due to Elizabeth I sending out pirates like Francis Drake to steal from Spanish shipping. Many historians say the Spanish Armada attacked because England was a "Protestant" country and Spain was Catholic, covering up the fact that the English government was guilty of State sponsored terrorism because it encouraged thieves like Drake to go steal Spanish gold for England.

Note # 25

Robert Glass Cleland writes in his *This Reckless Breed Of Men: The Trappers And Fur Traders Of The Southwest*, © 1977, that Jed Smith was *"a pathfinder…who deserves a place in national tradition equal in every respect to that accorded Lewis and Clark, Daniel Boone, Kit Carson, or any other American explorer."* On Index page xvi under Smith's name is the following: *"…leader of first expedition to reach Pacific Ocean, 55;"* Cultural bias aside, it would be interesting to do a comparative history of the documented achievements of Jed Smith and any number of people before him, including Pedro Fages, Gabriel Moraga, etc. It would be possible to document the achievements of Spanish explorers because they all kept journals/diaries, as did Lewis and Clark. What mountain men wrote journals/diaries during their travels?

Note # 26

This is indeed high praise when one considers that these men were active in the 19th century while the explorers from Spain were mapping much of the Western Hemisphere from California down to the southern tip of South America some three hundred years before. For an opposing view of mountain men and the fur trade see *Land Grab: The Truth About The Winning Of The West* by John Upton Terrell. See "Part Two: The Fur Trade in the West" which begins with: *"The acquisition of the United States of the immense Louisiana Territory opened the way for the spread throughout the West of an American industry which for dishonesty, destructiveness, exploitation, cruelty, immorality, criminal negligence, viciousness and avarice has no counterpart in western history. It was the fur trade."* It ends on page 178 with *"…The Mountain Men were the great explorers of the West, but they brought no improvements…The fur traders left to history only a bloodstained record of disgrace, dishonesty, unparalleled greed, violence, and destruction…"* No historiographer has explored these details.

Note # 27

Pattie doesn't explain, nor has any historian, how he acquired smallpox vaccine while trapping or while in jail. Andrew Rolle writes in his *California: A History*, 1963 edition, page 172, that the *Personal Narrative* "*...is a mine of often unreliable but always fascinating information.*" In the 1998 edition, page 79, Rolle says the vaccination episode was a "*tall-tale*" that "*may well be an utter fabrication*" but that some of the *Narrative* is "*reasonably verifiable.*" One can only wonder how much of "mountain man" history is "verifiable" for a dispassionate investigator.

Note # 28

See *Frontier Settlement In Mexican California: The Hijar-padres Colony And Its Origins, 1769-1835* by C. Alan Hutchinson.

Note # 29

Speaking generally, American historiography dictates that in the Hispanic Southwest almost every European should be labeled an "Anglo-American." So Germanic *Johann Suter* from Switzerland is "promoted" as an "Anglo-American" and a *Captain* to boot. He was never a "Captain" and the label "Germanic" isn't popular though the Angles who arrived in Britain in the fifth century were a Germanic tribe.

Note # 30

See the classic *With The Ears Of Strangers: The Mexican in American Literature* by Cecil Robinson. Robinson feels that Americans writing about the people of Mexico and the Southwest were telling more about themselves than their subjects.

Note # 31

See the essay "Alta California's Trojan Horse" by Doyce B. Nunis, Jr. in *Contested Eden*.

Note # 32

See pages 40-41 in *History Of Nevada* by Russell R. Elliott. Elliott's view is in direct contradiction to what some other writers have to say. In his book *CALIFORNIA*, David Lavender writes that the "Bidwell-Bartleson party...were a husky bunch...farm people who could handle wagons, livestock, and rough tools" but "...possibly saved from disaster by Thomas Fitzpatrick..." Andrew Rolle refers to John Bidwell as "*a prince among California pioneers*" but he doesn't state why. Nor is any mention made of the party being "illegals" in a foreign country. Is the message that Americans didn't have to obey Mexican law because California became American property anyway? Does Orwellian presentism hold true for most of this beginning period in American California history? Common sense dictates that twenty-year-old John Bidwell was not a frontiersman, had never been on the trail West so he had no experience, and suffering hardships because of inadequate preparation or lack of a leader don't constitute being categorized as an *heroic pioneer*. Is it possible he is remembered at all because he wrote a memoir about the journey, an account to which other writers could refer? Are the many accounts written in Spanish automatically disqualified?

Note # 33

See *Spanish Arcadia* by Nellie Van de Grift Sánchez. This item is a popular read and might evoke the charge of "idyllic" though it is based on solid historical research. The great H.E. Bolton himself proofed the manuscript. The reader must also be aware that positive aspects of Californio life are generally targeted with descriptions like "idyllic" or "halcyon days," etc., challenging the idea that pre-USA California life could be so wonderful. Is such denigration the result of the American takeover of California? What of Americans like Thomas Oliver Larkin who wrote just before his death: *"I begin to yearn after the times prior to July, 1846, and all their honest pleasures"*?

If we were to employ the principles of logic it could be pointed out that almost all American eye-witness observers of Spanish/Mexican California commented on the remarkable Californio hospitality. The Hispanic people of California were so generous that visitors were treated as special guests when in fact they were mere travelers going from one place to another. If Californio psychology permitted such genuine hospitality, is it not likely that the depictions of Nellie Van de Grift Sánchez are historically valid?

Note # 34

It is interesting to speculate as to who have been the greatest horsemen in the world. Would it be the Mongols? The Arabs? The Cossacks of central Asia? The gauchos? The Hispanos of New Mexico? The Comanches? Tejanos? Californios?

Note # 35

See Chapter 5 in *General M. G. Vallejo And The Advent Of The Americans* by Alan Rosenus.

Note # 36

How does one account for the contradictory or polar opposite views of "observers" like Richard H. Dana and William Heath Davis?

Note # 37

It would be interesting to investigate who these "foreigners" were. Some historians generally avoid information on Americans spreading diseases. For example, few people know that the Lewis and Clark expedition carried smallpox which all but wiped out the Mandan Indians.

Note # 38

Thomas Farnham wrote that Californios were a *"...pusillanimous race of men...unfit to control the destinies of that beautiful country."*

Essay: ON CALIFORNIA HISTORIOGRAPHY

Oscar Handlin writes in his *Truth And History*, Chapter 3, that the basic guiding tenets of American history include a belief in the special purpose of America, a sense of *mission* which promotes *Liberty*! and *Progress*!, reflected in *boosterism* and *"composition on an epic scale,"* as well as the tendency to write in terms of *"heroes and villains."* It follows that personalities like Jedediah Strong Smith (1798?-1831) would be described by authors like Andrew F. Rolle in his *California, A History*, Chapter 11, as the *"...pioneer who blazed a trail from the newly formed USA to southern California."* This *"Knight in Buckskin"* is described as being (in the 1820s) *"one of the earliest white men..."* to travel what was to become the Oregon Trail and *"...the first white person to reach California overland"* (on November 27, 1826). Rolle dedicates some five (5) pages to Smith's adventures and his *"...influence upon the early history of western America..."* Are these encomiums valid history?

A quick look at the historical record becomes not only necessary but crucial because, unlike New Mexico and Arizona, so much was written on California history in the 19th century. In 1774 **Juan Bautista de Anza** led the first successful overland expedition to California. Then he returned to Mexico where 240 colonists were gathered whereupon Anza led them to Monterey, California, with Joaquín Moraga leading the pioneers on the last leg of their journey to San Francisco. The settlers, now some 244 due to births, were present to found the presidio in San Francisco in September of 1776. Then what is the historical value of Andrew Rolle's statement cited above? Furthermore, a Scot named **Alexander Mackenzie** of the Northwest Company of fur traders crossed the American continent from east to west in 1793. **Lewis and Clark** made their much publicized western expedition, starting in St. Louis, in 1803-06. **Jedediah Smith** was active in the 1820s (well after Anza, Mackenzie, Lewis and Clark; and it must be stated Smith never made the claims with which various writers have endowed him). Compared to Anza, Mackenzie, Lewis and Clark, was Jed Smith as influential and heroic a personality as has been written? A number of authors have produced books about him but is this mostly the "boosterism" described by Oscar Handlin? In *Bolton And The Spanish Borderlands* edited by John Francis Bannon, H.E. Bolton is quoted (Chapter 15) as saying about Anza: *"First to open a route across the Sierras and first to lead a colony overland to the North Pacific shores, he was the forerunner of Mackenzie, Thompson, Lewis and Clark, Smith, Fremont, the Forty-niners…"* The venerable Bolton states that in all American history there are few who could rival, much less compare to the achievements of Anza. I agree with Bolton: there is no one with whom to compare Anza who was a frontier captain, Indian fighter, military governor of Sonora, overland explorer and colonizer of California, Governor and Indian fighter/diplomat in New Mexico (and what is now Colorado) who established the Comanche Peace, trail blazer from New Mexico to Sonora, as well as writer of invaluable historical journals used by historians to this day. It wouldn't be fair to compare Jed Smith to the Great Captain. If this causes a controversy it is certain neither Anza nor Smith are responsible for it but rather the *"heroes and villains"* tenets of American historiography.

If we were to indulge in comparative history it would be interesting to focus on Jedediah Smith and Gabriel Moraga, California's greatest soldier/explorer. If the matter could be studied dispassionately, who would wind up being a significant influence in California history? Donald C. Cutter edited *Diary Of Ensign Gabriel Moraga's Expedition Of Discovery In The Sacramento Valley, 1808*, and is about the only major work on Moraga. In contrast, M.S. Sullivan has written two books on Smith, D.L. Morgan wrote a biography on Jed, and others like R. G. Cleland and H.C. Dale have included him in various books, not to mention inclusion in a number of other general works and historical journals. A comparative study would be most interesting if it could be accomplished with minimal cultural bias. Students of California history would be the better for it. Other comparative studies could be suggested: the heroic missionaries Serra and Lasuén; 19th century lifestyles of Californios before 1850 and American society after 1850; mission business activities compared to American business practice after 1850; wealthy Californios compared to wealthy Americans after 1850; etc.

Arizona Society

TUCSON

The settlers who founded *San Agustín de Tucsón* came from the presidio of San Ignacio de Tubac some forty miles south of the new presidio. Tucson therefore became the northernmost reach of the Spanish Empire in what is now Arizona. The Tucson site was selected by **Hugo O'Conor** in 1775 and the first European pioneers, soldiers with their families, settled in 1776. While some had been born in Spain or in the Americas of Spanish parents, others represented the racial/ethnic mixtures typical of the frontier, which tended to equality because of dangers common to all. These frontier people were a breed of hardy pioneers, second to none in all of North America. They were products of Hispanic culture (religiosity, ranching, mining, horsemanship, etc.) as well as life in the desert which made them tough as well as resilient. If life could be harsh there were also their times of joy between drought and flood, war and peace, birth and death. Their settlement style, their building materials, their irrigation traditions and methods of farming had already been used for centuries. They moved into the edge of *Apachería* and knew that the Apaches were their enemies and the Pimas and Pápagos their allies. [See Note # 1. *Notes begin on page 238.*] They held on to their land and culture despite the terrible odds stacked against them.

LOCATION

Tucson was established because the Santa Cruz River would provide precious water for agriculture and pasture land for livestock. The garrison would also be able to strike at the western Apaches if it became necessary as well as protect the overland trail to California blazed by Juan Bautista de Anza. The Tucson garrison, valiant *presidiales*, campaigned from the Santa Catalina Mountains to the Chiricahuas, the Tonto Basin to the north and the San Francisco River to the east. (Between 1807 and 1811 a total of twelve military expeditions went out of Tucson.) Even with their Pima and Pápago allies *Tucsonenses* knew they were vastly outnumbered by the Apaches, who in many ways ruled on how these first European pioneers would survive. During times of peace life was generally good but things could turn bad with no warning. For example, in May of 1782 hundreds of Indians attacked Tucson and nearly destroyed it. Conversely, in 1793 some ninety peaceful Aravaipa Apaches settled in the area and were later joined by Pinal Apaches (in 1819). Other Apache settlements were established at other posts (Fronteras, Janos, Bacoachi, etc.) because there was no Spanish policy of extermination directed at hostile Indians.

AGRICULTURE/RANCHING

Tucson was never a wealthy community because, as Captain **José de Zúñiga** wrote in 1804: *"There is no gold, silver, lead, tin, iron, copper, or quarries of marble."* What it did have was fertile land nourished by the Santa Cruz river. Corn wasn't easy to grow because it seldom grew to maturity due to the lack of sufficient water in its later growth stages. The basic crop was wheat because it could be grown in the "winter" months and harvested at the beginning of summer. Herds of cattle (some 3,500 head), sheep (2,600), horses (1200), mules (120), and burros (30) were also crucial on this Hispanic agricultural/ranching frontier of some 1,015 people (which included Pimas and everyone living in San Xavier del Bac). The

Arizona frontier was similar to other areas of the Borderlands due to the scarcity of water, very real dangers from hostile Indians, and the absolute need for cooperation. Water, brought to agricultural land through *acequias* (ditches), was precious in the desert so its use was carefully regulated by the water judge (*zanjero*) and people cooperated with each other to keep the ditches clean and receive their fair share of irrigation water. Like other dry regions, irrigation was basic to the culture.

PIONEERS

Hispanic *Tucsonense* pioneers had surnames like Burruel, Castro, Comadurán, Díaz, Gallegos, García, González, Pacheco, Pérez, Pesqueira, Ramírez, Romero, Ruelas, Sosa, Telles, Zúñiga, etc., and lived in relative isolation from other Hispanic communities but were bonded to each other through hard work, cooperation, drought, flood, Indian hostilities, and especially a tremendous drive to survive on the harsh Arizona frontier. They learned to harvest edible portions of the nopal and saguaro. Mesquite pods were ground up to make *pinole*. *Mescal* was either made or imported. There was no coffee.

DRESS

During the hottest months of the year some men dressed in little more than a breechclout like the Indians. Otherwise they wore typical pants, shirts, jackets, etc., a poncho when necessary during the cooler months. *Teguas*, a sort of moccasin made from buckskin, were worn on the feet. Soldiers on campaign wore leather jackets called *cueras* for protection from hostile Indian arrows. Women wore long skirts made of cotton cloth, blouses, scarves, and shawls. There were no doctors so medicinal herbs and roots were used as curatives. Adobe style architecture was basic and all buildings were in the frontier style with no windows facing outside the presidio. Contact with other settlements came with pack trains from towns like Arizpe and San Ignacio.

ALLIES

The Hispanic pioneers of Tucson were allied with Pápagos to the west and Gila Pimas to the north because their common enemy was hostile Apache groups who attacked all three populations with impunity. Hispanics, Pimas, and Pápagos came to rely on each other because they understood the enemy could destroy them individually. But there were exceptions because all groups were encouraged to live peacefully. The "Manso Apaches," who decided they would no longer live by raiding, came to Tucson and settled along the western bank of the Santa Cruz river. Referred to as "Tonto Apaches" by their warlike brethren, they served as scouts for Tucsonense expeditions and provided much intelligence that helped greatly to prevent ambushes or when preparing for major battles. The various groups respected each other and together created a pioneer society that enabled them to survive, each on basically their own terms, but as allies. [See Note # 2.]

INDEPENDENCE

The struggle for Mexico to liberate itself from Spain didn't directly affect the people of Tucson. Independence, achieved by 1821, was extremely expensive in that a large percentage of Mexican citizens died in the struggle and the revolution bankrupted the country. The silver mining industry was all but destroyed. Further, after the revolution different groups struggled against each other for control of the country. Missions were neglected or abandoned. Presidios didn't have money with which to pay their soldiers. Significantly, neither was there money to spend on Indian affairs. Apaches began raiding again and toward the end of the 1820s Tucsonenses were on the brink of extermination. Then civilian volunteers stepped forward to safeguard their community. For example, in 1832 some 200 volunteers formed an expedition and took the war into Apache strongholds. Around seventy-one warriors were killed and some 216 stolen horses recovered. The pattern for attack and retaliation was now set in motion. Because of its remoteness Tucson wasn't a center for the American illegal immigrants referred to as "mountain men" though there were some unsavory types like James Kirker running guns to hostile Indians. The balance of power was altered when American traders brought in modern rifles to trade with the Apaches (for stolen livestock), who were now better armed than the Tucsonenses. In 1848 hostile Apaches ambushed an expedition led by presidial captain **Antonio Comadurán** and killed fifteen of his men. By this time everyone understood that Hispanic Tucson was outnumbered, over matched, and on the brink of extermination.

Arizona, a part of New Mexico, was on the way to California, which had been coveted by the USA for decades. [See Note # 3.] Tucson was not involved in the Mexican War of 1846-48 though Lieutenant Colonel **Philip St. George Cooke** and his Mormon Battalion passed through in 1846. In 1847 one Lt. Schoonmaker and sixty soldiers rode into Tucson on their way to meet General Kearny in California. He demanded surrender but had no cannon with which to attack the adobe presidio so, after getting a mule killed in a minor skirmish, he merely continued on his way to California. Tucson simply held no interest for the Americans.

The 1849 gold rush to California took many wayfarers through Tucson, including some 10,000 from Sonora alone, finally chipping away at its isolation. The biggest problem occurred when the Mexican government established a military colony and ordered that military personnel be given agricultural land for their subsistence. But almost all the good agricultural land was already being cultivated by settlers so innumerable disputes arose until the practice was rescinded. Soldier and settler factions were now easily identifiable in Tucsonense society. To make matters much worse, cholera epidemics broke out in 1850 and 1851. One hundred and twenty-two deaths from cholera were recorded in Tucson in 1851.

GADSDEN PURCHASE

The final blow to Mexican Tucson came on December 30, 1853, when the Treaty of Mesilla, known in English as the Gadsden Purchase, signed away another portion of northern Mexico for the sum of ten million dollars. The Mexican garrison vacated Tucson in 1856 but most Tucsonenses remained in the settlement. T. E. Sheridan writes that *"...they and their property came under the protection of the United States..."* but he also gives voice to the statements made by some people from Santa Ana, Sonora: *The Republic of the United States is liberal and philanthropic for its citizens but woe to anyone of a different race. Consider how the Californios are being treated...our brothers in New Mexico and Texas are also forced to drink from the bitter chalice...*

DISCUSSION Notes *for* ARIZONA SOCIETY

Note # 1

See *Los Tucsonenses: The Mexican Community In Tucson, 1854-1941* by Thomas E. Sheridan. See also Sheridan's *Arizona: A History*.

H.H. Bancroft writes in his one-volume *History Of Arizona And New Mexico* (Chapter 16, p. 372) that "No chronological narrative of early Arizona annals can ever be formed with even approximate accuracy and completeness, *for lack of data.*" This "lack of data" is especially puzzling because southern Arizona produced three of the greatest personalities in American history: Kino, Anza, and Garcés. Further, with the exception of *Los Tucsonenses* cited above, the Hispanic settlers of Arizona are seldom even mentioned, much less listed by name, by writers like Odie B. Faulk (*Arizona: A Short History*), Marshall Trimble (*Arizona: A Cavalcade Of History*), and to a lesser degree, Thomas E. Sheridan (*Arizona: A History*) who lists a few family names. It is also disconcerting that denigrating commentary seems to be so much more readily available than even basic information on Arizona Hispanic pioneers. For example, the Trimble item cited above (published by Treasure Chest Publications in 1989) says about the Coronado Expedition, page 53: "*The grand hopes and fond dreams of getting rich without working were dashed in 1542.*" How did Coronado, the first European explorer of the Southwest, project the idea of "*getting rich without working*"? On page 54 the reader is told that Spain had an "*insatiable quest for conquering new lands.*" Page 57: Niza caused Mexico City to go into a "*gold crazed frenzy.*" Page 59 says the *Llano Estacado* is translated as "Staked Plains" instead of the correct translation of "stockaded plains." The reader might get the impression that "*Spanish oppression*" (page 61) is the basic contribution to the Southwest because (page 34) "*...the Spanish tried desperately to impose their religion and culture...*" Is this mere denigrating "Tree of Hate" propaganda? By contrast, the ludicrous adventures of James Ohio Pattie are related as if he was "*another of the great pathfinders to explore Arizona*" (pages 78-79). We are told that Pattie's adventures are "*...a rather colored-up account...*" but then we are informed of the "*daring rescue of Jacova Narbona...*" which never happened and was a total creation of Pattie's editor Timothy Flint. Further, while Pattie was in California, we are told he got out of jail by inoculating "*thousands*" against smallpox because he just happened to have the vaccine with him while trapping in the mountains. Should these antics, judgmental commentary like Hispanics wanting to "get rich without working" and preposterous "mountain man" yarns be the basis for incipient Arizona History?

Note # 2

Hispanic frontier people were not driven to the extermination of Indian people merely because they were Indians. Extermination was never Spanish policy after Bartolomé de las Casas. This appears to be a problem for some historians so they often emphasize that "Spanish frontier communities" weren't really "Spanish" but rather a combination of various racial and/or ethnic groups, as if blood and not cultural heritage is the only ingredient that matters. Is the real problem the heritage of racism and the historical extermination/exile of native populations?

Note # 3

Thomas E. Sheridan writes in his Los Tucsonenses, Chapter 2, page 23: "*Missouri merchants blazed the Santa Fe Trail.*" The Santa Fe Trail was blazed by Pedro Vial and a couple of companions in 1792. While *Tucsonenses* is certainly the best I have encountered on the Hispanic people of southern Arizona, "boosterism" is woven into the fiber of American historiography to such an extent that even very able writers can't seem to avoid it. At what point does *misinformation* become *disinformation?*

CHAPTER **6**

Indian Affairs In The
Hispanic Southwest

NEW MEXICO

New Mexico was settled by Hispanic people in 1598 and as the oldest European colony in what is now the Southwest and the USA, New Mexico's Hispanos have had more dealings with Native American people than any other European based population living in the Southwest or the USA. Among the most "popular" issues regarding Indian people in New Mexico are the Acoma War, the St. Lawrence Day Massacre, and the Comanche War and Peace.

ACOMA WAR

The fight at Acoma was the first military struggle between European settlers and Native Americans in what is now the USA. (For specific details on the Acoma war see the section titled *Colony: New Mexico, 1598*.) When Governor Juan de Oñate was informed about the tragedy at Acoma and the loss of so many of his stalwart pioneers, including his nephew Juan de Zaldívar, he withdrew into his tent then prayed and wept the entire night. By the following morning when he addressed his men he understood that Hispanic New Mexico might well be exterminated if he didn't take proper action. His people numbered some 500, a large number of them women and children, while the Indians numbered in the scores of thousands. [See Note # 1. *Notes begin on page 243.*] Governor Oñate addressed his men the next morning and finished with "*Whatever comes, whether it be death, hardship, or suffering, we shall meet all as brave men who trust in the Almighty Creator…*" Oñate decided that all must return immediately to *San Juan de los Caballeros* (Knights of St. John) to prevent the colonists from being wiped out in another sneak attack. He had learned the lesson of wariness at the cost of his men's lives. *If he had sent a warning to his nephew, maybe all would still be alive!* During the seven day return journey to Knights of St. John scouts went ahead and brought up the rear to protect the expedition. Sentries kept watch at night for attack was possible if the thousands of Indians united to exterminate them. But they made it home without incident.

EPIC *of the* **Greater Southwest**

DISCUSSION

Governor Oñate quickly set up a tribunal to decide if a justified war could be waged against Acoma. [See Note # 2.] According to Dr. **Marc Simmons**, contrary to what *"many writers would have us believe,"* Spaniards weren't reckless or given to unprovoked reprisals. The King's law and Church doctrine required rational deliberation. A *"highly formalized and legalistic procedure"* was in place by this time and it had to be observed before launching a war. Representatives from the entire community were permitted to give testimony. The Franciscan friars stated that the Acomas had sworn allegiance to the King and had broken the law by ambushing his representatives but a war for revenge would be immoral and illegal. Other witnesses testified that war had to be waged for reasons like family safety and basic security. Further, the Acomas had not been provoked. It was a sneak attack, a premeditated ambush pure and simple. Everyone knew war was the only strategy that would preserve New Mexico for as Captain **Gerónimo Márquez** said, *"If Acoma isn't leveled and the Acomas punished, there will be no security in New Mexico and the province can't be populated with more colonists. The other Indians are waiting to see what happens at Acoma."* Governor Oñate made the binding decision: a war of no quarter would have to be waged and he would lead it. But the citizenry objected: they needed their governor to lead them out of the province if the war was lost at Acoma. As much as it bothered the valiant leader to stay home, he knew his people were correct. He selected his other nephew, **Vicente de Zaldívar**, to lead the offensive. The loss of kith and kin had not made Governor Oñate vengeful for part of Zaldívar's instructions were: *"Make more use of clemency than severity if it should turn out that the Acomas committed their crimes more from incapacity of reason than from malice…If you should want to show leniency after they are arrested you should seek all possible means to make the Indians believe that you are doing so at the request of the friar with your forces. In this manner they will recognize the friars as their benefactors and protectors and come to love and esteem them, and to fear us."*

Vicente de Zaldívar led seventy-two paladins to Acoma. After three days (January 22-24, 1599) of bloody fighting, the stronghold was destroyed. Many Acomas had to be taken into protective custody because surviving warriors were going through all houses, killing their own women and children so they would not be captured.

TRIAL

A trial was given Acoma survivors on February 9-12. Captain **Alonso Gómez Montesinos,** in charge of their defense, pleaded for clemency on the grounds that these captured Acomas were absent when the Spaniards were killed, that Indians weren't "civilized," that they should be acquitted, set free, allowed to go wherever they wished, and the Governor should order compensation for the expenses resulting from their arrest.

But in the end the Acomas were found guilty. *No Acoma was given a death sentence; 24 males* over the age of 25 were sentenced to have *puntas de pies* (*toes, not feet*) cut off (according to researcher/author Dr. E.J. Gallegos) and then must render 20 years of servitude; two Moquis (Hopis) in the fight were to have a hand (*fingertips?*) cut off then set free; males 20 to 25 years of age were condemned to slavery for 20 years; females over 12 years of age were condemned to slavery for 20 years. Governor Oñate then stated: "*All of the children under twelve years of age I declare free and innocent of the grave offense for which we punish their parents. And because of my duty to aid, support, and protect both the boys and girls ... I place the girls under the care of our father commissary, Fray Alonso Martínez, in order that he, as a Christian and qualified person, may distribute them in this kingdom or elsewhere in monasteries or other places where he thinks they may attain the knowledge of God and the salvation of their souls. The boys under twelve years of age I entrust to Vicente de Zaldívar Mendoza, my sargento mayor, in order that they may attain the same goal. The old men and women, disabled in the war, I order freed and entrusted to the Indians of the province of the Querechos where they may be supported and may not allow them to leave their pueblos...*"

HISTORIOGRAPHY

Unlike the many Indian wars east of the Mississippi, the Acoma War still throbs in American historiography. Juan de Oñate is usually depicted as "brutal" or "harsh" for the treatment of Acoma prisoners. The historical record must be considered dispassionately in order to arrive at valid conclusions. First of all it must be acknowledged that all source material was written by Spanish language participants and the most important is the work by Villagrá, himself a participant in the war. All records are in Spanish since the Acomas had no written language. Villagrá states the war was started because the Acomas attacked then killed Juan de Zaldívar and most of his men. Was the attack provoked? It is illogical that the very small number of Hispanic people in New Mexico wanted an Indian war within a year of the founding of their settlement. If Juan de Zaldívar had been looking for war he would not have gone to Acoma with a handful of soldiers. It must be concluded that the ambush came as a surprise to the Christians. Further, Acoma weapons were ready for the attack, proving premeditation, before Zaldívar went up to the stronghold, which was upon invitation of Acoma leaders. Put simply, the Christians were lured into a premeditated ambush.

After the sneak attack, the people in the little village of Knights of St. John officially declared war on the Acoma people. All discussion was made public and the decision was arrived at democratically: a war of no quarter. (Some writers have implied that well armed Spaniards should not have fought primitively armed Indians but such implications are generally reserved for Hispanic people, not English or American. Indeed, in the latter cases superior armament is often lauded as a sign of racial superiority and Indian primitivism.)

Due to a stiff dose of presentism in American historiography, punishments of Acoma prisoners have been roundly criticized by many writers. Is it forgotten that such punishments were part and parcel of the European legal system? While dismemberment is repulsive to the extreme in the present day, having a portion of the human body cut off was typical of those times. Further, what exactly was cut? Few investigators have access to documents written in 1599 and in the Spanish language. Primary researcher Dr. **Eloy Gallegos** has said that the dismemberment punishment was cutting off *puntas de pies*, toes, while various writers, including Hammond and Rey, have said it was "feet." [See Note # 3.] Besides the dismemberments, the guilty were also sentenced to twenty years of servitude.

There are more complications. How many Acomas were dismembered? **Paul Horgan** writes that the sentence was "*...all men of Acoma over twenty-five years of age to have one foot cut off...*" [See Note # 4.] Horgan doesn't provide a number and no sources are cited for the above information. **Edward H. Spicer** writes: "*The Spaniards captured five hundred Acomas who were sentenced to have one foot chopped off and to twenty years at hard labor.*" [See Note # 5.] Like Horgan, no specific source is cited by Spicer for this information. Dr. Marc Simmons writes in *The Last Conquistador* that **twenty-four** Acomas were actually sentenced to have a foot cut off. As mentioned above, Dr. Eloy Gallegos informed me during a personal interview that the sentence had to do with toes, *puntas de pies*, not feet. Further, on April 2, 1998, Dr. **John Kessell**, founder of the Vargas Project at the University of New Mexico, stated in a speech titled "A Foot for a Foot," that he and his colleague researchers have been unable to find a single document to verify that the dismemberment portion of the sentences were actually carried out. Archival documentation indicates that the friars, with or without the prompting of Oñate, went to the Governor with pleas to suspend the dismemberment, that Oñate was thereby encouraging the Pueblos to seek out Christian friars as protectors while saving face but instilling respect for Spanish law. Is it possible there were no dismemberments? Then what is the value of works like those mentioned above? It is historical fact that Acoma people resettled their stronghold starting around 1604 so if they escaped their twenty years of slavery they might never have suffered the dismemberments. Dr. Simmons writes: "*The Acomas proved more resilient and slippery for within a year or two most of them escaped their servitude, fled back to the rock, and rebuilt a new pueblo that remains occupied to this day.*" It is difficult to believe that hundreds of Acomas (footless?) could "flee" anywhere unless they were allowed to do so but it is a fact that Acomas were resettling their stronghold by 1604, as already mentioned. If leniency was given in the sentence for 20 years of slavery it is possible the friars "convinced" Oñate to suspend the dismemberments. Further, what use could be made of "footless" slaves? (The Hammond & Rey work states the sentences were carried out.) It must also be emphasized that Spaniards were the best record keepers in the world but not a single writer in the New Mexico of that period ever reported that he had seen a "footless Acoma." Such sights would certainly have been mentioned if Spicer or Horgan were correct that hundreds of Acoma men were punished by having a foot cut off. It must also be added that Oñate's enemies, who grew to be numerous as well as vociferous, never wrote about seeing any "footless" Indians in New Mexico.

Are English language writers using Spanish language documents to write about colonial New Mexico? Is it possible that some writers using the English language are not knowledgeable enough in using Spanish language documents? Translating from 16th century Spanish into English is a demanding art in and of itself. It would appear that that deciphering *puntas de pies* (toes) from a document should not be easily confused with simply *pies* (feet). But then there are accompanying erroneous bits of information that are just as disturbing. Dr. Spicer writes (1962) that 500 Acomas were sentenced to have a foot cut off while Dr. Simmons puts (1991) the number at 24. How can there be such a wide disparity? What sources are being used? Then Dr. Kessell and his researchers can find no original documentation to corroborate the dismemberments at all. Is it any wonder that the word *propagandistory* had to be created?

DISCUSSION NOTES *for* ACOMA WAR
Note # 1
Oñate estimated the Indian population at around 60,000 but modern writers have said the number was more like 40,000 or so. No one really knows the exact number. Whatever the ex-

act Pueblo figures, there were also thousands of Apache and Navajo groups away from the Río Grande Valley. Few writers have explored what marvelous courage it required for a small group of Hispanics to travel hundreds of miles away from the nearest Spanish settlement and make a life in the middle of Indian country. Such a feat is unparalleled in what is now the USA.

Note # 2
See Chapter 8 in *The Last Conquistador: Juan De Oñate And The Settling Of The Far Southwest* by Marc Simmons.

Note # 3
See *Don Juan De Oñate, Colonizer Of New Mexico, 1595-1628* by G.P. Hammond and A. Rey.

Note # 4
See Chapter 5, pages 241-42, in *Conquistadors In North American History* by Paul Horgan.

Note # 5
See Chapter Six, page 157, in *Cycles Of Conquest: The Impact Of Spain, Mexico, And The United States On The Indians Of The SouthwesT*, 1533-1960, by Edward H. Spicer.

JUMANO WAR

Little is known about the Amerindians referred to as Jumanos (Humanos). There were a few Jumano settlements located southeast of San Gabriel. These were similar to other Río Grande villages, *pueblos*, but the Jumano people also appeared to have ties with the eastern plains Apaches, with whom they traded and appear to have been allied. (It is possible there were two distinct Jumano groups, one group living a more settled village lifestyle while another was closer to the nomadic plains lifestyle.)

Sometime before 1605 Governor Oñate made the decision to send out an expedition to explore for the South Sea (Pacific Ocean). Vicente de Zaldívar was in charge but first he was assigned to acquire supplies from the three or four Jumano villages. The Jumanos decided not to help supply the expedition and further, they gave Zaldívar stones instead of grain. [See Note # 1. *Notes begin on page 245.*] He informed Oñate of the insult then went west.

Oñate decided he would teach the Jumanos a lesson they wouldn't soon forget. With some fifty men he went to the Jumanos and demanded cotton blankets. The Indians gave up a few then the Spaniards withdrew to make camp. The following day Oñate returned and informed the Jumanos they were going to be punished for giving Zaldívar stones to eat. Part of the village was set afire and some Indians on a rooftop were shot and killed. Two war captains were hung and when the interpreter came under suspicion of working against the Spaniards, he too was hung. Then Oñate returned to San Gabriel.

Jumano resentment continued to simmer. During the Christmas season of 1600, five Spaniards were riding by the Jumano villages when they were attacked by warriors who managed to slay two Christians. When word of the killings reached San Gabriel the colonists began to fear a general uprising like Acoma. Even the friars advised Oñate to nip the rebellion in the bud. A war council was held and it was decided to send Vicente Zaldívar at the head of a punitive expedition, which for reasons unknown didn't move until the spring of 1601.

Warriors came out to do battle but the Spaniards soon drove them back behind their protective walls. For the next six days there were bitterly fought skirmishes and even Zaldívar received a serious wound. When the village was taken it was burned and Zaldívar gave each of his men one Jumano male slave, thus ending the "Jumano War." [See Note # 2.]

No one really knows what happened to the Jumano villages after this period in history. As stated, the Jumanos had been influenced by the eastern groups of Apaches and it is possible they were absorbed by those plains groups in New Mexico as well as in Texas. [See Note # 3.] In Texas the Jumanos came to be referred to as "los Apaches Jumanos."

DISCUSSION NOTES *for* JUMANO WAR

Note # 1

See pages 150-52 in *The Last Conquistador* by Marc Simmons.

Note # 2

Later in the year, Fray Juan de Escalona, a bitter enemy of Oñate, wrote the viceroy that some eight hundred Jumano men, women, and children had been killed during the war. No other writers have corroborated Escalona's commentary.

Note # 3

See Chapter 9 in *The Indians Of Texas* by W.W. Newcomb Jr.

ST. LAWRENCE DAY MASSACRE

Most English language writers have referred to the Pueblo Indian uprising of August 10, 1680, as the "Pueblo Revolt." Writers using the Spanish language at the time used the phrase *el Día de San Lorenzo*, St. Lawrence Day. Authors like John Kessell, Paul Horgan, J. Manuel Espinosa, etc., have depicted the tragedy for what it was, a *massacre*, therefore the more valid historical title for this event is "the St. Lawrence Day Massacre of 1680." [See Note # 1. *Notes begin on page 250.*]

REVOLT or MASSACRE?

The uprising which erupted on August 10, 1680, was targeted at all Hispanic or Christian people living in New Mexico. Leaders, only one of which was Popé, ordered that no one was to be spared so non-combatant women, children, and the elderly were slain wherever encountered, making it a massacre of huge proportions. Dr. Kessell sets the tone for what happened: ...*The rebels fell on Father Velasco...where the naked bodies of Father Custos Bernal, two other friars, and a number of Spanish men, women, and children stared grotesquely without seeing. Back at Pecos, young Fray Juan de la Pedrosa, along with two Spanish women and three children, lay dead.* In short, the St. Lawrence Day Massacre was a typically sanguine frontier uprising.

Writers who promote "the Pueblo Revolt" as a struggle for *Liberty!* against oppression, as a blow for *Religious Freedom!* seldom depict the tragic scenes which were the essence of the St. Lawrence Day Massacre. There is no denying that New Mexico was experiencing serious problems, especially a terrible drought, and that Pueblo Indians had serious grievances against the government and the Christian clergy. But the crux of the matter is that the Pueblos became executioners for ordinary, unsuspecting Christian people. Especially vulnerable were those who lived in outlying farms and ranches, who had never done anything to the Indians but who had no chance to escape pent-up wrath. Typical of the massacre were the violent deaths of Petronila de Salas and her family of ten sons and daughters who were murdered in their own home by a roving Pueblo mob of "warriors." Petronila had three grown sons who, presumably, could respond in self defense, though the surprise attack could be a major factor in responding, but the rest of her children were *"grown daughters and the rest young."* Some thirty-eight (38) Hispanics were murdered at the hacienda of Tomé Domínguez, such was the element of surprise. Twenty-one friars died in the carnage, many of them brutally ridiculed or tortured before they were slaughtered in cold blood. [See Note # 2.] It is true that the New Mexico Christian clergy worked against various aspects of native religion where they conflicted with Christianity. Being Europeans, dancing with venomous snakes could not be tolerated, even if the ritual was intended to produce rain. [See Note # 3.] Additionally, one of the least publicized Pueblo complaints was that Christianity required monogamy and Pueblo men highly resented being restricted to one wife. They much preferred their traditional polygamy. This "grievance" was voiced during the massacre. A Tano Indian known as Pedro García gave the following notice to someone from Galisteo: *The Indians want to kill the Fathers and all Spaniards. They promise that the Indian who kills a Spaniard will get an Indian woman, whichever one he wants, as his wife. He who kills four Spaniards will take four, and he who kills ten or more will have that many women for wives…*

HISTORIOGRAPHY

New Mexican scholar **Luis Brandtner** has done a study on the victims of the St. Lawrence Day Massacre. [See Note # 4.] He states that some 350 or so Indian males were killed in various battles. Brandtner goes on to suggest that the pre-massacre population of New Mexico was "about 2000," not the 2800 figure estimated by C.W. Hackett or the 2300 estimated by France Scholes. [See Note # 5] Brandtner reports that some seventy-three (73) Spanish men of military age were killed by the Indians. He has identified 203 Spanish deaths by name: 61 men, 45 women, 68 children, and 29 of unidentified age or gender. Twelve (12) servants were also slaughtered, along with 21 captives, leaving some 144 massacre victims unidentified by name/gender/age/ethnicity, etc. It is likely that if the unidentified victims had been part of the military they would have been identified as missing so we can presume the unidentified were non-military civilians. Twenty-one (21) missionaries, non-combatants, were also slaughtered during the massacre. Among the Hispano families who suffered brutal losses would include those (names can have alternate spellings) of Anaya Almazán, Archuleta, Baca, Barba, Blanco de la Vega, Carvajal, Domínguez de Mendoza, Durán y Chaves (now Chávez), Gamboa, García Holgado, García de Noriega, Goitia, Fresqui, Gómez Robledo, Griego, Guadarrama, Heras, Herrera, Jiménez, Leyva (also Leiva), López, López de Aragón, López de García, Lucero, Lucero de Godoy, Luz, Nieto, Peralta, Pérez de Bustillo, Romero, Ramos, Salas, Torres, Varela, Zamora.

According to Brandtner's study, the New Mexican families with the greatest losses were as follows:

Juan Domínguez de Mendoza reported 66 deaths of relatives;

Tomé Domínguez de Mendoza, 38 deaths of Spanish relatives;

Diego Lucero de Godoy reported the deaths of 32 household members;

Catalina de Zamora reported more than 32 deaths of relatives.

Pueblo Indians like one **Bartolomé Naranjo** were also murdered in cold blood. Brandtner reports that some sixty-one (61) servants were either *killed or carried off* by the revolutionaries. Some eighty-eight (88) captives were freed when Diego de Vargas reconquered the province and there were a number of children born to women during their captivity, indicating that Pueblo men used female captives for sexual purposes. For example, **Juana de Apodaca**, unmarried at the time of the massacre and later found at San Juan pueblo, gave birth to a son and a daughter while a prisoner in the village. **Petrona Pacheco Nieto**, wife of Cristóbal Nieto, was also a captive at San Juan, along with five daughters and two sons (three of the eight being born while in captivity). Some fifty-four Indian captives, along with five mulattos (**María Rendón** gave birth to three daughters while in captivity), were also freed by the Vargas conquest.

As for casualties by region Brantner reports that some 70 Hispanic people and three friars died in the Taos area. Some 76 individuals and 5 friars died in the Río Abajo jurisdiction. Five friars were martyred by the Zuñi and Hopi in western New Mexico. In the Tanos villages (Galisteo, San Cristóbal, San Lázaro, etc.) some 13 Spanish settlers were murdered. In the Tewa areas (Santa Clara, San Juan, San Ildefonso, Tesuque, Pojoaque, Nambé, Jacona, Cuyamungue) 33 Hispanics and 3 friars were slaughtered, twenty of them in Pojoaque. [See Note # 6.] The ferocious carnage must have been beyond belief, especially since the civilian population had no warning of what was happening all over New Mexico: enraged Pueblos appearing suddenly and slaughtering every Hispanic man, woman, or child within their reach. Further, as has been suggested above, it has been written that of the more than 400 or so dead, some 300 were women and children. The loss of human life has been described as "staggering" for the place and time.

The "Pueblo Revolt" has been a popular topic for American writers. A few books will serve to review this literature. **Robert Silverberg** published (University of Nebraska Press) his *The Pueblo Revolt* in 1970. **Marc Simmons** writes in the Introduction that "*descendants*" consider the "*massive assault…as the 'First American Revolution.' Before it would be over, 21 Franciscan missionaries, more than 400 Spaniards, and an uncounted legion of Indians had perished.*" The venerable Dr. Simmons doesn't use the word *massacre* in any portion of the Introduction. Causes for the uprising are cited by Simmons as Spanish intolerance for native rituals like doing the Rain Dance, which required dancers to hold venomous snakes by the mouth and hand of all participants. The sight of so many dancers grasping snakes would repulse almost any European (or American) and Spaniards were no exception. Aside from certain aspects of native ritual, Dr. Simmons also cites interference in village life by civil and church officials, forced labor, taxation in the form of tribute, and "abuse of native women." European diseases and then terrible drought are also listed as causes of the rebellion. All these impelled the Pueblo people to weave "a net of conspiracy" to destroy their Spanish overlords.

The Silverberg work is 216 pages long. The first 110 pages comprise chapters on topics like "People of the Río Grande," "Coming of the Spaniards," "Spaniards Return," etc. As quickly as page 3 the reader is told that the Spanish conquest of the Americas was…*a cruel harvest for gold and gems as well as the bodies and souls of men. Indians were treated with chilling inhumanity…converted to Christianity, forcefully if necessary, and made into slaves. Those who would not accept the teachings of the meek Jesus were slaughtered like beasts. The gods and ceremonies cherished by the natives were forbidden. Indian chieftains of nobility or intelligence were put to death as potential troublemakers. Terror was Spanish policy. Whole tribes were exterminated by Spanish ferocity and diseases the Spaniards brought. The holocaust took millions of Indian lives, their martyrdom at the hands of Spain was one of history's darkest episodes.* [See Note # 7.]

Silverberg informs (page 69) his readers that mission gardens of the "Pueblo folk" contained orchards of fruits new to them like ...*pears, peaches, figs, dates, pomegranates, olive, cherries, quinces, lemons, oranges, nectarines.* The climate of New Mexico is not conducive to growing orchards of citrus fruits so this information is preposterous.

Chapter 7 is titled "The Day of Reckoning." Popé is introduced as an "embittered medicine doctor" who had a *"fiery love for the kachina faith"* for which he had been imprisoned and whipped. (No mention is made of his zest for polygamy.) This *"fierce and dynamic individual"* gave the impression that he had "dark powers" which caused people to respect and fear him. It took years to agree to the plans but they were so well laid that Spanish New Mexicans didn't learn about the uprising until the slaughter began. Pope was deadly serious: when his son-in-law, governor of San Juan Pueblo, refused to join the rebellion Pope had him stoned to death. Silverberg writes that *"...the Pueblo gods had decreed the death of every male Spaniard in New Mexico..."* though it is common knowledge that more women and children were massacred than men

"...(Chapter 8) in one glorious convulsion of wrath..."

After the "glorious convulsion" Popé became the supreme authority and took to behaving like a Spanish governor, even to *"...wearing a bull's horn on his forehead as a symbol of power..."* (A horn on the forehead is associated with the Comanche chieftain Cuerno Verde in 1779.) Civil war was not long in coming for the Pueblo people *"...had merely replaced a rational tyrant with an irrational one..."* Further, running out the Hispano population had not ended the drought and now fierce Apache raiders were on horseback. Silverberg reports that Pope died in 1688 and *"...he must be considered a potent figure in the history of the American Indian, one of the very few who actually succeeded in halting, if only for a while, the territorial advance of the European conquerors."* Silverberg's work doesn't reflect the information done by scholars like Luis Brandtner. In contrast to Brandtner's work, Silverberg uses no footnotes or citations for specific information (for example, where did he get the impression that oranges grew in New Mexico?), merely listing a Bibliography at the end of the book.

Andrew L. Knaut published (University of Oklahoma Press edition) his *The Pueblo Revolt of 1680* in 1995. Knaut laments in the Preface that *"collective Pueblo memory"* has been distorted by modern influences and that Spanish documentary sources *"...reflect all too faithfully the biases of Spanish observers rarely concerned with an accurate sense of the lives of their Pueblo vassals."* [See Note # 8.] The author postulates that Pueblo people opposed Spanish New Mexicans throughout the 17th century, not only the few years before the "Revolt." As with Silverberg, "massacre" isn't used to describe the tragedy and Dr. Knaut states frankly that his hope is to *"...breathe new historical life into the experiences of its central actors—the Pueblo Indians..."* It is stated that Governor Otermín estimated that of the 380 dead, 73 were adult males, and 21 missionaries had also been brutally slain. That some 300 women and children were massacred draws no comment, perhaps because Knaut's avowed focus is on the Pueblo Indians:*"...how* *can one make the Pueblo experience speak?"* [See Note # 9.]

Dr. Knaut's work appears to be a compilation of previous works done by other writers like Lansing B. Bloom, J. Manuel Espinosa, Charles W. Hackett, George P. Hammond and Agapito Rey, John Kessell, Rick Hendricks, and Meredith Dodge, etc., as well as many other "secondary" sources. With the Pueblo people being promoted as "heroes," Knaut provides predictable perspectives. For example, H.E. Bolton was unable to "Parkmanize" (i.e., popularize) the Borderlands because Bolton rarely ventured *"beyond his research into the nature of Spanish institutions…"* therefore failing to write sagas that were *"…as attractive to general readers as the Parkman classics."* No effort will be made to challenge the veracity of Knaut's perspectives but it is necessary to address what could be termed an Orwellian twist when comparing the "Pueblo Revolt" and Parkman's *The Conspiracy of Pontiac*. Popé and other Pueblo leaders are promoted as heroes fighting *Spanish oppression* while Parkman depicts Chief Pontiac as the *Satan of the Forest* for fighting the British. [See Note # 10.] Put succinctly, Indians living under Spanish rule ("European overlords") were heroic resistance fighters while those battling English or Americans were *treacherous savages*. The rest of Dr. Knaut's *Revolt* follows a familiar pattern. The conquistadores were "profit-hungry entrepreneurs," who employed "brutal acts of suppression" to justify God, Gold, and Glory. Vásquez de Coronado started it off then Oñate came in with settlers. The Pueblo people numbered (estimated) in the hundreds of thousands and diseases brought in by Spanish people soon cut them down to some seventeen thousand. The Spaniards themselves were to blame for the ambush at Acoma, a rebellion that was put down so harshly it included *"…all males over twenty-five years of age to have one foot cut off…and twenty years of servitude."* While there is no number given for "one-footed Indian slaves," the other Indians have to pay tribute but "Pueblo Cultural Endurance" is lauded and it is unnecessary to point out that Denominational Christianity isn't in the mix during that period of time. Spaniards are also blamed for "fueling animosity" between the Pueblo and Athapaskan groups. How was this done? Horses were stolen by Athapaskans and they could now raid the Pueblos more efficiently because of the Spanish horse. It is unnecessary to continue with the rest of the work for it proceeds in a similar vein.

Joe Sando, a native of Jémez Pueblo, published (Clear Light Publishers) *Pueblo Profiles: Cultural Identity through Centuries of Change* in 1998. Part I deals with the "Pueblo Revolt" which is now promoted as *"…the first successful American revolution against a foreign colonial power, Spain."* Popé (*Po-pay, Po-pyn*: "Ripe Squash") is now *"…a man of the people…about fifty years old…"* who had been born into a *"…life of subjugation."* The Spanish took food and wood without giving in return. While the Christians had a concept of Satan and Pueblo religion did not, the Pueblos were accused of "devil worship." [See Note # 11.] "Conversion by the sword" had not been successful because the Pueblos continued practicing their religion in secret.

Sando provides an *"imaginative re-creation"* of how the "Pueblo Revolt" was planned. Leaders from the Pueblos are sitting around a small fire in a large meeting room. Dialects are heard throughout the room. A leader makes his way to the fire and speaks: *Our grandfathers told us that when the "metal wearers" arrived one of them told a Tiwa man to hold his horse then proceeded to attack the man's wife…* Other leaders air their grievances. Then Popé tells how 47 medicine men were arrested, four were executed, the others whipped and imprisoned. He ends by saying, "I am for telling the Spaniards to leave our country or suffer the consequences."

As time went on Pueblo leaders continued to communicate. Isleta Pueblo was loyal to the Spanish so they were excluded from all plans for war. Popé was eventually chosen as principal leader. Malacate spoke at a gathering: *Tell the warriors that we are not bloodthirsty. Our only goal is to get the Spanish to leave our country and let us return to the ways of our grandfathers. We will ask them to leave and if they will leave, let them go peacefully. It is only if they absolutely refuse that we must use force...*

It must be pointed out that the foregoing is labeled an "imaginative re-creation" by author Sando. If anything at all is known about the "Pueblo Revolt" it is that it was a *surprise* uprising. Yet the reader is told that Spanish New Mexicans were advised ahead of time to "*leave the country...ask them to leave...go peacefully...persuade the Spaniards they must leave or be killed...Twenty-one Franciscan friars had been killed as were some 400 of the more resistant Spaniards.*" If this is history, the three-hundred or so dead women and children were "the more resistant Spaniards"? Fittingly, the chapter winds up with Popé telling everyone to "Go home and enjoy your families, the birds, the clouds, the mist, the rain...cleanse yourselves of the recent past." The basic message is that "*The tyrants had been driven from the lands of the pueblo people. The first American revolution had succeeded.*" [See Note # 12.]

DISCUSSION NOTES *for* ST. LAWRENCE DAY MASSACRE

Note # 1

See Chapter V, page 228, and Chapter VI, in *Kiva, Cross, And Crown* by John Kessell. Paul Horgan uses the word "massacred" on page 270 of his *Conquistadors In North American History*, as does J. Manuel Espinosa in his *The Pueblo Indian Revolt Of 1696*, page 34.

Note # 2

The 9/11 attack on the World Trade Towers in New York is very similar to the St. Lawrence Day Massacre. In New Mexico innocent people were slaughtered because Indians resented civilian and Church authorities. In the USA innocent civilians were slaughtered because terrorists hated the American government.

Note # 3

Marc Simmons has written in his *Spanish Pathways* volume that among the cultural reasons for resentment was that Christian missionaries could not tolerate "*...public dancing, handling of venomous snakes, wearing of masks, and the sprinkling of sacred cornmeal...*" It is difficult to believe that clerics objected to "corn meal." Masks might be termed hideous by individuals outside the culture. Some Christian denominations object to dancing to this day.

Note # 4

This unpublished study is available on the website www.nmhcpl.com

Note # 5

For the principal work on this tragedy see *Revolt Of The Pueblo Indians Of New Mexico And Otermin's Attempted Reconquest, 1680-1682*, by C.W. Hackett.

Note # 6

Luis Brandtner has done a superb study on this very difficult issue. Most students or general readers have never been exposed to studies like Brandtner's. One might well ask why these go unpublished.

Note # 7

Such perspectives aren't rare in English language historiography. See *Tree Of Hate: Propaganda And Prejudices Affecting United States Relations With The Hispanic World* by Philip Wayne Powell. He states in the Preface that "Spaniards" were the first "to feel the impact of the printing press as a propaganda weapon."

Note # 8

No citation is given for this statement, other than to say "the documentary record" reflects it. With no written documentation in any Pueblo language and all documentation written by Hispanics of the day, what impels Dr. Knaut to decide that "Spanish observers" were biased? Dr. Knaut obviously considers himself superior to "observers" of the day but what is the basis for such superiority? Is it culturally biased omniscience? Should we contrast Indian survival in New Mexico with extinction/exile east of the Mississippi? Contrast Dr. Knaut's book with *The Protector De Indios Colonial New Mexico* by C.R. Cutter.

Note # 9

Howard Zinn writes in his classic A People's History Of The United States that *"...in such a world of conflict, a world of victims and executioners, it is the job of thinking people, as Albert Camus suggested, not to be on the side of the executioners."* Would Dr. Zinn refer to August 10, 1680, as "The St. Lawrence Day Massacre" or "The Pueblo Revolt"? Who were the victims and who were the executioners? Contrast roles (victims/executioners) in the Custer battle at the Little Bighorn.

Note # 10

See *Francis Parkman, Historian As Hero: The Formative Years* by Wilbur R. Jacobs for a good introduction to Parkman's works and career. As has been mentioned elsewhere, it would be interesting to make a comparative study of Popé (1680) and Pontiac (1763).

Note # 11

Neither Sando nor any other member of the "Pueblo Revolt school" addresses the issue of polygamy, highly cherished by Pueblo men, nor does he mention punishments like cutting off the ears/noses of "adulterous" Pueblo women. Neither does he dwell on "rituals" like the Rain Dance which had participants holding venous snakes while they danced. It would be interesting to study actual Pueblo rituals of that day and time. For example, how often were snakes utilized in such rituals? European people are not prone to condone "snake rituals," even in the present day.

Note # 12

Thus is the St. Lawrence Day Massacre converted into the "Pueblo Revolt" in American historiography. As mentioned elsewhere, there were a number of bloody uprisings in 17th century Virginia and New England but they aren't promoted as efforts for Native American freedom. Popé's name is still heard in New Mexico (and an artist's conception of him is placed in Statuary Hall) while that of Metacom, King Philip, has been all but erased from the popular mind. (See *500 Nations* by Alvin Josephy, Jr.)

RECONQUEST OF NEW MEXICO

After the St. Lawrence Day Massacre of 1680 the Pueblo people of New Mexico reverted to traditional animosities and made war against each other. Zía, Jémez, Santa Ana, Taos, San Felipe, Pecos, Cochití, and Santo Domingo were in league against the Tanos, Tewas, and Picurís. The Acomas were hopelessly divided and fought each other. Apaches attacked some villages and not others. Utes attacked all of them.

BLOODLESS PEACE

Diego de Vargas Zapata Luján Ponce de Leon was appointed (in 1688) Governor and Captain General for the reconquest of New Mexico. [See Note # 1. *Notes begin on page 253.*] He arrived in El Paso, which at that time was southern New Mexico, in February of 1691. By August of 1692 Vargas had built up a small army (perhaps from 50 to 60 men) of "Leatherjackets" and some 100 tough Pueblo auxiliaries who knew they would be entering an area inhabited by some 25- to 30,000 Indians. Marching under the banner of Juan de Oñate, all headed north on August 12th and entered Santa Fe unopposed on September 11th. The Tupatú brothers from Picurís, Luis and Lorenzo, came in and Vargas won them over with a promise of pardon for all participants in the Massacre of 1680. Reinforced by 300 warriors from Picurís, an expedition went against Pecos Pueblo, the largest in New Mexico. Pecos leader **Juan de Ye** welcomed Vargas peacefully and there was no war. Indeed, Juan de Ye became a stalwart ally. The pattern was set for the rest of the province and there was no bloodshed anywhere. All Pueblos expressed a desire to be reunited with the Spanish king and his Christian God. Some 2,214 Indians, mostly children were baptized and some 60 to 80 captives were set free. It was now up to Vargas to recolonize northern New Mexico and he asked for some 500 families to populate this northern frontier.

WAR

In December of 1693 when Vargas arrived in Santa Fe with colonists the Tanos refused to vacate the Spanish settlement. Some twenty-one colonists died from the cold while Vargas tried diplomacy to resolve the situation. It failed so he finally led a military attack on the "City of the Holy Faith." In two days of bloody fighting Santa Fe is won back. Some 70 leaders who had refused to surrender before the battle are executed. Some 400 prisoners are condemned to ten years of servitude. Juan de Ye and his Pecos people are now the strongest allies of Vargas and his Christians. Other pueblos become allies against those villages which wish to make war. By January of 1695 the pacification of New Mexico is considered complete. But on June 4, 1696, various pueblos rise in a second rebellion, brutally murdering 21 soldier-settlers and five missionaries. [See Note # 2.] Pecos, Tesuque, San Felipe, Santa Ana, and Zía remain loyal. Taos, Picurís, Cochití, Santo Domingo, Jemez, and the Tewa villages have to be subdued militarily. By December of 1696 there is finally a lasting peace in Pueblo land.

NO EXTERMINATION

Diego de Vargas and the Reconquest of New Mexico are significant for a number of reasons. First and foremost, the Pueblo people were not exterminated out of revenge for the atrocities of the St. Lawrence Day Massacre of 1680. [See Note # 3.] New Mexico was recolonized with a European based people and the two groups, Pueblo and Hispanic became stalwart allies in defense of their homes and societies. European technologies related to the farm, the ranch, and mining, returned to New Mexico, the northern most reach of the far flung Spanish Empire.

ALLIANCE

While it is seldom mentioned by English language writers, the Hispano-Pueblo alliance of New Mexico is perhaps the most sterling American example of European and Native American people joining together as partners for the common good. The Pueblos developed their share of autonomy and a number of Pueblo leaders were to become well known in the province. At the base of the alliance was that Hispanic government respected the Pueblo peoples' right to their land, which included water rights, thus preserving them and their culture.

Just as important as not exterminating native people, Christianity and its civilizing efforts returned to the area under the guidance of the Franciscan missionary leader **Fray Francisco de Vargas**. Fray Francisco and his paladin missionaries provided an immense initiative toward preserving and including Native Americans as valued participants in New Mexican society. While it is true that Christianity continued to forbid Pueblo traditions like polygamy, dancing with snakes or human body parts like scalps, etc., the Pueblos were able to adjust to basic tenets of the Christian church.

Diego de Vargas was the "Last Conquistador" because after his time there was little need for military campaigns into unknown/unexplored lands. He has been variously described by Southwestern historians. **Warren A. Beck** has written in *New Mexico: A History of Four Centuries* that Vargas possessed "*...unbelievable energy and strength of character...courage so great that it verged on the foolhardy...capable of implacable cruelty toward the Indians...which was to prove costly to the Spaniards in the long run.*" **J. Manuel Espinosa** has written that "*...Vargas stands out as one of the great figures in the colonial history of Spanish North America...*" because he was bold and capable, winning Pueblo leaders to his cause through diplomacy or waging war when necessary. Additionally, though there were disagreements, Vargas respected Church leaders and they generally cooperated with him. The Hispanic world's valiant knight died on April 8, 1704, and on the day of his burial, as dictated in his will, twelve head of cattle and fifty measures of corn were given in his name to the poor people of Santa Fe.

Paul Horgan has written that Vargas and the Spanish conquistadores were endowed with "*Confidence amounting to genius...*" Unlike some conquistadores, Diego de Vargas was high born but he too valued glory in service of God and King. His entire being was one of courage, a multi-sided courage which enabled him to vow to return Spain and Christianity to New Mexico and not exterminate the perpetrators of the St. Lawrence Day Massacre of 1680 in the process. He was true to his promise and he did it with the Spanish sense of honor mirrored by Calderon de la Barca who stated: "*To the King we owe our life and fortune, but Honor is the patrimony of the soul and the soul belongs to God.*"

DISCUSSION NOTES *for* RECONQUEST of NEW MEXICO

Note # 1

See Crusaders Of The Río Grande: The Story Of Don Diego De Vargas And The Reconquest And

Refounding Of New Mexico by J. Manuel Espinosa.
Note # 2
See *The Pueblo Indian Revolt Of 1696 And The Franciscan Missions In New Mexico: Letters Of The Missionaries And Related Documents* by J. Manuel Espinosa.
Note # 3
Contrast this lack of retribution against New Mexico's Indians with those in Virginia of the Powhatan Confederacy or the tribes allied with King Philip in New England, who were virtually wiped off the face of the earth. While the 1600s might well be considered a brutal age, American retaliatory policy toward Indians continued in the West until Custer was avenged in the December 29, 1890, massacre of Sioux at Wounded Knee. See *500 Nations* mentioned above.

COMANCHE WAR & PEACE

The province of New Mexico was in dire straits when forty-two year old **Juan Bautista de Anza** was appointed Governor in 1777. When he rode into Santa Fe the following year there was no doubt in anyone's mind that he was a frontiersman of the first rank. Despite his heroic reputation as trail blazer and colonizer of California, he was unaffected when dealing with ordinary people, whether Hispanic, Indian, or African. Unlike some of his predecessors, Anza could tell the difference between a Navajo and a Pueblo upon meeting them. After conferencing with various New Mexican leaders, Anza understood that the Comanches would have to be dealt with first. These warlike people had all but destroyed Pecos Pueblo and they attacked with impunity almost at will wherever they wished. The most implacable Comanche leader was known as **Cuerno Verde** (Green Horn, because he wore a headdress with a horn on the forehead), often referred to as *"the scourge of New Mexico."* [See Note # 1. *Notes begin on page 257.*]

EXPEDITION NORTH

Anza had his 600 man army ready by mid-August of 1799. The Governor had to supply weapons and horses for some of his militiamen. There were hundreds of horses (three for each soldier; some 1800 head in all), vast quantities of food (enough for forty days), arms and ammunition (ten ball cartridge belts), and other supplies. The expedition moved northward on the afternoon of August 15. But this time the route was different. Previously expeditions in pursuit of raiding Comanches went through Pecos or east through Taos. Comanches were always able to discover their approach and escape on their fleet horses. Anza's strategy was to invade *Comanchería* from the north, since an attack would not be expected from there. So the little army went north through *San Juan de los Caballeros* (Knights of St. John), Ojo Caliente, etc., and into the San Luis Valley. Scouts were constantly on the move in and out of the expedition, alerting Anza with all kinds of information on enemy movement, terrain, water sources, pasturage, etc. Pushing ever northward, the expedition picked up some 200 Utes and Apaches who teamed up because they had their own scores to settle with Comanches. Now there were some 800 men and perhaps 2400 horses in the expedition. At times it was necessary to move at night to avoid detection. The weather was bitterly cold as they went over "rarely crossed" Poncha Pass. By August 28th they crossed the *Río Napestle* (Arkansas) in foggy/snowy weather. A herd of some fifty buffalo was encountered in the area of *El Capitán* (Pike's Peak) and the men were treated to fresh buffalo meat. By August 30 the expedition was in the Comanche homeland and extra precautions were taken (in the area of present Colorado Springs) by placing lookouts in strategic positions. On August 31scouts reported that dust clouds toward the east were being raised by the enemy in considerable numbers. Further, one of the scouts felt his tracks were probably discovered so Anza decided to attack immediately. They closed in from the center, left, and right as prearranged but the Comanches fled precipitously because the group contained more families than warriors. The fleeing warriors finally turned to fight in order that the rest could escape, eighteen valiant Comanches being killed and many others wounded. Most of the women and children were taken captive, along with some 500 horses. All goods and baggage, so much that a hundred horses couldn't carry it all, were captured. The Comanche encampment was described as containing some one-hundred-twenty tents. Prisoners were interrogated and it was learned that Cuerno Verde was raiding settlements in New Mexico, that everyone would gather to celebrate Cuerno Verde's victories. Anza resolved to march south in hopes of meeting Cuerno Verde as he returned to his homeland. Surprise would probably not be a real factor but scouts were ordered to travel a distance from the trail so Cuerno Verde would see no new tracks on it. On September 2nd most of the Ute warriors abandoned the expedition (in the area of present Pueblo) and headed for home without farewell. That afternoon scouts came in saying the enemy was approaching and seemed to be unaware of the army's presence. A preliminary battle was fought at sunset until the army got bogged down crossing a gully and the Comanches withdrew. It was cold and rain came down but the army spent the night there, ready to fight if the enemy attacked but they didn't.

BATTLE

The morning of September 3rd found the army confronted by Cuerno Verde and his warriors, some fifty in number. The chieftain now rode forward alone, his horse curveting as if to attract attention to its rider. Anza's plan was to throw a half circle of men against the Comanches while feigning a frontal retreat. But Cuerno Verde saw through the strategy and ordered his warriors to withdraw, counting on their swift horses to escape. But Anza had his reserve forces waiting in a gully, trapping the Cuerno Verde personal guard from all sides. The warriors quickly dismounted and made a brave stand to the last man. All died in the battle, including Cuerno Verde, his firstborn son, and four of his most famous captains. Others might have been killed or captured but Anza concentrated on Cuerno Verde because he was the avowed scourge who had killed hundreds of Hispanos and Pueblos then taken as many more prisoner only to execute them later. Cuerno Verde's death was a great victory. His own fearlessness was his downfall, taking on a large army of six hundred with the mere handful of warriors in his personal guard.

HOMEWARD

The expedition, always on guard, now headed south and home. The rest of the Utes departed for their country with their share of the booty. The expedition arrived in Taos on September 7, 1799 and learned that the Comanches, estimated at around 250, had indeed raided there. Santa Fe was reached on

September 10, 1799. The expedition had covered some 615 miles, had been gone for 26 days during which some 133 enemy Comanches had been killed or captured, in which total was Cuerno Verde himself, while Anza hadn't lost a single man.

HONORABLE PEACE

Governor Anza sent Cuerno Verde's headdress as a trophy to Commandant General Teodoro de Croix. While the battle had been won, the war wasn't over until a peace could be made. The Comanches now understood they had a real warrior leading New Mexico but they still attacked places like Pecos Pueblo. Anza forbade any trade with hostile Comanches but he let it be known that an honorable peace could be made whenever the warriors wanted to come to terms. He made it clear that all Comanche groups had to make peace or there would be none with anyone. [See Note # 2.]

ECUERACAPA

Representatives from the three major branches of the nation, Yupe, Yamparika, and Cuchanec, met in council and decided to send a leading chieftain, **Ecueracapa** (also known as *Cota de Malla*, Coat of Mail), to speak for peace in Santa Fe. First Ecueracapa sent emissaries to size up the situation: for four days they were feted then given gifts for Ecueracapa. Anza selected a return delegation, a Spaniard named José Manuel Rojo with 13 Pecos Indians, and sent them out of Santa Fe on January 3, 1786. Ecueracapa entertained the delegation so lavishly that they never stopped talking about it. In February the Comanches descended on the vicinity of Pecos Pueblo, but this time they merely put up their tipis in peace. Ecueracapa and a small entourage went into Santa Fe, with a full military escort, where Anza and town dignitaries were waiting to receive him as any other visiting chief of state, ordinary citizens applauding at every turn.

Ecueracapa, recognized among his own people for his abilities as warrior as well as diplomat, played his part to the hilt. His greeting of Governor Anza took several minutes. Finally he embraced the Spanish leader and rubbed faces with him as was customary among these "lords of the southern plains." Anza led the chieftain into the Palace of the Governors and through interpreters discussed peace terms. During a short break in the discussion Anza brought in a delegation of Ute chieftains (which included Moara and Pinto?). The two groups had been mortal enemies for decades and suddenly leaders were in the same room with Anza asking them to make peace for the good of all nations. This was risky business because the very name "Comanche" was a Ute word which meant *wants to fight me all the time.*" There were tense moments when each side accused the other of instigating war but when animosities cooled Ecueracapa conceded that peace was better than war. The Utes said they would keep the peace if the Comanches did. According to plains custom, the two groups then exchanged garments of clothing to show that they were indeed true friends. The conference lasted for three days, Ecueracapa and the Utes being feted throughout, church bells pealing in jubilation. Then Anza led everyone back to Pecos and the Comanche encampment. Some two hundred warriors greeted the Governor, crowding around him, embracing him, rubbing their faces on his, such was their "joy and delight." Anza, experienced frontiersman that he was, accepted their friendship in a sincere manner. He took a meal with the Comanche captains and was impressed by them. They seemed very healthy people, of happy disposition, many were good looking. These were warriors but also men of character, generous and honest. They were dressed in buffalo skins and painted their faces with red ochre, their eyelids in vermilion. Their long braided hair was adorned with anything that glittered or was bright.

STIPULATIONS

Peace terms were hammered out by all parties. The peace would be *permanent*. The Comanches could move closer to New Mexico and go to Santa Fe through Pecos. Pecos would be the official site for trading and prices would be regulated. Comanches would help fight the Apaches. All Comanche groups would have to agree to the treaty. Anza gave his personal sword and banner to Ecueracapa to show the rest of the nation. The Comanches dug a ceremonial hole in the ground then covered it up, thereby burying war forever. It was February 28, 1786.

TRADE FAIR

The following day a Trade Fair was held to celebrate the Comanche Peace. It happened to be Ash Wednesday so the Comanche captains accompanied Governor Anza while receiving ashes on the forehead. Anza decreed strict rules intended to prevent the Indians being cheated out of their goods and woe to any Christian who "played infamous tricks on them." Overseers were selected to keep a close watch on the trading and even troops were employed in that capacity so that everything proceeded in good order. Some 600 skins were traded, along with loads of meat, tallow, some horses and a few muskets, all to the Comanche's satisfaction.

TREATY OF PEACE

By April of 1787 the final treaty that included all three groups of the Comanche nation was finalized. The Comanche Peace would last for generations, despite the replacement of Anza in 1787 and the death of Ecueracapa in 1793 (even into the American period of Southwest history). Though real dangers still existed, plains travel was safer with the Comanches as stalwart brothers-in-arms. Ciboleros, mesteñeros, and comancheros could venture out to the plains to ply their professions. New Mexico's Hispanos were now staunch allies with the Pueblo as well as Comanche nations, feats which rank among the most marvelous in frontier history.

DISCUSSION NOTES *for* COMANCHE WAR & PEACE

Note # 1

See *Forgotten Frontiers: A Study Of The Spanish Indian Policy Of Don Juan Bautista De Anza, Governor Of New Mexico, 1777-1787* by Alfred Barnaby Thomas. This work supplies historians with much primary material and is more correctly "Spanish Indian Policy," not only that of the Great Captain. See also Chapter VII in *The Apache Frontier: Jacobo Ugarte and Spanish-Indian Relations in Northern New Spain, 1769-1791* by Max L. Moorhead.

Note # 2

For basic information on Comanches see *The Comanches: Lords Of The South Plains* by Ernest

Wallace & E. Adamson Hoebel. See also *Los Comanches: The Horse People, 1751-1845* by Stanley Noyes.

CEBOLLETA and the NAVAJO FRONTIER

Navajos referred to themselves as *Diné*, "The People," and *Dinétah* was the Navajo homeland. It is believed that in 1626 Fray Gerónimo de Zárate Salmerón was the first Hispanic to mention the *Apaches de Nabajú*. Fray Alonso de Benavides also wrote about them in 1630. Efforts to Christianize the Navajos met with no success.

Dinétah included lands in the Four Corners area, most of western New Mexico and eastern Arizona to the Colorado River. The Navajos were small scale farmers but they also raided Pueblo and Hispanic villages in the Río Grande Valley for plunder as well as women and children captives. Expeditions, comprised of Pueblos and Hispanics, were sent against the Navajos, the Christians also taking captives whenever possible. These punitive expeditions usually brought peace until more raids occurred. Raid and counter-raid characterized Navajo and Hispanic/Pueblo relations in New Mexico, each side taking slaves whenever possible. [See Note # 1. *Notes begin on page 260.*]

The most serious counter-raid began in August 11, 1705, when Captain **Roque de Madrid** led a force into an area in Dinétah which he called "*los Peñoles*." Roque's men fought Navajos wherever they encountered them, reportedly killing some thirty-nine warriors and capturing several women and children. Soon after the Navajos asked for peace talks but Governor Cuervo y Valdés didn't believe them because they had feigned desires for peace before. He sent out another expedition but the Navajos were able to elude it. Once more a delegation of Navajos asked for peace talks and this time they got them. A fragile peace was established. Part of the reason is possibly that by 1709 the Navajos were also being attacked by Utes and Comanches. Not even the numerous Navajo warriors could fight everybody.

The peace held until 1713 when Navajos raided San Ildefonso Pueblo. Captain **Cristóbal de la Serna** led some 50 presidial soldiers, 20 Hispano militiamen, and 150 Pueblo Warriors into Dinétah to retrieve stolen stock.

In 1714 Navajos raided Jémez Pueblo so Roque de Madrid led soldiers, militiamen, and some 212 Pueblos into Navajo land, reportedly killing some 30 Navajos, capturing seven, confiscating much corn and 110 sheep, much of which was given to the victims back in Jémez Pueblo. Another expedition went into Dinétah in October of 1716, led by Captain de la Serna.

The area north of Laguna Pueblo was known as *Cebolleta* (Wild Onion or Little Onion) and in 1748 it was there, "the place of the pagans," that missionaries decided to found a mission, with another to the southwest at Encinal. But in 1750 when builders from Laguna and Acoma were directed to work at the sites the Navajos refused to follow the example and bolted away from the area. The missions were abandoned soon after. Spanish stockmen were granted grazing rights in the Cebolleta area as far as Mount San Mateo (now referred to as Mt. Taylor). From 1753 until 1772 some land grants were awarded for Cebolleta lands. Navajos resented these grants because they were accustomed to grazing their own animals on them. In 1774 raids from Navajos and Apaches forced Hispanic settlers to withdraw. In 1785

Governor Anza was able to break the Navajo/Apache alliance.

In 1788 Governor de la Concha led a large expedition against the Gila and Mimbres Apaches. Of the 500 men there were Hispanic militia and Pueblo warriors from Acoma, Jémez, Santa Ana, Taos, Zía as well as some 20 Navajos. Some eighteen Apaches were killed and several captives were taken.

In 1796 the Navajos made peace with the southern Apaches and resumed raiding.

On January 31, 1800, Governor Fernando Chacón issued the Cebolleta (today Seboyeta) land grant of about 200,000 acres to 30 families from the Albuquerque-Atrisco area.

Marc Simmons has written that "New Mexico in the year 1800 was a remote and almost forgotten corner in Spain's New World empire." [See Note # 2.] The New Mexicans had long since become accustomed to shifting for themselves, wresting a living from poor, rain-deprived soils. What they had was mostly of their own creation because supplies from the south were few and far between. Even "savage Indian attacks had to be handled by the people with the aid of a skeleton garrison of royal troops." New Mexican Hispanos were "tough and hardy," inured to very real frontier dangers. Above all they were resilient, which enabled them to "absorb blow after blow" delivered to them, their families, their fields, herds and flocks, etc., by hostile Indians. They endured, rebuilt, and replanted.

Among the founding families of Cebolleta were those of Francisco Aragón; Domingo Baca; Josefa Baca; Marsial Baca; Antonio Chaves; Bicente Chaves; Juan Antonio Chaves; Juan Bautista Chaves; José Chaves; J. Santos Chaves; Salvador Chaves; Francisco García; Anastacio Gallego; Felipe Gallego; Juan Cristóbal Gallego; J. Gregorio Gallego; Manuel Gallego; Pablo Gallego; Román Gallego; Miguel Herrera (?); Juan Domingo Herrera; Gregorio Jaramillo; Javier Jaramillo; Diego Antonio Márquez; Bentura Peralta; Santiago Peralta; Juan J. Perea (?); Lorenzo Romero; Manuel Romero; Judás Satillanes…

The settlement was intended as a buffer to forestall Navajo raids on the Río Grande communities. Navajos living in the immediate area were forced out (to the present Cañoncito area) and the Hispano stockmen brought in their herds of horses, sheep, and cattle. By March the Navajos protested that Cebolleta was *their* grazing land but the new settlers responded by building a stone wall around their little village. Navajo raids began, building in intensity as time went by, but the "Cebolletanos" held on to their settlement. At times the women and children would be sequestered in a protected grotto that came to be dedicated to the *Virgen de Nuestra Señora de Lourdes*, commonly referred to as *Los Portales*.

In August of 1804 around a thousand Navajo warriors attacked Cebolleta with the intention of wiping it off the face of the earth. For days the little settlement was besieged. Villagers and their terrified domestic stock gathered in the fortified plaza to defend themselves from raining arrows and burning pitch-pine knots, the "flaming hand grenades" of the time. The town was besieged for several days and there were heroic feats of valor on both sides. Individual warriors tried to open the village gate to the plaza in order to overwhelm the defenders by sheer numbers.

Antonia Romero, who like the other women was helping with making bandages, taking water to the men, and trying to calm the terrified livestock, suddenly noticed that a Navajo had made it over the wall during a furious assault and was about to remove the bar from the gate. There was no time to scream the alarm so she picked up a heavy *metate* (grinding stone basin), arrows whizzing all about her, and hurled it at the foe, crushing the warrior's skull and saving the village from certain destruction, at least for the moment.

Domingo Baca and a group of paladins sallied out and in the hand-to-hand encounter which followed his abdomen was sliced open by a Navajo lance. The Cebolletanos retreated to the plaza, Baca's entrails hanging out but for his hands that kept them in place. His fellow defenders believed he was a goner but once in safety he put a pillow to his belly, lashed it in place, then returned to help throw back the assault by firing his musket. When the assault abated, he removed the pillow and *sewed up his* own *abdomen*. (Baca made a complete recovery and lived for many years thereafter.)

The Navajos finally called off the attack. It was reported they lost 22 men killed and about 50 wounded.

Virtually all of the Cebolletanos were wounded and their military corporal was dead. They knew it was just a matter of time before the Navajos returned for another assault on the tiny village and that would be the end of Cebolleta. After a town meeting they decided to abandon the settlement so they packed up their *carretas* and retreated to Laguna Pueblo for temporary security. [See Note # 3.]

Governor Chacón was quickly informed of the Cebolletanos heroic defense and their subsequent withdrawal to Laguna. He sympathized with the Cebolletanos plight but he knew it was illegal to abandon frontier outposts once they has been established. He referred the matter to the military commandant in Chihuahua. The commandant also sympathized but the law must be obeyed so he ordered the settlers back to Cebolleta, but this time to be escorted by Colonel **Antonio Narbona** and a troop of 30 well-armed soldiers from Chihuahua. Thus fortified, the Cebolletanos returned to their village.

In 1805 Navajos attacked Cebolleta once again but with the Chihuahua reinforcements they were driven off. On May 12, 1805, a peace treaty was signed in which Navajos relinquished all claims to Cebolleta lands. Captives were released by both sides. But raids and counter-raids become integral parts of the history of Cebolleta for the next half century or so.

Manuel Antonio Chaves, New Mexico's greatest 19th century frontiersman, was a product of Cebolleta on the Navajo frontier. [See Note # 4.] Other frontiersmen like **Chato Aragón,** "the marksman without peer," and the "enormously powerful" **Redondo Gallegos** also became famous for their heroics as they, and several other Cebolletanos, become part of New Mexican folklore and legend. But the frontier always took its toll. Navajos finally claimed the lives of Chato Aragón and Redondo Gallegos.

DISCUSSION NOTES *for* CEBOLLETA and the NAVAJO FRONTIER
Note # 1
See Chapter 2 in *Navajo Wars: Military Campaigns, Slave Raids, and Reprisals* by Frank McNitt.
Note # 2
See page 10 in the short volume *The Fighting Settlers Of Seboyeta* by the venerable Dr. Simmons.
Note # 3
See page 42 in *Navajo Wars* by Frank McNitt who describes the gallant Cebolletanos as "frightened settlers." Let us imagine that there might have been two fighting men in each of the thirty families. The odds would then be around 17 warriors to 1 Hispano. The "frightened settlers" (?) held on despite the odds. Marc Simmons writes that Hispano villages were all frontier settlements at one time or another "but perhaps the triumphs and tragedies of Seboyeta were experienced to

a greater or more intense degree."

Note # 4

See the biography *The Little Lion Of The Southwest: A Life Of Manuel Antonio Chaves* by Marc Simmons.

PINO OVERVIEW in 1812

Just before the end of the Spanish colonial period (1821), don **Pedro Bautista Pino**, New Mexico's delegate to the Spanish *Cortes* (Parliament), wrote his "Brief Exposition on the Province of New Mexico." It was published in Cadiz, Spain, in 1812 and Delegate Pino had this to say about New Mexico's Indians:

Giving gifts to the Indians has been immensely successful diplomacy…

Pueblo Indians *live in multistoried housing much like the people of Cádiz. Pueblo people wear clothes and shoes. The women are endowed with natural grace and beauty, dressing much like the ladies of Cádiz.*

Comanches *are known for their robust and graceful presence, a frank martial air, modest dress, particularly the women, and other commendable qualities. They are the most powerful militarily, accepting no quarter but granting it to those they conquer. They have been friendly to New Mexicans since the Comanche Peace was established by Governor Juan Bautista de Anza.*

Utes *are very interested in material goods and they will steal if necessary…*

Apaches *are a numerous people with several different bands. They are generally a traitorous people, warlike, and cruel. But they fear the brave and honorable Comanches.*

Navajos *are now given to farming and manufacturing since they fought Hispanos in the three-year war when don Fernando Chacón was governor. Their woolen goods are the most valuable in N.M., Sonora, and Chihuahua.*

Essay: ON NEW MEXICAN INDIAN AFFAIRS

Hindsight justifies the assertion that New Mexico's Hispanos were among the most successful of European populations to live as neighbors with Amerindian people. This might seem a contradiction because New Mexicans were also renowned Indian fighters. The difference is that New Mexicans fought when they had to and lived peaceably when they could. As a group they were not products of an Indian hating society. It is a little publicized fact that Indian extermination or exile was never an established public policy in New Mexico. Any number of excuses could have been used to exterminate Indians after the "Acoma War," after the "Jumano War," after the St. Lawrence Day Massacre, after resistance to the Reconquest by Vargas. Even if such an extermination/exile movement had gotten started, which it never did, missionaries would not have permitted it. The role of the Church in the preservation of Native American people has not been publicized by very many English language historiographers. Indeed, it is more common to find fault with missionary efforts than to laud them.

After the brutalities of the 17th century, perhaps the worst of which was the St. Lawrence Day

Massacre of 1680 in which unsuspecting Hispanic women and children were the principal victims, New Mexicans and Pueblo people became close allies against Amerindian raiders who targeted both groups. Indeed, warlike groups might well have exterminated both populations if the Pueblos and Hispanos hadn't united for the common defense. But defense was only one of the principal issues. New Mexican Hispano governmental authorities obeyed orders from their superiors in Mexico City and Madrid, Spain: Indians were accorded an inalienable right to their lands and Christian Hispanics were not permitted to take them. It was a well known fact that Pueblo Indians along the Río Grande River owned the best farmlands in New Mexico. That's why they had settled there. Hispanics weren't permitted to usurp them from Indian owners. Further, there was no subterfuge like withholding irrigation water to drive Indians from their land. Respect for Indian land holdings was an established part of Hispanic society.

As recounted above, New Mexican Hispanos could be sincere allies of settled Pueblo (village) Indians but they could also be stalwart friends to the warrior Comanches if they wanted to live in peace with New Mexicans. The alliance with Comanches, warrior masters of the southern plains, was as sterling an accomplishment as with the Pueblo villagers. It is true that trade was an important factor between the two people but even that would never have transpired as it did without mutual respect between the two groups. They kept their promises to each other. They helped each other out as fellow human beings. Among other things, the two groups were also master horsemen, ranked with the best in history, and each admired that.

Sincere alliances with Indians is part and parcel of Hispanic New Mexican history. If further proof is needed one can point to the contemporary existence of nineteen Native Indian villages in New Mexico, including San Juan where Hispanics first settled in New Mexico. While it is a little known fact, Comanches asked for lands in eastern New Mexico on which to make their permanent settlements. (The request was denied by American authorities.) What would the *Land of Enchantment* be like with Comanche villages in eastern New Mexico?

TEXAS Indian Affairs

Apachería encompassed what could be described as the desert Southwest but it would also have to include the grassy plains of the Texas Panhandle, the mountains of New Mexico and its Río Grande Valley, and then west into the Arizona desert. Apache raiders could also cast a shadow deep into Nuevo León, Coahuila, Chihuahua, and Sonora. [See Note # 1. *Notes begin on page 265.*] Hostile Apaches were a factor from the very founding of San Antonio in 1718. This also stemmed from the fact that Spaniards were friendly with the Tejas and other tribes of eastern Texas, who were bitter enemies of the Apaches. In 1720 the **Marques de San Miguel de Aguayo** tried to make peace with the Apaches but his overtures at conciliation were ignored. On August 17, 1723, Apaches raided the Presidio San Antonio de Bexar and made off with eighty horses. Captain **Nicolás Flores y Valdez** gave chase for some 130 leagues, fought a six-hour battle, killed some 34 Apaches, took some 20 women and children captive, and recovered 120 horses and mules.

MISSIONARIES as DEFENDERS

As was typical in all Spanish provinces, missionaries demanded the Indians be treated with kindness in order to convert and civilize them while military personnel demanded retributive punishment for killings or depredations. Father **Joseph González**, a padre at San Antonio de Valero, quarreled with Captain Flores y Valdez to the point that the captain was temporarily removed from command. Things quieted down from 1726-1730.

A highly critical factor beginning in the 1720s was the appearance of **Comanches** in Texas. Their aim was to drive the Apaches south out of their homeland and claim it for themselves, which they did. (The Spaniards then came to refer to the area as *Comanchería*.)

WAR and PEACE

On September 18, 1731, the Apaches made off with some 60 horses from the presidio's herd. A campaign was launched against them in October of 1732. Governor **Antonio Bustillo y Ceballos** led a command of some 217 men, sixty of whom were mission Indians, and fought a successful battle on the San Sabá River. A truce was signed in 1733 but more raids occurred during the years 1734-1738. Presidio Captain **José de Urrutia** led an expedition against the Apaches in 1739 and took many captives which could be sold into slavery but Father **Benito Fernández de Santa Ana** vehemently fought the effort. [See Note # 2.] The padres could not accept killing or enslavement as inducements to peace. They felt only patience and understanding could work.

Some 350 Apaches, which included women and children, attacked San Antonio on June 30, 1745. It was repelled with the help of 100 Indians from Mission Valero. The valiant Franciscans now felt that missionary efforts had to be extended beyond San Antonio to address hostility at its source. **Toribio de Urrutia** led a campaign (1745) against the hostile Apaches but Father Benito described it as merely another slave-hunting effort. The Sons of St. Francis wanted to found a mission in the Apache homeland itself.

The Apaches were being pressured relentlessly by the Comanches so the former decided to become friends with the Spaniards by way of obtaining help. A peace treaty was signed in San Antonio in 1749. The area around the San Sabá River was explored in 1753 and it was decided the site would make an excellent location for a mission. Apaches said they would come to live there if a mission was established. In 1756 a deposit of red iron ore was discovered in the area so now there was the lure of possible wealth. In Mexico City one **Pedro Romero de Terreros** volunteered to finance the San Sabá mission if his cousin Father **Alonso Giraldo de Terreros** was put in charge. It was agreed that a presidio and a mission would be founded and in April of 1757 the expedition set out with missionaries, soldiers and their families, mission Indians, some 1400 cattle and 700 sheep. Despite previous promises, Mission *Santa Cruz de San Sabá* didn't draw a single Apache neophyte. [See Note # 3.] On March 16, 1758, hundreds of hostile Comanches, Bidais, Tonkawas, and even Tejas surrounded the mission. The Indians were painted red and black for war and heavily armed with swords, lances, muskets. Fathers Terreros, Molina, and Santisteban had refused to leave and were in the mission. They tried to talk to the Indians but Terreros was shot and Santisteban decapitated at the altar. Victims were scalped, some decapitated, eyes were gouged out. Even oxen were killed in the rampage. The Indians took whatever they wished then set fire to the mission. Miraculously, Father Molina and some others went unnoticed and lived to get to the presidio.

Colonel **Diego Ortiz Parrilla** led a punitive expedition against the hostiles and a battle was fought on October 2, 1759. Several Indians were killed and some 149 captives were taken. A band of some 60 or 70 hostiles counterattacked on October 7, but they were repulsed and pursued through the woods until they came into view (on the south bank of the Red River) of a fort flying the flag of *France*. Parrilla's men opened fire on the fort but it was returned with vigor. Not being equipped for laying siege to a fort, Parrilla ordered a retreat. [See Note # 4.]

LOUISIANA to SPAIN

The 1763 Treaty of Paris which ended the French and Indian War transferred the Louisiana Territory from France to Spain. Charles III (1759-1788), one of Spain's most able monarchs, recognized that Frenchmen had forged strong bonds with most Indian groups so he directed administrators to employ Frenchmen as Indian agents wherever possible. Among the most famous was **Athanase de Mezieres** who served as diplomat to the northern tribes starting in 1770. [See Note # 5.] He negotiated successful treaties with a number of tribes.

APACHES and COMANCHES

The "New Regulations for Presidios" of 1772 decreed that only San Antonio and La Bahía be maintained. People living in east Texas were instructed to move to San Antonio and most of them complied. (Some were dissatisfied and returned east by 1774 and others founded the town of Nacogdoches in 1779.) Lipan Apaches continued to be the major threat to Texas settlements. In 1781 the Lipans settled their differences with the Mescaleros and other Apache groups. Reinforced, raiders bloodied the frontier with their depredations. For example, during June of 1784, some 46 people were killed by Apaches and around 600 horses and mules were stolen. Despite this menace to Hispanic society, Viceroy **Bernardo de Gálvez** would not order a war of extermination against Apache groups. He recognized Apaches as the principal enemies *"because of their treachery, warlike customs, stealing as a way of life, and their knowledge of our strength."* Attacks were met with counterattacks and settlers were required to help in all punitive campaigns.

While hostile Apaches were the main problem, Comanches were not far behind. Comanche attacks between 1783-1785 were deadly. Despite the bloodshed, official Comanche policy was "Peace by Persuasion" so Governor **Domingo Cabello y Robles** invited Comanche chieftains to Béxar in an effort to forge a peace. Three chieftains accepted the offer and signed a treaty stipulating that all hostilities would cease at once, which included all nations allied with the Spanish; Spanish captives would be ransomed exclusively by Spaniards; foreigners wouldn't be welcomed into Comanche villages; present friends and enemies would remain so; both parties would make war on the Apaches; annual presents would be made to all chiefs and leading tribal members. The "Texas Comanche Peace" lasted unbroken for some thirty years.

In 1804 an American named **John Sibley** was appointed by the USA to perform functions of an Indian Agent for the Comanches and Norteño tribes. Sibley sent **John House**, who had been with

Philip Nolan in his fourth expedition, with presents for the tribes, urging them to send representatives for a Grand Council (1805) in Natchitoches (now American territory due to the Louisiana Purchase of 1803). Sibley told those who assembled that the people of the USA were "native…white Indians" so they should ally themselves with the USA for their own benefit. Spaniards later advised the tribes not to listen to such blandishments, that the people of the USA would come in and take all their lands.

DISCUSSION Notes *for* TEXAS Indian Affairs

Note # 1
See *The Apache Frontier: Jacobo Ugarte and Spanish-Indian Relations in Northern New Spain, 1769-1791* by Max L. Moorhead.

Note # 2
See *Spanish Texas, 1519-1821* by Donald E. Chipman.

Note # 3
Chipman quotes (Chapter 8, page 160) one Robert S. Weddle saying that the history of "*San Sabá is one of Apache perfidy, Spanish gullibility, and the disastrous consequences of both.*" The Spanish missionaries were *gullible* because they wanted to missionize Apaches?

Note # 4
The expedition is generally depicted as a failure because of the retreat. T.R. Fehrenbach's *Lone Star* account of this episode is in Chapter 4 and titled "The Faith and the Failure: the Missions." *Failure* seems to be the bedrock litany for the Spanish era of Texas history as interpreted by some writers.

Note # 5
See *Athanase De Mezieres And The Louisiana-Texas Frontier, 1768-1780* by H.E. Bolton.

California Indian Affairs

UPRISING AT SAN DIEGO

When Hispanic people arrived to settle in California in 1769 there were large numbers of Indians in the area. They appeared friendly, even accompanying the newcomers as they went from place to place. But the Indians remained friendly only so long as there were gifts to dispense. When these ran out the Indians took to taking whatever they wanted and at least one sharp encounter took place because of that behavior.

Mission *San Diego de Alcalá* was moved some six miles from the presidio in order that neophytes might not suffer from the "bad example" set by soldiers, according to the missionaries. This proved to be a dangerous move because Indian leaders, especially the shamans, resented losing their authority to the hard-working missionaries.

At around one o'clock in the morning of November 5, 1775, the **Kumeyaay** Indians, numbering around 600, neophytes and gentiles in the mob, surrounded Mission San Diego and attacked from all sides.

One of the first to react to the commotion was Father **Luis Jayme**, thirty-five years old, who walked out of his quarters to try to restore order by talking to his charges, whom he loved sincerely. He raised his arms and said, "Love God, my children!" as was his custom. Instead of listening to him they fell upon Father Luis and dragged him away to a nearby arroyo. They stripped him naked then stabbed him countless times, his entire body riddled by sharp knives. Finally the Indians took turns clubbing him, so many times that his face was rendered unrecognizable. [See Note # 1. *Notes begin on page 269.*] Exalted by their victory over the non-combatant priest, they resumed their attack on Mission San Diego.

The church was looted then set afire. All buildings were then torched. The few soldiers on duty at the mission fired their weapons but it wasn't enough to stem the tide of rebellion. Father **Vicente Fuster**, who slept in a back building used as a storehouse, woke up and went outside to see flames everywhere, the air thick with arrows. Father Fuster made a dash across the grounds to where the four soldiers assigned to the mission were fighting back. He asked why this was happening but all were too busy to answer. They were forced to retreat into a room that was being built. A soldier shouted that they would need more powder, all the powder stored in the mission. Father Vicente remembered where it was and dashed next door, fetching the bag of powder from the room that was already on fire. Then he remembered that Father Luis Jayme's quarters were in the midst of the flames so he ran out once more in search of his fellow priest. He made it through the flaming door but Father Luis wasn't in the room so he dashed back to safety with the soldiers. The blacksmith Felipe Romero now ran up to the group. The other blacksmith, José Arroyo, had been killed by the rampaging Indians. Felipe had escaped the same cruel fate only because he was able to get his gun and shoot one of the Indians, after which the others quickly retreated. The flames were now getting very close to the small party of survivors so Father Vicente said, "Let's go to the cookhouse and make a barricade." They gathered their gear and raced to the three-sided cookhouse, a couple of soldiers being injured in the process. A barricade was quickly put together at the entrance but the Indians spied the survivors and focused their attack on the gallant little band. A veritable storm of arrows, large rocks, firebrands, even adobes, were hurled at the Christians. Father Vicente prayed "to God and Mary Most Holy" for their deliverance, vowing to fast nine Saturdays and honoring the Holy Mother with nine masses. Firebrands nearly got to the bag of gunpowder and a large rock hit Father Vicente on the shoulder, quite painful but not disabling.

All hoped daylight would come quickly in this eternity of danger. But then it appeared the Indians were also waiting for the dawn to make a final attack and wipe the mission and its inhabitants off the face of the earth. At dawn Father Vicente heard familiar voices, trusted men who had been at the mission, saying now was the time to destroy the Christians once and for all. They charged in but the soldiers fired their weapons at them, causing them to scatter. Now that the sun was up Christian Indians from nearby rancherías came in to help, chasing the rebels away from the mission. Father Vicente then asked if anyone had seen Father Luis. They hadn't so he told the neophytes to search for him, to go inform the authorities at the presidio, catch the horses and other scattered livestock, etc.

Father Vicente then received word that Father Luis had been found, dead. Full of grief and sorrow at the news, he took a group to bring in the cadaver. What he saw, a horribly mutilated body which indicated a death so cruel that it could be identified only by skin color and the tonsure on its head, caused Father Vicente to faint. He would have fallen on the mutilated corpse of his "Father Comrade" had not some Indian women caught him. They laid him on the ground, brought him water and bathed his temples until he regained consciousness. The mission being nothing but smoking ruins, all survivors were forced to seek asylum at the presidio

Father Serra at Carmel was deeply saddened at the loss of his fellow priest, a blacksmith, and a carpenter at San Diego. His only solace was the Christian belief that *The blood of the martyrs is the seed of the Church*. Governor **Rivera y Moncada** vowed he would bring the murderers to justice but Father Serra pleaded mercy for all attackers. As luck would have it, Captain Juan Bautista de Anza was in San Gabriel Mission on his way with settlers for San Francisco. So the Governor, Anza, and thirty-five soldiers went to investigate the situation in San Diego. Some of the perpetrators were brought in and given fifty lashes. One Indian died and another committed suicide. One Indian, named Carlos, came in and sought sanctuary in the church. The Governor demanded the padres give him up but Father Fuster refused so Rivera y Moncada took him by force, saying the building Carlos was in was not really a church. Fuster excommunicated the Governor and Serra upheld the excommunication so Carlos was returned to the padres. In order to make peace, Carlos was later released to the authorities but there is no record of any retribution.

YUMA MASSACRE

Two small colonies were planted on the Colorado River on the California side in the fall of 1780: Purísima Concepción and San Pedro y San Pablo de Bicuñer. Led by their renowned Chief (Olleyquotequiebe) **Salvador Palma**, the Yumas had been asking for missionaries to proselytize in their settlements at the junction of the Gila and Colorado rivers since Anza passed that way a few years before while blazing an overland route from Sonora to California. It is possible that to the Yumas the new Christian religion meant new and valuable gifts like metal tools, new foods, tobacco, colored beads, etc. They grew tired of asking that missionaries be sent to them and the irritation smoldered until it was ready to erupt in blood. When the settlements finally materialized trouble over land ownership began almost at once and now an additional irritant was that Spanish cattle roamed into areas where native crops grew, ruining items like mesquite plants.

In June of 1781 some forty families of settlers from Sonora used the Yuma crossing on their way to settle in California. Captain **Fernando Rivera y Moncada** was in charge of the eleven or so soldiers provided as an escort. The pioneers continued into California while Rivera y Moncada and his men encamped to allow their animals to rest and strengthen on good pasture land.

On July 17, 1781, **Father Garcés** was saying mass at Purísima Concepción when the Indians attacked in overwhelming numbers. Commandant Islas and all males were immediately killed. Fathers Garcés and **Barreneche** were spared because Palma had ordered the missionaries were to be brought to him.

Bicuñer was attacked by overwhelming forces at the same time as Purísima Concepción and totally destroyed. The two missionaries and all the men were immediately put to death at Bicuñer. Padre **Moreno** was decapitated. While the women and children were taken captive for enslavement at both places, all males were immediately shot or clubbed to death. [See Note # 2.]

Rivera y Moncada and his men were unaware of what was happening until the following day when the Yumas attacked them. The Christians were surprised but under Rivera y Moncada's leadership they mounted their horses and fought back with volleys from their guns. But the Indians threw themselves upon horses and riders, forcing the soldiers to the ground. They went into a sort of defensive trench but they knew there would be no rescue and they expected no mercy at the hands of the fierce Yumas, who preferred to kill rather than capture and who delighted in decapitating their dead enemies. They fought the mobs of Indians hand-to-hand until the Christians were overwhelmed by sheer numbers and wiped out to the last man.

Fathers Garcés and Barreneche made it through the night but on the 18th it is said a "Christian Indian deserter" from Altar demanded: *These are the worst! If these remain alive all is lost.* Garces and Barreneche were murdered on the spot. [See Note # 3.]

While the enslaved captives were later ransomed, the uprising had resulted in the deaths of some fifty-five Hispanics which included four Christian missionaries. Rivera y Moncada was on his way to retirement when he met his end at the hands of the Yumas. The colonists going through only a month or so before had narrowly missed the bloodbath. Punitive expeditions were mounted in 1781 and 1782 but they did little except ransom the captives. Palma and his Yumas were never chastised. No missions or villages were ever re-established on the Colorado River and California became more and more isolated from Mexico, not to mention Spain. Further, Commandant General Teodoro de Croix blamed Juan Bautista de Anza for the uprising, saying Anza had made promises that couldn't be kept, thus endeavoring to absolve himself from the responsibility which was primarily his, besmirching the Great Captain's reputation in the process.

CHUMASH REBELLION

The Chumash "Revolt" of 1824 had been planned for many months before it finally took place. It appears February 22, 1824, was set for a general attack on the missions of Santa Inés, La Purísima, and Santa Barbara while mass was being celebrated. According to tradition, an Indian was whipped on the 21st and because of that the revolt began spontaneously on Saturday instead of waiting for Sunday. Most of Mission Santa Inés was burned down though the church itself was spared. Military reinforcements arrived so the rebels went to La Purísima where, after a serious fight the garrison was forced to surrender. The priest and all soldiers and their families were permitted to leave.

At Santa Barbara the Indian leader **Andrés Sagimomatsee** convinced Father **Antonio Ripoll** that the Chumash were afraid the military garrison (who numbered all of three soldiers) would retaliate against them for the uprising at the other two missions. He asked Father Antonio to go to the presidio and get Commander **García y Noriega** to withdraw the garrison, which was done successfully. When Father Antonio returned to the mission the Chumash under Sagimomatsee were in control, as had been planned all along. The priest was able to negotiate a peaceful withdrawal of the three soldiers. When the presidio commander heard about the situation he attacked but was unable to dislodge the Chumash so his forces retired from the field. The Chumash saw their opportunity and fled some sixty miles into the hills. A Christian expedition was sent against them but it was unsuccessful in bringing the rebels

back to the missions. A larger expedition was sent later and with the promise of amnesty for all participants, the revolt ended. Three people who happened to be traveling from Los Ángeles were killed by the
Indians and seven Indians were later executed because of the unwarranted killings. [See Note # 4.]

DISCUSSION NOTES *for* CALIFORNIA Indian Affairs

Note # 1
See "1775: Rebellion at San Diego" in *Lands Of Promise And Despair* edited by R.M. Beebe and
R.M. Senkewicz.
Note # 2
See Chapter 26 in *A History Of California: The Spanish Period* by Charles E. Chapman.
Note # 3
See Chapter 4 in *Time Of The Bells* by Richard F. Pourade.
Note # 4
See "1824: The Chumash Revolt" in *Lands Of Promise And Despair*.

ARIZONA Indian Affairs

The first commander at the Tucson presidio, founded in 1776, was **Pedro Allande y Saabedra**
(Saavedra). By 1778 he had all of 77 soldiers in the fort. Their job was to protect settlers and guard the
missions, along with building the presidio itself. He led campaigns into hostile Apache territory in 1778.
On November 6, 1779, some 350 Apaches attacked Tucson but were again defeated. On May 1, 1782,
another 300 or so Apaches attacked when there were only 24 soldiers in the presidio but once more the
hostiles were repulsed. [See Note # 1. *Notes begin on page 270.*]

While the Pimas and Pápagos became Spanish allies, hostile Apaches didn't seem to be impressed
with peace. Commander Allande y Saabedra went on the offensive during the years 1783, 1784, 1785,
pushing as far north as the Gila River and Huachuca Mountains. His *soldados de cuera*, Leatherjackets,
carried muskets, pistols, lances, and short swords. A soldier also carried a shield (*adarga*) which could
deflect arrows and sometimes bullets, along with the thick leather jacket used for the same purpose.
Leather leggings completed the soldier's outfit.

Captain **Manuel de Echeagaray** campaigned with soldiers from Sonora (Santa Cruz and Altar) and
Tucson to the headwaters of the Gila River in 1788. In the same year acting Commander at Tucson
Pablo Romero went against hostiles for a whole month during which some forty-four were killed. These
expeditions into hostile territory were evidently successful because various Apache bands came in asking for peace. They were located in villages called *establecimientos de paz* (peace settlements) where they
were given weekly rations of corn, meat, tobacco, etc. The Apaches were permitted to keep their weapons as well as their tribal customs. Missionaries felt the latter was an impediment to Christianization,
along with soldier examples in card playing, dancing, swearing, gambling, etc.

Thirty-nine year old **José de Zúñiga** became Tucson commander in 1794 and took the field against
hostiles many times, going as far as the Zuñi pueblos in 1795.

By 1800 there was relative peace in Arizona and people could go about their business in ranching, mining, or farming. As of 1821 Captain **José Romero** was the commander at Tucson when it became Mexican territory. Captain Romero is especially remembered for reopening the Anza trail to California. That last commanders at Tucson were **José Antonio Comadurán** (1830-53) and **Hilarion García** (1853-56).

The period of peace ended in 1831 when Apaches renewed hostilities. Tucson and Tubac were attacked several times by as many as a thousand warriors but presidio walls provided refuge. Warfare once more ruled the frontier. At their wits end, authorities in Sonora supposedly instituted a scalp-bounty system, paying handsomely for hostile Apache scalps. [See Note # 2.] The Apaches were never conquered during the Spanish period of Arizona Southwest history.

DISCUSSION NOTES *for* ARIZONA Indian Affairs
Note # 1
See "Lancers for the King" in *Arizona: A Short History* by Odie B. Faulk.
Note # 2
A male Apache scalp supposedly was bought for 100 pesos, 50 for a female, 25 for a child. The drain on an already depleted treasury would have been phenomenal. Americans James Johnson and James Kirker were supposedly highly successful in murdering Apaches for their scalps. Kirker "reportedly" collected $100,000 in bounty money in 1839. This needs to be investigated. Further, unless Arizona/Sonora is a unique exemption, extermination of Indians was never official policy for Hispanics living in the Southwest.

Essay: ON THE SPANISH ERA

Hispanic people with intimate attachments to the culture of Spain were living in what is now called the "Southwest" as of 1598. Settlements in New Mexico were followed by those in Texas, California, and Arizona. The brave colonizers who came to live in these areas were the first European pioneers in these frontiers. Pioneering efforts were costly, especially in loss of human life, but Hispanics settled permanently in the Southwest.

Cabeza de Vaca and his three companions (Alfonso de Castillo, Andrés Dorantes, and Esteban from Morocco) traveled through much of Texas and possibly southern sections of New Mexico/Arizona during the years 1528-1536. In this dangerous yet marvelous odyssey, these four men were the first to cross the USA from east Texas to the Río Grande River then on to Culiacán, Mexico on the coast of the Pacific Ocean. Starting at Tampa Bay, Florida, these survivors shed light on how big the North American continent might be. There would be centuries of explorations.

The **Francisco Vásquez de Coronado** exploratory expedition was the greatest in the history of the Southwest, going from California to Texas then as far as Kansas. Vásquez de Coronado's captains earned their honored places in Southwest history. Perhaps the most stalwart was **Melchor Díaz** (described by Stewart Udall as "heroic," America's "first frontiersman," "our first mountain man"), a fearless, energetic "commoner." After the battle of Zuñi (Hawikuh), the Captain General told Díaz to go west into unexplored desert territory then south to locate the supply ships commanded by **Hernando de Alarcón**. It is believed Díaz explored up the mighty Colorado river for some fifty leagues. He became the first European to step onto California soil. **Pedro de Tovar** was the first to visit the Hopi (Tusayan) villages. In his retinue was "the fighting friar," fray **Juan de Padilla**. **García López de Cárdenas** and his men were the first to view the Grand Canyon (South Rim). **Tristán de Arellano** and his men were the first Europeans to see *El Morro* (Inscription Rock). **Hernando de Alvarado** and his men were the first Europeans to visit the Pueblo Indians of the Río Grande Valley and the first to see the immense herds of wild bison to the east of those settlements. Alvarado compared them to *"…fish in the sea."* Fray **Juan de Padilla** was in Alvarado's contingent and he was to be the first Southwest missionary to be martyred.

Exploration and trailblazing continued over the centuries. **Juan de Oñate** extended the Camino Real (*de Tierra Adentro*) from Mexico City to *San Juan de los Caballeros* (Knights of St. John) in northern New Mexico as of 1598 (the first road established by Europeans in what is now the USA and the longest for centuries). In 1601 Oñate explored the (Quivira) plains east of New Mexico and in 1604-05 he went west as far as the estuary of the Colorado River in the Gulf of California.

In 1774 Fernando Rivera y Moncada led a small party of colonists from Baja to Alta California. In the years 1774-76 Juan Bautista de Anza blazed an overland trail from Tubac, Arizona, to California then returned to lead colonists over it, his pioneers settling in San Francisco. Such trailblazing activities continued through the years and not only by civil authorities. In 1776 Father Francisco Atanasio **Domínguez** and Father Silvestre Vélez de **Escalante** took off from Santa Fe and explored almost two thousand miles of lands in Colorado, Utah, northern Arizona, and western New Mexico. In 1786-87 **Pedro Vial** blazed a trail from San Antonio to the Taovaya villages and on to Santa Fe. In 1787-88 **Jose Mares** went from Santa Fe to the Taovaya villages then on to San Antonio. In 1788-89 Pedro Vial opened another road from Santa Fe to Natchitoches to San Antonio then back to Santa Fe. In 1792-93 Vial blazed the Santa Fe Trail in a 2,279 mile roundtrip from Santa Fe to St. Louis, Missouri.

Major as well as minor events were written down by observers of the day so the legacy of an historical record is unsurpassed in any other section of the present USA, a record which included information on aboriginal groups as well as transplanted European pioneers who became native Southwesterners. It could be said that **Alvar Núñez Cabeza de Vaca** started it off with his *Los Naufragios* (Shipwrecks), first published in 1542. Written Southwest history definitely began with the Vásquez de Coronado Expedition of 1540-42. As official chronicler, **Pedro de Castañeda,** would have to be acknowledged as the "Father of Southwest History." **Gaspar de Villagrá** is the "Father of New Mexico History" for his *Historia De La Nueva Mexico*. As if that achievement wasn't enough, the *Historia* is written as an epic poem, making this founding chronicle of New Mexico the only such *epic* document in the history of the world. Padre **Eusebio Kino** is considered the historian of Pima land in Arizona. Padre **Agustin Morfi** is the "Father of Texas History" because of his *History Of Texas, 1673-1779*. (An inestimable debt is owed to Texas scholar **Carlos Castañeda** for his English translation of Morfi's bedrock Texas history.) Finally, the "Father of California History" is Padre **Francisco Palóu**, who chronicled the activities of missionaries, especially those of Father Serra, and the founding of missions, where European California got its start.

While the highly developed writers mentioned above created works that are used to this day (in translation, which has its pitfalls), innumerable other people wrote journals or kept diaries while exploring or campaigning, as required by Spanish authorities. Military men like **Roque de Madrid** in New Mexico wrote a journal of his march to Navajo country, **Juan Bautista de Anza** did the same for his trailblazing journey to California and his subsequent colonization to San Francisco, as well as campaigns like those to Cuerno Verde's Comanchería. Needless to say, missionaries like Benavides, Olivares, Salvatierra, Margil, Crespi, Font, etc., wrote down much of what was happening during their times and sent those documents to their superiors. History of the Spanish Southwest rests on a wealth of documentation written in the Spanish language for those who can utilize it.

For any number of reasons, Spanish missions have received much attention in Southwest history. While the California missions have been popularized more than others, missions existed throughout Spanish lands. In the Spanish mind, Christianity was the most priceless gift to New World people. Spain took seriously its responsibility to bring Christianity, and through it, European civilization, to aboriginal populations. Neither was a simple task for some Indians didn't even use clothes to keep warm nor did they have knowledge of basic technology like the wheel. No other countries took on such an awesome responsibility because they generally believed the "naked savages" were beyond redemption. Missionaries from Spain and the rest of Europe performed herculean feats in laboring with aboriginal populations who were mostly in the Stone Age of development compared to European standards. A significant number of missionaries were martyred for their efforts, the largest single tragedy occurring during the St. Lawrence Day Massacre of 1680 in New Mexico when twenty-one (21) missionaries were brutally slain in one single uprising. After the initial decades of the Spanish conquest, laws were in place to protect Native American groups and it is a matter of record that Indians in the Southwest were neither exterminated nor exiled from their native lands.

Agriculture took a giant leap forward with the arrival of Hispanic people in the "Southwest." Not only did they bring in basics like beef, pork, mutton, wheat, rice, etc., in time they introduced orchards of citrus fruits in California, *chile* (from Mexico) into New Mexico, and potatoes from South America. The basic aboriginal diet of corn, squash, and beans was thus phenomenally augmented.

Ranching became fully developed during the Hispanic era of Southwest history. Unknown east of the Mississippi or outside Spanish territories, by 1821 ranching was a basic Hispanic industry with a tried and tested body of practice and tradition like roundups and brandings. Begun by Juan de Oñate in New Mexico in 1598, herds of horses, cattle, and flocks of sheep came to be part of the Southwest Hispanic landscape. Products of a highly developed "horse culture," Hispanos, Tejanos, Californios, and Tucsonenses were among the best horsemen in the world who could be rivaled perhaps only by Arabs in the Old World and possibly Comanches in the New.

While there were no overwhelming gold or silver strikes in the Southwest during the Spanish period, Hispanics were as much a mining people as they were ranchers. The big "gold rush" in Mexico occurred in 1549 (yes, *three centuries* before the one in California) and a highly developed law of mines with its comprehensive rules and regulations were created to handle the industry. Hispanic miners from New Spain were to make their mark in the Southwest at a later time because of mining knowledge that had been built up over three centuries.

The frontier environment of the Hispanic Southwest promoted a society that tended to emphasize individual worth rather than European concepts of class which gave most societal fruits to the "high born" aristocracy. Frontier dangers weren't concerned with one's status at birth so race relations were more fluid than rigid.

Spanish legal concepts became basic to the Southwest. Indian groups were accorded legal rights to land and water. In English and American law, *when a man and woman became one in marriage, the man was the one*. Unlike their European and American sisters, Hispanic women had basic rights, including the power to own land without a husband automatically becoming the owner of it upon marriage. Furthermore, community property concepts emanated from the Hispanic Southwest, thereby acknowledging that a wife was an equal partner in all property accumulated during a marriage.

Thoroughly familiar with arid environments, Spanish law provided that no individual could own a water source. The legal code understood that if a water source was owned privately then all surrounding land was under the control of that person, which would destabilize society.

There were numerous Hispanic legacies in the fields of religion, architecture, art, music, theater, education, etc. The greatest contribution of Christianity in the Southwest was the preservation of Indian groups. Missionaries would not allow extermination of aboriginal populations, even after brutal uprisings. Christianity also paved the way for transmitting European culture, and survival, to Indians. For example, the Pueblo people of New Mexico became adept at functioning in the legal system. Mission architecture became famous throughout the southwest, the most famous being in California but those in Texas are also lasting contributions. In the Fine Arts, the earliest painting was done in New Mexico on the "Villasur Expedition" (Segesser Hide Painting) in the 1720s and the Texas "Destruction of Mission Santa Cruz de San Sabá" done after 1758. Both are of paramount historical as well as cultural value. "Santero Art" became a powerful movement in New Mexico at least by 1750. Father Serra collected a number of paintings (three of them done by the well known José de Paéz) in Mexico City and took them with him to the California missions. Religious theater presentations like *Las Posadas* and *Los Pastores* were well known throughout the Southwest, along with folk drama like *Los Comanches*. Music was always extremely popular and the art of the troubador was highly developed, engendering many songs and corridos which described love, courage, heroism, tragedy, the land, a favorite horse, etc.

The Spanish language became the *lingua franca* for the Southwest and numbers of Native Americans became proficient in it. Place names abounded with the arrival of Hispanic people, most of them remaining to the present day. The legacy of the Hispanic Southwest has been of inestimable value to countless people. (Negative effects and/or charges of the Hispanic colonization of the Southwest have been touched upon in the Notes sections and can be developed for discussion.)

CHAPTER 7

The Mexican War Of 1846-48

The Mexican War is as controversial as any in American history despite the fact that most historians assert that *Mexico started the war*. This view generally maintains that this "conflict" was the "inevitable" result of clashing cultures, American citizens claiming the Mexican government owed them money due to damages from civil wars, to America wanting California, the Texas boundary question, and "to the unwillingness of Mexican politicians to seek a peaceful solution…" while President Polk "sought every honorable avenue of settlement" until "Mexican troops attacked American soldiers…." [See Note # 1. *Notes begin on page 282.*]

SYNOPSIS

The Mexican War of 1846-48 had its beginnings decades before the shooting war started in April of 1846. In 1812 **Luis de Onís** wrote from Washington D.C. that the USA intended to take "…Texas, New Mexico, Chihuahua, Sonora, and the Californias…" [See Note # 2.] In 1819 when Spain and the USA fixed (Adams-Onís Treaty) the southwestern boundary at the Sabine River, **John Quincy Adams** informed the President Monroe cabinet that "the continent of North America is our proper dominion." In 1821 the Mexican committee on Foreign Affairs predicted that the USA would overrun Mexico like the German tribes descending on the Roman Empire. With Independence from Spain achieved in 1821, Mexico then became embroiled in two decades of revolution and counter-revolution. Without governmental stability reform could not take place. This played into the hands of foreign countries with designs on Mexico. The Monroe Doctrine of 1823, little more than a paper tiger at that time, warned foreign nations to stay out of the Western Hemisphere. In 1825 **Joel Poinsett** arrived as the American Minister to Mexico. His intrigues and general meddling in Mexican politics made him unpopular President Jackson recalled him in 1829, replacing him with the unsavory Anthony Butler until he too was recalled five years later. In 1828 General **Manuel Mier y Terán** wrote that the American strategy would be that of making preposterous demands, sending in adventurers to bolster ridiculous claims, discrediting local authorities, then "diplomatic maneuvering" to give everything credence. In 1829 President **Andrew Jackson** instructed Minister Poinsett to try to buy Texas, or portions thereof, for five million dollars. The offer was refused. In 1835 Jackson authorized Anthony Butler to try to buy the San Francisco Bay area along with Texas but it too was refused. By 1836 things had gotten to the point that Jackson informed Congress the situation "...would justify in the eyes of all nations immediate war."

In 1835 Mexican centralists led by **Antonio López de Santa Anna** drew up a new constitution which abolished almost all local autonomy. Federalists revolted in Zacatecas but the uprising was brutally squelched. In January of 1836 a special convention of Texians declared Texas to be independent of Mexico. Santa Anna would now have to teach the Texians a lesson. He easily captured the Alamo and Goliad but he executed all prisoners afterward. Then he advanced eastward after the ragged Texian forces. Believing the real war over, Santa Anna halted at San Jacinto where **Sam Houston** and his forces caught him by surprise on April 21, 1836, and destroyed his army. On the threat of being lynched if he didn't, Santa Anna signed a treaty that recognized Texian independence and the western boundary of Texas was now placed at the Río Grande River (instead of the Nueces River where it had always been). Further, the Texians argued that their western boundary "...included San Francisco Bay, the Pacific coast to the south, Lower California, and Sonora." [See Note # 3.]

The American press and most people supported the independence of Texas as a blow for *Freedom!* against *Mexican tyranny!* In this mix was the new availability of much Texas land, fertile and cheap. The faction-ridden Mexican government was unable to send in an army to end the "ramshackle" Republic of Texas. The population was about 30,000 in 1836 and nearly doubled by 1840 but the Republic was on the edge of bankruptcy, its paper money worth around 16.6 cents on the dollar. Its shaky foundation rested on land grants and promissory notes.

President **Martin Van Buren** continued to press the claims issue during his presidency, to no avail in Mexico City. Texian requests to be annexed to the USA were denied. **John Quincy Adams**, now a member of the House, accused Jackson and Van Buren of stirring up the claims question as a pretext for the annexation of Texas as slave territory.

In 1838 France declared a blockade of the Mexican Gulf coast until outstanding French claims were paid by the Mexican government. In November a French squadron bombarded and "conquered" the dilapidated island fortress of San Juan de Ulua. Mexico declared war on France but British diplomacy brought both sides to the conference table and a peace treaty was signed. The British now had the impression that while Mexico hadn't paid the money it owed, they were perceived in the role of *martyrs* while creditors were *assailants*.

New president of the Texas Republic **Mirabeau B. Lamar** (1839-41) endeavored to get Mexico to acknowledge Texian independence. He sent negotiators to Mexico City but in the spring of 1841 he also sent a military-commercial expedition to Santa Fe in hopes New Mexico might be interested in joining the Republic, thus channeling the rich Santa Fe trade into Texas. The "Texian Invincibles" got lost on the way, were attacked by hostile Indians, and wound up surrendering to Governor **Manuel Armijo**. All were taken to Mexico City and later **George W. Kendall** would describe the cruelty of the march in his *Narrative of the Texas-Santa Fe Expedition*, inflaming American public opinion against Mexico and reviving interest in Texas.

In 1842 Minister to Mexico Waddy Thompson suggested to President Tyler that Mexico might be willing to exchange Texas and California for the cancellation of all debts owed the USA. Continuing with his euphoric attitude, Thompson felt it was also possible the acquisition of (free) California might permit the annexation of (slave) Texas. Thompson was being naïve because Mexico was still resentful over American aid/interference in Texas. Then there occurred an incident which proved beyond a doubt what American intentions were. Commodore **Thomas ap Catesby Jones**, believing that the war with Mexico had started, entered Monterey Bay with two warships on October 19, 1842, and demanded the (astonished) garrison surrender immediately, which it did. Commodore Jones raised Old Glory at the fort and gave a stirring oration: *Inhabitants Of California! You have only to remain at your homes in pursuit of peaceful vocations to insure security of life, liberty, and property from the consequences of an unjust war, into which Mexico has plunged you. Those Stars and Stripes, infallible emblems of civil liberty now float triumphantly before you, and henceforth and forever will give you protection and security, to you and your children, and to unborn countless thousands....*" The next day Jones was informed by "reliable sources" like Thomas Larkin that there was no war. No war?! Yes, no war. Jones apologized to the Monterey authorities and the American flag was taken down in a solemn ceremony. To assuage the embarrassment the Americans held banquets and dances for the general public. The warships then "sheepishly" sailed away. [See Note # 4.]

John Charles Fremont, who was married to the daughter of "expansionist" Missouri Senator **Thomas Hart Benton**, led an exploratory expedition into the area west of South Pass in Wyoming in 1842. The following year Senator Benton helped Fremont with a second expedition, which set out from St. Louis and covered areas in what is now Utah, Nevada, and Oregon. Fremont's group was caught east of the Sierras and Lake Tahoe as winter set in but Fremont decided to cross the snow-covered mountains into California anyway. The men, unprepared for such a senseless venture, nearly perished from cold and hunger in the freezing mountains. They staggered into Sutter's fort on March 8, 1844, where they recovered from their brush with death in Sierra snows. They "explored" the Sacramento and San Joaquín valleys and into the Bay area. [See Note # 5.] The expedition was back in St. Louis by August of 1844 and Fremont's report on California was widely circulated in the USA, whetting American interest in the province.

In 1843 **John Quincy Adams** wrote in his diary that the movement was afoot "for a war of conquest and plunder from Mexico..." President Tyler avoided the Texas annexation issue at first but finally succumbed to the pressure that Britain might gain too much of a foothold there if the Texians weren't brought into the Union. Avid annexationist John C. Calhoun, leader of the Southern bloc in and out of Congress, was selected to lead the State Department which would create the treaty of annexation. But the treaty was rejected in the Senate.

President Tyler appointed **Wilson Shannon** as Minister to Mexico. Shannon promptly got into difficulties with his Mexican counterpart, **Manuel Crescencio Rejón**, a liberal who had lost his former admiration for the USA because he was now convinced that it wanted Texas as well as California. Shannon maintained that unless Rejón changed his tune America would break off diplomatic relations with Mexico (which strategy Shannon had never been instructed to invoke). By the end of his term Tyler was recommending annexation of Texas.

The election of 1844 brought the unknown Democrat **James K. Polk** to the presidency, a victory construed as in favor of "expansionism" (the slogan for taking the Oregon country was "Fifty-Four Forty or Fight!") and an "honorable" annexation of Texas (with "Remember the Alamo!" in the background).

Mexican Minister **Juan Almonte** packed up and went home to prepare his homeland for the war that he felt Polk would promote.

Beginning in August of 1845, President Polk kept a diary in which he recorded discussions and his personal reaction to various events. Polk favored the "reoccupation of Oregon" because American title to it was "...clear and unquestionable ...The world beholds the peaceful triumphs of the industry of our emigrants. To us belongs the duty of protecting them..." But it was Texas that was annexed in 1845 and American newspapers like the Washington *Union* reviled Mexico for "...her pretended rights and pretended wrongs...her insolence and stupidity...her absurd threats of war...she will exhaust what remains of our disposition to deal generously with her." Polk's Mexican policy has been described as "defiance and patronizing self-righteousness." [See Note # 6.] Polk wrote he would defend Texian title to the Río Grande boundary as claimed by Texians and verified by the "dictator" Santa Ana under threat of execution. The claim therefore took in half of New Mexico, including the town of Santa Fe, but it doesn't appear this bothered anyone in the Polk administration. In June of 1845 General **Zachary Taylor** was ordered to establish his army at a point on or near the Río Grande in order to repel any Mexican invasion of the territory. The fact that the Nueces River had always been the boundary of Texas was not a matter for concern because Santa Anna had signed the document specifying the Río Grande as boundary. Polk also sent orders to Commodore **John D. Sloat**, commander of the Pacific Squadron cruising the western side of the continent, that if he heard that the war with Mexico had started to immediately seize San Francisco and blockade all other ports as quickly as possible. In August of 1845 Polk wrote that America would "not be the aggressor upon Mexico..." for the only interest was to protect Texas. This theme seems to be mirrored by Polk's administration for Secretary of the Navy **George Bancroft** declared: "Our country can never extend its territory by conquest for the principles of our constitution preclude the possibility of governing a country against the will of its inhabitants. We know of no possible extension of our territory but by consent. We have no cause but for joy at the prosperity of all other states throughout the world and most especially of those upon our borders. Disclaiming not only the desire but the authority to make an increase of our territory by conquest, we can as little favor the introduction among us of wars or negotiations for a balance of power, as for any other antiquated form of policy, which is destined to vanish before the better influences of the increasing intelligence of mankind." [See Note # 7.] It was not long before secretary Bancroft would send American squadrons to assigned stations at Veracruz and Mazatlán.

John Slidell was sent to Mexico as a regular Minister Plenipotentiary, thus ignoring the fact that Mexico had broken off diplomatic relations with the USA over the Texas annexation issue. Foreign Minister **Manuel de la Peña y Peña** informed Slidell that he couldn't be received except to discuss the Texas issue. Another revolution broke out and Slidell wrote to Secretary of State Buchanan that Mexican government leaders were corrupt and ignorant. To President Polk he wrote that war was the only way to settle affairs with Mexico. On January 28, 1846, the Polk administration replied to Slidell: "Should the Mexican government finally refuse to receive you the cup of forbearance will then have been exhausted. Nothing can remain but to take the redress of the injuries to our citizens and the insults to our Government into our own hands...Every honorable effort should be made before a final rupture..." [See Note # 8.] Slidell made efforts to negotiate but he was informed his credentials would not be accepted. He then defended the USA against the accusations of seizing Texas, citing Mexico's inability to retake the province. While it was true the USA had a few warships off Mexican coasts and a small military force on the Río Grande it was Mexico who had been demanding a fight and was now refusing to negotiate. He asked for his passports and sailed out of Veracruz.

In March of 1846 General Taylor marched his troops toward Matamoros and once there established his base camp. General **Pedro Ampudia** arrived in Matamoros with reinforcements and sent Taylor a letter demanding that American forces withdraw back across the Nueces River, the boundary of Texas. Taylor now ordered the naval vessels to blockade the mouth of the Río Grande, an act of war, but described by Taylor as "a simple defensive precaution." General **Mariano Arista** now took charge and informed everyone that as far as he was concerned the American invasion had begun.

On **April 25, 1846**, Taylor sent out a reconnaissance patrol of some 63 men to search out enemy positions. At a large farm surrounded by high chaparral the Americans stopped to investigate and a Mexican force opened fire on the unsuspecting patrol which hadn't even bothered to post sentries. A number of Americans were killed and the rest taken captive. The next day Taylor reported the incident to the Polk administration, saying "Hostilities may now be considered as commenced." [See Note # 8.]

President Polk must have been elated. Texas had been annexed into the Union and Mexico had done nothing. An American army had been sent into "disputed" territory and the Mexicans had done nothing. The Río Grande was blockaded and still nothing! Polk had decided to ask Congress for a declaration of war due to Mexico's failure to pay its debts. [See Note # 9.] But when Taylor's men were attacked he had a patriotic cause for promoting the war and he stated: "The cup of forbearance had been exhausted even before the recent information from the frontier of the Del Norte. But now, after reiterated menaces, Mexico has passed the boundary of the United States, has invaded our territory and shed American blood upon American soil…As war exists, and notwithstanding all our efforts to avoid it, exists by the act of Mexico herself, we are called upon by every consideration of duty and patriotism to vindicate with decision and the honor, the rights, and the interests of our country." The call was now for troops to defend American territory and American honor. American patriotism was emphasized in the face of "Mexican treachery." According to Polk, it was necessary to "conquer the peace."

American public opinion was split. **Henry David Thoreau** denounced the war in his essay "Civil Disobedience." When a poll tax was levied to help with war expenses Thoreau refused to pay it and was jailed. **Ralph Waldo Emerson** visited him and asked: "Henry, what are you doing in here?" Thoreau replied: "What are you doing out there?" Poet **Walt Whitman** wrote in the Brooklyn *Eagle*: "Yes, Mexico must be thoroughly chastised! Let our arms now be carried with a spirit which shall teach the world that, while we are not forward for a quarrel, America knows how to crush as well as expand!" Boston Unitarian minister **Theodore Parker** criticized the war while he referred to Mexicans as "a wretched people, wretched in their origin, history, and character…" He felt the USA should definitely expand by the power of her ideas, her commerce, as befitted "…a superior race with superior ideas and a better civilization." [See Note # 10.]

Senator **Thomas Hart Benton** stated he would vote for money and men for defense, but he wouldn't support an aggressive war against Mexico. He stated that he didn't believe in the Río Grande boundary, that sending Taylor's army to that river tended to provoke a war, and war could be declared legally only by Congress. **Joshua R. Giddings** of Ohio stated that Polk had violated international law and moral justice. But the implication in Congress came out being that anyone opposed to the war was a disloyal American. Opponents countered that national patriotism was being exploited to promote a war of conquest for the ugly purpose of obtaining more slave territory for freedom-loving America.

Though Polk didn't really like him, he made General **Winfield Scott** supreme commander of American forces. Secretary of State Buchanan drew up a circular that stated emphatically that war wasn't being waged to acquire New Mexico and California. Polk told Buchanan to delete it and proclaimed: "We go to war with Mexico solely for the purpose of conquering an honorable and permanent peace…"

Congress authorized a call for 50,000 volunteers, apportioning quotas from the Ohio valley and Southern states, where there was much enthusiasm for the war. Texas and the states bordering the Mississippi are said to have furnished some 49,000 volunteers (out of an estimated final total of some 90,000 men under arms).

General Taylor's men fought the battle of *Palo Alto* on May 7, 1846, and declared victory the next day when they learned Mexican forces had evacuated the area. Taylor pursued and the battle of *Resaca de la Palma* was fought but superior American firepower caused the Mexican line to waiver then break down completely. American forces occupied Matamoros on May 18 and 19. Taylor couldn't control his men and soon the streets were filled with American "…drunks carrying bowie knives, rifles, and pistols, which they used at the slightest provocation." [See Note # 11.]

In May of 1846 General Taylor wrote a dispatch to the Adjutant General of the United States army in which he described the serious problem of desertion. Taylor wrote that Mexican authorities were offering inducements for soldiers to go to the other side, which was simple because all deserters had to do was swim the river at Matamoras [sic]. While war hadn't been officially declared yet, Taylor ordered (April 1 or so) that if any soldier(s) in the river refused to return when hailed by pickets, they were to be shot. At least two were shot dead.

The American public and Taylor's forces now considered their general a hero though critics said he knew little of strategy or tactics in deploying a large army. On May 30, 1846, Polk informed his cabinet that he intended to take California, New Mexico (which included what is now Arizona), and possibly other portions of northern Mexico in order to strengthen peace negotiations and provide an avenue by which Mexico would be able to pay for the costs of the war. Since "Mexico had started the war," it was only proper that Mexico pay the price.

It has been written that the two most grievous deficiencies of the Mexican army were its leadership and its firearms. While some officers had been trained in the European style, many were political appointees devoid of military tactical skill. The Mexican soldier was tough but all he had to fight with was old flintlock muskets discarded by the British army. Most of their cannon were old and inferior to American artillery. To boot, gunners had little training. The clincher was that the government was all but bankrupt and a new revolution always seemed to be around the corner. For example, in August of

1846, President Paredes was deposed by General José Mariano Salas who in turn asked Santa Anna to return to power to save Mexico once again. True to form, Santa Anna accepted.

American public opinion was either hot or cold, depending on whose newspaper was read. The Philadelphia *Public Ledger* advocated making General Winfield Scott the military governor of Mexico, allow some Mexican representation in Congress, and opening up the country to emigration from the USA and Europe… "Our Yankee young fellows and the pretty senoritas will do the rest of annexation, and Mexico will soon be Anglo-Saxonized and prepared for the confederacy."

Though they risked being accused of being traitors by giving "aid and comfort" to the enemy, some people spoke up against the war. A new member of the House, **Abraham Lincoln**, sponsored a "Spot Resolution" which demanded to know exactly where "American blood had been shed on American soil." Lincoln paid the political price for his sense of justice because he wasn't nominated for reelection. [See Note # 12.]

British newspapers reported the Mexican War as the result of "American greed and treachery." The London *Examiner* stated: "They have now got a Catholic Ireland in Mexico." But the British were exasperated by Mexican leaders who refused to forget past losses, stabilize the government and its finances, or prepare for the defense of the Mexican homeland. But not the British nor any other European power was about to intervene so President Polk was free to wage war as he saw fit.

While a popular motto pertaining to the Oregon country had been "Fifty-Four Forty or Fight!" directed against Great Britain, on June 15, 1846, Polk "compromised" the northern boundary of the USA at forty-nine degrees, thus avoiding a possible war with militarily powerful Britain. The USA could now direct its full energies against "treacherous Mexico" which just happened to be riddled by revolution and counter-revolution, making it comparatively "easy pickings."

General Winfield Scott landed his army of some 12,000 men in the vicinity of Vera Cruz in March of 1847 then set out toward Mexico City in what proved to be a "brilliant" campaign. In two weeks a sharp battle was won at the fortified pass of *Cerro Gordo*. In the group were Captains Robert E. Lee, George B. McClellan, and Lt. Ulysses S. Grant. General Scott later admitted that American soldiers, especially the volunteers, "committed atrocities to make Heaven weep and every American of Christian morals blush for his country. Murder, Robbery and rape of mothers and daughters in the presence of tied-up males of the families have been common all along the Río Grande." [See Note # 13.] Scott was not alone for Lt. **George C. Meade** also reported that the "American volunteers would drive husbands out of houses and rape the wives…They fight as gallantly as any men, but they are a set of Goths and Vandals without discipline, making us a terror to innocent people." [See Note # 14.]

Carey McWilliams relates that one **Lloyd Lewis** studied Mexican newspapers of the time and reported the view that American soldiers behaved like "…a horde of banditti, drunkards, and fornicators, vandals vomited from hell, monsters who defied even the laws of nature…shameless, daring, ignorant, ragged, foul-smelling, long-bearded men with hats turned up at the brim, thirsty with the desire to take our riches and beautiful women."

A stiff battle was fought and won on August 20, 1847, at *Churubusco*. Some 177 American soldiers were killed and around 879 wounded, casualties said to have been inflicted mostly by the artillery of the San Patricio Battalion made up of Catholic deserters, mainly Irish, from the American army. Some

3,000 Mexicans were captured, which included some 80 men from the San Patricio Battalion (also known as the "Irish Legion"). Of that number, 27 were sentenced to be executed by hanging (September 10, 1847) and 14 were sentenced to be stripped to the waist and to receive fifty lashes on their naked backs, then to be branded with the letter "D" high on the cheek bone near the eye. [See Note # 15.] One man, a leader named **John Riley**, was unconditionally pardoned. This raised a storm of protest but General Scott, who made the final decision, pointed out that when Riley deserted the USA had as yet not declared war. While desertion during wartime was punishable by death, during peacetime the Articles of War only required whipping and branding. The 26 deserters who fled after the official declaration of war were executed. The fourteen to be whipped and branded were tied to trees in front of the Catholic church at San Angel outside of Mexico City and fifty stripes were laid across their bloodied backs which quickly took on the appearance of raw beef. Then they were branded on the cheek with the letter "D" and drummed out of camp.

Peace Commissioner **Nicholas Trist** had been instructed to forge a peace along terms that the Río Grande was the boundary for Texas, New Mexico and California would be ceded to the USA, etc. Trist's efforts were rejected so on September 8, 1847, Scot marched into the blood bath that came to be known as *Molino del Rey*, storming Chapultepec hill five days later, defended to the last by its boy cadets of the military school. Soldiers rushed into the castle. A thirteen year old cadet was bayoneted to death by an American soldier. The last six cadets, Agustín Melgar, Juan Escutia, Fernando Montes de Oca, Vicente Suárez, Francisco Márquez, and Juan de la Barrera were the last to die by American hands, Juan Escutia wrapping himself in the Mexican flag and leaping to his death instead of waiting to be killed by the Americans. For all practical purposes, the Mexican War was over when the American flag was raised over Chapultepec Castle. Symbolically, the raising of Old Glory at Chapultepec was the signal at which the deserters from the San Patricio Battalion were executed.

There were sniper attacks against occupying American troops in Mexico City but General Scott turned heavy cannon on every building identified as having snipers and razed them to the ground. In Huamantla, a village some twenty-five miles from Puebla, Captain **Samuel Walker** of the Texas Rangers was killed by Mexican soldiers. General Lane loosed his men on the village, virtually destroying its civilian population in another of the major atrocities of the war.

Santa Anna resigned and months elapsed before anyone could be found to "negotiate" the dismemberment of Mexico. Nicholas Trist was recalled by Polk but Trist remained in hopes of forging a treaty that might be construed as honorable. Polk declared him an outlaw of the administration but the resultant **Treaty of Guadalupe Hidalgo**, which took almost half of Mexico and stipulated that the USA pay $15,000,000, was sent to the Senate for ratification. Now Democrats demanded that all of Mexico be annexed but this didn't win approval and after bitter debate the Trist Treaty was finally accepted. President Polk then did his best to denigrate General Scott, who had won the war, and Nicholas Trist, who had forged the peace, was fired by the State Department.

By the time of the Treaty of Guadalupe Hidalgo one **Ashbel Smith** orated that the "Mexican War was part of the mission…" that destiny had reserved for the Anglo-Saxon race and its duty to Americanize the entire continent…degenerate Mexico was fated for conquest…by the sword, that great civilizer that cleared the way "…for commerce, education, religion and all the harmonizing influences of morality and humanity…" One Lieutenant **Raphael Semmes** of the USN later wrote along the same vein: "The passage of our race into Texas, New Mexico, and California…" was the initial step southward for sweeping out an inferior people "and remove them (as a people) and their worn-out institutions from the face of the earth…for (the benefit of) letters, arts, and civilization." [See Note # 16] Mexican historian Josefina Zoraida Vázquez has written: "It was the final end of the dream, the end of the greatness of New Spain…"

The preliminary costs of the Mexican War included some 9,207 deserters and around 39,197 casualties from all causes, which included some 12,800 dead. Expenses for the war ran to perhaps $100,000,000, plus the $15,000,000 paid to Mexico with an additional $3,000,000 for claims settlements. The Whig *Intelligencer* concluded in exaltation: "We take nothing by conquest, Thank God!" President Polk's farewell message to Congress included: "Peace, plenty, and contentment reign throughout our borders and our beloved country presents a sublime moral spectacle to the world… While enlightened nations of Europe are convulsed and distracted by civil war or intestine strife, we settle all our political controversies by the peaceful exercise of the rights of freemen at the ballot box." [See Note # 17.]

It has been written that the land bludgeoned away from Mexico played a part in bringing on the Civil War. American slavery wasn't transplanted to the West but only because the areas weren't conducive to that kind of labor force. What did emerge from the Mexican War was military leaders who became more adept in the carnage of war. It would not be long before these propensities would be turned on each other in bloody civil war.

DISCUSSION NOTES *for* SYNOPSIS of the MEXICAN WAR

Note # 1
See pages 59-60 in *Arizona: A Short History* by Odie B. Faulk.

Note # 2
See Chapters 3 and 4 in *The Diplomacy Of Annexation: Texas, Oregon, And The Mexican War* by David M. Pletcher.

Note # 3
See page 89 in *The Diplomacy Of Annexation*.

Note # 4
See page 126 in *My History, Not Yours* by Dr. Genaro M. Padilla for the oration segment. The incident has been given an Orwellian softening because of its supposed "comic opera" character. David M. Pletcher writes on page 101 of his *Diplomacy Of Annexation*: "Authorized or not, Jones' attack on Monterey clearly showed American intentions toward California." On page 109 Pletcher writes concerning the Oregon question: "…American campaign for Oregon was typical of the extravagant demands, reckless assertions, disingenuous conduct, and…all those things which have on so many previous occasions tended to place American statesmen so low in the scale of morality."

Note # 5
As already documented, California had been explored by Hispanic Europeans long before Fremont. But the land was new to him and most Americans so is that why he is considered parochially?

Note # 6

See pages 253-4 in *Diplomacy Of Annexation*.

Note # 7

See Note 80, pages 307-8 in *Diplomacy Of Annexation* for assurance from Secretary of the Navy Bancroft that America would never extend its territory by conquest.

Note # 8

See the Pletcher volume, p. 365.

Note # 9

See page 561 in *The Oxford History Of The American People* by Samuel Eliot Morison.

Note # 10

See pages 154-57 in *A People's History Of The United States* by Howard Zinn.

Note # 11

See the Pletcher volume, page 463.

Note # 12

Long before the War Powers Act there have been examples of American presidents as Commander in Chiefs pressuring the nation to support a foreign war or risk being targeted as *traitors to America*. The War of 1812 is depicted as a national effort against British abuses but was the main thrust of Congress to conquer Canada for control of the land? In the Mexican War (1846-48) Senator Benton stated that only Congress could declare war but he understood that President Polk instigated the bloody affair by sending troops where they would be attacked, thus neutralizing the Constitution. Once "American blood has been shed on American soil" Benton and the Congress would have to "support the troops" or be branded as traitors in the eyes of the nation. The Spanish-American War of 1898 has been described as motivated more by "yellow journalism" than anything else. "Liberating" places like Cuba and the Philippines took only a few months but it took a couple of years to conquer the Filipinos who thought they were going to manage their own country once they got rid of Spain but American authorities felt they "weren't ready" for self-government so American liberators had to turn on the Filipinos. President Wilson "kept us out of war" (WWI) until after his reelection when it was decided America would have to "Make the World Safe for Democracy" by sending in American troops. American entry into WWII was initiated by the attack on Pearl Harbor so long as we don't consider the military help (Flying Tigers?) we were giving the Chinese against Japan. The "Korean Conflict" was merely a "police action" according to President Truman. Serious involvement in the Vietnam War is said to have been legalized by the Gulf of Tonkin Resolution based on a supposed "American blood on American soil" attack. President Reagan sent troops into Grenada to rescue some young people and President Bush (the Elder) felt compelled to push Saddam Hussein out of Kuwait because of its oil reserves, leaving the younger President Bush to bludgeon him out of Iraq because of his "weapons of mass destruction." Has the Constitution been observed in all these actions or is the Commander in Chief the real power in American government?

What have historians and the "Dixie Chicks" learned about "Freedom of Speech" in our

free society?
Note # 13
See pages 102-3 in the classic *North From Mexico* by Carey McWilliams. A few writers like McWilliams and Howard Zinn are rather unique among historiographers in that they are able to relate the Mexican side of the historical record at the risk of being charged with lacking patriotism or even *treason.*
Note # 14
The U.S.-Mexican War by Carol and Thomas Christensen, companion to the PBS television series, brings out information from Mexican writers of the day in a "powerful work" titled *Apuntes Para La Historia De La Guerra Entre Mexico Y Los Estados Unidos*, a copy of which I have been unable to acquire. *The Mexican War* by the Editors of Time-Life Books is a popular read that relies on valid documentation but not enough Mexican sources. By and large, however, it appears that inhuman brutality issues like the bombardment of the civilian population of Vera Cruz or branding of human beings or "Rape" are reserved for people other than American when reported by various historiographers. *Occupied America* by Rudy Acuña mentions "Rape" on page 26 when discussing Spanish colonial history. The topic isn't mentioned in the section "The Invasion of Mexico" starting on page 48, though he does quote participants like Grant and Meade remarking on the brutalities of American soldiers directed against "greasers." The illuminating *Foreigners In Their Native Land* by Dr. David J. Weber gives voice to many perspectives but American brutalities during the Mexican War aren't included. As might be expected, *The Far Western Frontier, 1830-1860* by Ray Allen Billington assures the reader (page 171) that "...Polk was no aggressive dictator..." and that he tried every legal means to acquire California and resorted to war only when all other means failed. And anyway the Mexicans wanted war and started it. *Chronicles Of The Gringos* edited by G.W. Smith and C. Judah don't discuss "Taylor's rapists" but they do mention "Mexican Barbarity" on page 105. Howard Zinn provides a more balanced introduction to the Mexican War in his *People's History Of The United States*, pages 152-59.
Note # 15
See pages 431-37 in *Chronicles Of The Gringos: The U.S. Army in the Mexican War, 1846-1848, Accounts of Eyewitnesses & Combatants* edited by George W. Smith and Charles Judah.
Note # 16
See the Pletcher volume, page 579.
Note # 17
See page 169 in Howard Zinn's *People's History*. For the quote by President Polk see page 40 in *Empire Express* by David H. Bain.

Essay: THE DRED SCOTT DECISION
The Declaration of Independence is a basic document in American history and therefore part of American psychology and character. It states, among other things: "*We hold these truths to be self-evident,*

that all men are created equal, that they are endowed by their Creator with certain unalienable rights, that among these are Life, Liberty, and the pursuit of Happiness."

Among the very few historians who have popularized an investigation behind the idealism of the Declaration, which can be traced to the ideas of John Lock, is Howard Zinn. He writes in his *A People's History of the United States* that "Indians, black slaves, and women" were "clearly omitted" from Declaration's idealism. Author Thomas Jefferson was himself a slave master and it is obvious he did not consider his slaves his equal. To put it bluntly, "Happiness" was intended for white males. Further, when a draft was created in Boston to battle the English there was a stipulation that people with enough money could pay a substitute to fight English tyranny. The poor would be *Patriots!* and go into the field of battle for *Freedom!* It would be interesting to investigate how many of the founding fathers actually took up arms. George Washington, Alexander Hamilton, etc., would certainly make the list.

It is difficult to understand the depths of American racism unless one studies African slavery. The work by Garry Wills titled *Negro President: Jefferson and the Slave Power* has to do with the pervasiveness of institution of slavery in the American psyche. For example, the center of American civilization would be Philadelphia but there was a law there that any slave who resided in that jurisdiction for six months was automatically free. Therefore, as of 1790, Washington, Jefferson, and Madison worked vigorously for establishing the District of Columbia as the seat of American government. There the Congress would have absolute authority. The land for D.C. had been ceded by the slave states of Virginia and Maryland so Southern legislators maintained the institution of slavery should forever be respected there. Slaveholders from the South could go to D.C. without risking loss of their black servants.

George Washington was very conscious of his status as slave master, refusing to advertise in the North if one of his slaves escaped. When he did go after escapees he did so by stealth, using government agents instructed not to create any kind of stir. While serving in Philadelphia as Secretary of State, Thomas Jefferson was very worried that his slave cook, James Hemings, trained at great expense in Paris, would run away. In an effort to keep him he began paying James a regular salary. During the effort to make D.C. the capital, James Madison asserted that Virginia would not have ratified the Constitution had it been made clear that Philadelphia might be the capital.

The District of Columbia was chosen as the seat of American government because it was part of a well established slave community, Alexandria. When the federal government moved in more than a fifth of residents were black slaves, many of them owned by legislators. The District became a strong slave trading center with chained slaves herded to the auction block at regular intervals. Unlike the centers of government in Europe, D.C. was placed where there was little cultural life but where slavery would not be challenged. Accommodations would be primitive but there would be no challenge to the twelve (12) slaveholding Presidents or various legislators who would lead the USA in the quest for freedom and progress.

How does the institution of slavery figure into the national psyche? Is the idea that "all men are created equal" central to American psychology and culture? Henry Steele Commager writes in his (edited) *Documents of America History* (pages 339-40) that the Dred Scott Decision of 1857 is *"probably the most famous in the history of the Court."* How ingrained is the Dred Scott Decision in the American character? Which is dominant, the Declaration or the Decision?

The basics of the Decision are as follows. Dred Scott, a Negro slave from Missouri, is taken into Illinois in 1834, a free State, and then to Wisconsin Territory where slavery was forbidden by the Missouri Compromise of 1820. When taken back to Missouri in 1846 he filed a lawsuit to have his freedom recognized by the courts. He believed that under American law he was now a free man.

The Dred Scott case made its way to the Supreme Court by1857 and the following opinion was rendered and articulated by Justice C.J. Taney:

• Dred Scott is neither a citizen of the U.S. nor of Missouri so he isn't entitled to go to court in the first place.

• In the opinion of the Supreme Court, Negroes "weren't intended to be included under the word citizens" as used by the framers of the Constitution, that they were "considered as a subordinate and inferior class of beings subjugated by the dominant race."

• Whether emancipated or not, Negroes are subject to the authority of the "dominant race" and have no rights or privileges except those which authorities in power might wish to grant them.

• The U.S. Constitution recognized "every person and every class and description of persons as citizens if they were so recognized by the States, but none other... it was formed by them, and for them and their posterity, but for no one else."

• Neither the Declaration of Independence nor the Constitution applied to "the class of persons who had been imported as slaves, nor their descendants, whether they had become free or not, and could not be included in the general words employed in that memorable instrument."

• By custom Negroes have been "regarded as beings of an inferior order, altogether unfit to associate with the white race, either in social or political relations, they have no rights that the white man is bound to respect, the negro might justly and lawfully be reduced to slavery for his benefit. This opinion is universal among civilized white people..."

How crucial is the Dred Scott Decision for a student of Southwest and/or American history? Which should be dominant when considering historical facts or when writing about them? If African-Americans were considered property, not human beings, what of other groups like Indians, Hispanics, Orientals, etc.? What should people targeted as minorities, which at one time or another included most immigrants, understand from the realities as well as the fantasies of American history?

The Mexican War In TEXAS

Despite the anarchy that reined in Mexico after independence in 1821, **Stephen F. Austin** wrote in 1829 that the government of Mexico was "the most liberal and munificent on earth" for emigrants. There is no evidence that his empresario activities had at its base a struggle between American and Hispanic people and their cultures for control of the continent. Austin might have been aware that in the 1820s Mexico was around 60% Indian, 22% *mestizo* (mixed), and some 18% European (white) Spanish. By contrast, Americans were 82% "white," and 18% African. The Indians had been exterminated or would soon be exiled to Oklahoma so America didn't rely on an Indian base as did Mexico. Despite the turmoil, Austin was able to hold on to his empresario grant and he brought in some 5,000 Americans into Texas with additional thousands of illegals filtering in. They came to refer to themselves as Texians and were soon categorizing Mexicans as *greasers*, despising them much as they did Africans or Indians.

When Kentuckian **Haden Edwards** came into east Texas with claims on the land Austin's colonists joined the fight against the declared "Republic of Fredonia" (December 20, 1826) and chased the *Fredonians* back across the American line (January, 1827). Various American newspapers reported the incident as a "handful of men against a whole nation!" or that "apostles of democracy" had been crushed. [See Note # 1. *Notes begin on page 291.*]

By around 1830 Mexico began to realize that Texians had no intention of becoming Mexicans but would ever hold themselves apart due to their feelings of "racial superiority." Further immigration from the USA was made illegal and Texians regarded this as a personal insult. The situation became worse when the period of being exempt from taxes expired and Texians were required to pay customs duties and other taxes, which they found "humiliating" because soldiers were sent to assure that the law was being obeyed.

Rebellion was at the threshold in 1831 when some illegal immigrants organized the town of Liberty and General **Mier y Terán** sent in troops under Captain **Juan Bradburn**, a Kentuckian by birth, to "abolish the community." Most Texians now considered Bradburn a "turncoat and racial traitor." Leaders like **William Barret Travis**, an illegal immigrant from Alabama, became firebrands for insurrection. In the summer of 1832 Texians made plans for an attack against Anahuac but their schooner was blocked by the fort at Velasco. Texians launched a ground assault that proved successful and the Mexican garrison was permitted to withdraw from Velasco. Then word came that a peace had been settled at Anahuac and the "war" was declared over. Nevertheless, rebellion was in the air because many Texians refused to be ruled by people they considered their racial inferiors. [See Note # 2.]

By 1833 committees of "safety" or "vigilance" were being formed by Texian leaders and in April a convention called by a central committee met to discuss options. Stephen Austin, considered too pro-Mexican, was deposed and **William H. Wharton** was selected as chairman. The convention articulated grievances, petitions, and an appeal for local government. It framed a state constitution. An illegal immigrant who had drifted into Texas, **Sam Houston**, was among those who came to the fore during the convention. But when it came to choosing who would present everything to the authorities in Mexico City the man chosen was Stephen F. Austin.

Acting President Valentín Gómez Farias received Austin cordially (1833) and agreed to present his petitions to the House of Deputies. Cabinet minister **Lorenzo de Zavala**, always friendly to Americans, informed Austin that the law forbidding further American immigration would be revoked. The Mexican government continued in turmoil, however, and when Austin met with Gómez Farias in September both men became angry. In a fit of pique, Austin wrote a letter supporting the creation of a government separate from that of Coahuila, which was construed as "treasonous" back in San Antonio and sent to Gómez Farias.

Austin spoke with Santa Anna in November and the latter agreed to most of the petitions presented: repeal of the immigration ban, better mail service, lightening tariff charges, etc., but no separation of Texas from Coahuila. Austin headed for home but when he stopped at Saltillo he was arrested on charges that he was plotting treasonous activities, returned to Mexico City and thrown into prison. (He wasn't released until December 25, 1834.) But progress was made when the Saltillo legislature passed a number of measures which helped Texas: naturalized citizens were enabled to engage in retail trade, Texas was allotted three representatives in the Coahuila congress, English was recognized for use in official business, trial by jury was instituted, and religious toleration was granted.

In April of 1834 Santa Anna returned to power and in October of 1835 he abolished the Constitution of 1824 and declared Mexico was now a centralist state, not federalist. The President and Congress now held all power and authority. A revolt in Zacatecas was brutally squelched. Lorenzo de Zavala fled to Texas.

A group of Texians, mostly newcomers who had no land or other prospects, was formed to resist Mexican inequities. William Barrett Travis was authorized to capture Anahuac, which he did, paroling the garrison there. This seemingly senseless act aroused almost everyone's ire and Travis was denounced "as a fool, a traitor, and a dangerous idiot." [See Note # 3.] In July of 1835 the majority of Texians expressed loyalty to Mexico in a letter to General Cos. Cos ordered that "hotheads" like Travis be arrested but no Texian supported the order. Cos then wrote that Texians were not really loyal to the Mexican Constitution.

The Texian population after 1830 has been estimated as about 30,000, which included some 3,000 African slaves. Rumor had it that a Mexican army would soon be invading Texas and Texians began to prepare for war if it came, calling for American reinforcements at every opportunity. The Constitution of 1824 would be upheld and the Cos army would be kept out of Texas. Austin wanted to negotiate with Cos while the "frontier element" in this "irregular army" wanted to fight. In time military command was passed to Colonel **Edward Burleson**. But problems continued: there was no artillery, no clothes for cold weather, and even food supplies were irregular. The only good note is that hundreds of men were pouring into Texas from the southwestern United States.

On December 5, 1835, **Ben Milam** led a foray against the Cos troops in San Antonio. On the third day of fighting Milam was shot dead but on December 10, Cos was forced to surrender. Burleson gave Cos the honors of war after he pledged never again to fight Texians. The little Texian army now controlled Goliad and the Alamo at Béxar.

There was now a distinct euphoria among Texians and the question was asked if the fight was to uphold the Constitution of 1824 or to declare independence from Mexico altogether. A document titled a "Consultation" had attacked Santa Anna tyranny, upheld the 1824 Constitution, but also stated Texas had a right to establish an independent government if the federalist system was discarded. [See Note # 4.] Texians weren't particularly interested in independence but apparently the newcomers were..

On January 3, 1836, Dr. James Grant and Colonel Frank Johnson were authorized to capture Matamoros because of its strategic location, its silver, and its "señoritas." [See Note # 5.] **James W. Fannin Jr.** was then appointed to take Johnson's place after the latter declined the command, though he later re-accepted it. But confusion and feuding over command finally prevented the attack. Indeed, chaos, dissension, and rivalry ruled the Texian government while most Texians merely went about their business.

Mexican cavalry rode into San Antonio on February 23, 1836. Learning that rebels were holed up in the Alamo mission, the "defenders" were advised to surrender or suffer the consequences. Passage in and out of the Alamo was permitted and all could half left if they had so chosen, but they didn't. **William B. Travis** was in nominal command of the rebels inside the Alamo but the **James Bowie** contingent would obey only their leader. The two struck up an immediate dislike for each other. [See Note # 6.]

For a time Travis and Bowie shared command in the Alamo because each had a significant following. When Bowie came down with pneumonia he publicly passed his authority to Travis. The now supreme commander stated he needed help but would never surrender. His famous motto was *Victory Or Death* and he answered the demand to surrender with a cannon shot, despite the fact that his small force was facing some 1,000 enemy soldiers. **Davy Crockett**, one of the "Tennessee Boys," asked for and got the assignment of defending the most dangerous area of the Alamo wall. The assault was made on **March 6, 1836** and it took some five hours of horrendous fighting to succeed, the defenders making good use of their marksmanship abilities. In the melee Mexican soldiers accidentally shot other soldiers, thus adding many "friendly fire" casualties to those dead and wounded. [See Note # 7.] It had required unbridled savagery but the Alamo fell to Santa Anna's victorious army and the word spread quickly. The cold blooded executions of Davy Crockett and six other now defenseless Alamo survivors were the beginning of the atrocities of the Mexican War. [See Note # 8.]

Rebel Texians now had nothing to cheer about. General **José Urrea** and his men marched on San Patricio and Goliad. In February of 1836 the few Texians at San Patricio were destroyed. James Fannin had some 500 men at Goliad but none were sent to rescue Travis at the Alamo, despite his urgent requests, which also went unheeded at the March 1, 1836, convention at Washington-on-the-Brazos when **Sam Houston** negated a motion to hasten to help the patriots at the Alamo. It was during this convention that Texas independence from Mexico was proclaimed. [See Note # 9.]

Urrea, the best general of the Texas war, surrounded Fannin's force in the area of Coleta (*Encinal del Perdido*) and attacked. Fannin was hopelessly outnumbered so he surrendered. Everybody marched back to Goliad in hopes of repatriation. But orders came in from Santa Anna that all "pirates" were to be executed immediately. Urrea protested to no avail and excepting a handful which had been hidden, the noble Fannin and his men were executed in this second atrocity of what would become the Mexican War.

Horrified by these atrocities, Texians deserted their homes and headed east. Men and not a few boys joined Sam Houston's army but the exodus was on and refugees numbered in the thousands. The rainy season caused additional hardship but even worse were the looters who grabbed whatever they could. Some men rode into settlements and shouted "The Mexicans are coming!!" then stole anything they could in the confusion.

Sam Houston, general of the army, felt there was little to do but retreat until he got to a position between the San Jacinto River and Buffalo Bayou. Santa Anna, with some 700-800 troops, pursued in the belief that for all practical purposes, the Texas war was over. Cos came into camp with his 400 men and now Houston was outnumbered with his 918.

On **April 21, 1836**, Houston's force marched on the dozing Santa Anna encampment. Incredibly, sentries had not been posted so the attack was a total surprise, despite it being the middle of the afternoon. At the distance of twenty yards some eight hundred rifles blasted into the unsuspecting, confused, dazed, then bleeding Mexican soldiers. A charge was made amid cries of "Remember the Alamo!" and "Take prisoners like the Meskins do!" The death trap was covered with blood and no mercy was shown until there were some 630 Mexicans dead in the field, the wounded being killed along with those who tried to surrender. When the bloodlust finally abated in the late afternoon, prisoners were taken and permitted to live.

Santa Anna himself was made a prisoner. While at Béxar the Commander in Chief would say "I neither ask for nor give quarter" but he changed his tune at San Jacinto where he saved his life by signing a peace document that gave away Texas with a boundary up to the Río Grande where it had never existed. Further, Santa Anna sent orders to his generals to retire from Texas, despite the fact that only the vanguard of the army had been destroyed and some 4,000 soldiers were still able to fight the estimated 1,500 Texians. [See Note # 10.] In time Santa Anna was given his freedom, perhaps because it was believed he would help the Texian cause more if alive than if dead.

The Mexican War grew out of the American annexation of Texas. President Polk had vowed to respect Texas boundaries so he sent General Taylor and his troops into Texian claimed territory in hopes that Mexican troops would retaliate and thus have a valid excuse to begin the war. As has been shone, the strategy worked. Some 5,000 Texians volunteered to fight during the war. Officers like John C. (Jack) Hays, Ben McCulloch, and Samuel H. Walker became well known for their prowess. There were no battles on Texas soil but Joe B. Frantz has written that "the Rangers" who crossed the Río Grande into Mexico with Taylor's troops were motivated by revenge for previous atrocities. [See Note #

11.] "Revenge became their watchword and no Mexican, regardless of age or sex, was safe. They gutted women, shot old men and children, and hanged civilians for no more offense than being there." After the victory at Buena Vista, "the Rangers got 'celebratin' drunk and picked fights with Taylor's regulars, causing a riot that "required several hundred military police and a troop of cavalry to control." Rangers under General Winfield Scott in Mexico City delighted in killing civilians. The Treaty of Guadalupe Hidalgo was accepted by Mexican authorities on February 2, 1848, and in April the Rangers were mustered out of the American army and sent back to Texas.

DISCUSSION NOTES *for* The Mexican War in TEXAS.

Note # 1
See page 164 in *Lone Star* by T.R. Fehrenbach.

Note # 2
See page 175 in *Lone Star*.

Note # 3
See page 186 in *Lone Star*.

Note # 4
See page 354 in volume 1 of *History Of Texas* by H. Yoakum, Esq.

Note # 5
See page 203 in *Lone Star*.

Note # 6
See page 64 in *Texas: A Bicentennial History* by Joe B. Frantz.

Note # 7
See page 51 in *With Santa Anna In Texas: A Personal Narrative Of The Revolution* written by José Enrique de la Peña, translated and edited by Carmen Perry.

Note # 8
See page 214 in *Lone Star* for the detail that Crockett might have survived the battle at the Alamo. See also page 53 in *With Santa Anna In Texas: A Personal Narrative Of The Revolution*. When this work first came out in 1975 it unleashed a storm of protest, due mostly to the fact that almost everyone believed that Crockett died in battle, not by execution afterward. Despite the fact that the De la Teja work is basically a stinging criticism of Santa Anna and his management of the Texas war, it has been denounced as a forgery, probably because of the Crockett detail. *La Rebelion De Texas* edited by Jesús Sánchez Garza of Mexico City is often cited by Carmen Perry and would make interesting reading for those who wish to explore further. Writing valid history is a perilous business in more ways than one and the intrepid Carmen Perry and Dan Kilgore, author of *How Did Davy Die?* have paid the price for their moral courage. More acceptable to popular belief has been *Defense Of A Legend* by Bill Groneman.

Note # 9
See page 94 in *Texas The Lone Star State* by Rupert N. Richardson.

Note # 10

See page 179 in *With Santa Anna In Texas*.
Note # 11
See pages 91-92 in his *Texas: A Bicentennial History*. The atrocities of the Mexican War have been so well covered up that the popular mind doesn't associate them with targeting "Mexicans" as a "minority" and its concomitant perils.

The Mexican War In NEW MEXICO

On May 11, 1846, President James K. Polk sent a message to Congress saying that war existed between the USA and Mexico, "…and notwithstanding all our efforts to avoid it, exists by the act of Mexico herself." In little more than a month the "Army of the West" under the command of Colonel **Stephen Watts Kearny** was mobilized at Fort Leavenworth, Kansas, and ordered to take New Mexico and California for the USA. The little army of some 1,648 men was ready to march westward as of June 21, 1846. [See Note # 1. *Notes begin on page 295*.] During the entire march there was no settlement or even a house to intrude on the prairie landscape. Kearny, now promoted to Brigadier General, became ill during the march and was unable to mount his horse even when partly recovered so he rode in a supply wagon and then in a spring wagon for a more comfortable ride.

MAGOFFIN

Kearny and his staff were in Bent's Fort by July 26, 1846, where the colonel met **James W. Magoffin** who presented him with a letter of introduction from Secretary of War W.L. Marcy. Kearny then decided to send Magoffin, a well known trader, to Santa Fe with a proclamation for New Mexicans and a letter for Governor Armijo. The proclamation said that Kearny was entering New Mexico "…with a great military force…" for the betterment of New Mexicans, who should remain peaceful in their homes and labors and they would not be molested by the American army because "they will be respected and protected in all their rights, both civil and religious. All those who shall take up arms and encourage or recommend resistance to the government of the United States will be looked upon as enemies and treated accordingly."

The letter to Governor Armijo, dated August 1, 1846, stated that because of the annexation of Texas to the USA the Río Grande river was now the western boundary of Texas (which included the eastern half of New Mexico as well as the city of Santa Fe itself), therefore American territory. Governor Armijo was advised to "…submit to fate…" and not put up a resistance in order to avoid bloodshed and the "…needless sufferings and miseries that may follow…"

ARMIJO

When Governor Armijo received Kearny's letter he convened a group of prominent men in order to decide on a course of action. Armijo was a business man, like most of those who met with him, and involved in the Santa Fe trade with various American trading firms. Colonel **Diego Archuleta**, the only professional soldier in the group, urged a strong military defense against the aggressor Americans. It was decided to resist the American juggernaut and on August 8, 1846, Armijo issued his own proclamation asking all New Mexicans to come to the aid of their homeland. On August 10th Armijo asked for an appropriation of $1,000 to maintain Archuleta's dragoons. It was granted then rescinded the next day. Armijo received Magoffin and Captain Cooke on August 12th, conferring with them in private. Of particular importance was Magoffin's discussions with Colonel Archuleta who was actually in command of New Mexico's professional soldiers. Magoffin apparently informed Archuleta that the USA claimed only the eastern half of New Mexico so the western part could come under Archuleta's control and to sweeten the deal Magoffin (he stated later) gave Archuleta a substantial bribe. [See Note # 2.]

On August 15th General Kearny addressed the people of Las Vegas, informing them that he was taking possession of the country. "We come amongst you as friends, not enemies, as protectors, not conquerors…not a pepper, not an onion shall be disturbed or taken by my troops…But listen! He who promises to be quiet and is found in arms against me, I will hang!"

Armijo had asked for volunteers to mass in the mountains east of Santa Fe through which the invaders would have to march. Once there, Colonel Archuleta and his professional troops informed Armijo they would not fight. They departed from the battlefield, taking their professional armaments with them. Armijo realizes that against modern weaponry New Mexican bravery would result in nothing but bloodshed so he tells all citizens to go home. He rides south to avoid being captured.

BLOODLESS CONQUEST

Americans enter Santa Fe unopposed and on August 19th General Kearny informs everyone on the plaza that Armijo is no longer governor, that he (Kearny) is, that they are no longer subjects of Mexico but rather citizens of the United States. On August 22, 1846, Kearny issues a proclamation that states *all* of New Mexico is now part of the USA, that anyone who took up arms would be considered a traitor and executed as such. The Mexican War was raging but declaring New Mexicans to be citizens of the USA was an effective strategy to sow terror in the population because patriots fighting in defense of their Mexican homeland could be charged with treason against the USA and executed. And of utmost importance, the subterfuge played on Colonel Archuleta had worked like a charm, enabling the Army of the West to take New Mexico without a fight.

In order to prevent mass communication, Kearny takes away the printing press of Father Martínez of Taos. He prints up the "Kearny Code" of laws drawn up by Francis P. Blair, a professional lawyer now functioning as Attorney General, by which New Mexico was to be governed. American **Charles Bent** is installed as Governor with **Donaciano Vigil** as Secretary. Fort Marcy, the first American military post in the Southwest, is established on a hill overlooking Santa Fe. Then Kearny and most of his soldiers depart (September 25, 1846) for the conquest of California.

ABUSE OF NATIVES

Charles Bent was married to an Hispana of the Jaramillo family but he had a low opinion of New Mexicans. He once implied that Hispanics should be enslaved, that they were not fit to be a free people, that "…they should be ruled by others than themselves." [See Note # 3.] But by October 9th even Governor Bent was protesting to Colonel Doniphan that American soldiers, the "rowdy, overbearing, insulting" Missouri Volunteers, were abusing the native population, "greasers," to the degree that people might even take up arms against their oppressors. [See Note # 4.] There are rumors that Diego Archuleta and Tomás Ortiz are plotting a general revolt but the plot is leaked, arrests are made and most of the conspirators flee south.

CHARGE OF TREASON

American authorities now believe they have to teach the populace a lesson. They arrest **Manuel Antonio Chaves** and the Pino brothers Nicolás and Miguel on charges of *conspiracy* while they are sitting under the portal of the Exchange Hotel. The Pinos are soon released but Colonel **Sterling Price** had been informed that Chaves was a dangerous frontier fighter that should be shot as quickly as possible, which is why he had been arrested in the first place on the trumped up conspiracy charge.

In January of 1847 Chaves, is charged with *treason against the USA*. Captain Angney is assigned to defend Chaves and the lawyer points out that his client is a citizen of Mexico, that the Mexican War is raging, that if he defends his homeland it is out of patriotism to Mexico, not treason to the United States. Angney further states that the USA would be forever disgraced if it executed a man for defending his country in time of need. Chaves is acquitted and released.

ASSASSINATION and REVOLT

Governor Bent believes the rebellion has been squelched and on January 19, 1847, he is at his home in Taos when a mob of insurgents, Hispanos and Native Americans led by Tomásito Romero from Taos Pueblo break into Bent's home and brutally murder the Governor in cold blood. The mob then attacks various others and succeed in killing Narciso Beaubien and Cornelio Vigil. They target Americans and one Elliot Lee is pursued until Father Martínez gives him sanctuary in his house, berating the mob all the while. [See Note # 5.] The revolt spreads and Americans are attacked in Mora and Arroyo Hondo.

On January 24, 1847, Colonel Sterling Price arrives in Taos with cannon and other arms of overwhelming force. Some 150 rebels are slaughtered. On January 25 Captain I.R. Hendley leads some eighty soldiers against the little town of Mora where some 150 rebels are supposed to be holed up. Hendley is killed in action but the Missouri Volunteers have no cannon so they retreat to Las Vegas. On February 1, 1847, Captain J.B. Morin leads 200 men and artillery against Mora, which is virtually destroyed. Hardly a building is left standing so the rebels would be unable to find shelter against the winter weather. There are other skirmishes but American firepower is victorious against basically bows and arrows. Rebels are pursued relentlessly. On July 5, 1847, three Mexican suspects are taken to Major B.B. Edmondson who is investigating the disappearance of four Americans sent to investigate the driving off of an American horse herd. The suspects refuse to answer any questions so Edmondson places a noose around the neck of one of them and lifts him into the air. After the third "lift" the man says the four were killed at the village of Los Valles. Edmondson takes his men and all artillery to Los Valles and destroys the little village. Then he sets fire to the rubble to make certain nothing can be salvaged. The insurrection against American authority is over by the end of July and it is decided to put captured rebels on trial for murder and treason against the USA.

Lewis H. Garrard, an eyewitness to events and later author of *Wah-to-yah And The Taos Trail*, described what was happening. "We strolled to the room in which were the condemned and other prisoners…" [See Note # 6.] According to Garrard, the group that would be executed after giving them a fair trial numbered "eighty or more." Some 280 soldiers were at the ready, a brass howitzer with its muzzle pointed at the door, in case there was any disturbance.

One of the people murdered was Narciso Beaubien so his father, **Carlos Beaubien**, was appointed as one of the judges, along with Joab Houghton. The rebels were found guilty and sentenced to death by hanging. At least six (6) were adjudged guilty of treason. The charge of treason against citizens of Mexico "raised some eyebrows" in Washington and President Polk explained to Congress that American military officials in New Mexico erred "in designating and describing the crimes of conquered Mexican inhabitants as treason against the United States." [See Note # 7.]

Though a member of a group whose intention it was to "travel to Taos and kill and scalp every Mexican to be found…" and a teenager at the time, Lewis Garrard was moved to write: "It certainly did appear to be a great assumption on the part of the Americans to conquer a country and then arraign the revolting inhabitants for treason…Treason indeed! The poor wretches…Men remanded to jail till the day of execution, they drew their serapes more closely around them and accompanied the armed guard….I left the room, sick at heart. Justice! Out upon the word, when its distorted meaning is the warrant for murdering those who defend to the last their country and their homes."

The Hispanos of New Mexico were never of a society who condoned murder, even during a riot, so it is difficult to ascertain how they felt about the executions. While relatives had to be heart broken, ordinary people only heard that "murderers had been brought to justice." The absolute destruction of villages like Mora had to rankle but now everyone realized that American brutality could be unleashed at any moment. The people had no way of knowing that Kearny's proclamation of American citizenship was illegal, even when enforced by military tribunals merely to rid the country of leaders who might want to protect it against invading Americans. It must also be pointed out that many New Mexicans, especially the powerful *rico* class, had had serious business dealings with Americans over the Santa Fe Trail and they generally wanted this commerce to continue. With all these perspectives to consider, it can be said that American military power now dominated New Mexico and there would be no more bloody uprisings in this phase of the Mexican War.

DISCUSSION NOTES *for* The Mexican War in NEW MEXICO

Note # 1
See *Turmoil In New Mexico, 1846-1868* by William A. Keleher. See also volume two in *Leading Facts Of New Mexican History* by Ralph E. Twitchell.

Note # 2
See pages 26-35 in *Turmoil In New Mexico* by William Keleher. There is no record that Armijo was bribed but various authors promote the idea, ignoring Archuleta altogether. Governor Manuel Armijo is perhaps the most denigrated individual in New Mexican history, perhaps because he was serving as governor when the USA took the country from Mexico.

Note # 3

See page 96 in *Seeds Of Discord: New Mexico In The Aftermath Of The American Conquest, 1846-1861* by Alvin R. Sunseri.

Note # 4

See page 134 in *New Mexico: A History Of Four Centuries* by Warren A. Beck.

Note # 5

The insurrection was led by Diego Archuleta at first then by Pablo Montoya, Manuel Cortez, Jesús Tafoya, and Pablo Chávez. All except Cortez were either killed in battle (as with Crockett after the Alamo battle, Montoya was murdered by the military immediately after the battle in which he participated) or executed in Taos. Historian Ralph E. Twitchell was later to write that Padre Martínez was the mastermind of the revolt, that he hated Americans and American institutions. New Mexico author Angélico Chávez, who investigated the Martínez historical record in his *But Time And Chance: The Story Of Padre Martínez Of Taos, 1793-1867*, suggests that Twitchell's information is bigotry, not history.

Note # 6

See page 193 in *Wah-to-yah And The Taos Trail*, © 1955 in paperback by Oklahoma University Press. It would be interesting to study the first edition of this book and compare it with the 1955 version.

Note # 7

See page 28 in *Wildest Of The Wild West* by Howard Bryan, who writes that some forty prisoners were sent to Santa Fe "to face military court martial on charges of treason..." and six were executed on August 3, 1847, on that charge. Warren A. Beck writes in his *New Mexico: A History Of Four Centuries*, pages 137-138, that some fifteen were sentenced to death, that only one (1) was executed for treason, and that "in accordance with the traditions of Anglo-Saxon justice, the leaders of the uprising were given a fair trial." Beck also states that prosecuting attorney Francis Preston Blair, a lawyer by profession, believed that General Kearny had granted American citizenship to all New Mexicans, thus providing the legal grounds for the treason charge. History proves that Kearny's strategy was very effective. First he was able to get Magoffin to bribe Col. Archuleta into not fighting as well as assuring him the USA wanted only the eastern half of New Mexico. With soldiers in control of population centers, Kearny then bestowed citizenship on New Mexicans in order to be able to charge them with treason, a capital offense, if they resisted the invasion of their homeland. It is now the role of historiography to make everything palatable on a moral plane.

The Mexican War in ARIZONA

The Mormon Battalion was mustered into service in Iowa Territory on July 16, 1846 and had some 486 men (accompanied by some 25 women and a number of children) when it reached Santa Fe. On October 13 **Philip St. George Cook** took command of the Battalion with orders from Kearny to open a wagon road to California. When they left Santa Fe on October 21 the troop had been trimmed down to 397 men (and five women). Guides were **Antoine Leroux** and **Pauline Weaver** who followed the trail south, as Kearny had done, then on to Guadalupe Pass, "the only wagon pass to the Pacific for a thousand miles to the south…" with much difficulty. [See Note #1.] Everyone was grateful when the little expedition reached the San Pedro River with its grass for the animals and shade for the soldiers.

The Battalion descended the San Pedro valley from the vicinity of (present) Bisbee to that of Benson. In the deserted rancho of San Pedro was fought the only real battle of the Mexican War on Arizona soil, against the fierce, wild bulls of the ranch. The soldiers, unfamiliar with a ranching environment, had never seen such cattle. From Benson the route took the expedition westward between the Santa Rita and Santa Catalina mountains.

When Cooke approached the vicinity of Tucson he was informed that Mexican troops had gathered there in order to do battle. In reality Commandant **Antonio Comadurán** had less than 150 soldiers in the village. Cooke sent a messenger into Tucson and some officers came out and arranged what could be described as an armistice. Cooke would be permitted to march unopposed so long as the Americans didn't come into Tucson. Cooke said those terms were unacceptable, that the garrison was to surrender and the town "thrown open to trade and refreshment for his men." [See Note # 2.] But when the terms were inspected back in Tucson they were rejected so the Americans marched forward prepared for battle. On December 17, 1846, the Mormon Battalion took possession of Tucson because the Mexican garrison had abandoned the place, taking many civilians with them. Cooke ordered the stores of food thrown open for his men, many of whom ate so much they became sick.

Cooke described Tucson as resembling Santa Fe in appearance, though not as developed. The people were friendly and came to trade foodstuffs with the soldiers.

On December 18 the Battalion continued its westward trek for there was nothing in Tucson to detain it. Descending the Santa Cruz and Gila Rivers, the Pima villages were reached within four days. The Pima Indians impressed the soldiers because of their kindliness and general habits. On January 7-8, 1847, the Gila-Colorado junction was reached and described as "…a picture of desolation." The Colorado was crossed on January 9 and the Battalion made its way across the desert to Warner's Ranch, suffering severely from thirst, heat, and hunger. On January 29, 1847, the expedition reached San Diego but the fighting in California was already over.

Cooke's route would become known as "Cooke's Wagon Road" and it would be used by thousands of westward bound emigrants.

DISCUSSION NOTES *for* ARIZONA in the MEXICAN WAR

Note # 1
See page 98 in *ARIZONA: THE HISTORY OF A FRONTIER STATE* by Rufus K. Wyllys.
Note # 2
See pages 62-63 in *ARIZONA: A SHORT HISTORY* by Odie B. Faulk.

The Mexican War in CALIFORNIA

For whatever reasons, California has always been entwined with myth and fable. The name itself first appeared in a 1510 (?) Spanish language novel of knight errantry, *Las Sergas de Esplandián* (The Exploits of Esplandián) written by Garcí Rodríguez de Montalvo. In the novel *California* is the name of an island inhabited by tall, bronze colored women referred to as *Amazons* and ruled by a queen named *Calafia*. There are no men on the island but there are pearls and much gold…what more was needed for a paradise on earth? [See Note # 1. *Notes begin on page 307.*]

Into the 19th century coastal California was described as a most beautiful place and, as already mentioned, coveted by visiting Americans like Richard Henry Dana and Thomas Farnham. [See Note # 2.]

It has also been mentioned that in 1842 Commodore Thomas Ap Catesby Jones "seized" Monterey because he thought the Mexican War was already in progress. Commodore Jones sheepishly "gave it back" then sailed away. The peaceful Californios, evidently unable to read the writing on the Manifest Destiny wall, didn't pay much attention to the incident and among the revolutionaries and counter-revolutionaries in Mexico City it apparently caused not a ripple. [See Note # 3.]

MOUNTAIN MEN

Trappers led by **Jedediah Smith** are said to have been the first Americans to "penetrate" California in their quest to acquire furs. These suffering "fourteen ragged, shaggy-bearded, half-starved, half-demented woodsmen from the East" stumbled into Mission San Gabriel on November 27, 1826. [See Note # 4.] Had it not been for the mission these "frontiersmen" might now be considered tragic figures (as are the members of the Donner Party.).

Trappers were not aware of themselves as the vanguard of American civilization and at the time people thought of them mostly as "white savages." Robert G. Cleland has written that the American fur trapper "…affected the destiny of nations, changed the continent's future, and gave future generations of Americans a tradition of heroic exploration comparable to that of the seamen of Elizabeth or the conquistadores of Spain." Robert Utley has written that while mountain men must have loved the "…adventure, freedom, independence, outdoor life, the challenge of hardship and danger…" their main reason for trapping was to make money. [See Note # 5.] The historical record shows that the ragged, suffering men in the Smith expedition went from disaster to disaster while trying to acquire furs in the lower Colorado basin. Like most mountain men, they were mostly unaware of what was happening politically and apparently they didn't leave any journals or diaries, though some mountain men created maps which served others who came later. It is documented history that the California missions and/or settlements enabled Jed Smith and his men to survive. [See Note # 6.] In time Smith and his men were ordered out of California but others followed.

FREMONT

More aware of the power of publicity was **John Charles Frémont** and he was to have a definite influence in California affairs. Frémont has been described as "The Pathfinder," "The Path Follower," an adept social climber, etc. [See Note # 7.] In 1836 prominent Joel Poinsett obtained a surveying assignment for Frémont. [See Note # 8.] Poinsett served as Secretary of War under President Martin Van Buren and the former helped organize (1838) the Army Corps of Topographical Engineers. Poinsett saw to it that Frémont, a civilian, was assigned to the Corps for its first expedition into the country between the upper

Mississippi and Missouri rivers. Frémont later said that the two years he spent working with the Corps and commander Joseph Nicollet were like attending "Yale and Harvard."

While in Washington D.C., Frémont met **Jessie Benton**, the "beautiful and brainy" 15-year-old daughter of Senator Thomas Hart Benton from Missouri. The Senator couldn't stand the handsome but penniless Frémont so Jessie and John Charles married secretly in October of 1841. When the Senator discovered the fact he was furious but in time he acquiesced because he loved his daughter. Benton and other senators pushed through an appropriation of $30,000 to map the Oregon Trail and when Joseph Nicollet couldn't lead it Benton succeeded in naming 29-year-old Frémont as commander. His mission was to "map and promote" the West (1842), in which he succeeded brilliantly. The 207-page report, dictated by Frémont and written by Jessie, was printed by Congress (1843) to the tune of 10,000 copies and widely disseminated. It was a sensation and the American public got the impression that going West was an exciting adventure. It was Frémont's report that also brought fame to guide **Kit Carson**, whom Frémont portrayed as the "Hawkeye of the West" though Kit was all but unknown in his adopted (after fleeing from his native Missouri) Taos, New Mexico. [See Note # 9.]

Another valuable member of Frémont's first expedition was the highly accomplished technician Charles Preuss, a hard working German who knew topographic science. It has been written that Carson did the guiding, Preuss the science, and Frémont "reveled in the glory of command."

Frémont's second expedition for the Topographical Engineers was to continue to the Oregon Territory to complete the monumental work of Charles Wilkes who during 1841-42 had gathered enough material to fill sixteen volumes. While in St. Louis (May, 1844) gathering equipment, Frémont bought to take with the scientific expedition a carriage-mounted howitzer that could fire twelve-pound cannonballs. Kit Carson wouldn't join the expedition until it got to Colorado so Frémont hired Broken Hand Fitzpatrick to guide him through what was basically a well-worn trail. The howitzer was used on buffalo herds when meat was needed. In September the expedition viewed the Great Salt Lake and by November (1844) they arrived in Fort Vancouver (across the Columbia River from present Portland, Oregon).

Frémont's orders were then to return whence he had come but instead he decided to lead his men into Mexican California. It was late November and though the winter was a relatively mild one, the Sierras were covered with snow. The "dauntless Pathfinder" forged ahead anyway, got lost despite having Carson and Fitzpatrick with him, his men suffering from the intense cold and from hunger which caused them to eat the horses. The situation was so bad that the howitzer had to be abandoned. On March 6, 1845, the expedition staggered into Sutter's Fort where everyone rested for three weeks and bought supplies, horses, and mules. They went south down the San Joaquín Valley then east from the Mojave River into Utah, following Jed Smith's old trail, picking up famous guide Joe Walker along the way. Walker guided the expedition across the Rockies to Bent's Fort. From there Frémont returned east across the prairie without getting lost. Back in Washington once again Jessie Frémont set to writing her husband's report and when it was published the 10,000 copies were snapped up immediately by an American public with an insatiable curiosity about the West.

Frémont's third expedition started in the summer of 1845, traveled up the Arkansas River, over the Continental Divide, across western Colorado and eastern Utah, into the Great Basin. Frémont's group went into the Sierra Nevada, crossing into what later would be known as Donner Pass, later uniting with the Joe Walker contingent. This was now a band of some 60 well armed Americans led by an Army officer in Mexico and Mexican authorities, well aware of how Texas had been subverted, ordered Frémont and his men out of California. Frémont protested that he was merely a surveyor but then he led his men to Gavilán Peak, planted the American flag for all to see, and dared the Mexicans to dislodge him. They ignored him but the men realized they would soon run short of supplies so after they days they abandoned the peak and headed for Oregon.

Joe Walker refused to continue with the group and he was later to describe Frémont in most unflattering terms, saying: "…An explorer! I knew more of the unexplored region fifteen years before he set foot on it than he does to this very day."

In Oregon Frémont received a messenger from Marine Lieutenant Archibald Gillespie which caused Frémont to lead his sixty men back to California though he still didn't know that Mexico and the USA were at war. The situation was serious: rumor had it that Governor Castro and the Californios were going to "drive all Americans out of the country, lay waste to their farms, raise the Indians against them, or destroy them altogether." [See Note # 10.]

BEAR FLAGGERS and SONOMA

At this time there occurred what is generally referred to as the "Bear Flag Revolt." On June 10, 1846, a band of well armed American illegal immigrants led by one Ezekiel "Stuttering Zeke" Merritt overtook a few Californio soldiers led by one Lt. Francisco Arce, herding some 170 horses from Sonoma to the Santa Clara Valley. Merritt's group "seized" the horses at gunpoint and told Arce and his men to go tell General Castro about it. [See Note # 11.] The stolen horses were sent to Captain Frémont's camp then the "Spartan band" of "heroes" decided to "surprise the fortress" of Sonoma and neutralize their "multitudinous hosts of enemies."

The Americans rode into "fortress Sonoma," which had no garrison, on the morning of June 14, 1846, while everyone was still sleeping. They surrounded the "Casa Grande" home of Mariano Vallejo and banged on the door with their pistols until a sleepy servant came to see what all the commotion was about. The men were a rather forbidding group to face so early in the morning. He was informed by these "uncouth and even ferocious" looking strangers, some 33 of them, to bring out General Vallejo, that everybody was under arrest. A couple of the men went inside the house. [See Note # 12.]

Wife Francisca Vallejo was very alarmed over the appearance of such rough looking banditti, most of them wearing torn, greasy hunting shirts, coyote-skin caps, and a number of them were barefooted. She begged her husband to escape through the back door but don Mariano said it would not be dignified. So he went out to meet the powder-keg "liberators," mostly because he had always gotten along famously with Americans.

The Vallejo parlor was handsomely furnished with beautiful chairs, sofas, mirrors, mahogany tables, and a beautiful piano, quite a contrast to "white Indians" waiting for him. [See Note # 13.]

Vallejo appeared, in full military uniform, and asked "To what happy circumstances shall I attribute the visit of so many exalted personages?" William Knight did his best at translating while Merritt stammered through the conversation. Vallejo quickly sized up the situation: violent Americans from the

Sacramento valley were trying to force the peaceful pro-American faction in Sonoma into violent action. He suggested that Jacob Leese, an Ohio merchant, might prove valuable in writing up the necessary documents if he was sent for, which was done. Salvador Vallejo and Victor Prudon were then brought into the parlor, under arrest. All three favored setting up California as an American protectorate. When Leese arrived he asked why Vallejo and the others had been "arrested" and the answer was that men wanted an independent California. Documents needed to be written out.

As discussion continued inside Vallejo's home, the men outside got a hold on a cask of brandy and began drinking in the plaza. There was no resistance, no soldiers, no Indians to fight...why not loot the place to make the effort worthwhile? The noise caught the attention of **Robert Semple** who "promised to kill" anyone caught looting. Semple, a six-foot-six illegal immigrant from Kentucky (who was to become California's first English-language newspaper editor and president of the constitutional convention) turned out being one of the main spokesman for this "burst of liberty" in northern California, ably assisted by **William Ide**.

Mariano Vallejo was informed that he and all leaders from Sonoma were now under arrest and required to sign the articles of capitulation before being "escorted" to Sutter's Fort. The genial Vallejo said he would sign the articles of capitulation so Semple and Jacob Leese set about to writing them.

Wine was passed around to everyone in the parlor and soon all except Mariano Vallejo were drinking heavily. Stuttering Zeke told Salvador Vallejo that he would put him in irons. It was now about 8:30 and the men outside complained that they "was hongery" so Vallejo had a beef killed to furnish them breakfast. The men and their horses smelled quite badly but they were served tea with sugar as proper for honored guests.

When John Grigsby went into Vallejo's parlor a couple of hours later he found something of a celebration going on. Merritt was almost asleep from the wine but he invited John to join him in a drink. Grigsby soon became part of the glass-eyed crowd.

The heroes in the plaza now chose William B. Ide, who didn't drink, to go see why the liberators inside were taking so long. Ide quickly saw what the liquor had done but the documents were just about ready for signing. The Bears signed a separate declaration which stated a government would be established on Republican principles, that no one who didn't take up arms would be taken prisoner, and property would not be destroyed or taken "unless necessary for our support."

When the Articles of Capitulation were taken to the freedom fighters outside they shouted their disappointment. They wanted something to show for their efforts and they wanted Vallejo as a prisoner. John Grigsby, not to steady on his feet, went outside to see why the men were yelling. "Have you got authority from Captain Frémont?" he yelled out. No one did but in the confusion there was a renewed call for looting while several exclaimed the revolt was worthless. William Ide then stepped forward, declaring he would leave his bones in this place before he ran like a coward. Was not everybody working for *independence from the treacherous Spaniards?* Then he stated: "We are robbers or we must be conquerors!" The crisis passed but only with the compromise that Vallejo and other leading citizens would be imprisoned at Sutter's Fort until Frémont decided what he wanted done with them. The Bear Flaggers also demanded eighty horses from Vallejo an sixty from Leese. Both complied but when Leese asked that his children's horses not be taken he was refused and told "We go in for good horses." Though an

American, Leese was also later "arrested" and imprisoned at Sutter's Fort,.

The Vallejo family and those of other inoffensive citizens realized they were in tremendous potential danger. The smelly liberators had deadly guns and under the influence of liquor they were capable of anything. Unknown to the Bears, Chief Solano, Vallejo's principal Indian ally, was in the Casa Grande and went undiscovered by the liberators. Solano suggested to Vallejo that once the Bears departed he could form a rescue force to free the Sonomans but the general wanted to avoid bloodshed so he refused the offer. Solano remained to safeguard Doña Francisca and the children after the prisoners were taken by the liberators, who had vowed that anyone trying to notify others of what had transpired "...were liable to be shot."

Casa Grande was searched and all arms and ammunition removed, along with nine cannon, 250 stands of arms, and "tons of copper, shot, and other public property...seized and held in trust for the public benefit." [See Note # 14.]

William B. Ide was left in charge of the group remaining behind at Sonoma and he decided to do some writing on his own to add to that of Semple. After all, the Bear Flag Republic, with its "high and holy aims," was being born and Ide had intended that there would be no taxation on free men, no compulsory military service or for any other service, and everything would be ruled by the people and their inalienable rights. The poorer Californios would be freed from the "peonage of the rancho system" and government would be taken "out of the hands of the leading families." [See Note # 15.] To symbolize the new republic, "plucky" William Todd created a flag when on a cotton cloth, perhaps one of Mrs. Vallejo's petticoats, was drawn, with berry juice, the symbol of the California animal that always "stands his ground:" the bear. Some of the heroes at first thought it was a pig. At the bottom was the inscription *California Republc* (which spelling was later corrected). Despite its artistic merit, the "flag" was hung in the plaza, cheered, and a toast was drunk to a free California.

The "benighted" Californios had to be educated to their new freedoms so Mariano Vallejo and later some 40-50 other "leaders" were taken to jail at Sutter's Fort. William Ide later addressed them on "man's inalienable rights to liberty and equality" as they sat sleepy, impassive, or bewildered in jail, for they had all surrendered to the new "authorities." The "Father of the Bear Flag Republic" told his very captive audience: We have come together to assure you of justice for all, not to rob you of your liberty nor deprive you of your property...as had been done in the past, and they were here only to be informed about true liberty. Resistance would be sheer folly because "We are few but we are firm and true." He spoke in English and most of the Californios understood very little of the grandiose freedoms which would soon be theirs though one "Spaniard" was moved at the mention of the name *Washington*.

When Frémont finally granted Mariano Vallejo an interview the American told the Californio that he was the prisoner of the Bear Flaggers, not the USA. Vallejo stated he had been led to believe that his home had been invaded by the Bears under orders from Frémont. Frémont said the prisoners would have to remain under guard until charges against the Californio government could be straightened out. All went to Sutter's Fort, the prisoners, including Jacob Leese, under guard.

John Sutter was unprepared to see his friends coming into his establishment as prisoners. Frémont ordered Sutter to incarcerate them, Sutter objected, then Frémont informed him that since he was a (naturalized) Mexican citizen it could be arranged to have him join his compatriots.

The four prisoners were given a room too small for four, with no mattresses or blankets, no water, and when a pot of soup was given them there were no utensils. Mariano's brother, Salvador, later wrote that the worst part of the experience was seeing how his brother was treated after years of hospitality to so many American, English, French, and Russian people. The abject ingratitude grieved Salvador greatly.

Sutter tried to make amends by relaxing with the prisoners, sometimes leaving them unguarded or sharing his meals with them, allowing them to stroll outside. When Frémont learned about this treatment he threatened to hang Sutter himself. Mrs. Vallejo wrote a letter to her husband and sent it with Julio Carrillo with a pass signed by Captain John B. Montgomery of the ship *Portsmouth*. Frémont ordered Carrillo imprisoned with Vallejo and the others. Nobody wanted to guard the friendly Californios so Frémont finally had to assign one of his own men, Edward Kern, to guard "the damned greasers" (who wouldn't be freed until August).

Frémont reached Sonoma on June 25, 1846, and organized his men and the Bear Flag rebels into a "motley" group calling itself the *California Battalion*. With the help of military leaders like Commodore Stockton, Sonoma and northern California was put under the American flag after the capture of Monterey on July 7, 1846.

Captain **William Mervine** was at the head of some 250 "marines and seaman" when they landed in Monterey. They took control of the custom's house, raised and cheered the American flag, then Commodore Sloat's proclamation was read: "I declare to the inhabitants of California that although I come in arms with a powerful force I do not come among them as an enemy of California. On the contrary, I come as their best friend, as henceforward California will be a portion of the United States and its peaceful inhabitants will enjoy the same rights and privileges as the citizens of any other portion of that territory…and the same protection will be extended to them as to any other state in the Union…" [See Note # 16.] As per instructions from Washington, Sloat was trying to win over the Californios, not conquer them militarily if he didn't have to. Perhaps he knew that General Castro had scarcely a hundred men under his command, very poorly armed men, who hadn't been paid for their services in a very long time.

On July 15, 1846, Commodore **Robert F. Stockton** arrived in Monterey and replaced Sloat. Stockton pursued a more aggressive policy, stating he would lead his forces inland against the "boasting and abusive chiefs" who refused to acknowledge American domination. He promoted Frémont to the rank of Major and with the "California Battalion of Mounted Riflemen" marched from Sonoma to San Diego looking for the enemy, which was never found, so the American flag was everywhere raised peacefully.

On August 13, 1846, American naval forces sailed into Los Ángeles and raised the American flag without opposition. Captain Archibald Gillespie was put in command of the fifty-man garrison at Los Ángeles and the naval force sailed out of the harbor. The Angelinos hadn't resisted but Gillespie felt he must assert his authority in order to prevent any sort of uprising. According to Josiah Royce, in the eyes of Gillespie and various other naval officers and men, including the California Battalion, especially its Bears, the Californios were "…a boastful and treacherous people, given to murder and pillage, an inferior race, a people to be suspected, to be kept down with a strong arm, and to be reminded constantly of their position as the vanquished." [See Note # 17.] He declared martial law and issued decrees that two Californios could not walk down the street together, that Californios could not hold gatherings in their houses, that all commercial businesses had to close down at sundown. The spark that ignited the people's revolt was the arbitrary arrest of a Californio. Gillespie's small garrison couldn't handle the overwhelming numbers of Californios who had been targeted by Gillespie's oppressive decrees. On September 23, Gillespie's garrison was attacked and totally surrounded on top of an L.A. hill. Gillespie decided to send one John Brown (Juan Flaco: Lean John, said to be the "Paul Revere" of California history) to tell Stockton to bring help before his force was annihilated.

Being thus informed of the revolt, Stockton in Yerba Buena (San Francisco) promised to make quick work of the uprising and its leaders. He had sent Captain Mervine and the ship *Savannah* (Rolle says the ship was the *Vandalia*) to San Pedro then Stockton himself set sail in the *Congress*. The Californios would be taught a lesson in warfare.

Back in Los Ángeles a flag of truce was sent to the Californios and the tyrannical Gillespie and his garrison were permitted to go board an American ship and withdraw. But when Gillespie saw Mervine and his 350 men landing in San Pedro on October 7, 1846, he immediately scraped the truce, joining his men to those of Mervine.

The new expedition quickly set out for Los Ángeles, anxious to cover themselves in military glory. In a skirmish known as the "Battle of the Old Woman's Gun," mounted Californios led by **José Antonio Carrillo** met Mervine's marines with fire from a single cannon, an "antique" four-pounder, and though they had very little powder their shots took a terrible toll on Mervine's men. The "treacherous" Californios always managed to wheel the cannon out of range from American rifles and Mervine decided the best strategy was to lead his marines back to the *Savannah* where the Californios couldn't reach them.

Commodore Stockton arrived at San Pedro but because he was short on supplies he sailed to San Diego where he made camp (November, 1846) and drove off some enemy Californios. Word was then received that General **Stephen Watts Kearny** and his Army of the West were arriving and that it too needed supplies. Gillespie and some 35 mounted soldiers were sent to help Kearny where he was camped in a place called San Pascual (near present-day Escondido). Gillespie reported to Kearny that a force of rebels led by **Andrés Pico** was a few miles distant, that perhaps the general might engage them.

General Kearny had been advised by a number of Americans, including Kit Carson, that the Californios were basically cowards, that they would sooner run than fight. Kearny received with some pleasure the news that Andrés Pico and his insurgents were in the vicinity. Kearny ordered that the rebel position be reconnoitered with special care that the element of surprise not be lost because he wanted to fight the "cowardly" Californios before they ran away.

Before dawn on December 6, 1846, the Army of the West, augmented by Gillespie's men, went in search of the enemy Californios, everyone hoping they would stand and fight instead of run away. Riding two abreast, the Americans were strung out in a long column. Suddenly the Californios were spotted holed up in a ravine. Shots rang out and Captain A.R. Johnston, leading the advance guard, fell dead with a bullet in his head. The mounted Californios now began a hurried retreat and the yelling Americans, including General Kearny, gave chase to cut off their escape. After a quick run of perhaps a mile the Californios wheeled about and met the exuberant Americans with lances leveled for attack.

Because of dazzling horsemanship the Californio lances took a fearsome toll on the Americans who minutes before had been spoiling for a real fight. Almost every American, including General Kearny, was wounded in this battle at San Pascual. Captain Moore, leader of the dragoons, happened across Andrés Pico and gave him a pistol shot which missed. He charged in with his saber but he was lanced several times, unhorsed, and killed.

Because the enemies were so close to each other the battle almost became one of hand-to-hand, the Americans with swords after they couldn't reload, the Californios with lances and their lariats, which they used with great skill to rope their antagonists and drag them to death. Master horsemen, the Californios maneuvered themselves so quickly they were all but immune from the charging Americans. The "mountain men" in the group "narrowly escaped death by their own comrades' hands." The tyrannical Archibald Gillespie was recognized, wounded three times, unhorsed, but "the unstoppable Gillespie managed to make it to the rear" (?) whereupon he helped bring one of the howitzers to the scene of battle. The Californios promptly captured one of the big guns and made off with it. Then the Californios rode away, the Americans not pursuing this time. [See Note # 18.]

In his official report to Washington Kearny claimed a victory at San Pascual (now said to be the largest armed conflict within the borders of California) because the Californios had abandoned the field of battle. To his wife he wrote: "We gained a victory but paid most dearly for it." Casualties were said to be 21 (or 22) killed, many more wounded, each with from two to ten lance thrusts. Fearing that the Californios might renew the attack the next day, Kearny sent away post haste to San Diego for reinforcements. His little army was now described (December 7, 1846) as "the most tattered and ill-fed detachment of men that ever the United States mustered under her colors." The Californios didn't return for another attack so Kearny's survivors were spared.

On November 14, 1846, an action took place at Rancho *La Natividad*. Some 100 of Frémont's men, led by Bluford "Hell Roaring" Thompson and Charles Burroughs met a contingent of Californios led by Joaquín de la Torre. The preliminaries had some fifty American rifles going against Californio muskets but when the fighting moved out of a wooded area into the open the Californio horsemen lured the Americans into a charge then turned and attacked. Several were killed/wounded on each side during the hand-to-hand fighting. American rifle fire caused the Californios to withdraw on their magnificent horses. The pattern was clear: American firepower from a distance would give victory to the Americans but the superb Californio horsemen had the advantage in close-up or hand-to-hand fighting. It was also evident that Californios didn't have modern weapons and that Americans didn't like hand-to-hand fighting.

The Californios had acquitted themselves well from September to December, 1846. They had captured Americans, expelled Gillespie then Mervine, and taken a grim toll at San Pascual and La Natividad. Commodore Stockton would accept no blame for any of these engagements, putting it on his subordinates and referring to San Pascual as an outright defeat. Furthermore, Stockton, Kearny, and Frémont were now at loggerheads as to who was the final American authority in California. While Kearny, recovering from his wounds, had the rank, Stockton had the men and matériel, and Frémont had influence back in Washington. Kearny stated that President Polk's instructions indicated that he would be governor of California. (Stockton would later appoint Frémont to that post.)

Calculating Kearny compiled a careful record for the future (which would include a successful court martial against Frémont).

Californios asked for a truce but Stockton demanded unconditional surrender. Stockton sent his men and Kearny gathered his recruited forces as all prepared to battle the some 500 Californios at the San Gabriel River on January 8, 1847. The marching Americans, formed in a hollow square, could see the Californios' lances and swords glistening in the sun. One group of master horsemen were led by Andres Pico, another by José Antonio Carrillo.

The battle commenced with the artillery exchanging shots, the Californios falling short of the mark due to inferior powder. The Americans charged across the river and on came the superb Californio horsemen. The Americans in the lead dropped to one knee and anchored their pikes or steel-tipped muskets at a forty-five degree angle on the ground, a standard tactic when being charged by cavalry. Then the order to *Fire!* was given and a sheet of flame illuminated the scene, lead and steel stopping the Californio charge and causing them to retreat back up a hill. Kearny ordered "Charge and take the hill!" which the Americans did but the Californio horsemen rode away and the Americans were powerless to catch them. The next day the Californios charged the Americans but were repulsed by heavy gunfire. The Americans then withdrew toward Los Ángeles. The Battle of Los Ángeles (also called the Battle of the Mesa) was ended.

On January 10, 1847, under a flag of truce, the city of Los Ángeles surrendered to American forces "if property and persons would be respected." Stockton accepted and Captain Archibald Gillespie, who had been the cause of losing the town in the first place, hoisted the American flag he had been forced to haul down in September of 1846.

While the Americans were not about to let their guard down, it was felt that everyone now was in favor of peace. Some believed Americans had goaded the Californios with charges of cowardice, precipitating a needless war. It was now obvious that Americans had superior weaponry and firepower while the masterful Californio horsemen could carry on an indefinite guerrilla warfare until all were exterminated. Commodore Stockton's demands of unconditional surrender were too harsh, Kearny was not trustworthy, so the Californios signed the **Treaty of Cahuenga** with John Charles Frémont on January 13, 1847. The treaty specified that public arms (artillery, etc.) would be surrendered, Californios would be permitted to return to their homes and obey the laws of the USA, life and property would be protected by American authorities, Californios could travel anywhere without validating documents, etc., and all would be citizens equal to those in the USA proper. It was a generous agreement. Without authority, Frémont had begun warfare in California and he had ended it in the same way.

Stockton and especially Kearny were livid that a "character" like Frémont had ended the war without their authorization. But the country was at peace and, much to Kearny's chagrin, Stockton wound up appointing Frémont as Governor. In a startling about-face, Frémont pursued a policy of reconciliation toward the Californios, appointing some to serve as advisers, hosting dances in the Californio style, and ingratiating himself to the people.

DISCUSSION NOTES *for* The Mexican War in CALIFORNIA

Note # 1

See pages 38-41 in *Books Of The Brave, Being an Account of Books and of Men in the Spanish Conquest and Settlement of the Sixteenth Century New World* by the powerful Irving A. Leonard. This valuable study shows that the conquistadores who came to the New World were avid readers of books.

Note # 2

How has this motivation been portrayed in the California historical record? Despite its polemical nature, this issue has to be addressed if one is to come to terms with reality. The book *My History, Not Yours* by Genaro M. Padilla elaborates on the issue of Spanish language documents translated into English by various English language writers. A case in point is the work "Occurrences in California" by Angustias de la Guerra Ord translated into English by Francis Price and William Ellison (as *Occurrences in Hispanic California*, published in1956). Dr. Padilla discovered that Angustias wrote: "*La toma del país no nos gustó nada a los Californios, y menos a las mujeres.*" In English this would translate as "The taking of the country [by the USA] didn't at all please the Californios, least of all the women." But the Price/Ellison translation has Angustias saying just the opposite: "*The conquest of California did not bother the Californians, least of all the women.*" Granted that Angustias de la Guerra Ord is not the most influential of historians for California but her mistranslated commentary has been quoted by powerful writers, including David J. Weber in his *Foreigners In Their Native Land*. It is certain that the good Dr. Weber was not trying to skew the historical record for he has spoken up against that malady in his marvelous book of essays titled *Myth And The History Of The Hispanic Southwest*. But all historians must research what has been written and Dr Weber supplies the following caption, evidently based on the Price/Ellison mistranslation, by Angustias' picture in his *FOREIGNERS*: "Some Mexicans resisted United States military occupation of the Southwest, but others probably agreed with Angustias de la Guerra Ord, who said that the conquest '*did not bother the Californians, least of all the women.*' An excerpt from her reminiscences appears in chapter III."

Reaction to this historiography can be a sobering experience. Not only must it be admitted that what we have believed is incorrect, what we were led to believe was a *conscious creation*. At best the mistranslation must now be considered as propaganda, not history, and if such techniques are being used on a relatively inconsequential narrative what does that imply for documentation of supreme importance? Further, one might well ask how much of "American History" is a "conscious creation"? How crucial would be a serious study of *1984* and/or *Animal Farm* by George Orwell?

Note # 3

For a serious study of American expansionist sentiment see *Manifest Destiny: A Study of Nationalist Expansionism in American History* by Albert K. Weinberg. The work brings out the stark truth that most influential Americans of the day honestly believed that God had decreed that all "inferior" races like Indians or Mexicans must be swept aside so that Americans could control the land and its destinies. It was not uncommon for people to say that Canada and Mexico should be taken for the liberty-loving USA, that the entire North American continent should belong to "the America favored by God" because then the land would be "used according to the intentions of the Creator," to quote Senator Benton of Missouri.

Note # 4

See page 118 in *California: A Literary Chronicle* by W. Storrs Lee. Smith's group is touted as having "accomplished the impossible–crossed the continent." As previously pointed out, Alexander Mackenzie crossed the continent in 1793 and the Lewis and Clark expedition did it in 1803-06. Let's not even mention the Coronado and De Soto expeditions of the *1540s*.

Note # 5

See the Prologue in *This Reckless Breed Of Men*, 1950, by R.G. Cleland. Robert M. Utley writes in *A Life Wild And Perilous: Mountain Men and the Paths to the Pacific*, 1997, that "this single generation of frontiersmen" wrote American history as trappers, explorers, discoverers, and expansionists. Is this the "boosterism" identified by Oscar Handlin? Is it a stiff dose of *presentism*? They might be promoted as having "made" history but which of them actually "wrote"? The only one that comes readily to mind is the hilarious J.O. Pattie, who was even "helped" by his editor Timothy Flint, who was certainly no Western frontiersman or pioneer.

Note # 6

Who would actually qualify as a *pioneer*? Smith and his men made it to Sutter's establishment so if they are "pioneers" what is Sutter? And what are the Californios who enabled Sutter?

Note # 7

See pages 156-174 in *The Trailblazers*, 1973, by the Editors of Time-Life Books, text by Bil (sic) Gilbert.

Note # 8

While serving as the first American minister to Mexico, Poinsett "discovered" the Christmas Eve Flower, *Flor de Noche Buena*, used in celebrating Christmas in Mexico. He brought the flower back with him after his tour of duty, calling it the *poinsettia* after himself. The Christmas Eve Flower, known now as the "poinsettia" among mono-cultural people, has since become part of the American Christmas celebration.

Note # 9

It was after the Frémont report that writers of "Dime Novels" used Kit Carson's name as a "heroic Indian killer" in the pulp fiction of the day. Being basically an unassuming type, Carson was disgusted by that fiction, which had no base in reality. Though he later led the American destruction of Navajo society, Kit Carson was never an "Indian killer" and before the Dime Novels he was not famous in New Mexico or anywhere else.

Note # 10

See pages 47-66 in *California: From the Conquest in 1846 to the Second Vigilance Committee in San Francisco* by Josiah Royce.

Note # 11

It is interesting to note that a quick review of this incident as related by some authors doesn't use the word "theft" nor do they focus on the fact that the 170 horses were government property being stolen by a gang of illegal immigrants. Josiah Royce writes that the "Americans *seized* upon the body of horses…" Andrew Rolle states in his *California: A History* (1963, p. 195) that "Merritt and his followers *intercepted* the horses…" David M. Pletcher writes in *The Diplomacy Of Annexation* (1973, p. 431) that "Americans *seized* a band of horses intended for Prefect Castro." Neal Harlow asserts in his *California Conquered* (1982, p. 97) that "the Americans surprised the party and *relieved* them of most of their animals." The incident took place without anyone knowing that war had been declared, so participants couldn't claim a state of war as rationale. So where does use of *seized, intercepted, relieved* put American historiography? What is the value of the historical record as written?

Note # 12

See page 160 in *California: A Literary Chronicle* by W. Storrs Lee.

Note # 13

See page 110 in *General M.G. Vallejo And The Advent Of The Americans* by Alan Rosenus.

Note # 14

See page 116 in the Rosenus volume. Americans of the day believed they could take anything they wished if they determined it was "for the public benefit." How have such motivations/actions been dealt with in American historiography?

Note # 15

See page 107 in *General M.G. Vallejo* by Alan Rosenus.

Note # 16

See pages 197-205 in A.F. Rolle's *California*, 1963.

Note # 17

See pages 147-156 in the Royce *California* volume.

Note # 18

See pages 182-92 in *California Conquered*, 1982, by Neal Harlow. The reader is prepared for the Battle of San Pascual by being told that the Americans "were in search of adventure." Their horses and mules had come all the way from New Mexico and were exhausted. American powder was wet due to a downpour the previous night. There weren't more than 85 men in the American attacking force. The Americans were strung out in a long column. When Kearny ordered a trot Johnston ordered "Charge!" and the dragoons were riding broken down mules. General Kearny was "calm as a clock." Gillespie was a "skilled and dauntless swordsman" who managed to make it to the rear (?) because "his assailant was eager to get away with his fine saddle and bridle."

Timeline: DENOMINATIONAL CHRISTIANITY

Tradition in the Southwest was that the religious would be responsible for Amerindian welfare. The American takeover of the Southwest was to bring with it the introduction of a seemingly myriad of

Christian sects. All claimed to be more properly based on the teachings of Jesus Christ who was cruci-fied under a notification which read "INRI," *Iesus Nazarenus Rex Iudaeorum*, "Jesus of Nazareth, King of the Jews." [See Note # 1 *Notes begin on page 313.*] It would prove difficult for the Indians to decide which religious sect was the most proper belief for their particular welfare. Teaching the basic tenets of Denominational Christianity would prove difficult but it might have been done as presented below.

Jesus of Nazareth gathered about him a group of followers, disciples who came to be known as *apos-tles* (sent ones), who would carry on his work concerning the "kingdom of God, forgiveness, and love." It was the Apostles who actually became the first "church" (from Greek *ekklesia*, church in English), calling their new movement "The Way" because Jesus Christ would lead his people to the Kingdom of God. These first Christians came to believe that the death, burial, and resurrection of Jesus, followed by the coming of the spirit at Pentecost, were divine events. To commemorate their beliefs, baptism and reenactment of the Last Supper with bread and wine became central ceremonies which renewed their covenant with God and with each other. The followers of Jesus were first called Christians (from the Greek *Christianoi*) in Antioch, Syria, at around A.D. 44 and after Jesus himself, Paul (Saul) structured the Christian Faith more than anyone else.

The Roman Empire persecuted Christians until it became Christian itself in A.D. 312. Christianity was removed from places like the catacombs and into palaces. The Church was now referred to as Catholic, i.e., universal, and Christians turned to their bishops for guidance in things spiritual. When the Germanic barbarians of northern Europe destroyed the Roman Empire in the West it was the Catholic Church that created the idea of *Europe* which included leadership roles in Law and the pursuits of knowledge and culture. The unifying concept of *Christendom*, begun under Charlemagne, Europe's greatest medieval king, tended to unite empire and church. The Bishop of Rome gained ascendance over other bishops and came to be addressed as "Pope." By the time of Innocent III (1198-1216) popes were like other world rulers and in time reformers accused them of corruption and demanded changes. These reformers have come to be known as *Protestants* because they *protested* against abuse and corruption in the Church.

Martin Luther is inextricably associated with The Reformation (1517-1648) in which old questions were answered in a new or different way from Catholicism. The questions are/were basically as follows: (1.) How is a person saved? (2.) Who has ultimate religious authority? (3) What is the church? (4.) What is true Christian living? Martin Luther espoused the idea that human beings are saved by their "faith in the merit of Christ's sacrifice." This seemingly innocuous belief was a most serious threat to orthodox Catholicism. If salvation is gained through faith in Christ alone, then priests and bishops are unnecessary. Further, the written/preached Bible requires no monks, no masses, and no prayers to saints. The Church is therefore insignificant because it is *Believers* who are the church. Since Martin Luther stated he didn't have to obey his bishop, Luther was excommunicated but his reforms were the foundation for Lutheranism. German rulers eagerly became Lutherans and took over rich church prop-erties with which they enriched themselves.

Luther translated the New Testament into the German language and liturgy became based on preaching and teaching God's Word instead of celebrating the sacrificial mass. Faith, conscience, and Scripture were the guiding lights to the reformed faith.

There were also problems. Though not sanctioned by Scripture, Luther abandoned celibacy and married Katherine von Bora, a former nun. German peasants also demanded to know where their brutal serfdom was sanctioned in Scripture. If it was not condoned in Scripture why was it so prevalent in society? Luther at first recognized their complaints but when violence erupted he sided with the German princes and nobles who crushed the revolt in 1525 at the cost of some estimated 100,000 lives. (Luther had written a pamphlet in support of the nobles: *Against the Thievish and Murderous Hordes of Peasants*. Many surviving peasants now considered Martin Luther a false prophet and returned to the Catholic Church or sought more radical movements of the Reformation.)

The German Reformation resulted in Evangelical Lutheranism (led by Luther and Melanchthon) and the Reformed Church (John Calvin, Ulrich Zwingli, John Knox). Lutheranism came to America basically from Germany and Scandinavia. At one time there were "150 Lutheran bodies in the U.S. but through consolidation, unification, and federation that number has been reduced to nine." [See Note # 2.]

It has been written that *Protestants* protested against various practices of the Catholic Church. It has also been observed that "protesters" also protested subsequent "protesters" in order to establish their own Christian sects. Following is an approximation of major Denominational Christianity in the Southwest and the USA [See Note # 3.] from which the Indians could choose if they had a choice:

LUTHERAN
American Lutheran
Apostolic Lutheran
Lutheran Brethren
Evangelical Lutheran
Free Lutheran Congregations
Lutheran Church–Missouri
Lutheran Church in America
Protestant Conference (Lutheran)

BAPTIST
American Baptist Association
American Baptist Churches/USA
 Baptist Bible Fellowship, International
Baptist General Conference
Baptist Missionary Association of America
Bethel Ministerial Association
Central Baptist Association
Conservative Baptist Assoc. of America
Baptist Church of Christ
Free Will Baptist
General Assoc. of Regular Baptist Churches.
General Baptist

General Conference of the Evangelical Baptist
Church
Landmark Baptist
National Baptist Convention of America
National Baptist Convention USA
National Missionary Baptist Convention of
America
National Primitive Baptist Convention of the USA
North American Baptist Conference
Primitive Baptist
Progressive National Baptist Convention
Reformed Baptist
Separate Baptists in Christ
Seventh Day Baptist General Conference
Southern Baptist Convention
United Baptist
United Free Will Baptist

BRETHREN
Brethren Church (Ashland)
Brethren in Christ Church
Church of the Brethren
Church of the United Brethren in Christ

Fellowship of Grace Brethren Churches
Old German Baptist Brethren
United Zion Church

CHRISTIAN CHURCH (Stone-Campbell Movement)
Disciples of Christ
Christian Churches and Churches of Christ
Churches of Christ
Christian Church of North America
Christian Congregation
Christian union
Church of Christ (Holiness) USA
Church of Christ, Scientist

CHURCH OF GOD
Church of God, Huntsville, Alabama
Church of God, Original
Church of God, Anderson, Indiana
Church of God, Cleveland, Tennessee
Church of God, Seventh Day
Church of God by Faith
Church of God in Christ
Church of God in Christ (International)
Church of God of Prophecy

EPISCOPAL/ANGLICAN
African Orthodox Church
Anglican Orthodox Church
Episcopal Church
Reformed Episcopal Church

FRIENDS (QUAKER)
Friends General Conference
Friends United Meeting (Five Years Meeting)
Religious Society of Friends (Conservative)

LATTER-DAY SAINTS (MORMON)
Church of Christ (Temple Lot)
Church of Jesus Christ (Bickertonites)

Church of Jesus Christ of Latter-Day Saints
Church of Jesus Christ of Latter-Day Saints (Strangite)
Reorganized Church of Jesus Christ of Latter-Day Saints

MENNONITE
Beachy Amish Mennonite Churches
Church of God in Christ, Mennonite
Conservative Mennonite Conference
Evangelical Mennonite Church
Fellowship of Evangelical Bible Churches
General Conference Mennonite Church
Hutterian Brethren
Mennonite Brethren Churches, General Conference
Mennonite Church
Old Order Amish Church
Old Order (Wisler) Mennonite Church
Reformed Mennonite Church
Unaffiliated Mennonite

METHODIST
African Methodist Episcopal Church
African Methodist Episcopal Zion Church
Christian Methodist Episcopal Church
Congregational Methodist Church
Evangelical Methodist Church
Free Methodist Church of North America
Primitive Methodist Church USA
Reformed Methodist Union Episcopal Church
Southern Methodist Church
Union American Methodist Episcopal Church
United Methodist Church

MORAVIAN
Moravian Church (Unitas Fratrum)
Unity of the Brethren

ORTHODOX (Eastern)

Albanian Orthodox Archdiocese in America
American Carpatho-Russian Orthodox Greek
Catholic Church
Antiochian Orthodox Christian Archdiocese of
North America
Bulgarian Eastern Orthodox Church
Romanian Orthodox Episcopate of America
Russian Orthodox Church
Serbian Eastern Orthodox Church in the USA
and Canada
Syrian Orthodox Church of Antioch
Ukrainian Orthodox Church of the USA

PENTECOSTAL
Assemblies of God, General Council of
Elim Fellowship
Independent Assemblies of God, International
International Pentecostal Church of Christ
Pentecostal Assemblies of the World
Pentecostal Church of God
Pentecostal Free-Will Baptist Church

Pentecostal Holiness Church, International
United Pentecostal Church, International

PRESBYTERIAN
Associate Reformed Presbyterian Church
Bible Presbyterian Church
Cumberland Presbyterian Church
Evangelical Presbyterian Church
Orthodox Presbyterian Church
Presbyterian Church in America
Presbyterian Church USA
Reformed Presbyterian Church of North America
Second Cumberland Presbyterian Church in the
United States

REFORMED
Christian Reformed Church in North America
Hungarian Reformed Church in America
Netherlands Reformed Congregations
Protestant Reformed Churches in America
Reformed Church in America
Reformed Church in the United States

DISCUSSION NOTES *for* DENOMINATIONAL CHRISTIANITY
Note # 1
See *Church History In Plain Language* by Bruce L. Shelley.
Note # 2
See page 177 in *Handbook Of Denominations In The United States* by Frank S. Mead and revised
by Samuel S. Hill.
Note # 3
The Southwest was historically a Roman Catholic area. What kind of impact has been made
by Denominational Christianity? Have the Denominationals focused on Amerindian welfare?
Have there been Denominational missionaries to rival Christian knights like Perea, Kino,
Margil, Serra?

CHAPTER 9

The Civil War in the Southwest

exas was the only area in the Southwest to side with the Confederacy. T.R. Fehrenbach has written that 95% of Texians didn't own any slaves. [See Note # 1. *Notes begin on page 319.*] But slavery was an integral part of the culture and ordinary Texians "feared a Negro insurrection as much as the slave master." Furthermore, white workers didn't want competition from free blacks, "freedmen," and no white Texian entertained notions that Negroes could be considered as equals. To even imply such belief would bring down a charge of "race treason" on the head of anyone with temerity enough to voice it.

The sectional conflict that was looming had the North in the role of crusaders and the South equating Negro slavery with "the American way of life." This left very little room for compromise. Most of the top leaders in Texas, including **Sam Houston**, believed in the Union. Though Houston was born in Virginia, matured in Tennessee, and rose to glory in Texas, he supported slavery and the Constitution but would not condone seceding from the Union.

WITCH HUNT ATMOSPHERE

John Brown raided Harper's Ferry on October 16, 1859 and Southerners now felt the North was conspiring to foment slave insurrections throughout the South. A "witch hunt" mentality began to dominate: anyone who had ever spoken against slavery was suspect and every Negro was seen as ready to rise up and kill whites. A sixty-year old preacher criticized the flogging of black slaves so members of his congregation tied him to a post and gave him seventy lashes, almost killing him. In Palestine, Texas, "dangerous books" were collected and burned in a public bonfire. A white supremacy group known as the Knights of the Golden Circle sprang up across the state. The Knights vowed to make the South safe for slavery and conquer Mexico in order to acquire more land. Vigilante committees were formed everywhere. Paranoia fed on paranoia and anyone who objected was a *traitor*.

SECESSION

Houston ran for the governorship in 1859 and won in a close election. In 1860 Houston came up with a plan to provoke a war with Mexico in order to avert civil war in the USA. He sent Rangers to the Mexican border and worked on securing financing for the expected war. But on November 8, 1860,

Abraham Lincoln was elected President and within a week South Carolina was on the path of secession, seceding as of December 10, 1860. In Texas Sam Houston was pressured to call a convention to declare secession. He fought it but finally had to acquiesce. On February 1, 1861, delegates voted to secede from the Union. Only eight Texians, including **James W. Throckmorton**, voted against secession. Among the "causes" for secession was that people in the North had become unfriendly to the South and "their beneficent, patriarchical system of African slavery, preaching the debasing doctrine of equality with all men, irrespective of race or color." [See Note # 2.] "Southern manhood" would never tolerate such odious, enforced equality. Secession was the only answer and many Southerners believed they could "whip the Yankees in a month." A chivalrous euphoria somehow colored the approaching conflict and few Southerners stopped to consider realities like the differences between the agrarian South and the industrial North. For example, they didn't consider that while Texans and most Southerners were proud of their weapons, all their firearms were manufactured by Yankees in the North.

HOUSTON DEPOSED

Governor Sam Houston was now required to take an oath of allegiance to the Confederacy. He refused, so on March 16, 1861, Houston was deposed, Lt. Gov. William T. Clark being appointed to take his place. While he was willing to turn the ground red with Mexican blood, the great Houston could not fight his United States of America nor could he turn against his beloved Texas. He faded from the scene and died in July of 1863.

It has been written that 90% of Texians "stood by the state" in the Civil War. Between 60,000 and 70,000 Texians were to render service in the war, around two-thirds of males of military age. Many believed the war would be a short one. [See Note # 3.] Texian authorities seized all Federal properties and Rangers under **John S.** (RIP) **Ford** and the **McCulloch** brothers **Ben** and **Henry** provided the militia muscle to keep them.

Stationed in San Antonio, Union Major General **D.E. Twiggs**, from Georgia, wrote to Washington for orders but received none. He had only 160 men in his command so when it was demanded that he turn over all Federal property he complied. His troops were permitted to march to the coast and depart but on April 12, 1861, Ft. Sumter was fired upon and with hostilities commenced the troops were declared to be prisoners of war. Some three million dollars worth of military stores were seized. In May a Texian army pushed into Oklahoma and captured three Federal forts (Arbuckle, Cobb, and Washita), causing Union soldiers to retreat all the way to Kansas. This assured that Texas would not be invaded by ground forces. [See Note # 4.]

Colonel **John R. Baylor** was charged with the defense of western Texas. He would handle the "Indian menace" but the gold fields of Colorado and California beckoned because the Confederacy needed money with which to prosecute the war. Baylor also had personal dreams of empire and the will to make them a reality.

INVASION OF NEW MEXICO

By May 1, 1861, it was rumored that Baylor "...*a fast stepping and energetic Texan if there ever was one.*" had recruited 1,000 "...*rough, tough and determined Texas riflemen...*" for the invasion of New Mexico, which would have to be conquered before the gold fields could be "liberated."

Part of the early Southern euphoria in favor of war was based on the fact that Southerners were among the top military leaders in the Union Army while few Northern generals could compare with men like Robert E. Lee. Most Southerners in the Army would not fight against the South. This became evident in New Mexico. On May 7, 1861, Captain **R.S. Ewell** resigned his Union commission in New Mexico and signed up with the Confederate forces (where he was to achieve the rank of Lieutenant General). On May 13, officers **T.T. Fauntleroy, W.W. Loring, H.H. Sibley** (inventor of the *Sibley tent* and later the *Sibley stove*) resigned their Union commissions and went over to the Confederacy. In June, officers **W.J. Longstreet** and **G.B. Crittenden** resigned their commissions and went over to the Confederacy.

On June 16, 1861, Union Col. Canby ordered Major **Isaac Lynde** to abandon Fort McLane (situated near the Santa Rita copper mines) and remove all government property and his Union command to Fort Fillmore.

On June 23, **Edward R.S. Canby** was appointed to head all military troops in N.M. (As fate would have it, the general of the Confederate army would be **H.H. Sibley,** Canby's brother-in-law.) Troops are disorganized and confused as to loyalties so his first task is to bolster morale because he feels the Confederacy will attack N.M. first in order to strike at the rich gold fields in California and Colorado.

July 1, 1861: Capt. Baylor and some 400 men, the Second Texas Mounted Rifles, reach Fort Bliss and are welcomed to El Paso by, among others, James Magoffin, who felt he had been ill-treated after helping the USA in its conquest of New Mexico during the Mexican War.

July 5: Major Lynde's Union command readies Fort Fillmore and is augmented by three more companies. Because the fort is surrounded by hills he writes to Canby saying the area can't be defended against cannon so Lynde asks for permission to abandon it. In the meantime he takes 380 men and marches to the outskirts of Mesilla where he demands an unconditional surrender of Baylor's invading force. There is a skirmish and Lynde orders a retreat to Fort Fillmore but he is convinced the fort can't be defended against Baylor's artillery so he decides to abandon it and retreat to Fort Stanton, some 154 miles to the northeast. Wagons are quickly loaded with supplies, ammunition, women and children. The departing men hear that kegs of hospital brandy and medicinal whiskey are to be left behind so many partake of the liquor on the spot and *most empty their water canteens and fill them with liquor.*

July 26: Fort Fillmore is evacuated and everyone retreats toward Fort Stanton. Heavy dust clouds inform Baylor of the evacuation so he sends a detachment to take over the abandoned Ft. Fillmore while the main body of his troops speed to intercept the retreating Union forces at San Augustín Pass. Union soldiers (described officially as "...*well disciplined and drilled troops...*") are literally dying of thirst in the July heat because they have had nothing but liquor to drink. They surrender to Baylor's force in exchange for water. Less than 200 Confederates capture nearly 700 Federal soldiers without firing a shot.

Upon hearing of Lynde's surrender to Baylor, troops at Fort Stanton set fire to all government stores and abandon it. A sudden rainstorm puts out the fire so people living in the area help themselves to supplies.

On August 2, 1861, Capt. Baylor issues a proclamation: All of N.M. south of the 34th parallel (the southern half of N.M.) is now the Confederate Territory of Arizona. The dream of a window on the Pacific might now be a reality if the South can win the war. Mesilla is designated the capital and Baylor appoints himself Governor.

August 8: Gen. Canby suspends the writ of habeas corpus throughout N.M. and issues *"an order to enable every commander to guard against the treasonable designs of persons disloyal to the government of the United States..."*

August 17: The Grand Jury of the United States District Court at Santa Fe issues 26 indictments for treason against the Union. Only one person in the group, **Manuel Barelas,** is Hispanic. *Twenty-five indictments are dismissed* but Manuel Barelas is found guilty and all his property is confiscated.

Summer/Fall, 1861: The Territory of N.M. raises five regiments of volunteers, a regiment of militia, a battalion of militia, three independent companies of militia which enlist for three months, as well as four independent cavalry companies enlisted for three months to fight in the Civil War, which in effect was another Texian invasion of New Mexico as in 1841. (Some 3,500 New Mexicans fought for the Union, out of a total population of 50,000, motivating Governor Connelly to pay tribute to a people *"so patriotic in nature"* because they had been with the USA only since 1846 and as yet hadn't even been granted the status of regular citizens in the American Union.)

November 18, 1861: Gen. Canby writes to the Paymaster General in Washington that regular troops hadn't been paid in 12 months and volunteers not at all. He must have money if he is to meet the Confederate threat and hostile Indians who, especially the **Navajos,** are causing much suffering with their depredations. *"Extermination by the sword or by starvation is our only remedy for the evils which they have caused and will continue to cause our people so long as there is one in existence..."*

December 20, 1861: Confederate Gen. **H.H. Sibley** addresses a proclamation to the people of N.M.: *An army under my command enters New Mexico to take possession of it in the name and for the benefit of the Confederate States ... we come as friends ... to liberate ... from the yoke of military despotism erected by usurpers upon the ruins of the former free institutions of the United States. Your persons, your families, and your property shall be secure and safe. All taxes are hereby abolished ... To my old comrades in arms ... drop at once the arms which degrade you into the tools of tyrants, renounce their service, and array yourselves under the colors of justice and freedom...* Sibley had some 2600 men with him, all Texians, and he was very mistaken if he thought New Mexican Hispanos would accept the invasion of their homeland by Texians.

CIVIL WAR BATTLES in NEW MEXICO

February 21, 1862: The Battle of Valverde begins soon after dawn, continuing throughout the day and into the next. [See Note # 5.] Union troops from Fort Craig march out to engage the Confederates, along with a full regiment of New Mexico Volunteers under **Kit Carson**, as well as two companies of Colorado troops, the *Pike's Peakers*. The Río Grande River separates the two armies and Union forces charge across the river as the Confederates open fire. Many Federal soldiers are killed or wounded but Company K makes it across with two 24 pounders and they fire on the Confederate position. The Southerners attack and counter-attack until Canby orders a retreat to Fort Craig, leaving the Confederates victorious in the field. Union officers, especially Gen. Canby, blame the New Mexico Volunteers for the defeat: *"...the battle was fought ... with no assistance from the militia and but little from the volunteers, who would not obey orders or obeyed them too late to be of any service..."* in an effort to get himself off the hook for the loss. [See Note # 6.]

Confederate General Sibley stops in Belén and demands $5,000 and "considerable" numbers of sheep and cattle for his troops from the *rico* **Felipe Chávez**. In return Chávez is given Sibley's IOU, which turns out to be worthless.

March 2, 1862: Confederate forces occupy Albuquerque but Canby has ordered that all government property be put to the torch and only smoking ruins remain when the town is taken without a fight. (Sibley's troops have "lived off the country" in their march from Valverde through Socorro, Peralta, etc., to Albuquerque, taking whatever they wished, causing much hardship among citizens who had something worth "commandeering.")

March 5: Governor Connelly and all Federal troops abandon Santa Fe, fleeing to Fort Union. Col. **Manuel Chaves** is ordered to gather militiamen and join the retreat.

March 23: The Confederates hoist their flag in the Santa Fe plaza without having to fire a shot. Two days later they march eastward intending to attack Fort Union.

March 27: A number of skirmishes take place: at a watering place known as Pigeon's Ranch; at Apache Canyon; at Johnson's Ranch; at Kozlowski's Ranch, amid beautiful mountain country or grassy meadows.

March 28: Scout Manuel Antonio Chaves guides Colorado troops, led by Methodist Preacher **J.M. Chivington** and also **J.P. Slough,** to the Confederate army's supply and ammunition train. The "Pike's Peakers" are guided down the mountain to the rear of the train, Chaves telling Chivington: *"You are right on top of them, Major."* In the distance opposing armies are engaged in the Battle of Glorieta Pass but the surprise move against the supply train captures/destroys all supplies. This turns out being the death blow for Confederate plans in the Southwest, including Baylor's Confederate Arizona.

April 15, 1862: Their supply train destroyed, Sibley's forces retreat to Texas, ending the Civil War in N.M. Conditions in N.M. are now very severe because of the destructive fighting. Confederate and Union forces alike have confiscated, pillaged, stolen, or burned at will if it served their purpose.

INDIAN FRONTIER

Despite Sibley's forced retreat, there was no Union invasion of Texas. The Baylor-Sibley invasion of New Mexico had disastrous results in the long term because now there was no one to hold the Indian frontier. By 1864 Comanche and Kiowa raiders had driven back Texian settlements as far east as Young County. Simply put, Texians couldn't fight the Civil War in the east while at the same time hold on to its western frontier. The biggest Indian battle of the War occurred at Dove Creek when Texians fought a pitched battle against Indians in January of 1865. This was a huge mistake because it turned out the Indians were Kickapoos, not Comanches, moving south out of Oklahoma for freedom in Mexico. They had done no raiding and furthermore were as well armed as the Texians. The Kickapoos mauled the Texian forces, who suffered heavy losses and were forced to retreat.

NAVAL BLOCKADE

The only real Union peril for Texas during the Civil War would come from the coast because the U.S. Navy had the ships and used them for a generally effective blockade. The Union blockade of the Texas coastline caused plantation families to make serious and sometimes painful adjustments. Unlike the

Mexican hacienda, which was basically a self-sufficient entity, the plantation system depended on outside entities for its survival. Cotton was still "king" but corn became more important. Uniforms could be made at in a home setting but that wasn't the case with firearms, which had always been bought from Northern manufacturers. Privations were borne with patriotic cheerfulness. One of the worst was a shortage of medicines, which Union officials placed on the list of contraband and were not permitted past the blockade.

WHITES NOT ATTACKED

Despite the hysteria of "black violence" and the constant specter of a "bloody slave revolt" before the War, there was not a single incident of violence against white Texians while the men were away fighting. Further, not a single white woman or child was assaulted/molested and there were fewer runaways during the War than in previous years.

BITTER REALITIES

By 1863 the early euphoria for war had vanished. Texas credit was now worthless at home and abroad. There was soaring inflation and currency was of no value. Resentment flared over many laws, including exemptions from the draft, which in effect exempted anyone with money enough to pay someone to fight in his place. But if ordinary people resisted their property could be legally confiscated. Martial law could be and was often declared by officials who wanted to show who was boss. Some Texians of German descent, some 65 men and boys led by a man called Tegener, decided to leave Texas for Mexico but they were overtaken on the road and massacred, those who lived to surrender being shot on the spot by order of one Lt. McRae.

"People's Courts" were set up to insure things like patriotism. In Gainesville (Cooke County) some forty men were accused and convicted of "talking against the South." All forty were executed by hanging.

A few champions had the courage to speak up against "lynch law" and other atrocities. **J.W. Throckmorton,** who had spoken passionately against secession, though now the Texian patriot served his beloved Texas as a Brigadier General, heard that another forty men had been sentenced to hanging in Grayson County. Throckmorton rode there and pleaded for "Anglo-Saxon justice," getting the court to liberate all but one.

The end of the tragic Civil War finally came but not before there was one more pitched battle in Texas. The "Cavalry of the West" led by John S. Ford, went into battle against Yankee forces controlling Brownsville. Texians consolidated their victory at Palmito Hill on May 13, 1865. No one knew at the time that General Lee had surrendered at Appomattox more than a month before. Like the Confederacy itself, all had been for naught except the patriotism, perhaps still best exemplified by Sam Houston, instilled by a love for Texas. [See Note # 7.]

DISCUSSION NOTES *for* CIVIL WAR in the SOUTHWEST
Note # 1
See "Part IV: The Confederacy and the Conquered" in *LONE STAR* by T.R. Fehrenbach.

See also Chapter 12 in *An Empire For Slavery: The Peculiar Institution In Texas, 1821-1865*, by Randolph B. Campbell.

Note # 2

Texian society was a product of the American South and these attitudes must be understood as basic attitudes of Southern culture, not of the West. Virginian Thomas Jefferson, who stated in the Preamble to the Constitution that "all men are created equal," was a slave master. Further, he fathered children with Sally Hemmings, herself the daughter of his father-in-law, John Wayles, a white slave master, and his black female slave. Whites fathering children with black females was common in the South, perhaps one of the "privileges" of being a slave master? Further, racial mixing has not been something that merely existed centuries ago. Strom Thurmond, the avowed segregationist Senator from South Carolina, had a daughter with his family's black maid. (To his credit, he supported his daughter with necessary expense money, though her existence wasn't revealed to the public until after Senator Thurmond's death.)

Note # 3

This was a grievous error for the American Civil War was one of the most brutal and sanguine on record, outdoing its precursor, the Mexican War, overwhelmingly. Union generals realized that the North had a much larger population so the brutal strategy, euphemistically presented as a "war of attrition," was to throw large armies into the field and let them annihilate each other because the South would run out of soldiers first. It has been written that perhaps 300,000 Northerners fell in battle while some 200,000 Southerners died in combat. A third of all Texian males were killed or incapacitated by wounds. It has been said that had there been no Mexican War over Texas, compromises might have been worked out during the era of sectional conflict.

Note # 4

See pages 183-98 in *Texas: The Lone Star State* by Rupert Norval Richardson.

Note # 5

See pages 145-49 in *New Mexico: A History* by Marc Simmons.

Note # 6

A.A. Hayes later wrote that Valverde was lost by mismanagement at the command level. J.W Ellis, a member of K Company in the battle, wrote that Canby had lost the battle by ordering a retreat. W.W. Mills also verified later that the fight went well for the Union until General Canby appeared on the scene. The "Mexicans" were branded as cowards or deserters despite their high casualty rates "...*always from Anglo pens--while conveniently overlooking any shortcomings exhibited by the Anglo soldiers...*" according to Jacqueline D. Meketa, author of *Legacy Of Honor: The Life Of Rafael Chacón, A Nineteen Century New Mexican.*

Note # 7

See Chapter 10 in *Texas: A Bicentennial History* by Joe B. Frantz. The author calls this chapter "The Tagalong Confederate." In it Frantz quotes Sam Houston upon leaving the Senate: Let my tombstone read: "He loved his country, he was a patriot; he was devoted to the Union....it shall be preserved."

Indian Affairs In The American Southwest

Indian Affairs in the American Southwest will be presented in the sequence of statehood. [See Note # 1. *Notes begin on page 328.*]

TEXAS

Texas was the first area in the Southwest to become part of the American Union and the first to have to address the "Indian Problem" on its frontiers as "Texians" then "Americans." [See Note # 2.] Few writers of Texas history give much time or energy to Indians in Texas but W.W. Newcomb, Jr. is an exception. [See Note # 3.] According to Dr Newcomb, Texas Indian policy promoted by the "white man" revolved around two choices for Native Americans: exile or extermination. [See Note # 4.] Dr. Newcomb also states that the Texas Indians were "exterminated or brought to the brink of oblivion by Spaniards, Mexicans, Texans, and Americans." [See Note # 5.] It is also stated that Indians fought other Indians in Texas into oblivion, cultural and otherwise, as for example Comanches against Apaches. A brief synopsis is provided below for the major groups of Texas Amerindians.

JUMANOS

The Jumano Indians are an example of groups that were absorbed by other Amerindians, specifically the Apaches, and henceforth known to Hispanics as *los Apaches Jumanos*. [See Note # 6.] Little is known about them, though it has been written that they were a pioneering people living to the east of the New Mexican pueblos. Their settlements might have been successful in prehistoric times and they might have had a rich, varied ceremonial and social life. Their native land was already arid so when drought struck it was a death blow, causing most to move away. It is possible they became bison hunters when their agricultural fields could not produce due to lack of water.

KARAKAWAS

The Karakawas, often referred to as "Cronks," more than any other Texas group tried to hold on to their way of life. They preferred their own gods, their own foods, and their own customs to the "blessings of civilization." They had no champions so they were exterminated by the Texans by around 1858.

LIPAN APACHES

The Lipans were the conquerors of the southern plains during the 17th century. They were hunters as well as gardeners until they were dispossessed by Comanches. They were greatly reduced in numbers and often attacked by the Comanches. They were basically friendly with the Texans. Head Chief Flacco was said to be a good friend of Sam Houston but in time these Apaches "became the skulking, beggarly riffraff of the Texas frontier." [See Note # 7.]

TONKAWAS

The Tonkawas were never a direct threat to the existence of Texas. Texans tried to get them to move away from the coastal areas during the 1820s but they were generally friendly and closely allied to English-speaking Texans, for whom they often served as scouts, even when the Texans were fighting other Indians. Amerindians additionally despised the Tonkawas because at one time they had been practicing cannibals. Under the authority of Sam Houston the Tonkawas were permitted to blend with the Lipan Apaches. [See Note # 8.]

CADDO

The Caddo people of east Texas were basically friendly people, also greatly reduced in numbers. Two centuries before Americans started coming into Texas the Caddoes had been a numerous, powerful people, products of a rich, theocratic society. It has been written that epidemics, not wars, caused the Caddoes to decline. By the time Americans came into Texas they hardly noticed Caddo existence.

WICHITA

The Wichita groups (Wacos, Tawakonis, etc.) were still warlike and allied to the Comanches. They were excellent farmers but they also hunted bison. They indulged heavily in tattooing their skin. While they were friends with various Comanche bands they were also close to the southeastern Caddoes.

KIOWAS

The Kiowa and Kiowa Apaches were also fearless warriors but their numbers were small. While they were allies of the Comanches they were not particularly active in Texas except along the outlying frontier.

EXILE or EXTERMINATION

Dr. Walter P. Webb has written that the "Bloody Years" of Texas Indian history were 1858-59. [See Note # 9.] In 1858 **John S. "Rip" Ford** was placed in command of all state forces with orders to subdue any hostile Indians. Some 1,100 friendly Indians were making a life for themselves in the Brazos Reserve reservation, farming and becoming "civilized." Ford waged war against Comanches and Indians from the Brazos Reserve were staunch allies who rendered "good and honorable service" to Texas. But rumors soon got started that the Reserve Indians were secretly conducting raids against the settlements and that the Indians would have to be driven from Texas or be exterminated.

Major **Robert S. Neighbors** defended the Indians against Texan wrath. But some Texans would not be satisfied until their demand was met that no Indians be permitted to live in Texas. When depredations occurred, the Reserve Indians were blamed and the public began to give credence to the charges. Two days after Christmas, 1858, some Texans led by Peter Garland stole into a sleeping camp of Caddos and Anadarkos, shooting everybody as they slept, killing four men and three women. Captain Ford was advised as to the situation but he refused to arrest the murderers, saying he was a military, not a civil official.

Indians in the Brazos Reserve realized they were being targeted by Texans who coveted their lands. John R. Baylor was among those who filled the frontier with rumors of Indian perfidy. He vowed he would destroy every single Indian, no matter the cost. On May 23, 1859, Baylor's men fought with the Reserve Indians.

On June 11, 1859, the order came for all Indians to remove themselves from the Brazos Reserve. They had been loyal to Texas by fighting its frontier enemies, by walking the "white man's road" in their farming, and now they had no choice but to pack up their goods and set out toward the Red River. It was either that or be killed because henceforth no Indian could have legal residence in Texas. As Dr. Webb has written: "No Indian had any business in Texas. If he came now it was at his own peril and it was the duty of any Texan to kill him…"

Major Neighbors wrote to his wife: "I have this day crossed all the Indians out of the heathen land of Texas and am now out of the land of the Philistines." When the paladin Robert S. Neighbors returned to Texas, stopping at Ft. Belknap, he was shot in the back by one Ed Cornett, a man Neighbors did not know. "Indian hating" included anyone who championed Indians.

COMANCHES

The various autonomous Comanche groups were a genuine power in Texas and Texans came to regard them with hatred and terror because they were strong enough to refuse to relinquish their freedoms and independence. [See Note # 10.] Comanches were the heralded warriors of the plains and capable of extreme courage. Every male was a warrior with little fear of death, at home in the plains country, the trail, or the war path. Comanches were master horsemen, vastly superior to their Texan enemies. Even after the Texans began using the Colt revolvers the Comanches on horseback were capable of confronting such superior firepower.

PARKER'S FORT

Comanches accused a man named Parker of stealing Comanche horses in 1836. In May a large party of Comanches and allied Kiowas attacked Parker's Fort, some seventy miles east of Waco, killed various people and took five captives. Among the captives was Rachel Plummer, who later wrote about her experiences as a captive. Another captive was nine-year-old Cynthia Ann Parker, who lived as a Comanche for some twenty-four years and was the mother of the great Chief Quanah Parker.

PEACE EFFORTS

In 1838 some 150 warriors went into San Antonio in an effort to establish peace with the Texans. A council was held but the Comanches demanded that a boundary line be established between "The People" and the Texans coming into Comanche territory. No one had the authority to make such a promise so the council was ended.

In 1838 when Mirabeau Lamar became president the policy was to "defeat, expel, or exterminate" all Indians in Texas. On February 15, 1839, Texans surprised an unsuspecting Comanche encampment near the mouth of the San Saba River. A number of Indians were killed but when warriors rushed to the rescue the Texans withdrew.

In the spring of 1839 a party of Rangers led by Captain Bird attacked Comanches on the Little River, tributary of the Brazos River in central Texas. The Texans charged into the Comanches but couldn't catch them when they fled. Seven Rangers, including Captain Bird, were killed before the Comanches withdrew, the brisk little fight ending at nightfall.

CHEROKEES

The first group of Cherokees arrived in Texas in 1822 when it was Mexican territory. As of August 15, 1831, the Cherokees were legal residents of Texas, Mexico, and owners of a specified tract of land. [See Note # 11.] In the empresario grant made later to David G. Burnet, Cherokee lands were specifically exempted from the Burnet grant. In 1835 Texan leaders of what was to be the Texas Revolution verified that Cherokees were in legal possession of Texas Cherokee land. But in 1838 Mirabeau Lamar became president and no promise to an Indian was binding on him. He ordered Colonel Burleson to be ready to enter Cherokee territory upon notification, orders which were also given to other military units. In 1839 "peace commissioners" were sent in to inform the Cherokees that they must leave their land and settlements in Texas. They would be paid for improvements, but not the land, which belonged to the Texas Republic. The Indians could go join their brethren in Arkansas. Cherokee Chief Bowles told the commissioners his people would not heed such advice because Texas was their home, legally and emotionally. Talks ended on July 15 and General Douglas was ordered to commence military action against the "savages." There was a fight the next day in which Chief Bowles was brutally slain. The retreating Cherokees were followed and the several villages along the trail were burned to the ground and cornfields were cut down. Cherokee land was marvelously productive and it would be now be owned by Texans. [See Note # 12.] The Cherokees were driven out of Texas in 1839 as their tribesmen had been herded out of the USA just a few years before.

COUNCIL HOUSE MASSACRE

On January 9, 1840, three Comanche chiefs rode into San Antonio under a flag of truce. They were directed to Texas Ranger Henry W. Karnes where they spoke for peace between Comanches and Texans. Karnes told them that before any peace treaty could be signed the Comanches would have to bring in all their white prisoners. The Comanches agreed and would return within twenty days to make the treaty.

Karnes immediately wrote a letter to the Texas Secretary of War, General Albert S. Johnston, alerting him as to what was happening, also saying that he could put no faith in any Indian promise. He didn't keep the Indians hostage because they were too few in number but he urged that peace commissioners be sent along with a strong body of troops for protection as well as provide a way to take all visiting Comanches hostage if necessary. President Lamar sent in three companies of infantry under Lt. Col. William S. Fisher.

On March 19, 1840, Comanche runners came in to announce the arrival of some twelve chieftains, along with numerous warriors, women, and children. The chiefs were taken to the Council House and the rest of the Comanches lounged outside. The chiefs were asked why they had brought in only one captive (a little girl named Matilda Lockhart; the Mexican captive, a little boy, "did not count," according to T.R. Fehrenbach) and one Muk-war-rah replied that's all they had at the time, that others were with other bands. Soldiers were then brought into the room and the chiefs were informed they would be held prisoners until all white captives were delivered up. If the Texans thought they could intimidate Comanches they were dead wrong. One chieftain, probably realizing that a trap had been laid, bolted for the door and when a soldier blocked his way, stabbed the Texan. The soldiers started shooting and the Comanches fought back with knives or their bows and arrows. The fight now spilled out into the yard but the Comanches didn't have a chance because the Texans were waiting for them. Some thirty-five Comanches were slaughtered, which included all the chieftains, three women, and two children. Twenty-seven were captured, over a hundred horses and large quantities of buffalo robes and various peltries were taken by the Texans, who lost some seven killed and eight wounded. One Comanche woman was put on a horse and released to return to her people to let them know that they must keep their word to return white hostages or they would suffer the consequences at the hands of Texans, which included the execution of all remaining hostages. The Texans didn't realize that they had just begun a war that would take nearly forty years to play out.

The Comanches retreated far out into the plains and were not heard of, the Texans believing the "savages" had been taught a lesson at San Antonio. Nothing happened until some 300 warriors rode to the outskirts of San Antonio but remained behind when Chief Isimanica rode into town with just one warrior at his side. At the plaza he stopped in front of Black's saloon and challenged anyone inside to come out and fight. Someone said that soldiers were at San José Mission if he wanted a fight. He rode there but the soldiers under Captain Read were not permitted to fight because they were observing a truce. The warriors rode off in disgust. Infuriated, one Captain Lysander Wells later called Read a coward which resulted in a duel in which both men died.

LINNVILLE

On August 8, 1840, hundreds of Comanches led by Chief Potsanaquahip, perhaps as many as 4-500, attacked the coastal town of Linnville, the seaport for San Antonio on Lavaca Bay. For some unexplained reason they weren't noticed until they were about two miles from town. They charged into town in a half-circle formation in order to surround the whole place. The Texans were so completely surprised they didn't even try to fight back, running to boats that were in the harbor, thus sailing out of Comanche reach. The Indians literally controlled the whole town, looting at will, then methodically burning buildings. The Texans watched from the safety of the sea and no effort was made to counter-attack. The

Comanches killed some 20-25 people and throughout the day loaded their some 2-3,000 horses and mules with all the plunder they could carry. They departed at nightfall and the Texans returned to their ruined town of Linnville.

It turned out that the invading Comanches had been spotted before Linnville and Rangers like Ben McCulloch and Adam Zumwalt and Indian fighters like John J. Tumlinson were on the march against the marauders.[See Note # 13.]

The Texans led by Tumlinson and McCulloch, some 125 well armed men, met the Comanches on August 9, the day after the sacking of Linnville, but they hesitated in taking on such a large group so the Comanches got away from the vicinity of Victoria.

Another group led by Lafayette Ward, Captain Matthew Caldwell, Captain James Bird, Ben McCulloch, General Felix Huston, Edward Burleson, decided to attack the Indians at Plum Creek where the Texans had brush to conceal them. By the time the Comanches saw the hated Texans it was too late to escape so they immediately formed for battle. As a preliminary, which was a cover to enable the huge horse herd to get away, some of the Comanches began curveting about in a display of horsemanship and some of the Texans, not to be outdone, did the same. A chieftain with a huge war bonnet came within rifle range and was felled by a Texan marksman and the battle began (August 12, 1840) in all its frontier fury. The Comanche horse herd stampeded and the warriors scampered away for their lives. When the smoke finally cleared it was estimated that from 60 to 80 Indians had been killed. Only one Texan was reported killed. [See Note # 14.] The Comanches never again attacked a Texas town.

ADOBE WALLS (First Battle)

The command led by Christopher "Kit" Carson reached the area of Mule Spring in the Texas Panhandle on October 24, 1864. Its purpose was to chastise the Comanches, Kiowas, and Cheyennes for depredations against American ranches and settlements. The Santa Fe Trail also had to be protected for it had become the lifeline to the West. Scouts reported a large Indian encampment some ten miles away and the soldiers marched in that direction. The Indian village turned out being some 150 lodges made of whitened buffalo skins. The Kiowa warriors put up a stiff resistance then withdrew down the Canadian River to a place near an old adobe building known as Adobe Walls, possibly the first trading post in the Texas panhandle, built then later abandoned by William Bent because he had no success in the Comanche trade. [See Note # 15.]

The soldiers corralled their horses in the Adobe Walls ruins while the Indians waited for reinforcements, which came to be hundreds of warriors, possibly as many as a thousand for a mile away there was a huge Indian village of some 500 lodges. The Indians made a charge but the mountain howitzers stopped them in their tracks. They had to reorganize but more and more Indians began appearing in the horizon. Carson was quickly finding himself in desperate straits. What if his supply train coming from Mule Spring was captured? Finally he issued the order to retreat toward Mule Spring in an effort to link up with the supply train. The Indians attacked from all sides, finally setting fire to the grass over which the soldiers were headed. The howitzers were once again used to disperse the attackers. Carson made it back to the Kiowa village just before sunset. The Kiowas were by then trying to load up their property to escape its destruction. The howitzers were fired into the village, causing the Indians to flee. The soldiers then helped themselves to whatever they wanted for there were many furs and much food, it being the Kiowas winter camp. Then the whole camp was put to the torch. After destroying the camp Carson's soldiers went out in search of the supply train which was located within a few hours, the Indians in full view but not attacking, probably due to the howitzers. The expedition headed back to Ft. Bascom on November 27, 1864, and got there without further incident. Disaster had narrowly been avoided, mostly because of dexterous use of the mountain howitzers and their explosive shells. While this winter expedition against "hostile" Indians didn't punish them as General Carleton of New Mexico had hoped, it did reduce the number of raids on wagon trains along the Santa Fe Trail. As was relatively common on the frontier, various bands of Comanches, Kiowas, and Apaches had signed a peace treaty with the USA, before the first battle of Adobe Walls. Neither Carson nor the Indians knew about the treaty which required that the Indians "…cease all acts of violence or injury to the frontier settlements, and to travelers on the Santa Fe road, or other lines of travel, and to remain at peace."

ADOBE WALLS (Second Battle)

It had been rumored that Indians would attack Adobe Walls on June 27, 1874. The fact that the Medicine Lodge Treaty (1867) guaranteed that no Americans would be permitted to go into Indian territory and slaughter the buffalo made no difference to hide men like Wright Mooar and John Webb. They went to Ft. Dodge and spoke with commandant Col. Richard I. Dodge, finally asking him point blank what the Army would do if they went into Texas for buffalo. Dodge replied: "Boys, if I were a buffalo hunter I would hunt where the buffalo are." [See Note # 16.] In the spring of 1874 the hunters loaded their wagons and set out for Texas. There soon followed a trader named A.C. Myers, a blacksmith named Tom O'Keefe, saloon-keeper Jim Hanrahan, trader and buyer Charlie Rath, and William Olds with his wife were to open a little restaurant.

The little settlement of sod and log houses was built on the Canadian River (in what is now Hutchinson County, Texas) about a mile from the old Adobe Walls. The illegal settlement became the center for the hidemen's wanton slaughter of buffalo, taking only the hides and tongues, leaving the rest to rot. To the Indians this was a criminal act.

The Indians decided to "rub out" the Americans at Adobe Walls. Between 5- to 700 hundred descended on the settlement at dawn on June 27, 1874. The brothers Shadler, Ike and Shorty, two freighters who had just brought in supplies and were leaving in the morning, were the first casualties of the Indian charge. Remaining were 27 defenders, one a woman, at Adobe Walls. Surprised at first, the Americans fought back and their superior weaponry drove the Indians back. Courageously, the Indians dashed in only to be shot by powerful guns from protected emplacements. A siege was now necessary but the native plainsmen soon wearied of it and began drifting away. By July 2, only four Americans had been killed, one in an accident, but the decision was made to abandon the settlement and everybody hightailed it back to Dodge City. [See Note # 17.]

PALO DURO CANYON

The Kwahadi Comanches had been able to maintain their independence on the *Llano Estacado*, the "Palisaded Plains," generally mistranslated as "Staked Plains." [See Note # 18.] The Kwahadis continued to live their lives on the plains while most other Indians had been forced onto reservations. In September of 1874 they had made their winter camp in Palo Duro Canyon, protected from wintery blasts so common on the plains. But on September 28 Colonel Ranald Mackenzie led his 450 soldiers (4th Cavalry) toward the sleeping encampment and got halfway down the trail before being sighted. The Comanches were taken by such surprise that they didn't attack while the soldiers were strung out along the trail leading to the canyon floor. Instead they fled in panic, abandoning all their possessions, including their large horse herd. Too late the warriors began to fight back but by then the soldiers were in the camp, setting it to the torch. Great bonfires were fed by robes, tanned hides, dried meat, etc., nothing being spared, the soldiers' weapons keeping the warriors away. The Comanche horse herd was next: Mackenzie gave the order to shoot the some 1,400 horses and mules so the Indians couldn't recapture them. The entire herd of panicked animals was methodically and ruthlessly shot down. With all their possessions destroyed, the Kwahadis now had no choice but to surrender or starve to death. In October they started going into Ft. Sill to surrender to the American Government.

DISCUSSION NOTES *for* TEXAS INDIAN AFFAIRS

Note # 1

Since the European-based Southwest was Hispanic beginning as of 1598, it is only natural that comparative history will play a role in understanding the Southwest as it exists today. The Notes sections will contain comparative history perspectives.

Note # 2

While it is understood that Texians formed their own independent Republic before American statehood in 1845, Texians were transplanted Americans who held typical American views concerning Indians. Being in Texas didn't change basic American attitudes toward Amerindians. Personality of Texian leaders was also a huge factor on the Texas frontier. Sam Houston, (technically the second) President of the Texas Republic (1836-38, and then again from 1841-44; after statehood he was Governor from 1859-61 until he was deposed for refusing to side with the Confederacy) was a rarity on the American frontier: he didn't hate Indians. Indeed, he went a long way in understanding the Amerindian mind and while president sincerely cared about Indian welfare. (It must be remembered that this was in the time when Texans referred to Indians as "red niggers.") The man who followed him in the presidency, Mirabeau B. Lamar (1838-41), was an avowed Indian hater who thought of Indians as "trespassing vermin," ran up a bill of $2,552,319 for "Indian Affairs," a huge sum in those days even for extermination of Indians. One of the first accomplishments of Houston's second term (1841-44) was a reversal of Lamar's Indian policy and he was to spend only $94,092 in the same department during his second term.

Note # 3

See *The Indians Of Texas: From Prehistoric To Modern Times* by W.W. Newcomb, Jr. See especially his Chapter 13.

Note # 4

The use of "white man" is an oblique or disingenuous circumlocution commonly used in American historiography. It enables the writer to avoid using "American" or in this case, "Texan." Atrocities against Indians are thus presented as perpetuated by a nondescript "white man." This historiographical pattern appears to be reserved for use basically when English-speaking people are involved.

Note # 5

Spaniards created the mission system, typically referred to as a failure by various Texas writers, in an effort to promote Native American welfare. Mexico gave citizenship to Indians who accepted Mexican suzerainty but was not in existence long enough in Texas to promote "extermination or oblivion." Is the text "extermination" commentary above a rationalization of "heroes and villains" historiography?

Note # 6

Dr. Newcomb says on page 335 of his book that "exposed to Hispanic civilization…" by the 19th century "the Jumanos, as we have seen, had been exterminated." On page 233 he states that between 1693 until after 1715 the Spaniards had no contact with the Jumanos and that the Jumanos had been absorbed by the Apaches. So where did the "extermination" take place or is this a strategy?

Note # 7

See page 131 in the Newcomb volume.

Note # 8

Newcomb writes on page 153 that the Tonkawas had been "mission-weakened." Would it be interesting to compare Spanish mission Indian policy with Texas Indian policy?

Note # 9

See Chapter 8 in his *The Texas Rangers*.

Note # 10

There is much literature on Comanches. To start off with see *The Comanches: Lords Of The South Plains* by Ernest Wallace and E. Adamson Hoebel; *Los Comanches: The Horse People, 1751-1845* by Stanley Noyes. For Comanches as little more than "brutal barbarians" see *The Texas Rangers: A Century Of Frontier Defense* by Walter Prescott Webb.

Note # 11

See page 264 in *History Of Texas* by H. Yoakum.

Note # 12

On page 272 Yoakum gives the reader a quote to describe the situation: "Perhaps the excuse offered by Cicero…is the best for us—that 'no people have a right to the soil who do not know the use of it.'"

Note # 13

See pages 55-63 in *The Texas Rangers* by W.P. Webb. The popular *Texas* history by R. N Richardson hardly mentions the Council House Massacre or the attack on Linnville. Further, Texas historians appear to project that no matter what the provocation, Indians were the "savages." There appears to be little sympathy in Texas historiography for the Amerindian, unless the Spanish period is being studied. What are the historiographical implications for such an observation?

Note # 14

War casualties are always reported by the victorious side.

Note # 15

See pages 102-07 written by Lawrence V. Compton in *Great Western Indian Fights* by Members of the Potomac Corral of the Westerners, University of Nebraska Press, 1960.

Note # 16

See page 183 in *The Long Death*, 1964, by Ralph K. Andrist. The author also points out that most American military officers, especially Sherman and Sheridan, believed that the quickest way to defeat the plains Indians was to exterminate the buffalo.

Note # 17

It is obvious that Americans respected no treaty made with Indians. Senator Ben N. Campbell from Colorado once wrote that the USA had made some 472 treaties with Indian groups and never kept a single one. Was the real purpose to force Indians into desperate situations so they would retaliate then the Military would have an excuse to exterminate them?

Note # 18

Popular myth has it that Spanish explorers put down stakes at various intervals to use as guideposts for the return journey. Common sense dictates that thousands if not hundreds of thousands of wooden stakes would have been necessary while journeying on the plains from Texas to Kansas, for example. Where would they have obtained the wood to make stakes? How would they have carried so many? From how far away could you find a stake driven into the plain? This nonsensical fable is due to a mistranslation of *llano estacado*, which means *palisaded* or *stockaded plains* because the tablelands in the far distance appeared to the Spanish to be stockaded or palisaded villages. But the "Staked Plains" mistranslation continues to this day.

CALIFORNIA

Robert F. Heizer has written that in California in 1846-48, the years of the Mexican War, there were some 100,000 Indians living in what was to be called the *Golden State*. He goes on to assert that between 1848 and 1870 around 50,000 California Indians "died." "Homicide…starvation…disease." are among the listed causes of death. [See Note # 1. *Notes begin on page 342.*]

The authorities offered eighteen (18) treaties to the California Indians during the years 1851-52 but Congress refused to ratify any of them, in effect leaving the Indians to the mercies of the State and people of California. Dr. Heizer points out that in 1850 the California legislature authorized the indenture of Indians, "a thinly disguised substitute for slavery—or the common practice of kidnapping Indian children and women, and openly selling them as servants." [See Note # 2.] Further, no Indian could testify against a white person in any American California court.

In 1853 some reservations were established but they failed because the Indians were inadequately supplied with food, clothing, housing, etc., and no protection was given them against American "settlers" who wanted Indian land. It has been said that "Indian Agents" in charge of the reservations were often so corrupt that money appropriated by Congress was rarely spent on the Indians. [See Note # 3.] Dr. Heizer asks: "Were there no champions of the Indians…?" Then he goes on to supply primary documentation like the following:

March 13, 1847: Fort Sacramento

George McKinstry, Sheriff of the Sacramento District, writes to Captain I.G. Hall, Commander of the Northern District of California, that Captain J.A. Sutter has a strong, effective Indian garrison, which he pays out of his own pocket, for protection against the "half-civilized Californians and the savage Indians…" but now he looks to the flag of the USA for protection. Americans are trying to bring in liquor for the Indians, something never done by Sutter.

March 17, 1847: Sonoma

George W. Harrison writes to Captain DuPont that recent "Indian difficulties" were caused by the "whites" because they "stormed the village and tried to take some of the Indians into servitude."

April 11, 1847: Los Ángeles

Col. R.B. Mason writes to don Manuel Arquisola asking that he require "one or two good men from each ranch" to join U.S. troops for an expedition against the "horse stealing Indians, repel their invasion…and pursue and destroy them."

July, 1847

Captain H.A. Naglee writes to Col. R.B. Mason that a decree is needed to prohibit "all persons from trespassing upon the Indians." Various "persons" are going into the villages, causing difficulties, get run out, then they "hasten to the settlements" to get friends to help them against Indian savagery. This is going to cause an Indian war if it isn't stopped.

May 16, 1850: Cantonment Far West

Captain H. Day writes to the Assistant Adjutant General that about ten "white men" made an unprovoked attack on an Indian camp for supposedly stealing/killing their cattle. Two Indians were killed and the next day the missing cattle were found. Indians then attacked two brothers, Samuel and George Holt, killing Samuel and severely wounding George. The Holts had always been friendly to the Indians but evidently the Indians held all "white men" guilty for what was happening to them. Miners have taken over the valley without caring that it is Indian Territory. Miners believe Indians must "discontinue their thieving and submit with a better grace to being shot down…"

June 1, 1851: Sonoma

Peter Campbell writes to the Commissioner of Indian Affairs that the "California Indian commonly called the digger Indians are the most abject poor, stupid and filthy tribe I have ever been acquainted with." Those who lived in the missions "are the most licentious." Some Indians know how to work but they are "inclined to theft."

March 7, 1852: Fort Miller

"White settlers" have taken up holdings by the streams for the purposes of agriculture and mining. The Indians there are friendly to them except for the *desparadoes* (sic) who infest some of the mining regions. These bad people oppress anyone weaker and the life of an Indian is held in the same regard as a wild beast.

It is curious that Indians and newly arriving Chinese immigrants have a definite aversion to each other. [See Note # 4.]

April 8, 1852: Sacramento

Governor John Bigler writes to General E. Hitchcock concerning hostilities in the counties Trinity, Klamath, Shasta, and Siskiyou. The trouble stems from the "savages…instinctive hatred toward the white race." This hatred is hereditary, passed on from "the live to the Son." Whites and Indians cannot live in close proximity with each other. The Federal government has not adequately protected the citizens of California. The hostile "mountain Indians, whose activity, sagacity, and courage has never been surpassed by Indians on the continent of America" have yet to be tamed and conquered. If the Government won't do the job then pay the bill and California will issue a call for volunteers to do it.

August 26, 1852: Fort Miller

Major G.W. Tatten writes to the Assistant Adjutant General that the cattle ordered to feed the Indians have not arrived. No beans have been delivered either. The Commissioner promising the Indians that they will be respected in their lands is now open to question. The treaty is good and should be ratified in Congress. If this doesn't happen then the treaty-making between the Commissioner and the Indians "is a mere farce."

December 31, 1853: Camp Wessells

Second Lt. John Nugens writes to Lt. T. Wright that the Indians living in the Four Creeks (Tulare) area number around 1,000. They suffer from "fever, ague and other fevers" due to their manner of living. Their principal food is fish, which is in fine abundance in the streams. They hunt deer and dress the skins for sale. They also have good supplies of acorns. They are friendly with the "whites" and have promised not to bother them.

December 31, 1853: Diamond Springs

Special Indian Agent E.A. Stevenson writes to Supt. of Indian Affairs T.J. Henley that his area holds some 8,000 Indians in perhaps 125 separate bands. Many are being ruined by the "vices of civilization." Around Buckeye Flat a couple of miners were living with two Indian women or keeping them as prostitutes. When village men went to retrieve their women the miners fired on them, killing one Indian and seriously wounding another. Since Indians were not allowed to testify in court against "whites" there was nothing legal the Indians could do.

The "poverty and misery" now existing among the Indians "is beyond description." Squaws are being driven to prostitution, "engendering diseases of the most frightful and fatal character." Indians are now afraid they will starve or fall victim to "the disease brought by the white men." In one camp nine Indian women were so far advanced in the disease that they couldn't even walk.

Liquor is another serious malady. When sober, most Indians want to do what is right but when drunk they will commit any act of crime, brutality, or violence. It is impossible to prevent them from getting liquor because so many Americans bring it to them and the Indians won't inform on them.

Game animals have been driven away by our thousands of mining people or killed for their own sustenance. Streams used to be filled with the finest salmon and other fish but miners have diverted the streams or filled them with so much sand that the fish have all but disappeared. And for the last three years even the acorns have disappeared. In their "superstition they blame the 'white man' for all these troubles." [See Note # 5.] Indians should immediately be removed to a protected reservation and they should receive desperately needed medical attention.

1853: Newspaper article, Sacramento

Smallpox is raging among the Indians, especially the children which are being "swept off in numbers." Smallpox has taken some 400 Indian victims in the past six months. Very few whites have come down with the disease.

February 24, 1854: Fort Miller

H.W. Wessells writes to E.D. Townsend that an "inoffensive Indian was barbarously murdered" by a white man at the Indian *rancheria*. The murderer escaped but a warrant is out for his arrest.

March 9, 1854: Fort Miller

Lt. LaRhett L. Livingston writes to Major W.W. Mackall that most of the troops stationed at Ft. Miller are suffering from venereal disease. Indians are contracting the disease and liquor is speeding their ruination. There are always disturbances "among drunken whites and Indians." Indian Agents do nothing about it. The Indians will be annihilated within a very short time if they are not removed from contact with the mining population.

March 26, 1854: Fort Jones

Lt. J.C. Bonnycastle writes to Commander G. Wright that the Indians of Scotts' Valley have asked to be put under the protection of American troops. Their chief, a man known as Bill, and the Indians are currently living in a cave in order to protect themselves against attacks from the "whites." Many of the Indians are sick with fever and Chief Bill has no way to transport them to the fort. The trouble started when the "citizens of Cottonwood" attacked them without provocation, the Indians driving them off handily when they fought back.

May 28, 1854: Fort Jones

Lt. J.C. Bonnycastle writes to Major General John C. Wool concerning the Indian disturbances begun when a Shasta Indian named Joe had "attempted an outrage on a white woman." Joe fled when some white men arrived but a message was sent to Chief Bill to surrender Joe unconditionally. Working through Indian Agent Rosborough Bill said he would comply so long as Joe was not hung. Bonnycastle replied he could not make such a promise and when Joe was not brought in he led his soldiers into the mountains to bring in the miscreant. During one encampment a couple of Indian headmen came in to parley, saying Joe would be delivered up so long as he wasn't hung. The offer was refused once again. The Indians pointed out that the white woman had not been hurt, that nothing had actually happened. Bonnycastle replied that the intention "was almost as culpable whether successful or not." The fact that Indian women were often run down by men on horses and raped didn't seem to enter into the picture.

While waiting for the Shastas to bring in Joe, word was received that a pack train in the Siskiyou Mountain had been attacked and one white man killed. It was concluded that an Indian known as Tipsha Tyee had committed the foul deed and the military force now turned its efforts toward him. Bonnycastle's Indian scouts, De Chutes from Oregon, indicated that six Indians were in the rogue band. Four of them appeared to be heading toward the cave occupied by Chief Bill and his people so Bonnycastle determined to pursue them also. Word was then received that Tipsha Tyee had made it to the Shasta camp and asked them to join in a war against the whites. Instead of agreeing, the Shastas killed Tipsha Tyee and took his scalp to show Bonnycastle as proof. The Shastas promised to bring Joe to Fort Jones when the whole band went there in a few days.

Captain Goodall was leading the Shastas, some 60 men, women, and children in all when at the Klamath Ferry a party of whites and the De Chute Indians opened fire on the Shastas. Two were killed instantly, three were wounded, including Chief Bill. A white man named Stuart rushed up to scalp Bill but the chief managed to fight him off until he was shot again, whereupon a man named Brickey scalped him then threw the body into the Klamath River. The De Chutes plundered the Shasta camp, also stealing four children, at least a half dozen horses and several guns. Despite these tragedies, the Shastas said they didn't blame all white men for such treachery, just those who perpetrated the foul act of cowardice, and that they recognized who they were. Bonnycastle asks that "the most severe measures be taken against the murderers."

October 19, 1854: Fort Humboldt

Lt. Col. Robert C. Buchanan writes to Major E.D. Townsend that State authorities wish Buchanan to take charge of two Indians who murdered "one of the citizens of the State." Citizens don't want to go to the expense of keeping the murderers until the next term of the District Court. The *Humboldt Times* is advocating the creation of a "Committee of Vigilance" to handle the situation, thereby ignoring the law.

December 12, 1854: Bodega

George Wooman writes to T.J. Henley that from 3-400 Indians "were distributed to labor among the settlers." The Indians earned from three to four thousand dollars, along with clothing and tools, all of which they took home with them after working from September to November. There is a "band of scoundrels" comprised of fugitive "Americans and Spaniards" who carry off Indian children and commit outrages upon the women. The military should run them out of the country.

March 25, 1855: Cow Creek

George Woman writes to T.J. Henley that because provision has not been made for the northern Indians, many have perished, "literally starved." As for the survivors, is there no law to prevent "certain persons" from taking Indians and their women against their will? There is a flourishing traffic in this business.

June 18, 1855: Diamond Springs

The Indians living in their *ranchoreis* (sic) are peaceful "but their condition is wretched in the extreme." They have to eat grass, seeds, acorns, pine nuts, clover, and insects. The women are prostitutes and many have contracted "disease" which they pass on with terrible consequences to the Indian communities. I have found some 50 that are dying of that awful disease. And they are all addicted to "firewater." They want to know when the Government is going to help them. I believe they will remove to a good reservation.

August 2, 1855: Fort Jones

F. Sorrel writes to E.D. Townsend that Indians of all ages and both sexes are being murdered wherever found. Two Indians visiting in Yreka were seized and executed simply for being Indians. There are now some 100 Indians seeking protection at this post. Notification has been received from Hamburg Bar on the Scott River that some 50 women and children have gathered there, that I should come retrieve them "but as my absence from the Post under these circumstances is deemed inadmissible I am obliged to relinquish them to their fate."

August 22, 1855: San Francisco

Affidavit of Charles L. Thurman sworn before J. Montgomery Peters, Judge of the 8th Judicial District: On August 22 Mr. Thurman saw William Maul, a man known by Thurman, go into the house where a harmless Indian boy named Billy (Emmashewyka, perhaps fourteen years old) was staying, grabbed Billy by the arm and when outside indicated that the boy had to run. Billy ran some ten steps whereupon William Maul aimed his rifle at Billy's back and shot him, the boy dying in about thirty minutes. Thurman also states that other men by the names of Usery, McClane, and Gillespie, also known to Thurman, were then walking with Maul, encouraging him in the deed.

August 23, 1855: Fort Jones

Captain H.M. Judah writes to E.D. Townsend that bands of white men, "too lazy or cowardly to scout in the mountains" (for hostile Indian groups) want to come here and slaughter the inoffensive Indians in the fort. Our friendly Indians are greatly alarmed.

September 15, 1855: Benicia

J.E. Wool writes to T.J. Henley that around 150 Indians, mostly women "whose husbands have been killed by the whites of California…" and children are now in the Military Reserve at Ft. Jones, and fed by Captain Judah. The whites appeared to be determined to exterminate "these miserable creatures."

1855: Newspaper Editorial, Sacramento

A war of extermination against Indians has started. Provocation and destitution must be considered because the "white man" has gone into Indian hunting grounds, driven off the game, destroyed their fisheries. Government policy has been miserable and if it had been different it would not have been necessary to slaughter the race. "The fate of the Indian is fixed." The advance of the "white man" means annihilation by diseases and the "evils of civilization."

January 31, 1856

Captain A.J. Smith writes to Colonel G. Wright concerning the difficulties of the whites at Cottonwood with neighboring Indians. The white miners waged an unprovoked attack on the Indians. Calling themselves "Squaw Hunters," the miners had vowed to take squaws by force if necessary. The whites attacked a cave and seven Indians were killed, three of whom were men. After the attack the whites withdrew and spread the word that the Indians were going to attack and plunder the white settlement. Some 28 men went out to meet the "invading" Indians but were turned back with four killed because the Indians were now ready to fight.

August 9, 1856: Benicia

Captain E.O.C. Ord writes to Major W.W. Mackall on the people of California. He says that in Los Ángeles "Americans and Mexicans are arrayed against each other." Mexicans are well armed and soldiers are needed to prevent a revolution. Indians are "servants of the whites." Any "justice of the peace" is legally enabled "to buy and keep Indian servants." [See Note # 6.] Pay for Indians averages to about six dollars a month. They ask about the promises made to them by Indian Agents and the moneys supposedly sent for them and "they fancy they are deprived of their rights." They resent having to give up their irrigable land to squatters and State authorities but since they can't testify in court they have no redress.

August 23, 1856: Mission San Diego

William A. Winder writes to Major W.W. Mackall that the Santa Isabel Indians have come in to complain that J.J. Warner, Sub Agent for this group of Indians, has informed them that all animals having no brands will automatically become his private property. Many of these Indians own horses and they have no branding irons with which to brand their new colts. I informed the chief that the Army would protect the Indians in their property. "This is just one of the many cases of injustice practiced upon these Indians."

1856: Newspaper article, San Francisco

Reservation "agents" and other "employees" are "nightly engaged in kidnapping the younger portion of the females, for the vilest purposes." These defenseless "Diggers" are prostituted by these "civilized monsters."

March 4, 1857: Klamath

Lt. C.H. Rundell writes to Lt. F.H. Bates that two men, "Squire" Lewis and "Texas" Lawson went to an Indian ranchería known as Wasch and "commenced abusing Indian Squaws." A mother tried to protect her daughter and Lewis stabbed her, along with the father of the girl. They took two other "squaws" and forced them to spend the night with them. The next day the men left the camp but I sent for a warrant for their arrest. When the two returned to Wasch the Indian women ran to the hills. This infuriated Lewis so he took a club and brutally beat an Indian boy with it. Soldiers were stationed to protect the Indians and Captain Young had to shoot Lawson. Squire Lewis was arrested and bound over for trial. If he is properly punished by the court he will be the first white man to have been brought to justice, "though his offense compared with others that have taken place on this river is a mere trivial matter" (by comparison).

September 1, 1857: Nome Lackee Reserve

Lt. M.R. Morgan writes to Major W.W. Mackall that more than 8,000 bushels of wheat have been harvested on this reservation. Some of the Indians from Yuba County are dissatisfied with reservation life, sometimes running away in squads. Some are caught and brought back. Where they used to live they got paid to work in farms or mines and they enjoy having money to spend, which they don't now.

The number of Indians here is around 800. There is much sickness here, even among the whites.

June 19, 1858: San Francisco

T.J. Henley writes to Charles E. Mix that "settlers" near Mendocino have "attacked, killed, or driven away all the Indians" and are attacking any Indians to be found in the valley or mountains. Indians are being shot without the slightest provocation by an expedition bent on destroying all the *rancheries* (sic) in the area. "I have of course no remedy for such outages."

November 1, 1858: San Francisco

J. Ross Browne sends affidavits to Commissioner of Indian Affairs Charles E. Mix. J.L. Clapp states in his affidavit: "The Indians have been mismanaged and the reservations have been a curse to the settlers because of the way they have been handled. Two thirds of the time the Indians are starving so they are forced to steal...or left to shift for themselves." H.A. Bostwick states that "public officers...have made the Indian Reservation their own private benefit."

November 14, 1858: Fresno Indian Sub-Agency

Various "citizens of Fresno and Tulare counties" write to M.B. Lewis why they have "removed" some 200 Indians from the area. First, the Indians have been killing great numbers of hogs and cattle. Second, Indians and "stock growing people" can't inhabit the same country. If the Indians return they will be dealt with harshly, *"as abide with us they shall not."* There are some "thirty mission Indians who are all daring and expert marauders" who will be dealt with "summarily" if they do not "peaceably retire."

1858: Tuolumne *Courier*, San Francisco

The Indians about the Columbia are absolutely miserable. Civilization has brought them "prostitution, intemperance, and vice, in their most revolting aspects." There is no one to look after or protect them. Why can't they be removed to a reservation where they can learn the "Christian ways of civilized beings"?

1858: Amador *Sentinel*, San Francisco

The Indians of Amador, El Dorado, and Calaveras counties have been totally neglected. They are the most miserable, degraded race of beings as ever existed. Besides their "slothful and filthy habits" they now have all the vices of the "white man." They are wracked with "loathsome diseases, the natural consequence of their contact with civilization."

1859: Napa *Reporter*, Sacramento

The Clear Lake tribe now numbers about 150. They have some one hundred acres under cultivation. Their land has been taken by "settlers" pre-emption claims. The tribe numbered some 10,000 in 1849 but today a mere remnant of 500 or so remain.

January 15, 1860: Pitt River Valley

Three white men (one of them, named Napoleon McElroy, had killed an Indian man and woman previously) were "murdered" in December of 1859 and a punitive force went out to even the score. The expedition came upon a group of Indians who had been living for a long time in a place called Roff's Ranch. The whites attacked and killed nine men, the others escaping. Women and children stayed behind, "trusting to confidence in the honesty of an American, whom they believed would not murder women and children." They were wrong. Throughout the day some forty Indian women and children were butchered by the Americans, splitting their heads open with hatchets.

May 31, 1861: Fort Bragg

Lt. Edward Dillon writes to Captain C.S. Lovell that "several parties of citizens" are engaged in "stealing or taking by force Indian children" for sale to any buyer. The pretense is that they were bought from the parents according to the law. Retaliatory raids can be expected and some calculating persons welcome the extermination of the Indians because of their depredations.

January 9, 1865: Daily Evening Bulletin

The Indian Department of California now consists of four reservations. For the first time in many years there is peace between the two races in California. Indians are "fast passing away and the least we can do for them is to prevent their ending from being hurried or violent."

MODOC WAR

The Modoc people lived around Lost River, a stream that ran into Tule Lake around the California/

Oregon border. "White settlers" decided they wanted that area so in 1864 a "treaty" was signed that re-quired the Modocs to move north to the Klamath reservation. [See Note # 7.] They weren't happy with the move and after a year **Captain Jack** (his real name was *Kientpoos*) led some 175 of his followers back to their original country. "Settlers" went into a near panic and demanded the Indians be removed once again. The Indian Bureau wasn't really concerned with the situation and Captain Jack said in 1867 that he would accept no annuities if it meant returning to the Klamath Reservation. [See Note # 8.]

In 1869 **Alfred B. Meacham** was appointed Indian Superintendent for Oregon. He was appalled at what he found on the reservation: gambling, polygamy, slave-holding. He issued orders against these and decreed that any white man living on the reservation with an Indian woman would marry her or give her up. This included Army officers who had "purchased" Indian girls. Shamanistic rituals were forbidden because they had caused various ritualistic murders of Indians. At the end of the year Meacham went to confer with Captain Jack and convinced him to return to the Klamath Reservation. The Klamath Indians, who outnumbered the Modocs 2-to-1, demanded forms of tribute from the Modocs and they taunted or harassed them while gathering wood, wild grain at the lake, or when fishing. Captain Jack went to the agency to complain but the agent wound up cutting off all rations for the tribe in April of 1870. The Modocs "could now go out and find their own food." Captain Jack once again led his people back to Lost River, this time with more people than the first. In order to retrieve the deserters, the Modocs were given lands of their own with their own agency called Yainax.

The "settlers" complained about the Modocs and their "vile ways." Captain Jack now demanded that a reservation, a tract six miles square, be given his people on Lost River by Tule Lake. Meacham thought it was a fair proposal, although several whites had ranches on some of the land.

In 1872 T.B. Odeneal replaced Meacham as Superintendent. Odeneal had orders to return Captain Jack and his followers to Yainax, by force if necessary. War talk was in the air, even among the Modocs. Odeneal went to Ft. Klamath and asked for troops to use against Captain Jack's people. Captain James Jackson led a company of soldiers to arrest Captain Jack, Scarfaced Charley, and Black Jim. The troopers entered Jack's village at around seven in the morning but they were spotted and some seventeen armed Indians were waiting for them. Suddenly a couple of shots rang out and the battle was on. The "settlers" who had joined the soldiers immediately ran away from the fight. When the shooting abated within five minutes, one soldier and one Indian were dead. The Indians fled and Jackson ordered the village burned.

On the other side of the lake a subchief named Hooker Jim and his warriors came upon some thir-teen uninvolved whites and killed them. No women or children were harmed. Moving with some of his men, Scarfaced Charley met some white ranchers whom he told to go home because he didn't want to see them get hurt. When all the Modoc warriors got together there were perhaps fifty fighters holed up in the Lava Beds, an area of chasms, caves, ridges, pits, etc., of lava. There might have been some 115 non-combatant Modocs with Captain Jack.

Lt. Col. Frank Wheaton, commander of the District of the Lakes, now sent reinforcements to put down the Modoc uprising, leading them himself. The Governor of Oregon issued a call for volunteers to help the Army and some sixty-five "patriots" signed up to quell the Indian menace. A rancher signed up another sixty-eight men, most of them Klamath Indians from the reservation.

Wheaton's job was most difficult because the Modocs could hide in the lava formations and shoot from behind marvelous cover. Rifle and/or artillery fire was relatively futile unless the "marauders" gave away their positions. On December 21, 1872, the wagons loaded with ammunition were spied then attacked (skirmish of Land's Ranch) by the Indians. The whole train would have been lost had not help come in the form of a half dozen mounted soldiers.

Christmas came and went. Wheaton was readying his some 300 men for the attack which would certainly destroy the Modocs. They would be attacked from east and west, then north and south, completely surrounding the hostiles.

On January 16, 1873, soldiers advanced through a heavy fog. The Modocs fired a few shots but the fog prevented anything close to good marksmanship. They retreated toward their main camp "Stronghold" where they danced and chanted during the night, the soldiers hearing it from an eerie distance. A trooper's reconnaissance party got close and the Modocs realized they would be attacked from the east and west.

The battle began the next day with howitzer shots, the troops moving forward in the cold, gray morning. The Modocs were at least a mile away so the artillery shots were useless. Then the Oregon volunteers, positioned between the cavalry and infantry, decided they didn't want to fight, thus leaving a wide, undefended gap between the two units. They got away from the scene of upcoming action and couldn't be induced to come back. Other Army units couldn't do anything because the fog was still too thick and the artillery remained silent for the same reason. Finally Major John Green jumped on top of a large rock and, in full view of the Indians, condemned his men as cowards for not charging in. A few men jumped up and got off a few shots but not enough to start the engagement. By the end of the day Wheaton called off the "attack." Many soldiers had already retreated in fright, though most hadn't seen any Modocs. Casualties were two killed and thirteen wounded. Outnumbered six to one, the Modocs hadn't lost a single warrior.

General **E.R.S. Canby**, commander of the Department of the Columbia, removed Wheaton from command and replaced him with Col. Alvin C. Gillem. Canby also sent in more soldiers until there were perhaps 700 and he himself went to the battlefield to scrutinize the situation.

Then someone came up with the idea that a Peace Commission might be the best way to end the "war." The commissioners would be Alfred Meacham, rancher Jesse Applegate, and Samuel Case of the Indian Bureau.

Captain Jack expressed a willingness to talk but two other whites would have to be appointed to the commission. This was done. Negotiations became difficult because Oregonians demanded the Modocs be tried for murdering the unsuspecting ranchers. Captain Jack still demanded a reservation on Lost River and the Army insisted that all Modocs remove to Indian Territory (Oklahoma). After almost two months of negotiations the impasse seemed irreparable and General Canby decided to continue the war. The Army tightened its grip on the Stronghold but Captain Jack sent word that he wanted to negotiate once more. New commissioners now included L.S. Dynar from the Klamath Agency and Reverend Eleasar Thomas, along with Meacham and General Canby.

Captain Jack reiterated his demand for land at Lost River and he also needed a promise that his men would not be punished for killing the ranchers. Canby could only promise "fair treatment" if the

Modocs surrendered. Once again the meeting ended in a hopeless deadlock.

On April 10, 1873, the Indians sent word they wanted to talk once again. Captain Jack wanted to end the war, even if it meant returning to the Yainax reservation. But a war faction had arisen in the Modoc camp and they would rather fight than lose their lands. They wanted to kill the commissioners, especially General Canby. Captain Jack spoke up against the plans and he was called a "Coward!" to his face. He would be deposed as chief so he said if they were serious about killing Canby he would do it himself.

On April 11, Good Friday, everyone came together to negotiate. Old proposals were rehashed. Finally Captain Jack pulled out a pistol and shot Canby in the face at point blank range. (Canby thus became the first and only American general to be killed by Indians.) Reverend Thomas was shot down immediately afterward. Alfred Meacham had felt something was going to happen so he pulled his derringer and ran, thus saving his life, though he was wounded. Then somebody yelled that soldiers were coming and the Modocs retreated to their stronghold.

Newspaper reporters picked up the story and the whole country was shocked. Whereas before many sympathized with the tiny band of Indians holding out against the Military now the cry was one of *extermination*. General Sherman was quoted as saying that "Treachery is inherent in the Indian character." He assigned General Jefferson C. Davis (not the Confederate president) to replace Canby and extermination is what was expected.

On April 15, Davis and a thousand soldiers approached the stronghold much as had been done before but again the soldiers stopped when the Modocs opened fire. Artillery shots were from too far away to do any good. By nightfall nothing had been accomplished. On the 16th the officers called for their men to retreat because the terrain was just too treacherous.

Captain Jack was now in complete command of his warriors but because his people had been cut off from the lake he ordered a withdrawal from the Stronghold. Let the Army come get them in the lava beds, if they dared. Come the Army did, some sixty-four soldiers headed to the top of a butte where they could place their artillery. The Modocs ambushed the column, the panic-stricken soldiers running to safety as quickly as they could. A company of infantrymen came to rescue their comrades but when they were fired on they turned tail and ran too. Some half dozen men with courage enough to help their fellows stood up to fight but they were immediately shot down. Twenty more were shot down from above. During a lull in the firefight Scarfaced Charley called out: "All you fellows that ain't dead had better go home cause we don't want to kill you all in one day."

A relief column was sent in but it got lost in the dark. The next morning it was discovered that some twenty-three soldiers were dead, nineteen wounded, and the relief column hadn't brought a doctor along to tend them.

The Modocs hadn't lost a single warrior but had acquired stores of supplies, including rifles and ammunition. But Captain Jack understood that his 165 people would run out of water if the war continued for a long time. He didn't know it, but he was now outnumbered twenty-to-one.

General Davis now sent out Captain H.C. Hasbrouck and his company of cavalry to hunt Modocs. They bivouacked in an area called Dry Lake and early the next morning the Modocs attacked while most of the soldiers were still sleeping. Two were killed immediately and a number wounded. But Hasbrouck was able to rally his men and turn the artillery on the Indians, causing them to abandon the field completely. One Indian had been killed but for some unknown reason the Modocs had loaded their supplies on pack horses, brought them to the attack, and these were captured by the soldiers. Morale got a boost for this was the first time the soldiers had actually won a skirmish.

The warriors began to quarrel among themselves and some fourteen warriors and their families departed from the battlefield. Captain Jack now had only thirty-three warriors and there were the many women and children to worry about.

The Modocs known as the Hot Creek band went to a friendly rancher and gave themselves up. They let out the word that they would help the Army find Captain Jack so he could give himself up. General Davis sent them in and they found an angry Captain Jack who told them they wouldn't let him surrender when he had wanted to but now they had turned traitor and they wanted him to give himself up, knowing full well what would happen. But Captain Jack really had no alternative. On June 1, 1873, he surrendered and the Modoc War was over.

Oregon screamed for Modoc blood. Four Modocs surrendered to the rancher Fairchild but when he was delivering them in a wagon to the Army some Oregonians stopped him and shot down all four in cold blood. It isn't known (or at least it hasn't been reported) if they were part of the group that had refused to fight the Modocs when the warriors were armed.

Modoc prisoners were taken to Ft. Klamath and put on trial on July 1, 1873. After a "fair trial" in which the Indians had no defense counsel, Captain Jack, Schonchin John, Boston Charley, Black Jim, Slolux, and Barncho were found guilty of murdering General Canby and Reverend Thomas. President Grant commuted the death sentences of Slolux and Barncho but the other four were hung. The rest of the Modoc tribe was sent to Oklahoma where their numbers dwindled as they adapted to civilized life.

DISCUSSION NOTES *for* CALIFORNIA INDIAN AFFAIRS

Note # 1

See *The Destruction Of California Indians*, 1974, Bison Book edition in 1993, by Robert F. Heizer. Numbers for Indian populations always vary greatly, depending on who is doing the estimating. In the Heizer volume, the "Introduction to the Bison Book Edition," Albert L. Hurtado writes that between 1848-1860 the California "Indian population plummeted from about 150,000 to about 30,000." It is often written that there might have been more than 300,000 Indians living in California when Hispanics founded the missions but that figure is also an estimate because no one ever counted all the Amerindians living in that large area and contemporary writers are making little more than "educated" guesses. It appears that figures also are related to who was in charge at the time, Hispanics or Americans. Numbers for Indians living in the missions, said to be some 13,000, should be credible only if original missionary sources are used. (See the Essay: On California Indian History at the end of this section.)

Note # 2

See the "Introduction" in the Heizer volume.

Note # 3

Concerning the quality of Indian Agents on the Western frontier see pages 167-69 in *The Long Death* by Ralph K. Andrist. It would be interesting to compare Roman Catholic missionaries and Indian Service personnel as "Indian Agents."

Note # 4

It would be interesting to see where these two groups, both viciously targeted by Americans, learned prejudice against the other.

Note # 5

Use of the phrase "white man" isn't peculiar to writers from Texas. The phrase is also a disingenuous term for how Indians actually referred to Americans. As far as I can tell, color seldom had anything to do with how Indians referred to newcomers from Europe. The Narragansetts referred to the pilgrims as *Awaunageesuck*, their word for *strangers*. *Youngis*, from whence derived Yankees, also meant *strangers*. The Shawnee used *Shemanese*, "long knives." The Sioux word for "American" is *wasichu* which signifies *greed*. All of these names are translated as "whites" by American historiographers but I have seldom found, "paleface" being a possible exception if some Amerindian group actually used it, an Amerindian group that actually referred to Americans as "whites." Skin color appears to be related only to American racism and its European antecedents.

Note # 6

Slavery is not generally associated with California as with the American South.

Note # 7

It seems to be a pattern that Americans taking Indian lands are referred to by the circumlocution "settlers." Further, it is seldom pointed out that surviving California Indians were forced onto miniscule reservation lands.

Note # 8

See Chapter 7 in *The Long Death* by Ralph K. Andrist.

Essay: ON CALIFORNIA INDIAN HISTORY

The Destruction Of California Indians is a litany of how the California Indians were destroyed in American California but, amazingly, very few of these monstrous tragedies have made it into popular reading. R.K. Andrist has written that "In no other part of the United States were the Indians so barbarously treated and so wantonly murdered." This is certainly not popular commentary. Indeed, most American would be shocked if they thought it was true therefore such information has been swept under the rug by historiographers. Where does morality enter into the American picture?

Let us take a quick look at Chapter 14 in *California: A Land of New Beginnings* by David Lavender. The chapter deals with "land problems, the treatment of foreigners, Indian affairs, and crime." He writes that "in spite of the good men and true…(who believed in) fair play…the story is among the most distressing reading in the nation's history." He warns the reader that "the squeamish may decide to skip this long chapter." On page 212 (titled "Hatred"), Mr. Lavender cites the work of S.F. Cook that between 1848-1870 the numbers of California Indians declined by 48,000, that "most…as in Spanish and

Mexican times" resulted from diseases. Further, that from 1851-60, "at least 1,000 Indian women…a group fairly limited in numbers…were raped so brutally that most of them died." (There is no Index citation for "Rape" in the Lavender work.) How could this happen? Because the California "settlers" made it a law that Indians or non-whites could not testify in court against a "white man." Americans making the laws were therefore exempt from prosecution so they could "take" any Indian woman without fear of legal reprisal. And if Indians decided to protect their women the Americans then felt justified in exterminating them.

The Black Legend enters the picture to subtlety "defend" American behavior by saying that "manhandling Indians is an old story…not uniquely American…as the Spanish conquistadors illustrate." There is no doubt that some conquistadores like Pizarro and Guzmán were destructive thugs but what is not pointed out is that the "thuggeries" were combated by Indian champions like Bartolomé de las Casas, Antonio Margil, Junípero Serra, etc. These champions made a difference and spearheaded reform measures that were in place even before Hispanics colonized New Mexico in 1598. [See *The Spanish Struggle For Justice In The Conquest Of America* by Lewis Hanke.]

While "conquistadors" like Pizarro and Guzmán were bloodthirsty killers and are portrayed as such, along with other conquistadores who weren't, Americans who committed the same kind of foul deeds are labeled "vigilantes" or "volunteers" or "enraged settlers," etc. For example, on February 25, 1860, "carefully rehearsed vigilantes" attacked four different villages of peaceful Indians, one in which a community dance was being held, and slaughtered some 188 to possibly more than 200 Indian men, women, and children…"babes, with brains oozing out of their skulls, cut and hacked with axes, and squaws exhibiting the most frightful wounds…" Who were the perpetrators of these savage deeds? *Vigilantes.*

In 1864 the Yanas tribe was accused of killing two white women so "volunteers swarmed in" and killed between 2-3000 Indians, men, women, and children. Who committed these heinous acts? *Volunteers.*

Didn't the California Indians have any champions? Some tried but they didn't get far. A young newspaper man named Bret Harte condemned the above atrocities in his newspaper and was "harried out of the county." No mention is made that American "frontier" society made no room for anyone who defended Indians (or *blacks* or *greasers* or any other group targeted in a particular section of the country).

Mr. Lavender ends the section by saying: "By 1900, of the 250,000 or so Indians who had lived in California when Cabrillo first saw the coastline, only 16,000 remained." How many California Indians were there in 1846? Under American rule which started in 1846, what happened to them by 1900? What did Cabrillo have to do with the American extermination of California Indians? Is this another Orwellian shroud?

Relating "unpleasant history" is no simple feat because retribution can be expected, foremost of which is making one's book unsaleable. But there are some American writers with ample moral courage. R.K. Andrist has written that California Indian "Women were brutalized by gang rapes; men were captured like animals…kidnapped children were treated as slaves." As has been indicated above, Robert Heizer documented the following points, succinctly presented here for review:

1. "Whites" used liquor (the most popular of drugs) as a weapon on the California Indians;
2. Whites did their utmost to enslave the California Indians;

3. Military expeditions against the Indians were encouraged;

4. Whites tried to provoke Indian wars;

5. Miners respected no Indian or his land;

6. "Settlers" almost always denigrated the Indians;

7. It was promoted that Indians "hated the white race;"

8. It was promoted that Indians and whites could not live in close proximity to each other;

9. Promises to the Indians were not kept; Indian health was very often not good;

10. Indian women were driven into prostitution by white miners;

11. Indian game animals were destroyed by white "settlers" and miners;

12. Settlers felt that all Indians should be removed to reservations;

13. Whites often murdered Indians in cold blood; talk of exterminating them was common;

14. California law stated that Indians could not testify in court against a white person;

15. "Lynch law" was often condoned against Indians;

16. Indians could be legally enslaved by whites;

17. Whites often targeted friendly Indians for extermination, avoiding avowedly hostile warriors generally living in the mountains;

18. Indian lands were taken by white squatters but if the Indians defended themselves the whites used it as reason for extermination;

19. Indian Agents often cheated the Indians out of supplies and funding;

20. Indian females were targeted by whites for sexual purposes; rape of Indian women was common but "white" courts were not permitted to hear Indian testimony;

21. Dissatisfied Indians often ran away from reservations;

22. White civilization has brought the Indians "prostitution, intemperance, and vice."

23. Indians don't have very many champions.

24. Slaughtering Indian women and children was common.

25. The reservation system was not working.

26. Indian people are fast disappearing "and the least we can do for them is to prevent their ending from being hurried or violent."

While this kind of history is generally shunned by American writers, it is a realistic insight into the popular idea of "How the West Was Won!" which also applies to the Southwest. It should likewise be kept in mind that wherever Spain established its laws, religion, and society, are various American writers using the Hispanic historical record to defocus from the American record?

NEVADA

While there were some twenty-seven tribal groups living in what is now Nevada the main groups are considered to be the Northern and Southern Paiute (also Pah Ute in Bancroft's work), the Shoshone and the Washo. They survived in this basically hostile land by hunting (deer, antelope, etc.), fishing (in lakes Tahoe and Pyramid), and gathering foods provided by nature.

The first European to go into (the southern tip of) Nevada was Father Francisco Garcés in 1776. It is thought that Jedediah Smith was the first American to enter Nevada, in 1826.

Serious troubles with the Indians didn't occur until the American "farmer and miner" went into Nevada to carve land out of traditional Indian territory. While Indians had raided "emigrant" wagon trains in the 1840s and the 1850s, serious problems didn't erupt into war until the Comstock Lode was discovered in the summer of 1859. The deluge of miners into the area caused the Paiutes and some of their Bannock allies to call a large council at Pyramid Lake in the spring of 1860. During the council news was received that because whites had captured and raped two Indian women, some Bannocks rescuing the women burned Williams Station and killed three whites in retaliation. [See Note # 1 *Notes begin on page 347.*]

While there are variations of why the attack was made on (James) Williams Station the basic story is that American miners were raping Indian women. Two young "squaws" were "captured" and taken to the Williams trading post where they were raped. Their husbands/friends went there on May 7, 1860, to rescue them but the Americans refused to free the women. A fight broke out and three "whites" were killed. The Indians set fire to the shanty buildings and two other whites died in the fire. [See Note # 2.]

Another version has it that a Paiute "buck and squaw" happened to stop at Williams. Some Americans pounced on the "buck," tied him up, then raped the "squaw." [See Note # 3.] When the "buck" was freed he went to ask for help of Little Winnemucca (whose real name was *Chiquito*) who gathered some warriors and attacked the Station.

At the Pyramid Lake council, chief Old Winnemucca (Poito) had been trying to avoid war with the Americans. War chief Young Winnemucca (Numaga) felt the same way. But when news of the killings and burnings at Williams Station came in Numaga said: "The Americans will now come. We must prepare."

James Williams, who had been absent on the seventh, returned to the Station on the eighth and saw the burned buildings and dead bodies. Without taking time to bury the bodies, he immediately fled to Virginia City and gave the alarm that Indians were on the warpath. The call was made for volunteers to exterminate the "savages." Around 105 volunteers signed on to do the job. They were an assortment of American miners, prospectors, professional gamblers, cutthroats, etc. They created a slogan: "An Indian for breakfast and a pony to ride." They believed the Indians wouldn't fight so the volunteers thought it would be "easy pickings" to plunder Paiute villages, kill a few braves and "capture" the "squaws." Major William M. Ormsby later took on general command of this "hell-bent outing of rollicking fun" expedition.

BATTLE at PYRAMID LAKE

The morning of May 12, 1860, found the Indian fighters along the Truckee River, following the trail of the Indians who had gathered at Pyramid Lake. From the plateau the volunteers spotted some Indians in the green bottom lands below. A narrow trail led down to the grassy meadows and the volunteers began descending, though one Abe Elliott said it would be suicide to be caught on the narrow trail. But nothing happened and the volunteers made it down without incident. Then a group of Indians was seen a short distance away and the order was given to attack. The jubilant Americans climbed on their horses and whooping wildly, charged at the Indians. It was now about four in the afternoon. The targeted

Indians disappeared but suddenly the volunteers were totally surrounded by Indians firing at them from behind every rock and sagebrush. Ambush! The Indians had suckered the Americans into a deadly encirclement. It was now the Indians turn to make their bloodcurdling yells amid a rain of arrows and bullets. Volunteer valor was quickly drained as Americans were shot out of their saddles. They retreated only to be attacked by another contingent of Indians under Chiquito who was waiting for them. Panic gripped the Indian fighters as they ran trying to escape. In the confusion the Indians always seemed to be on higher ground, shooting down into the volunteers. A one-legged man named Watkins stood with his crutch on the trail and "blazed away" at the Indians before he was killed. Chiquito and a man named Headly were in single combat until the American was shot down by other Indians.

The now panic-stricken, "every-man-for-himself" Americans tried to escape up the narrow trail but they got in each other's way and turned up being "easy pickings" for the Indians. Paiutes on horseback chased the retreating Americans, pouncing on them, then both crashing to the ground where the Americans were clubbed or tomahawked. Bancroft portrays one Indian's testimony, the implication being that he was a witness as to the end of the battle: "White men all cry a heap; got no gun and revolver, throw 'um away; no want to fight any more now; all big scare, just like cattle, run, run, run; heap cry, like papoose; no want injun to kill 'um any more." [See Note # 4.]

Major Ormsby's horse was shot out from under him but he was able to mount a mule in an effort to escape the disaster. His saddle came loose and he landed on the ground. Most of the Americans had already passed by in their own efforts to escape when Ormsby saw an Indian he thought he knew so he told him: "I am your friend." The Indian replied: "Too late now" and shot an arrow into him, killing him as Ormsby would have done had the Americans been victorious for they had come to exterminate the Indians. But the Indians had defended the invasion of their country and Americans had paid the price for their behavior. [See Note # 5.]

When news of the defeat reached the Comstock settlements people went into a panic. Ordinary Americans had favored extermination so would the Indians now come and exterminate them? Citizens of Silver City were so fearful they actually constructed a cannon out of *wood*. (Gratefully, it was never used.) A volunteer force of 549 was organized under Col. Jack Hayes and 207 regular soldiers under Captain Joseph Stewart were sent from California. The two groups united on May 31 and met the Indians in the vicinity of the mouth of the Truckee River. The battle didn't last long: some 160 Indians were killed while only two Americans fell in the short encounter. The remaining Indians dispersed and while there were sporadic attacks in the years to come the Indians of Nevada finally understood that war against the USA would end only in defeat and/or death for all Indians. Some two dozen military posts were established in an effort to "keep the peace." [See Note # 6.]

DISCUSSION NOTES *for* NEVADA INDIAN AFFAIRS

Note # 1
See pages 92-94 in *History Of Nevada* by Russell R. Elliott.
Note # 2
See Chapter 6 in *Great Western Indian Fights* by Members of the Potomac Corral of the

Westerners. The *History Of Nevada* volume by R.R. Elliott doesn't mention Americans raping Indian women, saying that the attack at Williams Station was "apparently in retaliation for the capture of two Indian women." *The Nevada Adventure* by James W. Hulse, intended for school use, states that "the men kidnapped two young Indian women and held them prisoner." *History Of Nevada, 1540-1888*, by H.H. Bancroft makes no mention of Americans raping Indian women, merely saying that "Captain Soo stole away from the council…and opening the war" by attacking Williams Station, as if the Indians attacked because they were…what? As might be expected from the foregoing, none of the books cited have an index entry for "Rape." (Compare this with Note # 8 in the *Discussion Notes For Californio Society* section.)

Note # 3

Does the language used in writing American history make a significant difference? Is there a propaganda effect between reading "a buck and squaw" as opposed to "an Indian man and woman"?

Note # 4

This portrayal should also be described as including American stereotypes as to how an Indian speaks. Amerindian leaders have often been described as possessing great oratorical powers, no inkling of which is even implied in this excerpt from Bancroft.

Note # 5

It appears that casualties are always subject to "interpretation." R.R. Elliott writes that of the 105 Americans, 76 were killed and most of the survivors wounded. *The Nevada Adventure* by James W. Hulse states that 76 Americans were killed in the battle of Pyramid Lake. The *Great Western Indian Fights* volume says 42 whites were killed, 30 missing, and 33 made it back to their towns, that the Indians claimed 46 Americans killed and "admitted to only three warriors wounded." Bancroft states in his *History Of Nevada* that 43 Americans were buried and "two weeks after the fight 60 persons were still missing."

Note # 6

None of the sources cited supply information on what, if any, retribution was taken on the Nevada Indians.

COLORADO

It is believed that the Cheyenne and Arapahoe nations had been closely allied for generations, certainly since they had arrived on the plains and become buffalo hunters. Both were brave in former wars against tribes like the Sioux and Crow. The Cheyenne were especially valiant. In 1835 trader **William Bent** (there were two Bent brothers: Charles and William; William had five children that were half Cheyenne) convinced the Cheyenne to move south in order to become trading partners at his Bent's Fort, situated in the area of present La Junta, Colorado. Those bands became known as Southern Cheyenne and Arapahoe. Their rich hunting range now included eastern Colorado, an area they shared with their now friends the Sioux, Kiowa, and Comanche, but not with their enemies the Utes to the west.

Americans started coming into the area when gold was discovered in the Rocky Mountains in 1858.

They came with slogans like "Pike's Peak or Bust!" and usually went out with "Busted, by Gosh." The Indians were friendly to the Americans. Little Raven, an Arapahoe chief, went into the mining camp which would grow into Denver and promised that his people would remain peaceful. An Arapaho camp was established close by. But one day when the warriors were gone a gang of American miners went into the Arapahoe camp and raped some of the women. [See Note # 1. *Notes begin on page 355.*] This was the beginning of enmity between Americans and Indians in Colorado. Further, when mining became a big business, ranchers, farmers, and other "settlers" came in and occupied the land. [See Note # 2.] They didn't consider it Indian land if "Anglo-Americans" wanted it. The *Rocky Mountain News* was among the "booster newspapers" who advocated that "…a few months of active extermination against the red devils" would settle the matter. [See Note # 3.]

TREATY MAKING

By 1861 the Cheyenne and Arapahoe had been pushed out of their beautiful mountain country right along with their game and the act was codified by a treaty (February 18, 1861) at Fort Wise on the Arkansas River. In return for giving up their hunting grounds they received the "sterile, sandy and useless" Sand Creek Reservation but with government annuities.

HUNGER & ANNUITIES

By 1863 both Cheyenne and Arapahoe groups were suffering from serious hunger and diseases sparked by malnutrition. While this was happening, their agent at Ft. Lyon, Samuel G. Colley, was diverting Cheyenne and Arapahoe annuities to his son Dexter, a trader who sold the annuities, sometimes back to the Indians who were supposed to have gotten them in the first place. There were no buffalo and game was almost non-existent. Out of desperation they attacked some wagon trains for food, without injuring any people.

BEGINNINGS of WAR

In April 11, 1864, a rancher named Ripley complained that Indians had taken some of his stock, which is possible, though it wasn't certain he had owned any to begin with. One Lt. Dunn and forty soldiers were sent to recover the animals, with Ripley along as guide. The expedition chanced upon a group of Indians driving some horses and Ripley claimed they were his. The Indians agreed to give up the horses but suddenly the situation turned violent and four soldiers were killed.

GOVERNOR EVANS

Colorado Governor John Evans had favored war against the Indians since the day he took office. The "Dunn fight" now gave him the opportunity to declare an Indian war. On April 18, 1864, word was received that Cheyenne warriors had chased "settlers" off their ranch on the South Platte and Major Jacob Downing with sixty soldiers were sent to punish them. They were unable to find the ranch, the settlers, or the Cheyenne. They returned to Camp Sanborn but they went out again at a later date to chastise the Cheyenne village at Cedar Canyon. The Americans shot down the surprised Cheyenne, killing some 26 and wounding 30…then "I burnt up their lodges and everything I could get hold of…we captured around 150 head of stock, which were distributed among the boys." Taking Indian stock and other items of value was a basic way to pay "volunteers" for attacking and defeating Indians on the frontier. [See Note # 4.]

CHIVINGTON and EAYRE

Governor Evans appointed his friend John Chivington, a Methodist minister, to command the Colorado Volunteers. Word got out that Indians had stolen some two hundred head of cattle from a government contractor so Chivington sent out Lt. George S. Eayre with a battery of artillery to chastise the Indians. He headed east, crossed into Kansas, and destroyed two Indian villages which had been deserted just before the soldiers appeared. The Americans destroyed both villages with all the food, robes, utensils, etc., stored there, and burned all tepees.

On May 16, 1864, Eayre chanced upon a camp of Cheyenne led by their chief Lean Bear, who rode out with his son to greet the soldiers. Their hands upraised in the universally understood sign for peace, the Americans let the Indians approach until they were at point blank range whereupon they were shot down in cold blood. The Cheyenne now came out of their village and attacked, killing four soldiers and wounding several others. A peace chief known as Black Kettle was able to stop the warriors from further efforts to annihilate Eayre's soldiers (who just happened to be way beyond their military jurisdiction).

WILLIAM BENT

Black Kettle sent a rider with a peace message for William Bent (brother of Charles), a good friend of the Cheyenne who had married two Cheyenne women, Owl Woman and then, upon her death, her sister Yellow Woman. Bent went to Chivington and advised him that the Indians wanted peace, not war. Chivington said he had no authority to make peace, that he was making war. Bent countered that if there was a general Indian uprising many innocent settlers and travelers along the Santa Fe and Oregon trails would be killed. Chivington replied they would have to take care of themselves.

ATROCITIES

On June 11, 1864, a settler named Ward Hungate, his wife, and their two young daughters were murdered, their ranch house burned, and their stock run off, this some twenty miles from Denver. The horribly mutilated bodies were hauled into Denver and put on public display. It was learned later that four young Arapahoes had committed the heinous deed but everyone now had proof that Indians were "murderers and cut-throats" fit only for extermination. Governor Evans issued a proclamation advising all Indians to report to various American forts to prevent them being "killed by mistake." Very few Indians went to the forts because it had been soldiers who had been doing the attacking.

William Bent became an indefatigable worker for peace. He arranged meetings between Cheyennes and military officers. He smoothed things over when meetings went awry. But events were on track to destroy the peace process. Stage stations and wagon trains were attacked. Indians destroyed ten wagons at Plum Creek on the Platte Trail with two women and two children taken captive. At Ewbank Station a family of ten was killed and mutilated. Ranches were being abandoned for fear of the "Indian menace," despite the Reverend Chivington's comment that the "settlers would have to take care of themselves."

3ᴿᴰ COLORADO VOLUNTEERS

Governor Evans sent out telegram after telegram, demanding that the Army be instructed to protect Coloradans from certain destruction. But the Civil War was raging and there were no troops to spare. His only alternative was to raise what came to be the 3ʳᵈ Volunteer Regiment to serve for one hundred days against hostile Indians. His orders to the 3ʳᵈ included "authorizing all citizens to pursue, kill and destroy the enemy wherever found."

William Bent was about the only person who still worked for peace. (Two of his sons, George and Charles, were somewhere in the Cheyenne camps.) Even Indian Agent Colley at Ft. Lyon wrote about the Indians: "There is no depending on any of them. I have done everything in my power to keep the peace. I think now a little powder and lead is the best food for them." But Major Edward W. Wynkoop reacted favorably when he received a letter stating that the Indians were willing to come in and discuss peace.

COUNCIL

On September 28, 1864, Wynkoop, Governor Evans, and Col. Chivington met with Cheyenne and Arapahoe leaders, Black Kettle acting as spokesman. The Indians wanted to live peacefully with the Americans but Evans told them they hadn't gone to the forts like he had advised them previously. Chivington told the chiefs that his style of fighting required that all enemies lay down their arms and submit. The Indians agreed to camp around the security of the fort but when they were instructed to move further away they chose an area on Sand Creek. They believed they were under the protection of the American government and they raised the American flag in the center of the little village.

CHRISTIAN PROGRESS

Governor Evans sincerely believed that "these savages couldn't continue to block Christian progress by their extravagant and inefficient use of land." [See Note # 5.] But now he was now totally embarrassed. He had demanded protection from Washington yet this young little Major Wynkoop had almost made peace with the "muderin' redskins." He had raised the 3ʳᵈ Colorado Volunteers "…to kill Indians and they must kill Indians." Then, for reasons historians haven't investigated, Governor Evans packed up his wife and family and left Denver for a two-month visit to Washington D.C.

SAND CREEK MASSACRE

At dawn on November 29, 1864, Col. Chivington instructed his force of some 750 men who were about to attack the encampment at Sand Creek: "Kill and scalp all, big and little; nits make lice…I shan't say who you shall kill, but remember our murdered women and children." The signal was given and the camp was shredded with fire from four twelve-pound howitzers. These exploding shells were what awakened the sleeping Indians. Then the Americans charged into the camp, shooting or cutting down every Amerindian in sight as they ran panic stricken. Black Kettle raised a white flag under the American flag.

Chief White Antelope refused to run and was heard to say that he and the chiefs were to blame for believing the Americans. At seventy years of age he sang his death song: *Nothing lives long, only the earth and mountains*, before he was cut down by American bullets.

Warriors tried to make a stand in an effort to protect the women and children. George Bent, son of William, was shot in the hip. Black Kettle had resolved to die like White Antelope but the warriors carried him away. They couldn't save his wife, who was shot seven times (but the indomitable woman lived to tell about it). Five "squaws" under a bank showed their breasts and begged for mercy but the American soldiers shot them down anyway. Another woman was lying on the ground with her leg broken. An American came up to her with a drawn saber and brought it down on the woman's arm as she tried to protect herself, breaking it. She turned over, raised her other arm, the soldier breaking that too with his saber. Then, the woman in absolute agony, he walked away without killing her.

A large number of squaws gathered in a protective hole sent out a little girl of perhaps six years of age with a white flag on a stick. She was immediately shot and killed. A mother with a baby in her womb was killed and cut open, the unborn sprawling at her side. Indian males had their sex organs cut off and the soldiers took a number of female genital scalps "…to make a tobacco pouch" out of them. [See Note # 6.] A little girl who had been trying to hide in the sand was pulled out by two soldiers and shot by both. With all these atrocities taking place, women with babes in arms killed their own babies so the Americans wouldn't subject them to more heinous tortures. The slaughter continued into the afternoon. Soldiers raped dead or dying squaws in relays while toddler Indian children were used for target practice by the victorious Americans.

Reverend Chivington sent a preliminary report before returning to Denver: "I at daylight this morning attacked a Cheyenne village of from nine hundred to a thousand warriors. We killed between four and five hundred. All did nobly." George Bent later testified that perhaps there had been around two hundred men in the camp, that of the 163 slain, 110 were women and children.

When they got back to Denver, Chivington and the 3rd Colorado Volunteers were received as "heroes and saviors of the frontier." The Denver *News* wrote: "Colorado soldiers have again covered themselves with glory!" and that "All acquitted themselves well." Chivington was now Denver's living hero and his highly sought political career was all but assured of success.

The nation-wide uproar over Sand Creek forced Congress to send in an investigative committee of three to Colorado. They arrived at Ft. Lyon in August, 1865, and called in witnesses, one of whom was Kit Carson. He testified that "Chivington and his boys were cowards and dogs." But it was not safe to contradict what people of the time wanted to believe about Sand Creek. Captain **Silas S. Soule** testified against Chivington in the inquiry. Soule was subsequently murdered on a Denver street and his assassin was never punished. [See Note # 7.] Whenever Denverites encountered the men holding the hearings they yelled out: "*Exterminate them! Exterminate them!*" [See Note # 8.]

AFTERMATH

Before Sand Creek there were always young, hot-headed Indians who went on the raiding trail in an effort to make a reputation. Most Indians and almost all Indian leaders did not desire war. After Sand Creek, all the plains Indians whether old, young, men or women, all wanted to make war against the heinous Americans, even if it was winter. These battles have been described as the biggest race war in the history of the USA. As usual, those not guilty of anything, like people in wagon trains or settlers in outlying farms, were the ones who bore the brunt of Indian retaliation.

Four years later the Government issued a report which stated that because of the Sand Creek Massacre the Americans had to fight the plains Indians with the monetary cost being some $30,000,000 (per year? Bishop H.B. Whipple of Minnesota wrote in 1880 that the "Indian wars have cost the United States $500,000,000"). About 8,000 troops had to be diverted from the South because of the Indian war. Hundreds of soldiers had died in battles, settlers had been butchered, and much property destroyed, all because of Colorado Indian haters who caused the Sand Creek Massacre.

UTES

Much of western Colorado was Ute territory so when "settlers" began moving into the San Luis Valley around 1852 the Utes resented the intrusion. This resentment flared into open warfare on Christmas Day in 1854 when the Utes killed some fifteen men at Ft. Pueblo then raided along the Arkansas River and the San Luis Valley. The Army had to come in to put a stop to the raids. During the 1860s mining developments weren't located in traditional Ute hunting grounds so there wasn't too much trouble. But by 1868 the tribe was "persuaded" to cede their lands from North Park to the San Luis Valley, thus opening it up for settlers. The "treaty" acknowledged that much of western Colorado was still recognized as Ute territory.

"THE UTES MUST GO!"

Some five years later the San Juan Mountains were found to contain precious minerals so in the Brunot Agreement Americans took control of the land. (The ceded land became the site for one mining rush after another in 1890-91, to Ouray, Rico, Telluride, Ophir, Silverton, etc.) With this successful dismemberment of Ute territory, Coloradans believed the rest of their land should also belong to Americans. Why should a third of Colorado remain "unproductive"? The feeling was that "these savage tribes are all waning and must finally become extinct, leaving their rich possessions to be occupied and developed by a more appreciative race." [See Note # 9.] In 1876 the Colorado Legislative Assembly petitioned Congress to remove the Utes to Oklahoma. In 1877 the *Ouray Times* was publishing articles that asked why "semi-barbarous" Utes were permitted to occupy land when "intelligent, industrious citizens" could use it so much better.

GOVERNOR PITKIN

In 1879 Governor Fred Pitkin stated that if the Ute Reservation could be extinguished the land would be thrown open for settlers and their homes. "My idea is that unless they are removed by the government they must be exterminated. I could raise 25,000 to protect the settlers in twenty-four hours. The State would be willing to settle the Indian problem at its own expense. The advantages that would accrue from the throwing open of twelve million acres of land to miners and settlers would more than compensate all the expenses incurred." [See Note # 10.] W.H. Vickers added that the Utes were "degenerates," and disagreeable neighbors who should be "banished to some more appropriate retreat than the garden of our growing state." A popular slogan was created and promoted by the *Denver Tribune*: "The Utes must go!" All that was needed to take action against the Utes was a reason. In reality an excuse would do.

NATHAN MEEKER

In 1878 Nathan Meeker was appointed as Indian Agent at the White River Agency. Meeker sincerely believed that the Utes could become farmers and that their agricultural society would preserve them. So he introduced the products of white civilization: steel plows, barbed wire, windmills, "proper" homes with stoves and bathtubs, etc. Meeker moved his operation to Powell Park where he ordered that the meadows be plowed for planting wheat. The meadows supplied the Utes with rich grass for their horse herds and they didn't want it plowed. A Ute named Johnson went in to see Meeker to have him stop the plowing permanently but the Agent told him "You have too many horses. You must kill some of them." Johnson, a powerful man, picked Meeker up, flung him to the floor, then walked away. Nathan Meeker promptly sent a message by telegraph that troops were needed at the Ute Agency.

SOLDIERS

Troops under Major Thomas T. Thornburgh arrived in the beautiful mountain setting. A Ute named Chief Jack dropped by to tell Thornburgh that troops were not needed so the major replied that he would leave his men at Milk Creek where they were and take only a half dozen to see what was bothering Meeker at Powell Park.

On the morning of September 29, 1879, the Utes were watching as the long column of soldiers didn't stop at Milk Creek as Thornburgh had promised. [See Note # 11.] A soldier spotted the Indians and then a rifle shot rang out. There was a moment of silence followed by a veritable hail of bullets. Thornburgh fell dead out of his saddle and ten more soldiers were killed before the battle ended. Four days later a company of Negro soldiers rescued the trapped troopers.

The Utes had sent word to their fellows at Powell Park that soldiers were headed there. They immediately attacked the Agency, Meeker falling with a bullet in the head. Ten other unsuspecting white men were murdered, all the women taken captive. All buildings were burned to the ground.

Chief Ouray was able to establish a sort of armistice and after twenty-three days the women captives were released, unharmed. The women stated they had not been molested by their Ute captors but later they changed their minds and said they had been outraged. Everyone was now convinced, if they weren't already, that *The Utes Must Go!* Rumors fueled the idea that a large scale Indian war would break out so militia forces were gathered and federal troops sent in. But nothing actually happened so in time an official investigation was ordered by the authorities in Washington.

FINAL TREATY

It was decided that the Ute leader known as Douglas was culpable for the whole affair so he received a sentence to Leavenworth Prison. No other Ute was punished. The real "punishment" would be taking the land from the Utes. The *Denver Times* stated: "Either they or we must go, and we are not going. Humanitarianism is an idea. Western Empire is an inexorable fact. He who gets in the way of it will be crushed." In 1880 Ute leaders signed a treaty where the Southern Utes would be restricted to a reservation on the La Plata River bridging northern New Mexico and southern Colorado. The other Ute groups would be removed to the Uintah Reservation in Utah. In 1882 Ute lands were opened to "settlers," who in fact had already moved in to claim the rich prize of Ute lands.

DISCUSSION NOTES *for* COLORADO INDIAN AFFAIRS

Note # 1
See page 73 in *The Long Death* by R.K. Andrist. Part III of this work is an excellent account on this portion of Colorado Indian history.

Note # 2
As previously mentioned, anyone taking over land belonging to Indians is automatically described as a "settler" in American historiography.

Note # 3
See page 75 in *Colorado: A History Of The Centennial State* by Carl Abbott, Stephen J. Leonard, and David McComb.

Note # 4
As in other areas, this also encouraged Americans to goad Indians into defending themselves, giving "whites" an excuse to begin a general Indian war in order to take Indian land, then deporting or exterminating the Indians.

Note # 5
See pages 38-40 in *Colorado: A Bicentennial History* by Marshall Sprague.

Note # 6
See pages 90-91 in *The Long Death*. Considered from the Native American point of view, the Sand Creek Massacre was the 9-11 of the Plains Indians tribes.

For perspectives contrary to R.K. Andrist and other citations see Chapter 13 in *Massacres Of The Mountains: A History Of The Indian Wars Of The Far West, 1815-1875* by J.P. Dunn, Jr. First published in 1886, Dunn states that among the 300 Indian dead, half were warriors, the rest women and children. He states that the "massacre" aspect has been "...exaggeration, much invective, much of misunderstanding, and much of wholly unfounded statement." Col. Chivington was an "uncompromising Union man" who led the destruction of the supplies needed for the Texan invasion of New Mexico during the Civil War. The Colorado troops at San Creek were composed of men who are "...prominent and respected citizens of Colorado now." Indians, including Cheyennes, were constantly attacking settlers and white women taken captive were raped time and again by men of the tribe. "The treatment of women, by any Indians, is usually bad, but by the plains Indians especially so." Dunn cites the case of one Lucinda Ewbanks who suffered under the Cheyenne, Sioux, and Black Foot. "They would bring in the scalps of the whites and show them to me and laugh about it," she later testified.

The people of Colorado wanted revenge because Indians had ruined their crops, run off their stock, burned their homes, had helped bury the mutilated dead, had heard the stories of women captives "...these men marched to Sand Creek, with the fire of vengeance in their hearts, and quenched it in blood."

Dunn ends the chapter by quoting Chivington's "courageous" words: "I stand by Sand Creek" and the author writes that "Sand Creek is far from being the climax of American outrages on the Indian as it has been called." Have the people of the East forgotten about the Pequots and the Conestogas? The Moravian Indians? The treatment of Cherokees and Seminoles? "…Your ancestors and predecessors were guilty of worse things than the Sand Creek massacre."

Note # 7

See page 107 in *A Colorado History*, 7th Edition, by Carl Ubbelohde, Maxine Benson, and Duane A. Smith. The authors state that Sand Creek is "unpleasant reading."

Note # 8

See pages 76-78 in *Colorado: A History Of The Centennial State*.

Note # 9

See page 124 in *Colorado: A History Of The Centennial State*.

Note # 10

See page 331 in *The Long Death*.

Note # 11

See page 95 in *Colorado: A Bicentennial History*.

UTAH

The principal Amerindian groups with historical ties to Utah are the Utes, Southern Paiutes, and Gosiutes (though there were also a few Navajos). The first known European-based people to make contact with them were the Rivera expedition to the Uncompahgre River in 1765, the Domínguez-Escalante expedition of 1776, the Arze-García expedition of 1813, and the many trips made by an interpreter and possibly Indian Agent named Mestas from New Mexico. [See Note # 1 *Notes begin on page 359.*] While they were followed by fur trappers and other "trailblazers" the two events that were totally to alter Utah Indian life were the defeat of Mexico by the USA in 1846-48 and the entry of Mormons into Utah in 1847. Mormons considered themselves "friendly and constructive" toward Indians but as Americans they appropriated any lands and the water needed for them so long as they could hold them. [See Note # 2.] In 1850 when Utah became an American territory, **Brigham Young** was appointed Territorial Governor and Superintendent of Indian Affairs. While the Book of Mormon identified Indians as a "chosen people," by November of 1850 he was working for removal of Indians away from projected Mormon settlements.

Brigham Young also sought to end the slave trade which had targeted basically the Paiutes. In 1852 he had a law enacted that permitted only "indentured servitude" and only Mormons could "buy" or "adopt" indentured servants. Churchmen were empowered to assure that indentured servants were being well treated.

In 1853 there occurred a series of clashes referred to as the "Walker War." Led by an Indian named Wahkara, anglicized into "Walker," the raids were over as of May, 1854.

UTES

Indian farms were started in central Utah in the 1850s but it didn't take them long to fail. Mormon leader Brigham Young asked his people to help the Indians with food but most of the newcomers considered them mere thieves. In 1849 some Utes stole some livestock, they were pursued by militia and four were killed. In 1850 another forty were killed under similar circumstances. The Utes had no alternative: it was either steal or starve. [See Note # 3.] The "whites" didn't concern themselves with the fact that they had taken all agricultural lands for themselves or that they hunted down most of the available game. Isn't that what Americans did everywhere else? Why should Utah be any different? Remove the savages!

By the winter of 1856 the Utah Utes were on the verge of starvation. Utah Indian lands were not respected by "settlers," who quickly started demanding that the Indians be removed, especially if the Indians fought to protect their property.

The Uinta River Valley was explored and when the area was declared "unfit for white settlement" it was given to the Indians. On October 3, 1861, President Abraham Lincoln set the area aside for the starving Utes and an Army post was established in 1862. The Congress got around to ratifying the grant on May 5, 1864, by which time many Utes had starved to death because there was not enough money for annuities during the Civil War.

In 1865 Indian Superintendent O.H. Irish made a treaty with the Utes living at Spanish Fork. The Government promised to pay $25,000 a year for ten years, $20,000 a year for the next twenty years, $15,000 a year for the next thirty years, if the Utes would immediately relinquish their lands and move to the reservation. They did and the treaty went to the Senate, which refused ratification in 1869. There would be no such payments as specified in the "treaty" and the vacated land was now in American hands.

The Utes wanted their own lands back. Under a leader named Black Hawk a series of guerrilla raids (which actually started as far back as 1847), referred to as the "Black Hawk War," turned out to be costly in life and property. But the Utes couldn't outlast the millions upon millions of Americans. Black Hawk died of tuberculosis in 1870. A peace chief, Tabby-to-Kwa (Child of the Sun), took over. He led the defeated but still reluctant Utes to the barren Uinta Basin, where absolutely nothing was waiting for them to help make the transition. Raids started up again until Brigham Young took them some seventy-five cattle. In exchange for their lands the Utes now received some beef, lard, bacon, flour, beans, sugar, salt, and soap. That is, when the annuities arrived.

The Uintah Reservation was of such poor quality that the first Indian agents refused to stay. In 1871 the energetic John J. Critchlow arrived at the Reservation and tried to teach the Utes to farm the land which had been judged too poor for white farmers. [It is often said that various Indian groups did not accept farming as a way of life. It is seldom pointed out that Americans appropriated good farming lands for themselves then "gave" the Indians lands which were not suited for farming. Then the "savages" were blamed for not wanting to become "civilized like the white man," thereby "proving" Indian inferiority and white superiority.] He started a sawmill, various trading posts, worked to enlarge cattle herds, started a day school, etc., and distributed supplies honestly.

Bowing to the 1879 Colorado pressures of "The Utes Must Go!" the White River Utes were forced onto the Uintah Reservation, putting more stress on an acknowledged poor reserve. In 1886 the Uintah Agency and the Ouray Agency were combined and the agent moved to Fort Duchesne. In 1887 the Dawes Act was passed in an effort to break up the reservation system. [See Note # 4.] Each Indian would received a certain amount of land, depending if he was the head of a family, single, orphan, etc., and any remaining land would revert to the Government, which would open it up for "settlers." When the valuable hydrocarbon mineral gilsonite was discovered on the reservation there was heard another demand that the Indians be *removed* for the betterment of all. The Uncompahgres lost much land to American settlers by 1898 and in 1905 the bulk of the reservation was opened up for American settlement by Congress.

Another way to get control of the land was through the availability of water. The Pahvants at Kanosh had some 3,200 acres and were legally entitled to 120 shares of water for that acreage. They were never able to get more than 20 shares, thereby rendering the land relatively "useless," whereupon they were beset by offers to buy the land. [See Note # 5.]

SOUTHERN PAIUTES

The Shoshonean Paiutes' homeland included extensive areas in southern Utah, northern Arizona, southern Nevada, and southeastern California. Their lifestyle included hunting, gathering, and farming. They were grouped in bands, not one nation, though they could unite for a particular project. They were slow to acquire the Spanish horse, at first killing it for food. Mounted Utes often raided them to capture women and children for the slave trade with New Mexico. The Domínguez-Escalante expedition of 1776 was probably the first European group to make contact with Paiutes. American trappers and explorers began entering the Paiute kingdom in the 1820s but the Mormons were the first to actually settle on their land. Hostile at first, the Paiutes became friendly in hopes they would get help against slave raiding. Believing that Indians had a special role as written in the Lamanities of the Book of Mormon, leaders wanted to put their beliefs into practice. The Southern Indian Mission was established at Fort Harmony in 1854 and proved very successful. Jacob Hamblin and Howard Egan became highly successful missionaries among the Paiutes.

Mormons sought to end the Ute-New Mexico slave trade and they were successful in that outright slavery was replaced with indentured servitude in which only Mormons could participate. The Paiute population had been shrunk by slavery, continued under indentured servitude, and European diseases always took their toll.

The first Southern Paiute Agency was established at Saint Thomas in 1869 and the Moapa Indian reservation in 1873. When valuable mineral deposits were discovered in the Meadow and Pahranagat valleys in the late 1860s and early 1870s the typical American clamor arose to remove the Paiutes from southern Utah. A treaty signed by Utah Paiutes in 1865 was used as the fulcrum for removing all Paiutes to the Uinta Basin. [See Note # 6.] In 1873 commissioners John Wesley Powell and George W. Ingalls recommended that all Paiutes be removed to Moapa, which was a pit of neglect and corruption. The Paiutes were all but forgotten by the Government and they were soon even more destitute. Though other lands were opened for Paiutes, Floyd A. O'Neil has written that "The United states government has also largely continued its traditional role of ignoring the Indians and their problems." [See Note # 7.]

GOSIUTES

Though difficult to conceive, the Gosiutes were even more destitute than the Paiutes. This small group of a few hundred people had no horses and in 1859 one writer described them as eating "crickets, ants, rats, and other such animals." [See Note # 8.] But they did utilize their desert environment to the fullest, harvesting wild vegetables, berries, roots, seeds, etc. On occasion there were communal rabbit hunts. Because food was so scarce each family moved about basically alone so there was no tribal development. The family lived in sagebrush wickiups.

But everything was to change starting in 1853 when American "settlers" came in and took over the best portions of land. There were raids against livestock and the settlers clamored for protection. In one serious incident a number of soldiers under Captain Absolom Woodward camped in Ibapah land near a group of Gosiute wickiups. The men were away hunting antelope so the soldiers raped various Gosiute girls before they moved on. When the men returned they decided to even the score and ambushed five soldiers, killing four, but the fifth returned to relate the story of "wanton murder."

Indian Agent Robert Jarvis tried to convince the Gosiutes to learn how to farm (1862-63) the American way. There was little success. A "treaty" gave the American president the right to remove Indians from their native lands and force them onto a reservation but the Gosiutes refused to remove to the Uinta Basin, saying they were afraid of the other Indians there and preferring their native Skull Valley. For some unexplained reason, probably due to their small numbers, the Gosiutes were forgotten by the Government. In 1912, perhaps a more humane period in American history, eighty acres were reserved for the Gosiutes in Skull Valley. The Deep Creek Reservation (in western Tooele County and eastern Nevada) was founded with some 34,560 acres in 1914. Some 17,920 acres were added to Gosiute land in 1919.

DISCUSSION NOTES *for* UTAH INDIAN AFFAIRS

Note # 1

See pages 27-59 in *The Peoples Of Utah* edited by Helen Z. Papanikolas.

Note # 2

See pages 358-59 in *Utah's History* by Richard D. Poll, Thomas G. Alexander, Eugene E. Campbell, and David E. Miller.

Note # 3

See *History Of Utah* by H.H. Bancroft.

Note # 4

See Document 315 in *Documents Of American History* edited by Henry Steele Commager.

Note # 5

It has been said that Indian dispossession in property, education, employment, etc., continues to this day.

Note # 6

The Government always assured the targeted Indians that after signing the treaty the acknowledged land would belong to the Indians *"as long as the grass grows, the water runs, the sun shines."* Regular cash payments were also promised for a specified number of years, which were to be in the form of annuities. As of 1871 the Government finally ended the hypocritical practice of making treaties with Indians. Senator Ben N. Campbell has written that of the 472 treaties made with Amerindian people the American government didn't keep a single one.

Note # 7

See page 49 in *The Peoples Of Utah.*

Note # 8

See page 54 in the Papanikolas volume above.

OKLAHOMA

While precontact Oklahoma saw a number of Amerindian groups on its lands, the Indians who first "made history" in the area were eastern Indians. Among the most important were the Cherokees, Choctaws, Chickasaws, Creeks, and Seminoles, generally referred to as the "Five Civilized Tribes." They were called "civilized" because they had basically adopted European material items like weapons, wagons, livestock, and food items. Intermarriage between British and Amerindian people was not uncommon. [See Note # 1 *Notes begin on page 366.*]

The history of Amerindian refugees forced into exile in Oklahoma had its beginnings when the Federal government decreed that a certain area was "Indian land." But Americans, generally referred to as "whites" or "white citizens," coveted fertile Amerindian lands and refused to abide by any law that protected Indian property. The states of Georgia, Alabama, and Mississippi proved particularly hostile to Amerindians within their borders, even declaring that federal law could not take precedent over state law.

CONCEPT of REMOVAL

Thomas Jefferson, acknowledged as "humane and tolerant," is generally credited with conceiving the plan that all Indians should be "removed" to lands west of the Mississippi, thus solving the problem of "troublesome Indian neighbors" in the States. This concept took hold in the American mind and ideas like protecting Indian property or educating the Indians for American citizenship fell by the wayside. Deportation of Indians would provide quick profits with the sale of Indian lands and those in a position to make money lobbied for removal. [See Note # 2.]

BASIC PATTERN

There was a basic pattern to exile of Indians from their native lands. The Cherokees will serve as the basic example. [See Note # 3.] In 1817 the Cherokees "ceded" to the USA around one third of their lands east of the Mississippi and in return they would be awarded "equal acreage" in Arkansas along the White and Arkansas valleys (where other Indians, the Osages, believed they owned the land, though the Cherokees didn't know that). The USA was treaty bound to furnish boats, vehicles, and provisions for the journey west. Indian leaders were generally treated royally in efforts to get them to sign but the ordinary Indian would receive a blanket and a kettle or beaver trap. "White intruders" would be put off the land by government forces. As with most Indian removal treaties, the 1817 document contained the stipulation *"until the same shall be ratified by the President and Senate of the United States, and duly promulgated."* [See Note # 4.]

American settlers living on Cherokee land in Arkansas "proved hard to remove" so in 1828 President J.Q. Adams decided to invite Cherokee leaders to Washington and get them to sign a treaty that would remove them even further west. The 1828 treaty included the stipulation that the new lands would be "…a permanent home, and which shall, under the most solemn guarantee of the United States, be and remain theirs forever—a home that shall never, in all future time, be embarrassed by having extended around it the lines, or placed over it the jurisdiction of a Territory or State, nor be pressed upon by the extension, in any way, of any of the limits of any existing Territory or State…" The Cherokees were to receive about seven million acres and they would cede all Arkansas lands to the USA, who would pay for improvements to boot. The new lands in the West came to be called Indian Territory, the beginning of what is now Oklahoma.

Choctaws and Chickasaws were also interested in finding suitable lands for their people so in 1828 Peter Pitchlynn of the Choctaws and Levi Colbert of the Chickasaw led a delegation to search for land in Indian Territory but their report stated it was not suitable.

ANDREW JACKSON

Indian-hating Andrew Jackson was elected to the presidency in 1828. There was no longer any attempt to settle things diplomatically: Indians would be deported to the West and that was that. In 1829 the State of Georgia annulled the Cherokee Nation constitution on the grounds that it was creating "a state within a state." This excuse was the cover by which Georgians sought to take Cherokee lands but President Jackson agreed with Georgia, thereby denying the Cherokees the protection which was theirs under federal law.

Also in 1829 gold was discovered on Cherokee land in northeastern Georgia and thousands of Americans were soon in the diggings, trampling on Cherokee crops or stealing Cherokee livestock if they needed food. In 1830 Congress passed the Indian Removal Act which supported Jackson's position. The Cherokees decided to go to court and their case went all the way to the Supreme Court. Chief Justice **John Marshall** declared that the Cherokee Nation had a legal right to its land. President Jackson remarked to the effect that *Marshall has made his decision now let him enforce it.*

DIVISION OVER REMOVAL

Speaking generally, full-blood Cherokees opposed removal while mixed-bloods felt there really was no other alternative. By 1835 the Ridge faction among the Cherokees (led Major Ridge, his son John, his two nephews Buck Watie and Stand Watie) was committed to removal. John Ross, a mixed-blood with one-eighth Cherokee, opposed removal unless an adequate sum, perhaps twenty million dollars, could be paid by the USA. Then the people might remove "to Spanish territory." [See Note # 5.]

The Ridge faction signed a removal treaty in 1835, the Treaty of New Echota. The time limit set for removal was May, 1838, and perhaps one-eighth of the nation had started westward by then. General

Winfield Scott and 7,000 troops arrived with orders to evict all Cherokees from Georgia. Some 17,000 Indians were rounded up, held in stockades, then forced to walk west, under military escort, with little concern for food or clothing.

FAMILY of MARTYRS

Many Cherokees resisted and some escaped. An elder named **Tsali**, known as Charley to the Americans, slew a soldier who had viciously jabbed his wife with a bayonet. Tsali, his wife, and their sons managed to escape from the stockade and joined other escapees in the forests and caves of the Smokey Mountains. General Scott now ordered that Tsali and his family be hunted down. Troops pursued them relentlessly through the mountains and in a skirmish two more soldiers were killed. Finally General Scott relented somewhat: if Tsali and his sons would give themselves up he would ignore the rest of the 400 Cherokees hiding in the mountains. Tsali, his three sons, and a brother turned themselves in. Adept General Scott ordered that a firing squad made up of Ridge treaty-party Cherokees execute the martyrs, which they did. [See Note # 6.] Despite such premeditated brutality, Scott held true to his promise and the other Cherokees (now recognized as the Eastern Cherokees) remained to live free in their mountains.

TRAIL OF TEARS

The Indian death march across America has been euphemistically referred to as the Trail of Tears. It was indeed a trail of *death* because Cherokees died in horrendous numbers, especially the young and the old. It has been said that about 4,000 of the 18,000 Cherokees who started never arrived in Indian Territory, victims of "hunger, exposure, sickness, or despair."

JOHN ROSS

The removal managed by the U.S. Army was recognized as exceptionally brutal. John Ross asked for authority to conduct the removals and it was granted. He organized thirteen different groups and he and his wife departed from Georgia with the last contingent. The journey generally took six months to complete. Even with Ross' more understanding leadership, the march was still a grueling one and Ross' wife was among those who died on the trail. Some groups of Cherokees managed to slip away in hopes of making it to Texas or Mexico.

Those Cherokees who made it to Indian Territory were beset with problems. The Ross and Ridge factions were now bitter enemies. On June 22, 1839, Major Ridge, John Ridge, and Elias Boudinot were assassinated. (The same fate was dealt to William McIntosh, Tustennuggee, and Sam Hawkins, Creeks who signed the Treaty of Indian Springs in which Creek land was ceded to the USA. As far as Cherokee history is concerned, it is thought that John Ross had nothing to do with the killings of the Ridge faction.)

RAW FRONTIER

In an effort to stabilize the situation John Ross was elected as Principal Chief of the Cherokee Nation. It was now he who would have to deal with American personalities like Secretary of War Joel Poinsett, General Matthew Arbuckle, and Superintendent William Armstrong. And at home violence was all too common, bitter animosity was simple to foment, and united government was mostly a dream. Adjustments were very difficult for a number of reasons. There were bitter memories over the thousands of family and friends that had died on the trails leading west or from pestilence on the steamboats that took some Indians part way. The new lands thrust on the people were valued at around one dollar per acre while the lands they had been forced to leave were now selling for as much as $100 per acre but the Government was not about to reimburse the difference. And a very basic, stark reality was the herculean challenge of creating absolutely new pioneer settlements with only large, destitute camps as a start.

HOMES in the WILDERNESS

The first homes were built with walls of peeled saplings set up between corner posts. The saplings were plastered with mud to improve on the barrier. In winter the place was heated by a round clay stove placed in the middle of the room, a smoke hole in the roof providing a way for smoke to escape. The roof consisted of shingle-like bark. There were no nails and about the only tool available was the hatchet. Cooking was done outside on open fires. Meat was roasted in the coals or ashes. Those with earthen pots could boil meat for soups and such.

FEDERAL MANAGEMENT

Among the greatest problems was Government management of Oklahoma Indian affairs. For whatever reasons, keeping order in the Indian nations was close to impossible for the Government. For example, when cash payments were disbursed to the Indians, American traders would bring in huge amounts of whiskey and other liquors but the Government did nothing, at least nothing that helped the Indians. Drunkenness became a major problem and blood feuds started or were settled while under the influence of whiskey. Treaties generally specified that Government authorities had the power to enforce laws but such stipulations were often ignored. Indeed, Congress wound up ignoring most Indian treaties when it came to voting agreed-upon appropriations for the tribes. Further, swindling the Indian nations out of their money, annuities, etc., became all but "standard operating procedure" for those in power.

EFFORTS to STABILIZE

In an effort to stabilize society, the Treaty of 1846 included the three main factions of the Cherokee Nation in Oklahoma: the Old Settlers, the Treaty Party, and the Ross Party. It reiterated that the Nation owned seven million acres of land west of Arkansas. All past crimes committed by Cherokees were now officially pardoned in an effort to assuage animosities. The law would protect everyone and the rights to protect peaceable assembly and to petition the government were guaranteed. The Government agreed to pay various indemnities, including $115,000 to members of the Treaty Party. The heirs of Major Ridge, John Ridge, and Elias Boudinot (who had been assassinated) would be paid $5,000 for each of the three. The Government would also pay for some damages made by American intruders. Collecting these awards was quite another matter and it turned out collections were almost impossible without attorneys and their handsome fees. In 1852 Col. John Drennen, Indian Superintendent for the Western District, paid attorneys fees of $70,369 to S.C. Stambaugh, Amos Kendall, and John Kendall, all from the money owed the Cherokees.

CIVIL WAR

When the Civil War broke out the Cherokees were of divided allegiance. It is believed that John Ross wished to remain neutral but the Nation became allied with the South though a number of Cherokees enlisted to fight for the Union. Federal troops were withdrawn from Indian Territory so the Confederacy held sway. The tribes could not have opposed the Confederates even if they had wished to.

There was great suffering in Indian Territory because of the Civil War. [See Note # 7.] At the beginning Indian Union families fled north while toward the end Confederate families fled south. All factions of the Five Civilized Tribes suffered great losses and especially among the Cherokee, Creeks, and Seminoles there was outright anarchy in their territories. A class of men now turned to living by raiding and they didn't really care which side they stole from. In October of 1862 William C. Quantrill brought his guerrilla raiders into the Cherokee Nation, further making it a region of terror and despair. It wasn't until September, 1863, that major fighting ended in Indian country. Stand Watie, an implacable enemy of Union Indians, continued his raids until 1865.

Union Indians had suffered greatly at the beginning and they would not forget those hardships. Confederate Indians made efforts to unite with Plains Indians as well as Union Indians in May, 1865, when they met at Camp Washita. Leaders of the Five Civilized Tribes met with chiefs of the Comanche, Caddo, Kiowa, Osage, and Cheyenne and promised to remain at peace with each other.

REVENGE

With the Civil War over it was now time for *revenge*. Kansas Senators Samuel C. Pomeroy and James H. Lane wanted to "relocate" Kansas Indians to what had been *Confederate* Indian Territory. If the Kickapoo, Osage, Ottawa, Potawatomi, Sac and Fox, Kansas, Iowa, Shawnee, etc., could be "persuaded" to remove to Indian Territory then their lands could be opened to American "settlers." That Indian Territory belonged exclusively to the Five Civilized Tribes was supposedly neutralized by their allegiance to the Confederacy. According to some American "statesmen" previous treaties were therefore null and void. (This was not a new development in American psychology. The same sentiments had been expressed, successfully, after the War of 1812.)

A council was convened on September 8, 1865, at Fort Smith. Commissioner of Indian Affairs Dennis N. Cooley informed the Indian delegates that their rights under the old treaties had been forfeited because of the Civil War and that new agreements were now required. Union Indians would remain protected but the "Nations had lost all their rights to annuities and lands." [See Note # 8.] Part of their lands would now be given to Indians from Kansas or elsewhere "as the Government may desire to settle thereon." John Ross strongly opposed giving up Indian lands but Elias C. Boudinot, the son of Buck Watie, denounced him bitterly. The council adjourned with the agreement to meet in Washington in 1866.

Secretary of the Interior James Harlan was determined that the Five Civilized Tribes must give up part of their land to make room for other Indians, indeed, all Indians who lived east of the Rocky Mountains. He frequently cited the "unprovoked war" of the Tribes against the USA and the Indians' *"flagrant violation of treaties which had been observed by us with scrupulous good faith."* (Emphasis added.)

During the Washington meetings in 1866 leader John Ross was too ill to attend and shortly died. American "statesmen" got what they demanded because the Indians really had little choice. In the eyes of the Americans, Indians "leaders" now became those who ceded tribal lands as demanded by Americans. Those who demanded that Indians had a legal right to their land were considered *troublemakers* and shunned by Government authorities, who controlled the money. During the proceedings it was suggested that all Indians unite under one government and that Indian Territory henceforth take on the name *Oklahoma*, which was Muskhogean for *Red People*. The Medicine Lodge Creek Treaty of 1867 entitled Comanches, Kiowas, and some Apaches to settle on Choctaw and Chickasaw land. Cheyennes and Arapahoes were assigned land in the Cherokee Outlet, later adjusted slightly by executive order, and then Wichitas, Caddoes, and Delawares were brought in by 1872, along with the Osage and Kansas groups. Within a few short years the Poncas, Otoes, and Missouris were brought in, along with smaller bands of Sac and Fox, Kaskaskias, Peorias, Miamis, Weas, Piankashaws, Nez Perce, Wyandottes, Ottawas, Modocs, etc. In short, any and all "peaceful" Indians were required to live in Oklahoma, away from Americans, or they could be declared hostile and attacked by the Army.

SHERMAN and SHERIDAN

The mood of American leaders was reflected by that of General Grant: It is necessary to protect Americans on the plains, "even if the extermination of every Indian tribe is necessary to secure such a result." General **William Tecumseh Sherman** said in 1868: "We have now selected and provided reservations for all, off the great road… all who cling to their old hunting grounds are hostile and will remain so till killed off…The more we can kill this year the less will have to be killed in the next war…The more I see of these Indians the more convinced I am that all have to be killed or maintained as a species of pauper. Their attempts at civilization are simply ridiculous." [See Note # 9.]

WINTER CAMPAIGN

Army personnel often held the belief that Indian raiders went into "peace camps" for the winter then came out to raid during the months when there was pasturage for their horses. General **Phillip Sheridan**, commander of the Southwestern Department, decided to wage a winter campaign (1868-1869) against the "hostile" Cheyennes with **George Armstrong Custer** in command. It was the first-ever winter campaign against the plains Indians so surprise would be the Army's basic advantage, along with their grain-fed horses. Because they were in winter camp, the Indians couldn't easily escape and their villages and supplies could be destroyed, thus forcing them toward starvation or their lands in Indian Territory. Sheridan's orders to Custer were explicit: any warrior not killed in battle was to be hanged; all women and children were to be taken prisoners; all villages were to be totally destroyed and all Indian horses killed.

BLACK KETTLE

Cheyenne Chief Black Kettle, who had narrowly escaped death at Sand Creek, had parleyed with General Hazen at Fort Cobb in an effort to assure his people's safety. Then he had made a winter camp, part of some 180 lodges, along the Washita River (near present Cheyenne, Oklahoma).

BATTLE of the WASHITA

Custer rode south from Fort Supply with his Seventh Cavalry, a large baggage train laden with supplies, with Osage and white guides who knew the country. The Cheyenne camp was located and the attack was to take place at dawn the following day, November 27, 1868. Daybreak came and no sentries had been posted by the Indians. The Seventh Cavalry, now some 800 men, charged into the sleeping camp from four directions, shooting anything that moved. The Cheyenne quickly saw what was happening and fought back with anything they could, even the women and young boys returning fire if they had guns. For Black Kettle it was Sand Creek all over again but this time he died fighting for his people. But the surprise attack had been most effective and after the initial desperate resistance the Indians were defeated. The village was then systematically destroyed.

It was soon learned that Black Kettle's village was merely the first in a series of winter camps along the Washita. Down the river were located villages of Cheyenne, Arapaho, Comanche, and Kiowa. Major Joel Elliott and some 19 of his men had pursued fleeing Indians and hadn't returned but Custer ordered an immediate retreat after some 875 captured Indian horses were slaughtered. As it turned out, Elliott and his men had all been killed but many soldiers resented Custer's refusal to go find them. [See Note # 10.]

The flamboyant Custer made a grand entry back at Ft. Supply, complete with the band playing the 7th's fight song, "Garry Owen."

Oklahoma Indians continued to lose their land under one guise or the other, to Government laws like the Dawes Act, to cattlemen, to the railroads, to squatters, etc. On the more positive side of the ledger the Indians of Oklahoma are credited with a number of firsts that no other Amerindians even approached. [See Note # 11.] Union Mission, the first Christian Denominational entity in Indian Territory, was established in 1821 for the Osages and later included the Creeks and Cherokees. The first church organization was Presbyterian, in 1830. Elections were being held in Oklahoma as early as 1831, the first public school law was passed in 1832, the Choctaws created the first constitution in 1834. The first book was printed at Union Mission in 1835. Choctaws built the first capitol in 1838, in Tuskahoma. The first newspapers, the *Cherokee Messenger* and the *Cherokee Advocate*, started publication in 1844. The first Masonic Lodge was chartered in 1848, at Tahlequah. Tahlequah also became the first incorporated town in Oklahoma in 1852.

DISCUSSION NOTES *for* OKLAHOMA INDIAN AFFAIRS
Note # 1
See page 89 in *Oklahoma: A History Of The Sooner State* by Edwin C. McReynolds. Racial mixing isn't something that is popularly acknowledged in American historiography, unless people other than Americans are involved. On page 91 McReynolds writes that "European influence upon the Choctaws…began with the De Soto expedition." As with typical American historiography, he relates how the Spanish required "carriers and women." His source appears to be *Narratives of the Career of Hernando De Soto* by Edward G. Bourne. One can only wonder if Bourne was using an original Spanish language source or was he merely quoting some other American writer? If the

latter, is this "History written according to somebody-said-that-somebody-said"?

Note # 2

On pages 111-12 McReynolds writes that Indians were not interested in American citizenship because what they really wanted was to preserve their own culture. How did Indian land and personal freedom enter into Amerindian psychology? McReynolds' assertion would make an interesting debate. Further, why were "Indian neighbors" labeled as *troublesome?* Would the issue boil down to Americans coveting Indian lands?

Note # 3

The word "removal" is commonly used for the exiling process and it appears "exile" is rarely utilized, *removal* being much softer than *exile.* The same could be said for *deportation.* Possibly inured to such phraseology in American historiography, the popular mind might not come to terms with the underlying tragedy of these events. "Removal" might be more properly understood if, for example, the population of San Francisco, California, was forced at the point of a bayonet to "remove" to the eastern flatlands of North Dakota. Would the people of San Francisco survive the "walk"? Would they refer to it as the "trail of tears"? How would they feel about being deported?

For a good introduction to the Cherokee "removal," see *Trail Of Tears: The Rise And Fall Of The Cherokee Nation* by John Ehle. For excellent history on the Civilized Tribes see the works of Angie Debo. McReynolds appears to rely heavily on her *The Road To Disappearance* about the Creeks as well as her *Rise And Fall Of The Choctaw Republic.*

Note # 4

As history would show, some Indians vacated their native lands, went West, then the Senate refused to ratify the treaty, thus having possession of the vacated land with no "legal" obligation to help Indians who removed to the West because the unratified treaty was not "legal." Does Christian morality enter into American Indian Affairs?

Note # 5

See page 154 in the McReynolds volume. The Indians understood that Spanish authorities were not anti-Indian.

Note # 6

See page 221 in *500 Nations* by Alvin M. Josephy, Jr.

Note # 7

See page 51 in *Oklahoma Memories* edited by Anne Hodges Morgan and Rennard Strickland.

Note # 8

See pages 229-31 in the McReynolds volume.

Note # 9

See pages 154-66 in *The Long Death.* In the contemporary popular mind sympathies toward the extermination of people are more associated with 20th century Europe.

Note # 10

R.K. Andrist writes that Custer didn't make an effort to search out or retrieve Elliott and his men, that henceforth some of his soldiers couldn't really trust him. On page 179 of *Great Westrn Indian*

Fights it is written that "A search was made for Major Elliot and his nineteen men…"
Note # 11
See pages 19-20 in *Oklahoma: Foot-loose And Fancy-free* by Angie Debo.

Timeline: KING OF THE PLAINS

Paleo-Indian hunters of some 10,000 years ago hunted the bison (buffalo) with stone-tipped weapons like the atlatl. Buffalo hunting got a little easier some 5,500 years ago with the introduction of the bow and arrow but the bison herds of North America prospered and grew to incalculable numbers. The first European settlers-turned-hunters were from the colony of New Mexico (founded in 1598). Led by **Vicente de Zaldívar**, sixty Spaniards went to the eastern plains and encountered bison for the first time (September-October, 1598). The chronicler of the expedition found the animals to be "as fishes in the sea," so "amazing…amusing…frightening that one never tires looking at them." The "wild and fierce" animals killed three horses and wounded forty before the New Mexicans decided it would be better to capture the calves for domestication. But the calves struggled so mightily they died from the exertion. Finally the animals were hunted down and butchered for the winter meat supply. The meat was described as superior to beef.

What has been referred to as the **Northern Herd** could be found as far north as Great Slave Lake in Canada to as far south as the Platte River, as far west as the Rockies, as far east as Minnesota. The **Southern Herd** ranged from the Platte River on the north, Rockies to the west, New Mexico and Texas to the south, to the east as far as the middle of Kansas.

Scholars have written that immense herds of buffalo existed from the plains all the way to Kentucky and Tennessee. Indeed, as late as 1750 there were relatively large herds in Pennsylvania. By the 1830s "it was doubtful that any wild bison were found east of the Mississippi River." [See Note # 1 *Notes begin on page 371*.] "European immigrants to America" targeted all wild game for extinction, organizing "game drives" to remove all wild animals permanently from the land they inhabited. In one such operation in Pennsylvania in 1760, one "settler" named Black Jack Schwartz and his fellows killed some 1,124 animals, including 111 bison, from which the tongues and a few of the better hides were taken. After slaughtering the animals, they were piled up and burned, the stench causing settlers from three miles around to vacate their cabins temporarily. [See Note # 2.]

The first trappers' "Rendezvous" was held around July 10, 1825, in Wyoming but an important aspect of it was that William H. Ashley brought in a wagon (drawn by mules) for the first time. By 1830 a report was made to the Secretary of War that wagons could be used on the plains. By the early 1840s the beaver had been all but exterminated so "entrepreneurs" looked for other sources of income.

These were the days of "master race" Manifest Destiny when Americans believed all of North America should belong to the United States. In the year 1840 Independence, Missouri, was the westernmost settlement in the United States. In 1841 the first American immigrant wagon train headed for California (which was still part of Mexico), in 1843 some one thousand immigrants in Joplin, Missouri, headed for the Oregon country. In 1844 the first message was sent via a telegraph line. In 1846 the USA decided to take northern Mexico for itself and after a bloody war Mexico "ceded" the land. In 1849 gold was discovered in California. It is reasonable to assume that all these caused traffic on the plains, traffic which would have a deadly bearing on the plains bison.

Explorers, hunters, trappers, frontiersmen, and early travelers usually commented on the remarkable numbers of buffalo. The animals meandered from northern Mexico, the plains of the USA, into Canada and Alaska. How many might there have been? No one knows, but a popular number is 60,000,000 (some say less, others say twice that number). Washington Irving, said to be America's first professional writer, described the killing of a buffalo, which was mostly for sport, in one of his travels. He also said: "We felt somewhat ashamed of the butchery..." [See Note # 3.]

Wagon train people going west also killed bison for meat. [See Note # 4.] Bulls were tough eating but cows were more tender. It became common knowledge that the hump was always good, as were the marrow bones, and the tongue approached being a delicacy. Plains Indians hunted bison, the "king of the plains," and made their living off them, including selling/trading buffalo robes. [See Note # 5.] It was not long, probably no later than 1840, before the bison were being killed by Americans for their tongues, hides, or merely for the "sporting thrill" of killing an animal. In 1867 officers of the Seventh Cavalry out of Ft. Hays in western Kansas held a competition to see which "team" could bring in the most buffalo tongues in one day's hunting. The winners brought in twelve tongues, the losers eleven, the meat left to rot on the prairie. As the Union Pacific laid rails across the Kansas and Nebraska buffalo country that summer of 1867, "sportsmen" took to shooting buffalo from open windows of passenger cars. [See Note # 6.] Needless to say, not even the tongues were taken.

The plains quickly filled with American hide hunters. [See Note # 7.] One James R. Mead decided to turn to buffalo hunting and over eight to nine years personally killed more than 2,000 bison, a small number compared to claims made by others. One James Stuart wrote about chasing buffalo into a water hole just for laughs. William Cody, later to become "famous" under the name of Buffalo Bill, was hired by the Kansas Pacific Railroad to bring in buffalo meat. It is said that during the 8-18 months of his employment he killed some 4,280 buffalo. Frank Collinson wrote that he had seen thousands of buffalo cows killed for the hides while their calves were left to starve to death or be killed by wolves. International "sportsmen" also wanted to hunt. One Sir George Gore led an expedition onto the plains that lasted three years.

Hunters from New Mexico, referred to as *ciboleros*, hunted mostly with the lance. Their parties were huge, sometimes comprised of two hundred men, and they could kill some fifty animals in a day. Then every part of the animal, including items like the hair and horns, was processed to take back to the New Mexican villages.

Americans taking buffalo for the hide alone probably didn't start as regular commerce before 1830. By the time railroads were crossing the plains in the 1860s it was big business. Wagon trains and railroads broke up the mega herds into four irregular parts: the Northern herd which extended from Canada into Montana, the Dakotas, and into Wyoming; the Republican (River) herd from Wyoming into Nebraska, Kansas, Colorado; the Arkansas herd which roamed from Nebraska to the Oklahoma Panhandle; and the Texas herd which ranged from Colorado, Kansas, Oklahoma, and into Texas. In 1860 it was estimated that there were some 28,000,000 bison on the Great Plains. By 1870 the estimate was at 15,000,000. The Southern Herd was basically wiped out between 1870-74. The Northern Herd was systematically annihilated between 1876-1883.

By the late 1860s the railroads could take hides and bison bones to market so the slaughter of buffalo accelerated. In 1868 Col. **Henry Inman** stated that between 1868-1881 in Kansas alone there was paid out around $2,500,000 for buffalo bones gathered from the prairies. According to Inman it would take about one hundred buffalo to make one ton of bones. At the usual payment of eight dollars per ton, the above sum represents some 31,000,000 dead buffalo. (One can only wonder as to how many pounds of buffalo meat was left to rot because of the hide hunters.) According to Harold P. Danz, J.L. Hill wrote in his *The Passing of the Buffalo* that in 1877 the Atchison, Topeka and Santa Fe railroad carried out some 25,443 robes, 1,617,600 pounds of meat, and 2,743,100 pounds of buffalo bones. [See Note # 8.]

By the summer of 1872 the new .50-caliber Sharps rifle was becoming a popular weapon of the hide hunters. [See Note # 9.] These powerful guns (there were also .44 and .45 models), some weighing as much as sixteen pounds, were too cumbersome for use in the saddle but they were excellent for use while standing. The "Sharps 50" could kill a tough buffalo bull at six hundred yards ("shoot today and kill tomorrow"). Hunters could down any number of buffalo because they kept such a distance between themselves and the animals, which didn't stampede as their fellows were shot down one by one. A hunter named R.W. Snyder is said to have killed 119 bison in one day with his Sharps 50.

There was some American resistance to the indiscriminate slaughter of buffalo. During the years of 1871-76 several bills were passed by Congress to protect the bison. None were successful. For example, when a suitable bill made it though Congress in 1874 President **U.S. Grant** killed it with a pocket veto (refusal to act on a bill). Grant's Secretary of the Interior **Columbus Delano** had previously written that "I would not seriously regret the total disappearance of the buffalo" because the Indians would come to realize that they had to become farmers. He was not alone. Col. **Richard Dodge** told his troops to "...kill every buffalo you can...every buffalo gone is an Indian gone." General Phil Sheridan said of the hide hunters: *These men have done more in the last two years and will do more in the next year, more to settle the vexed Indian question than the entire regular army has done in the last thirty years. They are destroying the Indians' commissary...it is a well known fact that an army losing its base of supplies is placed at a great disadvantage. Send them powder and lead, if you will...for the sake of a lasting peace, let them kill, skin and sell until the buffaloes are exterminated. Then your prairies will be covered with speckled cattle and the festive cowboy, who follows the hunter as a second forerunner to an advanced civilization."* When the Texas legislature in Austin was debating a bill to protect the buffalo, Sheridan appeared before a joint meeting of the House and Senate and advised them that "instead of stopping the hunters" they should give them a hearty thank you by creating a medal for each and every one of them. The medal should depict "a dead buffalo on one side and a discouraged Indian on the other." [See Note # 10.]

American "bone gatherers" collected bison bones and made huge piles close to the railroad tracks. For example, in the area of Grenada, Colorado, along the AT&SF right of way, there was a pile of bison bones 12 feet high, 12 feet wide, and half a mile long... "and this was but one of many." One bone-buying company estimated that between 1884-91 they bought the bones of "approximately 5,950,000 bison skeletons" and there were many such companies in the business. [See Note # 11.] This commerce lasted until the late 1880s to early 1890s.

Harold Danz cites Dr. William T. Hornaday as crediting "the man with a gun" for the destruction of the buffalo, along with "man's reckless greed, his wanton destructiveness, and improvidence in not husbanding such resources as come to him from the hands of nature, ready made." [See Note # 12.] Hornaday wrote that in 1887 it was estimated there were now some 1,091 bison remaining in the land mass of Canada and the USA, some 600 in the USA proper. Thus it was that the most numerous ruminant known to mankind was now in immediate danger of extinction.

Frank Mayer, a professional buffalo hunter toward the end of that era, might be said to be representative of the psychology of the day. He maintained that the Government cooperated with his actions, providing him with free ammunition, that he was *"…neither proud nor ashamed. At the time it seemed like a proper thing to do. Looked at from a distance (he died at the age of 104), I'm not so sure. The slaughter was perhaps a shameless, needless thing. But it was also an inevitable thing, an historical necessity…The buffalo didn't fit in so well with the white man's encroaching civilization. He didn't fit in at all, in fact. He could not be controlled or domesticated. He couldn't be corralled behind wire fences. He was a misfit. So he had to go."* [See Note # 13.]

DISCUSSION NOTES *for* Timeline: KING OF THE PLAINS

Note # 1

See page 90 in *Of Bison And Man* by Harold P. Danz. For basic information on buffalo with emphasis on the people who hunted them see *The Buffalo Hunters* by Mari Sandoz and *The Great Buffalo Hunt* by Wayne Gard.

Note # 2

It is obvious that the wanton slaughter of American wildlife did not begin in the West. One of the most notorious examples in the East was the extermination of the millions or perhaps billions of carrier pigeons. It has been written that "settlers" actually *dynamited* trees where they were roosting.

Note # 3

Dan L. Thrapp writes on page 212 of his *Conquest Of Apacheria* that the Apache leader "…Victorio was a toddler barely old enough to learn the delights of torturing such small birds and animals as fell into his clutches." Are such historiographical claims made to aid or hide the American cause?

Note # 4

Americans thoroughly resented Indians killing their cattle but it appears these same people didn't concern themselves with killing "Indian cattle," considering buffalo to be wild game not owned by Indians or anyone else. Manifest Destiny psychology is many-sided.

Note # 5

On pages 96-97 Harold Danz cites a quote attributed to Josiah Gregg (*"Commerce of the Prairies"*) that the Indians were most culpable for the reduction of bison numbers. Is such reportage another aspect of Manifest Destiny historiography?

Note # 6

See pages 64-5 in *The Great Buffalo Hunt* by Wayne Gard. It would be interesting to discuss the American concept of a "sportsman" as well as its use by American historiographers.

Note # 7

Wayne Gard has written that these hunters were "mighty men" who have a place "among the heroic figures of the early West...rugged pioneers who tamed the West...who followed the missionary, the explorer, and the fur trader." He also declares that "by depriving the hostile plains Indian of his food, garb, and shelter, he starved him into submission to the whites." This commentary could make for a most interesting discussion on what is "mighty" or "heroic," what missionaries he is referring to, and the American use of pervasive starvation as a weapon of war against the plains Indians, hostiles as well as non-combatants. Curiously, who was a "greater hero of the American West," the mountain men or the hide men? How "heroic" would the hide men have been if they had encountered innumerable grizzly bears instead of bison?

Note # 8

See page 110-11 in the Danz volume.

Note # 9

See page 97 in the Gard volume.

Note # 10

See page 215 in the Gard volume.

Note # 11

See page 358 in *The Buffalo Hunters* by Mari Sandoz.

Note # 12

See pages 112-14 in the Danz work. American historiography is now recognized as writing about "man" when something unpleasant has to be addressed in American history. Danz does state that Canadians believed the "buffalo extermination" strategy was the American way to deal with the "Sioux problem." When did morality enter into the picture when dealing with Amerindians?

Note # 13

See pages 115-16 in the Danz work.

New Mexico

PUEBLOS

James S. Calhoun, New Mexico's first American Indian Agent and first (1850) Territorial Governor, wrote that the Pueblo Indians were adept at utilizing legal channels for their grievances of encroachments on their lands. It did not take long for him to become "excessively annoyed" with their complaints. [See Note # 1 *Notes begin on page 385.*]

In 1851 Governor Calhoun's first message to the Territorial Legislature addressed "*...a proper disposition of our Pueblo friends. What should we do with them?*" They are in our midst, surrounded by our population "*and rightfully, in my opinion, without authority to mingle in our political affairs.*" Calhoun was fully aware that the Pueblos *"own portions of the richest valley lands in this territory and why should they be exempt from paying a just proportion of the taxes which must be raised to support the Territorial government?"* This would cause a problem because as tax paying residents *"…are you prepared to elevate them to full fellowship? I cannot recommend such a union. It is inevitable that they must be slaves (dependents), equals, or an early removal to a better location for them and our own people, must occur."* [See Note # 2.] Calhoun advised the Legislature that guidance should be asked of Congress. In the meantime, *I recommend that if any of the Pueblos should wish to abandon their separate existence as a people, that the laws of the territory be immediately extended over them, under such regulations as you may prescribe.*

J.S. Calhoun was a typical American of the period of Manifest Destiny in which Indians could not be considered as American citizens and further, if the Indians had good lands, the Indians should be "removed for their own benefit" as well as that of "American settlers." To make matters worse, Calhoun said that his political opponents and "evil disposed Mexicans and others" were starting rumors that Pueblo lands were going to be seized. [See Note # 3.]

In 1852 Calhoun decided to take a Pueblo delegation to Washington in order that President Millard Fillmore might hear their grievances. Though Calhoun died en route, President Fillmore heard their complaints: the price of food was too high, nomadic Indians constantly raided their villages, their water was being appropriated by "Mexicans," and agricultural implements as well as church ornaments were in very short supply. The visit was very successful for in the decade of the 1850s the American Congress approved their land claims and some $15,000 was appropriated for their needs. [See Note # 4.]

Governor **Abraham Rencher** (1857-61) was among the first to laud the Pueblo people as "superior in manufacturing and agriculture…to the coarse Mexican population." [See Note # 5.] As time would show, Pueblo people would find many champions among Americans from the East.

NAVAJOS

Stephen Watts Kearny entered New Mexico at the head of the Army of the West and took it for the USA. He had told the New Mexicans: "…the Apaches and Navajos come down from the mountains and carry off your sheep and your women whenever they please…My government will correct all this." [See Note # 6.]

On October 2, 1846, Kearny ordered **Alexander Doniphan** and his Missouri Volunteers to march into Navajo land and secure the peace or defeat the Diné in battle. Scouts from the Cañoncito Navajos led by **Cebolla**, also known as **Antonio Sandoval**, signed up as scouts. A small body of troops led by Captain John W. Reid went into Dinétah to make preliminary contact with the Navajos. These American soldiers were the first Bilagáana to encounter **Narbona**, one of the famed chieftains of the Diné. The Americans were impressed by the Navajos who were "of good stature," protecting themselves from the cold weather with blankets and wearing "panther-skin caps" plumed with eagle feathers. These "bold and fearless warriors" had many excellent horses and were superb horsemen, "lords of the mountain country." Their arms consisted basically of bows, arrows, and lances.

Narbona was a peace chief and he told Captain Reid that his people wanted peace with the American *Bilagáana*. But his words were not binding on the numerous other bands of Diné, most of whom wished to continue raiding the Pueblo and Hispano (*Nakai*, "group travelers") settlements of New Mexico.

Colonel Doniphan, as confident as Kearny, believed he could end Navajo depredations within thirty days if the Navajos wanted to fight but first he would call for a large council to discuss peace. The gathering took place at Bear Springs (east of Gallup, N.M.). **Zarcillos Largos** turned out being spokesman for the Navajos. He stated that he respected American soldiers but he saw no reason why he should not continue raiding the Mexicans. Doniphan explained that all people were now under the protection of the USA now that Americans had taken the country. Americans wanted peace with the Navajos too but if it was refused they would be given "powder, bullets, and steel." [See Note # 7.] Zarcillos Largos responded that the Diné had fought the Nakai for generations, plundering their settlements, along with those of the Pueblos, killing many and taking more prisoners. The Americans had no right to come in and order them to stop. Doniphan replied that the Mexicans no longer wished to fight, that they and the Navajos should start trading with the Americans in order that all might live well. Zarcillos Largos stated that the Diné would sign a peace treaty if indeed the USA was going to control the country permanently. But the signed peace treaty turned out being relatively worthless.

Pueblo and Hispanic settlements continued to be plundered by Navajo warriors from various bands since each band was sovereign and not bound by any other. The Navajo wars would continue for almost two decades more.

In September of 1847 Major Robert Walker and a battalion of Missouri Volunteers went out of Santa Fe to chastise the marauders. At Bear Springs they headed in a northwesterly direction until they got to Red Lake where they established their base camp. They located Cañon de Chelly but no Indians so they returned to Santa Fe.

In the spring of 1848, Col. Edward W.B. Newby resented the "frequent outrages" perpetrated by Navajo raiders against ordinary people living peaceably in their settlements. Not products of a horse culture, American soldiers in N.M. were still mostly infantry and mounted raiders eluded them almost without effort. So he decided to empower the native New Mexican "centaurs" to protect themselves and pursue any and all raiders, in this case Navajos and Apaches. [See Note # 8.] Newby also decided to march into Dinétah and put a stop to Navajo raiding. There were a number of small skirmishes and another worthless peace treaty was signed. Raiding from other bands continued as before.

In 1849 James S. Calhoun was appointed Indian Agent for New Mexico/Arizona Territory. He knew little about Indians or New Mexico but he worked with Col. John Washington to send in some 348 soldiers into Dinétah to teach the Navajos a lesson. Both believed that the Navajos must be chastised into submission or exterminated all together. In the area of the Tunicha Valley they were met by a delegation of Navajos, one of whom was the aged peace chief Narbona. During one of the talks someone on the American side made the claim that one of the Navajo warriors was riding a horse that that been stolen from him a few months earlier. Col. Washington ordered the horse be handed over immediately. Confusion set in and the Navajos now thought it must be some kind of a trap so they spurred their horses to get away. Washington ordered the mountain howitzer be fired at the fleeing Navajos. Peace chief Narbona was those among the dead.

Washington's troops pursued the Navajos into Cañon de Chelly where another peace treaty was signed on September 7, 1849. Like the others, it didn't bring peace. Raid and counter-raid continued as a way of life and the Americans were unable to do anything about it. Navajos targeted pueblos, towns, and ranches then Hispanics and Pueblos joined to attack Navajos in Dinétah.

In July of 1851 Col. Edwin V. Sumner arrived in N.M. as head of the Ninth Military District. Immediately he made plans to chastise the Navajo raiders. He led some 350 men into Dinétah. At Cañon Bonito he met a Navajo whom he asked to inform headmen to meet with him. Perhaps remembering what had happened to Narbona, no one came. He moved into Cañon de Chelly then realized that the area was excellent for an ambush so he withdrew. Before he returned to Santa Fe he left enough men at Cañon Bonito to build a fort which came to be called *Fort Defiance* because it was in the heart of Navajo country. When Sumner arrived in Santa Fe he learned that during his absence Navajos had raided various settlements at will.

When General James Carleton became military head of the Territory he decided to put an end to Navajo raids once and for all. He decided the only course of action would be to remove all Navajos from their native haunts. One of the major reasons for this strategy was that some people believed there were "vast deposits of gold, silver, and other valuable minerals" in Dinétah. It could be richer than California and all that stood in the way of "development" was a "bunch of savages." For General Carleton the Navajos were "aggressive, perfidious, butchers…" who understood only force because they could no more be trusted "than wolves." [See Note # 9.]

So General Carleton decided to send in an army under Colonel Christopher Carson to bring the Navajos to their new homeland, Bosque Redondo (Round Forest) by Ft. Sumner. Carson was instructed to hire "none but the best" New Mexican and Ute trailers available because "…we must have *real men* to do it." Carson's command, setting out in July, 1863, totaled some 1,000 men. [See Note # 10.] His orders were to kill the men when necessary and take all others prisoner "as punishment for their long continued atrocities." The reservation experiment at Bosque Redondo would be promoted under the name of "Fair Carletonia."

Carson's force made it to Ft. Defiance on July 20, 1863. Horses and other stock were in poor condition due to lack of water and pasture so the stream in that area was a welcome sight and all animals were allowed to feed on the Navajo wheat being grown there. The pattern for Carson's campaign was now set: Navajo food supplies would be taken or destroyed by the invading Bilagáana army. Sheep were seized wherever found and the Utes were permitted to take Navajo slaves as payment for their services. Back in Santa Fe, it appears that Carleton did not favor enslavement. At Bosque Redondo he would "be kind to the Navajos…teach their children how to read and write…teach them the arts of peace…the truths of Christianity." He directed that all prisoners be sent back to Santa Fe but it would take time to get those orders to Carson.

On July 23, 1863, Kit Carson himself led a scouting expedition deeper into Navajo land. In the area of Pueblo Colorado (present Ganado, Arizona), Ft. Canby was built. Another basic strategy was established: expeditions would be sent out to engage Navajo warriors and destroy all items that sustained them. The wheat crop turned out producing some 75,000 pounds though the corn was not very plentiful. The wheat was used for fodder over the winter.

Ft. Canby was relocated to Canon Bonito where the old Ft. Defiance had been. This now became base camp for all scouting forays against the Diné. The strategy was one of scorched earth: what couldn't be carried away was destroyed or burned. Fields of corn, wheat, pumpkins, beans, etc., were systematically plundered then destroyed. For example, on the way to Canon de Chelly a field of corn of perhaps a hundred acres was encountered. Stock was permitted to graze on it then the whole crop was trampled and burned. Peach trees were cut down. All rancherías (encampments) were destroyed, livestock taken or slaughtered, hogans burned. A war of death and destruction was thrust against all Navajos and no effort was made to distinguish between friendlies or hostiles. While very few warriors were killed in battle, the scorched earth policy would force the Navajos to starve, freeze to death in the cold, or turn themselves in for "relocation" to Bosque Redondo.

Conditions at Ft. Canby were exacerbated by various soldiers' "homosexuality, drunkenness, and whoring." [See Note # 11.] Major Thomas J. Blakeney, a friend of General Carleton, became unpopular with his soldiers and was even accused of setting up Navajos who had turned themselves in so they could be "shot while trying to escape."

Summer turned into fall and Carson's campaign continued. The thrust was now to capture as many Navajos as possible and send them to Bosque Redondo. Neither Carleton nor Carson approved of killing any Navajo who surrendered. At one time the Zuñis and Hopis were suspected of helping the Diné but the rumor turned out being false, the Pueblos being traditional Navajo enemies. The soldiers rarely even encountered the Dine but their homes, crops, and animals were seized or destroyed. Though hardly anybody realized it, the Navajo Nation was on the brink of defeat.

While the American "Indian fighters" rarely encountered Navajos, Navajos raided the horse herds at Ft. Canby seemingly at will during the fall of 1863. Despite the embarrassment, a winter scout was ordered by Carleton back in Santa Fe. The winter of 1863-64 turned out being one of great snow and this caused even greater hardship on the pursued Diné. Their lifeways were being shattered and most sunk into despair. They had little protection against the blizzards. Women and children were dying in the snows. Surrender was the only way to survive. They went in and told the Americans: "You have killed us and there is nobody left for you to kill. We have nothing. We are suffering. We want it to stop. We want peace."

Carson told all who surrendered that they had to go live at Bosque Redondo where they would have food and all the supplies they needed. These were alluring words to destitute Navajos. They would go. There was really no other choice.

On February 7, 1864, General Carleton reported to his superiors in Washington that Col. Carson's campaign against the Navajos was the "crowning act" of the colonel's life in fighting the savages, that because of it this would be *the last Navajoe war.*" But the situation would deteriorate because when thousands of Navajos surrendered at Ft. Canby and Ft. Wingate, Army personnel were not prepared to supply their needs. There were more Navajos than American authorities had expected and they quickly began to perish from starvation and disease. At Ft. Canby alone there were over 2,500 Navajos ready for "removal." Some 126 died while waiting. It was decided to get them as quickly as possible to Bosque Redondo. Healthy or not, the Diné were herded toward their new home in the east. As had occurred in the past with Americans dealing with Native Americans, Indians groups who had remained friendly with the Bilagáana were not exempted from the order of exile. The band of Cebolla, Antonio Sandoval, who had been loyal scouts for American troop movements (other Navajos had named them *Diné Ana'aii*, Enemy Navajo), were forced to Bosque Redondo without apparent American compunction.

There were few wagons so most of the Diné had to walk the more than three hundred miles to the Ft. Sumner area, always "under the guns of the soldiers." [See Note # 12.] Referred to as the "Long Walk" by American writers, it was considered a "death march" by Navajos who survived the ordeal. While American observers would not record them, Navajo witnesses later testified as to the atrocities perpetuated on them. There were not enough blankets to protect them from inclement weather on the journey and some froze to death. Many sickened and died because they were unaccustomed to provisions given them, especially bacon which they refused to eat because it came from an animal they considered to be unclean. Dysentery took its toll and diarrhea caused many deaths among babies, young children, and old people. Those who were too ill to keep up were either simply left behind or shot by soldiers to "put 'em out of their misery." [See Note # 13.] Some of the Navajo women were raped by soldiers who were supposedly there to protect them, the beginning of venereal diseases which were to become rampant at Bosque Redondo. Smallpox also became part of life at the Bosque.

Those who survived the journey to Bosque Redondo discovered that their enemies, the Mescalero Apaches, were already there. If the journey had not been prepared for, the destination had been even more neglected. There was not enough agricultural land for so many Indians. The few crops they could grow were victimized by "drought, flood, hail, and insects." [See Note # 14.] There wasn't enough grass for the sheep and goats then there was the ever present danger of raids from hostile Comanches and Kiowas. Whiskey peddlers and gamblers preyed on the Indians. Malnutrition quickly became a real problem. When supplies did arrive they were often spoiled, as flour filled with bugs, meat that was already putrid. Water was either bad or salty. Wood for cooking was quickly used up. Seeds were consumed and most of the land was unsuitable for the serious farming which was necessary to feed the thousands of Amerindians. Even Bishop Lamy, an avowed ally of the American occupation of New Mexico, was shocked by the human misery at Bosque Redondo.

General Carleton's "humanitarian experiment," which had been promoted as "Fair Carletonia," quickly took on the appearance of a concentration camp. Carleton hadn't intended that so now it was up to him to rectify the situation. Solution: give the responsibility to the Department of the Interior and its Superintendent of Indian Affairs, Michael Steck. But Superintendent Steck refused to become responsible for the Navajos, saying they were the Army's prisoners of war so Interior had no obligation there. A bitter feud now arose between Carleton and Steck, with most Americans taking sides all the way to Washington. Steck had opposed removing Navajos from their native land in the first place, opting for a smaller reservation somewhere in their own territory. Kit Carson sided with Carleton, saying it was foolish to believe that Navajos in their own country would stop raiding. Steck asserted that as much as half of the Navajo Nation still hadn't been rounded up. Carleton called Steck a *liar*. The fight between Steck and Carleton raged for two years until the spring of 1865 when Steck resigned in disgust. [See Note # 15.] While the bureaucrats fought, the Navajos froze and starved at "Fair Carletonia." Despite their misery, they constantly petitioned anyone who would listen to let them *return to their homeland* where they could take care of themselves.

In April of 1868, well known headmen like Manuelito, Barboncito, etc., went to Washington to ask for permission to lead their people back to their country. President Johnson decreed that a "peace commission" would decide the issue of repatriating the Navajos to Dinétah or sending them to Oklahoma

(Indian Territory). One of the commissioners was Indian-hating General William Tecumseh Sherman who visited Bosque Redondo and found it "…a mere spot of green grass surrounded by a wild desert…the Navajos were in absolute poverty and despair." It was apparent to all that Dinétah didn't hold mineral riches of gold and silver so on April 29, 1868, the peace commissioners informed the Diné they could return to Navajo land if they would forever walk the peace road. The Dine agreed. Anxious to forget these miseries, The People packed up their meager belongs and headed back to their homeland, thoroughly impoverished but elated to try to live in freedom once again. When they reached their beloved homeland their tears helped wash away past sorrows. They could never forget but once more they could sing:

> In beauty may I walk.
> All day long may I walk.
> Through the returning seasons may I walk.
> Beautifully will I possess again…
> With dew about my feet may I walk.
> In old age, wandering on a trail of beauty,
> Lively may I walk.
> In old age wandering on a trail of beauty,
> Living again may I walk.
> Let it be finished in beauty.

JICARILLA APACHES

When first encountered by Hispanic people in the 1600s the Jicarillas ranged from northeastern New Mexico to the southeastern slopes of the Rocky Mountains. As with most Amerindian groups, the advent of the Spanish horse changed Jicarilla lives as nothing else before or since. They hunted the buffalo along with deer, elk, mountain sheep, rabbits as well as gathered wild fruits, nuts, tubers, herbs, etc. When the Comanches became dominant in the southern plains they pushed the Jicarillas toward northern New Mexico's mountain country where they continued their hunting and gathering lifestyle but they also did a little farming. Governor Anza of New Mexico finally put a stop to their raiding by defeating the Jicarillas in battle in 1776 with a combined force of Hispano militia and Pueblo warriors. [See Note # 16.]

After 1848 American "settlers" began moving into Jicarilla lands, carving out sheep and cattle ranches, developing mines, building roads, etc., not concerning themselves with Jicarilla property rights. For example, among those establishing ranches in the Rayado Valley, deep in Jicarilla territory, were Kit Carson and Lucien Maxwell. [See Note # 17.] Army troops were stationed at the Rayado ranch for protection and they often chased Apaches who were generally too elusive for the soldiers. By 1850 the Jicarillas were unable to hunt and forage freely, becoming "trespassers" in their own country, hunted by American soldiers from Ft. Union and Ft. Burgwin.

In 1851 a treaty was made with Jicarilla headmen like Francisco Chacón which resulted in a Jicarilla agricultural program being started near Abiquiú. Funding for the experiment was soon terminated, forcing the disillusioned Jicarillas to fend for themselves, minus most of their lands. In 1854 the Jicarillas clashed with and defeated a troop of American dragoons but after that they were kept on the run until they realized they could not address their predicament in a military way.

By around 1875 all of New Mexico's Indians had their own reservation lands except the Jicarillas. In 1883 American authorities decided to do something about it so they sent the Jicarillas south to live with the Mescaleros in the Sierra Blanca region. This didn't work out so the Government decided on a Jicarilla reservation in north-central New Mexico. The soil was poor but perhaps the Jicarillas could make a homeland. In 1907 the Jicarillas were able to add some land to their reservation and began some cattle ranching. They suffered greatly from poverty, malnutrition, and disease, especially tuberculosis which caused an "alarming decline in population." By 1925 there were only around 625 Jicarilla Apaches.

MESCALERO APACHES

Mescaleros derived their name from the agave plant, *mescal*, which they used as an important part of their food supply. They lived much as did the Jicarillas, hunting and gathering. Their territory was between the rivers Pecos and Río Grande and south into Coahuila and Chihuahua. The Spanish horse changed their lives like nothing else because it facilitated hunting the buffalo, raiding, and warfare. Primary Mescalero targets were Pueblo and Hispano settlements in the Río Grande valley. Hispanos and Pueblos fought back so life was characterized by raid-and counter-raid in which horses, booty, and slaves were taken. When the Comanches became dominant in the southern plains the Mescaleros were squeezed between the two enemy groups.

By 1848 when the USA took over New Mexico the Mescaleros were now targeted by Americans who wanted Mescalero land for ranching and mining. After the Civil War, American troops led by Kit Carson forced some 450 Mescaleros to Bosque Redondo. [See Note # 18.] The first Amerindians in the concentration camp, they were required to help build Ft. Sumner. When thousands of enemy Navajos were herded into Bosque Redondo the Mescaleros fled to their native land in the Sierra Blanca. "Fair Carletonia" being a failure, the Mescaleros were not pursued, apparently.

In 1872 President U.S. Grant set aside the Sierra Blanca lands for the Mescalero people. They were in their own homeland but they were beset with problems like malnutrition because of the extermination of the southern buffalo herd. The Jicarillas were thrust into the reservation (1886-87) as were the Lipan Apaches and later the surviving Chiricahua (as of 1913). There were land losses and diseases brought by American settlers, and in time, American schools which demanded that Mescalero children forget their native culture and religion. In 1912 an effort was made to "remove" the Mescaleros from their land so Americans could have the use of it. After all, Grant had only given it them by executive order. Happily, in 1922 the American Congress confirmed a patent of land ownership to the Mescaleros.

MANGAS COLORADAS

The Mimbreño chieftain Mangas Coloradas (Red Sleeves; unaccustomed to other languages, Americans often referred to him as *Magnus Colorado*) is thought to have been born in the early 1790s. As an adult his strongholds were in the Mimbres mountains of southwestern New Mexico.

Mangas was a fearsome warrior, very tall, perhaps six-foot-five, had an extremely large head, could speak Spanish fluently, and was genuinely concerned for his people. Considered by some to be the greatest of Apache leaders, he and his people had fought the Hispanics of Mexico and the Southwest "forever." Mangas was no mere guerrilla raider. He was a brilliant war chief, strategist, and diplomat. While chief of the Mimbreño Apaches he sought alliances with other Amerindian people by marrying his daughter Tesalbestinay to Cochise of the Chiricahua, another daughter to the Navajo chieftain Manuelito, a third to Pedro, leader of a western Apache band of Coyoteros, and a fourth to Gianmatah of the Mescaleros. His hope was to form alliances and defend the Apache homeland.

In 1837 a man named **Juan José** was chief of the Mimbreños. An American named **James Johnson** and some twenty other Americans went on a scalp hunting expedition into Mimbreño country. Johnson made contact with a group of Mimbreños, in which was Juan José, and invited them to come in and receive presents. When the Apaches were together selecting what they wanted, Johnson gave the signal to fire the cannon into the assembled Mimbreños, most of them women and children. Juan José died in the carnage. Mangas' wife and three of his children were also among those slaughtered. The Americans then scalped the dead and took their grisly trophies for payment in Chihuahua. All Apaches were infuriated at the fiends who could do such a thing but Johnson and his men escaped.

Mangas Coloradas was selected chieftain after the death of Juan José. When Americans came into the Southwest in 1846 Mangas invited General **Kearny** to join with the Apaches to conquer Mexico once and for all. He wanted peace and friendship with the newly arrived Americans but this was not to be. Mangas Coloradas had no way of knowing what Manifest Destiny Americans intended for Indian people. Efforts at friendship with Americans were not reciprocated and the shedding of blood was not long in coming.

In 1861 Mangas went into a mining camp in southwestern New Mexico in an effort to persuade American miners to leave Chiricahua territory peaceably. Seeing this lone "injun" and apparently not knowing who he was, the Americans tied Mangas to a tree and whipped him brutally with a bullwhip. Then, after "teaching him a lesson," they let him go. It was not long before Mangas returned with his warriors and wiped out the entire mining camp. This was the beginning of the bloody Apache wars, brought on by a few American miners who thought Indians were no better than beasts. Americans would learn that hostile Apaches were among the most effective warriors in the Americas but because they proved so difficult to conquer Americans would denigrate them as a vicious, cruel people.

In 1862 Mangas and Cochise jointly led their warriors in an Apache Pass ambush against General James H. Carleton's California Column. Had it not been for the American troops being equipped with howitzers the Apaches might well have destroyed the Column. Mangas was seriously wounded so the ambush attack was called off. The chieftain was taken to a well known doctor in the Mexican village of Janos and given the limp body of Mangas. The doctor was told: *Make him well. If he dies this town will die.* The doctor worked on Mangas day and night until the chief pulled through.

In January of 1863 Mangas Coloradas once more tried to establish peace with the Americans. Under a flag of truce he was invited to come in and parley with the **Joseph Walker** group of miners working some diggings in the Santa Rita area by Silver City, New Mexico. Victorio and Nana pleaded with him not to go because they knew the "White Eyes" could never be trusted. Mangas went in under the white flag but the Americans seized him and delivered him to Colonel **Joseph R. West**, who had orders from Carleton to "punish" all Apaches. **Daniel Ellis Conner** of the Walker party overheard Col. West telling the soldiers who would guard Mangas: "Men, that old murderer has got away from every soldier command and has left a trail of blood for five hundred miles on the old stage line. I want him dead or alive tomorrow morning, do you understand? I want him dead." [See Note # 19.] That night while two soldiers guarded the dozing Mangas, the Americans were seen by Daniel Ellis Conner to be heating their bayonets in the camp fire. When the bayonets were burning hot the soldiers would touch them to the feet and legs of the "savage." Mangas finally sprang up and protested angrily whereupon the two soldiers fired point blank at the chieftain then pulled out their six-shooters and each fired two more shots into him. [See Note # 20.] Mangas was then scalped by the Americans after which his head was cut off and boiled in a pot so it could be sent to a phrenologist (who later stated the skull was larger than that of Daniel Webster). The official report said that Mangas Coloradas had been shot while the "savage" was trying to escape.

The betrayal, cold blooded murder, and mutilation of Mangas Coloradas would bring on sanguinary retaliation in brutal raids and genocidal counter-raids. While it is a documented fact that Americans depicted Apaches as fiends, it is logical to assume that Apaches felt the same way toward their new enemies because of brutish American behavior toward the Apaches. The mutilation of Mangas Coloradas set the pattern for similar atrocities committed by Apaches who before this time didn't even believe in taking scalps. [See Note # 21.]

VICTORIO

It is believed Victorio was a Mimbres Apache from southwestern New Mexico. There is no doubt that he was one of the greatest of Apache war leaders. [See Note # 22.] Victorio and his band had finally been permitted to settle legally at Warm Springs (Ojo Caliente), their homeland in southern New Mexico. The Indians liked it there but pressures from "white settlers" caused the Interior Department to order their removal to San Carlos which among all Apache lands was the most hated because there was no grass, no game, too much heat, too many insects, and the water was terrible. It was at San Carlos that Apaches first contracted malaria, the "shaking sickness." [See Note # 23.]

On March 20, 1877, John Clum was ordered to transfer the Warm Springs Apaches to San Carlos so he gathered his 102 Indian Police and went out on his mission. General Edward Hatch, commander of the Department of New Mexico, ordered out eight companies of the Ninth Cavalry to help in the removal. But Clum had learned that 250-400 "well armed, desperate Indians," including the "renegade" Gerónimo, were in the area of the Warm Springs agency, so he decided to deal with the "renegade" first.

Clum arranged a meeting with Gerónimo, soldiers hidden out of sight but ready to encircle the renegades at a given signal. Clum started by saying the Indians should "listen with good ears" and no harm would befall them. Gerónimo retorted that Clum should speak with discretion and no harm would befall Americans. So Clum gave the signal and soldiers swarmed out of their hiding places, weapons ready to fire. It was indeed useless to resist and Gerónimo "gave himself up." Shackles were riveted to his ankles and other Indians were also shackled.

Clum now received another explicit order: All Warm Springs Apaches, whether renegade or not, were to be removed to San Carlos. Clum asked for a parley with Victorio and after serious discussions he consented to remove to San Carlos with his some 453 men, women, and children (110 or so of which were with Gerónimo). The group made it to San Carlos by May 20, 1877. Victorio was made one of the Agency's council judges.

Due to continued feuding between the Army and Indian Service personnel, John Clum resigned in a huff as of July 1, 1877. Victorio and his people became unhappy, restless, and unsettled with the over-crowded, often hostile atmosphere at San Carlos. When H.L. Hart replaced Clum, supplies became short. The leader known as Poinsenay slipped into the reservation and showed all the booty he had taken in Mexico. One September night, led by Victorio and Loco, 310 men, women, and children, bolted out of San Carlos into the mountains of eastern Arizona and western New Mexico. A mixed group of Indian police, scouts, and volunteer Apaches gave chase but the "hostiles" escaped. They "lived off the land," stealing horses and cattle when possible, killing ranchers when necessary. After losing some 56 persons in various skirmishes, some 190 hostiles surrendered at Ft. Wingate, another 50 coming in later. No one knew what to do with them so General Hatch returned them to *Warm Springs*, which is all they had wanted from the beginning. There were no more Apache depredations in New Mexico, no cattle stolen, no prospectors harmed, no freighters or travelers attacked.

There were continued troubles at San Carlos but Victorio and his people paid no attention. Then the Interior Department decided the Warm Springs Apaches should be returned to San Carlos and asked the War Department to effect the transfer. On October 8, 1878, Captain F.T. Bennet and his Ninth Cavalry informed Victorio he would have to go back to San Carlos. Victorio asked why it was necessary. He stated his people had been born here, they loved their home and they didn't want to leave it. Then suddenly he and many warriors bolted for the mountains and made good their "escape." Some 169 remaining Indians, mostly noncombatants, were loaded in wagons and taken to Ft. Apache (December, 1878).

Freezing winter weather in the mountains made things difficult for Victorio and his "renegades" who had refused removal. By February, 1879, they had had enough so with great caution they returned to Warm Springs and pleaded to be allowed to stay there with their people. They said they would rather die than return to San Carlos. Lt. C.W. Merritt of the Ninth Cavalry said he would see what he could do. The bureaucrats decided the Mescalero Reservation might work out so Victorio and his people were sent there by June 30, 1879. Wives and children could be brought back from San Carlos.

In July an indictment charging Victorio and others with murder and horse stealing was brought at Silver City. Victorio and the Indians now became restive, wondering if they were ever going to be allowed to live in peace. When a judge and prosecuting attorney came on the scene Victorio and his people had had enough of American justice. As of September 4, 1879, when they fled the Mescalero reservation, it would be war unto death. [See Note # 24.]

Vengeance started immediately. The group headed for the Black Mountains, encountered and slew two unsuspecting sheepherders and stole their horses. They swept down on the horse herd of the Ninth Cavalry and stole some forty-six mounts. Now well mounted, they sowed fear and terror as they rode toward their stronghold near the headwaters of the Animas River some twenty miles from Hillsboro and forty south of Ojo Caliente. (Within a few months his band contained some 350 Chiricahuas and Mescaleros.)

On September 18, 1879, Victorio and some 150 of his "renegades" ambushed Captain Byron Dawson with his 46 soldiers and Navajo scouts. The Apaches were concealed so well that Americans rode right into the trap, Apaches shooting down into them from both sides of a small canyon. The cavalry sent for help and Captain Charles D. Beyer came with some 52 men, which included citizens from Hillsboro. The fight continued all day but the Apaches couldn't be dislodged. Beyer ordered a retreat as night began to fall, leaving Victorio in the field of battle. Eight Americans had been killed, a number wounded, fifty-three horses and mules abandoned, thirty-two others killed outright, baggage and other booty captured by the Apaches.

Cavalry units were ordered to the Black Mountains with orders to kill or capture the renegades. Another engagement was fought as the Apaches ascended their high mountain stronghold, daring the soldiers and their scouts to follow them. Several soldiers were killed as the battle turned into skirmishes. In one (October 13) incident some volunteers from Mesilla spied three loose horses and rode in to take them. They were ambushed, six men being killed. Later the Apaches attacked a wagon train, killing eleven men, capturing a woman and child, burning all the wagons. (It is possible the attack on the wagon train was directed by Juh, coming up from Mexico, not Victorio at all.)

Victorio had southwestern New Mexico in an absolute uproar. On October 22, 1879, the *Star* newspaper reported that Lt. Blocksom's Apache Scouts and men had been in a bloody fight with Victorio's renegades, losing some seventeen scouts and two soldiers. With seemingly everybody in the country out to get him, Victorio decided to escape into Mexico. It is said he had killed between 75 to 100 people. [See Note # 25.] Major Morrow continued the pursuit but when the two enemy forces got close to each other the Apaches counter-attacked so savagely that the Scouts/soldiers had to fall back to the main group. On one occasion in the high mountains the advancing soldiers were subjected to boulders crashing down toward them. Luckily, none were crushed by the large rocks.

Victorio decided to come back into New Mexico in January of 1880, probably because General Gerónimo Treviño was after him with some 400 men. Major Morrow and his forces were supposed to be waiting for the renegades but Victorio and his fighters evaded them easily, making it back to their stronghold in the Black Mountains. On January 12, 1880, Morrow's men caught up with the Apaches and a sharp fight ensued, lasting throughout the afternoon. At dark the Apaches raced toward the San Mateo Mountains. A week later another fight occurred. Victorio's warriors escaped but on February 3, 1880, there was another serious clash near the San Andrés Mountains. Morrow's forces chased the renegades up the sides of a canyon, driving them from crevice to ledge, to no avail. Victorio's warriors withdrew and Morrow didn't follow because his men were exhausted, ammunition was low, supplies nearly gone. A company under Captain L.H. Rucker was permitted to continue the chase for two more days. The soldiers unexpectedly came upon the Apaches in a canyon, took heavy fire, and when the Indians charged at the soldiers they retreated post haste, the pursuers now becoming the pursued. The Apaches took all abandoned rations, bedding, and supplies.

While more than a thousand men were after Victorio's band the Indians fought only in selected mountain sites where their guerrilla tactics, based on the realities of exhausting pursuit and occasional skirmish, proved most effective. The impregnable terrain was as crucial as the Apaches fighting prowess and proclivities for military strategy. The warriors were well armed and somehow possessed plenty of ammunition. American authorities came to believe that Apaches from the Mescalero Reservation were aiding the renegades so plans were made to disarm and dismount the Mescaleros.

It was learned that Victorio was camped in Hembrillo Canyon on the eastern side of the San Andrés Mountains. General Hatch formulated a plan by which the stronghold would be attacked from all sides while sealing off the escape route to Mexico. Captain Henry Carroll was to come in from the north by April 6, 1880, McLellan from the west, Hatch from the south, B.H. Grierson from the east. With this kind of manpower "the renegades wouldn't have a chance."

Carroll's men camped at Malpais Spring on the evening of April 5. The water flowed clear and inviting so the men and horses drank their fill but it was full of gypsum. By the following morning most everyone was seriously ill. The column continued their march into Hembrillo Canyon, where there was good water but also hostiles. The Apaches scampered for cover but quickly discerned that something was wrong with their enemy, who seemed to have no will to fight. They got between the soldiers and the water and fought ferociously. Two soldiers were killed and many wounded, including Carroll. The other American columns were now seen approaching and that saved Carroll's men because Victorio, this time almost out of ammunition, ordered a retreat, as it turned out, not to Mexico but the Black Range.

While it can't be said that Victorio was winning every engagement of the war, he certainly hadn't lost any. Though he killed more soldiers than they killed warriors, soldiers could be replaced in limitless numbers while every warrior killed was basically an irreplaceable loss. Despite their heroic resistance, the band was wearing down.

Most depredations in the Southwest were now blamed on Victorio and his people. At one point a rumor circulated that he would soon attack San Carlos itself. It was promoted that other Indian tribes were going over to Victorio, that soon the entire Southwest would be ravaged by desperate Indians who already outnumbered the forces under General Hatch. Major General John Pope, commanding the Department of Missouri, said the rumors were "greatly exaggerated."

A chief of scouts named "Captain" H.K. Parker was given permission to take his 60-75 Indians and pursue Victorio in May of 1880. General Hatch had told him: *Go out and kill an Indian or two so we can keep things stirred up until we can get our troops back into shape.* On Parker's second day out the renegade trail was identified and on May 23 the scouts reported the enemy camped at the headwaters of the Palomas River. The order was given to surround the encampment. At dawn the next day the hostiles found themselves receiving fire from all sides so they quickly forted up to make a defense but it is believed several warriors were killed or wounded. Night fell and the scouts shouted for the "squaws" to come out and surrender, they would not be harmed. The women openly laughed at them.

Parker then realized he was running low on ammunition, now at about five rounds per man, so he sent a runner to General Hatch, informing on his situation and emphasizing that he needed more ammo immediately. Help never came and Parker had to withdraw to Ojo Caliente. The Silver City *Southwest* wrote: "Is Hatch an imbecile? General, the blood of more than 500 citizens slain by merciless Apaches within the last twelve months calls for vengeance..." Citizens had to be protected and construction of the Southern Pacific railroad pushing across southern New Mexico could not be jeopardized.

With troops on his trail, Victorio and his band of some 160 warriors, with their women and children, made it into one of their favorite sanctuaries in Mexico. Now there was prepared the biggest manhunt in the history of the Southwest, to which was added civilian posses, Texas Rangers and hundreds of Mexican soldiers.

Mexican forces under Adolfo I. Valle skirmished with the hostiles at Ojo del Pino then the Apaches headed north of the border. Grierson spotted them passing near Ft. Quitman, sent for help, then tried to stop the hostiles with a skirmish. Victorio lost seven of his warriors. The hostiles slipped through as of August 4, 1880. But Grierson gave chase, got ahead of them, and laid an ambush at the waterhole the Indians needed. Sure enough, the hostiles straggled in for water. When the Indians were close enough, the soldiers opened fire and the hostiles scampered behind the surrounding rocks and other available cover. Realizing that there were very few soldiers after all, the warriors counter-attacked in an effort to gain the waterhole. Then two companies of soldiers swarmed unto the scene, rescuing their comrades and causing the Indians to retreat to higher ground. There was silence for a couple of hours, as if each side was waiting for the other to make a move.

At about four in the afternoon a supply train came into view. The train was apparently unaware of the fight at the waterhole so Victorio's men decided to attack and loot the wagons. To their great surprise the wagons were filled with troopers who jumped out with guns blazing. The warriors retreated precipitously and finally decided to return to Mexico where they could recuperate.

In time it was reported that Victorio had made his camp in Corral de Piedras. A price of $3,000 was put on his head. General Joaquín Terrazas was sent at the head of some one thousand troops to exterminate the marauders. Token American units were permitted to come in for the kill. For the first time, Victorio was really trapped.

It was reported that on October 14, 1880, Mexican troops had surrounded Victorio's people and all fighting ended on the 15th. Victorio was said to have been wounded many times then finally killed by a Tarahumari scout named Mauricio. An informant to Eve Ball says Victorio and his last few warriors fell on their own knives in order to avoid capture. [See Note # 26.] It was reported that seventy-eight Apaches had been killed, sixty of them warriors. Sixty-eight women and children were captured, along with some two hundred horses and mules. Some thirty Apaches escaped, old Nana among them.

DISCUSSION NOTES *for* NEW MEXICO INDIAN AFFAIRS

Note # 1
See pages 101-10 in *The Protector De Indios In Colonial New Mexico, 1659-1821* by Charles R. Cutter. According to Dr. Cutter, during the Spanish colonial period of New Mexican history "...there was never a successful or concerted effort in New Mexico to break up communal land-holdings of the various Pueblo groups." Then Dr. Cutter adds: "...the Pueblos were less successful in retaining their land base during the Mexican and early American periods."

Note # 2
See page 52 in *Seeds Of Discord: New Mexico in the Aftermath of the American Conquest, 1846-1861* by Alvin R. Sunseri.

Note # 3
While American writers like G.W. Kendall, Josiah Gregg, W.W.H. Davis, etc., had often made negative commentaries about "vile Mexicans," Calhoun's remarks might be the beginning of such sentiments expressed by American Territorial officials. It would be interesting to explore the

implications of "designated villains" in American society.

Note # 4

While it is obvious that Indian "removal" was an accepted American policy, if utilized with the Pueblo people it would portray the USA as "worse than vile Spain" because the "cruel" Spanish hadn't "removed" the Pueblo Indians. It is also worthy of note that the Federal Government spent such little money on Pueblo Indians while between 1850-65 it had to spent some $30,000,000 to fight the Plains tribes. It is also ironic that the "civilized" Pueblo people are often described as "docile" despite the fact that they produced warriors that were the equal of anybody on the frontier. It has been commented upon that if Indians fought for their land they were depicted as "savages" while those who didn't resort to warfare are described as "docile." Is it a de facto tenet of American historiography that no matter what Amerindian behavior was it is going to be denigrated?

Note # 5

This might well be the beginning of American efforts to drive a wedge between Pueblo Indians and Hispano New Mexicans. The "divide and conquer" strategy was used successfully against the Hispano/Comanche alliance.

Note # 6

See page 25 in *The Kit Carson Campaign: The Last Great Navajo War* by Clifford E. Trafzer. Author Trafzer refers to Kearny's remark as a "pompous promise" from someone "who little understood that the Indians were more than a match for the American troops."

Note # 7

See page 29 in the Trafzer volume.

Note # 8

Robert M. Denhardt states on page 114 of his *The Horse Of The Americas* that "contemporary observers termed the New Mexicans 'a race of centaurs.' " He adds that the greatest horsemen of the 17th and 18th centuries were the Arabs, the Comanches, and the Hispanos of New Mexico. One might well wonder about the 19th?

Note # 9

See page 76 in the Trafzer volume. The author describes one of Carson's officers, Captain Albert Pfeiffer, as having a reputation as "the most desperately courageous and successful Indian fighter in the West." It should also be pointed out that the Trafzer work does not contain a complimentary depiction of General Carleton. Surprisingly, invective against Kit Carson is rather restrained. On page 67 he also writes that Manuel Antonio Chaves "was a scourge" to the "Navajo Indians of Dinétah." For biographies on Kit Carson see *Dear Old Kit: The Historical Christopher Carson* by Harvey L. Carte; also *Kit Carson: Folk Hero And Man* by Noel B. Gerson. For the biography on M.A. Chaves see *The Little Lion Of The Southwest: A Life Of Manuel Antonio Chaves* by Marc Simmons.

Note # 10

David G. Noble says on page 126 of his *Pueblos, Villages, Forts & Trails* that Carson's men were

"New Mexican irregulars." While Carson led the First New Mexico Volunteer Cavalry, the campaign was basically an American Army affair by American soldiers.

Note # 11

See page 92 in the Trafzer volume.

Note # 12

See page 84 in *The Indian Frontier Of The American West, 1846-1890* by Robert M. Utley. Historian Utley writes that the "Long Walk" was "the eastward equivalent of the Trail of Tears by which Cherokees and others had journeyed westward…" It would appear that "Death March" is reserved for the 68-mile atrocity at Bataan.

Note # 13

See Chapter 6 in the Trafzer volume. Even Mr. Trafzer, who has recorded the Navajo point of view and appears sympathetic to it, uses the euphemistic phrase "Long Walk."

Note # 14

See page 85 in the Utley volume.

Note # 15

Steck went back to Washington where he discredited Carleton. Newspapers and New Mexicans criticized the general publicly. The Territorial Legislature sent a memorial to President Johnson asking for the general's removal. In April of 1867, Carleton was relieved of his command. His dream of "Fair Carletonia" ended. He left New Mexico and later died of pneumonia on January 7, 1873.

Note # 16

The best specific work on the military alliance between Hispanos and Pueblos is probably *Pueblo Warriors & Spanish Conquest* by Oakah L. Jones, Jr.

Note # 17

See pages 117-18 in the David G. Noble volume.

Note # 18

See page 122 in the Noble volume.

Note # 19

See page 111 in *Arizona: A Short History* by Odie B. Faulk.

Note # 20

See page 60 in *Arizona: A History* by Thomas E. Sheridan.

Note # 21

Few historiographers have written from this perspective. On page 20 of *Indeh*, an informant of Eve Ball states: "To an Apache the mutilation of the body is much worse than death, because the body must go through eternity in mutilated condition. Little did the White Eyes know what they were starting when they mutilated Mangas Coloradas." On the Apache side there had been very little mutilation before the atrocity performed on Mangas.

Note # 22

One can only wonder what Victorio could have accomplished had technology been on his side.

Note # 23

See page 37 in *Indeh*.

Note # 24

See pages 171-72 in *The Conquest Of Apacheria* by Dan L. Thrapp. Historiographers seldom point out that "Victorio the renegade" was a creature created by Washington bureaucrats. All he had asked for was to live in peace in his homeland.]

Note # 25

Joseulogio Márquez, eldest brother of the author's maternal grandfather, Justiniano Márquez, was among those New Mexicans in pursuit of and who skirmished with Victorio and his warriors.

Note # 26

See page 83 in *Indeh* by Eve Ball. Whatever the end of Victorio, American historiography has portrayed him as a pillaging, murdering hostile. Little attention has been given to his side of the story, which would have to begin simply with a man wanting to live in his native land and a Government that wouldn't let him.

Arizona

PIMAS

The Pima people had been friends to Europeans since the days of Father Kino. Hard working and skillful farmers, they developed into the agricultural producers of Arizona, selling their crops to Arizonans as well as miners going to California during the gold rush. They were immensely successful and independent. For example, by 1870 the Pimas were selling or trading more than three million pounds of wheat.

Americans started coming into Pima land when a stagecoach route was established through their territory as of 1857 and the Civil War caused an even greater influx. Americans settled around Florence, upriver from the Pima villages, and dug irrigation ditches that diverted water from the Gila River onto "American" farmland. Without respect for Indian water rights there could be no Pima agriculture so in 1873 Chief Antonio Azul led a delegation of his people to protest in Washington D.C. Government authorities declared the solution was simple: the Pimas should immigrate to Indian Territory in Oklahoma. The suggestion was refused. [See Note # 1. *Notes begin on page 402.*]

The matter of water rights was settled in 1887 when a large canal was constructed near Florence, permanently diverting the Gila River water onto "American" land. Without water Pima farmers and the O'odham in general became so destitute that by 1895 the Government had to start giving them rations on which to survive. The Pimas had gone from people who fed Arizona Territory to impoverished Indians who couldn't feed themselves.

APACHES

Probably no group of Amerindians struck more fear into the hearts of American "settlers" than the *Tindé*, Apache. It has been written that their environment had molded them into "one of the toughest human species the world has ever known, the Arabs of the New World." [See Note # 2.] Apache leaders often spoke for peace but if they were attacked they would retaliate with vengeance, thus establishing the brutish pattern of fiendish provocation and fiendish revenge with the greater focus on the latter. Consequently, Americans portrayed Apaches as cruel, torturing, blood-thirsty savages who deserved nothing but extermination. Their depiction as "fiendish savages" is so common that few individuals are aware of Apaches as mere people. [See Note # 3.]

Despite being fierce raiders, Apache leaders held their followers lives in high regard. They held strong religious, aesthetic, and social beliefs. Females were highly regarded. Clan and marital loyalties were taken seriously. Apache camps were places of wit and good cheer. The Tindé loved sports, gambling, and social activities. It could be said they had complex personalities because the deadly, merciless raider on the warpath could arrive at the campsite and become the mirthful lover who taught children how to capture beautiful, delicate butterflies then release them unharmed.

The various Apache bands preferred to establish their villages in mountain strongholds that could be easily defended. Women planted corn, beans, and squash where the land permitted. They excelled in basket making. They were also strong when it came to surviving in their environment. For example, special women could ride a horse almost as well as some of the men.

Government was democratic. Certain families were expected to produce chiefs but anyone with sufficient ability could get to be a chieftain if the people willed it.

Almost every Apache was a warrior. Raiding and the warpath was the warrior way. Males went through rigorous training from boyhood. One of their exercises was to go out on a hot day, fill your mouth with water, run a designated distance, then spit out the water to show none had been swallowed. They also trained by dodging arrows shot at them. Warriors became tough, accustomed to hardship, skilled in combat, incredibly observant, and masters in the art of concealment. They were master horsemen.

For all practical purposes, Apaches rejected efforts at Christianization. They raided the Pueblo (Indian village) and Hispano settlements in Arizona, the Río Grande valley in New Mexico and into Mexico, plundering them and taking slaves whenever possible. There was fierce retaliation but neither group ever succeeded in defeating the other. The most important leaders of the Tindé are generally considered to be Mangas Coloradas (see *New Mexico Indian Affairs* for the stories of Mangas and Victorio), Cochise, Victorio, Juh, Nana, and Gerónimo.

COCHISE

The best known of Apache chieftains was probably Cochise (1812-1874). He was born in the Dragoon Mountains of southeastern Arizona, the son of Chief Nachi and his wife Alope. Named *Cheis* (which denotes the strength and quality of oak, rather than the wood itself) at birth, he grew up as did all Apaches, wanting to be a hunter and warrior. At six he was given his first bow and arrows. He was trained in running, wrestling, endurance, horsemanship, and concealment. It was not long before he became a favorite in the tribe. He went on his first raiding trail in his early teens. His role was to wait on the warriors' needs. After the raid his father Chief Nachi gifted Cheis with a black stallion named *Intchi-dijin*, Black Wind. After another successful raid the boy was given the name of *Cochise*.

By the age of seventeen Cochise was already tall (sources vary from five-nine to six-two). During a raid on the Mexican village of Concurpe, Chief Nachi received such a serious wound that he died. Though only eighteen years of age, Cochise was selected as chieftain. One of his first decisions as chieftain was to invite Chief Mangas Coloradas of the Mimbreños to wipe out Concurpe. Mangas came with his warriors and Concurpe was so devastated by Apache vengeance that it was abandoned by its Mexican residents.

Cochise wanted peace between his Chiricahuas and the Americans from the United States. Mangas thought it was a tactical mistake. Cochise allowed stagecoach stations to be built on Chiricahua territory. Some of his tribesmen got paid to bring in firewood and grass at the coach stations.

As a mature man Cochise was of an imposing appearance. He was tall, broad-shouldered, deep chested, with a high forehead, straight nose and black eyes in an intelligent face. He was known for being neat and clean. Undisputed leader of the Chiricahuas, he was famous for his hunting as well as warrior abilities. Of a strong intellect, he spoke Spanish fluently. Of special importance, he wanted peace with the Americans.

In February of 1861 Cochise received a message from the stagecoach station at Apache Pass that an Army officer wanted to talk with him. Cochise gathered a few people, including some family members, and went. During the parley in a tent he was confronted by a young Lt. **George N. Bascom** and was told that Chiricahuas had stolen a boy and some cattle from a certain ranch and Bascom wanted them returned immediately. Cochise denied that the Chiricahua had the boy or the cattle but he promised to look for them. Bascom said all the Apaches were under arrest and soldiers came into the tent. Cochise quickly cut a hole in the tent wall and ran while the soldiers opened fire. The chief was wounded but he escaped. Most of the other Chiricahuas were held hostage.

Cochise gathered his warriors and took hostages of his own from the Butterfield Trail. He informed Bascom he would exchange prisoners. Bascom demanded the return of the stolen boy and cattle before hostages could be exchanged. Cochise blocked up Apache Pass with his warriors and attacked the stage station. Once more Cochise tried to exchange prisoners and once more Bascom refused, this time threatening to execute all hostages if his demands weren't met. Tragically, both sets of prisoners were finally executed.

Cochise now saw that Mangas Coloradas had been right all along and some of Cochise's own family was dead to prove it. He joined Mangas in an all out war (1861) against American miners, wagon trains, stage coaches, mail carriers, Bluecoats, Graycoats, etc. No American was safe in Apachería, thanks to Lt. Bascom. [See Note # 4.] To make matters worse, Union soldiers were withdrawn from Arizona to stop the Confederate invasion of the Southwest. Miners like Charles D. Poston were forced to close their mines and flee for their lives.

In 1862 Cochise and Mangas attacked the California Column led by General James Carleton. The warriors won the first skirmish in Apache Pass but American cannon, weapons new to the Apaches, turned the tide and the warriors were forced to withdraw.

Realizing the millions of Americans could not be defeated militarily, Mangas Coloradas once more tried to make peace with the Americans in 1863. Under a flag of truce he was made a prisoner then "shot while trying to escape." He was scalped then mutilated when his captors cut off his head and boiled down the skull.

Apache wars resumed in all their sanguine brutality. Cochise and his 300 or so warriors gripped the country from Arizona to the Mimbres Mountains of New Mexico in a vice of terror. Though the warriors were outnumbered by perhaps 100-to-1, guerrilla warfare raged, even where it was least expected. The tactics used by Cochise were acknowledged as brilliant and his followers were unswerving in their loyalty. For every Apache that died some twenty Americans followed him to the spirit world. General Carleton had one basic strategy: *exterminate every Apache*. The Pinal Apaches, who had never taken part in the Cochise war, were slaughtered because they were *Apaches*.

Finally the American government decided the war against the Apaches was costing too much money, not to mention American lives, so peace efforts were made. By the late 1860s Cochise knew he could never conquer the millions of Americans but he let it be known he would never leave his Dragoon Mountains. The Government suggested he move into an area of New Mexico but he refused. He would live in his homeland or die in it. If he had to take others with him he would do so. Everyone knew Cochise was a man of his word. The Government finally gave in and peace was made between General Howard and Cochise in 1872. The Chiricahua would continue to live in their native land and their Agent would be the paladin Tom Jeffords, close friend of Cochise. [See Note # 5.]

In the spring of 1874 Cochise became very ill and soon died. He had accomplished what few other Amerindian leaders had: his people remained in their homeland after an all-out war with the USA. [See Note # 6.] Though their valiant paladin Cochise was dead, the USA was not yet finished with the Chiricahuas.

CAMP GRANT MASSACRE

It was in February of 1871 that five elderly Apache women came into Camp Grant under a flag of truce. Their clothes in tatters, they were also starving. The old women were fed and treated well by the camp commander, First Lieutenant **Royal Emerson Whitman**. [See Note # 7.] The women said that others of their band were in miserable condition so Whitman told them they could come to Camp Grant for assistance. The Apache women informed their people that help was available through Whitman. Many Apaches came in, some 150 people, including **Eskiminzin**, chief of the Aravaipa Apaches, who declared for peace. Eskiminzin (called *Skimmy* by English speakers) told Whitman that his people had always lived along Aravaipa Creek from the San Pedro to the Galiuro mountains but now they had no home and were fearful the American cavalry would attack them. Whitman suggested the Aravaipa should go to the White Mountains but Eskiminzin said that was not his country and the people there would not accept them anyhow. Whitman told the chief he could bring in the rest of his people, that he would give them rations until he got orders from his superiors as to what to do. While Whitman was new to Camp Grant, he knew it would be an accomplishment to get Apaches off the warpath and on to designated lands. Other bands heard the news and Whitman offered them the same deal as he had the Aravaipas.

By March, 1871, there were some 300 Apaches at the post, soon 500, all living so peaceably they weren't even required to give up their weapons, which were very poor to begin with. The Indians camp was located about a mile from Camp Grant but because of water scarcity it was moved some five miles into the mountains where there was more water.

Whitman told the Apaches they would be protected so long as they behaved. The experiment was working. Everyone got along well. Whitman hired the Apaches to bring in hay and in two months they brought in some 300,000 pounds at one cent per pound. He also got some American ranchers to hire "his Indians" to work as field hands, for which they were also paid. Whitman suggested that some of the Apaches could hire on as scouts to go against the hostiles but the offer was refused. If Whitman wanted to fight the Mexicans they would hire on but now it was Whitman's turn to refuse, saying the two countries were now at peace.

Captain Frank Standwood arrived to take command of Camp Grant in April of 1871. The captain approved of and was thoroughly impressed with what Lt. Whitman had been able to accomplish. Then Standwood took most of the soldiers and headed south where Apache depredations were still taking place, leaving only 50 men at Grant.

Promoted by newspapers like the *Tucson Star* and the *Arizona Citizen*, there arose a groundswell of bias against "Whitman's Indians." American frontiersmen generally held the belief that all Indians should be exterminated and Arizona was especially virulent in that belief. **William Sanders Oury**, "a pillar of Tucson society and a veteran of the Texas war of independence," charged that several Americans had been killed by Whitman's Apaches during January of 1871. Such was the resentment against the "friendlies" that it did no good to point out that they had arrived at Camp Grant toward the end of *February*. It has also been written that those Americans who made a living off Army contracts didn't want peace because it would diminish their various businesses. Among ordinary people there were "staunch and honest citizens in Arizona…but their number was too few…and there were numerous cruel and depraved men." It has been asserted that "subtle intriguers" targeted the Apaches at Camp Grant as the fiends responsible for murders and depredations. These attitudes were promoted in the press of the day and Whitman was universally vilified.

A "Committee of Public Safety" was formed to confer with military authorities and ask for more protection for the five hundred or so "settlers." General Stoneman remarked that if there were that many Americans they should be able to take care of themselves. Committee members like Oury took this to mean that they could address the situation as they considered necessary. The last straw came in April when Apaches raided San Xavier and a few days later four Americans were killed by hostiles. The *Arizona Citizen* claimed the murderers must have come from Camp Grant but there wasn't any way to prove it. Meetings were held and various speakers orated they would settle matters themselves if the Army didn't. Some eighty men put their names on a list to take appropriate action but everything fizzled out within a couple of days.

One evening William Oury met his friend **Jesús María Elías** and the two decided to form a group of courageous men and put an end to the marauders at Camp Grant. Elías said he would ask help of his good friend Francisco, chief of the Pápagos, then he would go into the Mexican community for recruits. Oury said he would bring in some 80 "Anglo-Americans" who had spoken up courageously and signed up to fight.

On April 28, 1871, Oury and Elías were at the head of 140 men intent on wreaking vengeance. [See Note # 8.]

It is unknown if the "avengers" knew that Apache men were away hunting when they made it to the friendlies camp on April 29 and waited for the word to be given to attack at dawn. Once the attack started, the unsuspecting Apaches were clubbed, stabbed, raped, hacked to pieces, etc., heads split open even with rocks, then hideously mutilated. The Pápagos reportedly led the slaughter of their ancient enemies while the "Anglos" and Mexicans shot down any Apaches trying to escape.

Of the 85-144 Apaches killed, eight of them were men, the rest women and children. [See Note # 9.] None of the attackers were even wounded because the Apache men had been off on a hunting expedition. Some 27-29 surviving children were taken back to Tucson to sell as slaves "in Sonora." [See Note # 10.]

Lt. Whitman arrived on the scene and quickly saw that there was no use "for wagons or medicine." It appeared the entire camp had been surrounded for the dawn attack. So sudden and unexpected it was that no Apache sounded an alarm. Many women were shot while still asleep. The wounded who were unable to get away were clubbed until their brains spilled on the ground. Some had had their brains beaten out with stones. Those who had been shot were subsequently riddled with arrows. The bodies had been stripped of all clothing. Most of the dead had been horribly mutilated. Two attractive Apache women had obviously been raped then shot dead where they lay. One infant of perhaps ten months was shot twice and had a leg nearly hacked off. The entire camp had been put to the torch and dead bodies were scattered throughout. [See Note # 11.]

Miraculously, by kind acts like helping to bury the dead, the surviving Apaches still had faith in Lt. Royal Emerson Whitman. They understood that neither he nor the Army had committed the fiendish atrocity at Camp Grant. The Apache survivors showed tremendous concern for the captives that had been taken: "*Get them back for us. Our little boys will grow up as slaves and our girls, as soon as they are old enough, will be diseased prostitutes, making money for whoever owns them. Our women work hard and are decent women. They and our children have no diseases. Our dead you cannot bring to life, but those that are living we gave to you, and we look to you, who can write and talk and have soldiers, to get them back.*"

Led by the press, Arizonans lauded the "Indian fighters" for getting rid "*of about 144 of the most blood-thirsty devils that ever disgraced mother earth,*" according to William Oury. But the rest of the country was outraged and President Grant himself told Arizona Governor Safford that if the "Indian fighters" were not brought to trial he would put all of Arizona under martial law. A "solemn" trial was held and at the end the jury "deliberated" for some nineteen minutes before acquitting every defendant. The dead had been Apaches and no Arizona jury would convict anyone for killing Apaches, national public opinion be damned. Further, Arizonans went on the offensive. The *Arizona Citizen* made scurrilous attacks on Lt. R.E. Whitman, accusing him of being an on-and-off duty drunkard, a debauched scoundrel addicted to little more than vice, that his real interest in Indians was his yen for "dusky maidens" like the original ones who first arrived at Camp Grant (the five elderly, beseeching, tatterdemalion squaws). The Army seemed to take sides with Arizonans for it court martialed him three times: for conduct unbecoming an officer and a gentleman; for disobedience of orders, and such "catchalls," but was unable to convict him. Even the usually fair General George Crook seems to have considered the paladin Whitman as someone who shouldn't be in the Army.

President Ulysses Grant appears to have been sincerely moved by the murders of Apaches at Camp Grant. He caused a Peace Commission to be created in which a new, more Christian, peace policy could be utilized to help settle the western Indian problem. [See Note # 12.] Under the President's authority, a Quaker named **Vincent Colyer** arrived in Arizona intent on creating reservations for the Indians. On August 15, 1871, Governor Safford issued a proclamation requesting that Arizonans cooperate with Colyer and all such agents even if they held "erroneous opinions upon the Indian question and the condition of affairs in this Territory." Newspapers in Prescott and Tucson were not so receptive. Regarding Colyer, one editorial stated that Arizonans "…*ought, in justice to our murdered dead, to dump the old devil into the shaft of some mine, and pile rocks upon him until he is dead. A rascal who comes here to thwart the efforts of military and citizens to conquer a peace from our savage foe, deserves to be stoned to death, like the treacherous, black-hearted dog that he is.*" [See Note # 13.]

GENERAL GEORGE CROOK

(Lieutenant Colonel) George Crook arrived in Tucson in June of 1871. There are indications that Crook did not relish his Arizona assignment and after talking with Governor Safford, who could be said to represent the militant sentiment of Arizonans toward Apaches, his dislike for Lt. Whitman was strong, though the general still hadn't met Whitman. He sent out couriers that all officers in southern Arizona were to report to their new commander as quickly as possible. Crook thereby acquainted himself with knowledge of Arizona and the foe he was to fight. The wilderness did not make Crook uneasy nor did it make him coarse or inhumane. He did his best to study the Apaches, think like them, anticipate their behavior. He was a literate man, courteous, didn't use vulgar or obscene language, respectful of his junior officers and not shy about disagreeing with his superiors. He rarely wore his fancy uniforms. [See Note # 14.]

Crook was quickly convinced that soldiers would never conquer the Apaches. Neither would civilians, nor any combination of the two. He believed that *only Apaches could whip Apaches.* In August, 1871, Crook encountered the rancherías of Coyotero and White Mountain Apaches (some 500 people) led by **Capitán Chiquito**, **Pedro**, and **Miguel**. After many discussions he convinced various Apaches to enlist as scouts for the Army, which would also serve as an example that Apaches could be friends with the Americans. The first expedition that went out with **Apache Scouts** proved successful, "killing 7 warriors and taking 11 women prisoner." [See Note # 15.] The Apache Scouts quickly became an indispensable element in the Apache Wars.

On November 15, 1871, some seven Americans were killed, by Apaches it was said, known as the Loring Massacre (also the Wickenburg Massacre; at first it was thought it might have been the work of "white ruffians" or Mexicans). Crook continued readying his command for a general attack on all hostiles who were not on their assigned reservations by February of 1872. Then President Grant sent in Brigadier General Oliver Otis Howard as overall commander of the Department. Howard was an accomplished field commander but also a strong Christian interested in settling matters peacefully wherever possible. After the Wickenburg Massacre, Crook was permitted to go after hostile Indians and his expedition brought a permanent peace to western Apachería. Now he could turn his attention to the many hostiles to the east where within the past year there had been more than fifty raids and some forty murders attributed basically to Apaches. As of November 15, 1872, columns of soldiers were sent out to engage hostiles wherever found. Basic strategy was to burn all homes and supplies, forcing starvation in the cold weather, then fighting hostiles into submission where necessary. Hunt them down until all were killed or captured. Large engagements would be preferred to skirmish after skirmish. If the Indians wished to surrender it was to be accepted. Women and children were not to be killed if at all possible. Prisoners of either sex were not to be abused in any way. Encourage male prisoners to enlist as scouts because they would know where their fellows would be hiding. If soldiers wear out their horses then pursue the enemy on foot. If the hostiles weren't killed they were to be kept constantly on the move. The campaign was intended to be decisive and permanent. The Indians would be taught that Crook was their worst antagonist but if they wanted peace he would be their best friend. Fort Apache became Crook's preliminary headquarters from which he directed and coordinated his columns of junior officers, soldiers, and scouts. Indian Scouts were crucial in the operation of all columns and they were generally the first to engage the hostiles, sometimes waiting for soldiers to catch up. One Mike Burns later wrote that the Apache Scouts were "...reliable, endowed with great courage and daring...the soldiers were worth nothing." [See Note # 16.] Crook came to value his Apache Scouts above the Paiutes, Navajos, Maricopas, and Pimas.

The winter campaign was arduous but it would have been worse during the summer. Because the Apaches were comprised of many different bands the campaign had to continue until all hostiles understood that it was just a matter of time before the Americans caught up with them. Apache resistance was effectively broken and for the first time these indomitable people began to turn themselves in at the various military forts and spoke for peace. One Apache-Mohave chief named Cha-lipun (Americans rendered it *Charley-pan*) stated they were afraid of Crook ("Gray Fox") but even worse they now had to fight their own people as well. Crook told him this was the time to establish peace because the only alternative was war and death for the Apaches. [See Note # 17.] The Apaches would have to change some of their ways, like cutting off the noses of unfaithful wives, but on the other hand they would learn how to work and have "full bellies" all the time.

For all practical purposes, organized Apache resistance was broken by the Crook campaign of 1872-73. Delshay, leader of the Tonto Apaches, became the last holdout. He had reason to mistrust the Americans for previously his brother had been "shot while trying to escape" and Delshay himself had been shot merely for being an Apache. He surrendered because there was no rest anywhere and of his 125 warriors there were now left only 20.

George Crook was now a hero throughout Arizona and the *Miner* newspaper referred to him as the "Napoleon of successful Indian fighters." The Army promoted him to Brigadier General. [See Note # 18.]

JOHN CLUM

John Philip Clum arrived as the Indian Agent for San Carlos on August 8, 1874. (It is unknown how he reacted to the row of Indian heads displayed on the parade grounds.) Unlike some of his predecessors he was honest, willing to assume authority as well as responsibility. His enemies soon found him "presumptuous, belligerent, cocky and cantankerous" but Clum didn't worry about them.

When Clum first met Eskiminzin ("Skimmy") the Apache was in chains but after chatting the two became close allies, a friendship which would last for the rest of their lives.

John Clum's biggest problem at San Carlos, at least as he saw it, was the Military, which at first even refused to acknowledge Clum's authority. Reports had to be sent to far-away Washington before the matter was resolved in Clum's favor. The newspaper *Miner* reported: "The brass and impudence of this young bombast is perfectly ridiculous." But he set to work immediately, advising his charges that if they wanted to prevent sickness they could start by keeping their villages clean. He counted adult Indians daily and all Indians on Saturday when rations were distributed. He had the Indians designate policemen, organized a court system, with himself as the highest judge. He convinced his charges to turn in their weapons which were reissued only for hunting. Liquor was forbidden, and *tiswin* could not be manufactured at the agency. He tried to find work for those who wanted it and paid them for work on building projects at the Agency. Martin Sweeney helped Clum and the two worked well with the Indians, who numbered some 700.

The situation quickly became more complex. Washington bureaucrats decided that a "removal policy" would be best for Indians of the Southwest and that San Carlos would be the base for all related tribes of Arizona and New Mexico. Starting in February of 1875, some 1500 Indians from Verde were reassigned to San Carlos. There was a near battle between Tontos against Mojaves and Yumas at the Agency. There was feuding between military personnel and those in the Indian service. White Mountain and Coyotero Apaches were assigned to San Carlos and despite a few who refused to go, Clum now had charge of some 4200 Indians.

Despite the agreement with Cochise (now dead), it was decided the Chiricahuas ("Cherrycows" to Arizonans) should also be removed to San Carlos. They refused. It was said that this Chiricahua territory attracted "wild spirits" from other bands, that they raided in Mexico. Then Agent Tom Jeffords' beef ration was cut (because his charges had refused to remove to San Carlos?) so he told some of his Indians they would have to go hunt to make ends meet. There was a fight in the Dragoon Mountains and three Indians died. At a stagecoach station a couple of American whiskey peddlers were killed and robbed of their arms and ammunition. So finally John Clum was ordered to go to the Chiricahua Reservation, suspend Jeffords, and remove the Chiricahuas to San Carlos, if possible.

On or about June 5, 1876, Clum arrived at Apache Pass and parleyed with Chief Taza, who agreed to remove to San Carlos. Some sixty warriors and their families made it to San Carlos but some four hundred under Juh, Nolgee, and Gerónimo escaped into Sonora while perhaps two hundred others went to their familiar haunts in New Mexico. The Indian Bureau had now committed a great folly in removing the Chiricahuas from their treaty-sanctioned lands. The Apaches had done nothing to break the treaty made with General Howard and yet the Americans were taking away their reservation. Further, San Carlos was disliked and no proper substitute for their homeland. Finally, the Agency was overcrowded with groups hostile to each other.

John Clum believed he had been successful in concentrating the Western Apaches at San Carlos. The only ones missing were the Warm Springs Apaches under Victorio. With help from the U.S. Army, Victorio would be living in San Carlos in the near future. (See *New Mexico Indian Affairs* for the story of Victorio.)

JUH

The Nednhi have been described as the "bravest and fiercest of all Apaches" but also the most courteous. [See Note # 19.] Juh (also spelled Ju, Ho, etc.; pronounced *Ho*), though born a Bedonkohe, was the

Nednhi chieftain. Juh was a great chief who served his people, supplying their needs before his own. Juh spent a lot of time, sometimes months, at the Cochise reservation.

Because he lived mostly in the Sierra Madre (referred to by Apaches as the Blue Mountains) in Mexico, Americans heard relatively little about him compared to other Apache chiefs and leaders. Juh and his band traded for supplies and ammunition with Mexican people but he didn't trust them because they used *mescal* and *tequila* to get his men drunk then tried to kill them. These Apaches generally preferred to be on good terms with Mexican villagers so they could trade with them. Because of that Mexicans could usually go about in safety. Juh and other leaders could usually speak at least a little Spanish.

The "Pale Eyes" (Americans; commonly rendered as "White Eyes") from the east were always enemies and could not be trusted under any circumstances. At first the Pale Eyes were curiosities because they had so much hair on their faces and bodies, which sometimes was oddly missing on their heads. The Pale Eyes descended in hordes after gold was discovered in Apache country. That is why Juh made his stronghold in the Sierra Madre: he could not trust the "cruel and treacherous" Americans. [See Note # 20.]

Juh was in the fight against the California Column going through Apache Pass. He always said the Column would have been defeated had not the Americans used cannon, huge guns mounted on wheels, a terrible weapon new to Apaches, most of whom still fought with bows and arrows.

While Juh was in many fights and skirmishes against the Americans, he was proudest of the engagement (May, 1871) against Lt. Howard Cushing. The vow to kill Cushing began when some Mescalero families were camping in the Guadalupe Mountains while the men hunted for game. The warriors returned to find everybody dead, murdered by Howard Cushing and his soldiers. Then two women survivors were found, who were seriously wounded and couldn't walk. The horses had all been stolen by Cushing and his men. After the dead had been buried the injured women had to be carried back home on the backs of the warriors. The women said to leave them while they went to get horses but the men thought it would be too risky if Cushing happened to come back. After many arduous days, the women were returned safely to their homes.

Juh, while not a Mescalero, made it a point of honor to track down the murdering Cushing. [See Note # 21.] Cushing, who had been killing Apaches with wanton, savage impunity in Arizona, had made it his personal ambition to kill Cochise. It is possible he was unaware of Chief Juh but Juh was aware of him. He assigned scouts to track Cushing so as to learn where he was operating. Three times Juh's warriors skirmished with Cushing's soldiers, one of which occurred after the warriors had robbed a paymaster wagon taking money (silver dollars) to the White Eyes camp.

Around May 20, 1871, Juh finally engineered the Cushing fight in a canyon west of Tombstone. Juh placed a (very brave) Apache woman in a dry arroyo where Cushing and his men were sure to see her moccasin tracks. The White Eyes went in after her, Cushing coming up to give the command "Forward!" Sergeant John Mott, suspecting an ambush, later wrote that he told Cushing: "Lieutenant, do you think it prudent to go further?" [See Note # 22.] Cushing thought the Apaches had been routed and the remaining eight men could assuredly finish the job. The soldiers advanced some twenty yards when the Indians opened up on them and charged into the battle for hand-to-hand combat. Mott turned when he heard Cushing say: "Sergeant, I am killed, take me out, take me out." Cushing clutched his chest as he fell to the ground. Mott and another soldier picked the Lieutenant up by the arms to drag him away when he was again shot, this time through the head, and Howard Bass Cushing, "the southwestern army's most successful and energetic Indian fighter," was dead. Juh had fulfilled his vow.

There were many other fights and raids in which Juh and his warriors participated.

One day Juh and his men were returning from Casas Grandes where they had traded hides and jerked meat for ammunition, coffee, and blankets. As the men were riding single file along the Río Aros, the bank crumbled and Juh's horse shied suddenly to the side, pitching Juh into the river. The warriors immediately went into the waist-high water and brought him out, unconscious. The great Juh died that day and was buried on the banks of the Río Aros.

It was a sad caravan that returned to Juh's stronghold that night. The people then remembered the vision they had shared a long time ago: a cloud had descended and stopped in front of the opening of a big cave on the side of a mountain. Soldiers dressed in blue kept marching into the cave by the thousands. The medicine men said the Blue Coats represented the government of the United States which would exterminate the Apaches. Juh then stood up and said: "We must gather together all Apaches. We must bind them into a strong force, just as the soldiers are strong. With our courage and skill in fighting we must oppose the enemy who has driven us from our country. We must never give up. We must fight to the last man. We must remain free men or die fighting. There is no other choice." Juh was an inspiring leader even into Death.

NANA

In July of 1881 a group of warriors led by wily Nana, said to be around seventy years of age, crossed into southern New Mexico and made their way into the Sacramento Mountains. [See Note # 23.] In an ambush that went astray they wounded a soldier with the Ninth Cavalry led by Lt. J.F. Guilfoyle. Around the White Sands periphery they killed three Mexicans, one of them a woman. Guilfoyle's men reappeared and a skirmish ensued, neither side losing any men. Guilfoyle's "Negro soldiers" attacked Nana again on July 25, 1881, capturing horses, mules, and the Apaches' camp supplies. The flight and pursuit continued toward the west, presumably toward the San Mateo Mountains, the raiders killing another seven people on the way.

"White settlers" were now up in arms so they organized posses of "reckless, Indian-hating horsemen" to attack and exterminate the renegades. Some thirty-six "man-hunters" rode into the San Mateos without encountering the raiders. When they found a good spring of water and pasture for the horses they decided to rest up a bit. They got to talking, smoking, dozing, etc., under the large cottonwoods when suddenly the air was filled with savage warcries as the Apaches charged in to annihilate the hated Americans. In a few seconds eight "man-hunters" were seriously wounded, one was dead, and all their horses, 38 head, had been stampeded then captured by the warriors. On their way out of the canyon the Apaches killed a Mexican who happened by.

Lt. Guilfoyle caught up with the renegades at Monica Springs in the San Mateos on August 3, 1881. Nana managed to slip away. On August 11 Guilfoyle found that two more Mexicans had been killed and two women carried away near La Savoya (sic; La Cebolleta?).

General Hatch ordered every available soldier into the field and took over personal command. Hundreds of soldiers scoured the plains, canyons, mountains, etc., but the hostiles under Nana seemed to come out of their hiding place, strike their target, then disappear into the wilderness once more.

Captain Charles Parker struck the raiders on August 12 some twenty-five miles west of Sabinal. Parker suffered five casualties, one of them killed, but he reported killing four Indians before they retreated without a trace.

On August 16 Nana's band was in another fight, this time with Ninth Cavalry troopers. Lt. G. Valois reported he had met some "fifty" Indians at the Cuchillo Negro River. Two soldiers were killed, several wounded, then the Apaches disappeared.

Nana had barely evaded Valois when he ran into Lt. F.B. Taylor, also of the Ninth Cavalry. Nana fled into the Black Mountains, Taylor in pursuit but cautiously.

After ten fights in less than thirty days, with soldiers swarming everywhere, Nana decided to retreat into Mexico. On the way his warriors clashed with Lt. G.W. Smith and his patrol of some twenty Ninth Cavalry troopers. In a "severe fight" Lt. Smith was killed, as were four of his men, along with a civilian named George Daly who had wanted to fight the hostiles. Three other soldiers were wounded. Though the Americans later claimed victory, Nana's band held command of the battle field until they slipped into Mexico.

Nana's raid became somewhat legendary. The seventy-year-old leader directed his few warriors through more than a thousand miles of enemy territory, often covering *seventy miles*, sometimes a few more, in one day. They lived off the country, fought off professional American soldiers, and if they didn't win all of them outright they certainly didn't lose any. They killed anywhere from thirty to fifty of the hated Americans, wounded many more, captured two women, at least 200 horses and mules, eluded pursuit by a thousand soldiers and several hundred civilians. All this with a band that started out with fifteen warriors and never counted more than forty. Nana was a living legend. And more was yet to come.

SIKI

Among the captives taken at *Tres Castillos* where Victorio died were five women. Siki, daughter of the chieftain Loco, and four other women were taken to Mexico City where they endured captivity for three years. True to their warrior heritage, they planned to escape at the most propitious moment. When the opportunity presented itself they eased their way toward the desert country of northern Mexico, intending to make it to the Blue Mountains. With only a blanket and a knife between them, they experienced an adventurous, heroic odyssey which finally reunited them with Gerónimo's band in the Sierra Madre. (This feat is probably unparalleled in the history of women in the West.)

GERÓNIMO

The Apache who received the most notoriety was not a chief but the guerrilla raider known in English as Gerónimo (Spanish for *Jerome*). His real name was Gothlay (also Goth-lyka). Gerónimo was part of Juh's band and after his death, Naiche, son of Cochise, was elected chief for this group living in Mexico. Gerónimo was a respected shaman with powers which included foretelling the future. [See Note # 24.] But he was also a respected guerrilla fighter with obvious leadership qualities so Naiche listened to him.

General Crook was reassigned to command the Department of Arizona in September of 1882. By 1883 the USA and Mexico had signed a treaty that enabled continued pursuit across the international border when hostiles were being chased by soldiers from the other country. Raiders could no longer slam the border door on pursuing soldiers. Crook collected a contingent of some fifty soldiers with perhaps 200 Indian scouts and headed for the Sierra Madre strongholds in Mexico. The ranchería of Chato and Bonito was attacked but that was the only military engagement of Crook's campaign. The Apaches realized the armies of both the USA and Mexico could go after them no matter where so leaders, including Gerónimo, went in to parley with Crook.

Gerónimo finally told Crook he would bring in his people to San Carlos in Arizona. Crook really was in no position to take Gerónimo prisoner and return him by force. If he had tried the band would have scattered throughout the Blue Mountains and war would last forever. Crook was able to lead Nana, Loco, Bonito, and some 225 other Chiricahuas back to Arizona. Newspapers ridiculed Crook for believing Gerónimo.

In February of 1884, Gerónimo and his (Naiche) band came in and settled along Turkey Creek some fifteen miles below Ft. Apache. The skeptics were dumbfounded. Further, the Apaches took to cultivating the land, harvesting good quantities of wheat, corn, beans, potatoes, pumpkins, etc. Gerónimo himself became a successful farmer.

Incessant feuding between officers at Ft. Apache and the agents at San Carlos proved to be the cause for Apache discontent. Each group accused the other of abusing the Indians, in effect treating them as pawns to damage the opposing side. On May 17, 1884, Gerónimo, Naiche, Nana, and some 131 other Apaches fled the reservation for Sonora, Mexico.

Crook immediately organized another expedition, among which were Apache Scouts that now included former "renegades" like Chato. Crook finally held a parley with Gerónimo on March 25, 1886. This time Crook had been ordered to accept only unconditional surrender and the Chiricahuas immediate return to San Carlos. Crook also informed Gerónimo that he would have to be sent to Fort Marion (now *Castillo de San Marcos* National Monument) in Florida but after a couple of years he could return to Arizona. As soon as General Sheridan and President Gover Cleveland heard of the agreement they rejected it out of hand. Further, Crook was ordered to dismiss his Apache Scouts, to use only American soldiers from now on, that all Chiricahuas were to be shipped by railroad to Florida. General George Crook could not go back on his word so he asked to be relieved of his duties. His resignation was accepted and General Nelson Miles was sent to replace him. Gerónimo and his people bolted out of sight.

General Miles came in with some 5,000 soldiers, *fully one fourth of the entire U.S. Army*, with which to capture some 24 Apache warriors. Miles, with his walrus moustache and penchant for self-aggrandizement, was nothing if not a good politician. He kept newspapers informed on how the pursuit was going. With great fanfare and concomitant expense he erected some twenty-seven heliography stations to track the "hostiles" every move, proving that there was money to be made in capturing renegade Indians. Despite the technology, it was two Chiricahua scouts, Kayitah and Martine, who tracked Gerónimo to the Torres Mountains southeast of Fronteras. Gerónimo surrendered for the final time on September 4, 1886. For all practical purposes, the Indian wars of the American Southwest were finished.

President Cleveland invited Chato and some of his people to come to Washington and be honored for their service to the USA. Chato was presented with a silver medal and Cleveland asked him to take his people to Florida. Chato refused and asked for a document that would permit them to stay in Arizona. Cleveland gave him a paper that verified he had visited Washington, which Chato could not read. On the way back to Arizona Chato and the rest of the delegation were arrested at Ft. Leavenworth, Kansas, and charged with being *prisoners of war*. [See Note # 25.]

EXILE

General Crook had trusted the Apache Scouts and always remained loyal to them. General Miles and American authorities held contrary views. They believed Arizona would not be secure until all Chiricahuas were deported to Ft. Marion prison. Therefore all Chiricahuas, including the valiant Apache Scouts, even those from other groups married to Chiricahuas, were loaded in railroad cars and shipped east to Ft. Marion prison. [See Note # 26.] Chato wore the silver medal given him by President Cleveland when he was forced to board the train with the hostiles he had helped convince to surrender. Gerónimo and his band were among the last to go. By the end of 1886 there were some 500 Chiricahuas in Florida, the men at Ft. Pickens by Pensacola, the women at Ft. Marion on the Atlantic coast. [See Note # 27.]

General George Crook was incensed over the treatment given his Apache Scouts. He wrote that the Apache wars would still be raging without the Scouts, that Gerónimo would never have surrendered without the services of men like Chato, Kayitah, Martine, and countless others. He was furious that their reward from the USA should be a dungeon in Florida. President Cleveland and the War Department simply ignored him.

After some 119 exiles had died in the "dank, malarial, overcrowded prisons" in Florida the government moved them to Mount Vernon, Alabama. Crook visited them there on January 2, 1890. Chato came out and greeted the general very tenderly, taking him by the hand and struggling not to embrace him for Apaches didn't behave in such ways. Both old warriors were probably close to tears.

George Crook went to Washington to lobby for a bill which would permit the Chiricahua to settle at Fort Sill, Oklahoma. When he died in March of 1890 the bill died with him. The Apaches remained in the sweltering Alabama heat, dying in significant numbers, until 1894 when the Government decided it would be alright to send them to Ft. Sill after all. In Oklahoma they created a few villages as if they were back in their own homeland.

Nana died in 1896.

Gerónimo went into depression and took to drinking heavily. He often said it would have been better for him if he had died fighting. He passed away February 17, 1909.

After some 27 years as prisoners of war, Americans decided the Chiricahuas could be free people. In 1913 the Apaches were offered the choice of land in Oklahoma or land in the Mescalero Reservation in New Mexico. Of the 271 surviving Chiricahuas, 187 chose to return to New Mexico. It is unrecorded if the older Chiricahua Apaches, once described by General Crook as the "tigers of the human race," privately shed tears upon returning to a portion of their homeland. None were ever permitted into Arizona.

DISCUSSION NOTES *for* ARIZONA INDIAN AFFAIRS

Note # 1

See pages 97-99 in *Arizona: A History* by Thomas E. Sheridan.

Note # 2

See section 22 in *Historical Atlas Of New Mexico* by W.A. Beck and Y.D. Haase.

Note # 3

Apaches might be compared to the Vikings of the Old World. While the savage Norsemen raiders terrorized most of coastal Europe, movies and such have softened their image. With a few exceptions like *Blood Brother* by Elliott Arnold, this has not happened for the Apaches.

Note # 4

According to Odie B. Faulk, page 98 in his *Arizona: A Short History*, Bascom was commended by his superiors for his actions.

Note # 5

Marshall Trimble writes on page 116 of his *Arizona; A Cavalcade Of History* that many Arizonans criticized Jeffords as an "Indian lover."

Note # 6

Rufus K. Wyllys, author of *Arizona: The History Of A Frontier State* mentions Cochise a few times in his 408 pages but the impression is that the chieftain was an inconsequential player in Arizona history. Is Amerindian history an integral part of American historiography?

Note # 7

See pages 80-90 in *The Conquest Of Apacheria* by Dan L. Thrapp.

Note # 8

Thomas E. Sheridan writes on page 81 of his *Arizona: A History* that historiographers "fell into a common trap of Western history by making Anglos the leading protagonists in the drama even though most of the participants were O'odham or Mexicans." There are implications here beyond those of veracity. Arizonans of the day strived to be known as stalwart frontiersmen and "heroic" killers of Indians. This sort of reputation isn't very acceptable today so has the historical record been made more palatable "for modern readers"? H.H. Bancroft writes that *"40 citizens and 100 Pápagos from Tucson and vicinity marched out to the camp and killed 85, all women and children but eight, and captured some 30, who were sold by the Pápagos as slaves."* Sheridan writes that while 80 "Anglos" had signed up, the expedition of April 28 consisted of 92 Pápagos, 42 Mexicans, and 6 "Anglos." J.P. Dunn wrote: "It seems unjust to charge this wrong against the American people, for most of the perpetrators were Mexicans and Indians, and there were Americans nearby who would have given protection to the victims if it had been in their power." He goes on to say that "the offense of the people of Arizona was in defending it..."

Composition of the "avengers" expedition, then and now, would make for an interesting study. So would a comparison with Sand Creek (1864), where the blame was not fixed on "Pápagos and Mexicans."

Note # 9

The number of slaughtered victims varies with the writer. Bancroft states the number of Apaches killed was 85, all but eight were women and children. (As in Sand Creek in Colorado, the expressed belief was that *"Nits make lice."*) Odie Faulk says the number was 108 killed. Rufus K. Wyllys says the number was 108. J.P. Dunn writes that the dead/missing numbered 125. Dan L. Thrapp puts the number of dead at 144.

Note # 10

The Camp Grant atrocity took place in 1871. Mexico abolished slavery in 1829-30 yet we are told that Apache children were to be sold in Sonora, Mexico. Is Mexico being used as a convenient cover-up?

Note # 11

See pages 621-24 in *Massacres Of The Mountains* by J.P. Dunn.

Note # 12

See *New Hope For The Indians: The Grant Peace Policy And The Navajos In The 1870s* by Norman J. Bender for an introduction to this peace initiative. Basically, Denominational ministers would become Indian Agents and care for their charges under Christian principles.

Note # 13

See page 193 in *Arizona: The History Of A Frontier State* by Rufus K. Wyllys.

Note # 14

H.H. Bancroft writes (page 565) in his *History Of Arizona And New Mexico* that Crook was "the best Indian fighter of all, but by no means the only one...He fully understood the Indian character, exercised practical good sense in all he undertook, being unaffected by sickly sentimentalism on one side, or exterminating vengeance on the other." While there is no confusion about the "exterminating vengeance" comment, it would be interesting to investigate the psychology of "sickly sentimentalism" as applied by Americans toward realities involving Amerindians. Would this "sickly sentimentalism" be the "Indian lover" syndrome?

Note # 15

See page 100 in *Conquest Of Apacheria*.

Note # 16

See page 126 in Conquest Of Apacheria.

Note # 17

This was not mere rhetoric. It has been estimated that there had never been more than some 5-6,000 Apaches in the Southwest compared to the teeming 31 millions of Americans (as of 1860), not to mention the weaponry which characterized American "civilization."

Note # 18

The best books on George Crook are *On The Border With Crook* by John G. Bourke and of course *General George Crook: His Autobiography* edited by Martin F. Schmitt.

Note # 19

See page 5 in *Indeh* by Eve Ball.

Note # 20

See page 19 in *Indeh*.
Note # 21
See footnote 6 on page 26 of *Indeh* which states: *Cushing had killed more savages of the Apache tribe than any other officer or troop of the United States Army had done before or since.* Dan L. Thrapp writes in Chapter VI of his *Conquest Of Apacheria* that Cushing was the "Beau Sabreur of the border," that John G. Bourke, author of *On The Border With Crook*, described him as "the bravest man I ever saw."
Note # 22
See page 75 in *Conquest Of Apacheria*.
Note # 23
Dan L. Thrapp writes on page 212 of his *Conquest Of Apacheria* that Nana was a veteran raider "when Victorio was a toddler barely old enough to learn the delights of torturing such small birds and animals as fell into his clutches." Compare the tone of Eve Ball, author of *Indeh*, with that of Thrapp.
Note # 24
See page 93 in *Arizona: A History* by Thomas E. Sheridan.
Note # 25
See page 96 in the Sheridan volume.
Note # 26
Because of the genocidal images associated with W W II, it should be pointed out that the Apaches were not transported in freight or cattle cars. See *I Fought With Gerónimo* by Jason Betzinez (with Wilbur S. Nye) for an insider's view of the Apache story.
Note # 27
It appears not unusual for American historiography to minimize unpleasant history. For example, Marshall Trimble covers this episode on page 121 of his *Arizona: A Cavalcade Of History* by writing: "The two scouts, Martine and Kayitah, were imprisoned along with the renegade Chiricahua and sent to prison in Florida." [See the *Essay: Morality Aside* below.]

Essay: MORALITY ASIDE

One of the inescapable historical characteristics of the American Southwest is that it belonged to Spain for more than two centuries (and Mexico for some twenty-five years). The European base for Southwest history was/is written in the Spanish language. It has now been supplanted by use of English therefore translation from original Spanish documents is an integral factor for Southwest history until the 1800s. As every scholar knows, accuracy of translated documents can never be taken for granted, especially in a country like the USA where foreign language study is not particularly popular. Further, it can be shown that the tenets of American historiography have been applied to the whole of Southwest history, not just to the English language historical record begun in the 1800s. Therefore the Spanish **Black Legend** (*Leyenda Negra*) of cruelty, depravity, and fanaticism must be considered as having a possible role in much of what is written in English.

Take for example the title of an English language translation done on *Destrucción de Indias*, the reform piece written by **Bartolomé de Las Casas**. Cultural bias can be readily discerned by merely reading the title of the following London edition of 1689: *Popery truly Display'd in its Bloody Colours: Or a Faithful Narrative of the Horrid and Unexampled Massacres, Butcheries, and all manner of Cruelties, that Hell and Malice could invent, committed by the Popish Spanish Party on the Inhabitants of West India…composed first in Spanish by Bartholomew de Las Casas, a Bishop there, and an Eye-Witness of most of the Barbarous Cruelties; afterwards translated by him into Latin, then by other hands into High-Dutch, Low-Dutch, French, and now Taught to Speak Modern English.* [See Note # 1. *Notes begin on page 410.*]

English language historians/writers have superimposed their ideas on the history of the Spanish Southwest. More writers have been critical than positive, especially where Amerindians are concerned, despite the fact that more Indians were preserved under Spanish suzerainty, especially in New Mexico where there were relatively large numbers of Hispanic people, than under American rule. As an example of what is often written, let us elaborate on the commentary of Robert Silverberg's *Pueblo Revolt*, published by the University of Nebraska. [See Note # 2.] Among other things, Mr. Silverberg writes, and his work was published by a university press, that the Spanish friars introduced "*…orchards of fruit unfamiliar to the Pueblo folk: pears, peaches, figs, dates, pomegranates, olives, cherries, quinces, lemons, oranges, nectarines.*" With the slightest possible exception of the southernmost parts of New Mexico, "lemons, oranges, nectarines" don't grow in New Mexico. Where is Mr. Silverberg getting his information? Certainly not from New Mexico. (Is the rest of his work as accurate?)

Silverberg's book contains issues much weightier than citrus fruits, however. He informs the reader that the Spanish conquest of the Americas "*…was a cruel harvest, not only of gold and gems but of the bodies and souls of men.*" The Indians were "*treated with chilling inhumanity…converted to Christianity…turned into slaves…slaughtered like beasts. The gods and ceremonies the Indians cherished were forbidden…Terror became a routine instrument of Spanish policy…Whole tribes died out, shattered by Spanish ferocity and by the diseases the Spanish brought. The holocaust took millions of lives; the martyrdom of the Indians at the hands of Spain was one of history's darkest episodes.*"

How much historical validity is there to Silverberg's perspectives? Agriculture aside, there is no doubt there were horrendous atrocities at the beginning of the Spanish conquest beginning in 1492. Native inhabitants of the Caribbean Islands, like the fierce Caribs, found to be cannibals, were virtually exterminated. On the mainland Pizarro and Guzmán were little more than thugs who exterminated as the easiest way to effect a conquest. When word got back to Spain as to what was happening the government investigated and made laws intended to halt abuses. [See Note # 3.] What reforms were instituted? According to L.B. Simpson, the policies by which "*…Cortés achieved the pacification of New Spain with extraordinarily little bloodshed. Cortés became the idol of the Indian population. What is more important for the subsequent history of New Spain, the policy of Cortés was the policy of its rulers for three hundred years.*" [See Note # 4.]

It is only logical that the moral yardstick applied to Spain must be used for all other colonial powers, including England which dominated along the eastern seaboard. Englishmen founded Jamestown, Virginia, in 1607 (there were no women in the settlement) and exchanges between the races at the time have been described as *brutish*. And they continued that way. In 1763 during the Pontiac War, Lord **Jeffrey Amherst** told his subordinates to infect blankets with smallpox then give them to the Indians in order to quell the uprising. This was done and in a short time whole tribes, including non-combatants, were dying with smallpox sores all over Amerindian bodies. When has this been described as "chilling inhumanity" on the part of Amherst, his army, or his English nation? This hasn't been the standard way to approach English-American history but it is common when discussing Spanish lands. Why has such a double standard been permitted in American historiography? (One of the few to address this issue is Stewart L. Udall in his *Majestic Journey*.)

The focus must now be placed on the American Southwest because that is the nature of the work being presented. To use Mr. Silverberg's phraseology, have there been incidents of "chilling inhumanity" in the Hispanic Southwest (1540-1846)? **Vásquez de Coronado** made war on various Indian groups during his reconnaissance in force of the Southwest but nations were neither exterminated nor subject to exile from their native lands. The Acoma battle was a declared war caused by an Acoma Indian ambush. The St. Lawrence Day Massacre, referred to in English as the "Pueblo Revolt" though three-out-of-every-four dead were women and children, was a surprise uprising. There is no denying that the atmosphere in the Hispanic Southwest, particularly in Athabascan areas, was one of raid and counter-raid. At a later date, it could be asked if the Comanche war was justified and the answer would have to be in the affirmative because Pueblo and Hispanic people were on the brink of extermination due to Comanche raiders. (Pecos Pueblo died out because of Comanche raids.) All have been addressed in previous sections above for the reader to study at leisure. Which would fall under the Silverberg category of "*…history's darkest episodes*"? The reader can decide.

What happens when the same parameters are utilized for the American Southwest? Was it "*chilling inhumanity*" that caused the forcible deportation to Oklahoma of the Civilized Tribes and all Indians from east of the Mississippi? Was there "chilling inhumanity" at the Council House murders in Texas? At Sand Creek, Colorado? Camp Grant, Arizona? On the Washita in Oklahoma? Was the American destruction of California Indians a veritable *holocaust*? To delve deeper, have Americans even been made aware of the above? I will cite one example. *"It's Your Misfortune And None Of My Own:" A History of the American West* by Richard White (University of Oklahoma Press, 1991) is an excellent, informative book issued by a highly respected publisher. Written history begins with Spanish people, in this case Alvar Núñez Cabeza de Vaca, whom Richard White introduces on page four along with the phrase "*…the nature of the Spaniards.*" He also mentions Estevánico (sic). Vásquez de Coronado is introduced with "*Coronado exercised his cruelty…*" According to Mr. White, Coronado was merely a warning for the Pueblos that there were "*…storms brewing on the horizon. The storm broke in 1598 when Don Juan de Oñate…set out to fulfill his contract for the colonization of New Mexico.*"

What happens by the time *It's Your Misfortune And None Of My Own* gets to the American period of the Southwest? There are no Index entries for the Camp Grant Massacre nor for the Council House murders of Comanche chieftains. Mr. White doesn't ignore all the atrocities. After supplying background information, the Sand Creek Massacre receives the following coverage (p. 96): *In the slaughter that ensued, 105 Cheyenne women and children and 28 men died. Chivington's soldiers scalped and mutilated the dead Indian bodies, gathering "trophies" to take back to Denver. Soldiers stretched the genitals of dead women over their saddlebows or wore them as decorations on their hats.* Richard White makes no mention of *cruelty*, as he did with Coronado, nor does he describe the advent of Americans as a *storm*. (Since Spaniards are portrayed as *cruel* for fighting Indians, it can only be imagined what would be written if Spaniards had taken "female genitals" with which to decorate their helmets.) He does report (pp. 337-40) on the plight of California Indians but he says the atrocities were committed by "the whites." Who hunted Indians like animals? Whites. "Far more wrongs rested with the whites…" There were "…epidemics and white attacks…[Indian] children were stolen and their women removed." (We are not told if the "removal" was to make prostitutes out of them.) Who did all this? "Angry whites." It is perfectly acceptable to focus on "the nature of Spaniards" and "Coronado's cruelty" but if writing about the USA the closest one can get is "the whites." What has this done to the national psyche? Again, these matters have already been presented and the reader can decide.

The characteristics of American historiography (boosterism, Progress!, heroes versus villains, Liberty!, etc.) are as much principal players when discussing "American History" as the actual incidents that occurred. It must be pointed out that it isn't very acceptable to discuss negative Southwest history issues unless they pertain to Spain and Hispanic people. For example, smallpox and such European maladies are often presented as "Spanish diseases" by American writers. The Lewis & Clark expedition of 1803 inadvertently carried smallpox that decimated the Mandan Indians of the upper Missouri region. But that tragedy has never been associated with any terms like "American smallpox." Indeed, the popular mind doesn't even acknowledge that smallpox was carried by the Lewis & Clark expedition and to so state would probably evoke a charge of *revisionist* or worse from people accustomed to thinking of the expedition as strictly a heroic venture.

Perhaps the ultimate way to judge a colonizing power is to investigate what effect it had on native inhabitants. Roman Catholic missionaries were the paladin defenders of Indians in Spanish lands. The herculean champion Father Bartolomé de Las Casas, *Apostle to the Indians*, became famous (his opponents called him *infamous*, "the most hated man in the Indies") and is in a class by himself for his defense of Amerindians. His best known effort at reform was published (1552) under the title of *Very Brief Recital of the Destruction of the Indies*, and became the most translated European work of the day. Few tracts in history have had such far-reaching effects. [See Note # 5.] This paladin tradition was continued in the Southwest by sterling heroes like Benavides and Perea in New Mexico, Kino in Arizona, Margil in Texas, Serra and Lasuén in California, to name but a few. It must also be pointed out that these "Soldiers of the Cross" achieved what they did because they had a Government that would listen to them.

Who championed the Amerindians of the Southwest when it came under American domination? The established American tradition was one of deportation for all Indians. President Jefferson is "credited" with conceiving of the idea that Indians should be "removed" to lands west of the Mississippi River. Despite the Supreme Court ruling against the deportation, President Jackson had it carried out. It would have taken superlative courage to go against Jackson when the President disobeyed the ruling of the Supreme Court. Who championed the Indians?

Trying to help Amerindians in the USA carried with it the stigma of being an *"Indian lover"* which connotes being a *racial traitor*. Despite that very negative sentiment there were some Americans who had the courage to stand up for moral justice. **Robert S. Neighbors** (Texas) and **Silas S. Soule** (Colorado) tried and were murdered for it. General **George Crook** spoke up in favor of his Apache Scouts but he held no sway with his superiors and the Scouts were deported to prison in Florida alongside the "renegades" they helped capture.

Who in American society were responsible for Amerindian welfare? The Department of the Interior and later the Bureau of Indian Affairs appear to have been little more than a morass of self-serving bureaucracy. Most Indian Agents have been described as working for their own personal benefit instead of Indian welfare. Ordinary Americans living in areas where there were Indians often believed extermination was the only real solution for the "Indian problem." In all fairness, such sentiment was not new to the Southwest because it had been apparent from the earliest settlements along the eastern seaboard and went unchecked as soon as the "settlers" established military superiority. [See Note # 6.]

Bartolomé de Las Casas published his *Destrucción* treatise/book demanding reform in 1552. A related American effort could be said to be that of **Helen Hunt Jackson** in 1880 titled *A Century Of Dishonor*. Though the two can't be compared in scope or impact, both were efforts at reform in the treatment of Amerindians. [See Note # 7.] The Jackson work doesn't limit itself to the Southwest but it does relate information on atrocities like Sand Creek and Camp Grant. The Preface by Bishop **H.B. Whipple** is a searing condemnation worthy of Las Casas: "*...The American people have accepted as truth the teaching that the Indians were a degraded, brutal race of savages, whom it was the will of God should perish at the approach of civilization...It soothes conscience to cast mud on the character of the one whom we have wronged.*" He asserts that the "*Indian Bureau represents a system which is a blunder and a crime.*" What is the Amerindians status under domination of the USA: "*The Indian is the only individual with no right in the soil...no standing before the law...It may be doubted whether one single treaty has ever been fulfilled...Pledges solemnly made have been shamelessly violated. The Indian has had no redress but war. In these wars ten white men were killed to one Indian, and the Indians who were killed have cost the Government a hundred thousand dollars each.*"

Bishop Whipple contrasts the American situation with that of Canada where there were no Indian wars. [See Note # 8.] The impression is that Indians in Canada were considered British subjects recognized by the Crown while Indians in American territories were considered an enemy race with coveted lands.

Whipple also relates the story about the time when Alaska became American territory. An American army officer happened to go into a Greek Orthodox church and saw "on the altar a beautiful copy of the Gospels in a costly binding studded with jewels." The officer sought out the bishop and advised him that so valuable an item should not be left unguarded in church. The bishop remarked the Gospels had lain on the altar for seventy years without the slightest trouble because "the book is in God's house." The day after Alaska officially became American territory "the Gospel was stolen."

Bishop Whipple asserts that the deportation of the Cherokees and other Amerindian nations is "*...one of the darkest crimes ever committed by a Christian nation.*" Because solemn treaties have been ignored the Bishop says "*...the name of a white man is to the Indians a synonyme (sic) for liar.*" [See Note # 9.]

Julius H. Seelye from Amherst College (1880) writes in his "Introduction" to *A Century Of Dishonor* that "*...the Indian problem is not with the Indian, but with the Government and people of the United States.*"

Indians have been encouraged to remain in their "savage" state in order to negate citizenship status. Their ways of living have been denied them without providing anything to take their place. They have been shut into reservations "notoriously unfit for them" and even these lands were taken when someone could make a profit from it. *Civilization does not reproduced itself. It must first be kindled and can then only be kept alive by a power genuinely Christian.* Americans must set a Christian example and *"…we should be honest…exemplified in our own deeds."*

Hope springs eternal. In the "Author's Note" in *A Century Of Dishonor*, H.H. Jackson declares the *"American people, as a people, are not at heart unjust…they believe in 'fair play'…And as soon as they fairly understand how cruelly it has been denied to the Indian, they will rise up and demand it for him."* In the "Introductory" to her book Jackson sums up: *"There is but one hope of righting this wrong. It lies in appeal to the heart and conscience of the American people…What an opportunity for the Congress of 1880 to cover itself with a luster of glory, as the first to cut short our nation's record of cruelties and perjuries! The first to attempt to redeem the name of the United States from the stain of a century of dishonor."*

While many Americans meant well, hatred of Indians didn't abate because of Jackson's efforts of 1880. On December 29, 1890, the Sioux band led by Big Foot, ill with pneumonia, had surrendered to Major S.M. Whitside of the Seventh Cavalry. Reinforcements arrived at the site of Wounded Knee and Colonel Forsyth took overall command of the now 470 soldiers. Big Foot's people were ordered to surrender all their weapons but few were turned in so soldiers were ordered to search all teepees, which formed a semicircle, and belongings for weapons. Sioux women protested, some physically refusing to let their belongings thrown around by the soldiers. Perhaps forty guns were discovered and piled in the center of the village. A struggle broke out between a Sioux and a soldier then a shot rang out. "This was what the Seventh had been waiting for; this chance was too good to miss…It took two minutes to turn the camp into a burning shambles while the surviving Indians scattered in utter rout." [See Note # 10.] Soldiers opened fire with their Springfield rifles then the Hotchkiss guns situated on a little knoll let loose with their explosive shells into the Sioux camp. The soldiers fired at everybody, man, woman, child, even dogs and some horses. Indians trying to run away, as well as those who found cover (*"Come out. We do not make war on women and children."*) were shot down. Soldiers pursued and shot most of the Sioux they found. After the action an officer of the Seventh Cavalry was heard to say: "Now we have avenged Custer's death."

A burial detail arrived a few days later and threw some 144 Sioux bodies into a mass grave. Some 84 were men/boys, along with 44 women and 16 children. Many of the corpses were stripped of clothing by souvenir hunters. Some thirty-one "whites" were killed with thirty-three wounded. It has been said that most of the American casualties were victims of "friendly fire" because the Sioux basically had no guns. Wounded Knee became the last "Indian war" of the West.

The underlying tenets of American historiography continue to dominate and shape most events as related by American historians. For example, any time a group of "whites" was killed it is generally reported as a *massacre*. An atrocity by which Indians were destroyed is generally referred to as a *tragedy*. If culpability is a factor then it was the *white man* who was to blame. Why did he do it? Because Indians were in the way of the march of *civilization*. And so on. While Helen Hunt Jackson is representative of very few Americans, there have been individuals like Senator Ben N. Campbell of Colorado who once asserted that of the 472 treaties made by Americans with Amerindian groups, every single one was broken by the USA.

The Indian wars ended on December 29, 1890, with the massacre of a basically unarmed band of Sioux by the Seventh Cavalry. With some notable exceptions, American historiography promotes the Indian wars as *civilization* against *savagery*. It doesn't emphasize the deceit or covetousness of treaties used to take Indian land. Perhaps because of the death camps of the first part of the 20th century, it steers away from the sentiments of extermination directed at Amerindian people. The United States never produced a "Protector of the Indians" like Bartolomé de Las Casas. Indeed, it would be safe to say it never produced a Serra, Lasuén, Kino, Benavides, Perea, Margil, etc., the latter being humanitarian champions in the Southwest. Is it because American society would not permit it? Further, American historiography has laid no emphasis on what Dan L. Thrapp has expressed in the following manner: *"Nor is it the purpose of this book to argue the morality* (of American Indian wars), *its rights and wrongs…morality aside, and it was indeed, often cast aside…"*

DISCUSSION NOTES *for* Essay: MORALITY ASIDE

Note # 1

See pages 176-77 in *A History Of Latin America From The Beginnings To The Present*, 1955, by Hubert Herring. The *Destrucción* treatise by Las Casas was fed into the English propaganda machine and became the basis for the anti-Hispanic Black Legend in existence to this day. See *Tree Of Hate: Propaganda and Prejudices Affecting United States Relations with the Hispanic World*, 1971, by Philip Wayne Powell.

Note # 2

See page 3 in *The Pueblo Revolt*, Robert Silverberg, University of Nebraska Press, 1970.

Note # 3

See *The Spanish Struggle For Justice In The Conquest Of America* by Lewis Hanke, Little, Brown and Company, 1965.

Note # 4

See page 27 in *Many Mexicos* by Lesley Byrd Simpson, University of California Press, 1952.

Note # 5

Las Casas work was thus the first in modern polemics, along which would later be included *Uncle Tom's Cabin* by Harriet Beecher Stowe (said to have been one of the principal reasons for the start of the American Civil War) and the expose of French anti-Semitism *J'accuse* by Emile Zola.

Note # 6

See *500 Nations* by Alvin M. Josephy Jr.

Note # 7

Las Casas is a herculean figure in the early history of the Latin Americas. If Helen Hunt Jackson is remembered today it is mostly as the author of *Ramona*.

Note # 8

It would make for an interesting discussion to explore ideas as to why British people were so different in Canada and the USA with regard to their views on Amerindians. Why were there no Indians wars in Canada while there were so many in the USA?

Note # 9

The commentary by Bishop Whipple, though he employs "white man" for "American," is among the closest that an American writer has come to asserting sentiments like Robert Silverberg hurls against Spain and its people. Sioux chieftain Red Cloud referred to Americans as *thieves* and *liars* but in all of Southwest history I know of no general work that refers to Americans in such terms. The Sioux term for "American" is *wasichu*, which connotes *greed*.

Note # 10

See page 313-15 in *Great Western Indian Fights*.

Note # 11

See pages 366-67 in *The Conquest Of Apacheria*.

CHAPTER 11

Transcontinental Railroad

B uilding the American transcontinental railroad (1863-1869), a combination of the Union Pacific (which would be built toward the west from the Missouri River) and the Central Pacific (which would be built toward the east from Sacramento, California), was one of the USA's greatest ever achievements. While the trans-Canada railroad was a little longer (2,097 miles) and the Trans-Siberian railroad (5,338 miles) dwarfed both of them, the American road completed in 1869 was the first trans-continental system "…thus ensuring an empire of liberty running from sea to shining sea." [See Note # 1. *Notes begin on page 421.*]

It has been written that the first engines were used to haul coal in Britain in 1813. George Stephenson created the first steam-powered locomotive, called the *Rocket*, in 1829 and the first steam locomotive appeared in the USA in the same year. The first American steam locomotive, the *Tom Thumb*, designed and built by Peter Cooper in 1830, worked on a thirteen mile track between Baltimore and Ellicott's Mills, Maryland. It was around this time that people began talking about a transcontinental railroad to the Pacific.

ASA WHITNEY

Among the most important "dreamers" of the transcontinental railroad was Asa Whitney. He rode on the Liverpool and Manchester Railroad while in England in 1830 and later wrote the railroad would be of particular importance for America to grow to the Pacific Ocean. The ocean journey down and around Cape Horn was simply too long and fraught with too much danger.

Whitney wrote a document and gave it to Zadock Pratt, a legislator from upstate New York, to introduce it to the second session of the Twenty-Eighth Congress in 1845. It was titled: *Railroad From Lake Michigan to the Pacific: Memorial of Asa Whitney, of New York City, relative to the Construction of a Railroad from Lake Michigan to the Pacific Ocean.* The remarkable proposal was referred to the Committee on Roads and Canals where it was tabled. Undaunted, Whitney gathered a group of talented "gentlemen of high respectability and education" to inspect and partially survey a railroad route to the Pacific. They headed west from New York on June 2, 1845. By the first of July the group was at Pairie du Chien but they had been slowed because they couldn't find men to handle the heavy work associated with the little expedition. They also had trouble finding guides and, not being frontiersmen, they had no knowledge of the areas they were "surveying." The "gentlemen" did the best they could, even performing the required labor to keep moving west. They loved the rolling prairie country between the Mississippi and the Missouri, "…the finest country upon the globe…" All the Government had to do was supply the land and means with which to build the railroad.

As if to support such sentiments, one John L. O'Sullivan wrote in *The United States Magazine and Democratic Review*: "Our manifest destiny is to overspread the continent allotted by Providence for the free development of our yearly multiplying millions."

In 1846 Asa Whitney entrusted Illinois Senator Sidney Breese with a new memorial which was referred to the Committee on Public Lands. Among other things it also stated that the "numerous, powerful, and entirely savage" Indians (Sioux) were willing to sell land for the railroad. A Senate bill was drawn up on his proposal but then powerful Senator Thomas Hart Benton (Missouri) demanded the eastern terminus be located in St. Louis.

The Mexican War (1846-48) would rage and politics would take their toll in Washington but Whitney wouldn't give up on the dream of a transcontinental railroad. Gold was discovered in California and as the 49ers went west everyone agreed a railroad was absolutely necessary. Shortly there were *five* transcontinental plans being discussed in Congress, Whitney's among them. In 1849 Whitney published his *A Project for a Railroad to the Pacific*, the peak of his efforts. But nothing happened in Congress. He continued his efforts, which culminated in a two hour address to the House in January of 1851, on the importance of the Pacific railroad. Nothing happened.

Asa Whitney journeyed to England to try to attract funding but he wasn't successful there either. Almost bankrupt, the dream finally faded and Whitney resigned himself to the private life of a gentleman farmer. (He lived to see his dream realized by the hands of other people but nowhere was there a station or railroad line named in his honor. He died of typhoid fever in 1872.)

THEODORE D. JUDAH

In 1852 a group of Californians decided it would be profitable to build a railroad out of Sacramento in order to tap the rich mines of the lower Sierra Nevada slopes. One William T. Sherman resigned from the Army to work on building the line which would be called the Sacramento Valley Railroad. He traveled to New York to find the right engineer for the job and came up with twenty-eight-year-old Theodore Dehone Judah. Ted Judah discussed moving to California with his wife **Anna Ferona Pierce**, who understood that building a transcontinental railroad was her husband's primary goal in life. By April of 1854 they were on their way to Nicaragua from whence they would board a steamer bound for San Francisco. They arrived in May and proceeded immediately to Sacramento. By the end of the month Judah informed his superiors that a line could be built from Sacramento to Folsom for about $33,000 per mile. In February of 1855 actual grading began, the first rails were laid in August and a handcar carried a few individuals for the first-ever ride on a California railroad. The first locomotive, the *Sacramento*, arrived in August and everywhere was greeted with excitement. By February of 1856 the line was completed to Folsom.

In 1856 Ted Judah and his wife Anna made three ocean voyages back to Washington in efforts to convince the Government that it was the only entity large enough to motivate the creation of a transcontinental railroad. Only the Government had enough land, which could be given out as land grants, or enough money, by issuing bonds, to accomplish the feat. Judah was a masterful lobbyist. Anna was later to write: *Everything in his life, time, money, brains, was absorbed to the goal of a transcontinental railroad.* Some people thought he was crazy and they began to refer to him as *Crazy Judah.* But he continued to work through the years. In December of 1859 he was able to talk with President Buchanan who now favored a transcontinental railroad. In 1860 the Republican platform favored the project and the Republican candidate, a former railroad lawyer named Abraham Lincoln, did too.

A basic question constantly posed to Judah was How are you going to get a railroad across the Sierra Nevada mountains? He resolved to conduct his own survey so he could explain all details with first-hand facts. With Anna staying with friends in Sacramento, Judah went into the mountains to find the best routes and passes. He camped in the wilderness, slept in the open, cooked on a campfire, reclined sitting against a tree. He found the best routes, mapped them carefully, wrote his reports. His association with Daniel "Doc" Strong, a druggist from Dutch Flat, led to the birth of what was to be the Central Pacific.

Judah and Strong now needed investors to the tune of some $115,000. Various potential backers in San Francisco scoffed at the idea that a line could be built through the Sierra Nevada. What about the snow?! And Congress isn't doing a thing to help! Crazy Judah resolved never to bother with such people again so he packed his bags and took Anna back to Sacramento where he went to work immediately, talking to anyone who would attend his meetings. At one gathering there happened to be four men who were destined to be major players in the railroad project: Charles Crocker, Collis Huntington and his partner Mark Hopkins, and Leland Stanford (who would come to be known as "The Associates" or "The Big Four"). Crocker was running a dry-goods store, Huntington and Hopkins had a general store, and Stanford was also a shopkeeper. [See Note # 2.] Crocker and Stanford were active politically. None had any experience with railroads but all saw its economic potential. While a few shares were sold, Collis Huntington invited Judah to drop by and see him. When he did Judah had his money ($35,000) for a real survey. The Central Pacific Railroad of California incorporated into formal existence on June 28, 1861. The combined wealth of incorporators/directors totaled some $159,000 and neither the State of California nor the federal Government had a penny in the venture. Some people thought it was madness.

On November 27, 1861, Crocker, Huntington, Hopkins, and Stanford created articles of association for the Dutch Flat and Donner Lake Wagon Road Company. Judah was in Washington and probably didn't know about the new association but the group explained the road would help get supplies to the people who would be working on the railroad.

The Civil War was now raging but Judah did his best to lobby congressmen. The House passed the Pacific Railroad Bill on May 6, 1862. While it was extremely complicated, the bill called for the creation of a Union Pacific corporation which would build toward the west from the Missouri River while the Central Pacific would build toward the east from Sacramento. The telegraph would be built alongside the tracks. Each line would have a right of way of two hundred feet on each side of the railroad along with 6,400 acres per mile of track. There would be additional land for stations, shops, etc., as required, as well as timber, stone, earth, etc., materials necessary for construction. Capital stock would be a hundred thousand shares at $1,000 each (a hundred million dollars). Government bonds would be let at

$16,000 per mile of flat land, $32,000 for foothills, and $48,000 per mile through mountains. Advance money would be available through loans in the form of six percent government bonds which the railroads would have to sell to get the actual money. The Government would have to be repaid within thirty years. The entire transcontinental railroad would have to be completed by July 1, 1876, or everything would be forfeited to the Government. Ted Judah wired back to Sacramento: We have drawn the elephant. Now let us see if we can harness him.

UNION PACIFIC

The first meeting of the Union Pacific was held in Chicago in September of 1862. Samuel R. Curtis was selected temporary chairman, William B. Ogden was elected president, Henry V. Poor as secretary. But Thomas C. "Doc" Durant would soon be the dominant figure in the UP. They felt there might not be enough money to actually build the railroad, especially due to the first mortgage nature of the Government bonds. They were going to need promoters who could convince investors to buy into the deal. In the first four months of sales only forty-five shares were sold to eleven individuals, one of whom was Brigham Young (five shares). Grenville M. Dodge was sought to head the Union Pacific but he was a Union general in 1862 so he refused the proffered $5,000 yearly salary.

It was decided that Omaha, Nebraska, would be the eastern terminus for the Union Pacific and Durant, now officially vice-president of the UP, ordered that a proper ceremony be held to celebrate, and publicize, since the Central Pacific had done so some eleven months earlier. Chief Engineer Peter Dey reported it was a grand affair.

CRÉDIT MOBILIER

The UP was to become involved in shady (complex) business practices which culminated in the Crédit Mobilier scandal. The Crédit Mobilier was based on investors owning railroad stock as well as stock in the construction companies hired to build the actual railroad, thus enabling investors to contract themselves while being paid with Government loans in the form of UP stocks and bonds. (The CP did basically the same thing in California. The Big Four awarded a contract to Charles Crocker & Co. to supply all materials, equipment, buildings, etc., a "company" owned by the Big Four. It appears Ted Judah was not in on it.) Construction contracts brought windfall profits to those in the Crédit Mobilier, who were also the directors and large stockholders of the UP. It appeared that anything could be rationalized because people considered the transcontinental railroad as a wild-cat venture which could yield a great prize or a total defeat. In the meantime, the Government would have to come through with a better deal, which it did.

PACIFIC RAILROAD ACT OF 1864

President Lincoln, who loved railroads, signed this bill into law on July 2. It was what the UP and CP directors had been wanting. Among other things, the corporations could issue their own first-mortgage bonds in amounts equal to Government bonds. They were also empowered to collect money sooner than before, for example, by laying twenty miles of track rather than forty. Not only did the railroads get more land they also got the rights to coal, iron, and other minerals found on their land grants. Further, investors could now buy in for $100 instead of $1,000. The two rail lines would soon view construction as a race to get rich with the attraction of building a transcontinental railroad on the side. There were all sorts of fights and factions in both railroad groups. One of the greatest losses was the death of Theodore Judah who contracted yellow fever while crossing the Isthmus of Panama in 1863. On his tombstone his wife and companion Anna had inscribed "He Rests from his Labors."

CENTRAL PACIFIC and CHINESE LABORERS

It was very difficult to find Americans who would work for the less than $3 per day paid by the railroad. Some Irishmen were brought in but it wasn't long before they too would work just long enough to gather enough money for a try at the gold fields. In 1865 Charlie Crocker made something of an outlandish suggestion: why not hire Chinese laborers? Chinese?! Why, they were too light and too short for railroad work. Really? They had built the Great Wall of China, hadn't they?

It has been estimated there were some 60,000 Chinese in California by 1865, most of them males looking to make money then return to China. The Chinese population was large considering that in 1858 the California Legislature had banned Chinese immigration. When running for Governor, Leland Stanford referred to them as "that degraded race…the dregs of Asia." The State of California continued to discriminate against them in almost every way: Chinese were prohibited from obtaining American citizenship, they couldn't attend public schools, they couldn't vote, and they weren't permitted to testify in any court of law. They were not permitted to work on the "Mother Lode," and to work in a mine they were required to pay a "miner's tax" of $4 per person and a $2 water tax, along with a personal tax, a hospital tax, a school tax, and a property tax. It has been written the Chinese paid more than two million dollars in taxes. Any Chinese who "dared" to enter a new mining area would be beaten, robbed, sometimes killed by American miners.

The Chinese proved to be excellent workers, according to their bosses better than the "whites." [See Note # 3.] While they were relatively small physically, they moved with great agility and worked persistently at any task given them. They had a spirit of adventure, almost all could read and write, and were good at "figures." They worked well in teams (each had a "white," usually Irish, boss), took very few breaks, stayed healthy, and were so intelligent they learned quickly, even blasting into the mountains by using black powder (which Chinese had invented). They demanded and received their own foods: oysters, different kind of fish, abalone, oriental fruits, many different kinds of vegetables but especially rice, etc., bought from Chinese merchants in San Francisco. They were fond of fresh pork and chicken. They refused to drink water from streams, preferring tea. They bathed as often as they could, taking sponge baths daily if nothing else. In comparison, "whites" were reported as suffering from "hydrophobia" because they rarely bathed. [See Note # 4.] The Celestials didn't drink whiskey so fights were few. Some did smoke opium on Sunday, their day off, but it appears not to have been a serious vice because apparently it didn't interfere with their work week.

Unlike some workers, the Chinese proved to be "honest, industrious, steady, sober, painstaking" and it was soon believed the railroad would not have been built without them. [See Note # 5.] Despite their superior work ethic and the feats they accomplished, managers like Charlie Crocker referred to them as "Chinks." [See Note # 6.]

While building through the mountains was a dangerous, all-engulfing challenge, perhaps the most demanding stretch of railroad was "Cape Horn," a three mile area along the gorge of the North Fork cut by the American River. The river was from 1200 to 2200 feet below the projected railroad bed and the rock slope was at around seventy-five degrees. There would be no tunnels because the plan was to lay track on the side of the mountain which would be sculpted by blasting powder. (Some engineers thought even the idea was "preposterous.") Few knew that during the summer of 1865 a Chinese foreman had suggested that the "Celestials" (from *Celestial Kingdom*; China) were skilled in this type of work which had been done in the Yangtze gorges back home. No one else came up with ideas so the Chinese were assigned to the task. They set up a system by which Celestials were lowered in waist-high baskets, holes were hand-drilled in the rock then tamped in with explosives. The fuse was set and lighted then the workers yelled to be hauled up away from the explosion. There were accidents but the Central Pacific didn't keep statistics on how many Celestials were killed. Little by little a ledge was formed on which the railroad could be laid. Clearing the roadbed was just about as dangerous as the blasting. A two hundred foot roadbed had to be cleared to provide ample room and prevent trees, some were 150 feet tall, from falling on the tracks. It took until the spring of 1866 to make the roadbed and lay track around Cape Horn. The feat remains one of the most famous labors in the history of the CP and one of the greatest sights in the entire line.

Another unbelievable challenge was blasting into the mountain to form tunnels for the roadbed. The work was slow and very dangerous. There was room for only three men to work together: one would hold the drill against the granite rock while the other two swung eighteen-pound sledgehammers to hit the back end of the drill. (Drills were ordered in one hundred ton lots.) When the hole was large enough for significant blasting powder the three-man crew would fill it, set the fuse, light it and "run like hell" to get out of the way of the blast. It was slow work, sometimes one foot per day, despite men working round the clock. Enormous quantities of black powder were used up.

By the end of 1865 the Central Pacific had 54 miles of working track. Some twenty miles had been spiked that year, at the cost of $6,000,000. It was a staggering amount but not when one considers the Sierra Nevada terrain it had to go through.

The winter of 1865-66 turned out being one of the wettest on record. Up in the Sierras there was five feet of snow on New Year's Day. Snowstorms lasted until June. Despite this and other travails, including serious financial problems, the CP had more than ten thousand men working, eight thousand of them Chinese. Nitroglycerin, thirteen times more powerful than black powder was introduced. But it was also more dangerous to workers so its use was shortly discontinued.

The winter of 1866-67 brought some forty-four separate storms, worse than the year before. There were many accidents but the work crept along. The Summit Tunnel was completed by September of 1867 then it was on to Nevada to link up with the Union Pacific. Whoever went the fastest would make the most money so the race would get richer and richer for whoever covered the most ground with track.

UNION PACIFIC and the IRISH

Grenville Dodge had recommended that the Union Pacific follow the Platte River westward to the base of the Rocky Mountains. Engineer Peter Dey agreed it was the best route. The people of

Denver wanted the railroad through their town as did Brigham Young in Salt Lake City. The route through Cheyenne Pass (ultimately called Sherman Hill) was finally approved by President Lincoln on November 4, 1864. Among the most pressing problems for the UP was that it would have to lay track across lands the Indians believed belonged to them.

On November 29, 1864, there occurred the Sand Creek Massacre in Colorado. Retaliation was not long in coming. On January 7, 1865, Sioux, Cheyenne, and Arapaho warriors attacked Julesburg, Colorado, killing many people and burning all buildings. One Lt. Casper Collins "was found horribly mutilated…with over a hundred arrows in him." Engineer Samuel Reed reported to Doc Durant that merely conducting his surveys was dangerous due to "hostile Indians everywhere…" which would not change until they were either exterminated or rendered powerless. [See Note # 7.]

General Grenville Dodge was the commander of the Department of Missouri, comprised of all lands between the Missouri River and the Rocky Mountains. Dodge understood the Union Pacific couldn't be built with Indians on the warpath and his orders were to remove them from railroad lands. It is believed that while Dodge was leading his troops he was also looking for the best railroad route across the plains. The Civil War ended in April of 1865 so Dodge was able to return to railroad building, but not before he had offered the UP captive Indians for grading work.

The Union Pacific had typical problems but also those peculiar to the Great Plains. Track had to be laid over Indian land and the Indians, usually targeted as "savages," were not about to let it go without a fight in which many would pay with their lives. Amerindians hated the railroad because it split the buffalo herd in two since the animals would not cross the iron rails. The railroad also brought in many more people who had no respect for Indian land ownership. General John Pope, who replaced General Dodge, wrote: *The Indian no longer has a country. He must either starve or wage war to the death. The white man will drive off his game and dispossess him of his lands…His end is sure and dreadful to contemplate.*

The terrain had other serious problems. the plains didn't have trees so wood for ties, trestles, buildings, etc., had to be imported along with everything else.

Laborers were hard to get. Most of the recruits turned out being Irish immigrants with a sprinkle of second-generation Americans. [See Note # 8.] Some workers were young veterans of the Civil War. By 1868 they numbered around three thousand. The work was steady, paid $2.50 to $4 a day depending on the nature of the job, considered good for the time and place. The work was demanding pick-and-shovel type labor which developed tough hands and steel-like muscles. The basic food (coffee, soup, meat, potatoes, fruit, pies/cakes) provided was good and most of the men enjoyed living in the open air environment. The Irish could also become difficult if they weren't paid as promised, even threatening to strike.

HELL ON WHEELS

When the UP stopped at North Platte for the winter of 1866-67 a village of some five thousand people sprang up almost overnight. This happened all along the line wherever railroad workers had to stop because of the weather, to wait for more supplies, etc. These "Hell on Wheels" tent or shack cities contained gambling houses, brothels, saloons, hotels, music halls, a few restaurants, managed by a "wild and savage conglomeration." [See Note # 9.] Most of these establishments were run by "sharpers" from cities like

Chicago. The young men working on the railroad, far from home and family, had no where else to go so they became rather easy pickings for the sharks. The men spent their money on liquor, prostitutes, and gambling. No one was shy when it came to using firearms. Vice and crime were the disgusting and dangerous order of the day or night. According to one Samuel Bowles everybody was "…dirty, many filthy, and with the marks of the lowest vice; averaging a murder a day; gambling and drinking, hurdy-gurdy dancing and the vilest of sexual commerce the chief business and pastime of the hours." [See Note # 10.]

There was often a "Big Tent" for dancing. There was a bar on one side, a band at the other, gambling tables surrounding the dance floor. Women dressed in light clothes mingled with the customers. Men paid fifty cents a drink for (watered-down) whiskey, another fifty for "their girl" (who drank tea), and a dance was part of the deal. No one cared about anybody and there was no law that had to be respected. In Julesburg things got so bad that the Army had to come in to restore a semblance of order. Gamblers had taken up railroad lands without paying for them and they dared the Army to do something about it. Soldiers shot them down and henceforth no one took railroad land illegally in the vicinity of Julesburg. But no matter. "Hell on Wheels" moved on to Cheyenne, Wyoming.

ON TO PROMONTORY

The Union Pacific had started at Omaha, Nebraska, and laid tracks west to Grand Island, North Platte, Julesburg, Sidney, Cheyenne, Laramie, Rawlings, Green River, Evanston, before they got to Wasatch, Echo and Ogden in Utah. The CP owed some ten million dollars but in December of 1868 the Crédit Mobilier, the CP financial arm, paid (itself) stockholders almost three million dollars in dividends. Brigham Young had put his Mormons to work laying track in Utah but his men weren't being paid the three-quarters of a million dollars owed them. No matter what Young did, Doc Durant would not send the money. Despite not being paid, Young was able to keep the Mormons working on promises that they would get their money.

The Central Pacific had started at Sacramento, California, and worked east to Junction, Newcastle, Auburn, Clipper Gap, Dutch Flat, Emigrant Gap, Cisco, Summit, Truckee, Reno, Wadsworth, Winnemucca, Battle Mountain, Elko, Toano, and into Kelton in Utah. Money was scarce with the CP but not in the proportions that affected the UP.

Rivalry was keen. When the UP laid 4 ½ miles of track in one day the press, always ready for a good story, publicized the feat all over the country. Not to be outdone, the CP gathered materials and laid six miles in one day. The UP wouldn't come out second best so they worked by lantern light and laid eight miles. The CP managers decided they would put the record out of reach by laying ten miles in one day, but only when the UP would be closer than ten miles at the end of the CP ten mile stretch so they couldn't possibly lay more track to break the record. The ten mile record would depend on absolute organization beforehand. They waited until April 27, 1869, when the CP had fourteen miles to go and the UP nine miles of track to lay. (Charlie Crocker is said to have offered a $10,000 bet to Doc Durant that the CP would lay the ten miles of track in one day. It is said Durant took the bet.) A locomotive ran off the track on the 27th so the effort was made on the 28th. Various officials from both lines, including Durant, were on hand to watch. Even the usually calm Chinese workers were caught up in the excitement of the moment. A thousand men advanced the railroad one mile per hour. By 1:30 when the noon meal was served, six miles of track had been laid. By 7:00 p.m. ten miles and fifty-six feet of railroad track was complete and engineer Jim Campbell ran a locomotive over the new track at forty miles per hour to prove it had been done right. The workers laughed gleefully, patted each other on the back, cheered, sang songs. They had accomplished what no one ever had before and no one would again. (As far as it is known, Durant never paid Crocker the $10,000.)

Each line continued building toward the other, track beds even paralleling each other until it was decided the meeting point would be at Promontory, Utah. Promontory Summit, a mountain elevation of some 5,000 feet, was at the northern end of the Great Salt Lake. The circular basin area was a mile in width and relatively level so it would pose little problem for the railroad builders. Making the climb to the Summit was the challenge. Who would get there first? Both shared problems like the weather (snow storms and accompanying cold waves), attracting sufficient money, obtaining enough construction materials like railroad ties, rails, spikes, etc. In January of 1869 the CP had 35 ships going to San Francisco in which were included 18 locomotives.

Ill will broke out on one occasion. On the eastern slope of the Promontory Mountains the CP Chinese were grading to the east while the UP Irish were grading to the west. The Irish began jeering at the Chinese and got to tossing rocks at them. This got no response so the Irish attacked the Chinese with pick handles. Much to the Irishmen's surprise, the Chinese gamely fought back. So the Irish decided to settle the matter by setting off heavy powder charges which were sure to injure Chinese workers close by. Though none died, many Chinese were seriously hurt. A couple of days later the Chinese set off an explosion of their own, burying a number of Irishmen alive. That ended the "workers' war."

The Central Pacific reached the final summit on April 30, 1869. The new (but short lived) town of Promontory sprang up. The Union Pacific arrived shortly and all that was necessary was a proper ceremony to witness placement of the last 2500 feet of track. The big day was set for Saturday, May 8. It had to be delayed to May 10 because the UP delegation had been delayed by heavy rains. Unaware of the delay in Promontory, people in Sacramento and San Francisco celebrated on the 8th as scheduled. Parades in either town were the largest seen to that time.

May 10, 1869, started out near freezing but the sun quickly warmed things up for the five- to six-hundred people in attendance for the ceremony. Photographers recorded the event with many pictures. There was a squabble as to who should drive in the Golden Spike, Stanford or Durant, until they decided both would take alternate swings at it. At the first blow on the Golden Spike (a gift of David Hewes of San Francisco; the spike now resides at Stanford University) the telegraph informed the rest of the world that the first transcontinental railroad was a reality. Bells pealed and cannons boomed across the nation. There were fireworks, fire whistles, singing, etc., throughout the nation. Perhaps it was something of a healing process for the people who had fought and killed each other so savagely during the Civil War. Perhaps the transcontinental railroad running east and west into the American future was indeed a new beginning for a country that was whole once again.

As it turned out, Anna Ferona Judah, widow of Theodore Judah, spent the festive day in her home in Greenfield, Massachusetts. No one had thought to invite her to the final ceremony. Would she have attended? Who knows. May 10, 1869, would have been the Judah's 22nd wedding anniversary.

DISCUSSION NOTES *for* TRANSCONTIENTAL RAILROAD

Note # 1

See page 18 in *Nothing Like It In The World: The Men Who Built the Transcontinental Railroad, 1863-1869*, 2000, by Stephen E. Ambrose. The author also parallels some of the sanguine battles of the Civil War in which the "empire of liberty" was engaged in a death struggle over American black slavery. See also pages 9 and 16 in *Empire Express: Building the First Transcontinental Reailroad*, 1999, by David Howard Bain.

Note # 2

For the seamy side of how the railroad operated in California see *The Octopus: A History of Construction, Conspiracies, Extortion* by John Robinson.

Note # 3

See pages 207-8 in *Frontier Express*.

Note # 4

See page 162 in the Ambrose volume.

Note # 5

See pages 150-54 in the Ambrose volume.

Note # 6

See page 58 in *Trails Of The Iron Horse: An Informal History* by The Western Writers of America. None of the books consulted for the railroad section had a single Chinese foreman or worker designated by name. Could it be said that *American historiography is "of, by, and for" Americans?*

Note # 7

See page 130-33 in the Ambrose volume. The author makes no mention of the Sand Creek Massacre, implying that "savage" behavior *just happened*. David H. Bain does mention the Massacre several times in his *Frontier Express*. Should American historiography not give a complete picture? What are the differences between historiography, propaganda, or propagandistory?

Note # 8

Why was it so difficult to get Americans to work? Is the cherished "American work ethnic" in reality the "American immigrant work ethic"?

Note # 9

See page 23 in *Trails Of The Iron Horse* by The Western Writers of America.

Note # 10

See pages 218-19 in the Ambrose volume.

CHAPTER 12

Frontier Law and Order

Very few aspects of American culture have received more attention than "The West." Myth and legend have grown beyond mere fact while most of the facts conflict with the legends. While it has been said that "truth is stranger than fiction" it must also be said that fiction is often made more sensational and romantic than truth.

The frontier town in the West was born around activities like cattle ranching, mining, the railroad, cattle rustling, etc. More often than not it began with tents which gave way to wooden shacks which sometimes grew to a real town. The saloon-brothel-dance hall(s) was the most popular of American frontier institutions. Cowboys, miners, railroad workers, etc., gravitated to them because that's where the "action" was and there was no where else to go. Men could get "gloriously drunk," gamble, chase loose women, and use their guns if given sufficient excuse. [See Note # 1 *Notes begin on page 429.*] Some boasted that their town was the "wickedest, most wide-open town in the West" because the population was made up of gamblers, thieves, highwaymen, ruthless cutthroats, and "women of the underworld." The hard truth was that seamy activities like "drinking, whoring, and gambling" made for good economics. They brought money to town. [See Note # 2.]

CODE OF THE WEST

The behavior of men in the West was contradictory at best. On the chivalrous side the Code of the West dictated that a man's word was his bond, hospitality was a hallmark, a good horse was a man's most prized possession, and property was to be respected. A horse thief could expect to be hung from the first available tree when apprehended. A vile gunman or cheating gambler could be shot in front of witnesses who would immediately forget the matter as "good riddance." If a respectable citizen was the victim the killer could be hanged with or without a trial, real or mock.

There were twists in the Code of the West. It endorsed brute force and power decided most issues in a frontier town. The Sheriff devoted much of his time to politics. Deputy Sheriffs actually did the work of hunting down criminals. An enemy was never given a fair chance. Only a "fool" would pass up an opportunity to shoot an enemy in the back. Paid gunfighters stood guard over cattle, stage lines, or railroads. They could kill with relative impunity and this included ordinary citizens who got in the way of "progress." The one-on-one shootout was good fiction and little else. Citizens formed posses, the larger the better, and hunted down bad men. Vigilantes dispensed unofficial justice, mostly on the guilty but sometimes on the innocent. Lynch law was condoned by those with the power to lynch. The weak had no chance against the rich and powerful.

THE GUNFIGHTER

The popular mind invariably associates the gunfighter with the "wild West." A man adept with a gun could be on either side of the law and there are cases where individuals abandoned one side for the other. Gunfighters came from all walks of life but their shared identity was that they lived or died by the gun. Contrary to popular fiction, a gunfight was seldom a one-on-one battle on main street. Gunmen had few rules and personal honor wasn't one of them. One outlaw was quoted as saying; "Fair play is a jewel but I don't care for jewelry." Shooting your enemy in the back was a more common practice for man-killers, who could be divided into three groups: pathological killers (the most dangerous of all) who seemed to enjoy killing, courageous men (as a Sheriff) or villains who killed to defend themselves or their ill-gotten gains, men who killed in the heat of passion. [See Note # 3.] Killers were often soft spoken, had eyes of blue or grey, and generally they could trust only their six-gun. They had to have courage, experience, and the ability to act deliberately without hesitation.

The life of a gunfighter has been romanticized by entertainment media then and now. Unlike the devil-may-care attitudes promoted by pulp fiction and movies, the gunfighter lived a difficult existence which usually ended on Boot Hill. Frank James summed it up: "I've been hunted for twenty-one years, literally living in the saddle to escape. In that time I never had a day of peace. It was one long, anxious, eternal being on your guard. If I slept it was with an arsenal of guns at my side. If I heard the dogs bark louder than usual or horses in greater numbers than usual, I went for my guns. Have you any idea what kind of a life that is? No, you don't….you can't even go out and cut a stick of wood without looking around to see if somebody is there to kill you." [See Note # 4.] Frank James was a rarity for outlaws: he lived to old age.

Living a life of violence often came early in life. **John Wesley Hardin**, who is said to have killed 44 men, is said to have shot his first victim at the age of 15. **Billy the Kid** shot his first man at the age of 16. [See Note # 5.] Most people wanted nothing to do with such killers. When a number of them appeared in any one town the populace was generally terrified. Then as now, rumors spread like wildfire and most ordinary people were in awe as well as dread of "famous" (infamous) gunfighters because whatever the situation, they tended to "shoot first and ask questions later." If an innocent person died it was "tough."

While gunfighters were generally proud of their reputations as men who would kill, historical investigations assert that most reputations were more inflated than realistic. For example, it has been written that Wild Bill Hickok was the "most bald-faced liar among Western gunmen." While the "face-to-face shootout at high noon" seldom took place in the West, a real shootist had to remain cool in the midst of shooting at an enemy who was shooting at him. [See Note # 6.] Contrary to popular perception, a gunman was often a good mixer and rarely a solitary figure. Because of their instability, most were not suited for marriage so they consorted mostly with prostitutes. Gunmen usually had highly flawed character: overriding pride, arrogance, indifference to human life. They were generally driven by greed, jealousy, resentment, anger, and often fear. They were generally very common, not heroic personalities

Marksmanship and the quick draw were crucial for all gunfighters but, unlike media creations like the Dime Novel and later movies, gunmen considered themselves adept if they could hit an opponent at a distance of around fifteen yards with their long-barreled revolvers. A shooter practiced his draw constantly, several hours a day in some instances, but accuracy was still more important that speed. The "shootist" had to grab the gun securely while his thumb cocked the hammer and the weapon was aimed instinctively, then pulled the trigger, all in one lightning-quick movement. An experienced gunman shot at his opponent's gut whenever possible, unless it was an ambush.

Renowned gunfighters traveled about the West. Though they crossed paths many times, a real gunfighter rarely went against another. It was generally "lesser men" who wanted to tangle with gunfighters, as if wanting to "prove" themselves.

GUARDIANS of the LAW

It is ironic that the American popular mind has given more attention to outlaws than those who risked their lives to enforce the law. The enforcers were called Sheriff, Marshal, Ranger, but in essence they were men who could shoot straight with enough courage and nerve to carry out their tasks. While they often displayed valor and skill, most of their time was spent mundanely with paper work or activities like collecting taxes. The Sheriff generally had more power and prestige than any other officer. He had to be elected by the people so he needed political skills. Once in office he had the inside track on money-making schemes and he often succumbed to temptation. For example, at a time when a Sheriff's average monthly salary might have been around $150 a month, it has been said that Sheriff John Behan in Tombstone, Arizona, was raking in some $40,000 a year.

Sheriffs' jobs were usually unromantic and common. They had to serve legal papers, preside over the selling of delinquent properties, maintain the county jail, give testimony in court proceedings. Sheriff's also functioned as health, fire, and sanitation inspectors. They often had to collect taxes and license fees for places like saloons and brothels. Utah sheriffs maintained jails but also dog pounds. In Colorado they had to help fight forest fires. In Texas they had to pitch in to exterminate prairie dogs. In New Mexico they were required to help search for strayed livestock.

Keeping order in a frontier town was generally a constant challenge. It depended on the peace officer's reputation with a gun because very few people in a frontier town respected authority. Unlike creations of the media, then or now, a Sheriff (Marshall, Ranger) seldom was alone when in pursuit of a criminal. He always had help, whether professional or amateur. Indeed, some sheriffs preferred to have their Deputies do the tracking and gunfighting while they devoted their time and energies to politics and making money.

HIS HONOR The JUDGE

Taming the West ultimately resided with judges in court. At the beginning a judge could be anybody with a "decent" reputation in town, including saloon keepers. Early judges were often tradesmen with little to no legal training. Some were "bumblers, drunkards, and flamboyant eccentrics" like Roy Bean of Vinegaroon, Texas. [See Note # 7.] There were no courthouses so they held trials in stores, saloons, pool halls, etc. What there was plenty of was disdain and disrespect directed toward judges in general. Some judges were cursed out to their faces, pelted with rotten vegetables, spat upon with tobacco juice. Partisans of one faction or another were quick to show their firearms and bowie knives. Individual fist fights or out-and-out brawls often broke out in court. Judges who stuck it out were often as courageous as any lawman with a reputation.

In time reputable citizens saw the need for professional jurists and elected them to serve their communities. For all its failings, the District Court became the backbone for establishing law and order in the West. It handled cases related to train robbery, the mail, counterfeiting, selling liquor to Indians, etc., but also murder, rape, armed robbery, etc. Despite enormous distances in the West, a judge would often have to do plenty of "circuit-riding" to bring justice to outlying communities.

VIGILANTES

It often happened that bad men became the ruling force in a community and the only way citizens could fight back was to band together and enforce the law themselves. Sometimes they came together secretly, sometimes as posses, often as spontaneous mobs. Miscreants who fell within their power were usually hanged, shot, even burned to death, with or without a mock trial beforehand. Sometimes the victims were merely beaten or flogged. Sometimes the wrong people were killed or injured. Vigilance Committees have been accused of lawlessness on par with that of ordinary criminals. In their own defense, vigilantes asserted they were the only law where there was none. In some areas vigilantes were incorporated into standard legal processes. Stockmen, homesteaders, and range associations often hired men to protect their interests against rustlers and other thieves. Individuals of wealth never had trouble finding hired gunslingers. Stagecoach lines and finally the railroads brought in professional gunmen to combat road agents. The environment was the "law of the jungle" where only the most powerful would survive. Forces, good or bad, with the most powerful guns usually won most fights.

GREATEST GUNFIGHT IN THE WEST

Elfego Baca was born in Socorro, New Mexico, in 1865. His father, Francisco Baca, relocated his family to Topeka, Kansas, when Elfego was around a year old. So Elfego's early years were passed in Topeka. Elfego's mother died in 1872, then there followed the death of a sister and brother, all within a month or so. Elfego was sent back to Socorro to live with his Uncle Abdenago but it is unclear when this took place. One thing is certain: Elfego was fluent in English but he knew very little Spanish by the time he returned to Socorro. [See Note # 8.]

Elfego was nineteen years old in the fall of 1884 when he happened to go on an electioneering campaign (for Sheriff Pete Simpson of Socorro) to an area in southwestern New Mexico known as San Francisco, three small farming villages populated by Hispanic farmers and their families. English-speakers referred to the three little plazas as "Frisco." William R. Milligan operated a saloon-general store at what was called "Milligan's Plaza" (also Upper Plaza) by the cowboys who traded or drank there. The cowboys were mostly Texans and, always well armed, they delighted in "terrorizing the Mexicans," who seldom carried guns, for the cowboys' entertainment.

Deputy Pedro Sarracino related a story to Elfego that some half dozen cowboys had gotten hold of a Mexican called "El Burro" and said they were going to castrate him right there in the bar. [See Note # 9.] A man named **Epitacio Martínez** who happened to be present objected then begged them not to do the vile deed. After the Texans finished with "El Burro" they went after Martínez, tied him up and stood him against a wall then used him for target practice to see who was the best shooter. (Martínez was hit four times though none of the wounds were mortal.)

Elfego asked how Sarracino could allow such thuggeries but the Deputy said the Texas cowboys were so numerous they would retaliate by burning down the little villages if he arrested any of them. Elfego volunteered to put a stop to the lawbreaking so Sarracino deputized him. They rode to Frisco in a buckboard.

Baca and Sarracino spent a couple of days in Frisco before anything happened. On the third day Elfego was talking to the Justice of the Peace, a man named López, when a couple of Texas cowboys came into town. To announce their presence they were gleefully shooting at dogs, chickens, and cats with their six-shooters. Baca asked López why he tolerated such behavior. López said they were cowboys from the John B. Slaughter Ranch and they had scores of cowboys who would destroy Frisco if any of them were jailed.

The cowboys were gathering for drinks at Milligan's. Another group headed there when Elfego saw one man pistol whip another. Baca hollered for the ruffian to stop whereupon the latter shot a hole through Elfego's hat. The shooter, one **Charlie McCarty** (some sources say *McCarthy*) got away temporarily but when Elfego caught up with him he put the miscreant under arrest. The only persons available to help Baca were **Francisco Martínez, José Andrés Montoya, Patrociño Romero, José T. Montoya, Espiridión Armijo**, and **Francisco Naranjo**, "very brave men" because there were so many cowboys. The miscreant McCarty stayed in jail throughout the night.

The following morning Elfego decided he would take the jailed cowboy to the Upper Frisco plaza. A couple of friends told him there were perhaps a hundred cowboys waiting for him to go by. Elfego was not about to back down, whatever the numbers against him. But he didn't want to jeopardize innocent citizens so he had his friends pass the word around that all villagers were to gather at the church for safety in the event of trouble. In a short while there were some 125 people inside the church.

Elfego took McCarty to Milligan's Plaza only to learn that the Justice of the Peace now refused to put McCarty on trial. Milligan, who at first demanded the arrest, had by now also changed his mind because McCarty's cowboy friends were his best customers. Elfego said he would take McCarty to Socorro for trial. McCarty was placed under guard in a private home.

Elfego was talking to the JP (October 29, 1884) when a dozen or so cowboys rode up and demanded the immediate release of McCarty. All were heavily armed. The group was led by the Slaughter ranch foreman **Young Parham** [some sources say his name was Perham or Purham or Perryman]. Baca recognized one of the riders, a man named Wilson, so he greeted him with "Hello, Mr. Wilson." The man answered something to the effect of *Hello you little Mexican greaser son-of-a-bitch.* His handful of partisans behind him, Elfego told the cowboys he would give them to the count of three to get out of town. "One-two-three" said Baca as he opened fire on the cowboys, who had been going for their six-shooters. The cowboys all ran before Elfego's pair of blazing six-guns and those of his five or six friends standing with him. Parham's horse was hit and fell on Parham, injuring him so seriously that he died within a few days.

The cowboys hightailed it out of Frisco but when they were a safe distance away they stopped and decided to inform all "Americans" in the area that *Mexicans in Frisco were in revolt*. Riders fanned out in all directions and informed American citizens that four or five Americans had already been killed by the *greasers*, that all able bodied Americans were needed to quell the revolt and bring the Mexicans to justice! Now was the time to protect their women and children! All able bodied men should arm themselves and ride immediately to Frisco! Cowboys saddled their horses, grabbed their guns and ammunition, and rode to Frisco.

Elfego told his friends the cowboys would be back, to go protect the villagers who could fort up in the church if necessary. He went to the (empty) Sarracino house where he had stashed plenty of ammunition then raced to the nearby jacal (a house made of poles then plastered over) owned by one **Gerónimo Armijo**. Mrs. Armijo and a couple of kids were in there so Elfego told them to run quickly to the church, which they did. For whatever reason, the floor of the Armijo shack was almost two feet lower than the ground outside.

The next morning, October 30, 1884, scores of cowboys rode into the Frisco (Upper) Plaza. With them were James Cook, William French, a JP from outside the Frisco area, and Deputy Sheriff Dan Bechdolt. They were ready to fight but the "Mexican revolt!" was no where in sight. Most of them, numbering around 84 cowboys, gravitated toward Milligan's Bar and began drinking. A small delegation found out where McCarty was being held prisoner by Baca and his handful of supporters. They went and told Elfego to bring McCarty to Upper Plaza so he could be tried in front of a JP so as to put the matter to rest. Baca agreed and at the appointed hour appeared with his prisoner at the house designated for the hearing. Cowboys had gotten wind of the trial and streamed out of Milligan's Bar. One Sam Wilson was cursing at Baca during the entire walk to the house.

McCarty was found guilty of drunk and disorderly charges. He paid the fine of five dollars. Then he asked his gun be returned, which Baca had taken from him. But Elfego had exited the house immediately upon hearing the verdict. Outside there was a large group of angry cowboys so Elfego pulled his hat down and disappeared around a corner of the house. He walked hurriedly to the Armijo house where he found Mrs. Armijo preparing food to take to her family waiting for her on a nearby hill. Elfego told her to leave immediately, that the cowboys would be showing up any second. Mrs. Armijo left hurriedly and when she closed the door behind her she put a heavy padlock on it. Elfego hadn't eaten so he helped himself to the food on the stove.

Meanwhile the cowboys had returned to Milligan's Bar where one William B. "Bert" Hearne informed French that the JP had given him authority to arrest Baca for yesterday's shootings. Upon learning where Elfego was holed up, Hearne, French, and some others went to the Armijo shack and hollered for Baca to come out. There was no answer. "I'll get that greasing little Mexican out of there!" exclaimed Hearne as he started kicking the door violently. Two shots rang out and Hearne fell back, both shots hitting him through the flimsy door. (He died from his wounds that night.)

Upon hearing shots the cowboys made a beeline for the Armijo shack and scores of them surrounded the flimsy structure. Those who came within sight of Elfego's guns got a bullet through their hats. An excellent shot, he could have killed any number of them but evidently chose not to unless his own life had to be protected. The cowboys poured gunfire into the shack, bullets crashing through the thin walls, sending splintering wood and mists of plaster throughout the house. By lying still, below ground level, Elfego was able to stay out of the line of fire. It must have been quite an experience not to move as bullets whizzed throughout the shack, striking everything on all sides.

Villagers were watching from protected cover in the nearby hills but none came to help.

The cowboys shot from all sides, knowing a bullet would get *the greaser* sooner or later. But after every fusillade Elfego returned their fire. Several cowboys were wounded when they tried to close in on the shack.

Massive fusillades failed to silence Baca's guns. A makeshift clothes line was put up between houses in order to prevent Elfego from seeing the cowboys as they closed in for a better shot. It didn't work. One of the cowboys pushed in front of him what had been part of a cast iron stove but retreated hastily when Baca creased his scalp with a well aimed bullet.

Someone got the idea to burn down the shack so rags were soaked in kerosene, lighted, and thrown on the roof. A small fire was started but it went out before doing any serious damage. Toward the end of the day a wall collapsed because it had been weakened by so many bullet holes. Someone said the rest of the house could be brought down if a rope could be thrown around a main beam. But no one volunteered to get close enough for a rope to reach the structure. Night fell and cowboy guards were posted to make certain the greaser wouldn't escape during the night.

The following morning the cowboys returned to the shack, confident Baca had succumbed to the hail of bullets fired the previous day. Much to their chagrin, they saw a curl of smoke coming out of the chimney. Shortly they could smell coffee brewing and warm tortillas from the stove. Dead?! Hell, Baca was making breakfast. Enraged, the cowboys opened up with a terrible fusillade, which was continued at intervals throughout the day. But it was no use. Baca merely shot back, keeping the attackers at bay.

Late in the afternoon Deputy Sheriff **Frank Rose** from Socorro County came on the scene and agreed to take Baca to Socorro for trial if he could be persuaded to surrender. A brave Francisco Naranjo, accompanied by Cook, approached the shack and informed Elfego about the offer. Cook gave his word that Baca would not be harmed if he surrendered for trial in Socorro. Elfego said he would accept on the condition that he keep his guns. The condition was accepted.

Baca came out of the shack through a little window. He held a fully loaded six-shooter in each hand as he looked around suspiciously. The cowboys, who wanted to lynch him immediately, trained their rifles on Elfego but Cook reminded them he had given his word and anyway Baca would be hanged legally for sure.

Elfego Baca was escorted back to Socorro in a buckboard but he insisted his cowboy escort ride in front, not behind, the buckboard. He also held both guns in his hands throughout the ride. He was jailed in Socorro and charged with the killing of Hearne. A jury acquitted him of the charge. Another charge for the death of Young Parham was brought against Elfego but he was acquitted again.

When the thirty-three hour saga finally became known Elfego Baca achieved fame throughout New Mexico and the Southwest because of the gunfight in Frisco. Sources disagree as to how many cowboys died in that village, some say two, others four. At least eight were wounded. More than 4,000 bullet holes were later counted in the shack, 367 in the half-sized door alone, 8 bullet holes in a broomstick standing in a corner. The 33-hour siege had splintered everything inside the shack but no bullet touched Elfego or a statue of *Santa Ana*, St. Anne, which Elfego came to regard as his Guardian Angel. [See Note # 10.]

Elfego Baca became a living legend because of the Frisco fight. Three times he was charged with murder but acquitted each time. In his long and varied career he was a practicing attorney, private detective, Sheriff and Deputy Sheriff, County Clerk, newspaper publisher and editor, School Superintendent, Mayor, District Attorney. He died at home in Albuquerque at the age of 80 on August 27, 1945.

DISCUSSION NOTES *for* FRONTIER LAW AND ORDER

Note # 1
See page 34 in *The Gunfighters* by the Editors of Time-Life Books.

Note # 2
See page 188 in *The Wild West* by the Editors of Time-Life Books. For an introduction to prostitution in the West see *Soiled Doves: Prostitution In The Early West* by Anne Seagraves. It has also been said that some 50,000 prostitutes were working in the West. Besides "soiled doves," prostitutes were also referred to as "Demimonde," "fair but frail," "girls," "lady of easy virtue," "lady of the evening," "lady of the night," "painted lady," "old timer," "streetwalker." Brothels also had various labels: "bagnio," "bordello," "house," "crib," "Hog Ranch," "Boarding House," "Parlor House." Areas designated as places for prostitution were described as "Red Light District," "Skid Road," "Tenderloin."

Note # 3
See page 162 in *The Wild West*. See also Chapter Eight in *The Gunfighter: Man Or Myth?* By Joseph G. Rosa.

Note # 4
See page 14 in *The Wild West*.

Note # 5
See page 148 in *The Wild West*.

Note # 6
See page 37 in *The Gunfighters* volume. See also page 125 in the J.G. Rosa volume.

Note # 7
See page 142 in *The Gunfighters*.

Note # 8
James H. Cook wrote his version of the Baca gun battle in his 1923 volume, *Fifty Years On The Old Frontier*. William French, an eye-witness, wrote about it in his *Some Recollections Of A Western Ranchman* (1928).There are also various books on Elfego Baca. Kyle S. Crichton wrote *Law And Order Ltd., The Rousing Life Of Elfego Baca* (1928). Larry D. Ball wrote *Elfego Baca In Life And Legend* (Texas Western Press). A very handy short volume is *Incredible Elfego Baca: Good Man, Bad Man of the Old West* by the venerable Howard Bryan.

Note # 9
See page 21 in *Incredible Elfego Baca: Good Man, Bad Man of the Old West* by Howard Bryan.

Note # 10

It is a tribute to American psychology that the greatest gunfight in the West has been ignored almost out of existence. The usually reliable Leon Metz refers to Elfego as a "loud-mouthed *pistolero*," a "braggart," reportedly a "frontier Confidence man." But W.A. Beck really goes out to get Elfego Baca. On pages 172-3 of his *New Mexico: A History Of Four Centuries* Beck writes that many communities produced *"legendary gunmen"* and some are remembered as folk heroes instead of the violent ruthless killers that they were; in this latter category *"must be placed Elfego Baca."* According to Beck, Baca *"resented"* the treatment of Spanish-Americans at the hands of incoming Texans; the Texas cattlemen also targeted Mexican sheepherders *"who were powerless before the Texans' six-shooters."* (Beck doesn't inform the reader if the sheepherders were armed or unarmed.) W.A. Beck does quote Harvey Fergusson as saying that Baca's heroics deserve to be remembered but then states *"there are those who feel the facts have grown with the telling."* Perhaps in time the gunfight never really took place at all?

TEXAS Law & Order

It is probable that no group of law enforcers has received more notoriety than the Texas Rangers. First organized in 1835, they served Texas until 1935 and became part of history, folklore, and myth because the Ranger stood between ordinary citizens and Indian renegades, Mexican bandits, and American outlaws. [See Note # 1 *Notes begin on page 436.*] Because of the nature of the opposition and Texian (Southern) attitudes, conflicts were charged with the elements of racism as well as differing cultures. Indians like the Comanches held undisputed possession of the plains, Mexicans dominated along the southwest of Texas to the Río Grande, and English speaking Texians controlled what could be called the timbered areas. The Rangers were unique because, unlike their typical American heritage, they were mounted and pursued the enemy on horseback. Dr. Webb, a proud Texan himself, asserts unabashedly that the Texas Rangers could "ride like a Mexican, trail like an Indian, shoot like a Tennessean, and fight like the devil."

A Texas Ranger had to be intelligent, courageous, and relatively independent. His mind had to handle unexpected emergencies but he also had to plan ahead. Often he was impatient of discipline. He had to be bold but he also had to possess sound judgment. [See Note # 2.] Among the best known Texas Rangers were men like John C. Hays, Sam Walker, Ben McCulloch, John (Rip) Ford, Leander H. McNelly, along with Lee Hall, John Armstrong, John B. Jones.

JOHN C. HAYS

In 1841 the Texas Congress mandated the reorganization of frontier defenses and ordered the appointment of three new Ranger companies. The captains selected to command were John Coffee Hays, John Price, and Antonio Pérez. [See Note # 3.]

Jack Hays was born in Tennessee on January 28, 1817. He arrived in San Antonio, Texas, in 1837 or '38. He was short and his boyish good looks belied his energy and abilities. He worked as a surveyor.

He participated in the Plum Creek fight and in 1840 was made Captain for the San Antonio area, a territory in constant turmoil because of fear of an invasion from Mexico. In 1841 "Captain Jack" led an expedition to Laredo and informed the "Mexicans" (no names provided by Dr. Webb) there would be retaliation for all raids or robberies. It later took a short firefight to let the Mexicans know that Hays was a man of his word.

Hays also went after Indians. As a prelude to the Battle of the Llano, Captain Jack and some 35 Rangers cornered some 12 Indians and killed 10. Then they went after the main body of Indians and during the running gun battle Hays' horse got spooked and raced right through the escaping Indians. The Lipan chief Flacco (sic) thought Hays was making a charge so he raced after his leader, both riders coming out on the other side of the Indian lines then returning safely to the Ranger group.

In September of 1842 General Adrian Woll led an expeditionary force into the San Antonio area. Hays kept watch on enemy movements and reported the situation to the central government. On or about September 17 a bloody engagement took place with Woll's forces getting the worst of it. Hays' company was among those who pursued the retreating Mexicans.

In October of 1842 President Sam Houston authorized the invasion of Mexico under Brigadier General A. Somervell. An army of "adventurers" was recruited. They arrived in Laredo on December 8 and plundered the town. When Somervell returned the plunder and arrested ringleaders some two hundred men deserted and headed for home. The remaining army marched down river and took Guerrero. Insubordination grew to the extent that Somervell ordered everyone to return to Gonzales, thereby ending the expedition. Some 300 refused to obey, including Jack Hays, and continued under the command of William S. Fisher in what has come to be known as the **Mier Expedition.** Mexican forces were engaged in the little town of Mier, Fisher was wounded, and the Texians surrendered. The prisoners were marched to the interior as far as Monterey. In February of 1843 they were started on the road to Saltillo but the Texians escaped into the wilderness, a desert waste where no one knew the road home. They were soon without food or water in the arid, wild, rugged country. When Mexican patrols found them they were glad to surrender. To "teach the escapees a lesson" it was decided that one in ten would be executed by firing squad. But how would the unlucky ones be chosen? All were made to take a bean from a pot which contained seventeen black beans with the rest white. Those who drew a black bean were executed. Jack Hays was among the lucky ones who returned home. It was a fortuitous survival because in him was the mould of character and fiber for the Texas Rangers.

The Jack Hays era of Texas Ranger history saw the introduction of the Colt revolver. It is believed that Captain Jack acquired his first Colt around 1839. The weapon revolutionized frontier warfare, giving a huge advantage to its owner because he could fire five or six times without stopping to reload. During the Mexican War which started in 1846 each Ranger was equipped with two Colt revolvers.

SAMUEL H. WALKER

Sam Walker was a major player in bringing the Colt revolver to the Texas Rangers. President Houston sent Walker to New York to purchase arms for the new Republic. He met with Samuel Colt and made suggestions as to what was required on the battlefield. For one thing, the present Colt revolver was too light and flimsy for frontier fighting. The two went to the Colt factory to work on the gun. Within a month was produced a new model, the Colt Walker revolver, stronger, heavier, with a handle that was easier to grip. After other adjustments were made, including the addition of a trigger guard, it was indeed a deadly, dependable weapon that could be used without having to dismount from one's horse.

During the Mexican War which started in 1846 Walker and the Rangers were issued some 1000 six-shooters when they got to Vera Cruz. They used the new weapon to good advantage and they lived by one principle: *Take No Prisoners,* which often led to atrocities against unarmed people.

Walker and his men reached Perote, a third of the way between Vera Cruz and Mexico City, where Walker had been imprisoned during the Mier Expedition. When they went out of Perote the Rangers were attacked by Mexican forces and after the battle Sam Walker was found dead on the field. The Texians were saved by forces under General Lane. Then he loosed the Rangers on the civilian population of Huamantla. In one of the major atrocities of the Mexican War, the Rangers took their revenge for Walker's death by cold-bloodedly killing virtually everybody in the village.

BEN MUCULLOCH

Another of the most feared contingents during the Mexican War was the company led by Ben McCulloch. Born in Tennessee, McCulloch came to be trusted by General Taylor, at least more than he trusted any other Ranger company. Muculloch's Rangers sowed terror among the enemy during the war. Inactivity at the town of Reynosa earned the Rangers the reputation of being insubordinate. Because of atrocities committed by Rangers, General Taylor wrote: "…the mounted men from Texas have scarcely made on expedition without unwarrantably killing a Mexican…" He wanted no more Texas Rangers in his army. [See Note # 4.]

JOHN S. (Rip) FORD

On January 28, 1858, John S. Ford was commissioned Senior Captain of the Texas Rangers. (He got the nickname RIP because whenever one of his Rangers died in the line of duty, Ford always wrote "Rest In Peace," RIP) He was to be cooperative but he was the supreme commander of all State forces. It was pointed out to Ford that the Indian menace had to be addressed with great energy and immediate action. Ford decided to take the frontier war into Comanche territory, even if it was beyond the borders of Texas. Lead by friendly Indian scouts working for the Rangers, some 300 warriors under Iron Jacket were met and defeated (in what is now Oklahoma), Ford claiming to have killed some 76 Indians, and taking 18 women and children prisoners. A major significance of the battle was that the Indians now clearly understood they would be pursued into their own homeland if they raided in Texas. Tragically, some of the Indian scouts who figured so prominently in the victory were later gunned down while they were living peacefully on their reservation. Ford was directed to apprehend the murderers but the Ranger declined, saying he had no civilian authority while a military officer. Indian Superintendent **Robert S. Neighbors** resented Ford's refusal because everyone knew victory over the Comanches would not have been possible without the Indian scouts that had been gunned down while they slept. Major Neighbors paid the price for being an Indian champion. While at Fort Belknap one Ed Cornett shot him in the back, killing him in cold blood. It has been said that Rangers killed Cornett. But as of 1859 no Indians could reside legally in Texas.

FRONTIER BATTALION

The Texas Legislature created the Frontier Battalion, Texas Rangers, on April 10, 1874. The era of the citizen-Ranger was over and now the Rangers would be a professional, permanent body. The Frontier Battalion has been described as the "best organized and best disciplined Ranger unit of the 19th century…because of Major John B. Jones." [See Note # 5.] Jones was born in South Carolina but brought to Texas by his family in 1838. He fought for the Confederacy during the Civil War and was elected to the Legislature in 1868 (but denied his seat by Republicans). Unlike most Rangers, Jones neither smoked nor drank. He was addicted to coffee.

On the more professional side, Jones saw his role as Supreme Commander, placing Ranger companies where they were needed as he viewed the entire frontier. Henceforth Rangers would not exhibit casual attitudes toward dress, discipline, or following orders. Organization became crucial for success under Jones' leadership.

With the U.S. Army focusing on Indians or border bandits, the Rangers could concentrate on outlaws who targeted stagecoaches, trains, horse and cattle rustling.

Another serious problem in Texas society of the day was the blood feud, with the Civil War often at the root of it. There were various reasons for hatred: Southerner vs. Northerner, Republican vs. Democrat, Unionist vs. Secessionist, citizen vs. carpetbagger, white vs. black, white vs. Mexican, etc.

The "Mason County War" of 1875 could be said to be indicative of the Texas blood feud (among the most notorious were the Taylor-Sutton feud, Jaybird-Woodpecker feud, the Horrell-Higgins feud, the Shackelford County feud, etc.). Settlers of German origin had been predominantly pro-Union during the Civil War and were now prosperous stock raisers. "Anglo-Saxons," generally former Confederates and thought to be resentful of German prosperity, were accused of rustling German cattle. [See Note # 6.] Sheriff John Clark (of the "German" faction) arrested Lige Baccus (an "Anglo-Saxon") and some of his friends on charges of cattle rustling. A mob soon formed outside the jail and the Sheriff didn't have enough men to prevent the lynchings. This set off a series of killings that polarized the "Anglo-Saxon" and "German" communities. Everybody armed themselves for protection. The situation wasn't defused until John Jones himself took in some Rangers who quelled the hatred because they had no allegiance to either side.

LEANDER MCNELLY

On July 1, 1870, Leander McNelly became one of four captains in the (Gov. Davis) Texas State Police. McNelly had been born in Virginia, arrived in Texas around the age of sixteen and later fought for the Confederacy. He was soft-spoken, of a slight build made thin and frail by tuberculosis. A sometime lay preacher, he also had a reputation as a tenacious fighter who could resort to "throat-cutting, lynching, and the use of torture to obtain confessions." [See Note # 7.]

McNelly and his men were sent to DeWitt County to put an end to the vicious Taylor-Sutton feud which had kept the county in bloody violence for years. The Taylors were anti-Reconstruction while the Suttons were pro. Each group hard a large group of blood kin, extended family, and friends willing to fight the other faction. (Nineteen-year-old John Wesley Hardin was allied with the Taylor faction.)

Both groups were always heavily armed and indeed the environment was a reign of terror. For example, if a situation made it to court the witnesses were murdered before they could testify. By 1874 so many Taylor-Sutton leaders had died and survivors were so exhausted that an informal "truce broke out" that lasted for a couple of years.

In 1876 there occurred the pointless double murder of Dr. Philip Brassell and his son George. The Brassells had not been involved with either faction and so ordinary people had finally had enough, demanding Rangers be sent in again. McNelly, doing duty along the Mexican border, sent Jesse L. Hall and a contingent of Rangers to work with Judge Pleasants in bringing the murderers, Sutton devotees, to justice. Legal proceedings dragged on for years. Three were convicted of the Brassell murders but the decision was overturned on appeal. (The three moved to New Mexico to get away from Texas.)

McNelly and his men operated in the "Nueces Strip," the southernmost strip of Texas between the Nueces and Río Grande rivers. Bandits and cattle rustlers, American and Mexican, made it their hangout while stealing cattle and other goods before crossing into Mexico. Ranches were plundered and people murdered with impunity. McNelly and his Rangers made their presence known in 1875 when in the "McNelly Pronunciamento" he said for the Rangers there would be only two kinds of people: law-abiding or outlaws, and they intended to arrest or kill all outlaws.

McNelly understood that bandits could flee to safety across the river into Mexico. Though illegal, he determined he would pursue them. The Rangers came to the village of *Las Cuevas* where they heard many bandits were holed up. McNelly gave the order to kill all men, exempting non-combatants like old men, women, and children. Pistols blazing, everyone in view gunned down. When things finally quieted down a captured woman informed the Rangers they were in the ranch known as *Las Cachutas*, not Las Cuevas, which was about a half mile up the road. Some seven men had been killed and nine wounded, mistakenly.

The element of surprise for Las Cuevas now destroyed, some 300 Mexicans under Juan Flores Salinas, perhaps a third of them mounted, were prepared to meet McNelly's Rangers. The Texans dug in and a short firefight ensued. The following day a truce was declared and the Texans were advised to get out of Mexican territory. McNelly was able to bluff so successfully that, despite breaking international law, killing innocent people in the wrong village, and putting his Rangers in a situation where they could have been annihilated, he and his men were permitted to recross the river and some stolen cattle were sent after him.

OUTLAWS

The most infamous desperados to come out of Texas are generally considered to be John Wesley Hardin, John King Fisher, Ben Thompson, Bill Longley, and possibly Sam Bass. Inexplicably, some of these were considered almost like folkheroes and at times more "popular" than the lawmen who pursued them.

John Wesley Hardin, the son of a Methodist circuit preacher, claimed in his autobiography to have killed forty men, though other sources say it could have been twenty-seven or even twenty-one. (Western mythology being what it is, there is no way of knowing how many men died because of this killer.) Hardin was reputedly a quick-draw artist, described as the fastest draw in the West despite being a cross-draw. Ranger John B. Armstrong, known as "McNelly's Bulldog," finally apprehended Hardin in 1877, having to go get him in Florida. In 1877 the killer was convicted of murdering deputy

Sheriff Charles Webb and sentenced to twenty-five years in prison. He served sixteen, most of the last six studying Law. He went to El Paso to live where on July 19, 1895, he died after being shot in the back of the head. [See Note # 8.]

John King Fisher was a rustler-gambler-lawman during the 1870s. He was arrested several times on charges of rustling or murder but never convicted. By 1878 he claimed he had killed seven men, "not counting Mexicans." He decided to reform and by 1881was considered a "champion of law and order" when sworn in as a deputy sheriff in Uvalde County. He was gunned down in 1884 in the Vaudeville Variety Theater in San Antonio during a deadly brawl which also saw the demise of his friend Ben Thompson.

Ben Thompson was born in England, arrived in Austin, Texas, in 1849. He fought for the Confederacy but also engaged in serious gambling and whiskey smuggling. In 1881 he was elected Marshall of Austin, Texas, but gave up the job after he killed Jack Harris, owner of the Vaudeville Variety Theater in San Antonio. He was charged with the Harris murder but acquitted. Inexplicably, in 1881 Thompson attended a performance at the Vaudeville Variety Theater in San Antonio. Harris' two partners gunned down Thompson along with King Fisher.

It is said **William Preston Longley** learned how to use a gun before he was a teenager. He was expert at the fast draw, accurate and fearless in gunfights. He claimed to have killed thirty men in various fights. Due to his reputation as a fast draw, some gunmen sought him out to prove they were faster, but they weren't. Longley picked many a fight himself. He hated Yankee sympathizers, carpetbaggers, and black people. He fought Wilson Anderson (of Evergreen, Texas) in a duel and killed him. He fled to avoid prosecution but was captured within two years. Convicted for the Anderson killing, he was executed by hanging on October 11, 1878.

Sam Bass had a short criminal career of some four years. He robbed banks, trains, and stagecoaches. Born in Indiana, Bass arrived in Denton, Texas, in 1870. After working at this and that for several years, without showing much of a profit, Bass and a few gunmen decided to rob stagecoaches then trains. After operating in different parts of the country they robbed four trains in Texas. Ranger J. Peak lead a contingent of men who vowed to stop the Bass gang. Their break came in 1878 when Jim Murphy, member of the gang, came in and offered to deliver Bass if Murphy was given immunity from previous charges. A trap was set in July, 1878, for the projected robbery of the bank in Round Rock, Texas. The gang members were shot down, but Bass and one of his men were able to ride out of town. Sam Bass was quickly found, bleeding to death under a tree. He was taken back to town and a doctor called in but there was no hope. On July 21, 1878, the outlaw's 27th birthday, Sam Bass died.

All charges against Jim Murphy were dropped and he got the reward for Bass' capture. But he paid the price: his name became synonymous with *traitor* and even Ranger Jesse L. Hall said Murphy was "a veritable Judas in ever sense of the word."

END OF AN ERA

In 1918 State Representative **J.T. Canales** of Brownsville identified eighteen charges of abuse and corruption against the Texas Rangers, whom he said had been infiltrated by vile types as well as used for political purposes. He charged the Rangers would kill a man first then investigate afterward, that the

Rangers were there to intimidate or terrorize citizens. The Rangers set themselves up as judge and jury, shooting men without provocation, even when they were unarmed. There were incidents of extortion, pistol whippings and other tortures, and the massacre of innocents at the village of Porvenir could not be forgotten. (Some fifteen Mexican men and boys in Porvenir were routed out of bed at midnight and gunned down in cold blood by Texas Rangers who said they were hunting bandits.) In 1919 the Ranger force was reduced to four regular companies. In 1935 the Rangers were placed under the Department of Public Safety, ending their autonomy.

DISCUSSION NOTES *for* TEXAS Law & Order

Note # 1
See *The Texas Rangers: A Century Of Frontier Defense* by Walter Prescott Webb for the best known account of the Rangers.

Note # 2
It will be up to the reader to decide what is fact and what is mythology when studying the Texas Rangers. For example, Tejanos were products and heirs of an age old horse culture. They were master horsemen. English speaking Texians, not horsemen in their own country, needed time to acquire the art of horsemanship and it couldn't be done overnight.

Note # 3
See page 60 in *The Men Who Wear The Star: The Story of the Texas Rangers* by Charles M. Robinson III. It is obvious Tejanos like Antonio Pérez were an integral part of the Texas Rangers but Tejano Rangers haven't received much publicity. Robinson does little more than mention Antonio Pérez twice and the Webb volume merely states (p. 70): "…Captain Antonio Pérez, a daring Indian fighter and citizen from San Antonio."

Note # 4
See page 113 in the Webb volume.

Note # 5
See page 169 in the C.M. Robinson volume.

Note # 6
It is curious how people rationalize to divide themselves. "Anglos" (from Angles) and "Saxons" are German (Germanic) people.

Note # 7
See page 183 in the Robinson volume.

Note # 8
It is amazing how much coverage has been given to outlaws. See *Encyclopedia Of Western Lawmen & Outlaws* by Jay Robert Nash. This volume is handy for recounting short biographies and incidents involving lawmen and outlaws. Along the same lines are *The Authentic Wild West* by James D. Horan; *Cowboys And The Wild West* by Don Cusic. The latter includes movie and television personalities.

CALIFORNIA Law and Order

While a few outlaws like Joaquín Murrieta, Black Bart, and Tiburcio Vásquez have made it into the American popular mind, California lawmen have not received much publicity either in books or the entertainment industry. [See Note # 1. *Notes begin on page 445.*] The California gold rush beginning in 1849 started one of the most criminal periods in American history and California had an ample share of lawmen and law breakers, along with vigilantes.

VIGILANTISM

Were *vigilantes* law enforcers or law breakers who hid behind the law by taking it into their own hands? In San Francisco a "Committee of Vigilance" was formed in 1851 to combat what various individuals, mostly of the merchant class, thought was rampant crime and arson. If the authorities would not protect then the citizenry must. Among the first to organize the Committee were men like S.E. Woodworth, S. Brannan, E. Gorham, F.A. Woodworth, G.J. Oakes, F.S. Mahony, F.E. Webster, R.D. Davis, J.C. Ward, W.N. Thompson, W.H. Jones, R.S. Watson, etc. [See Note # 2.] The Committee set itself up as judge and jury because the authorities refused to confront the criminal element in San Francisco.

The most "notable" early case (1851) of vigilantism was against an Australian named Simpton (or John Jenkins; there is doubt as to the man's real name), part of a group known as the "Sydney (also Sidney) ducks." Simpton (Jenkins) waited until a shop owner named Virgin closed up shop for the day then broke into the business where, being a very strong man, he picked up the small safe, put it in a sack, then walked out into the street. For some reason Virgin returned to his place of business, passing Simpton on the way, and saw his safe had been taken. He raced back out into the street and hollered "Stop thief!" when he saw Simpton in the brilliant moonlight. Others quickly joined the chase but Simpton made it to his waiting boat with the safe. Various boatmen went after him but it was a returning John Sullivan who stopped Simpton's boat before he could get to his refuge in Sidneytown, a half mile away. Simpton threw the safe overboard as the other boatmen surrounded the big man, forcing him back to the wharf, where the thief was beaten. Someone suggested taking him to the Vigilance Committee since the authorities "would probably let him go" after paying a fine. He was taken by George Schenck to Committee head-quarters where members Oakes, Ryckman, McDuffee, etc., happened to be present. A general meeting was called by going to the nearest firehouse and striking the fire bell with a billet of wood, pausing, then striking again and again. Nervous over the recent fires that had plagued San Francisco, many citizens gathered to see what was happening. Some 80 of the 103 Committee members "reported for duty."

Inside headquarters no one was sure as to what to do next. A spirited discussion ensued until ship-master Captain Howard exclaimed: "Gentlemen, as I understand it, we came here to hang somebody!" That did it: a court was organized and all members were to be the jury. Schenck became the prosecuting attorney and the prisoner, who gave his name as John Jenkins, had to conduct his own defense. As far as everyone was concerned it was an open and shut case: Jenkins had been caught red handed. Rumors began floating about that the "Sidney ducks," a group of Australian ex-convicts, were going to try to rescue Jenkins, one of their own. There were two unanimous verdicts: guilty and the death penalty, since California law permitted the death penalty for robbery. About midnight the bell at the California Engine House began an ominous toll.

It was decreed the execution would take place in the moonlit plaza within the hour. Jenkins at first refused the services of a minister but then accepted, probably as a strategy for more time. But he was not intimidated and remained defiant to the end.

The Committee members, four abreast and twenty deep, each with a revolver, escorted Jenkins out to the plaza. Anyone trying to rescue Jenkins was treated to a gun barrel aimed at his head. A rope was thrown across a strong beam, the other end forming a noose around Jenkins' neck, and the man was pulled off the ground by various Committee members.

A coroner's inquest declared Jenkins had died from strangulation. Witnesses could not remember the names of those present at the execution and some feared for their own safety if they testified. There were those who felt the execution was cold blooded murder. But the newspapers wrote the act was really a blow for law and order, something that had been ignored by the authorities. The Committee made a statement as to their motives and the document carried the names of some 183 members (out of a total of 186). By so doing, they won immunity because most were respected, well-to-do members of the community. Additionally, they had strong support from newspapers and most of the public. Many others now joined the Committee. By June 13, 1851, the critical period was at an end. There were no more robberies (for a time) and on June 18 the *Herald* newspaper asserted: "This city is more free from crime than it ever has been within our recollection."

JUANITA

Downieville in Yuba County was a large mining camp and prosperous. Populated mostly by Americans, a big celebration was held for the 4th of July, 1851. In other words, almost everybody got drunk. Among them was a man named Cannon (also written as *Cannan*), a native of Scotland, but a "serious celebrant" anyway. He spoke a little Spanish so that night on the way home Cannon and some of his drunken cronies went by a shack where lived a "Mexican gambler and his 'woman' Juanita." [See Note # 3.] Cannon knocked on the door or knocked it down. Then Cannon forced his way into the house then went on his way or he raped Juanita, depending on what author one wishes to believe. [See Note # 4.]

It has been said that for California miners of the day there were only three kinds of women: a wife, a whore, and somewhere in between a "woman" who lived with a man. For whatever reason, Cannon, depicted as a "good hearted drunk," went back to Juanita's house early the following morning, accompanied by a friend. Perhaps he was hung over, still drunk, or merely going to apologize for the night before. Nobody knows.

According to Cannon's friend, Juanita came to the door and the two exchanged words, Cannon calling Juanita a *puta*. Juanita went back into the room and returned holding a long knife with which she suddenly stabbed Cannon in the heart, killing him instantly. Then she fled to the saloon where her gambler worked.

Word got out that Cannon had been murdered by "the Spanish bitch." Despite their hangovers, men formed into a mob. "She stabbed him!" "Hang her!" The puffy-faced vigilantes demanded justice as they went into the saloon and dragged out Juanita and the gambler, the latter of whom was quickly released since he had been away at the time of the murder. It was decided to give the woman a fair trial before she could be hung.

Juanita was uncowed by the some 500 American miners who wanted her dead. She was about twenty-three years old, small and slender, but "well set up" as described in miners' parlance. Her black hair hung in two thick braids and her dark eyes flashed defiantly. She was also three months pregnant.

No one in the woman-less mob hollered "Self defense!" or "Her honor was at stake!" but they were going to give her a "fair trial" if the mob would cooperate. One John Rose was selected to preside as judge, William Spear as public prosecutor, and a young bespectacled lawyer named Thayer was defense attorney. When Thayer finally got his chance to speak for the defense he was knocked down to the ground and kicked, ending his defense effort. The jury went out and returned with a *Guilty* verdict. One Dr. Cyrus D. Aiken then faced the mob and informed everyone that Juanita was three months pregnant. Three other "doctors" (which would make four doctors in one mining camp?) examined the young woman and said she wasn't pregnant, that Dr. Aiken was lying.

On July 5, 1851, Juanita was taken by the some 500 American miners to a nearby bridge where a scaffold was rigged up. Defiant to the end, Juanita's incomparable courage enabled her to put the noose around her own neck then she said clearly, "Adiós, señores" before she made her way into eternity. The *Star* newspaper later editorialized that it could not "…heartily approve of this hasty lynching of a woman but it expects the moral effect of the act to be on the whole good." [See Note # 5.]

LAWMEN

There was about as much "notable" gunplay in California as any other place taken over by Americans after the Mexican War. In 1854 Captain **Jonathan R. Davis** fought to the death with eleven (11) thieves who had shot down Davis' two mining companions on a mining trail near Placerville. Davis shot it out with the thieves, shooting seven of them and taking on three others in a knife fight, all of whom were killed by Davis. (The entire heroic episode was witnessed by other prospectors.) In 1867 the **Coates** and **Frost** families took their blood feud to the streets of Little Lake: six men died and three were wounded. In 1880 some seven men died in a fight between settlers and railroad people at Mussel Slough. These incidents have not made it into the popular mind, probably because the entertainment media hasn't focused on them.

Among the sterling lawmen of early California would be Sheriff Thomas Cunningham of San Joaquín County, John Thacker of Wells-Fargo, George Gard of the Southern Pacific Detective Force, and Isaiah Lees, Captain of the San Francisco Detective Force.

THOMAS CUNNINGHAM

Thomas was born in Ireland in 1838 and migrated to the USA with his family in 1848. He was apprenticed to a brother-in-law who worked in the harness-making business. In 1855 Tom went to California and settled in Stockton, a booming agricultural and mining area. By 1860 he went into the harness business for himself. He became active in community affairs and running as a Republican was elected Sheriff of San Joaquín County in 1872. The county had been a haven for criminals and escaped convicts but Tom let it be known things would be changing, starting immediately. And they did. He also proved himself a tough campaigner, becoming part of the posses which tracked outlaws like Tiburcio Vásquez (1874), Bill Miner and his gang of stage robbers (1881), and Black Bart (1883).

Sheriff Cunningham experienced many hazardous adventures during his long career. In one instance he was escorting a murderer named Winters to Stockton. When both stepped off the train, Winters dropped down and rolled under the railroad car, thinking Cunningham would run to the other side to catch him. Instead the Sheriff dove in after Winters. The two wrestled under the railroad car until Cunningham was able to pull Winters back out to the platform. Moments later the train started moving toward its next destination. Had the two remained under a minute more both might have been killed or seriously maimed.

Cunningham was a meticulous record keeper. By 1898 he had built up a "rogues gallery" of some 42,000 criminals with indexed information on each one kept in triplicate. He also had so many other articles like weapons and such that his office was considered along the lines of a private museum for law enforcement.

Cunningham believed in tough enforcement of the law but he didn't believe criminals should be treated inhumanely. He had vowed never to take a man's life unless it was absolutely unavoidable. Even hardened criminals came to trust him to the point that Tom Cunningham seldom had to use a gun when making an arrest.

After some 26 years of service Sheriff Cunningham retired from law enforcement. Friends and acquaintances asked him to open his own private detective agency but he declined because he felt there was a great difference between law enforcement from a sense of duty and motivation for personal gain. He died of a heart attack in 1900.

JOHN THACKER

Thacker was born in Missouri in 1837. He migrated to Nevada in the early 1860s and then to California around 1870. He began working for Wells-Fargo in 1875 and after a brief hiatus became a Lieutenant under James B. Hume, making investigation of crimes against Wells-Fargo his career. Thacker traveled all over the West during his investigations and like all Wells-Fargo agents, he worked with local law enforcement officers to help capture criminals.

Thacker also worked (with Hume) to compile the famous "Robbers Record," a list of all W-F robberies between 1870-84. The Record contained information on all criminals captured or killed, how much was stolen and/or returned, conviction data, etc. For example, during that period W-F lost some $415,312 to a wide assortment of thieves, spent nearly a million dollars waging war against them, but the record of capture and conviction (usually by local officials, who often resented Thacker's notoriety when they felt it was they who actually did most of the work) was notable.

John Thacker and other such agents were quickly on the scene of a robbery but they became especially instrumental in the investigative part of capturing thieves who preyed on W-F shipments. For example, he studied the Black Bart (alias of Charles E. Boles) robberies and helped identify who he actually was so he could be brought to justice. In 1888 two bandits robbed an express car at Clipper Gap east of the Sacramento area. Thacker and other agents studied the crime until they decided it had been committed by two brothers named Gordon, who later confessed. He did the same with stage robberies that took place in northern California in 1891 and those of Shasta County in 1892. In 1893 a couple of men surnamed Evans and Sontag were thought to be the culprits in a series of train robberies in which three lawmen were killed. Despite large rewards for their capture Evans and Sontag remained on the loose until Thacker came up with the strategy to keep a posse in the field, but out of sight, to patrol the trails used by the thieves. Shortly the posse ambushed the outlaws, who were badly wounded when they put up a fight.

When J.B. Hume passed away in 1903, John Thacker was appointed Chief Special Officer. He worked until 1907 when he retired. He died peacefully in his Oakland home in 1913. He was eulogized for his "grit and bravery" as well as using his intelligence for capturing criminals. His personal courage never had anything to do with "putting notches on his guns."

GEORGE E. GARD

This veteran law enforcement officer was born in Ohio in 1843 and arrived in California in 1859 with a cattle drive. After serving the Union during the Civil War, George settled in Los Ángeles. In 1869 he married Kate Hammel. In 1871 he joined the L.A. Police Department which then had six officers serving under the city marshall.

In 1871 a riot erupted in the *Calle de los Negros* section of town when a "white" mob targeted Chinese for lynching, succeeding in murdering nineteen Orientals, only one of which was thought to have had anything to do with the riot. Many more Chinese would have probably been taken by the rampaging mob had it not been for the efforts of Gard and fellow officer Emil Harris.

Gard was quickly recognized for his detective skills, which required "stability, sobriety, sound judgment, and common sense discretion." In 1881 he was appointed Chief of Police and in 1884 he was elected Sheriff, running on the Republican ticket. In 1890 President Benjamin Harrison appointed Gard as U.S. Marshall for the California southern district, which office he held until 1894.

George Gard's thirty year career had him working on many interesting cases. For example, when "noted" counterfeiter Ricardo Gonzales escaped from an L.A. jail he fled to Albuquerque then El Paso where he was waiting for money from some friends. While waiting, Gonzales took on the name of *José Crespo* and shaved his mustache. The package didn't come so he went to Chihuahua. When Gard learned "José Crespo" was waiting for a package at the Wells-Fargo office George hired a man to go to the boarding houses in search of "Crespo" to tell him a package was waiting for him at Wells-Fargo. When Gonzales went to the office to pick up his package an officer was waiting for him and arrested him on the spot.

In 1893 Gard joined forces with John Thacker to catch the bandits who had been robbing trains in late 1982. Good detective work pointed to Chris Evans and John Sontag as the robbers who also killed three lawmen who went after them. Gard and Thacker hand-picked a small posse that kept after the thieves until they were captured. Large rewards were offered for the malefactors and there could well have been serious gun play over who was going to collect, the posse or the Fresno and Tulare officers. Gard declined all reward money, giving it to the posse members.

Gard became Chief of Inspectors for the Southern Pacific Railroad after his days as Marshall. In March of 1895 the Oregon Express was robbed and Sheriff John Bogard was shot to death. A massive manhunt was launched. Gard, Jim Hume, and John Thacker stayed on the trail until Jack Brady and two guilty ex-convicts were caught.

During his final career years Gard established his own private detective agency. He succumbed to pneumonia in 1904.

ISAIAH W. LEES

Born in England in 1830, the Lees family migrated to the USA in 1831. Isaiah went to California in 1849, tried mining for a while but soon realized the rewards were more illusive than real. By 1852 he began to take an interest in police work and the following year he became a patrolman with the San Francisco Police. He showed exceptional abilities in following up clues so he drifted into detective work, a relatively new field for the time and place.

San Francisco was a tough town filled with "thugs, thieves, conmen, gamblers, outlaws," etc., as well as "election riggers and crooked politicians." In 1854 Lees and other officers were called to restore order at a political meeting. The officers were manhandled but order was restored. Some days later three of the provocateurs confronted Lees in a coffee house and started a fight. Isaiah fought them off and took the leader, a prize fighter known as Wooley Kearney, to jail. Kearney said he didn't care because Judge Alexander Wells would set him free. Sure enough, Judge Well did just that.

In 1856 there was so much crime and political corruption in San Francisco that vigilantes took over the city (as they had in 1851). In March, Lees and his superior City Marshall Hampton North got into a violent argument that saw Isaiah pull his knife on his boss. Lees was suspended from all duties until July.

Lees participated in many cases during his long career. His method was relatively simple: he would piece together all clues until the evidence fell into place. If he failed he would start again from the beginning. His detective work usually led to convictions. In 1856 a saloon owner was convicted of throwing acid in the face of his discarded mistress. In 1856 Isaiah foiled a plot to have Archy Lee, a former slave, returned to his former owner in the South. His investigations were successful in the Bonney case, the Visitación Valley murders, the La Meet killing, etc., but perhaps Lees' most popular investigation was the Chapman case. A group of Southerners tried to outfit the schooner *J.M. Chapman* as a privateer to attack or capture Union shipping around the California coasts. Lees was at the head of a boarding party that seized the *Chapman*, thus putting an end to its activities before they even began. With the nation gripped in bloody civil war, the incident made national headlines. There were also other cases which made only local headlines, as when Isaiah captured (1868) William "Jersey Gregg" Gray after a bruising, hand-to-hand encounter in which most of the windows of the railroad depot where the fight took place were busted out.

Isaiah Lees retired in 1900 after serving forty-seven years on the San Francisco police force. William Pinkerton referred to Lees as the "greatest criminal catcher the West ever knew." This most famous policeman in California history died December 21, 1902, and his funeral was one of the largest in San Francisco history.

OUTLAWS

It has been written that "crimes of violence" were all but unknown in Hispanic California prior to the American conquest. Carey McWilliams quotes various travelers as saying there was perfect security in California until the American conquest. After 1846 there appeared "bold and daring outlaws" with names like Louis Bulvia (sic), Antonio Moreno, Tomás Procopio Bustamante, Juan Soto, Manuel García, Juan Flores, Pancho Daniel, Tiburcio Vásquez, etc. California's most "noted" early "bandit" was **Joaquín Murrieta** (also rendered *Murieta*; it is possible no such single personality ever really existed). [See Note # 6.] Legend has it that Joaquín was born in 1832 in Sonora, Mexico, and came to California around 1849 during the Gold Rush. He brought his young wife, Rosa Felíz, as well as other members of his family. It is said that Joaquín was mining in Tuolumne County in 1850 when his claim was jumped by American miners who also raped his wife. He moved to Calaveras County where his brother was accused of being a thief and lynched by another group of Americans, who for good measure also gave Joaquín a terrible whipping. Joaquín finally took to defending himself whereupon he was declared a "bandit" by American authorities.

In January of 1853 the *Alta* newspaper published an article that "enraged" American miners were reportedly targeting "all Mexicans" in order "to exterminate the Mexican race from the country." Numbers of Mexicans were lynched by Americans calling themselves *vigilantes*. [See Note # 7.]

In April of 1853 the San Francisco *Herald* published an interview supposedly given by Joaquín himself in which he declared Americans had robbed him of some $40,000, that he had been oppressed and persecuted by most Americans. Turn around now considered fair play, Joaquín and his "scoundrel" friends began robbing American miners, travelers, and teamsters in the mining country, using his ranch in Niles Canyon as a base of operations.

The phantom-like Joaquín seemed to be able to turn up just about anywhere and often in places so far apart that it couldn't possibly have been the same man. The "Joaquín scare" could be described as *hysteria* when posses couldn't capture the "bandido mastermind," who somehow managed to escape over every horizon. But they often did "capture" or lynch Mexicans they encountered.

Despite so much publicity Joaquín's identity became beclouded. Even his surname, which started out as Murrieta, became variations like Muriati, Ocomorenia, Valenzuela, Botello, Boteller, Carrillo. A $1,000 bounty was put on Joaquín's head and Captain Harry S. Love was put in charge of the effort (with twenty men) to capture the outlaw once and forever. Just before the time limit was set to expire Love and his men encountered a group of "suspicious looking horsemen" at Panoche Pass and a "stirring" gunfight took place in which Joaquín and his second-in-command, Three-fingered Jack García, were killed. The Americans cut off Joaquín's head and García's hand as proof they had earned their bounty. The grisly trophies were placed in alcohol for preservation. The California Legislature gave Love $5,000 though the Los Ángeles *Star* wrote (June 25, 1853) that Love had taken "an available head" to collect the bounty, that Joaquín still lived. Bandit attacks continued until 1856.

"Joaquín's pickled head" became a museum piece in San Francisco until it was destroyed by the earthquake of 1906. [See Note # 8.]

Tiburcio Vásquez (c. 1835-1875), a native Californio, is generally depicted as a "notorious outlaw" though he stated he "had numerous fights in defense of what I believed to be my rights and those of my countrymen. I believed we were being unjustly deprived of the social rights that belonged to us." [See Note # 9.]

Vásquez was the product of "a respectable family," was literate in English as well as Spanish. At the age of nineteen he was declared an outlaw by American authorities when he and some friends got into an altercation at a dance in which Constable William Hardmount was killed. He was convicted of steal-ing horses in 1857 and sentenced to five years in San Quentin. In 1859 he participated in a successful mass escape in which a number of guards and prisoners were killed. He was in and out of prison over the next few years but by 1871 rode at the head of a gang that preyed on stagecoaches, trains where fea-sible, as well as outlying settlements. By 1873 there was a $3,000 bounty on Vásquez' head and Sheriff **Harry Morse** of Alameda County was commissioned by Governor Newton Booth to catch the bandit. This was done on May 14, 1874 and he was executed by hanging on March 19, 1875. It is said he met his death bravely.

Charles E. Boles (sometimes spelled *Bowles*), alias **Black Bart**, was born in England around 1828 but it is believed his family brought him to the USA around 1830. His father farmed in New York but the Gold Rush brought Charles to California in 1850. He didn't make any money despite the hard work. He drifted around the mid-West in 1854 then he married and settled down in Decatur, Illinois. He served the Union during the Civil War and was wounded several times. After the war Boles abandoned his wife and family and wound up back in California. He worked at different jobs, even school teaching.

On July 26, 1875, the unknown Black Bart robbed the stage traveling daily between Sonora and Milton, California. Wearing a mask, he jumped out in front of the horses and shouted at the driver: "Please throw down the box!" Pretending there were other thieves waiting in the bushes, Boles added: "If he dares to shoot, give him a volley, boys." The driver, a man named John H. Shine, saw a half dozen rifle barrels aimed at him from the bushes so he did as he was told and threw down the strong box. When he was told to drive on the driver did so then as he rode away he saw the "rifles in the bushes" were mere blackened sticks of wood.

Black Bart robbed other coaches and on one occasion left this (famous?) bit of doggerel:
I've labored long and hard for bread
For honor and for riches,
But on my corns too long you've tread
You fine haired sons of bitches.
Black Bart

Wells-Fargo Special Officer **James B. Hume** was assigned to investigate and stop these robberies (21 of them at this point), thus far by person or persons unknown. The method of operation was clear: wearing a flour sack as a mask, the robber always uses a double barreled shotgun, he was never vicious, he was always polite to passengers but especially to the ladies. It appears he gets to the robbery scene on foot and evidently escapes that way. He is never recognized at the scene of the robbery.

On July 13, 1882, a stagecoach was stopped by the shotgun wielding Black Bart but when he politely demanded the strongbox be thrown down the driver shot at him instead, wounding him slightly in the head. The outlaw managed to escape.

After four more holdups, on November 3, 1883, Black Bart was shot at while holding up the Sonora to Milton stagecoach. In his haste to escape, the robber dropped a handkerchief. Private Detective **Harry Morse** was assigned to run down this lead, the only one that had ever turned up. It was marked FXO7 and after checking out most of the laundries in San Francisco it was identified as belonging to one *Charles E. Bolton*, an alias for Charles E. Boles, who turned out being Black Bart. Boles was convicted of robbery and sentenced to six years in San Quentin. When he was released in 1888 he dropped out of sight and in time came to be considered something of a romantic California figure. But James B. Hume summed up: "If anyone thinks that a man who lets his wife struggle along in poverty while he lives comfortably off our express boxes is acting as a husband should toward his wife, why we differ in opinion…" [See Note # 10.]

DISCUSSION NOTES *for* CALIFORNIA Law & Order

Note # 1
See *Lawmen & Desperadoes: A Compendium of Noted, Early California Peace Officers, Badmen and Outlaws, 1850-1900* by William B. Secrest.

Note # 2
See pages 95-100 in *Committee Of Vigilance: Revolution in San Francisco, 1851,* by George R. Stewart for a longer list of names and valuable basic information.

Note # 3
No name is given for the gambler and Juanita's last name evidently went unrecorded/ignored. Is this typical American historiography related to seamy incidents?

Note # 4
Carey McWilliams reports in *North From Mexico* (p. 128) that O.C. Coy describes the situation as: "In keeping with the characteristics of her race, Juanita had a quick passion" with the miner (despite being three months pregnant?). George R. Stewart states in his *Committee Of Vigilance* (p. 155) that there was "some kind of incident at the gambler's house" then the revelers went on their way.

Note # 5
See page 294 in *California* by Josiah Royce.

Note # 6
See pages 129-31 in *North From Mexico* by Carey McWilliams, who quotes observers who maintain that Americans forced the Californios into banditry by taking their country, their land, and other personal property, that "lynching of Mexicans soon degenerated from a form of vigilante punishment for crime to an outdoor sport in Southern California." For specific information on Joaquín Murrieta see pages 246-51 in *Lawmen & Desperadoes.* See also pages 79-82 in *Decline Of The Californios* by Leonard Pitt.

Note # 7
It would be interesting to investigate the lynching aspect of the American California vigilante movement. Who was targeted and how many victims were there? How many race riots took place in California between 1850-1900? How was the extermination of California Indians accomplished during the American era?

Note # 8
What is the civilized rationale behind the preservation of human heads?

Note # 9

This quote is from the McWilliams volume cited above. It would be a daring work indeed to investigate if Californios were immorally despoiled of their lands and basic human rights after the American conquest. *California Controversies* by Leonard Pitt doesn't broach this issue. Neither does *Lawmen & Desperadoes Of Early California* by William B. Secrest.

Note # 10

See pages 48-52 in the *Lawmen And Desperadoes* volume.

OKLAHOMA Law & Order

While the American West has been described as a "legal and jurisdictional nightmare," Indian Territory was considered a "criminal's paradise." [See Note # 1 *Notes begin on page 451.*] Outlaws from Arkansas to the east, Kansas to the north, and Texas to the south and west sought refuge there after committing their villainous crimes. Scoundrels and murderers like the James and Dalton gangs roamed about Indian Territory, robbing and killing as they saw fit. The only permanent residents were some 50,000 Indians who had been forced out of their native lands east of the Mississippi. While each tribe had its own system of justice, final jurisdiction fell to the U.S. Court for the Western District of Arkansas. One judge and a few marshals were expected to enforce law and order over the some 70,000 square miles of outlaw-infested terrain whose "white" population consisted of "gamblers, prostitutes, whiskey peddlers, and well armed drifters."

ISAAC CHARLES PARKER

In 1872 one William Story was appointed to the Arkansas federal judgeship. In little over a year more than a hundred murders took place in Indian Territory and Story resigned, among other things to avoid impeachment from bribery charges. By 1875 the area was in such disarray there was talk of abolishing it altogether. Then a reputable individual, Isaac Charles Parker, stepped forward, actually *volunteering* to fill in as judge. Parker was only 36 years old but he already had a solid career in the public service, including being considered in Congress as "the Indians' best friend." A staunch Methodist, Isaac believed life was a constant struggle between good and evil, that Divine Justice decreed that evildoers be punished. President Grant made the appointment and Congress confirmed it with alacrity.

Parker, with his wife and two sons, arrived at Fort Smith on May 2, 1875. The judge made a good impression at the dock: he was six-feet tall, weighed around 200 pounds, a tawny mustache and goatee giving him a dignified demeanor. But could he tame Indian Territory? Could he really live in Ft. Smith with its 2,500 inhabitants and 30 saloons? Mrs. Parker confided to her husband that "We have made a mistake" but Isaac said the people needed them and they couldn't let them down. Court was in session within eight days of their arrival.

Parker's first court session lasted eight weeks and 91 defendants were brought before him. Eighteen were charged with the crime of murder and 16 were convicted. Eight received long prison sentences, one was killed while trying to escape, and six died on the gallows because they had committed crimes like murdering a cowboy for his fancy boots and saddle, killing a man for his pocket money, borrowing a Winchester from a friend then using it to shoot the owner, etc. Judge Parker didn't relish sentencing these men to hang but "It is the law" he told them and then, inexplicably, he wept.

Judge Parker had a huge gallows erected, one that could execute twelve people at a time. The executions were public at that time and some 5,000 people watched as the six murderers were marched up to the scaffold and executioner **George Maledon** sprang the long trap door that sent the malefactors to a quick death. The executions were publicized from coast to coast. Some criticized Judge Parker, especially in the East. The judge replied: "If criticism is due, it should be the system, not the man whose duty lies under it."

Judge Parker had been invested with exclusive jurisdiction and final authority over all crimes that took place in Indian Territory. There were no appeals to a higher court, other than a pardon or commutation from the President of the U.S. In the final analysis, Isaac Parker was the law. (Defending attorneys didn't like or appreciate the situation.)

Judge Parker was also authorized to hire some 200 deputy marshals, more than in any other state or territory. While Parker despised gunfighters he understood that "it took one to catch one" so sometimes he had to hire shady characters because instructions were "Bring them in, dead or alive." During Isaac's two decades at Ft. Smith, some 65 of his deputies died in the line of duty.

Parker's marshals patrolled throughout Indian Territory, usually in teams of four or five men equipped from a wagon that served as headquarters, arsenal, kitchen, dormitory, and jail when necessary. These teams could be given a specific assignment or they could be "on the scout" for lawbreakers. The deputies made every effort to bring the accused back for trial because they were paid two dollars for each arrest and nothing for a corpse unless the outlaw happened to have a price on his head. Deputies were empowered to collect and keep fines for some types of illegal behavior so some of them took to planting "evidence" like stolen items or booze in someone's wagon then collect the fine for it. This caused many people to turn against Parker's deputies, even to the point of helping the lawbreakers by giving them food and ammunition. Deputies were easy to identify because their horses were shod while those of ordinary people weren't. Many people were also against acting as witnesses because they feared retaliation and few could afford the time necessary to go to Ft. Smith to give testimony. Waiting around for trial was also difficult.

Shootouts involving deputies were generally short and brisk. One fierce firefight took place at Rabbit Trap Canyon near Tahlequah against the elusive Ned Christie, a train robber, horse thief, and whiskey peddler. Sixteen deputies cornered Christie in his log fort built on the rim of a cliff-sided canyon. The deputies opened up on the building when Christie and fellow outlaw Archie Wolf refused to surrender. The desperadoes returned their fire in the standoff. The following morning a wagon was made into a moving barricade. When the deputies got close enough they lobbed sticks of dynamite into the stronghold. It exploded in flames. Archie Wolf somehow managed to escape but Christie died in a blaze of gunfire as he ran from the flaming ruins.

Isaac Parker served on the Ft. Smith school board, championed the establishment of a school for black children, and helped local charities. He entertained at his home and always had a bag of candies for children he met on the street. But the passion of his life was his Court. It is said he worked from

8:30 in the morning until nightfall, six days a week. Sometimes he even held night sessions. (He was not concerned for his personal safety because many a time he would walk the mile home, unarmed, in the dark.) Parker moved his trials with as much dispatch as possible, which was often criticized by defense attorneys. In one case involving five men, one of whom was the "ferocious" Rufus Buck, accused of rape and murder, the five were found guilty of rape on one day and murder on the next. All were sentenced to hang (twice) and George Maledon's nooses did their work (once was enough).

Ironically, one of Judge Parker's most exasperating antagonists was "leather-faced" Belle Starr. The press made her somewhat of a "favorite criminal" because she "sold copy." Myra Belle Shirley, later known as Belle Starr, was born in Missouri but when her family moved to Texas and she became old enough she started to hang out with outlaws. She bore Cole Younger a daughter, a son with horse thief Jim Reed, then married a handsome Cherokee bandit named Sam Starr. She organized, planned, and fenced for rustlers, horse thieves, and bootleggers who sold liquor to the Indians. She made money and she often used it to get her people out of jail. Outlaws liked her because she liked them. Judge Parker was finally able to jail her for a short time but this didn't change her in the slightest. In 1886 when Sam Starr was shot to death Belle took up with Blue Duck who later murdered a farmer in cold blood. Parker sentenced him to hang. Belle hired the best lawyers available and sent them to Washington where President Grover Cleveland commuted the death sentence to life in prison. When her son by Jim Reed was sentenced to six years in prison for horse stealing Belle once more sent her attorneys to Washington and got the President to issue a full pardon. For better or for worse, Belle Starr was gunned down by ambush in 1889, allegedly by her new husband, Jim July.

By 1889 it was apparent that the case load at Ft. Smith was simply too heavy for any one court. Further, Congress now made it possible for the U.S. Supreme Court to hear appeals from those sentenced in Parker's court. Parker commented: "I have no objection to appeal. I favor the abolition of the death penalty, provided there is a certainty of punishment, whatever it may be, for in the uncertainty of punishment following crime lies the weakness of our halting justice system."

The year 1889 also brought another disappointment to Judge Parker for "Boomers" were given permission to take up properties in the "Unassigned Lands" in Indian Territory. Some 50,000 Americans poured into the 1.8 million acre tract then looked around to getting more Indian land under their ownership. Parker protested that Indians had been given guarantees that their lands would be theirs forever. In 1890 Oklahoma Territory was established and the phrase "Twin Territories" came into existence.

In 1896 Congress removed Indian Territory from Judge Parker's jurisdiction. Parker's methods came under increased fire, especially by an ambitious lawyer named J. Warren Reed. Time and again Parker's decisions were taken to the Supreme Court under "bills of exception" or "writs of error." Some 50 of Parker's 78 death sentences were appealed and the Supreme Court reversed and remanded 37 of them. Parker stated: "During the twenty years I have engaged in administering the law here, the contest has been one between civilization and savagery, the savagery being represented by the intruding criminal class." He was still unswayed by "flimsy legal technicalities."

In July of 1896 Isaac Parker became ill and had to stay in bed. Unknown to anyone outside his immediate family, he had long been a diabetic. Now he was also suffering from exhaustion. He was not in court in September to hear his clerk say: "*The Honorable District and Circuit Courts of the United States for the District of Arkansas, having criminal jurisdiction of the Indian Territory, are now adjourned, forever. God bless the United States and the honorable courts."*

In November, 1896, at the age of fifty-seven, Judge Parker died. It is said he looked seventy. In his 21 years on the Ft. Smith bench he had heard some 13,490 cases, 9,454 of which resulted in convictions or guilty pleas. This "Hanging Judge" had sent a total of 160 villains to the gallows and his death evoked mixed reactions. Tributes rolled in from all over the country for the funeral of Isaac Charles Parker, who was eulogized as the "greatest judge in the history of the West."

OKLAHOMA GUARDSMAN

As mentioned above, lawmen seldom challenged gunmen on a one-to-one basis because they understood thieves, murderers, back shooters, and bushwhackers followed no rules of sportsmanship. Teamwork improved the chances of bringing an outlaw to justice and a famous triumvirate of lawmen in Oklahoma (also referred to as the "Three Guardsmen") was comprised of Henry Andrew "Heck" Thomas, Christian "Chris" Madsen, and William Mathew "Bill" Tilghman (pronounced *Tyman*).

Henry Andrew "Heck" Thomas (1850-1912) was one of the West's most effective lawmen. Born in Athens, Georgia, during the Civil War he served as a courier though he was only twelve years old. When he became of age he joined the Atlanta police force and won the reputation as a fearless fighter. He and his wife moved to Texas in 1875, worked as a guard for the Texas Express Company, promoted to Detective within a year. He led posses that captured members of the Sam Bass gang. By 1885 he became a bounty hunter, capturing the murderous brothers Jim and Pink Lee. In another incident he recaptured the Lee brothers and gave them a chance to surrender, as was his custom. The Lees fired on Thomas whereupon the lawman killed both of them in the shootout that followed.

Toward the end of 1875 Heck Thomas was appointed Deputy U.S. Marshall at Ft. Smith, Arkansas, which was under the jurisdiction of "Hanging Judge" Isaac Parker. During those years some fifteen officers of the law died in the line of duty in Indian Territory. Thomas brought in numerous outlaws, single-handedly when necessary.

Christian "Chris" Madsen was born in Denmark. He fought for Garibaldi and in the French Foreign Legion in Africa before he decided to come to America in 1870, lured by tales of gold strikes and Indian wars. He joined the U.S. Cavalry and fought in the West against the Sioux, Cheyenne, Nez Perce, Utes, Bannocks, etc. Then he became one of Judge Parker's lawmen for Indian Territory.

By the age of twenty-three **William Mathew "Bill" Tilghman** (1854-1924) was a Deputy in Dodge City, Kansas, under sheriff Charlie Bassett. He was appointed City Marshall for Dodge City in 1884, serving for two years. He helped to establish and enforce the "No Guns in Dodge" rule. His Marshall's badge in Dodge, two $20 gold pieces hammered artistically, was famous throughout the Western frontier. He moved to Oklahoma Territory to work for Judge Parker.

While they worked against outlaws in general, the Guardsmen especially wanted to catch Bill Doolin, "king of Oklahoma outlaws," and his gang members.

William M. Doolin (1858-1898) was born in Arkansas and arrived in Indian Territory in 1881. He worked as a cowboy, was quiet, tough, and quick with his gun. After being in the group that killed two deputies in Coffeyville, Kansas, Doolin joined the Dalton gang. He wasn't with the gang when most were killed while trying to rob the two Coffeyville banks on October 5, 1892.

In 1893 Doolin married (a preacher's daughter) and organized his *Oklahombres*, considered one of the most notorious outlaw gangs in the West. For three years the Oklahombres robbed banks, trains, and stagecoaches. On May 30, 1893, Doolin and three of his cutthroats robbed a train near Cimarron, Kansas. A large posse led by **Chris Madsen** surprised them and a wild gunfight ensued in which Doolin got a bullet in the foot. The thieves made good their escape under the cover of darkness.

On September 1, 1893, the Doolin gang (Doolin, Bill Dalton, Dan Clifton, George Weightman, George Newcomb, and Jack Blake) was holed up in the "outlaw" town of Ingalls, drinking in the Ransom and Murray saloon. Unknown to them, lawmen had entered the town and were watching as the gang members sat down to a game of poker. Newcomb happened to go out into the street to check on the horses. A Deputy named Dick Speed fired on Newcomb and the element of surprise was lost. A battle royal ensued as the gang members fired on the lawmen. Stray bullets killed a boy watching the fight and another citizen was felled by a bullet in the chest. During a lull a deputy yelled out for Doolin to surrender. "You go to hell!" replied Doolin and the fighting erupted once more.

The Oklahombres dashed out of the saloon to get at the horses at the livery stable, firing all the while. Bill Dalton had his horse shot out from under him. He was a sitting duck standing in the street until Doolin rode up from out of nowhere, pulled him up behind the saddle and raced out of town amid a hail of bullets.

The Oklahoma Guardsmen and their posses pursued the Oklahombres across five different states. Heck Thomas, Chris Madsen, and Bill Tilghman, already considered the greatest lawmen of the day, would not give up. There seemed to be a grudging admiration between the two groups. It is said that Doolin saved Tilghman's life one night when the Oklahombres arch killer "Red Buck" Weightman was prevented from shooting the lawman from ambush.

In another incident the gang had just eaten a large breakfast at a certain man's farmhouse. When Doolin stepped outside he saw Tilghman's posse coming down a distant hill. Doolin told the farmer *the rest of the posse* would soon be at the farmhouse, that they would want a good breakfast too, and the second group would pay the farmer for his generous hospitality. The Oklahombres rode away. When Tilghman and his posse rode up, yes, they needed breakfast, and when told about the financial "arrangement," Tilghman paid the farmer in full.

One by one the Oklahombres were shot down by pursuing deputies. Doolin's own end was close at hand when he rode into Eureka Springs, Oklahoma, in December of 1895. Bill Tilghman tracked him to a bath house. One story has it that Doolin was permitted to get out of the bathtub, unarmed, whereupon he challenged Tilghman to a fist fight, winner get out of town. Bill Tilghman put down his gun belt and the two men duked it out until Doolin lay unconscious. When he awoke Tilghman put him under arrest.

The famous lawman and the infamous outlaw went to Guthrie, Oklahoma, to await the court session. Thousands crowded the railroad station to see the pair, Tilghman signing autographs and letting photographers take pictures. But the story wasn't ending yet because six months later Doolin led a mass jail break in which he and some 37 other prisoners got away. Doolin then seemed to have vanished into thin air but in reality he had made it to Mexico. It is said he hid out at the ranch of American writer Eugene Manlove Rhodes. [See Note # 2.] But he was missing his wife and child so he decided to go fetch them. On August 25, 1896, he was approaching his father-in-law's farmhouse where his family had been staying. Unknown to Doolin, the house was being staked out by Heck Thomas and a posse of deputies. Doolin was walking in front of his horse as he approached the house, rifle in hand. Thomas hollered out for Doolin to surrender but Doolin raised his rifle which was promptly shot out of his hands. He pulled his six-gun and got off two shots before he was felled by a shotgun blast from a deputy and several bullets from Heck Thomas. The lawman was the toast of Oklahoma and Bill Doolin was the last of the Oklahombres.

DISCUSSION NOTES *for* OKLAHOMA Law & Order

Note # 1
See pages 142-164 in *The Gunfighters* by the Editors of Time-Life Books.
Note # 2
See page 107 in the *Encyclopedia Of Western Lawmen & Outlaws* by J.R. Nash.

NEW MEXICO Law & Order

It has often been said that **Patrick Floyd Garrett** was the most famous sheriff in the Southwest. [See Note # 1. *Notes begin on page 457.*] As might be expected, some people considered Garrett a true hero while others villainized him.

Pat Garrett was born in Chambers County, Alabama, on June 5, 1850. The family moved to Louisiana in 1853. As he got older he worked on usual farm chores: plowing, planting, hoeing, harvesting, etc. While he didn't have much formal schooling he did learn to read and write. The Civil War and Reconstruction destroyed the fortunes of the Garrett family. His mother, Elizabeth Ann Jarvis Garrett, died in 1867 at the age of thirty-eight, his father died in 1868. It is said Pat questioned organized religion. He left Louisiana in January of 1869 and wandered westward into Texas. He created a buffalo hunting partnership in the 1870s, becoming the outfit's hunter. He liked guns and chose to use a Winchester in his work. He could kill from 60 to a 100 buffaloes in a day but by 1877 the buffalo hide business was dwindling. An argument between Pat and one of his partners resulted in the partner's death and Comanches were attacking hunters' camps. By 1878 the buffalo hunting venture was abandoned and Garrett rode into the Ft. Sumner, New Mexico, area.

Pat got on well with the basically Hispanic population, who often referred to him as *Juan Largo* (Long John) because of his six-foot-five height. He sincerely liked Hispanic people and loved their *bailes*. There are indications that Garrett might have married Juanita Gutiérrez, who died shortly after the wedding, then he married Apolinaria Gutiérrez, probably Juanita's sister, on January 14, 1880. They had several children together. Just as important, Pat wanted to become an *hombre* to be reckoned with in New Mexico.

He worked as a bartender in Beaver Smith's saloon and heard all about the incidents of the Lincoln County War. It is said that Pat got to know Billy the Kid. Word got out about Garrett's perseverance and bravery in chasing down some marauding Comanches. Two well known citizens from Roswell, New Mexico, **John Chisum** and Captain **Joseph C. Lea**, approached Pat with the idea of moving to Roswell and running for Sheriff. Pat consented, won the nomination, and the election in November of 1880.

BILLY the KID

Firmly under American domination, New Mexico territorial politics were as corrupt as anywhere else in the USA. Crooked politicians bent on getting rich ruled almost everywhere while outlaws terrorized citizens, especially those in southeastern New Mexico. Among these outlaw thieves, cutthroats, and rustlers was **Billy the Kid** and his "gang," which included Dave Rudabaugh, Charles Bowdre, and Billie Wilson. The latter's specialty was passing counterfeit money, generally used to buy cattle, which brought the Federal government into the area.

Sheriff Garrett came under much pressure to capture or kill the thieves to stop the lawlessness. He formed a posse and intermittently kept on their trail. On November 20, 1880, the Kid's gang burglarized two stores in White Oaks. Some citizens took some shots at them but the gang rode away and holed up at the "Whiskey Jim" Greathouse ranch. Greathouse sold cheap whiskey, his customers were usually outlaws, and the horses in his corrals were often stolen. The Kid's gang boasted some 18 men when Deputy James Carlyle rode up with a posse. During negotiations Carlyle was shot, no one knows by whom (Billy later said it was "friendly fire" from his own posse men), and when he died the posse retreated to White Oaks.

Governor Lew Wallace put up a $500 reward for the capture of "Bonney, alias "The Kid." **Charles Siringo** led a group from the Texas Panhandle who intended to capture Billy. **Frank Stewart**, a deputy U.S. Marshal, also brought in another group of Texans to capture the outlaw who had been stealing so many Texas cattle. Pat Garrett was approached with the idea of all three groups uniting to capture the thieves but Garrett decided to select various men and chase the outlaws only with them while the others waited until they were needed.

It turned out the outlaws (the principals of which were Billy, Tom O'Folliard, Dave Rudabaugh, Charles Bowdre, Billie Wilson, Tom Pickett) were in Ft. Sumner but when Garrett and his men got there they learned the thieves had gone to the Thomas Wilcox ranch some twelve miles away. Using one Juan Gallegos as a double agent, the outlaws were misled into thinking the posse had gone to Roswell. When the outlaws came into town to celebrate the trap was set. In the brief gunfight that followed Tom O'Folliard was shot and killed but the other outlaws got away to the Wilcox ranch where they stole supplies and hit the escape trail, despite the threat of snow.

The two groups met at an abandoned rock house in a place called Stinking (Sinking?) Springs. The plan had been to kill Billy the Kid but Garrett was the only one who could recognize him on sight. He told his posse that the Kid wore a broad-brimmed sombrero with a bright, Irish-green hatband. But when Charlie Bowdre appeared in the doorway he was shot and the wounds quickly proved mortal.

The outlaws were trapped and they knew it as the day wore on. Dave Rudabaugh was chosen to wave a white handkerchief and discuss surrender terms: all would lay down their arms if Garrett would guarantee not to shoot any of them. Pat agreed. The outlaws were taken to Ft. Sumner then to Las Vegas on the railroad before taking them to John Sherman, the U.S. Marshal in Santa Fe.

Despite an angry mob that wanted to lynch Rudabaugh, the outlaws were ensconced in jail. Billy was interviewed by a reporter of the Las Vegas *Gazette* and the article was published on December 28, 1880. The Kid depicted as little more than a "mere boy," five-feet-eight inches tall, weighing maybe 140 pounds, two protruding front teeth, clear blue eyes "with a somewhat roughish snap," friendly manner, all in all looking like a school boy. Then the reporter turned to Dave Rudabaugh, who was noted for never bathing and for being the most calloused member of the gang who, incidentally, had unnecessarily killed a jailor during the Webb prison break of April 2, 1880.

Garrett had to face an angry mob clamoring for Rudabaugh's hide when he escorted his prisoners to the railroad station. He got the outlaws on the train but then citizens boarded the locomotive and stopped its progress. Garrett and Frank Stewart drew their revolvers and the crowd back down a bit. Another deputy marshal, one J.F. Morley, offered his assistance so Garrett sent him to A.F. Robinson, chief engineer for the Santa Fe railroad. Robinson looked at the angry mob from his second story office window and told Morley the lawmen could have the train but they'd have to run it themselves. Morley went back to the locomotive, started pulling on this lever and that, and all felt good when the train chugged out of Las Vegas. By the time they made it to Santa Fe the whole Territory was cheering for Pat Garrett and his two marshals.

Dave Rudabaugh was sentenced to hang but before the execution could be carried out he escaped (December 3, 1881) and made it to Mexico. His behavior there was so brutal that natives finally shot him to death.

Billy tried contacting Governor Wallace but the Governor ignored him. What Wallace really wanted was a better appointment out of New Mexico, not interviews with a thieving rustler charged with murder. [See Note # 2.] On March 28, 1881, Billy the Kid was transferred to Mesilla to stand trial for several murders. His court appointed attorney turned out being Albert J. Fountain. The trial was quick and a guilty verdict decreed that Billy be executed for the killing of Sheriff William Brady. *William Bonny*, alias *William Antrim*, alias the *Kid*, was sentenced to "*be hanged by the neck until his body be dead*" on May 13, 1881, and that the prisoner be delivered to Sheriff Garrett in Lincoln for the execution.

The Kid was delivered to Garrett and jailed on the second floor of the old Murphy-Dolan store. J.W. Bell and Bob Olinger were assigned to guard the prisoner. On April 28 Olinger had morning duty then was relieved at noon by Bell while Olinger went to have lunch at the restaurant across the street. The Kid told Bell he needed to use the outhouse so he went into the privy where a gun had been hidden for him. When he returned up the stairs, gun in hand, he ordered Bell to surrender then struck him on the head with the gun. Bell fell down the stairs as two shots rang out, one of them hitting and killing Bell. The Kid hobbled across the floor to grab Olinger's shotgun, which was still loaded, then waited at the open window. The shots had been heard by everyone, including Olinger, who raced toward the building only to see his own shotgun just before it roared out in his death. Billy ordered the caretaker to remove his shackles and the frightened man complied. He walked out of the building, jumped on a horse and galloped out of sight.

Though Pat Garrett hadn't been present when the Kid killed his guards and escaped, the Sheriff was somehow blamed for the escape. Pursuit ended up empty and it was said Garrett would never capture the Kid a second time. There was also trouble in gathering posses for Hispanic people somehow aligned themselves emotionally with the Kid and non-Hispanics were afraid of retribution, besides asserting that "Garrett rustled as many cattle as Billy ever did." [See Note # 3.] Pat even threatened to resign if he didn't get more citizen support. Governor Wallace once more put up a $500 reward for the Kid's capture. Most people felt Billy had fled to Mexico but, incredibly, *the Kid returned to Ft. Sumner* and hid out when he wasn't courting Paulita Maxwell. Paulita's brother Pete Maxwell finally got word to Garrett that the Kid was right under their noses. Pat didn't believe Billy could be that dumb but it turned out to be true.

A posse was recruited and all rode to the outskirts of Ft. Sumner on July 14, 1881. It was decided to watch the home of Celsa Gutiérrez, another of the Kid's girlfriends, because it was next to a peach orchard that provided cover. Around midnight Garrett and two deputies, John Poe and Thomas "Tip" McKinney, made their way to Pete Maxwell's house. A fresh quarter of beef was hanging on the north porch of the porch of the Maxwell home. While the deputies waited outside, Garrett entered the house into what proved to be a bedroom. A startled Pete Maxwell woke up and the two were talking in low voices when they heard the Kid's voice outside. Billy had noticed Poe and McKinney but no one recognized anybody because the Kid asked "¿Quién es? ¿Quién es?" (Who is it? Who is it?). Suddenly he darted into the Maxwell bedroom and asked, "Pete, who are those fellows outside?" Due to the darkness he was totally unaware that Pat Garrett was sitting on the bed. Then Billy's eyes adjusted slightly and he became aware of another person in the room. He had his gun cocked and ready but he asked Maxwell: "¿Quién es? ¿Quién es?" Garrett fired twice, the first shot killing the young gunman instantly, the second bullet burying itself in the wall. Billy the Kid was indeed dead but his legend was just getting started.

FOUNTAIN MURDERS

On February 1, 1896, Colonel Albert J. Fountain and his nine-year-old son Henry disappeared without a trace in the White Sands. Reward money for bringing the killers to justice got to over $12,000 and Pat Garrett, living in semi-retirement in Uvalde, Texas, was asked to return and solve what was considered a real murder mystery. He brought his family to Las Cruces, New Mexico, and bought a home there. Governor Thornton hired Pat to handle the Fountain disappearances and waited for the proper time to get him elected as Sheriff of Doña Ana County. He also wrote for a Pinkerton man to come in to help. A detective named J.C. Fraser was assigned to the case.

Fraser wanted indictments immediately against Oliver Lee, Bill McNew, James Gililland, and Bill Carr, but Garrett cautioned they would have to wait until he was Sheriff, which came about in April of 1896. Inexplicably, Garrett took no decisive actions and in 1898 new Governor Otero encouraged him to act on any leads he might have. On April 2, 1898, Pat went to Judge Frank Parker and requested warrants for the arrests of Oliver Lee, Jim Gililland, Bill Carr, and Bill McNew for the murder of nine-year-old Henry Fountain. McNew and Carr were jailed immediately because Garrett was hoping they would confess and implicate Lee and Gililland. The confessions never came.

Lee and Gililland were hiding out so Pat gathered a posse and pursued them to a place called Wildly Well. In the early morning of July 12, 1898, the posse circled the (only) house and Garrett burst inside and ordered a sleeping figure to throw up his hands. Mary Madison woke up and screamed when she saw a gun in her face. Her husband and three children then awoke with a start, as did a stranger named

McVey who had arrived a couple of hours earlier. Garrett demanded to know where Lee and Gililland were but there was no answer.

McVey was caught trying to signal someone on the roof so it became obvious the wanted men were on it, providing them with a good angle to defend themselves against the posse. Garrett hollered out for Lee and Gililland to surrender but a firefight broke out and lasted some two minutes. The men on the roof had the advantage and one of Garrett's men had been hit.

Pat told Oliver Lee to surrender but Lee declined, saying Garrett intended to shoot him. Pat promised not to, saying he would only take him into custody. Lee told Pat the posse was in a bad predicament, that if Garrett withdrew his men they wouldn't get shot. The Sheriff yelled back "OK!" and the posse retreated. One of his men, Kent Kearney, died from his wounds. It has been said the shootout at Wildly Well was the most humiliating experience of Pat Garrett's career. Be that as it may, one man was dead, two fugitives were on the loose, and the Southwest was in an uproar, split in pro- or anti-Garrett factions.

Albert Bacon Fall would be attorney for the defendants and it was he whom Garrett feared the most because he was a brilliant lawyer and had much courtroom experience in defending outlaws. Pat was indeed overmatched because Albert Fall was able to have a new county created (January 30, 1899) , naming it *Otero County* in honor of the sitting governor. Garrett thus lost jurisdiction over the Fountain investigation when George Curry became Sheriff.

Writer Eugene Manlove Rhodes was host to Lee and Gililland in March of 1899 and it was Rhodes who "negotiated" their surrender to Sheriff Curry. It was finally agreed to hold court in the "neutral" site of Hillsboro on May 25, 1899.

The trial was a sensational event and Western Union wires, strung up just for the proceedings, reported all events almost as they were happening. For eighteen days, Hillsboro was the focus of the entire Southwest.

Governor Otero had appointed Tom Catron as Special Counsel for the prosecution. While undisputedly a brilliant lawyer, Catron also was considered the kingpin of the nefarious Santa Fe Ring. Defense Attorney Albert Fall used the strategy of "the little guys against the big guys," which was sure to score with the men on the jury. Pat Garrett was a leading witness for the prosecution. Prisoners Lee and Gililland exuded confidence, acting more like celebrities than men accused of murder, when they talked to members of the press. (One reporter wrote that Oliver Lee could read Greek and Latin.)

The prosecution was quickly in deep trouble when some of their witnesses failed to appear. Defense attorney Fall cut aggressively into all adverse testimony, underscoring that these witnesses were sworn enemies of the defendants. Only Pat Garrett remained unshaken while on the witness stand, even getting in a few barbs of his own. But it was all for naught: the jury found the defendants *Not Guilty*.

Was the verdict "an appalling miscarriage of justice"? León Metz has written that there is no doubt the Fountains were murdered but for years there was a "chain of silence" on the matter. [See Note # 4.] Jim Gililland came to be considered the "talker" in the predicament. Perhaps it was because he is supposed to have said that nine-year-old Henry Fountain was *nothing but a half-breed, no better than a dog.* Many years later a young cowboy named Butler Oral "Snooks" Burris bought the Gililland ranch and Burris was in his company quite often. While the two were out riding one day Gililland pointed to a rock under which he said the Fountain bodies had been buried some twenty years before. Burris said nothing and in time, especially when Gililland was drinking heavily, he admitted to the Fountain murders, describing them in detail. He told how he, McNew, and Oliver Lee had chased the fleeing wagon carrying Fountain and his son. The three gunmen raced alongside and shot many times at Fountain. When the wagon finally stopped Fountain jumped out but was dead when the riders got to him. Young Henry was still alive so the three men drew straws to see who would kill the boy. Gililland drew the short straw. Six-foot-four Jim Gililland took his knife from his pocket, opened it, walked over to the terrified youngster, grabbed his black hair to pull his head back, and *"cut the little feller's throat."* [See Note # 5.]

"GREATEST NEW MEXICAN"

Despite a bleak financial outlook, Pat Garrett continued his role as an active lawman. On July 3, 1896, he also became a U.S. Deputy Marshal. His finances didn't improve and it really wasn't his fault. For example, by 1900 the county owed him some $4,000 and the only way he got the money coming to him was to keep $3,000 in tax collections in order for the county to file suit, thus airing the matter. Garrett won the case, with Albert Fall representing him. But Pat had had enough and declared he would not run for another term, the salary being too meager, the job too demanding, the authorities too ungrateful. He went to El Paso where in December of 1901 President Theodore Roosevelt nominated Garrett for the post of Customs Collector and he was confirmed. There were some grating incidents in El Paso and Garrett wasn't reappointed in 1905. He returned to his (neglected) ranch east of Las Cruces (coincidentally the area where the Fountains had been murdered) and in 1906 there were rumors he would reopen the Fountain investigation on his own. It was mere rumor but people thought it might be happening.

In March of 1907 Garrett leased part of his land holdings to one Jesse Wayne Brazel, who wanted to raise goats on it, though Pat didn't know that. When he found out he made efforts to nullify the contract with Brazel and the matter landed in court. The matter dragged on and in 1908 Brazel agreed to cancel the lease if his 1200 goats were bought at $3.50 a head. It was agreed a buyer would be sought then later Brazel asserted he had some 1800 goats, not 1200. Finding a buyer would now be much harder.

On February 29, 1908, Garrett and Carl Adamson climbed into a buggy pulled by two horses and headed out to meet Brazel on the "disputed" land. When they caught up with Brazel the atmosphere was decidedly cool. A stop was made along the road and when Garrett got down from the buggy and turned his back *"a bullet slammed into the back of his head."* A second shot got him in the stomach.

Who murdered Pat Garrett? Was it Brazel or Adamson? Brazel, never considered a gunman, "confessed," was tried for the crime, but found not guilty by reason of *self defense.*

Rumor had it that there had been a conspiracy to kill Pat Garrett and the names associated with that rumor have been Oliver Lee, Carl Adamson, W.W. Cox, Jim Miller, Albert B. Fall, etc., along with Wayne Brazel. (León Metz believes Brazel did it.)

Patrick Floyd Garrett was laid to rest on March 5, 1908, in the Las Cruces Odd Fellows Cemetery. He was later moved to the Masonic Cemetery and his tombstone was inscribed *Garrett.* There is no other monument for this paladin lawman whom President Theodore Roosevelt described as "the first man to introduce law and order" into New Mexico, to which Pat Hurley added that Garrett was "the greatest New Mexican."

THE LEGEND

Pat Garrett wrote *The Authentic Life Of Billy The Kid*, thus getting the legend started. Ash Upson, Pat's faithful friend, did the actual writing and created the fantasy sections of the story (first fifteen chapters). Garrett's contributions (last eight chapters) have been proven to be historically accurate. But it was the romanticized *Saga Of Billy The Kid* by Walter Noble Burns that made "the Kid" a permanent part of Southwestern folklore because starting in 1926 it became a tremendous bestseller. It portrayed Billy the Kid as something of a chivalrous hero while it tended to depict Pat Garrett as an establishment tool. The Kid came out heroic because on paper he "embodied youth, nobility, humanity, romance, and tragedy." [See Note # 6.] The fantasy found its way into poetry, movies, television, even music. As if construing fantasy into history wasn't bad enough, the real hero, lawman Pat Garrett, the most famous of brave Southwestern sheriffs, had his life ended in a tragedy as unfair as the romanticized mythology which gives him little justice. (See *Essay: On Myth & Media in the American West* at the end of the Law & Order sections.)

DISCUSSION NOTES *for* NEW MEXICO Law & Order

Note # 1

See page 80 in *Desert Lawmen: The High Sheriffs Of New Mexico And Arizona, 1846-1912*, by Larry D. Ball. For a reliable biography (and much related bibliography) on Garrett see *Pat Garrett: The Story Of A Western Lawman* by the inimitable León C. Metz.. For an excellent study of Albert Fountain and Albert Fall see *The Two Alberts: Fountain And Fall* by Gordon R. Owen.

Note # 2

See page 169 in *Billy The Kid: A Short And Violent Life* by Robert M. Utley.

Note # 3

See page 96 in *Pat Garrett* by Leon Metz.

Note # 4

See pages 227-33 in his *Pat Garrett* volume.

Note # 5

Mariana Pérez Fountain, who bore Albert twelve children, had not wanted her husband to take his last fateful trip to Lincoln alone so she suggested he take some neighbors with him for added protection. Albert said he needed no protection. So Mariana demanded he take nine-year-old Henry because *"They wouldn't take a chance on hurting a little boy."* Mariana was obviously unfamiliar with the workings of American racism or the psychology of "Nits make lice" as played out in Colorado and much of the American West. How naïve are people targeted by racism in the present day?

Note # 6

See pages 200-01 in *Billy The Kid* by Robert M. Utley. The author sums it up quite well: "What society made of the Kid told more about society than about the Kid."

ARIZONA Law & Order

While there were comparatively few people in Arizona it didn't escape the violence which engulfed the Southwest after the Mexican War and intensified after the Civil War. Once the Apaches were defeated militarily and the Chiricahua deported to Florida, many Americans began to fight each other for control of power, resources, scarce women, etc. By 1880 Tombstone was a large scale producer of silver and was considered a "bonanza town" for a few short years by its some 15,000 people. [See Note # 1. *Notes begin on page 461.*] There were also all kinds of feuds, duels, and shootings among the inhabitants. "Law and order" was indeed limited.

GUNFIGHT at the OK CORRAL

The simmering feud between the Earp brothers and the Clanton-McLowery (also McLowry or McLaury) gang finally became deadly on October 26, 1881. [See Note # 2.] The Earps, with their friend Doc Holliday, were told that some men were waiting for them at the OK Corral. The three Earp brothers, Wyatt, Morgan, and Virgil, were lawmen so they and Holliday walked to the OK Corral where they found Ike and Billy Clanton, Frank and Tom McLowery, and Billy Claiborne. Sheriff John Behan, considered partial to the Clantons, tried to prevent the meeting but Wyatt ordered him to step aside and Behan complied. Marshall Virgil Earp ordered the men in the Corral to put up their hands because they were under arrest for wearing their guns in town. Despite the warning, guns were drawn and the two groups blasted into each other for some seconds. Morgan, Virgil, and Holliday were wounded. Billy Clanton as well as Tom and Frank McLowery were killed. Billy Claiborne was wounded but he managed to get away. Only Wyatt Earp emerged unscathed. [See Note # 3.]

Tombstone was divided as to deciding if the OK Corral affair was cold blooded murder or a fair fight. Sheriff Behan brought charges against the Earps but a hearing ruled in their favor because they had been trying to disarm their opponents in accordance with the city ordinance banning guns in town. The matter didn't end there because a few weeks later Virgil Earp was shot from ambush, crippling him permanently, and the following March, Morgan Earp was shot to death, also from ambush. Sheriff Behan did nothing to bring the bushwhackers to justice so (presumably) Wyatt and Holliday shot and killed the (three) men responsible. Wyatt then left Cochise County forever.

JOHN SLAUGHTER

John Horton Slaughter arrived in Arizona in 1878. A cattleman, he bought a large ranch in 1884. In 1887 the "tough, no-nonsense" Texan became Sheriff of Cochise County. [See Note # 4.] Slaughter seldom allowed his adversaries to make the first move. He always advised his deputies to *fire first and then yell Throw up your hands!* He had only one message for rustlers: *Get out or get killed.* His critics often charged that Sheriff Slaughter killed fugitives then didn't report their deaths. The psychology of the day also permitted "summary acts of justice against Hispanos and Mexican citizens" like one Juan Soto and robbers merely designated as *Geronimo* and *Federico.*[See Note # 5.] To his credit, Sheriff Slaughter never hurt an insane prisoner, one of whom bit him seriously while he was escorting her to a sanity hearing.

PERRY OWENS

Elected Sheriff of Apache County in 1877, Perry Owens, often referred to as "Commodore" because he was named after Commodore Perry, went to Holbrook to arrest Andy L. Blevins (alias Cooper) on September 6, 1887. Well known for his shoulder length hair and buckskin clothes, Perry walked up to the house and informed Blevins he was under arrest on a rustling charge. Blevins pulled a gun and slammed the door shut whereupon Perry shot him through the door. Sam Blevins, Andy's sixteen-year-old younger brother, then started shooting and Perry killed him with his Winchester. John Blevins, another brother, was wounded (though he later recovered). The Blevins women inside the house were screaming hysterically as their men were being killed. Mose Roberts, who had merely been visiting in the home, was also shot dead when he attempted to escape through a window.

The carnage over serving a warrant for rustling brought much negative attention to Commodore Perry. His political fortunes dimmed though he continued in law enforcement, being appointed Sheriff for the newly formed Navajo County in 1895.

GRAHAM-TEWKSBURY FEUD

Many rustlers and outlaws had drifted into Arizona by the 1880s because large cattle ranches had been established and law enforcement hadn't really taken hold. Rancher Jim Stinson, who used a "T" brand that could be easily altered, tired of his cattle winding up on other ranches. He accused the Graham family of cattle rustling but when the case went to court no witnesses appeared (a common occurrence in the West). Stinson's foreman, John Gilleland, good friend of the Graham family, openly declared it was the Tewksbury families who had done the rustling. The two families then made accusations against each other and even got into some shooting scrapes. On September 2, 1887, Andy Blevins (alias Cooper) and members of the Graham family raided the Tewksbury ranch. Bill Jacobs and John Tewksbury were killed from ambush. Two weeks later Graham supporters spied Jim and Ed Tewksbury, along with **Jim Roberts**, camped at Rock Springs. Roberts, who became "top gun" in this so called "Pleasant Valley War," and later a well known lawman, saw the ambush coming and called out to the Tewksbury brothers. All three were excellent shots and when the smoke cleared one Graham partisan was dead and a number wounded.

Unknown to the men fighting at Rock Springs, a large posse was converging on the area to arrest the leaders from both sides. The posse gathered at Perkins' Store then laid a trap they hoped would snare the Grahams first. John Graham and Charlie Blevins rode up, sensed a trap, then tried to flee out of range. But a shotgun blast killed Charlie Blevins and rifle fire brought down John Graham. The posse then rode over to the Tewksbury ranch where no resistance was offered. The whole matter was taken to court but once more no witnesses dared appear. All charges were dropped against both sides.

By 1892 Tom Graham and Ed Tewksbury were the last fighters left in the feuding families. Tom went to Tempe and developed a farm there. On August 2, 1892, Graham was shot and killed by (allegedly) Ed Tewksbury and one John Rhodes, in the outskirts of Tempe. The two were charged with murder but Rhodes couldn't be placed at the scene of the crime and Tewksbury was released on a technicality. Ann Graham, Tom's widow, then tried to shoot her dead husband's assailants. The Pleasant Valley War finally ended and it has been said that some 50 people, many of them innocent victims, died in those few years.

THE APACHE KID

His real name was *Zenogalache* but Americans knew him as the *Apache Kid* (1867-1910?). He was taken to the San Carlos reservation at an early age. There he met Al Sieber who "educated the boy" and taught him how to use firearms. [See Note # 6.] When the Kid was old enough, Sieber got him appointed into the Apache Government Scouts which served with the U.S. Cavalry. The Scouts worked as reservation policemen when arrests had to be made from among the Apache population.

It is said the Kid murdered an Indian who had killed his father many years before. Sieber ordered the arrest of the Apache Kid but when he came into San Carlos he was at the head of some ten heavily armed followers. Sieber ordered the other policemen to put the Kid in the guardhouse but a shootout ensued. Sieber was wounded in the leg and the Kid's gang thundered out of the agency. A price was put on the Kid's head and he became a wanted man. The gang rode for Mexico. On the way they stole horses and supposedly killed two Americans, Bill Diehl and Mike Grace.

He eluded capture for two years. Once captured he was given a "quick trial" and sentenced to hang. The Kid maintained he hadn't killed Diehl or Grace, that the killings were done by some of his followers. Petitions went to Washington and President Grover Cleveland granted him a pardon.

Inexplicably, soon after his release the Apache Kid conducted more raids on freight wagons through-out the Territory. Drivers were murdered and all goods stolen. Sheriff Glen Reynolds of Gila County got together a huge posse and managed to capture the Kid. He was sentenced to prison but en route to Yuma Prison the Kid and his friends broke free, shot and killed his guards (November 1, 1889), Sheriff Reynolds, and one Bill Holmes.

In time six of the Kid's gang were captured and sentenced to hang. Two were executed but the other four avoided the hangman by committing suicide in their cells. In retribution, the Apache Kid went on a murderous rampage. In one incident he stopped a covered wagon in which a woman, son, and baby were traveling to meet the husband. He shot the woman and son but didn't harm the baby. All civilians as well as the military were now up in arms and literally hundreds of volunteers vowed to bring in his head. But no one was able to claim the $5,000 reward.

For several years the Kid and his renegade band of Apaches raided freight lines and ranches in Arizona, New Mexico, and northern Mexico. In 1894 Edward A. Clark, who had been a partner of Bill Diehl years before, claimed to have shot the Kid and his wife. The body of an Apache woman was found by the corral where the couple had been trying to steal horses. A trail of blood lead out to the sur-rounding hills but no other bodies were ever found. Strangely, attacks on settlers and ranches came to a halt. Was the Apache Kid dead or had he merely moved on? Later the story came out that a posse led by Charles Anderson cornered the Kid near Kingston and killed him on September 10, 1905. Another story had it that the Apache Kid escaped into the mountains of Mexico where he lived until 1910 when he supposedly died of consumption.

ARIZONA RANGERS

Modeled after the Texas Rangers, the Arizona Territorial Legislature created the Arizona Rangers in 1901 to bring law and order to border towns and remote areas of the Territory. Burt Mossman, a tough Scotch-Irish personality who had been with the Hashknife Outfit when rustlers nearly drove it bankrupt, was selected as Captain. The Rangers consisted of only fourteen men but during its first year the lawmen put some 125 criminals in jail while having to kill only one thief. Only one Ranger, Carlos Tafolla (Tafoya), lost his life. Gangs led by men like Bill Smith and George Musgrove were forced to leave Arizona altogether. The notorious Agustín Chacón (who supposedly killed some 29 men) was captured in Mexico and brought back to Arizona where he was executed. It has been said the Rangers had a "working arrangement with the notorious Rurales of northern Mexico." [See Note # 7.]

Tom Rynning became Captain in 1902 and the Ranger force was increased to 26 men. The Ranger image was tarnished when they were used as strike breakers at the Morenci mines.

The third (and last) Captain was Harry Wheeler. In 1904 a bandit by the name of Joe Bostwick walked into the Palace Saloon in Tucson and ordered everyone to throw up their hands. Everyone complied but one man standing close to the door managed to escape where he fortuitously ran into Harry Wheeler, who was told a robbery was taking place. Wheeler stepped through the swinging doors. Bostwick saw him and turned slightly to fire just as Wheeler's gun fired twice. Bostwick missed but Wheeler got him with both shots, Bostwick dying the next day. Wheeler told a reporter that he hadn't intended for such an incident to happen, that the gunman had given him no choice.

The Arizona Rangers were disbanded by law in 1909.

DISCUSSION NOTES *for* ARIZONA Law & Order

Note # 1

See page 220 in *Arizona: The History Of A Frontier State* by Rufus K. Wyllys.

Note # 2

See *And Die In The West: The Story of the O.K. Corral Gunfight* by Paula Mitchell Marks. It has never been decided what the gunfight was really about. Most writers claim there were several reasons, including who would control the prostitution industry in Tombstone.

Note # 3

Because of the attention given to the bloodshed at the OK Corral, the popular mind has come to believe that this gunfight, which didn't last 33 seconds, was the most dramatic encounter in American frontier history. (This is the same kind of hype that made an obscure Billy the Kid "the West's most famous outlaw.") It would be interesting to compare the 33-hour shootout of Elfego Baca against some 84 gunmen with the OK Corral fight.

Note # 4

The biography on John Slaughter was written by Allen A. Erwin and is titled *The Southwest Of John H. Slaughter, 1841-1922: Pioneer Cattleman and Trail-Driver of Texas, the Pecos, and Arizona and Sheriff of Tombstone.*

Note # 5

See page 197-98 in *Desert Lawmen* by Larry D. Ball.

Note # 6

See pages 10-11 in the *Encyclopedia Of Western Lawmen & Outlaws* by Jay Robert Nash.
Note # 7
See pages 179-81 in *Arizona: A Cavalcade Of History* by Marshall Trimble.

CHAPTER 13

Statehood and Americanization of the Southwest

S igned in 1848, the Treaty of Guadalupe Hidalgo officially ended the Mexican War which brought the "American Southwest" into existence. Various states were carved out of that immense territory but they became States in the Union at different times and for varying reasons, in the following chronological order: Texas – 1845; California – 1850; Nevada – 1864; Colorado – 1876; Utah – 1896; Oklahoma – 1907; New Mexico – 1912; Arizona – 1912. The quest for statehood is as interesting as it was different from State to State.

TEXAS STATEHOOD and SOCIETY

Texas is the only State in the Union that had been an independent country before becoming a State. The *Lone Star Republic* was declared after the defeat of Santa Anna at San Jacinto. While Mexico never reconciled herself to losing Texas, it couldn't muster the military power to take it back from Texian control, though it was always a possibility in both the Mexican and Texian mind. Texians, the overwhelming majority of whom emanated from the USA, therefore sought to become part of the American Union in order to maintain their independence from Mexico and obtain American protection.

As cultural products of the American South, Texians creating the Lone Star Republic adopted a Constitution which stated in part:

1. *Citizenship*: All Africans and all Indians and their descendants are not citizens of the Texas Republic (1836).

2. Slavery is made legal.

3. Emigrants may legally bring their slaves into Texas.

4. No clergy may serve in the Legislature nor may be President.

5. All shall enjoy equality before the law. [See Note # 1. *Notes begin on page 474.*]

ANNEXATION

Texians were adamant that if they worked to join the Union the USA should admit them to statehood and also promise protection if Mexico should invade. During negotiations two additional points emerged: Texas could be divided into four states and the Texian navy vessels would become property of the USA. The treaty was accepted by Texian authorities on April 12, 1844, and sent by President Tyler to the Senate for ratification. Much to Texian dismay, the Senate rejected the treaty. [See Note # 2.] The people of Texas, "with a proud though wounded spirit," turned to their Lone Star Republic for comfort but they were also bolstered by Americans who maintained the nomination of James K. Polk boded well for Texian aspirations for statehood.

In June of 1844 President Houston was informed of renewed hostilities by Mexican general Woll. But James K. Polk was elected to the American presidency and he clearly favored annexation of Texas. One of the final acts of President Tyler was to push through the resolutions for annexation which passed the House in February of 1845 and the Senate in March. On June 23, 1845, the Texian Congress approved the joint resolutions, then created a State constitution, and the people approved it. Texas was now part of the American Union. The first Governor was J. Pinckney Henderson, the first Senators were Sam Houston and Thomas J. Rusk.

SLAVERY

President Lamar's 1839 extermination of Indians campaign had met with significant success, thus opening up the east and northeast sections of the territory for white American settlement. About 90% of immigrants came from the Southern States. It has been said that half of the families who came to Texas arrived from Alabama and Tennessee. [See Note # 3.] Many also came from Georgia and Mississippi. As in the Old South, Texas economic life was based on a slave plantation reality where white men gave the orders and "chattel" black men did the work. [See Note # 4.]

The new wave of "Texans" prospered because they had two advantages to utilize: plenty of land and black slaves to work it. Between 1850 and 1860 the white population increased by some 171%, the African slave population by some 213%. Enslaved blacks, some 182,000 people, were perhaps one-third of the entire Texas population. It should also be pointed out that "one drop" of African blood made a person an African. [See Note # 5.]

PLANTERS

Planters, in reality a semi-leisure class who never called themselves farmers, were at the apex of Texas society. Planters had enough money to hire a white overseer who actually supervised the work of slave Africans. They were a small class numbering perhaps some 2,000 families. Of these, some fifty-four owned a hundred or more slaves. Outside the planter class most slave owning Texans held five or less Africans in bondage.

NATIVE and FOREIGN BORN

By 1860 there were some 43,422 "foreign born" people living in Texas. According to T.R. Fehrenbach, this "foreign" number included the some 12,000 Tejanos who are treated with an Orwellian twist because, while born in Texas, they had not been born citizens of the USA. Europeans came from Germany, France, Austria, etc., and traders/merchants emanated from northern states like New York and Pennsylvania. Economic and political control quickly passed out of Tejano hands into those of the new immigrants who proved more vigorous and "enterprising" than Tejanos. This occurred even in south Texas despite the fact that Tejanos possessed numerical superiority. [See Note # 6.]

AN OPPOSING VIEW

Texas historians like Yoakum, Richardson, and Fehrenbach provide rather consistent "Remember the Alamo!" views when writing their histories. There are various Texas historians who provide contrary perspectives. David Montejano does not promote the idea that it was the "energy and initiative" of new Texans that made them winners. Indeed, it was more the use of force, violence, and fraud that caused Tejanos to give up their lands. [See Note # 7.] Tejanos, even those who had favored the Texas Revolution, were driven out of colonies like Austin and DeWitt. A case in point is Juan Seguín, hero of San Jacinto, who was threatened that he and his whole family would be murdered if they remained in Texas. (They fled to Mexico in 1842.) Other prominent families were also forced to leave and their vacated lands were "purchased" by Texans. From 1837 to 1842 some thirteen "American" buyers took over some 1,368,574 acres of land from some 358 Tejanos. On the grounds that they were "horse thieves and consorters of slave insurrections," Tejanos were driven out of Austin in 1853 and 1855, from Seguín in 1854, from Matagorda and Colorado counties in 1856, from Uvalde in 1857. Some Texans wrote that Mexicans shouldn't be permitted to own firearms. Some considered Tejanos as "vermin to be exterminated." [See Note # 8.]

TEJANO TEAMSTERS

Mexicans dominated the freighting business between San Antonio and the Gulf Coast ports. Texans wanted this lucrative business for themselves so in the summer and fall of 1857 Tejano teamsters were attacked by masked raiders. Some seventy-five Tejanos were murdered during that time. A troop of Rangers started frequenting the trade routes in order to put a stop to the murders but none of the murderers were ever identified or arrested. Tejano cart men abandoned their business and freighting costs increased by 30%.

LIVESTOCK INDUSTRY

Realizing that they were being targeted for violence, Tejano rancheros moved from their ranchos to the protected towns of the Río Grande. The Texas Republic saw an opening and declared all Tejano livestock to be public property. Texans then took to raiding for animals below the Nueces River and the word "cowboys" came to be applied to the thieves.

EMANUEL DOMENECH

A French clergyman named Abbé Emanuel Domenech, ministering in the Lower Valley in 1848, wasn't impressed with the English speaking population of the area. He observed: "Americans of the Texian frontiers are, for the most part, the very scum of society—bankrupts, escaped criminals, old volunteers…"

He described the Texas Rangers as "the very dregs of society and the most degraded of human creatures." He also mentioned it was beyond belief how Tejanos would accept the brutality directed at them with such "imperturbable meekness." [See Note # 9.]

JUAN CORTINA

The typical portrayal of Juan Nepomuceno Cortina (sometimes spelled Cortinas) is that he was a "soldier, bandit, cattle thief, murderer, and mail robber." [See Note # 10.] Charles W. Goldfinch is among the few English language writers to portray Cortina, affectionately known as *Cheno* to his people, as a warrior for social justice for Hispanics in Texas. [See Note # 11.] In contrast to the conventional portrayal, Goldfinch postulates that Cheno might well have been *a champion, a hero and a noble avenger for his people, the Robin Hood of the Río Grande.* [See Note # 12.]

Estefana and Trinidad Cortina had three children, the eldest being Juan Nepomuceno. "Cheno," as he came to be known, was born on May 16, 1824. Trinidad was the *alcalde* (mayor) of Camargo. The family was part of the landed gentry and when Trinidad died sometime in the 1840s, Estefana maintained her inherited portion of the Espíritu Santo Grant where she established a large ranch known as Rancho Del Carmen.

The entire area emphasized ranching as a way of life although suitable areas were planed in cotton, sugar cane, corn, and beans. Wealth was measured by one's number of horses and cattle. Everyone grew up on horseback and boys especially developed themselves into superlative horsemen.

It has been written that Juan got into trouble while in various schools due to his temper. Because he couldn't remain very long in any one school he grew up, it is said, without being able to read or write. It is possible that such things have been written by Cortina's enemies but few deny that Cheno quickly became a leader among his friends, composed mainly of vaqueros and such. He seemed to be suited for the outdoor life of the cowboy but he also attended dances and social functions with everybody else. Juan was a popular personality.

In 1826 the village of Matamoros was officially organized and named a city in 1836. It was the largest in the area until surpassed by its sister city, Brownsville, Texas.

From the time that Texas declared its independence from Mexico in 1836 the area between the Nueces and the Río Grande became one of violence and cattle rustling. When Tejanos withdrew from the area many Texans conducted raids (the notorious "cowboy raids") for acquiring livestock. They also took cattle from Tejano ranchers who remained on the periphery of this "no man's land." Racial hatred became part of the area culture. With American victory in the Mexican War the boundary of Texas expanded to the Río Grande.

There was real cultural shock for Hispanics. For example, religion was not much of a factor in American life. As one frontier poet phrased it, the American West was:

Whar (sic) the grass grows and the water runs,
And the sound of the Gospel never comes.

Additionally, due to a virulent Texan racism, Tejanos were being targeted as an inferior, sub-human species referred to as *greasers*.

Hispanics like Cheno Cortina were products of a society that sought to bring Amerindians into the

Christian fold, establish ranching as a basic industry, and create stable communities. There was genuine freedom in Hispanic culture but basic respect had to be a part of character, which tended toward a moral society. Each person had a place and a duty with responsibilities and privileges determined by birth or enterprise. Cortina was born to the social class that provided leadership and his talents were those for the military. There is no valid evidence that he rustled cattle or smuggled contraband items as did various personalities of the age.

Cortina accepted a job with the U.S. Quartermaster's Corps. One of his duties was to supervise the wagon masters and teamsters when they needed to change mules/horses. The rule was that animals could not be taken from the stock herd without first acquiring permission from the person in charge. On one shift when Cortina was the official on duty a wagon master "helped himself" to new animals without asking permission. Cortina told the man he must first have permission to do so whereupon the Texan said something to the effect that he didn't need permission from a *greaser* and struck out at Cheno. Cortina defended himself by pummeling the wagon master and would have choked him to death had not some onlookers pulled him off the bleeding Texan. A few days later there was another similar argument and when the military took the side of Texans who refused to ask for permission to change animals, Cortina and some of his friends resigned.

Cortina took up residence in Brownsville, dedicated himself to ranching, married the widow Rafael Cortés (Cortez), had two daughters, Felicitas and Faustina. There was much trafficking in stolen cattle on both sides of the border and it is possible Cheno might have been involved in some of it. [See Note # 13.] Due to a supposed cattle rustling incident **Adolphus Glavecke** became Cortina's bitter enemy, despite the fact that Glavecke was married to one of Cheno's relatives.

Brownsville grew and American lawyers came into possession of much land when various Texans laid claim to Tejano lands and took the matter to court. In 1857 Cortina and his cousin Antonio Tijerina took the lead in exterminating some Amerindian raiders who were preying on the Brownsville vicinity. But the situation in Brownsville was one where Tejanos were not in positions of authority. Worse still, brutalities directed at Mexicans were winked at by most authorities to the degree that killing Tejanos was "no crime and mistreating them an every day pastime." [See Note # 14.] While Cortina was of the upper-class and more or less immune from such treatment, he came to realize that he could not be elected to any political office of importance in Texas. So he decided to move to Mexico to pursue his ambitions. But it was not to be, at least not yet.

In July of 1859 Juan Cortina rode into Brownsville on business. He happened to see Marshall **Bob Shears** in the process of arresting an inebriated ranchero, who happened to have worked previously at his mother's ranch. Marshall Shears commenced to beat the drunk on the head with the butt end of his pistol. Cortina rode up and told Shears he knew the offender, that he would take him home to sleep it off. Shears, who didn't know Cortina, replied with something like: *What is it to you, you damned Mexican!* Cheno's temper flared so he drew his gun and fired a warning shot. Shears still wouldn't release his prisoner so Cortina shot the marshall in the shoulder. He reached down for the drunk, lifted him up behind his saddle, and the two rode out of town.

Immediately there was talk of riding after Cortina and arresting him but no one did. It appears no action was taken by the Brownsville authorities.

On September 28, 1859, there was a ball in Matamoros to celebrate the Mexican holiday. Though ready to leave for the interior of Mexico, Cortina attended the ball. As the evening wore on the topic of conversation among the *bravos* was how many Tejanos had been killed by Texans like Morris, Neal, etc. A group, led by Cheno, went over to Brownsville in search of the men responsible for so many killings. Shots were soon being fired everywhere and a jailor named Johnson was killed.

Cortina led his men into the Alexander Werbiski store and bought all the arms and ammunition in stock. He paid for all items then distributed them among his men if they had none of their own.

Morris and Neal were found and shot to death. Shears and Glavecke managed to hide so they couldn't be found. When a man named García was killed by mistake, Cortina called off his men and all rode out of town. There had been no looting of any kind.

Two days later Juan Cortina published his first proclamation (*Pronunciamiento*, reproduced here in summation):

To the Inhabitants of the State of Texas and the City of Brownsville

Our object in Brownsville has been to chastise the heretofore unpunished villainies of our enemies. Orderly people and honest citizens are inviolable to us in their persons and interests. These have no need to fear us. We target only those who persecute and rob us for no other reason than we are of Mexican origin. We have united to put an end to these oppressions. Those charged with the authority to protect us are in fact the villains who oppress us. Three of them have died at our hands, all criminal, wicked men, notorious among our people due to their hateful deeds.

Some villains hid out so we could not bring them to justice. Now we are being portrayed as bandits and looters. The record is clear: no outrages have been committed on the city of Brownsville. No vandalism has occurred, no house was robbed or burned down. No one has been molested. One innocent man, Viviano García, has died, due to a lamentable accident.

The Mexican community has suffered from the machinations of men like Deputy Sheriff Adolph Glavecke who in collusion with a multitude of lawyers have sought to acquire the land owned by Mexican people. This is not a supposition but a reality. We will no longer tolerate them in our midst because they threaten our tranquility and welfare. All truce between them and us is at an end. Many of our families have been forced to return to Mexico as strangers begging for asylum. Innocent persons shall not suffer but our personal enemies shall not possess our lands until they have fattened it with their own gore.

Our cherished hope is that the government will prosecute the villains who are forcing injustice upon us. [See Note # 15.]

Juan Nepomuceno Cortina
September 30, 1859

While "piteous pleas for aid" were being sent to Austin and Washington, a posse was formed in Brownsville and sallied out in search of Cortina. They were unable to find him but they did "capture" an old man named Tomás Cabrera who had been in on the Brownsville raid. When Cheno heard of this he delayed his departure (to Tampico, Mexico) and demanded that Cabrera be released or he would burn down the town. Some 100 Texans in Brownsville were willing to fight but they also requested and received Mexican troops from Matamoros in order to "capture the bandit Cortina." The "Brownsville Tigers" and the Mexican troops engaged Cortina and his men in what proved to be a disastrous defeat for the Texans and their allies. They even lost their artillery to Cortina's men.

Cheno now offered to withdraw his men and leave the country if Cabrera was released. On November 10, 1859, the night after the arrival of Tobin's Rangers in Brownsville, elderly Tomás Cabrera was taken out of jail and lynched "by an unknown mob." [See Note # 16.]

On November 12, two days after the murder of Cabrera, Brownsville Texans were bombarding the authorities in San Antonio with news that "the bandit Cortina" was at the head of some one thousand *Mexicans* who had taken the city of Brownsville, killed all the Americans, and was now marching on Corpus Christi. (One H.C. Miller is supposed to have witnessed Cortina "put all prisoners to the sword.")

Cortina and his men ambushed a party of Rangers under Lieutenant Littleton. Three Rangers were killed and one captured. On November 22 Tobin and his Rangers attacked Cortina but, Cheno's men being armed, the Rangers were routed and forced to flee ignominiously to the safety of Brownsville.

Word spread that Juan Cortina had now defeated two "armies" sent against him. Hundreds of other aggrieved Tejanos now flocked to his banner.

On November 23, 1859, Cheno published another proclamation (provided here in summation from the J.D. Thompson volume cited above):

To The Mexican Inhabitants Of The State Of Texas!

I hope that my words may offer you a degree of consolation in the midst of your adversity. History teaches us that we must resist our enemies with a firm spirit. We have grievous cause that impels us to use force to remedy our despair. We confront persons so overcome with prejudice that those of us who love liberty are branded as bandits. I am ready for the combat.

The Mexican people of this region are honorable and dedicated to their work. They love peace and recognize it as crucial to their labor. They believe in equality, humility, simplicity, etc., and perhaps suffer from an excess of goodness. But they are surrounded by malicious and crafty monsters who rob them and hate them.

When the State of Texas became a part of the Union there came upon us a plague of vampires in the guise of men who scattered themselves in our settlements. Their only capital was corrupt hearts and perverse intentions. Some, brimful of laws, promised to be our friends and pledged to protect us against attacks from the rest. Others got together secretly and sought to take our lands or burn our houses. We trusted our land titles to some and then they refused to return them on one pretext or another, always with a smile on their faces.

Mexicans! We have been robbed of our property, thrown into jail, chased and hunted like wild beasts, murdered with impunity. These monsters live by the adage *Kill them for the greater will be our gain!* It would appear that justice has fled from this world. We are here by the whim of the oppressor and at any time we can be jailed or "shot while trying to escape." These criminals believe we are unworthy to belong to the human species. Our courtesies are considered as admission of inferiority to their superiority. But now our race of people, filled with gentleness and inward sweetness, gives now the cry of alarm.

Mexicans! The law exists to protect all but they are used for evil and injustice by certain judges and hypocritical authorities bent on avarice and other evils. All of you know of which I speak.

Mexicans! It is time to break the chains of your slavery. The Lord has given you and me powerful arms to combat our enemies. You may count on my cooperation.

We demand that Mexican people be permitted to live their lives as does everybody else.

We demand that the laws be enforced.

We demand that governor-elect Sam Houston give us legal protection.

Mexicans! Peace be with you! Inhabitants of Texas: keep in mind the Holy Spirit which proclaims: *Thou shalt not be the friend of the passionate man, nor join thyself to the madman, lest thou learn his mode of work and scandalize thy soul.*

Juan N. Cortina

November 23, 1859

There was expressed sentiment that a real possibility existed for a major revolt so U.S. Army troops were readied to be sent to Texas from as far away as Kansas and Virginia. When the truth of the situation was discovered troops under Major Heintzelman were ordered to Brownsville, reaching the city on December 5, 1859. He had with him some 122 officers and men. Captain Ricketts added 48 artillerymen and some 200 Rangers under Tobin and Ford rounded out the army which was to face Cortina and his men, which Heintzelman estimated to number from 350-500.

The two groups skirmished at Río Grande City and Cortina was forced to retreat, at first taking his cannon but later having to abandon them. (Heintzelman estimated that sixty of Cortina's men were killed while Ford put the estimate at close to two-hundred.) Cortina retreated down the Mexican side of the river and established a camp at a place known as *La Bolsa*. Ford crossed into Mexico and drove Cortina's men away. Ford was to invade Mexico several times in pursuit of Cortina, who was all but finished as a military threat. He took refuge in the Burgos mountains but the Texas Rangers continued to invade and pillage along the border on the premise that they were in pursuit of "Cortina and his bandits." When the Civil War broke out Cortina returned to the border but when Confederates attacked the ranch where he was staying he was forced to leave Texas once more. [See Note # 17.]

NEWSPAPERS

It has been reported that by 1860 there were some seventy-one newspapers in Texas, that the 100,000 circulation and that of other print publications reached perhaps ninety-five percent of the white population. Themes were more political than focusing on the dissemination of information concerning factual events. Journalism could also be dangerous work. William C. Brann was shot down in cold blood in Waco, Texas in 1898. [See Note # 18.] Editorial writing was a major part of any publication and most people valued reading, especially including the Bible. Literacy, schools, and school teachers were highly prized, though real public education was not established in Texas before the Civil War.

RECONSTRUCTION

Texans in 1865 were a suffering lot. They had given their all for the Civil War and had been soundly thrashed. The economy was in ruins. Planters were impoverished and their black slaves who had done the work were now free because on June 19, 1865, General Gordon Granger of the Union Army landed in Texas and proclaimed American authority over Texas was restored and blacks were now free. (June 19th thus began the famous *Juneteenth* tradition of celebrating African-American freedom.) Texans took their defeat bitterly and tended to blame the former African slaves for their troubles. When thousands of occupying Union troops turned out to be Negroes, racial hatred became almost tangible.

Occupation was to last nine long years and blacks abandoned the plantation lands they had worked. Freedmen's Bureau offices had herculean tasks and whites resented them bitterly. Texans had no intention of permitting full citizenship for the "impoverished, illiterate, and unskilled horde of Negroes…" whom they considered to be racially inferior. The new Texas constitution enabled blacks to hold property but they were denied the right to vote and they still could not testify in court against a white man. [See Note # 19.] So-called "black codes" were passed by the legislature and these laws effectively put black workers back on plantations. "More than a few blacks were beaten or murdered" by white Texans. [See Note # 20.] The First Reconstruction Act, passed in by Congress in 1867, declared "black codes" to be illegal and required civil rights like Negro suffrage (although it was legally denied in most Northern states). People who came in from out of state were derogatorily referred to as *carpetbaggers* because it was considered they were so poverty stricken where they came from that they put all their belongings in a bag then went to Texas looking for some kind of "get rich quick" scheme. *Scalawags* was the term used for southern Republicans and connoted feelings akin to "native traitor." Amid charges of fraud, E.J. Davis became Governor of Texas in 1870. It has been said nine-tenths of white Texans detested the Davis administration and all the years of "carpetbagger rule" which have been described by historians like T.H. Fehrenbach as corrupt and extravagant. Massive resistance to carpetbagger rule was clearly discernible by 1871. Further, armed desperadoes became the ruling power in various Texas counties. The State Police included Negroes and racist Texans would never submit to them, thus adding to the breakdown in law and order. Shooting a black policeman made a man somewhat of a hero. Martial law was frequently declared.

Governor Davis ran for reelection in 1873. His opponent was Democrat Richard Coke, a Confederate veteran. Whites rode into black neighborhoods and threatened to kill anyone who voted. There was "terror, intimidation, and murders…" in Texas. [See Note # 21.] Coke won so Davis charged election irregularities and fraud. The Texas Supreme Court invalidated the entire election. The Democrats, who had won almost every office, simply ignored the Court and took their posts. Davis requested that Federal troops be sent in but President Grant refused. Davis directed the local militia to keep order but the militiamen went over to the Coke side. Once more he asked for Federal troops and once more was denied. Davis finally gave up his office on January 19, 1874. Amid the mighty roar of men singing "The Yellow Rose of Texas," Coke's men took over at Austin. Political wars were to continue as a reality and problems like a bad economy didn't go away but at least "backroom" Texas politicians, not carpetbaggers, were at the helm of State government.

SHARECROPPING

The "Negro problem" was handled through the system of sharecropping, a form of tenantry in which a worker tilled someone else's land for a share, from one-third to one-half, of the yield. The land owner kept the books and often "deducts" made sizeable cuts into the worker's share. While thousands of "poor whites" were sharecroppers, Africans had few other avenues by which to make a living. Further, the black Texan was generally poor, illiterate, and hated by white Texans, especially including the class of poor whites. An identifiable caste system was in place by the decade of the 1890s. Ironically, the Fourteenth and Fifteenth amendments became the law of the land but the rights they granted were not guaranteed or enforced by Federal power. "Jim Crow" laws built around devious strategies like the poll tax or "grandfather clauses" effectively neutralized Federal dictates. In effect, racial segregation shrouded by the hypocrisy of "separate but equal" became the de facto law of the land.

KU KLUX KLAN

The "white supremacist" KKK first appeared in East Texas around 1921. It targeted African-Americans but also Catholics and Jews. [See Note # 22.] By 1922 the Klan was involved in local politics and in 1924 it ran one Felix Robertson of Dallas for governor.

The KKK also took up vigilantism against people it didn't like: criminals, individuals of loose morals, "uppity niggers," drifters, Mexicans, prostitutes, etc. People were dragged into the woods at night, given a "trial" under a flaming torch, then sentenced to flogging or some such punishment. Victims were threatened into not talking about what had happened and very few refused to comply. While the Klan could terrorize the powerless, it didn't have the strength to move against anyone in the power structure of Texas society. Without real popular support, the KKK simply faded away.

GREAT DEPRESSION

While the Depression which started in 1929 was devastating throughout the country it wasn't quite a serious in Texas because ownership of corporate stocks wasn't common. Texans didn't much believe in Wall Street or the power of industrialization to improve life. Further, many Texans were already poor in 1929 and it has been said the drought and dust storms of the 1930s did more damage than the Depression.

Behind their "folksy" image, Texas politicians like John Nance Garner, Sam Rayburn, and Lyndon Johnson began or gained influence during the Democratic administration of Franklin D. Roosevelt. They were highly successful in bringing money and federal establishments to the State of Texas.

SPINDLETOP

The Texas economy improved spectacularly after the 1920s due to discovery of huge petroleum reserves. The first significant field was Spindletop (1901) at Beaumont on the Mexican Gulf coast. This was followed by Petrolia (1904), Electra (1911), etc., until oil was discovered under the majority of Texas counties. Landowners across the State made money and an adage was coined: *A few oil wells make ranching a fine business.* (The "new rich" Texas oilman became a somewhat stereotypical figure.) By 1928 Texas was the national leader in oil supply and this led to an industrialization heretofore unknown in the Southern states. Other natural resources like salt, sulphur, limestone, gypsum, aluminum, magnesium, tin, etc. contributed to economic development. There were still millions of head of cattle on Texas pasture lands and processing shrimp became big business on the Gulf coast.

CIVIL RIGHTS

Historian T.H. Fehrenbach has written that "…civil rights for the non-peer group were forced down the Texan throat from outside." [See Note # 23.] In the racist mind, rights were for Texans, not "non-peer" groups like Mexicans or Africans.

Reminiscent of South Africa, there were three caste systems in Texas which governed whites, Mexicans, and Africans. Excepting voting rights, Mexicans were discriminated against much like blacks. There were slight variations: while white intermarriage with blacks was against Texas law, marriage to a Mexican, while legal, was *unthinkable*. White students would certainly not attend "black" schools, or vice versa, but there was no problem if "Latinos" went there. There were also some night clubs, bars, theaters, barber shops, restaurants, etc., which would not serve Mexicans because they so chose.

Some believed that Mexicans became "good Americans" if they served in the military. Thousands served, most were excellent soldiers, and many were highly decorated, some with the Congressional Medal of Honor. One valiant soldier was **Arturo Músquiz** who had fought the Nazis in Europe and paid the price for it. During a serious firefight, shrapnel had shattered his cheekbone, blinded him in one eye, made him deaf in one ear, and almost lost the power to speak. When he returned home to his West Texas town his uniform had five ribbons on it, including the Purple Heart. He went into a local restaurant and was informed *We don't serve Mexicans here.* [See Note # 24.]

It has been said that blacks emigrated out of Texas in large numbers. Those who remained were forced to contend with a rigorous caste system shrouded by "separate but equal" hypocrisy. When segregation and discrimination were barred by law in 1964 it gave impetus to de facto segregation. Integration was an idealistic goal but in effect Texas society continued to be racist by polarizing on both sides, white and black, and would remain so. If this is difficult to understand, it can be pointed out that Texan Lyndon B. Johnson, an avowed segregationist before he ascended to the presidency, became the undeniable champion of civil rights legislation in the USA.

With Lyndon Johnson, certainly one of the most powerful of American presidents, leading the way, Texas society was affected by the civil rights movement. In 1968 San Antonio, Corpus Christi, and Austin adopted an open housing ordinance. In 1969 the legislature worked to throw out the segregationist laws passed in 1957 requiring segregation in schools, sporting events, transportation facilities, etc. Legal segregation was ending in Texas. The Voting Rights Act of 1975 was among the most important final measures.

Henry Cisneros became the first Hispanic since Juan Seguín to be elected Mayor of San Antonio. Cisneros went on to serve in House of Representatives. The San Antonio Convention Center bears his name.

The Tejano culture of the past is now a sterling tourist attraction for the entire State. In 1998 the cover of the El Paso telephone directory had a *conquistador* in full armor as well as Mexican folk dancers. Today the **Institute of Texan Cultures** in San Antonio is promoted as "emphasizing the contributions of the 27 ethnic groups that helped settle Texas."

DISCUSSION NOTES *for* TEXAS STATEHOOD and SOCIETY

Note # 1

There is no doubt that Texas was culturally a creation of the American South. See *The Constitution And Government Of Texas* by Frank M. Stewart and Joseph L. Clark.

Note # 2

See pages 425-44 in volume Two of *History Of Texas* by H. Yoakum.

Note # 3

See page 285-87 in *Lone Star* by T.R. Fehrenbach, who says the settlers were "red-necks or yeoman farmers" who "wanted to get away from the slave plantations."

Note # 4

T.R. Fehrenbach writes (p. 84) that "Anglo-Americans" were heirs of the Enlightenment, "inherently liberal...optimistic...rational." He confronts the institution of African slavery by asserting "No one was less fitted by rationale to make human chattels of other men than Anglo-Americans..." Why was African slavery so accepted (that it took the bloodiest war in American history to abolish)? Because it was "horribly complicated by economics, social factors, and race." Is this studied historiography or masterful propagandistory?

On page 306 Fehrenbach continues to write that "few of the Founding Fathers of the United States, from ethical reasons, favored human slavery." How so? Even "...George Washington experienced qualms. Just as the Englishman was poorly fitted by his law, ethic, and experience to 'make a slave of any man,' Americans were similarly badly suited to hold Negroes in bondage." How realistic is such commentary? The English were the slave traders of the Western world as already mentioned in previous sections. Eight of the first twelve American Presidents were slave owners. It has been proven by DNA testing that Thomas Jefferson had children with his black slave named Sally Hemmings. Any number of African-Americans have claimed blood ties to George Washington. So what is T.R. Fehrenbach about?

It also appears that Fehrenbach believes the Scotch-Irish are "Anglos" (though he also uses labels like Anglo-Celts, Nordic, Anglo-Saxon, Teutonic, etc.; he doesn't use the umbrella term *Germanic*), the supposedly racially superior entities of the 19th century in which Germans, French, Irish (Catholics), etc., aren't included. It would be interesting to compare the use of American "Anglo" in the 19th century with that of German "Aryan" in the 20th.]

The new wave of "Texans" prospered because they had two advantages to utilize: plenty of land and black slaves to work it. Between 1850 and 1860 the white population increased by some 171%, the African slave population by some 213%. Enslaved blacks, some 182,000 people, were perhaps one-third of the entire Texas population. It should also be pointed out that "one drop" of African blood made a person an African. By contrast, in the Hispanic Americas there was the concept of "dominant blood" which acknowledged human behavior exhibited throughout the world, including the USA. Hispanic racial mixing provided a sort of democratic social mobility which was decried as intolerable under the tenets of American racism. There was considerable racial mixing in English speaking lands but historians don't focus on it because they would be ostracized in their field. English racial mixing is kept out of focus by concentrating on Hispanic mixing.

Note # 5

In the Hispanic Americas there was the concept of "dominant blood" which acknowledged human behavior exhibited throughout the world, including the USA. Hispanic racial mixing provided a sort of democratic social mobility which was decried as intolerable under the tenets of American racism.

Note # 6

Fehrenbach writes (p. 289) this happened because Tejanos "remained politically inert as individuals…" along with the "patronizing attitude of the rancheros, whose ignorance of and impatience with the vagaries of American law and political practice completed their decline." It would be interesting to investigate if Orwellian forces were at work in the Texas society of the day. Were Tejanos consciously targeted by the Government for dispossession of political power, their land, their self respect? Fehrenbach appears to assert that the "Hispanic legacy" didn't include things like initiative which, of course, the newcomers had in abundance. Fehrenbach doesn't investigate how the Government operated to take Tejano land and put it in Texan hands.

Note # 7

See *Anglos And Mexicans In The Making Of Texas, 1836-1986* by David Montejano.

Note # 8

See pages 28-29 in the David Montejano volume.

Note # 9

See page 32 in the *Anglos And Mexicans In The Making Of Texas, 1836-1986* volume.

Note # 10

On page 152 of *Texas: The Lone Star State*, Rupert Richardson writes him off as "the bandit Cortinas." T.H. Fehrenbach gives "Cortinas" much more attention in his *LONE STAR* but it is more as the "Red Robber of the Río Grande" than anything else. On page 512 Fehrenbach also asserts that Cortina "…carried a grudge against Americans and was bitter about the American conquest of his native land." (Was it American or Texan oppression that Cortina fought against?) On page 139 of his *TEXAS*, Joe B. Frantz writes that Cortina was "a natural bandit and natural leader…a living folk hero…he remained true to his one love: cattle stealing."

Note # 11

See *Juan N. Cortina, 1824-1892: A Re-Appraisal* by Charles W. Goldfinch.

Note # 12

This dichotomy is crucial when studying Texas history because one or the other interpretations of Cortina cannot be valid history. That will bring on a serious question: which is propaganda and which is History? How then must one consider the works of historians like those mentioned above, as well as those of J. Frank Dobie, J. Fred Rippy, Dr. Walter Prescott Webb, etc.? What implications will the answer have for Texas society in general?

Note # 13

There is no valid proof that Cortina did or did not. The message of Texas history is that targeted groups continue to be targeted to the present day when "History" is written. It is also a corollary that personalities like King and Kennedy are generally not subjected to such scrutiny.

Note # 14

See page 40 in *Juan Cortina* by Charles W. Goldfinch.

Note # 15

See pages 14-18 in *Juan Cortina And The Texas-Mexico Frontier, 1859-1877* edited by Jerry D. Thompson.

Note # 16

T.R. Fehrenbach writes in *Lone Star*, p. 514, that "Webb wrote that Tobin and his men were a sorry lot...street sweepings that so often were the first to join an expedition to the Río Grande... Their first official act in Brownsville was to storm the jail and lynch a captured 65-year-old Tomás Cabrera..."

Note # 17

The saga of Juan Cortina hasn't really been investigated from Hispanic perspectives. Such a work would be as interesting as the tales of Robin Hood in England. Has this not been done due to cultural bias? What light would it shed on Texan historiography?

Note # 18

See *Fighting Words: Independent Journalists In Texas* by James McEnteer.

Note # 19

See pages 398-99 in *Lone Star*.

Note # 20

Is it possible that in the final analysis, "American democracy" is defined by who has control of the Government? Is that Democracy or *Oligarchy*?

Note # 21

See page 429 in *Lone Star*.

Note # 22

See *War, Revolution And The Ku Klux Klan*, a study by Shawn Lay on the KKK in El Paso where a large population of Hispanic Catholics prevented the Klan from winning widespread acceptance.

Note # 23

See page 713 in *Lone Star*. This edition was published in 1983.

Note # 24

See page 4 in *Latin Americans In Texas* by Pauline R. Kibbe. On page 228 author Kibbe enumerates "the shortcomings of Latin Americans" which tend to weaken them in American society: exaggerated individualism and disinterest in cooperating with each other; separation from each other because of envy and other pettiness; collaborators who work for the status quo; inability to identify and combat "divide and conquer" strategies. It is possible to add that many Latinos don't combat the racist forces which keep them down, as if ignoring them would solve the issue.

CALIFORNIA STATEHOOD and SOCIETY

It has been reported that of the some 4,000 to 10,000 (sources vary) non-Indian population of California in 1845, around 700 were non-Hispanic American or English people. Perhaps half of the English-speaking Californians were Hispanicized Mexican citizens who had put down roots in California. The other half has been described as disparaging Mexican California and stating openly that the USA would soon take over the country. [See Note # 1. *Notes begin on page 505.*] After the Treaty of Cahuenga (January, 1847) ended the Mexican War in California the national Congress made no move to establish a government so the territory was ruled by military governors. Americans wouldn't tolerate military rule for long and by the spring of 1847 there was an identifiable movement to form a constitutional convention. The gold rush brought in another 2,000 immigrants by January of 1849 and these added their voices to self-determination and an end to military rule. (By mid-1849 San Francisco alone had a floating population of some ten to thirty thousand people.) Preparations were made for constitutional convention members to meet in Monterey in September of 1849. Nine Californios would be part of the convention. Miners, evidently busy in the diggings, were not represented at all.

Due to the nature of Spanish-speaking Californio society, there had been no need for restaurants, hotels, saloons, etc., so delegates had to find lodgings and meals on their own. True to traditional Californio hospitality, Monterey's upper class Hispanic families opened their homes to convention delegates. [See Note # 2.]

The constitutions of Iowa and New York were used as basic guides for the California constitution which would be created. Delegates leaned toward strict regulation of corporations and prohibition of banks distributing paper notes to serve as money. Other matters were omens of what was to come: a motion was made to ask for immediate statehood for northern California (where most Americans lived) while requiring territorial status for southern California (where most Californios lived). But the most explosive issues proved to be those related to African slavery. For example, everyone agreed that slavery should be declared illegal but there were those like **Morton Matthew McCarver** (Kentucky born) who believed that "free Negroes" should be prohibited from entering California. McCarver stated that contacts between whites and blacks only served to degrade the white race. [See Note # 3.]

Suffrage was granted to "Every white male citizen of the United States…twenty-one years of age." Californio **Pablo de la Guerra** commented that Mexican law had not denied citizenship to Indians and Negroes, and what of dark skinned Californios (because they spent so much time outdoors)? **Charles Botts** stated the vote could not be given to "those objectionable races." [See Note # 4.] Delegates finally skirted around the issue by introducing a provision that stated "nothing herein contained shall be construed to prevent the Legislature…from admitting to the right of suffrage Indians, or descendants of Indians, in such special cases as such a proportion of the legislative body may deem just and proper." Delegates didn't want to run the risk of having the constitution rejected by Congress so controversial issues of the time were put off until a future day of reckoning. (Los Ángeles delegate Manuel Domínguez, a mestizo, was eight years later prohibited from testifying in a San Francisco court on the grounds of his race, so the California constitution ended up with strong racist overtones.)

Another controversial issue was setting the state's eastern boundary. The first proposal had the eastern boundary taking most of Nevada. Some delegates favored an "extended boundary" whose eastern line would go into Wyoming, Colorado, and New Mexico. It was finally decided that the Sierra Nevada (summit) formed a natural boundary for the eastern limit of California.

Statehood was granted to California on September 7, 1850. The first Governor was Peter H. Burnett, the first Senators were John Charles Frémont and William M. Gwin.

GOLD RUSH

The first person to discover gold in California was one **Francisco López**. This happened on March 9, 1842, in Santa Feliciana canyon some forty miles from Los Ángeles. [See Note # 5.] Miners flocked in from Sonora but gold deposits proved shallow and were soon exhausted. (As it turned out the rich deposits were in the interior, not by the coast.)

Some years later John Sutter had hired **James Marshall** to build a sawmill on the South Fork of the American River around forty-five miles from his New Helvetia fort. On January 24, 1848, Marshall happened to notice some shiny flecks that glittered in the earth. He picked up some of the larger grains and sacked them into a handkerchief. The next day he went to Sutter and in a great state of agitation showed his find. (The Senate accepted the Treaty of Guadalupe Hidalgo, which would officially end the Mexican War, on March 10, 1848.) This was the beginning of a new California, Sutter's doom, and a dream that would be a nightmare for most get-rich-quick miners.

While Sutter tried to keep the discovery quiet but the effort was futile. One Sam Brannon filled a bottle full of gold dust then went to San Francisco where he paraded up and down the street yelling *Gold!! Gold from the American River!!* By May of 1848 men were leaving their ordinary jobs for "the diggins" as the news spread south. By July there were some four thousand would-be miners scrambling about for gold which they found as dust, flakes, pebbles, and even fist-sized nuggets. Thousands more would soon join them as gold fever struck. (It has been estimated that by the end of 1848 perhaps six to ten million dollars worth of gold had been mined in California.) The New York Herald wrote on December 9, 1848: "*The gold region in California! Startling discoveries! The El Dorado of the old Spaniards is discovered at last...*" It seemed that gold hysteria had gripped the entire country. Many Americans, "poets, philosophers, lawyers, brokers, bankers, merchants, farmers, clergymen..." sold their belongings to finance the journey to California.

The would-be "49ers" formed brotherhoods, companies, societies, associations, etc., and crowded ports from Boston to Charleston in hopes of getting on a boat headed for the 18,000 mile journey to California around Cape Horn. Some of the boats weren't sea worthy and some crews were totally incompetent. During the five to eight month voyage there were dangers from mutiny, lack of food and water, vicious feuds, etc., and many dead bodies were cast into the sea.

Thousands more decided to try the route through the Isthmus of Panama. Most were destroyed by mosquitoes, infernal heat, putrid water and food. To make matters worse, cholera broke out along the trail to the west coast port where the "Argonauts" hoped to board a boat for San Francisco. Most of those who finally made it had little to no money so they had to live by their wits when they finally arrived.

Uncounted thousands came overland on routes like the Santa Fe Trail. They brought all kinds of gear with them, items suggested by guide books, much of which had to be abandoned along the trail when excess weight of wagons threatened to cripple their oxen, mules, or horses. These would-be 49ers paid the price for being so unacquainted with frontier lands: some drowned trying to cross rivers or large streams, some got lost or fell into gullies and canyons, and many shot each other during fights. "As if their own incompetence were not enemy enough…" cholera was a menacing presence and hundreds if not thousands died from the dread disease. [See Note # 6.] Crude wooden markers dotted the trail where were buried those who succumbed to rigors of the trail. One J.L. Stephens of Ohio wrote: *Hardships of the overland route to California are beyond conception. Time is spent in care and suspense, anxiety, fear of losing your animals and being left to walk with your gear on your back, having to beg for food, fear of being left in the mountains to starve or freeze to death…and a thousand other dangers you don't realize until you are on the way…* [See Note # 7.]

It has been written that some 90,000 people arrived in California during 1849. The gold rush thus became one of the biggest mass migrations of people in all history. It has also been said the gold rush was basically over by 1852 when some 23,000 (disillusioned?) people departed from the Golden State.

THE DIGGINGS

According to Leonard Pitt, some 1300 Californios mined for gold in the bonanza year of 1848. [See Note # 8.] But troubles began when "fist swinging Oregon Yankees" entered the area and refused to believe that Californios were now American citizens merely because of the Treaty of Guadalupe Hidalgo. Posters began to appear at the diggings, warning foreigners that they had no right to be there so they had better leave immediately. Things escalated when "some Yankees" accused five "foreigners" of stealing five pounds of gold. Friends of the accused denied the charge but took up a collection, gathered five pounds of gold, and delivered it in an effort to placate the accusers. American miners, numbering in the hundreds, demanded a trial after which the two men accused of the theft were lynched. The area was henceforth named *Hangtown*.

Attacks on Californios and "foreigners" (many were from Chile and Sonora, Mexico; the Sonorans were excellent miners because mining had been part of their heritage since 1549) increased to the point that native Californians gave up mining activities. **Mariano Vallejo**, who had a long history of being friendly to Americans, described the 49ers as mostly "wicked" men. **Hugo Reid** characterized them as "*…vagabonds from every quarter of the globe…scoundrels…rascals from Oregon, pickpockets from New York, Mexican thieves, gamblers…assassins manufactured in Hell…Judge Lynch with his thousand arms, thousand sightless eyes, and five-hundred lying tongues.*" [See Note # 9.]

While Hispanic miners were being targeted for violence, their laws and methods were being utilized because Americans were not a mining people by tradition. For example, before 1848 there was no body of American mining law in existence. The mining codes of Spain and Mexico were translated into English and used in California (and the West). In his book *The Big Bonanza*, Dan De Quille (pseudonym of William Wright) listed three pages of Spanish mining terms that were taken into English, such as *bonanza, placer, batea, arrastra*, etc.[See Note # 10.]

Miners from Sonora were especially adept at finding gold deposits and they knew the techniques with which to extract them. Jealous Americans, ex-army officers, clergymen, lawyers, business men, etc., were soon attacking them with the intention of driving them away from the diggings. One Persifor F. Smith, an American general, orated that all non-citizens were trespassers. Self-appointed vigilantes, who resented competition from the foreigners, drove out over a thousand Mexicans, Chileans, Peruvians, etc., from the areas around Sutter's Mill and the Sacramento River. Many wound up in San Francisco (where they were attacked by a notorious gang known as the "Hounds").

Another strategy with which to drive out foreigners was the Foreign miners' Tax Law of 1850. Credited to **Thomas Jefferson Green**, a Texan, the law required that all non-citizens pay a $20 per month fee to acquire a mining permit. Some 4,000 foreigners gathered in the vicinity of Sonora Town to protest the unfair, exorbitant tax, to no avail. Some four hundred Americans marched to Columbia Camp, said to be the foreigners' headquarters, and collected the tax from those who could pay and chased all others away. The two Frenchmen credited with starting the whole mess were arrested, fined $5 for *treason*, then released.

Most if not all crimes in the diggings were blamed on the *greasers* (which term also included the native Californios). In a series of robberies and murders the weapons left on the scene were *riatas* (sic), and everyone knew they were used only by "greasers." At a public meeting American miners voted almost unanimously to require all foreigners to turn over their weapons to American authorities and apply for permits of good conduct. Anyone not complying would be run out of the diggings. (Leonard Pitt writes that from 5- to 15,000 Hispanic miners, suppliers, freighters, etc., were forced out of the southern mines.) With the *bandidos* gone, life could be secure once more.

But the "doctrine of trespass" and the Foreign Miners' Tax Law backfired: when Spanish-speaking miners were driven from the gold fields the gold supply dropped to the point that merchants suffered serious losses in business. For example, crowbars selling for $8 now went for as little as fifty cents. Thousands of dollars were being lost every day so the merchants began a movement to rescind the Miners' Tax, which was achieved in early 1851. Merchants publicized the fact that the diggings were open again, that Hispanics could now return and work for American patrons. Few returned because they now had first-hand experience with the many facets of American racism. The Californios didn't return to work the mines either.

DOWNIEVILLE

Lynch law and lynch courts could strike at any place during this time of California history. A Mexican woman known as Juanita was lynched in Downieville in 1851 after an incident involving her possibly being raped by an American named Cannan, though the incident hasn't been reported with anything approaching unanimity. Josiah Royce has written that Juanita was living with her *Spanish paramour… All reports make her a woman of beauty, considerable intelligence and vivacity, and a still youthful appearance.* Carey McWilliams quotes Owen C. Coy as saying: "In keeping with the characteristics of her race (sic), Juanita had a quick passion" with Cannan. Andrew F. Rolle says she was "an evil Mexican woman." Leonard Pitt describes Juanita as "a Mexican prostitute." So depending on the author, Juanita was someone's common law partner, a woman of easy virtue, or a vile prostitute. [See Note # 11.]

The basic story from the American side appears to be as follows: a man named Cannan and his (drunken) partying friends went by Juanita's house and Cannan "sort of stumbled into the door" and broke it down. Cannan picked up a scarf that had been lying on the floor then the Americans went on their way. Cannan returned the following day, possibly to return the scarf (?), apologize for the night before (?), or who-knows-what. Juanita's man came to the door and "seemed angry." Cannan supposedly was calm but Juanita became angry, grabbed a knife and stabbed Cannan to death.

News of the killing spread throughout Downieville and the Americans miners organized a "popular court." When Juanita and her man were brought before the court the big crowd voiced its excitement. Some shouted "Hang 'em!" Others said "Give them a trial!" while others added "Give them a fair trial and then hang 'em!" A man named Thayer objected to the impending violence and the crowd told him to "desist" if he valued his own safety. Cannan's witnesses, none of whom could speak or understand Spanish, related what happened as they saw it. [See Note # 12.] It is unknown what Juanita's defense was (evidently she didn't speak English and the judge, jury, or mob didn't speak Spanish) but she called one Dr. Aiken who testified she was three months pregnant. Amid cries of *"Hang her!"* the jury, composed of men with names like Burr, Reed, Woodruff, etc., found her guilty and sentenced her to death by hanging. A gallows was improvised and Juanita walked quietly to her execution. The Star newspaper stated in an editorial that while *it couldn't heartily approve of the hasty lynching of a woman, the act would have a good moral effect on the community.*

NATIVE AMERICANS

As has already been described in the "Indian Affairs" section, American miners believed Indians were deserving of little more than extermination. The English speaking 49ers demanded wars of extermination and the new California government did whatever possible to accommodate them. [See Note # 13.] Miners held no respect for Indian land, overran their hunting and gathering grounds, rode into villages and shot anyone in sight "for sport," seized and carried off women to be used as concubines. [See Note # 14.]

Federal authorities sponsored treaties that would have established reservations for California Indians but the State legislature lobbied against them so the Senate refused to ratify provisions for California Indian reservations. Indians were therefore at the mercies of American 49ers, business interests, and the State government. Between 1848 and 1860 the Indian population went from some 150,000 to perhaps 30,000, such was the American effort at extermination. (Alvin Josephy writes that the Indian population continued to decrease until about 1900.) There were also those who demanded that surviving Indians "should be removed beyond the limits of civilization," it didn't matter where.

Amerindian survival was indeed an heroic feat in the face of brutal violence directed at all Indians. It has been written that in the years 1851-1860 "at least" a thousand women were so brutally raped that they *died.* Some 3,000 to 4,000 Indian children were kidnapped and sold into slavery. Indian women were often forced to live with American miners in order to supply sexual favors. Numbers of them were forced into prostitution to make money for mere survival. [See Note # 15.]

The California legislature enacted a law which prohibited non-whites from testifying in court against whites. While it also outlawed slavery it permitted Indians to be arrested on almost any charge, including idleness, and fined. If the Indians couldn't pay the fines then anyone who paid it was entitled to get the Indian to work for him until the amount of the fine was paid off. This indentured servitude was the equivalent of enslavement for Indians who fell into the clutches of the legal system because the day they finished paying off their debt they were arrested again on similar charges. And their testimony was illegal in a court of law so they really couldn't defend themselves in any situation involving American white men.

CALIFORNIOS

Despite the professed idealism of the Treaty of Guadalupe Hidalgo and the commentary by Secretary of State Buchanan (who asserted that there would be "*...protection in the free enjoyment of their liberty, property and religion, these would be amply guaranteed by the Constitution and laws of the United States*), the Hispanic people of Mexican California were more or less destroyed by the American takeover of the country. [See Note # 16.]

The American takeover of California was at first welcomed by a few Californios like the stalwarts Mariano Vallejo and Juan Bandini who believed the USA offered a "brilliant future." It didn't take long for disenchantment to set in. Despite the writings of Leonard Pitt to the contrary, among the most vocal in expressing their discontent were the women interviewed by Bancroft's field researchers. [See Note # 17.]

Rosalía Vallejo (Leese) had nothing but contempt for the individuals known as the "Bear Flaggers." She considered them lawless criminals and when they even stole various items from the Vallejo household she felt vindicated in her assessment of men whom she considered to be nothing more than well armed *cholos* (convicts). Her esteem went even lower when John Charles Frémont asked her to deliver a seventeen-year-old Indian servant girl for use by one of his officers in the barracks. Rosalía refused and continued to protect the girl.

While her husband was imprisoned in Sutter's Fort, Francisca Vallejo continued managing Mariano's ranchos. While not at first as hostile as her sister-in-law Rosalía, Francisca finally had to complain that the Americans were stealing Vallejo cattle and horses, the latter among the best in the country. [See Note # 18.] Doña Francisca also came to hate the Bear Flaggers and refer to them as *banditti*.

Apolinaria Lorenzana (*La Beata*, The Blessed) who became a well known teacher and nurse, testified how the Americans had swindled her out of her ranch lands.

Perhaps the best known of Californio women is **María de las Angustias de la Guerra**. [See Note # 19.] She was described as a woman of striking feminine beauty by R.H. Dana in *Two Years Before The Mast*. But María de las Angustias proved herself as more than just beautiful when, with "...a fearless presence of mind and socially knowledgeable..." she lamented Hispanic California as the "passing away of something loving and dear" in her *Ocurrencias en California*. Like so many other natives, the American takeover impoverished her and her Santa Barbara family. Further, at least one part of her writings have been subverted by mistranslation, according to Dr. Padilla. María de las Angustias wrote: "*..la toma del país no nos gustó nada a los Californios, y menos a las mujeres...*" which translates "the taking of the country did not please us Californios, and even less the women." According to Dr. Padilla, Francis Price and William Ellison translated it to read: "the conquest of California did not bother the Californians, least of all the women," exactly the opposite of what she said. [See Note # 20.] It is quite possible that María de las Angustias is recognized to this day for something she never said and to which she would have objected strenuously were she alive.

Ironically, among the Californio women who have most come to life in American culture is the fictionalized Señora **Gonzaga Moreno**, a personality out of the novel *Ramona* written by a genuine Yankee from Massachusetts, **Helen Hunt Jackson**. Jackson portrayed Señora Moreno as *So quiet, so* *reserved, so gentle an exterior never was known to veil such an imperious and passionate nature, brimful of storm, always passing through stress; never thwarted, except at the peril of those who did it; adored and hated by turn, and each at the hottest…How did this grandmotherly type feel about Americans? Any race under the sun would have been to the Señora less hateful than the Americans. She had scorned them in her girlhood when they came trading to post after post. She scorned them still…* [See Note # 21.]

MARIANO VALLEJO

It has been written that Mariano Vallejo of Sonoma was the best representation of a pro-American Californio. He started out as a soldier under the Mexican government and due to his abilities he advanced in rank and acquisition of land. By the age of twenty (1827) he was a Second Lieutenant (*alférez*) at the San Francisco presidio and a member of the *Diputación* (legislative body). In 1833 Governor José Figueroa assigned him to form a settlement in the interior and it came to be known as *Sonoma*. In 1835 he was appointed Commandant-General of Alta California. He has been described as perhaps the most powerful man in California by 1836.

In the 1840s Mariano Vallejo and his wife Francisca, parents of sixteen children, built up an estate that would encompass some 175,000 acres of land, thousands of cattle and fine horses, luxury homes and furnishings, a complete retinue of ranch hands and servants, perhaps the best library in California with books on history, science, the classics, etc., and enough money to provide schooling for his children in the eastern USA. He consistently loaned money to family, friends, and acquaintances. He was a pillar of Californio society, admired and respected by seemingly everybody.

A well educated man for the time and place, Mariano believed in the freedoms espoused by the USA. Even his first rude awakening, that of being imprisoned by the Bear Flaggers for such an extended period of time (some six weeks from June to August, 1846) that the six-foot Vallejo weighed under a hundred pounds by the end of his incarceration, did not seem to cool his ardor for American annexation, so long as the ludicrous Bear Flaggers were not in charge. (A son named **José Altamira**, whom Mariano had adopted, began to develop a fierce hatred of Americans when he learned of his father's imprisonment.) Upon Mariano's release he rid himself of his Mexican army uniforms and awaited "the cultural advances, economic opportunities, and splendid future" he expected under American rule. [See Note # 22.]

Realities were not encouraging. He found he had lost some thousand cattle and six hundred horses, along with valuable household items stolen by Fremont and his men along with the Bear Flaggers. To boot, his 350 acres of wheat had also been ruined. His only alternative was to work to get things back to normal and at this point in time he felt it would be better to remain aloof from political life. He wrote a letter to Thomas Oliver Larkin in which he stated he was interested only in farming/ranching activities, not in a position with the new government being formed. "As a private individual I will do what I can for the prosperity of the country." (He would be a delegate to the constitutional convention in 1849 and he was elected state senator in the same year. On September 9, 1850, California was admitted to the Union as the thirty-first state.) When other Californios began fighting (fall of 1846) the American invaders, Vallejo remained neutral.

By January of 1847, Vallejo's situation was as bleak as the weather. Frémont's men continued to rustle Californio livestock, including Vallejo's. But Americans wanted land and Mariano Vallejo owned lots of it, some of which he intended to sell them. He deeded a five-square-mile parcel of land on the Carquinez Straits to Robert Semple and Thomas Larkin with the hope the two would develop a port which would bring great value to his inland holdings. To the U.S. government he submitted a bill of $117,875 for the losses suffered during the war. (In 1855 he was compensated with $48,700.)

When James Marshall discovered gold on January 24, 1848, Mariano Vallejo was one of the first men outside of Sutter's Fort to learn about the rich strike. Salvador, Mariano's brother, went into the gold field and extracted a small fortune. But by 1849 the diggings were dangerous because Americans treated the Californios as trespassing *greasers* to be handled with violence.

Aside from the violence directed at "greasers and other foreigners," Vallejo and all Californios had to deal with cultural changes. The population grew at a phenomenal rate: 92,000 by 1850, a whooping 250,000 by the end of 1852. Mariano remarked on the differing nationalities now in California: Australia contributed "swarms of bandits dedicated to robbery and assault…France sent lying men and corrupt women…Italy send musicians and gardeners…Chile sent desirable laborers but some were addicted to gambling and drinking…China sent men who wanted to make money and return to China… but all paled in comparison to the 'torrent of shysters who came from Missouri and other states of the Union.' Upon arrival they 'assumed title of attorney' and began to divest Californios of their lands and homes…these legal thieves, clothed in the robes of the law, took from us our lands and our houses…" [See Note # 22.]

Mariano offered to donate significant land and money if the state capitol would be built at the town of Vallejo. A number of other sites were also considered but Sacramento was finally chosen in 1855. This was a huge disappointment for Mariano.

Mariano Vallejo opted not to run for another term as state senator. The militant squatters in his district would probably not have elected him so he withdrew from state government. He moved his family away from the hectic Sonoma plaza to a new residence a quarter mile away that came to be known as *Lachryma Montis*. The new house was a happy place but times were getting bad. By 1855 the gold rush was definitely fizzling: a cow worth $90 in 1852 sold for $16 in 1856. Cattle rustling and a serious drought in the late 1850s all but destroyed the Californio rancho system. Mariano Vallejo was forced into selling or mortgaging his land. American squatters tore down his fences, milked his cows during the night, stole his horses and cattle. Like the other Californios and their families, the Vallejos were traveling the roads of impoverishment and injustice, especially because of the U.S. Land Commission charged with adjudicating land titles. (See the chapter on Land Tenure.)

By the 1860s, Mariano's losses were surpassing his gains (like those of most other Californios throughout the State). While in public he was generally cheerful, in private he aired his disappointments. He now saw American society as more obsessed with money than personal freedom. He was everywhere losing to American lawyers and squatters who respected nothing except what they wanted. When visiting in New York he thought the people were "money mad." Upon his return to California he saw that money avaricious Americans, "hardened into an obsession with getting and hoarding money…" had overturned his world of family, kinship, civility. [See Note # 23.] He realized that Californios were being denigrated in the English language press so in 1867 he began writing his memoirs in an effort to portray California as it had honestly been. He had some 900 pages written when a fire destroyed his house on the Sonoma plaza, destroying the entire manuscript along with his some 12,000 books. It must have seemed that all Hispanic California was doomed.

Fortuitously, one ray of hope appeared in the person of **Enrique Cerruti**, one of H.H. Bancroft's field researchers in 1874. Cerruti sincerely wanted to record Mariano's perspectives on California history. For months Cerruti and Vallejo began to labor on (the five volume work that would become) *Recuerdos históricos y personales tocante a la alta California*. [See Note # 24.] This was just the beginning. There were two or three trunks full of documents, too many for Cerruti to copy alone so he asked Mariano to permit him to take the papers to San Francisco where Bancroft's people could copy each one carefully. Wary because he had been betrayed so many times before, Mariano Vallejo nevertheless consented to *give* all his historical documents to H.H. Bancroft. These papers (and those of a few others) were the way to preserve eternally the realities of Hispanic California and Vallejo and Bancroft fully understood that. [See Note # 25.] Further, while Bancroft was the writer of History, Vallejo was the embodiment of it and both men seemed to realize that too. After so much injustice, Mariano Vallejo had found a way to bequeath his eternal legacy to California.

An added joy turned out being going into the homes of other Californios who possessed official or family documents that could buttress his memoir. In the company of friends from Monterey, Santa Barbara, etc., the Californios talked long into the night, sharing documents and memories of halcyon days. Mariano was happy again when he visited his old friends, he was happy to write the truth about Hispanic California, happy to be researching and writing his people into historical significance. In December of 1874 he wrote to Platón: "My historical works continue their majestic march…" In 1875 he added: "…the truth impartially written so it can serve posterity as a guide." [See Note # 26.] He was able to speak from personal experience. For example, Vallejo was able to compare the Californio deputies of 1827 to Americans in the California Legislature of 1874. Californios considered it an honor to serve and took no pay for representing constituents. His estimate of the American legislators was that they were out to enrich themselves at the expense of the people they were supposed to be serving… "passing laws designed to make them rich, lying whenever it suits their ends, selling their votes to the highest bidder." [See Note # 27.]

Mariano Vallejo was a product of an Hispanic California which prided itself on generosity, hospitality, and ranchero economics. American California was now controlled by courts of law (which targeted Californio land), dog-eat-dog mistrust, and stingy people who cared only for themselves. Mariano projected a calm personality in public but he aired his grief in private when he wrote to his children, especially his son Platón (Plato).

While displaying outward equanimity, inside he was "burning in an abysmal inferno of griefs that have poisoned my blood." [See Note # 28.] It must have been immensely difficult to remember a magnificent Californio past while enduring dispossession in the American present (1870s).

Vallejo's custom of delegating authority to others, a feature of Californio culture, proved injurious when the people whom he trusted turned out working for themselves instead of Vallejo interests. He was able to hold on to his beloved Lachryma Montis estate (228 acres) and the home comforted him in old age. Unfortunately, his faith in historian H.H. Bancroft also turned into disappointment. When a crucial meeting of Californio leaders took place, described by Vallejo in his *Recuerdos*, Bancroft's published work expressed the sentiment that Vallejo's work was "…not only the most extensive but the most fascinating…like the works of Bandini, Osío, Alvarado, Pico and the rest…a strange mixture of fact and fancy." Vallejo wrote that if the *Recuerdos* weren't accurate history to send it back but like his land, the work now "legally" belonged to someone else: H.H. Bancroft, and he could use it or not as he saw fit.

Mariano Vallejo spoke often on California's Hispanic legacy, which he always referred to as a sterling pioneer achievement. Despite reversals in fortune, sometimes condemning the *ingratitude* of some American friends, he maintained his dignity and family as best he could. He died on January 18, 1890. Flags flew at half mast in his honor. [See Note # 29.]

COMMITTEE OF VIGILANCE OF SAN FRANCISCO

The American frontier in the West has often been characterized as lawless. California was no exception. The town of San Francisco in 1851 was wracked by thieves, thugs, and assorted hoodlums. A group known as the *Hounds* (also "Regulators") terrorized the city, seemingly at will. In a section referred to as Sydney Town, former convicts from Australia, called *Sydney Ducks*, lived by thievery, murder, and strong arm tactics. Worse still, authorities in charge of law enforcement appeared disinclined to address the situation. This gave rise to vigilantism: ordinary citizens banded together to enforce laws ignored by authorities. While "vigilance committees" believed they were "champions of justice," they have also been associated with *mobocracy* and *lynch law*. There are also definite patterns of racial prejudice/hatred, generally referred to euphemistically as *nativism* in standard historiography, in the workings of American vigilantes. For example, on July 15, 1849, the Hounds held a "patriotic parade" in San Francisco. Then groups made the rounds of bars where they demanded free liquor and if they didn't get it they smashed windows. They turned their attention to some Chilean families living in tents, brutally beating numbers of them, even opening fire on some. [See Note # 30.]

Indignant merchants, property owners, and civic leaders like **Sam Brannan** got together to form their own tribunal because they knew the authorities would take no action. In a citizens' court they found various Hounds guilty of disturbing the peace and banished them from San Francisco.

Lawlessness continued: in February of 1851 a well known merchant named Jansen was assaulted in his own store and the contents of his safe burglarized. The community finally roused from its lethargy and on June 10, 1851, the Committee of Vigilance of San Francisco was organized. **William T. Coleman**, a young merchant, became one of its leaders. Many others signed up, men with names like Woodworth, Gorham, Oakes, Mahony, Webster, Davis, Ward, Thompson, Jones, Watson, Winter, King, Mellus, Huie, Howard, Stevenson, Payran, Lammot, Ryckman, McDuffee, etc. The vigilantes soon numbered in the hundreds because citizens were fed up with lawlessness. Their headquarters became the Monumental Fire Engine House and the signal to gather was ringing the fire bell.

A Sydney Duck named John Jenkins broke into a shipping office and audaciously walked down the street carrying the strongbox he had stolen. When vigilantes tried to stop him he threw the strongbox into the bay. Jenkins was finally taken into custody and given a trial. He was found guilty and sentenced to be hung by the neck until dead. He was taken out and hung from a hastily erected scaffold.

On July 11, 1851, the fire bell summoned everyone to the trial of another Sydney Duck, one "English Jim" Stuart, a career criminal. He was found guilty and hung aboard a ship anchored in the bay.

Charges were brought against Samuel Whittaker and Robert McKenzie, two known Sydney Duck criminals. They confessed and were condemned but Sheriff Jack Hays, the former Texas Ranger, was able to get them into his jail for safety. The vigilantes were able to abduct them and shortly Whittaker and McKenzie were executed by hanging as some 6,000 people looked on. [See Note # 31.]

Most newspapers endorsed the actions of the vigilantes but the real power emanated from the people as represented by the Committee membership which numbered some 600 at one time. For the legal authorities to bring charges of murder against members it would have had to indict so many people there might well have been an armed rebellion. All told the Vigilance Committee hanged four men, whipped one, deported fourteen, handed over fifteen to the authorities, found some forty-two innocent. Activities ceased in June of 1852.

It has also been pointed out that San Francisco vigilante activities encouraged people in the interior of the State, especially the mining camps. Lynch courts were active and foreigners were often victims, as in the lynching of Juanita at Downieville. So-called vigilantes also used their mob power to chase foreigners out of the gold fields. White thieves, murderers, prostitutes, etc., were also targeted and a presumption of guilt was generally enough to get a conviction which could result in whipping, ear cropping, or execution.

FRANCISCO P. RAMÍREZ

One of the several newspapers that were popular during the latter 1850s was *El Clamor Público* whose editor was a twenty-year old named Francisco Ramírez. Unlike most newspapers, *El Clamor Público* was able to articulate the views of native Californios. [See Note # 32.] These editions appeared during the years 1855-1859, described as the most violent years in all of California history. Hispanophobia reached a peak during these years and *El Clamor Público* was generally the only publication openly to confront this racism.

Little is known about Francisco Ramírez. [See Note # 33.] He was a practicing Catholic, quite rational in his thinking with secular leanings. It is possible he attended school in Mexico. While Francisco exhibited the typical fervor of youth, he owned no land or cattle and probably wasn't a product of the upper classes, though he was fluent in Spanish, French, and English. His experience in newspaper work was gathered while working for the Los Angeles *Star*. It appears he was repelled by some of the Star's racist editorials so he quit his job in June of 1855 and began publishing his own Spanish-language weekly devoted to Hispanic themes. For the years 1855-59 Ramírez wrote, edited, and published his *El Clamor Público*. The weekly was intended to appeal to all Latin Americans as well as Frenchmen who numbered some 400 in Los Ángeles alone. Americans also seemed to read it with interest, even advertising in it to get (what they referred to as) "the serape trade."

Young Ramírez wasn't afraid to criticize but he also endorsed democratic ideals espoused in the American Declaration of Independence and Constitution. [See Note # 34.] His weekly was dedicated to moral and material progress, law and order, popular government, peace, civil rights, etc. He believed in California and its brilliant future because it had the beauties of Switzerland and the fertility of the Nile Valley. During his four years of publication he editorialized on myriads of topics from prostitution to anti-Catholicism, Manifest Destiny to filibusterism, etc., and most unusual for the time and place, he denounced slavery and the restrictions which some Americans wanted to place on free Negroes. For the time and place, this was downright *radical*. [See Note # 35.]

The Los Ángeles Star accused Ramírez of exaggerating the plight of Hispanics in California while at the same time it editorialized comments like *"...Last Saturday night the tendencies of our Mexican population toward armed riot, scuffling and robbery, seemed to develop completely."* Ramírez protested including all Mexican people when a small group did something wrong. This kind of courage raised the ire of L.A. Assemblyman Joseph L. Brent in 1857 when he accused Ramírez of "...disseminating sentiments of treason and antipathy among the native population." Francisco replied that speaking up against injustice was not treason to the USA. He also added that the many of the laws now in force were "...hypocritical, unfair, and even brutal to the Spanish-speaking..." Americans weren't living up to their own Constitution, not even to ordinary standards of decency. American California didn't appear to hold life sacred and charged that all kinds of outrages were permitted against Latin Americans. Ramírez asserted that American lawyers, sheriffs, judges and jurymen violated their nation's high ideals. There were plenty of good laws but little will to put them into effect. Authorities often refused to prosecute, courts often ignored the intent of the law, and criminals went free on mere technicalities.

Francisco was not shy about expressing himself on subjects few others would broach. For example, on one occasion he wrote: "World history tells us that the Anglo-Saxons were in the beginning thieves and pirates, the same as other nations in their infancy...the pirate instinct of old Anglo-Saxons is still active." [See Note # 36.]

As a "crusading editor" Francisco Ramírez brought out myriads of topics, including Hispanic history like Francisco López being the first to discover gold in California. He criticized the policy of targeting Mexicans for violence in the diggings, condemned lynchings and kangaroo courts. He berated Californios for staying with the Democratic Party (Francisco was a Republican) when all it did was take them for granted. Further, in the election of 1856 Ramírez could not support James Buchanan because the former Secretary of State "...had expressed vicious sentiments toward non-Anglo-Saxons, in particular opposing the annexation of Texas because its Negroes and dark-skinned Mexicans might mingle with too much liberty there." Francisco felt that Democrats openly condemned Latin Americans and Negroes as a matter of policy. So he supported John Charles Frémont for the presidency (who lost).

Ramírez lauded the virtues of work. He detested the seemingly ubiquitous American saloons, gambling halls, and brothels. He constantly supported public education and asserted that *educating our children* should be a top priority. Furthermore, *girls* should also be included in educational endeavors. As with his stance on civil rights, this was indeed *radical* for the place and time because Americans held women virtually on par with chattel. He believed the English language should be learned now that California was under American domination. He considered English absolutely essential in order to protect Californio lands, stock, and ranches from American sharpers who were fleecing Hispanos. He spoke up for publishing new laws also in Spanish instead of only English. How could Spanish speaking Californios understand the laws if they couldn't read them? The Legislature refused (this in 1857 when speaking English was relatively new).

At the end of 1859 Francisco Ramírez printed his last issue of *El Clamor Público*. He went to Mexico where he became the official printer for the state of Sonora (1860-62). In 1864 he was back in Los

Ángeles serving as postmaster. In 1865 he was appointed official state translator. In 1872 he edited the Spanish language weekly *La Crónica* for a time then the record is unclear as to his activities.

AGRICULTURE

The citrus fruit industry got its start when the Franciscan missionaries introduced fruit trees into mission gardens. Cattle raising continued as the basic California industry along with the raising of wheat and cotton. After the American takeover citrus fruits like oranges, lemons, tangerines, and grapefruit took on greater importance.

William Wolfskill, a trapper from Kentucky, planted two acres of oranges in the Los Ángeles area in 1841. He was successful in selling his oranges so he expanded his operation to seventy acres. In 1877 he sent a trainload of oranges to St. Louis via the Southern Pacific Railroad. The oranges arrived in good condition and Wolfskill made a handsome profit. He continued to export his crops, one shipment netting him some $23,000, and other growers began to follow his example by expanding their acreages.

In 1870 one (Judge) **John Wesley North** bought (on credit) some four thousand acres of hilly, desert-like terrain in the Riverside area. He launched a promotional campaign to bring in settlers from Michigan and Iowa. A few immigrants settled the area in 1871 and commenced planting thousands of orange seedlings.

In 1873 **Luther Calvin Tibbets** and his wife **Eliza** introduced the "Washington Navel" orange which in fact emanated from the Bahía, Brazil, area. [See Note # 37.] Eliza nurtured the cuttings they had brought to California and in time the meaty, juicy, Navel orange spread throughout the citrus areas and became the most popular variety of orange.

Large scale growers soon recognized the need to organize because middlemen (speculators, commission agents, railroad companies, etc.) were taking most of the profit. A loose cooperative was formed by growers in 1893, which grew into the Southern California Fruit Growers Exchange in 1895 and developed into the California Fruit Growers Exchange in 1905. One of the organization's major accomplishments was to convince the American public that a glass of orange juice was an integral part of an American breakfast. Oranges came to be identified with California and a popular saying became "Oranges for health; California for wealth."

A number of valley "garden spots" were discovered in California: Livermore, Napa, Salinas, San Luis, Napa, San Bernardino, etc. Spanish missionaries had introduced both black and green olives during mission days. Olive oil was essential for California cuisine and olive production has grown to the present day.

Walnuts were also first grown by the mission padres and the industry has continued to expand as has the production of almonds. French and Italian prunes were introduced into the Santa Clara Valley. Peaches, apples, cherries, apricots, pears, grapes, plums, etc., also became important crops as California agriculture became a bread-basket for the nation. [See Note # 38.]

Luther Burbank carried on agricultural experiments from 1875 until his death in 1926. His autobiography, *The Harvest Of Years*, provides many details which were later used to increase California agricultural production. This production also gave rise to a powerful canning industry.

As with most basic California crops, the mission padres were the first to introduce vineyards and the wine industry. German immigrants founded Anaheim in 1857 and planted some 400,000 vines.

In 1851 a Hungarian named **Agoston Haraszthy** introduced the zinfandel grape into Sonoma. Two Frenchmen, **Etienne Thée** and **Charles Lefranc** founded the Almaden Vineyards at Los Gatos. In 1858 one **Charles Krug**, founder of the first German language newspaper on the West coast, bought land from Haraszthy, planted vines, then two years later moved to the Napa Valley where he founded a winery which became famous.

By the 1880s the largest number of grape acreage was owned by the Italian-Swiss Agricultural Colony at Asti. Founded mostly by Italians, whose heritage included excellent wine production, this colony prospered after the first lean years.

California wines became well known throughout the world as vineyard acreage increased dramatically. The Prohibition era halted this flourishing industry but it resumed upon repeal of the law.

RACE PROBLEMS

Immigrants from all over the world contributed to the development of California. It would be logical to assume that such an environment would soften the American tendency toward racism but this was not the case in California. As has already been mentioned, Native Americans were all but exterminated, the few survivors being placed on miniscule reservations. Hispanics, including native Californios but especially those from Mexico, were often targeted for violence. But no group was more mistreated than Orientals, especially the Chinese.

The first group of Chinese arrived in 1847 and by 1865 it is said there were some 60,000 in the state. They had the same motivation as everybody else: they wanted to make money, especially in the gold fields. Not wanting the competition, Americans passed laws to discourage them. They were barred from working on the Mother Lode. They were forced to pay a $2 per head miner's tax even to work the tailings, a $2 water tax, a $2 school tax, a hospital tax, an additional personal tax, and a property tax. (It has been written that Chinamen paid some two million dollars in taxes.) They could not become citizens, could not attend public schools, could not vote, and couldn't testify in court. If any Chinese dared to enter a new mining field the Americans would beat them, rob them, sometimes kill them. It was considered recreation to fight the Chinese, cut off their pigtails (which meant death in China), and to abuse them generally. [See Note # 39.] The expression, "Not a Chinaman's chance" became indicative of an impossible situation. They were called *coolies* (unskilled labor), an expression picked up by the British in India and passed on to Americans. Politicians vied with each other as to who hated Chinamen the most. While running for governor in the 1862 election Leland Stanford referred to Chinese as the dregs of Asia and stated: *The Chinese Must Go!* He won the election. [See Note # 40.]

It has been said the Chinese were hated for their virtues. They were more honest than Americans, more hard working, reliable, sober, and caring over how they did their work. They saved their money and kept working. They could read and write, they possessed a certain spirit of adventure, and they learned quickly. No one wanted to hire an Irishmen, German, Englishman, Italian, etc., if they could get a Chinese. Americans resented their successes. As of 1858 the California legislature banned all Chinese immigration but they came anyway.

By 1867 "anti-coolie clubs" were strong enough to take the law into their own hands and punish any

Oriental while law enforcement merely looked on. In December of 1867 a number of Chinese were brutally driven out of French Corral in Nevada County and their cabins destroyed. Some 27 Americans were arrested for the mob violence, 26 were acquitted and one man was fined $100. On October 23, 1871, some twenty Chinese were massacred in a Los Ángeles race riot. American authorities ignored the killings because Chinese were generally regarded as "vicious, depraved, pagans," the "Yellow Peril," threats to "Christian values and Republican government." [See Note # 41.]

When the USA took over Hawaii in 1898 large numbers of Japanese and Chinese entered the USA. By 1910 there were some 71,000 Japanese in the country and Californians voiced their anti-Japanese sentiments. The *Asiatic Exclusion League of San Francisco* was created in 1905. In 1906 the San Francisco Board of Education recommended that Japanese and Chinese students should attend their own schools, separate from those of whites, but the recommendation was not acted upon due to the earthquake disaster of that year. The *Japanese and Korean Exclusion League* was founded and it advocated separate schools for Orientals. The Japanese government protested vigorously and President Theodore Roosevelt ordered his Attorney General to see to it that Orientals in California were treated like all other Americans. But agitation continued.

Japanese were charged with being "ambitious, aggressive, alert, acquisitive, efficient, shrewd, conniving," etc. Further, they weren't content with mere labor. They soon bought land for themselves and became highly productive farmers. Americans didn't like the competition so in 1913 the California legislature passed the Webb Act (California Alien Land Act) that worked to deny certain Japanese immigrants the right to own land (i.e., "Aliens not eligible for citizenship may inherit or devise real estate only as prescribed by treaty..."). The Japanese government formally protested the discrimination once more. In California the Webb Act was neutralized by Japanese leasing land from "regular" citizens. Large truck-farms were developed in which the Japanese grew lettuce, celery, beans, tomatoes, strawberries, etc. Americans continued to fear the Japanese as real economic threats.

RAILROADS

The Central Pacific was considered by many Californians to be the "third party" in State politics. It was charged that the railroad operated basically free from control or regulation. Railroad lobbyists worked assiduously to maintain the Southern Pacific monopoly on rates and services. For example, when the Legislature was in session in Sacramento, lobbyist William F. Herrin saw to it that all legislators were provided with free weekend round-trip tickets to San Francisco for the entire session. Most newspapers were also friendly to railroad interests because the railroad men understood the value of controlling public opinion. Farmers, ranchers, and small shippers resented the railroad, charging that large or favored shippers were given under-the-table rebates.

The "Colton Letters" were made public in 1883. The letters consisted of some 213 business letters written by Collis Huntington to David D. Colton, a close business associate of Huntington, Stanford, and Crocker. When Colton died in 1878, his widow was dissatisfied with the settlement offered for her husband's efforts. She sued and the "Colton Letters" were used in court to show how Huntington had corrupted state and national officeholders to get his legislation passed. When published by the San Francisco *Chronicle* and the New York *World* the letters exposed Huntington's successful use of money to promote legislation favorable to the railroad. In 1887 Huntington was called before the United States Railway Commission. He stated that his efforts served the people of California, that he "*practiced the usual methods known among business men to accomplish certain objects…My record as a business man is pretty well known among business men and there is nothing in it I am ashamed of.*" [See Note # 42.] It also came out that the **Big Four** (Charles Crocker, Collis Huntington, Mark Hopkins, and Leland Stanford, each of whom amassed fortunes in excess of $50,000,000) had voted themselves huge dividends but no attempt had been made to pay the government loans used to acquire these fortunes.

Hopkins died in 1878, Crocker in 1888, Stanford in 1893. Huntington lived until 1900 and his fortune was estimated at around $70,000,000. It was said his railroads could have connected the North and South poles, that he could travel from Virginia to San Francisco without stepping off his own railroad lines. He owned timber lands, sawmills, steamship lines, coal mines, etc. Through it all he maintained that his railroad was basically a public service to the people of California and America. He continued to state publicly that no impropriety had occurred during his lobbying efforts, that he operated under prevailing business ethics.

Under the guidance of **William Randolph Hearst**, the San Francisco *Examiner* targeted Huntington with cannonades of criticism, questioning his honesty, exposing his vindictiveness, his lack of concern for everything except his railroad. The cartoons accompanying the *Examiner* articles, like the one with Huntington leading the Governor around on a leash, did as much damage as the articles themselves.

The "Free Harbor Fight" (1893-96) was one of the few defeats suffered by the Collis Huntington interests. A deep harbor was needed in the Los Ángeles area and Huntington favored Santa Monica because the Southern Pacific controlled all railroads going into it. A "Free Harbor League" group was created to direct all government funding to build the harbor at San Pedro, away from railroad interests. After a three year battle led by Senator Stephen M. White, San Pedro was chosen as the deep harbor site for Los Ángeles.

Collis Huntington's nephew, Henry E. Huntington, sold the Southern Pacific to E.H. Harriman (who ran it much as Huntington had). Perhaps in an effort to erase past stigmas, the nephew founded the magnificent *Henry E. Huntington Library and Art Gallery* in San Marino, one of the greatest libraries in the West.

POLITICS and GOVERNMENT

By 1900 it appeared that Californians and the American people were ready to reform all levels of government. Charles Evans Hughes became known as a reformer in New York, Robert M. La Follette in Wisconsin, etc. **Lincoln Steffens**, who spent his boyhood in Sacramento and became the best known of the *muckrakers*, published a series of articles which exposed corruption in city after city. Later collected under the title of *The Shame Of The Cities*, Steffens documented how business interests were immorally allied with politicians for the material gain of both.

In San Francisco the Union Labor Party was voted in and **Eugene E. Schmitz**, a theater musician, was installed as mayor in 1902. The real power was held by one **Abraham Ruef**, a "shrewd" lawyer who started out as a reformer but who turned opportunist. Schmitz and Ruef collected bribes, blackmailed and extorted money from businesses under the guise of protection, forced businesses to purchase licenses to sell liquor or cigars, operate gambling halls, bilked French restaurants which fronted for prostitution, forced municipal employees, utilities companies, streetcar owners, etc., to pay kickbacks. Ruef and Schmitz were so successful they planned to run for Senator and Governor.

SAN FRANCISCO EARTHQUAKE and FIRE

At 5:16 a.m. on April 18, 1906, a massive earthquake hit along the San Andreas Fault from Cape Mendocino in northern California to Salinas in the south. The loud rumbling was followed by horrendous creaking and grinding as buildings separated from their foundations. Bricks cascaded into the street and those that didn't fall were on the verge of doing so. Electric wires hit the ground and started fires that rampaged in every direction. Firemen and myriads of volunteers attached fire hoses to hydrants but no water came out because water pipes had been busted by the quake. (It was also learned later that a number of fire hydrants had never even been hooked into the city water system.) Despite so much human effort, the fires spread for three days and two nights before the tragedy was brought under control. Now looking like a war zone, some four square miles had been destroyed, over five hundred city blocks, including banks, churches, businesses, etc. The property loss was estimated at $200,000,000 and some 452 people had perished. There were some 300,000 homeless people to help and for weeks they had to live in Army tents wherever they could be set up. Relief came in from all over the world and the Red Cross helped in the distribution of food and medicine.

The San Francisco earthquake caused a massive rebuilding program but it also motivated a drive to end corrupt city government. Graft prosecutions were spearheaded by Francis J. Heney, William J. Burns, Fremont Older, and Rudolph Spreckels. The prosecutions lasted more than two years. It was no simple process. The house of a principal prosecution witness was blown up. Documents needed in court were stolen by persons unknown. One prospective juror shot Prosecutor Heney in the head, almost killing him.

Abe Ruef was finally sentenced to 14 years on a charge of bribery. He served four-years-seven-months. Mayor Schmitz' prison sentenced was reversed by the state Supreme Court due to a technicality. Fremont Older became convinced that, while front men like Ruef had been caught, others just as guilty as he had gotten off scot free. [See Note # 43.]

California in general and Los Ángeles immediately profited from the prevailing spirit of municipal reform. Under the leadership of Dr. John Haynes and other civic minded Angelinos, the Los Ángeles charter included the measures of initiative, referendum, and recall. Mayor Arthur C. Harper was re-called in 1907, the first use of recall in the USA. Governor Gray Davis was recalled in 2003 and replaced by body-builder/actor Arnold Scharzenegger.

HUBERT HOWE BANCROFT

It is doubtful that any American historian produced more books than Hubert Howe Bancroft. His "The History Company" compiled thirty-nine volumes, some 30,000 pages, which ranged from Alaska to Latin America. Dr. Charles E. Chapman has written that *Bancroft's works constitute the greatest single achievement in the history of American historiography.* [See Note # 44.]

Bancroft, an independently wealthy bookseller and publisher from San Francisco, operated his workshop between 1875 and 1890. He was able to hire talented interviewers, researchers, collectors, writers, etc., to compile his thirty-nine volumes. While it is generally agreed that Bancroft had a directing hand in every volume, other staff writers did much of the work. For example, **Henry Labbeus Oak** is thought to have written most of the *California* and *North Mexican States* volumes. It is unfortunate that Bancroft did not assign specific credit to specific writers but there is no doubt the workshop produced a wealth of history volumes under his direction and personal effort. His multi-volume works are titled as follows: *The Native Races; History of Central America; History of Mexico; History of the North Mexican States and Texas; History of Arizona and New Mexico; History of California; History of Nevada, Colorado, and Wyoming; History of Utah; History of the Northwest Coast; History of Oregon; History of British Columbia; History of Alaska; California Pastoral; California Inter Pocula; Popular Tribunals; Essays and Miscellany; Literary Industries.* As indicated, these compilations stand alone in scope and stature, unequaled in American historiography. Bancroft's books are quoted by almost everyone writing about the West. His works on California have been unsurpassed to this day.

Among other historians who have earned their niche in California historiography are Herbert E. Bolton, Charles E. Chapman, Alfred L. Kroeber, Herbert. I. Priestley, Robert G. Cleland, John W. Caughey, Henry R. Wagner, Carl Wheat, etc.

OIL INDUSTRY

While there is no basic agreement as to where California's first significant oil discovery was made it is verifiable that an oil well was drilled in Humboldt County, near Petrolia, in 1861. By 1864 the price for crude oil in Pennsylvania had gone from $3 to $14 per barrel. Two companies in Philadelphia and New York formed the Philadelphia & California Petroleum Company and drilled the first well in southern California in 1865. The California Star Oil Company began drilling in the 1870s. Most efforts were not profitable and few companies survived the speculation stage of the industry.

Profitability in oil began in the early 1890s when **Lyman Stewart** and **Edward L. Doheny** became active. Stewart and his partner, Wallace L. Hardison, suffered through lean years while prospecting for oil but with T.R. Bard the men formed the Union Oil Company in 1890 and in 1892 discovered the marvelous "Wild Bill" well in Adams Canyon (Ventura County). Within a few years Union Oil dominated the California industry.

Edward L. Doheny arrived in Los Ángeles in 1892 and with a friend named Charles A. Canfield leased a certain city lot on which a driller brought in a well that produced 45 barrels a day. Within the next five years some 2,300 wells were drilled in the Los Ángeles area. By 1897 production was at 1,400,000 barrels per year and by 1902 it was 9,000,000. The greatest California oil strikes were made (1920) at Huntington Beach and at Santa Fe Springs (1921) and Signal Hill. As in the gold rush, a few people got rich while most got nothing.

Surplus oil soon glutted the market. Other markets had to be found and one proved to be the railroads converting from the use of coal to fuel oil. Another important breakthrough was paving with asphalt. The greatest development was using gasoline for motor cars.

Scandal became part of oil development in California. For example, Ed Doheny wanted the Elk Hills reserves so he sent his "old friend" Secretary of the Interior **Albert B. Fall** $100,000. (Because he ruled at Interior, Fall controlled the Elk Hill reserves and the Teapot Dome area in Wyoming.) In 1923 Fall and Doheny were indicted for bribery and conspiracy to control national resources. In 1928 Albert B. Fall was convicted of taking Doheny's bribe. Ironically, Doheny was found not guilty of giving Fall a bribe.

CONSERVATION

John Muir has been described as the most popular of California naturalists. Born in Scotland, he was educated in the United States then spent much of his life roaming the California back country. He soon became influential in defending forests like the magnificent redwoods and Sequoias, the mountains, and all kinds of wildlife. One person whom he influenced greatly was President Theodore Roosevelt. Muir died in 1914 but his books remained popular. Other prominent naturalists would include the brothers Joseph and John Le Conte, David S. Jordan, and Clarence King.

California created a State Conservation Commission in 1911 and the State Water Commission in 1913. Conservation practices made serious advances in the science of reforestation because lumber companies had denuded great areas of forest lands. In 1924-25 alone the California Forest Protective Association is said to have planted some million and a half young redwoods, Douglas firs, spruce, cedar, etc.

National and State parks were also developed during these years and the movement took root. Between the two World Wars some twenty-two national forests were created, along with four national parks, eight national monuments, and some 150 State recreational areas.

LABOR & MANAGEMENT

It has been written that the labor movement in California began with the American takeover and has been "convulsed by violent struggles." The struggle has been described as responsible for "the marked political instability of California." [See Note # 45.]

Laboring people valued joint action when confronting Management so the latter formed "associations of employers" with which to combat "federations of unions." Sailors in the San Francisco area are said to have been the first (1850) to organize. California labor was also active in politics and the Union Labor Party dominated San Francisco politics for some ten years. Indeed, by 1900 San Francisco was the stronghold of trade unions in the USA, probably the most highly organized city in the country. The power base was small shopkeepers, much of the rural population, and various white-collar workers. Chinese were restricted to low paying, undesirable jobs but wages in many other jobs were high. The threat of Asiatic competition is said to have unified Labor. [See Note # 46.] The threat from Chinese and Japanese people, real or imagined, drove many Californians to align themselves with the working class (so long as they weren't Oriental workers).

Foreign born workers brought their organizational knowledge to California. German brewers, bakers, etc., organized unions immediately. Men from Scandinavia formed the Sailors' Union. When a particular activity boomed, high wages were demanded and usually obtained, despite serious conflict. Seasonal laborers involved in harvesting, canning, processing, etc., were more vulnerable because their employment would expand or contract depending on the season. For example, agricultural crops had to be picked, processed, and shipped at specific times. Employers didn't want labor problems during these peak periods so they opposed organized labor actions in general.

The urban centers of San Francisco and Los Ángeles dominated California economic life. The struggle between organized capital and organized labor had its seamy underside. Ship owners in San Francisco used *crimping* methods ("procuring sailors through fraud, decoy, violence, etc.;" the term *shanghai* originated in San Francisco, not China). It is said these "strong-arm tactics" encouraged radicalism among working people. The socialist International Workingmen's Association was important in the 1880s. From 1905-1920 the Industrial Workers of the World played a key role. The Communist Party was a factor from 1920-1940 and the Socialist Party was strong in Los Ángeles. It came to be that Labor spoke for great numbers of Californians even if they were not directly a part of the Labor movement.

Carey McWilliams has written that there were various important "major labor-capital battles in California." From 1886 to 1893 Management worked to destroy the power of labor unions. In 1886 a serious waterfront strike brought on virtual warfare between employers and workers. In 1890 there was a bitter fight between the Iron Trades Council (workers) and the Engineers' and Foundrymen's Association (employers). The Board of Manufacturers and Employers, and all-inclusive employers group, was formed in 1891 with the intention of breaking up unions. Also in 1891 the Coast Seamen's Union was formed to cover the entire Pacific Coast. Directed from San Francisco, it had agents in every port. In 1893 the unions lost ground when a bomb exploded in front of a non-union boarding house, killing some eight men and wounding many others.

A second round of violent struggle began in July of 1901 when waterfront workers struck once more. Harbors were crippled for three months, some five men were killed and perhaps 300 assaulted. Both sides exhausted themselves but the unions emerged stronger from the battles.

In 1910 there were strikes by brewery workers, metal workers, and street railway workers. The Merchants' and Manufacturers' Association sponsored an anti-picketing ordinance (which inspired all other such ordinances in the country). By July 16, 1910, some 470 workers had been arrested but juries acquitted them without exception.

On October 1, 1910, the Los Ángeles Times building was dynamited and twenty-one men lost their lives in the explosion. Most people in Los Ángeles turned against the unions when the community learned the tragedy was union sponsored.

In 1916 longshoremen went on strike and bottled up millions of dollars in exports. A bomb went off on July 22, 1916 ("Preparedness Day bombing"), and ten people were killed. When it was learned that strikers had set the bomb, San Francisco voted in an anti-picketing ordinance. The cause of labor was thus set back for at least twenty years in California.

INDUSTRIAL WORKERS of the WORLD

The "revolutionary" organization known as the *wobblies* became involved in a free speech issue. By 1910 the Industrial Workers of the World had eleven locals in the State and some 1,000 members. One Frank Little, an organizer from Fresno, was arrested and jailed on October 16, 1910, after an outdoor meeting in which he spoke. In subsequent meetings as many as 50 people were arrested. Fire hoses were used on the prisoners in order to make them stop singing in jail. (Wobbly headquarters were burned down.) after six months mediation procedures were finally put in place and those arrested were set free.

On January 8, 1912, San Diego adopted an ordinance which limited free speech. While the wobblies had only some 50 members there as many as 5,000 people demonstrated against the ordinance. Many were arrested, one Michael Hoy was "kicked to death while in jail," while one Joe Mikolash was shot and killed. Police and vigilantes rounded up demonstrators, beat them with clubs and fires hoses, drove them out of town. Governor Hiram Johnson finally sent in an investigator who corroborated the fact that free speech was the central issue, thus vindicating the wobblies.

While the wobblies utilized anti-Oriental prejudice, they did have significant influence in the plight of seasonal workers in California. On August 13, 1913, there occurred the Wheatland "hop pickers" riot in which four people were killed. The subsequent investigation exposed facts like the following: some 2,800 hop pickers, of diverse nationalities, had been recruited by ads to work on a large agricultural ranch. Many were women and children. Once on the scene, workers were informed wages would vary from day to day. The promised bonus was actually a "hold-back" which would be forfeited if the worker quit employment. Daily earnings were from 90 cents to $1 per hour. There were eight (8) toilets for the some 2,800 people and no separate toilets for females. The riot started when uniformed law officers tried to break up a protest meeting which the wobblies had called on the ranch.

The Wheatland Riot marked a significant beginning of intense labor strife in the California agricultural industry. It brought national attention to the plight of farm workers and exposed the "festering cancer" of farm labor problems in the Golden State.

GREAT DEPRESSION

Beginning with the stock market collapse in October of 1929, the American economy began a downward spiral. While the administration of Herbert Hoover maintained that *prosperity is right around the corner*, unemployment spread throughout the nation. Californians responded to Franklin Delano Roosevelt during the 1932 presidential election and FDR easily took the state on election day.

Roosevelt's "New Deal" was launched around concepts like the "Three R's:" Relief, Recovery, Reform. While programs were being put into place formerly prosperous industries, farms, housing developments, etc., were going bankrupt. [See Note # 47.] Worried depositors took their money out of banks and many were on the verge of failing. On March 2, 1933, Governor James Rolph, Jr., ordered the closing of all banks for a three day "holiday" then extended it for another three.

During the years 1935-39 some 350,000 migrant workers, the "Okies" and "Arkies," descended on California looking for work. Their plight was described by John Steinbeck in his well known *Grapes Of Wrath*. Already pressed Californians passed a law which closed the border to migrants (overturned by the Supreme Court in 1941, long after the unconstitutional law had done its job). At least a third of all Mexicans in California were rounded up and deported to Mexico. It has been written that the deportees numbered from 500,000 to 600,000 people. [See Note # 48.] Filipinos were also targeted as in the Watsonville riot of 1930 and Salinas in 1934.

The Great Depression also gave birth to "utopian schemes" like the *Technocracy* espoused by one Howard Scott, where "technical experts" would be in control of government and industry. Crusading author and journalist **Upton Sinclair** advocated a monthly pension ($50) for all widows, the aged, and physically handicapped. He also espoused graduated inheritance and income taxes, taxes on unused land, etc. In 1934 Dr. Francis E. Townsend proposed a monthly pension of $200 for every person sixty years of age or older, an amount which had to be completely spent within a three month period. It has been said that utopian schemes like those mentioned above were symptomatic of the crushing despair of the Depression years.

Organized labor also had serious troubles. **Harry Bridges,** an Australian-born longshoreman, attracted much attention in San Francisco when he emerged as a labor leader in the 1930s. His enemies considered him a radical, even a Communist. His leadership was authoritarian but effective. In 1934 he led a strike that virtually shut down the ports from San Diego to Seattle. Arbitration was difficult, even when President Roosevelt tried for a settlement. On July 5, 1934, violence erupted in San Francisco when police used tear gas against picket lines. Two picketers were shot to death and more than a hundred men were injured. As a show of solidarity and protest, some 150,000 workers in various fields stopped work for three days. "Bloody Thursday" paralyzed San Francisco like it hadn't been since the earthquake of 1906. The governor called out the National Guard, some 5,000 men, "to protect state property." [See Note # 49.] In 1836 demands were made that Harry Bridges be deported. The Dies Committee on Un-American Activities charged that many unions were under Communist leadership, etc., and it was charged that Bridges himself was a Communist using the unions for purposes of the Communist Party. Bridges was vindicated in court and he retained his power along the Pacific Coast. There was hope: by the end of the 1930s the two sides understood that cooperation was more mutually beneficial than strikes and violence.

It has been said that **William Randolph Hearst** is also representative of the Depression years. Born into a wealthy family in San Francisco in 1863, Hearst attended Harvard and at the age of twenty-four was given the San Francisco *Examiner* to manage, which he made the most powerful newspaper on the west coast. A reformist-crusader while young, as he aged he came to believe that unions were ruining the country, that State and national government was getting too strong, that New Dealers were dangerous, etc. He came to own some thirty newspapers (which, it has been said, thrived on "yellow journalism), thirteen magazines, many radio stations, etc. He built his San Simeon estate as the headquarters for his operations. Famous guests from the movies, literature, art, music, public affairs, etc., were often Heart's guests at San Simeon, which was more like a museum than a home. In 1935 his fortune was estimated at some $200,000,000. It is said that Orson Welles' 1940 film "Citizen Kane" was based on William Randolph Hearst.

HOLLYWOOD and the MOVIES

It is highly probably that the most famous of all California industries is the making of motion pictures. Movies are considered basic Americana and have exerted inestimable influences throughout the country and the world. [See Note # 50.]

The rapid industrial expansion and subsequent urban growth that took place in the early 20th century saw the rise of nickelodeon entertainment in America (as well as France, England, etc.). Though technically crude, nickelodeon "movies" were enjoyed by immigrants and working classes. There was a definite need for mass entertainment and technological advances were on the way.

Invention of the motion picture camera is usually accorded to **Thomas A. Edison** (and his workshop of inventors). Their Kinetoscope machine was first exhibited in the 1893 World's Fair in Chicago. Film production developed basically around New York and New Jersey.

During the 'teens and 20s feature-length pictures broke away from previous entertainment styles and emphasized uplifting themes like the value of home and family, Christian behavior, patriotism, etc. An assortment of small, competing enterprises in time merged into a few very dominant corporations. The cinema flourished as it developed into a highly efficient industry. The USA emerged as the leading producer and distributor of popular movie fare and Hollywood became a fixation in the popular mind.

In 1887 **Harvey H. Wilcox** registered his 120-acre ranch just northwest of Los Ángeles. His wife **Daeida** named it *Hollywood*. In 1903 Hollywood is incorporated as a municipality and the Hollywood Hotel is built. In order to be assured of a water supply, residents of Hollywood vote to become a district of Los Ángeles in 1910. (The Hollywood population is around 5,000). Eastern film companies are discovering the southern California climate and sending film crews to work there. In 1911 the Horsley brothers, owners of the Centaur Film Company in New Jersey, convert a tavern and grocery store at the corner of Sunset Boulevard and Gower St. into the first movie studio in Hollywood. In December of 1913 the first feature-length western made in Hollywood, "The Squaw Man," is begun. Various filming groups merge and studios are slowly enlarged. **D.W. Griffith** makes "The Birth of a Nation" in 1915 and "Intolerance" in 1916. Producer **Louis B. Mayer** arrives in California in 1918 and builds a small studio the following year when the population of Hollywood has grown to some 35,000 people.

Many of the famous movie producers emanated from rather unglamorous backgrounds, often under girded by financial insecurity. It has been written that William Fox was a cloth sponger from New York's East Side. Marcus Loew and Adolph Zukor worked in penny arcades. Lewis J. Selznick had a small jewelry business. Carl Laemmle managed a clothing store. Samuel Goldwyn was a glove salesman. Louis B. Mayer was a junk man. [See Note # 51.] It has been said that the commercialism of movies was tied to the early beginnings of these producers because commercialism almost always triumphed over artistic goals. The colossal and stupendous was a money-maker so that's what producers shot for. It is also possible the drive for glamour came from such depths. For example, "stars" had their names changed from the ordinary to something befitting the kings and queens of glamour. Harry Lillis Crosby became *Bing Crosby*, Frances Ethel Gumm became *Judy Garland*, Margarita Carmen Cansino became *Rita Hayworth*, etc.

One of the basic technological innovations that catapulted movie success was the addition of a sound track to movie film. "The Jazz Singer," starring song-and-dance man Al Jolson, was a smashing success and studios had to get on the "talkie" bandwagon. Some did so reluctantly because there was an ingrained belief that "Movies should be seen and not heard." Dialog and music added unparalleled dimensions to movies.

The movie industry of the 1920s caught the fancy of America and the world. The "star system" developed personalities like Charlie Chaplin, perhaps the best known film actor of all time, Mary Pickford, "America's Sweetheart," Rudolph Valentino, Greta Garbo, John Gilbert, Will Rogers, Gloria Swanson, etc. People wanted to know about the stars and their private lives so a tremendous gossip/paparazzi industry sprang up. Any star's scandal became fair game. Some people protested that films were often charged with glorifying "crime, corruption, violence, and sex." Groups of Americans were scandalized by various goings-on and sentiment for proper morality became so strong that producers formed the Motion Picture Producers and Distributors Association. **Will H. Hays** was brought in to serve as watchdog to guard against the inclusion of objectionable material in movies. The "Hays Office" has been described as only partially successful. It is a fact that in its heyday, Hollywood produced some 90% of American films and 65% of the entire world's.

Among the more powerful studios in Hollywood were Columbia, Fox/20th Century Fox, Paramount, RKO, United Artists, Universal, Warner Brothers, and Metro-Goldwyn-Mayer.

Columbia: The letter "C" could be said to be significant in *Columbia*. Most importantly it stands for the brothers Cohn, Jack and Harry, co-founders and leaders of Columbia from 1924 until the mid 50s. Harry Cohn has been described as a "brash, tough, New York street kid" who grew up to run the California studio while Jack managed the New York office. "CBC" was the original name for the filming company. Frank Capra was the studio's leading director in the '30s. Comedy was Columbia's most popular/successful type of movie. Coca-Cola took over the studio in the '80s. Among its grand successes were "It Happened One Night" in 1934, "From Here to Eternity" in 1953, "On the Waterfront" in 1954, "Lawrence of Arabia" in 1962, "Kramer Vs. Kramer" in 1979.

Fox/20th Century Fox: William Fox was the founder and sole owner of this studio up until 1930. He had operated a penny arcade then opened a nickelodeon in New York in 1904. Fox built up his business then in 1916 went to California where he contracted Tom Mix and Buck Jones for western movies. William Fox was also an innovator in sound film with his Fox Movietone. Fox merged with 20th Century in 1935 and production chief Daryl F. Zanuck dominated the studio until about 1970. Zanuck hired and marketed stars like Tyrone Power and Betty Grable ('40s), Marilyn Monroe ('50s), etc. The studio produced movies in color as well as black-and-white with directors like John Ford, Elia Kazan, Joseph Mankiewicz, etc.

Paramount was formed in 1916 when Adolph Zukor merged his "Famous Players Film Company" with the group headed by Jesse Lasky then took over the Paramount distribution company. Due to Zukor's "shrewd, aggressive, and enterprising" approach to the move business, Paramount became the country's most successful studio. The studio's Gloria Swanson emerged as the leading female star in the '20s. Rudolph Valentino also made highly profitable movies like "The Sheik" (1921) and "Blood and Sand" (1922). When sound technology arrived Paramount quickly made the transition. The Depression greatly affected revenues until Barney Balaban became president in 1936. The studio recovered from the Depression and produced good successes in the '40s, winning Best Picture Oscars for "Going My Way (1944) and "The Lost Weekend" (1945). In 1949 it was forced to sell off its theaters and the 50's were only moderately successful for Paramount. The giant conglomerate Gulf-Western took over the studio in 1966. Paramount invested in television production, thereby avoiding the huge losses experienced by some other studios. It had huge hits in "The Godfather" (1972) and "The Godfather: Part II" (1974).

RKO, an acronym for Radio-Keith-Orpheum Corporation, came into being as a direct result of the introduction of sound. In 1821 a small British-owned company named Robertson-Cole decided to build a small studio in Hollywood, reorganized as film Booking Offices of America (FBO) in 1922, then functioned as a distributor and small-time movie producer. David Sarnoff and the Radio Corporation of America (RCA) purchased FBO in 1928 then merged with Keith-Albee-Orpheum to create RKO which was intended to utilize RCA's highly developed (for the time and place) sound technology . It functioned as a top production/distribution/exhibition studio which produced "King Kong" (1933), the Astaire-Rogers musicals, and "Citizen Kane" (1941). RKO was purchased by Howard Hughes in 1948 who then unloaded it in 1955. In 1957 RKO was converted for television production. In 1958 the studio was purchased by Lucille Ball and Desi Arnaz for their Desilu Productions.

United Artists was formed when producer-stars Mary Pickford and Douglas Fairbanks ("the world's most famous married couple"), Charlie Chaplin and famed director D.W. Griffith created the new studio in an effort to control the production and distribution of their movies. (Stars were not generally credited with business sense and Metro president Richard Rowland is supposed to have quipped: *So the lunatics have taken charge of the asylum.*) It was a struggle because only Fairbanks was free to make pictures, the others still under contract to other studios. Joseph Schenck was hired to manage UA in 1924, to attract new stars and promising producers (like Walt Disney, Darryl F. Zanuck, Alexander Korda). Quality films were produced in the '30s but RKO declined in the '40s when independents left the studio. However, there were hits like "High Noon," (1952), "Marty" won the Best Picture Oscar in 1955, "West Side Story," (1961), "It's A Mad, Mad, Mad, Mad World," (1963). In 1967 the Transamerica Corporation took over the company then sold it to Kirk Kerkorian and MGM in 1981. The MGM/UA was formed. In 1985 Ted Turner bought both companies then sold them back to Kerkorian with the proviso that Turner retain all film and television libraries, movies which are now shown on his cable network.

Universal was founded by New Yorker Carl Laemmle when his Independent Motion Picture Company merged with a number of smaller filming entities. In 1915 he bought a 230-acre site north of the Hollywood Hills, named it Universal City, and began making films under the direction of young Irving Thalberg, who managed the studio for two-and-a-half years. His most successful project was "The Hunchback of Notre Dame" (1923). Many other films were made, mostly undistinguished. Universal was slow to adopt the new technology of sound but it won an Oscar for "All Quiet on the Western Front" (1930). The studio gathered strength through the'40s. In 1946 Universal merged with International Pictures to form Universal-International. By the '70s U-I was considered an industry leader as well as important in television production. The Music Corporation of America (MCA) accomplished its takeover of the studio in 1962. In 1973 "The Sting" was awarded the Best Picture Oscar. Among its other hits have been "E.T. The Extra-Terrestrial (1982) and "Out of Africa" (1985).

Warner Brothers was incorporated in 1923, began experimenting with sound by 1925, and released the smash hit "The Jazz Singer" in 1927. The brothers, Albert, Harry, Sam, and Jack, had tried various jobs when in 1904 Sam got the idea of opening a nickelodeon, their first experience in "show business." In 1918 the brothers were successful with their first major feature, "My Four Years in Germany," filmed in New York. They went to Hollywood in 1919 and opened a small studio. By 1923 they released the successful Rin-Tin-Tin series.

The brothers hired young producers like Darryl F. Zanuck, Hal Wallis, Henry Blanke, and leading director Ernst Lubitsch.

In 1925 Warner Brothers was producing quality musical shorts. When spoken dialog for movies was discussed Harry Warner is supposed to have said: *Who the hell wants to hear actors talk?* He changed his mind after "The Jazz Singer" and its success revolutionized Hollywood and the movie industry, leading the way to 100% *talkies*. Warner Brothers continued to experiment with 3-D, Cinemascope, and programming for television. It merged with Seven Arts Productions in 1967 then was taken over by the Kinney National Corporation in 1969. Among its great hits were "The Life of Emile Zola," "Casablanca," "My Fair Lady" (Best Picture, 1937, 1943, 1964, respectively), and "Gremlins" (1984).

Metro-Goldwyn-Mayer, the biggest and most powerful of all Hollywood studios, was founded by merger (of Metro Pictures, Goldwyn Pictures, and Louis B. Mayer Productions) in 1924. Its formation marked the beginning of the "studio era" and the "star" system flowered. MGM was the top studio as of the 1930s and no one else could match it for quality or loyalty of its stars because, it is said, at MGM the stars came first. Further, it was also able to retain top technicians in various fields. Surprisingly, it was slow to make the transition to sound but when the decision was made no cost was spared, which quickly produced hits like "The Broadway Melody." The three-strip Technicolor process was first used in 1938 in super hits like "The Wizard of Oz" and (co-production) "Gone With the Wind" (winner of *ten* Oscars; said to be the all-around most profitable film of all time), both released in 1939. The peak years were the 1940s and MGM's Culver City studios had grown from its original forty acres to some 187 with six different lots used for filming. The musical ("Gigi" won *ten* Oscars in 1958) became its most popular type of film (although there were other super-successes like "Ben-Hur," 1959, winner of a record *eleven* Oscars). Arthur Freed headed the musical unit and "the rest is history" which could be recounted by the numbers of Academy Awards received by Cedric Gibbons, Preston Ames, Roger Edens, Lennie Hayton, Adolph Deutsch, Andre Previn, Johnny Green, Irene Sharaff, Walter Plunket, Alan Jay Lerner, etc., not to mention the well known stars like Fred Astaire, Judy Garland, Gene Kelly, etc. At the heart of it all was the music of giants like Irving Berlin, Richard Rodgers, Jerome Kern, George Gershwin, Cole Porter, Frank Loesser, Harry Warren, etc, along with the poetic lyrics of people like Lorenz Hart, Ira Gershwin, Oscar Hammerstein II, Dorothy Fields, Johnny Mercer, etc. MGM musicals were truly an uplifting gift to America and the world.

As indicated above, the movie industry's supreme, though mundane, rival turned out being television. Indeed, television came to dominate the film industry, which wound up producing television films for survival. While television proved basically a commercial medium that could create celebrities, it would never approach the grandeur of the Silver Screen and its famous stars like Charlie Chaplin, Rudolph Valentino, Clark Gable, Eleanor Powell, Fred Astaire, Rita Hayworth, etc.

While movies have always been fantasy, an escape from reality, Hollywood promoted a standardized American culture, setting examples in dress, home living, married or single life, entertainment, personal behavior, etc. [See Note # 52.] While always intended to make money, on occasion there were created artistic, enduring films. There are movies which still bring people into theaters and send them home marveling at this truly indigenous American art form. Needless to say, there are also many efforts which pander to vulgarity, employ obscene language, emphasizing the crudity of culture based on the money-making lowest common denominator.

WORLD WAR II

The bombing of the military installation of Pearl Harbor in Hawaii on December 7, 1941, caused the USA to enter World War II. [See Note # 53.] Speaking economically, the war was a tremendous boost for California. Training camps for the military, aircraft factories, shipyards, etc., had to be built and just about anybody who wanted a job could find one. The "bum blockade" against Okies and Arkies was lifted and defense workers poured into the State. Towns expanded seemingly overnight. For example, the little town of Vallejo had a population of some 20,00 in 1941 but by 1943 it had 100,000. Government money built new housing developments which necessitated infrastructure like highways, streets, lines for water and sewer systems, schools, transportation, etc.

Military training sites brought in hundreds of thousands of sailors, airmen, soldiers, marines, etc. Military posts became like cities. Los Ángeles and San Francisco became major embarkation centers.

Heavy industry was introduced on a massive scale. Steel mills did a landslide business. Ship building installations received huge appropriations from the federal government. Industries converted to the manufacture of tanks, jeeps, munitions and other war materiel. The aircraft industry grew at especially enormous rates and the Douglas and Lockheed plants became the cornerstone of American air superiority. (At the height of the war Lockheed employed some 90,000 persons.) It must also be pointed out that war industries didn't replace California agricultural production, which remained strong.

One of the basic tragedies on the California home front was the "relocation" of Japanese Americans away from the west coast. [See Note # 54.] Worry over security had caused the State Legislature to pass statutes like the Dilworth Anti-spy Bill, the Tenney Anti-Subversive Bill, the Slater Anti-Sabotage Act. A lone Japanese submarine surfaced near Santa Barbara and fired a shell in 1942. On February 25, 1942, a newspaper reported that Los Ángeles had been bombed the night before, that anti-aircraft fire had been used against enemy planes. In reality there were no enemy aircraft in the California skies but people were scared.

Military authorities believed the Japanese in California, many of them second generation Nisei, were a danger to American military installations. President Franklin D. Roosevelt finally signed the order that deported Japanese-Americans from California. Some 112,000 were forced to leave The Golden State, despite the property loss of some $365,000,000 when Americans, who had long envied Japanese agricultural success, bought up their properties at forced-sale prices. The Japanese were not charged with any crime. Being considered potential enemies was enough for deportation. No American defender, in or outside the Government, stood up against this violation of guaranteed constitutional rights. [See Note # 55.] Indeed, the San Francisco *Examiner* said: "*Herd 'em up, pack 'em off and give 'em the inside room in the badlands. Let us have no patience with the enemy or with anyone whose veins carry his blood.*" Some Japanese were sent as far away as Utah or Wyoming where they had to live in "internment camps" surrounded by imprisoning barbed wire. [See Note # 56.]

Race riots have been a part of California history since the American takeover and the war years were not to prove an exception. In June of 1943 some eleven sailors reported to police that they were attacked by a large number (the sailors said they were outnumbered 3-to-1) of Los Ángeles hoodlums. On June 4, 1943, some 200 sailors hired a fleet of taxicabs to cruise them to East L.A. where the "Mexican hoods" could be found. When a Mexican boy wearing a zoot-suit was sighted the first cab stopped and the sailors pounced on the zoot-suiter. The unsuspecting victim was left beaten and bleeding on the pavement. The scene was reenacted a few times until the taxicabs were met by police and the Shore Patrol. One sailor informed the police: "*We're out to do what the police have failed to do; we're going to clean up this situ-*

ation. Tonight we might have marines along."

The L.A. press had a field day with "Sailor-Zooter Clash" stories. On June 5th scores of marines joined sailors as they walked through downtown L.A. four abreast, ordering zoot-suiters to shed their "drapes" by tomorrow or they would pay the price. Some twenty-seven Mexican teenagers were on a street corner and promptly arrested by the police and charged with suspicion of this-or-that. The servicemen continued on their way.

Some sailors went into a bar and inspected everyone's clothes. Two zoot-suiters drinking beer at a table were ordered to shed their clothes. One refused and he was beaten brutally, after which his clothes were ripped to shreds.

On the night of June 6, 1943, the police knew the servicemen would find the *troublemakers* so they followed them as they cruised through L.A. The servicemen beat up all Mexican males they encountered then the police arrived and arrested the brutally beaten victims. By morning of the 7th some 44 Mexican boys, all seriously beaten, were in jail and under arrest. [See Note # 57.]

The L.A. press milked the story, thus encouraging more involvement in the serious rioting of June 7 and 8. The newspapers said the zoot-suiters were planning massive retaliation, that sailors would have their brains beaten out with hammers, that an army of 500 zooters was getting ready for combat… On June 7, 1943, thousands of servicemen and civilians walked through downtown and beat up every zoot-suiter they could find. The attacks spread to Negroes and Filipinos. One African-American was taken from a street car and had an eye gouged out with a knife. Club-swinging policemen went on the attack and arrests were made wholesale. A crippled teenager who asked why he was being arrested was hit three times on the head with a policeman's nightstick before he crumpled to the pavement. In another incident a Mexican woman screamed that her son had done nothing. She was struck across the jaw with a nightstick, almost dropping the baby she was holding in her arms. When Al Waxman pleaded with the police to stop the rioting he was told it was a matter for the Shore Patrol…

The newspapers printed large, half-page photographs of Mexican boys stripped of their clothing, laying on the pavement, often bleeding profusely, with jeering mobs of men and women around them. The rioting spread to the suburbs and continued for two more days. The Eagle Rock *Advertiser* editorialized: *"It is too bad the servicemen were called off before they were able to complete the job…Most of the citizens of the city have been delighted with what has been going on."* The L.A. City Council passed an ordinance that made the wearing of a zoot-suit a misdemeanor.

The riots attracted international attention to the point that official Washington made its presence felt. While the newspapers had been using headlines like "Zoot Suiters Learn Lesson in Fight with Servicemen!" the cry now turned into one for "Peace" and "Unity." The Los Ángeles *Times*, which had hailed the riots for their "salutary" and "cleansing" effects, now maintained that no particular group had been targeted, that at no time were Latin Americans condemned as a race.

CESAR CHÁVEZ

On September 8, 1865, the Agricultural Workers Organizing Committee, led by Filipino workers, struck against the grape growers of the Delano area in the San Joaquín Valley. Cesar Chávez emerged as a principal leader. Born in 1927 in Yuma, Arizona, his was the life of a migrant farm worker. In 1940 he moved to San José, California, met and married Helen Fávila. He was influenced by Father **Donald McDonnel** into educating himself. (He later stated that learning how to read changed his entire life.) Father McDonnel also introduced him to **Fred Ross** of the Community Service Organization. Chávez became an organizer for the CSO and learned grassroots strategies. In 1962 he moved to Delano and began to create the National Farm Workers Association with the help of other organizers like **Dolores Huerta** and **Gil Padilla**.

By 1964 the NFWA was on its feet financially and by 1965 it had some 1,700 diverse (UAW union members, civil rights workers, Catholics, Protestants, etc.) members. The end of the bracero program was a big factor in the NFWA's success. The *boycott* also proved to be a most effective strategy: supporters were encouraged against buying grapes. Starting in 1966 the big growers began signing contracts with the NFWA. An important exception was the Di Giorgio Corporation who wanted their workers to be represented by the Teamsters union instead of the NFWA. An election was set for August 30, 1966.

Charges of communist infiltration were made against the NFWA. They couldn't be substantiated but the union's financial resources were used up for various reasons. Chávez had no choice but to merge into the United Farm Workers Organizing Committee (UFWOC). The situation was now one of charges and counter charges but when the election came the UFWOC was chosen to represent the field workers.

In 1967 the largest producer of table grapes in the USA, Giumarra Vineyards Corporation, was targeted for unionization. Giumarra used other companies' labels to get around the boycott so the union ordered a boycott of all California grapes. The boycott spread into Canada and Europe. Each side had its partisans. For example, the Defense Department bought millions of pounds of grapes for American soldiers fighting in Vietnam. [See Note # 58.] Finally, a settlement was made with the UFWOC in 1970.

The 49ers are of a bygone era, military-industrial contracts come and go, but California agriculture exerts a constant presence. Cesar Chávez earned his niche in history because he was able to achieve what no one else had ever accomplished: unionization of agricultural workers in California.

DISCUSSION NOTES *for* CALIFORNIA STATEHOOD and SOCIETY

Note # 1
See page 20-21 in *Founding The Far West: California, Oregon, and Nevada, 1840-1890* by David Alan Johnson.

Note # 2
This demonstration of Californio hospitality is proof that Hispanic California was indeed more a land of heart's desire than backward, materialistic, oppressive, or brutal in nature. English language literature abounds with commentary that Californio life has been overly "romanticized." Is such strategy necessary to offset historical realities relating to how California came to be part of the USA?

Note # 3
See page 111 in *Founding The Far West*. With regard to historiography, is it a penchant for utilitarian expressions of English-speaking American writers that Americans in California are generally

referred to as *Yankees*, even if they were from the Southern states? Do the same principles hold true for use of *Anglo*? *Protestant*?

Note # 4

See Chapter Four in *Founding The Far West* for a discussion on the dilemma of "freedom loving Americans" who believed denying freedom to "objectionable races" was good for the community.

Note # 5

See page 134 in *North From Mexico* by Carey McWilliams.

Note # 6

See Chapter 5, "The Fools of '49," in *California: An Illustrated History* by T.H. Watkins.

Note # 7

It is startling to consider that the first European travelers were on this scene in 1540-42 with Coronado. It would be interesting to compare the first entrada with those motivated by the California gold rush. Were these 49ers pioneers, as they are so often referred to, or actually tragic players on the frontier? How can cultural bias be neutralized to arrive at historical truth?

Note # 8

See Chapter III, "Greasers in the Diggings: Californians and Sonorans under Attack" in Leonard Pitt's *The Decline Of The Californios: A Social History of the Spanish-Speaking Californians, 1846-1890*.

Note # 9

Owen C. Coy wrote in his *Gold Days* that the 49ers were basically law-abiding, decent folks.

Note # 10

On page 141 of *North From Mexico*, Carey McWilliams quotes Owen C. Coy, author of *Gold Days*, as saying that the California mining codes are an example "of the extraordinary capacity of the Anglo-American for self-government." Such strategies aren't new to students of Southwest history because we have already seen that some historiographers write that English speaking Texans are creators of the ranching industry in the West.

Note # 11

Who is credible? Is this merely an example of the "heroes and villains" structure of American historiography? Does American History depend on valid documentation or on who is writing it? The Downieville incident would have to be studied seriously in order to learn what forces actually took the life of Juanita and so many other Hispanics in California. It has been said that more Hispanics were lynched in California than blacks in the South.

Note # 12

See page 293 in *Calfornia* by Josiah Royce. The possibility of rape or even consensual sex isn't mentioned by Royce, although it is mentioned or alluded to by writers like Coy and Pitt.

Note # 13

See *The Destruction Of California Indians* by Robert F. Heizer.

Note # 14

See page 347 in *500 Nations* by Alvin M. Josephy Jr. It is a highly cherished tenet of American historiography that "Anglo-Saxons" didn't approve of "racial mixing." For example, Leonard Pitt writes (page 14) in his *Decline Of The Californios*: "..the Anglo-Saxon's generalized fear of racial mixture." This popular mythology falls by its own weight when studying American frontier history. Indian women in California were kidnapped expressly for sexual purposes. Further, it has been said that some 80% of African Americans have white American ancestry. DNA tests have proved that Thomas Jefferson fathered children with Sally Hemmings (herself the product of a white slave master father and his black slave), his mulatto slave. Many African-Americans claim George Washington as a direct line ancestor. George Orwell wrote: "Truth is Treason!" so such historical facts have been taboo.

Note # 15

See page 213 in *California: Land of New Beginnings* by David Lavender. Lavender is quoting from the work of Sherburne F. Cook in these passages but he includes commentary like "The tribes... already crushed by the Spanish and Mexicans, sank deeper into apathy." Is this a typical strategy in American historiography?

Note # 16

See page 84 for Buchanan's quote in *The Decline Of The Californios* by Leonard Pitt. Such commentary is not unparalleled in American history: slave master Thomas Jefferson wrote in the Declaration of Independence that "all men are created equal."

Professor Pitt wrote in the Preface of *Decline* that California's Hispanic people were too small in number and "*culturally too backward to contribute to mankind much that was new or original...I see this as an instance of the worldwide defeat of the relatively static, traditionalist societies by societies that were oriented to technology and the ideal of progress.*" Technological progress is wonderful but weaponry leading to the Manhattan Project isn't a measure of civilization. Was the technology in reality militant aggression coupled with the development of superior weaponry? Are super-weapons (for the time and place) the real "technology and progress" Professor Pitt is lauding? What was the nature of the new *progress*, a change in land ownership? Is such dog-eat-dog commentary an Orwellian cover-up for the morality of Manifest Destiny? Is Dr. Pitt's commentary guided by the George Orwell adage "*Truth Is Treason*"?

Note # 17

See page 23 in *Decline*: "...many California women seem to have been more favorably disposed toward the Yankees than were their men." Professor Pitt quotes Thomas Farnham as saying it was because of "the Yankee's superior romantic prowess" and even supplies a bit of doggerel written up for the WPA in 1941: *Already the senoritas* (sic)/ *Speak English with finesse./ "Kiss me! Say the Yankees,/ The girls all answer "Yes!"* Would it be worthwhile to investigate such historiography? Or would it be called historiography?

Note # 18

See page 28 in *Decline* where William B. Ide proclaims to the Hispanic people of California that the Bear Flag movement was the beginning of "industry, virtue and literature" for them.

Note # 19

See Chapter 4, which is about Californio women, in *My History, Not Yours* by Dr. Genaro M. Padilla. In later life María de las Angustias married a man named *Ord* so American writers usually refer to her by that name although she carried it for a relatively short period of time.

Note # 20

See page 149 in the above cited Padilla volume. The accuracy of translations is a major pitfall in Southwest history, or to quote Padilla: "…there is evidence of mistranslation that subverts intent." The serious student of Southwest history must always ask: How faithful is the translation? While Ph.D.s are definitely serious, how often have they "spoken out" about mistranslations that "subvert intent"? There have been very few paladins like Dr. Padilla.

Note # 21

It has been said that Helen Hunt Jackson (1830-1885) wrote the novel *Ramona* in an effort to expose the injustices that were taking place in California, much like Harriet Beecher Stowe had done for the southern slaves in *Uncle Tom's Cabin*. The former, which went into some 150 printings, proved almost as popular as the latter. *Uncle Tom's Cabin* has been described as one of the most influential books ever published in the USA since it has been linked to the reasons for the Civil War. Though very powerful in its day, *Ramona* caused no such maelstrom.

Note # 22

See pages 167-68 in *General M.G. Vallejo And The Advent Of The Americans* by Alan Rosenus.

Note # 22

See page 200 in *General M.G. Vallejo* by Alan Rosenus.

Note # 23

See Chapter 3 in *My History, Not Yours* by Dr. Genaro Padilla.

Note # 24

The *Recuerdos* contained almost a thousand pages on the social, political, cultural, and familial history of Hispanic California from 1879 to 1850. As Dr. Genaro Padilla has written, works like these should be made accessible through publication. Of inestimable value, why have they not been published? Would they refute popular historiography? Would American psychology permit it?

Note # 25

Bancroft wrote in 1890: *I was literally speechless with astonishment and joy when Cerruti told me "General Vallejo gives you all his papers." Besides the priceless intrinsic value of these documents…the example would double the benefits of the gift.*

Note # 26

Dr. Genaro Padilla writes that the Californios were aware of the denigration they and their country was being subjected to in English language publications. The Californios realized they had been dispossessed but apparently they also understood they were being maligned into an unmarked grave.

Note # 27

See page 99 in *My History*.

Note # 28

See page 87 in the *My History* volume.

Note # 29

On pages 234-35 of *General M.G. Vallejo*, Alan Rosenus writes that in 1921 a vote was taken in the Bay Area to select who would be placed in Statuary Hall in Washington, D.C. to represent the State of California. Mariano Vallejo got 4,417 votes; Junípero Serra, 3,341; Thomas Starr King, 1,837; Bret Harte, 1,174. Representing California in Statuary Hall to this day are Thomas Starr King and Junípero Serra. According to Andrew F. Rolle, T.S. King lived in California from 1860 until his death in 1864.

Note # 30

See Chapter 17 in *California: A History* by Andrew F. Rolle.

Note # 31

Were the vigilantes right or wrong? Much has been written on this subject. See *Committee Of Vigilance: Revolution in San Francisco, 1851. An account of The Hundred Days when certain citizens undertook the suppression of the criminal activities of the Sydney ducks* by George. R. Stewart. For a differing view see *San Francisco's Reign Of Terror* by John Myers Myers.

Note # 32

See Chapter XI, "El Clamor Público: Sentiments of Treason" in *Decline Of The Californios* by Leonard Pitt. It would be interesting to investigate the use of "Treason." George Orwell also wrote "Truth is Treason!" in his *1984*.

Note # 33

A.F. Rolle makes no mention of Ramírez or his newspaper in the Index of his *California*. The same is true for the *California* of D. Lavender. In his *Occupied America* Rodolfo Acuña refers to Ramírez as "a young Chicano," this in the years 1855-59, and he devotes a couple of pages to Ramírez' work.

Note # 34

As Howard Zinn has written in his *A People's History Of The United* States, the Declaration of Independence has never been the law of the land. Its idealism has often been part of American psychology.

Note # 35

It would be interesting to explore the psychology of enslaving Africans and exterminating Amerindians while espousing that "all men are created equal." Or would it be too dangerous?

Note # 36

See page 148 in *Occupied America* by Rudolfo Acuña.

Note # 37

It would appear that the "Washington Navel orange" is in reality the Brazilian orange. So why do writers refer to it as the former instead of the latter?

Note # 38

It is difficult to distinguish history from propaganda in American historiography. For example,

John S. Hittell wrote in his *The Resources Of California* that a field of one hundred acres produced a crop of 90,000 bushels of barley (in 1853). He said he had seen potatoes that weighed from four to seven pounds each, cabbages that were seven feet wide, onions of twenty-two inches in circumference, and "a three-year-old red beet that weighed 118 pounds."

Note # 39

See pages 150-53 in *Nothing Like It In The World* by Stephen E. Ambrose.

Note # 40

Regarding the transcontinental railroad, Stanford later wrote to President Andrew Johnson that the Chinese were peaceable, patient, industrious people. "Without the Chinese it would have been impossible to complete the western portion of this great national highway."

Note # 41

See page 378 in *California: A History* by Andrew F. Rolle. Despite all the efforts to ostracize them, the Chinese were also charged with refusal to assimilate into American culture. Then there was the old charge: "All they do is have kids!." Has racism changed in the present day?

Note # 42

See pages 444-47 in California by A.F. Rolle. Would it be fair to observe that control of the government is often crucial in amassing a personal fortune? What are the implications of the phrase "Robber Barons"?

Note # 43

Is the judicial process any different today? Does the legal system exist for the benefit of those who can pay for it?

Note # 44

See pages 498-500 in *A History Of California: The Spanish Period* by Charles E. Chapman. A.F. Rolle refers to Bancroft as "…the best of California's amateur chroniclers." Perhaps this means that Bancroft didn't have a Ph.D. in History? How do "academic" volumes on California compare with those written by Bancroft? Rolle also asserts that Bancroft was "*highly romantic about California, as his Californias Pastoral (1888) especially demonstrates.*" Does being impressed with Californio society somehow neutralize the writer? Are the vilifiers more acceptable? Why/why not?

Note # 45

See Chapter 8 in *California: The Great Exception* by Carey McWilliams.

Note # 46

Is historian Howard Zinn (*A People's History Of The United States*) correct when he states that racism is basic to American society? The first European colonists on the east coast banded together against the Indians, whites passed laws to enslave Africans, Americans united to take Mexican land, etc., all such unity under girded by racism?

Note # 47

Contemporary students seldom understand the depths of the Great Depression. Perhaps it can be described succinctly by saying that "The Depression was a time when a loaf of bread cost a nickel and you didn't have a nickel to buy it."

Note # 48

See pages 220-21 in *Occupied America* by Rodolfo Acuña. Would it be accurate to say that American racism consistently targets groups which have the least power in American society?

Note # 49

It is curious that Government forces consistently seem to side with Management. What chance do ordinary people have when the Government sends government troops against them?

Note # 50

There are myriads of works relating to the movie industry and its "stars." The following are suggested for starters: *The Hollywood Story* by Joel W. Finler; *Hollywood Musicals* by Ted Sennett; *Great Movie Actresses* by Philip Strick; *A History Of Movie Musicals: Gotta Sing, Gotta Dance* by John Kobal; *The International Film Encyclopedia* by Ephraim Katz. It would be interesting to discuss the concepts related to the "star system," "stars," and "celebrity."

Note # 51

See page 545 in *California* by Andrew F. Rolle.

Note # 52

It would be interesting to investigate how much the American penchant for fantasy has worked its way into American historiography. Was Wyatt Earp really a hero as he is so often portrayed in movies? Has the Alamo been endowed with heroic myth?

Note # 53

Few writers have investigated why the Japanese bombed Pearl Harbor. Would it be considered *unpatriotic*? What are the implications in bombing a military target as compared to civilian targets?

Note # 54

It would be interesting to compare the use of concepts like "Japanese Relocation" and "Indian Removal" in American historiography. Are they accurate? Are they Orwellian euphemisms? Why or why not?

Note # 55

How powerful is the Dred Scott Decision in the contemporary American psyche?

Note # 56

See page 267 in *Occupied America* by Rodolfo Acuña.

Note # 57

See pages 244-58 in *North From Mexico* by Carey McWilliams.

Note # 58

See pages 351-53 in *Occupied America* by Rodolfo Acuña.

NEVADA STATEHOOD and SOCIETY

Popularly known as *Washoe* (for the Washoe Indian tribe), Nevada was among the most sparsely settled regions in the West before the 1859 silver strike. There was a "massive wave of humanity" rushing to

Washoe in the spring and summer of 1860 because of the rich silver deposits. Rough mining communities like Virginia City, Gold Hill, Silver City, etc., began to form, populated by hordes of people intent on finding their "pot of gold" quick riches. As in California, people who came in to sell food and supplies to the miners generally made more money than the miners themselves. Within a few short years it was apparent to everyone that a government had to be created.

Nevada became a territory in the spring of 1861. One of the problems in Nevada government was that people came in looking for riches and went out when they succeeded or failed. They didn't much care about government. However, the majority of people sided with the Union against the Confederacy. Nevada statehood was desired for a number of reasons. Most people agreed that citizenship in a State provided more status than in a Territory. Another important factor was that the Union needed Nevada's silver to fight the seceded Confederate states. Further, President Lincoln needed additional votes in Congress to secure passage of the antislavery amendment. It was a real worry that a two-thirds majority might not be achieved in each house so Lincoln could use more Republican (Nevada) votes in Congress.

On November 2, 1863, delegates met to create a constitution for the "State of Washoe." Bribery was found to be a most effective strategy in getting what the rich wanted, the will of the people being as nothing when compared to money from the wealthy. Though the situation was one of brutality, there were those who poked it with humor. For example, upon the occasion of writing the 1863 constitution and already on his way as a humorist, Samuel Clemens (Mark Twain) convened his own rump convention, called the *Third House*. Clemens castigated William Stewart by saying "*...if you can't add something fresh to it, or say it backwards, or sing it to a new tune, you simply have got to simmer down for a while...Gentlemen, you have discussed a subject which you know nothing about, spoken on every subject but the one before the House, voted without knowing what you were voting for, or having any idea what would be the general result of your action...*" [See Note # 1. *Notes begin on page 518.*] The 1863 effort was rejected by the voters because it supposedly served the interests of San Francisco capitalists instead of workingmen, small mine owners, prospectors, merchants, farmers, ranchers. Another writing effort was made a few months later.

On July 4, 1864, thirty-five men convened in Carson City to write a constitution. Among the central figures in the new constitutional convention were John North, William M. Stewart, John Anderson Collins, Charles De Long, Thomas Fitch, and John Neely Johnson. The first mild controversy was over what to name the new state. The Spanish language *Nevada* won out over Washoe, Humboldt, or Esmeralda. While not controversial in that day and time (despite the idealism of the Declaration of Independence, the U.S. Constitution did not grant all Americans the right to vote), women, blacks, Indians, and Orientals were denied the right to vote. A poll tax was made legal.

Representatives from the ranching and mining interests were easily distinguishable at the convention and self-interest was basic to all votes. There was especially angry debate on four central points:

1. Loyalty oath to the Union: Safely in Nevada and far from the Civil War, the constitution writers were fervently patriotic. There were several impassioned speeches that decried "*...those in whose veins runs no blood save that which is black as hell with the taint of treason.*" [See Note # 2.] The committee recommended the loyalty oath be adopted but on the final vote the loyalty oath was struck out.

2. Subsidy for the construction of the Pacific railroad: Leland Stanford, former governor of California and president of the Central Pacific, hurried to Carson City in an effort to have the state issue railroad

subsidy bonds, *solely* to his Central Pacific line. Delegate Thomas Fitch proved an able point man for the railroad and most delegates favored it. A state subsidy was authorized.

3. Taxation of existing mines instead of on extracted ore: The failed 1863 constitution had provided for "taxation of all property, both real and personal, including mines and mining property…" A motion was made to delete the portion referring to *mines*. The next day, Francis Kennedy, sponsored an amendment that said "…excepting mines and mining claims, the proceeds alone of which shall be subject to taxation." In the debate which followed it was pointed out that mining corporations would get by without paying significant taxes, that the tax burden would rest solely with ranchers and businessmen. Maneuvering got the Article on Taxation passed with Kennedy's amendment intact.

4. The state court system issue was hottest over the provision for the impeachment of judges. Many delegates felt the provision was necessary because of the prevalence of bribery "and other forms of persuasion." Cynically, it was said it would be harder to bribe senators and assemblymen than a few judges. Mining delegates were opposed and in the end the provision was voted down.

The constitutional convention adjourned on July 27, 1664. The new constitution was approved by the voters and on October 31, 1864, President Lincoln issued the proclamation that made Nevada a State in the Union. Republicans were victorious almost everywhere so **H.G. Blasdel** was chosen as Nevada's first Governor, **William M. Stewart** and **James W. Nye** were its first Senators in Congress, **H.G. Worthington** the first Representative in the House. Territorial status had begun on March 2, 1861, and by 1864 it still had the smallest population of any State but Nevada was now an integral part of the Union.

COMSTOCK LODE

Hubert H. Bancroft has written that the discovery and development of the Comstock Lode is "to a great extent," the basic history of Nevada. [See Note # 3.] One of the first paying efforts was the Candelaria Mining Camp discovered in May of 1845. Five miners from Mexico, **S. Aruña, José Rodríguez, Antonio Rojer, Ventura Beltrán,** and **Francisco Pardo,** controlled mining interests in Candelaria, Nevada, until Americans and Europeans pushed them out.

American miners, most of them from California, were looking for gold when they went to Nevada and it has been estimated that from 1850-59 some $642,000 of the precious metal was taken out of the Gold Canyon area by 100 to 180 miners. Having no extensive heritage in mining, while they were looking for gold they were bothered by the *black sand* which got in their way. For example, **Patrick McLaughlin** and **Peter O'Riley** were looking for gold in Six-Mile Canyon when they ran into a ledge of heavy stone with a decided bluish cast. They didn't know what it was so they ignored it. They were looking for gold. One **Henry Paige Comstock** came on the scene with the assertion that he and his partner Emanuel Penrod had already made a claim on the area. Comstock has been described by some as a "lazy, half-mad, loud-spoken trickster" but Dan De Quille portrays him in softer hues. [See Note # 4.] In order to avoid trouble, a four-way partnership was worked out. The men were panning for gold one day when a Mexican miner (unnamed) happened by when Comstock was complaining that the *blasted blue stuff* sure made it hard to isolate the gold. The Mexican miner became very excited and started yelling *¡Mucha plata! ¡Mucha plata!* (*A lot of silver! A lot of silver.*) It took a while for the English speaking miners to realize that one of the richest silver mines in the world had been discovered. [See Note # 5.]

Americans knew next to nothing about mining silver. Indeed, there wasn't even a national mining law in existence in the USA until 1866 when Nevada Senator William M. Stewart got one passed. Americans hired Spanish-speaking Hispanic miners and learned techniques (how to use the *arrastra*, etc.) and vocabulary (*bonanza, placer,* etc.) from them. De Quille wrote: "*There were, undoubtedly...many old and skillful Mexican miners–skillful after the fashion of mining in Mexico--and with what our people were able to learn of these men, and what they soon themselves discovered, it was not long before very good work was being done...*"[See Note # 6.] There were various important Hispanic miners on the Comstock. For example, **Gabriel Maldonado** was part owner of the "Mexican Mine" in 1860-61. Maldonado used knowledgeable Mexican miners to develop a more advanced system of extracting ore on the Comstock. Until he sold his share of the mine he was considered one of the wealthiest men in Virginia City. **Manuel San Pedro** had learned about mining and business practices while traveling in the Latin Americas. He arrived in Virginia City in 1861 and later owned the rich *Está Buena* mine. San Pedro helped to organize the Union Mining District, later founded the town of Grantsville, and in 1877 founded the Alexander Mining company with James B. Cooper. [See Note # 7.]

The bonanza years from 1864-81 gave growth to lavish and colorful Comstock towns. For example, Virginia City attracted men and women, but mostly men, from all over the world. (In the census taken in 1875 there were some 19,528 people in the Comstock communities and 13,415 of them were male.) In the years 1876-77, more than $75,000,000 worth of ore was taken out of the mines around Virginia City. [See Note # 8.] The two mines known as the "Big Bonanza" brought out some $101,157,490 worth of ore in the years 1873-82. It has been written that from 1859-82 the Comstock yielded some $292,726,310 worth of ore. [See Note # 9.]

However, great wealth also engendered recklessness which led to corruption in politics and the judiciary. In the final analysis, few men got rich. As in California, ordinary mining men often had high hopes of striking it rich, intense moments of ecstatic expectation, then bitter disappointment. Further, most miners weren't equipped to do the heavy work required to make a mine pay. Corporations and "the bank crowd" took over.

MORMON TOWNS

The Latter-Day Saints began founding towns in Nevada in the 1860s. Most Mormons were very industrious and took no part in the rowdy behavior so common in the mining camps. One serious problem arose when the settlers asserted they were living in Utah, not Nevada, so they refused to pay taxes (in what authorities called Lincoln County, Nevada). The confrontation was solved in 1870-71 when an official survey proved the settlements were in Nevada. The Mormons moved back into Utah proper. In 1880 some Mormons returned to the disputed area, revived the town of Overton, reestablished St. Thomas, and the former St. Joseph became known as Logandale.

Led by **Edward Bunker**, Sr., in 1877 settlers from Santa Clara, Utah, moved into the fertile Virgin Valley. The first spring and summer were spent digging an irrigation canal and preparing the land for communal planting. Bunkerville, their first permanent town, was established. In time, vegetables, grain, and cotton yielded well. Mills were established in order to process flour, molasses, cotton. The communal effort was ended in 1881.

Speaking generally, miners came to Nevada to make fast money then enjoy life with it. By contrast, Mormons came to make homes and stay to live. Mining towns like Eureka, Pioche, Hamilton, etc., were usually "men's towns," rowdy and violent, full of saloons and gambling rooms. Mormon towns like Panaca, Overton, Bunkerville, St. Thomas, etc., were generally quiet and efficient with no saloons or gambling. While miners enjoyed much personal freedom, they often had an impermanent "freebooter" feeling about them because they could leave at any moment. Mining towns usually had a few lavish homes owned by the wealthy, while most other people lived in cabins or shacks. Mormon settlers built modest but comfortable homes. When the mining booms were done, the towns took on aspects of typical family living. That is, those that survived because for every town that remained during the depression years of 1881-1900 there were five that didn't.

TONOPAH

James Butler was a rancher in the Monitor Valley who also worked as a part-time prospector. Like most Nevada miners, he emanated from California. In 1900 he decided to do some prospecting in the desert referred to as the Southern Klondike. On May 19, 1900, he found some "rich-looking" rocks, loaded some on his mule, then continued his little jaunt. When he returned he gave the samples to **Tasker L. Oddie**, a young attorney, who said he would have the assay done for free. The test was made in a high school and the ore proved to be rich in gold and silver to the tune of about $300 a ton.

Butler, Oddie, and a merchant named Wilson Brougher went out and did some mining, though they really didn't have proper mining equipment, not even a tent to stay in. They were able to extract two tons of ore and when they finally got it to a smelter their payment amounted to $500, the beginning of their millionaire careers. Hundreds of men began to arrive.

Butler, Oddie, and Brougher leased small portions of the land to miners who promised to pay them one-fourth of all proceeds. Everyone trusted Butler and he trusted the miners working the mines. Unlike other diggings, not a single lawsuit was ever filed between the two parties.

A new town came into being and Butler called it *Tonopah* in honor of the Indians. The name would become famous throughout the West and the town proved as productive and more peaceful in nature than other boom towns. After the depression years, Tonopah ushered in a new chapter in Nevada mining history. Butler would become a millionaire and Oddie would become Governor and a U.S. Senator.

In 1901 James Butler sold his mining interests to eastern investors. He wound up one of the few Nevada prospectors who actually became wealthy from his discovery. While the later town of Goldfield proved to be unbelievably rich, Tonopah has to be considered one of the most unique boom towns in the history of the West.

LAS VEGAS

The first non-Indian to go through the Las Vegas Valley was a teenager from New Mexico named **Rafaél Rivera**. This courageous young man was a part of the history making expedition led by **José Antonio Armijo** that started out from Abiquiú, New Mexico, on November 7, 1829, intent on blazing a new trading route to California. [See Note # 10.] Armijo kept a terse diary on the journey while he crossed the desert areas which had first be traveled by Franciscan priests Garcés, Domínguez, and Escalante. On December 25, 1829, Armijo recorded that he had sent out a reconnaissance party to look for a shortcut and water sources. Evidently a knowledgeable scout, despite his scant seventeen years, Rafaél pushed out on his own.

On January 1, 1830, he recorded that Rafaél Rivera had not returned with the reconnaissance party. On January 4th he sent out a search party but Rafaél wasn't located.

Rafaél found his way back to the Armijo caravan by January 7th, 1830. He related how he had originally traveled in a southwesterly direction from the caravan, winding up in the foreboding Black Canyon (now the site of Hoover Dam). He traveled west (from present-day Henderson) and saw the snow-capped Spring Mountain Range so he knew there would be plenty of water some place, along with game for meat. He studied the Las Vegas Valley. He avoided the lava rock plain and traveled west along (what is now called) the Las Vegas Wash. Continuing westward, he discovered the "Little Spring of the Turtle" (Cottonwood Springs) where he and his horse rested. The young New Mexican trailblazer encountered Indians from the Cucha Payuches and Hayatas villages during his journey. He continued westward to Stump Spring then Resting Springs (near Tecopa, California) and finally to the Armagosa and Mojave Rivers (Barstow area). Now he had to return and find the Armijo caravan, guessing correctly that it would be traveling along the Las Vegas Wash. He was located it on January 7. He was exhausted from his incredible, solitary, thirteen-day journey of some 506 miles, but after a couple of days rest he was ready to hit the trail once more.

Led by Rafaél Rivera, the caravan entered the Las Vegas Basin and continued west (through present East Las Vegas). They traversed Cottonwood Springs, over Mountain Springs Pass, etc., until they hit the Mojave River and on to San Gabriel Mission. The journey from New Mexico had taken some 86 days and the trade route became a popular one under the name of the *Old Spanish Trail*.

The railroad came to Las Vegas in 1905 and Clark County was established in 1909. Prosperity from Tonopah and Goldfield benefited Las Vegas' growth for a time. Of more permanent importance was the large supply of underground water from artesian wells.

When the automobile age arrived it turned out that Las Vegas was conveniently located between Salt Lake City and Los Ángeles so the town became a favorite stopping-point for early motorists. While the population was a mere 5,165 in 1930, legalized gambling made it one of the fastest growing communities in the USA. By around 1985 there were some 15,000,000 tourists visiting Las Vegas every year. The permanent population of Clark County was more than 600,000 people by 1990.

Las Vegas has become the "tourist-gambling" mecca of the West and the USA, a rival to Hollywood, New York, and Paris for the tourist dollar. Easily accessible from southern California as well as air travel from all over the world, Downtown areas and "The Strip" are lined with sumptuous casinos which, as in the days of the Old West, invite tourists to try their luck at quick riches.

CIVIL RIGHTS

The Nevada Constitution echoes passages from the Declaration of Independence with regard to the equality of all men and God-given "inalienable rights." This idealism notwithstanding, equality proved to be as difficult in Nevada as in the rest of the USA. For example, Indians, African-Americans and

Orientals were denied the right to vote in Nevada until 1880. Women's suffrage would take even longer but under the leadership of women like **Anne Martin**, females were granted the right to vote as of 1914.

The federal government established Indian reservations like Pyramid Lake and Walker Lake. Subsequently, lands were reserved for Paiutes and Shoshones but in most cases there was not enough land on which Native Americans could make a living. Native Americans have been relegated to menial labor for most of Nevada history. There began to be improvements in the 1960s but progress has been slow for the first Nevadans.

While African-Americans were very few in number in the early days, blacks were skillful cowboys and ranch hands. Few were permitted to work in the mines or in skilled trades after the mining booms. Most often they worked as maids, janitors, cooks, etc. This began to change in the 1940s due to WW II. Change came slowly in the '50s and '60s. Ironically, while many popular Las Vegas entertainers were of African descent, these same headliners were not permitted to enter the casino through the front doors nor would hotels rent to black people. In 1965 the Nevada Legislature finally passed a law which made it illegal to discriminate on the basis of race or religion. **Woodrow Wilson** was the first African-American to be elected (1967) to the Legislature but problems remained because most black communities were still impoverished.

Orientals, especially the Chinese, were brought over by railroad companies in the 1860s. When railroad construction ended in 1869 many Chinese sought work in the mines but whites banded together to keep them out, by violent force when necessary. Race riots broke out, as in Carson City. In the 1870s and '80s the Legislature passed laws aimed at removing Orientals from Nevada.

Chinese people lived peacefully where they didn't threaten the jobs of whites. They were excellent, industrious, energetic workers who quickly learned many trades, though most whites wanted them as cooks or laundrymen. Equality came slowly toward the end of the 20th century.

ATOMIC TESTING

Because of its sparse population, the Nevada Proving Grounds were chosen for atomic testing in December of 1950. Between 1951 and 1955 some forty-five atomic devices were tested. Sometimes the blasts could be seen from hundreds of miles away. Minor damages like broken windows were compensated by the government but Nevadans worried about radioactive fallout. Testing was halted for two years during which equipment and techniques were improved. The establishment of Yucca Mountain as a national nuclear waste repository site continues to be a virulent controversy in the 21st century.

SAGEBRUSH REBELLION

It has been written that members of the Nevada Legislature began the controversy of objecting to the federal government owning most of the "public land" in Nevada. [See Note # 11.] Referred to as the "Sagebrush Rebellion," some Nevadans maintain that the State should own State lands, not the federal government. While no claim has been made on federal military bases, Indian reservations, national forests, test sites, etc., some Nevadans assert that unappropriated land should belong to Nevadans. Further, there are those who have argued that the extensive land holdings of the federal government in the West put the area in a competitive disadvantage with the East where the land can be taxed to generate income for growth. [See Note # 12 See page 567.] The thrust was to have the Feds cede unappropriated lands to Nevada. The movement weakened in the 1980s and has not been successful.

DISCUSSION NOTES *for* NEVADA STATEHOOD and SOCIETY

Note # 1
See pages 82-3 in *Founding The Far West* by David A. Johnson.

Note # 2
See pages 218-30 in *Founding The Far West* by David A. Johnson.

Note # 3
See page 92 in *History Of Nevada, 1540-1888* by Hubert Howe Bancroft.

Note # 4
See pages 62-64 in *History Of Nevada* by Russell R. Elliott. Dan De Quille writes that Comstock was known as "Old Pancake" by his familiars, an exceedingly generous man to everyone. He also mentions that Comstock finally committed suicide in 1870. See chapters VI and IX in his *The Big Bonanza*.

Note # 5
See page 138 in *North From Mexico* by Carey McWilliams. McWilliams derived this information from Chapter IV of *The Big Bonanza* by Dan De Quille (William Wright), who has the Mexican miner saying "Mucho plata!" Despite this error in elementary Spanish grammar, De Quille does provide "Appendix: Mexican Mining Terms" at the end of his very well known and highly regarded work on Nevada mining.

Note # 6
See pages 85-6 in *The Big Bonanza* by Dan De Quille.

Note # 7
See pages 8-12 in *Hispanic Profiles In Nevada History: 1829-1991* by M.L. Miranda and Thomas Rodríguez. Of the other works cited herein for Nevada history, only Bancroft mentions miners like Maldonado. What does that fact say to the student of Southwest history?

Note # 8
See page 109 in *The Nevada Adventure* by James W. Hulse.

Note # 9
See page 134 in *History Of Nevada* by Russell R. Elliott.

Note # 10
See *Hispanic Profiles In Nevada History: 1829-1991* by M.L. Miranda and Thomas Rodríguez.

Note # 11
See page 289 in *The Nevada Adventure* by James W. Hulse. It has been asserted that the federal government owns more than half of the land in Western states like Nevada and New Mexico. These Government properties are always referred to as "public domain" or "public land."

Note # 12
See page 567 in *"It's Your Misfortune And None Of My Own:" A New History Of The American West* by Richard White.

COLORADO STATEHOOD and SOCIETY

Colorado became a Territory on February 28, 1861, beginning a status that has been described as "a colony of the United States" until 1876. [See Note # 1. *Notes begin on page 528.*] Territorial officers were appointed from Washington D.C. The Colorado Delegate to Congress could participate in debates but was not permitted to vote on any issue. People in Colorado as well as in Washington favored or opposed statehood depending on how the status would affect them personally. Those who favored *statedom* asserted the benefits would be those of home rule, local pride, encouragement for eastern capital to come in for the mining industry, and bona fide representation in Congress.

On July 4, 1864, delegates to a constitutional convention met at Golden but then adjourned to Denver because it had better facilities. Those who favored statehood, mostly Republicans, had control of the convention. A slate of candidates was put forth for new offices required under statehood. For example, Col. **John Chivington** was tabbed for Representative. Many whose names were not on the ballot became disenchanted and ended up opposing statehood. Further, Democrats didn't want to see three more Republican votes in Congress. Federal taxes became an issue. The statehood movement was defeated when the constitution was rejected by the voters.

Another constitutional convention was called in the spring of 1865. The voters passed the new constitution by less than two-hundred votes but they did reject a proposal for African-American suffrage. Leaders now called for an election of state officers. Three parties, Republican, Democrat, and a group calling itself the Sand Creek Vindication Party, nominated candidates. Republicans captured most offices. The bad news was that Washington, now led by President Andrew Johnson, wasn't interested in Colorado statehood. Additionally, Republicans weren't pleased with the rejection of black suffrage by Coloradans. The congressional investigation of the Sand Creek Massacre and eventual removal of Governor Evans were also serious negative factors.

Colorado Territorial history appears to be a "scurry and scramble...for the spoils of office." [See Note # 2.] Graft and corruption were not rare. The "Denver ring," led by **John Evans** and **Jerome Chaffe**, continued to work for statedom. The "Golden gang," led by **Henry Teller**, worked against it. A new enabling act for statehood was passed in 1866 but President Johnson vetoed it on the grounds that the Colorado population wasn't large enough.

The seat of Territorial government alternated between Denver and Golden until 1867 when the Denver site became permanent. The election year of 1868 brought some hope for statehood. Evans and Chaffee informed a congressional committee that Colorado's population was now between 75-100,000 while Teller said there were no more than 30,000 (the 1870 census would put the figure below 40,000). As it turned out, statehood would remain a dead issue until 1876 and "carpetbagger" territorial government, complete with a "revolving door" governorship (three men held the office in one three-year period), would continue until then.

In 1876 Republican leaders in Congress decided they could use Colorado's (projected) three electoral votes. An enabling act linking Colorado and New Mexico was created. The New Mexico (Democrat) bill failed, but Colorado passed on March 3, 1875. Coloradans then selected thirty-nine delegates (24 Republicans, 15 Democrats) to create a constitution. Most provisions were agreed to without difficulty. Controversy was stirred over how to determine the state's authority in regulating economic activity. Miners and ranchers needed capital investment but it was felt corporations shouldn't be given a free hand in dominating the state. Basic compromises avoided rigid regulation or a lack of restrictions. No provision was made for the establishment of a railroad or public utilities commission. Debates over reference to God finally ended with mentioning "a profound reverence for the Supreme Ruler of the Universe." School lands debate centered on whether or not to include parochial schools or only public schools. Denominational Protestants clashed with Roman Catholics and the vote was to deny aid to any sectarian institution. It was decided women could be permitted to vote in school district elections but nowhere else. After some eighty-seven days of work, the constitutional convention adjourned on March 14, 1876. The voters ratified the effort and President Grant declared Colorado statehood on August 1, 1876. It's three Republican electoral votes were crucial in the disputed election between Samuel Tilden and Rutherford Hayes because Hayes won by *one vote*. Colorado became known as the "Centennial State" because it achieved statehood during the USA's one-hundredth anniversary.

The first Colorado Governor was John Routt, the first Senators (appointed) were Jerome Chaffee and Henry Teller, the first Representative was (Democrat) Thomas Patterson.

EARLY EXPLORATIONS

The first well documented penetration of what is now the Centennial State occurred in 1706 when the renowned **Juan de Ulibarrí** led a rescue mission into the territory (Colorado east of Pueblo and Colorado Springs) of the Cuartelejo Apaches. [See Note # 3.] Scores of Picurís had fled New Mexico after the 1696 uprising and had been subsequently enslaved by the Apaches. New Mexico Governor Cuervo y Valdés sent Ulibarrí to take the Picurís out of slavery and return them to their village. It took some time to gather the Picurís from outlying rancherías, the area being explored (and *El Capitán* peak possibly being identified at this time) until the refugees were returned to New Mexico.

The next significant exploration of Colorado came in 1776 under the leadership of two priests, Francisco Atanasio **Domínguez** and Silvestre Vélez de **Escalante**. [See Note # 4.] With this expedition was the noteworthy **Bernardo de Miera y Pacheco**, well known as an engineer, merchant, Indian fighter, government agent, rancher, artist, and, of particular importance in this expedition, cartographer. The Domínguez-Escalante expedition route traversed and described (with comments like"...*stopped to observe the latitude by the meridian of the sun...it was good land, with facilities for irrigation and everything else necessary for three or four settlements...*") much of western Colorado before going into Utah.

In August of 1779, the incomparable **Juan Bautista de Anza** led his New Mexican soldiers, settlers, and Pueblo auxiliaries into Colorado for a showdown with Comanches led by **Cuerno Verde**. [See Note # 5.] In order not to alert the Comanches by marching on the eastern side of the Sangre de Cristo Mountains, Anza led his force northward through the San Luis Valley then crossed toward the east at (present) Wilkerson Pass then Ute Pass, then on to (present) Colorado Springs, from where could be seen *El Capitán*, where the expedition turned south to encounter the Comanches. While his journal is concerned basically with the campaign, much of it describes the Colorado landscape. [See Note # 6.]

In 1806 there appeared the spy expedition of **Zebulon M. Pike**. Sent by the scheming General James Wilkinson, ostensibly for geographical exploration, Pike was to report on how feasible would be an American invasion of New Mexico. [See Note # 7.] The Rocky Mountains were sighted in November and some of his men were sent to climb the highest peak but they were unable to do so because of the snow. (Pike never climbed "Pike's Peak," some sources saying he got no closer than twenty miles from it.) Being unfamiliar with the exigencies of high mountain travel, the Americans didn't even have proper winter clothing and their supplies were running low. A breastwork of logs was erected around the site of modern Pueblo and later the suffering expedition crossed into the San Luis Valley. Spanish soldiers took the bedraggled group into custody and on to Santa Fe and Chihuahua where the Americans were released in 1807. Pike's report was printed in 1810 and became popular reading for Americans who previously had known nothing of what was to become Colorado and "The West."

The Long Expedition of 1820 was the next American thrust into Colorado. **Stephen H. Long**, native of New Hampshire and graduate of Dartmouth College, and his group first viewed the Rockies in July. From (present) Colorado Springs, the young scientist **Edwin James**, who would write the record of the expedition, decided to climb the great peak to the west. James and two of his men accomplished the feat. Long named it "James' Peak" in honor of this first American achievement. (Promotion, perhaps encouraged by alliteration, finally settled on "Pike's Peak," though the historical honor belongs to Edwin James and before that to whoever named it *El Capitán*.)

A direct result of the Long Expedition was the erroneous description of eastern Colorado and the plains as the "Great American Desert." Obviously unacquainted with the geography of the West, Long compared the *"vast plains"* to *"the sandy deserts of Africa...uninhabitable by a people depending on agriculture."* Americans came to believe the rich grasslands of the high plains were like the Sahara Desert. [See Note # 8.]

MINING

The mining industry has been of paramount importance in the development of Colorado. In 1859 the "Pike's Peak gold rush" was promoted by merchants and popular guidebooks. It has been estimated that some 50,000 people reached the goldfields but most were quickly disappointed by the demanding work and small returns. Many came to agree with Mark Twain's definition of a gold mine: *a hole in the ground owned by a liar.* But then men like George A. Jackson, John H. Gregory, Wilkes Defrees, etc., uncovered the first lode mine that proved the existence of Pike's Peak gold. Towns were virtually emptied as hordes of gold seekers, popularly referred to as *59ers*, rushed to the diggings.

The town of **Leadville** began its silver boom in 1877 and within a year it boasted some 120 saloons, 115 gambling houses, 35 brothels, and 31 restaurants. [See Note # 9.] By 1880 its silver production was valued at $11.5 million and Leadville silver-lead smelters were considered the most productive in North America. Among the more spectacular mines was the *Little Pittsburgh*. The city was choked by smoke, the streets were strewn with filth, and housing ranged from canvas to rickety but everyone agreed that any kind of house in the land of silver was better than a mortgaged mansion anywhere else.

Leadville thrived on its bonanza spirit and was variously described as *wild, fast, roaring, eager, fierce,* etc. Banking made good profits, as did saloons. In 1880 it was reported that the 249 Leadville saloons took in some $4,000,000. Fortunes were also made in real estate. For example, some lots went from a value of $25 to $5,000 in six months. Town government was feeble but efforts were made to build hospitals, schools, churches, etc. People tended to gather by ethnicity: Irish, German, Scandinavian, Cornishmen, blacks, etc.

As with all mining communities, Leadville boom turned to bust at the end of 1880. The final bonanza in Colorado was at Cripple Creek during the 1890s.

CATTLE INDUSTRY

It has been written that **John C. Dawson** trailed the first herd of Texas cattle into Colorado in 1859. The best known cattle routes coming into the state were the Dawson Trail and the Goodnight Trail. Large herds started coming as of 1864-65 and the "bonanza days of the open range" began. Once the Indians were bludgeoned away from their ancestral properties, the rich grasslands became "public domain" for cattle to feed on.

Like prospecting for gold, the cattle industry was risky business. While the cost of trailing cattle in from Texas was around $1 per head, many variables could come into play: number of animals (2-3,000 being considered the best size), branding them for the trail (road brand), number and abilities of cowboys (due to ancestral legacies, Hispanics were the most experienced) and horses, trail conditions, availability of water, weather (storms could be disastrous), Indians/homesteaders met on the trail, health-disease of the cattle, stampedes, etc.

In 1880 a steer could be bought in Texas for around $9.30 and sold in Colorado for $14.50 so various men worked for the profit. The cattle kings in Colorado included John Wesley Iliff, John Wesley Prowers, and James C. Jones. The best known corporate ranching outfit was the Prairie Cattle Company organized in 1881.

As with mining lore, ranching was basically a new industry to people coming into Colorado. For example, it was not until 1885 that a centralized system for brands was required by state government. The death knell of open range ranching began in 1874 with the creation of barbed wire fencing. Another serious contributing factor was overstocking the range, though cattlemen blamed sheepmen for destroying the grasslands. The fact that many sheepmen were Hispanic enabled English-speaking cattlemen to vent their traditional American racism against targeted minorities. [See Note # 10.]

AGRICULTURE

The San Luis People's Ditch was started on April 10, 1852 by the area's Hispanic pioneers who emanated from New Mexico. This was the beginning of Colorado agriculture by non-Indian people. English speaking settlers who had depended on rainfall "were doomed" when they crossed the one hundredth meridian because rain was not dependable for agricultural production on the high plains. Irrigation was an absolute necessity for farming, in which case a 160-acre homestead might be more land than one farmer could work. The alternatives were grazing or dry farming, in which 160 acres weren't enough.

The Homestead Act (1862), the Timber Culture Act (1873), and the Desert Land Act (1877) were efforts in national land policy and use but they often resulted in fraud. Further, the new English speaking immigrants had to learn new water law because riparian rights from humid areas of the USA were now inapplicable in the arid West. The **Doctrine of Prior Appropriation** (water could be diverted but users along a flow of water would be guaranteed enough water for their needs) was made into law and part of the State Constitution.

David K. Wall is thought to have been among the first successful farmers north of San Luis. In 1859 he diverted water from Clear Creek at Golden in order to irrigate a couple of acres of vegetables. He made a profit and others quickly followed his lead.

Residents of Greeley formed a community effort in 1870. By pooling their resources they were able to build larger and longer canals that provided water for lands above the riverbeds. Other cooperatives were soon formed.

Corporate farming activity took hold between 1870-80 because irrigation systems might well be lucrative investments. The Colorado Mortgage and Investment Company, better known as the **English Company,** constructed the Larimer and Weld Canal, just one of the various corporation projects (which would include the Otero, Fort Lyon, Bessemer, Bob Creek).

Experiments were made with new crops. It was learned that alfalfa (first planted in Colorado in 1863) from Mexico could produce three cuttings in one year. Mennonite farmers brought in hard red winter wheat which proved acceptable after 1881 when milling techniques were improved. Potatoes proved successful. By 1890 some 2,000 railroad cars full of potatoes were being shipped out. A wet cycle developed during the 1880s, encouraging new farmers to come to Colorado and till the soil. When a terrible drought hit in the 1890s farm production failed and "the only crop was bankrupts."

Not everything was bust. The sugar beet industry grew stronger in the early 1900s when the Great Western Sugar Corporation and the Holly Sugar Company were created through mergers. Farmers raised some 108,000 acres of beets in 1909 and 166,000 acres by 1919. Beet sugar has served as a reliable cash crop and processed beet pulp has been engineered as livestock feed. Between 1900 and 1940 the Great Plains and plateau took their rightful place as producers of Colorado wealth.

IMMIGRANT LABORERS

The first laborers to work in the sugar beet fields have been described as German/Russian immigrants. When more stoop labor was needed, Hispanos were brought in from New Mexico to do the "bunching, thinning, hoeing, and harvesting." While it has never been explained why Americans were not hired for such work, the sugar corporations went into border towns like El Paso, Texas, to bring in workers from Mexico. [See Note # 11.]

Between 1915 and 1930 anywhere from 2,000 to 15,000 workers were brought into Colorado. By 1927 some 60% of sugar beet workers were Hispanic. In the Platte Valley the permanent resident population of Mexican people had increased from 3,000 to some 11,000. The 1930 Census revealed that Colorado now had some 13,000 residents who had been born in Mexico and some 28,000 Hispanos from New Mexico.

The large companies delivered workers to the farmers who in turn were expected to provide fair wages, housing, and facilities. In the boom years of 1920-23, the average family earned around $1,000 annually. During the Depression years it was perhaps half that.

RACISM

Though immigrants were needed to do the work that Americans wouldn't do, Mexican immigrants were regarded at best as "a necessary evil." By the 1920s a virulent prejudice excluded or segregated Mexicans from Colorado swimming pools, movie houses, restaurants, and other such public places. Newspapers and law enforcement officials portrayed them as "natural criminals." The same discrimination applied to jobs, housing, schools, etc. The situation could be said to be summed up by the school Superintendent of Weld County in the 1920s: "...*respectable people do not want their children to sit along side of dirty, filthy, diseased, infested Mexicans.*" It was said that "*Anglo pupils enjoyed taunting the greasers...teachers assumed that Mexican children had no capacity for learning...*" While some Coloradans believed the Hispanos from New Mexico weren't as "inferior" as those from Mexico, all were basically lumped together in the "Anglo" mind. [See Note # 12.] In 1965 the *Crusade for Justice* was founded by former world-class boxer **Rodolfo (Corky) Gonzales** in order to combat the forces of racism in Colorado and the Southwest.

African-Americans in Colorado during the 1920s-30s were channeled into jobs traditionally reserved for them: railroad porter, waiter, household servant, unskilled labor, janitor. Discriminatory housing practices decreed that only blacks could rent to blacks. Social services were guided along the same lines. For example, the Denver Parks Department prohibited blacks from swimming pools except on Wednesday at the downtown Curtis Street pool. The black family income in 1940 was 62% that of a white family while the Hispanic family survived on less than half of black family earnings.

The Bureau of Indian Affairs began encouraging Native Americans to move to large cities and by 1970 Denver had some 4,104 Indians from various tribes living there. Their median family income in 1970 was $7,163, even less than that of Hispanic families. Few Utes decided to pull up stakes and move to urban environments.

In summation of Colorado racism, all "*can be thankful that Denver, Pueblo, and Colorado Springs escaped full-scale rioting during the hot summers of the 1960s.*"

LABOR and CAPITAL

In 1899 there was created the mega-corporation known as the **American Smelting and Refining Company**. The gigantic combination, capitalized at some $65 million, included most of the significant smelter works in Colorado. One exception was the Guggenheim smelter at Pueblo but by 1901 they too joined the trust and were soon in a position to control it.

Labor had no choice but to organize in the face of such corporate power. The **Western Federation of Miners** gained strength. The **United Mine Workers of America** organized workers in the coal mines. The struggle between management and labor often focused on the hiring of non-union labor: management wanted them for work, especially to break a strike, while labor unions were determined to drive them off. Battles were fought in the General Assembly as well as mining sites. Each side sponsored legislation which would protect them. For example, labor wanted the right of collective bargaining while management demanded that it should not be required that unions be recognized. Among significant strikes were those at Cripple Creek in 1903-04 and the coalfields in 1910-14.

The Cripple Creek strike started out as a gesture of sympathy for the mill workers at Colorado City, where ore was processed. Then mill workers demanded the reduction of the 12 hour day to 8 hours and the gold miners went out on strike to support them. Non-union laborers were imported so union members barricaded the roads and tracks going into the gold fields. Mine owners called on the governor who promptly dispatched militiamen to Cripple Creek. The strike continued and each side resorted to "raw and brutal" violence to attain its goals. [See Note # 13.] On June 6, 1904, the railroad station at Independence was dynamited, resulting in thirteen deaths and many wounded among nonunion workers. Each side blamed the other for the atrocity but the popular mind blamed the union. The strike was ended when owners reopened the mines with nonunion labor.

In 1914 the United Mine Workers made a concerted effort to improve their situation. They demanded recognition of their union, a 10% increase in wages, enforcement of the eight-hour work day, improved health and safety regulations, the right to select their own houses, restaurants, and doctors (instead of those chosen by the company). The typical pattern evolved: strikers were replaced with nonunion labor, union men fought their entry into the coalfields, the governor sent in the militia. On April 20, 1914, militiamen drove the miners out of Ludlow Station. Five miners and one militiaman were killed but a fire started in the tent colony in which two women and eleven children perished. (Henceforth the event would be referred to as the *Ludlow Massacre*.) A veritable war continued for ten days as "burnings, dynamitings, and murders" ruled the day. Governor Elías Ammons decided the situation was beyond his control so he asked President Woodrow Wilson to send in federal troops, who finally quieted the situation. While a few concessions were won by the miners, the UMW lost because bargaining rights were denied it and the owners instituted a company union. There was no way to win so long as mine owners could control the government and its forces.

POLITICS

Republicans controlled every legislature in Colorado until the 1890s, making the Democrats a minority party that enjoyed only an occasional victory. Among the most influential men were Thomas Bowen, Jerome Chaffee, George Chilcott, Horace Tabor, Henry Teller, and Casimiro Barela, who is seldom written about in comparison with other Colorado leaders.

Casimiro Barela was born (1847) in Taos, New Mexico and went into what is now Colorado in 1866. He became active in the politics of Las Animas County, won a seat in the House of Representatives in 1871 then the Senate in 1876 where he served continuously until 1912. He has been referred to by some as "Father of the Colorado Senate." [See Note # 14.]

A "classic political struggle" unfolded in 1882-83 when Henry Teller vacated his Senate seat to become Secretary of the Interior. Of the various seekers for the office, Thomas Bowen and Horace Tabor were the strongest candidates. Bowen, a native of Arkansas, finally won the six-year term and went on to become known as "Washington's finest poker player." [See Note # 15.] Legislators in 1889-90 "scandalously squandered appropriations" and political corruption appears to have been the rule until the 1890s.

Weary of shady politicians, in 1892 Coloradans elected Populist **Davis H. Waite** to the governor's chair and Populists John C. Bell and Lafe Pence as Representatives to Congress. With the aid of a few

Democrats, Populists could control the state Senate while Republicans had a one-vote majority in the House. The Populists stood for an eight-hour work day, employers' liability laws, protection for child labor, etc., "paternalism for the common people." [See Note # 16.]

Silver was the foundation of the Colorado economy but in 1893 the price of silver continued to fall, forcing mining and smelting works to shut down. To make matters worse, a severe drought developed in agricultural areas. A full economic crash hit Colorado in July of 1893 and there were bank closures, business failures, foreclosures on property, workers were let go, etc. Governor Waite summoned the Legislature into special session and suggested various relief measures, which were shot down.

The Cripple Creek gold fields were still booming so many went there looking for work. With so much surplus labor on hand the mine owners could do pretty much as they pleased. The Western Federation of Miners called a strike early in 1894. Soon there were three armed camps in the goldfields: union strikers, the sheriff and his deputies, and the state militia. Governor Waite led a taskforce that saw the WFM settle with the mine owners and bloody violence was narrowly averted.

In the national election of 1896, Colorado "silverites" went strongly for William Jennings Bryan who wanted to "save the country from crucifixion upon the cross of gold." But McKinley was elected President, the death knell of silver as the foundation of Colorado's economy.

Colorado politics have been described as volatile and confused. For example, in 1904 Democrat Alva Adams was elected to the governor's chair. The Republican legislature yelled *election fraud*. They were able to declare enough vacancies in the legislature to unseat Adams, replacing him by Republican James H. Peabody, who had promised to resign immediately after taking office in order to put in Lt. Gov. (Republican) Jesse F. McDonald, who finally served as Governor of Colorado.

Weary of the (perceived) alliance between big money and the politicians it could buy, the beginning of the 20th century finally brought on interest in reform. In 1907 the Colorado General Assembly created the state's first civil service statute. It also enacted the first effective railroad commission to represent the public's interest in the workings of railroads.

John F. Shafroth (from Missouri) was elected Governor in 1908 and 1910. His platform called for various different reforms and his administrations brought out much progressive legislation. Among his major achievements were providing for initiative (in which citizens could initiate amendments to the constitution or any statute) and referendum (where voters could accept or reject statutes enacted by the legislature). Other progressive measures also included enactment of a primary election law, an election registration law, creation of a tax commission, a campaign expenses law, regulation of child and female labor, an eight-hour day for certain hazardous employment, creation of a conservation commission, and inspection acts which targeted factories and coal mines.

Reformers generally referred to themselves as *Progressives* and many did excellent work. For example, when **Robert W. Speer** became major of Denver he expanded the city's park system, built new boulevards, viaducts, sewer systems, etc. Judge **Ben Lindsey** created a *Juvenile Court* in order to manage juvenile offenders separately from adult criminals. **Emily Griffith** established an *Opportunity School* to fulfill the needs of children as well as adults in day as well as night classes in both academic and vocational studies. Speaking generally, progressives were an assortment of individuals working for prohibition, crusading journalists, ambitious politicians, determined private citizens, etc., following the dictates of their own consciences as Colorado was transforming itself from a rural to an urban state.. [See Note # 17.]

In 1912 there were four candidates for Governor: a Progressive, a Democrat, a Republican, and a Socialists. (Democrat Elías Ammons won.) Colorado voters defeated the proposed ban on the manufacture and sale of liquor but they did approve a constitutional amendment that provided for judicial recall. In 1913 the seventeenth amendment to the Constitution required that Senators in Congress had to be elected by the people instead of being appointed by state legislatures.

In 1919 the "red scare" anticommunist movement was identifiable in Colorado. It was charged that strikes were fomented by *Bolsheviks*. Headquarters for the Industrial Workers of the World in Pueblo was raided. In Denver a city ordinance was passed against any person speaking in such a way as to incite to "rebellion."

For a time the Ku Klux Klan gained ascendancy in Colorado. This "anti-foreign, anti-Catholic, anti-Jewish, anti-Negro" organization became a dominant force in state politics under the leadership of *Grand Dragon* Dr. **John Galen Locke** of Denver starting in 1924. The Klan has been described as controlling Governor Clarence J. Morley as well as the House. Strongest in Denver, the Klan was able to direct boycotts against Catholic and Jewish businesses. On Monday nights cross burning sessions were held at the summit of Lookout Mountain near Golden. The KKK began to decline as of the summer of 1925 but there "remains an ugly stain on the history of the state." [See Note # 18.]

When John J. Roche died in 1927, his daughter **Josephine Roche** inherited his holdings of the Rocky Mountain Fuel Company, the coal mining concern. The other owners were horrified when Josephine stated that coal miners' grievances were legitimate. Disgruntled stockholders threatened to sell their shares if the mines were unionized. Josephine bought them out. In 1828 an historic labor agreement was signed while other mine owners looked forward to Josephine's falling flat on her face. This was a real possibility because there was serious competition from oil and natural gas, not to mention the high wages Josephine had promised to pay. But the miners themselves rallied around her, selling coal on their own under the slogan of "Buy from Josephine!" Production rates soared to the degree that the Rocky Mountain Fuel Company became the most popular coal supplier in the state.

The Great Depression hit Colorado as hard as elsewhere but World War II finally ended it. Boom returned to Colorado with the creation of military installations as well as a number of scientific developments. The Denver Arms Plant (1941) employed some 20,000 people in the manufacture of munitions. The Rocky Mountain Arsenal, specializing in chemical weapons, employed some 15,000. Farms and factories now had markets paying good prices. Colorado's population increased and land values went up.

While Coloradans had little choice in the matter, the Granada Relocation Center was created on some 11,000 acres in the Arkansas Valley near the town of Granada. Japanese-Americans were deported from their homes and properties along the west coast and forced into the "detention" camp. The "detainees" began arriving in August of 1942 and the peak population got to be around 7,500, the overwhelming number of them citizens of the USA. As in the rest of the country, the "internees" had no one to champion them or the injustice they had to endure. [See Note # 19.]

Patricia Schroeder became Colorado's first woman in the national House of Representatives when she won the election of 1972. Ben Nighthorse Campbell was elected to the Senate in 1992 when better than 75% of Coloradans voted.

As with most Southwestern states, tourism is basic to Colorado because of its natural Rocky Mountain beauty. The environment does have problems, however, due to disasters like that at Summitville where toxic chemicals contaminated the water supply, and/or radio-active waste and similar pollution left behind by entities like Rocky Flats.

DISCUSSION NOTES *for* COLORADO STATEHOOD and SOCIETY

Note # 1
See the chapter titled "Carpetbagger's Kingdom" beginning on page 133 in *A Colorado History* by Carl Ubbelohde, Maxine Benson, Duane A. Smith.

Note # 2
See pages 138-39 in *A Colorado History*.

Note # 3.
See pages 137-38 in *Quest For Empire* by Donald Cutter & Iris Engstrand. See also page 201 in *Spain In The Southwest* by John L. Kessell.

Note # 4
See *Without Noise Of Arms* by Walter Briggs.

Note # 5
See Chapter 15 in *Bolton And The Spanish Borderlands* by John Francis Bannon. Bolton described Anza as *"…a man of heroic qualities, tough as oak, and silent as the desert from which he sprang…it is difficult to find anyone in Anglo-American annals with whom to compare him."*

Note # 6
See *The Diary Of Juan Bautista De Anza: Campaign of 1779 Against the Comanches*, translated by Alfred B. Thomas, Expounded upon by Ronald E. Kessler.

Note # 7
See page 121 in *It's Your Misfortune And None Of My Own: A History Of The American West* by Richard White.

Note # 8
It would be interesting to compare the "desert" description of the plains with that made almost three centuries before by members of the Coronado Expedition. See *Coronado: Knight Of Pueblos And Plains* by Herbert E. Bolton.

Note # 9
See page 102 in *Colorado: A History Of The Centennial State* by Carl Abbott, Stephen J. Leonard, David McComb. The book *A Colorado History* by Carl Ubbelohde, Maxine Benson, and Duane A. Smith additionally supplies (page 159) "17 barber shops, 51 groceries, 4 banks" but makes no mention of brothels.

Note # 10
See page 344 in the Richard White volume …*The American West* where he writes: "Like so much other economic violence, these conflicts often had racial, religious, and ethnic overtones."

Note # 11

See chapter 15 on "Plural Society" in *Colorado: A History Of The Centennial State*. As an aside, it has been observed that the "Protestant Work Ethic" is one of America's most cherished tenets but there seems to be an ironic pattern when difficult work needs to be done: *bring in immigrants*. Why did Americans refuse to labor on the railroad, agricultural fields, etc.? What kind of jobs are demanded by Americans and/or the "Protestant Work Ethic"?

Note # 12

While *racism* is just a word to some, to understand its realities it should be pointed out that in 1940, according to the *Centennial* volume quoted above, for every 1,000 live births in Mexican families, 205 babies died soon after birth. How can a civilized society condone such tragedy? Is it acceptable because of the "Master Race" complex?

Note # 13

See page 247 in *A Colorado History*.

Note # 14

José E. Fernández wrote *Forty Years As A Legislator, Or The Biography Of Casimiro Barela* in 1911. This biography is all but unknown to most students of Southwest history. Perhaps that will change now that New Mexican scholar A. Gabriel Melendez has translated the work into English (published by UNM Press).

It must also be pointed out that the Colorado histories by Sprague and Ubbelohde/Benson/ Smith don't even mention Barela, who served Colorado for some forty years. While the Abbott/Leonard/McComb *Colorado: A History Of The Centennial State* (see pages 41-49) does provide basic information on Barela it paves the way by saying that *"to Americans"* the Mexican farmers of southern Colorado where a *"shiftless…degraded race…their agriculture slovenly and without signs of thrift…Penitent Brothers were strange to Anglo-Americans…who had the normal Anglo-Saxon disregard for dissimilar cultures…for they were products of the rapid progress of civilization…who would replace Hispanics because they were ignorant and debased to a shameful degree."* There are many questions that should be asked when confronted with this type of historiography and the attitudes it conveys. Is Casimiro Barela being ignored or denigrated in comparison to other political leaders of Colorado? Is it abject racism to consider an entire group as a "degraded race"? Is racism being condoned by this kind of historiography? Is this racism being perpetuated by Orwellian techniques?

While it is possible that leaders like Thomas Bowen, Jerome Chaffee, George Chilcott, Horace Tabor, Henry Teller, etc., were from various Germanic ethnic groups (or did they/their families change their ethnic names upon arriving in the USA in order to be accepted?), how is it that all are considered *Anglo* (Angles were only one of the various Germanic tribes)? Marshall Sprague postulates that an Anglo in Colorado is a white person of "whatever European origin." Many Hispanic people are of "European origin" so would that make them *Anglos*? How can Latin people like the French or Italians be *Anglo*? Does this strategy in effect become a *master race* concept for American racism? What are the similarities/contrasts between *Anglo* (or Anglo-Saxon) as used in 19th century America and *Aryan* in 20th century Europe? What of America in the 21st?

The largest ethnic groups in the USA have been identified as German, Italian, Irish, and Austrian. On occasion all these groups have been targeted by racism but in the modern era American racism has been described as particularly virulent toward Indians, blacks, Hispanics, and Orientals. What is required for citizens of the USA to be considered *Americans*?

Note # 15

See page 208 in *A Colorado History*.

Note # 16

See pages 141-42 in *Colorado: A History Of The Centennial State*.

Note # 17

See page 253 in *Colorado...centennial State*.

Note # 18

See page 286 in *A Colorado History*.

Note # 19

It appears this tragedy was not founded on anything other than another national "scare" and an opportunity to usurp Japanese-American properties. There has been not a single incident uncovered relating to Japanese-Americans not being loyal to the USA. It would be interesting to discuss the civil rights of targeted groups when said groups are considered to be "security risks" or whatever label is in fashion at the time. What groups would or would not be targeted in the present era?

UTAH STATEHOOD and SOCIETY

The State of Deseret was organized in 1849 and hope was expressed that statehood would soon follow. Deseret was a well-functioning, theocratic entity which continued to operate for some two years.

The Organic Act for the creation of Utah Territory was signed on September 9, 1850. The staffing and organization of Territorial government wasn't complete until August of 1851. Problems were immediate because by late September three high ranking appointees "packed their carpetbags" and returned East. [See Note # 1. *Notes begin on page 537.*] Other officials were appointed but they were often (described as) "misfits" in Utah. The executive department continued in Mormon hands until 1858 when Brigham Young was replaced by Alfred Cumming.

By 1869 some 80,000 converts had arrived in Utah, more than enough to qualify for statehood. But problems continued between the "gentile" federal government and Latter Day Saints of Utah. In 1870 William H. Hooper stated: "The Mormons are the most vigorously lied about people on earth." Over the years seven official appeals were made for statehood but demands for separation of Church and State and abolishment of polygamy remained serious obstacles. Progress began to be made by the Manifesto of 1890 which called for the end of plural marriages and a withdrawal of the Church from partisan politics. In 1891 the Mormons dissolved their "People's Party" and divided among national parties. In 1894 Congress passed an enabling act for Utah statehood. Delegates numbering 107 met and within two months created a constitution, which the federal government accepted and which was ratified overwhelmingly by the people. On January 4, 1896, President Gover Cleveland declared Utah a State in the American Union. Heber M. Wells was elected Governor.

EARLY EXPLORATIONS

It is no longer believed that members of the Coronado Expedition of 1540-42 (in the person of García López de Cárdenas) crossed into Utah. It appears that the first penetration of European-based people came in 1765 with a small expedition headed by the resourceful **Juan María Antonio Rivera**. With Rivera were Gregorio Sandoval, Antonio Martin, Andrés Sandoval, and a Ute interpreter named Joaquín (or Juanchinillo). [See Note # 2.] Hispanics being a mining people, the Rivera expedition was on the lookout for signs of silver when they crossed into Utah northeast of Montecello and into what is now Moab, Utah.

That basic honor of extensive Utah exploration by non-Indians is accorded to the Domínguez-Escalante group of 1776. **Francisco Atanacio Domínguez** and **Silvestre Vélez de Escalante** were two Franciscans from New Mexico who got permission to blaze a trail from Santa Fe to the missions of California. Among the ten-man (starting) group was the stalwart **Bernardo Miera y Pacheco** and the trusted **Juan Pedro Cisneros**. Father Domínguez was the leader of the expedition as well as Father Vélez de Escalante's superior.

The Domínguez-Escalante expedition set out on July 29, 1776, and entered what is now Utah on September 11. The "wayfarers" described the Utah Valley in glowing terms, that it had excellent pastures, abundant water in streams and rivers, good climate, mountains rich in timber, etc. Miera y Pacheco drew a map which included the Great Salt Lake.

The explorers continued south by southwest. A snowstorm struck around October 8th and soon the travelers were dangerously low on provisions. The quest for Monterey had to be abandoned. They made it back to Santa Fe by January 2, 1777, after journeying some 2,000 miles in their 158-day odyssey which explored what would be called the **Great Basin**. The Domínguez-Escalante journal was the first to describe the flora and fauna of Utah, along with its native inhabitants. (It has been said that, after Spanish authorities, the great Baron Alexander von Humboldt was one of the first scholars to utilize the Domínguez-Escalante journal.)

Fur traders and mountain men trappers pushed into Utah around the year 1824 in their quest for pelts (from which were made beaver felt hats). **Peter Skene Ogden** led the large contingent from the (British) Hudson Bay Company, **Jedediah S. Smith** became the best known American trapper, with **Etienne Provost** (pronounced *Provo*) becoming the best known French-Canadian trapper (working out of Taos, NM). In 1837 **Antoine Robidoux** (from NM) built a trading post on the west fork of the Uinta River (by present White Rocks). [See Note # 3.] All of these men followed existing trails or blazed new ones in Utah.

In 1841 the **Bartleson-Bidwell** Party is credited with bringing the first wagon train into Utah. (The wagons would be abandoned in favor of pack animals before the group made it to California.) **John Charles Frémont** came into Utah in 1843, 1845, and 1853. [See Note # 4.] While Frémont was often following trails blazed by others (therefore referred to as a "Pathmarker" by some), he did traverse regions which had not been written about before and he was adept at self-promotion. Published in 1845, his *"Report of the Exploring Expedition to the Rocky Mountains in the Year 1842, and to Oregon and North California in the Years 1843-44,"* most of which is said to have been written by his wife **Jessie Benton**, was to have a crucial influence on the Latter-day Saints of 1847.

MORMON PIONEERS

The *Church of Jesus Christ of Latter-day Saints* was organized in 1830. Converts to the Church came from the USA as well as Europe. They were persecuted and forced to leave their communities in New York, Ohio, Missouri, and finally Illinois. After the murder (1844) of founder Joseph Smith, **Brigham Young** led the Mormon migration to the Great Basin beginning in 1847. Young had read Frémont's glowing report of the area and decided this would be the nucleus of the *Kingdom*. Though the Great Basin turned out being more desert than Garden of Eden, the call was sent out to gather to *Zion*. Within about two decades there were some 80,000 Mormons living in some 300 settlements in or around the Great Basin. These settlements embraced an area extending some one thousand miles from north to south, some eight-hundred from east to west. Brigham Young qualifies as one of America's greatest pioneering leaders for he served as head of the colonization, the directing hand behind the founding of settlements, president of the Church, the first governor of Deseret and the Territory of Utah, head of the Nauvoo Legion militia, as well as regional superintendent for Indian Affairs.

CONFRONTATION

As of 1857 President James Buchanan appeared to be convinced that Mormon Utah was in a state of rebellion. Federally appointed officials had charged that Mormons had no respect for non-Mormons, that Indians were being alienated, that necessary records were being destroyed instead of put into the hands of government officials, that government by the Mormon priesthood was despotism, etc. Buchanan appointed **Alfred Cumming** (from Georgia) as Utah governor and ordered General William S. Harney to organize a military force to escort Cumming to Salt Lake City. Harney was replaced by Col. Albert S. Johnston while advance units were under the temporary command of Col. Edmund B. Alexander. Ahead of them was sent Quartermaster Corps Captain Stewart Van Vliet to make arrangements for food and forage.

News that an invading American army was on its way ran through Utah. Mormon leaders, perhaps remembering previous persecutions, decided to resist if American troops forced their way into the Territory. Fiery rhetoric was heard everywhere as the Nauvoo Legion was mustered. Captain Van Vliet arrived to consult with Mormon leaders as of September 7, 1857. He discerned that Mormons were not in rebellion but they would be prepared to defend themselves if necessary. He was unable to make quartermaster arrangements so he returned to the expeditionary force and then went on to Washington where he advocated a peaceful reconciliation.

Amid the fiery preaching and general warlike atmosphere there appeared the **Fancher-Baker Train** of immigrants to California. Led by Alexander Fancher and Captain John T. Baker, the train was composed of some thirteen families from Arkansas and a group of horsemen (the latter of whom called themselves the *Missouri Wildcats*). Adolescents under the age of sixteen outnumbered the men, and the eighteen infants ranging in age from six days to six months outnumbered the women.

Expecting an American military invasion, Mormons refused to sell supplies to the Fancher-Baker Train. Words and threats were exchanged on both sides and then the immigrants went on to **Mountain Meadows** where they decided to rest their animals. Between September 7-11, 1857, they camped at Mountain Meadows, some thirty-five miles southwest of Cedar City on the trail to California. Meanwhile, Mormon leaders back at Cedar City decided to attack the train before it could make it to California and return to invade the Territory from that side.

Historians differ as to what role Indians had in the Mountain Meadows Massacre. Some say they were responsible for the massacre. Stewart Udall, who has a solid reputation for veracity, writes that Indians had no part at all in the tragedy. [See Note # 5.] Mormon militiamen under the leadership of Major **John D. Lee**, some disguised as Indians, attacked the Fancher-Baker Train. Wagons were circled and a fight ensued though it ended in stalemate. Then a fifty-man force of Iron County militia appeared on the scene. It was decided all immigrants had to be exterminated, except the infants. Under a white flag of truce, the immigrants were approached and promised safety "from the Indians" if they would surrender all guns to the Iron County militia then the train would be escorted to Cedar City. The infants would proceed first, then the women and children, then the men. The train leaders accepted the terms and the caravan began its way back to Cedar City. At a prearranged signal each militiaman shot the unarmed, defenseless immigrant male closest to him until all were dead, then the soldiers went up to the women and adolescents, shooting them all in cold blood. [See Note # 6.]

Bodies were dumped into hastily dug graves. The infants were given out to Mormon families. The booty of wagons, horses, oxen, cattle, and personal valuables were given to local Church leaders. Militia leaders spread the word that Indians had massacred the immigrants, sparing only the infants who were "sold" to Mormons.

Brigham Young didn't want the tragedy to injure the Church so he had a trusted *apostle* investigate the entire incident. The report supported the Indian massacre story and further, some in the immigrant party might have been connected with the persecutions of Mormons in Missouri and Illinois. All militia leaders were cleared, except John D. Lee.

Federal officers later came in to claim the surviving infants and gather facts for their own report. The true story came out from a guilt-ridden militiaman: there had been no Indians, just militiamen. When the word got out that militia leaders would be arrested they fled to mountain hideouts.

The Civil War came and went but the Mountain Meadows Massacre would not go away. In an effort to placate public opinion, Brigham Young had John D. Lee excommunicated. Lee would be the scapegoat for Mountain Meadows. In 1874 Lee was captured and brought to trial. He was found guilty, taken to Mountain Meadows and executed by firing squad in 1875.

POLYGAMY

The Mormon Church sponsored the institution of plural marriage and had been practiced secretly by the leadership before migrating to Utah. [See Note # 7.] It was made public in 1852 and the practice was sensationalized in American media.

Mormon theology postulated that plural marriage solved many social problems. Through "The

Principle," all women could have the opportunity for marriage and childbearing. Widows could have another chance to enter into family life. Young women coming in from abroad could marry instead of being forced into burdensome domestic service or immoral prostitution. Leaders pointed out that there was no prostitution in Mormon settlements, quite a contrast from the situation in *gentile* communities. [See Note # 8.]

No one really knows what percentage of Mormons were actually involved in plural marriages. It has been said that some 10% of males were polygamous, that the majority of that ten percent took only one additional wife, though some of the leaders had more than twenty women "sealed" to them. It was felt that at times the percentage went as high as 20%, as in the years 1856-57 and in 1882.

Polygamy was intended only for Mormons who were faithful and active in the Church. Some members rejected plural marriage, for any number of reasons, including that the first wife had to give her permission. Some wives refused, some acquiesced grudgingly, and some favored the institution. [See Note # 9.]

It was customary to have separate homes or living quarters for each wife and her children. (This worked against the practice because it was too expensive for most people.) Husbands divided their time between their families. (Some leaders had wives in various settlements.) While some wives managed their households basically on their own, it was common for the wives of one man to associate in order to share necessary labors, especially housekeeping and babysitting. The children all related to each other and referred to other wives as "aunts." Jealousy could erupt very easily and often wives competed with each other through cooking, sewing, etc., the children or budgetary management. Pioneering was extremely difficult and Stewart L. Udall relates that Louisa (Bonelli) Hamblin once commented to a granddaughter: "*I was not happy unless I was miserable, for I knew nothing except hardships…as Jacob Hamblin's squaw…*" referring to how difficult life was for Indian and Mormon women. [See Note # 10.]

The overriding characteristic of plural marriage was that it was not legal under American law and American society was not going to change. This drove the institution underground, making it more difficult for Church regulation. On the home front, polygamy was expensive and few men had enough money to support plural families. Pressures mounted.

WOODRUFF MANIFESTO of 1890

By 1890 everyone could read the writing on the wall: polygamy had to end for Utah to become part of the American Union. On September 25, 1890, President **Wilford Woodruff** wrote in his journal: "*I have arrived at a point in the history of my life as President of the Church of Jesús Christ of Latter-day Saints where I am under the necessity of acting for the temporal salvation of the Church…and now, I publicly declare that my advice to the Latter-day Saints is to refrain from conducting any marriage forbidden by the law of the land.*" Mormons gathered in general conference on October 6, 1890, and unanimously approved the Woodruff Manifesto. At first the move was doubted by certain leaders in Washington but it was proven to be genuine. The road to statehood was secure.

NEW IMMIGRATION

Whereas Mormons arrived basically from northern Europe, southern and eastern Europeans came to Utah in the Territorial and/or early statehood years. They were Greek, Italian, Yugoslavs (Croats, Slovenes, Serbs, Dalmatians, Herzegovinians, Bosnians, etc.), and some from the Middle East. These immigrants were recruited to labor on the railroads and/or in the mining and smeltering centers in and around the Salt Lake Valley. A typical pattern emerges: these laborers were segregated from whites and discriminated against in housing and wages. Working conditions are invariably described as dangerous with employers taking no responsibility for the risks. Maimings and deaths were not rare. There were no unions nor workmen's compensation. Immigrants lived in "Greek Towns, Lebanese Towns, Bohunk Towns, Wop Towns, Little Italies," etc. [See Note # 11.]

Agents who recruited workers proved to be crucial in the economy of the day. Perhaps the best known was the Greek **Leonidas G. Skliris**, "Czar of the Greeks," a *padrone* (labor boss/agent) who wielded great power in Utah and the West. Skliris advertised for workers in Greek newspapers in the USA as well as Greece and Crete. Thousands of Greeks responded and came to work on the railroads and coal mines of Utah and the West. Skliris became immensely wealthy because he collected fees from everyone. Indeed, he hired workers and if they went out on strike, as Yugoslavs and Italians often did, he hired strikebreakers. Predictably, all strategies were used to control workers, including setting one ethnic group against another, even factions of the same ethnicity against each other, for the benefit of management. The power of Skliris wasn't broken until 1912 when he was forced to leave Utah. The restrictive immigration laws of 1821 and 1824 immediately began to diminish the supply of immigrant labor in Utah.

New immigrants were easy to recognize because they were usually darker skinned than the Mormon populace, a dark skin somehow associated with ethnic/racial inferiority in the American psyche. [See Note # 12.] They were criticized for reading foreign language newspapers, for belonging to Eastern Orthodox or Roman Catholic churches, sending money "back home," and generally refusing to *Americanize*. (Succeeding generations became acculturated and foreign influences were all but gone by WW II.) There were instances of violent repression of immigrants, as when a Greek in Price, Utah, was nearly lynched when he took a "white girl" for a ride in his new car. The Ku Klux Klan attacks of 1924 caused immigrants to unite against such injustice, neutralizing Klan power, though a black man named Robert Marshall was lynched in 1925.

RESOURCES

Beginning in 1847 the base for Utah's economy was agricultural. Between 1890 and 1920 there arose agri-business as well as corporate mining and manufactures. During those decades agricultural acreage grew from 1.3 million to 5 million acres. Diversified farming was typical and there were increases in the production of wheat, fruits and vegetables, livestock, etc, but among the most significant crops was the introduction of sugar beets. The industry became a good cash crop in Utah.

Mining was the leading export industry. Coal mining became very important and Utah coal production topped one million tons for the first time in 1900. Copper mines were also developed and proved quite profitable. Copper and lead smelters were stimulated by World War I, though farmers protested that emissions of sulphur dioxide injured their crops. Labor was unable to unionize workers in large corporations like American Smelting and Refining, Utah Copper, and Utah Fuel.

Milling, meat packing, and canning also became important industries. By the end of 1919 Utah was a major exporter of flour with Ogden at the center of the industry, as it was in canning and meat packing.

URBANIZATION

By 1970 around 80% of Utah's population was living in urban environments like those of Salt Lake City, Provo, and Ogden.

There have been a number of factors which promoted the growth of **Salt Lake City**. It quickly became a supply source for the California gold rush of 1849. It functioned as a receiving station for thousands of entering Mormon immigrants so it became the hub of Mormon culture. It became a center for religious life then also political, civil, and commercial influences. As it became the largest city in the intermountain area it prospered as a regional commercial and business metropolis.

Ogden grew because of the transcontinental railroad and branch lines that were built in the 19th century. The railroad also facilitated growth due to war industries brought in by WW II.

Provo grew rapidly in the mid 19th century then abated until the Ironton Works brought in jobs in the 1920s. World War II brought in defense industries and population increased some sixty percent.

MINORITIES

It has been said that identifiable minorities have made progress toward equality but that Utah society, described as a microcosm of American society, has had difficulties in accepting them as equals. [See Note # 13.] By *identifiable* is generally meant Indians, blacks, Hispanics, and Orientals. These groups have characteristics in common which are said to single them out: physical characteristics like skin color, texture of hair, etc.; their cultural patterns aren't from northern Europe; they weren't immigrants in the sense of leaving northern Europe forever; excepting Orientals, these groups had been conquered or enslaved in America; Amerindians and Hispanics share the loss of their native lands to the American Government. Finally, these minorities truly have had very small population numbers in Utah.

In 1887 the **Dawes Severalty Act** (General Allotment) was passed under the guise of promoting Indian welfare but in effect to acquire more Indian land for "white settlement." Indians were opposed because they realized they would lose much of their land. The Government forced it on them anyway. For example, in 1905 allotments were made to individual Utes, many of whom refused them, then remaining lands were "opened to white settlement." Also in 1905 President Theodore Roosevelt withdrew some 1,100,000 acres of reservation land and created the Uintah National Forest Reserve. In 1909 another 56,000 acres were taken for the Strawberry Valley reclamation project. In summation of the refusal to acknowledge Amerindians as owners of their land, Ute properties in the Uinta Basin went from 4,000,000 acres to around 360,000. Lawsuits have been filed and compensation has been awarded in efforts to undo the injustices of the past.

African-Americans have never had large numbers in Utah, though their history goes back to the Mormon founding. Blacks were generally treated as they were in the rest of the USA. For example, though still not a State in the Union, in 1851 the Utah territorial legislature passed laws to protect the American institution of slavery. In 1862 Congress abolished all slavery in American territories. But changes in American society were very slow in coming. For example, marriage between blacks and whites was against Utah law until 1963. Priesthood in the Mormon Church was denied to blacks until 1978. Among African-Americans remembered in Utah history are men like Green Flake, Hark Lay, Oscar Crosby, Albert Williams ("Speck"), Isom Dart, and Nat Love.

It has been said that **Hispanics** are Utah's largest identifiable minority. Historically, their greatest influence has been in leaving early place names and in more recent years they have been an important part in livestock operations as well as for labor in fields, orchards, sugar factories, canneries, etc.

Immigrants from Mexico have also arrived to labor in industrial environments like mills, smelters, and railroads. At times Mexicans were used as strikebreakers and during the Great Depression they were deported. Around 1965 it was said there were some 8,000 workers from Mexico in Utah.

Japanese-Americans didn't arrive in significant numbers in Utah until Executive Order 9066 (March 27, 1942) deported all Japanese from the West Coast. The Central Utah War Relocation Center, referred to as *Topaz*, brought some 8,000 Japanese-Americans into the State. They were forced to live in tar-paper barracks and were permitted to do only farm work. By law they were banned from owning land.

The Japanese in Topaz published a newspaper, managed schools, held art classes for adults, etc. **Mike Masaoka** became a spokesman for his *Issei* and *Nisei* (first and second generation Japanese-Americans, respectively) people. When WW II was over some 5,000 Japanese remained to live in Utah.

DISCUSSION NOTES *for* UTAH STATEHOOD and SOCIETY

Note # 1

See page 250 in *Among The Mormons* edited by William Mulder and A. Russell Mortensen. The term *carpetbagger* has been used to describe federal officials in the histories of Texas, Colorado, and now Utah.

Note # 2

See pages 170-73 in *Quest For Empire* by Donald Cutter & Iris Engstrand.

Note # 3

Among the more written-about mountain men are Jim Bridger, James Clyman, Thomas Fitzpatrick, Hugh Glass, Moses Harris, David E. Jackson, Daniel T. Potts, Jedediah Smith, Milton G. Sublette, William L. Sublette, John H. Weber, etc., with an occasional Jim Beckwith (James P. Beckwourth) thrown in. (See *Breeds And Half-breeds* by Gordon Speck.) Speaking generally, less is written about men like the incomparable Manuel Lisa ("Father of the American Fur Trade"), Mariano Medina of NM and Colorado; and French-Canadians like Provost and Robidoux. Despite the impression that Americans were *the* mountain men, it appears there were more French fur traders than any other nationality. See *The American Fur Trade Of The Far West* (2 vols.) by Hiram M. Chittenden.

Note # 4

See pages 73-79, plus the map on 728, in *Utah's History* by Richard D. Poll, Thomas G. Alexander, Eugene E. Campbell, and David E. Miller.

Note # 5

See pages 63-73 in *Forgotten Founders*. It can be observed that trying to blame Indians for white violence goes back at least to the Boston Tea Party.

Note # 6

See *Mountain Meadows Massacre* by Juanita Brooks. Could it be observed that, speaking generally, the disregard for the value of human life in the American West is seldom explored by American historiographers?

Note # 7

See pages 289-92 in *Utah's History*.

Note # 8

It has been written that as many as 50,000 prostitutes were working the American West. What are the implications for American society?

Note # 9

See *Isn't One Wife Enough?* by Kimball Young.

Note # 10

See pages 56-57 in *The Forgotten Founders* by Stewart L. Udall.

Note # 11

See page 456 in *Utah's History*. For more detailed information see *The Peoples Of Utah* edited by Helen Z. Papanikolas.

Note # 12

Historiographers seldom point out that the darker-skinned Greeks and Romans were founders of Western civilization. Lighter skinned Northern Europeans were not civilizers in the ancient world. Indeed, Germanic tribes finally conquered Rome and plunged Western Europe into the Dark Ages. Is it tantamount to *treason* to say so?

Note # 13

See Chapter 34 in *Utah's History*. See also chapters 1, 3, 10, 14 in *The Peoples Of Utah*.

OKLAHOMA STATEHOOD and SOCIETY

Oklahoma has been described as a paradox because of images evoked when one discusses the State and its people. The *Grapes of Wrath* has given us an image of poverty stricken *Okies* but on the other side of the coin there are highly accomplished Oklahomans like **Sequoyah** who gave the Cherokees an alphabet with which to write their language, humorist **Will Rogers**, the greatest of American athletes in **Jim Thorpe**, and world class historian **Angie Debo**. Then there are many engaging personalities like **O.C. Brown** who emanated from Oklahoma and earned their own brand of renown among their circle of friends and acquaintances.

EARLY HISTORY

The first Europeans to enter (what is now) *Oklahoma* (Choctaw for *"land of the red people"*) were in 1541. The Francisco Vásquez de **Coronado** and Hernando **De Soto** expeditions into Oklahoma mark the beginning of history written in a European language. [See Note # 1. *Notes begin on page 543.*] These

Hispanics went through various sections of Oklahoma. They never linked up. After these expeditions the area passed back and forth between the Spanish and French until 1803 when the USA made the Louisiana Purchase, thus sealing American ownership of Oklahoma.

In a very real sense, Oklahoma history begins with various groups of Native Americans. **Thomas Jefferson** wanted the Cherokee, Choctaw, Chickasaw, Creek, and Seminole nations, the "Five Civilized Tribes," to "relocate" to the West so that American settlers could have all Amerindian lands east of the Mississippi River. Tribal groups that sided with Tecumseh and the British, known as "Red Sticks," during the War of 1812 were targeted for violence. When Indian-hating **Andrew Jackson** became President in 1828 their fate was sealed. Jackson signed the Indian deportation bill on May 28, 1830. This began the violent uprooting of Amerindians living east of the Mississippi. The Cherokees filed a lawsuit and the Supreme Court ruled in their favor. President Jackson ignored the Court's ruling and used the Army and state militias to deport all Indians who refused to go West on their own. Some Amerindians were driven off their native lands "like cattle." It has been written that of the estimated 18,000 Cherokees some 4,000 died in stockades or on the "Trail of Tears" to Oklahoma. [See Note # 2.] Upon arrival the survivors now had to contend with the Osage Nation because the Osage believed the land belonged to them.

Many Amerindian deportees had died on the trail or in the pestilence of steamboats. Further, pioneer settlement in virgin land was invariably an ordeal. [See Note # 3.] Survivors knew that the developed lands they had been swindled out of were much more valuable than the raw territory they were forced into (the former valued at $100 per acre while the latter went for under *one dollar*). The first homes were very crude structures. Land had to be cleared and fenced for agriculture. Heavy labor was ceaseless. And when they had something to trade, where were the markets? Finally, the federal government often forgot about guarantees made in original treaties. Making a new life was as complex as it was demanding.

Eastern Oklahoma became known as "Indian Territory." The tribes set up their governments, the Choctaws writing the first constitution in 1834. Deportation of the Five Civilized Tribes was more or less complete by 1840. Towns were founded, newspapers and books were published, farms and livestock took hold. The plantation system reappeared and it is said there were some 7,000 black slaves living with the Tribes.

Some Americans married into tribal groups and gained property rights. Mixed-bloods became a factor in tribal politics. Some Americans continued to covet rich Indian lands in Indian Territory. For example, in 1857, the territorial governor of Kansas demanded the removal of the Five Tribes from eastern to western Oklahoma lands. During the 1860 presidential election William H. Seward maintained that if elected he would remove the tribes completely out of Indian Territory.

CIVIL WAR and RECONSTRUCTION

The Five Civilized Tribes initially followed a policy of neutrality at the onset of the Civil War. But when Union forces evacuated the forts in Indian Territory the Southern element became dominant, especially in southern areas of the territory. Cherokee leader **John Ross** advocated neutrality but the area became a Southern sphere of influence with some Indian regiments fighting for the Confederacy. Those who remained loyal to the Union were targeted for violence and many were driven from their homes. Some

19,000 people became refugees. To make matters worse, irregulars from Kansas also conducted raids into the territory.

During the Reconstruction period victorious Union authorities used tribal efforts to help the Confederacy as an act of treason that negated former treaties with the USA. In 1865 federal negotiators demanded the abolishment of black slavery and the surrender of a huge slice of land (on which to settle the Indians of Kansas). The Indians were dismayed at such harsh demands but the government forced them to accept the loss of lands in central and western Oklahoma. Caddoes, Delawares, Kickapoos, Modocs, Osages, Shawnees, and several other tribal remnants were forced into Indian Territory. There were also pressures to permit American settlers into the land.

LAND RUSHES

Americans demanded opening Indian Territory to American settlement. **David L. Payne**, a leader of this so-called "Boomer movement," led several expeditions into Oklahoma to acquire land. Between 1889 and 1906 there were a series of land rushes to "unassigned lands" in Indian Territory. In the 1889 there were some two million acres up for grabs with perhaps 50,000 people participating. "Sooners," people who set out before the official starting time and intent on creating towns, often grabbed up the best town lots.

ORGANIC ACT

The legislation that created the first typically American political system in Oklahoma was signed on May 2, 1890. Appointments for important offices came from Washington and the law now provided that land be provided for homesteaders. The issue of single or duel statehood was not settled. Indians wanted their own state in order to protect their land ownership. But Americans targeted the "un-American" custom of community land ownership, asserting it would hinder Indian advancement.

DAWES ACT

In 1893 Congress created the three-member Dawes Commission to force the Indians into receiving individual allotments of tribal land. As a bonus, Indians would be given American citizenship and the federal government would acquire ownership of all lands not allotted to individuals. This began "the long process of Indian land theft." Historian **Angie Debo** is among those who describe this land swindle from the perspectives of Indians. [See Note # 4.]

SEQUOYAH CONVENTION

A meeting was called to fight single statehood. Known as the Sequoyah Convention, it was held in August of 1905 in Muskogee. **Pleasant Porter**, a Creek chief, was chosen to lead the group. A constitution was created. A memorial was then sent to Congress requesting that Indian Territory be admitted as a State. It was to no avail. On June 16, 1906, President Theodore Roosevelt signed the Hamilton Statehood Bill (Oklahoma Statehood Act) into law, negating the concept of twin statehood.

One-hundred and twelve delegates, 55 from each section with two representatives from the Osage, met to create a constitution. Progressive ideas were on the upswing and Democrats were able to capitalize on them. Voters approved the constitution and on **November 16, 1907**, Oklahoma became the 46th State in the American Union. Charles N. Haskell was elected Governor, Robert L. Owen and Thomas P. Gore were selected for the Senate.

NATURAL RESOURCES

Mining for coal and zinc in eastern Oklahoma had become important in the state but it became famous with the opening of the great oil fields: Glen Pool (1905), Cushing (1912), Healdton (1913), etc. A few individuals became immensely rich and boom towns sprang up. Tulsa experienced spectacular growth because of the oil boom. From 1907 to 1928 Oklahoma was the largest oil producing state in the Union (and has remained among the top four ever since). Oilmen like Robert S. Kerr were to become political leaders.

POLITICS

Democrats, allied with the Progressive movement, were triumphant in most elections after statehood. Then the Progressives split into two camps: one seeking orderly changes to insure economic progress (described as the merchant-banker-lawyer-landlord crowd), the other wanting immediate reforms to benefit impoverished groups (the landless or debt-ridden farmers) that had been left behind. This struggle would often become explosive.

The Socialist Party grew remarkably and in the 1914 elections received almost 20% of the vote, electing some half-dozen state legislators and many local officials. But Socialists were often considered unpatriotic. They were targeted for violence and the Ku Klux Klan became part of the scene in the 1920s.

The 1921 Oklahoma legislature brought Republicans to power in such numbers that they were able to impeach elected Democrats. Society was also in deep trouble, attested to by the bloody riot in Tulsa in 1921 where some 36 African-Americans were killed and scores were left homeless when their homes were set afire. These activities encouraged the **Ku Klux Klan** on the right and the Farmer-Labor Reconstruction League on the left. As in the rest of the country, blacks were often victims of American violence and lynch law. White supremacy was basic in Oklahoma and Jim Crow laws kept African-Americans in the bondage of second-class citizenship.

John C. "Our Jack" Walton was elected to the governorship on January 8, 1923. The coalition that elected him quickly began to unravel but Walton proved himself a master of "rough and tumble politics." Talk of impeachment filled the air so Walton decided to take on the Ku Klux Klan as a diversionary measure. He declared martial law in Okmulgee and Tulsa counties, suspended the authority of city police and county sheriffs, and suspended the right to a writ of habeas corpus. Rebellion was in the air so Walton declared martial law throughout the state. When a grand jury was called to investigate impeachment charges Governor Walton brought in some 6,000 guardsmen to prevent the meeting. They also turned away members of the state legislature. Legislators were able to get authorization to call themselves into session, despite Walton's efforts to stop it. In October of 1923 Walton was suspended from office and Lt. Gov. Martin E. Trapp became governor. Among Trapp's achievements is that he sponsored a law which made it illegal to wear a mask, the nation's first anti-mask law.

DUST BOWL and the GREAT DEPRESSION

Freakish weather conditions set in during the 1930s. Oklahoma prairie land had been plowed for agricultural needs so when a severe drought set in there was no grass to hold the soil in place. Fierce winds blew and dust storms obscured the sun as Oklahomans came to realize there was no force that could change their reality. Land abuse, drought, and floods destroyed agribusiness. With the Great Depression the oil industry was all but neutralized. Without agriculture or oil the state was destitute.

OUT-MIGRATION

Though the Dust Bowl hit a number of states and the Great Depression everywhere, no state saw its citizens leave in the numbers recorded in Oklahoma. Between 1935-40 some 284,000 native born white Oklahomans abandoned the state. It has been said some 94,000 moved to California while 68,000 went to Texas. [See Note # 5.] **Woody Guthrie**, a native of Okemah, composed and sang songs about the refugees fleeing the Dust Bowl. Though unintended, **John Steinbeck** "fixed the Okie image" in the American consciousness with his *Grapes of Wrath*.

WORLD WAR II

Oklahoma received a share of government contracts and military installations like Tinker Air Force Base. Governor **Robert S. Kerr** (1943-47) is generally credited with encouraging the federal government to locate federal projects in Oklahoma. He also replaced the instability of "Wild West politics" with sound business practices. His philosophy was one of modernization and economic development. Succeeding governors followed Kerr's example and became leaders in the style of corporate executives who concerned themselves with budgetary items and attracting new industry to Oklahoma.

RACE RELATIONS

School desegregation came to Oklahoma in the 1950s. Though a Jim Crow society, state legislators decided to obey rather than defy decisions of the Supreme Court. This broke ranks with the Deep South where the choice was made for massive resistance. Governor Raymond Gary (1955-59) led the attack on segregated schools. He once said: *"I grew up in Little Dixie but as an active Baptist and believer in the Scriptures I have never understood how persons can call themselves Christians and believe that God made them superior because they were born with white skins."* Compliance with federal directives was not immediate but overall acceptance was a contrast to the rest of the South.

ECONOMIC RECOVERY

During the 1950s some 200,000 people left Oklahoma to explore better prospects elsewhere. Leaders realized that among the keys to economic recovery were better planning, recruitment and development of industry, promoting a positive business climate, etc. As the economy improved in the 1960s people stopped leaving the state. While agriculture and petroleum remained as basics, other mainstays were added. Federal government spending in Defense became significant, accounting for some 220,000 jobs between 1950-68. The manufacturing sector, the wholesale and retail trades, and services expanded significantly.

Oklahoma was no longer a "Wild West" frontier nor dependent on a "boom or bust" economy. This is not to say it couldn't happen again. For example, the 1973 Arab oil embargo resulted in a boom for Oklahoma oil. The natural gas industry also became very profitable. By around 1980, the average income of Oklahomans nearly reached the national average for the first time since statehood. The boom ended in 1982 when oil prices crashed. There were bank failures and many bankruptcies. But by 1990 many believed Oklahoma was once more on the road to recovery. The engaging "Okie spirit," down to earth yet open to contemporary knowledge-intensive industries of the high tech world, will face reality with a zest for living, wherever it finds itself. [See Note # 6.]

DISCUSSION NOTES *for* OKLAHOMA STATEHOOD and SOCIETY

Note # 1

Considering the time and place, the Coronado and De Soto Expeditions are perhaps the greatest efforts of their kind in the history of what is now the USA. Except for H.E. Bolton and some of his school of historiography, few writers express that kind of sentiment. Why is that? For possible answers see "The Epic of Greater America" in *Bolton And The Spanish Borderlands* edited by John Francis Bannon.

Note # 2

See page 38 in *Oklahoma Politics And Policies: Governing the Sooner State* by David R. Morgan, Robert E. England, and George G. Humphreys.

Note # 3

Chapter 8 in *Oklahoma: A History of the Sooner State* by Edwin C. McReynolds. Has the American treatment of Indians ever really been acknowledged?

Note # 4

See page 45 in *Oklahoma Politics And Policies*. Among Angie Debo's famous works are *The Rise And Fall Of The Choctaw Republic*; *And Still the Waters Run: The Betrayal of the Five Civilized Tribes*; *The Road To Disappearance*; Oklahoma: Footloose and Fancy-Free; *The Five Civilized Tribes*; A History of the Indians of the United States. Could it be expected that Debo's work might be described as *controversial*?

Note # 5

See page 54 in *Oklahoma Politics And Policies*.

Note # 6

See Chapter 10 in *Oklahoma: Foot-loose and Fancy Free* by Angie Debo for thoughts on the personalities of "Okies" and "Sooners." The work was published in 1949 but it still rings basically true. For a compilation of personal recollections see *Oklahoma Memories* edited by Anne Hodges Morgan and Rennard Strickland.

NEW MEXICO STATEHOOD and SOCIETY

New Mexico, which also included Arizona until 1863, was given territorial status by the **Organic Act**

of 1850. Americanization encountered situations which hadn't been faced anywhere else. The main reason was that the relatively large New Mexico population was almost entirely Hispanic and Pueblo Indian, not to mention the unconquered tribes like the Apache, Navajo, Comanche, etc. The 1850 census, not considered very accurate, stated there were some 56,984 non-Indians in New Mexico, of which some 550 were non-Hispanic, mostly American and French. Texas and California had been engulfed by massive American immigration but what could such small numbers of Americans in New Mexico do with so many "alien" New Mexicans who lived in such an "alien" culture? Control of the government had to be the key.

As required by the Organic Act, a bicameral legislature was created (elected) and all governors would be appointed by the President of the USA. [See Note # 1. *Notes begin on page 557.*]

While the Organic Act acknowledged commitment to the stipulations of the Treaty of Guadalupe Hidalgo by which the Southwest legally became American territory, it also contained avenues typical of American society. For example, voting rights were guaranteed to all white males 21 years of age or older…"*but the qualifications of voters and of holding office at all subsequent elections shall be as prescribed by the legislative assembly…*" [See Note # 2.] The Legislature could thereby restrict voting rights and/or prevent targeted people from holding office if it so desired. However, the difference in New Mexico was that Hispanic people comprised the overwhelming majority of citizens. It was not a New Mexican cultural tenet to target groups of people for exclusion, discrimination, or segregation so the Organic Act was thwarted in imparting the overt workings of American racism into Hispano society.

American leaders prepared for most eventualities, however, when something new was added to the territorial mix in New Mexico, something which had never happened in any American territory: the national Congress had to approve all legislation before it could become law. Territorial status has been equated with colonialism in other areas so it follows that New Mexico was now definitely a colony under the thumb of the USA through its carpetbagger governors and federal military might.

American societal pressures continued to be exerted. For example, Indians had never been citizens and could not vote in any part of the USA. By contrast, New Mexico's Pueblo Indians had the legal right to vote under Mexican law. The right was taken away by American authorities when they convinced the Pueblos to accept ward status, which they did in 1851. Americans also made efforts to legalize African-American slavery but the majority-Hispanic Legislature rejected the move.

PREVIOUS AMERICAN COMMENTARY on NEW MEXICO

Various American personalities had been and later came into New Mexico. In 1841 **George W. Kendall**, editor of the *New Orleans Picayune* newspaper, had been with the invading "Texian Invincibles" captured by Governor Armijo. Kendall experienced the cruel march to Mexico City and later wrote about New Mexicans in his *Narrative of the Texan-Santa Fe Expedition*, which was widely read in the States. While he lauded the beauty of Mexican women and the superlative talents of *arrieros* (muleteers), he denigrated just about everything else. [See Note # 3.]

Susan Magoffin, who wrote an account of traversing the Santa Fe Trail, was charmed by the manners and civilities of the people of New Mexico. Among other things, she wasn't impressed by a Catholic church service she witnessed.

Josiah Gregg wrote the very popular *Commerce of the Prairies* in which he remarks that New Mexicans are master horsemen, remarkable for their manners and politeness, make the best hot chocolate in the world, highly skilled goldsmiths and silversmiths, etc., but have "*inherited much of the cruelty and intolerance of their ancestors, and no small portion of their bigotry and fanaticism…they have no stability except in artifice…the Romish faith is not only the religion established by law, but the only one tolerated by the constitution, a system of republican liberty wholly incomprehensible to the independent and tolerant spirits of the United States.*"

Matt Field wrote an enduring account of his travel on the Santa Fe Trail (see *Matt Field on the Santa Fe Trail* edited by John E. Sunder). Published in the New Orleans Picayune, he made commentaries like the following: the "mud city" of Santa Fe looks like mole hills from a distance but he comes to be impressed by adobe architecture…blankets woven in New Mexico are "sometimes really beautiful"…the "dark-eyed señoritas are more delightful than the exhilaration of the wine bowl"…the card game of *monte* is a passion in Santa Fe…everyone smokes, including the women…dancing is a passion and few Americans can dance even the waltz compared to the Hispanos…"

Richard H. Weightman, elected Delegate to Congress in 1851, stated that violence was not part of elections until "Anglos" came into the picture. He accuses the Houghton political faction (proponents of territorial status; the "Alvarez faction" favor statehood) of creating rumors of impending revolt in order to win political appointments from Washington. He adds that New Mexicans are being described as unfit for self-government only to defeat the statehood movement.

W.W.H. Davis, the first U.S. Attorney in New Mexico and author of *El Gringo, or New Mexico and her People*, observes that New Mexicans are fine horsemen, sheep dogs are remarkably well trained, everybody smokes, the people are "swarthy," illiteracy is as rampant as prostitution, burial expenses are exorbitant, priests are leaders in vice, New Mexicans are incompetent when it comes to the workings of democracy and in general "*lack the stability of character and soundness of intellect that give such vast superiority to the Anglo-Saxon race over every other people.*" [See Note # 4.] Davis disappeared from New Mexico after being charged with embezzling federal funds. (His book is in circulation to this day.)

TERRITORIAL GOVERNORS

The first was **James S. Calhoun** (1851-52), a native of Georgia who had served previously as the first American Indian Agent for New Mexico. [See Note # 5.] He appointed Hispanos to government posts, causing strong resentment from Americans who wrote to the President Fillmore that Calhoun was protecting the Mexican population in the perpetuation of *murder*, that… "*there is no hope for the improvement of our territory unless Americans rule it…the spirit of Mexican rule must be corrupt, ignorant, and disgraceful in a territory of the United States.*"

In his first address to the Legislature Governor Calhoun stated, among other things, that "*The relations between masters and peons should be distinctly defined…*" Calhoun also asked the Legislature to bar free black people from the territory, saying "Free negroes are regarded as nuisances in every State and territory in the Union, and where they are tolerated, society is most degraded. I trust the legislature will pass a law that will prevent their entry into this territory. The disgusting degradation to which society is subjected by their presence is obvious to all and demands a prohibitory act of the severest character…"

[See Note # 6.] Governor Calhoun didn't know what to do with "...*our Pueblo friends, who own portions of the richest valley lands in this Territory. Why exempt them from taxes? Are you prepared to elevate them to full fellowship: I cannot recommend such a union. But it is inevitable, they must be slaves, dependents, equals, or removal to a better location for them and our people must occur...*" [See Note # 7.] As Calhoun stated, the Pueblos owned some of the best agricultural lands in the state and such a situation had never been tolerated by Americans. But New Mexico was different. What would the world say if Americans expropriated Pueblo lands and deported all Amerindians to Indian Territory? Especially since the *cruel, greedy Spaniards* had not done so. The Pueblo people were not deported (but later efforts would be made to take their land).

Henry Connelly was governor (1861-66) during the Civil War. He had to call for volunteers to defend the land against an impending Confederate invasion. Some 3,500 New Mexicans signed up to fight for the Union, motivating Connelly to pay tribute to a people "so patriotic in nature." He was aware that the Hispanos had been taken into the USA only as of 1846 and as yet hadn't even been granted citizenship.

Among the more infamous governors was **William A. Pile** (1869-71). A Methodist preacher, Pile had been in the Army, which is how he wound up in New Mexico. While no one can be certain as to motivation, though it might have been related to destroying land titles, Governor Pile ordered that a certain room full of archival documents be disposed of by selling them to merchants and grocers for wrapping paper, dumping the remainder out into the street. A wood hauler named Eluterio Barela happened by, recognized the value of the archival documents, and rescued those which had been flung into the street. When word got out many irate citizens demanded the return of all documents and the end of Pile's administration.

Governor **Marsh Giddings** (1871-75) had a very low opinion of Hispanic people, saying that they should be governed by people "other than themselves." New Mexicans didn't like him either.

The administration of Governor **Samuel B. Axtell** (1875-78) has been described as one of "corruption, fraud, and murder." [See Note # 8.] Things were so bad that Axtell was summarily removed from his duties.

It has been said that Governor **Louis "Lew" Wallace** (1878-81) spent most of his time in New Mexico finishing up his novel, *Ben-Hur*.

One territorial governor who couldn't be described as a carpetbagger was **Miguel "Gillie" Otero** (1897-1906), a native New Mexican. The appointment by President McKinley, unanticipated, was the first of its kind for territorial New Mexico and quite possibly the entire Southwest. [See Note # 9.]

RELIGIOUS LEADERSHIP

Political leaders were neutralized with the American takeover so there remained basically only native priests as leaders of the people. In 1851 Frenchman **Jean Baptiste Lamy** arrived in Santa Fe as Vicar Apostolic of NM. With him was his lifelong friend **Joseph Projectus Machebeuf**. The basic strategy of the two French priests was to replace native Hispanic clergymen, the best known of which was Father **Antonio José Martínez**. [See Note # 10.]

Lamy and Machebeuf began to write to their friends that they suspected the native priests were "horrible lechers" who didn't wish to reform. This was construed by the Frenchmen as defiance. Reverend

Machebeuf is especially critical of NM society with its "dancing and gambling, etc.," and people begin to resent him. Padre Martínez wrote to Lamy that vicar Machebeuf's suspension of priests wasn't legal under canon law. In time Machebeuf is accused of publicizing secrets of the confessional. Lamy considers the charges as "malicious calumny" and demands proof. Probate Judge Ambrosio Armijo of Albuquerque writes to Lamy demanding Machebeuf's removal. The letter is signed by some 950 heads of families.

Lamy writes that native clergy are in open rebellion when in fact the problem was Machebeuf and accusations relating to the confessional, which Lamy never mentioned.

People wrote to the Pope Pius IX to have Machebeuf removed from NM. Letters are also written by NM legislators. The Pope summons (1856) Machebeuf to Rome to answer the accusations. In his refutation Machebeuf charges that New Mexicans are "ignorant and vicious," lacking in education and little accustomed to governing themselves, etc., their legislators are *ignorant men, corrupt, dishonest,* that Padre Gallegos of Albuquerque lives with a prostitute, etc. No one appears in person to speak for the other side so Machebeuf is exonerated. He returns to NM but Archbishop Lamy finds ways to keep Machebeuf on the road, away from the controversy stirred up in NM. In time Machebeuf states the Southwest is *une petite Auvergne* with three quarters of the priests Frenchmen, Lamy in charge of ecclesiastical life in NM, Salpointe in Tucson, and himself as Bishop of Denver.

Numbers of Hispanics fell away from the French church brought in by Lamy and the American conquest. For example, Padre José Manuel Gallegos of Albuquerque became a member of the Episcopal Church after his excommunication. Americans supported Lamy's efforts, many of which were laudable once Machebeuf was away, and Lamy of necessity had to rely on American good will, whether or not it defeated Hispanic welfare. Numbers of Hispanics fell away from the Catholic Church. [See Note # 11.]

CIVIL RIGHTS

With W.W. H. Davis as interim Governor in 1856, American authorities were finally successful in passing laws against African-Americans in NM. For example, blacks living in NM were required to post $200 to insure good behavior and the ability to support themselves. A free black could not remain in NM for more than thirty days. Intermarriage of blacks and whites was now against the law. Newly freed black people must leave NM within thirty days of manumission. The Slave Code Act of 1859 added to the situation, despite New Mexican outrage. At the outbreak of the Civil War all these hateful laws, common in Southern states, were rescinded.

LAND TITLES

In 1860 one **Juan Batista Vigil** charged that Surveyor General **W. Wilbar** is not fulfilling his duty under the stipulations of the Treaty of Guadalupe Hidalgo. The treaty stated that land titles would be respected but the opposite proved to be the case. Authorities gave reasons for not acknowledging land ownership: farming lands existing in relatively narrow strips in order to touch a water source were not compatible with basic rectangular surveys used in the USA; communal ownership of land was not traditional in the USA; living in towns while owning outlying lands wasn't condoned in American law, which required residency to prove title, etc. The issue of land titles was allowed to drift by American authorities because it played into their hands when they sought to obtain title to lands they coveted; etc.

For example, the heirs of the San Joaquín land grant, some 400 people, petitioned the Surveyor General for confirmation of their land, some 184,000 acres. The petition was ignored for *seventeen years*. (When a survey is finally done in 1878 the acreage is set at 473,000 and Americans owned most of it.) By 1861 only 17 Pueblo land claims and 19 town or private claims had been approved.

SANTA FE RING

It could be said that New Mexico's introduction to American democracy came through the Santa Fe Ring. Territorial New Mexico has been characterized as an association of rings but it is generally agreed the Santa Fe Ring was the most powerful. [See Note # 12.] The Ring was a network (not a card-carrying association or club) of mostly Americans, especially lawyers, who were "ambitious, unscrupulous" carpetbaggers arriving in New Mexico after the Civil War. They were Republicans and Democrats, governors, judges, Surveyors General, newspaper editors, etc. It has been written that "almost every governor of New Mexico from the late 1860s to 1885 was a member of the Santa Fe Ring." [See Note # 13.]

Thomas B. Catron is generally described as the most powerful member of the Ring. Catron and S.B. Elkins are "credited" with creating the idea that every heir to a land grant owned a share in it, therefore he could sell those shares if he so desired. While that fantasy was never part of Hispanic land grant law or procedure, the lawyers were able to validate the ruse in American courts because judges were members of the Ring. Catron became one of the largest land owners in the USA.

Other well known Ring ("land grabbers") personalities were Stephen B. Elkins, Henry L. Waldo, L. Bradford Prince, Charles H. Gildersleeve, William C. Thornton, Max Frost, Joseph G. Palen, Samuel B. Axtell, Robert H. Longwill, Antonio Joseph, Alonzo B. McMillan, Alois B. Renehan, Charles Catron (son of T.B. Catron), etc. These are only a few of the individuals involved and a case could be made that almost anyone in a position of power became part of the network if money was the lure. Morals never appeared to enter the picture. Fraud, corrupt court hearings involving crooked lawyers and judges, even the "murder for hire" of Reverend Franklin J. Tolby, a Methodist minister, were typical devices used by the Ring. [See Note # 14.] For example, the carpetbaggers would go to a land grant heir and "buy" his share of the common lands (which could not be done under the laws of Spain or Mexico since common lands were owned by the entire community; today this would be like buying someone's "share" of a city park), thus making themselves "heirs" in the targeted grant. Then they would file a suit to partition the grant so that each heir would have their own private land, "American style." (This was considered part of "Americanization" and those who rejected Americanization were described as ignorant in the extreme. Social pressures, though described as a form of mental cruelty, were effective.) Litigation would prove as expensive as it was prolonged, the lawyers doing the gaining. For example, by the time the grant in question was surveyed as required by law, it had grown immensely from the grant as it was in the beginning. This didn't bother most judges because they would be getting some of the land under adjudication.

A basic strategy was to file a lawsuit against "Unknown Heirs." No one living on the targeted grant was ever served with papers stating the land was under adjudication. Where a public notice was required by the court, lawyers colluded with newspaper editors to print the said notice in *one copy* of the newspaper, the lawyer keeping that copy for use in court when the victims being put off the land asserted no such notice had ever been published. In some land fraud prosecutions all evidence in legal files "mysteriously" disappeared. [See Note # 15.] The corruption and immoral collusion brought into American NM was of such unimaginable proportions that Hispanic New Mexican land grant heirs were little more than sitting ducks on a stage directed by crooked American lawyers, judges, and government officials. Typically, no American champions arose to combat the immorality of what went on. On the contrary, it was common to "get in on the action." To add insult to injury, when Hispanos protested the fraud and corruption they were accused of *not knowing how to function in the American democracy.*

Though NM was in a colonial status to the USA, word of such rampant corruption finally reached Washington. In 1885 **Edmund G. Ross** was appointed Governor and **George W. Julian** as Surveyor General. Edmund Ross had already proved his personal courage by casting the crucial dissenting vote in the impeachment (1868) of President Andrew Johnson. He was ruined in Washington D.C. so he took the opportunity to come to the Southwest when it presented itself.

George Julian was of the same ilk. He was told that the office of Surveyor General would be even more difficult than that of governor. From a native NM perspective, Julian fought the speculators who had swindled Hispanos out of their lands but he fought just as hard to defeat genuine claims made by Hispanic people. In his quest to acquire land for the government, euphemistically referred to as the *public domain*, the guarantees of the Treaty of Guadalupe Hidalgo were so ignored they might as well not have existed at all. As has been mentioned before, there were no American champions to defend those Hispanics targeted for dispossession of their ancestral lands.

After familiarizing himself with the situation in NM, Governor Ross wrote: "*The curse of this Territory is rings…*" He said there were cattle rings, public land stealing rings, mining rings, etc. He described how "a few sharp, shrewd Americans" had entered NM, ingratiated themselves to native people then, saying they were lawyers, proceeded to take over existing grants while manufacturing titles to others, all the while "*swelling their holdings to colossal dimensions*" and seeking Congressional recognition. They possessed some legal knowledge but much more "*cheek and an unusual quantity of low cunning and astuteness that always had an inclination to run in a crooked direction.*" Santa Fe was the seat of American corruption and it didn't matter which party was in power because all worked to get control of the land and its resources. The Ring tried to win Ross and Julian to its side but failed so it worked diligently to get them removed from NM. This too failed but the Legislature fought Governor Ross at every turn. Ross was against statehood for NM so long as it was under the thumb of the nefarious Santa Fe Ring.

QUEST FOR STATEHOOD

As Robert W. Larson has written: "New Mexico remained a territory the longest." The first bill to give NM territorial status was introduced in 1848 but it wasn't granted until 1850. Memorials asking for NM statehood were frequent. Among the major thrusts for the movement was writing the constitution of 1872. Resentment peaked against Governor Marsh Giddings. His son William was beaten senseless on a Santa Fe street and the governor referred to the people of Santa Fe as "…the lowest class on God's earth…" Charges of corruption were in the air and the constitutional vote was declared null and void due to light voter turnout. New Mexicans never knew if the constitution was accepted or defeated because Giddings declared everything "nugatory."

There are various fantasies associated with New Mexico's saga toward statehood. For example, the

"Elkins Handshake" is an enduring fable. The story goes that in 1876 Delegate to Congress **Stephen B. Elkins** walked in on a passionate oration by (Michigan) Rep. J.C. Burrows denouncing attacks by Southerners on the civil rights of black people. Elkins went up to Burrows and shook his hand in congratulations, in full view of the Southerners who subsequently voted against NM statehood out of revenge. The story has attracted attention from some historiographers but the fact of the matter is that the idea of revenge was invented more than two decades after the handshake actually took place. At the time it meant nothing and was not a reason for denial of NM statehood.

Diverse motivations were always involved in New Mexico's quest for statehood. For example, **Susan Wallace**, wife of Governor Lew Wallace (1878-81), was against NM becoming a state because *"...the Americans would bear the taxes and the Mexicans hold all the offices—it is not in the interest of the white men to bring that about."* [See Note # 16.]

In 1888 Rep. William M. Springer, Democrat of Illinois, sought to secure statehood for NM and three other territories. One of the suggestions made in the bill was to have New Mexico change its name to *Montezuma* in order to avoid confusion with Old Mexico.

Partisanship was always a factor when Southwestern territories sought statehood but there was a new element in New Mexico's quest. Eastern and Midwest newspapers bitterly criticized the inclusion of NM because of race. The Chicago *Tribune* referred to Hispanic New Mexicans as *"...not American, but Greaser, persons ignorant of our laws, manners, language, and institutions."* New Mexicans were portrayed as *"...lazy, shiftless, and grossly illiterate and superstitious."* [See Note # 17.]

The **Struble Report** made by Isaac S. Struble (R-Iowa) presented the book *El Gringo, or New Mexico and her People* by W.W. Davis to corroborate New Mexican inferiority, along with extracts from reports by former governors like Lew Wallace. The Senate dropped NM from consideration for statehood.

A convention gathered (1889) to create a constitution and a document was hammered out despite problems with political, religious, and cultural issues, including "Mexican domination" of government. Charges were rampant that the effort was a "land grabbers constitution." It was decisively rejected by voters on October 7, 1889.

In 1894 **Thomas B. Catron** was Delegate to Congress. Because his land holdings would become more valuable he was committed to statehood. Catron was aided by his old friend **S.B. Elkins**, now Senator from West Virginia. Elkins' political enemies now fought Catron also. Both were *"...charged with being land robbers. Catron especially was slandered, being called a 'political freebooter' seeking to achieve his own selfish ends...Catron's controversial past had caught up with him, and at a most inopportune time."* [See Note # 18.]

In 1902 W.S. Knox of Massachusetts introduced an **Omnibus Bill** which would grant statehood to New Mexico, Arizona, and Oklahoma.

Senator **Albert J. Beveridge** (R.-Indiana) opposes statehood, except for Oklahoma, because New Mexico's insufficient population is Spanish, they know little English, illiteracy is high, and the land too arid. Beveridge believes the Southwest to be a *"backward area...not equal in intellect, resources or population to the other states in the Union"* because its people are "stifled" by their Indian and Spanish heritage, therefore not *"sufficiently American in their habits and customs."* [See Note # 19.]

Senator **Matthew S. Quay** (R.-Pennsylvania) attacks Beveridge's argument and spearheads passage of the statehood bill, presenting a number of arguments to contradict Beveridge's: thousands and thousands of new immigrants to America are permitted in without an English language requirement; New Mexico's population is larger than that of some other territories at the time of admission; no people were more loyal during the Civil War than New Mexicans... But on March 4, 1903, the statehood bill is defeated by use of parliamentary maneuvers.

On the opening of Congress on December 5, 1904, President Theodore Roosevelt calls for the admission of NM and Arizona as one state (and Oklahoma and Indian Territory as one unit). Residents of NM and of Arizona have never petitioned for jointure. Jointure debate rages in Congress. *"New Mexico's predominantly Spanish-speaking population and Arizona's Anglo majority seem to many an incompatible combination..."*

The Pittsburgh *Times* is quoted in the El Paso *Times* as referring to *"the citizens of New Mexico as a mongrel population too ignorant and lazy to assume the privileges of full citizenship..."*

An editorial in the Las Vegas *El Independiente* warns New Mexicans that they are presently being written out of the Southwestern historical record and that a vote for jointure will only speed up the process.

New Mexicans vote for jointure, Arizonans reject it, thus ending the movement forever.

On January 14, 1910, Representative Edward L. Hamilton (R-Michigan) introduces an act, referred to as the **Hamilton Bill**, to enable NM and Arizona to form separate governments and become states "on equal footing with other States." Senator Beveridge inserts an amendment that requires close federal government supervision of any proposed constitution. This has never been done with any other state, contradicting the enabling act which calls for New Mexico's entry into the union "on an equal footing with the other states." State land allotment is reduced (also a departure from procedures used with other states).

Senate restrictions include the issue of language: *"Whereas the House Bill permitted the teaching of languages other than English, the Senate version provided that schools should be conducted in English and struck out the provision 'that nothing in this act shall preclude the teaching of other languages in said public schools.' The Senate version requires state legislators as well as state officers to read, write, and understand the English language sufficiently well enough to conduct the duties of office without aid of an interpreter..."*

On June 20, President Taft signed the (Hamilton Bill) Enabling Act of 1910: New Mexicans can now form a government. There are glaring restrictions in the Act. For example, despite the fact that the territorial legislature has never prescribed a literacy or language requirement for the right to vote or hold office in NM, the national Congress stipulates in the Enabling Act: *That said state shall never enact any law restricting or abridging the right of suffrage on account of race, color, or previous condition of servitude, and that ability to read, write, speak, and understand the English language sufficiently well to conduct the duties of the office without the aid of an interpreter shall be a necessary qualification for all state officers and members of the legislature.*

In September of 1910, one-hundred Delegates were elected to the Constitutional Convention. There were 71 Republicans and 29 Democrats chosen to write the constitution. Categories in the hundred include: 32 attorneys, 20 stockmen, 14 merchants, 7 farmers, 6 small businessmen, 4 saloonkeepers, 3 bankers, 3 physicians, 3 editors, 3 territorial officers, 2 county officers, 1 college president, 1 mining man, 1 lumber man. Spanish-speaking delegates (32) are a sizable part of the Convention and the *New York Sun* remarks the proceedings will resemble *"…some bullfight in a Mexican village."*

Hispanic delegates provide for laws, and those speaking only English acquiesce to them, which insure voting rights for everyone in the following stipulations: *The right of any citizen of the state to vote, hold office or sit upon juries, shall never be restricted, abridged or impaired on account of religion, race, language or color, or inability to speak, read or write the English or Spanish languages except as may be otherwise provided in this constitution and the provisions of this section and of section one of this article shall never be amended except upon a vote of the people of this state in an election at which at least three fourths of the electors voting in the whole state, and at least two thirds of those voting in each county of the state shall vote for such amendment.*

Separate schools by race or ethnicity are made illegal, specifically stating that children of Hispanic descent shall never be denied *"the right and privilege of admission and attendance in the public schools…and they shall never be classed in separate schools."* (The *El Paso Times* warns the constitution will be rejected by Congress because it doesn't provide for separation of the races.)

Women are permitted to vote (only) in School Board elections.

A bill of rights is enacted: *"The rights, privileges and immunities, civil, political and religious, guaranteed to the people of New Mexico by the treaty of Guadalupe Hidalgo shall be preserved inviolate."*

However, there is one more hurdle to overcome because Congress has required an English literacy qualification for voting and/or office holding.

Unless the Treaty of Guadalupe Hidalgo was to be disregarded altogether, which would cause vociferous censure from the international community, the English language stipulation was the only leverage available to neutralize Hispanic political strength and fortify "Anglo" privilege in NM. Framers of the constitution refer to the American guarantee of voting rights then state (Article XXI) *"…and in compliance with the requirements of the said act of congress, it is hereby provided that ability to read, write…shall be a necessary qualification…"* in order to get the Congress to accept the constitution.

Charles Spies, "an able legislative draftsman and political strategist," commends the creators of the constitution, telling them: *"…You have by its provisions guaranteed the equal protection of the law to every citizen of New Mexico; you have preserved the religious, political, social, and civic rights to every one of our citizens, and placed them beyond the power of assault from any source whatsoever."*

On November 21, 1910, the New Mexico Constitution is adopted by the Convention.

January 21, 1911: New Mexican voters ratify the proposed Constitution.

February 24: President Taft approves the NM Constitution.

March 1: The House approves the NM Constitution. When the Constitution gets to the Senate, Robert Owen of Oklahoma objects to NM being admitted without including Arizona's admission, causing Congress to meet in an extra session. The Flood Resolution is added, providing *"…for the submission of amendments by a majority…"* which would destroy the guarantees of equality for Hispanics.

August 15: President Taft vetoes the Flood Resolution.

August 21: President Taft signs a compromise resolution which insures NM statehood if voters accept it.

November 7: New Mexicans ratify the Constitution and elect State officials.

January 6, 1912: At 1:35 p.m., President Howard Taft signs the proclamation making New Mexico the 47th State of the Union, and says, "*Well, it is all over. I am glad to give you life. I hope you will be healthy.*" The effort has taken almost 64 years. [See Note # 20.] Carpetbaggers are in control of NM with William C. McDonald (from New York) as Governor; the first two (appointed by the Legislature) Senators Thomas B. Catron (Missouri) and Albert B. Fall (Kentucky); national Representatives are George B. Curry (Louisiana) and Harvey B. Fergusson (Alabama).

SINCE STATEHOOD

Pancho Villa, or probably a remnant of his men because Villa himself was never seen, stage a predawn raid on Columbus, NM, on March 9, 1916. General John J. Pershing leads a punitive expedition into Mexico but the effort is futile because Villa isn't captured or even seen.

"The People's Champion" **Ezequiel C. de Baca** is elected as Governor in 1917. He dies some 49 days later on February 18, 1917, of what is described as "pernicious anemia." [See Note # 21.]

Mabel Dodge (Sterne, later Luhan) arrives in Taos in 1917 and becomes a central figure in attracting artists and activists to Taos (and Santa Fe). Among the many guests in her Taos home is one **John Collier** who becomes enamored of Taos Pueblo community life.

José Dolores López is credited with beginning the NM woodcarving industry in the 1920s.

In 1922 Senator **Holm Bursum** introduced the **Bursum Bill** which would, he informs Congress "*...quiet title to lands within Pueblo Indian land grants...*" and that the Indians themselves favor the move. Though the bill remained unpublicized in NM, John Collier informs the Pueblo people that the real motive was to separate Indians from their land. **Pablo Abeita** of Isleta is elected to the post of Executive Secretary of the All Indian Pueblo Council to fight the Bursum Bill.

Artists, writers, etc., from Taos and Santa Fe join the fight to protect Pueblo lands. The Bursum Bill is unmasked and recalled but the Senate comes up with the Lenroot Bill which launches investigations of individuals like Mabel Dodge Luhan, Mary Austin, Alice Henderson. The Pueblo Lands Act is passed in 1924 in an effort to acknowledge Pueblo lands recognized by Spain and Mexico. (But there would be other efforts to grab Pueblo land.)

The **Middle Rio Grande Conservancy District** is organized in 1923 but it lacks necessary funding to begin reclamation projects (until 1930).

Mary Austin settles permanently in Santa Fe in 1924. A nationally known personality, sometimes referred to by her friends as "God's Mother-in-Law," she devotes much of her time and energy to preserving and celebrating the Amerindian and Hispanic cultures of NM.

Camilo Padilla relocates his magazine *Revista Ilustrada* to Santa Fe in 1925. This most popular magazine, published for some 26 years, is tailored for New Mexicans with articles from Europe and Latin America. It also offers for sale popular books written by international authors like Hugo, Dumas, Verne, Cervantes, Isaacs, Lizardí, as well as New Mexicans like Benjamin Read, Eusebio Chacón, Aurelio Espinosa, etc.

Willa Cather publishes her *Death Comes for the Archbishop* in 1927. It goes on to become the best-selling book in the history of NM, despite its denigration of personalities like Fr. Martínez of Taos and Manuel Antonio Chaves (New Mexico's greatest frontiersman).

Russian artist **Nicolai Fechin**, "*The Modern Michelangelo,*" comes to live in Taos in 1927. His art wins national and international awards too numerous to mention.

The **University of New Mexico Press** is founded in 1929. Though in the middle of the Hispanic Southwest, the Press does not appear to pride itself on publications which focus on New Mexican Hispanic history and/or culture. In the *PASO POR AQUI* series (1989) volume *Critical Essays on the New Mexican Literary Tradition, 1542-1988*, editor Erlinda Gonzales-Berry writes in the Introduction: "...*New Mexican Hispanic writers have been virtually ignored in mainstream literary histories of the Southwest.*"

While realities are stark at UNM Press, "hope springs eternal." Upon reading enthusiastically that the 2003 UNM Press release of *The Biography of Casimiro Barela*, translated by A. Gabriel Meléndez, was part of the series titled *Recovering The U.s. Hispanic Literary Heritage*, a series launched in 1992, it was subsequently learned that the effort emanates from the University of Houston and is directed by Nicolás Kanellos... "founder-director of Arte Público Press, the oldest and most accomplished publisher of U.S. Hispanic literature." Other university presses seem to want to capitalize on Hispanic themes. For example, Northwestern University press has begun a series entitled *Latino Voices* which include fiction and non-fiction items addressing the Latino experience in the USA.

Personalities like **E. Boyd** and **Georgia O'Keefe** arrive in NM in 1929.

In the 1930s there are ever increasing numbers of impoverished migrants, especially from Oklahoma, entering NM looking for work. The Great Depression has thousands of New Mexicans out of work and the Legislature limits the employment of nonresidents on public works projects to 15%. Native New Mexicans are living in dire poverty because they have been swindled out of their grazing lands and there is little demand for wage labor. Some federal officials even challenge their right to federal relief, charging that the predicament was caused by soil exhaustion, insufficient farm land, long-term unemployment, etc., for which the government isn't responsible. Storekeepers refuse credit unless people sign affidavits that they are starving. New Deal programs are welcomed in NM.

In 1931 the **New Mexico Quarterly** is funded at the University of New Mexico.

The **University of New Mexico** is accused of discriminating against Hispanics. In 1932 one J.J. Clancy, a teacher at Antón Chico, accuses UNM President James Zimmerman of hypocrisy for lauding students from Latin America while treating NM Hispanics like foster children. For example, Hispanics are not permitted into fraternity/sorority organizations, a situation that endures into the 1940s.

Clyde Tingley is elected as Governor in 1935. Upon the untimely death of Senator Bronson Cutting, Tingley appoints Dennis Chávez (1888-1862) to take his place, where he serves for the rest of his life. Some individuals excoriate Tingley for permitting an Hispanic into the power structure of NM.

In 1936 **Patrociño Barela** of Taos wins national acclaim during a WPA show sponsored by the Museum of Modern Art in New York. There are some 171 artists in the show, Barela has eight pieces in it, more than any other artist, two of which are featured in the exhibition's catalog. Pat Barela is hailed by the New York *Times* and Time Magazine as the outstanding artist of the entire show. Several New York galleries clamor to represent Barela's work. Vernon Hunter, director of the NM Federal Art Project, states he will not permit the "exploitation" of Patrociño Barela, preventing galleries from direct contact with him, without Pat knowing about it. Hunter's efforts are effective: Barela never knows he is America's greatest wood sculptor and his work is forgotten outside NM.

In 1941 the **200ᵗʰ Coast Artillery** from NM is taken to the Philippine Islands where later the entire

American Army is forced into surrender. Many New Mexicans are on the Bataan Death March. Among those who survive the March but die in prison camps is **Adelardo Sánchez** from Belén.

Among individuals who become nationally famous during WW II is **Ernie Pyle**, who decides to settle in Albuquerque. He receives the Pulitzer Prize in 1944 and his *Brave Men* is published in 1945. (He dies on April 18, 1945, in the battle for Okinawa.) **Bill Mauldin** becomes the most famous cartoonist of WW II. He is awarded the Pulitzer Prize in 1945 and 1959.

Medal of Honor awardees (all wars) associated with New Mexico include Daniel Fernández, Joe R. Martínez, Hiroshi Miyamura, Harold Moon, Louis Rocco, Alejandro Ruiz, José E. Valdez, Kenneth Walker, Alexander Bonneyman, Robert McDonald, Franklin Miller, Francis Oliver, Robert Scott, Ebin (Eben) Stanley, Raymond J. Murphy.

The top-secret **Manhattan Project** is created in (what is now) Los Alamos in 1942. Among the international scientists working on the development of the atomic bomb are Robert Oppenheimer, Niels and Aage Bohr, Enrico Fermi, Victor E. Weisskopf, Emilio Segre, Stanislaw M. Ulam, Edward Teller, I.I. Rabi, John Von Neumann, Hans A. Bethe, etc. On July 16, 1945, the world's first atomic bomb is exploded at *Trinity Site* on the White Sands Missile Range, launching the Atomic Age of modern history.

In 1943 **Miguel Archibeque** leads the movement to have the Penitente Brotherhood officially recognized by the Catholic Church.

The **New Mexico Boy's Ranch** is founded in 1944. **Girls Ranch** is founded in 1982.

The **Roswell Incident** takes place on July 2, 1947. Rancher W.W. Mac Brazel hears an explosion that doesn't sound like thunder so the next day he rides out and encounters debris unlike anything he has ever heard of, including dead bodies of creatures three to four feet tall, heads larger than torsos, hairless, slanted eyes widely spaced apart. A military vehicle speeds into the scene and orders that nothing be discussed with anybody. All debris is gathered up and the Military publicizes that it was merely a downed weather balloon.

In 1951 during the Korean War, **Hiroshi H. Miyamura** from Gallup is in a bloody hand-to-hand combat that later earns him the Congressional Medal of Honor.

Reies López Tijerina founds the *Alianza Federal de Mercedes* in 1962. The purpose of the organization is to recover the land grants which had been swindled away from Hispanic New Mexicans. The issue continues to smolder. In May of 1967 there is an armed raid on the Tierra Amarilla courthouse and the media depicts it as a full blown revolution. The National Guard enters the scene with 350 Guardsmen plus some 150 law enforcement officers, two M-42 tanks, jeeps equipped with machine guns, etc., along with helicopters and a spotter plane, all intent on capturing the nineteen (19) suspects. None are caught until they walk up to authorities and turn themselves in.

At the age of twelve **Nancy López** from Roswell wins the New Mexico Women's Amateur Tournament in 1969. She wins her first professional tournament at the age of twenty-one then goes on to dominate the LPGA. It has been said she is the most recognized professional athlete to come out of NM

Rudolfo Anaya goes to a California publisher to publish his *Bless Me, Ultima* in 1972. It goes on to become a gigantic best-seller and ranks second only to *Death Comes to the Archbishop* in the history of New Mexican publishing.

One of the worst prison riots in American history begins on February 2, 1980, at the Santa Fe State

Prison. By the time the prison is taken back from inmates, thirty-three men are dead.

Arturo G. Ortega founds the Hispanic Culture Foundation in 1983.

Raymond G. Sánchez is elected to the state House of Representatives in 1970 and is elected Speaker in 1983, a post which he holds almost into the new millennium.

Manny M. Aragón is elected to the State Senate in 1975 and serves into the new millennium.

In 1994 the NM Legislature appropriates $12,000,000 to start the creation of the (National) **Hispanic Culture Center** in Albuquerque. In time J. Ronald Vigil is selected as the first Director and Edward Luján is chosen as Chairman of the Board of Directors. The Center is slated for its grand opening in 1998, the 400th anniversary of the founding of Hispanic NM.

By 1996 Indian casinos are operating in a number of reservations.

Three New Mexicans have been selected to serve as Ambassadors of the United States: **Frank V. Ortiz** (from Santa Fe), **Mari-Luci Trujillo** (from Las Vegas), and **Ed Romero** (from Albuquerque; to Spain in 1998).

The **New Mexican Hispanic Culture Preservation League** was formed in 1998. Vidal and Millie Santillanes are among the the driving personalities behind the organization which becomes a community force under the leadership/activism of Gene Hill, Robert Rodríguez, John and Conchita Lucero, Frank Osuna, Dolores Márquez, Richard Quintana, Rozanne Chávez Hurst, Pátryka Chávez de Tachick, George Lopez, Polly Cisneros de la Serna, Orae Domínguez, Carlos Cordova, Smokey Sanchez-Davis, etc. The League was created to "*...end the defamation of Hispanic culture and history...oppose negative stereotyping, racism, prejudice and bigotry of all kinds whether overt or covert...and promote an appreciation of our Hispanic New Mexican heritage and culture.*" The League has devoted itself to combat denigrating historical and cultural items. For example, it has stated that the "cutting off of feet" after the Acoma war was a mistranslation of "cutting off toes," which was probably never even carried out but was merely a way to have to Indians go to the missionaries so they could speak up for the Indians and thus become their champions. It was also pointed out that if the Europeans had been Englishmen the entire Acoma people would have been exterminated as the English did those along the eastern seaboard.

The League protested *New Mexico Magazine* publishing a letter ("Oñate was a terrorist," July, 1998 issue, page 7) from one Kathleen Thompson of Royal Oak, Missouri, in which Oñate is referred to as "*...that old terrorist. How utterly insulting to the Indians of New Mexico! The conquistadores were the disciples of the Spanish Inquisition, driven by power, greed and religious fanaticism...*" The League pointed out that, unlike Missouri, NM still has its Native Americans living within the State. It was also stated that if founders like Sam Houston, Davy Crockett, etc., were referred to in such terms by the Texas State magazine, the editor and its writers would be lynched or tarred and feathered before being run out of Texas.

In 1998, Hispanic New Mexico's 400th anniversary, the calendars released by *New Mexico Magazine* and the Office of Cultural Affairs didn't even bother to mention that 1998 was New Mexico's 400th "birthday." The only one that did was "Calendar of the Great Southwest, New Mexico Edition," produced by Rubén Sálaz M., which was supported by the HCPL.

The League spoke with the Director of the **Department of Tourism** when it learned that the brochure "El Camino Real," disseminated throughout the State by the Tourist Bureau, asserted that "*When the Indians, who had been mistreated by the Spanish colonists, organized the Pueblo Revolt of 1680...*" This information ("Text by Michael E. Pitel") belies the historical fact that the surprise uprising was referred to in Spanish as *"el Día de San Lorenzo,"* the *St. Lawrence Day (Massacre)* in which out of the some 400 dead a full 300 were noncombatant women and children. The State of New Mexico is therefore promoting anti-Hispanic racism through its "El Camino Real" brochure.

In early 2001 the **Museum of New Mexico** presented what it called the *CyberArte* Exhibit. It is common knowledge that the Virgin of Guadalupe is venerated by millions of Roman Catholics as the Patroness of the Americas. Despite that fact the focal point of *CyberArte* was a female figure wearing a bikini in a Virgin of Guadalupe context. League members attended the protest rallies along with hundreds of other New Mexicans. Despite being urged to do so by so many people and highly popular elected officials, the Museum of New Mexico hierarchy refused to take down the sensationalistic piece. Rumor has it that Museum officials remarked to various delegations of New Mexicans *"We're here to educate you…you people have a third grade education…"* When the Bill Richardson administration took office **Rubén Smith** was appointed as Director of the Office of Cultural Affair. The paladin Smith fired the Museum Director but then various forces in the Santa Fe area united to demand the ouster of Smith.

Anti-Hispanic racism is a pervasive foe but the quest for dignity and respect of New Mexico's Hispanic people continues through efforts like those of the HCPL, the Hispanic Genealogical Research Center, the Hispanic Roundtable, etc.

DISCUSSION NOTES *for* NEW MEXICO STATEHOOD and SOCIETY

Note # 1

Though New Mexico statehood wasn't achieved until 1912, it is interesting to note that while the term *carpetbagger* is used in other Southwestern states to describe territorial officials who came in from other parts of the country, there is not a single volume consulted for this section which uses "carpetbagger" to describe American officials in New Mexico. What are the implications for American historiography and culture?

Note # 2

See pages 51-52 in *Politics In New Mexico* by Jack E. Holmes.

Note # 3

See Chapter 2 in *With The Ears Of Strangers: The Mexican in American Literature* by Cecil Robinson.

Note # 4

The *Foreword* of the Matt Field volume states he "…is also one of the more enlightened and tolerant Anglos to have traveled the Trail." This brings up a necessary discussion point: if Matt Field was "one of the more enlightened and tolerant Anglos…" who were the unenlightened or intolerant? No English language writer during this period of New Mexico history has been described as racist, unenlightened, or intolerant by any subsequent English language writer. Indeed, the opposite is generally the case. For example, New Mexican scholar Angélico Chávez considered Josiah Gregg an absolute racist yet the *Commerce of the Prairies* edition edited by Max L. Moorhead states "Josiah Gregg best served posterity…" by writing about the West for "subsequent generations forever in his debt... Gregg's masterpiece is packed with prairie lore and human adventure...Historians, ethnologists, naturalists, and bibliophiles have cherished it for generations."

Harvey Fergusson wrote of W.W.H. Davis and his book: "Had he been consciously working as the agent of posterity, Mr. Davis could hardly have done better...because he was critical rather than imaginative...For all these reasons, his book is one of the best books about nineteenth century New Mexico."

What is credible when reading about New Mexico and her people when being described by someone from east of the Mississippi? What bearing does this have on the statehood movement and/or contemporary New Mexicans?

Note # 5

See *New Mexico's Troubled Years: The Story of the Early Territorial Governors* by Calvin Horn for information on the first ten governors.

Note # 6

Though the product of a slave culture, Calvin Horn describes Calhoun as the "Vanguard of Democracy." How does democracy mix with slavery? The very public but little publicized Dred Scott Decision was still a few years away.

Note # 7

It must be remembered that America had deported all its Native Americans from east of the Mississippi. In American rationale, why shouldn't the Pueblo people suffer the same fate as the Civilized Tribes?

Note # 8

See pages 173-97 in *New Mexico's Troubled Years* by Calvin Horn.

Note # 9

See *My Life On The Frontier, 1864-1882*, the autobiography of Miguel Antonio Otero. First published in 1935, a reprint was released in 1987 by the University of New Mexico Press. The "Introduction" by Cynthia Secor-Welsh is quite puzzling and the rest of the work bears investigation.

Note # 10

For contrasting views on the struggle between Hispanic and French priests in NM see pages 249-54 in *New Mexico: A Brief Multi-history* by Rubén Sálaz Márquez. Material is drawn from *But Time And Chance* by NM scholar Angélico Chávez and *Lamy Of Santa Fe* by Pulitzer Prize winner Paul Horgan.

Note # 11

To my knowledge, this falling away has never been investigated by scholars. I believed it also occurred in Texas and Colorado, if not the entire Southwest.

Note # 12

See Chapter 9 in *New Mexico's Quest For Statehood, 1846-1912* by R.W. Larson.

Note # 13

See page 39 in *Land, Water, and Culture: New Perspectives On Hispanic Land Grants* edited by Charles L. Briggs & John R. Van Ness.

Note # 14

See page 110 in *Translating Property: The Maxwell Land Grant and the Conflict over Land in the American West, 1840-1900* by María E. Montoya. For the view that "The famous Santa Fe Ring was a logical and sometimes brilliant combination of able men..." see Chapter 6 in *The Far Southwest, 1846-1912, A Territorial History* by Howard R. Lamar.

The Santa Fe Ring appears to wield power to this day. For example, though the Ring dominated territorial New Mexico, no publisher has issued a book on the subject. If an accurate book is ever done it will attract tremendous, possibly dangerous attention.

Note # 15

For an introduction to land grant fraud see *The Public Domain In New Mexico, 1854-1891* by Victor Westphall. Of special importance is *Land Grants & Lawsuits In Northern New Mexico* by the stalwart Malcolm Ebright.

Note # 16

See page 140 in the R.W. Larson volume.

Note # 17

See page 148 in the R. W. Larson work.

Note # 18

See page 187 in the R.W. Larson book.

Note # 19

Senator Beveridge has been described as *"wrong for all the right reasons"* by W.A. Beck, author of *New Mexico: A History Of Four Centuries*. Beck also relates the tale that an investigation committee brought back the story that a county superintendent of schools *"expressed amazement"* when he was told that *"Christopher Columbus* was dead." How does such material come under the heading of History?

Note # 20

R.W. Larson sums up by asking: **"Why was NM so long denied statehood..."** despite increasing numbers of New Mexicans determined to rise above the colonial or second-class citizenship of territorial status? Scrutiny reveals... a small population, not developed economically...Factional strife and political discord...NM was never considered in the same light as other territories... because of a *...strong prejudice toward the Spanish-speaking, Roman Catholic people of NM...that was thus the major obstruction to the territory's statehood aspirations...a most unfair bias against a people labeled by one congressman 'a race speaking an alien language' and not representing the 'best blood on the American continent'...the Catholic religion provoked the prejudice and dislike of a predominantly Protestant nation.* It can be observed that an instinctive *distrust of New Mexico's essentially Hispanic and Indian people* and culture was *"the last and most durable brick added to the strong wall of opposition that prevented the territory from becoming part of the Union until 1912.* Dr. Larson has proved himself a master of American historiographical language in this summation.

Note # 21

While Hispanos overwhelmingly constitute the largest ethnic group in NM, only five Hispanics have been elected to the governor's chair (out of thirty governors): Ezequiel C. de Baca, Octaviano Larrazolo, Jerry Apodaca, Toney Anaya, and Bill Richardson. As of the end of 2003, not a single member of New Mexico's Congressional delegation is an Hispanic New Mexican.

ARIZONA STATEHOOD and SOCIETY

From 1850 to 1863 Arizona was the western part of New Mexico Territory. Arizona citizens didn't wish to be dominated by legislators in faraway Santa Fe so they constantly petitioned Congress for separate status. Most Americans in Arizona emanated from the South and for a time during the Civil War, the area was part of the Confederacy. Union forces quickly won it back to the Union then placed the area under Army rule to assure that Arizona's rich mineral resources would not fall to the South.

ARIZONA TERRITORY

On February 20, 1863, Arizona was declared a Territory. One of the basic objections to making Arizona a Territory was that it didn't have enough population. [See Note # 1. *Notes begin on page 566.*] According to the 1864 census, there were some 4,187 non-Indians in Arizona, the overwhelming majority of them Hispanic. (It has been said the Indians numbered some 30,000.)

With Territorial status granted in 1863, it was said "…government arrived in Arizona before the citizens did." After the War many Confederates moved to Arizona. The second largest group of Americans was the Mormons who settled in northern areas of the territory. It can be observed that diversity was basic because of Hispanics living around the Tucson area, Southerners gaining recognizable dominance, and Mormons in the north, not to mention Amerindian groups.

In 1864 **Charles Debrille Poston**, called the "Father of Arizona," was elected Territorial Delegate. With Southern sympathizers and former Confederate soldiers residing in the Territory, federal territorial officials were not welcomed nor treated in a friendly manner. Mormons, who arrived in large numbers in the 1870s, also resented the federal government for past grievances, especially as concerned polygamy. Officials appointed by the President, governors (16 of them until statehood), secretaries, judges, etc., were not a part of Arizona cultures so they were viewed as *carpetbaggers*. Territorial newspapers in the 1860s-70s often expressed their contempt for Legislators, charging their basic job was "picking up their $4 a day plus mileage…" Editorials didn't mince words: "*As long as Arizona is the political dumping ground for the riffraff of eastern ward healers, aided by the scattering local scum of the earth, so long will the home maker and property holder be burdened with taxes and more taxes…*" By 1868 the Legislature convened only once every two years. Until 1876 the Governor could veto any act passed by the Legislature. As in the other Territories, the Delegate to Congress could not vote on any issue.

During the 1860s and most of the 1870s the territory was controlled by a fairly nonpartisan group call "The Federal Ring." Comprised of Republicans, Democrats, federal officials, prominent merchants, and Hispanic leaders from Tucson, unity was needed and achieved to combat hostile Indian groups, acquire federal aid, attract investment capital to develop mineral resources, build roads, bridges, schools, hospitals, etc.

PHOENIX

Around 1870 a new village was established on the banks of the Salt River, tributary of the Gila, by settlers who cleaned out some of the canals left by the Hohokam. An Englishman named **Darrell Duppa** marveled at the Hohokam canals and predicted the new settlement would rise "Phoenix-like" from the ashes of the old civilization. So the name *Phoenix* was given the new village and in time it witnessed spectacular growth. [See Note # 2.]

By 1884 the Santa Fe and Southern Pacific transcontinental railroads crossed the territory. Population increased from some 9,658 in 1870 to around 40,000 in 1880, and by 1900 there were some 122,931.

HISPANIC ARIZONANS

The Hispanic citizens of Tucson were true frontiersmen, equally at home with the lariat and frontier weapons of the day as well as business account books. They founded some of the largest ranches, established the largest businesses, and held the most important political offices. Families like Otero, León, Pacheco, Elías, Ruelas, Telles, etc., had lived in the area since Spanish colonial times. They were peerless as frontiersmen and Indian fighters. Other family groups like those of Esteban Ochoa, Leopoldo Carrillo, Mariano Samaniego, the Aguirre brothers, etc., arrived from (what is now) northern Mexico. [See Note # 3.]

It is quite possible that Tucson's most distinguished personality in the 1870s was the diminutive **Estevan Ochoa**, a highly successful freighter, merchant, and philanthropist. He and his wife **Altagracia**, "gracious, hospitable, soft-spoken," lived in perhaps the finest home in that frontier community, a home noted for splendid hospitality and "Hispanic courtliness and sophistication." Visiting dignitaries often dined and/or lodged at the Ochoa home rather than go to a hotel.

Don Estevan was from Chihuahua and had been a part of his brother's freighting business to Independence, Missouri. During those perilous treks across desert and plains Estevan learned about freighting, fighting off hostile Indians, and surviving until the next waterhole. He also became fluent in English. At the age of 28 he started his own business in Mesilla, New Mexico, in partnership with another pioneer, Pedro Aguirre. The partnership ended in 1859 so Estevan went into business with Pinckney R. Tully. Together they created one of the largest, most diversified, and successful business enterprises in the Southwest. Freighting was the basic service offered in this frontier for there was no other way to supply army posts, ranches, mines, and businesses until the railroad was completed.

Hispanic Mexicans were heirs to the legacy and techniques of Spanish pack trains. One **Joaquín Quiroga** brought in his pack train (from Yuma to Tucson) laden with goods in February of 1856. When wagon trains became necessary, various Tucsonenses like the Aguirre brothers, Leopoldo Carrillo, Sabino Otero, Mariano Samaniego, etc., invested heavily and became masters of the business. After the Civil War freighting was big business in frontier Arizona.

Tully, Ochoa, & Company was among the largest of freighting companies. It employed hundreds of men and owned more than $100,000 worth of equipment. Its business network ranged as far east as Philadelphia. By 1875 it was the second largest business in Tucson, handling some $300,000 worth of commerce per year. It's general mercantile store was also one of the largest with subsidiaries throughout the Arizona frontier. It was also strong in mining and sheep raising. It owned its own copper mine and purchased (1874) some 4,500 sheep in New Mexico to bring to Arizona. By the early 1880s the flocks numbered some 15,000 animals.

Estevan Ochoa was undoubtedly one of southern Arizona's most successful businessmen. Through it all, he maintained a reputation of the highest personal honor. His integrity was never questioned because he would fill an agreed upon contract even if he lost money on it. Because of his honesty he was elected to and served in the territorial legislature during the 1860s and '70s. In 1875 he was elected Mayor of Tucson. Further, he was a champion of public education, even when the Church fought the movement because it has always controlled the schools. Private religious education continued as a choice in Tucson because well-to-do Hispanics considered themselves exponents of "culture and civilization," a contrast to the "unaccountable bad manners" of Anglos in general, their children in particular.

Ochoa and all other freighters were dealt a death blow by the railroad which chugged into Tucson in November of 1880. Freighters simply couldn't compete with the lower rates offered by the railroad.

Mariano Samaniego was born in Sonora in 1844, moved to Mesilla, New Mexico, in the early 1850s, graduated from St. Louis University in 1862. He became a formidable personality in the worlds of Arizona business as well as politics. At the peak of his career in the 1890s he was described as the most powerful Hispano in Tucson. While he ran wagon trains he also invested heavily in stage lines, ranching enterprises, which boomed in the 1880s, and a large saddle and harness shop. Politically he served in territorial, county, and city government posts for almost thirty years. In 1886 he was appointed to the University of Arizona's Board of Regents. Among other posts, he served as president of the Arizona Pioneers' Historical Society.

Described as a "transitional figure," Don Mariano witnessed a large influx of Americans due to the railroad. As more and more Americans arrived, Hispanic voting power was diluted and few Americans would vote for "Mexican" candidates.

Leopoldo Carrillo (1836-1890) arrived in Tucson from Sonora in 1859. Within ten years he was a powerful businessman described as "Tucson's foremost urban entrepreneur" who did as much as anyone to develop the town in the 1870s and '80s. He built the town's first ice cream parlor, the first bowling alley, etc. He owned a large feed stable, owned some one hundred rental homes, and leased good farm land to Chinese truck farmers. According to the 1870 census Don Leopoldo was worth about $70,000, making him the wealthiest man in Tucson.

Around 1885 Carrillo decided to open a resort. His creation became known as *Carrillo's Gardens*, some eight acres of rose gardens, different kinds of trees, and man-made lakes. The Gardens have been described as "Tucson's crowning glory," the center of social life where most prominent as well as ordinary citizens held their formal parties, enjoyed the luxurious saloon, dance pavilion, hot baths, picnicking, boating, etc., in the midst of this magnificent oasis in the desert.

Leopoldo Carrillo had the reputation of being a "tough businessman" so he never became as popular as Ochoa or Samaniego.

Pedro Aguirre was a Chihuahua *hacendado* who moved to New Mexico in 1852. He had four sons: Epifanio, Pedro, Conrado, and Yjinio, all of whom learned their freighting skills on the Santa Fe Trail. The lessons could be costly: Epifanio died in an Apache ambush in 1870. The other three Aguirre brothers did very well in the fields of ranching, freighting, and managing stage lines.

Sabino Otero was acknowledged as the "cattle king of Tubac." Born in 1846, Sabino inherited a small farm from his grandfather and enlarged it into one of the larger ranches in all of southern Arizona. At his death his estate was worth $308,743.

As the frontier waned there emerged new Hispanic personalities who became well known in southern Arizona. They were men like Ignacio Bonillas, Carlos Velasco, Fernando Laos, Carlos Jácome, Federico Ronstadt, etc., city dwellers emerging as a middle class.

Large corporations began moving into Arizona Territory as of 1880. Railroads like the Southern Pacific, Phelps Dodge, the Aztec Land and Cattle Company, etc., soon dominated territorial business and life. Like everyone else, Hispanic Arizonans had to find their place in that world.

HASH KNIFE OUTFIT

Completion of the railroad had given the Arizona cattle industry a boost. The Aztec Land and Cattle Company was formally organized in New York City on January 3, 1885. It bought some 1,058,560 acres (at fifty cents an acre) from the railroad. It also bought some 32,000 cattle to get things started.

Captain **Henry Warren** (from Texas) registered the Hash Knife brand for stock on June 2, 1885, in Apache County, Arizona. (There were five allied Hash Knife cattle outfits in the late 19th century: three in Texas, one in Montana, and one in Arizona.) A permanent business office was established in Holbrook. Texas cattle started arriving by rail in the summer of 1886.

Because it was allowed the privilege of choosing which sections it would buy, the company controlled all water sections of grazing land in northeast Arizona. Further, by choosing alternate numbered sections of land the Company could prevent anyone from crossing its property, thereby controlling another million acres of land along the railroad right-of-way between Holbrook and Flagstaff. It was charged Hash Knife cowboys threatened to kill anyone who tried to use public domain lands for grazing of stock not of the Hash Knife. [See Note # 4.]

Hash Knife cowboys have been described as *"roughshod cowboys and undesirables…with criminal records in Texas and New Mexico…terrorizing Mormon settlers…taking part in the Pleasant Valley War between cattlemen and sheepmen though it wasn't their fight…waylaying and murder practiced by both sides."* Most used a first name only and when a family name was needed it was often "Smith."

The Aztec Land and Cattle Company was easily the biggest operation in the Arizona cattle industry, "a law unto itself," as well as the largest ranch in the West outside of Texas. [See Note # 5.]

STATEHOOD

Arizonans regularly petitioned for statehood. Points made were that territorial rule had already been too long, there was a large population and economic development was good, home rule was an intrinsic American right, etc. Without the customary go-ahead from Congress, a constitution was created in 1891 and approved by voters. Congress didn't accept it.

In 1906 Congress passed a statehood bill joining Arizona with New Mexico. Arizonans objected on the grounds that "Anglo-Saxon" Arizona was totally different from "Hispanic" New Mexico. While New Mexicans okayed it, voters in Arizona rejected jointure. In 1910 Congress passed and President

W.H. Taft signed an Enabling Act for creating a constitution. Among the stipulations was that both President and Congress had to approve the constitution.

Voters selected 41 Democrats and 11 Republicans for the constitutional convention which convened in Phoenix in October of 1910. Lawyers, ranchers, miners, and merchants comprised the membership. Only three individuals were native Arizonans. **George W.P. Hunt** was selected as president. After some sixty days of work the final document was approved. Aspects of direct democracy like initiative, referendum, and recall (judicial recall was removed in 1911 at the behest of President Taft, then reinstated in 1912 when Taft was voted out of office) proved popular. It worked against abuse by corporations and contained protections for workers. The constitution also provided for relatively easy ways for revision of constitutional laws.

As was typical wherever Americans went, voting rights were for white males only. Women, blacks, Hispanics, and Indians were denied the right to vote. Even after statehood the Legislature worked against "the ignorant Mexican vote" by requiring a literacy test in English, which was still being used into the 1960s to restrict the Hispanic, black, and Indian vote. [See Note # 6.]

President Taft proclaimed Arizona a State, the 48th in the Union, on February 14, 1912. George Wiley Paul Hunt ("*Old Roman*") was elected Governor (*seven* times between 1912 and 1932). Elected to the Senate were Henry F. Ashurst and Marcus A. Smith. Carl Hayden won the lone House seat. (Hayden served seven terms in the House then seven in the Senate before retiring in 1969.)

It has been said Arizona's long territorial period engendered hostility toward the federal government and entrenched a streak of Arizonan tenacity and contrariness.

ARIZONA WOMEN

Arizona women were given the right to vote in 1912. In 1914 **Rachel A. Berry** (House) and **Frances W. Munds** (Senate) were elected to State offices. In 1915 **Katherine Stinson** established air mail service into Tucson and **Nellie T. Bush** became the first and only female to pilot a riverboat on the Colorado River. Subsequently she served in the Legislature for sixteen years. **Lorna Lockwood** served for fourteen years on the Arizona Supreme Court and in 1965 became Chief Justice, the first woman to do so in the USA. [See Note # 7.]

GREAT DEPRESSION

The perilous times of the 1930s hit Arizona as hard as the rest of the nation. Mining and farming were devastated, properly values fell, State and local revenues dwindled in the face of greater demands to help the indigent. But it also brought on a conservative one-party regime that didn't begin to fade until after WW II. The "one-party system" has been described as very responsive to lobbyists for the "three Cs: copper, cotton, and cattle." Well funded lobbyists wooed State lawmakers with the "three Bs: beefsteak, booze, and blondes" in the Adams Hotel in downtown Phoenix. One-party (Democrat) politics weren't really dead until reapportionment in 1966. That year marks a watershed in Arizona politics because Republicans took control of both the House and Senate for the first time in State history. Since that time political parties have become more competitive, there has been more pluralism, significant modernization, a focus on economic development, etc.

VOTING RIGHTS ACT of 1965

The Arizona legislature didn't repeal the literacy test statute until 1972, despite the Voting Rights Act. The State also became subject to the Act's "pre-clearance" requirements. This requires Arizona to get federal approval of any legal change that affects minority voting rights, the only non-Southern State (excepting Alaska) required to do so. Through it all, Arizonans maintain there are no more biased against minorities than people in the rest of the USA.

BARRY GOLDWATER

Along with Carl Hayden, Barry Goldwater is among Arizona's best known politicians, running for President against Lyndon Johnson in 1964. He carried Arizona by a narrow margin but it has been said Goldwater represents the "friends and neighbors" views of Arizonans. Goldwater believed in personal freedom, whether that meant joining a union or having an abortion. Senator Goldwater attacked Reverend Jerry Falwell when the latter challenged the suitability of Sandra Day O'Connor for a place on the Supreme Court because she held a pro-choice stance on abortion. Goldwater asserted: "I think every good Christian ought to kick Falwell right in the ass…I'm sick and tired of political preachers telling me that if I want to be a moral person I have to believe as they do…I will fight them every step of the way…"

EVAN MECHAM

A recall effort was directed against Gov. Mecham in 1987. Led by individuals like Ed Buck and Naomi Harward, it was a diverse grassroots movement empowered by thousands of volunteers. Workers gathered some 391,738 signatures to force a recall election (to be held in May of 1988). As it turned out, the election wasn't needed because when Mecham took office in 1987 he canceled the paid holiday in honor of slain civil rights leader Reverend Martin Luther King. The cancellation caused such heavy national criticism to be directed at Arizona that Mecham proclaimed an unpaid Sunday observance for Dr. King. He also asserted he favored the King holiday but could not make it a paid holiday because the State couldn't afford it.

Mecham's troubles snowballed. Legislators accused him of not consulting them on legislative matters, the media focused on appointments made to unsavory cronies, party members began encouraging him to resign, etc. Mecham charged that his detractors were "militant liberals and homosexual lobbyists." He refused to resign but then an investigation showed he had received an unreported loan of $350,000 from a certain developer. The Attorney General took the matter to the Grand Jury and Mecham was indicted on six felony charges. The House impeached Mecham on February 5, 1988 and the Senate convicted him of obstructing justice. He was put out of office.

But the damage had been done: conventions canceled their bookings in Arizona and the National Football League threatened to move the (1993) Super Bowl out of Tempe into Pasadena, which it did. The Legislature then decided to try to make repairs by declaring a paid King holiday and making Columbus Day an unpaid holiday. Italian-American organizations were now upset, demanding that both holidays be paid. The issued was given to voters, *who voted it down*. All told it was said Mecham's original cancellation of the King holiday had cost Arizona some $400 million in tourism.

Secretary of State Rose Mofford (of "the white beehive hairdo") was thrust into the governor's chair, the first female to govern Arizona. In 1990 she stated she would not seek reelection.

Fife Symington, a former real estate promoter, was elected Governor in 1991. Arizona had budgetary problems, a major corruption scandal in the Legislature, and still no King holiday. During Symington's first term there surfaced rumors that he had been involved with the failed savings and loan scandals. He won a second term but then word got out that he had to declare bankruptcy. In 1996 a federal grand jury came down with an indictment, twenty-three counts of fraud, extortion, lying under oath, etc. Within a short time Symington was battling almost everyone. He resigned in September of 1997 after being convicted of bank fraud and wire fraud (felonies which had nothing to do with the governorship). But through it all Symington was thought to be less of an embarrassment than Mecham.

Though Arizona has grown in new industries, jobs, "snowbirds," tourism, etc., population has been described as transient. In 1990 there were 3.7 million people living in the State and by the beginning of the new millennium there were 4.8 million. Influences from out-of-state are still resisted. Some Arizonans pride themselves in being a "loner State." Federal projects are sought but not federal influence. Constantly promoting "States' rights," it has also be written that "...*minorities have to struggle continuously for inclusion in politics, voters have had little choice in elections, and citizens complain about a closed policymaking process limited a special few meeting behind closed doors...and official corruption...*" [See Note # 8.]

DISCUSSION NOTES *for* ARIZONA STATEHOOD and SOCIETY

Note # 1

See Chapter 2 in *Arizona Politics & Government* published by the University of Nebraska Press.

Note # 2

By 1990 Phoenix would have a population of more than two million people. See *Phoenix In The Twentieth Century: Essays in Community History* edited by G. Wesley Johnson, Jr., for a good introduction to the history of Arizona's largest city.

Note # 3

See Chapter 3 in *Los Tucsonenses: The Mexican Community in Tucson, 1854-1941* by Thomas E. Sheridan. Sheridan refers to the latter group as "immigrants from northern Mexico" as if the area had not been recently bludgeoned away from Mexico. This might be an adroit use of presentism because "American Tucson" at this time was little different from "Sonoran Tucson." To his credit, Sheridan does write that "Sam Hughes, Charles Meyer" were also ("Welshmen, Irishmen, and German") immigrants. But in keeping with the tenets of Southwestern historiography, Sheridan generally refers to the English-speaking in Arizona as "Anglos," despite the fact there were so many differing ethnicities involved. What is the intent here of this American-style historiography? Is the use of "Anglo" the standard structure of racism to promote superiority/inferiority?

Note # 4

See pages 57-59 in *The Hash Knife Brand* by Jim Bob Tinsley.

Note # 5

See page 136 in *Arizona: A History* by Thomas E. Sheridan.

Note # 6
See Chapter 5 in *Arizona Politics And Government*.
Note # 7
See pages 235-36 in *Arizona: A Cavalcade of History* by Marshall Trimble.
Note # 8
See page 196 in *Arizona Politics And Government*.

Essay: MYTH & MEDIA in WESTERN HISTORY

How can one decide what is History and what is myth when studying the American West? What is valid History and what is media promotion, cultural hype, or propaganda? [See *Myth And The History Of The Hispanic Southwest, Essays* by David J. Weber for an interesting introduction to this type of subject.]

For a number of reasons, much of what has been written on "The Wild West," including many dearly held beliefs, simply doesn't hold up under investigation. Paul Bunyanesque yarns abound when it comes to various topics, especially including "gunfighters" and others portrayed as *heroes* in Hollywood movie creations. For whatever reasons, most of them probably commercial ("if it bleeds, it leads" is in vogue to the present day), *killers* have been heroicized and *killing* during the "Wild West" has taken on the aura of heroic activity. (One can only ask why this would be so, considering that serial killers like Ted Bundy and Jeffrey Dahmer aren't looked on as heroes in the modern day.) Further, a student could get the impression that killers were grand personalities because they seem to get more attention, often sympathetic, than the sheriffs and marshals charged with defending society and its citizens.

Some killers were outlaws while others worked within the law. How historically accurate is the lore on Western personalities? "Bat" Masterson (William Barclay) is "credited" with shooting twenty-some men but the true record is that he shot next to no one and may have actually killed (heroic?) only *one person*. He preferred to talk his outlaws into surrendering and was quite successful at it. "Wild Bill" Hickok (James Butler) claimed to reporter Henry M. Stanley to have killed "over a hundred (white) men." In reality the actual number was *four*. William B. Secrest, author of *Lawmen & Desperadoes*, has written that the "famous" Hickock/McCandles Gang fight was mostly fictional. Billy the Kid became "famous" after his death because he supposedly killed twenty-one men, one for each year that he lived. In reality he killed four men (and one might well ask why *killing* is such an accomplishment in the American psyche).

Western "gunfights," especially the one-on-one shootout on main street, were definitely more fiction than fact. Indeed, it would be interesting to study how many men were shot in the back as compared to a face-to-face encounter. Was "back shooting" actually basic to the *Code of the West*? Was there really such a Code?

If the ranch or mission would be representative of the Hispanic West, what would be the most pervasive symbol of the American West? Quite possibly the *saloon*. [See *Saloons Of The Old* West by Richard Erdoes.] Saloons supplied about the only entertainment on the American frontier, from dogfights to theater presentations by Sarah Bernhardt or Edwin Booth. The saloon was about the only change in routine, a place for "drinking, dancing, and whoring." The American westerner was a drinking man.

Drinking was a sign of manhood. If men got drunk together it seemed to establish a kind of bond, whether they were "crying or singing drunk." Drinking was happiness for lonely cowboys, railroaders, sheepherders, miners, etc. Drinking was about the only way to make up for the loneliness, hardship, monotony. Contrary to popular opinion, men on a drunk usually didn't fight because a fight meant you had to know what you were doing or you could suffer serious injury.

The saloon was a microcosm of American democratic society: egalitarian for persons considered white, whether rich or poor, but inimical to targeted groups considered inferior. Some blacks with money to spend might be permitted in a saloon, especially if they were noted badmen or gamblers. Blacks who entered with a crew of cowboys or railroaders were also tolerated so long as they didn't get "uppity." Soldiers from nearby forts were not welcome because, rightly or wrongly, they were suspected of infecting prostitutes with venereal diseases. Chinese were rarely welcomed in a white man's saloon and those who dared enter ran the risk of losing their lives, literally.

It could be said that saloons had their code of behavior. For example, waitresses and prostitutes were accepted but respectable women were generally not welcome in the typical western saloon. Men wore their hats whether or not women were present. Real men drank their liquor "straight and in a tin cup." They were quick to buy another man a drink and a buy back was expected. It was an insult to refuse a drink when offered.

Privacy was respected. Men generally used only a first name and it was not proper to ask his surname or where he came from. A man's (or woman's) past was nobody else's business. "Minding your own business was good life insurance."

News was often made in saloons or at least discussed there. Journalists frequented saloons to acquire news copy.

What is the message here as far as American historiography is concerned? How much Western historiography is documented History and how much is historicized fiction promoted as History? Is it mere propaganda? We read that the American "mountain men" were *some of the most important men in American History…* "who were destined to live for generations in the history and heroic tradition of the race…" [See *This Reckless Breed Of Men* by Robert Glass Cleland.] Is that History or chauvinistic boosterism? Neither Jedediah Smith nor Kit Carson ever claimed the fame with which they have been endowed by succeeding generations of writers.

Jedediah Smith has been referred to as the greatest of mountain men. Understanding that Jed Smith never claimed fame, what exactly did Jed accomplish? Trapping for furs? The "first American" to go from Bear Lake (situated on the northern boundary of Utah) to the California missions? This is *heroic*? How so?

Kit Carson was unknown in New Mexico and the USA before Frémont "discovered" him. When he became one of the guides for John Charles Frémont (1845-46; there were other guides), who depicted him as the "Hawkeye of the West," Carson got the attention of eastern writers. As everyone knows, Hawkeye never existed except in the pages written by James Fenimore Cooper (though it is said Cooper might have used Daniel Boone as a model). Kit Carson was compared to a non-existent fantasy yet he became *famous* due to the Dime Novel genre that used his name in that "pulp fiction." Carson himself referred to the books as nonsense that weren't even worth reading because they were no where close to the truth. [For "a stirring biography of one of America's great folk heroes" see *Kit Carson: Folk Hero And Man* by Noel B. Gerson. For a more down to earth account see *Dear Old Kit: The Historical Christopher Carson* by Harvey Lewis Carter.] One can only wonder how much is fact and how much has been editorially added for effect in this genre of Western "heroics." It is recorded that Carson was once given a book that showed him on the cover as "clobbering Indians with one hand and rescuing a woman with the other." Kit is supposed to have remarked: "That thar may be true but I hain't got no recollection of it." [See page 271 in *The Wild West* by the Editors of Time-Life Books.]

Neither Jed Smith nor Kit Carson left a significant written record of their activities. (Indeed, Kit Carson was as illiterate in his native English as well as in his adopted Spanish.) Various writers have expounded on their "feats" but how accurate are they as History? Have they been inflated by said writers to give them a grandeur that didn't exist in reality? Consider the *Narrative Of James Ohio Pattie* as an example. Timothy Flint, Pattie's editor, freely added to the *Narrative* to make it more *interesting*. It is certain Flint added the incident where Pattie and a handful of mountain men rescued the daughter of a former governor of New Mexico while the "cowardly New Mexicans" refused to help. The entire incident was fantasy, totally invented by Flint, but the storyline goes on to describe how the rescued damsel proved to be so *grateful*. Another ludicrous episode has it that while in California, Pattie came out of the mountains where he had been trapping only to learn about a smallpox epidemic. He just happened to have smallpox vaccine with him (after a stint of fur trapping in the mountains?) and heroically, he vaccinated thousands of Californios, earning their undying gratitude. No one has bothered to ask how a trapper would have smallpox vaccine in his possession. Is the Pattie work mere fabrication? Today the *Narrative* is often described as a series of tall tales but it is promoted as historical nonetheless. After all, it is about the only work that came from a mountain man (or was it mostly ghosted by his editor Timothy Flint?).

What about the general history of the American West? Who were the explorers? The *pioneers*? A pioneer is "a person who goes before, preparing the way for others." Was everybody who went West from the States a *pioneer*? Truth be told, the Amerindians were the first pioneers and Hispanic people were the first European pioneers but American historiography rarely admits those historical facts. American writers promote the Orwellian idea that the people who came *last* are the pioneers. It is also interesting to note that when various people are written about they are unabashedly boosted, up to and including being given titles like "Captain."

Who should be considered as major historical figures of what is now the American West? According to historian H.E. Bolton, Juan Bautista de Anza is in a class by himself when it comes to bona fide achievement. If various American writers are credible, this-or-that American personality was "a legend in his own time." For example, according to David A. Johnson, one Lansford Hastings, thirty years old in 1849, "was known nationally as a trailblazer and guide…" [See page 111 in Johnson's *Founding The Far West*.] Hastings enjoyed *national fame*? This was the Lansford Hastings associated with the Donner Party disaster because they took the deadly cutoff he had recommended to them? Lansford was a *hero* nevertheless? Is it an additional stretch to say that the tragic innocents in the Donner Party were *pioneers*? Were they not actually *victims*? Those who died paid the supreme price because they were led by incompetents who understood little about the frontier and its dangerous realities. Can dead victims be described as *pioneers?* What about those who survived through *cannibalism?* It must also be pointed out that to ask such questions involves the distinct possibility of retribution in various forms so American writers don't discuss it.

Indian welfare under American domination is also a subject generally avoided by historiographers of the West. While there is great concern for Amerindians during the Spanish/Mexican eras, under American suzerainty the topic is decidedly unpopular except by a very few like Angie Debo. It follows that very little is known about the various native nations who populated the West. For example, it comes as a surprise to most Americans that the Sand Creek Massacre in Colorado caused the worst retaliatory race war in the history of the USA because most Americans have no knowledge of this unprovoked massacre of a peaceful Indian encampment. Further, the Indian nations who retaliated for Sand Creek are generally portrayed as *savages* who fought for no reason other than their savagery. Is genocide less odious if *heroes* like Custer practice it? Why is it impossible to present both sides of an issue? George Armstrong Custer is often promoted as heroic but the Indians who fought him considered him a "killer of women" who fell in battle the first time he faced hostile warriors at the Little Bighorn. Why do some portray Custer as heroic? Does it really have to do with the plight of Amerindians at the hands of the USA? Must 19th century genocide be avoided in order to deflect comparison with the genocidal 20th century?

Various English language writers have written about Spain in (what is today) the Southwest. Speaking candidly, with a few exceptions like the Boltonian school of writers, most of what is written about Spain and Mexico is decidedly negative. The people of Spain are portrayed as *cruel, greedy, superstitious fanatics* while those of Mexico are depicted as *mongrelized sub-humans*. These convenient denigrating stereotypes cloud the historical scene. Why, so that the USA can enter as the *heroic knight* on the white charger of *Democracy!* and *Liberty!?* In the final analysis, negative stereotyping is counter-productive because historical truth will out no matter how serious the effort to obfuscate. Some Americans are drawn to the study of History and they recognize valid truth despite the standard spin required in typical American historiography. For example, when it comes to Spanish history as interpreted by many English language writers, author/researcher Dr. Eloy Gallegos has asserted he accepts very little until he can investigate original documentation in its original Spanish. Speaking candidly, anyone who studies Southwest history would have to agree there is much to what Dr. Gallegos says. For example, the Catholic missions are often depicted by American Denominational Christian writers as centers of *disease* instead of the promoters of Christianization and European technological civilization centers which they were. Further, while disease is a component of the human condition, it isn't an integral part of typical American Southwest history unless the Spanish period is being studied. Perhaps that is why some students do not feel good about studying History: all too often it is more "heroes and villains" propaganda than History.

It has been said that Americans acquire their sense of History from Hollywood movies. A steady diet of "The Alamo" or "Gunfight at the OK Corral" isn't conducive to a sense of reality. No line was ever drawn in the sand at the Alamo, Hollywood fantasy notwithstanding. The sharpshooters inside the Alamo actually killed some sixty (60) Mexican soldiers and wounded some one-hundred and twenty (120) others, not the "epic" hundreds claimed in movies. Travis didn't consider Crockett and Bowie to be heroes, saying they had been drunk their entire time in the Alamo. Yet there are people who will fight the validity of this reality.

Stewart L. Udall writes that the "Hollywood dream machine" has made Wyatt Earp into a hero which he never was in life. (See Udall's *The Forgotten Founders*.) Earp lived in Tombstone, Arizona, for some four years (1878-82) then fled to Colorado "to avoid prosecution for several ambush murders." Udall quotes historians who have investigated the thirty-second OK Corral "fight" and assert that "Billy Clanton and the McLaury brothers were unarmed" during the fight. It is said the Earp brothers and Doc Holliday were in actuality "erstwhile gamblers and pimps…" instead of frontier heroes.

It is time to state that the "Wyatt Earp approach to history" has distorted the true history of the Texas, California, Nevada, Colorado, Utah, Oklahoma, New Mexico, and Arizona. The *first* American to ride into the Southwest on a sorrel horse was not automatically a hero, American historiography notwithstanding. Neither were the Spanish pioneers "a cruel, greedy, fanatic lot." Be advised that if one departs from the standard morality of "The winners write the history (or phrased another way: *The winners weave the Orwellian fabrication*)," presenting valid History is the most dangerous field of study in American society.

CHAPTER 14

Land Tenure

There is no more crucial natural resource than land. Southwestern land ownership is therefore a most important aspect for study. While land ownership is always complicated, it is especially so in the Southwest since at one time it was the northern half of Mexico.

The Treaty of Guadalupe Hidalgo, negotiated on the Mexican side by statesmen like **Manuel de la Peña y Peña**, officially ended the war on February 2, 1848. Articles IX and X deserve special mention. Article IX states specifically that Mexican people living in the territories shall be

"...incorporated into the Union of the United States, and be admitted at the proper time (to be judged of by the Congress of the United States)...to the enjoyment of all rights of citizens of the United States according to the principles of the Constitution; and in the mean time, they shall be maintained and protected in the enjoyment of their liberty and property, and secured in the free exercise of their religion without restriction..." Article X stated in part: "All grants of land made by the Mexican Government or by the competent authorities, in territories previously appertaining to Mexico, and remaining for the future within the limits of the United States, shall be respected as valid, to the same extent that the same grants would be valid, if the said territories had remained within the limits of Mexico..." [See Note # 1 *Notes begin on page 582.*] Article X was not acceptable to the Senate because it contained ample guarantees for land ownership so it was deleted from the Treaty. As a conquered nation still under the threat of American guns, the Mexican government had little choice in the matter. But there were assurances like those of Secretary of State **James Buchanan** who stated: "...*And here it may be worthy of observation that if no stipulation whatever were contained in the Treaty to secure to the Mexican inhabitants and all others protection in the free enjoyment of their liberty, property and the religion which they profess, these would be amply guaranteed by the Constitution and laws of the United States. These invaluable blessings, under our form of Government, do not result from Treaty stipulations, but from the very nature and character of our institutions.*" [See Note # 2.] Following is a brief description of land ownership and adjudication for the states of Texas, California, New Mexico and Arizona. [See Note # 3.]

TEXAS

Texas historian David Montejano has written that *"Mexicans in Texas, especially above the Nueces, lost considerable land through outright confiscation and fraud. Below the Nueces, however, the experience of displacement was more complex…"* [See Note # 4.] Part of the complexity emanated from cultural views of land ownership. To the Tejano, land was generally considered family patrimony, the basis for lifestyle. To the Texan, land was there to use for making money through ranching. Acquiring land was crucial and morality was not part of the mix, at least as compared to outright intimidation or legal fraud. T.R. Fehrenbach has also written: *"There is some truth that many Mexican landowners, especially the small ones, were robbed in south Texas by force, intimidation, or chicanery. But what is usually ignored is the fact that the hacendado class, as a class, was stripped of property perfectly legally, according to the highest traditions of U.S. laws."* [See Note # 5.]

There appears to be no dearth of "force, intimidation, or chicanery" when studying land ownership history in Texas. For example, records indicate that Henry Kinney of Corpus Christi defrauded "his friend" Blas Falcón out of his land. Mifflin Kenedy fenced in the lake owned by Eulalia Tijerina because the King Ranch had to be assured of a water supply. It was said that land owning neighbors of the King Ranch somehow seemed to *vanish* as the Ranch continued to grow. The Texas Rangers were often accused of acting as King's "strong-arm agents."

Racism and cultural conflict enter the picture. American and Europeans who coveted the land portrayed Mexican rancheros as employing primitive methods, that the rancheros lacked enterprise, were inefficient, lazy, ignorant. When rancheros were in situations that demanded money, caused perhaps by drought or cattle market fluctuations (in 1885 a steer brought in $35 while in 1887 it was worth $5), they took to mortgaging their land, which accelerated their land loss.

The **Miguel Gutiérrez** family of Nueces County can serve as a brief case study. In 1878 **Richard King** got 2,000 acres from Gutiérrez for what the legal record describes as "valuable considerations." (According to Montejano, entries like "sufficient," "taxes," "indefinite," were obviously acceptable in legal records.) In 1880 (Miguel had passed on by this date) some 17,872 acres of his *Gutiérrez Santa Gertrudis* grant were auctioned off at a sheriff's sale to pay for tax arrears, King buying the property by paying $240. In 1881 María Gutiérrez sold the remainder of the grant to King, some 24,354 acres, for $4,000. As can be discerned, the loss by the Gutiérrez family was a windfall for King and his life-long associate **Mifflin Kenedy**. As of 1913 the King Ranch held some 540,000 acres in its private domain and taxes didn't appear to be a problem.

Between 1850 and 1900 Texas land ownership, along with concomitant lifestyles, shifted from Tejano to Texan. For example, in Cameron County in 1892 non-Spanish surnamed individuals owned better than 1.2 million acres, more than four times the acreage held by Spanish-surnamed rancheros. An elite group of eighteen Texans owned a total of more than a million acres and some twenty-eight others held at least 100,000 acres. By contrast, of sixty-nine Tejano land owners, only three had large spreads and forty-two owned less than 2,560 acres, small acreage for a Texas ranch. Further, when land changed hands, it was from Tejano to Texan.

It could also be said that the standard of living in South and West Texas shifted away from what it had been before the Mexican War. In 1850 the Latino population was comprised of around 34% farm and ranch people, 29% skilled laborers, 34% manual laborers. By 1900 Latino farm and ranch people were 16% of the population, skilled laborers 12%, manual laborers 67%. It is obvious that Tejanos had been displaced by Texans between 1850 and 1900. [See Note # 6.]

CALIFORNIA

Leading Californios like **Mariano Vallejo** had favored annexation to the USA. In one of his famous speeches he stated: "*...When we join our fortunes to hers, we shall not become subjects but fellow-citizens, possessing all the rights of the people of the United states...We shall have stable government and just laws. California will grow strong and flourish, and her people will be prosperous, happy, and free...*" [See Note # 7.] Few people listened to **Antonio María Osio**, author of *The History of Alta California*, who warned that the Stars and Stripes "...alleged to be the symbol of liberty, but that was actually a lie. It belonged to an oppressor who displayed arrogance against the weak." [See Note # 8.]

The **Land Law of 1851** set the tone for the adjudication of California land titles. It was conceived and promoted by Senator (from California) **William Gwin**. He stated explicitly that he had no intention of harming Californio land titles, that the "happy and contented race" of Californios was now assured of an American "prosperous and glorious future." This was required window-dressing because in reality Gwin's bill called for a vigorous investigation of all Californio land titles, without exception, with the burden of proof completely on the claimant. Unpublicized in Hispanic California, Senator Gwin believed Californio land titles were basically fraudulent but for the record he stated that his bill would not cause Californios to be "distressed, oppressed or frightened." [See Note # 9.] Despite covert opposition from California's other Senator, **John C. Frémont**, and open opposition from his father-in-law Thomas H. Benton from Missouri, who denounced Gwin's efforts, even saying Gwin might be assassinated, the Gwin bill passed easily. [See Note # 10.] In brief, Gwin's bill established the **Board of Land Commissioners** which would judge the validity of all land titles. As Senator Gwin later stated, the effort was to have Americans homestead on Californio lands, thus forcing the Californios to resettle on "public lands," which meant lands controlled by the government. The Land Commissioners would rule on the validity of land titles, if a claimant disagreed he could take the case to District Court and all the way to the Supreme Court if necessary. Most importantly, rejected land claims would throw the land into public domain status, whereupon Americans could claim it for homesteading.

Americans coveted Californio land holdings. "Settlers" charged that for some 200 Californio families to own some 14 million acres of land was simply *unfair*. Many other charges were constantly leveled at Californio land owners: there had been no surveys and boundaries overlapped in bewildering fashion; lands were given to Californios after the USA took over; Californios were basically a lazy, shiftless lot; they didn't use the land properly, letting their cattle herds increase wildly; it was incoming Americans who had given new value to California land...so it should belong to the new "hardy immigrants...industrious settlers." In the view of covetous American squatters, the Gwin Bill didn't go far enough. Furthermore, if the courts didn't give them the land there were other ways to get it.

Though they had no knowledge of the American court system, as products of Hispanic culture and tradition the Californios felt they could prove their land titles. At the very least, "common knowledge" assured them that their ranches had been in existence for longer than necessary to perfect their titles.

Further, they had been the first European colonists in California, they had labored as soldiers for rights to the land, they had built homes and raised herds of cattle, etc. All these things were more important than papers. There had always been plenty of land, so no one had to go without, lie, or forge papers to get some.

American courts were a new experience for Californios. While the judges and juries of squatters were bad enough, the most vicious were the lawyers who would stoop to any means to win a case. Land law attorneys, numbering around 50 and referred to by Dr. Pitt as *"mostly shysters who lacked not only honesty but also knowledge and experience,"* quickly came to represent "Yankee justice" as Californios were stripped of their lands, losing to the juries or the lawyers they had to depend on. There were some American lawyers who asked for real justice. These few were Elisha O. Crosby, Carey Jones, Joseph L. Brent, Henry Halleck, Henry Hittell, etc., but they were the exceptions to the immoralities of early American California courts.

With Americans like Senator Gwinn making the rules, the struggle was all but impossible, its greatest strength being that Californios couldn't recognize what was happening: the land would be taken from them by hook or crook. They went into litigation expecting justice and usually exited impoverished. A basic strategy was to string out the hearing on a single claim, sometimes by months, often years. The average length of time a Californio landowner had to wait for his land patent to be granted was seventeen (17) years. [See Note # 11.] During delays American squatters often decided to take over their parcel of land and force their eviction in court where squatters comprised the jury. In April of 1853 Senator Gwin replaced two of the three Land Commissioners, thus causing another long delay while the new members learned the ropes, which only benefited the "industrious settlers," for whom Gwin was working and which the Californios never recognized, despite their growing miseries.

American "settlers" did what they could to acquire rancho land. Believing that there is strength in numbers, "Settlers' Leagues" were formed. League lawyers filed third party suits in order to intimidate litigating claimants with additional counterclaims, injunctions, or writs. After the land law took effect squatters refused to pay any kind of rent, asserting that nobody owned the land unless the Land Commission acknowledged ownership. When the opportunity availed itself the Americans took Californio cattle, horses, crops, etc., for themselves or for sale in places like San Francisco. Californio orchards were cut down, Californio crops like wheat were burned down, stray cattle were shot down then processed for meat, Californio vaqueros were chased off, outlying buildings were destroyed, trails were fenced, gates were blocked.

Americans felt no qualms about taking whatever they wanted. Walter Colton, alcalde of Monterey, was visited on afternoon by an American woman who demanded a permit to cut timber on a Californio's land. Colton asked the woman if her husband had rented the land. No. Was there an agreement with the Californio owner? No. Colton then asked her why she had a right to cut timber on another person's land? She replied: *Right sir, have we not taken the country?* [See Note 12.]

Attorneys pretending to befriend the Californios were able to acquire their land, generally using the Land Law as a subterfuge. American swindlers were able to ingratiate themselves to the Californios and ensnare them out of their wealth. For example, Horace Carpentier, Edson Adams, and James Moon were able to take over the 19,000 acre *Rancho San Antonio* (later the town of Oakland) from the Vicente

Peralta family. Carpentier got Peralta to sign a lease that was actually a mortgage against the Peralta rancho. When Vicente Peralta refused to honor the mortgage, which he never would have signed had it not been presented by his "friend," Horace Carpentier "bought" the property at a sheriff's sale. And it was all "legal" under American law.

Another way that Americans could get land was to marry a widow with a large estate. The bereaved widow was often in a tangled web of debt, litigation, tax liens, and ranch management problems. When someone appeared who might be able to help her out of her serious dilemmas it was often an American who quickly put the land under his name as required by American law. It was then no rarity to get rid of the wife.

Another way for Americans to gain Californio land was through money lending. Lawyers had to be paid and few Californios had ready cash. When the mortgage couldn't be paid the money lender took over the land.

One of the most tragic episodes propelled by the American takeover of California involved the **Nicolás Berreyesa** family. Nicolás owned *Rancho Milpitas* near San José. A charming swindler named James Jakes ingratiated himself to Nicolás and his three sons then advised them to approach the Land Law by squatting on their own Rancho Milpitas. Jakes even hired a surveyor to mark off a plot for each of the four Berreyesas. Believing they were protecting their land under American law, the Berreyesas followed through. James Jakes then went to the land office, declared Rancho Milpitas as vacated property and claimed it for himself. Don Nicolás sued for the return of his ranch but American authorities informed him everything had been done "legally," and was required to pay $500 in court costs.

When another American "benefactor" took a neighboring ranch from its owner and had a survey done that included Berreyesa land, Nicolás went to court once more but lost again. (The "benefactor" became rich and was later elected to the State Legislature.)

Nicolás Berreyesa took his legal fight all the way to the Supreme Court but then he learned his attorneys had disappeared from Washington along with all his original, irreplaceable documents. Nicolás could not believe the misfortunes that had befallen him and his family with the American takeover.

The son Nemasio, owner of a quicksilver mine that was coveted by Americans, was seized one night and lynched near San José. Two other Berreyesa family members were lynched in 1854 and 1857. The murderers were never identified or brought to justice.

Three of the Berreyesa brothers were so harried by squatters that they went insane. Don Nicolás finally told his family to move to Mexico while time permitted. They didn't, hoping their litigation would be positive in District Court. In 1869 Judge Ogden Hoffman ruled against the Berreyesas, citing that they had squatted on their own property. Nicolás died in 1873, a broken man. In 1876 the Supreme Court upheld Hoffman's decision. The some seventy members of the Berreyesa family, once powerful in the Californio tradition, were now without a foot of land and virtually without money.

The Board of Land Commissioners operated from January of 1852 until March of 1856. The task was herculean in nature, to be sure, but mostly because the real intent was to separate Californios from their land. Dr. Pitt mentions trustworthy people like Thomas Larkin, Abel Stearns, William Hartnell, etc., who could have acted as friends of the court and who in very little time could have identified all the well known ranchos owned by Californios. But an atmosphere of complexity and confusion lent itself to Americans taking over Californio land "legally." This self-righteousness was important so that American character could not be called into question. [See Note # 13.] This continues into the present day because historical literature contains assertions by Alan Rosenus that *"Mariano Vallejo treasured California's Americanization"* while Genaro Padilla writes that Vallejo *"…felt the military officers had treated him with the greatest disrespect; no leniency had been extended to him, nor was it their desire to deal justly with him; he thought the methods adopted by the U.S. law agents were calculated not to further justice but to defeat it by dilatory and expensive litigation."* [See Note # 14.]

NEW MEXICO

European (Hispanic) land ownership goes back further in New Mexico than any other area of the Southwest or the USA. Unlike other parts of the country, the cataclysmic event in New Mexico land ownership was the American takeover due to the Mexican War of 1846-48. It was not only that a differing system of laws would be in effect but also a totally different society with overt as well as covert motivations. A couple of brief land grant histories will serve to illustrate land tenure in New Mexico.

LAS TRAMPAS

The Las Trampas grant is one of the oldest continuously inhabited community grants in northern New Mexico. It was made to twelve (12) heads of families in 1751 by Governor Tomás Vélez Cachupín as part of his Indian defense policy. The leader of the twelve petitioners was fifty-seven-year-old **Juan de Argüello** (who lived to the age of ninety-five; his wife was Juana Gregoria Brito). Among the 12 heads of families were presidio soldiers as well as descendants of stalwart Tlaxcalan Indians who had come with the Spaniards from Mexico, and Melchor Rodríguez, son of Sebastián who had been Vargas' drummer and herald. The deed to the land was made by Alcalde Juan José Lobato on July 1, 1751. Each pioneer would receive a private plot of land as well as rights to *pastures, wood gathering, water, and watering places.* [See Note # 15.]

In 1771 some 500 Comanches attacked the settlement of El Valle on the grant. Numerous pioneers lost their lives defending against the Comanche attack. In 1776 the population of the grant was some 278 souls. In 1781 a smallpox epidemic caused the deaths of some 31 adults and 23 children. Despite the adversities, the villages of Las Trampas, Ojo Sarco, Chamisal, Llano, and El Valle were on the grant by 1846.

Surveyor General William Pelham found the Las Trampas grant to be genuine so he recommended confirmation to Congress, which it did on June 2, 1860. A survey was made in 1876 and some 46,000 acres were included in the grant. Commissioner N.C. McFarland of the General Land Office stated the eastern boundary of Las Trampas was overlapping into the Santa Bárbara grant. In 1885 William Sparks set aside the first survey and ordered a new one which found that the grant contained 28,000 acres. (A patent was issued for this greatly reduced acreage in 1903.)

In 1900 Las Trampas heir **David Martínez Jr.** needed money so he decided to file a suit (along with four other heirs) to partition the grant and be paid for their individual shares of land. This had been illegal under Spanish/Mexican law but now under American domination it was a sure way to get at the common lands even when just one heir petitioned for it. **Alonzo B. McMillan** was their attorney in the action. The suit named five individual defendants, not all the living heirs of the original "Trampas

Twelve," i.e., the hundreds of people living in the Trampas grant villages of Ojo Sarco, Cañada de los Alamos, Las Trampas, El Valle, Chamisal, and El Llano who were the bona fide heirs. Martínez certified under oath that he didn't know any other heirs on the grant and the court and all attorneys accepted his statement. Therefore permission was gotten from the court to place a legal notice in the (English language) Taos *Cresset* newspaper informing *"unknown heirs"* about the action. The ruse worked: no one answered the notice because no one read the notice or heard about the legal action. Since there was no answer to the lawsuit, the partition attorney now got a default judgment to force the sale of the grant. Put another way, New Mexican land owners were not permitted the right of due process. Everything was decided upon only by the handful of individuals intent on taking the land and they were able to keep their actions secret.

The Court appointed **Ernest A. Johnson** as referee to determine who were owners of the grant, how much of the grant was common land, and what was each owner's fractional interest in the common lands. Referee Johnson asserted that 650 acres were private land and the rest was commons subject to partition. Everyone involved took great care that citizens living on the land would not be informed about what the Court was doing, especially that only 650 acres out of the 28,000 were exempt from sale.

Judge **Daniel H. McMillan**, substituting for judge **John R. McFie** entered an order for partition and appointed a board of commissioners to divide the common lands. Commissioners reported that due to the nature of the land and large number of heirs, who at first were acknowledged as "unknown," a partition was impossible. People living on the Las Trampas grant would therefore not get their "individual percentage share" of land, as was common in the "American way," one of the original arguments in favor of partition.

Judge McFie returned to the bench and ordered the sale of Las Trampas common lands, which was the entire grant minus 650 acres. With hardly anyone knowing what was happening the only bid at sale was $5,000 by **H.F. Raynolds** and the lands are sold to him. Attorney Alonzo B. McMillan is awarded one-fourth of the net proceeds. Further, McMillan has been buying interests in the common lands from various heirs and now asserts he owns 10.6% of the grant, for which he must be paid.

A suit is filed by **Alois B. Renehan** to set aside the sale of the Trampas grant because the buyer, *H.F. Raynolds, turns out to be Alonzo McMillan's law partner.* McMillan, Raynolds, and Referee Johnson's assistant Amado Chávez are accused of conspiring to buy the land for about 18 cents per acre because they could then turn around and sell it at $1.50 per acre. It is also charged that *Referee Johnson has accepted a bribe to go along with the scheme.* [See Note # 16.]

Judge McFie sets the sale aside and orders a new one which is scheduled for February of 1903. As ludicrous as it may seem, the entire matter is still a well kept secret, only a handful of people being involved. Española merchant and sheepman **Frank Bond** bids $17,000 and is given title to the land. Attorney Alonzo McMillan gets his fee of around $4,200. David Martínez Jr. nets about $200. Villagers average about $25 for their "sale share" but the *fact that it is for sale of their common lands is hidden from them because they are temporarily allowed continued use of the lands.*

In 1907 Frank Bond sold the grant to the **Las Trampas Lumber Company** owned by four Albuquerque businessmen. Villagers finally realize their lands have been sold when they are informed they can no longer use grant lands as before. They hire **Charles Catron**, son of T.B. Catron, to get their land back, beginning a new round of litigation.

In 1908 the Las Trampas Lumber Company filed a quiet title suit to clear title for the land bought from Frank Bond. **Alois B. Rcnehan** is attorney for the Lumber Co. *as well as for some of the villagers, who are defendants in the suit.*

In 1911 Charles Catron filed an answer to the quiet title suit. 1913 the suit is settled out of court between Catron and Renehan with the following stipulations: Villagers receive deeds to their private tracts of land and easement for all irrigation ditches; they retain "use rights" for grazing and wood gathering; they sign quitclaim deeds to the Lumber Co. for what had been Trampas common lands; La Trampas Lumber Co. receives the villagers' quitclaim deeds *which make no mention of "use-rights,"* which the Company grants to all villagers via an individual agreement with each one. Villagers believe they have the same use-rights as before and the Lumber Company has a title that has been cleared of Las Trampas use-rights.

Unknown to anyone, except perhaps Charles Catron, Attorney Renehan now inserted a stipulation into the final settlement agreement: "…neither this contract nor any contract delivered pursuant hereto by said company is to be acknowledged or recorded." Under American law a document that is not notarized cannot be recorded and an unrecorded document is not binding. Therefore, Renehan guaranteed that villager "use-rights" were nonexistent before the law while all villagers possessed written documentation from the Lumber Co. that "guaranteed" their traditional use-rights. Catron and Renehan have settled the quiet-title suit by supplying documentation to villagers that they will have perpetual "use-rights" to their common lands while at the same time supplying the Lumber Co. with official court documents that showed the land to be unencumbered by "use-rights," enabling a Lumber Company sale whenever desirable.

In 1914 Judge **Thomas Lieb** (it is unknown if he was aware of what had transpired) signed a decree quieting the title to the Las Trampas grant. Charles Catron is awarded a fee of $5,500. In 1926 the Las Trampas Lumber Co. declared bankruptcy.

In 1926 the United States purchased the Trampas lands and villagers filed their "use-rights" documents with the Government. They are turned over to the Forest Service in Albuquerque for advice. The Forest Service questions attorney Alois B. Renehan who informs it that no "use-rights" agreement exists.

When Charles Catron is questioned he states that the "use-rights" documentation is in the court file but the Forest Service can't locate it. Since the use right agreements are not recorded nor referred to in the court decree, the Forest Service concludes "…*they are without any effect.*" But villagers are lulled with the subterfuge that matters can be "*worked out.*"

Traditional practices are permitted until 1915-1930 when the Forest Service restricts villager use rights. Grazing fees are charged, herds are limited and permits required. Unable to graze stock without paying onerous fees, villagers look to others ways to make a living.

The Great Depression smothers American society and wage labor is more difficult to come by. Stock animals don't exist in sufficient numbers to make a living for most village families. There is hunger in the land.

In 1967 the Tierra Amarilla Courthouse raid caused the Forest Service to be a little more conciliatory in the needs of Trampas villages but little changes in substance.

In 1971 at a meeting held in Peñasco local residents demand that their use right agreements be honored. The Forest Service replies that the documents aren't legal therefore there is no obligation on its part.

In 1981 Ben E. Domínguez, José Paz López, and Ron Maestas are cited for gathering firewood without a permit in the Carson National Forest. They claim the right to take wood under their use-right agreements, which are introduced at the trial but are not recognized as germane to the charges at hand.

JACONA

In 1702 Governor Pedro Rodriguez Cubero made the Jacona land grant to Ignacio Roybal. Ignacio had been recruited in Spain by Diego de Vargas and in New Mexico he enlarged his land holdings and became well known in politics. His son, Santiago Roybal, was sent to Mexico City for his education and upon graduation from the seminary he returned as Vicar of Bishop Crespo in Durango. Ignacio died in 1756 but the Jacona population slowly continued to grow. By 1874 there were some fifty (50) families living on the grant. [See Note # 17.]

Surveyor General James K. Proudfit recommended to Congress that the Jacona grant of some 40,000 acres be confirmed to the heirs of Ignacio Roybal. Congress ignored the recommendation and it fell to the Court of Private Land Claims (established in 1891) to adjudicate it, finally acknowledging it as belonging to the heirs. Another survey was ordered and now the grant contained only 7,000 acres, a great difference from the 40,000 of the 1878 survey.

Jacona attorney **Napoleon B. Laughlin** didn't contest the second survey. Instead he filed a personal lawsuit that would bring him ownership of one-third of the grant or a cash equivalent. Whereas Laughlin had been the attorney for Jacona heirs, defendants in Laughlin's lawsuit are now described as "unknown heirs" of the original grantee. As "required by law," legal notice was published in an English language newspaper, which it could be assumed very few Spanish-speaking New Mexicans could read. [See Note # 18.] No living people are named as defendants and no one is served in person, especially not the people living on the Jacona land being targeted for takeover by Laughlin and the court. Once more, due process isn't permitted by the American legal system, only taking the land under the guise of law.

By 1908 Laughlin's legal notice goes unheeded and unanswered so he petitioned the court for a default judgment. The court grants his request to partition or sell the Jacona land grant. The Referee appointed by the court is (probably) Laughlin's secretary. The Referee's report contains a list of 170 "heirs" of Ignacio Roybal, heirs which were "unknown" according to the previous action, but now Laughlin is included as a one-third owner of the grant as payment for his confirmation fee and for handling the partition suit. The case is given to Commissioners for recommendations, which wind up being to sell the grant. This was typical strategy because

commissioners were always chosen from among friends of the court and the lawyers involved.

Judge **McFie** ordered that Jacona be sold to the highest bidder.

A resident of the grant, **Cosme Herrera,** somehow discovered that the people's land was being sold from under them, without their participation or knowledge. He rallies the villagers, collects $15 from each of them, and *buys the Jacona land grant.* The lawyers/judges get their money and Herrera is awarded the land whereupon he deeds it over to Jacona villagers.

Villagers establish a three-man commission to administer the grant but as time goes by some villagers forget to pay their share of the taxes and the commission has no funds to pay them. In 1919 a deed is executed under which 110 individuals agree to partition common lands among themselves. Each person gets title to about 60 acres of common land and is individually responsible for the taxes on it. In 1928 some forty-six villagers (from the 1919 action) have not kept up with their taxes so a suit is filed, by those who are up to date, to declare that those forty-six have forfeited their interest in the Jacona grant and said interests should now pass to the plaintiffs. The court grants their petition and a deed is delivered to them. In summation, had it not been for Cosme Herrera the Jacona land grant would have been lost to the descendants of the original pioneers through the machinations of corrupt American lawyers and judges.

ARIZONA

With the ending of hostilities against the Apaches the Pápago/Hispanic alliance weakened and the two groups found themselves at loggerheads in the 1880s because in 1874 President U.S. Grant had set aside some 71,000 acres around Mission San Xavier exclusively for Pápago use. Hispanics had lived in the area for some thirty to forty years but they were informed they would have to move or they would be forcibly evicted by U.S. marshals. Tucson's leading newspaper, *El Fronterizo*, put out by Carlos Velasco, also charged that the improved properties of evictees were being taken over by Americans. [See Note # 19.]

Arizona history shows that small farm and ranch operations were no match for large land and cattle corporations or land speculators who could control the government. Former citizens of Mexico were also kept ignorant of new American laws which often permitted unscrupulous Americans to "jump" properties held by descendants of Spanish speaking pioneers. For example, one American rancher wanted the land (300 acres) of some Mexicans who worked for him so he told them he, their benefactor, would pay the taxes on their land. Once he did so he put the land under his name and had the sheriff evict the people from "his" acreage.

The Arizona Rangers used an effective trick to remove Mexicans from the land. A Ranger would put hides in a rancher's corral then walk up to the owner and accuse him of cattle rustling, proof being the hides with another brand. If there was any resistance the rancher could be hung on the spot.

The prominent **Yjinio Aguirre** had a close call with American claim jumping. One day his son Higinio was in a bar when he overheard some Americans asking if there were any available ranches in the area. One answered that Aguirre's *El Rancho de San Francisco* had no patent on it, thus ripe for the taking. The son rushed home to his father and informed him that the ranch could be taken if they didn't act quickly. Aguirre didn't believe any law could take his land because he had worked so hard for it. The son cited cases he knew of Americans jumping on other ranches. The old pioneer said he would use his gun and fight but in the end he gave his son permission to file the Aguirre claim on their own land.

Large ranchers like Yjinio Aguirre or Bernabé Robles were able to compete but small holders like Emilio Carrillo and José Moreno generally wound up selling their land to the big corporations. The small farm and ranch quickly became a thing of the past.

DISCUSSION NOTES *for* LAND TENURE

Note # 1

See page 190 in *The Treaty Of Guadalupe Hidalgo: A Legacy of Conflict* by Richard Griswold del Castillo.

Note # 2

See page 168 in *Foreigners In Their Native Land: Historical Roots of the Mexican Americans* edited by David J. Weber.

Note # 3

See Chapter 9 in *Tejano Legacy: Rancheros and Settlers in South Texas, 1734-1900* by Armando C. Alonzo for a brief introduction to this topic.

Note # 4

See Chapter 3 in *Anglos And Mexicans In The Making Of Texas, 1836-1986* by David Montejano.

Note # 5

See page 510 in *Lone Star* by T.R. Fehrenbach. Do Secretary of State James Buchanan and brilliant historian Fehrenbach appear to see eye to eye? If landowners can be "stripped of property perfectly legally," what is the American value of the Treaty of Guadalupe Hidalgo? Are there any implications for American character and/or American historiography?

Note # 6

See pages 62-63 in *The Tejano Community, 1836-1900* by Arnoldo De León.

Note # 7

See pages 90-91 in the biography *General M.G. Vallejo and the Advent of the Americans* by Alan Rosenus.

Note # 8

See page 462 in *Lands Of Promise And Despair* edited by Rose Marie Beebe and Robert M. Senkewicz. Is it ironic that Native Americans like Red Cloud of the Sioux made much the same statement?

Note # 9

See Chapter 5 in *The Decline Of The Californios: A Social History of the Spanish-speaking Californians, 1846-1890* by Leonard Pitt.

Note # 10

How much did the American Senate value or respect its Treaty of Guadalupe Hidalgo obligations? What are the consequences (or the fruits) of ignoring treaties? Henry Clay orated that Californios deserved consideration but "enterprising citizens," meaning Americans, deserved more. It must be pointed out that these events transpired before the Dred Scott Decision.

Note # 11

See page 219 in the biography *General M.G. Vallejo and the Advent of the Americans* by Alan Rosenus.

Note 12

See page 193 in the *General M.G. Vallejo* volume by A. Rosenus. Is the woman's reasoning logical: if the USA could take the northern half of Mexico didn't Americans have the right to take whatever they wished? Is this "master race" psychology? It would be interesting to compare it's tenets to those of "Manifest Destiny."

Note # 13

See page 89 in *Decline Of The Californios*. This need for respectability appears to be a steady tenet in historiography. For example, Professor Paul Gates is reported as writing that the "settlers" deserved better than they got, that the Californios received more benefits than they deserved, that they lost their lands because of their own incompetence. Henry George disagrees and states bluntly that American California land history is one of *"greed, perjury, corruption, spoliation, and high handed robbery."* Each writer thus opens avenues for a school of California land history. The reader will have to decide who has truth on his side.

Note # 14

See page 233 in *General M.G. Vallejo* and page 108 in *My History, Not Yours* by Dr. Genaro Padilla.

Note # 15

See Chapter 7 in *Land Grants And Lawsuits In Northern New Mexico* by Malcolm Ebright.

Note # 16

A study about American lawyers during the Territorial period would make interesting reading.

Note # 17

Chapter 11 in *Land Grants & Lawsuits In Northern New Mexico* by Malcolm Ebright.

Note # 18

What caused members of the legal profession to operate in this fashion in New Mexico? Were judges as crooked as the attorneys? Was the legal profession that adept at working for its own good? Was New Mexico "The Land of the Enchanted"? Is it possible to be "legalistically lawless"? How might "industrious American settlers" reacted if they were targeted in this situation?

Note # 19

See pages 70-74 in *Los Tucsonenses* by Thomas E. Sheridan.

CHAPTER 15

Education In The Greater Southwest

P ublic school education in the USA is often attacked as mediocre, underachieving, watered down, etc. Teachers are often denigrated overtly or covertly and generally blamed for the lack of achievement. There are also those who believe the institution of public education is no worse than the legal or medical industries, no worse than various other cornerstones of American society.

It must be pointed out that the Education industry in the USA is totally dominated by Administration. Teachers, teachers' unions, the community or School Boards do not run the schools. Underachievement is often blamed on teachers, students, the community, insufficient financing, etc., but most of the time failure can be traced to Administration. This sounds like a harsh indictment and it must be admitted that causes of failure are seldom found on only one doorstep. It is true that some Americans use the public schools as a baby sitting service and some parents believe the schools should help raise their kids. In the final analysis, the people in charge must bear the burden of failure though the consequences of this insidious failure will be suffered by others in the years to come, Administration thereby escaping direct or immediate responsibility.

Why are public schools considered such a failure by so many Americans? Despite the standard rhetoric of "Excellence in Education," the basic thrust of American public education is for athletics and "good times." This sounds quite radical, yes, but any honest professional working in the education industry will admit to that reality. For example, the football coach might be removed if the team isn't successful as demanded but when was the English teacher ever fired because students were functional illiterates after four years of "studying" English? Further, the schools are unable to foster a respect for work. Indeed, it appears to do just the opposite. Administration is well aware of these realities but few educational "leaders" have the will to challenge the status quo. (Among the exceptions have been stalwarts like Philip Grignon and Tony Trujillo.) Why "rock the boat" when it is so much easier to collect your ample paycheck for attending the breakfast meeting, the luncheon, the conference? Enron style executives are nothing new in Education because looting the school district can be accomplished by those holding the purse strings. There is no doubt that Americans spend fantastic amounts of money on public education. By and large, Administration decides how it will be spent and in the educational chain Administration needs come first, though this is never admitted, and anyone who tries to reform the situation is a *troublemaker.*

A glaring basic failure is that public schools haven't even been able to promote the privilege/responsibility of voting. It is often said that at least 50% of Americans never bother to vote. Why don't the schools promote the habit of voting by having school-wide elections from the First Grade on up through graduation at least once a year? Citizenship receives much lip service yet some half of all Americans don't feel it's their responsibility to function in this aspect of democracy. And the schools don't seem interested enough to do something about it by training young people into the voting habit. Further, what about promoting respect for work? The work ethic is not cherished, if it ever was. Administration isn't concerned? Are they working for that promotion, a higher paying job in another district, finishing work on that next degree, or mostly appearing to be working?

It would be difficult to find a school district that has been more criticized for being top heavy with administrators than the Albuquerque Public Schools of Albuquerque, New Mexico, the largest school district in the State. Often described as the "Good Ole Boy System," APS could be an example of *No Administrator Left Behind.* The "minority" population is the largest in the district but minorities like Hispanic and Native American generally rank at the bottom academically while the non-minority students rank consistently high, even when compared nationally. This pattern has been the same for basically half a century.

In previous years the District was broken up into Areas with a Superintendent for each Area, along with various associates and/or deputies, all of whom received very handsome salaries for hanging around the office. (Later the Area Superintendents were discontinued and the areas were referred to as Complexes.)

It will be recalled that upon the retirement of one APS superintendent he gave his secretary a $10,000 increase in salary.

At one period in time a number of upper level administrators were provided with cars "because they have to attend meetings at all hours."

To "better serve the community" the Albuquerque Administration bought itself an expensive ($12,000,000) office building in order to house administrative staff during a time when newspaper articles were focusing on school buildings with leaky roofs. All was sanctioned by the School Board.

In 2003 there were four (4) Superintendents leading the School District at the same time, all hired by the School Board upon direction from the Administration. When some new School Board members demanded a return to the single superintendent structure the person selected to lead APS, who had been one of the previous four, hired two associate superintendents as well as a "Chief of Staff," who had been one of the four former superintendents for the District. Salaries for the superintendents are among the highest in New Mexico *"because you have to pay them if you want good people."* The superintendents also have a designated "Spokesman" for the school district. (A call was made to the Albuquerque Public Schools Spokesman on February 17, 2004, at 11:55 a.m. The recording stated *Today is February 16 and we are closed for Presidents' Day. Please leave a message and I will return your call when I return to work on the 17th.* The call was returned at 2:00 p.m. on the 17th.)

EDUCATIONAL RANKINGS in the SOUTHWEST

The following rankings are from the Morgan Quitno Press volume titled *Education State Rankings, 2003-2004*. The information in brackets is as follows: the first figure pertains to national rank while the second figure provides the percent/amount pertaining to the specific State. "NA" indicates "Not Available."

Percent of Expenditures Used for Administration, 2001 (National Average = 2%):
Oklahoma [12 – 2.8%]; New Mexico [19 – 2.5%]; Arizona [35 – 1.7%]; Nevada [37 – 1.6%]; Texas [37 – 1.6%]; Colorado [42 – 1.4%]; Utah [47 – 1%]; California [50 – 0.8%].

Expenditures Per Pupil, 2001 (National Average = $413):
California [7 – $485]; Colorado [21 – $421]; Nevada [23 – $413]; New Mexico [33 – $362]; Texas [37 – $354]; Oklahoma [43 – $319]; Arizona [49 – $290]; Utah [50 – $280].

NEA Estimated Average Classroom **Teacher Salaries**, 2003 (National Average = $45,822):
California [1 – $56,283]; Nevada [23 – $41,795]; Colorado [26 – $41,275]; Arizona [27 – $40,894]; Texas [30 – $40,001]; Utah [37 – $38,413]; New Mexico [45 – $36,687]; Oklahoma [47 – $34,854].

Estimated **Pupil-Teacher Ratios**, 2003 (National Average = 15.7 Pupils per Teacher):
Arizona [1 – 20.9 Pupils per Teacher]; Utah [2 – 20.8]; California [3 – 19.8]; Nevada [6 – 19]; Colorado [11 – 16.6]; Oklahoma [23 – 15.4]; New Mexico [27 – 15.1]; Texas [30 – 14.6];

Average **Class Size in Elementary School**, 2000 (National Average = 21.2):
Arizona [1 – 24.5]; Utah [4 – 23.7]; Colorado [5 – 23.2]; California [8 – 22.7]; Nevada [24 – 20.7]; New Mexico [32 – 19.9]; Oklahoma [41 – 18.6]; Texas [42 – 18.5].

Average **Class Size in Secondary Schools**, 2000 (National Average = 23.4):
California [1 – 28.1]; Utah [3 – 27.1]; Nevada [4 – 27]; Arizona [6 – 25.6]; Colorado [12 – 24]; New Mexico [17 – 23.4]; Texas [27 – 22.2]; Oklahoma [32 – 21.5].

Highest **Reading** Scores in the Southwest for **Fourth Graders**, 2002 (National Average = 217):
Utah [12 – 222]; Texas [28 – 217]; Oklahoma [34 – 213]; Nevada [36 – 209]; New Mexico [37 – 208]; California [41 – 206]; Arizona [41 – 205]; Colorado [NA].

Highest **Reading** Scores for **Eighth Graders**, 2002 (National Average = 263):
Utah [24 – 263]; Oklahoma [26 – 262]; Texas [26-262]; Arizona [34 – 257]; New Mexico [37 – 254]; Nevada [40 – 251]; California [41 – 250]; Colorado [NA].

Highest **Writing** Scores for **Fourth Graders,** 2002 (National Average = 153):
Texas [17 – 154]; California [33 – 146]; Nevada [34 – 145]; Utah [34 – 145]; New Mexico [38 – 142]; Oklahoma [38 – 142]; Arizona [42 – 140]; Colorado [NA].

Highest **Writing** Scores for **Eighth Graders**, 2002 (National Average = 152):
Texas [16 – 152]; Oklahoma [23 – 150]; California [31 – 144]; Utah [33 – 143]; Arizona [37 – 141];
New Mexico [39 – 140]; Nevada [41 – 137]; Colorado [NA];

Highest **Mathematics** Scores for **Fourth Graders**, 2000 (National Average = 226):
Texas [5 – 233]; Utah [18 – 227]; Oklahoma [23 – 225]; Nevada [29 – 220]; Arizona [33 – 219];
California [38 – 214]; New Mexico [38 – 214]; Colorado [NA].

Highest **Mathematics** Scores for **Eighth Graders**, 2000: (National Average = 274)
Texas [21 – 275]; Utah [21 – 275]; Oklahoma [25 – 272]; Arizona [27 – 271]; Nevada [29 – 268];
California [34 – 262]; New Mexico [37 – 260]; Colorado [NA];

Highest **Science** Scores for **Fourth Graders**, 2000 (National Average = 148):
Utah [12 – 155]; Oklahoma [17 – 152]; Texas [26 – 147]; Nevada [32 – 142]; Arizona [33 – 141];
New Mexico [36 – 138]; California [39 – 131]; Colorado [NA].

Highest **Science** Scores for **Eighth Graders**, 2000 (National Average = 149):
Utah [14 – 155]; Oklahoma [22 – 149]; Arizona [26 – 146]; Texas [28 – 144]; Nevada [30 – 143];
New Mexico [34 – 140]; California [37 – 132]; Colorado [NA].

Estimated **High School Graduation**, 2003 (National Rate = 67.2%):
Utah [2 – 85.5%]; Oklahoma [13 – 75.6%]; Colorado [24 – 71.5%]; Arizona [26 – 71.3%];
California [29 – 70.8%]; Nevada [37 – 63%]; Texas [39 – 62.1%]; New Mexico [41 – 61%].

High School Dropout Rate, 2000 (National Rate = 4.8%)
Nevada [6.2%]; New Mexico [6%]; Oklahoma [5.4%]; Texas [5%]; Utah [4.1%]; Arizona [NA];
California [NA]; Colorado [NA].

Teen Birth Rates, 2001 (National Rate = 45.3% **Births per 1000** Women Aged 15 to 19):
Texas [2 – 66.5%]; Arizona [3 – 65.3%]; New Mexico [4 – 64.5%]; Oklahoma [8 – 58%];
Nevada [12 – 56.4%]; Colorado [20 – 45.7%]; California [22 – 45.2%]; Utah [30.38.2%].

Percent of Children Living in Poverty, 2001 (National = 15.8%):
New Mexico [2 – 24.6%]; Arizona [8 – 21.2%]; Texas [9 – 20.9%]; Oklahoma [10 – 20.3%];
California [17 – 15.8%]; Utah [31 – 12.3%]; Colorado [39 – 10.1%]; Nevada [44 – 8,7%].

ACT Average Composite Score, 2003 (National Average Score = 20.8):
California [17 – 21.5]; Arizona [20 – 21.4]; Nevada [25 – 21.3]; Utah [25 – 21.3];
Oklahoma [35 – 20.5]; Colorado [42 – 20.1]; Texas [42 – 20.1]; New Mexico [45 – 19.9].

Average **Verbal SAT** Score, 2003 (National Average Score = 507):
Oklahoma [10 – 569]; Utah [12 – 566]; Colorado [19 – 551]; New Mexico [20 – 548];
Arizona [27 – 524]; Nevada [35 – 510]; California [43 – 499]; Texas [47 – 493].

CHAPTER 16

A Personal Tour
Of The Greater Southwest

The Greater Southwest is a tourist's paradise. One could spend the rest of his life "on tour" and there would still be so much to see. Following is a list of personal recommendations, mostly in the "Not To Be Missed" category because a complete list would take a volume by itself.

Texas is the second largest State in the Union and because it is associated historically with the cattle industry it has been emphasized in movies about cowboys, ranching, and the West. While Texas has many attractions, including the huge *12 Travelers* bronze sculptures being developed in El Paso, San Antonio would still be the place to begin a tour of Texas. The San Antonio Missions and the Institute of Texan Cultures would be a good beginning to familiarize oneself with the State of Texas.

California is much more than the home of the American movie industry and its celebrities. The ocean is of incomparable beauty for those who love the sea. The mountains are among the most awesome in the USA. The giant sequoias and redwoods cast an eternal spell on their surroundings. While California is full of wonders, don't neglect the missions where the Golden State got its start and still represent the heart and soul of historical California.

Nevada is mostly harsh desert country but in the city of Las Vegas it has one of the major destinations for people from all over the world. Its architecturally magnificent casinos are man-made wonders, especially when all lit up at night. Vegas can be said to be the entertainment capital of the USA.

Colorado has the unequaled, breath-taking grandeur of the Rocky Mountains. While nothing can compete with the mountains, San Luis, Colorado, is the site of the life-like bronze sculptures known as *Shrine of the Stations of the Cross*. Created by sculptor Huberto Maestas, the Shrine overlooks the San Luis community and at the top of the hill is the artistic *Capilla de Todos los Santos*, All Saints Chapel. The bronze sculptures rank with any in the world for artistic merit as well as in spiritual feeling and should not be missed when in southern Colorado.

Utah is full of natural wonders but Salt Lake City and the Great Salt Lake dominate the State. If at all possible, don't miss the Mormon Tabernacle and do your utmost to hear the Mormon Tabernacle

Choir, certainly one of the world's best known large choirs. To hear the Choir sing the "Hallelujah Chorus" from Handel's *Messiah* would be among the musical thrills of a lifetime.

Oklahoma is crossed by the famous Route 66. Oklahoma City has a number of things to see especially if one is interested in cowboys. Live cattle auctions can be seen in the Oklahoma City Stockyards historic district. World class art collections are available in the National Cowboy and Western Heritage Museum. (Not to be missed is the collection of some 300 saddles.) Great art is also held at the Gilcrease Museum of Art in Tulsa. In Norman one finds Oklahoma University and its Oklahoma University Press, probably the best known press in the Southwest, especially famous for the volumes it has produced on Native Americans. No other State in the Southwest has such a famous musical as *Oklahoma!* to its credit and seeing it at least once is a must.

New Mexico is unique in that it has a living cultural base derived from Amerindians, Hispanics, and typical American institutions. Hispanic-Americans comprise the largest ethnic group in the State and this fact has been crucial in the development of New Mexico culture. There are nineteen (19) very popular Pueblo Indian villages in the State, some of which have built casinos which attract tourists from throughout the country.

Santa Fe, the "City Different," is a favorite destination for people from all over the world. Don't miss the Spiral Staircase in the Loretto Chapel.

The largest city is Albuquerque, where one will find the tremendous bronze sculptures by Sonny Montoya and Betty Sabo known as the *Entrada Monument* which commemorates the European founding of New Mexico and the Southwest. Not to be missed is the Hispanic Cultural Center, a unique effort which commemorates the Hispanic presence in New Mexico, the Southwest, the USA, and the world. The Roy Disney Theater at the Center is a marvel all by itself. The developing History Gallery celebrates the history of New Mexico, the Southwest, the USA, with representatives from the Hispanic world (Don Quijote, María Felix, Bartolomé de Las Casas, etc.).

Arizona has the unparalleled Grand Canyon as its enduring tourist attraction. Sedona is a picturesque mountain town which, it has been said, has mystical qualities. The saguaro cactus is unique in the USA so don't miss the Saguaro National Monument. Not to be missed is Mission San Xavier del Bac, the peerless "White Dove of the Desert."

Annotated Basic Bibliography

As mentioned previously, Oscar Handlin wrote in his *Truth in History* (see especially Chapter 3: "A History of American History") that historians must recognize "the social and intellectual constraints under which they operate." Added to that is that the land itself is always a basic factor, especially such a different environment as the Southwest, along with the fact that Hispanic people had established a permanent presence there as of 1598, while Amerindian societies had been there for thousands of years.

Dr. Handlin writes that from the beginning "Americans believed in a special purpose to their experience as a people." He doesn't equate this with master race psychology and very few societies have asserted themselves in those tones. The personality of the people coming into a new land and encountering a new environment along with Amerindian and Hispanic populations would be crucial in interpreting the significance of all incidents and/or events.

Handlin states that European immigrants to American shores found "an all but empty continent…" This is basic American historiography and could be debated vigorously because there were millions of Amerindians residing in what is now the USA. It has become crucial to assert that the native population was miniscule so as not to have to address the extermination of Indians, something never acknowledged in standard historiography.

What of the *American* personality as it became accustomed to North America? It is common to describe European immigrants becoming Americans as *restless*. This implies the people involved were looking to do great things. New Americans were on a *heroic*, perpetual *quest*. This gave American historiography the tenet of *boosterism*. Whatever Americans did or tried to do was *heroic* or nearly so. A basic goal was *Liberty!* and *Progress!* was not far behind. The mission of America was *Freedom!* based on *Democracy!* Anything or anybody who stood in the way was villainous, so American historiography adopted a structure of *heroes* and *villains*. Though Dr. Handlin doesn't discuss it, this meant that Americans were the heroes and anyone outside the fold might well be villainous if they didn't "affirm the virtues and glorious destiny of the United States…" because it "guarded the liberties of the world." Tyranny, whether in society, religion, heritage, etc., as judged by Americans, was the enemy of the American *mission*.

Manifest Destiny became justification for just about anything done by Americans of the 19th century but its roots began with the landing of English immigrants on the eastern seaboard. African indentured servants were made slaves by law, "for their own good," and Indians were exterminated for the common good because under native control the land was *unproductive waste*. This has not been addressed by historiographers.

With such values and precedents, it is easy to understand why American historiography has been criticized, in some quarters, for a lack of objectivity, a willingness to glorify instead of presenting documented veracity, even embellishing a lack-luster narrative into something heroic to the point that the incident is *unparalleled in human affairs.*

With all this in mind, the following miniscule bibliography is presented so that students might investigate a slice of American historiography and/or react to points raised in the brief commentaries provided.

Acuña, Rodolfo. *Occupied America: A History of Chicanos.* New York: Longman, 2000.

This expensive volume is heavily researched, full of information and appears intended for the college classroom. It's layout and design are poor and the work is replete with typos, more in keeping with a "garage publication" than an item produced by a major publisher, which it is. It appears that the "*Occupied*" in the title refers to any European group in the Americas but not to any Amerindian groups who came into areas and displaced other Amerindians." The label *Chicano* doesn't exist in any historical documents but Dr. Acuña utilizes it as if it had been there when Spaniards arrived in 1540.

Who are the "Chicanos"? The author doesn't say but it appears it is whomever he admires. He has no admiration for the "Hispanos of New Mexico" whom he targets as victims of the "*fantasy heritage*" which impels them to "*hold on to the fable that they are Spaniards.*" While it would be possible to discuss the ethnic labeling used in the Southwest, Dr. Acuña doesn't address the "Anglo fantasy" that has European immigrants all belonging to an "Anglo" ethnicity. Apparently that isn't something to discuss but it is proper to denigrate the "Hispanos of New Mexico" because they think they are *Spanish.* One might well ask why the *Anglo fantasy* is acceptable to Dr. Acuña but not the *Spanish,* if either or both are fantasies.

Race mixing appears to be as much a hang-up with Chicanos as it is with the Ku Klux Klan, the former lauding it while the latter disparage.

One is exposed to much research in this book but the portions on New Mexico are often based on ordinarily accepted stereotypes promoted by typical American racism and Chicanos, neutralizing its worth. It is hoped the other sections of *Occupied* are more reliable.

Beebe, Rose Marie and **Senkewicz, Robert M.** (eds.) *Lands of Promise and Despair: Chronicles of Early California, 1535-1846.* Santa Clara: Santa Clara University Press, 2001.

This book is rich in perspectives provided by people who actually lived in California during the years mentioned in the title. It also provides views of visiting Americans, like R.H. Dana, who in effect told more about themselves than Californios of the day. But the bias of visitors like Dana have become an important element in what is generally perceived as California history, articulated by the editors as "*...sometimes without realizing it, we give foreign authors* [note: including Americans] *the last word about Spanish and Mexican California.*"

This book is refreshing. The introductory pieces at the beginning of each segment are valuable historiography by themselves. This book provides primary materials for students, researchers, or writers interested in what people of the day said, recorded, or acted upon.

Chapman, Charles E. *A History of California: The Spanish Period*. New York: The Macmillan Company, 1921.

This work is an authoritative popular history and has endured the test of time. Among other things, Chapman believes Hispanic California history is an integral part of American history and his writing shows it. Chapman is referenced by many authors and rightly so because his work is a bright spot in American historiography.

Cutter, Donald, and **Engstrand, Iris.** *Quest for Empire: Spanish settlement in the Southwest*. Golden, Colorado: Fulcrum Publishing, 1996.

These two university professors have collaborated on a marvelous book which acknowledges that the Hispanic Southwest is an integral part of American history. Heroes like Oñate, Kino, Anza, etc., are discussed for their accomplishments and little known personalities like Gabriel Moraga are introduced into the historical record. The "Bibliographic Essay" at the end of each chapter provides a wealth of sources for anyone who wants to investigate further.

While Dr. Cutter has a work called *Diary of Ensign Gabriel Moraga's Expedition of Discovery in the Sacramento Valley, 1808*, a popular history is needed on Gabe Moraga because during his forty-one year career as a California soldier he was on 42 expeditions/campaigns. It would appear there are many Southwest Hispanic items/themes that need to be explored.

Cleland, Robert Glass. *This Reckless Breed of Men: The Trappers and Fur Traders of the Southwest*. Lincoln: University of Nebraska Press, 1950.

The heroes in this work are the mountain men who trapped beaver while they "*...affected the destiny of nations, changed the future of a continent, bequeathed to later generations of Americans a tradition of heroic exploration comparable to that of the seamen of Elizabeth or the conquistadores of Spain.*" Is this History or boosterism? Elizabeth's pirates were explorers? Spanish conquistadores went from California/Kansas in the north to as far south as the tip of South America but the beaver men in the trans-Mississippi fur trade rank with them as explorers because they used Taos and Santa Fe as a base? We are told that "Ewing Young, William Wolfskill, Miguel Robidoux, Peg-leg Smith, George Yount, Old Bill Williams, Ceran St Vrain, and a dozen others are familiar to every student of the fur trade..." except they didn't do much writing. One of the few who actually wrote was James Ohio Pattie (along with his editor Timothy Flint), the "hero" who makes himself or his father "*the leading figure in other men's adventures and accomplishments.*"

Dary, David. *Cowboy Culture: A Saga of Five Centuries*. New York: Alfred A. Knopf, 1981.

There is much basic information in this work and a plethora of information on the English speaking cowboy, the "Texian" being of foremost interest to the author. One would almost get the impression that ranching and "cowboy culture" was a "Texian" creation. The first chapter is on "Spanish Roots," with Cortés, the first leader to bring horses to the North American continent, being villainized as a "Black Legend" figure. A chapter is devoted to "The California Culture" then *Tejano Culture* is totally ignored while we are treated to "The Texian Culture" which, directly or indirectly, takes up the rest of the book. The reader isn't told that Tejanos were conducting cattle drives to Louisiana at least by the 1770s, but he is informed that James Taylor White (whose real name was *Le Blanc*) "*...may have been the first white man to drive cattle from Texas to New Orleans.*" J.T. White arrived in Texas in 1819 or 1823 then took up ranching. The way this information is written it would appear that Tejano ranchers and cowboys didn't create ranching in Texas but that is inaccurate History.

Denhardt, Robert Moorman. *The Horse of the Americas*. Norman: University of Oklahoma Press, 1947.

The author has command of a broad historical base. Spaniards brought the first horses to the Americas and Denhardt has the moral fortitude to trace equine history from those beginnings. He declares that Spain had the best horses in Europe and their stamina was increased in the Americas. These horses came into what is now the USA through Florida, New Mexico, Texas, and California. Further, Denhardt states unequivocally that the greatest horsemen in the world were the New Mexicans, the Comanches, and the Arabs.

Ebright, Malcolm. *Land Grants & Lawsuits in Northern New Mexico*. Albuquerque: University of New Mexico Press, 1994.

This is perhaps the most important work written on New Mexico land grants. The material is professionally documented yet very readable. Especially impressive is the honesty with which Dr. Ebright presents the historical record. For example (p. 38): "*Corruption of public officials and dishonesty of claimants under U.S. land laws...It was not unusual for enterprising Anglos to wrest from Hispanos their land grant property through fraud or manipulation of the land laws...Hispanos never conceived their community grants were in jeopardy because under their laws and customs, the common lands could never be sold...*"

Fehrenbach, T.R. *Lone Star: A History of Texas and the Texans*. New York: American Legacy Press, 1983.

This complex work is awesome, exhilarating, philosophical, chilling, and disgusting. "Race" is a major player in these pages. (The author could have no knowledge that DNA breakthroughs have shown that popular concepts of race have no scientific basis whatever. Indeed, genome scientists now state all human DNA is 99.9% exactly the same for the entire human species.) Who are the Texans? Anglo-Celts, of course. When necessary they're Anglo-Saxons, Anglo-Teutonic, Anglo-Nordic, etc., until they become "old stock" Anglo-American. The important thing is to be "Anglo" when writing American history, at least in the English language in the American Southwest. The fantasy dictates that one mustn't be Germanic, from *Germanicus*, also referred to as northern Europeans to distinguish them from Latin groups, which is what the above mentioned groups are, for then one would be targeted with anti-German bias.

As judged by author Fehrenbach, the Texan proved "superior" to the other inhabitants of Texas because he was "*able to exterminate Indians, conquer the Mexican, and the black man was already his slave.*" It appears Texas and the South will ever be shaped by the Civil War, apparently a never ending conflict for Southerners. The author must be credited for almost considering various viewpoints: while he states emphatically that the Texas Rangers were successful because they were "ruthless killers," Ranger L. H. McNelly "*...never told a Mexican twice to do something...*" pilgrim.

Gutiérrez, Ramón A. and **Orsi, Richard J.** (eds.). *Contested Eden: California Before the Gold Rush.* Berkeley: University of California Press, 1998.

Well documented essays by a number of writers comprise this volume on California history. Some of the essayists like Steven W. Hackel and Lisbeth Haas seem out of place in this hispanophobic work. For example, Hackel writes that Crown economic initiatives promoted sea otter hunting, hemp production, and bringing in skilled artisans from Mexico, that many American writers from early California *"…were often anti-Catholic, Hispanophobic…"* Lisbeth Haas cites Genaro Padilla's classic *My History, Not Yours*, where the quote of María de las Angustias de la Guerra, translated by Francis Price and William Ellison, has her saying "…the conquest of California did not bother the Californians, least of all the women" while an accurate translation of what she said is just the opposite: *"…the taking of the country did not please the Californios at all, and least of all the women."* (Is it any wonder that the former can be described as "propagandistory"?) The hispanophobic essays are "academically" well researched and will appeal to hispanophobes interested in pursuing American "Tree of Hate" historiography. It is a wonder that such animosity can find a publisher.

Jackson, Helen Hunt. *A Century of Dishonor: A Sketch of the United States Government's Dealings with some of the Indian Tribes.* New York: Indian Head Books, 1993.

Champions like Roger Williams and Helen Hunt Jackson who pleaded for justice for Native Americans are few and far between in American history, mere voices crying in the wilderness. Helen Hunt Jackson believes that "the Indian problem is not with the Indian, but with the Government and people of the United States…It is to our own unspeakable disgrace that we have so often failed therein." In a nutshell, American Indian policy was to set aside Indian treaties whenever the American government wanted to. Senator Ben N. Campbell of Colorado has written that of the 472 treaties made with Indians not a single one was kept. The work of H.H. Jackson has fallen on deaf ears though she writes that "the American people, as a people, are not at heart unjust."

Kessell, John L. *Spain in the Southwest: A Narrative History of Colonial New Mexico, Arizona, Texas, and California.* Norman: Oklahoma University Press, 2002.

_____. *Kiva, Cross, & Crown: The Pecos Indians and New Mexico, 1540-1840.* Tucson: Southwest Parks and Monuments Association.

Dr. Kessell has few peers when it comes to utilizing Spanish language documentation. His *Kiva, Cross, & Crown* is certainly in a class by itself as far as colonial New Mexico is concerned.

Spain in the Southwest is puzzling at best. While Dr. Kessell relates honestly "If we select the facts to fit preconceived stereotypes, we can make the story come out rather the way we want, which is the nature of propaganda, not history." But the work also contains a streak which permits commentary like "…invading Spaniards did possess impressive advantages…but they too had to urinate. Try as they might, not even white men could hide so familiar an urgency." The human condition is universal, granted, but why is it necessary to preface one's work with an acknowledgement of bodily functions? (Is there a work on America's Founding Fathers that relate to bodily functions? I haven't encountered any such work.) Is there an inimical element here, not found in *Kiva*, indicated by commentary like "...missionaries stood out on New Spain's contested northern frontier as boldly in the late 18th century as they ever had...Missions were cheap." Therefore the real issue wasn't Christianization but merely financial? Why were there no missions on the American frontier if they were so cheap?

The work is full of valuable information though it appears there is reliance from Dr. Kessell's previous works. The material laced with denigration is worrisome.

Lamar, Howard R. *The Far Southwest, 1846-1912, A Territorial History.* Albuquerque: University of New Mexico Press, 2000.

This reprint is full of information but laced with master race tenets of Manifest Destiny common to American historiography. It's a deft weave. For example, when the American Army entered New Mexico, "...*Kearny declared that the Americans had no hostile purpose in mind but came only to occupy.*" It was much better for the Army to encounter no resistance while it took the country, which was proper because Americans believed God had chosen them to rule the continent.

First published in 1966, the revised edition still doesn't reflect the historical fact that Diego Archuleta and his professional soldiers were bribed into not resisting.

When the Taos Rebellion of 1847 was put down by hanging the *traitors*, Lamar doesn't dwell on the justice of hanging Mexican citizens for treason against the USA in the midst of the raging war with Mexico.

When writing about the atrocity Sand Creek Massacre against peaceful Indians in Colorado, the author maintains that "*Chivington, for all his critics was but a part of the juggernaut of civilization...the Indian question had to be settled, for 'civilization must rule this continent' Sand Creek was but a major step in the Americanization of Colorado. What history would never condone was Chivington's method of taking that step.*" Are atrocities like taking female Indian genital scalps and shooting down Indian toddlers being equated with *civilization*? Are all the bases covered? Is there a George Orwell award in the field?

León, Arnoldo de. *They Called Them Greasers.* Austin: University of Texas Press, 1983.

This penetrating work probably has few equals in its honesty in handling the subject of racial/ethnic prejudice in Texas. While the ugliness of prejudice is common in all the American Southwestern states, only the University of Texas has had the courage to publish such a work under its imprint. León asserts that famous writers of Texas history, men like E.C. Barker, W. P. Webb, and R. N. Richardson, were guided by serious biases against Indians, blacks, and Mexican people as well as "*serious deficiencies of research.*" Further, he states succeeding writers have "*followed their mentors' paths.*" I agree with León, but it must be said that Texas writers are merely following the pattern set by American historiographers in general: hypistory is what people seem to want.

Greasers explores the abject racism and bigotry of the people who founded "American" Texas. In Chapter 2, titled "Niggers, Redskins and Greasers," León writes that color (skin pigmentation) is held by Texas (American) racists to signify good or evil with "white" signifying everything good, and "colored" everything vile. As penetrating as the whole work is, León still uses "Anglo" to signify Texans or anyone considered "white," thus grouping people so that there exists a fantasy in people's minds of a "superior white majority" as well as an "inferior colored minority." Neither does León explore the idea that the "superior white Texans" were united by their fear and hatred of Indians, blacks, or Mexicans, who had to be "vile" so the land could be taken from them. It would appear that Texans found Mexicans lacking in almost everything positive but possessed of almost everything degenerate. Except the Mexican women of course, who were not as filthy, ignorant, backward, superstitious, cowardly, treacherous, idle, avaricious, etc., as the "mongrel" males of the species. (Obviously, it was males doing the writing.) As always, bigotry and prejudice directed against minorities, buttressed by horrific brutality and violence, found wide support among Texans. There were no champions rising up to defend basic human rights of targeted people in Texas any more than there were in Nazi Germany.

Intended or not, this work depicts American Texas as the apartheid South Africa of the USA but were places like American California any better?

Margolin, Malcolm. *Monterey in 1786: Life in a California Mission: The Journals of Jean François de La Pérouse*, 1989.

This short volume about a Frenchman who visited with Spanish missionaries provides no supporting documentation of any kind in French, Spanish, or English. The work isn't on the positive side when discussing Hispanic California. No documentation needed?

McReynolds, Edwin C. *Oklahoma: A History of the Sooner State*. Norman: University of Oklahoma Press, 1954, 1964.

Don't try to find the meaning of "Sooner" in the Index. Inexplicably, it wasn't included. (In Oklahoma history, "Boomers" were "settlers" who lobbied for the takeover of "Indian lands" and the "Sooners" went into designated lands "sooner" than anyone else.) This volume might be an introduction to the history of Oklahoma but it leaves one wanting to explore the whys and wherefores of any number of events. It would appear that controversial issues, like taking "surplus" Indian lands for "white" settlement, are given a rather wide berth. It would make an interesting volume to compare history of the Pueblos in New Mexico to the Five Civilized tribes which were exiled to Oklahoma.

McWilliams, Carey. *North From Mexico: The Spanish-Speaking People of the United States*. New York: Greenwood Press, 1948, 1968.

_____. *California: the Great Exception*. Santa Barbara: Peregrine Smith, Inc., 1949, 1976.

The author isn't chained to the standard tenets of American historiography. McWilliams will present the dictates of valid history, popular or not, and controversy is of little importance. For example, he asserts *"the term Anglo is used as a catchall expression to designate persons who are neither Hispano nor Indian…Anglo and Hispano are the heads and tails of a single coin, a single ethnic system, each having meaning only as the other is implied, defining a relationship…the term Anglo is essentially as meaningless as the term Hispano…"* This concept alone would motivate an excellent discussion in any Southwest classroom. It could also be explored as to which group is benefited or denigrated by use of those terms.

Whether one agrees or not with what he writes, Carey McWilliams has been a champion right along with historians like H.E. Bolton.

Annotated Basic Bibliography

Meléndez, A. Gabriel. (trans.) *The Biography of Casimiro Barela by José Emilio Fernández.* Albuquerque: University of New Mexico Press, 2003.

This is an important work for a number of reasons. First it is a biography of a most important Southwestern personality, Casimiro Barela. The work is representative of a body of knowledge that has been ignored to the verge of nonexistence. Translation into the English language hasn't resulted in the loss of original value. Further, the Notes sections are as valuable for the historical record as the text itself. The Hispanic past has been denigrated or shrouded in *propagandistory* (to coin a word).This situation has been recognized by the University of Houston and an effort is being made to remedy it under the title of Recovery of U.S. Hispanic Literary Heritage Project. Much needs to be done. A work on the Santa Fe Ring is needed. Dr. Meléndez is the paladin who could do it.

Montejano, David. *Anglos and Mexicans in the Making of Texas, 1836-1986.* Austin: University of Texas Press, 1987.

This excellent volume is full of well documented information. Montejano supplies wide perspectives because he is capable of discussing aspects of Texas history that are often glossed over in the standard cycle of historiography written by Webb, Richardson, Fehrenbach, etc. Montejano's work is crucial to understanding Texas history, past and present. He also addresses the land dealings that dispossessed so many Tejanos.

Montoya, María E. *Translating Property: The Maxwell Land Grant and the Conflict over Land in the American West, 1840-1900.* Berkeley: University of California Press, 2002.

The crucial issue of land ownership is addressed in this work and sooner or later those who were dispossessed by means fair or foul will recognize what has happened. Though this study concerns itself with the Maxwell land grant, Dr. Montoya addresses a number of land issues, as for example how Hispanic women were denied property rights when the USA took over the Southwest. She provides an honest portrayal of the Santa Fe Ring. She points out that the land was taken over under the guise of "the American way" while in effect it was merely dispossession. What would happen if land history became serious study?

Mora, Jo. *Trail Dust and Saddle Leather.* New York: Charles Scribner's Sons, 1946.
_____. *Californios.* Garden City, N.Y.: Doubleday and Co., 1949.

Mora's books are based on what he saw and experienced personally. He wrote the text (and did his own illustrations) so that the reading public would get the real feel of what it was like to work cattle in the West. For a personal approach to his subject Mora could be said to rival J. Frank Dobie. *Trail Dust* and *Californios* are often cited by other writers, though it is often mentioned they contain no corroborating footnotes.

Sheridan, Thomas E. *Arizona: A History.* Tucson: University of Arizona Press, 1996.

This relatively short volume is probably the best recent history of the "Grand Canyon State." The author is often able to write about "controversial" issues that are generally omitted in run-of-the-mill or "chamber of commerce" histories.

Simpson, Lesley Byrd. *Many Mexicos.* Berkeley and Los Angeles: University of California Press, 1952.

If for any reason your bookshelf could hold only one book on Mexico it should be this one. Simpson tells both sides of an issue, refreshing for American historiography which deals with Spain, Hispanic people, or the Catholic Church. Yes, Guzmán was a thug and Cortés was human but of heroic stature unparalleled in the Americas. The work is an excellent introduction to the culture which would be encountered in the Borderlands.

Stuart, David E. *Anasazi America.* Albuquerque: University of New Mexico Press, 2000.

Written with the "research assistance of Susan Moczygemba-McKinsey," considering that these pages emanate from archaeological and/or anthropological research it must be said the work is one of exuberance. Enthusiasm is a wonderful characteristic so long as it doesn't color one's findings. The achievements of the Anasazi are promoted in bold relief in this volume but the book also contains Orwellian techniques which could be construed as cover-up. The author knows precontact populations didn't have the knowledge of building with adobe until Hispanics settled New Mexico so he writes that the Indians built with *"poured adobe."* Cannibalism among the Anasazi is never mentioned. It comes as no surprise that the villains in the book are "the Spanish," which is typical "Black Legend" or "Tree of Hate" literature.

People from east of the Mississippi were brutish frontiersmen where Indians were concerned. Among the worst were the Scotch-Irish who exterminated aboriginal populations with horrible brutalities. Descendants of easterners often come to New Mexico, find Native American groups that were preserved by "the Spanish," then proceed to vilify "the Spanish." Is this a form of Orwellian catharsis? It is possible the information on the Anasazi is accurate but there is no doubt that the information on New Mexico's Hispanic people in Chapter 9 is hispanophobic and unreliable. The latter casts doubts on the former, thus causing this reader to question the entire work.

Terrell, John Upton. *Land Grab: The Truth about "The Winning of the West."* New York: The Dial Press, 1972.

Studying this work is best described as a sobering experience. There is no romanticism here because Terrell pulls no punches. For example, he writes that the American fur trade industry… "which for dishonesty, destructiveness, exploitation, cruelty, immorality, criminal negligence, viciousness and avarice has no counterpart in western history. While the mountain men were often courageous heroes…"*the industry they represented was without a redeeming quality, and wherever they went corruption, disease and ruination were sure to follow."* How about the cattle kings of the fabled West? *"The Cattle Barons were despots and tyrants who held their domains not by legal right but by force of arms and criminal violence…The cattlemen ruling the western grass seas paid few if any taxes, owned little or no real property, cared not for civic responsibility, and looked only to their personal aggrandizement and were loyal only to themselves…Fantasy and folklore survive where reality and history are interred, and there is no preventive, no cure, for inherent stupidity…"*

These ideas should be discussed in every survey course for the West or the Southwest.

Trimble, Marshall. Arizona: *A Cavalcade of History.* Tucson: Treasure Chest Publications, 1989.

Annotated Basic Bibliography

This informative work is an account of many interesting people and the episodes which made them worthy of inclusion in this state history. Most could be described as "surface" historical happenings intended for consumption by the popular culture.

Udall, Stewart L. *The Forgotten Founders: Rethinking the History of the Old West.* Washington: Island Press, 2002.

_____. *Majestic Journey.* Santa Fe: Museum of New Mexico Press, 1987.

Stewart Udall can be counted upon to provide broad perspectives in his historical works. Unlike so many historiographers using the English language, he is untouched by Black Legend bias. His work is well documented and refreshing, giving hope to American historiography. Works like *Forgotten Founders* and *Majestic Journey* should be required reading for all Southwest history classes.

Van de Grift Sánchez, Nellie. *Spanish Arcadia.* Los Angeles: Powell Publishing Company, 1929.

This delightful volume is hardly recognized by many historiographers, possibly because it is mostly positive. The author portrays Californios as real people who enjoyed, suffered, lived and died, etc., but were the freest and happiest of mortals on earth, until the American takeover. Perhaps that is why some writers refer to this volume as "idyllic," thereby implying it existed only in fantasy. The seed has been sown: is it possible the American conquest actually ruined the beautiful society of the Californios? Would it be treason to explore that idea?

Webb, Walter Prescott. *The Texas Rangers: A Century of Frontier Defense.* Austin: University of Texas Press, 1935, 1965, 1995.

_____. *The Great Plains.* Boston: Ginn and Company, 1931.

The work of the venerable Dr. Webb is basic to Texas history. While an independent personality, Webb is first and foremost a Texan and it could be said that his "patriotism" doesn't permit him to rely, for example, on Tejano history for foundations of the cattle industry. It would appear that Dr. Webb believes Texas got its real start when people came in from the USA. Though Dr. Webb is detached enough to write that the Texas Rangers were often ruthless killers, he is much better known for lauding their efforts in establishing Texian civilization. On the plains the Spanish, who created the institution of ranching, were "failures," of course, as were the Mexicans. This school of thought colors Texas history and therefore lowers it to mere propaganda. Tejano historians, not to mention those of the Southwest, have much to write about.

The reader will have to decide if Dr. Webb's work is credible in the light of impartial investigation.

Weber, David J. *The Spanish Frontier in North America.* New Haven and London: Yale University Press, 1992.

_____. *Myth and the History of the Hispanic southwest: Essays by David J. Weber.* Albuquerque: University of New Mexico Press, 1988.

_____. *New Spain's Far Northern Frontier: Essays on Spain in the American West, 1540-1821.* Dallas: Southern Methodist University Press, 1979.

_____. *The Mexican Frontier, 1821-1846: The American Southwest Under Mexico.* Albuquerque: University of New Mexico Press, 1982.

_____. *Foreigners in Their Native Land: Historical roots of the Mexican Americans.* Albuquerque: University of New Mexico Press, 1973.

Dr. Weber perhaps is among the few writers who could be classed as being *the* contemporary historian of the Southwest. A prodigious researcher, the Notes sections to works like *Spanish Frontier* run over a hundred pages and could very well stand alone, such is their importance to the student.

One problem that surfaces in Dr. Weber's longer works is that he includes vast quantities of materials and their concomitant points of view, whether positive or negative, accurate or inaccurate. Dr. Weber isn't hispanophobic but many of his quoted materials are, as in citing "religious history" written by a person who portrayed New Mexico missionaries as "fools for Christ." To quote that kind of denigration might give it credence in the minds of some, a credence that fosters negative bias. It can be observed that such descriptions are reserved for Catholic missionaries but Dr. Weber doesn't point that out.

Epilogue

EPIC OF THE GREATER SOUTHWEST has come a long way. The historical road is seldom smooth and Southwest history has been no exception. Biographer José E. Fernández wrote in 1911 that *History holds in its bosom the good and evil acts of human beings: the first so that we might imitate them, the latter so we can avoid their repetition.* Human personality is a factor in everything and as far as American historiography is concerned it appears the historical record is still greatly influenced by entertainment from movies/television and controlled by and large through Manifest Destiny. For example, movies on themes like the Alamo or the seconds-long gunfight at the OK Corral, more fantasy than History, appear to enjoy a never ending popularity while almost everything Spanish is denigrated, even promoting the missions as places of "European diseases" instead of the civilizing efforts that they were. Undoubtedly *Epic* will be interpreted through those prisms but valid American scholarship will be somewhere in the mix and discovered by some champions.

Thucydides wrote some four hundred years before the birth of Christ that "*...if he who desires to have before his eyes a true picture of the events which have happened, and of the like events which may be expected to happen hereafter in the order of human things, shall pronounce what I have written to be useful, then I shall be satisfied. My history is an everlasting possession, not a prize composition which is heard and forgotten.*"

It is hoped the Traveler will be sustained by *Epic* and continue on the quest, inspired.

Index

Abeita, Pablo 553
Abortion 3
Abreú, Ramón 149
Academy Awards 502
Acoma 21, 37
Acoma War 40
Adams, John Q. 274, 275, 276
Adelantado 30
Adobe Walls 326, 327
African-American 536
Agriculture 272
Aguirre, Pedro 562
Aguirre, Yjinio 581
Alarcón, Martín de 50, 163
Albuquerque Public Schools 585
Alburquerque 130
Alcalde Mayor 107
Alexander VI, (Pope) 65
Alexandria 285
Amador, J.M. 221
Amar a Dios 221
Ambassadors 556
Ambush (Acoma) 38
American California 485
American personality 591
American racism 177
American Revolution 60
American Smelting and Refining Co. 524
Amherst, Sir Jeffrey 24, 406
Ampudia, Pedro 278
Anasazi 1
Anaya, Rudolfo 555

Andrist, R.K. 344
Anglo 14
Anglo fantasy 592
Anglo-Celts 182
Angustias de la Guerra Ord 307, 482
Annexation 464
Anti-coolie Clubs 490
Anza 13, 58, 80, 89, 143, 234, 520, 528
Anza's departure 88
Apache Kid 460
Apache Pass 390, 397
Apache peace 167
Apache Scouts 394, 400, 401
Apache wars 380
Apachería 262
Apaches 51, 52, 67, 81, 82, 86, 89, 101, 235, 389
Apostle to Texas 76
April 30, 1598 33
Aragon, Chato 260
Aragon, Manny M. 556
Archibeque, Miguel 555
Archuleta, Diego 292, 293, 294, 296
Arellano 19, 23
Argüello, Concepción 208
Arista, Mariano 278
Arizona Citizen 393
Arizona Rangers 461
Arizona Territory 560
Arizona women 564
Arizonac 81, 106
Arkansas herd (buffalo) 369
Armijo, (Gov.) Manuel 151, 162, 292

Index

Armijo, Antonio 149, 275
Armijo, José Antonio 515
Army Corps of Topographical Engineers 298
Army of the West 304
Arriero 136, 172
Asiatic Exclusion League of San Francisco 491
Assimilation 67
Associates (The) 414
Atomic testing 517
Attorneys 575
August 10, 1680 116
Austin 300 173
Austin, Mary 553
Austin, Stephen F. 173, 287
Authentic Life of Billy the Kid 457
Avengers expedition 402
Averse to labor 229
Axtell, Samuel B. 546

Baca, Domingo 260
Baca, Elfego 425
Baca, Ezequiel C. De 553
Ball, Eve 404
Bancroft, George 277
Bancroft, H.H. 485, 493
Barela, Casimiro 525
Barela, Patrociño 554
Barelas, Manuel 317
Barreiro, Antonio 149
Bartleson-Bidwell Party 531
Bascom, George N. 390
Basketmakers 2,4
Bass, Sam 435
Battle for Santa Fe 125
Battle of Los Ángeles 306
Battle of Old Woman's Gun 304
Battle of Palo Alto 279
Battle of Resaca de la Palma 279
Battle of Valverde 317
Battle Pyramid Lake 346

Battle Washita 366
Bear Flag Republic 302
Bear Flag Revolt 300
Bear Flaggers 483
Beaubien, Carlos 295
Beck, Warren A. 253, 296
Belle Starr 448
Bent, Charles 293
Bent, George
Bent, William 348, 350, 351
Benton, Jessie 299
Benton, Thomas Hart 276, 279
Bering, Vitus 13
Bernalillo 34
Berreyesa, Nicolás 576
Beveridge, (Sen.) Albert J. 550
Bexar/San Antonio 52
Beyer, Charles D. 383
Bidwell, John 214
Big Foot 409
Big Four (The) 414, 492
Big tent 419
Bigotes 21
Billington, Ray Allen 284
Billy the Kid 423, 452
Birth of a Nation 499
Bishop Lamy 377
Bishop of Rome 310
Black Bart 444
Black Kettle 350, 352, 365, 366
Black Legend 17, 61, 73, 344, 405
Blood brothers 402
Blood feud 433
Bloody years 322
Board of Land commissioners 574
Bolton, H.E. 15, 73
Bond of community 53
Bond, Frank 578
Bone gatherers 370
Books 222

Books of the Brave 307
Boots 98
Bosque Grande de Dona Luisa 130
Bosque Redondo 375, 376, 377
Bouchard, Hippolyte de 207
Bowie, James 289
Bowles, Chief 324
Boyd E. 554
Boys' Ranch 555
Brann, William C. 470
Brantner, Luis 246
Brazil 9
Brazos Reserve 323
Bridge, Harry 498
Brooks, Juanita 538
Brothers of our Father Jesús 153
Brown, John 315, 323
Brownsville 466
Bryan, Howard 296
Bucareli, (Viceroy) 57, 85
Buchanan, James 279, 572
Buffalo 36, 368. 418
Buffalo Bill 369
Buffalo hunting 368
Bulls and bears 224
Bulto 134
Burbank, Luther 489
Burleson, Edward 289
Bursum Bill 553
Business and Honor 216
Bustamante, Josefa 143
Butler, Anthony 274
Butler, James 515

Cabeza de Vaca 270
Caborca 71
Caddo 322
Calhoun, James S. 372, 545
California Battalion 303
California Code 187

California Indians 56, 182, 183
California missionaries 185
Californio diet 220
Californio hospitality 505
Californio lifestyle 215, 223
Camino Real 131
Camp Grant Massacre 391
Campbell, (Sen.) Ben N. 360, 410
Canales, J.T. 435
Canary Island colonists 102, 166
Canby, Edward 316, 340, 341
Cannibals 28
Canon de Chelly 374
Cape Horn 478
Captain Jack 339
Caravan 113
Caribs 405
Carleton, James 375
Carpetbagger rule 471
Carrasco, José M. 145
Carrillo, J. Antonio 304, 306
Carrillo, José Ramón 225
Carrillo, Leopoldo 562
Carson, Christopher "Kit" 299, 317, 375
Cascarón Ball 226
Castañeda, Carlos E. 77
Castañeda, Pedro de 19
Castro, General 300
Cather, Willa 553
Catron, Charles 578
Catron, Thomas B. 548
Cattle 95, 96
Cattle drive (first) 102
Cattle ranching 170
Cebolla (Antonio Sandoval) 373
Cebolleta (Seboyeta) 258
Celestials 416
Census 1790 144
Centaurs 141
Central Pacific 412, 416, 419, 491

Index

Centralists 178
Century of Dishonor 408, 409
cerro Gordo 280
Cerruti, Enrique 485
Chaco Anasazi 3
Chaco Canyon 3
Chaco phenomenon 5
Champlain 12
Chaplin, Charlie 499
Chapman, Charles E. 94
Chapultepec Castle 281
Charo 401
Chaves y Castillo, Mariano 150
Chaves, Manuel Antonio 147, 294
Chávez, Cesar 504
Chávez, Felipe 318
Cherokees 324, 360
Chicanos 592
Chichimeca 28
Children (Precontact) 6
Chimayó Revolution 151
"Chinaman's chance" 490
Chinese laborers 416
Chinks 417
Chipman, Donald E. 181
Chiricahuas 390, 396, 400, 401
Chivington, J.M. 318, 350, 519
Christendom 310
Christian Knights 190
Christmas Eve Flower 308
Chumash Indians 194, 195
Chumash Rebellion 268
Church & State 113
Churubusco 280
Cíbola 19
Ciboleros 138, 369
Cisneros, Henry 473
Cisneros, Juan Pedro 531
Civil Rights 473, 516
Civil War (American) 364

Civilian ranching 104
Claim jumping 581
Cleland, Robert G. 298
Climate 3
Clothing styles 220
Clum, John 381, 395
Cochise 380, 389
Cody, William 369
Coke of the West 422
College of Santa Cruz de Querétaro 75, 76
Collier, John 553
Colorado River 87
Colorado Volunteers 350
Colt revolver 431
Colton letters 491
Colton, Walter 217, 223
Columbia (studio) 500
Columbus 8, 9
Colyer, Vincent 394
Comadurán, Antonio 297
Comanche bread 140
Comanche Peace 92
Comanchería 263
Comancheros 139
Comanches 67, 89, 101, 132, 146, 262, 323
Commerce of the Prairies 156
Committee of Public safety 392
Committee of Vigilance 486
Communist Party 496
Compañia Volante 177
Comstock Lode 513
Comstock, Henry P. 513
Conchos River 30
Concurpe 390
Confederate Indian Territory 364
Confederate Territory of Arizona 316
Conformity 7
Connelly, Henry 546
Conner, Daniel Ellis 381
conquer the peace 278

Conservation 495
Conspiracy of Pontiac 249
Cooke, Philip St. George 296
Cooke's Wagon Road 297
Cooking technique 3
Cooperation 7
Co-parent relationships 168
Córdova, Vicente 177
Corney, Peter 207
Coronado 11, 18, 20, 24, 97, 270, 406, 538
Cortes 26, 95
Cortina, Juan 466, 475
Cos, General 288
Council House Massacre 324
Court trial 41
Courtship and marriage 218
Coy, Owen C. 480
Credit Mobilier 415
Crespi, (Fray) Juan 60
Cripple Creek 526
Crocker, Charles 414
Crockett, Davy 289
Croix, Teodoro de 170
Crook, George 394, 400, 408
Crouching tigers 37
Crusading editor 488
Cubero 130
Cuerno Verde 90, 91, 143, 254, 520
Cuervo y Valdés, Francisco 130
Cunningham, Thomas 439
Cushing fight 397
Cushing, Howard 397
Custer, George A. 365
Customary Law 106, 150
CyberArte Exhibit 557

Dana, R.H. 214
Danz, Harold 371
Dark ages 538
Davis, E.J. 471

Davis, Jonathan 439
Davis, William H. 219, 221, 223, 226, 545
Dawes Act 366,540
Dawes Severalty Act 536
Dawson Trail 522
Dawson, Byron 383
Dawson, John 522
De Soto 27, 538
Dead Man's Route 33
Deaths (Precontact) 6
Debo, Angie 540
Denhardt, Robert M. 161, 373
Denominational Christianity 311
Denver News 352
Denver Ring 519
Desertion 112
Destruction of California Indians 342, 343
Dewitt, Green 178
Díaz, Melchor 19, 20
Dime Novel 424, 568
Diné 373
Discontent (NM) 43
Dissidents (NM) 43
District of Columbia 285
DNA 179, 507
Doctrine of Prior Appropriation 523
Dodge, Col. Richard 327, 370
Dodge, Grenville 418
Dodge, Mabel 553
Domenech, Emanuel 465
Domínguez, F.A. 13, 89, 143, 192, 520, 531
Domínguez, Tomé 246
Domínguez-Escalante Expedition 143
Don (de origen noble) 29
Doniphan, Alexander 373
Donner Party 569
Doolin, William 449
Downieville 438, 480
Drake, Francis 12, 16, 231
Dred Scott 286

Index

"drinking, dancing, and whoring" 556
Dunn, J.P. 402
Durán y Chaves, Fernando 101
Durán, Narciso 195
Dust Bowl 542

Earp brothers 458
Eastern Cherokees 362
Eayre, George S. 350
Echeagaray, Manuel de 269
Echeandía, J. M. 208
Ecueracapa 92, 258
Edison, Thomas A. 498
Education 150
Education industry 584
Education State Rankings 586
Edwards, Haden 287
El Capitán 91, 131, 255
El Clamor Público 487
El Morro 44
El Paso 116
El Turco 22
Elías, Jesús M. 392
Elizabeth I (Queen) 16, 231
Elkins Handshake 550
Elkins, Stephen B. 550
Emerson, Ralph Waldo 278
Encomienda System 65
England 9
English Company 523
Escalante 13, 143, 520, 531
Escudero, José 147
Escudero, Manuel Simón 147
Eskiminzin 391, 395
Españoles Mexicanos 126
Estevan 11
Eufemia (Doña) 32, 40
Evangelical Lutheranism 311
Evans, John 349
Exposición 145

Extended family 157

Fages, Pedro 57, 186
Fair Carletonia 377
Fall, Albert B. 455, 494
Familial attachments 217
Fancher-Baker Train 532
Fannin, James W. 289, 290
"fantasy heritage" 592
Farfán de los Godos 30
Farmers (Precontact) 5
Father of Arizona 560
Father of California 55
Father of New Mexico 50
Father of NM History 271
Father of Southwest History 271
Father of Texas History 171, 271
Faulk, Odie B. 73
Fechin, Nicolai 553
Federalists 178
Fehrenbach, T.R. 181
Field, Matt 152, 545
Fifty-Four Forty or Fight 276, 280
First Christmas (NM) 39
First reconstruction Act 471
Fisher, John King 435
Five Civilized Tribes 360, 364
Flor de Noche Buena 308
Florida 10
Flying squadron 177
Font, (Fray) Pedro de 85, 86, 88
Foot for a Foot 243
Ford, John S. (RIP) 315, 322, 432
Foreign Miners Tax of 1850 480
Foreigners in Taos 148
Fort Fillmore 316
Fort Marion 400
Fort Sumner 377
Fountain murders 454
Fountain of Youth 15

Fountain, Albert J. 454
Fountain, Mariana Pérez 457
Fox/20th Century Fox 500
Fraile de los Pies Alados 74
Franciscan missionaries 66
Franciscans 55
Franklin Intelligencer 148
Freighting 172
Fremont, John C. 276, 298. 302, 306, 531, 568, 574
French Church 547
Friar of the Winged Feet 74-75
Fronteras 81
Frontier Battalion 433
Frontier hardships 79
Frontier living 112
Frontier social mobility 78

Gadsen Purchase 237
Gallegos, Dr. Eloy 26, 160, 242, 570
Gallegos, Redondo 260
Gálvez, Bernardo de 77, 264
Game animals 333
Game drives 368
Garces, F.H. 13, 58, 82
Gard, George 441
Gard, Wayne 372
Garrard, Lewis 294, 531
Garrett, Patrick F. 451, 456
Garry Owen 366
Garza, Carlos de la 177
Gavilán Peak 300
Gente de razón 218
German Reformation 311
Gerónimo 381, 399, 401
Giddings, Joshua R. 279
Giddings, Marsh 546
Gila River 19
Gillespie, Archibald 300, 303
Girls Ranch 555

Glavecke, Adolphus 467
Gold Fields 315
Gold Rush 478
Golden gang 519
Golden Spike 420
Goldwater, Barry 565
Gómez Farias, Valentín 288
Gonzales, José 151
Gonzales, Rudolfo (Corky) 524
Goodnight Trail 522
Gosiutes 359
Gothlay 399
Governmental structure (NM) 132
Graham-Tewksbury Feud 459
Grant, Ulysses S. 278
Grapes of Wrath 538
Gray Fox 395
greasers 284, 287, 294
Great Captain 143
Great Depression 472, 497, 510, 564
Great Houses 5
Greatest Gunfight in the West 425
Greatest New Mexican 456
Gregg, Josiah 156, 545
Griffith, D.W. 499
Griffith, Emily 526
Grizzlies 225
Guardia Victoriana 177
Guardians of the Law 424
Guerra, Maria de las Angustias de la 307, 482
Guerra, Pablo de la 477
Gulf of Tonkin Resolution 283
Gunfight at the OK Corral 458
Gunfighter 423
Gutierrez, Miguel 573
Gwin, William 574

Hacendados 98
Hamilton Bill 551
Handlin, Oscar 227, 233, 591

Index

Hand-to-hand fighting 305
Hanging Judge 449
Hardin, John Wesley 423, 434
Harper's ferry 314
Harte, Bret 344
Hash Knife outfit 563
Hawikuh 19
Hayes, Will H. 500
Hays, John C. 430
Hearst William R. 492, 498
Heizer, Robert 330
Hell-on-Wheels 419
Hemings, James 285
Hemmings, Sally 320
"heroes and villains" 506
Herrera, Cosme 580
Hijar-Padrés Colony 210
Hispanic California 485
Hispanic Culture Center 556
Hispanic Culture Preservation League 556
Hispanic miners 479, 514
Hispanics 537
Hispanics of NM 592
Hispano-Pueblo alliance 253
Historia de la Nueva Mexico 113
History of Texas 171
Hohokam 2
Hollywood and the Movies 498
Hollywood dream machine 571
Holy Week
Hong Kong 16
Honor 46
Hopi 37, 91
Hopkins, mark 414
Horgan, Paul 253
Hornaday, William 371
Horned saddle 97
Horse Culture 96
Horse racing 224
Horses 53

Hospitality 219
Hotchkiss guns 409
Hounds 486
Houston, Sam 275, 288, 290, 314
How the West was Won 345
Howard, Oliver Otis 394
Hudson, Henry 12
Huizar, Pedro 168
Humanitarian experiment 377
Hume, James B. 444
Hungate, Ward 350
Huntington, Collis 414, 491

Ide, William 301, 302
Illegal immigrants 176, 209
Immoral soldiers 57
Imparting Christianity 68
Indian Agents 331
Indian cowboys 104
"Indian lover" 408
"Indian problem" 321
Indian Removal Act 361
Indian Territory 361, 539
Indian welfare 570
Industrial Workers of the World 496
Infant mortality 167
Infanticide (Precontact) 3
Inman, Henry 370
Inscription Rock 112
Institute of Texas Cultures 473
Interior Provinces 79
Irish immigrants 418
Irish Legion 281
Irving, Washington 369
Isabel (Queen Elizabeth) of Spain 65
Isimanica (Chief) 325
Isleta Pueblo 22
Isthmus of Panama 478
Iturbide, Agustin 208

Jackson, Andrew 274, 361, 539
Jackson, Helen Hunt 408, 409, 482
Jacona 580
James, Frank 423
Jamestown, Va. 406
Japanese & Korean Exclusion League 491
Japanese-Americans 537
Jayme, (Fray) Luis 59, 266
Jazz Singer 499
Jefferson, Thomas 285, 360, 539
Jeffords, Tom 391, 396, 402
Jesus of Nazareth 310
Jicarilla Apaches 378
Johnson, Ernest A. 578
Johnson, James 380
Jointure 551
Jolliet 13
Jolson, Al 499
Jones, Thomas ap Catesby 276
Jornada del Muerto 33
Juanita 438, 480
Juárez, Andrés 114, 115
Judah, Ana Ferona 420
Judah, Theodore 413, 416
Judges 424
Juh 397
Julian, George W. 549
Jumano War 42, 244
Jumanos, 321
Juneteenth 471

Karakawas 322
Karnes, Henry 324
Kearny, Stephen W. 292, 304, 373
Kendall, George W. 155, 162, 275, 544
Kenedy, Mifflin 573
Kessell, John 48, 243
Kickapoos 318
Kilgore, Dan 291
King, Martin Luther 565

King, Richard 573
King, Thomas Starr 509
Kino, Eusebio 69, 71, 72, 105
Kiowas 322, 326
Klamath Reservation 339
Knaut, Andrew 248
Knight, William 300
Knights of St. John 35
Knights of the Golden Circle 314
Ku Klux Klan 472, 527, 541
Kwahadi Comanches 327

La Pérouse, Jean Francois de 190
La reata 98
La Salle 13
La Sevilleta 146
Labor & Management 495
Lachryma Montis 485
Lamar, Mirabeau 275, 324, 328
Lamy, (Bishop) Jean B. 546
Land Grants 106
Land law of 1851 574
Land rushes 540
Land titles 547
Land usage 129
Largo, Juan 451
Larson, Robert W. 549, 559
Las Casas 18, 25, 66, 405, 407
Las Sergas de Esplandián 298
Las Trampas 577
Las Vegas 515
Las Vegas Basin 516
Lasuén, Fermín F. 187
Laughlin, Napoleon B. 580
Lawmen 439
Laws of the Indies 69
Leadville 521
Leatherjackets 63, 205
Lee, John D. 533
Lee, Oliver 454

Index

Lees, Isaiah W. 442
Lewis and Clark 14, 234, 407
Lewis, Lloyd 280
Life in California 192
Lincoln, Abraham 280, 314
Lingua franca 273
Linnville, TX 325
Lipan Apaches 264, 322
Llano Estacado 48
Loewen, James W. 73
London Examiner 280
Lone Star Republic 463
Lone Star: A History of Texas and the Texans 181
Long Expedition 521
Long Walk 377, 387
Longley, William P. 435
López de Cárdenas 20
López, Francisco 478
López, José Dolores 553
Lorenzana, Apolinaria 482
Loring Massacre 394
Los Ángeles 60
Los Naufragios 271
Los Valles 294
Louisiana Territory 264
Lummis, Charles F. 25, 45, 109
Luther, Martín 310
Lutheranism 310

Machebeuf, Joseph P. 546
Mackenzie, Alexander 13, 234
Mackenzie, Ranald 328
Madariaga, Salvador de
Madison, James 285
Madrid, Roque de 130, 258
Madsen, Christian 449
Magellan 10
Magoffin, James W. 292
Magoffin, Susan 544

Mail carriers 151
"make the world safe for Democracy" 283
Manchola, Rafael A. 178
Mangas Coloradas 379
Manhattan Project 555
Manifest Destiny 373, 591
Manje 72
Manso Apaches 236
Margil de Jesús, Antonio 74, 163
Margolin, Malcolm 62
Marques de San Miguel de Aguayo 262
Marquette 13
Márquez, Gerónimo 36, 39, 43, 45
Marriage 218
Marshall, James 478
Marshall, John 361
Martin, Anne 517
Martínez Jr., David 577
Martinez, Father J.A. 294, 546
Martyr (first in California) 59
Martyr (first in the Southwest) 24
Martyrdom 59, 66
Mason County War 433
Mass graves 6
Matamoros 278, 289, 466
Mauldin, Bill 555
Mayer, Frank 371
Mayer, Louis B. 499
McCulloch, Ben, Henry 315
McLowery-Clanton 458
McMillan, Alonzo B. 577
McMillan, Daniel H. 578
McNelly, Leander 433
McWilliams, Carey 280
Meacham, Alfred B. 339
Meade, George C. 280
Meats 7
Mecham, Evan 565
Medal of Honor 555
Medicine Lodge Treaty 365

Meeker, Nathan 354
Meketa, Jacqueline 320
Mendinueta, Pedro F. de 89
Mendoza, Antonio de 18, 97
Menéndez de Aviles 11
Merienda (picnic) 226
Merritt, Ezekiel 300
Mervine, William 303
Mescalero Apaches 379
Mesta 96, 97
Metro Goldwyn Mayer 502
Miera y Pacheco, Bernardo 142, 520
Miera y Terán, Manuel 274
Milam, Ben 289
Miles, Nelson 400
Mimbreño Apaches 380
Mining 272
Mission complex 68
Mission expenses 67
Mission Indians 193
Mission life 67, 191
Mission ranching 104
Missionaries 69
Missionization 114
Missions 183
Missions and Raiders 166
Missouri Volunteers 294
Mixed parentage 52
Miyamura, Hiroshi 555
Modoc War 339
Mogollon 2
Molino del rey 281
Monetary exchange 132
Monroe Doctrine 274
Monterey 57, 88, 207
Monterey Bay 57
Moqui 37
Mora 294
Moraga, Gabriel 205
Moraga, José Joaquín 85

Moreno, Gonzaga 482
Morfi, Juan Agustín 171
Morgan Quitno Press 586
Mormon Battalion 296
Mormon Church 533
Mormon pioneers 532
Mormon towns 514
Mormons 530
Morse, Harry 444
Mountain Meadows Massacre 533
Mountain Men 209, 232, 298, 537, 568
Muckrakers 492
MuCulloch, Ben 432
Muir, John 495
Murrieta, Joaquín 443
Museum of New Mexico 557
Músquiz, Arturo 473
Mustangers 137
My History, Not Yours 508

Naiche 400
Nana 385, 398, 401
Naranjo, José 130
Narbona 373
Narrative of the Texas-Santa Fe Expedition 275
Naufragios (Los) 271
Navajo raiders 374
Navajos 146, 258, 317, 375
Navel blockade 318
"necessary evil" 524
Negro slavery 182
Negroes (free) 477
Neighbors, Robert S. 323, 408, 432
Neve, Felipe de 60
New Deal 497
New Helvetia 214
New Mexican Hispanic Culture Preservation League 556
New Mexico 28
New Mexico Constitution 552

Index

New Mexico Quarterly 554
New Spain 96
Ninth Cavalry 382
Niza, Marcos de 11
"no guns in Dodge" 449
"no-quarter war 39
Norsemen 8
Norteño Indians 167
North From Mexico 445
Northern herd (buffalo) 368, 369
"not a pepper not an onion" 293

O'Conor, Hugo 77, 79
O'Keefe, Georgia 554
O'Sullivan, John L. 413
Ochoa, Estevan 561
Ogden 536
Ogden, Peter S. 531
Oil industry 494
Ojo Caliente 381
Okhe 34
Oklahoma 365
Oklahoma Guardsmen 449
Oklahomans 538
Oklahombres 450
"old settlers" 363
Old Spanish Trail 149
Omnibus Bill 550
Oñate colonists 110
Oñate, Juan de 100, 113, 240
Onís, Luis de 274
Opium War 16
Oregon Yankees 479
Ortega, Arturo G. 556
Ortiz, J. Simon 49
Orwell, George 14
Orwellian 15
Osio, Antonio M. 574
Otero, Sabino 563
Oury, William Sanders 392

Outlaws 434, 442
Overland to California 82
Owens, Perry 459

Pacific Ocean 44
Pacific Railroad Act (1864) 415
Packtrains 136
Padilla, Camilo 553
Padilla, Genaro 508
Padilla, Juan de 21, 24
Padres as ranchers 102
Páez, José de 58
Paiute 345
Pale Eyes 397
Paleography 48
Palma, (Chief) Salvador 83, 87, 267
Palo Duro Canyon 327
Palóu, Francisco 187
Pápagos 236
Pápagos 70
Paramount (studio) 500
Parker (Quanah) 323
Parker, Cynthia Ann 323
Parker, H.K. 384
Parker, Isaac Charles 446
Parker, Theodore 278
Parker's Fort 323
Pasó por aquí 44
Pathmaker 531
Patrón 158
Pattie, James Ohio 210
Pearl Harbor 502
Pecos (pueblo) 23, 82
Peña y Peña, Manuel de la 277, 572
Penitente Brotherhood 153
People's courts 319
Peralta, Pedro de 45
Perea, Estevan de 115
Pérez Serrano, Ana María 82
Pérouse (La), Jean François de 190

Pérouse 62
Perry, Carmen 291
Philadelphia 285
Philadelphia Public Ledger 280
Philip II 34
Philip IV 50
Picnic (merienda) 226
Pico, Andrés 304, 306
Picurís 130
Pierce, Anna Ferona 413
Pike, Zebulon M. 145, 521
Pike's Peak 91
Pile, William A. 546
Pima 70, 236, 388
Pimería Alta 70
Pinal apaches 391
Pino, Pedro B. 145, 261
Pioneers 163, 196, 210, 236
Pious Fund 67
Pit houses 4
Pitkin, Fred 353
Pitt, Leonard 482, 507, 509
Plantation slavery 229
Planters 464
Pletcher, David M. 282
Plum Creek 326
Poinsett, Joel 274, 298
Poinsettia 308
Polk diary 277
Polk, James K. 276, 292
Polygamy 114, 533
Pontiac War 406
Pony Express 151
Popé
Portolá, Gaspar de 55, 56, 184
Portugal 8
Poston, Charles Debrille 560
Pottery 4
Powell, William W. 17, 48
Prat, Pedro 223

Presidente 58
Presidios 77, 205
Preuss, Charles 299
Price, Sterling 294
Prince of Comancheros 141
Printing press 149, 251
Proclamation (Cortina) 468, 469
Promontory (Utah) 420
Pronunciamiento 468
propagandistory 474
Prostitutes 429
Prostitution 333
Protector of the Indians 115, 410
Protestants 311
Provo 536
Puaray 34
Pueblo Bonito 5
Pueblo Indian rituals 115
Pueblo Revolt 406
Pueblo-Hispanic alliance 131
Pulp Fiction 308
Puntas de pies 41, 241
Pyle, Ernie 555

Quanah Parker 323
Quantrill, William C. 364
Queen of Missions 193
Querétaro 75
"quick riches" 512
Quintana, Miguel de 135
Quivira 22

"race of centaurs" 141
Race problems 490
Race riots 503
Racial identities 168
"racial traitor" 408
Racism & Slavery 176
Racism 285
Raiding 131

Index

Ramírez, Francisco 487
Ramiréz, José Antonio 194
Ranch house 216
Ranch industry 52, 71, 99, 272;
  in NM 99; in TX 101; in CA 103;
  in AZ 105
Rangers (TX) 291
Rape 228, 280, 284, 344, 348
Raped by soldiers 377
Raynolds, H.F. 578
Reconquest (NM) 252
Reconstruction 471
Recopilación de las Leyes 107
Recuerdos 485
Reducciones 68
Regulations (of 1772) 77
Regulators 486
Reid, Hugo 479
Religious leveling 168
Relocation 503, 511
"Remember the Alamo" 276, 290, 465
Removal (Indians) 360, 367, 386, 511, 539
Removal policy 396
"Rendezvous" (trappers) 368
Renehan, Alois B. 578
Republican herd (buffalo) 369
Reredo 134
Reserve Indians 323
Resigned (Oñate) 44
Respect 217
Retablo 134
Revenge (TX Rangers) 291
Rezanov, Nicolai 208
Rhodes, Eugene Manlove 455
Ridge faction 361
Riley, John 281
Rivera de Moncada 58, 87
Rivera, Juan M.A. 531
Rivera, Pedro 51
Rivera, Rafaél 149, 515

RKO (studio) 490
Robidoux, Antoine 531
Robinson, Alfred 192, 221
Robledo, Pedro 31, 33
Roche, Josephine 527
Rocky Mountain News 349
Rodeo 99
Rolle, Andrew F. 71m 233m 480
Romero, Antonia 259
Romero, Vicente 141
Rope 98
Rosas, Luis 115
Ross Party 363
Ross, Edmund G. 549
Ross, John 362, 539
Roswell Incident 555
Roybal, Santiago 133
Royce, Josiah 480
Rubric 221

Saavedra, Pedro Allande y 269
Saga of Billy the Kid 457
Sagebrush Rebellion 517
Salary (frontier posts) 78
Salas, Juan de 115
Salas, Petronila de 246
Salmon 333
Saloon-brothel-dance hall 422
Saloons 568
Salt Lake City 536
Samaniego, Mariano 562
San Agustín de Tucson 63
San Antonio de Valero 51
San Antonio frontier 167
San Carlos 381, 382, 396
San Diego 56, 265
San Fernando de Bexar 51
San Francisco
San Francisco earthquake 493
San Gabriel 42, 44

San Jacinto 275, 290
San Juan Basin 4, 7
San Juan Bautista 50
San Juan de los Caballeros 35
San Juan Pueblo 34
San Luis People's Ditch 522
San Miguel de Aguayo 163
San Pascual 305
San Patricio Battalion 280, 281
San Xavier del Bac 71
Sanchez, Raymond 556
Sand Creek Massacre 351, 407
Sand Creek Reservation 349
Sando, Joe 249
Sandoval, Antonio 373, 376
Santa Anna 178, 275, 288, 290
Santa Bárbara 30, 193
Santa Cruz River 235
Santa Fe Ring 548
Santa Rita Mine 145
Santero 134
Santero Art 133
Santiago (St. James) 40
Santuario de Chimayó 145
Scalp Dance 131
Scalp hunting 380
Schwartz, Black Jack 368
Scorched earth" 376
Scotch Irish 182
Scott, Winfield 279, 280
Secession 315
Secularization (missions) 209
Seelye, Julius H. 409
Segesser Hide Painting 132
Seguín, José Erasmo 172
Seguín, Juan N. 173, 177, 465
Semmes, Raphael 282
Semple, Robert 301
Serape trade" 487
Sergas de Esplandián (Las) 298

Serna, Cristóbal de la 258
Serra, Junípero 13, 55, 57, 184
Settler's Leagues 575
Seventh Cavalry 366
Sevilleta (La) 146
Shanghai 496
Sharecropping 472
Sharps rifle 370
Shears, Bob 467
Sheep 100
Sheep ranching 136
Sheridan, Phil 25
Sheridan, Philip 365
Sherman, William T. 365
Sibley, H.H. 316, 317
Sierra Blanca 379
Siki 399
Silverberg, Robert 247, 405
Simmons, Marc 45, 48, 50, 241
Simpson, L.B. 405
Sinclair, Upton 497
Siringo, Charles 452
Sixty Years in California 219
Skliris, Leonidas G. 535
Sky City 21
Slaughter, John 458
Slave Code Act (1859) 547
Slavery 464
Slidell, John 277
Sloat (Commodore) 303
Smallpox 144
Smallpox 333, 407
Smith, Ashbel 281
Smith, Jedediah 209, 234, 298, 531
Socialist Party 496
Socorro 34
Solano (Chief) 302
Soldados de cuera 205
Soldados de cuera 63
Soldiers of the Cross 407

Index

Soldiers of the Cross 66
Sopote 22
Soule, Silas S. 352, 408
South Sea 44
Southern herd (buffalo) 368
Southern manhood 315
Southern Paiutes 358
Spanish customary law 106, 150
Spanish Trail 149
Spicer, Edward 242
Spindletop 472
Spot Resolution, 280
Spurs 98
St. Lawrence Day Massacre 100, 116, 245, 406
Staked Plains 48, 327, 330
Stanford, Leland 414
Steck, Michael 377
Stockton, Robert F. 303
Struble Report 550
Studios (Hollywood) 500
Subsistence farming 169
Sugar beets 535
Sutter, John 213, 302
Sydney Ducks 486
Symington, Fife 566

Tafoya, José 141
Tahlequah 366
Tallow 215
Taney, (Chief Justice) C.J. 286
Taos Trade Fair 132
Tarabal, Sebastian 85
Tejano system of justice 172
Tejano teamsters 465
Tejano water law 172
Teodoro de Croix 79, 80
Terán, Manuel Miera y 274
Texans 176, 287
Texan-Santa Fe Expedition 155
Texas herd (buffalo) 369

Texas racism 466
Texas Rangers 177, 430
Texas Revolution 178
Texas writers 54
Textile production 154
Thacker, John 440
Thanksgiving (NM) 47
The Associates 414
The Big Four 414
The Jazz Singer 499
"The Utes must go!" 354
Thomas, Henry A. "Heck" 449
Thompson, Ben 435
Thompson, Waddy 275
Thoreau, Henry David 278
Thrapp, Dan 410
Three Guardsmen 449
Three Years in California 217
Throckmorton, J.W. 319
Thurmond, Strom 320
Tibbets, Luther C. 489
Tierra Amarilla Courthouse Raid 579
Tiguex Province 22
Tiguex villages 23
Tijerina, Reies López 55
Tilghman, William M. "Bill" 449
Tindé 389
Tingley, Clyde 554
Tombstone (AZ.) 458
Tongues (buffalo) 369
Tonkawas 322
Tonopah 515
Town Council 53, 100
Trade (on SF Trail) 147, 156
Trade Fair 115, 131
Traditions 115
Trafzer, Clifford 386
Trail of Tears 362, 539
Trampas (Las) 577
Trappers' "Rendezvous" 368

Travel routine 86
Travis, William B. 287, 288, 289
Treaty of 1846
Treaty of Cahuenga 306
Treaty of Guadalupe Hidalgo 281, 572, 582
Treaty of Indian Springs 362
Treaty of New Echota 362
Treaty Party 363
Tree of Hate 17
Trist, Nicholas 281
Trobadores 158, 159
Tsali 362
Tubac 81
Tuberculosis 379
Tucson 235
Tucsonense pioneers 236
Tucsonenses 63
Tully, Ochoa & Co. 561
Tupatú 116
Two Years Before the Mast 214

Udall, Stewart 20, 24, 26, 45, 159, 406, 534, 571
Uintah Reservation 355, 357
Ulibarrí, Juan de 130, 520
Union Mission 366
Union Pacific 412, 415, 418, 419
United Artists 501
United Mine Workers of America 524
Universal Studios 501
University of New Mexico 554
Urrea, José 289, 290
U.S. Cavalry 148
Use-rights 579
Utes 353

Vaca, Cabeza de 270
Vaccination 145
Vallejo, Francisca 300
Vallejo, Mariano 216, 300, 302, 479, 483, 574
Vallejo, Rosalía 482

Vallejo, Salvador 223
Van Buren, Martín 275
Van de Grift Sánchez, Nellie 223
Vancouver, George 190, 194
Vaquero Apaches 36
Vargas Colonists 117
Vargas, Diego de 116, 252
Vásquez, Tiburcio 443
Vázquez, Josefina Zoraida 282
Velasco (Viceroy) 29
Vélez Cachupín, Tomás 142
Venereal diseases 377
Vera Cruz 280
Veramendi, Fernando de 169
Verbal skills 158
Vespucci, Amerigo 14
Vial, Pedro 13, 144
Victorio 381
Vigilantes 425
Vigilantism 437
Vigil, Donaciano 293
Vikings 8, 402
Villa de Béxar 163
Villa de San Antonio de Bexar 51
Villa, Pancho 553
Villages (Precontact) 4
Villagrá, Gaspar de 36, 46
Villalobos, Gregorio de 95
Villareal, Enrique 177
Villasur Expedition 131
Voting Rights Act (1965) 565

Wah-To-Yah and the Taos Trail 294
Waite, Stand 364
Walker War 356
Walker, Joe 299, 300
Walker, Samuel 281, 431
Wall, David D. 523
Wallace, Lew 546
Wallace, Susan 550

Index

War of attrition 320
War Powers Act 283
Warner Brothers 501
Wars of extermination 481
Washington navel orange 489, 509
Washington-on-the-Brazos 290
Washoe 511
Weapons 78
Weapons of mass destruction 283
Webb Act 491
Weber, David J. 73
Wedding day 218
Weddings 148
Weightman, Richard H. 545
Western gunfights 567
Western living 216
Whig Intelligencer 282
Whipple, Bishop H.B. 408
Whiskey 363
White eyes 380, 397
"white man" 328, 343
"white savages" 298
Whitman, Royal Emerson 391
Whitman, Walt 278
Whitman's Indians 392
Whitney, Asa 412
Wichita 322
Wickenburg Massacre 394
Wild Bill Hickok 423
Wild cattle 53
Williams Station 346
Winter campaign 365
Wobblies 496
Wolfskill, William 489
Women (Precontact) 6
"women of the underworld" 422
Woodruff Manifesto 534
Workers War 420
World War II 502
Wounded Knee 409

Wynkoop, Edward 351

Yanas tribe 344
"Yankee justice" 575
Ye, Juan de 116, 125, 252
Yoakum, H. 176
Young, Brigham 356, 357, 532
YRFF Cycle 54
Yuma Massacre 267
Yuma Nation 83

Zacatecas 28
Zaldivar 29
Zaldívar, Vicente 31, 36, 39, 368
Zarcillos Largos 374
Zavala, Lorenzo de 288
Zinfandel grapes 490
Zinn, Howard 285, 509
Zoot-suiters 503
Zuni 19, 37
Zúñiga, José de 235, 269
Zutucapán 37